COMPLETE ADVANCED LEVEL MATHEMATICS

Mechanics

Martin Adams • June Haighton • Jeff Trim

STANLEY THORNES

First published in 2000 by
Stanley Thornes (Publishers) Ltd
Delta Place
27 Bath Road
Cheltenham
Glos GL53 7TH

A catalogue record for this book is available from the British Library.

ISBN 0 7487 3559 3

00 01 02 03 04 / 10 9 8 7 6 5 4 3 2

The publishers are grateful to the following for permission to use copyright material:
Brooklands Museum Trust Limited, photograph, p.136
Blackpool Pleasure Beach, photographs, pp227, 256
Big Bang Promotions Limited (T/A UK Bungee Club), p293

All other photographs, including cover, from STP Archive

Every effort has been made to contact copyright holders. The authors and publishers apologise to anyone whose rights have been overlooked and will be happy to rectify any errors or omissions at the earliest opportunity.

Typeset by The Alden Group, Oxford
Printed and bound in Italy by STIGE, Turin

Contents

About the Authors

- **Martin Adams** is in charge of Mechanics at a school in Hampshire. He is an Assistant Examiner for a main Examination Board and has also worked as a Key Stage 3 marker. He has previous teaching experience in Wiltshire.

- **June Haighton** was formerly an Associate Lecturer at a college in Cheshire. She has many years teaching experience and her wide-ranging work has previously included the development of published Advanced Level Mathematics, as well as other materials.

- **Jeff Trim** is Head of Mathematics at a school in Reading. He has a wide range of teaching experience and has been involved in supervising initial teacher training students at Reading University. He has also led support courses on Advanced Level Mathematics for experienced teachers.

Examination Papers

We are grateful to the following Awarding Bodies and Examination Boards for permission to reproduce questions from their past examination papers:

- Assessment and Qualifications Alliance (AQA), including Northern Examinations and Assessment Board (NEAB), and Associated Examination Board (AEB).
- The Edexcel Foundation, including University of London Examinations and Assessment Council (ULEAC).
- Oxford, Cambridge and RSA (OCR), including University of Cambridge Local Examinations Syndicate (UCLES), Oxford & Cambridge Schools Examination Board (OCSEB) and Mathematics in Education and Industry (MEI).
- Northern Ireland Council for the Curriculum, Examinations and Assessment (NICCEA)
- Welsh Joint Education Committee (WJEC)

All answers and worked solutions provided for examination questions are the responsibility of the authors.

Introduction

Complete Advanced Level Mathematics is an exciting new series of mathematics books, Teacher Resource Files and other support materials from **Stanley Thornes** for those studying at Advanced Level. It has been developed following an extensive period of research and consultation with a wide number of teachers, students and others. All the authors are experienced and practising teachers and, in some cases, Advanced Level Mathematics Examiners. Chapters have been trialed in schools and colleges. All the requirements for complete success in Advanced Level Mathematics are provided by this series.

This book covers all the requirements for **Mechanics** from all the latest Advanced Level Specifications and course requirements for AS and A Level mathematics. It will provide you with:

- Material that builds on work done at GCSE level, where appropriate.
- Comprehensive coverage and clear explanations of all Mechanics topics and a skills.
- Numerous exercises and worked examples with questions and clear diagrams.
- Precise and comprehensive teaching text with clear progression.
- Margin notes that provide supporting commentary on key topics, formulas and other aspects of the work.
- In text highlighted 'hints' to assist with important areas, such as specific calculations in worked examples and key formulas.
- Margin icons for topics requiring the use of a graphical calculator or computer. Topics that can be developed with IT are included throughout.
- A comprehensive list of formulas that students need to know, with chapter references, and a full index.

Chapters in this book contain a number of **key features**:

- **What you need to know** sections covering prerequisite knowledge for a chapter.
- **Review** sections with practice questions on what you need to know.
- **Worked Examples** and supporting commentary.
- **Technique** and **Contextual Exercises** to give thorough practice in all Mechanics concept areas and skills.
- **Consolidation A** and **B Exercises**, which include actual examination questions, to build on the work in a chapter and provide practice in a variety of question types.
- **Applications and Activities** as a support to coursework.
- A **Summary** of all the key concepts covered.

Companion volumes for ***Pure Mathematics*** (0 7487 3558 5) and ***Statistics*** (0 7487 3560 7) and a ***Mechanics Teacher Resource File*** (0 7487 3562 3) are also available in this series.

1 Principles of Mechanics

What is mechanics? Mechanics is the mathematical study of how objects move and how structures are held together. The mathematics allows designers to predict how objects will move and to make structures which are safe. A roller coaster ride gives an example of both these branches of mechanics.

The roller coaster cars move around the track. At different points on the track the cars will move at different speeds. The part of mechanics concerned with motion is called **dynamics**. Using dynamics, the speed of the cars on the track could be predicted.

Kinematics
Dynamics includes the study of forces. When motion is studied without considering forces it is called kinematics.

The roller coaster track gives an example of a structure. It is important to make sure that the structure is strong enough to do its job. Different parts of the track will need to be stronger than others. By studying the structure, this information can be worked out. The study of structures in mechanics is called **statics**. This is because *static* means stationary or not moving.

Think of four examples where dynamics could be used and four examples where statics could be used.

1.1 Mathematical Modelling

The modelling process

The task of designing a roller coaster ride is a complicated job. To be able to complete this task, the designer needs a lot of information. To get this information questions need to be asked. What type of roller coaster is it going to be? How fast will it travel? How many people will it carry? How many loops will it have? How long is the ride to last? What area of land is available? At this stage, the problem is being **defined**. This stage is achieved by asking questions.

There will be some questions that cannot be answered. How much will the roller coaster cars weigh? The answer to this question will vary. It will depend on how many people the roller coaster is carrying. The people will weigh different amounts. By making assumptions, these problems can be resolved. Each person can be assumed to weigh 70 kg and the roller coaster cars can be assumed to be full of people. This stage sets up the **model** by making assumptions. These assumptions provide the information necessary to solve the problem using mathematics. Other assumptions can be used to help simplify the problem. This will make the problem easier to solve.

Next, mathematics is used to solve the problem. This could be to find how fast the roller coaster cars will travel or how strong the track needs to be at a certain point. This is called the **analysis** stage.

Once the analysis has been completed, the results need to be checked. Do the answers make sense? How do the results compare with current roller coasters? This stage is called **interpretation** of the results.

Even when this stage has been completed, the problem has not been solved totally. Remember the modelling stage when the *assumptions* were made? These assumptions can now be modified to check that the roller coaster will work under different conditions. This is carried out by asking other questions. Will the roller coaster still work if it is empty? What happens if everyone weighed 50 kg? This is a repeat of the definition of the problem. So the modelling process is a *circular* one.

The following flowchart shows the circular nature of the modelling process.

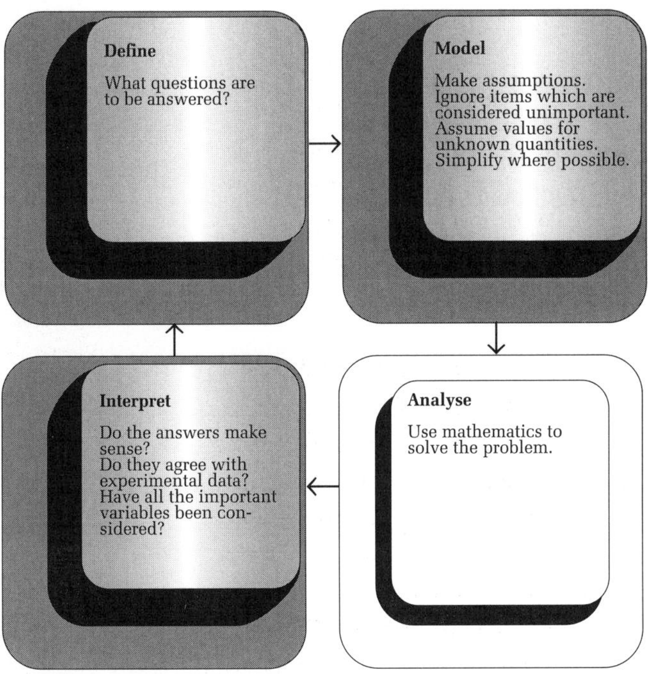

This modelling process is not only used in mechanics. It is used in everyday life. Think about how this process could be used when organising a party.

This four stage process will be called the **DMAI** model throughout this book. These letters stand for the **D**efine, **M**odel, **A**nalyse and **I**nterpret stages. This is the simplest structure for mathematical modelling.

Each stage of the DMAI model will be noted in the margin with an icon. This is the smallest number of stages for the modelling process. However, some mathematicians do prefer a longer and more detailed set of stages.

The particle model

The particle model ignores the size and shape of an object. The object's mass is treated as if it acts at one single point. This is one of the most common assumptions made when solving problems. It will help to simplify the problem and so make it easier to solve.

A 2 kg bag of peas could be modelled as a particle. This would be like replacing the bag by a single point of mass 2 kg. Although this appears ridiculous, it means the size and shape of the bag can be ignored. This assumption is valid when the size of the bag is small compared to the distance the bag travels, as in the following instance. If the bag is dropped from the top of a tower block, its size would not be very significant. However, if it is dropped from a ground floor window its size would be important.

2 kg

By treating the object as a particle, its air resistance must also be ignored. There are times when ignoring the physical effect of air resistance would simplify the model too much.

In the mathematical model of a particle, it has no area and so it cannot collide with the molecules in air. So the particle will not be slowed down.

Get two pieces of paper which are the same size. Crush one of the pieces into a ball. What do you think will happen when both pieces are dropped from the same height? Try this experiment to confirm your ideas. Try to explain the outcome. The *ball* shape hits the floor first. The ordinary sheet floats unpredictably to the floor. Air resistance has a significant influence on the sheet of paper and so a particle model would not be appropriate.

Another disadvantage of using the particle model is that it ignores some types of motion. To illustrate this, place a pencil on a table. What happens to the pencil if you push it at points A, B or C? Why not try this now.

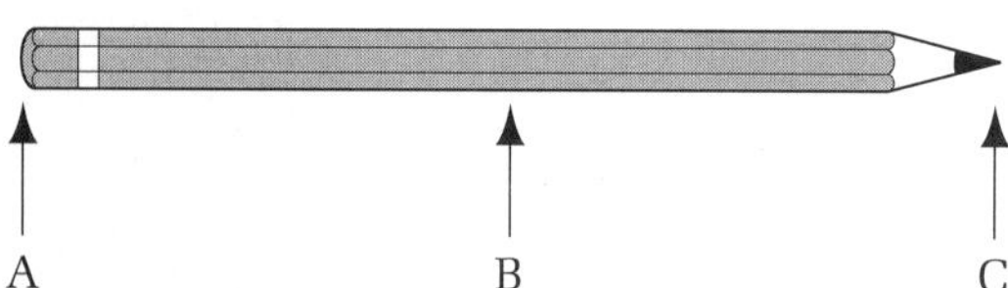

The pencil will move away from you but the effect in each case is *not* identical. When you push the pencil at A, it moves forwards and it spins. The spin or rotation of the pencil is clockwise. When you push the pencil at B, it moves forwards with little or no spin. When the pencil is pushed at C, it moves forward and rotates anticlockwise. If the pencil is modelled as a particle then it is replaced as a single point and the size and shape of the pencil would be ignored. The single point is only big enough to be pushed at one position. This means the particle will only move forwards and it will have no spin.

The particle's motion is the same (approximately) as when the pencil is pushed at its centre. Therefore, the particle model will *ignore any spin or rotation* of the object. In some situations, spin can be a major effect and should not be ignored. For instance, the game of snooker depends on the skill of the players to make the balls spin. Footballers spin the ball to make it swerve and a slice or hook shot in golf is caused by the ball spinning.

1.1 Mathematical Modelling
Exercise

Contextual

1 The analysis of walking is an area to which dynamics could be applied. List three other examples of dynamics.

2 The analysis of the structure of a playground slide is an area to which statics could be applied. List three other examples of statics.

3 Write down the four stage process for mathematical modelling that will be used in this book.

4 Describe how you would plan a party using the DMAI process.

5 Can the objects in the following situations be modelled as particles?

- **a** A car travelling along a motorway from Birmingham to Glasgow at a constant speed.
- **b** A snooker ball hit with back spin.
- **c** A boomerang being thrown.
- **d** A marble dropped from a height of 2 m above the ground.

6 A tennis ball is served in a match. The ball is modelled as a particle. State one advantage and one disadvantage of this model.

7 A golfer hits a golf ball with slice. Give a reason why the golf ball cannot be modelled as a particle.

8 A shuttlecock is served in a game of badminton. Explain why a particle model alone could not be used to represent the shuttlecock.

Applications and Activities

1 The following activities could be modelled:

a a bus journey into town
b a walk to a local beauty spot
c a day out at a theme park
d a school trip to a power station.

Carry out some of these activities to check your model's predictions for actual times, expenses, and so on.

Summary

- The modelling process consists of four stages: define, model, analyse and interpret.

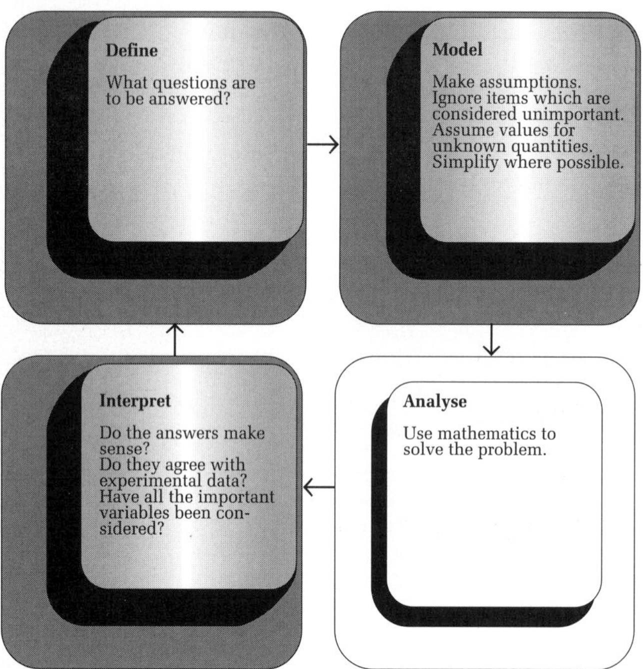

- If we model an object as a particle, we ignore the size and the shape of the object.
- Air resistance is zero in the particle model.
- The particle model ignores any spin or rotation of the object.

2 Forces

What you need to know

- How to use formulas to find unknown quantities.
- How to use standard form.
- How to use proportion and variation to find an equation.

Review

1 a $a = \dfrac{400}{b^2}$

i Find a when b is 10.

ii Find b when a is 10.

b $d = \dfrac{efg}{h^2}$

i Calculate d when $e = 5, f = 8, g = 6$ and $h = 2$.

ii Work out the value of e when $d = 200, f = 5, g = 4$ and $h = 7$.

iii Determine h when $d = 50, f = 10, e = 25$ and $g = 5$.

c $r = kv^2$

i Find k if $r = 405$ and $v = 9$.

ii Determine r if $k = 7$ and $v = 4$.

iii Find v if $r = 1250$ and $k = 0.5$.

2 a Write the following numbers in standard form:

i 193 000 000

ii 0.000 162

b Write the following numbers without using standard form:

i 2.37×10^6

ii 1.59×10^{-5}

3 a y varies linearly with x. If $y = 10$ when $x = 2$, find an equation relating x and y.

b y varies with the square of x. When $x = 4$, y is 160. Work out the equation between x and y.

c y is directly proportional to the square of x. When x is 5, y is 50. Find an equation between x and y.

2.1 Force

What is a force? The term force is a difficult one to define precisely. When you push or pull an object, you have applied a force. You often see the result of this force causing the object to move.

A shopping trolley needs to be pushed to start it moving. You would pull the trolley to stop it moving forwards or to make it move backwards. In both these cases, you have applied a force.

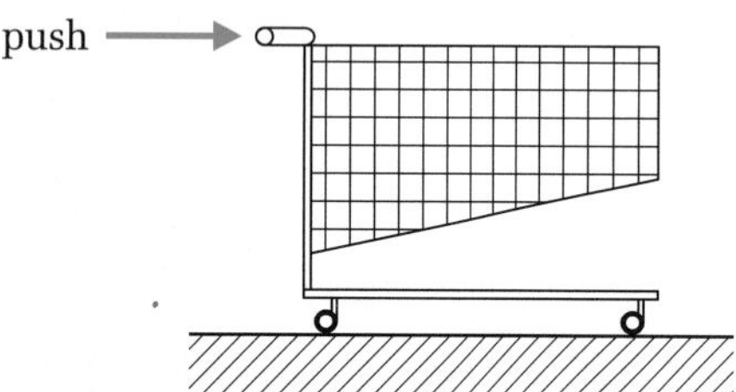

A force will not always cause motion; it can be used to prevent motion. When a shopping trolley is on a slope, it will roll down the slope. To stop this from happening, the shopping trolley will need to be held. In holding the shopping trolley you must apply a force.

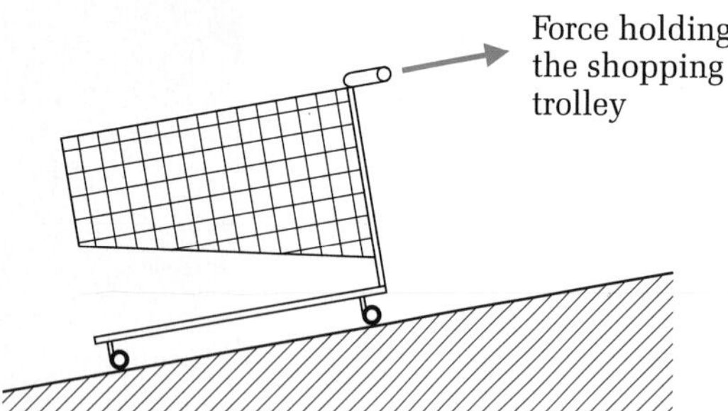

Roll a marble along a table. Hit the marble from the side with a ruler. Try to hit it at right angles to its direction of motion as shown in the diagram. What happened to the marble? The marble has changed direction. The force you applied with the ruler must have caused this change of direction.

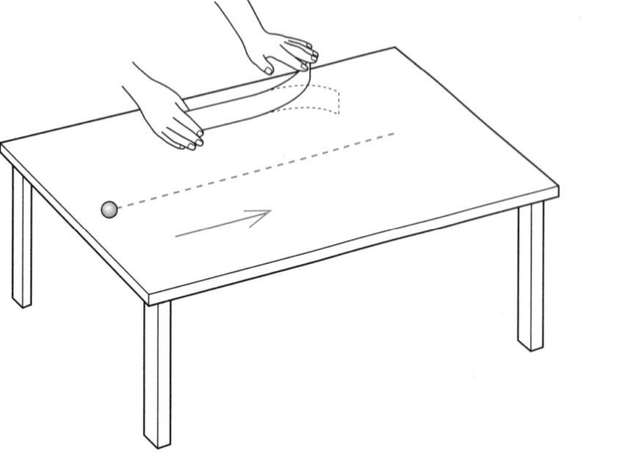

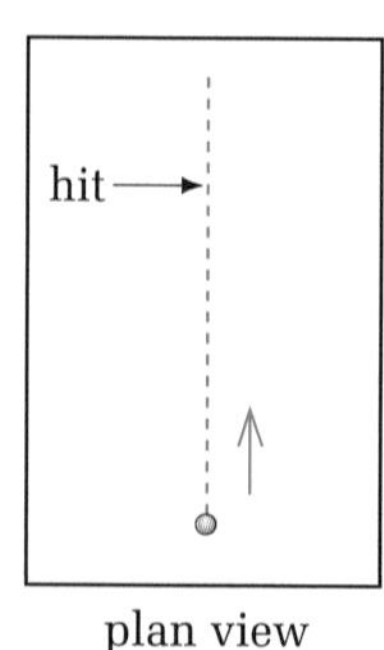

plan view

In a cricket or rounders match, the bat or baton is used to apply a force to the ball. This force causes the ball to change direction.

A force is most easily defined in terms of the effects it causes.

- A force can cause an object to *speed up* or *slow down.*
- A force can *prevent* an object *from moving.*
- A force can *change* an object's *direction of motion.*

Types of forces

There are two main types of forces:

1. forces of attraction
2. contact forces.

Forces of attraction act at a distance. When a ball is dropped it falls faster and faster towards the ground. This speeding up must be caused by a force. This attraction force due to gravity is called **weight**. Other forces of attraction are caused by magnetism and electricity.

Contact forces occur when objects are touching each other. When a book is at rest on a table there must be a force preventing the book from falling. This force is the contact force between the table and the book.

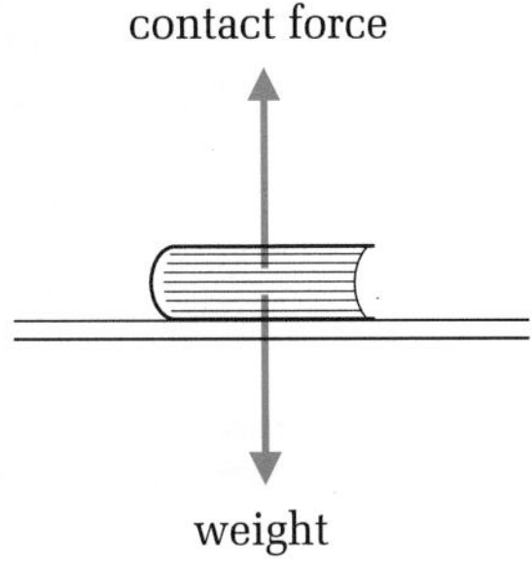

→ represents a force. The direction of the arrow gives the direction in which the force acts.

The SI unit of force is the newton (N). A force meter or newton meter can be used to measure the size of a force.

2.2 Universal Law of Gravitation

The Moon orbits the Earth. The Moon is continuously changing its direction to stay in its circular orbit. This changing of direction must be caused by a force. This force must be a *force of attraction* because there is no contact between the Earth and the Moon. In 1687, Sir Isaac Newton (1643–1727) described his work on this force of attraction. His predictions led to the development of a formula to be able to calculate this force of attraction between different masses. The formula is now called the **universal law of gravitation.**

Isaac Newton (1643–1727)
Newton's great achievement was to show that mathematics can be used to state a set of laws that explain so much about our universe. During 1665–1666, when he was forced home from Cambridge University, which had to close during the plague of that time, he conducted his famous experiments on the spectrum, he invented the reflecting telescope, he observed the Moon and the planets, and he developed his law of gravitation and his laws of motion.

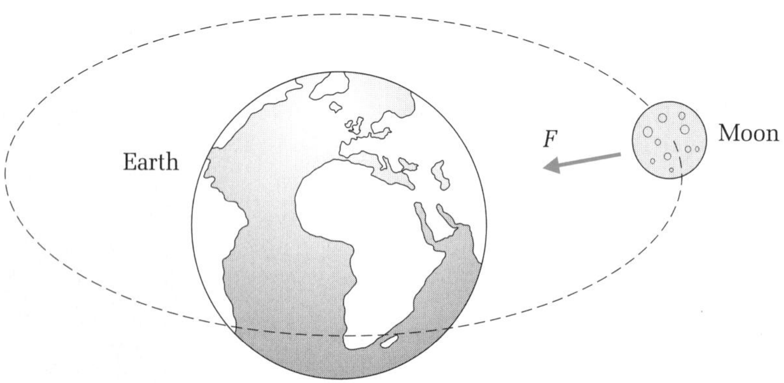

The universal law of gravitation is given by the formula:

$$F = \frac{Gm_1m_2}{d^2}$$

What the letters stand for is detailed below:

- F force of attraction between the two masses (N);
- G universal gravitational constant ($6.67 \times 10^{-11}\ \text{kg}^{-1}\ \text{m}^3\ \text{s}^{-2}$);
- m_1 mass of one of the objects (kg);
- m_2 mass of the other object (kg);
- d distance between the centres of the two masses (m).

The universal gravitational constant always has a value of $6.67 \times 10^{-11}\ \text{kg}^{-1}\ \text{m}^3\ \text{s}^{-2}$, provided **SI units** are used.

This constant is the constant of proportion in the formula.

Overview of method

In the worked examples the following method will be used to solve the problems.

Step ① Summarise the information given.

Step ② Write down the formula.
Step ③ Substitute the numbers into the formula.
Step ④ Calculate the unknown quantity.

Break the calculation into stages. Make sure you store the answer to each stage on your calculator.

This will keep your answer as accurate as possible.

Example 1

Calculate the force of attraction between the Earth and the Moon. The mass of the Earth is 5.98×10^{24} kg, the mass of the Moon is 7.38×10^{22} kg and the distance between their centres is 3.84×10^{8} m. Take $G = 6.67 \times 10^{-11}$ kg^{-1} m^3 s^{-2}.

Solution

$G = 6.67 \times 10^{-11}$ $d = 3.84 \times 10^{8}$ ◀ ① Summarise the information.
$m_1 = 5.98 \times 10^{24}$ $F = ?$
$m_2 = 7.38 \times 10^{22}$

$$F = \frac{Gm_1m_2}{d^2}$$ ◀ ② Write down the formula.

$$F = \frac{6.67 \times 10^{-11} \times 5.98 \times 10^{24} \times 7.38 \times 10^{22}}{(3.84 \times 10^{8})^2}$$ ◀ ③ Substitute the numbers into the formula.

$F = 2.00 \times 10^{20}$ N ◀ ④ Find F.

Example 2

Calculate the force of attraction on a mass of 1 kg at the surface of the Earth. The mass of the Earth is 5.98×10^{24} kg and the radius of the Earth is 6.38×10^{6} m. Take $G = 6.67 \times 10^{-11}$ kg^{-1} m^3 s^{-2}.

Solution

$G = 6.67 \times 10^{-11}$ $m_1 = 5.98 \times 10^{24}$ $m_2 = 1$ ◀ ① Summarise the information.
$d = 6.38 \times 10^{6}$ $F = ?$

$$F = \frac{Gm_1m_2}{d^2}$$ ◀ ② Write down the formula.

$$F = \frac{6.67 \times 10^{-11} \times 5.98 \times 10^{24} \times 1}{(6.38 \times 10^{6})^2}$$ ◀ ③ Substitute the numbers into the formula.

$F = 9.80$ N ◀ ④ Find F.

Example 3

Venus has a mass of 4.78×10^{24} kg and the Sun has a mass of 1.99×10^{30} kg. The force which keeps Venus in orbit around the Sun is 5.44×10^{22} N. Calculate the distance between the centres of the Sun and Venus. Take $G = 6.67 \times 10^{-11}$ kg^{-1} m^{3} s^{-2}.

Solution

$G = 6.67 \times 10^{-11}$ $\quad F = 5.44 \times 10^{22}$ ◀ ① Summary.

$m_1 = 4.78 \times 10^{24}$ $\quad d = ?$

$m_2 = 1.99 \times 10^{30}$

$$F = \frac{Gm_1m_2}{d^2}$$ ◀ ② Formula.

$$5.44 \times 10^{22} = \frac{6.67 \times 10^{-11} \times 4.78 \times 10^{24} \times 1.99 \times 10^{30}}{d^2}$$ ◀ ③ Substitute.

Multiply by d^2.

$$5.44 \times 10^{22} \times d^2 = 6.67 \times 10^{-11} \times 4.78 \times 10^{24} \times 1.99 \times 10^{30}$$

Calculate RHS (right hand side) of the equation.

$$5.44 \times 10^{22} \times d^2 = 6.34 \times 10^{44}$$

Divide by 5.44×10^{22}.

$$d^2 = \frac{6.34 \times 10^{44}}{5.44 \times 10^{22}}$$ ◀ ④ Find d.

$$d^2 = 1.17 \times 10^{22}$$

Take the square root to find d.

$$d = 1.08 \times 10^{11} \text{ m}$$

2.2 Universal Law of Gravitation

Exercise

Technique

Take $G = 6.67 \times 10^{-11}$ kg^{-1} m^3 s^{-2} where necessary.

1 The masses of two bodies are 4×10^6 kg and 5×10^4 kg. The distance between their centres is 2×10^4 m. Calculate the force of attraction between the two masses.

2 The force of attraction between two masses is 3.67×10^{24} N. The mass of one of the bodies is 5.98×10^{24} kg and the distance between them is 1.50×10^{11} m. Find the mass of the other body.

3 The masses of two bodies are 8×10^{10} kg and 4×10^5 kg. The force of attraction between the two masses is 2×10^{-4} N. Find the distance between the two masses.

Contextual

Take $G = 6.67 \times 10^{-11}$ kg^{-1} m^3 s^{-2} where necessary.

1 The mass of the Sun is 1.99×10^{30} kg and the mass of the Earth is 5.98×10^{24} kg. The distance between their centres is 1.50×10^{11} m. Calculate the force of attraction between the Earth and the Sun, assuming the orbit is circular.

The orbit of the Earth is really elliptical. This is caused by the forces of attraction of all the other planets on the Earth.

2 The Moon has a mass of 7.38×10^{22} kg and a radius of 1.74×10^6 m. Determine the mass of an object on the surface of the Moon if the force it experiences is 160 N.

3 Mars has a mass of 6.55×10^{23} kg and the Sun has a mass of 1.99×10^{30} kg. The force which keeps Mars in orbit around the Sun is 1.67×10^{21} N. Find the distance between the centres of the Sun and Mars, if the orbit is assumed circular.

2.3 Weight

When an apple falls off a tree it accelerates towards the Earth. This acceleration must be caused by a force. This force is the force of attraction of the Earth on the apple. This force is known as the **weight** of the apple.

The universal law of gravitation can be simplified for objects on or near the Earth's surface. In the formula some of the variables will remain constant near the Earth's surface.

$$F = \frac{Gm_1m_2}{d^2}$$

- G is always constant.
- m_1 is constant for the mass of the Earth.
- d is very close to being constant.

The distance between the centres of the masses will be approximately equal to the radius of the Earth. This is because the object will be close to the surface of the Earth. This means that $\frac{Gm_1}{d^2}$ is constant provided that the distance between the object and the Earth's surface stays small compared to the radius of the Earth. For objects close to the Earth's surface, the law of gravitation becomes:

$d \approx$ radius of the Earth

$$F = mg$$

$m = m_2$ and $g = \frac{Gm_1}{d^2}$.

The diagram shows the weight of the object acting downwards. This leads to the formula for the weight of an object.

Note, from the units of G, m and d, it can be shown that the units of g are m s^{-2}. These are the units of acceleration, a measure of how fast the speed is changing (see Chapters 4 and 6).

g

weight = mg

weight = mg

Notation
m = mass of the object (kg).
g = acceleration due to gravity (m s^{-2}).
⟶⟫ represents an acceleration.

The units m s^{-2} stand for metres per second per second. An acceleration of 10 m s^{-2} means that the object will speed up by 10 m s^{-1} every second.

The value of g must be constant because $\frac{Gm_1}{d^2}$ will be constant. The value of the **acceleration due to gravity** (g) can be calculated by working out the value of $\frac{Gm_1}{d^2}$.

$G = 6.67 \times 10^{-11}$ $\quad d = 6.38 \times 10^6$

$m_1 = 5.98 \times 10^{24}$ $\quad g = ?$

Note the acceleration due to gravity is written in italics.

$$g = \frac{Gm_1}{d^2}$$

$$g = \frac{6.67 \times 10^{-11} \times 5.98 \times 10^{24}}{(6.38 \times 10^6)^2}$$

$$g = 9.8\,\mathrm{m\,s^{-2}}\ (2\ \mathrm{s.f.})$$

The value of g is $9.8\,\mathrm{m\,s^{-2}}$. This is the value that this book will use throughout, unless a different value is stated. The value of $g = 10\,\mathrm{m\,s^{-2}}$ will sometimes be used to make the calculations easier. In such a case, the question will make it clear that you should use $g = 10\,\mathrm{m\,s^{-2}}$.

Some examination boards use $g = 9.81\,\mathrm{m\,s^{-2}}$.

Overview of method

The method can be broken down into three steps. These steps will be used when solving the worked examples.

Step ① Write down the formula.
Step ② Substitute the numbers into the formula.
Step ③ Find the unknown quantity.

Example 1

Find the weight of the following masses:

a 10 kg **b** 10 mg **c** 2 tonnes.

Solution

a weight = mg ◀ ① Write down the formula.
weight = 10×9.8 ◀ ② Substitute the numbers into the formula.
weight = 98 N ◀ ③ Find the weight.

b 10 mg = 0.01 g = 0.000 01 kg
weight = mg
weight = $0.000\,01 \times 9.8$
weight = 0.000 098 N

Convert mg into kg (SI units). Remember 1000 mg = 1 g and 1000 g = 1 kg.

c 2 t = 2000 kg
weight = mg
weight = 2000×9.8
weight = 19 600 N

Convert tonnes (t) into kg (SI units). Remember 1000 kg = 1 tonne.

Example 2

Find the mass of an object if its weight is 120 N. (Take $g = 10\,\mathrm{m\,s^{-2}}$.)

Solution

weight = mg ◀ ① Write down the formula.
$120 = m \times 10$ ◀ ② Substitute the numbers.
$m = 12$ kg ◀ ③ Find m.

Divide by 10.

2.3 Weight
Exercise

Technique

1 Taking $g = 10\,\text{m}\,\text{s}^{-2}$, find the weight of the following masses:

a 7 kg   **b** 200 kg   **c** 2 g
d 10 tonnes   **e** 40 mg

g stands for grams because the quantities are masses.
Remember the abbreviation for tonnes is t.
Remember $g = 9.8\,\text{m}\,\text{s}^{-2}$ unless otherwise stated.

2 Find the weight of the following masses:

a 32 kg   **b** 347 kg   **c** 25 g
d 7.5 tonnes   **e** 12 mg

3 Taking $g = 10\,\text{m}\,\text{s}^{-2}$, find the mass of the objects whose weight is given below:

a 170 N   **b** 0.03 N
c 12 kN   ◀ 1 kN = 1000 N

4 Find the mass of the objects whose weight is given below:

a 49 N   **b** 0.196 N
c 980 kN   ◀ 1 kN = 1000 N

Contextual

1 Taking $g = 10\,\text{m}\,\text{s}^{-2}$, find the weight of:

a a car, which has a mass of 1.5 tonnes
b a bag of sugar, which has a mass 0.5 kg
c an insect, which has a mass of 15 mg.

2 Calculate the weight of:

a a lorry of mass 40 tonnes
b a loaf of bread, which has a mass of 800 g
c a feather of mass 50 mg.

Remember $g = 9.8\,\text{m}\,\text{s}^{-2}$ unless stated otherwise.

2.4 Contact Forces

A table touches the floor at four points. At each one of these points there will be a contact force. The contact forces act at right angles to the floor. These forces are called the **normal reaction** forces. In general, the normal reaction forces will always act at *right angles to the continuous surface*.

Normal means *at right angles* or perpendicular.

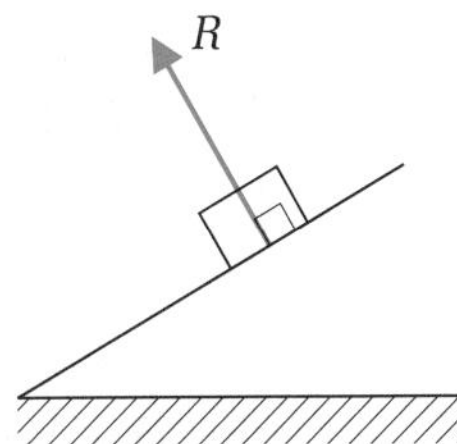

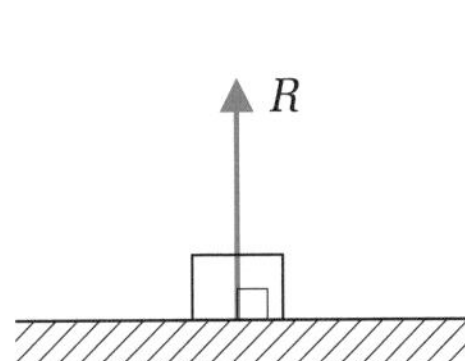

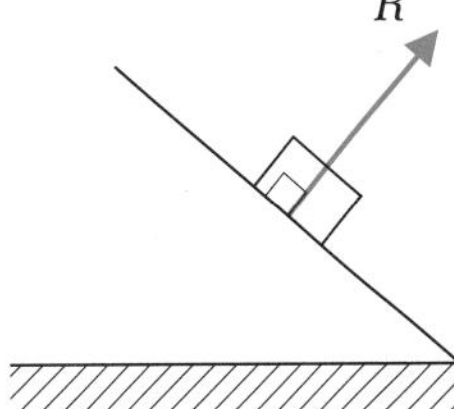

The table is difficult to draw in three dimensions (3D). Does the table have to be drawn in 3D? A two dimensional (2D) drawing could be used to represent the table. This means the reaction forces at two *feet* can be replaced by a single reaction force.

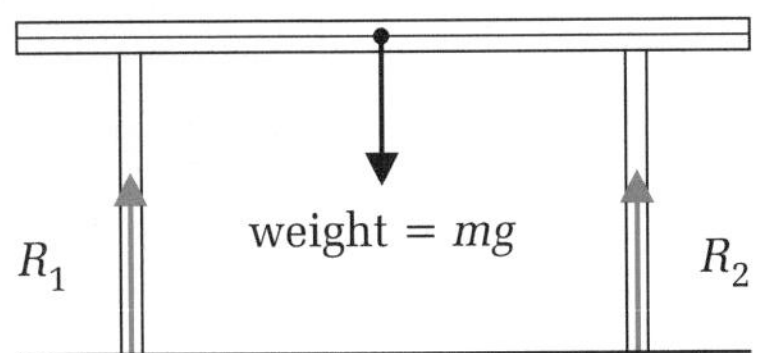

How could you model the contact force on a stationary car? The car cannot be modelled as a particle when it is stationary because its length will be important. This is shown by drawing two reaction forces.

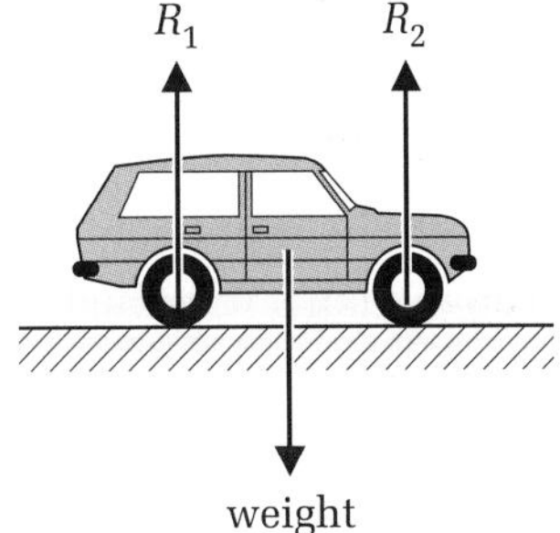

When the car travels a distance much longer than its length, it can be modelled as a particle. The diagram shows the weight and contact force if the car is treated as a particle.

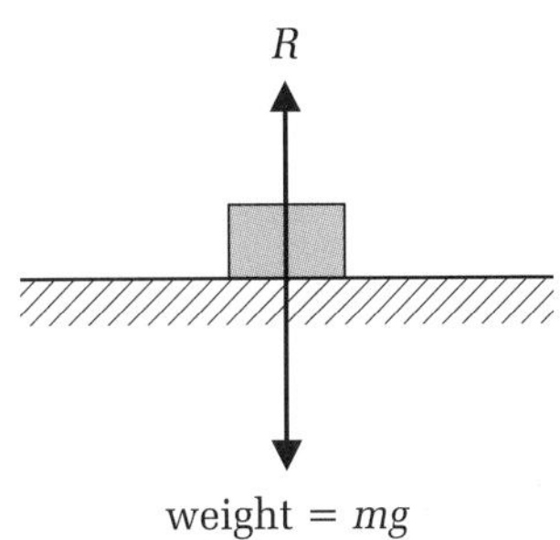

Friction

When a child goes down a slide, friction will oppose motion. The child can be modelled as a particle because the slide is much longer than the length of the child. The diagram shows the forces acting on the child.

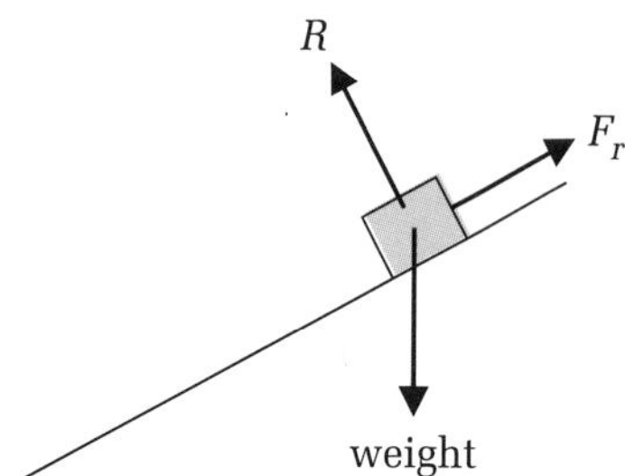

weight = mg
normal reaction = R
friction = F_r

F_r is used to represent friction. This avoids confusion since F will be used for a general force.

Friction will act parallel to the surfaces in contact.

If the slide is wet the child will not move down the slide. In this case, the water makes the clothing 'stick' to the slide and so the frictional force is increased. The frictional force is now big enough to prevent the child from moving down the slide. *When the slide is wet, the frictional force must be bigger.* Friction can still act even if there is no motion.

In other cases, water will reduce the frictional force. A car can slide on a wet road because the tyre is prevented from touching the road by a thin film of water.

Friction has a tendency to oppose motion at the point or surface of contact. Friction can prevent objects from moving, but without it most motions that we experience would be impossible. Try walking on a sheet of ice where there is little friction between your shoes and the ice.

Friction will be modelled in greater depth in Chapter 9. For the moment, you should be able to draw a frictional force on a diagram.

If surfaces are said to be **smooth** the frictional force can be ignored. If two surfaces are described as **rough** then a frictional force will act.

Friction and reaction forces

When an ordinary ladder is set up, it touches the floor and the wall. A diagram to model the situation is shown. Notice that there are *two* reaction forces because the ladder touches *two* surfaces. The diagram is drawn in 2D because the ladder is symmetrical and it is easier to draw.

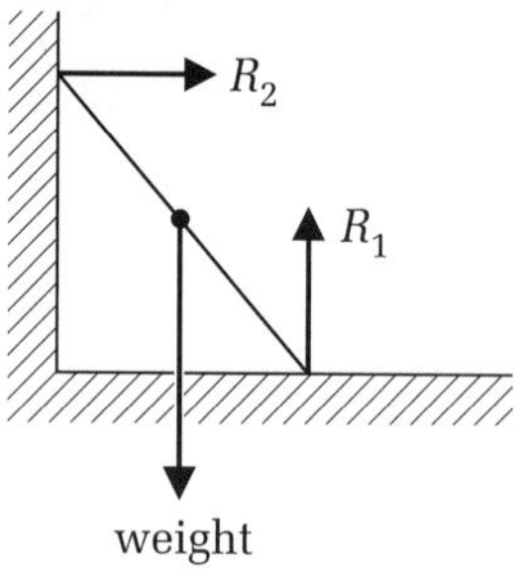

This diagram does not show all of the forces.

For a ladder resting against a window sill:

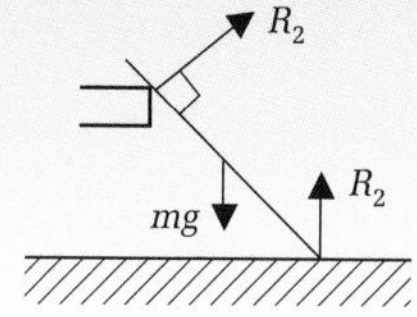

If the ladder slips, in which direction will it move? The surfaces between the ladder, the floor and the wall will be rough. Frictional forces will act to oppose motion. A complete diagram showing all the forces is drawn below.

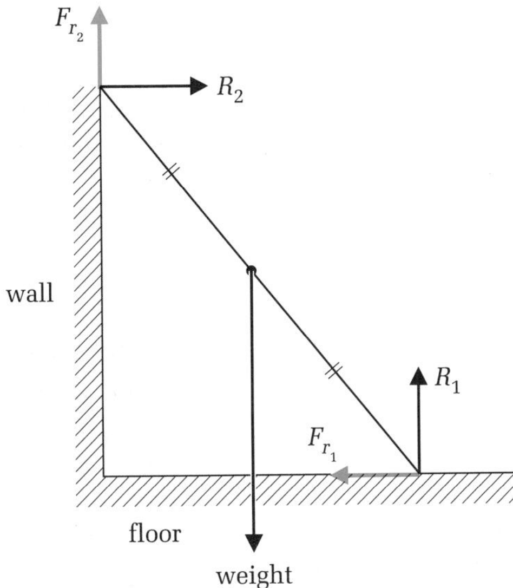

The ladder is assumed to be **uniform**. Uniform, in this situation, means the weight of the ladder can be assumed to act at its centre as shown. This centre point is called the **centre of mass**.

Centres of mass will be covered in Chapter 14.

Why do you think that ladders cannot be modelled as particles? The length and shape of the ladders are important when solving ladder problems. The distance between the points of action of the forces also matter.

Tension and thrust

A piece of string is tied to a conker and the other end of the string is held. How can this situation be represented? There must be a force preventing the conker from falling. The only thing in contact with the conker is the string. The string must be providing an upward force on the conker. This force is called a **tension**.

A string is normally assumed to be **light** and **inextensible**. Light means that the mass of the string is so small that it can be ignored. Inextensible means the string cannot be stretched.

If you held the conker like this for a very long time your arm would get tired. This is because your hand is being pulled down by the string.

Your arm is also supporting its own weight.

Notice that the tension in the string must act **inwards** towards the centre of the string from both ends. Tension occurs when the other forces are acting to try to **stretch** the string.

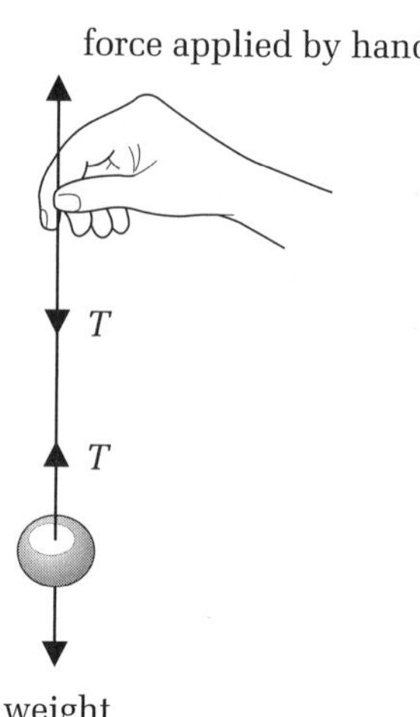

The weight of the bridge acts to compress the supports. The supports must produce a reaction. This reaction is called a **thrust**. Notice that the thrust in the supports acts **outwards** from the centre of the support towards the ends. Thrust occurs when the forces are acting to try to **compress** the support.

A string cannot resist compression. It will go slack and so a string cannot produce a thrust.

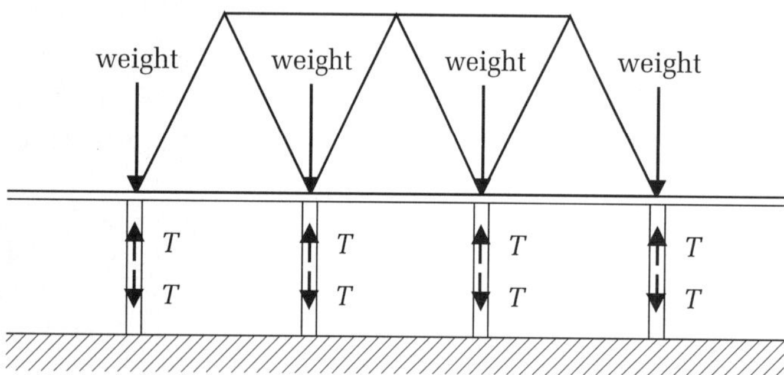

Air resistance

In 1992, Chris Boardman won Olympic gold in Barcelona. He used a specially designed bicycle and wore an aerodynamic helmet. These helped reduce the effect of air resistance. Air resistance is caused by the molecules in air hitting a moving object. This resistance opposes motion.

If a cyclist is modelled as a particle the forces acting are weight, normal reaction, air resistance and the cyclist's applied force.

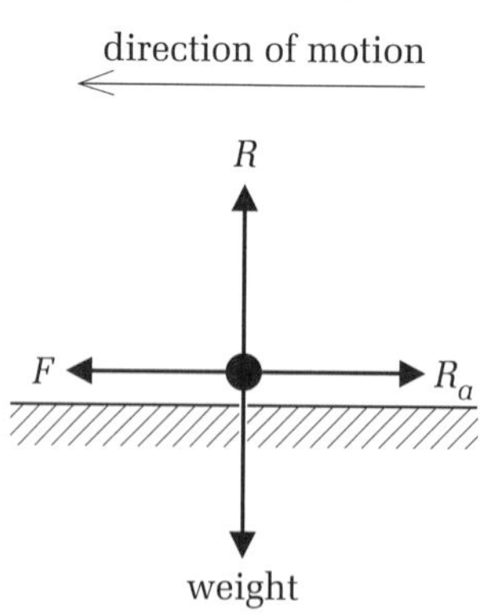

Notation

R = normal reaction

mg = weight

R_a = air resistance

F = force produced by cyclist

If the object is not moving then air resistance must be zero. This assumes that there is no wind. Two mathematical models for air resistance forces will be met later in this chapter.

Overview of method

The steps involved in drawing clear force diagrams are listed below.

Step ① Draw a clear 2D diagram of the situation.
Step ② Mark on the weight of the object.
Step ③ Mark on all **normal reactions**. These forces always act at right angles to the continuous surface. Mark on all other forces such as tension and friction.

Example 1

A car of mass 1000 kg is stationary on a horizontal driveway. Draw a diagram to represent the weight and normal reactions acting on the car.

Solution

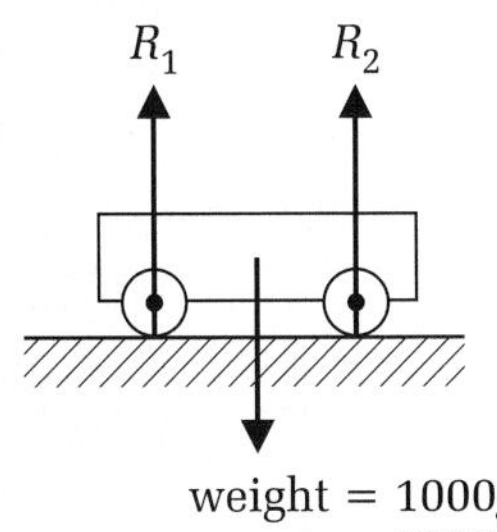

weight $= 1000g$
$= 9800$ N

◀ ① Diagram.
◀ ③ Normal reactions.
◀ ② Weight.

weight $= mg$
weight $= 1000 \times 9.8$
weight $= 9800$ N

Example 2

A book of mass 0.5 kg is placed on a table which is inclined at 10° to the horizontal. By treating the book as a particle draw a diagram showing the weight, normal reaction and friction.

Solution

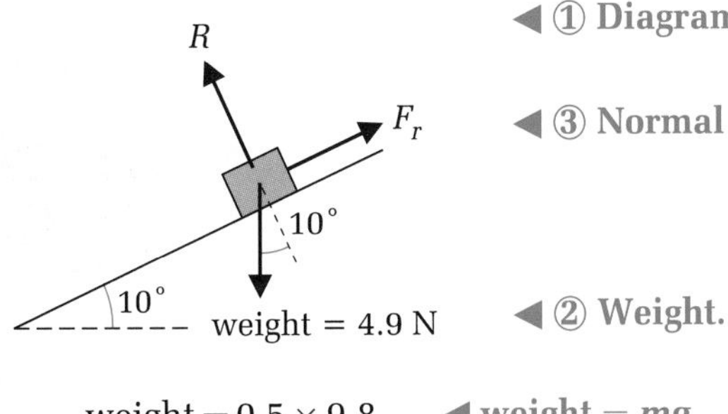

◀ ① Diagram.
◀ ③ Normal reaction and friction.
◀ ② Weight.

weight $= 0.5 \times 9.8$ ◀ weight $= mg$
weight $= 4.9$ N

Normal reaction acts at right angles to the table.
Friction prevents the book from sliding down the table.
The frictional force acts parallel to the table.

Example 3

A car is towing a caravan along a straight horizontal road. Air resistance can be neglected because the vehicles are travelling slowly. Mark on all the other forces acting on the car and caravan if:

a the vehicles are speeding up

b the vehicles are slowing down.

Solution

a

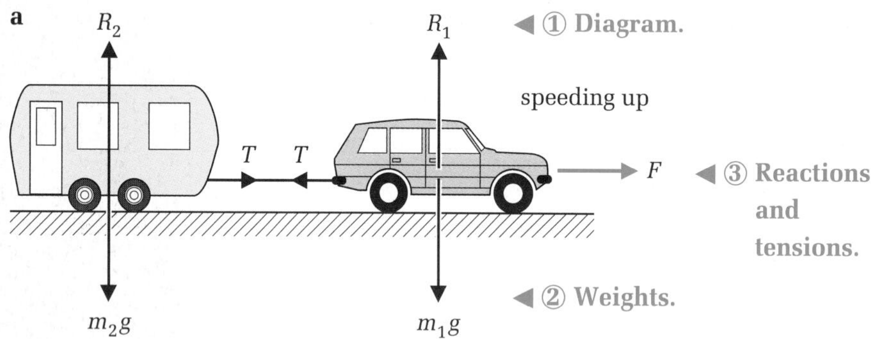

◀ ① Diagram.

◀ ③ Reactions and tensions.

◀ ② Weights.

The force in the towbar must be a tension. The caravan must be pulled to speed it up.

b

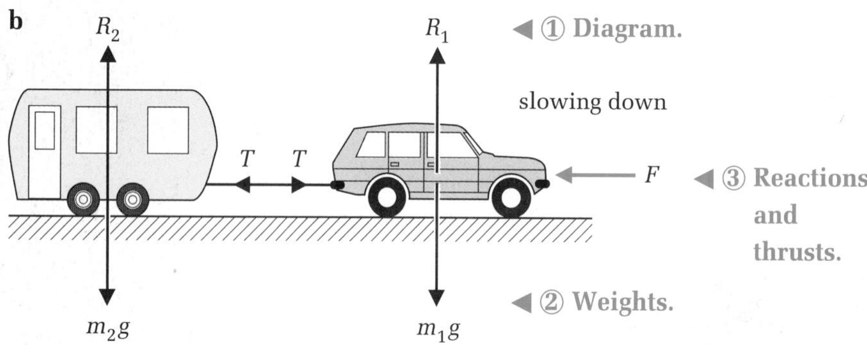

◀ ① Diagram.

◀ ③ Reactions and thrusts.

◀ ② Weights.

The caravan must be pushed to slow it down. The force in the towbar must be a thrust.

2.4 Contact Forces
Exercise

Contextual

1 For each of the following situations, draw a diagram showing all the forces:

a a lift supported by a cable
b a child sliding down a slide
c a crate resting on a horizontal floor
d a woman standing inside a lift supported by a cable.

2 **a**

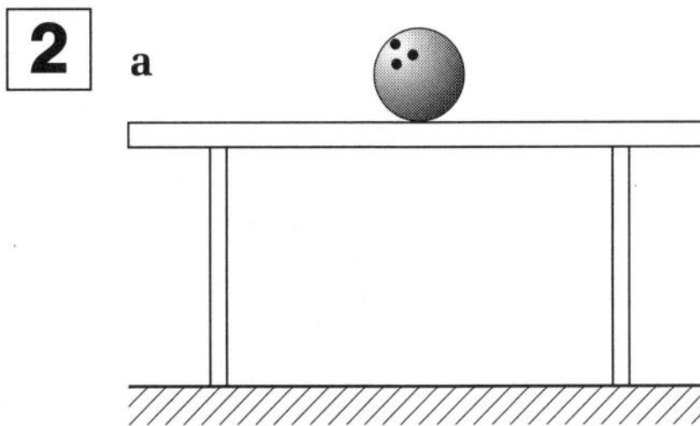

b

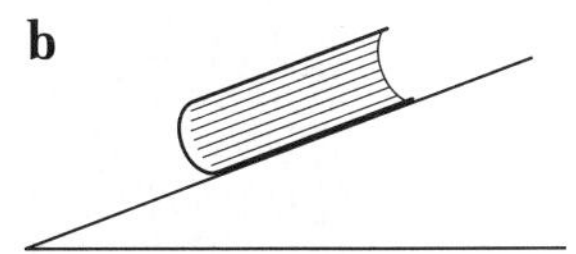

c

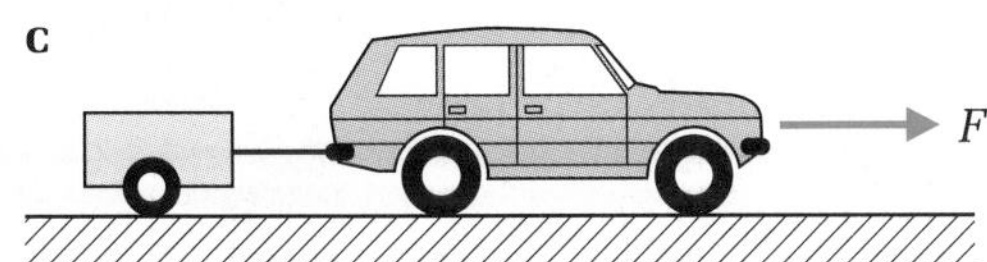

Copy each of the diagrams. Mark on all the forces.

3 A concrete sphere of mass 30 kg is placed on top of a pillar for decoration. Draw a diagram showing the forces acting on the sphere and pillar. Is the force in the pillar a thrust or a tension?

2.5 Modelling Resistance Forces

If you put your hand out of the sunroof of a moving car, what do you feel? If the car goes faster, what happens? If the car slows down, what happens? When you put your hand outside the car you feel the air pushing your hand backwards. If the car goes faster, the push you feel on your hand increases. When the car goes slower you feel the push on your hand decrease. These forces are all caused by air resistance. The air resistance must depend on the speed with which the object (in this case your hand) is travelling. The actual relationship between air resistance and speed is complicated. However, *as the speed increases, the air resistance increases.* The relationship between air resistance and speed can be assumed to be **proportional**.

The symbol for *directly proportional to* is $\propto$.

There are two models commonly used for air resistance.

1. Air resistance is proportional to speed. This can be written in symbols as $R_a \propto v$.
2. Air resistance is proportional to the speed squared. In symbols, this relationship is $R_a \propto v^2$.

$R_a =$ air resistance and $v =$ speed

The proportional symbol ($\propto$) can be replaced by an equals sign if a constant of proportion is introduced. This means:

$R_a \propto v$ becomes $R_a = k_1 v$

and $R_a \propto v^2$ becomes $R_a = k_2 v^2$

k_1 is a constant.

k_2 is another constant. This will be different from k_1.

You will normally be told which model to use. If you are not, then use $R_a \propto v$ for slow speeds and $R_a \propto v^2$ for high speeds.

These two resistance models can also be used when the object is moving in liquids and not in air.

Example 1

An object travelling at $10\,\text{m s}^{-1}$ experiences an air resistance force of 30 N. By modelling the resistance as proportional to speed, find an equation for the resistance.

Solution

$R_a \propto v$ ◀ Air resistance is proportional to speed.

$R_a = kv$

k is the constant of proportion.

$30 = k \times 10$

Divide by 10.

$k = 3$

$R_a = 3v$ ◀ Replace k in the equation.

Example 2

A particle travelling at $60\,\text{m s}^{-1}$ experiences a resistance force of 1800 N. The resistance varies with the square of the speed. Determine:

Varies means the same as changes proportionally.

a the model for resistance
b the resistance force if the particle travels at $100\,\text{m s}^{-1}$
c the speed when the resistance force is 1250 N.

Solution

a $R_a \propto v^2$ ◀ **Air resistance is proportional to speed squared.**

$R_a = kv^2$

Change into an equation.

$1800 = k \times (60)^2$

k is the constant of proportion.

$1800 = k \times 3600$

$k = 0.5$

Divide by 3600 to find *k*.

$R_a = 0.5v^2$ ◀ **Replace *k* in the equation.**

b $R_a = 0.5v^2$

$R_a = 0.5 \times (100)^2$

$R_a = 0.5 \times 10\,000$

$R_a = 5000\,\text{N}$

c $R_a = 0.5v^2$ ◀ **Use the equation for air resistance found in a.**

$1250 = 0.5 \times v^2$

Replace R_a by 1250.

$2500 = v^2$

Divide by 0.5.

$v = \pm 50$ ◀ **Remember ± sign.**

$v = 50\,\text{m s}^{-1}$

Take the square root to find the speed.

In this case, the positive square root is taken because the speed must be a positive number.

2.5 Modelling Resistance Forces

Exercise

Technique

1 A resistance force is proportional to speed. The resistance force is 200 N at a speed of 5 m s^{-1}. Determine:

a the equation for the resistance force
b the resistance when the speed is 7 m s^{-1}
c the speed when the resistance is 300 N.

2 A resistance force varies with the square of the speed. The resistance is 25 000 N at a speed of 50 m s^{-1}. Find:

a the equation which models the resistance force
b the speed when the resistance force is 36 000 N
c the resistance force when the speed is 35 m s^{-1}.

Contextual

1 A car travelling at 15 m s^{-1} experiences a force caused by air resistance of 2250 N.

a Give two possible models for the air resistance.
b Find the equations for these air resistance models.
c Which one is the better model to use at low speeds?

2 A ball bearing is dropped into a container full of oil. The ball bearing experiences a resistance force of 0.05 N when it is moving at 0.2 m s^{-1}. The resistance force varies with speed. Find:

a the equation to model the resistance force.
b the speed of the ball bearing if the resistance force is 0.1 N.
c the resistance force if the speed of the ball bearing is 1.5 m s^{-1}.

Applications and Activities

1 The unit of force is the newton, which is named after Sir Isaac Newton. Try to find out more about the life and works of this physicist, astronomer and mathematician. Produce a short report with your findings.

Summary

- A force can cause an object to speed up or slow down.
- A force can prevent an object from moving.
- A force can change the direction of motion of an object.
- Newton's universal law of gravitation states

$$F = \frac{Gm_1m_2}{d^2}$$

- An object of mass m has weight $= mg$, where g is the acceleration due to gravity ($g = 9.8\ \text{m s}^{-2}$).
- The two models for air resistance forces are

  1. Air resistance is proportional to speed

     $$R_a \propto v$$

     This is used when v is small.

  2. Air resistance is proportional to speed squared

     $$R_a \propto v^2$$

     This is used when v is large.

- Tension is caused by stretching and thrust is caused by compression.

3 Vectors I

What you need to know

- How to recognise and use angle properties of common shapes.
- How to simplify expressions given in surd form.
- How to use Pythagoras' theorem for right-angled triangles.
- How to use sine, cosine and tangent to solve right-angled triangles.
- How to plot points using Cartesian coordinates.

Review

1 **a**

State the size of angle x.

b

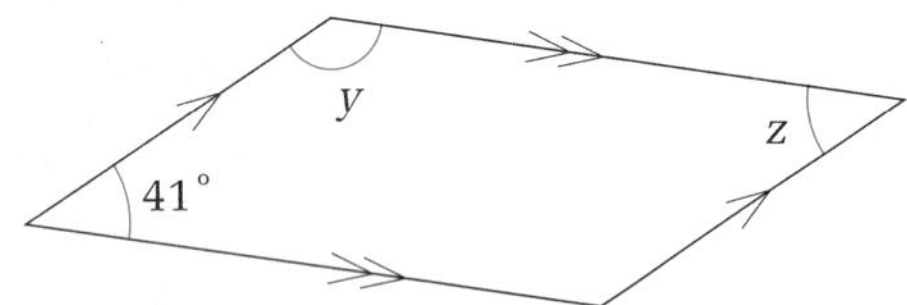

Name this quadrilateral and state the size of angles y and z.

c Two sides of a quadrilateral are known to be equal and parallel. Name the quadrilaterals it could be.

d For a regular hexagon, work out:
i the internal angle
ii the external angle.

2 **a** Write $\sqrt{50}$ in the form $a\sqrt{2}$.
b Simplify $\dfrac{8}{\sqrt{2}}$.
c Simplify $\sqrt{45}$.
d Express $6\sqrt{2}$ as a single surd.

3 **a**

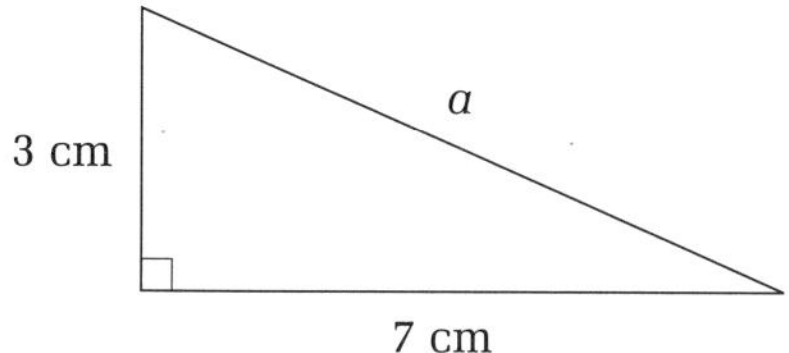

Give the length of a in surd form.

b

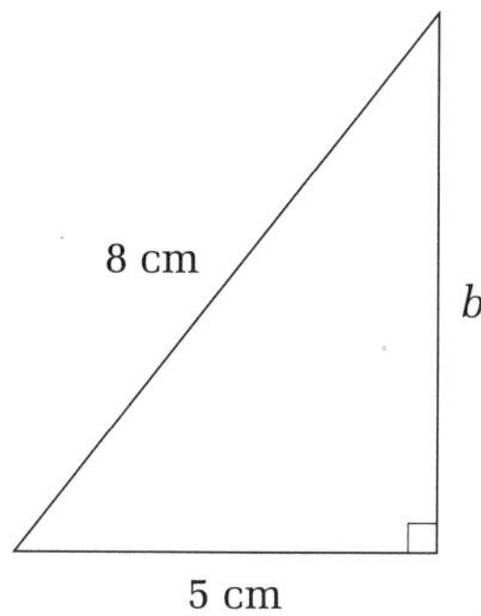

Calculate b to three significant figures.

4 **a**

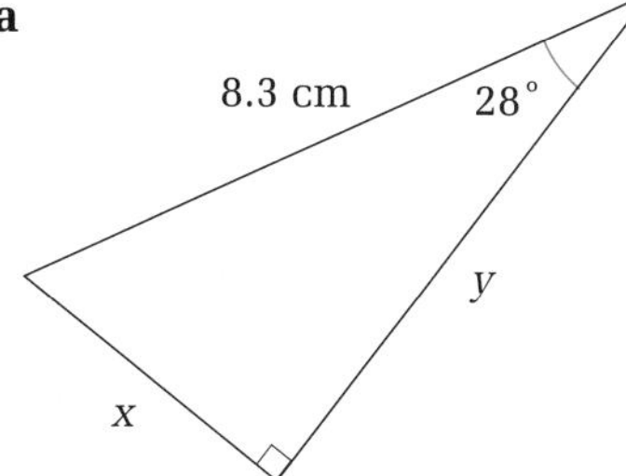

b

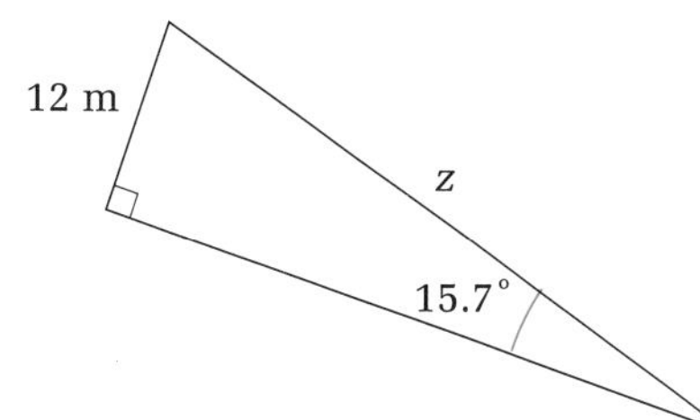

Calculate the missing sides, x, y and z, in the triangles given.

5 Draw axes such that $-3 \leq x \leq 4$ and $-2 \leq y \leq 4$.
Plot the triangle ABC where A is (3, 4), B is (−2, 1) and C is (1, −2).

a What is the area of triangle ABC?
b What is the midpoint of AB?
c What is the length of AC?

3.1 Scalars and Vectors

Some quantities can be described by a single number.

A mass of 15 kg

A time of 20 seconds

One piece of information is enough to describe them fully. These are called **scalar** quantities. Other quantities cannot be described by just one piece of information.

To tell someone how to get from Birmingham to Carlisle, one piece of information is not enough. To describe this fully, a **distance** and a **direction** are both required.

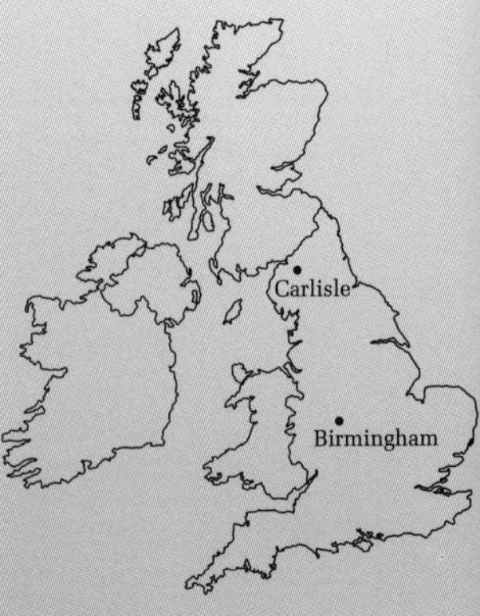

This diagram shows a speed of $10\,\text{m}\,\text{s}^{-1}$ on a bearing of 076°.

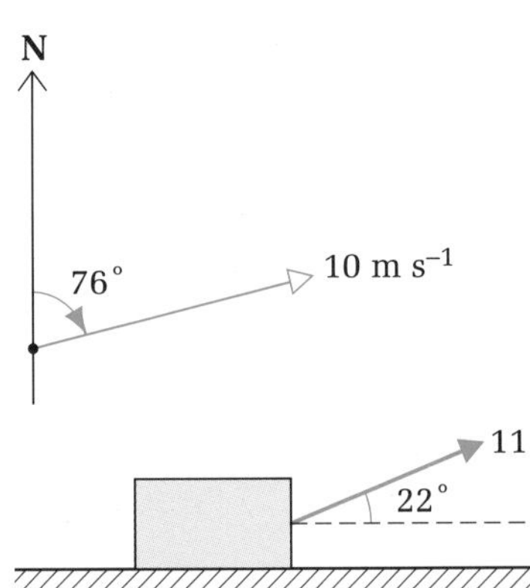

$\text{m}\,\text{s}^{-1}$ can be written as m/s and means 'metres per second'.

The force of 11 newtons acts to the right at an angle of 22° above the horizontal.

11 N

22°

To describe the above situations fully, both a **magnitude** and a **direction** have to be stated. These are known as **vector** quantities.

Magnitude is the size of something.

Displacement and velocity

If a person drives 3 km, then this is the **distance** driven. This is a **scalar** quantity. If the same person drives 3 km due west, these *two* pieces of information can be put together to make a **vector** quantity. This vector quantity is called **displacement**.

When the displacement is stated relative to a fixed origin, it is known as a **position vector**.

Due west means travelling towards the west.
Displacement means a distance in a specified direction.
Displacement is only the same as distance when the motion is always in the same direction with respect to an origin.

Consider an aeroplane travelling at 300 km h^{-1} on a bearing of 215°. Taken together, this information is the **velocity** of the aircraft. Velocity is a vector quantity because it has a **magnitude** and **direction**.

km h^{-1} is the index notation for km/h or 'kilometres per hour'.

Velocity is an example of a **free vector**. The velocity vector is not tied to a specific place in space. It is true of the aircraft, wherever it is, as long as it travels at this velocity.

Velocity is defined as speed in a specified direction.

The **magnitude** of the velocity of the aircraft would be 300 km h^{-1}. This is the same as the **speed** of the aircraft. Speed is a **scalar** quantity.

Alternatively, velocity can be defined as the rate of change of displacement.

Column vectors

A woman walks 400 m due east and then 300 m due north around a park. How could this displacement be represented? The woman will be treated as a particle. This means the size of the woman can be neglected. This is a reasonable assumption because the size of the woman will be small compared to the distances she has walked.

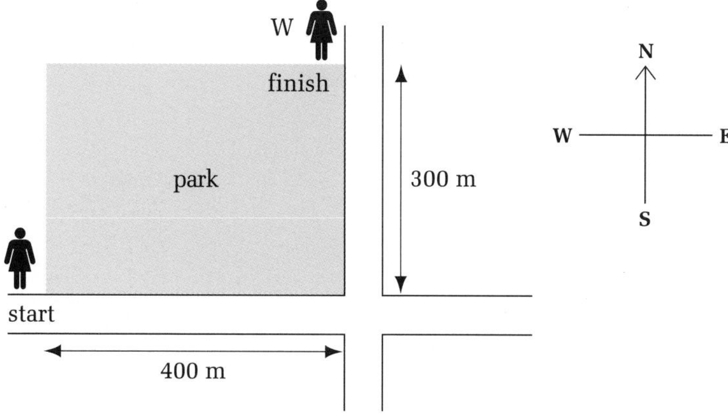

One way of representing this displacement is to use a coordinate system. The point W is the final position of the woman.

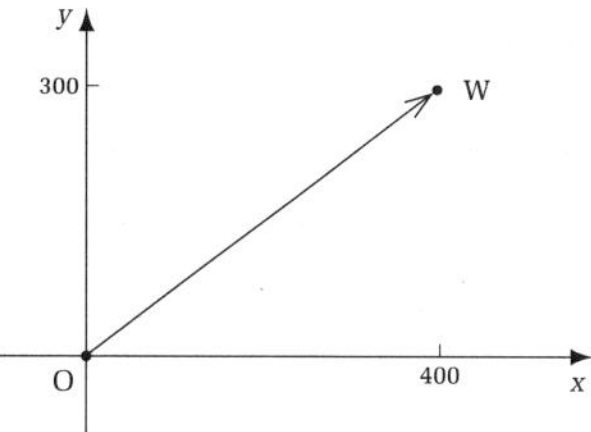

The arrow represents the position vector of the woman at W.

When the woman is at W, her **position vector** can be stated as a **column vector**:

$$\begin{pmatrix} 400 \\ 300 \end{pmatrix} \text{ m}$$

The units are written outside the brackets.

Notice that the x component is given first and the y component is written underneath. The top number indicates the distance in the easterly direction and the bottom number is the distance in the northerly direction.

Unit vectors

Another way of writing vectors is to use the letters **i** and **j** to represent vectors parallel to the axes.

$$\mathbf{i} = \begin{pmatrix} 1 \\ 0 \end{pmatrix} \qquad \mathbf{j} = \begin{pmatrix} 0 \\ 1 \end{pmatrix}$$

When letters are written in bold type, it means that they represent vector quantities. You should write them as $\underline{i}$ and $\underline{j}$. This is because underlining a letter is much easier than writing it in **bold**.

i can be considered as *one step* in the *x*-direction and **j** as *one step* in the *y*-direction. This means that both these vectors have a magnitude of **one**. This is the reason they are called **unit vectors**.

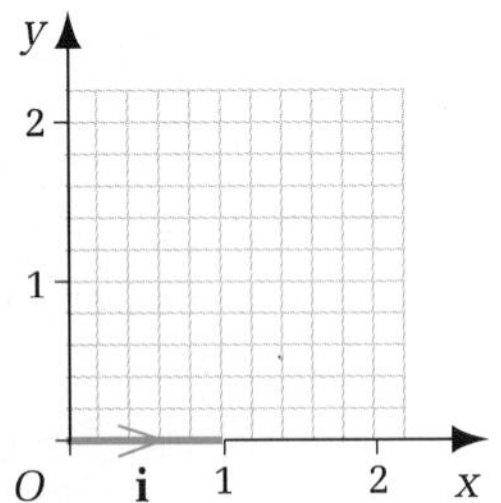

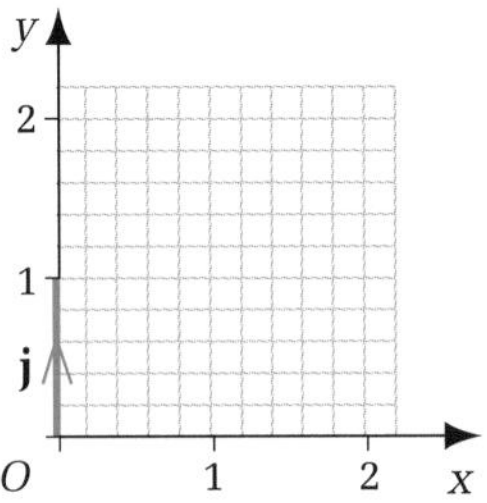

The position vector of the woman at W could be given as:

$(400\mathbf{i} + 300\mathbf{j})$ m

Units are written after the bracket.

Vectors in three dimensions

Both column and unit vectors can be used to represent three dimensional quantities. The diagram shows the directions of the unit vectors. Notice that the three vectors are at right angles to each other. The vectors are said to be **perpendicular** vectors.

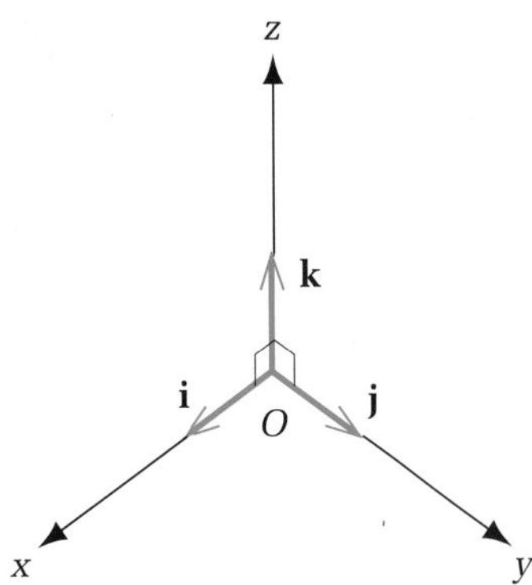

In three dimensions, the unit vectors are:

$$\mathbf{i} = \begin{pmatrix} 1 \\ 0 \\ 0 \end{pmatrix}, \qquad \mathbf{j} = \begin{pmatrix} 0 \\ 1 \\ 0 \end{pmatrix}, \qquad \mathbf{k} = \begin{pmatrix} 0 \\ 0 \\ 1 \end{pmatrix}$$

So the vector **k** is one step in the *z*-direction.

Example 1

Change the column vectors into unit vector form.

Unit vector form is also called **component** form.

a $\begin{pmatrix} 5 \\ 8 \end{pmatrix}$

b $\begin{pmatrix} -6 \\ 7 \\ 2 \end{pmatrix}$

Solution

a $\begin{pmatrix} 5 \\ 8 \end{pmatrix} = 5\mathbf{i} + 8\mathbf{j}$

b $\begin{pmatrix} -6 \\ 7 \\ 2 \end{pmatrix} = -6\mathbf{i} + 7\mathbf{j} + 2\mathbf{k}$

It is therefore quite straightforward to change a column vector into unit vector form and vice versa.

Example 2

Draw the following position vectors:

Remember *position vectors* start from the origin.

$$\mathbf{p} = \begin{pmatrix} 2 \\ 1 \\ 3 \end{pmatrix} \quad \mathbf{q} = \begin{pmatrix} -2 \\ 0 \\ -3 \end{pmatrix}$$

Solution

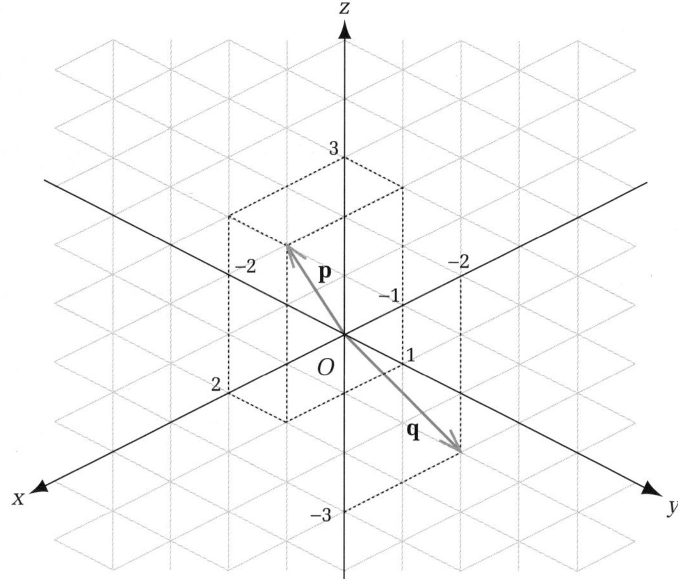

3.1 Scalars and Vectors
Exercise

Technique

1 Draw an arrow on a grid to represent each of the following vectors:

$\mathbf{a} = \begin{pmatrix} 3 \\ 7 \end{pmatrix}$ $\qquad$ $\mathbf{b} = \begin{pmatrix} 5 \\ -12 \end{pmatrix}$

2 Draw an arrow on a grid to represent each of the following position vectors:

$\mathbf{a} = 11\mathbf{i} + 3\mathbf{j}$ $\qquad$ $\mathbf{b} = -11\mathbf{i} - 13\mathbf{j}$ $\qquad$ $\mathbf{c} = -7\mathbf{j}$.

3 Represent the following three dimensional position vectors on isometric dotted paper:

$\mathbf{a} = 2\mathbf{i} - 8\mathbf{j} - \mathbf{k}$ $\qquad$ $\mathbf{b} = \begin{pmatrix} -2 \\ -4 \\ -5 \end{pmatrix}$

4 Convert the following vectors into unit vector form:

$\mathbf{a} = \begin{pmatrix} -7 \\ -4 \end{pmatrix}$ $\qquad$ $\mathbf{b} = \begin{pmatrix} -3 \\ -2 \\ -4 \end{pmatrix}$

5 Convert the following vectors into column vector form:

$\mathbf{a} = 11\mathbf{i} + 3\mathbf{j}$ $\qquad$ $\mathbf{b} = 5\mathbf{i} - 17\mathbf{j}$ $\qquad$ $\mathbf{c} = -7\mathbf{j}$ $\qquad$ $\mathbf{d} = 6\mathbf{i} - 11\mathbf{j} + 7\mathbf{k}$

Contextual

1 $\mathbf{a} = (6\mathbf{i} + 10\mathbf{j})$ km $\qquad$ $\mathbf{b} = (-2\mathbf{i} - 5\mathbf{j})$ km

The vectors given are in unit vector form, where **i** is a unit vector due east and **j** is a unit vector due north. Convert each displacement vector into column vector form.

2 $\mathbf{a} = \begin{pmatrix} 18 \\ 12 \end{pmatrix}$ m $\qquad$ $\mathbf{b} = \begin{pmatrix} -7 \\ 2 \end{pmatrix}$ km

Convert each displacement vector into unit vector form.

3.2 Addition, Subtraction and Scalar Multiplication of Vectors

To add or subtract column vectors the corresponding x and y components are added or subtracted.

Addition: $\begin{pmatrix} x_1 \\ y_1 \end{pmatrix} + \begin{pmatrix} x_2 \\ y_2 \end{pmatrix} = \begin{pmatrix} x_1 + x_2 \\ y_1 + y_2 \end{pmatrix}$

Subtraction: $\begin{pmatrix} x_1 \\ y_1 \end{pmatrix} - \begin{pmatrix} x_2 \\ y_2 \end{pmatrix} = \begin{pmatrix} x_1 - x_2 \\ y_1 - y_2 \end{pmatrix}$

Vectors written in unit vector form follow a similar approach.

Addition: $(a_1\mathbf{i} + b_1\mathbf{j}) + (a_2\mathbf{i} + b_2\mathbf{j}) = (a_1 + a_2)\mathbf{i} + (b_1 + b_2)\mathbf{j}$

Subtraction: $(a_1\mathbf{i} + b_1\mathbf{j}) - (a_2\mathbf{i} + b_2\mathbf{j}) = (a_1 - a_2)\mathbf{i} + (b_1 - b_2)\mathbf{j}$

Multiplication of unit and column vectors by a scalar follows the rules for multiplication of brackets.

A scalar is just a number not a vector.

$$c\begin{pmatrix} x_1 \\ y_1 \end{pmatrix} = \begin{pmatrix} cx_1 \\ cy_1 \end{pmatrix}$$

$d(a\mathbf{i} + b\mathbf{j}) = ad\mathbf{i} + bd\mathbf{j}$ ◀ **Expand the brackets.**

Example 1

$\mathbf{a} = \begin{pmatrix} 7 \\ 1 \end{pmatrix}$ and $\mathbf{b} = \begin{pmatrix} 2 \\ -3 \end{pmatrix}$

Work out $\mathbf{a} + \mathbf{b}$ and $\mathbf{a} - \mathbf{b}$.

Solution

$$\begin{aligned} \mathbf{a} + \mathbf{b} &= \begin{pmatrix} 7 \\ 1 \end{pmatrix} + \begin{pmatrix} 2 \\ -3 \end{pmatrix} \\ &= \begin{pmatrix} 7 + 2 \\ 1 + (-3) \end{pmatrix} \\ &= \begin{pmatrix} 9 \\ -2 \end{pmatrix} \end{aligned}$$

$$\begin{aligned} \mathbf{a} - \mathbf{b} &= \begin{pmatrix} 7 \\ 1 \end{pmatrix} - \begin{pmatrix} 2 \\ -3 \end{pmatrix} \\ &= \begin{pmatrix} 7 - 2 \\ 1 - (-3) \end{pmatrix} \\ &= \begin{pmatrix} 5 \\ 4 \end{pmatrix} \end{aligned}$$

Example 2

If $\mathbf{p} = \begin{pmatrix} 1 \\ 7 \end{pmatrix}$ and $\mathbf{q} = \begin{pmatrix} -1 \\ -7 \end{pmatrix}$, find $\mathbf{p} + \mathbf{q}$.

Solution

$$\mathbf{p} + \mathbf{q} = \begin{pmatrix} 1 \\ 7 \end{pmatrix} + \begin{pmatrix} -1 \\ -7 \end{pmatrix}$$

$$= \begin{pmatrix} 0 \\ 0 \end{pmatrix} \text{ or } \mathbf{0}$$

The zero vector is written $\mathbf{0}$ and is the vector whose components are all zero.

In 3D, $\mathbf{0} = \begin{pmatrix} 0 \\ 0 \\ 0 \end{pmatrix}$

Example 3

If $\mathbf{a} = 2\mathbf{i} - 4\mathbf{j}$, write down $6\mathbf{a}$, $12\mathbf{a}$ and $-\frac{7}{2}\mathbf{a}$.

Solution

$$6\mathbf{a} = 6(2\mathbf{i} - 4\mathbf{j}) = 12\mathbf{i} - 24\mathbf{j}$$

$$12\mathbf{a} = 12(2\mathbf{i} - 4\mathbf{j}) = 24\mathbf{i} - 48\mathbf{j}$$

$$-\frac{7}{2}\mathbf{a} = -\frac{7}{2}(2\mathbf{i} - 4\mathbf{j}) = -7\mathbf{i} + 14\mathbf{j}$$

Example 4

$\mathbf{a} = 5\mathbf{i} - 10\mathbf{j} + 3\mathbf{k}$ and $\mathbf{b} = 7\mathbf{i} - 3\mathbf{j} - \mathbf{k}$. Work out $\mathbf{a} + \mathbf{b}$, $\mathbf{a} - \mathbf{b}$ and $2\mathbf{a} - 3\mathbf{b}$.

Solution

Vectors with three components obey the same rules of addition and subtraction as vectors with two components. So corresponding components are added or subtracted.

$$\mathbf{a} + \mathbf{b} = (5\mathbf{i} - 10\mathbf{j} + 3\mathbf{k}) + (7\mathbf{i} - 3\mathbf{j} - \mathbf{k})$$
$$= 5\mathbf{i} + 7\mathbf{i} - 10\mathbf{j} - 3\mathbf{j} + 3\mathbf{k} - \mathbf{k}$$
$$= 12\mathbf{i} - 13\mathbf{j} + 2\mathbf{k}$$

$$\mathbf{a} - \mathbf{b} = (5\mathbf{i} - 10\mathbf{j} + 3\mathbf{k}) - (7\mathbf{i} - 3\mathbf{j} - \mathbf{k})$$
$$= 5\mathbf{i} - 7\mathbf{i} - 10\mathbf{j} + 3\mathbf{j} + 3\mathbf{k} + \mathbf{k}$$
$$= -2\mathbf{i} - 7\mathbf{j} + 4\mathbf{k}$$

$$2\mathbf{a} - 3\mathbf{b} = 2(5\mathbf{i} - 10\mathbf{j} + 3\mathbf{k}) - 3(7\mathbf{i} - 3\mathbf{j} - \mathbf{k})$$
$$= 10\mathbf{i} - 20\mathbf{j} + 6\mathbf{k} - 21\mathbf{i} + 9\mathbf{j} + 3\mathbf{k}$$
$$= 10\mathbf{i} - 21\mathbf{i} - 20\mathbf{j} + 9\mathbf{j} + 6\mathbf{k} + 3\mathbf{k}$$
$$= -11\mathbf{i} - 11\mathbf{j} + 9\mathbf{k}$$

Multiplying by a constant means each component is multiplied by that number.

3.2 Addition, Subtraction and Scalar Multiplication of Vectors

Exercise

Technique

1 $\mathbf{a} = \begin{pmatrix} 3 \\ 7 \end{pmatrix}$ $\mathbf{b} = \begin{pmatrix} -11 \\ 0 \end{pmatrix}$ $\mathbf{c} = \begin{pmatrix} -2 \\ -9 \end{pmatrix}$ $\mathbf{d} = \begin{pmatrix} 5 \\ -12 \end{pmatrix}$

Find:

a $\mathbf{a} + \mathbf{b}$ b $\mathbf{c} - \mathbf{a}$ c $\mathbf{d} - \mathbf{a}$

2 $\mathbf{a} = 11\mathbf{i} + 3\mathbf{j}$ $\mathbf{b} = -2\mathbf{i} + 0.3\mathbf{j}$ $\mathbf{c} = 5\mathbf{i} - 17\mathbf{j}$
$\mathbf{d} = -11\mathbf{i} - 13\mathbf{j}$ $\mathbf{e} = -7\mathbf{j}$

Determine:

a $\mathbf{a} + \mathbf{e}$ b $\mathbf{d} - \mathbf{b}$ c $\mathbf{c} + \mathbf{a}$

3 $\mathbf{r} = \begin{pmatrix} 2 \\ 3 \end{pmatrix}$

a Write down the following vectors in column vector form:
$2\mathbf{r}$ $3\mathbf{r}$ $5\mathbf{r}$ $\frac{1}{2}\mathbf{r}$ $-\mathbf{r}$ $-2\mathbf{r}$

b Show these vectors on a sketch.

c What do you notice about all of these vectors?

4 $\mathbf{s} = -4\mathbf{i} + 8\mathbf{j}$

Write down:

a $2\mathbf{s}$ b $10\mathbf{s}$ c $-\frac{1}{2}\mathbf{s}$ d $-25\mathbf{s}$

5 $\mathbf{p} = 2\mathbf{i} - 8\mathbf{j} - \mathbf{k}$
$\mathbf{q} = 6\mathbf{i} - 11\mathbf{j} + 7\mathbf{k}$
$\mathbf{r} = -9\mathbf{i} + \mathbf{j} + 3\mathbf{k}$

$\mathbf{s} = \begin{pmatrix} -7 \\ 0 \\ -9 \end{pmatrix}$ $\mathbf{t} = \begin{pmatrix} 6 \\ 1 \\ -2 \end{pmatrix}$ $\mathbf{u} = \begin{pmatrix} -1 \\ -1 \\ 10 \end{pmatrix}$

Determine:

a i $-4\mathbf{r}$ ii $2\mathbf{p} - 3\mathbf{r}$ iii $5\mathbf{q} + 2\mathbf{r}$

b i $10\mathbf{u}$ ii $4\mathbf{t} + 2\mathbf{u}$ iii $10\mathbf{u} - 12\mathbf{s}$

3.3 Magnitude and Direction of Vectors

An alternative way of describing a vector is to state its length and its direction.

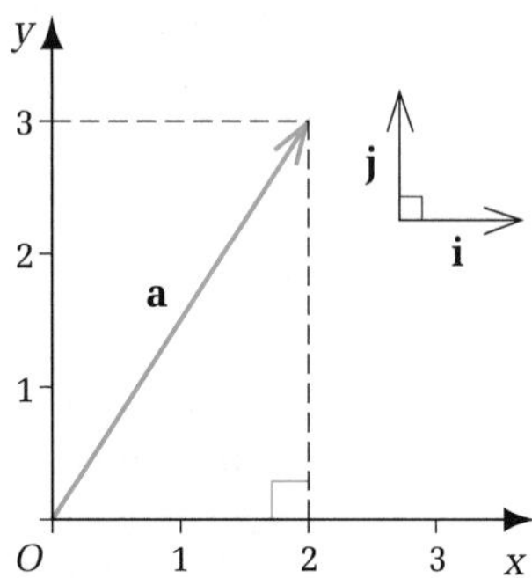

The vector $\mathbf{a} = 2\mathbf{i} + 3\mathbf{j}$ can be represented as shown. The length of the vector is called its **magnitude**. The magnitude of vector **a** can be written as either $|\mathbf{a}|$ or a. The magnitude of the vector **a** can be calculated using Pythagoras' theorem.

$|\mathbf{a}|^2 = 2^2 + 3^2$ — Pythagoras' theorem.

$|\mathbf{a}| = \sqrt{2^2 + 3^2}$ — Square root.

$|\mathbf{a}| = \sqrt{4 + 9}$ — $2^2 = 4$ and $3^2 = 9$

$|\mathbf{a}| = \sqrt{13}$

$|\mathbf{a}| = 3.61$ (3 s.f.) or $a = 3.61$

Notation
$|\mathbf{a}|$ = magnitude (or size) of a vector **a**.
a = magnitude or size of the vector **a**.

The direction of the vector can be found by using trigonometry.

$$\tan\theta = \frac{\text{opp}}{\text{adj}}$$

$$\tan\theta = \tfrac{3}{2}$$

$$\theta = \tan^{-1}\left(\tfrac{3}{2}\right)$$

or $\arctan\left(\tfrac{3}{2}\right)$

$$\theta = 56.3^\circ \text{ (1 d.p.)}$$

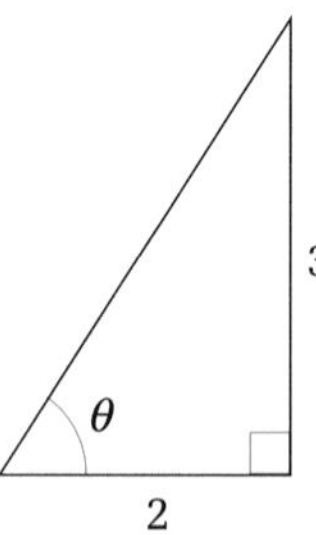

Vector **a** has a magnitude of 3.61 and its direction is 56.3° measured anticlockwise from the **i** direction.

Overview of method

To convert column vector form or unit vector form into a magnitude and direction use these three steps.

Step ① Always draw a diagram.
Step ② Use Pythagoras' theorem to find the magnitude.
Step ③ Use the inverse tangent to calculate the angle.

Example 1

Work out the magnitude and direction of $\begin{pmatrix} -5 \\ 2 \end{pmatrix}$.

Solution

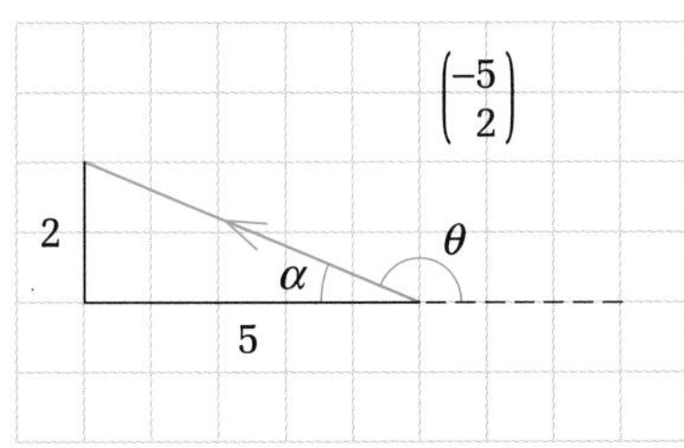

◀ ① Diagram.

Make sure your initial sketch is reasonable.

$$\text{hyp}^2 = 5^2 + 2^2$$

◀ ② Use Pythagoras' theorem.

$$\text{hyp}^2 = 25 + 4$$

Square root.

$$\text{hyp} = \sqrt{29}$$

$$\text{magnitude} = 5.39 \text{ (3 s.f.)}$$

$$\tan \alpha = \tfrac{2}{5}$$

$$\alpha = \tan^{-1}\left(\tfrac{2}{5}\right)$$

◀ ③ Use inverse tangent to calculate the angle.

or $\alpha = \arctan\left(\frac{2}{5}\right)$

$$\alpha = 21.8°$$

$$\theta = 180° - 21.8°$$

Angles on a straight line add up to 180°.

$$\theta = 158.2° \text{ (1 d.p.)}$$

Check: The angle θ looks as if it should be obtuse on the initial sketch above.

It is the convention to give the direction of a vector on the x–y plane as the angle it makes with the positive direction of the x-axis. This is positive when measured anticlockwise and negative when clockwise.

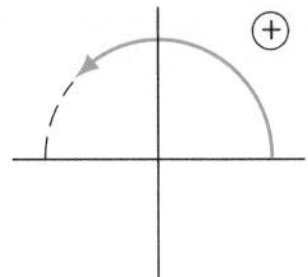

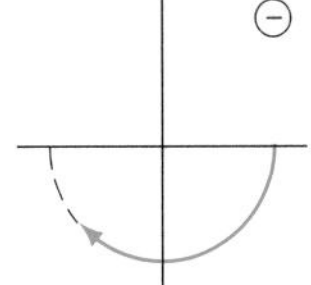

Example 2

If the position vector $\mathbf{b} = 11\mathbf{i} + 4\mathbf{j}$, what is b^2?

Solution

$$\mathbf{b} = 11\mathbf{i} + 4\mathbf{j}$$

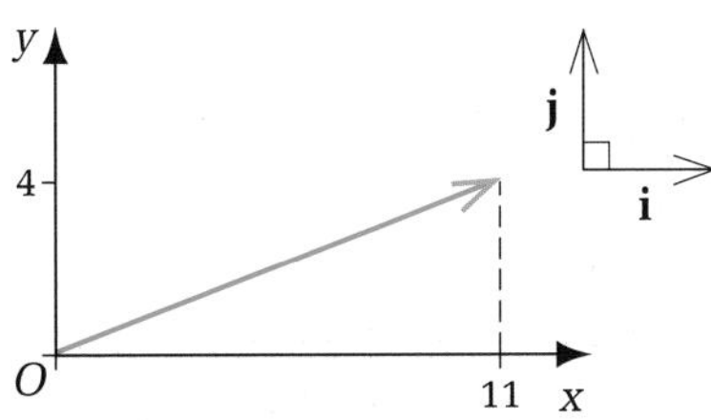

◀ ① Diagram.

$$|\mathbf{b}| = \sqrt{11^2 + 4^2}$$

◀ ② Use Pythagoras' theorem.

$$b = \sqrt{137}$$

$$b^2 = 137$$

b is the magnitude of vector $\mathbf{b}$.

Example 3

If $\mathbf{d} = a\mathbf{i} + b\mathbf{j} + c\mathbf{k}$ then find $|\mathbf{d}|$ and the angle it makes with the $\mathbf{i}$, $\mathbf{j}$ plane.

Solution

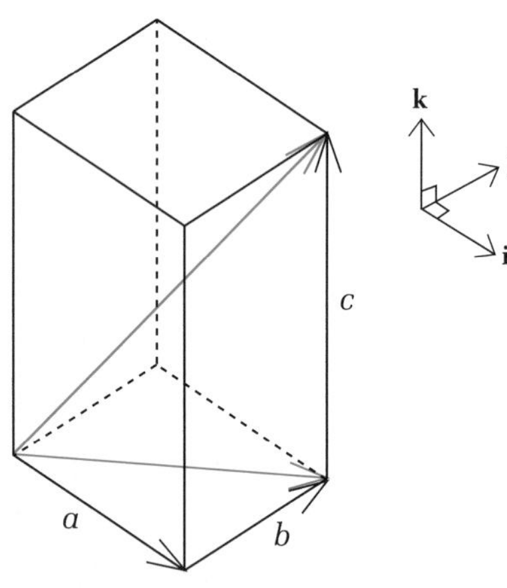

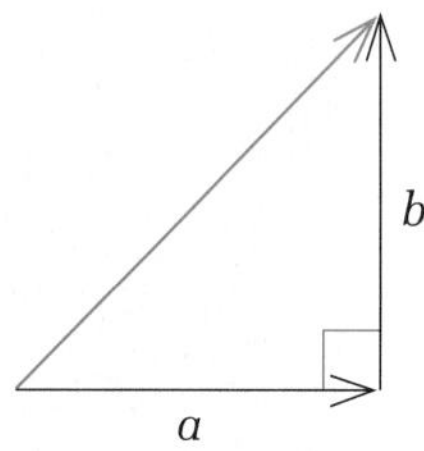

◀ ① Diagram.

This triangle is part of the horizontal base (of the cuboid above).

magnitude $= \sqrt{a^2 + b^2}$

◀ ② Pythagoras' theorem.

$$|\mathbf{d}| = \sqrt{\left(\sqrt{a^2 + b^2}\right)^2 + c^2}$$

$$|\mathbf{d}| = \sqrt{a^2 + b^2 + c^2}$$

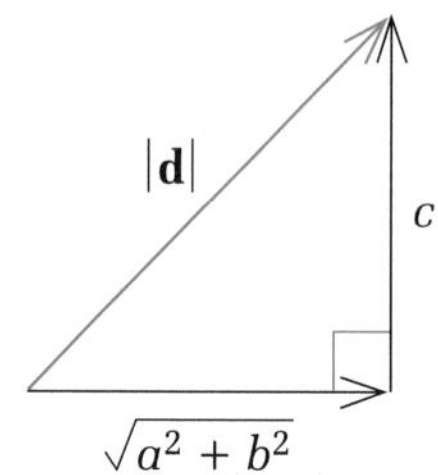

Really a version of Pythagoras in 3D.

▼ ③ Use inverse tangent to find the angle.

$$\tan\theta = \frac{c}{\sqrt{a^2 + b^2}}$$

$$\theta = \tan^{-1}\left(\frac{c}{\sqrt{a^2 + b^2}}\right)$$

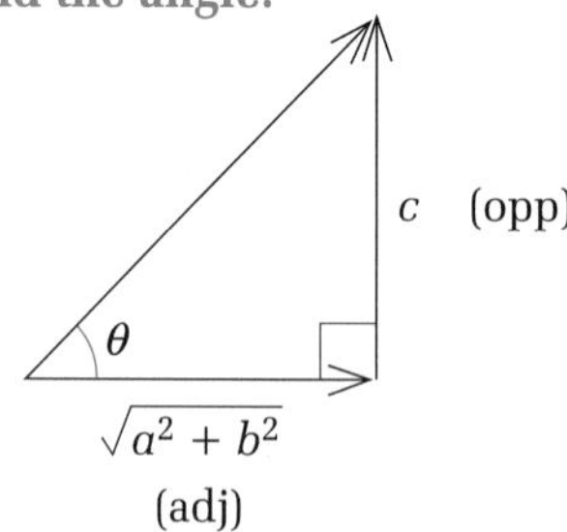

or $\theta = \arctan\left(\frac{c}{\sqrt{a^2+b^2}}\right)$

3.3 Magnitude and Direction of Vectors

Exercise

Technique

1 Find the magnitude and direction of each of the following vectors:

$$\mathbf{p} = \begin{pmatrix} 16.5 \\ -11.2 \end{pmatrix} \quad \mathbf{q} = \begin{pmatrix} 0 \\ -13.7 \end{pmatrix} \quad \mathbf{r} = \begin{pmatrix} -3.05 \\ 21.2 \end{pmatrix}$$

$$\mathbf{s} = \begin{pmatrix} 6.3 \\ 19.1 \end{pmatrix} \quad \mathbf{t} = \begin{pmatrix} -2.1 \\ -11.8 \end{pmatrix} \quad \mathbf{u} = \begin{pmatrix} 0.87 \\ 0.16 \end{pmatrix}$$

2 Calculate the magnitude of each of these vectors, and the angle it makes with the vector $\mathbf{i}$:

$\mathbf{a} = 12\mathbf{i} + 6\sqrt{2}\mathbf{j}$ $\quad \mathbf{b} = \sqrt{32}\mathbf{i} - \sqrt{32}\mathbf{j}$ $\quad \mathbf{c} = -0.06\mathbf{i} - 0.32\mathbf{j}$
$\mathbf{d} = 629\mathbf{i} + 31\mathbf{j}$ $\quad \mathbf{e} = -8.2\mathbf{i}$

3 $\mathbf{c} = 3\mathbf{i} + 4\mathbf{j} - 9\mathbf{k}$ and $\mathbf{d} = -2\mathbf{i} - 6\mathbf{j} + 10\mathbf{k}$

Work out:

a $|\mathbf{c}|$ **b** $|\mathbf{d}|$ **c** $|(\mathbf{c} + \mathbf{d})|$

Contextual

1 Calculate the length and bearing of each of these displacement vectors:

a 6.3 km due east, 5 km due south
b 1.4 km due east, 4.2 km due north
c 10.2 km due west, 2.7 km due north.

2 Calculate the magnitude and bearing of each of these displacements given in column vector form.

$$\mathbf{a} = \begin{pmatrix} 18 \\ 12 \end{pmatrix}\text{m} \quad \mathbf{b} = \begin{pmatrix} 35 \\ -84 \end{pmatrix}\text{km} \quad \mathbf{c} = \begin{pmatrix} -6\sqrt{2} \\ -6\sqrt{2} \end{pmatrix}\text{m}$$

3 Five forces are defined as follows:

$\mathbf{F}_1 = 26\mathbf{i}\,\text{N}$ $\quad \mathbf{F}_2 = (2\mathbf{i} + 38\mathbf{j})\,\text{N}$ $\quad \mathbf{F}_3 = (-12\mathbf{i} - 18\mathbf{j})\,\text{N}$
$\mathbf{F}_4 = (-16\mathbf{i} + 3\mathbf{j})\,\text{N}$ $\quad \mathbf{F}_5 = -21\mathbf{j}\,\text{N}$

Calculate the magnitude of each force.
For the forces $\mathbf{F}_2$ to $\mathbf{F}_5$ state the angle they make with $\mathbf{F}_1$, measured anticlockwise.

3.4 Parallel Vectors

When any vector is multiplied by a scalar, a vector parallel to the original vector is formed. This means $3\mathbf{a}$ will be *three* times as long as the vector $\mathbf{a}$. This provides a formula for parallel vectors.

The number in front of $\mathbf{a}$ is the length scale factor.

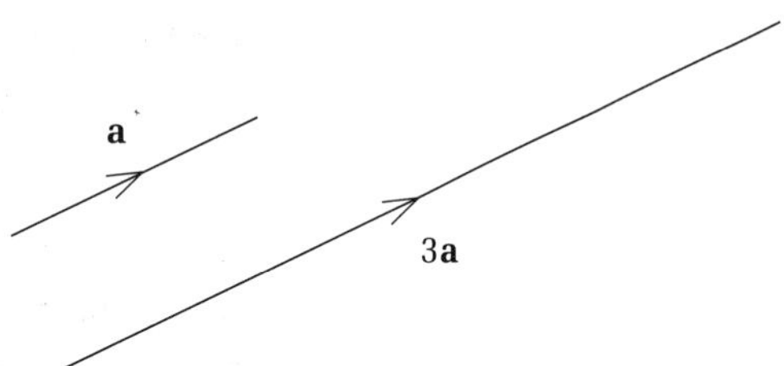

If $\mathbf{b} = k\mathbf{a}$ then $\mathbf{b}$ and $\mathbf{a}$ are parallel vectors.

Notation
$\mathbf{a}$ and $\mathbf{b}$ are vectors.
k is just a number (scalar).

Unit vector

Two vectors which are parallel must have the same direction. To test for this situation, the **unit vectors** of each can be found. A unit vector has a magnitude of *one* and so it really gives just the **direction** of the vector.

A unit vector can be found by dividing the original vector by its magnitude. A formula to show this calculation is:

$$\hat{\mathbf{a}} = \frac{\mathbf{a}}{|\mathbf{a}|}$$

Notation
$\hat{\mathbf{a}}$ represents the unit vector of $\mathbf{a}$.
$|\mathbf{a}|$ is the magnitude of the vector $\mathbf{a}$.

Example 1

If $\mathbf{p} = \begin{pmatrix} 1 \\ 3 \end{pmatrix}$, write down $2\mathbf{p}$, $4\mathbf{p}$, $-\frac{1}{2}\mathbf{p}$ and $-3\mathbf{p}$. What do you notice?

Solution

$$2\mathbf{p} = 2\begin{pmatrix} 1 \\ 3 \end{pmatrix} = \begin{pmatrix} 2 \\ 6 \end{pmatrix}$$

$$4\mathbf{p} = 4\begin{pmatrix} 1 \\ 3 \end{pmatrix} = \begin{pmatrix} 4 \\ 12 \end{pmatrix}$$

$$-\tfrac{1}{2}\mathbf{p} = -\tfrac{1}{2}\begin{pmatrix} 1 \\ 3 \end{pmatrix} = \begin{pmatrix} -\frac{1}{2} \\ -1\frac{1}{2} \end{pmatrix}$$

$$-3\mathbf{p} = -3\begin{pmatrix} 1 \\ 3 \end{pmatrix} = \begin{pmatrix} -3 \\ -9 \end{pmatrix}$$

The '×' sign is optional, e.g. $2 \times \begin{pmatrix} 1 \\ 3 \end{pmatrix}$ or $2\begin{pmatrix} 1 \\ 3 \end{pmatrix}$

All four vectors are parallel. This is because they are in the form $k\mathbf{p}$ where k is a scalar.

A sketch will show that these vectors are parallel.

Example 2

If $\mathbf{a} = 3\mathbf{i} - 4\mathbf{j}$, determine:

a the unit vector of $\mathbf{a}$

b the vector parallel to $\mathbf{a}$ with a magnitude of 17.

Solution

a $|\mathbf{a}|^2 = 3^2 + 4^2$

$|\mathbf{a}| = \sqrt{3^2 + 4^2}$

$|\mathbf{a}| = \sqrt{9 + 16}$

$|\mathbf{a}| = \sqrt{25} = 5$

$\hat{\mathbf{a}} = \dfrac{\mathbf{a}}{|\mathbf{a}|}$ ◀ Write the formula for a unit vector.

$\hat{\mathbf{a}} = \dfrac{3\mathbf{i} - 4\mathbf{j}}{5}$

$\hat{\mathbf{a}} = 0.6\mathbf{i} - 0.8\mathbf{j}$

b parallel vector $= \hat{\mathbf{a}} \times 17$

$= (0.6\mathbf{i} - 0.8\mathbf{j}) \times 17$

$= 10.2\mathbf{i} - 13.6\mathbf{j}$

Pythagoras' theorem.

Square root.

Calculate the squares.

Take the square root of 25.

Substitute the values into the formula.

$\hat{\mathbf{a}}$ represents the unit vector in the direction of **a**.

Multiply the unit vector by 17.

Expand the brackets.

Example 3

$\mathbf{a} = \begin{pmatrix} -0.5 \\ 2.3 \end{pmatrix}$ $\mathbf{b} = \begin{pmatrix} 2 \\ -9.2 \end{pmatrix}$

Are vectors **a** and **b** parallel?

Solution

The unit vectors of both **a** and **b** can be found.

$|\mathbf{a}| = \sqrt{0.5^2 + 2.3^2}$

$= \sqrt{5.54} = 2.354$

$|\mathbf{b}| = \sqrt{2^2 + 9.2^2}$

$= \sqrt{88.64} = 9.415$

$\hat{\mathbf{a}} = \begin{pmatrix} -0.5 \\ 2.3 \end{pmatrix} \div 2.354$

$= \begin{pmatrix} -0.2124 \\ 0.9772 \end{pmatrix}$

$\hat{\mathbf{b}} = \begin{pmatrix} 2 \\ -9.2 \end{pmatrix} \div 9.415$

$= \begin{pmatrix} 0.2124 \\ -0.9772 \end{pmatrix}$

$\hat{\mathbf{a}} = -\hat{\mathbf{b}}$

The vectors are therefore parallel.

$\hat{\mathbf{a}} = k\hat{\mathbf{b}}$ where $k = -1$.

Example 4

For what value of t are these two vectors parallel?

$$\mathbf{d} = (t\mathbf{i} + 4\mathbf{j}) \qquad \mathbf{e} = (11\mathbf{i} - 7\mathbf{j})$$

Solution

For parallel vectors:

$$\mathbf{e} = k\mathbf{d}$$

$$11\mathbf{i} - 7\mathbf{j} = k(t\mathbf{i} + 4\mathbf{j})$$

$$11\mathbf{i} - 7\mathbf{j} = kt\mathbf{i} + 4k\mathbf{j}$$

j components:

$$-7 = 4k$$

$$\tfrac{-7}{4} = k$$

$$k = -1.75$$

i components:

$$11 = kt$$

$$11 = -1.75t$$

$$\tfrac{11}{-1.75} = t$$

$$t = -6.29 \text{ (3 s.f.)}$$

3.4 Parallel Vectors
Exercise

Technique

1 Find the unit vectors for each of the following vectors.

$\mathbf{a} = \begin{pmatrix} 3 \\ 7 \end{pmatrix}$ $\mathbf{b} = \begin{pmatrix} -11 \\ 0 \end{pmatrix}$ $\mathbf{c} = 11\mathbf{i} + 3\mathbf{j}$ $\mathbf{d} = -2\mathbf{i} + 0.3\mathbf{j}$

2 $\mathbf{a} = \begin{pmatrix} -7 \\ 4 \end{pmatrix}$ $\mathbf{b} = -11\mathbf{i} - 13\mathbf{j}$

a Find the vector parallel to **a** but with magnitude 20.

b Find the vector parallel to **b** but with magnitude 7.

3 Which of these vectors are parallel?

$\mathbf{a} = \begin{pmatrix} 0.1 \\ 0.7 \end{pmatrix}$ $\mathbf{b} = \begin{pmatrix} -1 \\ -7 \end{pmatrix}$ $\mathbf{c} = \begin{pmatrix} -0.05 \\ -0.03 \end{pmatrix}$ $\mathbf{d} = \begin{pmatrix} -10 \\ 70 \end{pmatrix}$

$\mathbf{e} = \begin{pmatrix} 60 \\ 420 \end{pmatrix}$ $\mathbf{f} = \begin{pmatrix} 1 \\ 7 \end{pmatrix}$ $\mathbf{g} = \begin{pmatrix} -1 \\ 7 \end{pmatrix}$ $\mathbf{h} = \begin{pmatrix} 6 \\ -42 \end{pmatrix}$

4 For what value of t are these two vectors parallel?

$\mathbf{r} = (3\mathbf{i} + t\mathbf{j})$ $\mathbf{s} = (9\mathbf{i} - 12\mathbf{j})$

5 For what value of t are these two vectors parallel?

$\mathbf{c} = (t\mathbf{i} - 8\mathbf{j})$ $\mathbf{d} = (7\mathbf{i} - 10\mathbf{j})$

3.5 Vector Algebra

A single letter on its own (with no other notation), is not sufficient to describe or denote a vector. In algebra, *single* letters stand for numbers. Numbers are **scalar** quantities. Vectors need *two* numbers to describe their two parts, either x and y components or their magnitude and direction. A letter in bold type, **a**, indicates a **vector quantity**. However, this is not the only way to write a vector.

You should write **a** as $\underline{a}$.

Position vectors

The position vector of the point A gives the displacement of the point A from the origin, O. The position vector of the point A can be written as $\overrightarrow{\mathrm{OA}}$. This way of writing the vector is called end point notation. This is because the points at each end of the vector are used to describe it. The vector **a** is often used to represent the position vector of the point A. It is common, therefore to see the statement:

$$\overrightarrow{\mathrm{OA}} = \mathbf{a}$$

$\overrightarrow{\mathrm{OA}}$ is a position vector represented by the length of the line OA with a direction indicated by the letters O to A.

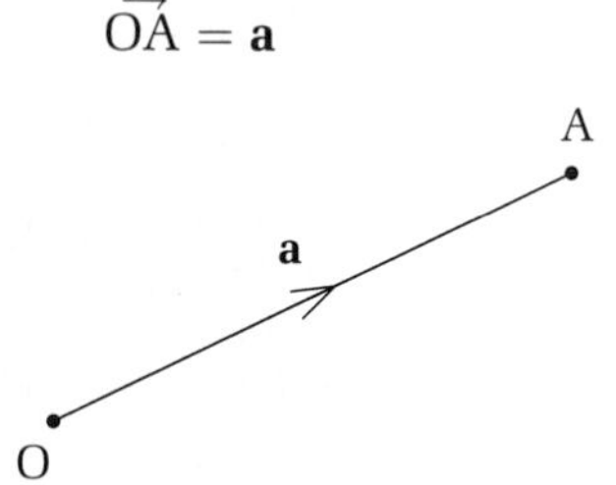

The lengths (or magnitudes) are also related.

$|\overrightarrow{\mathrm{OA}}| = |\mathbf{a}| =$ the length of the position vector of the point A.

$OA = a =$ the distance of the point A from O.

Recall that $|\mathbf{a}|$ represents the magnitude of the vector **a**.

The order of the letters is very important. $\overrightarrow{\mathrm{OA}}$ *does not have the same meaning as* $\overrightarrow{\mathrm{AO}}$.

$$\overrightarrow{\mathrm{AO}} = -\overrightarrow{\mathrm{OA}}$$
$$\overrightarrow{\mathrm{AO}} = -\mathbf{a}$$

$\overrightarrow{\mathrm{OA}}$ and $\overrightarrow{\mathrm{AO}}$ are the same length and parallel but act in opposite directions.

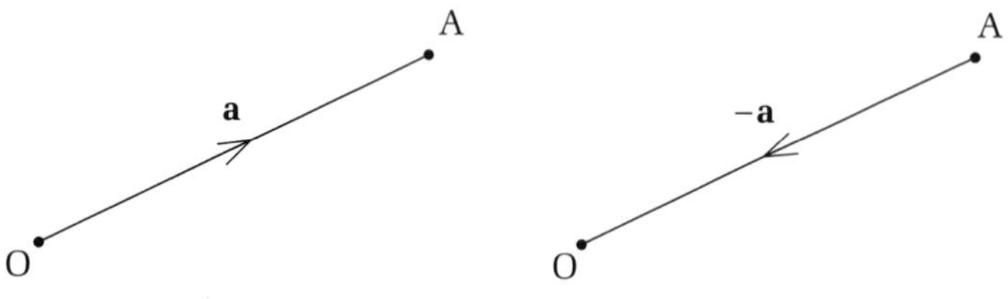

Addition of vectors

When two or more vectors are added, the answer is called the **resultant**. The **resultant** of two vectors is equivalent to the first vector followed immediately by the second vector.

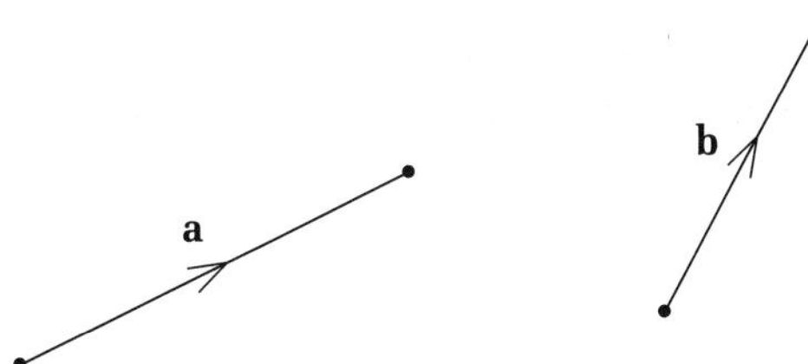

To find the resultant of vectors **a** and **b**, the tail of vector **b** must join to the head of vector **a**. The resultant (**a** + **b**) is the direct vector from the tail of vector **a** to the head of vector **b**.

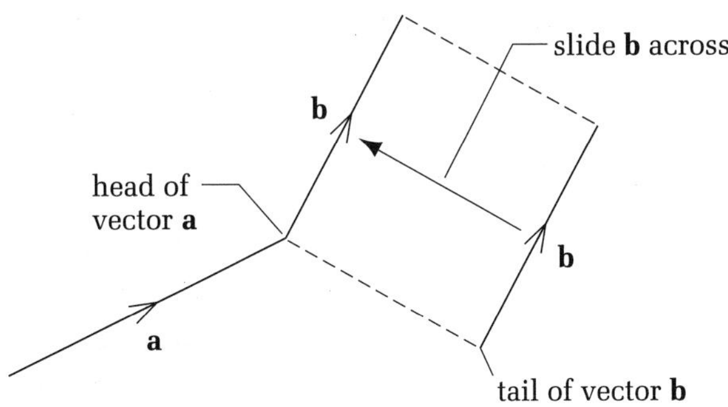

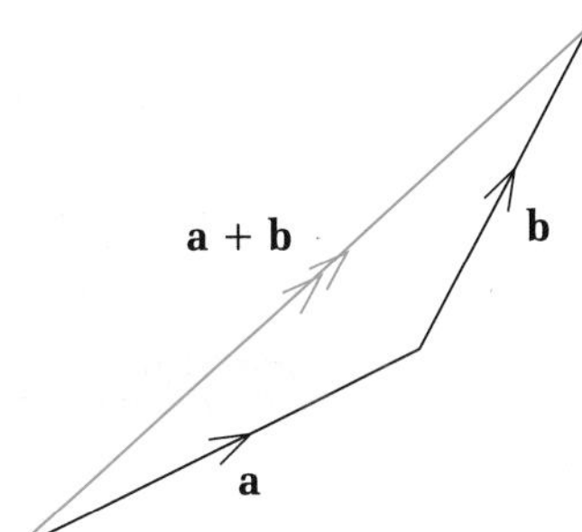

A double arrow is used to indicate the **resultant** vector.

Subtraction of vectors

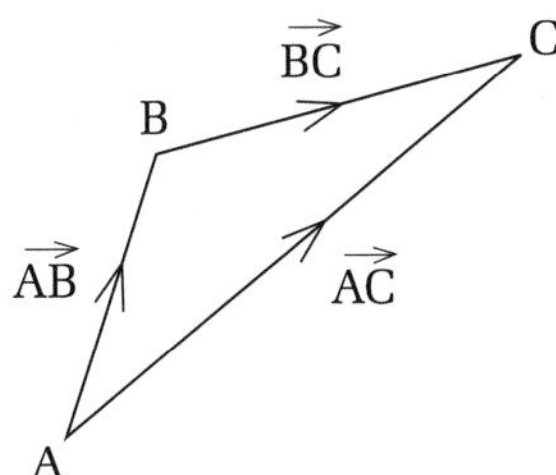

This diagram shows
$\overrightarrow{AC} = \overrightarrow{AB} + \overrightarrow{BC}$

$\overrightarrow{AB} + \overrightarrow{BC} = \overrightarrow{AC}$

head tail

answer

It is also true that $\overrightarrow{BC} = \overrightarrow{BA} + \overrightarrow{AC}$

$\overrightarrow{BC} = -\overrightarrow{AB} + \overrightarrow{AC}$

$\overrightarrow{BC} = \overrightarrow{AC} - \overrightarrow{AB}$

Since $\overrightarrow{BA} = -\overrightarrow{AB}$

This is **vector subtraction**.

The parallelogram rule for addition

To add **a** and **b**, imagine travelling along vector **a** and then along vector **b**. Two general vectors **a** and **b** are drawn.

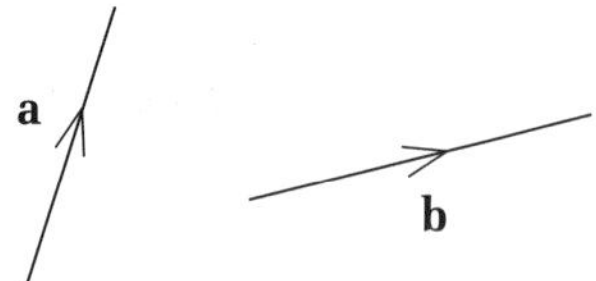

The vectors are added to form **a** + **b** by attaching the tail of vector **b** to the head of vector **a**.

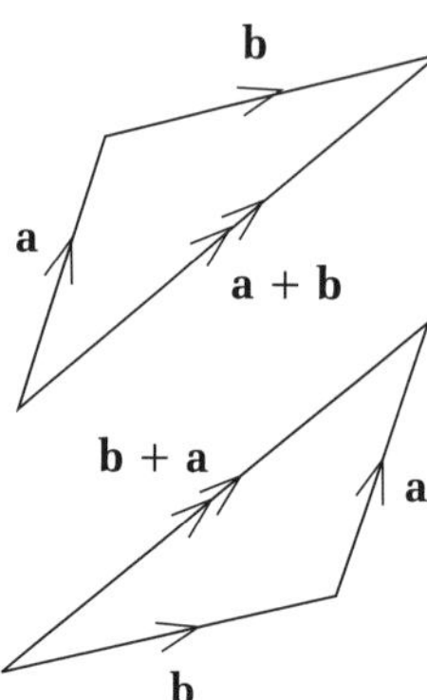

The vectors are added to form **b** + **a** by attaching the tail of vector **a** to the head of vector **b**.

What do you notice about the result of these two additions? Is the addition of vectors commutative?

Does **a** + **b** = **b** + **a**?

Both these additions can be shown on one diagram. The two pairs of equal vectors make a parallelogram. The diagonal is **a** + **b** or **b** + **a** depending on the route taken to C.

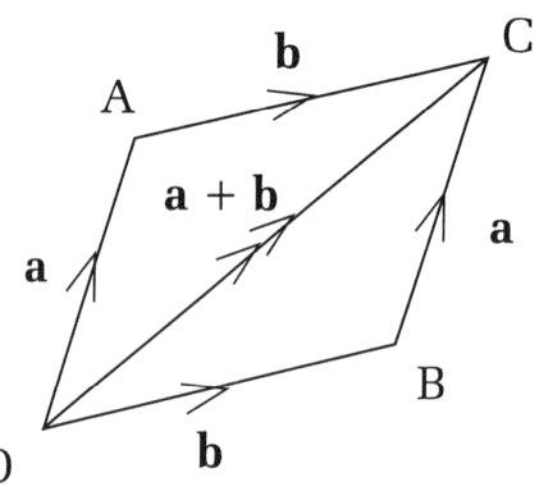

This is the parallelogram rule for the addition of vectors.

So vector addition is always commutative and a + b = b + a.

Zero vector

More than two vectors can be added by forming a polygon.

Consider this triangle:

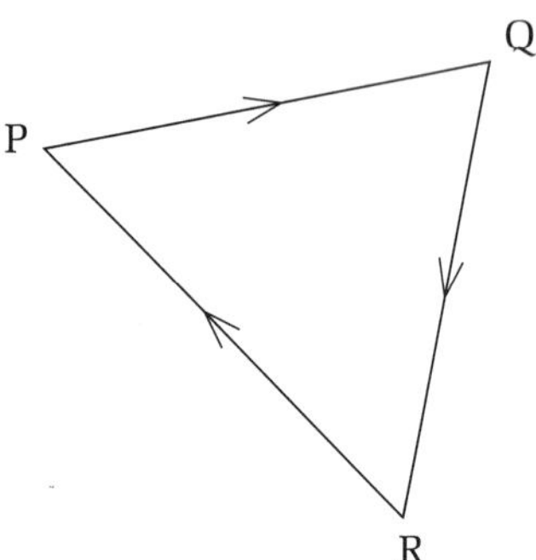

$\overrightarrow{PQ} + \overrightarrow{QR} + \overrightarrow{RP}$ must be equal to zero as the overall journey results in a return to the starting point. This is written as:

$$\overrightarrow{PQ} + \overrightarrow{QR} + \overrightarrow{RP} = \mathbf{0}$$

Or $\mathbf{0} = \begin{pmatrix} 0 \\ 0 \end{pmatrix}$ for 2-dimensional vectors.

The zero is in bold type to indicate it is a vector.

The vector from A to B

Let $\mathbf{a} = \overrightarrow{OA}$ and $\mathbf{b} = \overrightarrow{OB}$

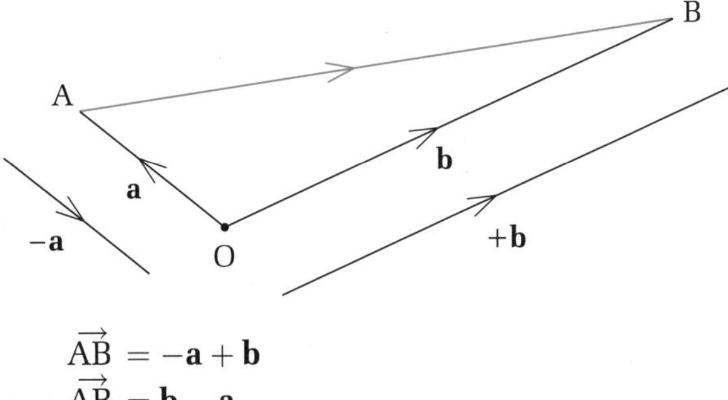

Going against an arrow means **a** will be negative.

$$\overrightarrow{AB} = -\mathbf{a} + \mathbf{b}$$
$$\overrightarrow{AB} = \mathbf{b} - \mathbf{a}$$

$\overrightarrow{AB}$ is always drawn from point A to point B.

Example 1

A student has written the following *incorrect* vector statement.

$$AB = \mathbf{b} - \mathbf{a}$$

Explain why this statement is *wrong* and then write it correctly.

Solution

AB is a scalar quantity (the magnitude of $\overrightarrow{AB}$) and $\mathbf{b} - \mathbf{a}$ will be a vector quantity. A scalar quantity cannot equal a vector quantity.

A possible correct statement is:

$$\overrightarrow{AB} = \mathbf{b} - \mathbf{a}$$

Example 2

$\overrightarrow{OD} = -4\mathbf{i} - 3\mathbf{j}$ and $\overrightarrow{OE} = 10\mathbf{i} + t\mathbf{j}$.
Find the value of t which makes D, O and E collinear.

Solution

Collinear means all the points must be in a straight line.

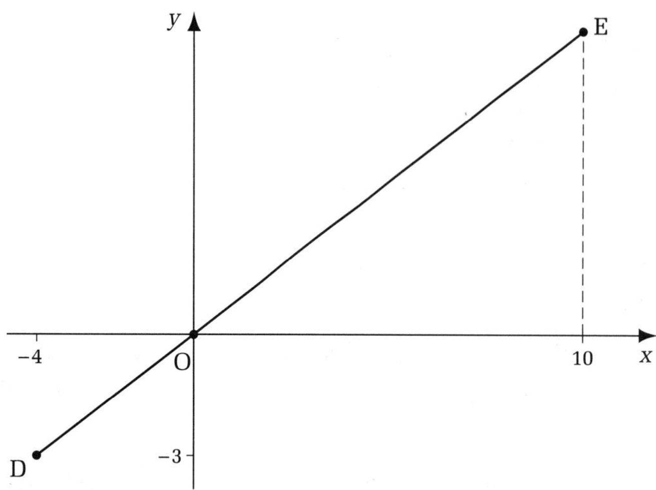

From the diagram the line $\overrightarrow{OD}$ and $\overrightarrow{OE}$ must be parallel to form a straight line.

$$\overrightarrow{OD} = k\overrightarrow{OE}$$ ◀ **Condition for parallel vectors.**

$$-4\mathbf{i} - 3\mathbf{j} = k(10\mathbf{i} + t\mathbf{j})$$

Expand the brackets.

$$-4\mathbf{i} - 3\mathbf{j} = 10k\mathbf{i} + kt\mathbf{j}$$

i component:

The **i** components must be equal.

$$-4 = 10k$$

Divide by 10.

$$k = -0.4$$

j component:

The **j** components must be equal.

$$-3 = kt$$

Replace k with -0.4.

$$-3 = -0.4t$$

Divide by -0.4.

$$t = 7.5$$

An alternative method of solution would be to find expressions for the magnitude of each vector and then use the fact that

$$|\overrightarrow{OD}| + |\overrightarrow{OE}| = |\overrightarrow{DE}|$$

when the points are collinear.

3.5 Vector Algebra
Exercise

Technique

1 There is a mistake in each of the following vector statements. Find the mistake and then write the correct version of each statement.

a $a = 2\mathbf{i} + 5\mathbf{j}$ b $|a| = \sqrt{29}$ c $\mathbf{b} = -2\mathbf{i} - 5\mathrm{j}$ d $\mathbf{a} + \mathbf{b} = 0$

e $\mathbf{a}^2 = 29$ f $AB = \mathbf{b} - \mathbf{a}$ g $b = -\mathbf{a}$ h $\overrightarrow{\mathrm{OA}} = a$

2 If $\mathbf{a} = 3\mathbf{i} + 7\mathbf{j}$ and $\mathbf{b} = 2\mathbf{i} - \mathbf{j}$, complete these questions, leaving your answers where necessary in surd form:

a $a =$ b $|\mathbf{b}| =$ c $b^2 =$ d $|(\mathbf{a} + \mathbf{b})| =$

e $a^4 =$ f $\mathbf{a} + 2\mathbf{b} =$ g $a \times b =$

$|(\mathbf{a} + \mathbf{b})|$ can also be written $|\mathbf{a} + \mathbf{b}|$.

3 ABCD is a square. Which of the following statements are *true* and which are *false*?

a $\overrightarrow{\mathrm{AB}} = \overrightarrow{\mathrm{CD}}$

b $\overrightarrow{\mathrm{AD}} = \overrightarrow{\mathrm{BC}}$

c $\overrightarrow{\mathrm{AD}} = -\overrightarrow{\mathrm{DA}}$

d $\overrightarrow{\mathrm{AD}} = \overrightarrow{\mathrm{AB}} + \overrightarrow{\mathrm{CD}}$

e $\overrightarrow{\mathrm{AB}} + \overrightarrow{\mathrm{DC}} = \mathbf{0}$

f $|\overrightarrow{\mathrm{AB}}| + |\overrightarrow{\mathrm{BC}}| = |\overrightarrow{\mathrm{AC}}|$

g $\overrightarrow{\mathrm{AC}} = \overrightarrow{\mathrm{BD}}$

h $|\overrightarrow{\mathrm{AC}}| = |\overrightarrow{\mathrm{BD}}|$

Label the vertices (corners) A, B, C, D consecutively around the square.

4 ABCD is a parallelogram. A has position vector $\binom{-1}{3}$, $\overrightarrow{\mathrm{AB}} = \binom{5}{2}$ and $\overrightarrow{\mathrm{AD}} = \binom{-1}{-4}$.

a What are the position vectors of B, C and D?

b Give the vectors $\overrightarrow{\mathrm{AC}}$ and $\overrightarrow{\mathrm{BD}}$.

c Show that $\overrightarrow{\mathrm{AB}} = \overrightarrow{\mathrm{DC}}$.

5 Given that $\overrightarrow{\mathrm{OA}} = (-2\mathbf{i} - 3\mathbf{j})$ and $\overrightarrow{\mathrm{OB}} = (5\mathbf{i} + t\mathbf{j})$, determine the value of t when the points O, A and B are collinear.

Collinear means all the points will be in a straight line.

6 a $\mathbf{p} = 7\mathbf{j} - 8\mathbf{k}$ and $\mathbf{q} = 11\mathbf{i} + \mathbf{j} - \mathbf{k}$. Calculate $|\mathbf{p}|$, $|\mathbf{q}|$ and $|\mathbf{p} + \mathbf{q}|$, giving your answers to three significant figures.

b In general $|\mathbf{a}| + |\mathbf{b}| \geq |\mathbf{a} + \mathbf{b}|$. Why is this so? When will $|\mathbf{a}| + |\mathbf{b}| = |\mathbf{a} + \mathbf{b}|$?

7 $\overrightarrow{\mathrm{AB}} = 6\mathbf{i} - 8\mathbf{j}$ and $\overrightarrow{\mathrm{AC}} = -18\mathbf{i} + 24\mathbf{j}$.

a Calculate $|\overrightarrow{\mathrm{AB}}|$ and $|\overrightarrow{\mathrm{AC}}|$.

b If $|\overrightarrow{\mathrm{BC}}| = 40$, what can be said about the points A, B and C? Calculate BC to show that this is true.

8 $\overrightarrow{\mathrm{DE}} = 10\mathbf{i} - 24\mathbf{j}$ and $|\overrightarrow{\mathrm{DF}}| = 46$. Determine the two possible values of $|\overrightarrow{\mathrm{EF}}|$ given that D, E and F are collinear.

Consolidation

Exercise A

1 The diagram shows two forces, of magnitudes 4 N and 5 N, acting at right angles to each other at a point O. Calculate:

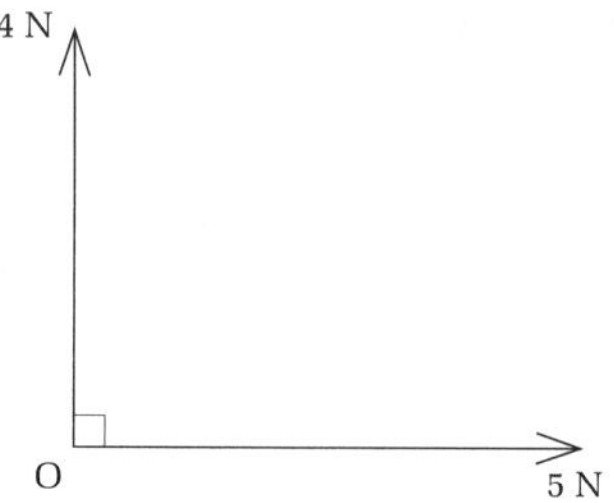

a the magnitude of the resultant of the two forces

b the angle that the resultant makes with the force of magnitude 5 N. *(UCLES)*

2 Two forces (measured in newtons) are acting at a point. They are denoted by the column vectors $\binom{4}{-1}$ and $\binom{0}{5}$ referred to the usual rectangular axes. Find the magnitude of their resultant and the angle that this resultant makes with the positive x-axis.

A further force of magnitude 5 N is applied so that the resultant of all three forces is denoted by the column vector $\binom{0}{a}$. There are two possible values of a. Find these two values and in each case find the direction of the force of 5 N referred to the positive x-axis. *(MEI)*

3 The vectors **a**, **b** and **c** are: $\mathbf{a} = 8\mathbf{i} + \mathbf{j} - 4\mathbf{k}$, $\mathbf{b} = \lambda\mathbf{i} + (\mu + 2)\mathbf{k}$ and $\mathbf{c} = \mathbf{j} + \mathbf{k}$.

a Find the magnitude of the resultant of **a** and **c**.

b Find the values of λ and μ if $\mathbf{a} - \mathbf{c} = 2\mathbf{b}$. *(NICCEA)*

4 A force **R** acts on a particle, where $\mathbf{R} = (7\mathbf{i} + 16\mathbf{j})$ N. Calculate:

a the magnitude of **R**, giving your answer to one decimal place.

b the angle between the line of action of **R** and **i**, giving your answer to the nearest degree.

c The force **R** is the resultant of two forces **P** and **Q**. The line of action of **P** is parallel to the vector $(\mathbf{i} + 4\mathbf{j})$ and the line of action of **Q** is parallel to the vector $(\mathbf{i} + \mathbf{j})$. Determine the forces **P** and **Q** expressing each in terms of **i** and **j**. *(ULEAC)*

Exercise B

1 The force $\mathbf{R}$ is given by the vector $6\mathbf{i} + 2\mathbf{j}$, where the units of force are newtons. $\mathbf{R}$ is the resultant of a force $\mathbf{P}$ parallel to $\mathbf{i}$ and a force $\mathbf{Q}$ parallel to $\mathbf{i} + \mathbf{j}$. Find the magnitudes of $\mathbf{P}$ and $\mathbf{Q}$. *(UCLES)*

2 A particle is acted on by two forces, $\mathbf{F}_1$ and $\mathbf{F}_2$, where $\mathbf{F}_1 = (6\mathbf{i} - 9\mathbf{j})$ N and $\mathbf{F}_2 = (-\mathbf{i} - 3\mathbf{j})$ N. Calculate:

a the magnitude of $\mathbf{F}_1$
b the angle between $\mathbf{F}_1$ and the direction of $\mathbf{i}$
c the resultant of $\mathbf{F}_1$ and $\mathbf{F}_2$
d the magnitude of the single force, $\mathbf{F}_3$, which satisfies the equation $\mathbf{F}_1 + \mathbf{F}_2 + \mathbf{F}_3 = \mathbf{0}$.

3 The vector $\mathbf{a}$ is given by $\mathbf{a} = (\lambda + 5)\mathbf{i} - 2\mathbf{j} + (\lambda - 4)\mathbf{k}$. Find the values of λ if the magnitude of $\mathbf{a}$ is 15 units. *(NICCEA)*

4 Three forces $(\mathbf{i} + \mathbf{j})$ N, $(-5\mathbf{i} + 3\mathbf{j})$ N and $\lambda\mathbf{i}$ N, where $\mathbf{i}$ and $\mathbf{j}$ are perpendicular unit vectors, act at a point. Express the resultant in the form $a\mathbf{i} + b\mathbf{j}$ and find its magnitude in terms of λ.

Given that the resultant has a magnitude of 5 N, find the two possible values of λ. Take the larger value of λ and find the tangent of the angle between the resultant and the unit vector $\mathbf{i}$. *(AEB)*

Applications and Activities

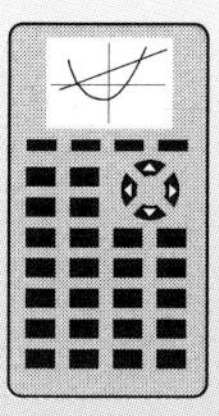

You can use a graphical calculator to convert between formats.

magnitude and direction $\longleftrightarrow$ components.

1 Convert these column vectors to magnitude and direction:

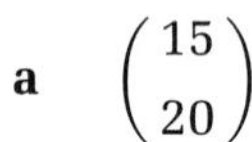

a $\begin{pmatrix} 15 \\ 20 \end{pmatrix}$ **b** $\begin{pmatrix} -5 \\ -12 \end{pmatrix}$ **c** $\begin{pmatrix} -7 \\ 16 \end{pmatrix}$

d $\begin{pmatrix} -1 \\ -1 \end{pmatrix}$ **e** $\begin{pmatrix} 11 \\ 10 \end{pmatrix}$ **f** $\begin{pmatrix} 19 \\ -4 \end{pmatrix}$

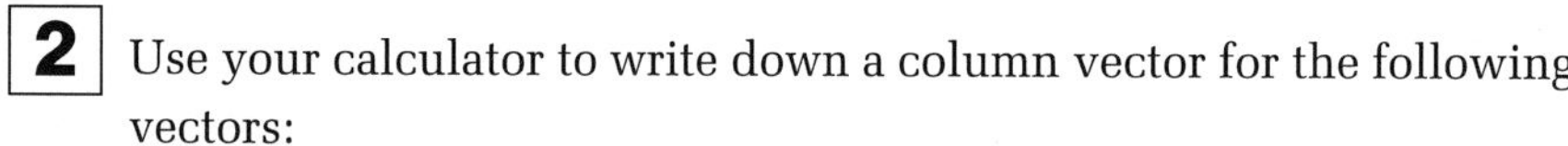

2 Use your calculator to write down a column vector for the following vectors:

a magnitude 40; angle 53.1°
b magnitude $\sqrt{8}$; angle 135°
c magnitude $4\sqrt{3}$; angle 210°
d magnitude 16.5; angle 312.5°

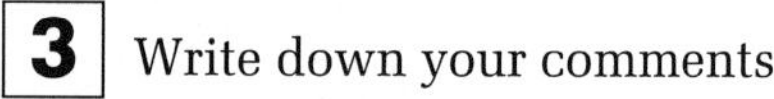

3 Write down your comments.

Summary

- A scalar quantity has magnitude but no direction. Examples are distance, speed, time, mass.
- A vector quantity has magnitude and direction. Examples are displacement, velocity, acceleration, force, weight.
  Vector quantities must also satisfy the parallelogram rule of addition.
- Vectors can be represented in the following ways:

  $\underline{a}$ $\quad$ $\mathbf{a}$ $\quad$ $\overrightarrow{\mathrm{OA}}$ $\quad$ $a\mathbf{i} + b\mathbf{j}$ $\quad$ $\begin{pmatrix} a \\ b \\ c \end{pmatrix}$

- The magnitude of a vector is a scalar quantity.
  The magnitude of $\mathbf{a}$ is $|\mathbf{a}|$ or a.
- Two vectors $\mathbf{a}$ and $\mathbf{b}$ are parallel if $\mathbf{b}$ is a scalar multiple of $\mathbf{a}$, that is, if $\mathbf{b} = k\mathbf{a}$, for some constant k, then $\mathbf{a}$ and $\mathbf{b}$ are parallel.
- Vectors can be added and subtracted. The resultant of $\mathbf{a}$ and $\mathbf{b}$ is the vector which represents $\mathbf{a}$ followed by $\mathbf{b}$.

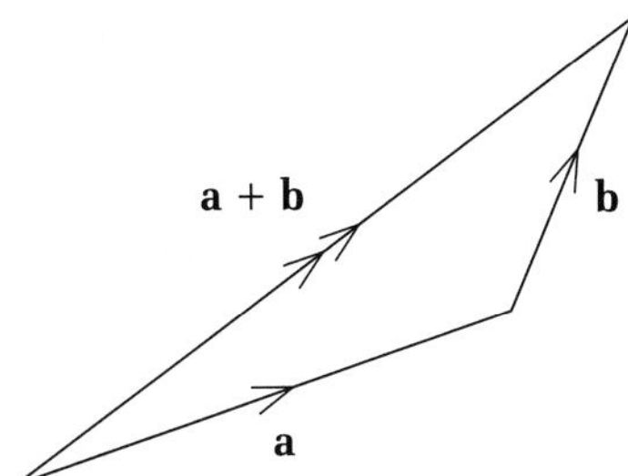

- When three points are collinear, vectors joining any combination of two points will be parallel.

4 Travel Graphs

Travel graphs are sometimes called kinematics graphs.

What you need to know

- The difference between a scalar and a vector.
- How to calculate the gradient of a straight line.
- For a body travelling at constant speed, speed $= \dfrac{\text{distance}}{\text{time}}$.
- average speed $= \dfrac{\text{total distance travelled}}{\text{total time taken}}$
- How to find the area of a trapezium using $\frac{1}{2}(a+b)h$.
- The rules of indices.
- The equation of a straight line is $y = mx + c$ where m is the gradient and c is the y-intercept.
- What is meant by the particle model.

Review

1 State whether the following quantities are scalars or vectors:

a a speed of 70 mph
b a distance of 4 km on a bearing of 120°
c a speed of 15 mph to the south.

2

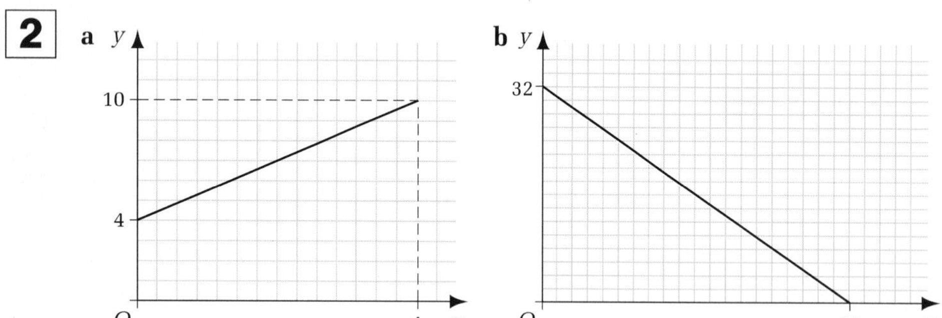

Find the gradient of each of the lines shown in the diagram.

3 A cyclist travels 200 m in 16 s. Find her speed in m s^{-1}, assuming it is constant.

4 A car travels 32 miles on the motorway in half an hour and then 3 miles in a built-up area in a quarter of an hour. Find the average speed.

5 Calculate the area of each trapezium.

a

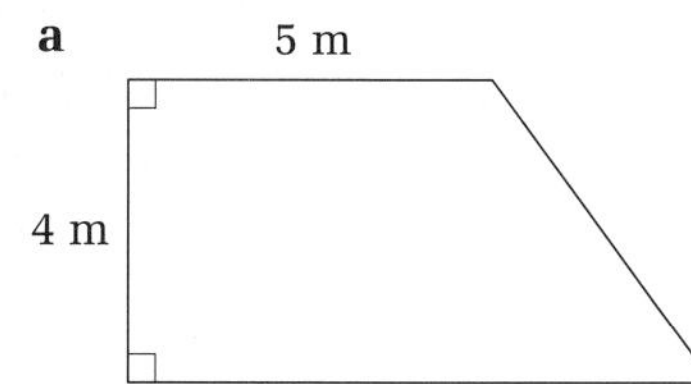

b

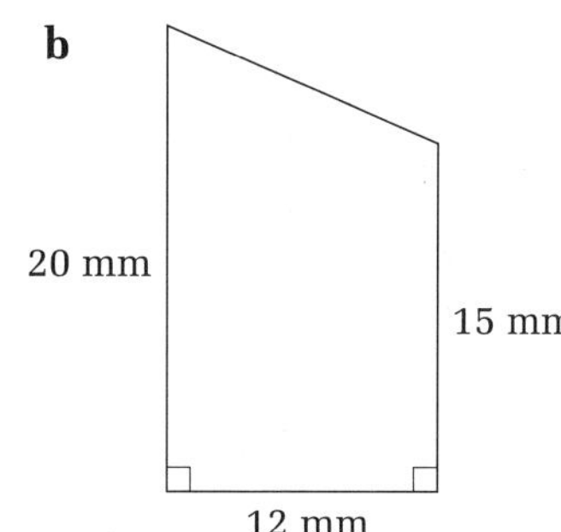

6 Use the rules of indices to simplify:

a $a^2 \times a^5$ **b** $\frac{b^3}{b^8}$ **c** $(f^4)^6$ **d** $(x^6)^{\frac{1}{2}}$

e $y^4 \div y^4$ **f** $p^2q^{-3} \times pq^2$ **g** $\frac{x^{-1}y}{xy^{-2}}$ **h** $(ab^{-1}c^{-2})^2$

7 **a** Write down the values of the gradient and intercept of the following straight lines:

i $y = x + 5$ **ii** $y = 5 - 2x$

b **i**

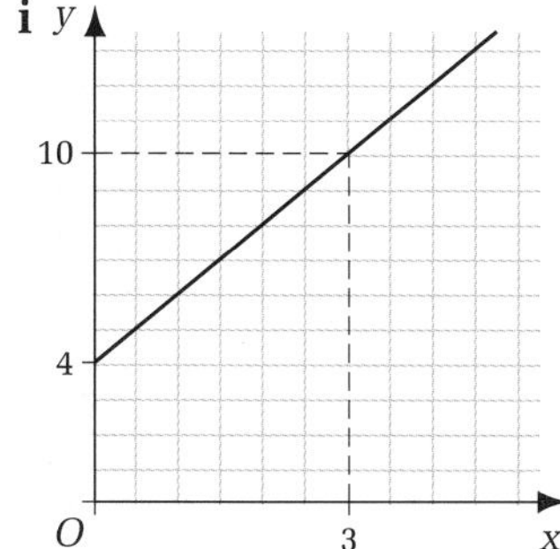

ii

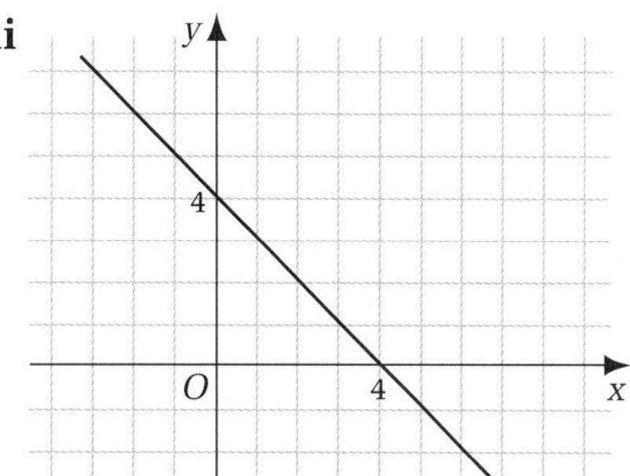

Find the equation of each line shown in the diagram.

8 Write down two characteristics of an object which are ignored when it is modelled as a particle.

4.1 Distance–Time Graphs

Suppose a bus sets out from a bus station and takes 20 seconds to travel a distance of 100 metres, through busy traffic, to the first bus stop. It stops there for 7 seconds to pick up passengers and then travels another 150 metres in 10 seconds to the next bus stop. This journey can be shown on a distance–time graph.

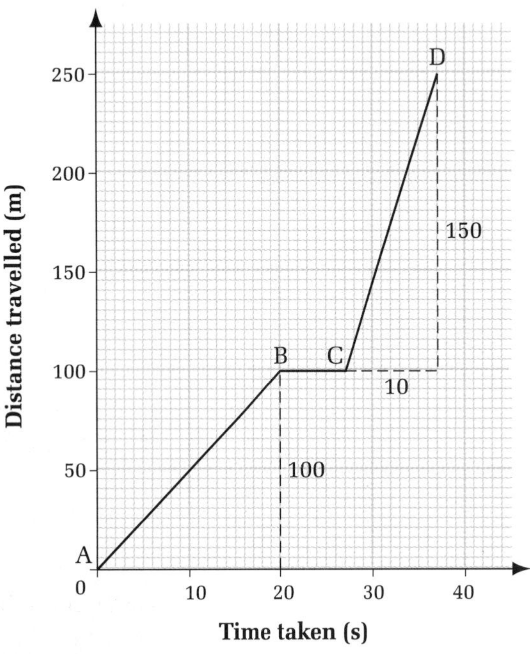

Notice **time** is always shown on the ***x*-axis** and **distance** on the ***y*-axis**.

We can use the distance–time graph to calculate the speed of the bus. We assume that the bus is a particle and that it travels at a constant speed when in motion.

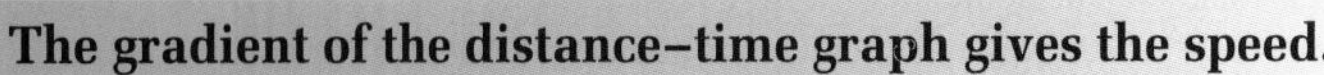

The gradient of the distance–time graph gives the speed.

$$\text{gradient} = \frac{\text{up}}{\text{across}} = \frac{\text{distance}}{\text{time}} = \text{speed}$$

The distance–time graph can now be used to calculate the bus's speed.

For section AB, $\quad \text{speed} = \text{gradient}$

$$= \tfrac{100}{20}$$

$$= 5\,\text{m}\,\text{s}^{-1}$$

For section BC, $\quad \text{speed} = \text{gradient}$

$$= \tfrac{0}{7}$$

$$= 0\,\text{m}\,\text{s}^{-1}$$

The speed is zero because the bus is **stationary**.

For section CD, $\quad \text{speed} = \text{gradient}$

$$= \tfrac{150}{10}$$

$$= 15\,\text{m}\,\text{s}^{-1}$$

The speed of the bus is greater from C to D than from A to B. How can you tell this from the graph? The *speed is greater* when *the gradient is steeper* on the distance–time graph.

Can you think of any way in which the graph is unrealistic? A *sloping straight line* on a distance–time graph indicates that the object is moving at a *constant speed*. It is unlikely that the bus will do this. Changing gears and moving through traffic will mean the bus changes speed as it goes along. It will also need to slow down gradually as it reaches the first bus stop. The graph suggests the bus stops abruptly. An accurate graph for this motion, would be a curve. However, by assuming the bus travels at constant speed, the mathematical analysis is much easier. Finding the gradient of a curve is more difficult. By calculating the gradient of the straight line, the *average speed* of the bus has been found.

Converting units of speed

In 1969, an Anglo–French company unveiled Concorde. This was the world's first supersonic civilian aircraft. In fact Concorde has a maximum cruising speed of $2179\,\text{km}\,\text{h}^{-1}$; about twice the speed of sound.

Supersonic means that the aircraft can fly faster than the speed of sound.

When solving real life problems it is often necessary to convert $\text{km}\,\text{h}^{-1}$ into $\text{m}\,\text{s}^{-1}$ and vice versa. This process can be completed in stages.

$$\begin{aligned} 2179\,\text{km}\,\text{h}^{-1} &= 2\,179\,000\,\text{m}\,\text{h}^{-1} \\ &= 2\,179\,000 \div 60\,\text{m}(\text{min})^{-1} \\ &= 36\,316.7 \div 60\,\text{m}\,\text{s}^{-1} \\ &= 605\,\text{m}\,\text{s}^{-1}\ (3\text{ s.f.}) \end{aligned}$$

Convert km to m by $\times$ 1000.
Distance travelled per minute = distance travelled per hour $\div$60.
Concorde will travel *less* distance in 1 minute than in 1 hour so *divide* by 60.
Distance travelled per second = distance travelled per minute $\div$ 60.

These steps may be combined.

To convert $\text{km}\,\text{h}^{-1}$ to $\text{m}\,\text{s}^{-1}$, $\times \frac{1000}{3600}$

To convert $\text{m}\,\text{s}^{-1}$ to $\text{km}\,\text{h}^{-1}$, $\times \frac{3600}{1000}$

Overview of method

To help solve distance–time graph problems, the method can be broken down into steps.

Step ① Sketch the distance–time graph (unless one is given).
Step ② Split the distance–time graph into different sections.
Step ③ Use speed = gradient of distance–time graph $= \dfrac{\text{distance}}{\text{time}}$

or use average speed $= \dfrac{\text{total distance travelled}}{\text{total time taken}}$

Example

A train travels at 50 km h^{-1} for 25 seconds before stopping at signals. After waiting for 15 seconds it travels on at 80 km h^{-1}.

a Sketch a distance–time graph for the first minute of this journey using metres on the distance axis and seconds on the time axis.

b Find the average speed in km h^{-1}.

Solution

a The distance travelled and time taken are needed for each part of the journey.

For the first part, convert the speed to m s^{-1}: ◀ ② **Split into different sections.**

Convert km h^{-1} to m s^{-1} by $\times \frac{1000}{3600}$.
Store the *exact* value in the calculator's memory.

$$50 \text{ km h}^{-1} = 50 \times \frac{1000}{3600}$$
$$= 13.\dot{8} \text{ m s}^{-1}$$

Using distance = speed × time

This is a rearrangement of speed $= \frac{\text{distance}}{\text{time}}$

$$\text{distance} = 13.\dot{8} \times 25$$
$$= 347.\dot{2} \text{ m}$$

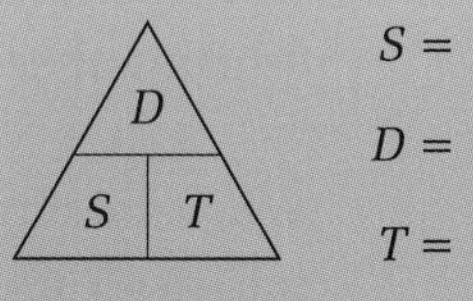

$S = \frac{D}{T}$

$D = S \times T$

$T = \frac{D}{S}$

Remember the speed triangle

The train then stops, so in the next 15 seconds the distance travelled is zero.

For the last part of the journey, convert the speed to m s^{-1}:

Convert km h^{-1} to m s^{-1} by $\times \frac{1000}{3600}$

$$80 \text{ km h}^{-1} = 80 \times \frac{1000}{3600}$$
$$= 22.\dot{2} \text{ m s}^{-1}$$

The time for this part is:

$$60 - 25 - 15 = 20 \text{ seconds}$$

Using distance = speed × time

This is a rearrangement of speed $= \frac{\text{distance}}{\text{time}}$

$$\text{distance} = 22.\dot{2} \times 20$$
$$= 444.\dot{4} \text{ m}$$

$$\text{total distance travelled} = 347.\dot{2} + 444.\dot{4}$$
$$= 791.\dot{6} \text{ m}$$
$$= 792 \text{ m (to nearest metre)}$$

The graph can now be sketched. 

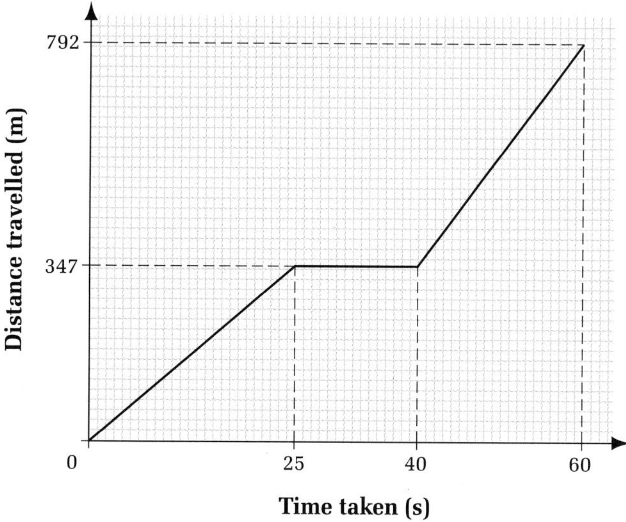

b A total distance of $791.\dot{6}$ m was travelled in 1 minute.

$$\text{average speed} = \frac{\text{total distance travelled}}{\text{total time taken}}$$

◀ ③ Use average speed.

$$= \frac{791.\dot{6}}{1}\ \text{m(min)}^{-1}$$

$$= 791.\dot{6} \times \frac{60}{1000}\ \text{km h}^{-1}$$

$$= 47.5\ \text{km h}^{-1}$$

The average speed was $47.5\ \text{km h}^{-1}$.

Total distance is in metres and time is in minutes. Units of speed must be m(min)^{-1}. Convert into km h^{-1} by $\times \frac{60}{1000}$

4.1 Distance–Time Graphs
Exercise

Technique

1 Convert the following speeds to km h^{-1}:

a $64\,\text{m s}^{-1}$ **b** $140\,\text{m(min)}^{-1}$

2 Convert the following speeds to m s^{-1}:

a $160\,\text{km h}^{-1}$ **b** $85\,\text{km h}^{-1}$

3 **a**

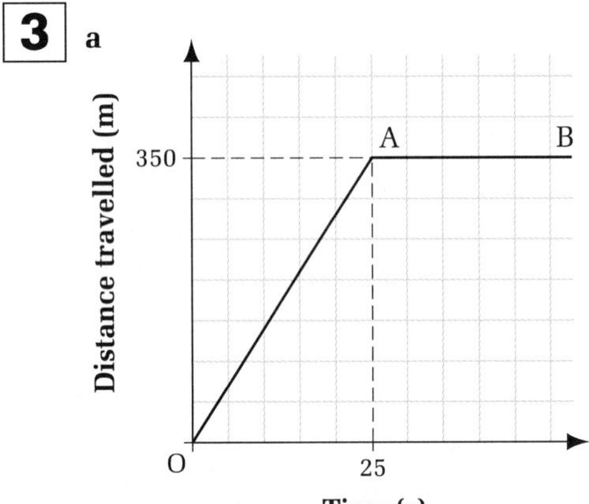

b

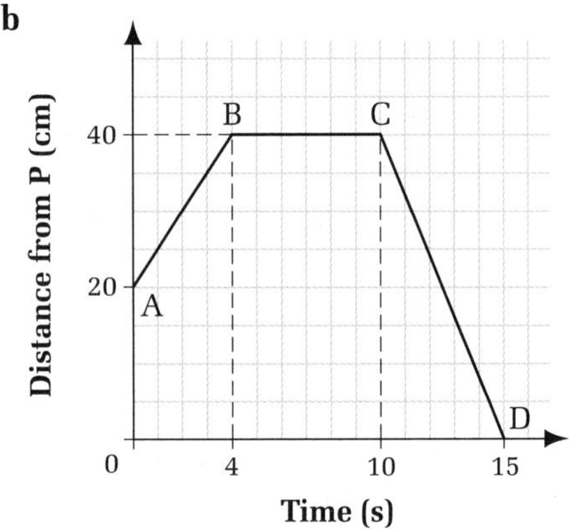

Remember speed is always a positive quantity.

Find the speed for each section of these distance–time graphs.

4 A moving object travels 150 m in 20 s, followed by 240 m in the next 15 s.

a Sketch a distance–time graph using metres on the distance axis and seconds on the time axis.

b Find the speed in each section in:
i m s^{-1} **ii** km h^{-1}

c Find the average speed in:
i m s^{-1} **ii** km h^{-1}

Contextual

1 **a** A sprinter runs at $9.6\,\text{m s}^{-1}$. Convert this speed to km h^{-1}.

b A skier travels 450 metres down a slope in one minute. What is the speed in km h^{-1}?

2 **a** A Formula One car travels at $320\,\text{km h}^{-1}$. What is this speed in m s^{-1}?

b Sally walks at a speed of $6.5\,\text{km h}^{-1}$. Convert this speed to m s^{-1}.

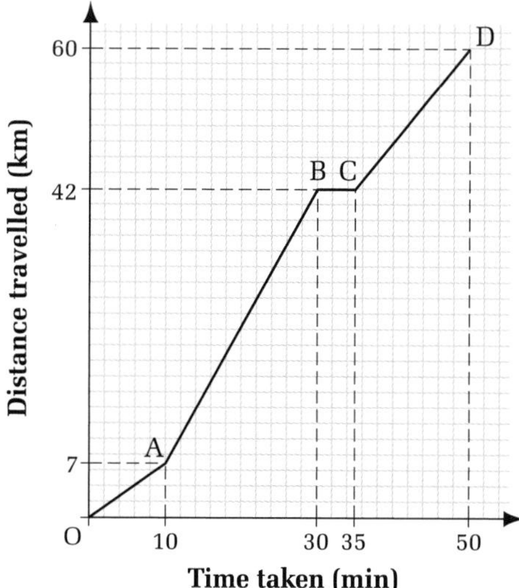

The graph shows a salesman's journey to a meeting. He drives from his office in town to the nearest motorway junction. On leaving the motorway he stops for petrol and then completes his journey along country roads.

a Find the speed in each section of the journey in km h^{-1}.
b Find the average speed in km h^{-1}.

On the way to the local shops, Sam stops for 2 minutes to talk to a neighbour. The distance from Sam's house to his neighbour's is 150 m and the total distance to the shops is 480 m. Sam walks at 2.5 m s^{-1}.

a Sketch a distance–time graph of Sam's journey to the shops using metres on the distance axis and minutes on the time axis.
b Find the average speed for the journey in km h^{-1}.

5 In a Land's End to John O'Groats trip, a car travels at a speed of 80 km h^{-1} for the first 400 km and then at 110 km h^{-1} for the next 3 hours. After stopping for an hour and a half for a rest and petrol, the car completes the remaining 670 km in a further 7 hours.

a Find the average speed during the last part of the journey in:
i km h^{-1} **ii** m s^{-1}
b Find the average speed during the whole journey in:
i km h^{-1} **ii** m s^{-1}

4.2 Displacement–Time Graphs

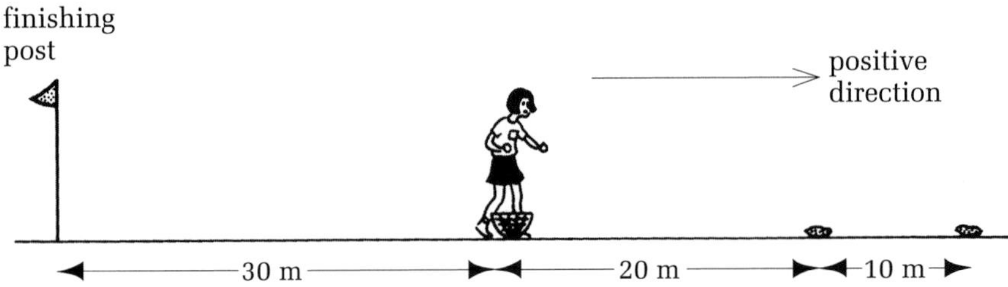

Jane is competing in a bean bag race at a primary school. Starting from the basket she collects the bean bags one at a time and puts them in the basket. Then she runs to the finishing line. Jane runs at a constant speed of $2\,\text{m}\,\text{s}^{-1}$.

To show the *direction* of motion, *displacement* from the basket can be used instead of distance.

Displacement is distance in a specified direction.

This means that displacement is a vector that gives the *direction as well as the distance travelled.*

10 km is a distance whereas 10 km north is a displacement.

The displacement–time graph for Jane's bean bag race is shown. Displacement has been measured from the basket. A *positive* displacement means that Jane is on the bean bag side of the basket. A *negative* displacement means Jane is on the finishing line side of the basket. A point on the graph shows exactly where Jane is at that particular time.

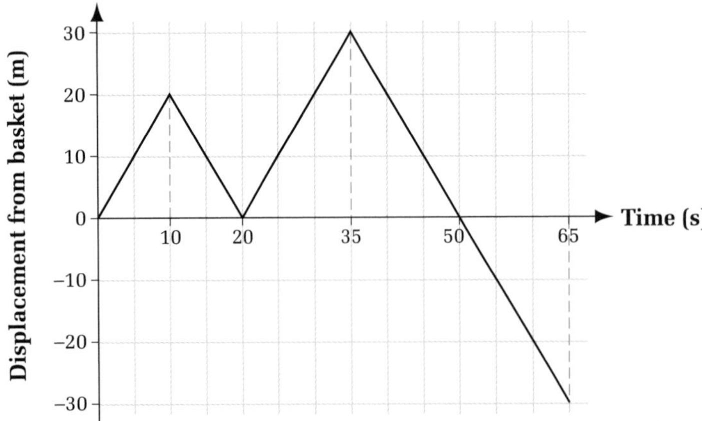

There are two abbreviations for displacement–time graph. The first uses the symbols for displacement and time. So **x–t graph** means a displacement–time graph. The second abbreviation takes the form of coordinates. This means a **(t, x) graph** is also a displacement–time graph. The first coordinate is the quantity which is drawn horizontally and the second coordinate is the quantity on the vertical axis.

Note that x is now on the vertical axis.

Velocity

Velocity is the rate of change of displacement with time.

The gradient of the displacement–time graph gives the direction of motion as well as the speed. The **gradient** of a displacement–time graph gives **velocity**.

$$\text{gradient} = \frac{\text{up}}{\text{across}}$$

$$\text{velocity} = \frac{\text{displacement}}{\text{time}}$$

Alternatively, velocity can be defined in terms of speed.

Velocity is speed in a specified direction.

Velocity is a vector and so consists of a magnitude (speed) and direction.

In the first part of the bean bag race when Jane is going for the first bean bag:

$$\begin{aligned}\text{Jane's velocity} &= \text{gradient of the displacement–time graph}\\ &= \tfrac{20}{10}\\ &= 2\,\text{m s}^{-1}\end{aligned}$$

In the next section when Jane returns to the basket:

$$\begin{aligned}\text{Jane's velocity} &= \text{gradient}\\ &= \tfrac{-20}{10}\\ &= -2\,\text{m s}^{-1}\end{aligned}$$

The negative sign indicates that she is now moving in the *opposite direction*.

Throughout the race Jane ran at a constant speed of $2\,\text{m s}^{-1}$ but her velocity varied because the direction varied. In everyday speech the words speed and velocity are used as if they mean the same thing. Mathematically, they are different. **Velocity** is a **vector** having direction as well as magnitude. **Speed** is a **scalar** having magnitude but no direction. Average speed and average velocity are also different. Here are the definitions.

$$\textbf{average speed} = \frac{\textbf{total distance travelled}}{\textbf{total time taken}}$$

$$\textbf{average velocity} = \frac{\textbf{total displacement}}{\textbf{total time taken}}$$

In the bean bag race:

$$\begin{aligned}\text{total distance} &= 20 + 20 + 30 + 30 + 30\\ &= 130\,\text{m}\\ \text{total time taken} &= 65\,\text{s}\\ \text{average speed} &= \tfrac{130}{65}\\ &= 2\,\text{m s}^{-1}\end{aligned}$$

◀ Use average speed $= \frac{\text{total distance travelled}}{\text{total time taken}}$

As Jane travelled at $2\,\text{m s}^{-1}$ throughout the race this is no surprise!

Now consider the average velocity. When the race started Jane was by the basket and when the race ended she was a distance of 30 m from the basket in the negative direction. For Jane's race the total displacement is -30 m.

Total displacement can also be found by adding the displacements for each part.
$20 + (-20) + 30 + (-30) + (-30) = -30$

$$\text{average velocity} = \tfrac{-30}{65} \quad \blacktriangleleft \text{ Use average velocity} = \frac{\text{total displacement}}{\text{total time taken}}$$

$$= -0.462\ \text{m s}^{-1}\ (3\ \text{s.f.})$$

This is not the same as the average speed of $2\ \text{m s}^{-1}$.

In all the examples which follow the motion is in a straight line. One direction along the line is taken as positive and the opposite direction as negative.

Example

A particle moves along a straight line so that its displacement, x metres, from a fixed point O on the line at time t seconds is given by:

$$x = -3t \text{ for } 0 \le t \le 4 \text{ and } x = 2t - 20 \text{ for } 4 \le t \le 15$$

Often x is used to denote displacement and t, as usual, denotes time. The motion of an object may be modelled using a formula relating x and t.

a Find the displacement of the particle from O when:
  i $t = 2$ **ii** $t = 10$

b Sketch the (t, x) graph for the motion.

c Find the velocity of the particle:
  i for $0 \le t \le 4$ **ii** for $4 \le t \le 15$.

d Find the total distance travelled in the 15 seconds of motion.

e Find the average velocity.

Solution

a **i** When $t = 2$, $x = -3t$

$$x = -3 \times 2$$
$$x = -6$$

displacement $= -6$ m

ii When $t = 10$, $x = 2t - 20$

$$x = 2 \times 10 - 20$$
$$x = 0$$

displacement $= 0$ m

b A (t, x) graph is a displacement–time graph in which *the displacement x is on the vertical axis* and the *time t is on the horizontal axis*. The equations $x = -3t$ and $x = 2t - 20$ are both linear equations. They both represent straight line segments. It is useful to find the start and end of each line segment.

A straight line segment is part of a straight line.

For $x = -3t$: when $t = 0$, $x = 0$ $x = -3 \times 0$

when $t = 4$, $x = -12$ $x = -3 \times 4$

For $x = 2t - 20$: when $t = 4$, $x = 2 \times 4 - 20$

$x = 8 - 20$

$x = -12$

when $t = 15$, $x = 2 \times 15 - 20$

$x = 30 - 20$

$x = 10$

Note the equations agree that $x = -12$ when $t = 4$.

The sketch shows the (t, x) graph of the motion.

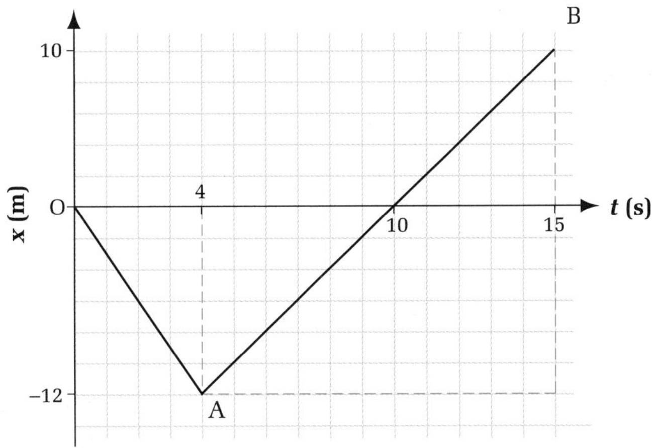

Check the answers for part **a** using the graph.

c **i** In section OA, velocity = gradient

$= -\frac{12}{4}$

$= -3 \text{ m s}^{-1}$

ii In section AB, velocity = gradient

$= \frac{22}{11}$

$= 2 \text{ m s}^{-1}$

In each case the gradient is equal to the coefficient of t in the equation of the line segment.

Compare each equation with $y = mx + c$.

d Adding the distance travelled in each section gives:
total distance travelled = 12 + 22 = 34 m

e Total displacement = −12 + 22 = 10 m
When $t = 0$, the displacement $x = 0$. When $t = 15$, the displacement $x = 10$.

Comparing the start and end points on the graph also gives the total displacement.

$$\text{average velocity} = \frac{\text{total displacement}}{\text{total time taken}}$$

$= \frac{10}{15}$

$= 0.667 \text{ m s}^{-1}$ (3 s.f.)

4.2 Displacement–Time Graphs

Exercise

Technique

a

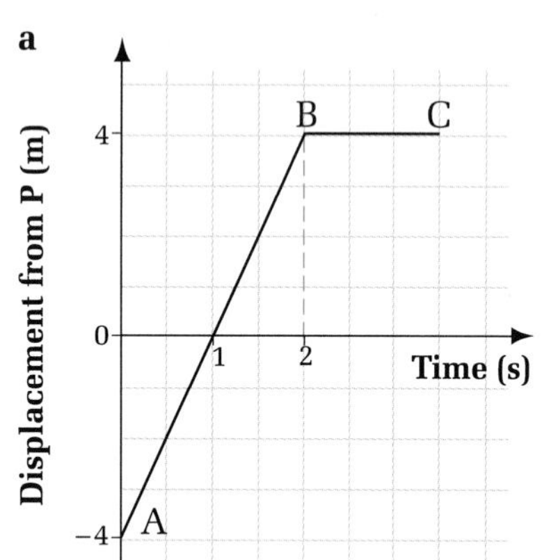

b

P is a fixed point.

Find the velocity in each section of the journeys shown in the displacement–time graphs.

2 Draw a sketch of the displacement–time graph for each of the following journeys. In each case, the body starts from a fixed point P and moves in a straight line. Your vertical axis should show displacement from P.

a A body takes 5 seconds to travel 18 m in the positive direction.

b A body moves 25 km in the positive direction in 2 hours. It stops for half an hour and then travels 50 km in the negative direction in the next 3 hours.

3 **a**

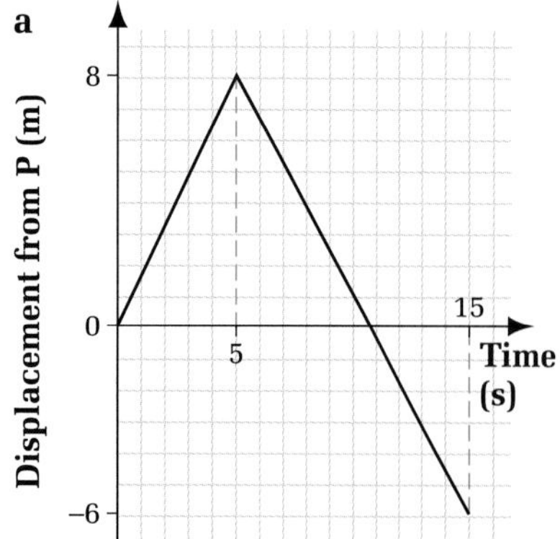

b

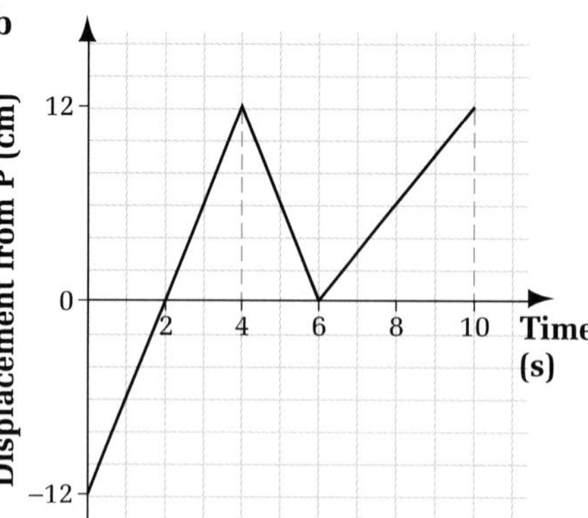

For each displacement–time graph, find:

i the average speed **ii** the average velocity.

4 a

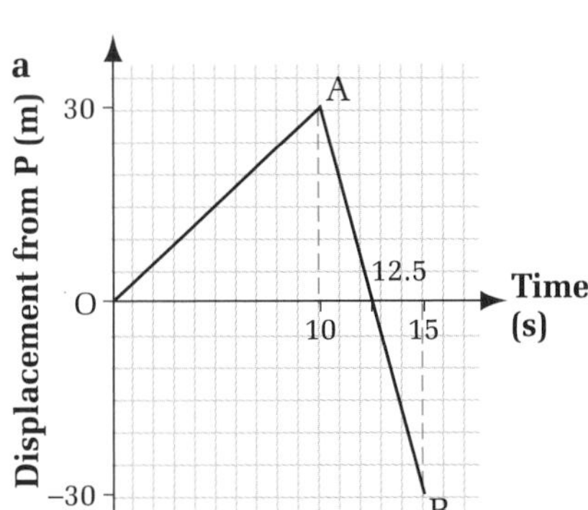

b

BC crosses the time axis at approximately 26 s.

For each of the displacement–time graphs:

i find in which section the speed is greatest

ii sketch a distance–time graph, using distance from P.

5 For the following models x is in metres and t is in seconds.

a $x = 4t$ for $0 \le t \le 10$

b $x = 2t$ for $0 \le t \le 5$

$x = 15 - t$ for $5 \le t \le 10$

c $x = 7 - t$ for $0 \le t \le 4$

$x = 3$ for $4 \le t \le 6$

$x = 21 - 3t$ for $6 \le t \le 10$

For each part:

i sketch a (t, x) graph

ii find the velocity in each part of the journey

iii find the total distance travelled.

A (t, x) graph means draw t along the horizontal axis and x along the vertical axis.

Contextual

1 A bucket is used to collect water from a well. The bucket is lowered at 0.8 m s^{-1} from the top of the well and it takes 6 seconds to reach the water. After collecting water for 2 seconds the bucket is returned to the top of the well at a speed of 0.3 m s^{-1}.

a Sketch a displacement–time graph using upwards as the positive direction and displacement from the top of the well.

b What is the average speed of the bucket?

c What is the average velocity of the bucket?

2 Kate and Vic stand 6 metres apart and kick a ball backwards and forwards to each other. After Kate kicks the ball it travels at a constant speed of 6 m s^{-1} and after Vic kicks the ball it travels with a constant speed of 4 m s^{-1}. Sketch a displacement–time graph (using displacement from Kate) to show the motion of the ball starting from a kick by Kate and ending when she receives the ball again.

3

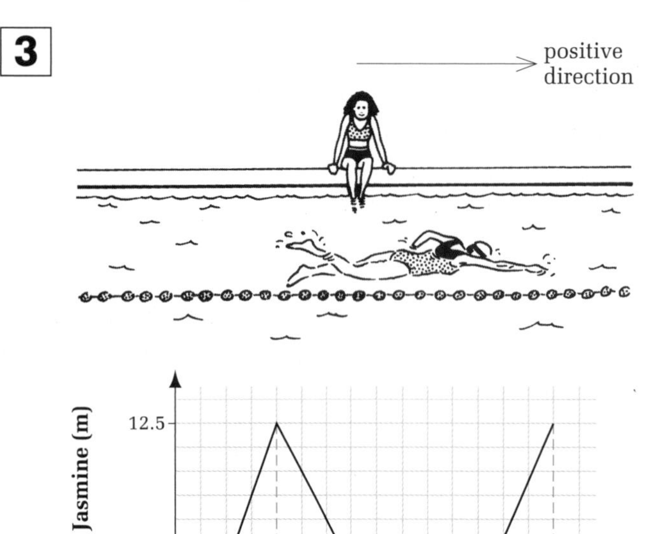

Jasmine sits half-way along the side of a swimming pool watching her friend Sonja swim lengths. The sketch shows a displacement–time graph of Sonja's motion with displacement measured from Jasmine's position. Use the sketch to answer the following questions.

a How long is the pool?
b What was Sonja's velocity during each length?
c How far did Sonja swim altogether?
d What was Sonja's average speed?
e What was Sonja's average velocity?
f In what ways do you think the graph is unrealistic?

4

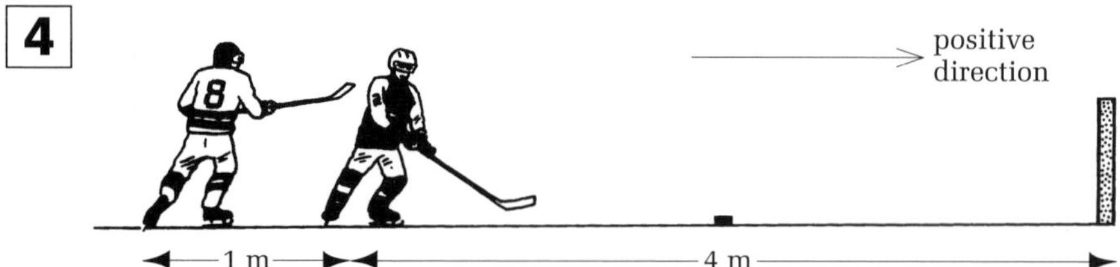

In a game of ice hockey Jeff is 4 m away from the barrier when he hits the puck. It travels at $10\,\mathrm{m\,s^{-1}}$ to the barrier and rebounds at $8\,\mathrm{m\,s^{-1}}$. Jeff misses the puck on the rebound and it travels on to an opposition player who is standing 1 m behind Jeff. Assume neither player moves whilst this happens. Stating any other assumptions you make:

a sketch a displacement–time graph of the puck's motion, using displacement from Jeff on the vertical axis with the positive direction from Jeff to the barrier;
b find the average velocity of the puck.

5 Two lifts P and Q travel in adjacent lift shafts. Each lift travels upwards at $1.5\ \mathrm{m\,s^{-1}}$ and downwards at $2\ \mathrm{m\,s^{-1}}$ between floors which are 3 m apart. The building has a ground floor, first floor and second floor. It also has a lower ground floor where there is an underground car-park. At the beginning of each day, lift P is situated on the ground floor whilst lift Q is on the lower ground floor.

One morning, lift P takes a passenger to the second floor, stops for 4 seconds and then returns to the ground floor. At the same time as P leaves the ground floor, lift Q leaves the lower ground floor and travels to the second floor, stopping at each intervening floor for 3 seconds. Use a displacement–time graph to answer the following questions (taking upwards as positive).

Hint: draw an accurate graph on graph paper.

a Find when and where the lifts pass each other.

b For each lift find:

i the average speed; **ii** the average velocity.

4.3 Speed–Time and Velocity–Time Graphs

The picture shows a sprinter running a 100 metre race along a straight track. He takes 1 second to reach a speed of $9\,\mathrm{m\,s^{-1}}$ and runs at this speed for $9\frac{1}{2}$ seconds. During the last second of the race, he throws himself forward and his speed increases to $11\,\mathrm{m\,s^{-1}}$ as he crosses the finishing line.

A speed–time graph can be used to model this example. The sprinter is modelled as a particle and he is assumed to speed up at a constant rate.

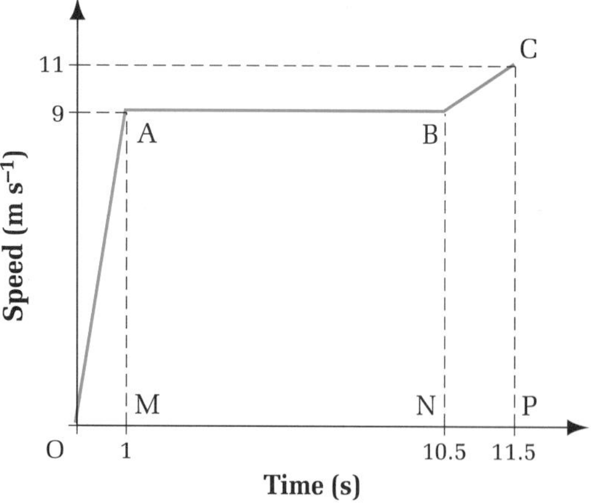

Time is shown on the *horizontal axis* and *speed* is plotted on the *vertical axis.*

The speed–time graph looks similar to the distance–time graphs used earlier, but now it is the change in *speed* as time passes which is shown. In section OA the speed increases from $0\,\mathrm{m\,s^{-1}}$ to $9\,\mathrm{m\,s^{-1}}$. The sprinter is **accelerating**.

In section AB, the speed remains at 9 m s^{-1}. On a speed–time graph a *flat line* represents *uniform (constant) speed.* During the last section, BC, the sprinter accelerates again.

All the motion takes place in the same direction. Defining this as the positive direction, a velocity–time graph can be drawn.

Velocity has *direction* as well as magnitude.

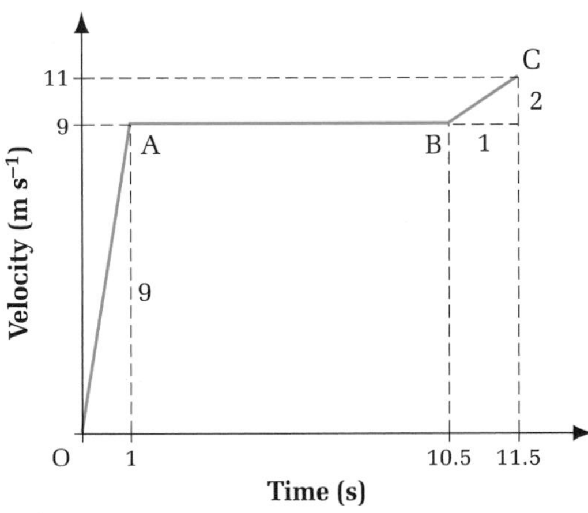

This graph looks exactly the same as the speed–time graph. Sections OA and BC still show acceleration and section AB now shows constant (uniform) velocity. On a velocity–time graph a *flat line* represents *uniform (constant) velocity*. When **velocity is uniform** both the **speed and direction of motion remain unchanged**.

Velocity–time graph can be abbreviated to v–t graph or (t, v) graph. The (t, v) abbreviation means that time is plotted along the horizontal axis and velocity along the vertical axis.

Acceleration

Acceleration is the rate at which velocity is increasing.

It has direction as well as magnitude and so it is a *vector* quantity.

$$\text{acceleration} = \frac{\text{increase in velocity}}{\text{time taken}}$$

Acceleration is given by the gradient of the velocity–time graph.

For straight line segments, the acceleration is uniform (constant).

If velocity remains positive, it is equal to the speed, giving:

$$\text{acceleration} = \frac{\text{increase in speed}}{\text{time taken}}$$

Using the velocity–time graph for the sprinter:

$$\text{In section OA, acceleration} = \frac{\text{increase in velocity}}{\text{time taken}}$$

$$= \tfrac{9}{1} = 9 \text{ metres per second per second}$$

If he carried on at this rate of acceleration the sprinter would increase his velocity by $9\,\text{m}\,\text{s}^{-1}$ every second.

After 1 second his speed would be $9\,\text{m}\,\text{s}^{-1}$. After 2 seconds his speed would be $18\,\text{m}\,\text{s}^{-1}$. After 3 seconds his speed would be $27\,\text{m}\,\text{s}^{-1}$, and so on.

The units of acceleration are usually abbreviated to $\text{m}\,\text{s}^{-2}$ and read as 'metres per second squared'.

$$\text{In section BC, acceleration} = \frac{\text{increase in velocity}}{\text{time taken}}$$

$$= \tfrac{2}{1} = 2\ \text{m}\,\text{s}^{-2}$$

The acceleration is greater at the start of the race than at the end. The *acceleration is greater* where the line on the velocity–time graph *has a greater gradient.*

In the flat section AB, acceleration $= 0\,\text{m}\,\text{s}^{-2}$

$$a = \frac{\text{increase in velocity}}{\text{time taken}}$$
$$= \tfrac{0}{9.5} = 0\,\text{m}\,\text{s}^{-2}$$

Distance and displacement

Look again at the central section (AB) of the speed–time graph for the sprinter. The sprinter is travelling at a constant speed of $9\,\text{m}\,\text{s}^{-1}$ for 9.5 seconds.

$$\text{distance} = \text{speed} \times \text{time}$$

$$\text{distance} = 9 \times 9.5 = 85.5\ \text{m}$$

For a body travelling at constant speed.

This is equal to the area of rectangle ABNM.

The area under a speed–time graph gives the distance travelled.

Applying this fact to sections OA and BC gives:

$$\text{distance travelled in section OA} = \text{area of triangle OAM}$$

$$= \tfrac{1}{2} \times 1 \times 9$$

$$= 4.5\,\text{m}$$

area of triangle $= \frac{1}{2} \times \text{base} \times \text{height}$. Notice the units will be in m ($\text{s} \times \text{m}\,\text{s}^{-1}$).

$$\text{distance travelled in section BC} = \text{area of trapezium BCPN}$$

$$= \tfrac{1}{2}(9 + 11) \times 1$$

$$= 10\,\text{m}$$

area of trapezium $= \frac{1}{2}(a + b)h$

$$\text{total distance} = 4.5 + 85.5 + 10 = 100\,\text{m}$$

In this example, the velocity–time graph could be used instead. The area under the graph would represent the displacement. As the motion is all in the same direction, the displacement is equal in magnitude to the distance travelled, 100 metres.

The area between a velocity–time graph and the time axis gives the displacement.

Speed–time and velocity–time graphs are not always identical. If the direction of motion changes, they are different.

The sketch shows a dog chasing a ball. The dog accelerates to a velocity of $8\,\text{m}\,\text{s}^{-1}$ in two seconds, runs at this velocity for 4 seconds and then slows down and stops to pick up the ball. On the way back to its owner it accelerates to a speed of $6\,\text{m}\,\text{s}^{-1}$ and reaches its owner after a total time of 18 seconds. Here is a velocity–time graph for the dog's motion.

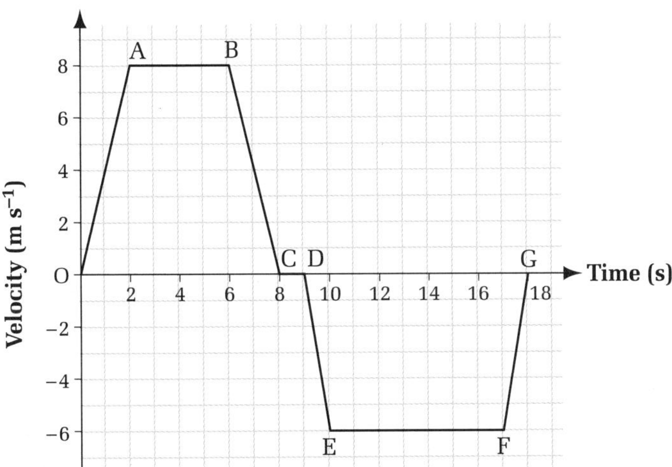

The speed–time graph would look like this:

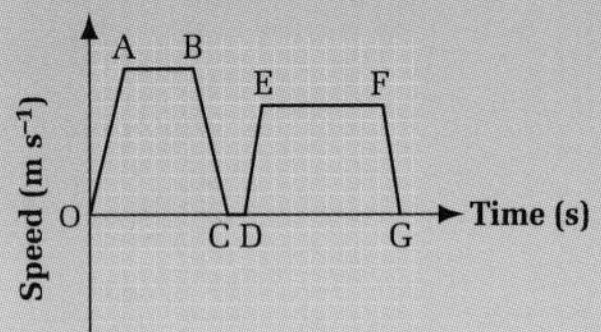

Compare the two graphs.

The fact that the dog changes direction after retrieving the ball is shown by the velocity being negative for the last part of the motion.

What was the dog's acceleration in each part of the motion? The dog's acceleration is given by the gradient of the velocity–time graph.

For section OA, acceleration $= \frac{8}{2} = 4\,\text{m}\,\text{s}^{-2}$

For section BC, acceleration $= \frac{-8}{2} = -4\,\text{m}\,\text{s}^{-2}$

The acceleration is positive when the velocity is increasing.

The acceleration has a negative value because the velocity is decreasing. The dog is slowing down. The rate at which the velocity is changing can be given by writing:

$$\text{acceleration} = -4\,\text{m s}^{-2} \text{ or deceleration (retardation)} = 4\,\text{m s}^{-2}$$

A negative acceleration is often called **deceleration** or **retardation**.
The word deceleration (or retardation) means the acceleration will have a negative value.

Most questions involving acceleration will have positive velocities only. However, occasionally you may need to interpret results when the velocity is negative. In this case, explaining the acceleration values is a bit trickier.

For section DE, acceleration $= \frac{-6}{1} = -6\,\text{m s}^{-2}$

Remember the velocity is now negative.

The acceleration is again negative but this time the dog is not slowing down. When the acceleration and velocity are both negative, the speed is increasing but in a *negative direction*.

For section FG, acceleration $= \frac{6}{1} = 6\,\text{m s}^{-2}$

The acceleration is in the opposite direction to the velocity and the dog is slowing down.

When the velocity and acceleration have the same sign the speed is increasing.
When the acceleration and velocity have opposite signs the speed is decreasing.

Each graph used in this section has consisted of straight line segments. This means the acceleration in each section is uniform (constant). This is a simplified model of what really happens. More realistic graphs would have curved sections with the velocity changing more gradually. But curves are more difficult to analyse so the motion will continue to be modelled with straight line segments for the time-being.

Overview of method

Step ① Sketch the v–t graph (unless it is given).
Step ② Make sure the axes are labelled and the units noted.
Step ③ Select and apply the formula or formulas to answer the question.

$$\text{displacement} = \text{area under the } v\text{–}t \text{ graph}$$

$$\text{acceleration} = \text{gradient of } v\text{–}t \text{ graph}$$

$$\text{average velocity} = \frac{\text{total displacement}}{\text{total time}}$$

$$\text{average speed} = \frac{\text{total distance}}{\text{total time}}$$

Example 1

① and ② are already complete.

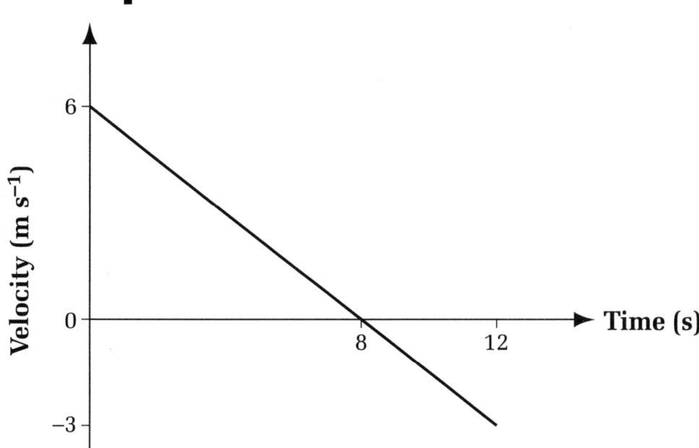

Use the velocity–time graph to:

a find the initial velocity
b find the final velocity
c find the acceleration
d find the total displacement
e find the total distance travelled
f find the average velocity
g find the average speed
h sketch a speed–time graph.

Solution

a initial velocity $= 6\ \text{m s}^{-1}$

b final velocity $= -3\ \text{m s}^{-1}$

Read the values directly from the graph.

c Using the first 8 seconds of motion, the acceleration is given by the gradient of the velocity–time graph. ◀ ③ **acceleration = gradient of v–t graph.**

acceleration $= -\frac{6}{8} = -0.75\ \text{m s}^{-2}$

Alternatively, use all of the motion.
$a = -\frac{9}{12} = -0.75\ \text{m s}^{-2}$

The acceleration is constant. A graph of acceleration against time would look like this.

d

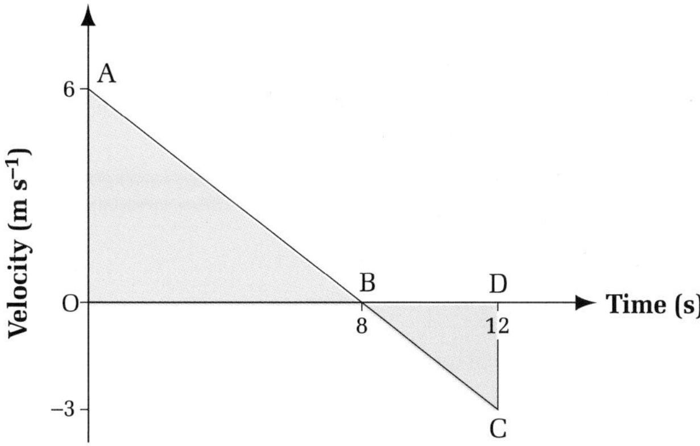

Displacement during first 8 seconds of motion is given by the area of triangle OAB. ◀ ③ **displacement = area under the v–t graph**

displacement$= \frac{1}{2} \times 8 \times 6 = 24$ m

Displacement during the last 4 seconds of motion is given by the area of triangle BCD.

displacement $= -\frac{1}{2} \times 4 \times 3 = -6$ m

Total displacement $= 24 - 6 = 18$ m

The displacement is negative because the velocity is negative. The area is *below* the time axis.

e Total distance travelled $= 24 + 6 = 30$ m

f average velocity$= \dfrac{\text{total displacement}}{\text{total time}} = \frac{18}{12} = 1.5 \text{ m s}^{-1}$

g average speed$= \dfrac{\text{total distance}}{\text{total time}} = \frac{30}{12} = 2.5 \text{ m s}^{-1}$

h

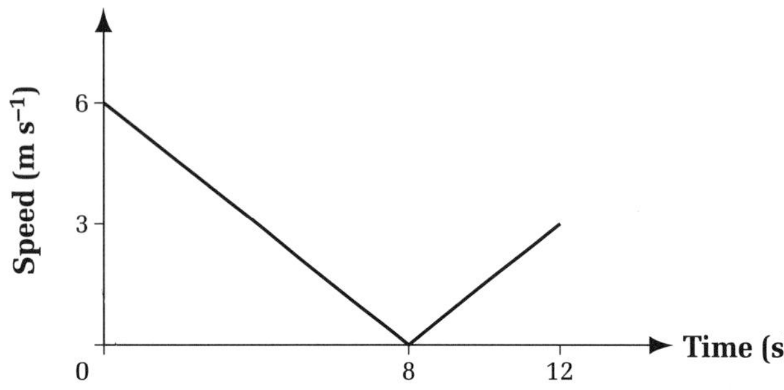

Notice that the speed on the speed–time sketch is always positive.

Example 2

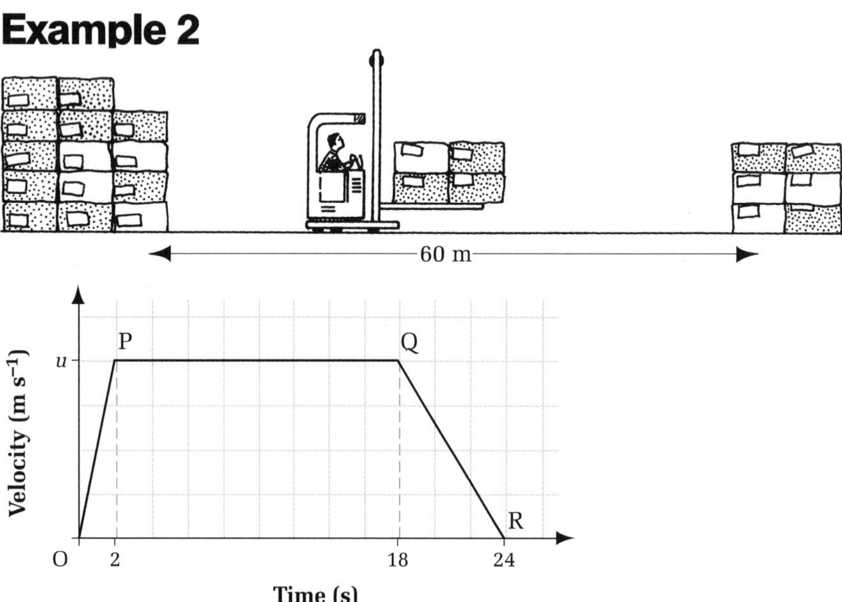

The sketch shows the velocity–time graph for a fork-lift truck as it transfers goods from one part of a warehouse to another. Find the value of u if the truck travels 60 metres.

Solution

Displacement is given by the area of trapezium OPQR. ◀ ③ displacement = area under the v–t graph.

① and ② are already completed. Displacement = 60 m.

area of trapezium OPQR = 60

$$\frac{(16 + 24)u}{2} = 60$$

area $= \frac{1}{2}(a + b)h$

$$20u = 60$$

Divide by 20.

$$u = 3$$

4.3 Speed–Time and Velocity–Time Graphs

Exercise

Technique

1 **a**

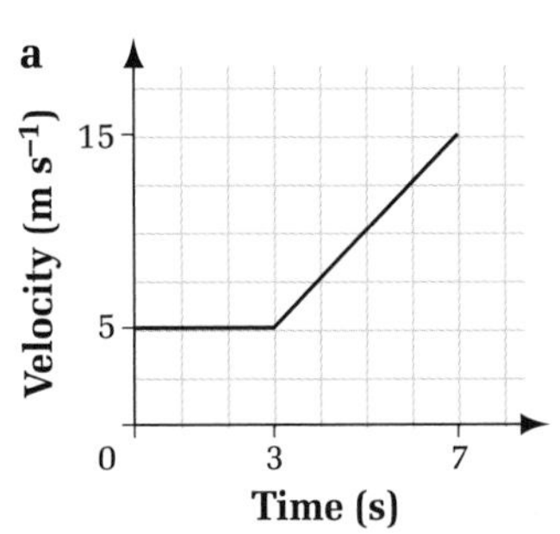

b

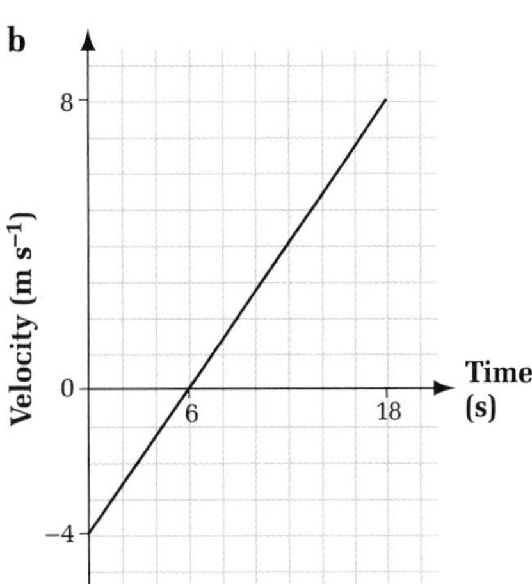

c

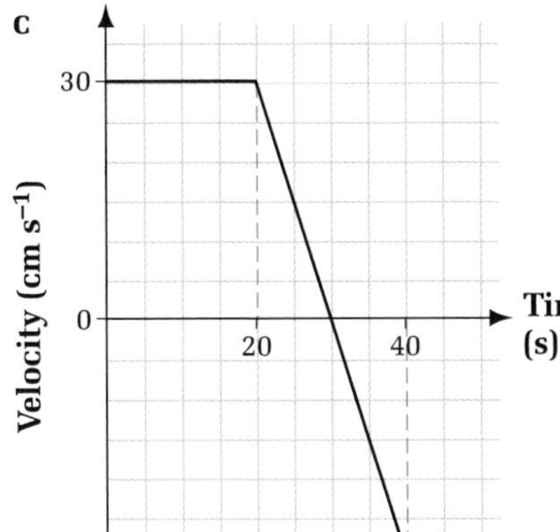

d

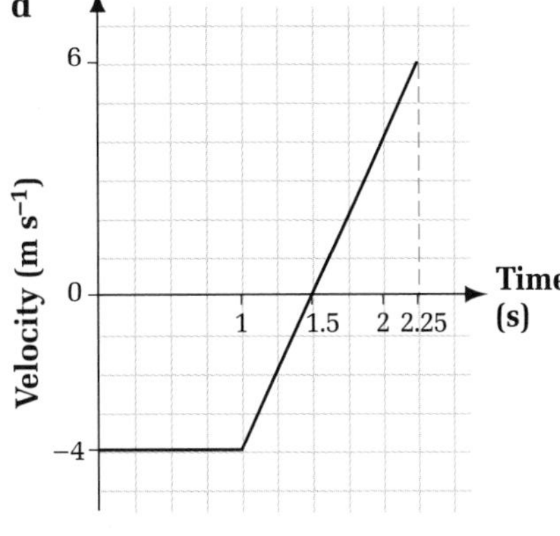

For each of the velocity–time graphs, find:

i the initial velocity
ii the final velocity
iii the total displacement from the starting position
iv the total distance travelled
v the acceleration in sections where the velocity changes.

2 A particle starts from rest and accelerates to a speed of $12\ \mathrm{m\,s^{-1}}$ in 6 s. The particle then travels at constant speed for 8 s before decelerating to rest in 4 s. Assuming that all the motion is in one direction along a straight line:

a sketch a speed–time graph for the motion
b calculate the distance travelled, acceleration and deceleration of the particle.

3 An object travels in a straight line with constant velocity $15\ \text{m s}^{-1}$ for 40 s. It then accelerates to a velocity of $20\ \text{m s}^{-1}$ in the next 25 s.

a Sketch a velocity–time graph.

b Calculate the distance travelled by the object.

c Find the average speed.

4 A body starts from rest and travels in a straight line, accelerating to a speed of $8\ \text{cm s}^{-1}$ after 2 s. After travelling at this speed for 3 s it decelerates, coming to rest after a further 4 s. It then moves in the opposite direction reaching a speed of $6\ \text{cm s}^{-1}$ after another 3 s.

a Sketch a (t, v) graph for the motion.

b Calculate the displacement of the body from its starting position at the end of the motion described.

c What is the total distance travelled by the object?

d Calculate the acceleration of the body in each part of the motion.

5 The velocity–time graph shows the motion of a body which travels a total distance of 100 m.

a Find the value of T.

b Find the acceleration.

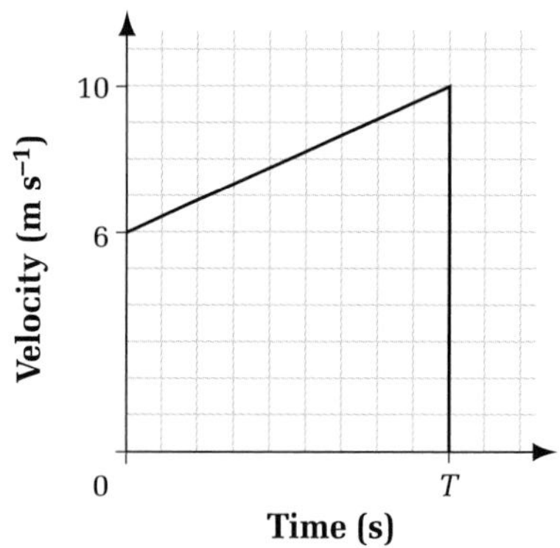

6 The motion of a particle is modelled by the (t, v) graph. If the total distance travelled is 28 m, find:

a the value of u

b the acceleration in each part of the motion.

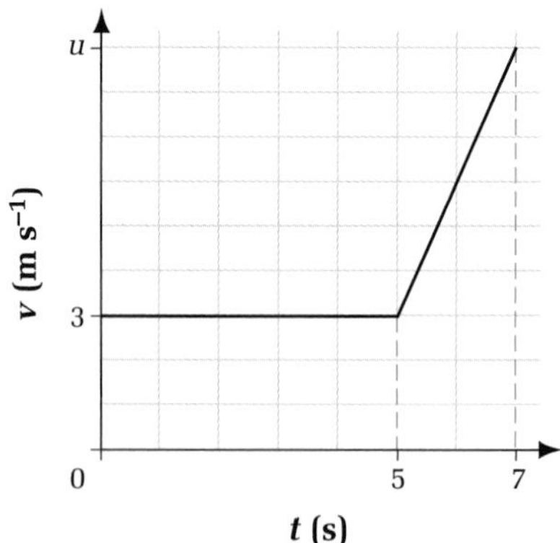

Contextual

1

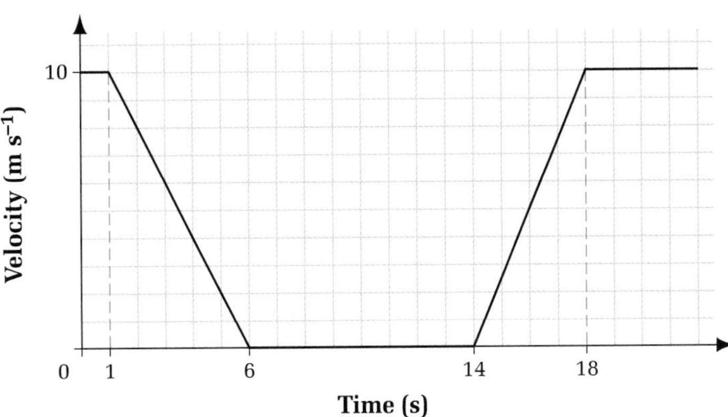

The sketch models the velocity–time graph of a bus as it stops to pick up passengers at a bus stop.

a Calculate the retardation of the bus.
b Calculate the acceleration of the bus.
c For how long is the bus stationary?
d How far does the bus travel while decelerating?
e How far does the bus travel while accelerating?

2 The sketch models the motion of a ball which is thrown up into the air and then caught.

a Describe the motion briefly.
b Calculate the acceleration.
c Find the height reached (above the point where the ball starts).

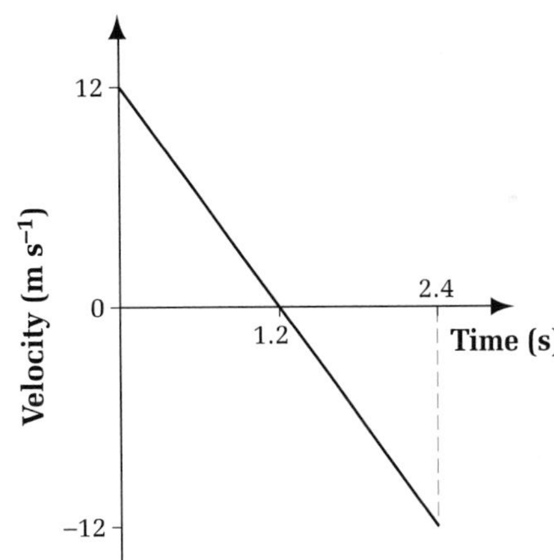

3 A coach accelerates from rest to a velocity of 15 m s^{-1} in 6 s and travels at this velocity for 8 s before stopping at a road junction. The total time taken is 20 s. Assume the motion is in a straight line and the acceleration and deceleration are uniform.

a Sketch a velocity–time graph.
b Find the acceleration.
c Find the deceleration.
d Find the total distance travelled.

4

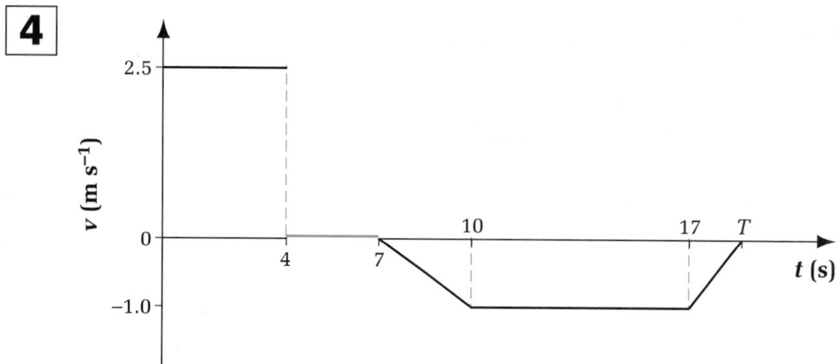

Note the dashed line at $t = 4$ indicates a sudden change in velocity from 2.5 m s^{-1} to 0 m s^{-1}.

Sally goes to a garden centre to pick up some gravel that she has ordered. The (t, v) graph shows the journey as she walks from her car to collect the gravel and pulls it back on a trolley to the car.

Assume the distance she pulls the gravel back to the car is exactly the same as the distance she walks from the car to the gravel.

a How far is it from the car to the gravel?
b How long did it take Sally to load the gravel onto the trolley?
c Find the value of T.

5

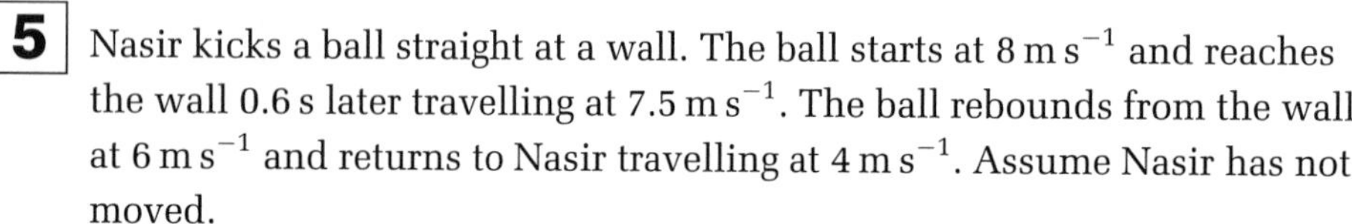

Nasir kicks a ball straight at a wall. The ball starts at 8 m s^{-1} and reaches the wall 0.6 s later travelling at 7.5 m s^{-1}. The ball rebounds from the wall at 6 m s^{-1} and returns to Nasir travelling at 4 m s^{-1}. Assume Nasir has not moved.

a Sketch a velocity–time graph for the ball's motion with the positive direction towards the wall.
b Find the distance between Nasir and the wall.
c Find the time taken for the ball to return from the wall to Nasir.

6 The velocity, v m s^{-1}, of a battery operated toy racing car is modelled by:

$v = 0.5t$ for $0 \le t \le 4$, (t in s)
$v = 2$ for $4 \le t \le 10$,
$v = 6 - 0.4t$ for $10 \le t \le 20$.

a Sketch the (t, v) graph for this motion.
b Describe briefly what happens, giving the times at which $v = 0$.
c Find the total distance moved by the car.
d Find its displacement from its initial position at the end of the motion.

4.4 Dimensional Analysis

The units in an equation can be used to check whether the equation is correct. They can even be used to predict what a formula is going to be.

There are four main metric units of length: millimetres, centimetres, metres and kilometres. These can be abbreviated to mm, cm, m and km. This variety of units for measuring length can be confusing. To simplify matters, the letter **L** is used to represent *all* the different measurements of **length**.

Capital, non-italic letters are used for the dimensions so that they are not confused with variables.

Length is called a **dimension**. The other dimensions used in mechanics are mass and time. The symbol for **mass** is **M** and **time** is **T**. The method of converting an equation into these symbols is called **dimensional analysis**.

Finding the dimensions of a quantity

To convert a quantity into its dimensions, it is useful to look at its units. For example, speed is measured in metres per second or $\mathrm{m\,s^{-1}}$. The dimensions of speed are $\mathrm{LT^{-1}}$. The L represents the metres and the T the seconds. There is a shorthand way to write this down.

$$[\text{speed}] = \mathrm{LT^{-1}}$$

The square brackets mean that the dimensions of speed are being taken. The brackets will distinguish dimensions from equations.

Sometimes the dimensions of a quantity can be found from an equation which relates it to other quantities. The following examples and exercises use a variety of equations. You may be familiar with some and not others. Most will be explained more fully, later in the course.

Using dimensional analysis to check an equation

The method of dimensions can be used to check whether equations are correct. The dimensions must be the same for each term in the equation otherwise it will not work.

Overview of method

Step ① Write down the dimensions of each quantity in the equation.
Step ② Substitute the dimensions into each side of the equation.
Step ③ Numbers can normally be assumed to be dimensionless.
Step ④ Use the laws of indices to simplify.
Step ⑤ Check that dimensions of each term in the equation are the same.

Example 1

a What are the dimensions of acceleration?

b Use the equation:

force = mass × acceleration

to find the dimensions of force.

Solution

a Acceleration is measured in m s^{-2}. The dimensions of acceleration are LT^{-2}.

$[\text{acceleration}] = \text{LT}^{-2}$

b $[\text{force}] = [\text{mass}] \times [\text{acceleration}]$

$[\text{force}] = \text{M} \times \text{LT}^{-2}$

$[\text{force}] = \text{MLT}^{-2}$

Note the dimensions of force are needed later in the section.

Example 2

In the equation $v^2 = u^2 + 2as$, u and v are both velocities, a is acceleration and s is displacement. Show that this equation is dimensionally correct.

Solution

$[u] = \text{LT}^{-1}$ $\quad [v] = \text{LT}^{-1}$ ◀ ① Write down the dimensions of all the quantities in the equation.

$[a] = \text{LT}^{-2}$ $\quad [s] = \text{L}$

$$v^2 = u^2 + 2as$$

Taking dimensions of the equation:

LHS $[v^2] = (\text{LT}^{-1})^2 = \text{L}^2\text{T}^{-2}$ ◀ ② Substitute the dimensions.

RHS $[u^2] + [2as] = (\text{LT}^{-1})^2 + (\text{LT}^{-2})(\text{L})$ ◀ ③ The number 2 is dimensionless.

$= \text{L}^2\text{T}^{-2} + \text{L}^2\text{T}^{-2}$ ◀ ④ Use laws of indices to simplify.

The dimensions are the same for all three terms and so the equation is *dimensionally correct*. Although dimensional analysis suggests the equation may be correct, it does not prove it. In particular, the number 2 in the equation cannot be confirmed as being correct using dimensions.

Using dimensional analysis to predict a formula
Overview of method

Step ① Consider which quantities may be relevant to the situation.

Step ② Write down a possible formula using powers of these quantities.

Step ③ Include a constant as the formula may involve a number which cannot be worked out by dimensional analysis.

Step ④ Change all quantities to their dimensions.

Step ⑤ Use the laws of indices to simplify.

Step ⑥ Equate the powers of each dimension in turn.

Step ⑦ Solve these equations to give the powers in the formula.

Example 3

A simple pendulum can be made from a length of string and a mass. The time for the pendulum to complete one oscillation is called the time period. The time period could depend on the length of the string, l, the mass of the object, m, and the acceleration due to gravity, g. A possible formula for the time period of a simple pendulum is thought to be:

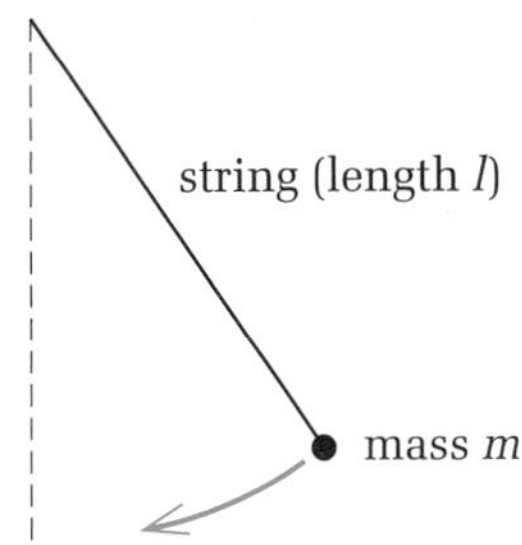

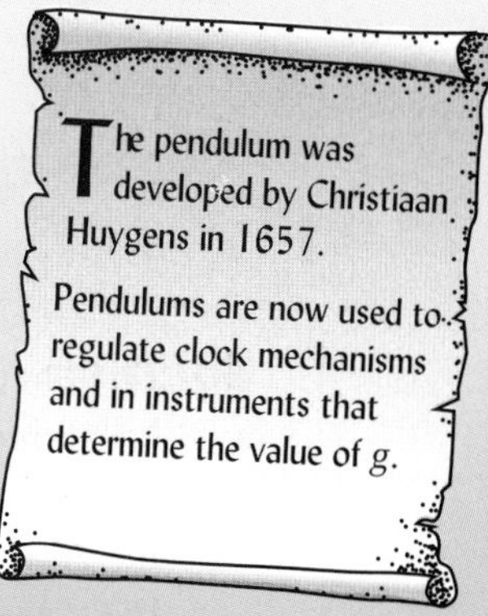

$$\text{time period} = k \times l^a \times m^b \times g^c$$

Use dimensional analysis to predict a possible formula for the time period.

The time period for a simple pendulum is the time it takes to swing back and forth once.

Solution

Step ① has been completed for you in the question.

$$\text{time period} = k \times l^a \times m^b \times g^c$$ ◀ ② Write a possible formula. ③ Include a constant k.

$[\text{time period}] = \text{T} \quad [l] = \text{L} \quad [m] = \text{M} \quad [g] = \text{LT}^{-2}$

The powers of l, m and g are not known so letters are used.
④ Change all quantities to their dimensions.

There are no lengths or masses on the left hand side of the equation. Consider the dimensions of both sides of the formula.

$$\text{LHS } [\text{time period}] = \text{M}^0\text{L}^0\text{T}^1$$

$$\text{RHS } [k \times l^a \times m^b \times g^c] = \text{L}^a \times \text{M}^b \times (\text{LT}^{-2})^c$$ ◀ ⑤ Use the laws of indices to simplify the expressions.

$$= \text{L}^a \times \text{M}^b \times \text{L}^c \times \text{T}^{-2c}$$

$$= \text{L}^{a-c} \times \text{M}^b \times T^{-2c}$$

For T, $\text{T}^1 = \text{T}^{-2c}$ ◀ ⑥ Equate the powers of each dimension.

$1 = -2c$ ◀ ⑦ Solve these equations.

$c = -\frac{1}{2}$

For L, $\text{L}^0 = \text{L}^{a+c}$

$0 = a + c$ ◀ Use $c = -\frac{1}{2}$ from above.

$0 = a - \frac{1}{2}$

$a = \frac{1}{2}$

For M, $\text{M}^0 = \text{M}^b$

$0 = b$

The formula becomes:

$$\text{period} = k \times l^a \times m^b \times g^c$$ ◀ Use $a = \frac{1}{2}$, $b = 0$ and $c = -\frac{1}{2}$.

$$\text{period} = k \times l^{\frac{1}{2}} \times m^0 \times g^{-\frac{1}{2}}$$

$$\text{period} = k \times l^{\frac{1}{2}} \times g^{-\frac{1}{2}}$$

$$\text{period} = k \times \sqrt{l} \times \frac{1}{\sqrt{g}}$$

$$\text{period} = k\sqrt{\frac{l}{g}}$$

Remember $m^0 = 1$.
$l^{\frac{1}{2}} = \sqrt{l}$

$g^{-\frac{1}{2}} = \frac{1}{\sqrt{g}}$

4.4 Dimensional Analysis Exercise

Technique

1 a Write down the dimensions of:

i area　　ii volume.

b Use the method of dimensional analysis to determine which of the following formulas could be correct, where A = area, V = volume, r = radius, d = diameter, and h = height:

i $A = \pi r^2$　　ii $V = \pi r^2 h + 2\pi dh$

iii $A = 4\pi r^2 - 2\pi rh$　　iv $V = 4d^2h + 72dh^2 - 3d^3$

2 a Using density = mass ÷ volume, find the dimensions of density.

b Using momentum = mass × velocity, find [momentum].

c Using work = force × distance, determine the dimensions of work.

d Using power = force × velocity, find [power].

e Using kinetic energy = $\frac{1}{2}$ × mass × (speed)^2, find [kinetic energy].

f Using pressure = force ÷ area, determine the dimensions of pressure.

Remember [force] = MLT^{-2}

3 In the following equations u and v are velocities, a is acceleration, s is displacement and t is time. Check that the equations are valid using the method of dimensional analysis.

a $v = u + at$　　b $s = \frac{1}{2}(u + v)t$

c $s = ut + \frac{1}{2}at^2$　　d $s = vt - \frac{1}{2}at^2$

In questions 4 to 6, m is mass, v is velocity, g is acceleration, t is time and h is height.

4 Use dimensional analysis to determine whether $mv = mgt$ is a possible equation.

5 A possible equation is thought to be $mgh = km^a v^b$, where k is a dimensionless constant. Use dimensional analysis to predict a and b.

6 A possible equation is thought to be $mg = kv^a$, where a is a constant. Find the dimensions of k when:

a $a = 1$　　b $a = 3$

7 The universal law of gravitation gives the formula:

$$F = \frac{Gm_1m_2}{d^2}$$

where F is force, m_1 and m_2 are masses and d is distance. Find the dimensions of the gravitational constant G.

Consolidation

Exercise A

1

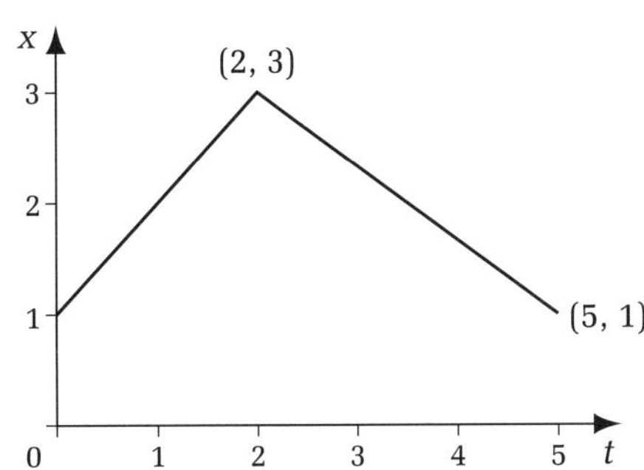

A snooker ball is moving in a straight line. Its displacement is x metres at time t seconds. For $0 \leq t \leq 5$ the (t, x) graph consists of two straight line segments as shown in the diagram. Find the velocity of the snooker ball:

a when $t = 1$ **b** when $t = 3$.

Describe briefly what could have happened when $t = 2$. *(UCLES)*

2 A car driver wishes to test her brakes. She drives in a straight line along a horizontal road. At time $t = 0$ seconds her car is moving with constant speed $13\ \text{m s}^{-1}$. At time $t = 0.65$ seconds she gently applies the brakes and the car comes to rest after a *further* 2.1 seconds. Assuming that the deceleration of the car is constant:

a sketch a velocity–time graph which models this entire manoeuvre;
b show that the total distance the car moves from time $t = 0$ until it comes to rest is 22.1 m. *(NICCEA)*

3

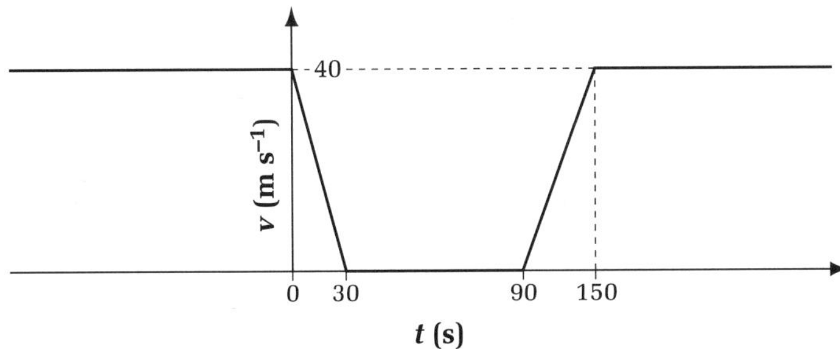

An express train stops at a station during its journey. The velocity–time graph shows a simple model of the motion of the train as it approaches the station, stops and then leaves.

a Find:
  i the constant deceleration of the train from full speed to rest in the station
  ii the constant acceleration as the train moves away from rest at the station back to full speed

iii the time spent in the station
iv the distance travelled during deceleration
v the distance travelled during acceleration.

b On Sundays the train does not stop and so continues through the station at full speed. Find the time saved.

c The original graph shows a simple model of the movement of the train. What adaptation would you make to the graph to make the model a little more realistic? *(MEI)*

4 Show that the impulse equation $Ft = mv - mu$ is dimensionally correct. *(NICCEA)*

[force] = MLT^{-2}

Exercise B

1

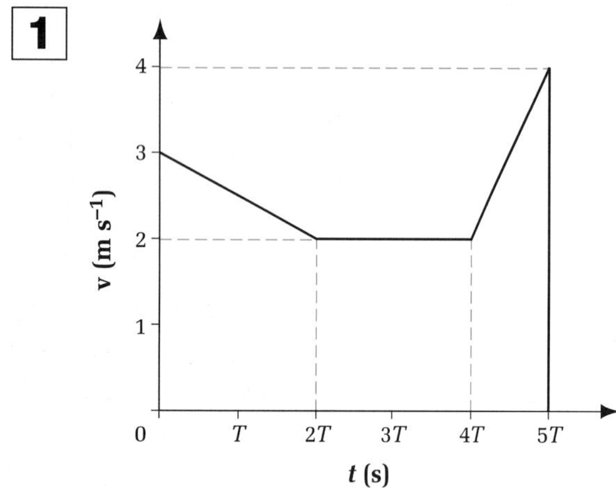

The v–t graph shows the speed of a particle during the course of its motion from time $t = 0$ to $t = 5T$ seconds. Given that the total distance travelled by the particle is 48 m, calculate:

a the value of T

b the initial retardation of the particle. *(UCLES)*

2

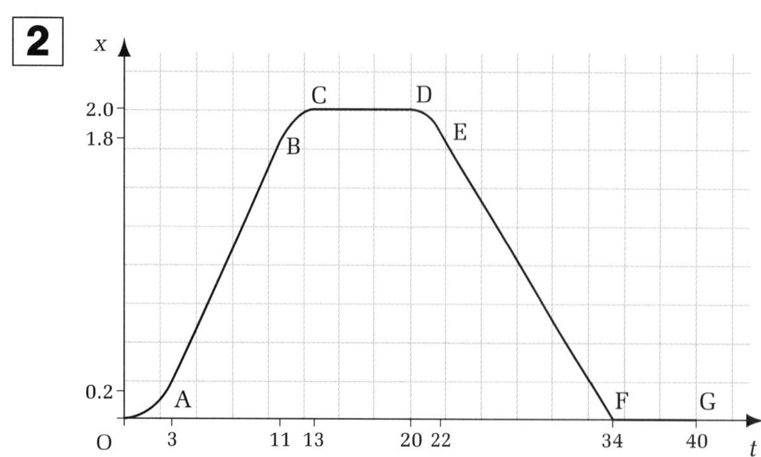

The (t, x) graph of a toy train moving on straight rails is as shown in the diagram. The distance x is measured in metres and the time t in seconds. The coordinates of the points marked are A (3, 0.2), B (11, 1.8), C (13, 2.0), D (20, 2.0), E (22, 1.8), F (34, 0), G (40, 0). The lines AB, CD, EF and FG are all straight line segments. Find the speeds when $t = 5$, $t = 15$, $t = 25$. Sketch the (t, v) graph and describe, in words, the motion of the train for $0 \leq t \leq 40$.

(UCLES)

3 A train accelerates from rest at a station A with constant acceleration of 2 m s^{-2} until it reaches a speed of 36 m s^{-1}. It then cruises at this speed for 90 s before braking to stop at the next station B. The line from A to B is straight. During the braking period the train decelerates with constant deceleration 3 m s^{-2}.

a Sketch a speed–time graph to illustrate this information.

b Find the total time taken for the train to travel from A to B.

c Find the distance from A to B.

(ULEAC)

4 P, Q, R and S are points, in that order, on a straight line and Q is the mid-point of PS. A particle travels from P to R at constant speed $V\text{ m s}^{-1}$, then retards uniformly so that it comes to rest instantaneously at S. It reverses direction at S and accelerates uniformly so that it reaches a speed of $V\text{ m s}^{-1}$ at R. It then travels at a constant speed $V\text{ m s}^{-1}$ towards P.

Assume that the negative acceleration is unchanged at S.

The time taken for the particle to travel from P to S is 7 s, and the time for it to travel from S to Q on the return journey is 4.5 s.

a Sketch the velocity–time graph for the motion of the particle as it travels from P to S and returns to Q.

b Calculate the time taken for the particle to travel from P until it reaches R for the first time.

c Calculate the ratio of the distance *PR* to the distance *PS*.

(UCLES)

Applications and Activities

1 Sketch the distance–time graph of a journey that you have made recently.

2 Sketch a distance–time graph and a speed–time graph for the following situations:

a a marble rolling across a table
b a trolley travelling down an inclined slope
c a book sliding along a table.

3 Sketch displacement–time graphs and velocity–time graphs for different modes of transport.

Summary

- Speed is the rate of change of distance with time. It has magnitude but no direction.
- Displacement is distance in a specified direction and is a measure of position.
- Velocity is the rate of change of displacement with time.
- Acceleration is the rate of change of velocity with time.
- We can convert units of speed from m s^{-1} to km h^{-1} using $\times \frac{3600}{1000}$.
- We can convert from km h^{-1} to m s^{-1} using $\times \frac{1000}{3600}$.
- If a velocity is uniform then it is constant (it does not change) and the speed and direction of motion remain the same.
- Uniform acceleration means that the acceleration is constant.
- The area under a speed–time graph gives the distance travelled.
- The area between a velocity–time graph and the time axis gives the displacement.
- The magnitude of the acceleration is given by the gradient of the velocity–time or speed–time graph.
- $\text{average speed} = \dfrac{\text{total distance}}{\text{total time}} \qquad \text{average velocity} = \dfrac{\text{total displacement}}{\text{total time}}$
- Dimensions are used to check equations and to suggest possible formulas.

5 Vectors II

What you need to know

- How to use trigonometry and Pythagoras' theorem for right-angled triangles.
- How to construct accurate scale drawings.
- How to add and subtract vectors expressed in column vector or component form.
- How to use the sine and cosine rules for any triangle.
- How to use Cartesian coordinates in three dimensions.
- How to find the magnitude of a vector.
- How to determine whether two vectors are parallel.

Review

1 **a**

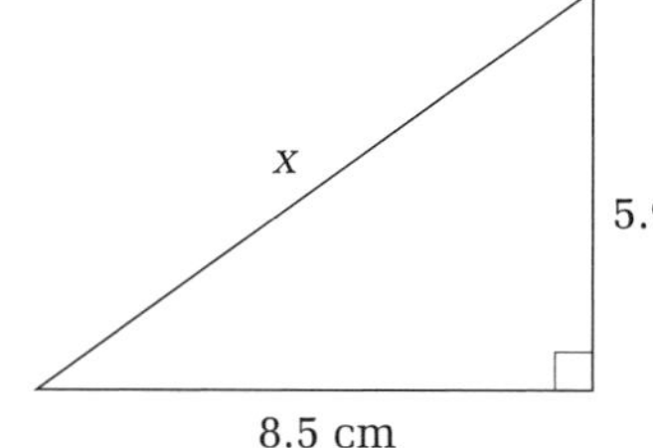

Calculate the length x.

b

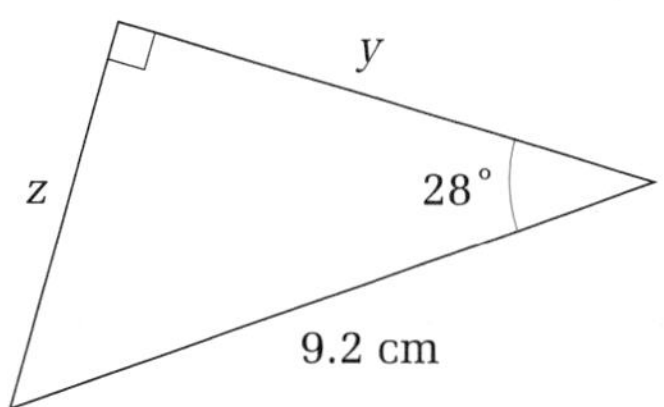

Calculate y and z.

2 **a**

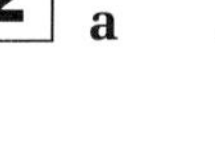

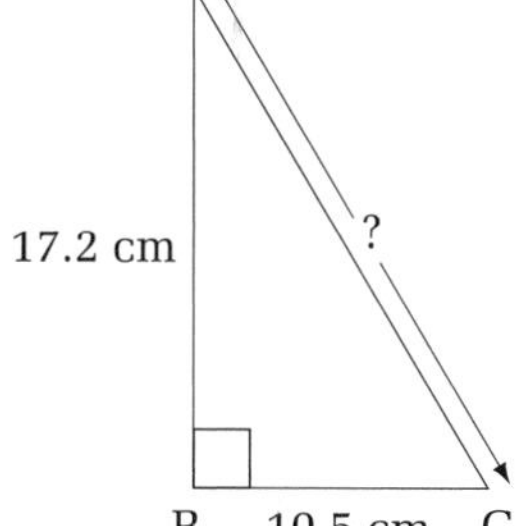

b

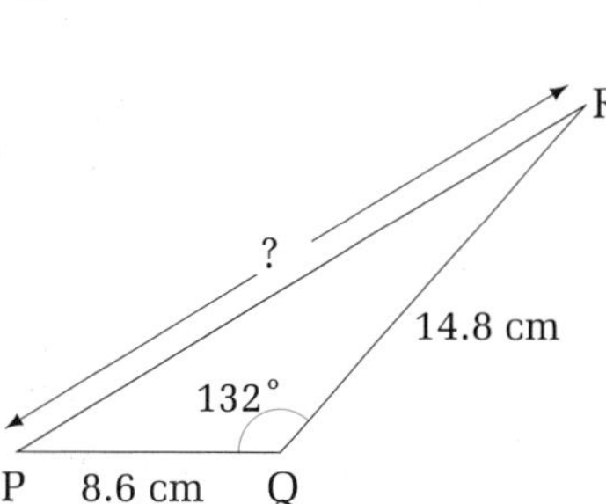

Draw both of these triangles to scale. Measure the lengths indicated, on your diagrams.

3 a $\mathbf{a} = 6\mathbf{i} - 8\mathbf{j}$, $\mathbf{b} = -3\mathbf{i} - 2\mathbf{j}$

Write down $\mathbf{a} + \mathbf{b}$ and $\mathbf{a} - \mathbf{b}$.

b $\mathbf{p} = \begin{pmatrix} 6 \\ 7 \end{pmatrix}$ $\mathbf{q} = \begin{pmatrix} -12 \\ 2 \end{pmatrix}$

Write down $\mathbf{p} + \mathbf{q}$ and $\mathbf{p} - \mathbf{q}$.

4 a

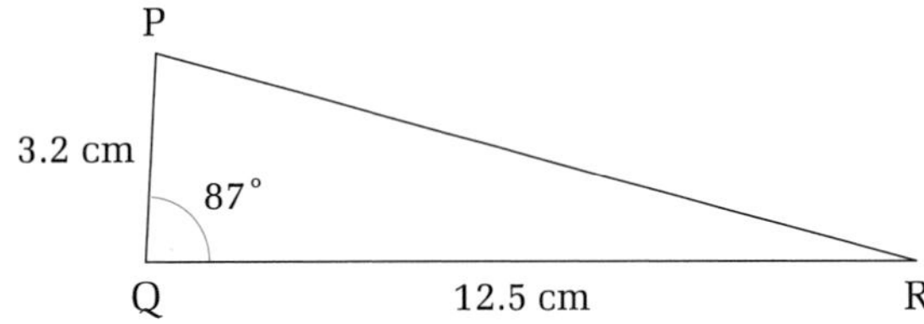

Use the cosine rule to calculate the length PR.

b

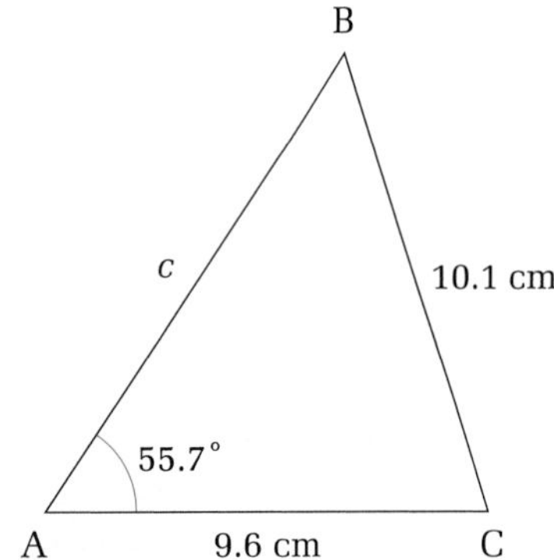

Use the sine rule to find:

i angle B

ii side c.

c

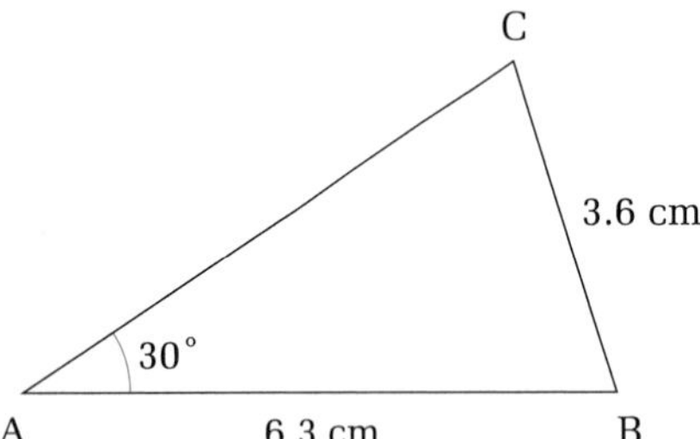

i Use the sine rule to find the two possible values of angle C.

ii If angle B is known to be less than 45°, which is the correct answer for C?

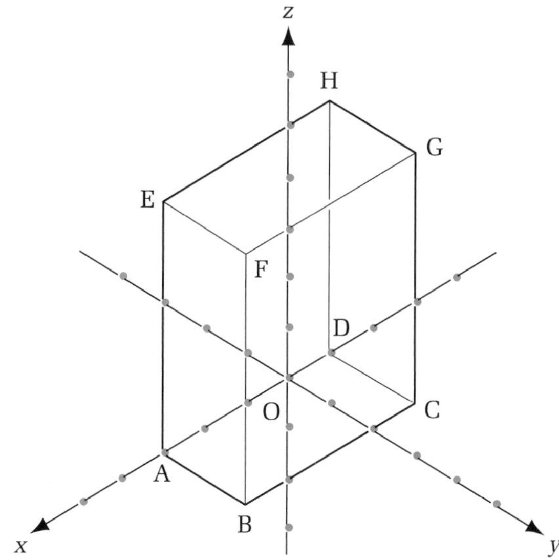

If A is the point (3, 0, 0), B is the point (3, 2, 0), *BC* is 4 units and *BF* is 5 units, write down the coordinates of the remaining vertices of cuboid ABCDEFGH.

6 Giving your answers in surd form where necessary, calculate the magnitudes of the following vectors:

$\mathbf{a} = 12\mathbf{i} - 16\mathbf{j}$ $\quad\mathbf{b} = -3\mathbf{i} + 9\mathbf{j}$ $\quad\mathbf{c} = \begin{pmatrix} 5 \\ -6 \end{pmatrix}$ $\quad\mathbf{d} = \begin{pmatrix} 8 \\ -15 \end{pmatrix}$

7 $\mathbf{a} = \begin{pmatrix} 2 \\ -5 \end{pmatrix}$ $\quad\mathbf{b} = \begin{pmatrix} -7 \\ 3 \end{pmatrix}$ $\quad\mathbf{c} = \begin{pmatrix} 14 \\ -6 \end{pmatrix}$ $\quad\mathbf{d} = \begin{pmatrix} 4 \\ 10 \end{pmatrix}$

Determine which two of these vectors are parallel.

Resolving Vectors into Perpendicular Components

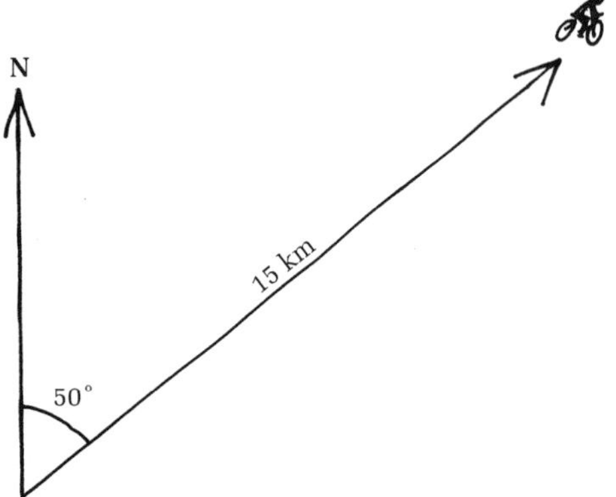

Notice that the length of the line indicates the magnitude of the vector.

After one hour a cyclist is 15 km from the starting point, on a bearing of 050°. The cyclist has travelled approximately north east, but how far north and how far east has the cyclist gone? To answer this question the magnitude and direction must be converted into column vector form or **i** and **j** form. The cyclist is treated as a particle. The displacement could be drawn to scale to find out the distances the cyclist has travelled to the north and to the east.

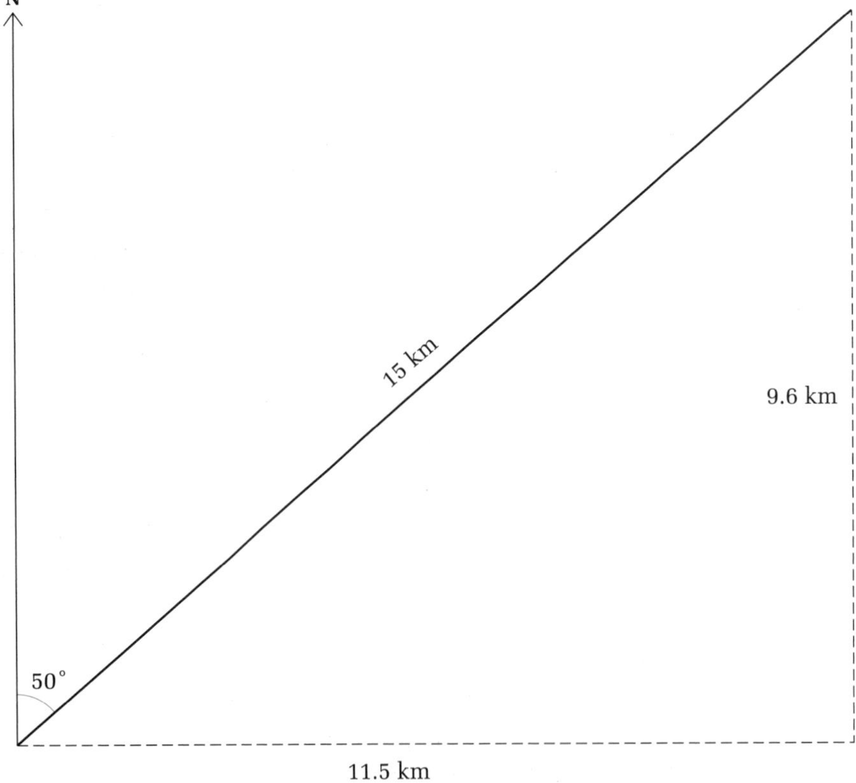

Scale 1 cm : 1 km

However, a more accurate solution can be obtained by using trigonometry.

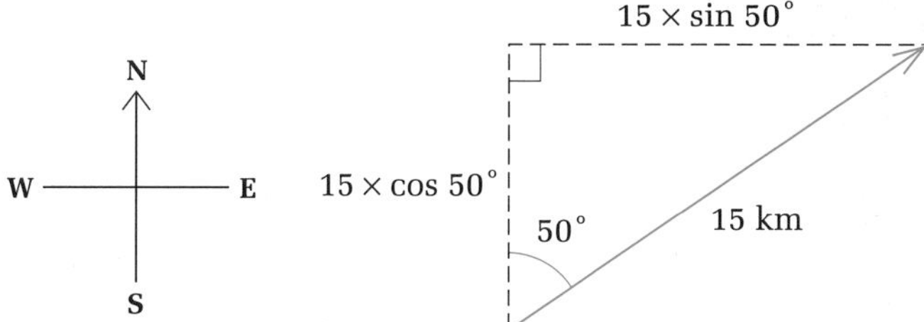

This can be remembered as 'the cos is on the line next to the angle'. Alternatively, it can be remembered as 'the cos is *with* the angle'.

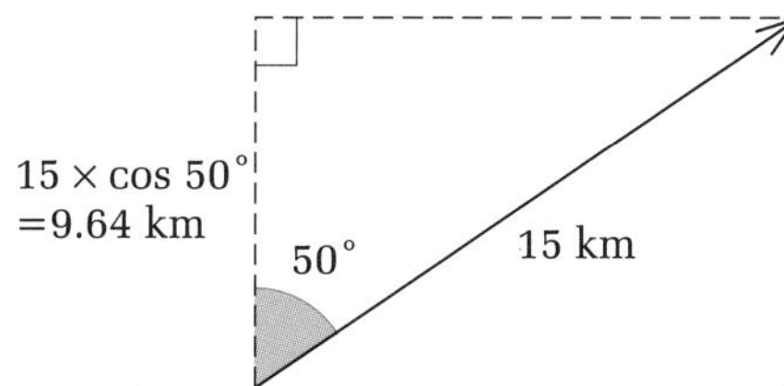

'The sin is on the line opposite the angle' or alternatively, 'sin is *not with* the angle'.

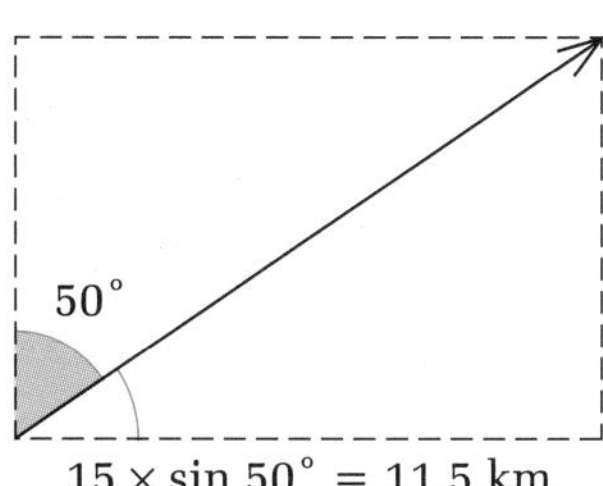

The displacement of the cyclist is 11.5 km due east *and* 9.64 km due north. These two numbers are called the **components** of the displacement vector. This process of converting a magnitude and direction vector in this way is called **resolving into perpendicular components.**

The components will always be at 90° to each other.

Column vectors and unit vectors

The total displacement of the cyclist is 11.5 km due east and 9.64 km due north. However this seems a rather long winded way of writing this down. Instead, the displacement can be written as a column vector or in unit vector form.

$$\begin{pmatrix} 11.5 \\ 9.64 \end{pmatrix} \text{km or } (11.5\mathbf{i} + 9.64\mathbf{j}) \text{ km}$$

The appropriate units are written after and outside the vector brackets.

Using surd form

Sometimes a vector will be expressed using surd form. This is usually because during the calculation the surds will cancel to give an *exact* answer. For these kinds of questions the following table of common results will be useful.

θ	$0°$	$30°$	$45°$	$60°$	$90°$
$\sin\theta$	0	$\frac{1}{2}$	$\frac{1}{\sqrt{2}}$ or $\frac{\sqrt{2}}{2}$	$\frac{\sqrt{3}}{2}$	1
$\cos\theta$	1	$\frac{\sqrt{3}}{2}$	$\frac{1}{\sqrt{2}}$ or $\frac{\sqrt{2}}{2}$	$\frac{1}{2}$	0
$\tan\theta$	0	$\frac{1}{\sqrt{3}}$	1	$\sqrt{3}$	undefined

You need to memorise these results.

Plot the graph of $\tan\theta$. What happens when $\theta = 90°$?

Overview of method

The following steps can be used to convert a magnitude and direction into components or column vector form:

Step ① Always draw a diagram.
Step ② Use trigonometry to separate the vector into two perpendicular components.

Sometimes it makes better sense to choose the **i** and **j** directions to fit the question, rather than automatically making them either horizontal and vertical or east and north. To resolve a vector into components which are **parallel** and **perpendicular** to a given direction, a clear diagram showing the angles involved needs to be drawn.

Example 1

Express, in column vector form, the vector with magnitude $5\sqrt{2}$, making an angle of $+45°$ with the x-axis.

Solution

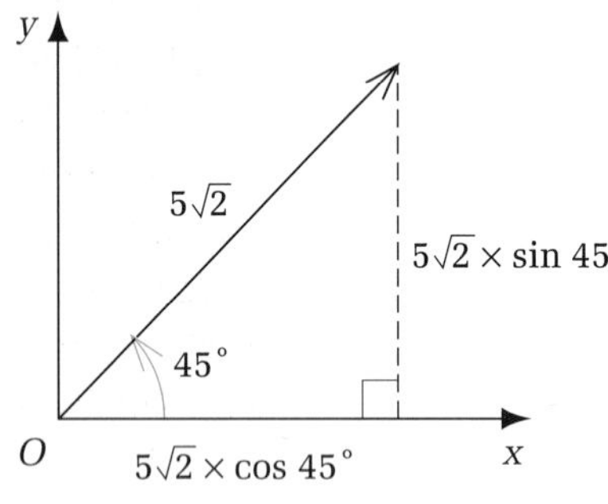

◀ ① Draw a diagram.
◀ ② Use trigonometry to resolve the vector.

Resolve →

$$x \text{ component} = 5\sqrt{2} \times \cos 45° = 5\sqrt{2} \times \frac{1}{\sqrt{2}} = 5$$

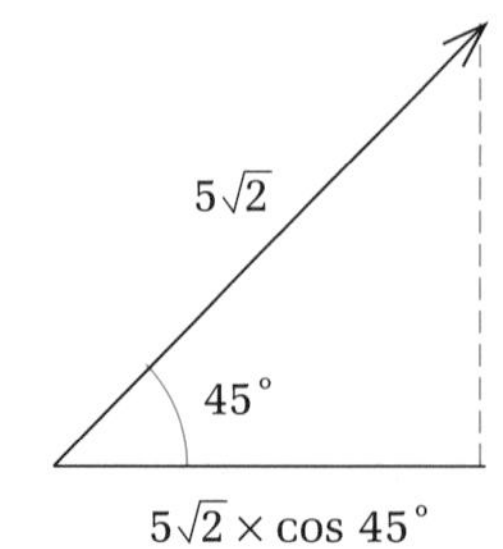

Notation
→ is shorthand for horizontal.
cos is next to the angle or with the angle.
$\cos 45° = \frac{1}{\sqrt{2}}$
$\sqrt{2}$ cancels.

Resolve ↑

$$y \text{ component} = 5\sqrt{2} \times \sin 45°$$
$$= 5\sqrt{2} \times \frac{1}{\sqrt{2}}$$
$$= 5$$

So the column vector is $\begin{pmatrix} 5 \\ 5 \end{pmatrix}$.

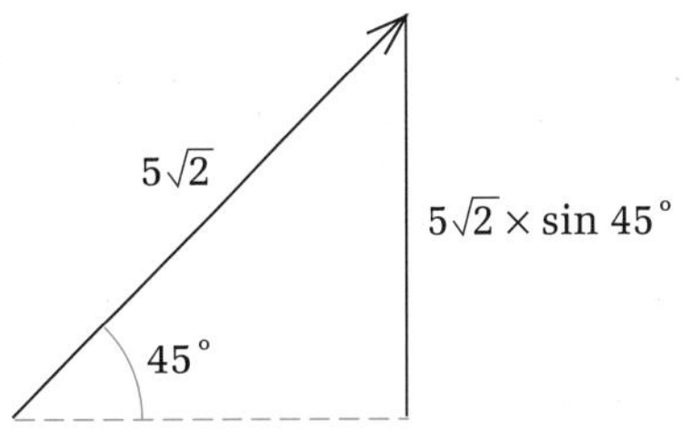

Notation
↑ is shorthand for vertical.
sin is opposite the angle or not with the angle.
$\sin 45° = \frac{1}{\sqrt{2}}$
$\sqrt{2}$ cancels.

Example 2

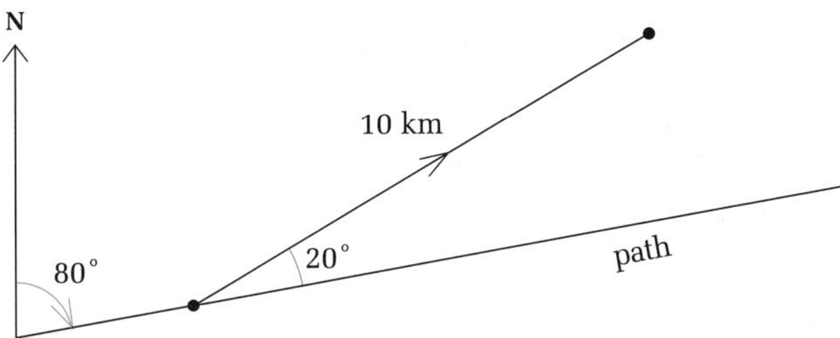

The displacement vector of a cyclist who has departed from a cycle path is shown.

a How long is the shortest route back to the path?

b If the cyclist now returns directly to the path, how far is she from the point where she was last on the path?

Solution

It makes sense to choose our directions for **i** and **j** to be parallel and perpendicular to the path.

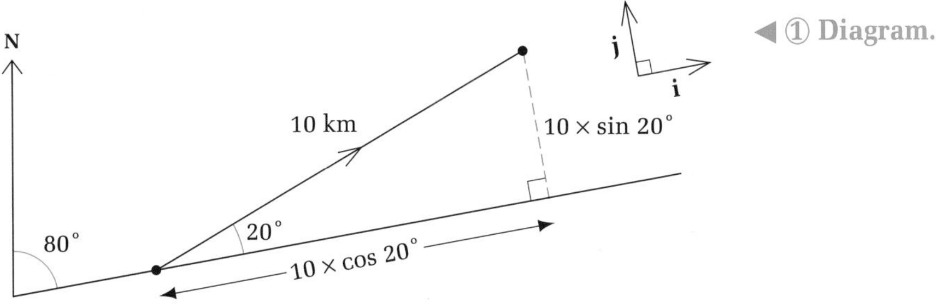

◀ ① Diagram.

It will be of no benefit at all to resolve the displacement vector into components due east and north. Drawing **i** and **j** on the diagram in this way indicates that you will be resolving into components in these directions.

Resolve // to the path:

$$10 \times \cos 20° = 9.40 \text{ km}$$

◀ ② Use trigonometry.

Notation
// is used as shorthand for *parallel*.

Resolve ⊥ to the path:

$$10 \times \sin 20° = 3.42 \text{ km}$$

Notation
⊥ is used as shorthand for *perpendicular*.

a The direct route back to the path is 3.42 km.

b At this point she will be 9.40 km from the point where she departed from the path.

Example 3

The mass of a crate is 10 kg. The crate rests on a slope inclined at 25° to the horizontal. Express the weight force in components parallel and perpendicular to the plane, as indicated by **i** and **j**.

Solution

Remember that *weight* is the force acting downwards due to the action of gravity. Taking $g = 9.8\,\text{m s}^{-2}$,

$$\text{weight} = 10 \times 9.8 \qquad \blacktriangleleft \text{ weight} = \text{mass} \times g$$

$$= 98\,\text{N}$$

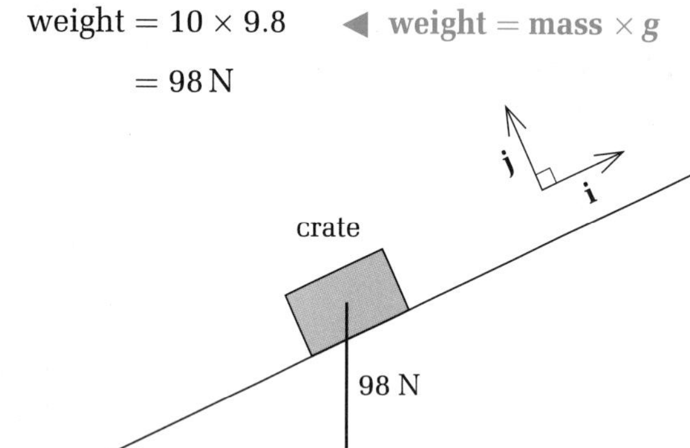

On the following diagram, you can see how the required angles have been calculated, using angle properties.

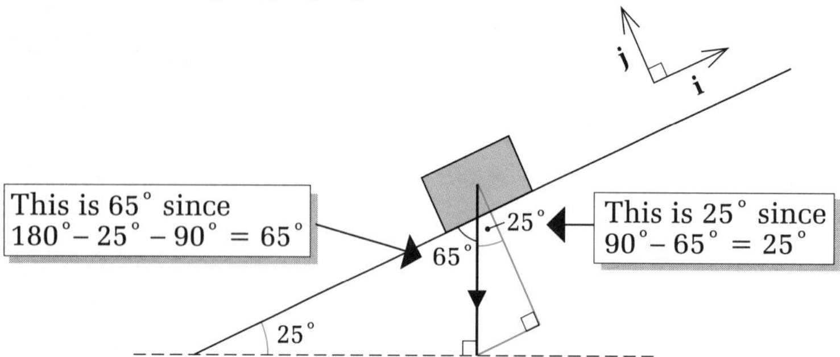

This leads to the following simplified diagram:

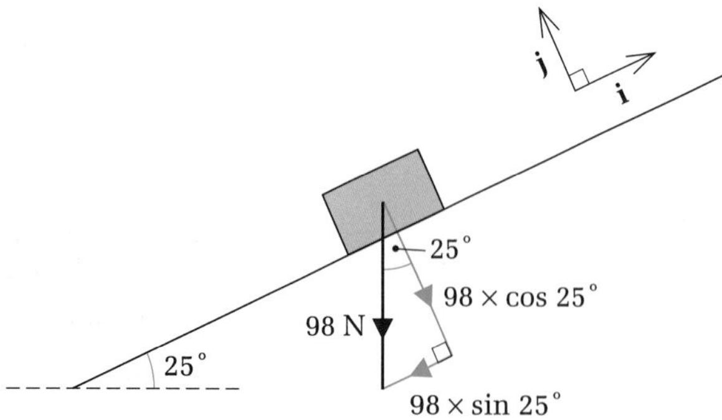

The weight of the crate can therefore be expressed as:

$(-98 \sin 25°\mathbf{i} - 98 \cos 25°\mathbf{j})\ \text{N} = (-41.4\mathbf{i} - 88.8\mathbf{j})\ \text{N}$ or $-(41.4\mathbf{i} + 88.8\mathbf{j})\ \text{N}$

Both components are negative, since they act in the opposite directions to **i** and **j** as they are shown on the diagram.

5.1 Resolving Vectors into Perpendicular Components

Exercise

Technique

1 Represent each of the following vectors as a column vector, by resolving into x- and y-components.

Remember $+38°$ means anticlockwise.

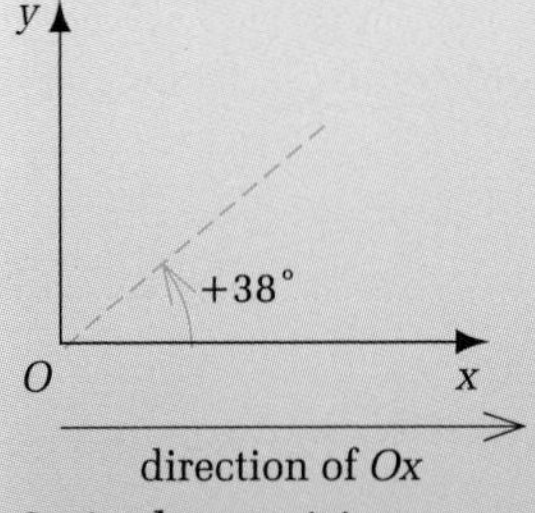

Ox is the positive x-direction.

a 8.7 units, $+38°$ from Ox
b 11.9 units, $+72°$ from Ox
c 5 units, $-25°$ from Ox
d 18 units, $+142°$ from Ox
e 0.72 units, $+212°$ from Ox
f 65.2 units, $-163°$ from Ox
g 10 units, $+255°$ from Ox
h 43 units, $+317°$ from Ox

2

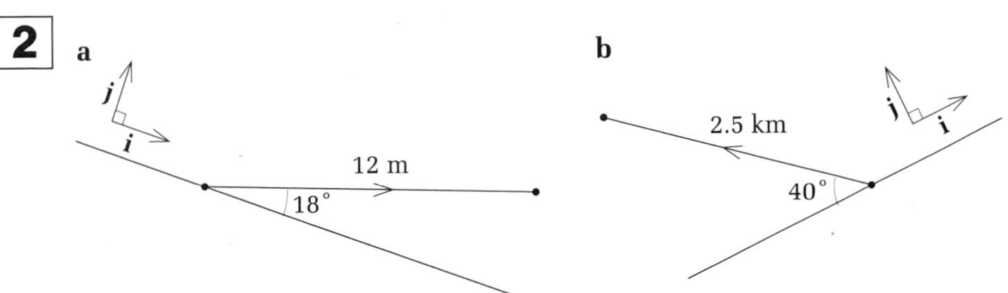

Express each displacement vector in terms of the unit vectors **i** and **j**, whose directions are shown.

3

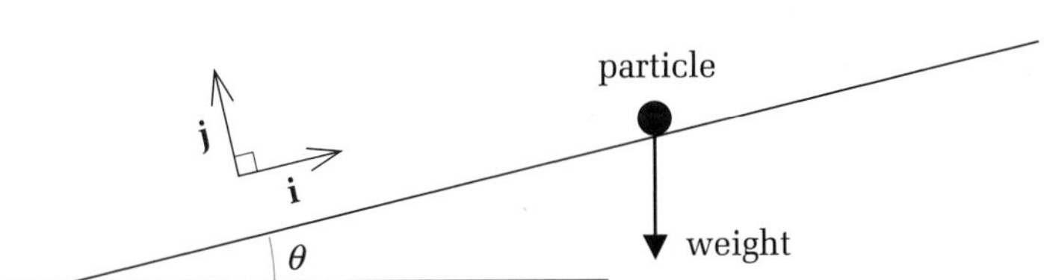

A particle of mass m is placed on an inclined plane, as shown. Express the weight in terms of **i** and **j**, where **i** is a unit vector up the plane and **j** is a unit vector perpendicular to the plane, when:

Remember to calculate the weight first. Use $g = 9.8\,\text{m s}^{-2}$ unless otherwise instructed.

a $m = 8\,\text{kg}$, $\theta = 10°$
b $m = 16\,\text{kg}$, $\theta = 15°$
c $m = 25\,\text{kg}$, $\theta = 5°$

4

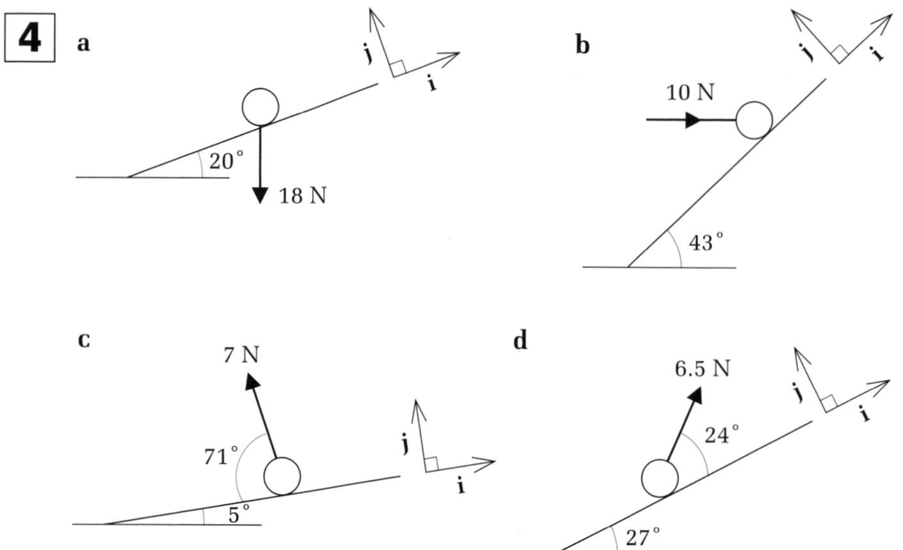

Express the force vectors in terms of components parallel and perpendicular to the planes shown.

Contextual

1

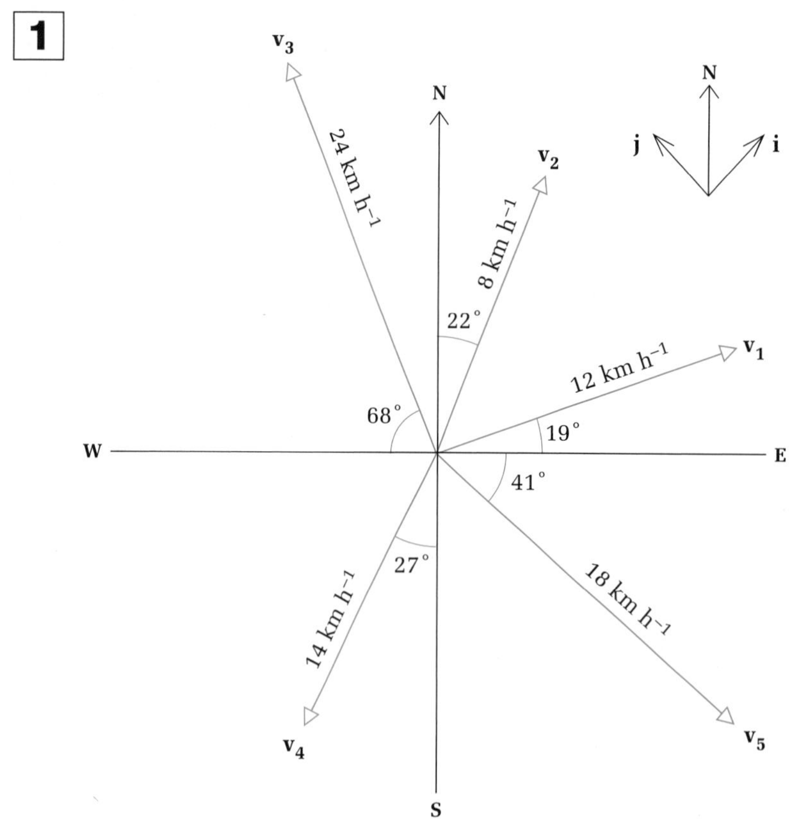

Resolve these velocity vectors into components in the directions shown.

i points due NE and **j** points due NW. Take care with the sign of each component.

km h^{-1} (kilometres per hour) is occasionally written as kmph.

2 A ferry sails out of harbour on a bearing of 197°. It is travelling at a speed of 64 km per hour. Convert this velocity vector into a column vector. (Assume that the x-direction is due east and the y-direction is due north).

3

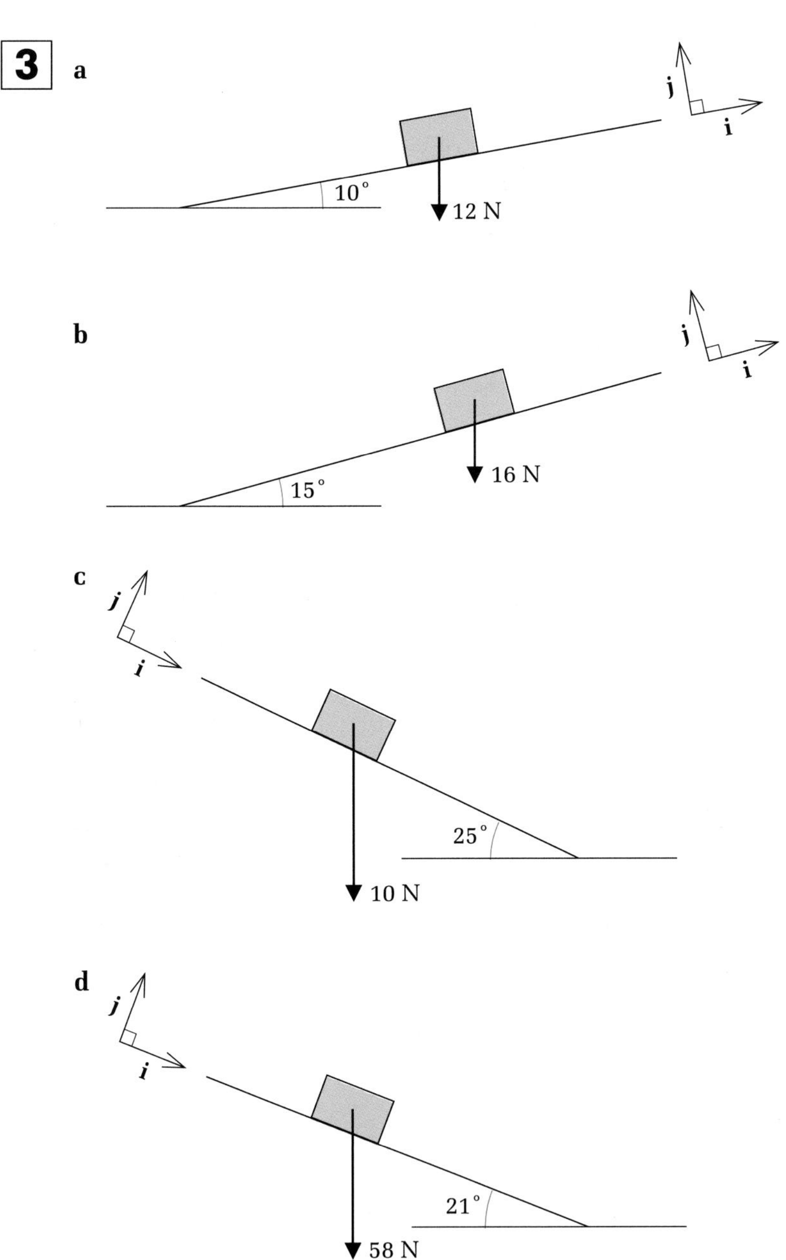

Each of these diagrams show the weight of a box on a slope acting vertically downwards. Resolve this weight force into components parallel and perpendicular to the plane, as indicated.

5.2 Resultant Vectors using Scale Drawings

One of the approaches to finding the resultant of vectors in magnitude and direction form is to draw a scale drawing and measure the resultant vector. This has the advantages of being relatively easy and of giving a good overall understanding of the situation. The principal *disadvantage* is that the accuracy of the solution depends entirely upon the accuracy of the diagram. This method can be used to add any number of vectors, but every additional vector is a new source of error. The best guidance is to draw the diagrams as large as possible.

Using a sharp pencil also helps.

Example

A motor boat sails out from the harbour a distance of 6 km on a bearing of 195°. It then changes course to 282° for 7.5 km.

a What is its distance and bearing from the harbour?

b What course should it set for the return journey?

Solution

Scale 1 cm : 1 km

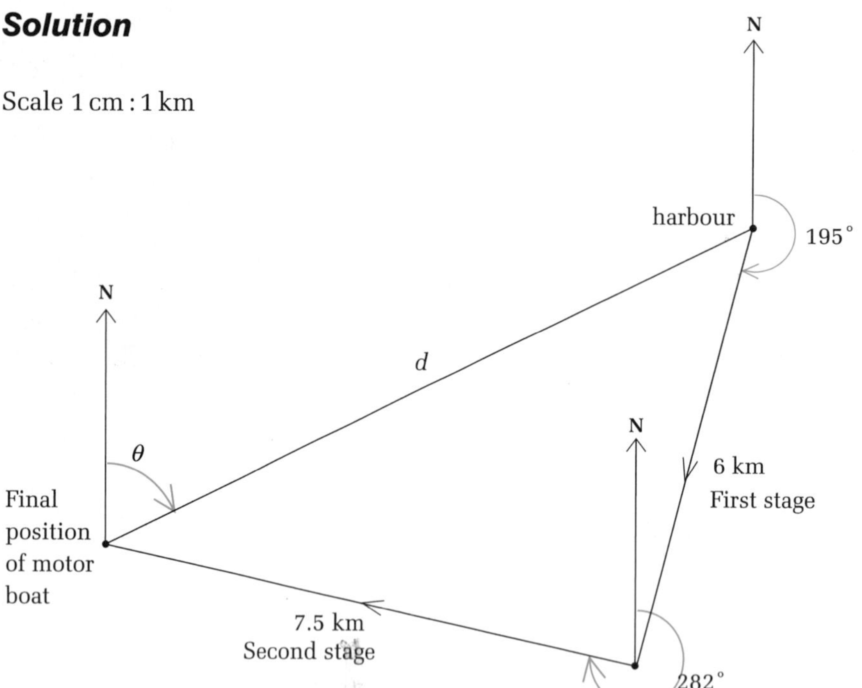

d and θ are to be measured from the scale drawing.

Remember vectors are joined head to tail.

a An answer such as $\theta = 65°$ and $d = 9.8$ km is about as accurate as can be expected from a scale drawing of this size. The motor boat is now 9.8 km from the harbour on a bearing of 245°.

$a = 180 - 65 = 115°$ (interior angles)

$b = 360 - 115 = 245°$

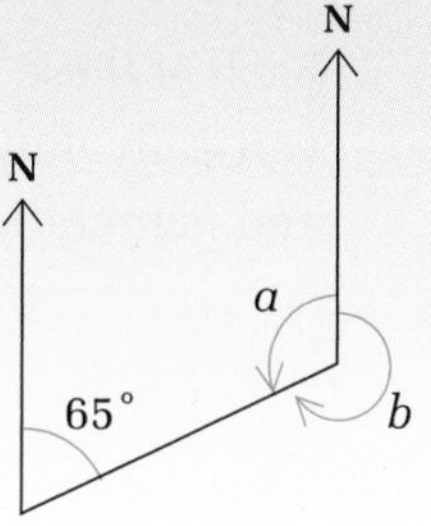

b The direction for the return course is 065°.

5.2 Resultant Vectors using Scale Drawings

Exercise

Technique

1 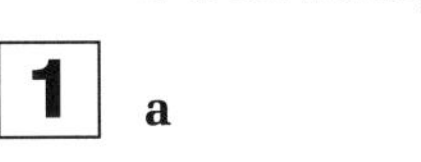

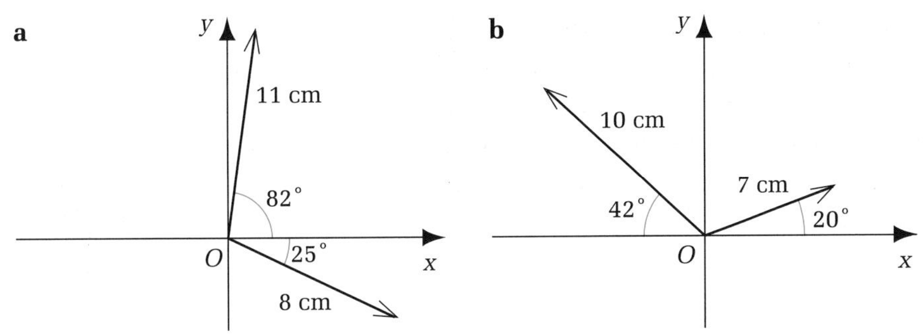

Find the resultant of each of the pairs of vectors given, by drawing a scale diagram. (Give your answer as a length and an angle from the *Ox* direction).

Remember to join the vectors head to tail.

2 Find the resultant of these two vectors:

$\mathbf{v}_1$ magnitude 12 units, direction 120°

$\mathbf{v}_2$ magnitude 8 units, direction 15°

Remember angles are measured anticlockwise from the *x*-axis.

3

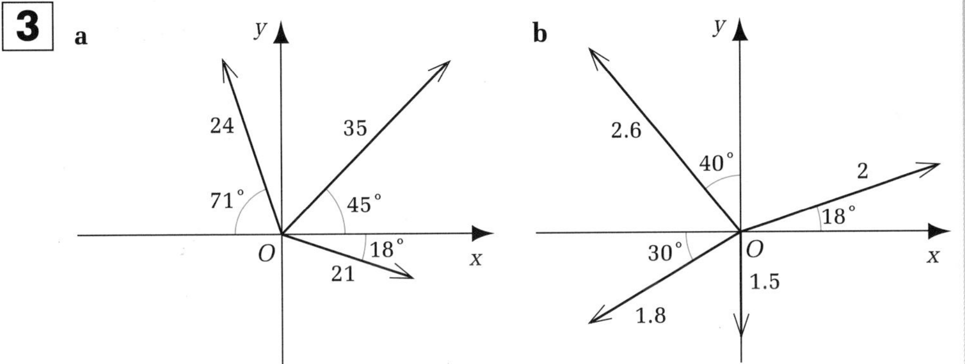

Use a scale diagram to find the resultant of each set of vectors shown. (Choose your scale with care).

Remember to join the vectors head to tail. This is called the polygon rule of addition.

4 A particle moves 10 km on a bearing of 150° and then 15 km on a bearing of 300°. Determine the displacement of the particle from its starting position.

5.3 Resultant Vectors using Trigonometry

The resultant of two vectors can also be found by using the sine and cosine rules. The main advantage of this method is that your answer will be more accurate than the answer obtained by scale drawing. Always draw a quick sketch as this will confirm your answers (or otherwise). This particularly matters where the inverse sine function is used, as there are usually two answers in the range of 0° to 180°. The diagram will make it clear which one is required.

$\sin\theta = 0.5 \Rightarrow \theta = 30^\circ$ or $\theta = 150^\circ$

Example

A motor boat sails out from the harbour a distance of 6 km on a bearing of 195°. It then changes course to 282° for 7.5 km.

a What is its distance and bearing from the harbour?

b What course should it set for the return journey?

Solution

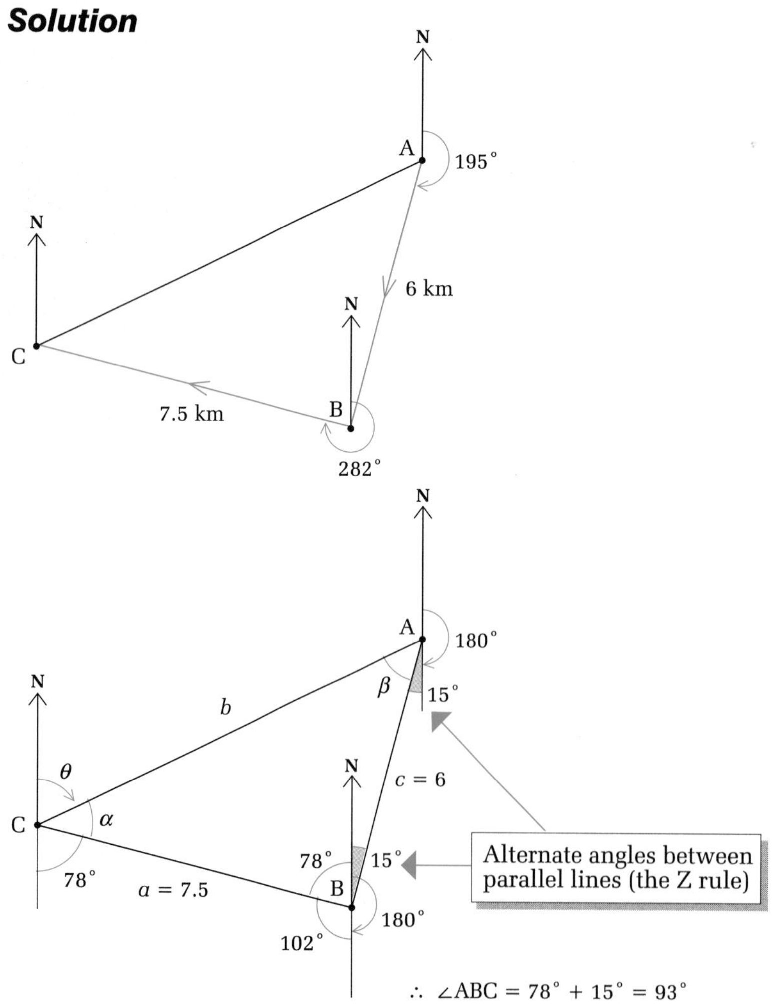

When using the sine and cosine rules, label the vertices and edges of the triangle of vectors to avoid confusion. The bearings will be used to calculate an internal angle.

a By the cosine rule:

$b^2 = c^2 + a^2 - 2ca\cos B$ ◀ **Substitute the values.**

Key the RHS (right hand side) into the calculator and press $\sqrt{x}$.
Store the fully accurate answer in the calculator's memory.

$b^2 = 6^2 + 7.5^2 - 2 \times 6 \times 7.5 \times \cos 93°$

$b = 9.85\,\text{km}$ (3 s.f.)

Use the sine rule to find α

$\frac{\sin\alpha}{6} = \frac{\sin 93°}{9.85}$ ◀ **Use the fully accurate answer for *b* here, *not* 9.85.**

$\sin\alpha = \frac{6 \times \sin 93°}{9.85}$

Calculate the RHS and key $\sin^{-1}$.

$\alpha = 37.5°$

$\theta = 180° - 78° - 37.5°$

$= 64.5°$

The bearing from the harbour:

$\beta = 180° - 37.5° - 93°$

Angles in a triangle.

$\beta = 49.5°$

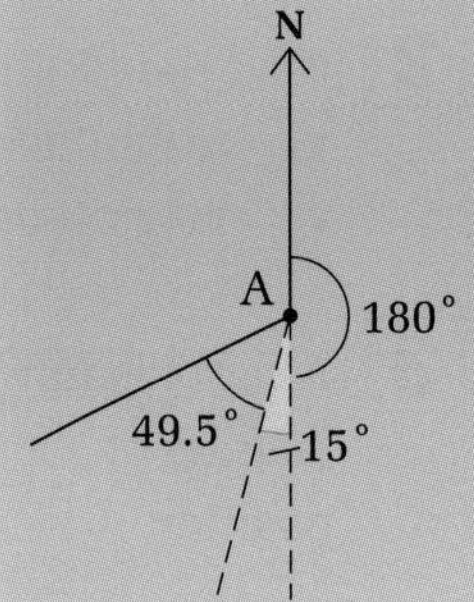

bearing $= 49.5° + 15° + 180° = 244.5°$ (1 d.p.)

b The bearing of the return journey is 064.5° (using θ).

5.3 Resultant Vectors using Trigonometry

Exercise

Technique

1

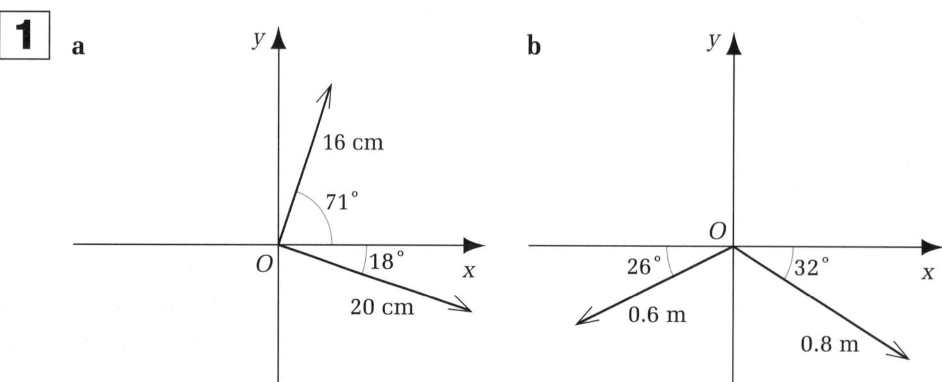

Find the resultant of each of the given pairs of vectors, by using trigonometry. (Give your answer as a length and an angle from the *Ox* direction).

Remember to join vectors head to tail.

2 Find the resultant of these two vectors:

$\mathbf{v}_1$ magnitude 9 units, direction 160°

$\mathbf{v}_2$ magnitude 7 units, direction 25°

3 A particle travels a distance of 200 m due west and then 450 m on a bearing of 320°. Calculate the displacement of the particle from its initial position.

Contextual

1 A rabbit leaves its warren entrance and hops 30 m on a bearing of 115°, where it stops by a bush. It then hops 24 m on a bearing of 225° to stop by a ditch. Use the sine and cosine rules to find the resultant magnitude and bearing of the rabbit's outing so far.

2 A submarine starts from its base. It travels on a heading of 080° for 7 km and then it changes course to a heading of 170° for a distance of 8 km. Determine:

a the distance of the submarine from its base

b the heading the submarine must set to return to base using the shortest route.

3 During an orienteering event, a woman runs 1.5 km on a bearing of 250° and then 0.8 km on a bearing of 100°. Find the direction she must take to return to her initial position. If the woman heads in this direction, what distance must she cover to return to her starting position?

5.4 Resultant Vectors using Resolving

Adding vectors in column vector form or **i**, **j** form is more straightforward than scale drawing or using the sine and cosine rule. The sine and cosine rule would have to be applied repeatedly for more than two vectors. By splitting each vector into two perpendicular components, the resultant can be found more easily.

Overview of method

Step ① Draw a large diagram.
Step ② Label all components of vectors.
Step ③ Calculate the overall x and y components to give the resultant.
Step ④ If required, convert this to magnitude and direction form.

Use your calculator as efficiently as possible, to minimise rounding errors.

Example

The movements of an armoured tank in a desert are plotted at five minute intervals by a spy satellite. These are the four observed stages of its journey:

First stage:	1.3 km, due north
Second stage:	1.1 km, due north-east
Third stage:	2.0 km on a bearing of 125°
Fourth stage:	0.9 km on a bearing of 102°

At the end of the fourth stage, what is its distance and bearing from its original position?

Solution

This time, all the measurements and components are shown on one diagram.

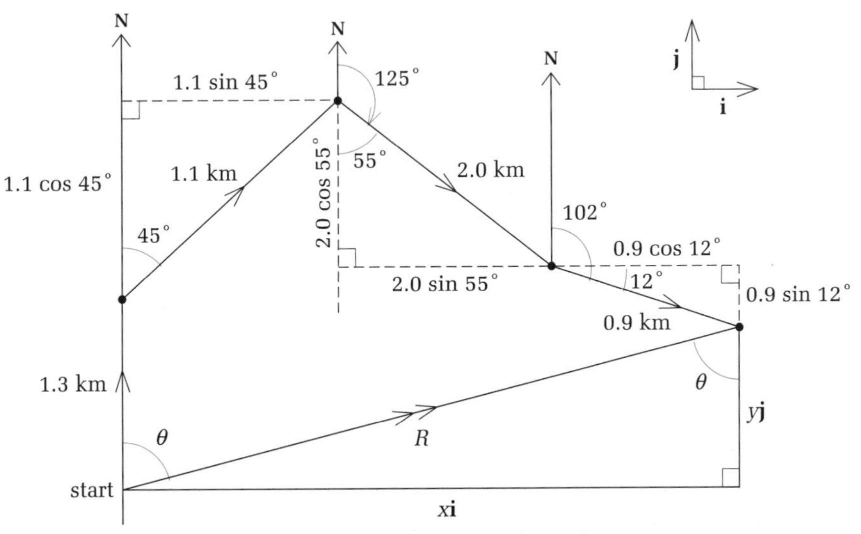

◀ ① Draw a large diagram.

◀ ② Label all the components of vectors.

All the calculations can now be done in one step, with no loss of accuracy.

Resolve → $1.1 \sin 45° + 2.0 \sin 55° + 0.9 \cos 12° = 3.30$

This will be the **i** component.

Resolve ↑ $1.3 + 1.1 \cos 45° - 2.0 \cos 55° - 0.9 \sin 12° = 0.744$

This will be the **j** component.

$\mathbf{R} = (3.30\mathbf{i} + 0.744\mathbf{j})$ km

$|\mathbf{R}| = \sqrt{3.30^2 + 0.744^2}$

Use the exact answers from the calculator's memory.

$R = 3.38$ km

$\tan\theta = \frac{3.30}{0.744}$

$\theta = \tan^{-1}\left(\frac{3.30}{0.744}\right)$

or $\arctan\left(\frac{3.30}{0.744}\right)$

$\theta = 77.3°$

The tank is 3.38 km from its starting point, on a bearing of 077.3°.

5.4 Resultant Vectors using Resolving

Exercise

Technique

1 **a**

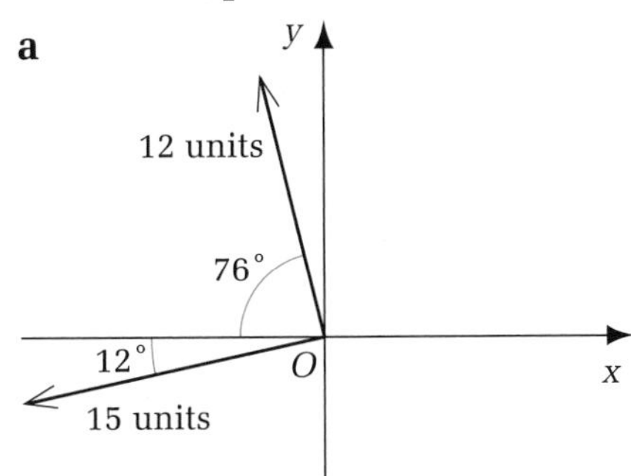

b

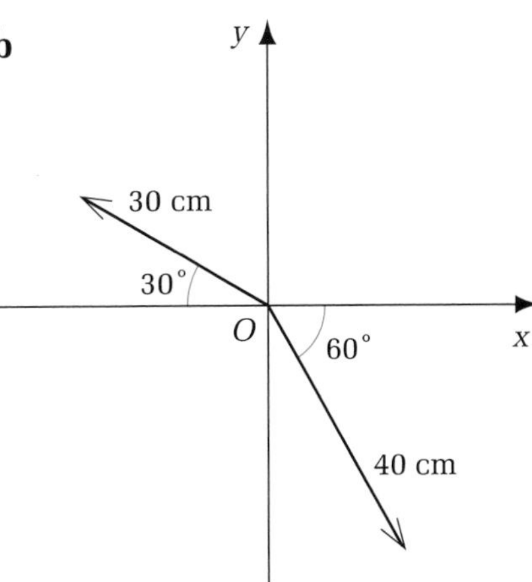

Find the resultant of each of the pairs of vectors given, by using resolving. (Give your answer as a length and an angle from the Ox direction).

2 Calculate the resultant of these two vectors:

$\mathbf{v}_1$ magnitude 25 units, direction 70°

$\mathbf{v}_2$ magnitude 14 units, direction 310°

3 **a**

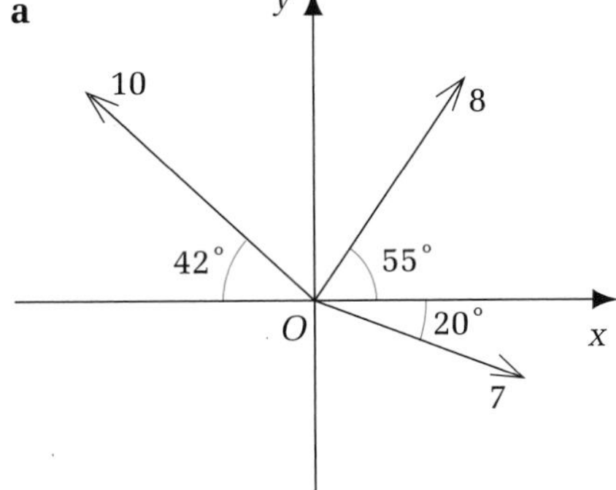

b

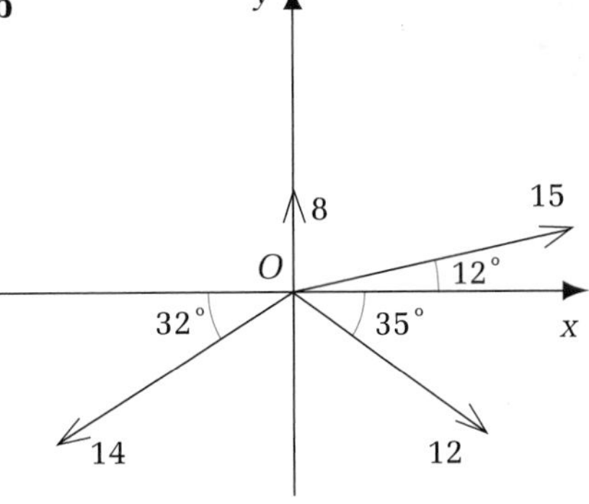

Convert the vectors into the form $x\mathbf{i} + y\mathbf{j}$ and then give the resultant of each set of vectors in this form.

4 Calculate the magnitude and bearing of the resultant of the following vectors:

3 units due west; 4 units due north-east; 7 units due north;
5 units due south-west; 6 units due east.

5.5 Parametric Vectors

Consider the following position vector, containing the variable t.

$$\mathbf{r} = \begin{pmatrix} 3t \\ 10 + \frac{1}{2}t^2 \end{pmatrix}$$

or $\mathbf{r} = 3t\mathbf{i} + (10 + \frac{1}{2}t^2)\mathbf{j}$

What will be the corresponding vector for each of the values of t from 0 to 5? What does the path of the particle, whose position vectors we have calculated, look like on a graph?

Subscripts can be used to indicate which value of t is being used. So $\mathbf{r}_2$ will be the position vector corresponding to $t = 2$.

The 2 in $\mathbf{r}_2$ is called a **subscript**. The 2 in t^2 is called a **superscript**.

$t = 0 \quad \mathbf{r}_0 = \begin{pmatrix} 0 \\ 10 \end{pmatrix} \qquad t = 3 \quad \mathbf{r}_3 = \begin{pmatrix} 9 \\ 14\frac{1}{2} \end{pmatrix}$

$t = 1 \quad \mathbf{r}_1 = \begin{pmatrix} 3 \\ 10\frac{1}{2} \end{pmatrix} \qquad t = 4 \quad \mathbf{r}_4 = \begin{pmatrix} 12 \\ 18 \end{pmatrix}$

$t = 2 \quad \mathbf{r}_2 = \begin{pmatrix} 6 \\ 12 \end{pmatrix} \qquad t = 5 \quad \mathbf{r}_5 = \begin{pmatrix} 15 \\ 22\frac{1}{2} \end{pmatrix}$

These can be shown on a graph, but note that the axes are x and y, corresponding to the components of the vectors. The letter t is *not* one of the axes. Instead, t values have been indicated at the end of the relevant vector. The variable vector $\mathbf{r}$, is dependent upon the value of t. In this situation, t is referred to as a **parameter**. A parameter is a variable which takes specific values.

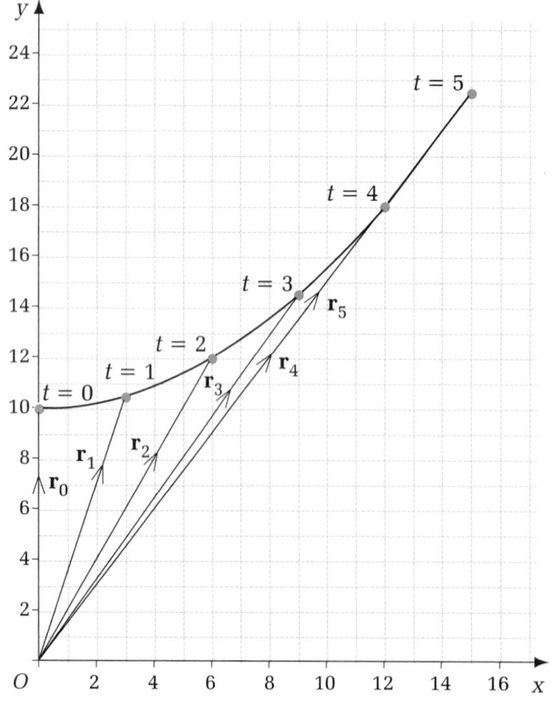

The end point of each vector represents the position of the particle at the time shown. The curved line joining the end points is the **locus** of the particle.
The equation of this locus can be determined as follows:

$\mathbf{r} = \begin{pmatrix} 3t \\ 10 + \frac{1}{2}t^2 \end{pmatrix} = \begin{pmatrix} x \\ y \end{pmatrix}$

$x = 3t \qquad y = 10 + \frac{1}{2}t^2$

$t = \frac{x}{3}$.

So $y = 10 + \frac{1}{2}\left(\frac{x}{3}\right)^2$

$y = 10 + \frac{x^2}{18}$

i.e. the locus is a parabola

Example 1

For what value of t is the vector $2t\mathbf{i} - 6\mathbf{j}$ parallel to $\mathbf{i} - 3\mathbf{j}$?

Solution

For two vectors to be parallel, one must be a constant multiple of the other.

$$2t\mathbf{i} - 6\mathbf{j} = k(\mathbf{i} - 3\mathbf{j})$$

$$2t\mathbf{i} - 6\mathbf{j} = k\mathbf{i} - 3k\mathbf{j}$$

For two vectors to be equal, the **i** components must be equal and the **j** components must be equal.

$$2t = k \qquad [1]$$

$$-6 = -3k \qquad [2]$$

Equation [2] becomes:

$$-6 = -3k$$

$$\tfrac{-6}{-3} = k$$

$$k = 2$$

Substituting into equation [1], $2t = k$

$$2t = 2$$

$$t = 1$$

Example 2

Write an expression for the magnitude of vector $\mathbf{p} = \begin{pmatrix} t \\ 2t+1 \end{pmatrix}$.

For what value(s) of t is $|\mathbf{p}| = \sqrt{13}$?

Solution

Using Pythagoras' theorem, as usual, for the magnitude gives:

$$|\mathbf{p}| = \sqrt{t^2 + (2t+1)^2}$$

Use $|\mathbf{p}| = \sqrt{13}$ and expand brackets.

$$\sqrt{13} = \sqrt{t^2 + 4t^2 + 4t + 1}$$

Square both sides.

$$13 = 5t^2 + 4t + 1$$

Subtract 13.

$$0 = 5t^2 + 4t - 12$$

Factorise the quadratic equation.

$$0 = (5t - 6)(t + 2)$$

Solve by making each bracket equal zero.

$$t = \tfrac{6}{5} \text{ or } t = -2$$

5.5 Parametric Vectors Exercise

Technique

1 A point P moves such that:

$$\overrightarrow{OP} = 2t\mathbf{i} + (15 - t^2)\mathbf{j}$$

Sketch the path of P for $0 \le t \le 5$, showing clearly where P will be for integer values of t.

2 The path of a point Q is given by the expression:

$$\overrightarrow{OQ} = \begin{pmatrix} t+3 \\ t^2 \end{pmatrix}$$

Determine what the equation of the locus of Q will be by sketching this path.

3
- **a** For what value of k is $3k\mathbf{i} + (10 + k)\mathbf{j}$ parallel to the vector $6\mathbf{i} - 38\mathbf{j}$?
- **b** For what value(s) of λ is $\lambda^2\mathbf{i} + 2\lambda\mathbf{j}$ parallel to $2\mathbf{i} + 2\mathbf{j}$? Comment on your answer.

4 $\mathbf{v} = \begin{pmatrix} t^2 - 3 \\ 5 - 2t \end{pmatrix}$

Calculate the magnitude of $\mathbf{v}$ when:

a $t = 0$ **b** $t = -3$ **c** $t = 2.5$

5 The vector $\mathbf{a}$ is given by $\mathbf{a} = 2t\mathbf{i} + (t + 3)\mathbf{j}$
- **a** For what values of t is $|\mathbf{a}| = 2\sqrt{2}$?
- **b** Show why $|\mathbf{a}| > 0$ for all values of t and find the least value of $|\mathbf{a}|$.
- **c** If $\mathbf{b} = (t - 2)\mathbf{i} + 4t\mathbf{j}$ find, to three significant figures, the values of t for which $|\mathbf{a}| = |\mathbf{b}|$.

Hint: use completing the square.

5.6 The Scalar Product

The multiplication of a vector by a scalar has been met already. The **scalar product** is a method of multiplying *two vectors* together to get a scalar answer. The answer is a single number, *not* a vector. It is defined as follows:

See Section 3.2.

$\mathbf{a.b} = ab \cos \theta$

Remember: $a = |\mathbf{a}|$ and $b = |\mathbf{b}|$.
The dot is the symbol for the scalar product. So it is also called the **dot product**.

where θ is the angle between the two vectors **a** and **b**, if they stemmed out from the same point as shown.

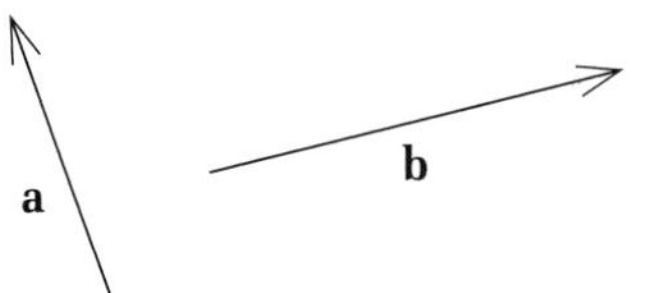

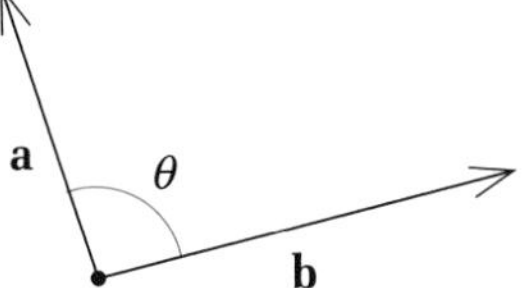

Example 1

Find the scalar product of **a** and **b** as shown in the diagram, if $|\mathbf{a}| = 5$ and $|\mathbf{b}| = 7$.

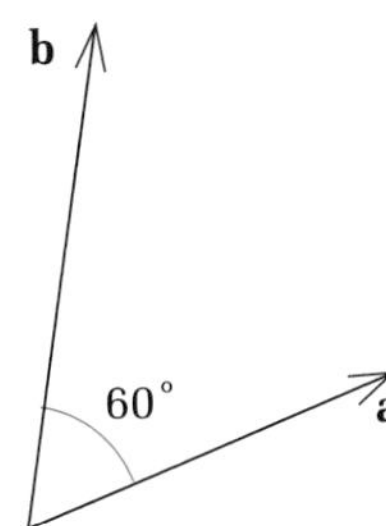

Solution

$$\begin{aligned}\mathbf{a.b} &= |\mathbf{a}|\,|\mathbf{b}|\cos\theta \\ &= 5 \times 7 \times \cos 60^\circ \\ &= 35 \times \tfrac{1}{2} \\ &= 17\tfrac{1}{2}\end{aligned}$$

The scalar product of unit vectors

Since $|\mathbf{i}| = |\mathbf{j}| = |\mathbf{k}| = 1$ and the angles between any pair are either 0° or 90°, several important relationships can be found.

$$\begin{aligned}\mathbf{i.i} &= 1 \times 1 \times \cos 0^\circ \\ &= 1\end{aligned}$$

$|\mathbf{i}| = 1$ and $\cos 0^\circ = 1$

Similarly $\mathbf{j.j} = 1$ and $\mathbf{k.k} = 1$.

$\cos 90^\circ = 0$

$$\begin{aligned}\mathbf{i.j} &= 1 \times 1 \times \cos 90^\circ \\ &= 0\end{aligned}$$

Similarly $\mathbf{i.k} = 0$ and $\mathbf{j.k} = 0$.

Commutativity

As ordinary multiplication is commutative:

$$\begin{aligned} \mathbf{a}.\mathbf{b} &= ab\cos\theta \\ &= ba\cos\theta \\ &= \mathbf{b}.\mathbf{a} \end{aligned}$$

$$\Rightarrow \mathbf{a}.\mathbf{b} = \mathbf{b}.\mathbf{a}$$

Commutative means that the same answer is obtained even if the order is reversed. For example, $4 \times 3 = 3 \times 4 = 12$

Scalar product is **commutative**.

Scalar product of vectors in component form

From the properties already established for **i** and **j** unit vectors above, the following result can be deduced.

$$(a\mathbf{i} + b\mathbf{j}).(c\mathbf{i} + d\mathbf{j}) = ac + bd$$

If the brackets on the left hand side are multiplied out:

$$\begin{aligned} (a\mathbf{i} + b\mathbf{j}).(c\mathbf{i} + d\mathbf{j}) &= a\mathbf{i}.c\mathbf{i} + a\mathbf{i}.d\mathbf{j} + b\mathbf{j}.c\mathbf{i} + b\mathbf{j}.d\mathbf{j} \\ &= ac\mathbf{i}.\mathbf{i} + ad\mathbf{i}.\mathbf{j} + bc\mathbf{j}.\mathbf{i} + bd\mathbf{j}.\mathbf{j} \\ &= ac(1) + ad(0) + bc(0) + bd(1) \\ &= ac + bd \end{aligned}$$

◀ $\mathbf{i}.\mathbf{i} = \mathbf{j}.\mathbf{j} = 1$ and $\mathbf{i}.\mathbf{j} = \mathbf{j}.\mathbf{i} = 0$

Scalar product obeys *multiplying out the brackets* rules. This is called the distributive property.

Similarly, in column vector form:

$$\begin{pmatrix} a \\ b \end{pmatrix}.\begin{pmatrix} c \\ d \end{pmatrix} = ac + bd$$

These properties can be extended to three dimensions as follows:

$$(a\mathbf{i} + b\mathbf{j} + c\mathbf{k}).(d\mathbf{i} + e\mathbf{j} + f\mathbf{k}) = ad + be + cf$$

$$\begin{pmatrix} l \\ m \\ n \end{pmatrix}.\begin{pmatrix} p \\ q \\ r \end{pmatrix} = lp + mq + nr$$

The magnitude of a column vector, or a vector in component form, can be worked out by Pythagoras' theorem. This allows the angle between any two vectors to be calculated.

This is the main use for the scalar product.

Overview of method

Step ① Find the magnitudes of the two vectors.
Step ② Calculate the numerical value of the scalar product.
Step ③ Substitute this information into $\mathbf{a}.\mathbf{b} = ab\cos\theta$.
Step ④ Rearrange and solve to obtain θ.

Example 2

Find the angle between $\mathbf{a} = \begin{pmatrix} 1 \\ 7 \\ -3 \end{pmatrix}$ and $\mathbf{b} = \begin{pmatrix} 5 \\ 0 \\ -2 \end{pmatrix}$.

Solution

Magnitudes:

$$|\mathbf{a}| = \sqrt{1^2 + 7^2 + (-3)^2}$$
$$= \sqrt{59}$$

◀ ① Find the magnitudes.

$$|\mathbf{b}| = \sqrt{5^2 + 0^2 + (-2)^2}$$
$$= \sqrt{29}$$

Calculate:

$$\mathbf{a}.\mathbf{b} = \begin{pmatrix} 1 \\ 7 \\ -3 \end{pmatrix} . \begin{pmatrix} 5 \\ 0 \\ -2 \end{pmatrix}$$

◀ ② Calculate the scalar product.

$$= 5 + 0 + 6$$
$$= 11$$

Substitute:

$$\mathbf{a}.\mathbf{b} = ab\cos\theta$$
$$11 = \sqrt{59}\sqrt{29}\cos\theta$$

◀ ③ Substitute into a.b $= ab\cos\theta$

$$\frac{11}{\sqrt{59}\sqrt{29}} = \cos\theta$$

Divide by $\sqrt{59}\sqrt{29}$

$$\theta = \cos^{-1}\left(\frac{11}{\sqrt{59}\sqrt{29}}\right)$$

◀ ④ Solve for θ.

or $\arccos\left(\frac{11}{\sqrt{59}\sqrt{29}}\right)$

$$\theta = 74.6° \text{ (1 d.p.)}$$

5.6 The Scalar Product
Exercise

Technique

1 Find the scalar product of the following pairs of vectors.

a $\mathbf{a} = \begin{pmatrix} 5 \\ -7 \end{pmatrix}$ $\mathbf{b} = \begin{pmatrix} 3 \\ 2 \end{pmatrix}$

b $\mathbf{c} = \begin{pmatrix} 12 \\ 0 \end{pmatrix}$ $\mathbf{d} = \begin{pmatrix} -1 \\ 16 \end{pmatrix}$

c $\mathbf{e} = \begin{pmatrix} -6 \\ 3 \\ -2 \end{pmatrix}$ $\mathbf{f} = \begin{pmatrix} 4 \\ 8 \\ -4 \end{pmatrix}$

2 Find the numerical value of **a.b**, if:

a $\mathbf{a} = 3\mathbf{i} - 4\mathbf{j}$ and $\mathbf{b} = -\mathbf{i} - 4\mathbf{j}$
b $\mathbf{a} = 6\mathbf{i} + 2\mathbf{j}$ and $\mathbf{b} = -\mathbf{i} + 3\mathbf{j}$
c $\mathbf{a} = \mathbf{i} + \mathbf{j} + \mathbf{k}$ and $\mathbf{b} = \mathbf{i} + \mathbf{j} + \mathbf{k}$

3 Calculate $ab\cos\theta$ to three significant figures if:

a $|\mathbf{a}| = 3$, $|\mathbf{b}| = 5$, $\theta = 60°$
b $|\mathbf{a}| = 9$, $|\mathbf{b}| = \sqrt{27}$, $\theta = 172°$
c $|\mathbf{a}| = \sqrt{33}$, $|\mathbf{b}| = \sqrt{14}$, $\theta = 16°$

4 By using the scalar product, find the angle between each of these pairs of vectors.

a $\mathbf{a} = \begin{pmatrix} 1 \\ 5 \end{pmatrix}$ $\mathbf{b} = \begin{pmatrix} 3 \\ 7 \end{pmatrix}$
b $\mathbf{a} = 2\mathbf{i} + 8\mathbf{j}$ $\mathbf{b} = 2\mathbf{i} + 6\mathbf{j}$
c $\mathbf{a} = 5\mathbf{i} - 4\mathbf{j}$ $\mathbf{b} = -2\mathbf{i} - 6\mathbf{j}$

Sketch each pair of vectors to confirm that your answers are reasonable.

5 Calculate the size of the angle between each of these pairs of vectors:

a $\mathbf{a} = 2\mathbf{i} + 3\mathbf{j} + \mathbf{k}$ $\mathbf{b} = -\mathbf{i} - 5\mathbf{j} + 7\mathbf{k}$

b $\mathbf{a} = \begin{pmatrix} 0 \\ 7 \\ 11 \end{pmatrix}$ $\mathbf{b} = \begin{pmatrix} 8 \\ -8 \\ 8 \end{pmatrix}$

5.7 Uses of the Scalar Product

Perpendicular vectors

If **a** and **b** are non-zero perpendicular vectors then $\theta = 90°$.

Non-zero means neither $\mathbf{a} = \mathbf{0}$ nor $\mathbf{b} = \mathbf{0}$

$$\mathbf{a}.\mathbf{b} = ab\cos 90°$$

$$\mathbf{a}.\mathbf{b} = 0$$

Since $\cos 90° = 0$.

So for any perpendicular vectors, $\mathbf{a}.\mathbf{b} = 0$.

$$\mathbf{a}.\mathbf{b} = 0 \Leftrightarrow \mathbf{a} \perp \mathbf{b}$$

Notation

$\Leftrightarrow$ means *if and only if*

Example 1

For what value(s) of t is the vector $2t\mathbf{i} + (t+6)\mathbf{j}$ perpendicular to $t\mathbf{i} - 7\mathbf{j}$?

Solution

For perpendicular vectors:

$$(2t\mathbf{i} + (t+6)\mathbf{j}).(t\mathbf{i} - 7\mathbf{j}) = 0$$

Multiply corresponding components together. Expand the brackets.

$$2t^2 - 7(t+6) = 0$$

$$2t^2 - 7t - 42 = 0$$

◀ This does not factorise so use the quadratic formula.

$$t = \frac{7 \pm \sqrt{7^2 - 4 \times 2 \times (-42)}}{2 \times 2}$$

$$t = \frac{7 \pm \sqrt{49 + 336}}{4}$$

$$t = \frac{7 \pm \sqrt{385}}{4}$$

$$t = 6.66 \quad \text{or} \quad t = -3.16$$

Alternative for perpendicular vectors:

$$m_1 = \frac{-1}{m_2}$$

$$\frac{t+6}{2t} = \frac{-1}{\left(\frac{-7}{t}\right)}$$

$$\frac{t+6}{2t} = \frac{t}{7}$$

$$7(t+6) = 2t^2$$

$$7t + 42 = 2t^2$$

$$0 = 2t^2 - 7t - 42$$

The component of one vector in the direction of another

The scalar product enables the component of one vector in the direction of another vector to be found but without having to find the angle between them.

Example 2

What is the component of $\mathbf{a} = \begin{pmatrix} 2 \\ 7 \end{pmatrix}$ in the direction of $\mathbf{b} = \begin{pmatrix} 8 \\ 1 \end{pmatrix}$?

Solution

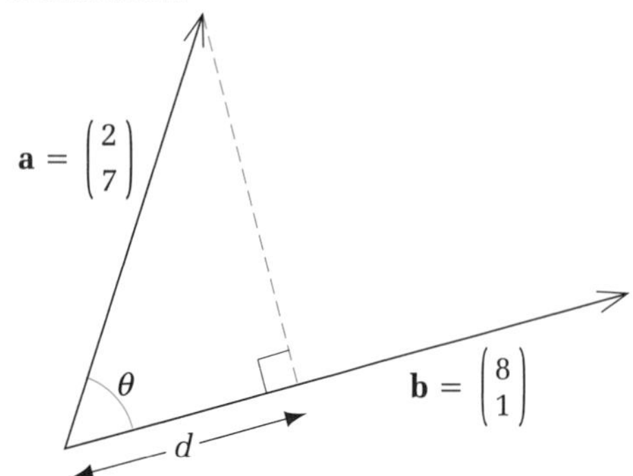

Resolving **a** into components // and ⊥ to $\begin{pmatrix} 8 \\ 1 \end{pmatrix}$.

d is the component of vector **a** in the direction of vector **b**.

$$d = a\cos\theta$$

Resolve vector **a**.

$$d = a\cos\theta \times \frac{b}{b}$$

Multiply by $\frac{b}{b}$ to obtain $ab\cos\theta$.

$$d = \frac{ab\cos\theta}{b}$$

Replace $ab\cos\theta$ with **a**.**b**.

$$d = \frac{\mathbf{a}.\mathbf{b}}{b}$$

For this formula **a**.**b** and b need to be found.

$$b = |\mathbf{b}| = \sqrt{8^2 + 1^2}$$
$$= \sqrt{65}$$

$$\mathbf{a}.\mathbf{b} = \begin{pmatrix} 2 \\ 7 \end{pmatrix} . \begin{pmatrix} 8 \\ 1 \end{pmatrix}$$
$$= 16 + 7$$
$$= 23$$

Use $d = \frac{\mathbf{a}.\mathbf{b}}{b}$

$$d = \frac{23}{\sqrt{65}}$$
$$= 2.85 \ (3 \text{ s.f.})$$

The elegance of this method is that θ does not need to be found.

Looking at the diagram, since $b = \sqrt{65} = 8.06$, the answer for d seems reasonable.

5.7 Uses of the Scalar Product Exercise

Technique

Identify the pairs of vectors, from those listed below, which are perpendicular.

$\mathbf{a} = \begin{pmatrix} 5 \\ 3 \end{pmatrix}$ $\mathbf{b} = \begin{pmatrix} -1 \\ 3 \end{pmatrix}$ $\mathbf{c} = \begin{pmatrix} 11 \\ -3 \end{pmatrix}$ $\mathbf{d} = \begin{pmatrix} -7 \\ -8 \end{pmatrix}$

$\mathbf{e} = \begin{pmatrix} -64 \\ 56 \end{pmatrix}$ $\mathbf{f} = \begin{pmatrix} -6 \\ 10 \end{pmatrix}$ $\mathbf{g} = \begin{pmatrix} 36 \\ 132 \end{pmatrix}$ $\mathbf{h} = \begin{pmatrix} 27 \\ 9 \end{pmatrix}$

2 a

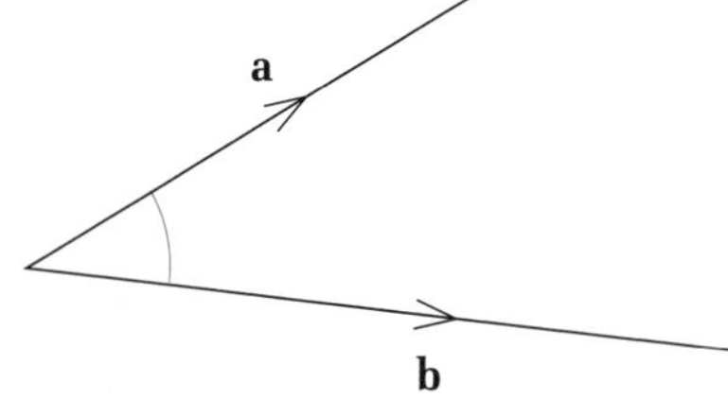

Find the magnitude of the component of **a**, in the direction of **b**, where $\mathbf{a} = 4\mathbf{i} + 2\mathbf{j}$ and $\mathbf{b} = 6\mathbf{i} - \mathbf{j}$.

b Similarly, find the magnitude of the component of $\mathbf{c} = -2\mathbf{i} + 5\mathbf{j}$ in the direction of $\mathbf{d} = -\mathbf{i} - 7\mathbf{j}$.

3 $\mathbf{v} = \begin{pmatrix} t+2 \\ 5 \end{pmatrix}$

a For what value of t is **v** perpendicular to the vector $\begin{pmatrix} 1 \\ 2 \end{pmatrix}$?

b For what value of t is **v** perpendicular to the vector $\begin{pmatrix} 10 \\ -17 \end{pmatrix}$?

c If $\mathbf{s} = \begin{pmatrix} 2t \\ t-3 \end{pmatrix}$, for what values of t are **v** perpendicular to **s**?

4 $\mathbf{a} = 4\mathbf{i} - 3\mathbf{j}$ and $\mathbf{b} = t\mathbf{i} - 2t^2\mathbf{j}$

a What is the angle between **a** and **b** when:

i $t = 1$ ii $t = 5$

b For what value of t is the angle between **a** and **b** equal to 90°?

5 Find the values of λ for which the angle between $\mathbf{i} + 3\mathbf{j} + 2\mathbf{k}$ and $2\mathbf{j} + \lambda\mathbf{k}$ is:

a 90° b 60°

Consolidation

Exercise A

1 Three forces $5\mathbf{i} + 4\mathbf{j}$ N, $7\mathbf{i} + 11\mathbf{j}$ N, $8\mathbf{i} + 6\mathbf{j}$ N act at a point. Find:

a the resultant of the forces in the form $a\mathbf{i} + b\mathbf{j}$

b the magnitude of the resultant

c the cosine of the angle between the resultant and the vector $\mathbf{i} + 3\mathbf{j}$.

(WJEC)

2

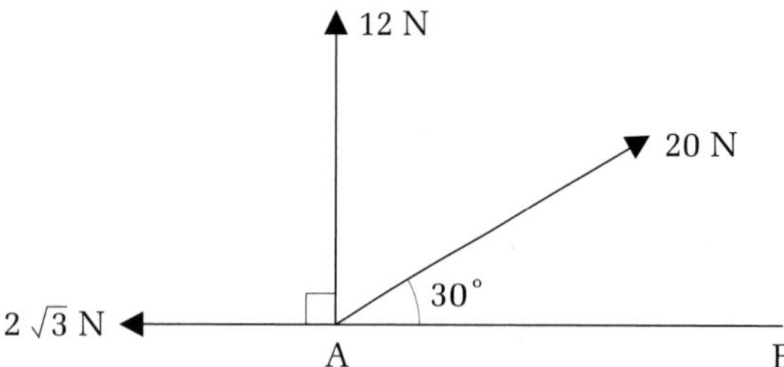

Three forces with magnitudes $2\sqrt{3}$ N, 12 N and 20 N act at the point A in the directions shown on the diagram. Calculate the magnitude of the resultant force and the angle that its direction makes with AB.

(WJEC)

3 An expedition travels from the base camp at A to a new point B, which is 25 km from A on a bearing of 072°.

a Write their displacement vector, $\overrightarrow{AB}$, as a column vector where the top component is the distance in km travelled due east and the bottom component is the distance travelled due north.

The expedition travels on from B to C, which is 32 km from B, on a bearing of 195°.

b Write $\overrightarrow{BC}$ as a column vector.

c Find in column vector form the displacement vector $\overrightarrow{AC}$.

d Calculate the distance and bearing of the direct return journey, $\overrightarrow{CA}$, that will take them back to the base camp, giving the distance to three significant figures and the bearing to the nearest degree.

Exercise B

1

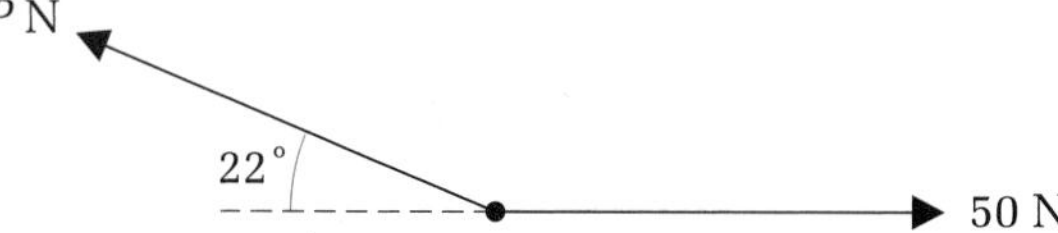

Forces of magnitudes 50 N and P N act on a particle in the directions shown in the diagram. The resultant of the two forces is at right angles to the direction of the force of magnitude 50 N. Find P.

(UCLES)

2 A particle is acted on by two forces $\mathbf{F}_1 = 5\mathbf{i} - 6\mathbf{j} + 2\mathbf{k}$ and $\mathbf{F}_2 = -3\mathbf{i} + 5\mathbf{j} - 6\mathbf{k}$

a Find the resultant force on the particle in vector form.

b Find the angle between the forces $\mathbf{F}_1$ and $\mathbf{F}_2$.

3

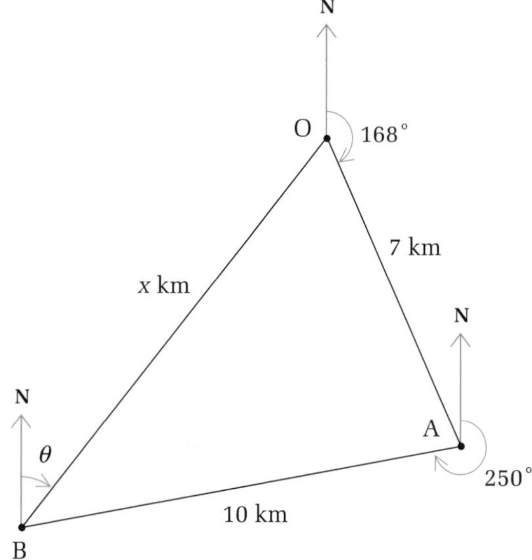

The diagram illustrates the movements of a group of walkers in the moors.

a They walk first from O to A. Taking $\mathbf{i}$ and $\mathbf{j}$ as unit vectors in directions due east and due north respectively, write $\overrightarrow{OA}$ as a vector in component form.

b They subsequently walk from A to B. Write $\overrightarrow{AB}$ as a vector in component form.

c Hence find $\overrightarrow{OB}$ in vector form.

d They now wish to plan their return journey. What is the distance x km and the bearing $\theta°$?

Applications and Activities

1 Design a mountain rescue game that uses vectors.

2 Design a set of cards using parallel vectors. Card games such as snap and matching the parallel vector cards can then be played.

3 Write computer programs or programs for a graphical calculator to:

a add two vectors together
b find the unit vector of any vector $a\mathbf{i} + b\mathbf{j}$
c find the length of a vector using the sine rule
d find the length of a vector using the cosine rule.

Summary

- Vectors can be resolved into two perpendicular components.
- The resultant of two vectors can be determined by resolving, and the *magnitude* and *direction* can be found from a scale drawing or by using the sine and cosine rules.
- The resultant of more than two vectors can be determined by resolving, using the polygon rule of addition to complete a scale drawing or by repeatedly applying the sine and cosine rules.
- The scalar product is

  $$\mathbf{a.b} = ab\cos\theta$$

  where θ is the angle between the two vectors **a** and **b**.
- If the scalar product of two vectors is zero then the vectors are perpendicular and vice versa.

6 Uniform Acceleration

What you need to know

- The definitions of displacement, speed, velocity and acceleration.
- How to calculate the displacement and acceleration from a velocity–time graph.
- How to use formulas to find an unknown quantity.
- How to solve quadratic equations by factorising.
- How to solve quadratic equations using the quadratic formula.
- How to simplify surds.
- How to add vectors in column and **i**, **j**, **k** forms.
- How to find the magnitude of a vector.

Review

1 Copy and complete the following table of definitions.

Term	Definition	SI unit	Vector or scalar
Displacement			
Speed			
Velocity			
Acceleration			

2 A car joins a straight motorway with a speed of $20\,\text{m s}^{-1}$ and accelerates to a speed of $30\,\text{m s}^{-1}$ in 20 seconds.

a Sketch a velocity–time graph.
b Find the acceleration of the car.
c Calculate the distance travelled by the car.

3 **a** If $c = d + ef$, find c when $d = 2$, $e = 7$ and $f = 4$.
b If $a = \frac{1}{2}(b + c)d$, find b when $a = 21$, $c = 4$ and $d = 7$.
c If $w^2 = x^2 + 2yz$, find x when $w = 26$, $y = 4$ and $z = 12.5$.
d If $d = eh + \frac{1}{2}gh^2$, find h when $d = -80$, $e = 0$ and $g = -10$.

4 Solve the following equations:

a $t^2 - 7t = 0$ **b** $t^2 - 5t - 50 = 0$ **c** $t^2 = 4t + 12$

5 Solve the following equations, giving your answers correct to three significant figures:

a $x^2 + 10x + 2 = 0$ **b** $x^2 = 8x + 10$ **c** $3x^2 + 4x - 5 = 0$

6 Simplify the following surds:

a $\sqrt{50}$ **b** $\sqrt{27}$ **c** $\sqrt{64} \times \sqrt{28}$ **d** $\dfrac{\sqrt{98}}{\sqrt{128}}$

7 Given $\mathbf{a} = \begin{pmatrix} 4 \\ -2 \end{pmatrix}$, $\mathbf{b} = \begin{pmatrix} -3 \\ 2 \end{pmatrix}$, $\mathbf{c} = 4\mathbf{i} + 5\mathbf{j} - 7\mathbf{k}$ and $\mathbf{d} = -2\mathbf{i} + 3\mathbf{j} - 4\mathbf{k}$, find:

a $\mathbf{a} + \mathbf{b}$ **b** $4\mathbf{b}$ **c** $\mathbf{c} + 2\mathbf{d}$

Remember to underline vectors.

8 Given $\mathbf{a} = \begin{pmatrix} 4 \\ -2 \end{pmatrix}$, and $\mathbf{b} = -2\mathbf{i} + 3\mathbf{j} - 4\mathbf{k}$, calculate:

a $|\,\mathbf{a}\,|$ **b** $|\,\mathbf{b}\,|$

6.1 Uniform Acceleration Formulas

When the acceleration does not change, it is said to be **uniform** or **constant**. To make sure the acceleration is uniform, two conditions must be met. The conditions are:

1. the size or magnitude of the acceleration must be constant
2. the direction of the acceleration must be in a straight line.

If the direction was changing then the acceleration would no longer be constant. This is because acceleration is a vector quantity and so both the magnitude and the direction of the vector must remain the same.

In this section you will study kinematics in one dimension.

When a car joins a motorway, it already has an initial speed. The driver will press the accelerator and the vehicle will speed up. How long would it take for the car to accelerate to its final speed? So far, the only way of analysing this situation is to draw a speed–time graph. This method can be time consuming and so an alternative method using formulas may be quicker. The car can be modelled as a particle and the acceleration can be assumed to be constant. If the car is travelling along a straight motorway, the speeds can now be treated as velocities because the direction of motion is assumed to be the same. By using letters to represent the variables, the uniform acceleration formulas can be derived.

By modelling the car as a particle, its size and shape can be ignored.

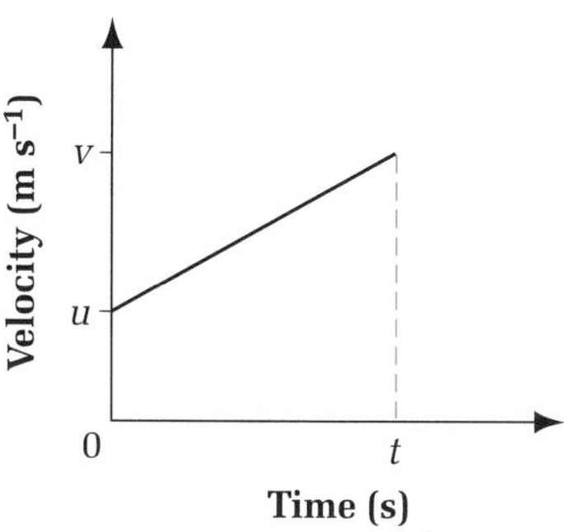

Notation
u = initial velocity (m s^{-1})
v = final velocity (m s^{-1})
a = acceleration (m s^{-2})
t = time (s)
s = displacement (m)

The graph shows the car with initial velocity, $u\ \text{m s}^{-1}$, accelerating uniformly to a final velocity, $v\ \text{m s}^{-1}$. The time taken for this change in velocity is t seconds. The acceleration being uniform means the velocity–time graph is a straight line. The gradient of the graph will give the acceleration of the car.

$$a = \frac{v-u}{t}$$ gradient $= \frac{\text{up}}{\text{across}}$

$$at = v - u \quad [1]$$ Multiply by t.

$$v = u + at \quad [2]$$ Add u.

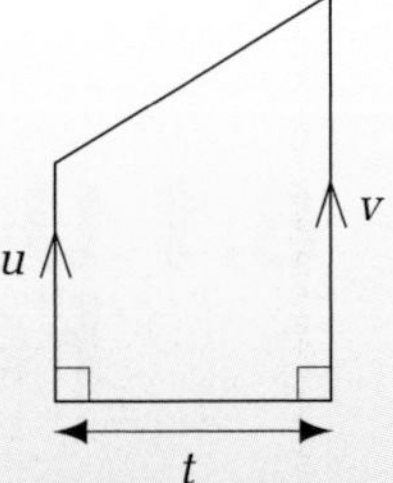

Next, the displacement s metres, will be given by the area under the graph. The shape of the graph is a trapezium.

$$s = \tfrac{1}{2}(u + v)t \qquad [3]$$

By using equations [1], [2] and [3], two other formulas can be found. First of all, replace v in equation [3] using equation [2].

$$s = \tfrac{1}{2}(u + v)t$$ ◀ **Replace v with $u + at$.**

$$s = \tfrac{1}{2}(u + u + at)t$$

$$s = \tfrac{1}{2}(2u + at)t$$

$$s = ut + \tfrac{1}{2}at^2$$

By replacing u by $v - at$ then $s = vt - \tfrac{1}{2}at^2$ is obtained.

The next formula is derived by replacing t in equation [3]. To do this, equation [1] must be rearranged to find t first.

Rearrange equation [1] by dividing both sides by a.

$$at = v - u$$

$$t = \frac{v - u}{a}$$

Write down equation [3].

$$s = \tfrac{1}{2}(u + v)t$$ ◀ **Replace t with $\frac{v - u}{a}$.**

$$s = \tfrac{1}{2}(u + v)\left(\frac{v - u}{a}\right)$$

Multiply by $2a$.

$$2as = (u + v)(v - u)$$

Notice the brackets expand to give the difference of two squares.

$$2as = v^2 - u^2$$

$$v^2 = u^2 + 2as$$

The four formulas which have been derived are:

$$v = u + at$$

$$s = \tfrac{1}{2}(u + v)t$$

$$s = ut + \tfrac{1}{2}at^2$$

$$v^2 = u^2 + 2as$$

These formulas must be **memorised**.

Additional formula: $s = vt - \tfrac{1}{2}at^2$

These formulas can only be used when the *acceleration is constant* (or is assumed constant). These equations are really vector equations and so v, u, a and s should be written as **v**, **u**, **a** and **s**. The vector notation is omitted for most cases.

For two and three dimensional motion the vector notation will need to be used. In these situations, the displacement, velocities and acceleration can either be in column vector form or **i**, **j** and **k** form.

To help you to choose the correct equation use the table on the next page. The equation needs to be the one that contains only the data you have and the quantity you need to calculate. Sometimes it is easiest to choose the formula by looking at the quantity you do not need. Look at the crosses in the table.

	s	u	v	a	t
$v = u + at$	✗	✓	✓	✓	✓
$s = \frac{1}{2}(u + v)t$	✓	✓	✓	✗	✓
$s = ut + \frac{1}{2}at^2$	✓	✓	✗	✓	✓
$v^2 = u^2 + 2as$	✓	✓	✓	✓	✗

In general, do not work out quantities that you are not asked for in the question. This will save you time and reduce the chance of mistakes. All the equations need u. If you are not given u then you will have to find u first. This will mean you cannot avoid using two equations.

Overview of method

Step ① State the positive direction.

A clear sketch is the easiest way.

Step ② Summarise the information given.

Step ③ Select one (or sometimes two) of the formulas. Use the table given to help you.

Step ④ Substitute the numbers.

Step ⑤ Calculate the value required.

Example 1

Find the final velocity, if the initial velocity is $2\ \text{m s}^{-1}$, the acceleration is $4\ \text{m s}^{-2}$, and the time of travel is 5 s.

This s stands for seconds.

Solution

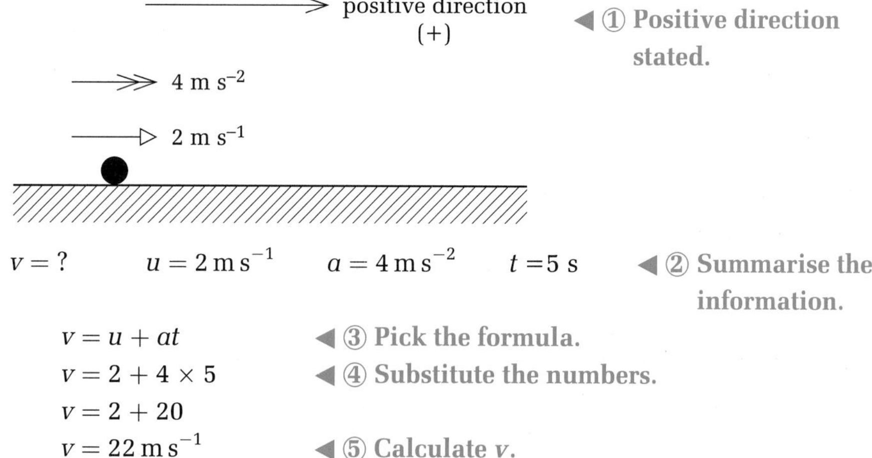

◀ ① Positive direction stated.

Notation

⟶ represents a displacement.

⟶▷ represents a velocity.

⟶≫ represents an acceleration.

$v = ?$ $\quad u = 2\ \text{m s}^{-1}$ $\quad a = 4\ \text{m s}^{-2}$ $\quad t = 5\ \text{s}$ ◀ ② Summarise the information.

$v = u + at$ ◀ ③ Pick the formula.

$v = 2 + 4 \times 5$ ◀ ④ Substitute the numbers.

$v = 2 + 20$

$v = 22\ \text{m s}^{-1}$ ◀ ⑤ Calculate v.

The equation $v = u + at$ is chosen since s is neither asked for nor given.

Example 2

Find the initial velocity, if the acceleration is $3\ \text{m s}^{-2}$ and the time taken to travel 10 m from the starting position is 4 s.

Solution

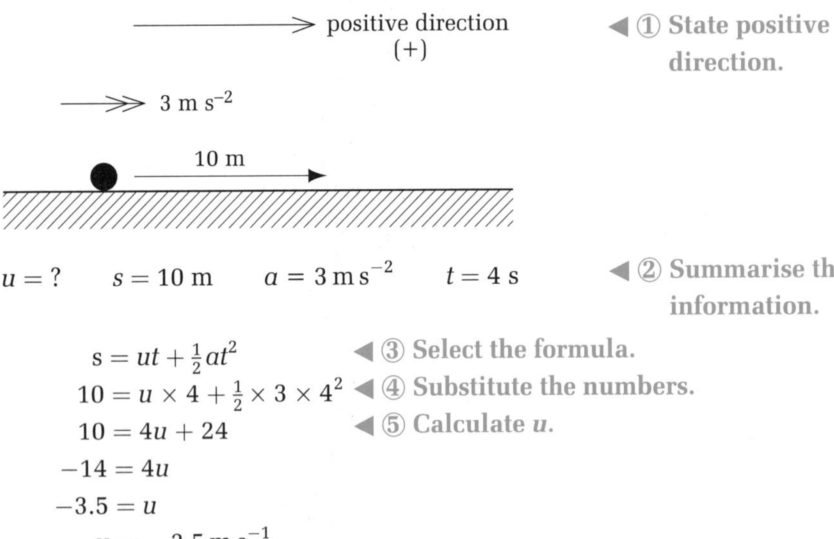

◀ ① State positive direction.

$u = ?\qquad s = 10\ \text{m}\qquad a = 3\ \text{m s}^{-2}\qquad t = 4\ \text{s}$

◀ ② Summarise the information.

$$s = ut + \tfrac{1}{2}at^2$$ ◀ ③ Select the formula.

$$10 = u \times 4 + \tfrac{1}{2} \times 3 \times 4^2$$ ◀ ④ Substitute the numbers.

$$10 = 4u + 24$$ ◀ ⑤ Calculate u.

$$-14 = 4u$$

$$-3.5 = u$$

$$u = -\ 3.5\ \text{m s}^{-1}$$

Subtract 24.
Divide by 4.

If the initial speed of the particle was required, the answer would be $3.5\ \text{m s}^{-1}$.

The negative sign must be left off because speed is a scalar.

Example 3

A car travels with a constant speed of $42\ \text{m s}^{-1}$ along a straight motorway. It passes a stationary police car which sets off in pursuit of the speeding vehicle 2 s later. The police car accelerates at $6\ \text{m s}^{-2}$. How long after being passed does the police car take to draw level with the other car? Leave your answer in surd form.

$42\ \text{m s}^{-1}$ is approximately 95 mph.

Solution

When the cars draw level, they must have covered the same distance. Their displacements must be equal. So expressions for the displacements of both cars need to be found.

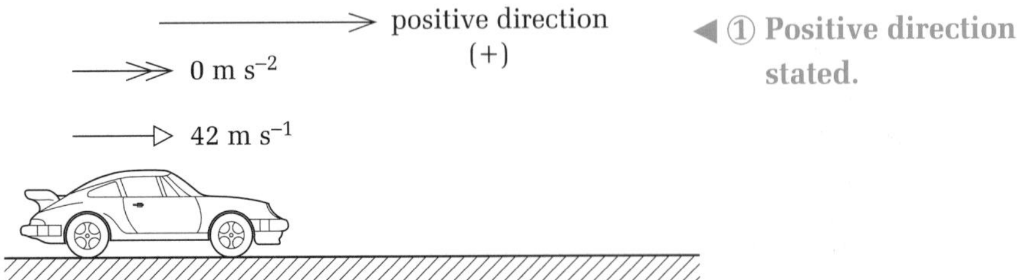

◀ ① Positive direction stated.

Let the time for the cars to draw level be T.

$u = 42\,\text{m s}^{-1}$ $\quad a = 0\,\text{m s}^{-2}$ $\quad v = 42\,\text{m s}^{-1}$ $\quad t = T$ $\quad s = ?$ ◀ ② **Summary.**

$s = ut + \frac{1}{2}at^2$ ◀ ③ **Formula.**

$s = 42T + 0$ ◀ ④ **Substitute.**

$s = 42T$ ◀ ⑤ **Find an expression for *s*.**

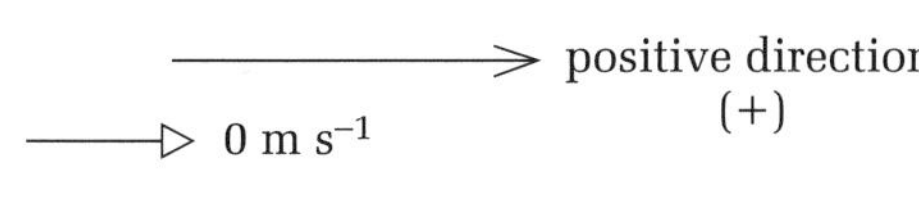

6 m s^{-2}

The police car is in motion for 2 seconds less than the first car.

$u = 0\,\text{m s}^{-1}$ $\quad a = 6\,\text{m s}^{-2}$ $\quad t = T - 2$ $\quad s = ?$

$$s = ut + \tfrac{1}{2}at^2$$
$$s = 0 + \tfrac{1}{2} \times 6 \times (T-2)^2$$
$$s = 3(T-2)^2$$

The cars will draw level when the displacements are equal.

$$42T = 3(T-2)^2$$

Divide both sides by 3.

$$14T = (T-2)^2$$

Expand the brackets.

$$14T = T^2 - 4T + 4$$

Rearrange.

$$0 = T^2 - 18T + 4$$

Quadratic equation does not factorise.

$$T = \frac{-b \pm \sqrt{b^2 - 4ac}}{2a}$$

Substitute the numbers into the quadratic formula.

$$T = \frac{-(-18) \pm \sqrt{(-18)^2 - 4 \times 1 \times 4}}{2 \times 1}$$

$$T = \frac{18 \pm \sqrt{324 - 16}}{2}$$

$$T = \frac{18 \pm \sqrt{308}}{2}$$

$\sqrt{308} = \sqrt{(4 \times 77)}$ $= 2\sqrt{77}$.

$$T = \frac{18 \pm 2\sqrt{77}}{2}$$

$$T = 9 \pm \sqrt{77}$$

$$T = 9 + \sqrt{77}$$

The police car is still at rest when $T = 9 - \sqrt{77}$.

6.1 Uniform Acceleration Formulas

Exercise

Technique

1 The descriptions below are for particles travelling in a straight line with uniform acceleration.

- **a** Find the final velocity, if the initial velocity is 5 m s^{-1} and the acceleration is 4 m s^{-2} for a time of 7 s.
- **b** Find the final velocity, if the initial velocity is 50 m s^{-1}, the distance travelled is 180 m and the acceleration is -2.5 m s^{-2}.
- **c** A particle accelerates from an initial speed of 4 m s^{-1} to a speed of 10 m s^{-1} in a time of 3 s. Work out the distance travelled.
- **d** A particle initially travels with a velocity of 3 m s^{-1}. It accelerates at 1.5 m s^{-2} for 50 s. Calculate the distance travelled.

2 A particle moves 350 m in 50 s along a straight line. If its initial velocity is 2 m s^{-1} and the acceleration is constant, calculate:

- **a** its final velocity
- **b** its acceleration.

3 A body accelerates from rest at 3 m s^{-2} along a straight line. If its final velocity is 21 m s^{-1}, find:

- **a** the time taken
- **b** the distance covered.

4 A particle accelerates at 4 m s^{-2} along a straight line. The initial velocity is 8 m s^{-1}. Find the time taken if the distance travelled is 24 m.

5 An object accelerates uniformly from 2 m s^{-1} to 10 m s^{-1} along a straight line. During this acceleration the object travels 48 m. Work out:

- **a** the time taken
- **b** the acceleration of the body.

6 An object decelerates uniformly at 4 m s^{-2} along a straight line. If the body has travelled 200 m and its initial velocity is 50 m s^{-1}, find:

- **a** the time taken
- **b** the final velocity.

7 A body accelerates at 2 m s^{-2}. Its initial velocity is 2 m s^{-1}. Leaving your answers in surd form, find:

- **a** the time taken for the body to travel 10 m from its starting position
- **b** the time taken for the body to travel 20 m from its starting position.

8 A particle X, travels with a constant velocity of 6 m s^{-1} along a straight line. It passes a particle Y which is stationary. One second later particle Y accelerates at 2 m s^{-2}. How long after being passed does it take for particle Y to draw level with the particle X? Leave your answer in surd form.

Contextual

1 A car travelling along a straight motorway overtakes a lorry by accelerating from $20\,\text{m s}^{-1}$ to $25\,\text{m s}^{-1}$. This overtaking manoeuvre takes 10 s. Calculate the acceleration of the car assuming it is constant throughout.

2 A roller coaster is accelerated along a straight track, from rest to $28\,\text{m s}^{-1}$ over a distance of 100 m. How long does it take for the roller coaster to travel this distance? Work out the acceleration of the roller coaster. Leave your answers as fractions.

3 An aeroplane lands on a runway at $60\,\text{m s}^{-1}$. If the plane takes 1.5 km to come to rest, calculate:

- **a** the time taken for the aircraft to stop
- **b** the acceleration of the plane (assuming it is constant).

4 A train accelerates at $0.5\,\text{m s}^{-2}$ along a straight track. It covers 0.5 km and has a final velocity of $25\,\text{m s}^{-1}$. Find, in surd form:

- **a** the initial velocity of the train
- **b** the time taken to travel the 0.5 km.

5 A roller coaster descends a straight slope. Its speed at the top of the slope is $2\,\text{m s}^{-1}$ and its acceleration down the slope is $5\,\text{m s}^{-2}$. If the slope is 50 m long, find (leaving your answer in surd form):

- **a** the time of descent
- **b** the final velocity of the roller coaster.

6 A lorry brakes to stop at a red traffic light. The initial speed of the lorry is $10\,\text{m s}^{-1}$ and the distance covered while braking is 120 m. Work out the deceleration the brakes cause. State any assumptions you have made.

7 A car travels with a constant speed of $40\,\text{m s}^{-1}$ along a straight motorway. It passes a stationary police car which sets off in pursuit of the speeding vehicle 1 s later. The police car accelerates at $4\,\text{m s}^{-2}$. How long does it take for the police car to draw level with the other car? Leave your answer in surd form.

6.2 Free Fall Under Gravity

Cochem Castle in Germany has a well to provide the castle with fresh water. To show how deep the well is, the tour guide pours some water into the well. The splashes of the water reaching the bottom of the well can be heard 5 seconds later. The tourists gasp in astonishment.

Why does the water accelerate in the first place? The acceleration is caused by the attraction of the Earth on the water and is called the acceleration due to gravity. The value of the acceleration varies slightly around the Earth's surface but it can be taken as $9.8\ \text{m s}^{-2}$ to two significant figures. Sometimes, a value of $10\ \text{m s}^{-2}$ is used to make the calculations easier. This introduces an error of about 2%. This is normally acceptable because of the other errors present and the assumptions being made.

$g = 9.8\ \text{m s}^{-2}$ or $g = 10\ \text{m s}^{-2}$, where g is the acceleration due to gravity.
% error
$= \dfrac{10 - 9.8}{9.8} \times 100$
$= 2.04\%$

In this book, the value of the acceleration due to gravity will be taken as $9.8\ \text{m s}^{-2}$ unless the question states a different value is to be used.

The tourists know the well sounds deep, but how deep is it? To answer this question the uniform acceleration formulas can be used to calculate the depth. We can assume that the water starts from rest and that the acceleration due to gravity is $10\ \text{m s}^{-2}$. Air resistance will be ignored and the water will be modelled as a particle.

$g = 10\ \text{m s}^{-2}$ is an appropriate assumption because only an estimate of the depth of the well can be calculated.

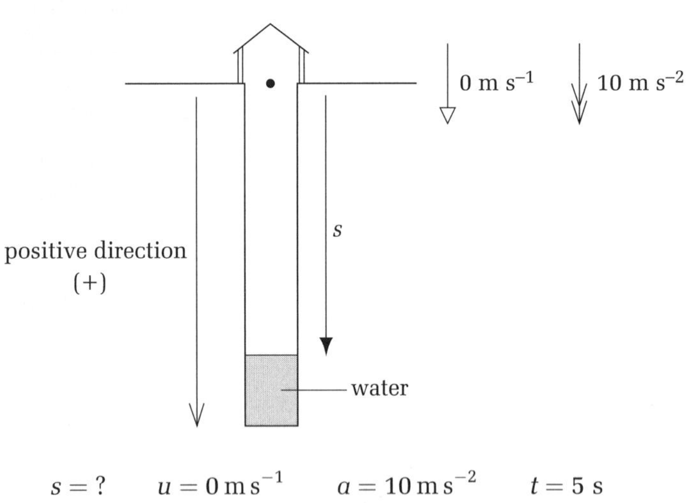

$s = ?$ $u = 0\ \text{m s}^{-1}$ $a = 10\ \text{m s}^{-2}$ $t = 5\ \text{s}$

$s = ut + \frac{1}{2}at^2$

$s = 0 + \frac{1}{2} \times 10 \times 5^2$

$s = 125\ \text{m}$

So the well is about 125 m deep. This depth can only be approximate due to the assumptions being made and the accuracy of the measurements.

Overview of method

Step ① Draw a clear diagram.
Step ② State a positive direction.
Step ③ Mark on the displacements, velocities and accelerations.
Step ④ Use the uniform acceleration formulas.

Example

A ball is thrown vertically upwards with a speed of $14\,\mathrm{m\,s^{-1}}$. Calculate:

a the maximum height the ball will reach above its starting position
b the time the ball takes to reach its maximum height.

Solution

◀ ① Diagram.
◀ ③ Mark on displacements, velocities and accelerations.
◀ ② Positive direction stated.

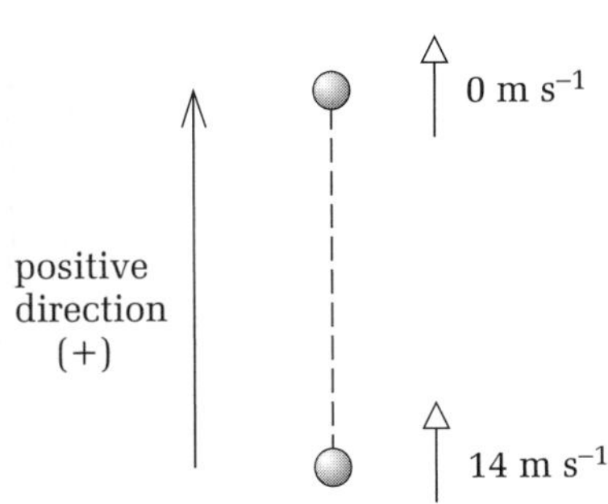

↓ $9.8\,\mathrm{m\,s^{-2}}$ or ↑ $-9.8\,\mathrm{m\,s^{-2}}$

a $u = 14\,\mathrm{m\,s^{-1}}$ $\quad a = -9.8\,\mathrm{m\,s^{-2}}$ $\quad v = 0\,\mathrm{m\,s^{-1}}$ $\quad s = ?$

Upwards is positive so downward acceleration is negative.

The maximum height will be reached when $v = 0\,\mathrm{m\,s^{-1}}$. This will be the point where the ball will stop before falling back down again.

$v^2 = u^2 + 2as$ ◀ ④ Use the uniform acceleration formulas.

Substitute values.

$0 = 14^2 + 2 \times (-9.8) \times s$

$0 = 196 - 19.6s$ — Add $19.6s$.

$19.6s = 196$ — Divide by 19.6

$s = 10\,\mathrm{m}$

b $u = 14\,\mathrm{m\,s^{-1}}$ $\quad a = -9.8\,\mathrm{m\,s^{-2}}$ $\quad v = 0\,\mathrm{m\,s^{-1}}$ $\quad t = ?$

$v = u + at$

$0 = 14 + (-9.8) \times t$

$0 = 14 - 9.8t$ — Add $9.8t$.

$9.8t = 14$ — Divide by 9.8.

$t = 1\frac{3}{7}\,\mathrm{s}$ — $\frac{14}{9.8} = \frac{140}{98} = \frac{10}{7} = 1\frac{3}{7}$

6.2 Free Fall Under Gravity
Exercise

Technique

1 An object is dropped from a height of 98 m above the ground. Find:

- **a** the time taken for the object to hit the ground
- **b** the velocity of the ball when it hits the ground.

2 An object is thrown vertically upwards with a speed of $24\,\text{m}\,\text{s}^{-1}$. Taking $g = 10\,\text{m}\,\text{s}^{-2}$, find:

- **a** the maximum height the object reaches
- **b** the object's velocity when it returns to its starting position
- **c** the object's speed when it returns to its starting position
- **d** the time taken for the object to return to its starting position.

3 A particle is dropped. The particle hits the ground with speed $50\,\text{m}\,\text{s}^{-1}$. Taking $g = 10\,\text{m}\,\text{s}^{-2}$, calculate:

- **a** the height from which the particle was released
- **b** the time taken for the particle to hit the ground.

4 An object is thrown vertically upwards. It takes 7 s to return to its original position. Taking $g = 10\,\text{m}\,\text{s}^{-2}$, calculate:

- **a** the speed of projection (initial speed)
- **b** the maximum height reached by the object.

5 A particle is projected vertically upwards with a speed of $19.6\,\text{m}\,\text{s}^{-1}$.

- **a** Calculate the time taken for the particle to:
  - **i** reach 14.7 m above its starting point
  - **ii** be at 14.7 m above its starting point for the second time.
- **b** How long will the particle be above 14.7 m?

6 An object is thrown vertically downwards with a speed of $14\,\text{m}\,\text{s}^{-1}$. Taking $g = 10\,\text{m}\,\text{s}^{-2}$, calculate:

- **a** the distance travelled in 17 s
- **b** the object's speed after 17 s.

7 A particle is thrown vertically upwards with speed $20\,\text{m}\,\text{s}^{-1}$. Two seconds later another particle is thrown vertically upwards from exactly the same place. Its initial velocity is also $20\,\text{m}\,\text{s}^{-1}$. How long after the first particle was projected, do the two particles collide? (Take $g = 10\,\text{m}\,\text{s}^{-2}$.)

Contextual

1 A diver steps off a 10 m high diving board. Calculate:

a the time taken for her to enter the water
b the speed with which she enters the water.

2 A stone is dropped from a cliff top. The stone hits the beach below after 2.5 s. Taking $g = 10\,\mathrm{m\,s^{-2}}$, find:

a the height of the cliff
b the speed with which the stone hits the beach.

3 A football is kicked vertically upwards. It takes 4.9 s to return to its starting position. Find:

a the speed of projection of the football
b the maximum height the football reaches.

4 A parachutist steps out of an aeroplane and her parachute opens 3 seconds later. Taking $g = 10\,\mathrm{m\,s^{-2}}$, determine:

a the vertical distance she has fallen when her parachute opens
b her vertical speed when her parachute opens.

State any assumptions you have made.

5 In a game of netball the umpire throws the netball vertically upwards from a height of 1.2 m. A player catches the ball 0.8 s later at a height of 2 m. Taking $g = 10\,\mathrm{m\,s^{-2}}$, determine:

a the speed with which the umpire threw the ball
b the speed of the ball when it was caught.

6 A diver jumps off a 5 m high diving board. The diver enters the water 1.5 s later. Taking $g = 10\,\mathrm{m\,s^{-2}}$, work out;

a the speed he generates in his jump
b his maximum height measured from the top of the diving board
c the speed with which he enters the water.

7 A basketball is thrown vertically upwards at a hoop. The maximum height of the ball is 3 m. If the ball was thrown at a height of 1.5 m, calculate:

a the initial velocity of the ball
b the time taken for the ball to return to 1.5 m.

6.3 Vectors and Uniform Acceleration Formulas

In this section you will study kinematics in two and three dimensions.

The bomb is given an initial horizontal velocity by the aircraft. The bomb then falls under gravity and is slowed down by air resistance. The bomb moves in two or three dimensions and so vectors need to be used to model the bomb.

Sir Barnes Wallis (1887–1979)
British aeronautical engineer who invented the bouncing bomb in 1943. These bombs were used to destroy the Ruhr dams in Germany during World War II.

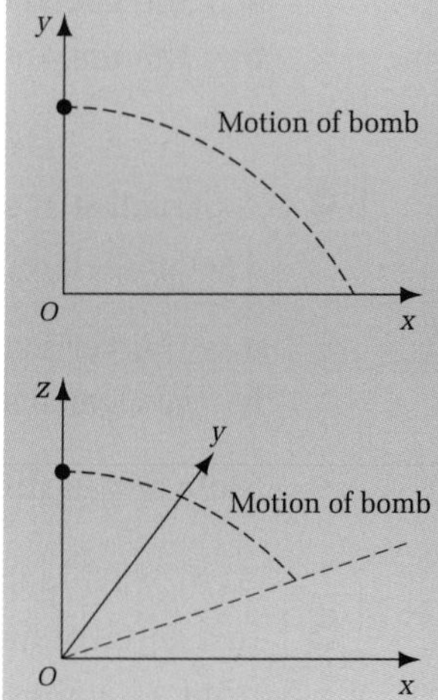

Overview of method

The method for solving vector problems with uniform acceleration can be broken down into steps.

Step ① Summary of the information.
Step ② Select the vector formula.
Step ③ Substitute the vectors into the formula.
Step ④ Calculate the unknown quantity.

Example 1

An aircraft has an initial velocity of $(90\mathbf{i} + 90\mathbf{j})\,\text{m s}^{-1}$ and a final velocity of $(100\mathbf{i} + 100\mathbf{j} + 30\mathbf{k})\,\text{m s}^{-1}$. The time taken for this change to occur is 100 s. Find:

a the constant acceleration of the aircraft, in **i**, **j** and **k** form
b the magnitude of the acceleration
c the vertical height that the aircraft has risen.

Solution

a $\mathbf{u} = (90\mathbf{i} + 90\mathbf{j})\,\text{m s}^{-1}$ $\quad\mathbf{v} = (100\mathbf{i} + 100\mathbf{j} + 30\mathbf{k})\,\text{m s}^{-1}$ ◀ ① Summary.
$t = 100$ s $\quad\mathbf{a} = ?$

$$\mathbf{v} = \mathbf{u} + \mathbf{a}t$$ ◀ ② Select the formula.

$$100\mathbf{i} + 100\mathbf{j} + 30\mathbf{k} = 90\mathbf{i} + 90\mathbf{j} + 100\mathbf{a}$$ ◀ ③ Substitute.

$$100\mathbf{i} + 100\mathbf{j} + 30\mathbf{k} - 90\mathbf{i} - 90\mathbf{j} = 100\mathbf{a}$$ ◀ ④ Calculate a.

$$10\mathbf{i} + 10\mathbf{j} + 30\mathbf{k} = 100\mathbf{a}$$

$$\mathbf{a} = (0.1\mathbf{i} + 0.1\mathbf{j} + 0.3\mathbf{k})\,\text{m s}^{-2}$$

b

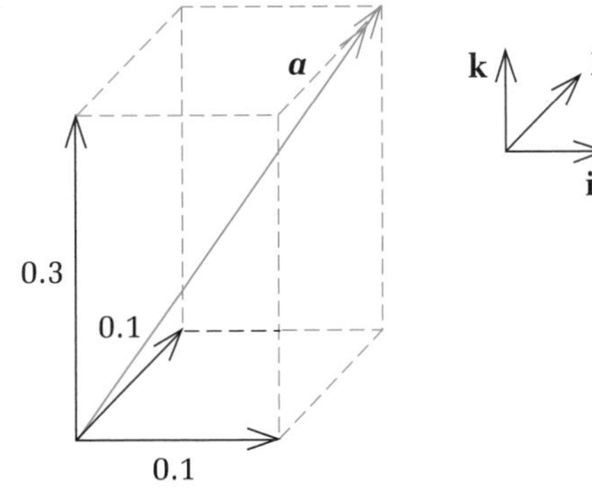

$|\mathbf{a}| = \sqrt{0.1^2 + 0.1^2 + 0.3^2}$

$|\mathbf{a}| = \sqrt{0.11}$

$|\mathbf{a}| = 0.332\ \text{m s}^{-2}$ (3 s.f.)

Recall finding the magnitude of a three dimensional vector using Pythagoras' theorem.

c $\mathbf{u} = (90\mathbf{i} + 90\mathbf{j})\ \text{m s}^{-1}$ $\mathbf{v} = (100\mathbf{i} + 100\mathbf{j} + 30\mathbf{k})\ \text{m s}^{-1}$ ◀ ① Summary.

$t = 100$ s $\mathbf{s} = ?$

$\mathbf{s} = \frac{1}{2}(\mathbf{u} + \mathbf{v})t$ ◀ ② Select the formula.

$\mathbf{s} = \frac{1}{2}(90\mathbf{i} + 90\mathbf{j} + 100\mathbf{i} + 100\mathbf{j} + 30\mathbf{k}) \times 100$ ◀ ③ Substitute the vectors.

$\mathbf{s} = 50 \times (190\mathbf{i} + 190\mathbf{j} + 30\mathbf{k})$ ◀ ④ Calculate s.

$\mathbf{s} = (9500\mathbf{i} + 9500\mathbf{j} + 1500\mathbf{k})$ m

So vertical height = 1500 m

k represents the vertical direction.

Example 2

An object has an initial velocity of $\begin{pmatrix} 5 \\ -2 \\ 7 \end{pmatrix}$ m s^{-1} and a final velocity of $\begin{pmatrix} -15 \\ 18 \\ -15 \end{pmatrix}$ m s^{-1}. The final displacement of the particle from its initial position is $\begin{pmatrix} -100 \\ 160 \\ -80 \end{pmatrix}$ m. Work out the time taken to reach that position.

Solution

$$\mathbf{u} = \begin{pmatrix} 5 \\ -2 \\ 7 \end{pmatrix} \text{m s}^{-1} \quad \mathbf{v} = \begin{pmatrix} -15 \\ 18 \\ -15 \end{pmatrix} \text{m s}^{-1} \quad \mathbf{s} = \begin{pmatrix} -100 \\ 160 \\ -80 \end{pmatrix} \text{m} \quad t = ?$$

◀ ① Summary.

$$\mathbf{s} = \frac{1}{2}(\mathbf{u} + \mathbf{v})t$$

◀ ② Select formula.

$$\begin{pmatrix} -100 \\ 160 \\ -80 \end{pmatrix} = \frac{1}{2}\left[\begin{pmatrix} 5 \\ -2 \\ 7 \end{pmatrix} + \begin{pmatrix} -15 \\ 18 \\ -15 \end{pmatrix}\right] t$$

◀ ③ Substitute vectors into equation.

$$\begin{pmatrix} -100 \\ 160 \\ -80 \end{pmatrix} = \frac{1}{2}\begin{pmatrix} -10 \\ 16 \\ -8 \end{pmatrix} t$$

Compare vectors on both sides. The vector on the RHS of the equation is multiplied by 10 to get the one on the LHS. Therefore $\frac{1}{2}t = 10$.

$$\frac{1}{2}t = 10$$

◀ ④ Calculate t.

$$t = 20 \text{ s}$$

6.3 Vectors and Uniform Acceleration Formulas

Exercise

Technique

1 A particle moves with a velocity of $(9\mathbf{i} - 12\mathbf{j})\ \mathrm{m\,s^{-1}}$. Determine the speed of the particle.

2 A body with an initial velocity of $(-4\mathbf{i} + 5\mathbf{j})\ \mathrm{m\,s^{-1}}$ accelerates at $(2\mathbf{i} + 8\mathbf{j})\ \mathrm{m\,s^{-2}}$ for 3 s. Calculate:

- **a** the displacement of the body from its original position
- **b** its final velocity
- **c** its final speed.

3 A particle accelerates from $(6\mathbf{i} + 7\mathbf{j} - 14\mathbf{k})\ \mathrm{m\,s^{-1}}$ to $(20\mathbf{i} + 28\mathbf{j} - 49\mathbf{k})\ \mathrm{m\,s^{-1}}$ at $(2\mathbf{i} + 3\mathbf{j} - 5\mathbf{k})\ \mathrm{m\,s^{-2}}$. Calculate:

- **a** the time taken
- **b** the displacement from the initial position.

4 An object accelerates from $\begin{pmatrix} 3 \\ -1 \end{pmatrix}\ \mathrm{m\,s^{-1}}$ to $\begin{pmatrix} 5 \\ 3 \end{pmatrix}\ \mathrm{m\,s^{-1}}$ in 2 s. Determine:

- **a** the acceleration of the object in column vector form
- **b** the displacement of the object from its starting position.

5 A particle accelerates from $\begin{pmatrix} 2 \\ 4 \\ 6 \end{pmatrix}\ \mathrm{m\,s^{-1}}$ to $\begin{pmatrix} 20 \\ -20 \\ 42 \end{pmatrix}\ \mathrm{m\,s^{-1}}$. During this acceleration, the particle's displacement changes by $\begin{pmatrix} 132 \\ -96 \\ 288 \end{pmatrix}$ m. For how long did the acceleration last?

6 A body's displacement is changed by $\begin{pmatrix} 3 \\ -3 \\ 9 \end{pmatrix}$ m in 3 s by an acceleration of $\begin{pmatrix} 2 \\ -4 \\ -4 \end{pmatrix}\ \mathrm{m\,s^{-2}}$. Find:

- **a** the body's initial velocity
- **b** the body's initial speed (in surd form)
- **c** the body's final speed (in surd form).

Contextual

1 An aircraft has an initial velocity of $(10\mathbf{i} - 20\mathbf{j})\ \mathrm{m\,s^{-1}}$ and a final velocity of $(15\mathbf{i} - 30\mathbf{j} - 20\mathbf{k})\ \mathrm{m\,s^{-1}}$. The aircraft accelerates uniformly and it takes 10 s for it to complete this acceleration. Determine:

a its acceleration

b the decrease in the vertical height of the aircraft during this acceleration.

2 A long jumper has an initial velocity of $(9\mathbf{i} + 4\mathbf{k})\ \mathrm{m\,s^{-1}}$ and her acceleration is $(-0.5\mathbf{i} - 10\mathbf{k})\ \mathrm{m\,s^{-2}}$. She remains in the air for 0.8 s. Find:

a her final velocity

b her final speed

c the horizontal distance she covers.

3 A sky diver has an initial velocity of $\begin{pmatrix}30\\40\\0\end{pmatrix}\ \mathrm{m\,s^{-1}}$ and a final velocity of $\begin{pmatrix}20\\35\\-45\end{pmatrix}\ \mathrm{m\,s^{-1}}$. The acceleration of the sky diver is $\begin{pmatrix}-2\\-1\\-9\end{pmatrix}\mathrm{m\,s^{-2}}$. Find:

a the time taken for this change in velocity

b the displacement of the sky diver from the starting position.

4 A hot air balloon changes its displacement by $(-360\mathbf{i} + 540\mathbf{j} - 210\mathbf{k})$ m in 30 s. Its acceleration can be assumed to be constant throughout its motion at $(-\mathbf{i} + 2\mathbf{j} - \mathbf{k})\ \mathrm{m\,s^{-2}}$. Determine the initial velocity of the balloon.

5 A long jumper has an initial velocity of $\begin{pmatrix}10\\4\end{pmatrix}\ \mathrm{m\,s^{-1}}$. His acceleration during his jump is $\begin{pmatrix}-1\\-10\end{pmatrix}\mathrm{m\,s^{-2}}$ and the jump lasts for 0.8 s. Find:

a his final velocity

b his final speed

c the horizontal distance he travels.

Consolidation

Exercise A

1 A car is moving along a straight road with uniform acceleration. The car passes a check-point A with a speed of 12 m s^{-1} and another check-point C with a speed of 32 m s^{-1}. The distance between A and C is 1100 m.

a Find the time, in seconds, taken by the car to move from A to C.
b Given that B is the mid point of AC, find, in m s^{-1} to one decimal place, the speed with which the car passes B.

(ULEAC)

2 Two humps are to be installed on a road to prevent traffic reaching speeds greater than 12 m s^{-1} between the humps. Assume that:

- the speed of the cars, when they cross the humps, is effectively zero;
- after crossing a hump, they accelerate at 3 m s^{-2} until they reach a speed of 12 m s^{-1};
- as soon as they reach a speed of 12 m s^{-1}, they decelerate at 6 m s^{-2} until they stop.

a A simple model ignores the lengths of the cars. Use this to find the distance between the humps.
b One factor that has not been taken into account is the length of the cars. Revise your answer to **a** to take this into account, giving your answer to the nearest metre. You must state clearly any assumptions that you make.

(AEB)

3 A ball is projected vertically upwards with an initial speed of 14.7 m s^{-1}. Find:

a its greatest height
b the time taken to reach its greatest height
c its speed 2 seconds after projection.

(WJEC)

4 A batsman hits a cricket ball which bounces for the first time on the boundary line. The vector $\binom{1}{0}$ is the unit vector in the horizontal direction and $\binom{0}{1}$ is the unit vector in the vertical direction. The origin is at the batsman's feet. The ball has initial displacement $\binom{0}{1}$ metres, acceleration $\binom{0}{-9.8} \text{ m s}^{-2}$ and initial velocity $\binom{15}{24} \text{ m s}^{-1}$.

a Find expressions for the velocity and displacement t seconds after the ball has been hit.
b When the ball hits the ground the displacement is given by $\binom{x}{0}$ metres. Find the value of t when this happens and deduce the distance to the boundary.

c A fielder is now put on the boundary line so that the ball will be stopped if it is not more than 3 metres above the ground when it passes his position. On the assumption that the horizontal component of the initial velocity remains at $15\ \text{m s}^{-1}$, find the minimum vertical component of the initial velocity for the ball to go over the fielder. *(MEI)*

Exercise B

1 A particle P is projected vertically upwards, with speed $16\ \text{m s}^{-1}$, from a point at ground level. Ignoring air resistance, calculate the maximum height reached by P. (Take $g = 9.81\ \text{m s}^{-2}$.) *(UCLES)*

2 A stone is thrown vertically upwards with a speed of $10\ \text{m s}^{-1}$. Two seconds later, a second stone is thrown vertically upwards from exactly the same point with a speed of $10\ \text{m s}^{-1}$. Calculate the time at which the stones collide.

3 A sack of mass 7 kg is at point O on a cliff-top and joined by a slack rope to a point A, 25 m vertically above O. The sack is thrown at $4\ \text{m s}^{-1}$ horizontally from O. Thus, taking O as the origin, x-axis horizontally in the direction of the throw and y-axis vertically upwards, A has a position vector $\binom{0}{25}$ m and the initial velocity of the sack is $\binom{4}{0}\ \text{m s}^{-1}$.

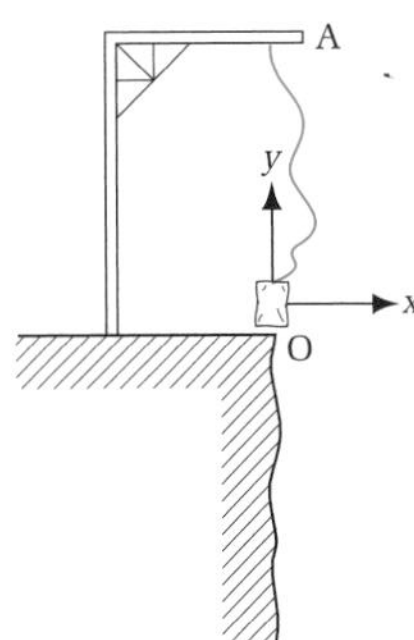

a Find, as column vectors
 i the velocity
 ii the position vector of the sack after t seconds, while the rope remains slack. (Take $g = 10\ \text{m s}^{-2}$.)

b Show that when the sack reaches 25 m below O its position vector is $\binom{4\sqrt{5}}{-25}$ m, and that its velocity is then in a direction directly away from A. *(OCSEB)*

4 Show that a speed of $72\ \text{km h}^{-1}$ is equivalent to $20\ \text{m s}^{-1}$.
A racing car, moving with constant acceleration along a straight stretch of track, passes a fixed marker A with speed $72\ \text{km h}^{-1}$. Two seconds later it passes a second fixed marker B. Given that the distance AB is 45 metres, find the acceleration of the car.

A third marker C is situated near the end of this section of track. Given that the speed of the car as it passes C is $216\ \text{km h}^{-1}$, find the time taken by the car to travel from A to C. *(NEAB)*

Applications and Activities

1

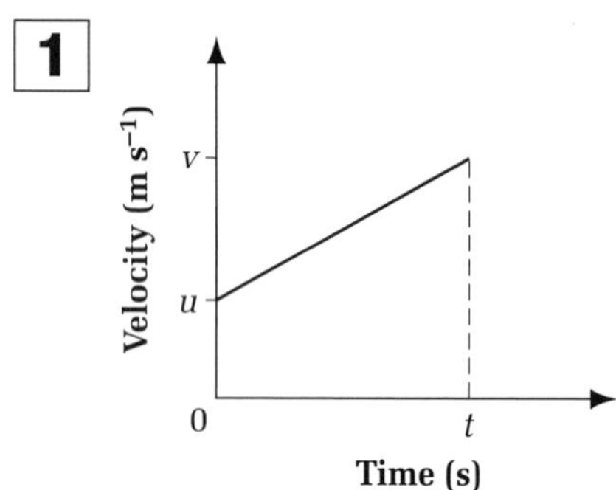

Use the graph to find a formula for:

a the acceleration, a, and hence the final velocity in terms of u, a and t
b the displacement, s, in terms of u, v and t.

Using your equations from parts **a** and **b**, derive:

c the displacement in terms of u, t and a
d the final velocity in terms of u, a and s
e the displacement in terms of v, t and a.

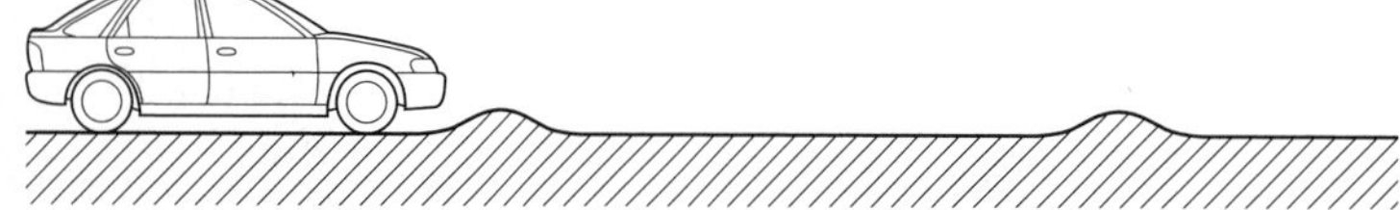

Sleeping policemen can be used to control the speeds of cars. Work out the distance between two sleeping policemen to keep the traffic speed below 30 mph. State any assumptions that you make.

3 By dropping different objects, calculate estimates for the acceleration due to gravity. Try to explain why they are not all exactly the same.

4 A ball rolls down a slope. By measuring the time taken for the ball to travel different distances, work out the acceleration of the ball. State any assumptions that you make.

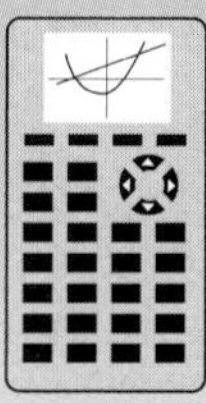

Graph plot (t, s)
$x_{min} = 0$ $x_{max} = 5$
scl $= 1$
$y_{min} = 0$ $y_{max} = 1$
scl $= 0.2$
Try to fit a curve to your points.

Summary

- The four uniform acceleration formulas are:

$$v = u + at$$
$$s = \frac{1}{2}(u + v)t$$
$$s = ut + \frac{1}{2}at^2$$
$$v^2 = u^2 + 2as$$

- The two conditions that must be met (or assumed to be met) before the uniform acceleration formulas can be applied are:

1. the size or magnitude of the acceleration must be constant
2. the direction of the acceleration must be in a straight line.

- During free fall under gravity the acceleration is the acceleration due to gravity, $g = 9.8\,\mathrm{m\,s^{-2}}$.

- The three uniform acceleration formulas for two and three dimensional problems are:

$$\mathbf{v} = \mathbf{u} + \mathbf{a}t$$
$$\mathbf{s} = \mathbf{u}t + \frac{1}{2}\mathbf{a}t^2$$
$$\mathbf{s} = \frac{1}{2}(\mathbf{u} + \mathbf{v})t$$

Additional equation:
$\mathbf{s} = \mathbf{v}t - \frac{1}{2}\mathbf{a}t^2$

7 Equilibrium

What you need to know

- The meanings of the words rotation, enlargement, reflection and translation.
- Pythagoras' theorem for right-angled triangles.
- Sine, cosine and tangent for right-angled triangles.
- How to find the resultant of two or more vectors.
- How to use the sine and cosine rules for any triangle.

Review

1 The following descriptions of transformations describe an enlargement, a rotation, a reflection and a translation. Which is which?

a moves without turning
b changes size but not shape
c turns but stays the same size
d the lines joining corresponding points on object and image have a common perpendicular bisector.

2 **a**

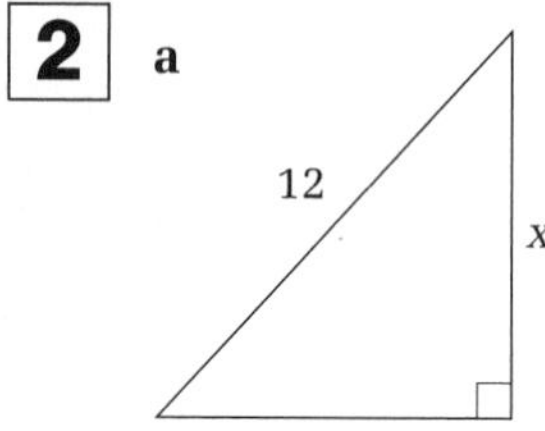

b

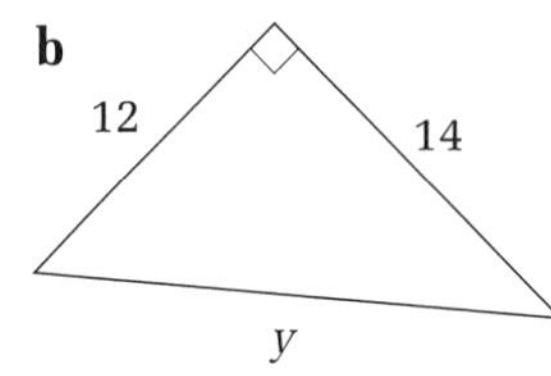

Calculate the lengths of the sides indicated, leaving your answers in surd form.

3

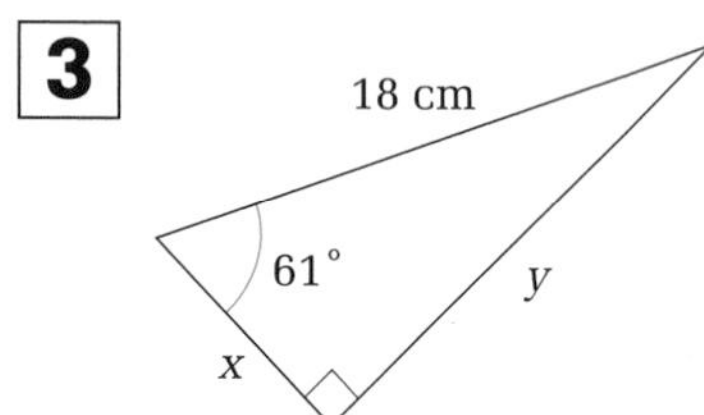

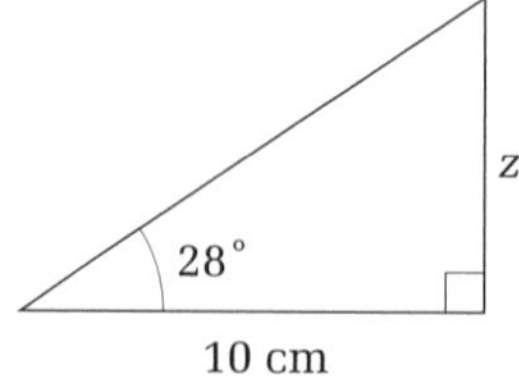

Calculate x, y and z.

4 **a** $\mathbf{a} = \begin{pmatrix} 5 \\ -2 \end{pmatrix}$ and $\mathbf{b} = \begin{pmatrix} -3 \\ -4 \end{pmatrix}$. Calculate $\mathbf{a} + \mathbf{b}$ and draw a sketch to illustrate your answer.

b What is the sum of a vector of length 5 units, due south west and a vector of length 11 units on a bearing of 100°? Give your answer as a length and bearing.

c

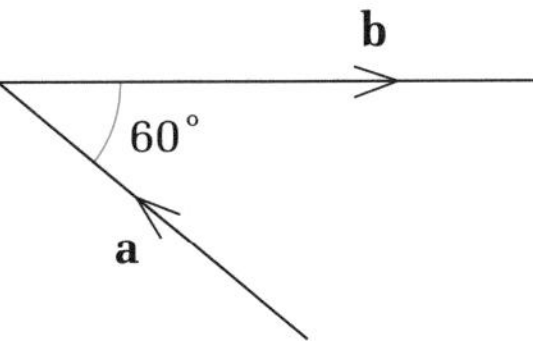

Calculate the sum of **a** and **b**, where $|\mathbf{a}| = 5$ units and $|\mathbf{b}| = 11$ units, stating the length of $\mathbf{a} + \mathbf{b}$ and the angle this vector makes with **a**.

5 **a**

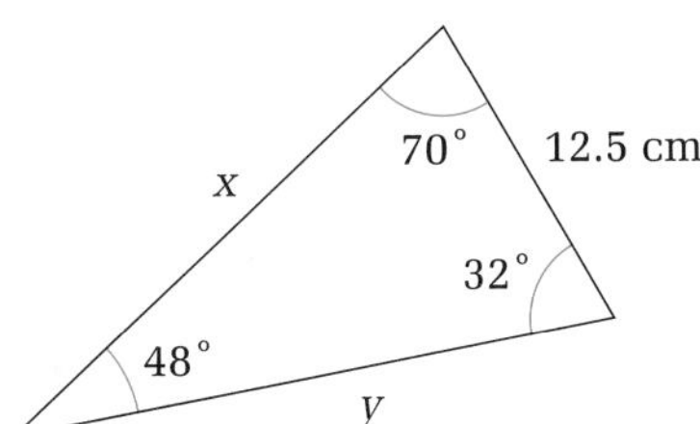

Find the lengths of the sides marked x and y.

b

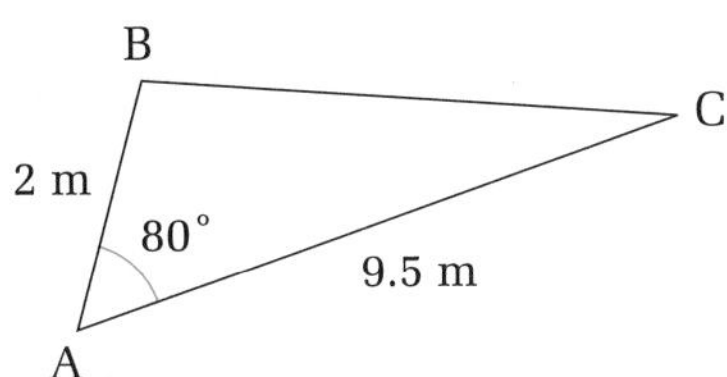

Calculate the length BC.

c

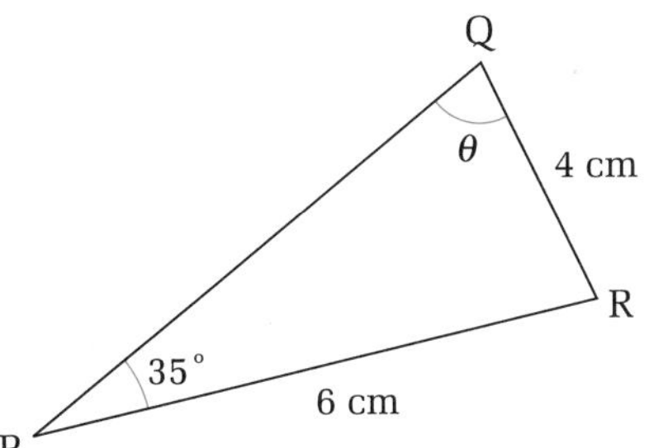

Find the two possible values of θ. In both cases state the third angle and the length of PQ.

1 Equilibrium under Concurrent Forces

Equilibrium

Equilibrium is the name for the state where a number of forces are *in balance*. A set of forces acting on a particle will either cause a change in its motion or no change. When there is no change in motion, a particle is said to be in **equilibrium**. Clearly there would be no change if no forces at all were involved. However, there are cases where a number of forces are acting, but the overall effect is the same as if no force is acting.

This is linked with Newton's first law (section 8.1).

For equilibrium the **resultant** of the forces acting must be zero. This gives the mathematical method for dealing with equilibrium problems. The sum of the forces will equate to zero if the system of forces is in equilibrium. For the four forces acting on a particle:

$\mathbf{F}_1 + \mathbf{F}_2 + \mathbf{F}_3 + \mathbf{F}_4 = \mathbf{0}$, for the particle to be in equilibrium.

Remember bold letters denote vector quantities.

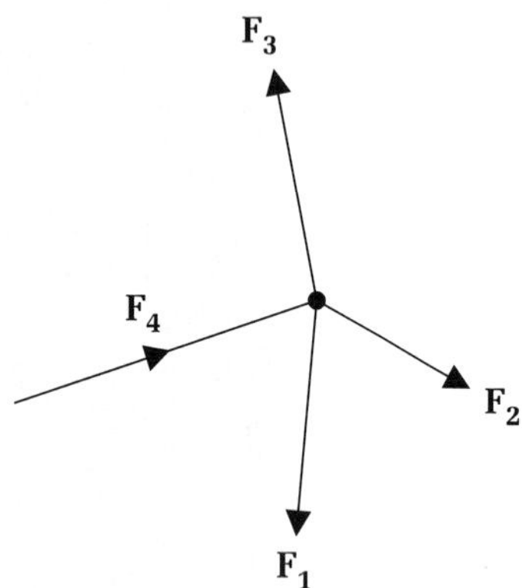

There are two types of equilibrium. When an object is stationary and remains so under the action of several forces, this is described as **static equilibrium**. Alternatively, an object may be moving with constant velocity and continues to do so under the action of the set of forces. This is referred to as **dynamic equilibrium**. In both cases the *resultant force equals zero*. The resultant force is found by adding all the forces acting on the object together. The fact that the resultant force is zero means the forces must cancel with each other.

Concurrent forces

The word **concurrent** means *acting at the same point*. When concurrent forces are referred to, the forces are all acting at the same point. If an object is modelled as a particle then all the forces acting on the object are considered to be acting concurrently.

Recall that a particle is a point object. See section 1.1.

Column vectors and unit vectors

When the forces are given in column or unit vector form, the forces can be added together to find the **resultant force**. This resultant force must be zero for the particle to be in equilibrium.

Overview of method

The following steps will be used to solve the worked examples.

Step ① Add the forces and put equal to zero.
Step ② Solve the vector equation.

Example 1

An object is in equilibrium under the action of the following three forces:

$$\begin{pmatrix} 2 \\ 7 \end{pmatrix} \text{N}, \begin{pmatrix} a \\ -11 \end{pmatrix} \text{N and} \begin{pmatrix} 4 \\ b \end{pmatrix} \text{N}$$

Calculate a and b.

Solution

$$\begin{pmatrix} 2 \\ 7 \end{pmatrix} + \begin{pmatrix} a \\ -11 \end{pmatrix} + \begin{pmatrix} 4 \\ b \end{pmatrix} = \begin{pmatrix} 0 \\ 0 \end{pmatrix}$$

◀ ① Vector equation is equal to zero for equilibrium.

$$\begin{pmatrix} a+6 \\ b-4 \end{pmatrix} = \begin{pmatrix} 0 \\ 0 \end{pmatrix}$$

$a + 6 = 0$ ◀ ② Solve the vector equation (x component).

$a = -6$

$b - 4 = 0$ ◀ ② Solve the vector equation (y component).

$b = 4$

The value of a has to be negative to balance out the 2 and 4 in the other two forces.

Example 2

Three forces, $\mathbf{F}_1$, $\mathbf{F}_2$ and $\mathbf{F}_3$ are in equilibrium. If $\mathbf{F}_1 = 12.5\mathbf{i} + 18.7\mathbf{j}$ N and $\mathbf{F}_2 = -22.0\mathbf{i} - 4.6\mathbf{j}$ N, what is $\mathbf{F}_3$ and what angle does it make with the positive x-direction?

The required angle will be measured *anticlockwise* from the x-axis.

Solution

For equilibrium:

$(12.5\mathbf{i} + 18.7\mathbf{j}) + (-22.0\mathbf{i} - 4.6\mathbf{j}) + \mathbf{F}_3 = \mathbf{0}$ ◀ ① Vector equation.

$-9.5\mathbf{i} + 14.1\mathbf{j} + \mathbf{F}_3 = \mathbf{0}$ ◀ ② Solve the equation.

$\mathbf{F}_3 = 9.5\mathbf{i} - 14.1\mathbf{j}$

Add $9.5\mathbf{i}$ and subtract $14.1\mathbf{j}$.

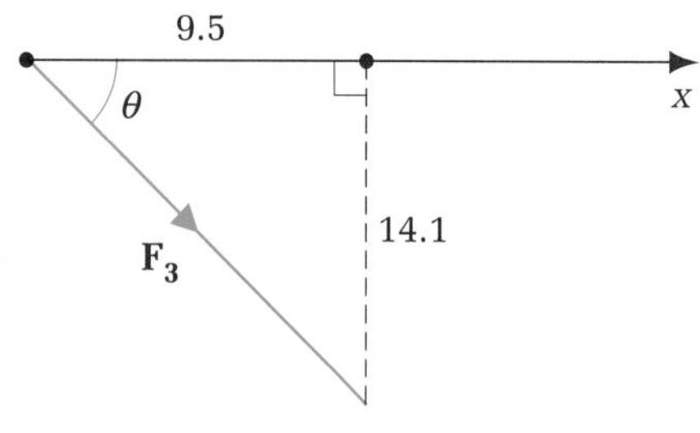

Use trigonometry to find the angle; adj = 9.5, opp = 14.1.

$\tan\theta = \frac{14.1}{9.5}$

$\theta = \tan^{-1}\left(\frac{14.1}{9.5}\right)$

$\theta = 56.0°$

or arctan $\left(\frac{14.1}{9.5}\right)$

The reflex angle measured anticlockwise from the x-axis should now be calculated.

$\alpha = 360° - 56.0°$

$\alpha = 304.0°$ (1 d.p.)

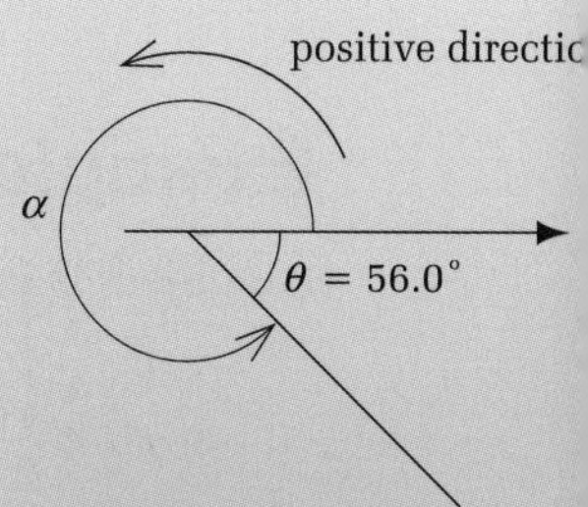

The positive direction for angles is anticlockwise.

Example 3

A body is in equilibrium under the action of forces: **P** N, (3**i** + 4**j** − 7**k**) N and (2**i** − 4**j** + 3**k**) N. Express **P** in component form and find the angle it makes with the z-axis.

Solution

The resultant will equal zero because the body is in *equilibrium*.

Equilibrium is stated in the question.

$\mathbf{P} + (3\mathbf{i} + 4\mathbf{j} - 7\mathbf{k}) + (2\mathbf{i} - 4\mathbf{j} + 3\mathbf{k}) = \mathbf{0}$ ◀ ① Add forces and put equal to zero.

$\mathbf{P} + (5\mathbf{i} - 4\mathbf{k}) = \mathbf{0}$ ◀ ② Solve the equation.

$\mathbf{P} = (-5\mathbf{i} + 4\mathbf{k})$ N

Subtract (5**i** − 4**k**).

P is in the x-z plane so this plane can be drawn on its own.

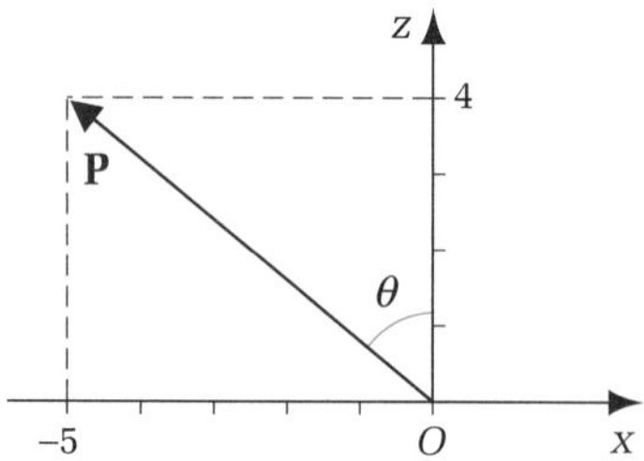

The y-axis is perpendicular to the x-z plane and points into the page of the book.

θ is the angle with the z-axis:

Use trigonometry.

$\tan\theta = \frac{5}{4}$

$\theta = \tan^{-1}\left(\frac{5}{4}\right)$

$\theta = 51.3°$ (1 d.p.)

or arctan $\left(\frac{5}{4}\right)$

7.1 Equilibrium under Concurrent Forces

Exercise

Technique

1 A particle is in equilibrium under the action of the following three forces:

$$\begin{pmatrix} 14 \\ -6 \end{pmatrix} \text{N}, \begin{pmatrix} 3 \\ 11 \end{pmatrix} \text{N and} \begin{pmatrix} a \\ b \end{pmatrix} \text{N}$$

a Find a and b.
b What is the magnitude of this third force?

2 A particle is at rest in equilibrium under the action of the three forces $(7\mathbf{i} + 2\mathbf{j})$ N, $(c\,\mathbf{i} - 5\mathbf{j})$ N and $(-3\mathbf{i} - d\mathbf{j})$ N.

a Find c and d.
b Calculate the magnitude of each force to three significant figures.

3 Forces of $12\mathbf{i}$ N and $(-8\mathbf{i} - 16\mathbf{j})$ N act on a particle. A third force $\mathbf{P}$ is to be added in order to produce equilibrium.

a Find $\mathbf{P}$ in the form $a\mathbf{i} + b\mathbf{j}$.
b Calculate the magnitude of $\mathbf{P}$ and the angle it makes with the positive $\mathbf{i}$ direction.

4

$$\mathbf{F} + \begin{pmatrix} 6 \\ 19 \end{pmatrix} + \begin{pmatrix} 8 \\ -3 \end{pmatrix} = \mathbf{0}$$

a Find $\mathbf{F}$ in column vector form.
b Calculate the magnitude of $\mathbf{F}$.
c Find the angle $\mathbf{F}$ makes with the x-axis.
d Draw a sketch of this triangle of forces in equilibrium.

5 A particle is at rest under the action of the four forces $(5\mathbf{i} + 19\mathbf{j})$ N, $(12\mathbf{i} - 15\mathbf{j})$ N, $-14\mathbf{j}$ N and $(a\mathbf{i} + b\mathbf{j})$ N.

a Find the values of a and b.
b Calculate the magnitude of the force $(a\mathbf{i} + b\mathbf{j})$ N.
c Determine the angle between $(a\mathbf{i} + b\mathbf{j})$ N and the $\mathbf{i}$ direction.

6 A body is acted on by the following forces: $20\mathbf{i}$ N, $(-11\mathbf{i} - 8\mathbf{j})$ N, $(3\mathbf{i} - 14\mathbf{j})$ N and $(-7\mathbf{i} + 17\mathbf{j})$ N. The addition of a fifth force, $\mathbf{P}$, brings about equilibrium.

a Find $\mathbf{P}$ in the form $x\mathbf{i} + y\mathbf{j}$.
b Calculate the angle $\mathbf{P}$ makes with the $20\mathbf{i}$ N force.

7 The action of the following three forces on a body results in equilibrium: $(-9\mathbf{i} + \mathbf{j} - 7\mathbf{k})$ N, $(3\mathbf{i} + 10\mathbf{k})$ N and $(a\mathbf{i} + b\mathbf{j} + c\mathbf{k})$ N.

- a What are the values of a, b and c?
- b Calculate the magnitude of $(a\mathbf{i} + b\mathbf{j} + c\mathbf{k})$ N.

8 A particle is in equilibrium when acted upon by these three forces: $\mathbf{Z}$ N, $(18\mathbf{i} - 6\mathbf{j} + 9\mathbf{k})$ N and $(2\mathbf{i} - 2\mathbf{j} - 7\mathbf{k})$ N.

- a Find $\mathbf{Z}$ in unit vector form.
- b By using the scalar product, find the angle $\mathbf{Z}$ makes with each of the other two forces.

Contextual

1 The lower part of a radio mast is held in equilibrium by three horizontal cables. The cables can be assumed to be light. The tension forces in two of the cables are $(10\mathbf{i} - 2\mathbf{j})$ N and $(-5\mathbf{i} + 6\mathbf{j})$ N.

- a State the third tension in the form $a\mathbf{i} + b\mathbf{j}$.
- b What is the magnitude of the tension in the third cable?
- c What angle does the third cable make with the $\mathbf{i}$ direction?

2 The tensions in four telephone wires attached to a telegraph post are $(17\mathbf{i} - 9\mathbf{j})$ N, $(-11\mathbf{i} + 6\mathbf{j})$ N, $(-3\mathbf{i} - 18\mathbf{j})$ N and $(a\mathbf{i} + b\mathbf{j})$ N. The four forces are in equilibrium.

- a Find the values of a and b.
- b Calculate the magnitude of $(a\mathbf{i} + b\mathbf{j})$ N.

3 A tent pole is held in equilibrium by guy ropes whose tensions are $(3\mathbf{i} + 5\mathbf{j} - 8\mathbf{k})$ N, $(-2\mathbf{i} - \mathbf{j} - 5\mathbf{k})$ N and $\mathbf{P}$ N. The thrust in the tent pole is $20\mathbf{k}$ N.

- a Express $\mathbf{P}$ in the form $a\mathbf{i} + b\mathbf{j} + c\mathbf{k}$.
- b Find the magnitude of $\mathbf{P}$.
- c What is the angle between the force $\mathbf{P}$ and the tent pole?

4 Four children are playing a four-way tug of war. Two skipping ropes have been knotted in the middle and each child is holding an end of one rope. The ropes are **not** at right angles. They prepare to take the strain before the competition begins. Three of the forces exerted are: $18\mathbf{i}$ N, $(3\mathbf{i} - 14\mathbf{j})$ N and $(-\mathbf{i} + 12\mathbf{j})$ N.

- a What must the fourth force be, to achieve equilibrium?
- b Calculate the angles between the ropes, showing them clearly on a sketch.
- c Which force has the smallest magnitude?

7.2 Equilibrium and the Triangle of Forces

What is the least number of forces that can produce equilibrium?

The body is modelled as a particle acted on by a force **F**.

A body is acted on by just *one force*, **F**. The resultant force must be equal to this applied force **F**. For the body to be in equilibrium, the resultant force must be zero and so the force **F** must be zero.

$|\mathbf{F}| = 0$ for equilibrium

This is a trivial solution and means no force is applied.

This means that a particle cannot be in equilibrium if just one force is acting.

If *two forces* are acting, where must the second force be placed in order to keep the body in equilibrium? The two forces must be equal in magnitude and act in opposite directions.

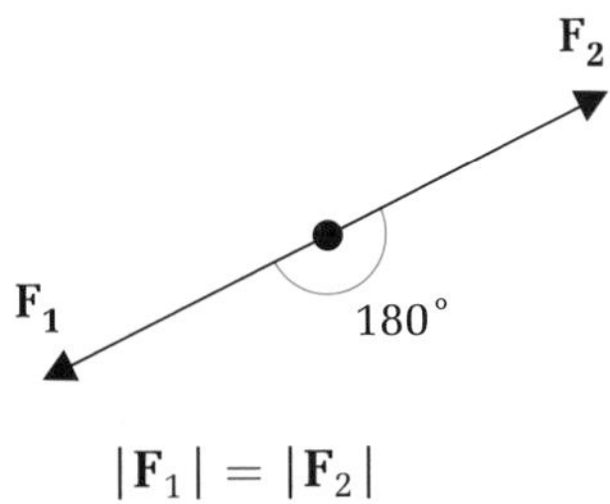

Vectors with equal magnitudes and opposite directions means $\mathbf{F}_1 = -\mathbf{F}_2$.

$|\mathbf{F}_1| = |\mathbf{F}_2|$

If the action of a set of *three forces* on an object produces equilibrium, the resultant force must be zero. A set of three vectors whose sum is zero can be shown as a triangle of vectors where the three arrows follow round in order.

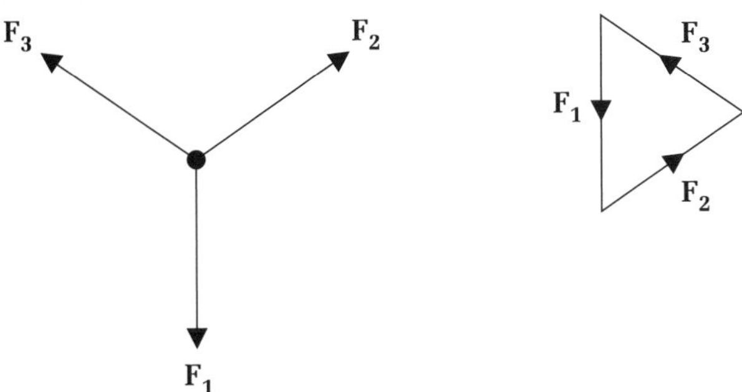

Compare this with adding three vectors using the polygon rule where the resultant is zero.

In a similar way, three forces can be drawn to form a triangle. Then, the geometry of the triangle can be used to answer the questions. A scale drawing of the vector triangle could be made, with geometrical equipment. The required information could then be measured from the diagram. As with all scale drawings, the accuracy is improved by choosing the largest sensible scale.

Overview of method

Step ① Draw a rough freehand sketch first.
Step ② Choose a suitable scale.
Step ③ Accurately construct the known parts of the force triangle.
Step ④ Measure the required information, remembering to convert lengths.

Sometimes only a sketch of the triangle of forces is required.

Use the freehand sketch to determine a scale which will produce the largest diagram that will fit on your page.

Example 1

A Christmas decoration is suspended by two wires. Two equal tension forces in the wires each act at 110° to the weight force. Sketch a force diagram and the associated triangle of forces.

This example only requires a sketch to be drawn.

Solution

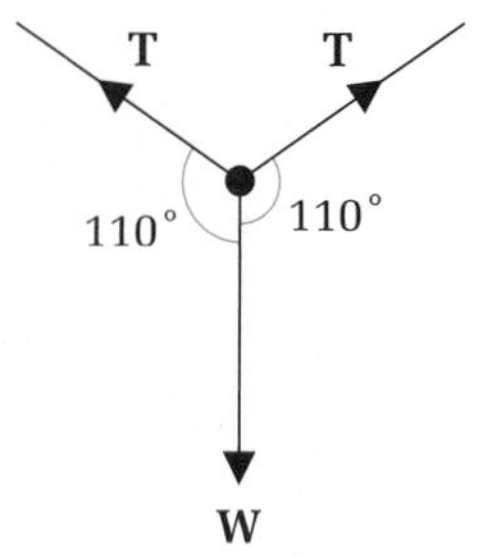

The decoration is represented by a dot, for a particle.

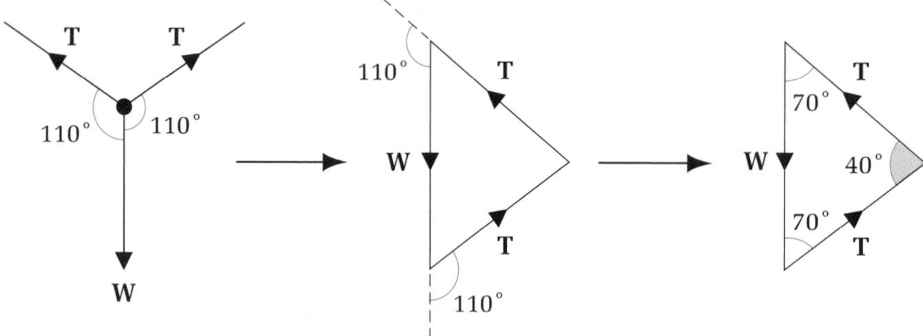

Keep the same angles when you move the forces. Calculate the interior angles by subtracting from 180°. The third angle of the triangle must be 40°.

Example 2

A force of 15 N acts at 85° to a force of 20 N. By scale drawing, determine the magnitude and direction of the force which must be added to produce equilibrium.

Solution

◀ ① **Rough sketch.**

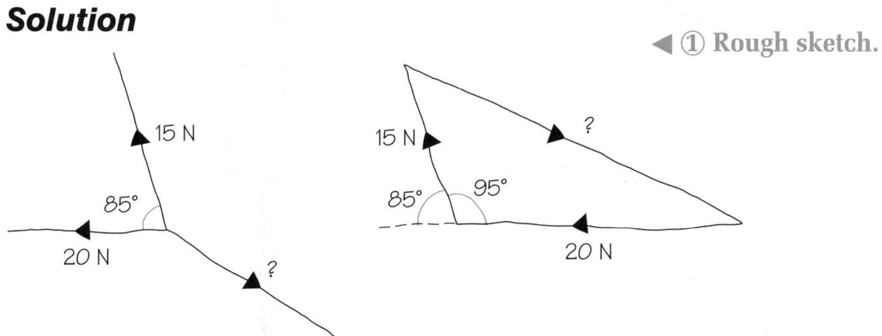

A scale of 1 cm to 2 newtons seems reasonable.

◀ ② **Choose a suitable scale.**

Now carefully construct the angle of 95° and the lengths, to scale.

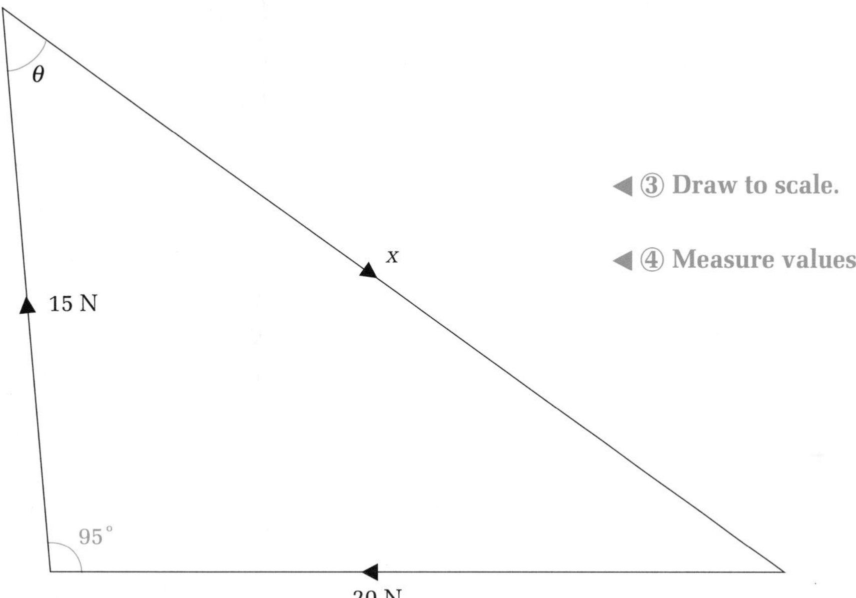

◀ ③ **Draw to scale.**

◀ ④ **Measure values.**

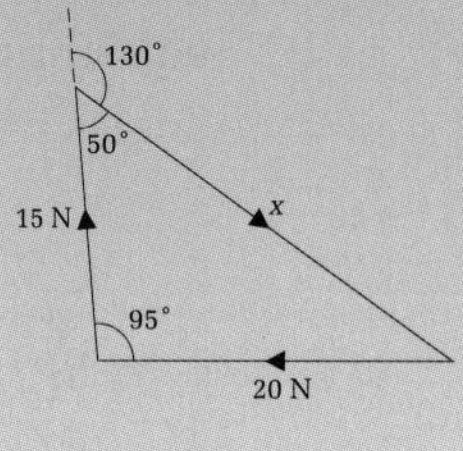

$180^\circ - 50^\circ = 130^\circ$

Measure x and θ.

$x = 26.0$ N and $\theta = 50^\circ$

The third force has magnitude 26.0 N and acts at an angle of 130° to the 15 N force.

7.2 Equilibrium and the Triangle of Forces

Exercise

Technique

1 a Draw a force diagram for a particle of mass 5 kg, at rest in equilibrium on a horizontal plane.

b How many forces are acting?

c What is the magnitude of each force?

2 A particle is acted upon by four forces, as shown. All forces have non-zero magnitudes. If $\mathbf{F}_1 + \mathbf{F}_2 + \mathbf{F}_3 + \mathbf{F}_4 = \mathbf{0}$, what can be said about the particle?

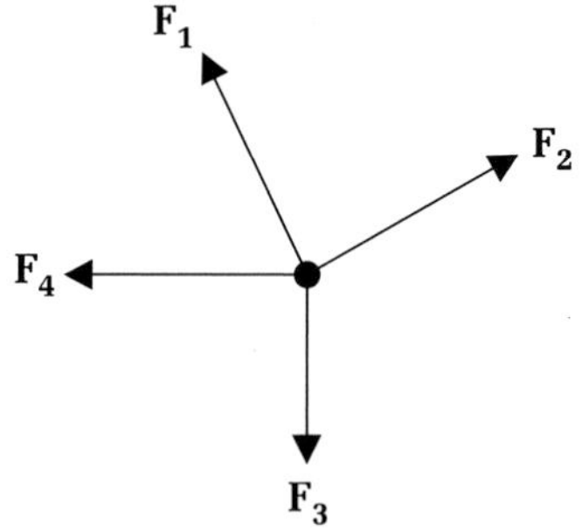

3 a Draw the force triangle corresponding to these three forces, if they are in equilibrium. Remember to label the angles carefully.

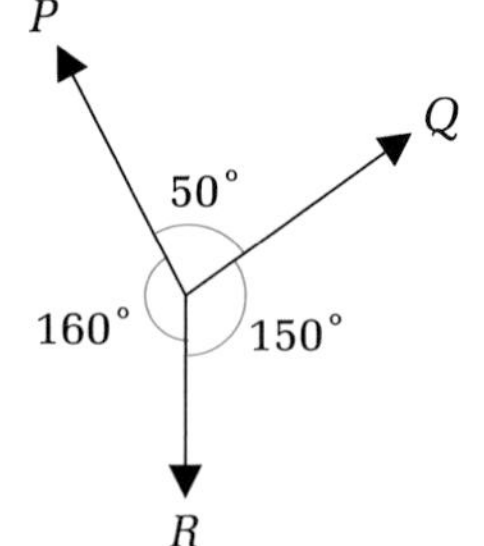

b Draw the force diagram corresponding to this triangle of forces. Label the angle between each pair of forces.

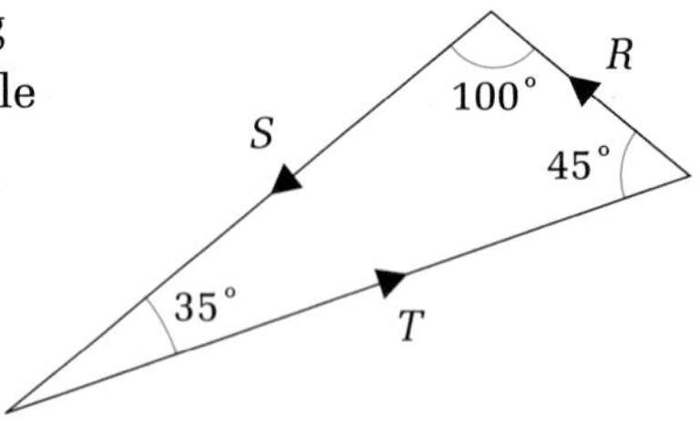

4 A particle is acted upon by three forces. These are: a force vertically downwards of W newtons, a force of P newtons acting at 150° to W, and a force of Q newtons acting at 100° to W.

a Draw a force diagram of this situation.

The particle is in static equilibrium.

b Draw an appropriate triangle of forces, labelling all the internal angles.

5 A particle is in equilibrium under the action of three forces. One has magnitude 7.4 N. A second, of magnitude 11.3 N acts at 67° to the first force.

a Draw this triangle of forces to scale.

b From your diagram, find:

i the magnitude of the third force

ii the angle between the direction of the third force and the 7.4 N force.

6 Three forces, of magnitudes 280 N, 175 N and 160 N, are in equilibrium. By choosing a suitable scale and using a pair of compasses, draw a suitable triangle of forces. Determine from your diagram the angles between the lines of action of the three forces, correct to the nearest degree.

Contextual

1 An object sinks through water at constant speed.

a Draw a diagram of the forces acting.

b The mass of the object is 10 kg. What are the magnitudes of the forces acting?

c What assumptions have been made?

2

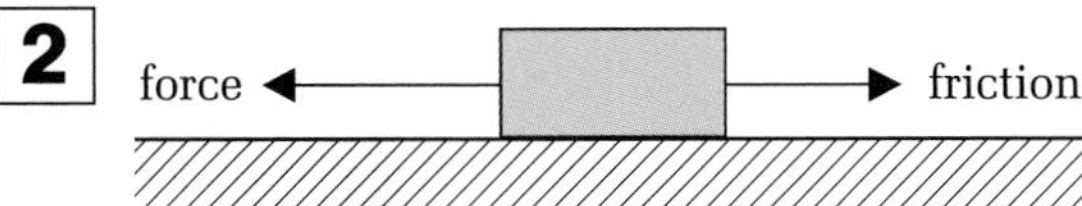

A crate of mass 40 kg is at rest on a horizontal surface. A force is applied by pulling on a horizontal rope.

a Complete the force diagram.

b The crate is pulled along at a constant velocity, and the force applied is 10 N. What can be said about the magnitude of the friction?

c What are the magnitudes and directions of the other two forces?

3 A microphone is suspended over a concert platform by two wires, each inclined at 20° to the horizontal.

a If each wire has the same tension, T newtons, draw a fully labelled force diagram.

b Convert this into a triangle of forces, labelling all the internal angles.

4 As part of a sculpture, a metal ball of mass 2.6 kg is supported by two light rods. One rod is inclined at 38° above the horizontal, and the magnitude of the thrust in it is 30 N. Find, by scale drawing, the magnitude of the thrust in the second rod, and the angle it makes with the horizontal.

7.3 Trigonometry and the Triangle of Forces

Scale drawing is one method for solving triangle of forces problems. However a more accurate solution can be obtained by using trigonometry. It is important to draw a clear diagram of the triangle of forces with all the lengths and angles correctly calculated. The next steps will depend upon whether one of the angles is 90° or not. If the triangle contains *one right angle*, all the calculations will involve simple trigonometry or Pythagoras' theorem. If *none of the angles is 90°*, then the sine rule or the cosine rule will be used instead.

Overview of method

Step ① Draw a clearly labelled diagram.
Step ② Apply trigonometry, Pythagoras' theorem or sine and cosine rules.
Step ③ Solve to find the required information.

Example 1

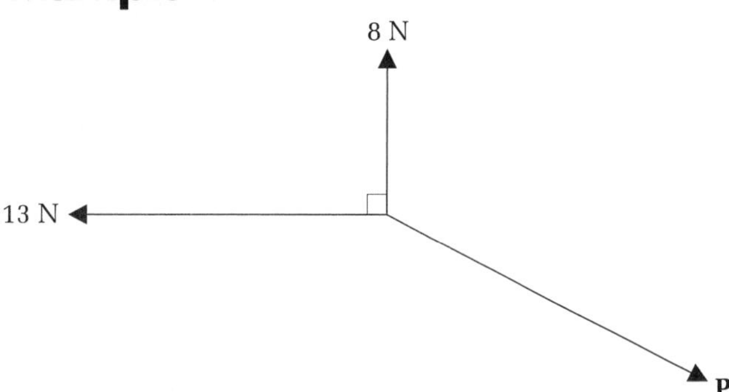

A particle is in equilibrium under the forces shown. Calculate the magnitude and direction of the force **P**, stating the angle it makes with the 13 N force.

Solution

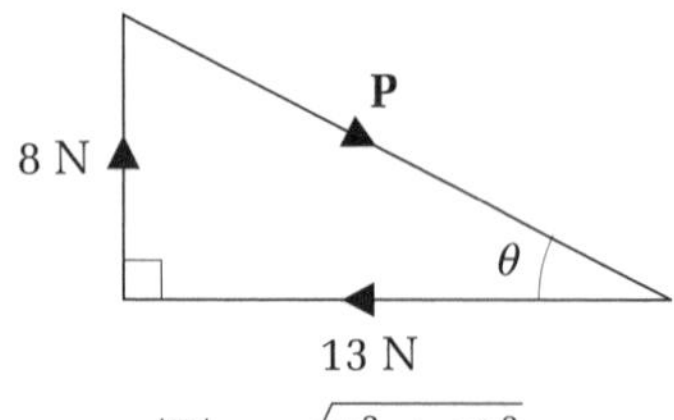

◀ ① Diagram for the triangle of forces.

$$|\mathbf{P}| = \sqrt{8^2 + 13^2} = \sqrt{233} = 15.3\,\text{N}\,(3\,\text{s.f.})$$

◀ ② Use Pythagoras' theorem.

$$\tan\theta = \tfrac{8}{13}$$
$$\theta = \tan^{-1}\left(\tfrac{8}{13}\right)$$
$$\theta = 31.6^\circ \ (1\text{ d.p.})$$

◀ ③ Use trigonometry to calculate the direction.

or $\arctan\left(\frac{8}{13}\right)$

Referring to the original diagram:

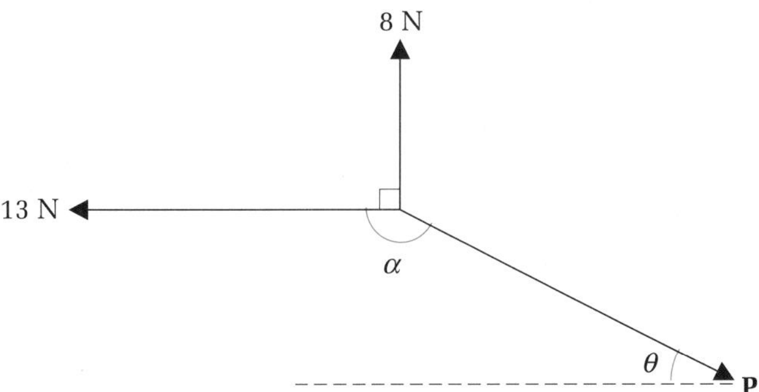

$\alpha + \theta = 180°$

$\alpha = 180° - \theta$

$\alpha = 148.4°$ (1 d.p.)

Angles between parallel lines such as α and θ are called Allied angles and sum to 180°.

P has magnitude 15.3 N and acts in a direction 148.4° anticlockwise from the 13 N force.

Example 2

Three forces, with magnitudes 8, 11 and 15 N, are in equilibrium. What are the angles between them?

Solution

This time the triangle of forces can be drawn first.

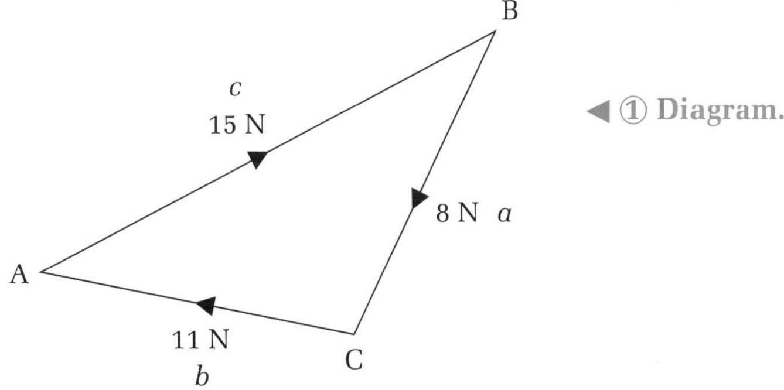

◀ ① Diagram.

The sides and vertices have been labelled for convenience.

By the cosine rule:

◀ ② Use the cosine rule.

$$\cos A = \frac{b^2 + c^2 - a^2}{2bc}$$

$$\cos A = \frac{11^2 + 15^2 - 8^2}{2 \times 11 \times 15}$$

◀ ③ Solution.

Insert values.

$$\cos A = 0.8545$$

$$A = \cos^{-1}(0.8545)$$

$$A = 31.3° \text{ (1 d.p.)}$$

or arccos(0.8545)
Use exact value.
Once again, store the exact answer for later use.

Now by the sine rule:

$$\frac{\sin B}{11} = \frac{\sin A}{8}$$

$$\sin B = \frac{11 \times \sin 31.3^\circ}{8}$$

$$B = \sin^{-1}\left(\frac{11 \times \sin 31.3^\circ}{8}\right)$$

$$B = 45.6^\circ \text{ (1 d.p.)}$$

Or you could use the cosine rule again.

or $\arcsin\left(\frac{11 \times \sin 31.3^\circ}{8}\right)$

Using the angles in a triangle:

$$C = 180^\circ - 31.3^\circ - 45.6^\circ = 103.1^\circ \text{ (1 d.p.)}$$

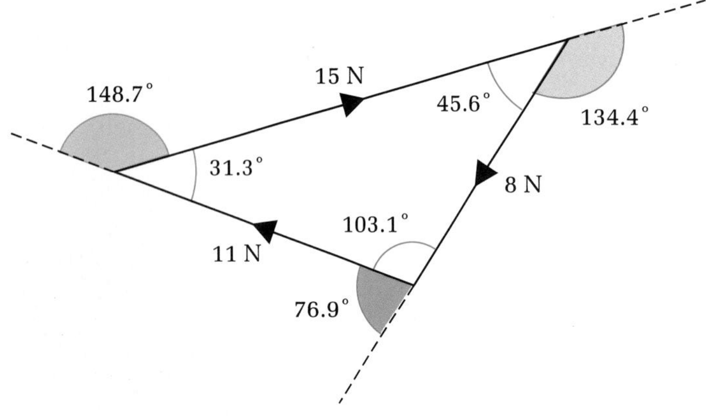

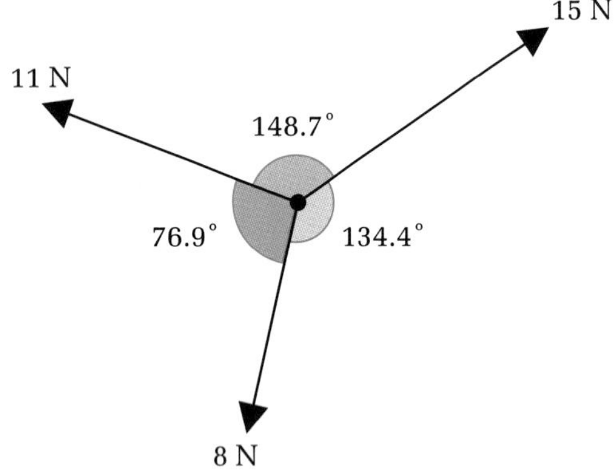

Angles between the forces are 76.9°, 148.7° and 134.4° as shown.

7.3 Trigonometry and the Triangle of Forces

Exercise

Technique

1 **a**

8 N

15 N

W

b

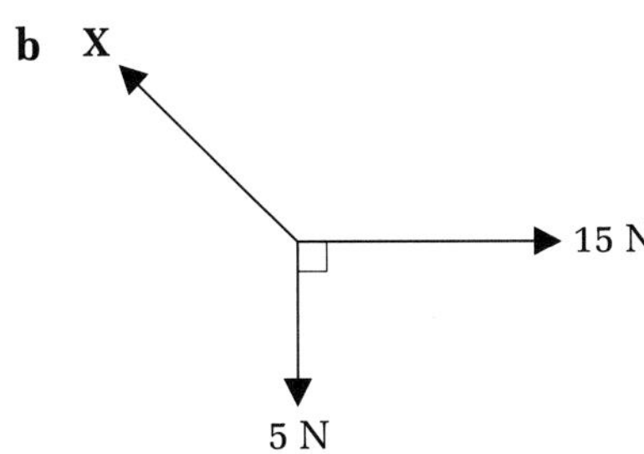

Each diagram shows a particle in equilibrium under the action of three forces. Find the magnitude of the unknown force in each case, together with the angle it makes with the 15 N force.

2 For this triangle of forces in equilibrium, find the magnitude of **X** in surd form and the angle with the 18 N force, correct to one decimal place.

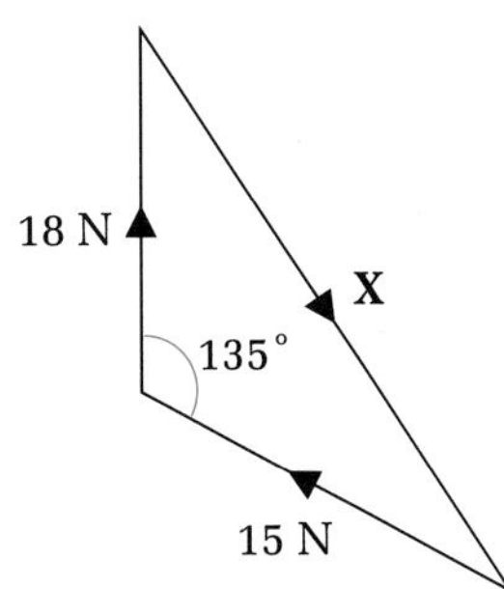

The required angle will be obtuse. It will be the angle between the directions of these two vectors.

3 A particle is at rest in equilibrium under the action of forces of magnitude 23 N, 18 N and 12 N. Find the angles between their lines of action.

4 The three forces shown hold a particle in equilibrium.

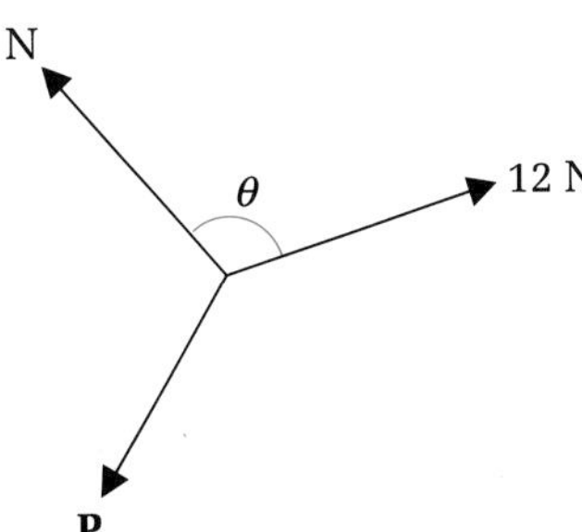

a What is the magnitude of **P** when:

i $\theta = 60°$

ii $\theta = 90°$

iii $\theta = 120°$

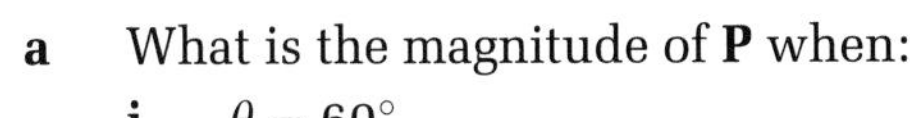

b What is the value of θ when:

i $P = 10$ N

ii $P = 16$ N

iii $P = 18$N

Contextual

1 A crate is being pulled along horizontal ground at a constant speed by two horizontal ropes at 90° to each other. There is a horizontal resistance force. The tension in one rope is 14 N and the tension in the other is 12.5 N. What must be the magnitude of the resistive force, and what angle does it make with the 14 N force?

2 Two children are holding one end each of a skipping rope. Their dog is holding part of the rope in his teeth and is pulling away from them. The three forces are temporarily in equilibrium. The angle between the two parts of the rope is 75° and the two tensions are 8 N and 11 N.

a What is the magnitude of the force exerted by the dog?
b What angle does this force make with the 8 N force?

3 As part of an experiment, three students attach force meters to a metal ring and exert forces that keep the ring in equilibrium. The forces are noted to be 6.8 N, 8.2 N and 5.9 N. What must be the angles between these forces?

4 A spider of mass 0.03 g is at rest in equilibrium part of the way along a single thread of silk. The angles betwen the silk thread and the weight force are 85° and 107°. Determine, by using the sine rule, the tensions in each part of the silk.

5 A parachute jumper descends with a constant velocity for a certain part of his motion. Three forces are acting; the weight of the man (including his equipment), the tension due to the parachute, the force of the air current (acting in a horizontal direction). If the mass of the man is 95 kg and the air current produces a force of 150 N, what is the magnitude of the tension and its angle from the vertical direction?

7.4 Lami's Theorem

For three-force problems, a force diagram is replaced almost immediately with a triangle of forces. It would be more convenient if the mathematical method worked for the original force diagram.
Where three concurrent forces are involved it has been necessary to use the trigonometrical formulas to calculate the unknown forces or angles in our vector triangle. The following method allows that to be done without the need to redraw the picture first.

Lami's theorem

For the forces P, Q and R, at angles α, β and γ, as shown:

$$\frac{P}{\sin(\alpha)} = \frac{Q}{\sin(\beta)} = \frac{R}{\sin(\gamma)}$$

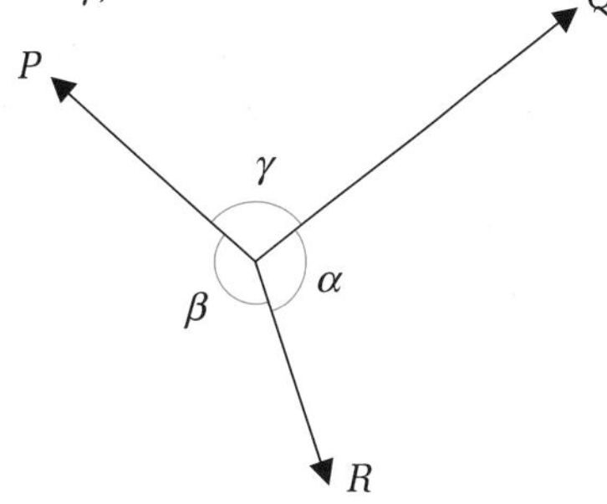

Notice that the formula pairs each force with an angle. In each case, it is the only angle the force is *not* touching or the force and 'paired' angle are opposite each other.

This formula is similar to the sine rule from which it can be derived.

This formula only applies for systems of *forces* that are *in equilibrium*.

Overview of method

Step ① Draw a clear force diagram.
Step ② Substitute the known values into Lami's theorem.
Step ③ Rearrange a pair of terms where three values are known, to solve for the other value.

If all three terms contain an unknown value, then a different method should be used.

Example

An object is held in equilibrium by three forces, as shown. Use Lami's theorem to find α and X.

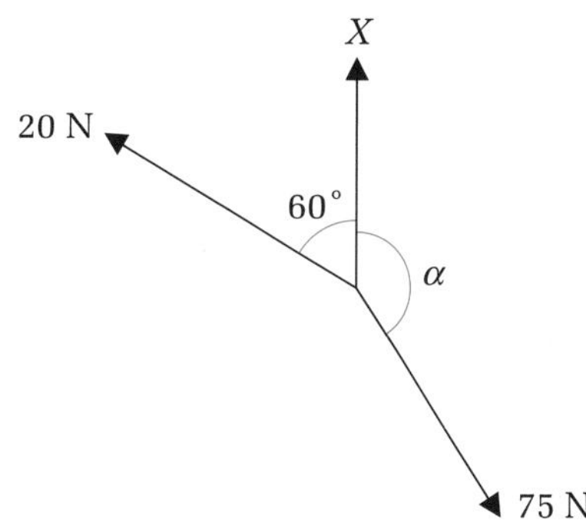

Solution

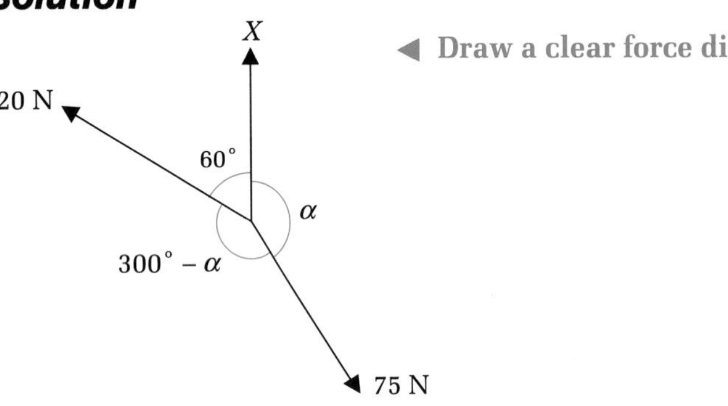

◀ Draw a clear force diagram.

$360° - 60° - \alpha$
$= 300° - \alpha$

The angle between the 20 N and 75 N forces is $(300° - \alpha)$.
Using Lami's theorem:

$$\frac{X}{\sin(300° - \alpha)} = \frac{20}{\sin\alpha} = \frac{75}{\sin 60°}$$

◀ ② Substitute into Lami's theorem.

$$\frac{20}{\sin\alpha} = \frac{75}{\sin 60°}$$

◀ ③ Solve for α.

Multiply by $\sin\alpha$ and $\sin 60°$.
Divide by 75.

$$20 \times \sin 60° = 75 \times \sin\alpha$$

$$\frac{20 \times \sin 60°}{75} = \sin\alpha$$

$$0.2309 = \sin\alpha$$

$$\alpha = 13.4° \text{ (1 d.p.)}$$

$\sin^{-1}(0.2309)$
or arcsin (0.2309)

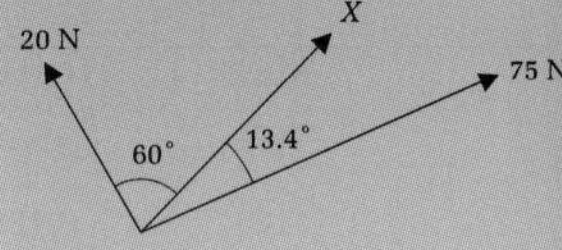

This angle cannot possibly produce equilibrium, since α must be bigger than 90° to produce equilibrium. Another solution can be obtained from a sketch of the sine curve.

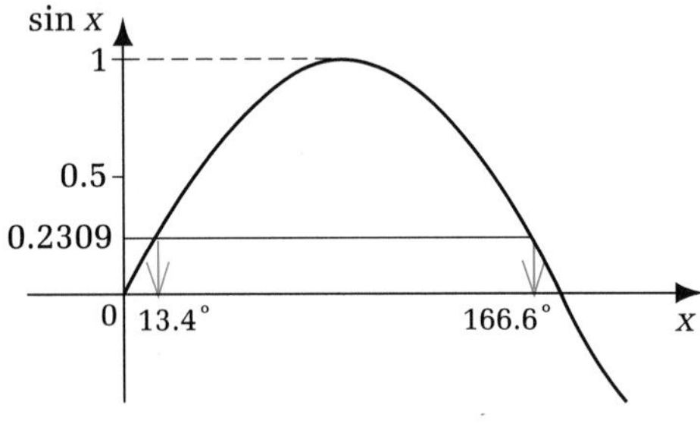

$$\alpha = 180° - 13.4° = 166.6°$$

Store the exact value of α.

Now solve for X:

$$\frac{X}{\sin(300° - \alpha)} = \frac{75}{\sin 60°}$$

Multiply by $\sin(300° - \alpha)$.

$$X = \frac{75 \times \sin(300° - 166.6°)}{\sin 60°}$$

$\alpha = 166.6°$ but use the stored value.

$$X = \frac{75 \times \sin 133.4°}{\sin 60°}$$

$$X = 63.0\,\text{N (3 s.f.)}$$

7.4 Lami's Theorem
Exercise

Technique

1 **a**

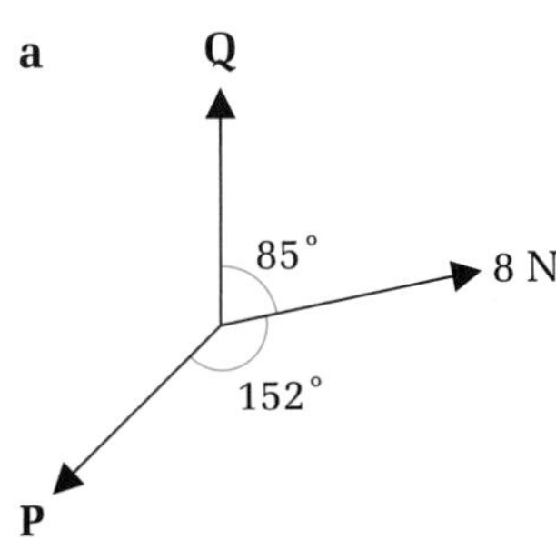

b

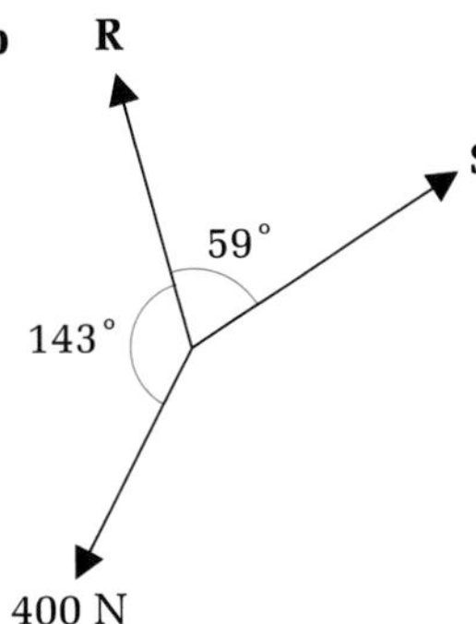

For each system of forces in equilibrium, use Lami's theorem to calculate the magnitudes of the forces marked with letters.

2 A body is in equilibrium under the action of three forces, as shown.

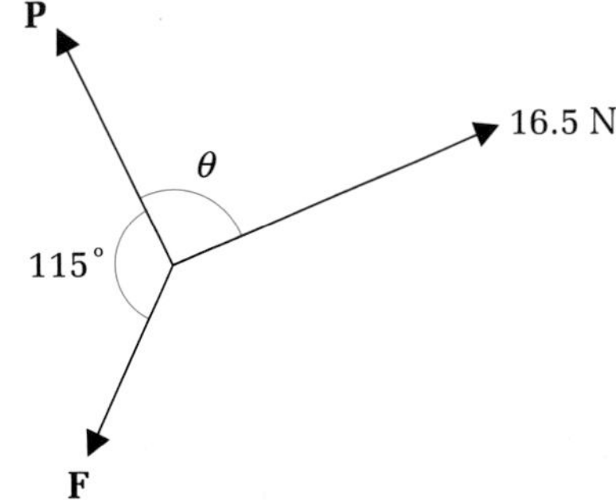

a Calculate the magnitude of **F** when:
 i $\theta = 50°$
 ii $\theta = 80°$
 iii $\theta = 100°$

b Calculate θ when:
 i $F = 12$ N
 ii $F = 18$ N
 iii $F = 6$ N

3 A force of 38 N is in equilibrium with two others, whose lines of action are at 118° and 132° to the 38 N force. What are the magnitudes of the other two forces?

4 Calculate $|\mathbf{Y}|$ and $|\mathbf{Z}|$, when:

a $|\mathbf{X}| = 190$ N
b $|\mathbf{X}| = 46$ N

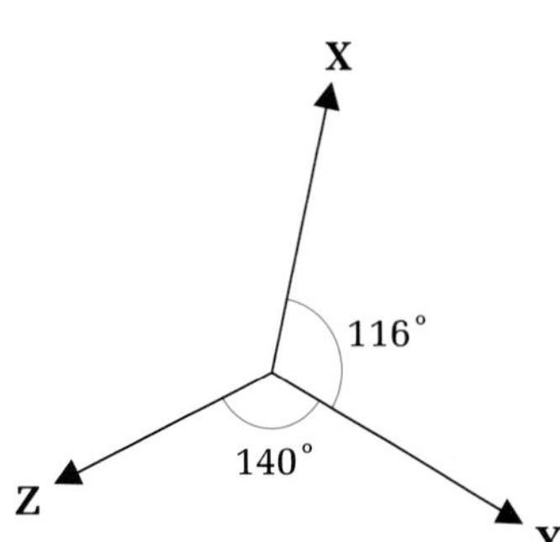

Contextual

1 Two children are playing on a simple swing made from a rubber tyre on the end of a rope. One child helps the other to start swinging by pulling the tyre to one side.

a The tyre has a mass of 50 kg and the child seated in the tyre has a mass of 20 kg. What horizontal force is needed to hold the tyre in equilibrium so that the rope is at 25° to the vertical? What will be the tension in the rope?

b The two children swap places and the mass of the child who is now on the tyre is 35 kg. If the rope is only deflected to 20° from the downward vertical to attain the starting equilibrium position, what is the magnitude of the horizontal force and the tension in the rope?

c What assumptions have been made in modelling this situation?

2 A camper has set up a torch in his tent by attaching it to the horizontal ridge pole, using two pieces of string. The lengths of string from the torch to the ridge are 28 cm and 21 cm. They are tied to the ridge pole so that their ends are 35 cm apart.

a Calculate the angles the two strings make with the vertical direction.

b If the mass of the torch is 300 g, what will be the tensions in the two strings?

c Before going to sleep, the camper hangs his watch on the end of the torch. If the mass of his watch is 15 g, what are the two tensions in the strings?

3 As part of a rescue operation, a man is lowered on a cable, down a cliff face. At one point in his descent, he rests in equilibrium, so that the cable is at an angle of 3° to the vertical. His legs are braced against the rock face at an angle of 65° to the cliff. The tension in the cable is 870 N.

a What is his mass?

b What is the magnitude of the thrust in his legs?

7.5 Resolving Forces

Another method for solving three force problems is to resolve the three forces into perpendicular components. Since the working definition of equilibrium is that the sum of the forces must be zero, it follows that the sum of the components in any direction must also be zero.

This method is applied by calculating the components in two convenient *perpendicular directions*. The sum of the components in a particular direction can then be equated to zero. In other cases it may be easier to equate the components to the *left* and the components to the *right* (or *up* and *down*, as appropriate). This is particularly useful when two of the forces are at right angles to each other, then only one force needs to be resolved into components.

Overview of method

Step ① Draw a force diagram.
Step ② Choose suitable perpendicular directions.
Step ③ Resolve each force into components in these directions.
Step ④ Write an equation for each direction, either equating the forces or letting their sum be zero.

Example 1

For the three forces in equilibrium shown here, find the magnitudes of **P** and **Q**.

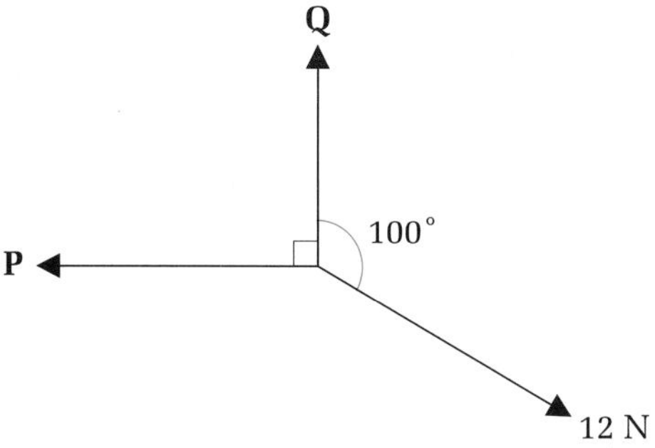

Solution

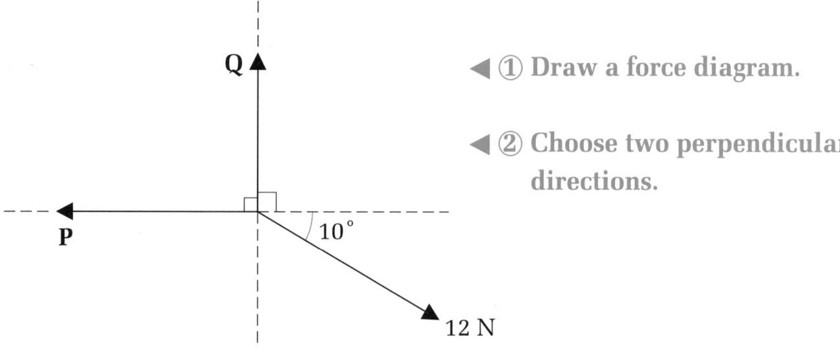

◀ ① Draw a force diagram.

◀ ② Choose two perpendicular directions.

Resolve → ◀ ③ Resolve horizontally.

$12\cos 10^\circ - P = 0$ ◀ ④ Write an equation.

$12\cos 10^\circ = P$

$P = 11.8\text{ N (3 s.f.)}$

cos is with the angle

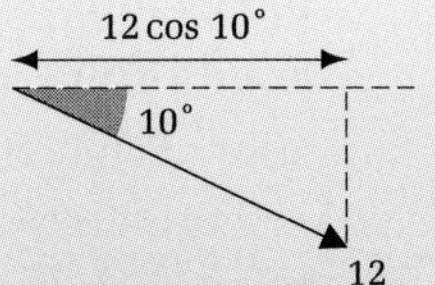

Resolve ↑ ◀ ③ Resolve vertically.

$Q - 12\sin 10^\circ = 0$ ◀ ④ Write an equation.

$Q = 12\sin 10^\circ$

$Q = 2.08\text{ N (3 s.f.)}$

sin is not with the angle

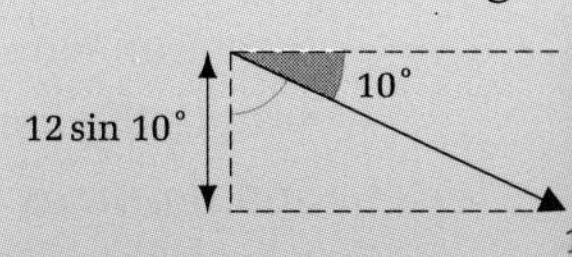

Example 2

For the three forces in equilibrium shown, find the exact magnitudes of X and Y.

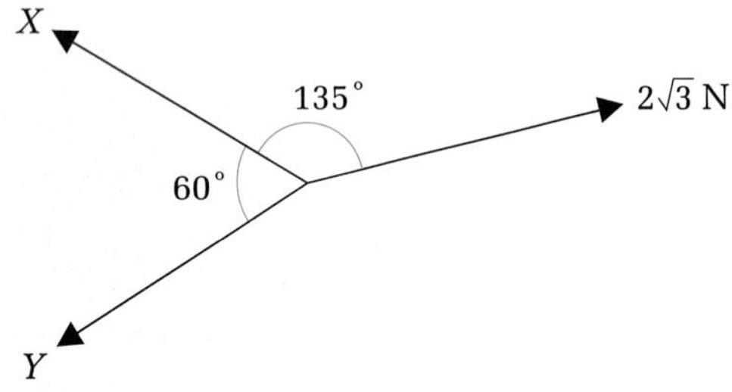

Solution

As none of the forces are horizontal or vertical, all three forces would need to be resolved if these directions were chosen. Instead pick directions which are parallel and perpendicular to one of the unknown forces. The benefit of this is that one of the two equations will contain only one unknown.

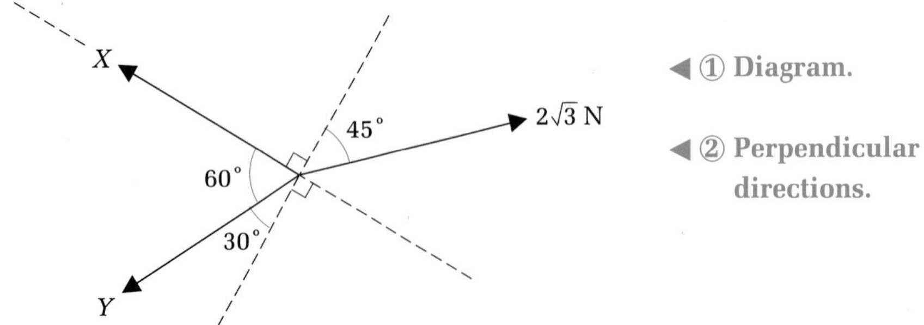

◀ ① Diagram.

◀ ② Perpendicular directions.

Directions chosen are parallel and perpendicular to force X.

Resolving // to X ↖ ◀ ③ **Resolve parallel to force X.**

$X + Y\sin 30° = 2\sqrt{3}\sin 45°$ ◀ ④ **Write an equation.**

Remember sin is not with the angle.

$$X + Y\left(\frac{1}{2}\right) = 2\sqrt{3}\left(\frac{\sqrt{2}}{2}\right)$$

sin $30° = \frac{1}{2}$ and sin $45° = \frac{\sqrt{2}}{2}$

$$X + \tfrac{1}{2}Y = \sqrt{6} \qquad [1]$$

Resolving ⊥ to X ↗ ◀ ③ **Resolve perpendicular to force X.**

$Y\cos 30° = 2\sqrt{3}\cos 45°$ ◀ ④ **Write an equation.**

cos is with the angle

$$Y\left(\frac{\sqrt{3}}{2}\right) = 2\sqrt{3}\left(\frac{\sqrt{2}}{2}\right)$$

cos $30° = \frac{\sqrt{3}}{2}$ and cos $45° = \frac{\sqrt{2}}{2}$

$$Y = 2\sqrt{3}\left(\frac{\sqrt{2}}{2}\right) \times \frac{2}{\sqrt{3}}$$

Multiply by 2 and divide by $\sqrt{3}$.

$$Y = 2\sqrt{2}$$

Substitute this value into equation [1].

$$X + \tfrac{1}{2}Y = \sqrt{6}$$

Equation [1].

$$X + \tfrac{1}{2} \times 2\sqrt{2} = \sqrt{6}$$

Replace Y and simplify.

$$X + \sqrt{2} = \sqrt{6}$$

Subtract $\sqrt{2}$.

$$X = \sqrt{6} - \sqrt{2}$$

$$X = \sqrt{2}(\sqrt{3} - 1)$$

Take out a common factor of $\sqrt{2}$, since $\sqrt{6} = \sqrt{2} \times \sqrt{3}$.

Four or more forces

The best way to add four or more forces is by resolving each force into two perpendicular components. Depending on the circumstances, it may be appropriate to choose *horizontal* and *vertical* components. However, particularly where objects on sloping planes are involved, it may be simpler to resolve into components perpendicular and parallel to the plane. Rather than having to add all the forces, written either as column vectors or with **i** and **j** unit vectors, the sum of the components in any direction can be equated to zero. Sometimes it is easier to write equations for the components which must balance in each direction.

forces *left* = forces *right* and forces *up* = forces *down*.

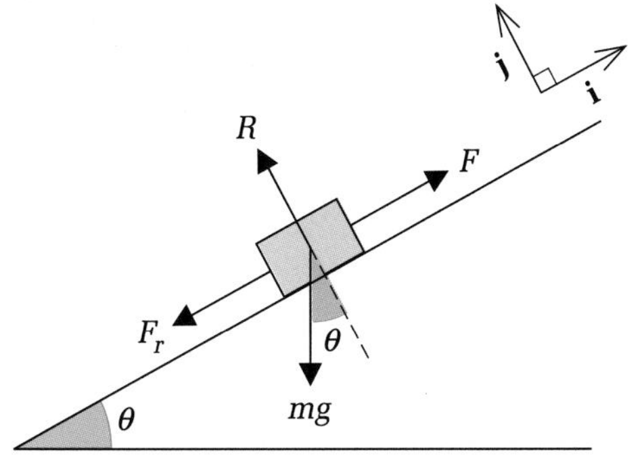

Example 3

For this system of forces in equilibrium, find the magnitude of P and the angle α.

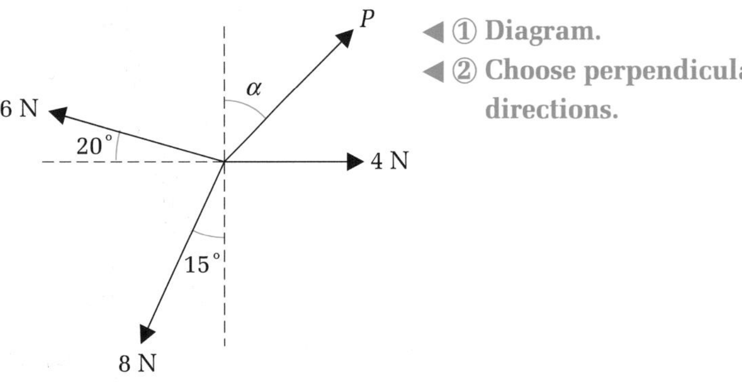

◀ ① Diagram.
◀ ② Choose perpendicular directions.

Think of each force in terms of its components. Remember cos is with the angle, sin is not with the angle.

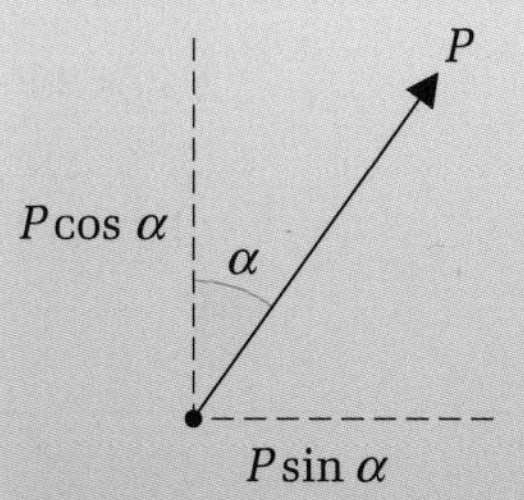

Solution

Resolve → ◀ ③ Resolve horizontally.

$$4 + P\sin\alpha = 6\cos 20° + 8\sin 15°$$ ◀ ④ Equate forces.

$$P\sin\alpha = 6\cos 20° + 8\sin 15° - 4$$

$$P\sin\alpha = 3.709 \quad [1]$$

Subtract 4. Calculate RHS. Store exact value in calculator.

Resolve ↑ ◀ ③ Resolve vertically.

$$P\cos\alpha + 6\sin 20° = 8\cos 15°$$ ◀ ④ Equate forces.

Subtract 6 sin 20°. Calculate RHS.

$$P\cos\alpha = 8\cos 15° - 6\sin 20°$$

$$P\cos\alpha = 5.675 \quad [2]$$

Store exact value in calculator.

Divide equation [1] by equation [2]

$$\frac{P\sin\alpha}{P\cos\alpha} = \frac{3.709}{5.675}$$ ◀ Use exact values.

P cancels and $\frac{\sin\alpha}{\cos\alpha} = \tan\alpha$

$$\tan\alpha = 0.6535$$

$$\alpha = \tan^{-1}(0.6535)$$

$$\alpha = 33.2° \text{ (1 d.p.)}$$

or arctan(0.6535) Store exact value.

Use equation [2]

$$P\cos\alpha = 5.675$$

Divide by cos α.

$$P = \frac{5.675}{\cos\alpha}$$

$$P = \frac{5.675}{\cos 33.2°}$$

Use exact values.

$$P = 6.78 \text{ N (3 s.f.)}$$

7.5 Resolving Forces
Exercise

Technique

1 The three forces shown are in equilibrium.

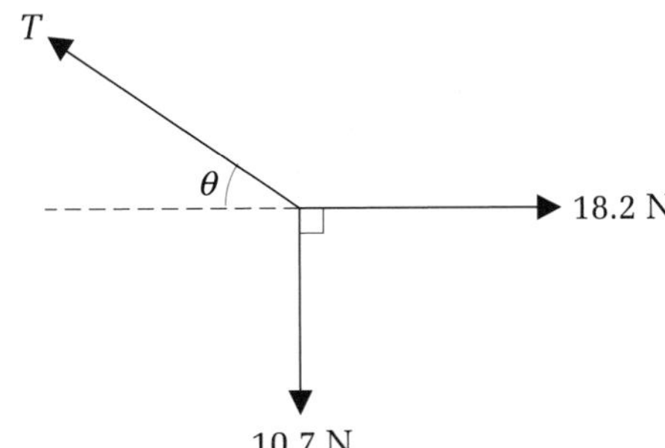

- **a** By resolving horizontally, write down the value of $T\cos\theta$.
- **b** By resolving vertically write down the value of $T\sin\theta$.
- **c** Using your previous answers, find θ and T.

2 Find the magnitude of **X** and the angle α if the forces are in equilibrium.

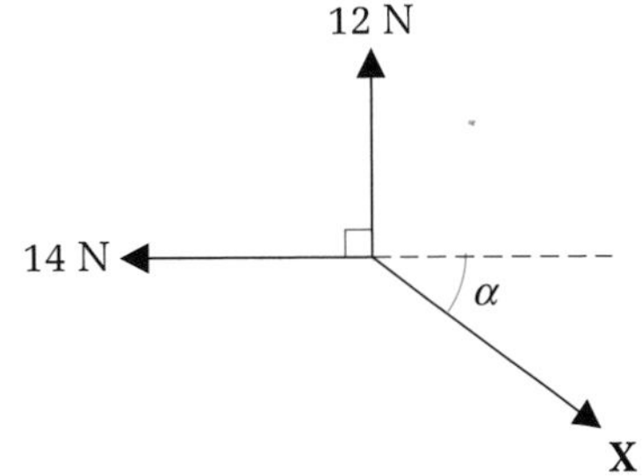

3 These three forces are in equilibrium. Calculate X and Y for the following values of θ:

- **a** $\theta = 120^\circ$ **b** $\theta = 135^\circ$
- **c** $\theta = 140^\circ$ **d** $\theta = 170^\circ$

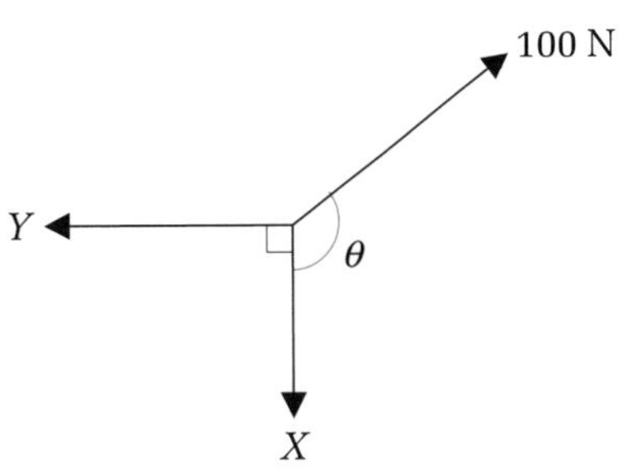

4 A particle is at rest in equilibrium under the action of three forces, as shown.

- **a** By resolving perpendicular to **X**, find the magnitude of **Y**.
- **b** By resolving parallel to **X**, find the magnitude of **X**.

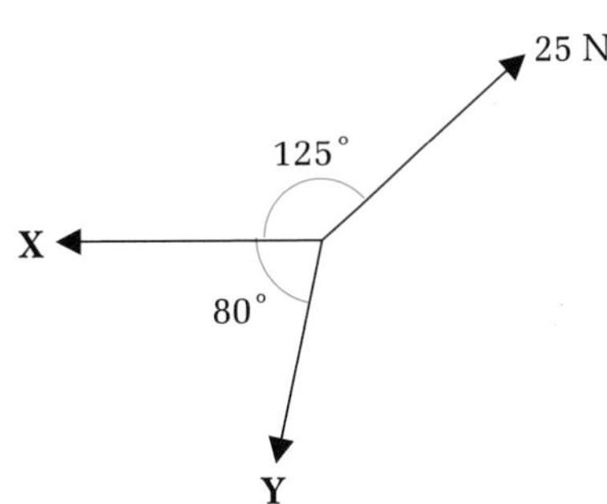

5

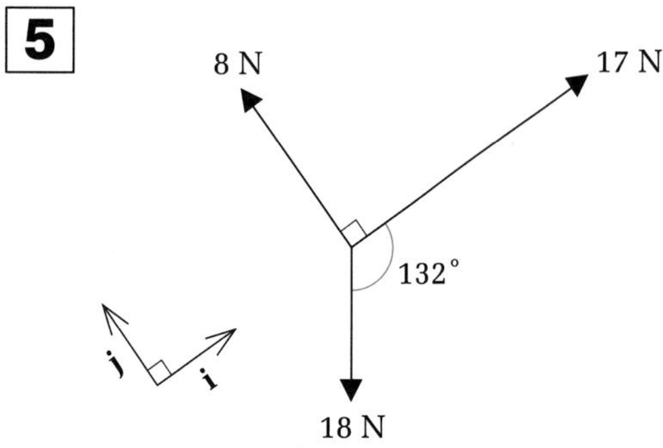

By resolving the three forces shown into components in the **i** and **j** directions, show that they are *not* in equilibrium.

6 Two forces are acting on a particle; **P** has magnitude 37 N and acts at an angle of 63° to **Q**. A third force of magnitude 60 N is added to the system to keep the particle in equilibrium.

a What is the angle between **Q** and the third force?
b What is the magnitude of **Q**?

7

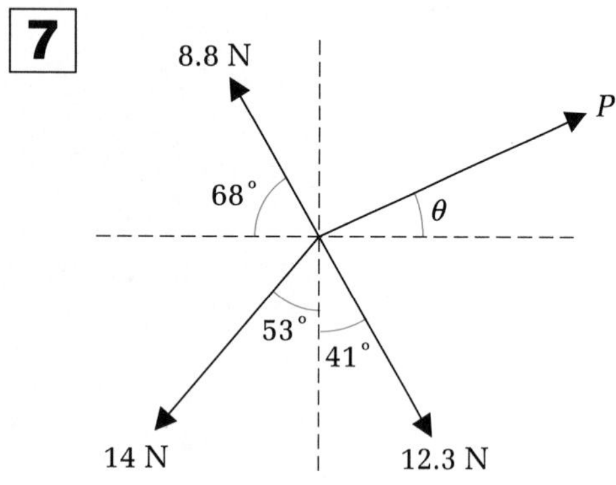

A particle is at rest in equilibrium under the action of the four forces shown. Find P and θ.

8

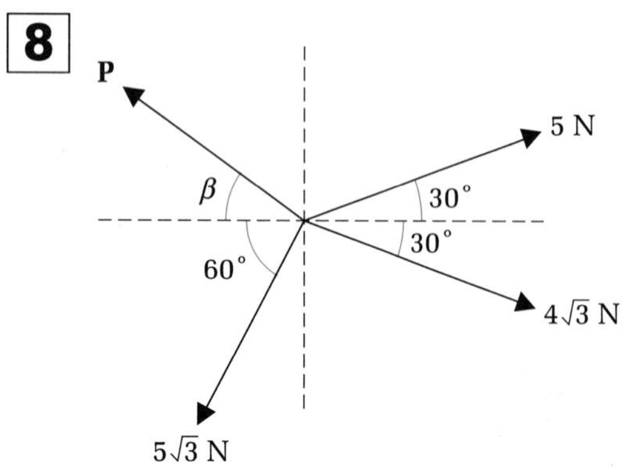

Calculate the magnitude of **P** in surd form, and β to the nearest degree, if these four forces are in equilibrium.

Contextual

1 Two cables of length 3 m and 7.2 m are used to suspend a sign, of mass 1.2 kg, from a horizontal ceiling. The cables are attached to the ceiling a distance of 7.8 m apart. Find:

- **a** the acute angles that the cables make with the vertical
- **b** the tensions in the cables.

2 A girl, of mass 40 kg, sits on a playground swing with her feet on the ground. The rope of the swing makes an angle of 10° with the downward vertical. Her legs make an angle of 60° with the horizontal. Calculate the thrust in the girl's legs and the tension in the rope. State any assumptions you have made during your analysis.

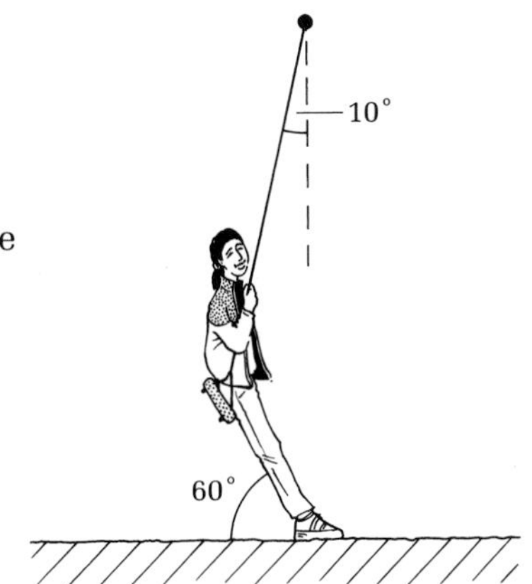

3 A 50 kg sack of coal is being lowered on a rope. In order to ensure it reaches the ground in the correct position, it is pulled aside by a horizontal force. For a few seconds the sack is held at rest in equilibrium, at which point the magnitude of the horizontal force is 118 N.

- **a** What is the magnitude of the tension in the rope?
- **b** What angle does the rope make with the vertical direction?
- **c** If the horizontal force had been 150 N, what would the tension and angle of the rope have been?

4 A hanging basket has been suspended from a boom outside a shop. The mass of the hanging basket is 7.5 kg. Find the magnitudes of the forces **X** and **Y**.

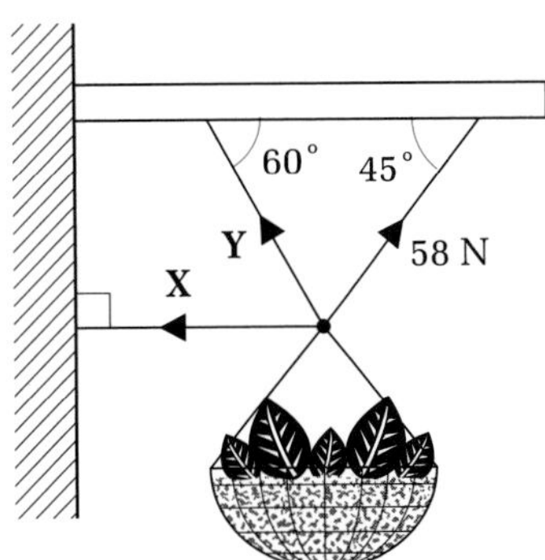

Consolidation

Exercise A

1

P

110°

Q

30 N

A particle is in equilibrium under the action of the three coplanar forces shown in the diagram. Find P and Q.

(UCLES)

2

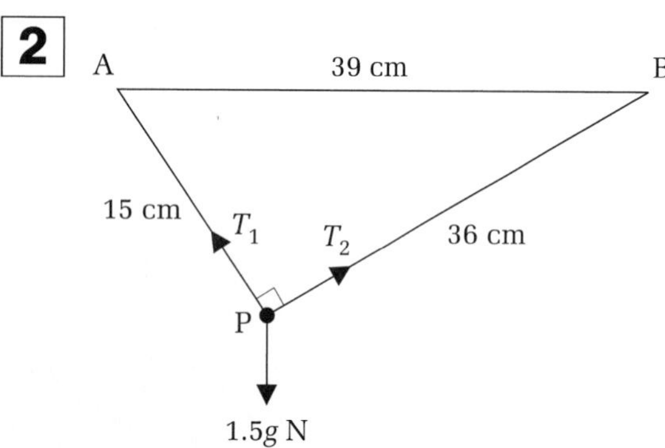

A particle, P, of mass 1.5 kg, is attached to two strings, AP and BP. The points A and B are on the same horizontal level and are 39 cm apart. The strings AP and BP are inextensible and of length 15 cm and 36 cm respectively. The particle hangs in equilibrium with $\angle APB = 90°$. The figure shows all the external forces acting on the particle. Find the tension, in newtons, correct to one decimal place, in each of the strings AP and BP.

3

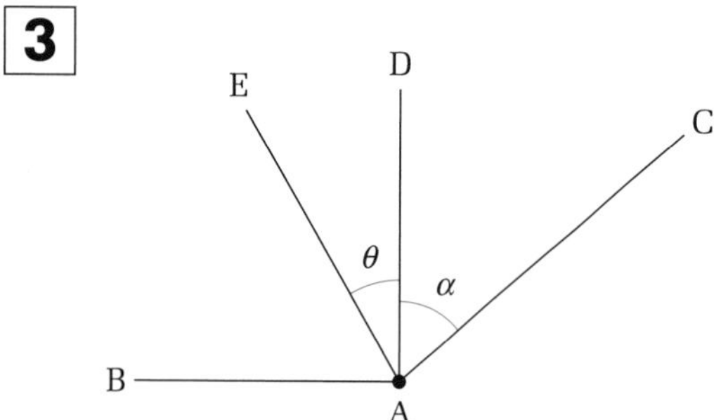

A particle of weight 75 N is hanging in equilibrium at a point A supported by four strings AB, AC, AD, AE, all in the same vertical plane. The string AB is horizontal and the tension in AB is 13 N; the string AC makes an angle α with the vertical, where $\sin \alpha = \frac{12}{13}$, and the tension in AC is 26 N; the string AD is vertical and the tension in AD is 5 N; the string AE makes an angle θ with the vertical and the tension in AE is T N. Find the values of T and θ.

(WJEC)

Exercise B

1 Three forces $\mathbf{F}_1$, $\mathbf{F}_2$ and $\mathbf{F}_3$ act on a particle and $\mathbf{F}_1 = (-3\mathbf{i} + 7\mathbf{j})$ N, $\mathbf{F}_2 = (\mathbf{i} - \mathbf{j})$ N, $\mathbf{F}_3 = (p\mathbf{i} + q\mathbf{j})$ N.

a Given that this particle is in equilibrium, determine the values of p and q.

The resultant of the forces $\mathbf{F}_1$ and $\mathbf{F}_2$ is $\mathbf{R}$.

b Calculate, in newtons, the magnitude of $\mathbf{R}$.

c Calculate, to the nearest degree, the angle between the line of action of $\mathbf{R}$ and the vector $\mathbf{j}$.

(ULEAC)

2

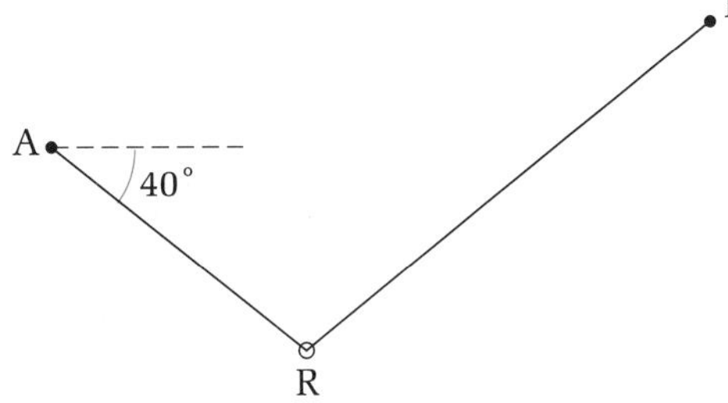

A small smooth ring R of mass 0.1 kg is threaded on a light string. The ends of the string are fastened to two fixed points A and B. The ring hangs in equilibrium with the part AR of the string inclined at 40° to the horizontal, as shown in the diagram. Taking $g = 9.81\ \text{m s}^{-2}$, show that the part RB of the string is also inclined at 40° to the horizontal, and find the tension in the string.

(UCLES)

Smooth means there is no friction and the tensions will be equal.

3

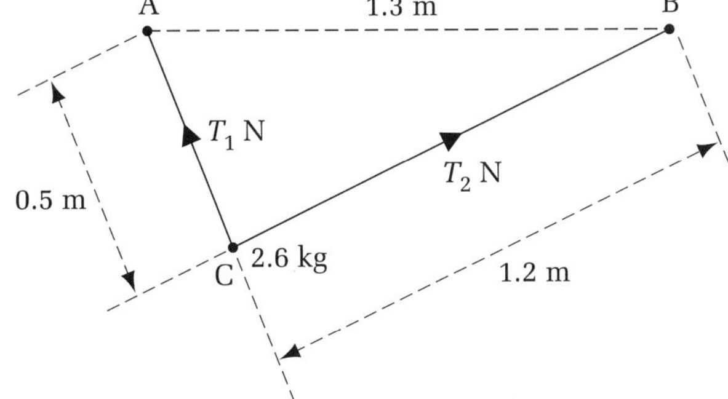

The diagram shows a particle of mass 2.6 kg, suspended at C by light inelastic strings attached to fixed points A and B which are at the same horizontal level, where $AC = 0.5$ m, $BC = 1.2$ m and $AB = 1.3$ m. The tensions in AC and BC are T_1 N and T_2 N respectively. Taking $g = 9.81\ \text{m s}^{-2}$:

a show that angle ACB is a right angle

b find the value of T_1 and of T_2.

(UCLES)

Applications and Activities

1

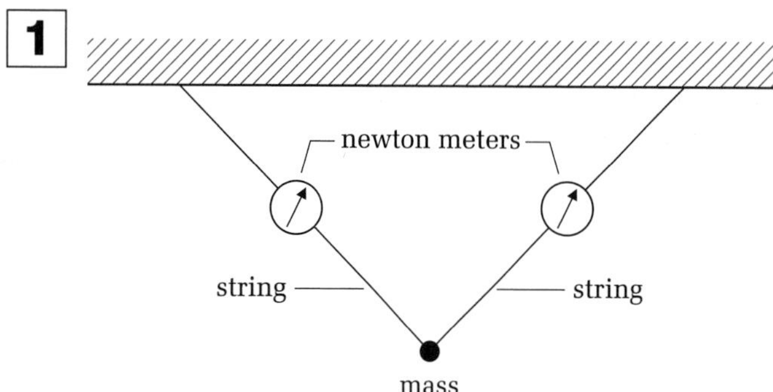

Tie two pieces of string onto a mass. Attach them to two fixed points via two newton meters as shown in the diagram. The newton meters measure the tensions in the strings. How does this compare with the theory on equilibrium?

2

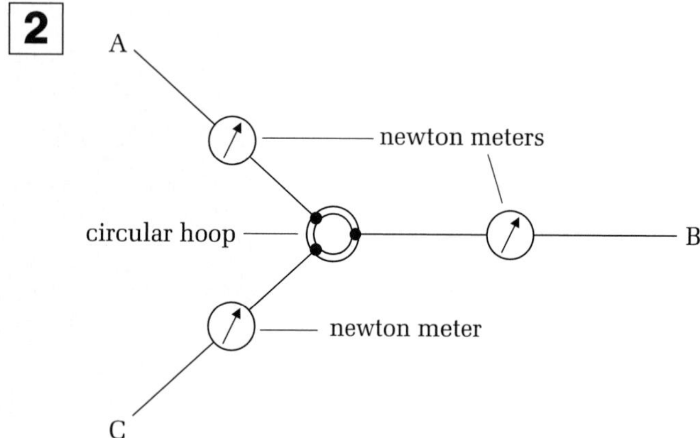

The equipment in the above diagram can be used to experiment with three forces in equilibrium. With a person pulling each of the strings at A, B and C, keep the hoop in equilibrium. Record the readings on the newton meters and the angles between the strings. By using calculations, should the hoop be in equilibrium? Why is this system not really three forces in equilibrium?

Summary

- When an object is stationary and remains so under the action of several forces then it is in **static equilibrium**.
- When an object is moving with constant velocity and continues to do so under the action of a set of forces then it is in **dynamic equilibrium**.
- **Concurrent** means acting at the same point.
- If the resultant of a set of forces acting on an object is zero then the object is in equilibrium.
- For a system of forces in equilibrium the sum of the components in any direction is zero.
- Equilibrium problems may be solved using the following methods:

  1. scale drawing
  2. trigonometry
  3. Lami's theorem
  4. resolving into perpendicular components.

8 Newton's Laws of Motion

What you need to know

- How to resolve a force into two perpendicular directions.
- How to find the resultant of forces which are perpendicular.
- How to use **i** and **j** vector notation.
- How to apply the uniform acceleration formulas.
- How to solve simultaneous equations.
- How to find the weight of a mass.
- The values of $\sin x$, $\cos x$ and $\tan x$, where x can be $30°$, $45°$ or $60°$.

Review

1 **a** 50 N, 30°; **j**, **i**

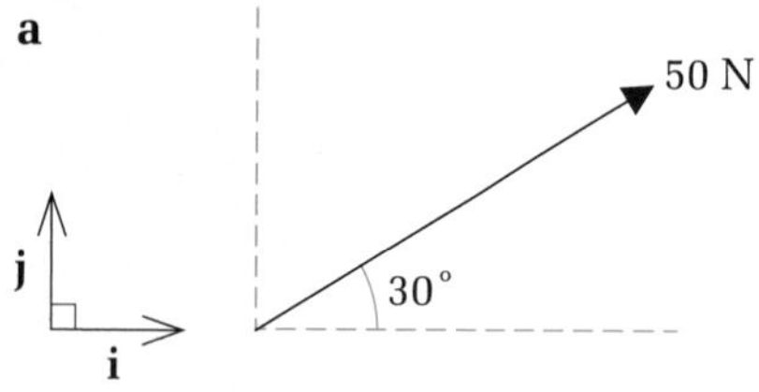

b 45°, 65 N

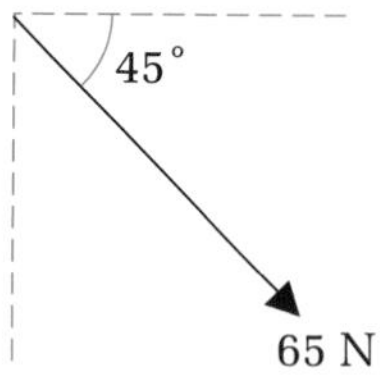

Resolve the forces into horizontal and vertical components, writing your answers in the form $a\mathbf{i} + b\mathbf{j}$.

2 **a** 5 N, 12 N

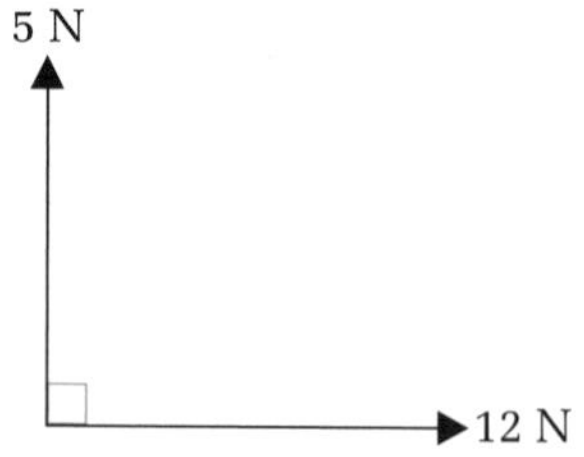

b 5 N, 6 N, 3 N, 1 N

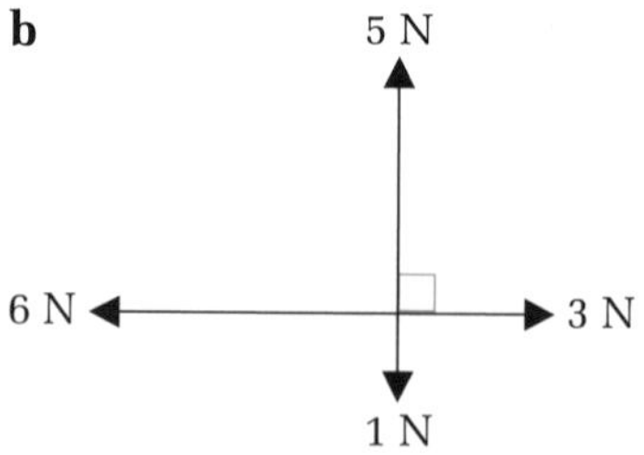

Find:

i the magnitude of the resultant force

ii the angle between the resultant force and the horizontal direction.

3 $\mathbf{a} = 5\mathbf{i} + 2\mathbf{j}$ and $\mathbf{b} = -3\mathbf{i} + 7\mathbf{j}$. Express the following vectors in the form $x\mathbf{i} + y\mathbf{j}$:

a $\mathbf{a} + \mathbf{b}$ b $2\mathbf{b} - \mathbf{a}$ c $5\mathbf{a} + 6\mathbf{b}$

4
- a Write down the uniform acceleration formulas.
- b A cyclist increases her velocity from $2\,\mathrm{m\,s^{-1}}$ to $7\,\mathrm{m\,s^{-1}}$ in 2 s. Calculate the acceleration of the cyclist, if it is assumed to be constant.
- c A stone is dropped under the effect of gravity. Find the time taken for the stone to fall a distance of 5 metres.
- d A car accelerates from $2\,\mathrm{m\,s^{-1}}$ to $10\,\mathrm{m\,s^{-1}}$ with an acceleration of $2\,\mathrm{m\,s^{-2}}$. Work out the distance travelled.
- e A train starts from rest and accelerates to a speed of $15\,\mathrm{m\,s^{-1}}$ in a time of 30 seconds. Find the distance travelled.

5 Solve the following simultaneous equations:

a $T = 5a$, $60 - T = 7a$ b $50 - T = 3a$, $20 + T = 4a$

6 Calculate the weight of the following masses:

a 5 kg b 100 g c 2 tonnes

7 Write down the exact values for:

a $\tan 45°$ b $\cos 60°$ c $\sin 45°$
d $\tan 60°$ e $\cos 30°$ f $\sin 30°$

8.1 Newton's First Law

In 1686 Newton published *Philosophie Naturalis Principia Mathematica*. In this he detailed the three laws of motion that form the basis of this chapter.

A stationary spacecraft in deep space will stay stationary unless it uses its engines to move. A meteor travelling in deep space will continue to travel at exactly the same speed and in the same direction. These are examples of Newton's first law.

Deep space means that there are no planets close enough to attract the spacecraft.

Newton's first law

Newton's first law states that a body will continue to remain at rest or move at constant speed in a straight line unless an external force makes it act otherwise. In reality, there will almost always be external forces acting on a body.

An extension of Newton's first law can be used when a body is at rest or moving at a constant velocity under the action of external forces. The resultant of these external forces must be zero.

Constant velocity is the same as constant speed in a straight line.

Inclined forces

During an aeroplane's ascent not all the forces are horizontal and vertical. How could an aeroplane's ascent be modelled? The aeroplane is assumed to ascend at a constant velocity. The lift force will act perpendicularly to the wings. There will be a thrust force acting in the direction of motion and air resistance will oppose motion.

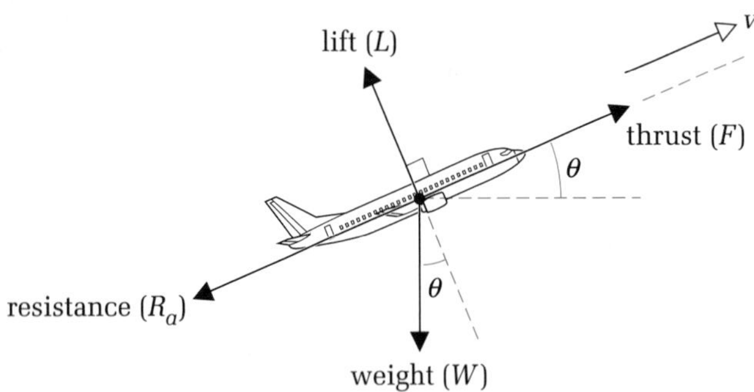

The diagram shows this model for the aircraft's ascent. Three of the forces are acting parallel or perpendicular to the direction of motion. By choosing these two directions, only the weight force needs to be resolved into *two* components. If vertical and horizontal directions were chosen, the lift, thrust and resistance forces would need to be resolved.

These forces are the *lift*, *thrust*, and *resistance*.

Resolve // to the direction of motion ↗

// means *parallel*.

$$F - R_a - W\sin\theta = 0$$

sin is not with the angle.

Resolve ⊥ to the direction of motion ↖

$L - W\cos\theta = 0$

⊥ means *perpendicular*

cos is with the angle.

Overview of method

Step ① Sketch a clear diagram showing all the forces.
Step ② Resolve into two perpendicular directions.
Step ③ The resultant forces in both directions must equal zero if the particle is at rest or moving at constant speed in a straight line.

Constant velocity is the same as constant speed in a straight line.

The forces are normally resolved horizontally and vertically or parallel and perpendicular to a surface. This is the same process as was used for static and dynamic equilibrium.

See Section 7.5.

Example 1

A car of mass 800 kg is travelling at a constant velocity of $30\,\text{m s}^{-1}$ along a level road. The resistance to motion is 1500 N. Taking $g = 10\,\text{m s}^{-2}$, determine:

a the force produced by the engine
b the normal reaction acting on the car.

Solution

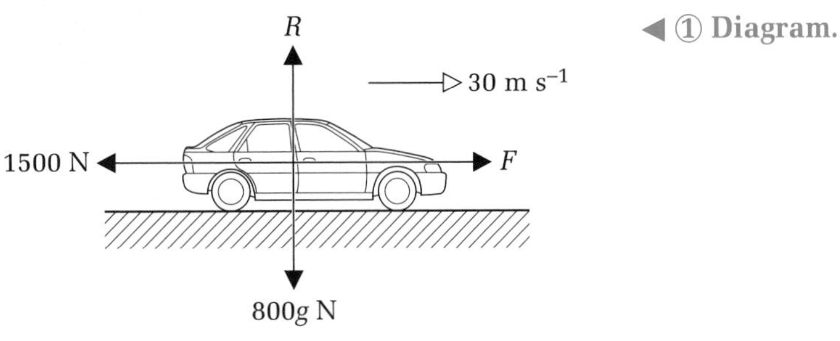

◀ ① Diagram.

Notice that all the forces are marked on the diagram.

a Resolve →

$F - 1500 = 0$

$F = 1500$ N

◀ ② Resolve. To the right is positive.
◀ ③ Resultant force must be zero.

b Resolve ↑

$R - 800g = 0$

$R = 800g$

$R = 8000$ N

Upwards is positive. Resultant force is zero because the car does not move vertically. $g = 10\,\text{m s}^{-2}$

Example 2

A trunk is pulled across a horizontal floor by a force of 50 N inclined at 30° above the horizontal. The trunk has a mass of 40 kg and travels with a constant velocity. Determine the *exact* values of:

a the resistance to motion
b the normal reaction.

Solution

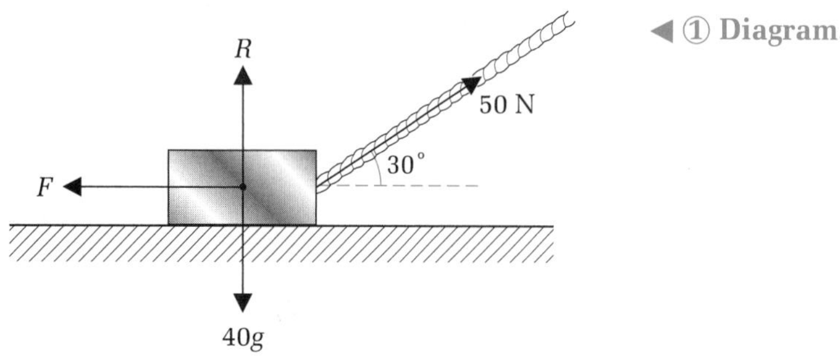

◀ ① Diagram.

a Resolve → ◀ ② Resolve. Most forces are horizontal and vertical.

$50\cos 30° - F = 0$ ◀ ③ Resultant force equals zero.

$50 \times \frac{\sqrt{3}}{2} - F = 0$

$25\sqrt{3} - F = 0$

$F = 25\sqrt{3}$ N

b Resolve ↑

$R + 50\sin 30° - 40g = 0$ ◀ *R* stands for normal reaction force.

$R + 50 \times \frac{1}{2} - 40g = 0$

$R + 25 - 40g = 0$

$R = (40g - 25)$ N

F is used here for resistance.
$\cos 30° = \frac{\sqrt{3}}{2}$
$50 \times \frac{\sqrt{3}}{2} = 25\sqrt{3}$, since $50 \div 2 = 25$
sin is not with the angle.
$\sin 30° = \frac{1}{2}$
Add $40g$ subtract 25.

Example 3

An object of weight 20 N is suspended by two cables, as shown in the diagram. Find the tension in each of the cables.

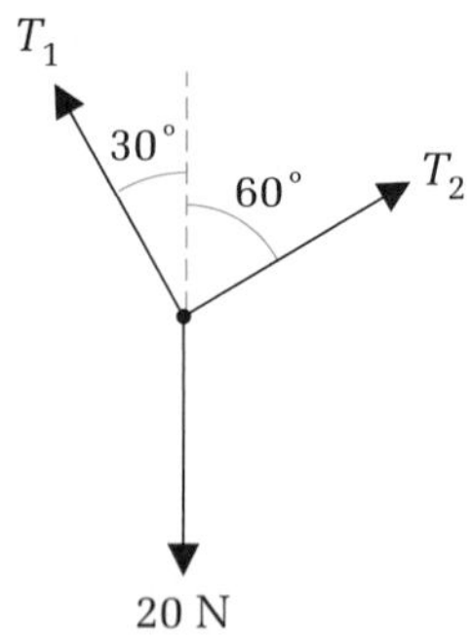

Solution

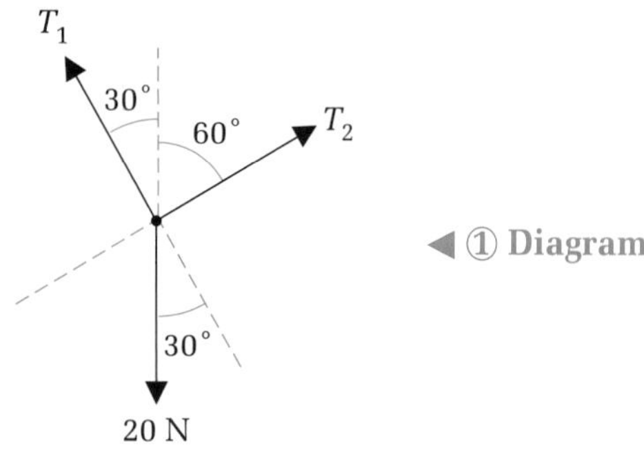

◀ ① Diagram.

It is easier to resolve parallel and perpendicular to T_1 because T_1 and T_2 are at right angles. This means that only the 20 N weight is resolved. Resolving horizontally and vertically would mean that both T_1 and T_2 would need to be resolved.

Resolve // to T_1 ◀ ② Resolve.

$T_1 - 20\cos 30° = 0$ ◀ ③ Resultant is zero. — cos is with the angle.

$T_1 - 20 \times \frac{\sqrt{3}}{2} = 0$ — $\cos 30° = \frac{\sqrt{3}}{2}$

$T_1 - 10\sqrt{3} = 0$ — Add $10\sqrt{3}$.

$T_1 = 10\sqrt{3}$

$T_1 = 17.3$ N (3 s.f.)

Resolve ⊾ to T_1

$T_2 - 20\sin 30° = 0$ — sin is not with the angle.

$T_2 - 20 \times \frac{1}{2} = 0$ — $\sin 30° = \frac{1}{2}$

$T_2 - 10 = 0$ — Add 10.

$T_2 = 10$ N

Example 4

An aeroplane of mass 300 tonnes during ascent travels at a constant velocity of $100\,\text{m s}^{-1}$. Its angle of ascent is 10° to the horizontal. The thrust produced by the engines is 9000 kN. Work out:

900 kN = 900 000 N

a the lift force acting on the wings

b the resistance to motion.

Solution

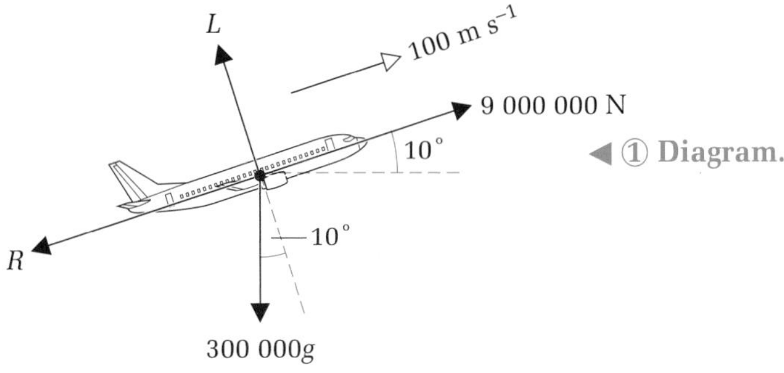

◀ ① Diagram.

a Resolve ⊾ to direction of motion. ◀ ② Resolve.

$L - 300\,000g\cos 10° = 0$ ◀ ③ Resultant force is zero. — cos is with the angle.

$L - 2\,895\,335 = 0$

$L = 2\,900\,000$ N (3 s.f.)

$L = 2900$ kN

b Resolve // to direction of motion.

$9\,000\,000 - 300\,000g\sin 10° - R = 0$

$9\,000\,000 - 510\,526 - R = 0$

$R = 8\,490\,000$ N (3 s.f.)

$R = 8490$ kN

8.1 Newton's First Law
Exercise

Technique

1 **a** R, F, 8 N, 16 N **b** 10 N, 5 N, S

The objects shown are at rest. Find the magnitudes of the forces marked with letters.

2 **a** **b**

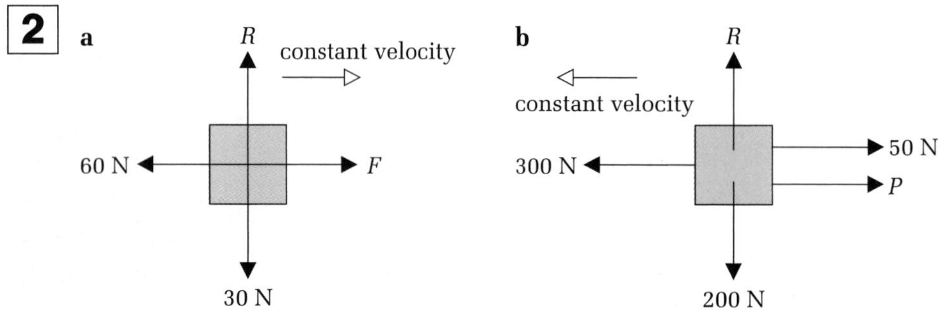

The particles shown are moving with a constant velocity. Determine the sizes of the lettered forces.

3

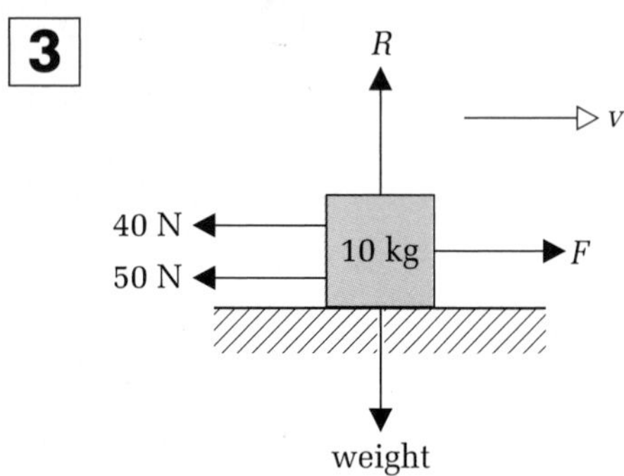

The block in the diagram has a mass of 10 kg and it is moving with a constant speed v m s^{-1} in a straight line. Calculate the magnitudes of F and R.

4 Three forces act on a body initially moving at 3 m s^{-1}. The forces are $(-6\mathbf{i} + 2\mathbf{j})$ N, $(7\mathbf{i} - 5\mathbf{j})$ N and $(-\mathbf{i} - \mathbf{j})$ N. Work out the force that needs to be added to keep the body moving at a constant velocity of 3 m s^{-1}.

5 A particle of mass 15 kg is pulled along a horizontal plane at a constant speed in a straight line. The applied force of 20 N acts at an angle of 20°. Find the resistance to motion.

6 A mass of 5 kg is pulled up a plane inclined at 30° to the horizontal. The mass travels with a constant velocity up the plane and the force acts parallel to the plane. The resistance to motion is 10 N. Taking $g = 10\,\text{m s}^{-2}$, determine:

a the magnitude of the applied force

b the normal reaction, leaving your answer in surd form.

Contextual

1 An empty lift, of mass 1000 kg, goes up at a constant speed during part of its motion.

a Draw a diagram showing the forces acting on the lift.

b Find the tension in the cable.

2 A trapeze artist of mass 60 kg sits motionless on a simple bar of mass 5 kg. The bar is held by two vertical cables, one at each end of the bar. Assume the cables are light and that the artist sits in the middle of the bar.

a Draw a clear diagram of the forces involved.

b Calculate the tension in each cable.

3 A box of mass 10 kg is pulled across a horizontal floor by a 50 N force, which is applied horizontally. The box moves at a constant speed in a straight line. Find:

a the normal reaction acting on the box

b the magnitude of the resistance to motion.

Magnitude means the size or value.

4 A trunk of mass 27 kg is pulled by a 80 N force inclined at 30° above the horizontal. The trunk moves at a constant velocity over a horizontal floor. Work out the *exact* size of the resistance to motion.

5 A person slides down a straight water chute. During part of the motion, the person travels at a constant speed. The chute is inclined at 45° and the mass of the person is 70 kg. Calculate the magnitude of the resistance to motion.

6 A pantomime fairy of mass 40 kg is held at rest above the stage by a harness and two cables. Each cable is inclined at 45° to the vertical. The cables can be assumed light and inextensible. Determine the tension in each cable.

7 An aircraft, of mass 14 tonnes travels at a constant velocity of $90\,\text{m s}^{-1}$ during its ascent. The thrust produced by the engines is 500 kN and the angle of ascent is 15°. Calculate:

a the lift force acting on the wings

b the size of the resistance to motion.

8.2 Newton's Second Law

In ice hockey, the puck can be accelerated from rest by pushing it with a hockey stick. The external force applied by the stick will cause the puck to accelerate. How do you get the hockey puck to accelerate twice as fast? The logical answer would be to apply twice the force. This is also the correct answer if there are *no resistances to motion*. This means that as the *overall* force increases, the acceleration will increase. This observation was first written down by Newton and it is called Newton's second law.

Newton's second law

Newton's second law states that a resultant force acting.on a body produces an acceleration which is proportional to the resultant force.

Notation
$\mathbf{F}$ = resultant force or overall force (N)
$\mathbf{a}$ = acceleration (m s^{-2})
k = constant of proportion
$\mathbf{F}$ and $\mathbf{a}$ are vectors.

This relationship can be written as:

$\mathbf{F} \propto \mathbf{a}$ or $\mathbf{F} = k\mathbf{a}$

If SI units are used the equation becomes:

$\mathbf{F} = m\mathbf{a}$

Notation
m = mass (kg)

Notice that the constant of proportion (k) changes into m. This is not just a coincidence. The newton (N) is defined as the force causing a mass of 1 kg to accelerate at 1 m s^{-2}. This formula is only valid when the mass remains constant. If the mass varies, an alternative definition of Newton's second law is used. This states that the resultant force acting on a body is proportional to the rate of change of *momentum*.

See Chapter 13 for momentum.

Often, only the size of the force or acceleration is required. In these circumstances the equation can be written as:

$F = ma$

F is the magnitude of $\mathbf{F}$
a is the magnitude of $\mathbf{a}$

Overview of method

Step ① Draw a clear diagram showing all the forces.
Step ② Mark on the direction of the acceleration.
Step ③ Apply Newton's second law, $F = ma$.

Example 1

A toy horse on wheels of mass 4 kg is pulled along by a taut piece of string. The string remains horizontal and the tension in it is 8 N. The resistances to motion are negligible. Find:

a the acceleration of the horse
b the normal reaction.

Solution

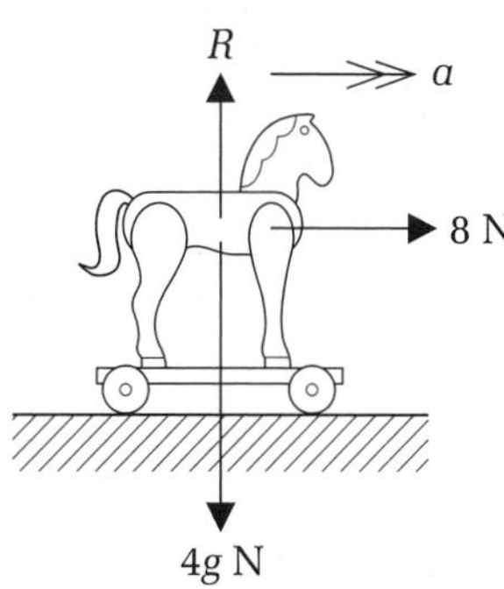

◀ ① Diagram.
◀ ② Acceleration.

a Apply $F = ma \rightarrow$

◀ ③ Newton's second law. To the right is positive.

$F = ma$

$8 = 4a$ — Substitute the numbers.

$a = 2\,\text{m}\,\text{s}^{-2}$ — Divide by 4.

b Resolve ↑ — Upwards is positive.

$R - 4g = 0$ — Resultant force must equal zero because there is no vertical motion.

$R = 4g$

$R = 39.2$ N — $4g = 4 \times 9.8 = 39.2$

Example 2

A lift has a mass of 600 kg and holds three people, of masses 75 kg, 45 kg and 80 kg. Taking $g = 10\,\text{m}\,\text{s}^{-2}$, determine the tension in the cable when the lift is travelling upwards and decelerates at $0.5\,\text{m}\,\text{s}^{-2}$.

Solution

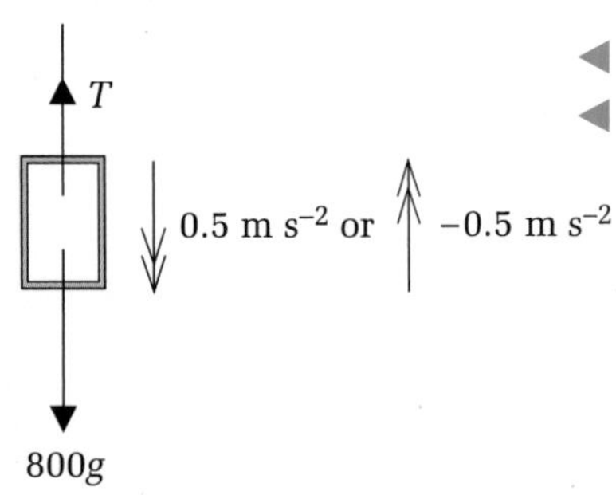

◀ ① Diagram.

◀ ② Acceleration acts downwards.

Total mass of lift and people:
$600 + 75 + 45 + 80 = 800$ kg.

Apply $F = ma \uparrow$ ◀ ③ Use $F = ma$ in the direction of motion.

$T - 800g = 800a$

$T - 8000 = 800 \times (-0.5)$

$T - 8000 = -400$

$T = 7600\,\text{N}$

Remember, the lift is travelling **upwards**.
$g = 10\,\text{m s}^{-2}$ and $a = -0.5\,\text{m s}^{-2}$

Add 8000.

Example 3

A force of $(28\mathbf{i} - 49\mathbf{j})$ N is applied to a particle of mass 7 kg. Calculate:

a the acceleration of the particle

b the magnitude of the acceleration.

Solution

a Apply $\mathbf{F} = m\mathbf{a}$

Use vector equation.

$28\mathbf{i} - 49\mathbf{j} = 7\mathbf{a}$

$\frac{1}{7}(28\mathbf{i} - 49\mathbf{j}) = \mathbf{a}$

$\mathbf{a} = (4\mathbf{i} - 7\mathbf{j})\,\text{m s}^{-2}$

Divide by 7.

b $\mathbf{a} = 4\mathbf{i} - 7\mathbf{j}$

$|\mathbf{a}| = \sqrt{4^2 + (-7)^2}$

$|\mathbf{a}| = \sqrt{16 + 49}$

$|\mathbf{a}| = \sqrt{65}$

$|\mathbf{a}| = 8.06\,\text{m s}^{-2}$ (3 s.f.)

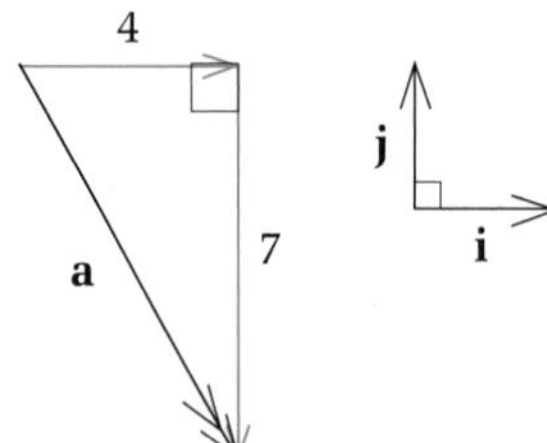

Draw a diagram of the acceleration vector.
Use Pythagoras' theorem.

8.2 Newton's Second Law
Exercise

Technique

1 What force is needed to accelerate a particle of mass 10 kg at $0.7\,\text{m}\,\text{s}^{-2}$?

2 A force of 18 N is applied to an object of mass 5 kg. Find the acceleration of the object.

3 A body accelerates at $5.3\,\text{m}\,\text{s}^{-2}$ when a force of 20 N is applied to it. Calculate the mass of the body.

4 An object of mass 500 g is pulled along a smooth horizontal surface by a horizontal force of 3 N. Find the acceleration of the object.

5 A particle has a mass of 3 kg and has an acceleration of $(4\mathbf{i} + 5\mathbf{j})\,\text{m}\,\text{s}^{-2}$. Work out the resultant force acting on the particle.

6 A force of $(2\mathbf{i} - 3\mathbf{j})$N acts on an object of mass 100 g. Calculate the acceleration of the object.

7 A force of $(-4\mathbf{i} + 10\mathbf{j})$ N acts on a body to produce an acceleration of $(-12\mathbf{i} + 30\mathbf{j})\,\text{m}\,\text{s}^{-2}$. Determine the mass of the body.

8 A particle of mass 50 g experiences a resultant force of $(5\mathbf{i} + 10\mathbf{j})$ N. Calculate:

- **a** the acceleration of the particle
- **b** the size of the acceleration
- **c** the direction of the acceleration.

9 A 7 kg mass accelerates at $(-3\mathbf{i} - 4\mathbf{j})\,\text{m}\,\text{s}^{-2}$. Find:

- **a** the overall force acting on the mass
- **b** the magnitude of the force
- **c** the direction of the force.

10 An object of 4 kg is initially at rest on a smooth horizontal surface. The object is pulled by a horizontal force of 20 N for 2 seconds and then by a force of 10 N for a further 4 seconds.

- **a** Calculate the accelerations for both parts of the motion.
- **b** Determine the speed of the object when the force changes.
- **c** Work out the total distance travelled when the object has been in motion for 6 seconds.

Contextual

1 A crate has a mass of 30 kg and it is pulled along a smooth horizontal surface by a horizontal cable. The acceleration of the crate is $0.4\ \text{m s}^{-2}$. Determine the tension in the cable.

Smooth means there is no friction between the surfaces.

2 An empty lift cage has a mass of 800 kg. It accelerates upwards at $2\ \text{m s}^{-2}$.

a Calculate the tension in the cable.

Two passengers each of mass 65 kg enter the lift at the next floor. Assume the tension in the cable cannot exceed the value calculated in part **a**.

b Find the maximum upwards acceleration of the lift.

3 A car's engine can produce a force of 3000 N. The car has a mass of 600 kg. Work out the maximum acceleration of the car along a flat, straight road. State *one* key assumption you have made.

4 A roller coaster is accelerated at $12\ \text{m s}^{-2}$ by a force of 50 000 N. Work out the mass of the roller coaster. State *two* key assumptions you have made.

5 A car of mass 800 kg accelerates from rest to $30\ \text{m s}^{-1}$ in 5 seconds. The resistances to motion are assumed constant at 800 N. Determine:

a the acceleration of the car

b the *overall* horizontal force acting on the car

c the force produced by the engine.

6 A sports car has a mass of 1200 kg and its engine can produce a force of 9000 N. At a speed of $10\ \text{m s}^{-1}$ along a flat straight road, the resistance to motion is 1800 N. Calculate the maximum acceleration of the car at $10\ \text{m s}^{-1}$.

7 An aircraft has a mass of 150 tonnes and accelerates at $4\ \text{m s}^{-2}$ along a runway. The resistance to motion is 200 kN. Find the thrust produced by the engines.

8 A jet aircraft of mass 100 tonnes accelerates from $5\ \text{m s}^{-1}$ to $105\ \text{m s}^{-1}$ in 50 seconds. The resistance to motion is 75 kN and can be assumed constant. Determine:

a the acceleration of the aircraft

b the force produced by the engines.

8.3 $F = ma$ and Inclined Forces

What happens to the car's speed if the car starts travelling up a steep hill? The car will slow down unless the driver makes the engine produce more force by pressing down on the accelerator pedal. With very steep hills even this will not stop the car from decelerating. This deceleration must be caused by an additional force opposing motion. A mathematical model of a car on an inclined road will help show this extra force which opposes motion. The car's mass is m kg and the effect of air resistance will be ignored. The road is inclined at $\theta°$ to the horizontal.

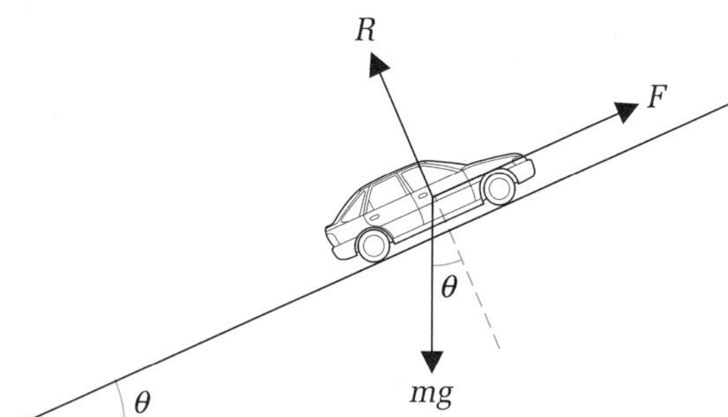

There are three forces acting on the car. Force F is parallel to the plane and R is perpendicular to the plane. By resolving in these directions, only the weight of the car needs to be resolved. This simplifies the problem.

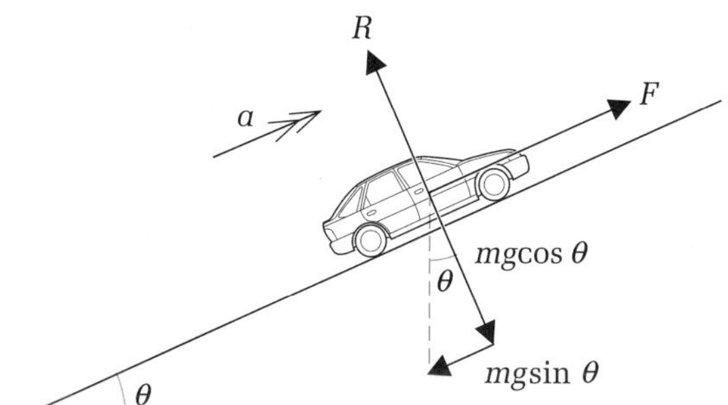

Remember cos is with the angle, sin is not with the angle.

When the weight of the car is resolved into two components, one of the components acts to oppose the motion of the car. This component is $mg\sin\theta$.

Apply $F = ma$ // to the plane ↗

$$F - mg\sin\theta = ma$$

$mg\sin\theta$ will always act down the plane if the angle of inclination is $\theta°$.

The weight component $mg\sin\theta$ is the additional force that opposes motion.

Resolve ⊥ to the plane

$$R - mg\cos\theta = 0$$
$$R = mg\cos\theta$$

Add $mg\cos\theta$.
$R = mg\cos\theta$ if no other forces ⊥ to the plane are involved.

Overview of method

Step ① Draw a clear diagram showing all the forces.
Step ② Apply $F = ma$ in the direction of motion.
Step ③ Resolve ⊥ to the direction of motion if the normal reaction needs to be found.

Resultant force ⊥ to the direction of motion equals zero.

Example 1

A toy cat on wheels has a mass of 3 kg. The cat is pulled along by a taut string inclined at 30° above the horizontal. The cat is accelerated at 3 m s^{-2}. Calculate the *exact* tension in the string.

Solution

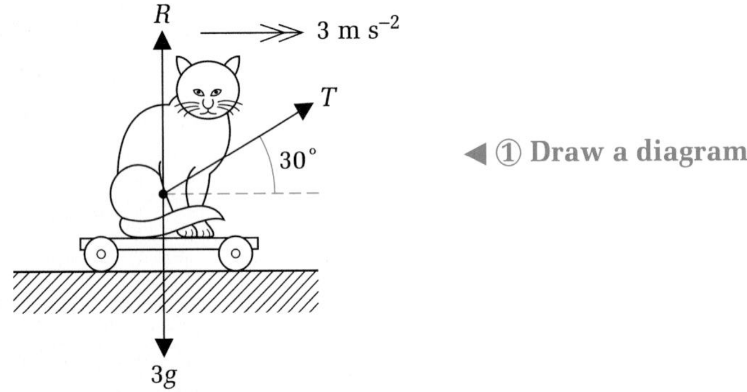

◀ ① Draw a diagram.

Apply $F = ma \rightarrow$

◀ ② Apply $F = ma$ in the direction of motion.

$$F = ma$$

$$T\cos 30° = 3 \times 3$$

$$T \times \tfrac{\sqrt{3}}{2} = 9$$

$$T = 9 \times \tfrac{2}{\sqrt{3}}$$

$$T = \tfrac{18}{\sqrt{3}}$$

$$T = \tfrac{18}{\sqrt{3}} \times \tfrac{\sqrt{3}}{\sqrt{3}}$$

$$T = \tfrac{18\sqrt{3}}{3}$$

$$T = 6\sqrt{3}\text{ N}$$

$\cos 30° = \frac{\sqrt{3}}{2}$
Multiply by 2 and divide by $\sqrt{3}$ to find T.

Rationalise the denominator.

Example 2

A car of mass 1 tonne accelerates at 2 m s^{-2} up a slope inclined at 5° to the horizontal. Find the force produced by the engine if the resistances are constant at 1500 N.

Solution

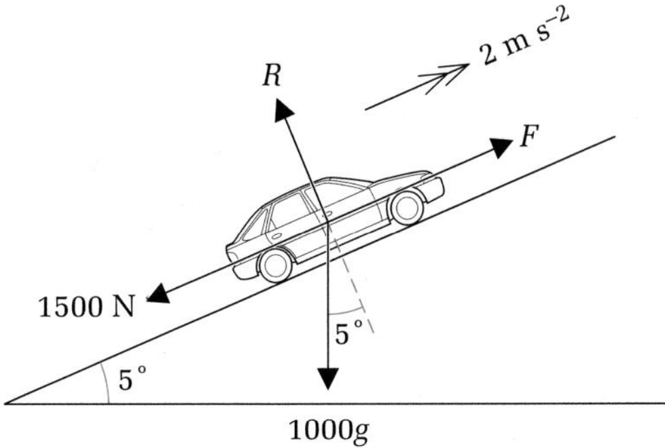

Apply $F = ma$ // to the plane ↗

$$F - 1000g\sin 5^\circ - 1500 = 1000 \times 2$$
$$F - 854.1 - 1500 = 2000$$
$$F = 4354.1$$
$$F = 4350 \text{ N (3 s.f.)}$$

*mg*sin θ always acts down the slope.
Add 854.1 and 1500.

Example 3

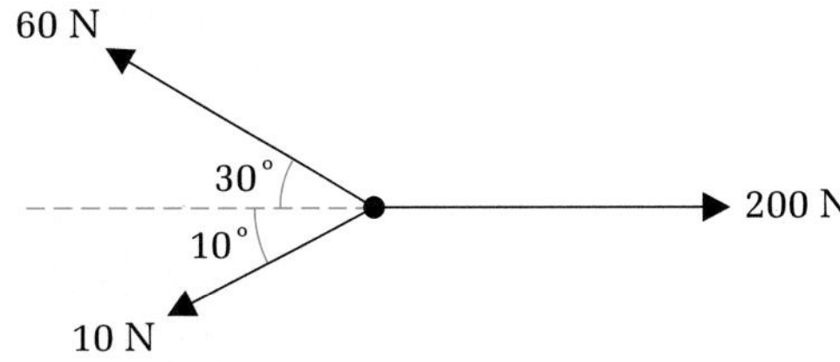

The forces acting on a 10 kg particle are shown. All the forces are horizontal. Work out:

a the magnitude of the overall force acting on the particle
b the magnitude of the acceleration of the particle
c the direction of the acceleration.

Solution

a Resolve ↑ $60\sin 30^\circ - 10\sin 10^\circ = 28.3$
Resolve → $200 - 60\cos 30^\circ - 10\cos 10^\circ = 138.2$

These horizontal and vertical **vector** components give the overall force:

$\mathbf{F} = 138.2\mathbf{i} + 28.3\mathbf{j}$

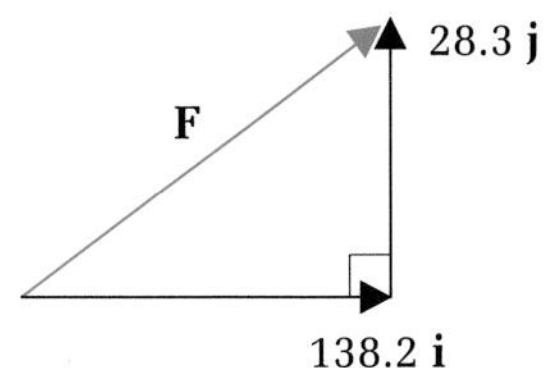

Using Pythagoras' theorem

$F^2 = 28.3^2 + 138.2^2$
$F^2 = 19\,895$
$F = \sqrt{19\,895}$
$F = 141$ N (3 s.f.)

Remember to store exact values in calculator.

b Use $F = ma$ ◀ ② **Apply $F = ma$ in the direction of motion.**

$F = ma$
$141 = 10a$
$a = 14.1\ \text{m s}^{-2}$ (3 s.f.)

F = magnitude of **F**.
Divide by 10.

c The direction of the acceleration must be the same direction as the force.

$\mathbf{F} = m\mathbf{a}$

The mass m is a scalar so **F** and **a** must be parallel vectors.

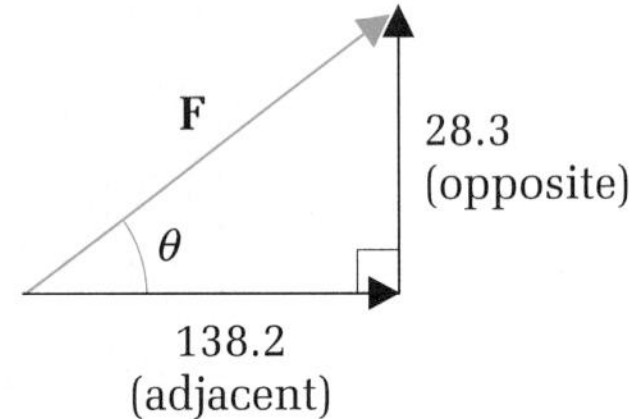

Using trigonometry,

$$\tan\theta = \frac{28.3}{138.2}$$

$\tan\theta = 0.2045$
$\theta = \tan^{-1}(0.2045)$
$\theta = 11.6°$ (1 d.p.)

Use tan in case a mistake was made when calculating the magnitude.

or arctan (0.2045)

The direction of the acceleration is 11.6° from the 200 N force towards the 60 N force.

8.3 $F = ma$ and Inclined Forces

Exercise

Technique

1 **a** **b**

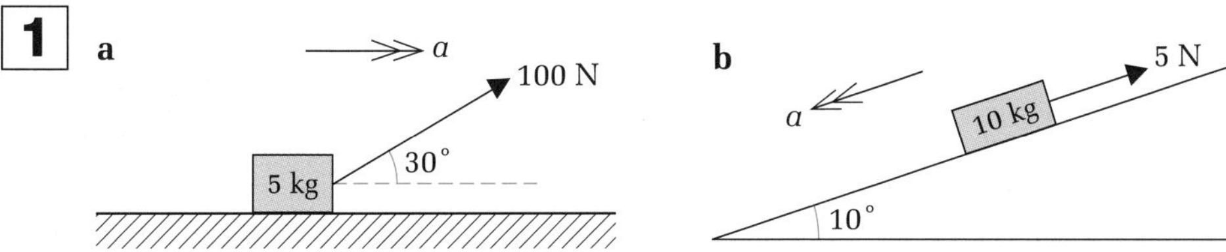

Find the acceleration of the masses shown.

2 **a** **b**

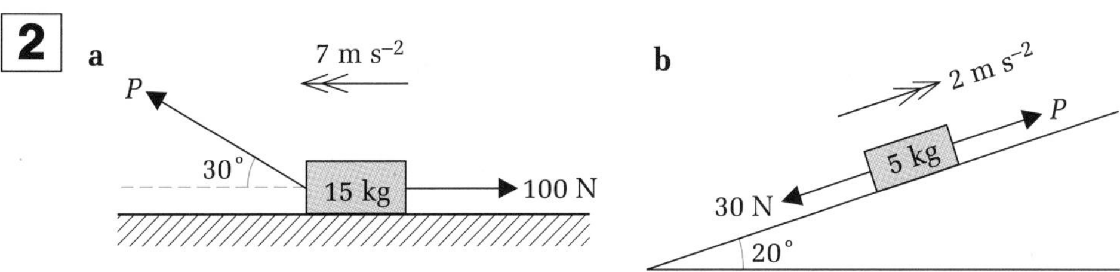

Work out the value of the force P.

3 **a** **b**

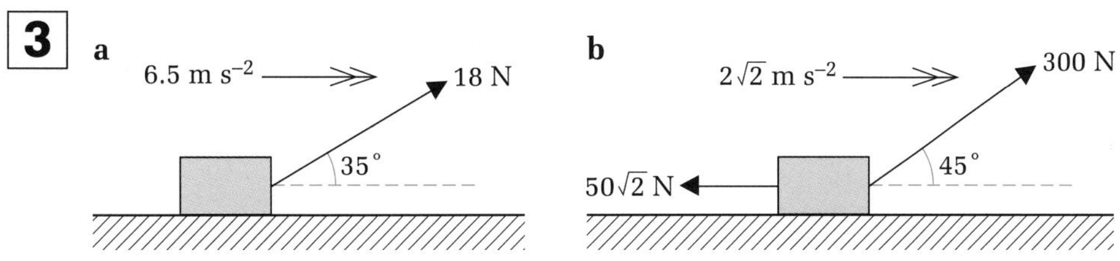

Determine the masses of the objects shown.

4 A particle of mass 5 kg is pulled up a smooth slope inclined at 30° to the horizontal. The applied force has a value of 50 N and acts parallel to the slope. Calculate the acceleration of the particle.

5 An object of mass 20 kg slides down a slope inclined at 45° to the horizontal. The resistance to motion is 60 N and acts parallel to the slope. Taking $g = 10\text{ m s}^{-2}$, determine the value of the acceleration of the object in surd form.

6 A particle of mass 100 grams is projected up a smooth inclined slope with an initial speed of 19.6 m s^{-1}. The slope is inclined at 20° to the horizontal. Find:

a the deceleration of the particle

b the distance travelled up the slope before the particle comes to rest.

7 A body has a mass of 30 kg and is accelerated up a slope inclined at 30° to the horizontal. The acceleration of the body is $3\,\text{m s}^{-2}$ and the frictional resistance is 300 N. Calculate the force parallel to the slope causing this acceleration.

8 **a**

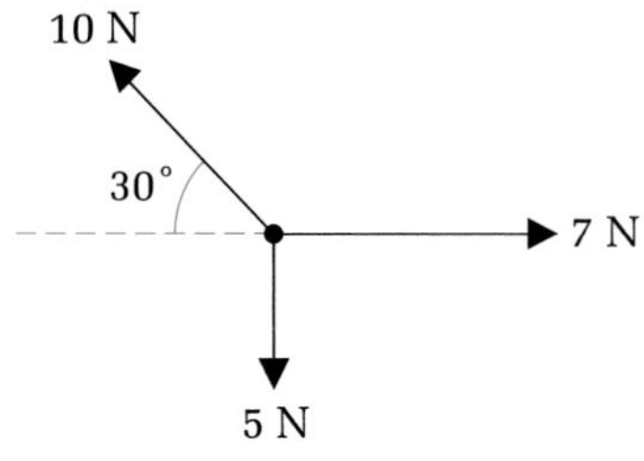

10 N, 30°, 7 N, 5 N

Particle of mass 2 kg

b

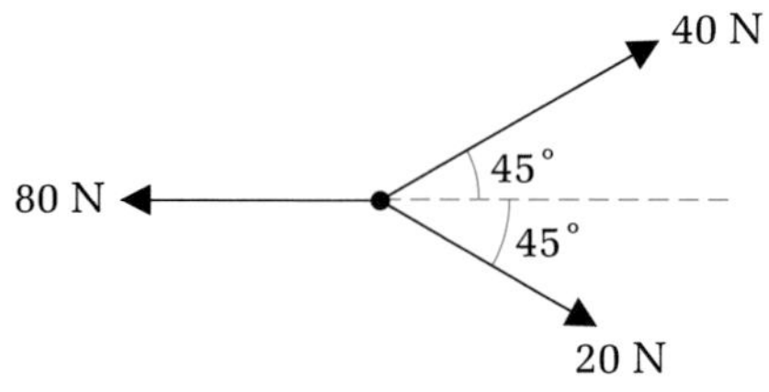

40 N, 45°, 80 N, 45°, 20 N

Particle of mass 4 kg

The particles are viewed from above and all the forces are horizontal. Calculate in each case:

- **i** the magnitude of the overall force
- **ii** the magnitude of the acceleration
- **iii** the direction of the acceleration.

Contextual

1 A car has a mass of 1.2 tonnes. The resistance to motion is 800 N. The car accelerates at $2\,\text{m s}^{-2}$ up a straight road inclined at 5° to the horizontal. Determine the force produced by the engine.

2 An aircraft of mass 60 tonnes ascends at an angle of 10° to the horizontal. The thrust produced by the engines is 200 kN and the resistance to motion is 50 kN. Find the acceleration of the aircraft.

3 A cyclist of mass 70 kg on a bicycle of mass 10 kg freewheels down a slope. The slope is inclined at 30° to the horizontal and the resistance to motion is 50 N.

- **a** Calculate the acceleration of the cyclist.
- **b** The initial speed of the cyclist at the top of the slope was $2\,\text{m s}^{-1}$ and the slope was 50 m long. Work out the speed of the cyclist at the bottom of the slope.

4 A car of mass 900 kg accelerates *down* a straight inclined slope at $4\,\text{m s}^{-2}$. The resistance to motion is 1200 N and the slope is inclined at 8° to the horizontal. Taking $g = 10\,\text{m s}^{-2}$:

- **a** draw a clear diagram showing all the forces
- **b** calculate the force produced by the engine.

8.4 Newton's Third Law and Connected Particles

Sir Frank Whittle (1907–1996)
Designed and flew the first British jet aircraft.

In a jet engine, fuel is burnt and this heat is used to accelerate the exhaust gases. The action of forcing the exhaust gases *backwards* causes a force on the engine *forwards*. This is an example of Newton's third law.

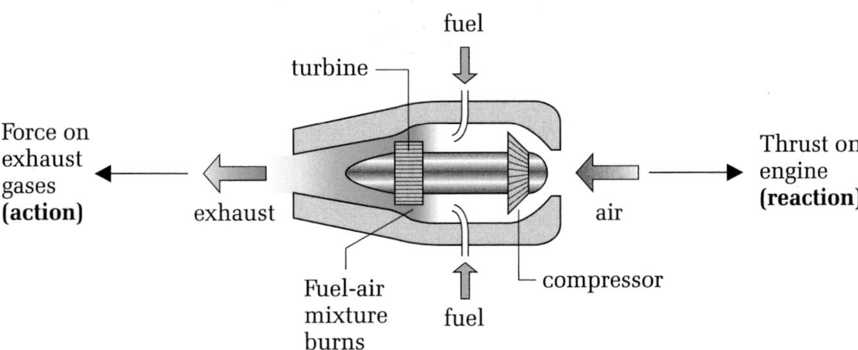

Newton's third law

Newton's third law states that for every action there is an equal and opposite reaction.

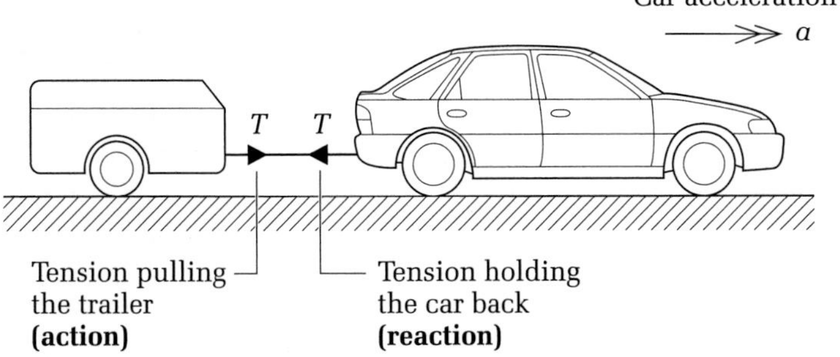

When a car pulls a trailer, the trailer is pulled forwards by the tension in the towbar (action). This action causes an equal, but opposite reaction. The towbar exerts a backwards force on the car. The diagram shows that the tensions act inwards from the ends. When the car brakes, the trailer is slowed down by the thrust in the towbar (action). This thrust acts to push the car forwards (reaction).

When the direction of acceleration is opposite to motion, the car is decelerating.

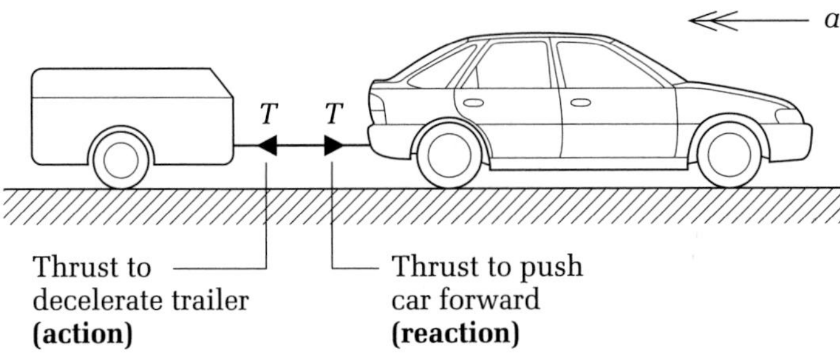

Notice that thrust acts in an opposite direction to tension.

Newton's third law will always involve *two equal forces* acting in *opposite directions*, on *two different bodies.*

Pulley systems

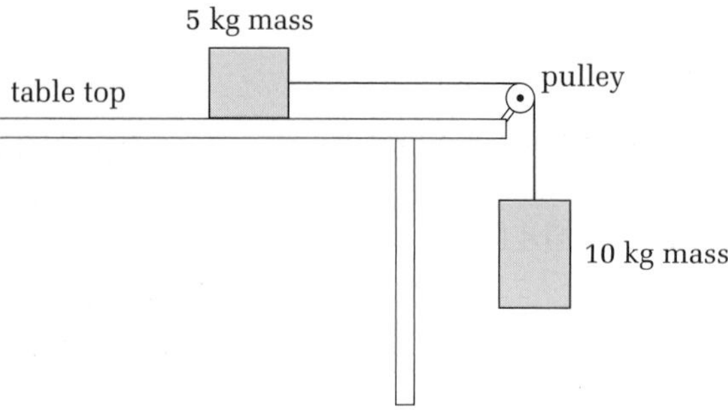

What do you think will happen when the masses are released? The 10 kg mass will accelerate the 5 kg mass on the table via the tension in the string. This action causes a tension to slow the 10 kg down. These two tensions are another example of Newton's third law. The tensions will be equal in magnitude if the pulley is smooth.

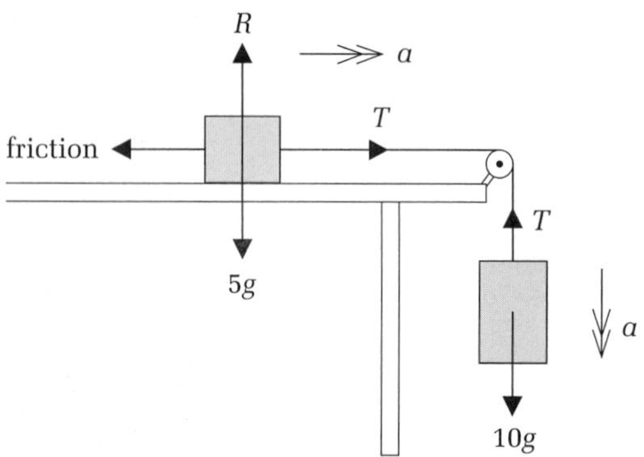

The two equal forces act at right-angles in opposite directions along the string.

Connected particles

The car and trailer problem and the pulley system are both examples of connected particle systems.

How do you think the acceleration of the car and the acceleration of the trailer compare? The acceleration of the car and trailer must be the same. If this were not the case the towbar would either be stretched or compressed.

This would actually happen in the real towbar but to a *very* small extent.

How do you think the acceleration of the 10 kg mass and the acceleration of the 5 kg mass compare? In the pulley system the masses must have the same acceleration as long as the string remains *taut* and it is not *stretched*. The tension on either side of the pulley will have the same size (but opposite direction along the string) provided the pulley is smooth. This means that to analyse real systems several assumptions need to be made:

- The string (or towbar) is *light* and *inextensible*. This means that the connected particles will have the same magnitude of acceleration.
- The string will remain *taut* throughout.
- The pulley is *smooth* and *fixed* and therefore the tension in the string will remain the same on each side of the pulley.

The string slides smoothly over the smooth fixed pulley.

Overview of method

Step ① Draw a clear force diagram.
Step ② Apply $F = ma$ to each particle in the direction of motion.
Step ③ *Add* the equations together. This will eliminate the tensions. Evaluate the acceleration.
Step ④ Use an equation to find the tension in the string.
Step ⑤ Use the other equation to check the answer.

Eliminate means cancel out.

This last step is a recommended safeguard.

Example 1

A car of mass 800 kg pulls a trailer of mass 200 kg. The force produced by the engine is 4000 N. The resistances acting on the car and trailer are 600 N and 300 N respectively. Calculate:

a the acceleration of the car and trailer
b the tension in the towbar.

Solution

◀ ① Draw a diagram.

Mark on forces and acceleration.

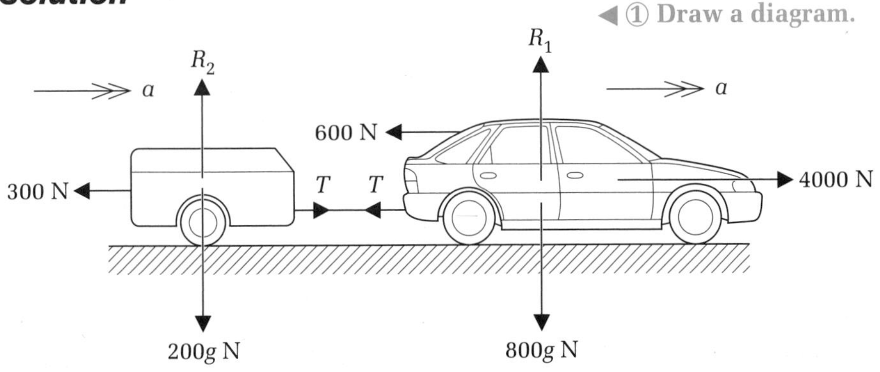

a Apply $F = ma$ to the car → ◀ ② Apply $F = ma$ in the direction of motion.

$$4000 - T - 600 = 800a$$
$$3400 - T = 800a \quad [1]$$

To the right is positive.

$4000 - 600 = 3400$

Apply $F = ma$ to the trailer → ◀ ② Apply $F = ma$ in the direction of motion.

$$T - 300 = 200a \quad [2]$$

Add equations [1] and [2]. ◀ ③ Add the equations to eliminate T.

Add corresponding sides of the equations. $-T + T$ cancel.

$$3400 - T + T - 300 = 800a + 200a$$
$$3400 - 300 = 1000a$$
$$3100 = 1000a$$
$$a = 3.1\ \text{m s}^{-2}$$ ◀ ③ Evaluate a.

Divide by 1000.

b Use equation [2] ◀ ④ Use equation [2] to find the tension.

$$T - 300 = 200 \times 3.1$$
$$T - 300 = 620$$
$$T = 920\ \text{N}$$

Substitute the value of a.
Add 300.

Check using equation [1] ◀ ⑤ **Check the answers using equation [1].**

$3400 - T = 800a$

LHS: $3400 - T = 3400 - 920 = 2480$ RHS: $800a = 800 \times 3.1 = 2480$ correct

Equation [1]. Replace T with 920 and a with 3.1

Example 2

A particle of mass 6 kg rests on a smooth horizontal plane. It is connected by a light inextensible string passing over a smooth pulley at the edge of the plane to a particle of mass 8 kg hanging freely. Find the acceleration of the system and the tension in the string.

Solution

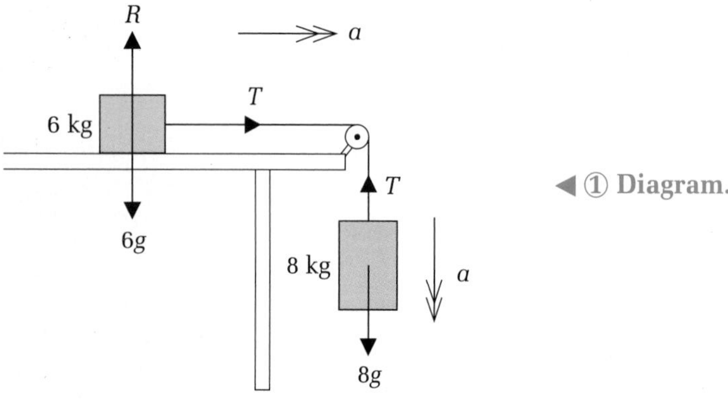

◀ ① **Diagram.**

Apply $F = ma$ to 8 kg ↓ ◀ ② **$F = ma$ in the direction of motion.**

$$8g - T = 8a \quad [1]$$

Apply $F = ma$ to 6 kg →

$$T = 6a \quad [2]$$

The plane is smooth so only T acts horizontally on 6 kg mass.

Adding equations [1] and [2], ◀ ③ **Add the equations to eliminate T.**

$$8g - T + T = 8a + 6a$$
$$8g = 14a$$
$$a = \frac{8}{14}g$$
$$a = \frac{4}{7}g$$
$$a = 5.6\ \text{m s}^{-2}$$

$-T + T$ cancels. Divide by 14.

Simplify fraction.

Using equation [2], ◀ ④ **Use equation [2] to find T.**

$$T = 6a$$
$$T = 6 \times 5.6$$
$$T = 33.6\ \text{N}$$

Substitute for a.

Check, using equation [1] ◀ ⑤ **Use equation [1] to check answers.**

$8g - T = 8a$

LHS: $8g - T = 8 \times 9.8 - 33.6 = 44.8$ RHS: $8a = 8 \times 5.6 = 44.8$ correct

Use the values for T and a.

Example 3

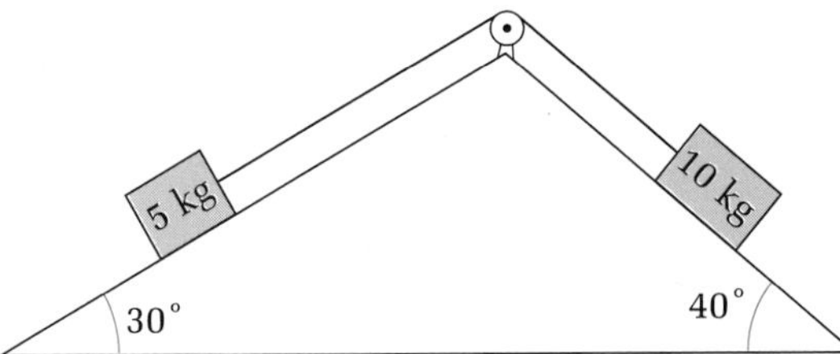

Two masses of 10 kg and 5 kg are connected by a light inelastic string passing over a fixed smooth pulley as shown in the diagram. The surfaces are both smooth and the system is released with the string taut. Determine the acceleration of the system.

Solution

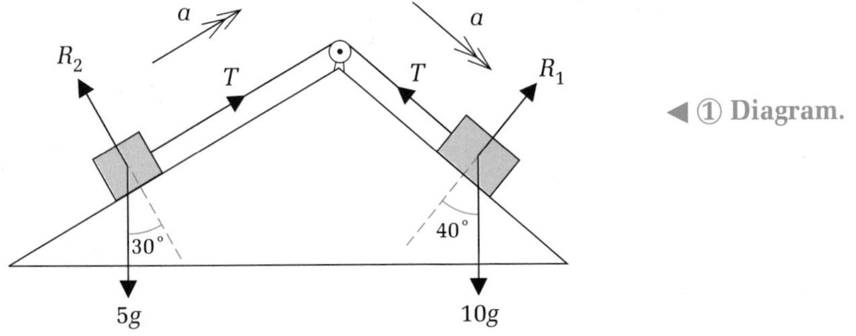

◀ ① Diagram.

The weight forces are not acting in the direction of motion. These forces need to be resolved into two components.

Apply $F = ma$ to 10 kg mass // to plane ↘ ◀ ② $F = ma$ in the direction of motion.

$$10g\sin 40^\circ - T = 10a$$
$$62.99 - T = 10a \quad [1]$$

Store the value for 10gsin 40° in calculator.

If you are unsure about the direction the masses will move in, choose a direction and stick to it. If your choice is incorrect, a will turn out to be negative, indicating that the direction of motion is opposite to your chosen one.

Apply $F = ma$ to 5 kg mass // to plane ↗

$$T - 5g\sin 30^\circ = 5a$$
$$T - 24.5 = 5a \quad [2]$$

Store value for $5g\sin 30^\circ$ in calculator.

Add equations [1] and [2] ◀ ③ Add equations.

$$62.99 - T + T - 24.5 = 10a + 5a$$
$$38.5 = 15a$$
$$a = 2.57\ \text{m s}^{-2}$$

Use stored values for 10gsin 40° and 5gsin 30°.

The tension is not required in this case.

8.4 Newton's Third Law and Connected Particles

Exercise

Technique

Assume the pulleys are smooth and fixed in questions 1, 2 and 3. The strings can be assumed to be light and inextensible.

1 a

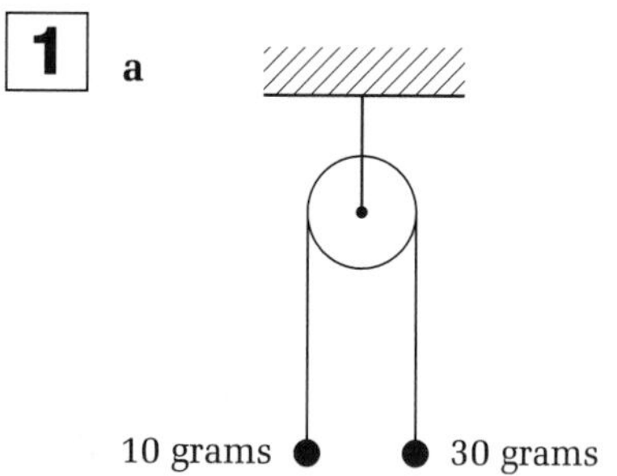

b

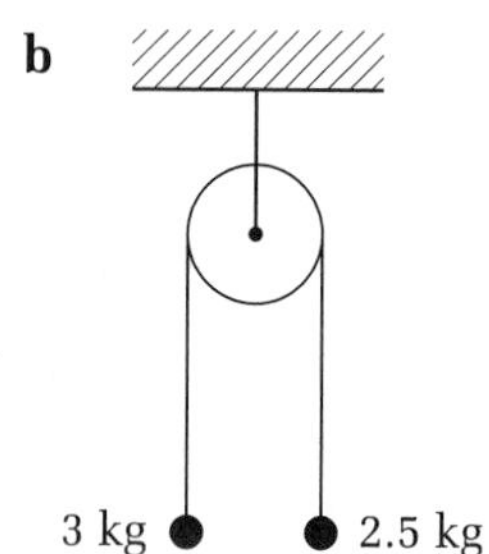

Find:

a the acceleration of the particles

b the tension in the string.

2 a b

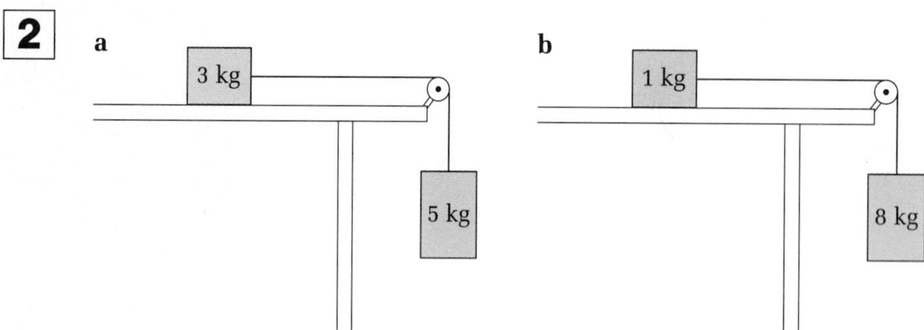

Work out the acceleration and tension in the string when the systems are released from rest. The surfaces are smooth.

3 a b

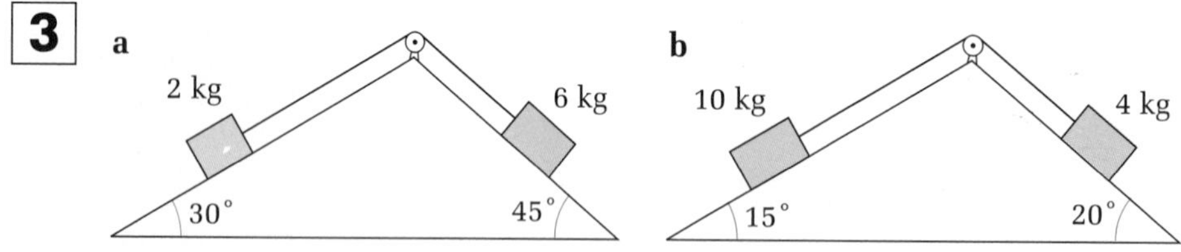

Calculate the acceleration of these systems. The surfaces are smooth.

4 A body of mass 5 kg is lying on a smooth table. It is connected by a light inextensible string to another body of mass 3 kg. The string passes over a smooth fixed pulley at the edge of a table and the 3 kg mass hangs freely. The string is taut and the system is released from rest. Find the acceleration of the system and the tension in the string.

5 A body of mass 6 kg lies on a plane inclined at 30° to the horizontal. It is connected by light inextensible string, running over a fixed smooth pulley, to a body of mass 10 kg which is hanging freely.

a Supposing there is no friction involved, find the acceleration of the body up the plane.

b If there is a frictional force of 8 N acting along the plane, what is the acceleration now?

Contextual

1 A car, of mass 1000 kg, tows a caravan of mass 700 kg along a straight horizontal road. The force produced by the engine of the car is 3500 N and the resistances to motion acting on the car and caravan are 650 N and 320 N respectively. Determine:

a the acceleration of the car and caravan

b the tension in the towbar.

The car and caravan travel up a hill of inclination 7° to the horizontal. Assuming that the resistances stay constant:

c draw a clear force diagram for this situation

d write equations of motion for the car and caravan

e calculate the acceleration of the car and caravan.

2 A tow truck of mass 5200 kg tows a car of mass 2300 kg. They are travelling at a constant speed of 20 m s^{-1} along a straight horizontal road. The tow truck brakes with a force of 7000 N. Work out:

a the deceleration of the tow truck and car

b the thrust in the towbar

c the length of time taken for both vehicles to come to rest.

Thrust will act in the opposite direction to tension.

3

A roller coaster is accelerated by means of a pulley system as shown. The total mass of the cars is 1500 kg and the mass hanging freely is 5000 kg. The system is released from rest. Air resistance and frictional forces can be ignored. Assume the pulley is smooth and fixed and the wire is light and inextensible. Determine:

a the tension in the wire

b the acceleration of the cars.

The cars are accelerated for a distance of 100 m. Calculate:

c the final velocity of the cars

d the time taken.

Consolidation

Exercise A

1 The diagram shows a man of mass 70 kg standing in a lift and carrying a suitcase of mass 8 kg in his hand. The magnitude of the contact force between the man and the floor of the lift is R newtons and that between the suitcase and the man's hand is S newtons. Take $g = 10\text{ m s}^{-2}$.

a **i** Show, in a diagram, the two forces acting on the suitcase.
ii Show, in a further diagram, the three forces acting on the man.

b Calculate the values of R and S when the upward acceleration of the lift is 2 m s^{-2}.

(NEAB)

2 A car of mass 850 kg is moving, with an acceleration of 1.4 m s^{-2}, along a straight horizontal road. The engine of the car produces a total forward force of magnitude X newtons and there is a horizontal resisting force of magnitude 450 N. Find X.

(UCLES)

3

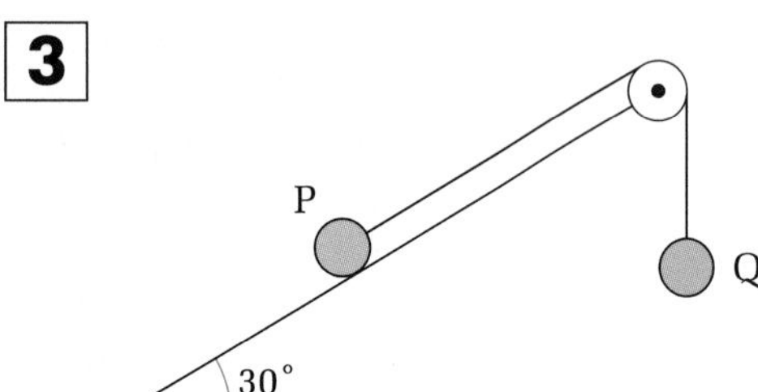

The diagram shows two particles P and Q connected by a light inextensible string which passes over a smooth pulley at the top of a smooth plane inclined at 30° to the horizontal. The masses of P and Q are $3m$ and $2m$, respectively. Initially P is held at rest on the plane, Q hangs freely and the inclined part of the string is parallel to a line of greatest slope of the plane. The system is then released. Find:

Assume the pulley is fixed.

a the acceleration of the particles in terms of g
b the tension in the string in terms of m and g.

(NEAB)

Exercise B

1 A woman of mass 60 kg is standing in a lift.

a Draw a diagram showing the forces acting on the woman, namely her weight and the normal reaction of the floor of the lift on her.

Find the normal reaction of the floor of the lift on the woman in the following cases:

b the lift is moving upwards with a constant speed of $3\ \text{m s}^{-1}$

c the lift is moving upwards with an acceleration of $2\ \text{m s}^{-2}$ upwards

d the lift is moving downwards with an acceleration of $2\ \text{m s}^{-2}$ downwards

e the lift is moving downwards and slowing down with a retardation of $2\ \text{m s}^{-2}$.

Retardation is deceleration.

In order to calculate the maximum number of occupants that can safely be carried, the following assumptions are made: the lift has mass 300 kg; all resistances to motion may be neglected; the mass of each occupant is 75 kg; and the tension in the supporting cable should not exceed 12 000 N.

f What is the greatest number of occupants that can be carried safely if the magnitude of the acceleration does not exceed $3\ \text{m s}^{-2}$?

(MEI)

2 A body of mass 5 kg is placed at rest on a smooth horizontal surface. Three forces, **P**, **Q** and **R**, all measured in newtons, are applied, where $\mathbf{P} = 3\mathbf{i} + 4\mathbf{j}$, $\mathbf{Q} = 2\mathbf{i} - 7\mathbf{j}$ and $\mathbf{R} = -5\mathbf{i} + 3\mathbf{j}$.

a Show that the mass remains at rest.

The force **R** is now removed. Find:

b the resulting force on the mass and the magnitude of this force

c the acceleration of the mass in the form $x\mathbf{i} + y\mathbf{j}$ and the velocity after 10 seconds.

The force **Q** is now also removed.

d Find the new acceleration and give the formula for the velocity t seconds after the removal of **Q**.

e Find the number of seconds that elapse after the removal of the force **Q** before the mass is moving parallel to the vector **i**.

(OCSEB)

3 Pat and Nicholas are controlling the movement of a canal barge by means of long ropes attached to each end. The tension in the ropes may be assumed horizontal and parallel to the line and direction of motion of the barge as shown in the diagrams.

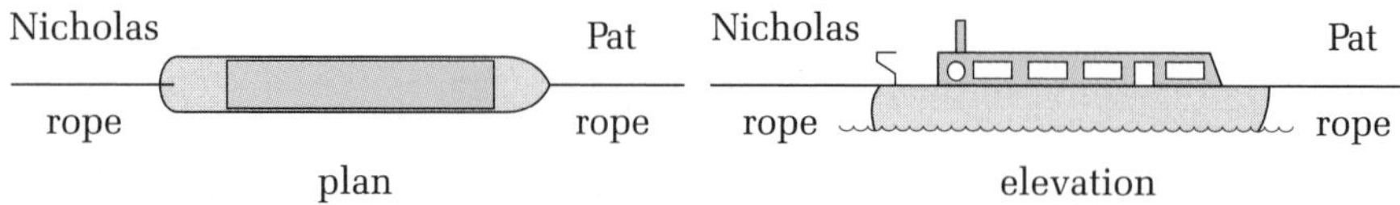

The mass of the barge is 12 tonnes and the total resistance to forward motion may be taken to be 250 N at all times. Initially Pat pulls the barge forwards from rest with a force of 400 N and Nicholas leaves his rope slack.

a Write down the equation of motion for the barge and hence calculate its acceleration.

Pat continues to pull with the same force until the barge has moved 10 m.

b What is the speed of the barge at this time and for what length of time did Pat pull?

Pat now lets her rope go slack and Nicholas brings the barge to rest by pulling with a constant force of 150 N.

c Calculate:

- **i** how long it takes the barge to come to rest
- **ii** the total distance travelled by the barge from when it first moved
- **iii** the total time taken for the motion.

(MEI)

4 A crate P containing blocks of wood has a total mass of M kg, $(M > 85)$. The crate is connected to a counterweight Q, of mass 85 kg, by a rope which passes over a fixed pulley. Initially the counterweight is held in contact with the ground, as shown in the diagram. The counterweight is released. In the ensuing motion both the crate and the counterweight move vertically.

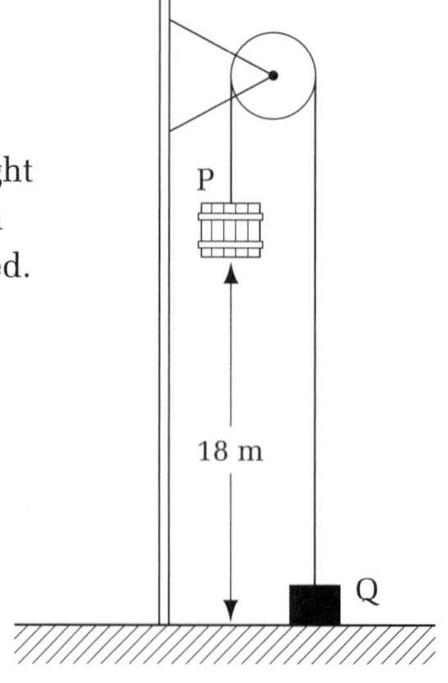

The following modelling assumptions are made: the crate and the counterweight are considered as particles; the rope is light and inextensible; the pulley is smooth; there is no air resistance. Given that the crate reaches the ground in 7.5 s and taking $g = 9.81\,\text{m s}^{-2}$:

a show that the acceleration of the crate is $0.64\,\text{m s}^{-2}$

b calculate the value of M.

(UCLES)

Applications and Activities

1

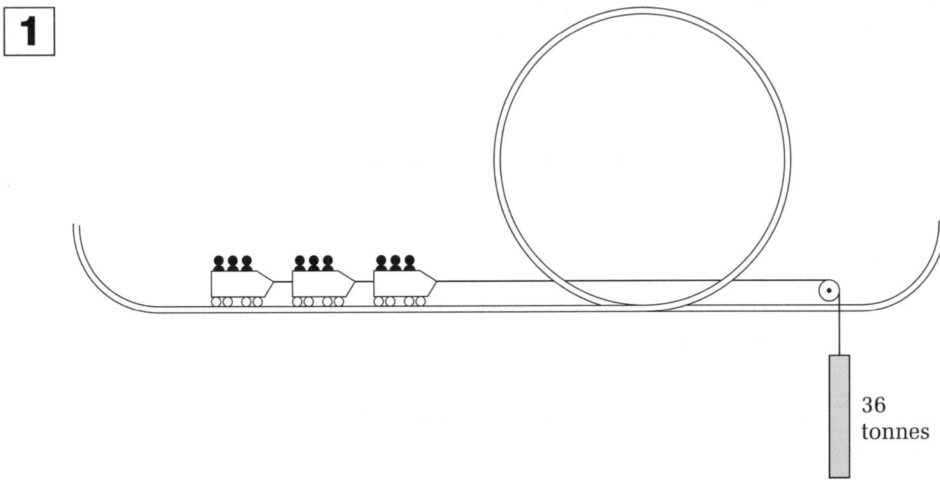

A roller coaster uses a pulley system to accelerate the cars. The unloaded roller coaster cars weigh 5.25 tonnes and the 36 tonne mass is used to accelerate the cars. The roller coaster can carry a maximum of 28 people. Use a mathematical model to calculate the acceleration of the roller coaster cars. State any assumptions that you have made. Validate your method using an experimental model.

2 A simple pulley system can be used to raise and lower loads from one level to another. Use a mathematical model to find the acceleration of the masses. Test this model by using an experiment.

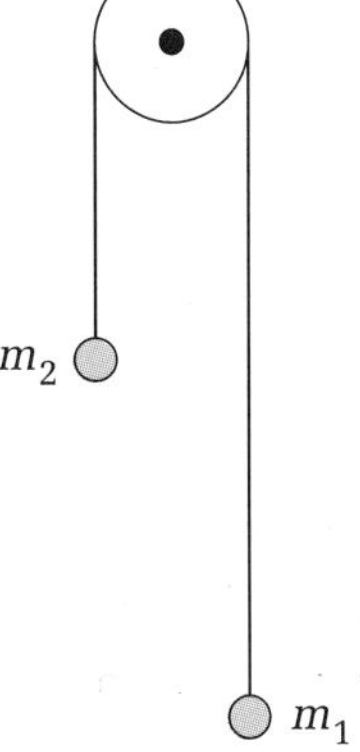

3 A trolley is placed on an incline and released. Use a mathematical model to calculate the acceleration of the trolley. Compare your results with an experimental model. What happens if you use a ball instead of a trolley?

Summary

- Newton's first law states that a body will continue to remain at rest or move at constant speed in a straight line unless an external force makes it act otherwise.
- Newton's second law states that a resultant force acting on a body produces an acceleration which is proportional to the resultant force. (Mass assumed constant.)
- The formula that is related to Newton's second law is

  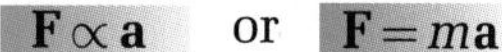

  $\mathbf{F} \propto \mathbf{a}$ or $\mathbf{F} = m\mathbf{a}$

  when SI units are used and the mass is constant.
- Newton's third law states that for every action there is an equal and opposite reaction.

9 Friction

What you need to know

- How to apply Newton's laws of motion.
- The value of sin x, cos x and tan x where x can be 30°, 45° and 60°.
- How to solve connected particle problems.
- How to apply Lami's theorem and triangle of forces.
- How to use the uniform acceleration formulas.

Review

1 Use Newton's laws of motion to solve the following problems. Take $g = 10\text{ m s}^{-2}$ where required.

a

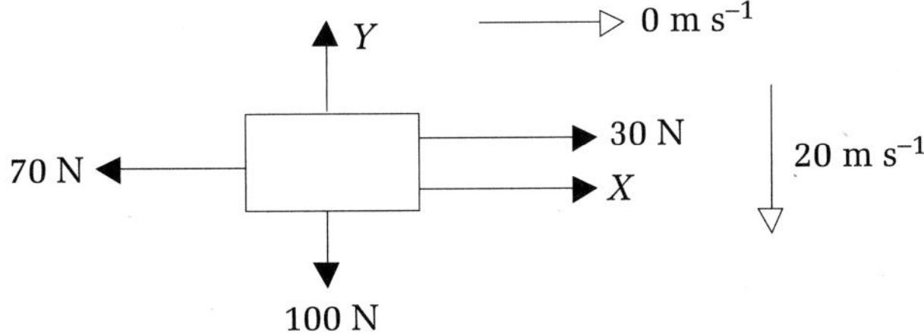

Find X and Y.

b

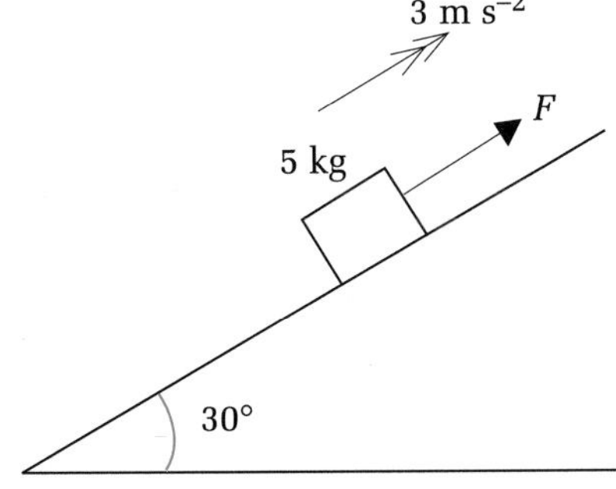

Find F.

2

A	30°	45°	60°
Sin A			
Cos A		$\frac{\sqrt{2}}{2}$ or $\frac{1}{\sqrt{2}}$	
Tan A			

Copy and complete the table giving exact values.

3 **a**

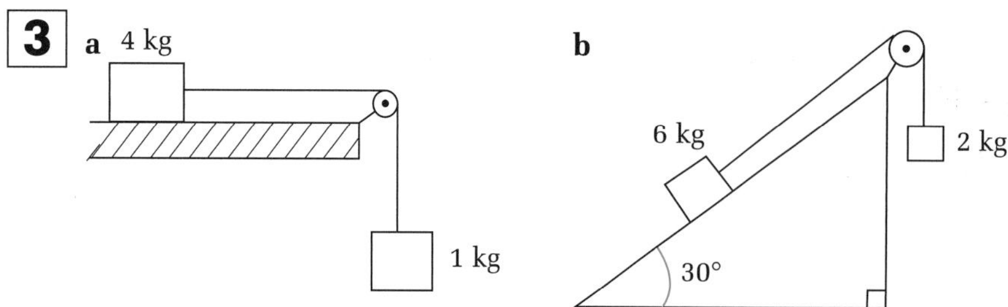

Taking $g = 10\,\text{m}\,\text{s}^{-2}$, calculate the acceleration and the tension in the string for the connected particle systems shown. Assume that the planes and the pulleys are smooth.

4 **a** Use Lami's theorem to solve the following problems given that the forces are in equilibrium:

i

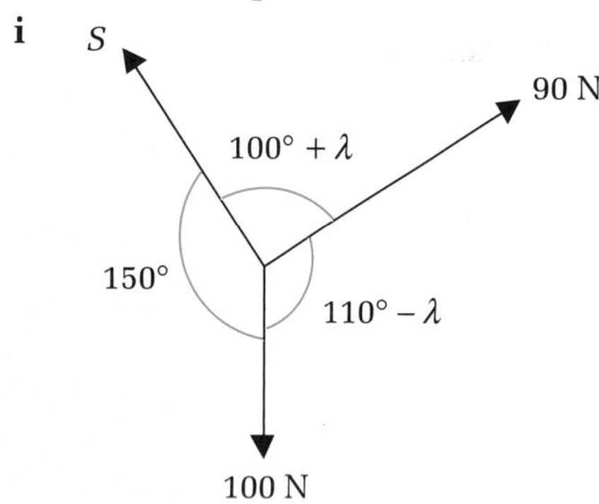

Find λ and S (λ is acute).

ii

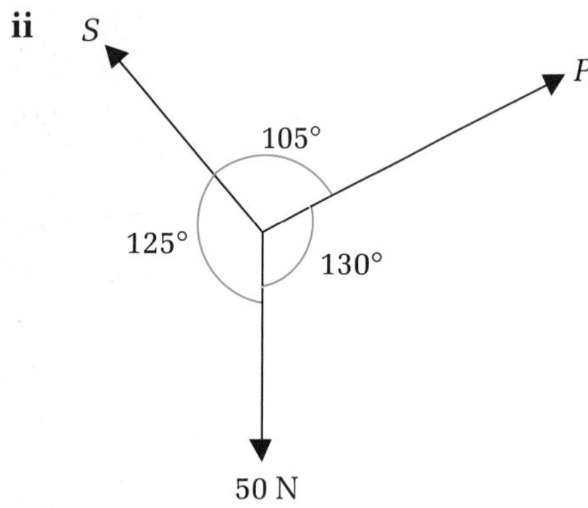

Find S and P.

b Use the triangle of forces to solve the following problems:

i

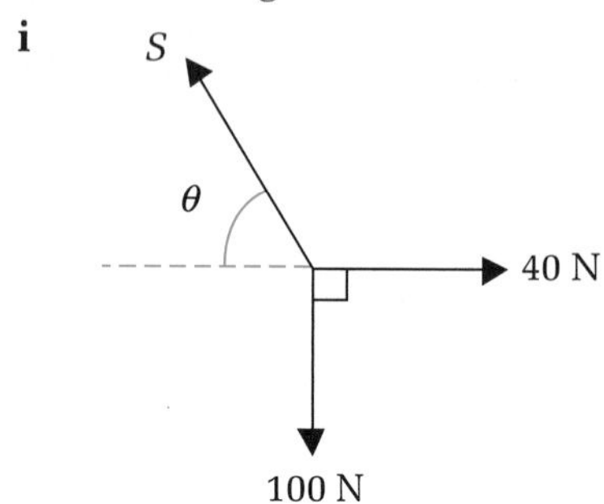

Find S and θ.

ii

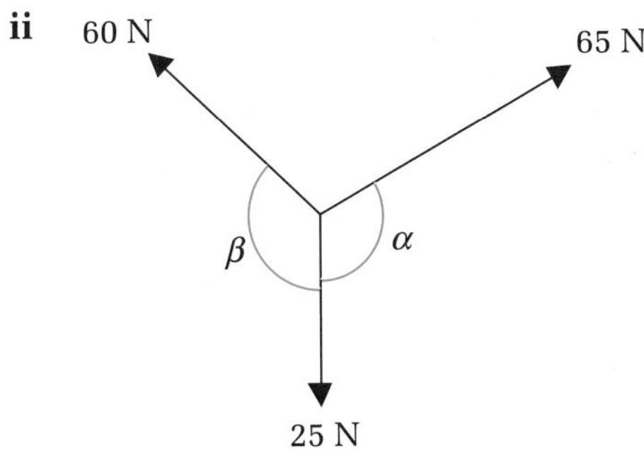

Find α and β.

5 **a** An ice puck has an initial velocity of $2\,\text{m}\,\text{s}^{-1}$. It covers a distance of 20 m before coming to rest. Find the acceleration of the ice puck.

b A bead is dropped into a container of oil. The bead takes 2 seconds to travel to the bottom of the tank. The tank is 1 metre deep. Calculate the acceleration of the bead assuming it is constant throughout.

c A car accelerates from $10\,\text{m}\,\text{s}^{-1}$ to $20\,\text{m}\,\text{s}^{-1}$ whilst covering a distance of 500 m. Calculate the time taken.

d A lorry decelerates to rest at $2\,\text{m}\,\text{s}^{-2}$. This deceleration takes 4 s. Calculate the lorry's initial velocity.

Additional pure

For this chapter you will also need to know a relationship between sin x, cos x and tan x.

$$\tan x = \frac{\sin x}{\cos x}$$

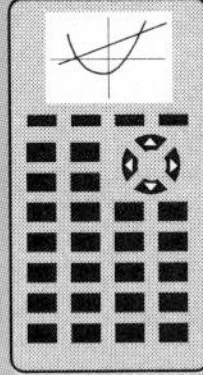

This relationship can be shown on a graphical calculator.

$x_{min} = 0$, $x_{max} = 360$, $x_{scl} = 90$

$y_{min} = -10$, $y_{max} = 10$, $y_{scl} = 1$

Graph $Y1 = \dfrac{\sin x}{\cos x}$

Graph $Y2 = \tan x$

9.1 Friction on a Horizontal Plane

If a book is placed on a table and given a push what happens? The book slides across the table, slows down and then stops. Why does it stop? The book must have an external force acting on it to slow it down. The force must act to *oppose motion*. This force is known as **friction**.

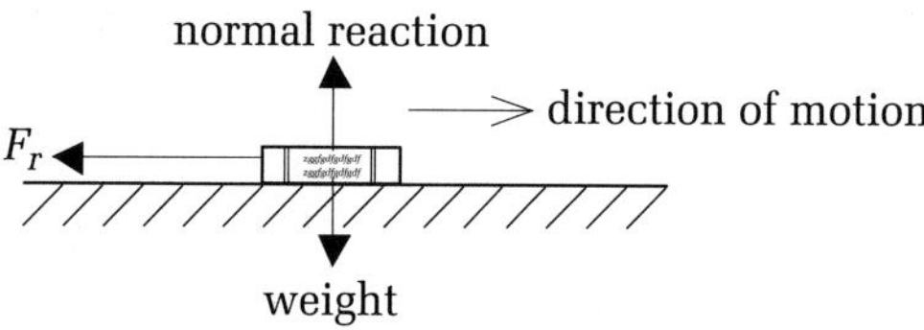

In this book, F_r is used to represent friction (F is used to represent a general force). Remember, friction has a tendency to oppose motion at the point or surface of contact.

What happens to the book if the applied force is slowly increased? The book does not move if a very small force is applied. The force can be increased until it reaches a certain value. Once the applied force exceeds this value the book will move. The frictional force (F_r) must have a maximum value.

What happens to the frictional force if the weight of the book acting on the table increases? The frictional force increases. This is caused by a larger force acting on the table's surface.

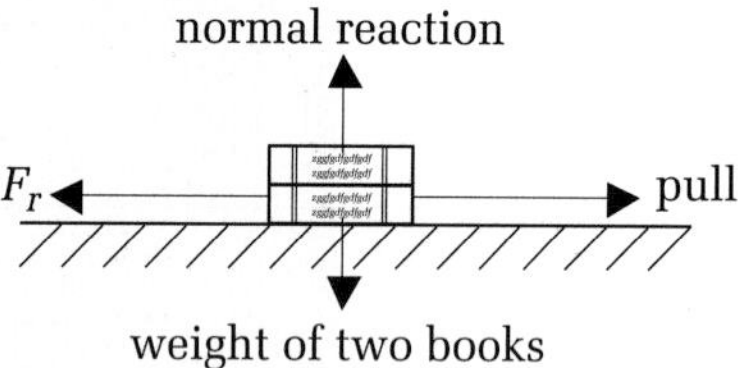

The normal reaction force (R) between the table and the book must be the same as the force pushing down on the surface. In this case the normal reaction is the same as the weight of the book, but this is not always the case. When the applied force is inclined or the surface is inclined, the normal reaction will not equal the weight of the object. These situations will be covered later in this chapter.

Newton's third law.

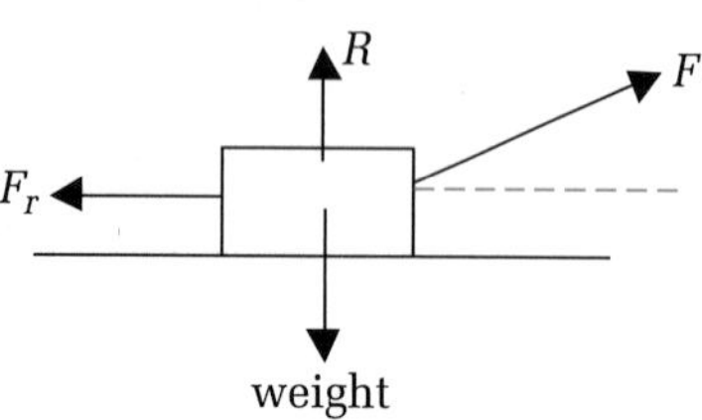

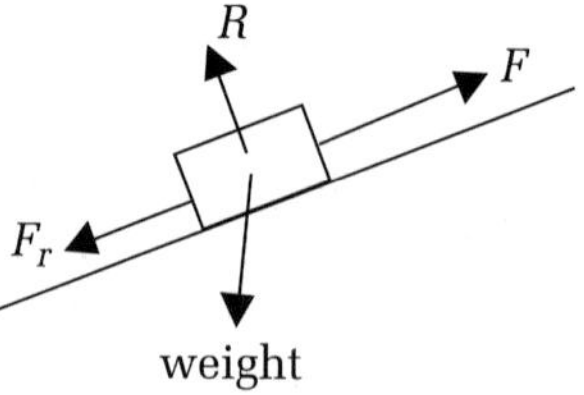

The model for friction

In summary, friction depends on

- the surfaces in contact
- the normal reaction force.

Friction does *not* depend on the *surface area*.

The coefficient of friction

The coefficient of friction gives a measure of the **roughness** of the surfaces. This number changes depending on which surfaces are in contact. The symbol used for the coefficient of friction is μ (pronounced mew). To work out the frictional force the following formula is used:

$$\boldsymbol{F_r \leq \mu R}$$

Notation
F_r = frictional force
μ = the coefficient of friction
R = normal reaction force between the surfaces
The inequality sign shows that the value of friction can increase up to its maximum value ($F_r = \mu R$).

The possible values of the coefficient of friction are given by the inequality:

$$\mu \geq 0$$

Problems involving friction

When an object is on a rough surface there are three possible events that can happen. The object will stay at rest, will be just about to move or will accelerate. When an object is *just about to move* the frictional force has reached its maximum value. If the applied force is increased any more the book will accelerate. The book is said to be in **limiting equilibrium**. In this case the frictional force must equal its maximum value *and* the frictional force must balance the applied horizontal force.

It should be noted that, in practice, the coefficient of friction is different for static and dynamic problems.

Overview of method

Step ① Draw a clear force diagram.
Step ② Resolve the forces vertically to find R.
Step ③ Use $F_r \leq \mu R$.
Step ④ Apply $F = ma$ horizontally when the object is moving (or assumed to be moving) *or* resolve the forces horizontally when the object is stationary.

Sometimes, Steps ③ and ④ will be swapped depending on the information that is given. If you are asked to find the coefficient of friction, it is often easier to use Step ③ after Step ④.

Example 1

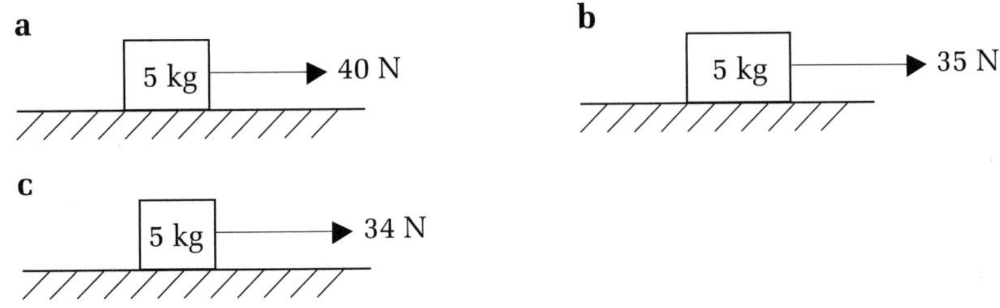

The coefficient of friction between the masses and the surface is $\frac{5}{7}$. Find the value of the frictional force in each case and determine if the mass will remain at rest, be in limiting equilibrium or accelerate.

Solution

a

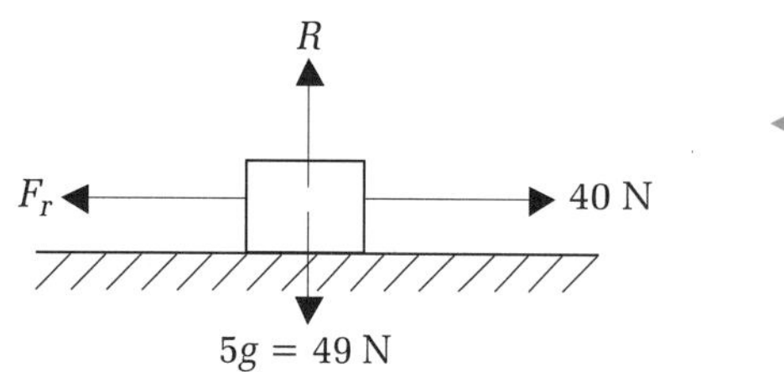

◀ ① Draw a clear diagram showing all the forces.

Resolve ↑ ◀ ② Resolve the forces vertically to find R.

$$R - 49 = 0$$
$$R = 49 \text{ N}$$

Using $F_r \leq \mu R$, ◀ ③ Apply $F_r \leq \mu R$.

$$F_r \leq \tfrac{5}{7} \times 49$$
$$F_r \leq 35 \text{ N}$$

From the question, $\mu = \frac{5}{7}$.

The frictional force cannot equal 40 N so the mass will accelerate. Since the mass will move, F_r must equal 35 N.

Compare F_r and the applied force (40 N). The frictional force cannot prevent motion.

b

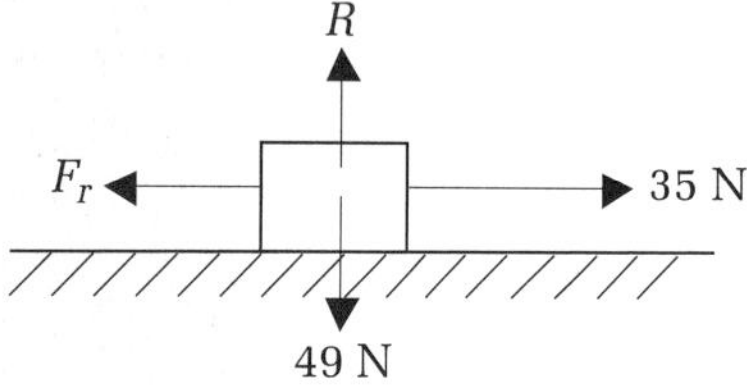

$F_r \leq 35$ N ◀ From part a.

$F_r = 35$ N

When $F_r = 35$ N, friction will just prevent motion from taking place. The object must be in limiting equilibrium.

Compare F_r and 35 N. This time friction can prevent motion.

c

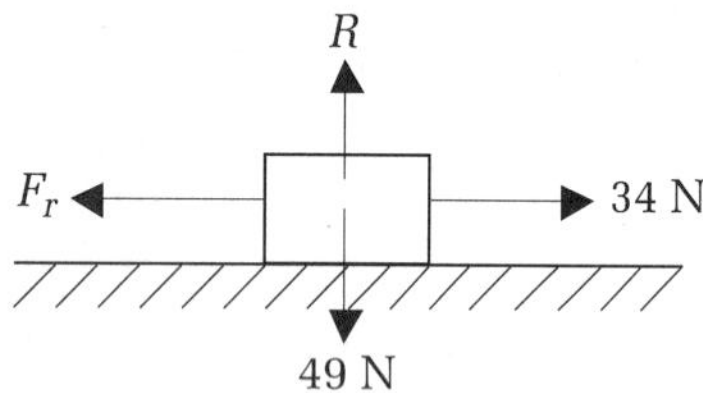

Same as in **a**.

$F_r \leq 35$ N ◀ From part a.

The object will remain at rest. This time the frictional force only needs to equal 34 N to prevent motion.

Example 2

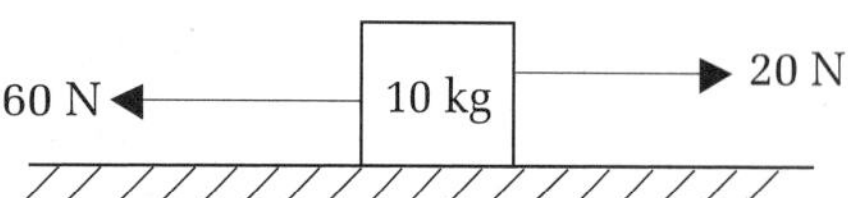

Taking $g = 10 \text{ m s}^{-2}$, find the acceleration of the mass shown in the diagram. The coefficient of friction is 0.3.

If the mass accelerates, it will move in the direction of the 60 N force (to the left). Friction will act to oppose this motion (to the right).

Solution

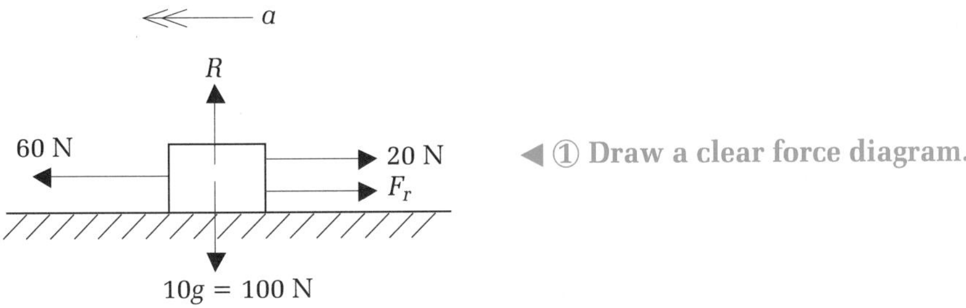

Resolve ↑ ◀ ② Resolve the forces vertically to find R.

The direction arrow refers to the diagram.

$$R - 100 = 0$$
$$R = 100\,\text{N}$$

Using $F_r \le \mu R$, ◀ ③ Apply $F_r \le \mu R$.

$$F_r \le 0.3 \times 100$$
$$F_r \le 30\,\text{N}$$

$\mu = 0.3$ from the question.

Assuming that the mass will accelerate, $F_r = 30$ N.

Apply $F = ma \leftarrow$ ◀ ④ Apply $F = ma$ to the 10 kg mass.

The arrow refers to the direction of motion on the diagram.

$$60 - 20 - F_r = 10a$$

$F_r = 30$ N

$$40 - 30 = 10a$$
$$10 = 10a$$

Divide by 10.

$$a = 1\,\text{m}\,\text{s}^{-2}$$

Example 3

A box of mass 3 kg sits on the load bay of a pick up truck. The coefficient of friction between the load bay and the box is 0.5. Taking $g = 10\,\text{m}\,\text{s}^{-2}$, find out whether the box slides off when the pick up truck accelerates at $6\,\text{m}\,\text{s}^{-2}$.

Solution

Friction is the force which prevents objects from sliding about in car boots or in the back of vans. If the vehicle accelerates too quickly, then the objects will slide around because friction will have reached its maximum value and so cannot prevent them from sliding.

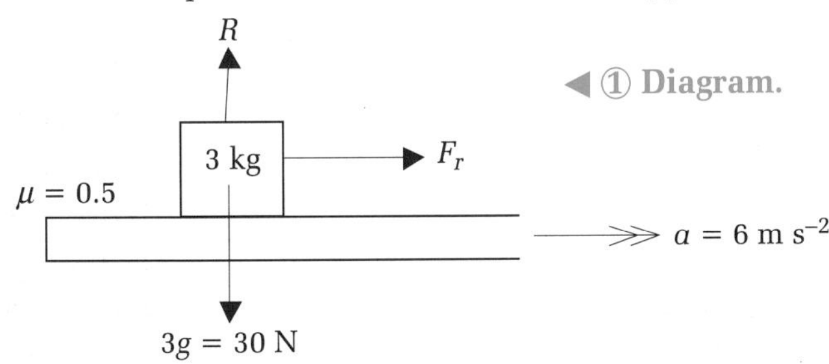

The box will move to the left if it slides so friction acts in the opposite direction (to the right).

Resolving ↑ ◀ ② Resolve vertically.

$R - 30 = 0$

$R = 30$ N

Applying $F_r \leq \mu R$, ◀ ③ Apply $F_r \leq \mu R$.

$F_r \leq 0.5 \times 30$

$F_r \leq 15$ N

$\mu = 0.5$ from question.

From the diagram, the only force that can accelerate the box *with* the truck is friction. If the frictional force cannot provide this accelerating force then the box will not be able to accelerate as fast as the truck. This will mean the box will slide off the back of the vehicle.

$a = 6 \text{ m s}^{-2}$

Applying $F = ma$ → ◀ ④ Apply $F = ma$.

$F_r = 3 \times 6 = 18$ N

$F_r \neq 18$ N so the box will slide off the truck.

For this truck, the maximum value that friction can take is 15 N. The value of 15 N is obtained from the inequality $F_r \leq 15$ N above.

Example 4

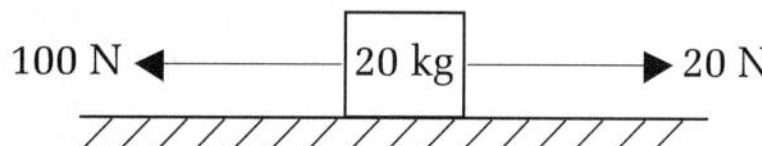

Find the value of the coefficient of friction for the mass in the diagram.

Solution

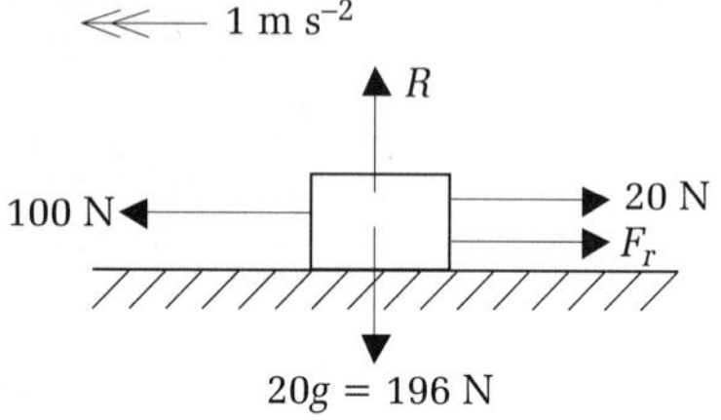

◀ ① Diagram.

weight = $20g$
weight = 20×9.8
weight = 196 N

Resolving ↑ ◀ ② Resolve vertically.

$R - 196 = 0$

$R = 196$ N [1]

Applying $F = ma$ ← ◀ ④ Apply $F = ma$.

Arrow refers to direction of motion on the diagram.

$100 - 20 - F_r = 20 \times 1$

$100 - 20 - F_r = 20$

$60 = F_r$

$F_r = 60$ N [2]

Using $F_r \leq \mu R$, ◀ ③ Use $F_r \leq \mu R$.

$F_r = \mu R$

$60 = \mu \times 196$

$\mu = \frac{60}{196}$

$\mu = \frac{15}{49}$

The question asks for μ so $F_r \leq \mu R$ is used last. Since 20 kg is moving, $F_r = \mu R$. Use [1] and [2] to replace F_r and R.

9.1 Friction on a Horizontal Plane

Exercise

Technique

1 Draw a clear force diagram for each of the following situations:

a A mass of 4 kg resting on a rough horizontal plane.

b A mass of 10 kg being pulled by a force P across a rough horizontal surface. The mass is being accelerated at $3\ \text{m s}^{-2}$.

c A mass of 5 kg being pulled by a force P across a rough horizontal surface. The mass is travelling at a constant velocity of $2\ \text{m s}^{-1}$.

2

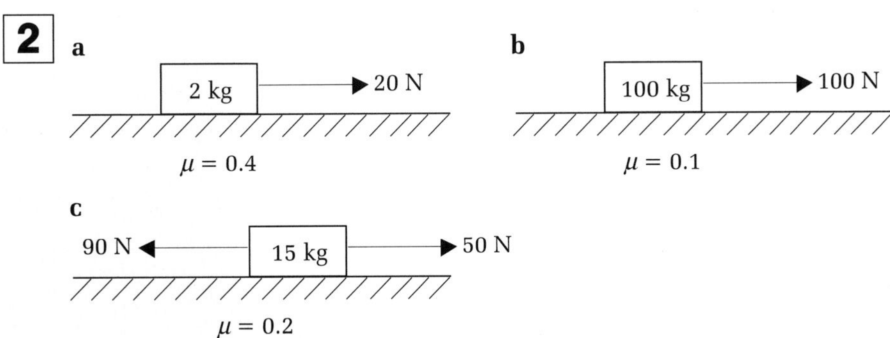

State whether the mass will remain at rest, will be in limiting equilibrium or will accelerate. Taking $g = 10\ \text{m s}^{-2}$, find the value of the frictional force.

3

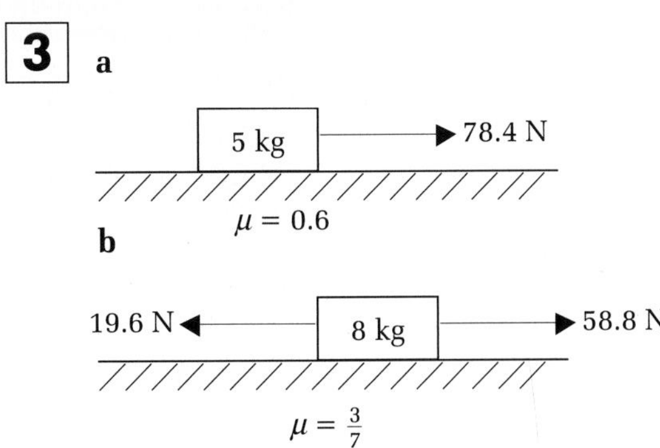

Work out the acceleration of the masses shown.

4

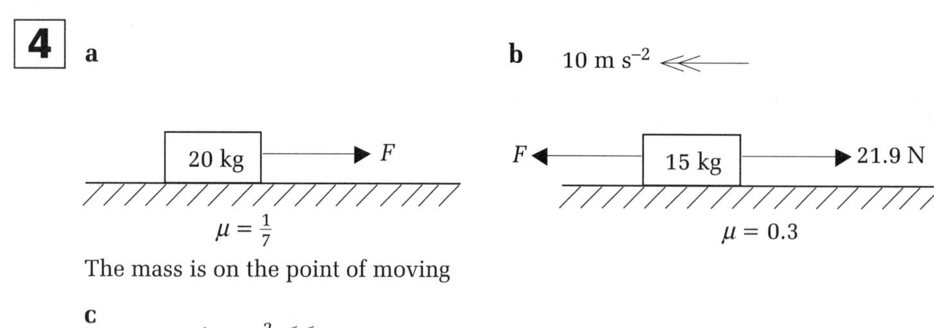

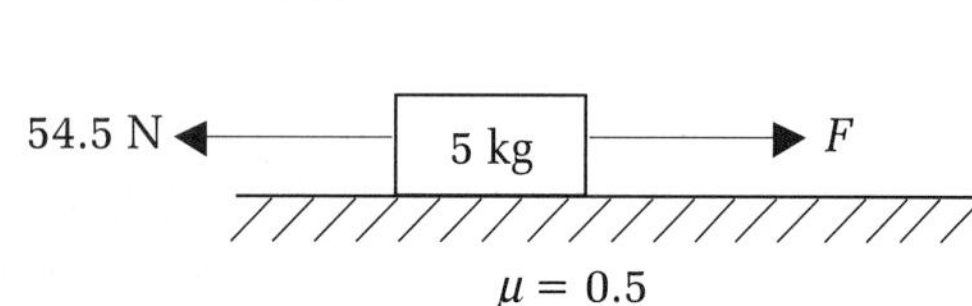

Find the force labelled F in the diagrams.

5

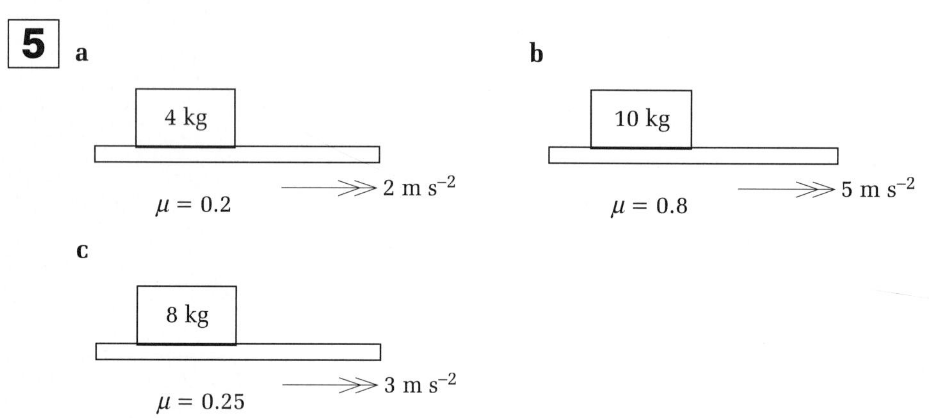

State whether the objects will remain on the surface or slide off. Give the value of the frictional force in each case. Take $g = 10\,\text{m}\,\text{s}^{-2}$ for this question.

6

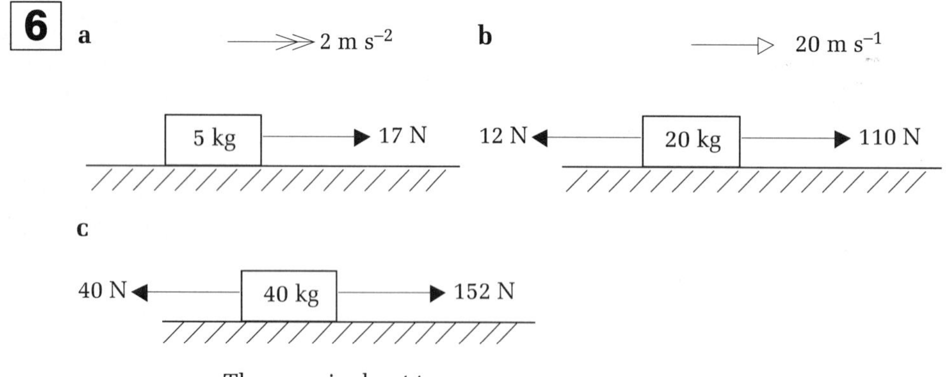

Determine the value of the coefficient of friction for the situations shown. Give your answers as fractions.

7 A mass of 12 kg is pulled along a rough horizontal surface at a steady velocity. The coefficient of friction between the surface and the mass is 0.2. Taking $g = 10\,\text{m}\,\text{s}^{-2}$, calculate the value of the horizontal force pulling the mass.

8 An object of weight $5W$ newtons is placed on a rough horizontal surface. A force of $4W$ newtons is applied to the object horizontally. The object is just on the point of moving. Show that the coefficient of friction between the object and the surface is $\frac{4}{5}$.

Contextual

1 A sledge of mass 120 kg is pulled across the snow by a team of huskies. The surface is horizontal and the coefficient of friction between the sledge and the snow is 0.2. Taking $g = 10\,\text{m}\,\text{s}^{-2}$, calculate the force the dogs must produce to:

a pull the sledge at a constant velocity
b accelerate the sledge at $0.7\,\text{m}\,\text{s}^{-2}$.

2 A car of mass 1200 kg brakes sharply and skids along a straight horizontal road. The coefficient of friction between the tyres and the road is $\frac{13}{14}$. Find:

a the value of the frictional force
b the deceleration of the car.

3 A lorry of mass 5760 kg brakes sharply and skids along a horizontal road. The deceleration of the lorry is $7\,\text{m}\,\text{s}^{-2}$. Taking $g = 10\,\text{m}\,\text{s}^{-2}$, calculate:

a the frictional force
b the coefficient of friction between the tyres and the road.

4 A maths teacher leaves his briefcase on top of his car. The mass of the briefcase is 4 kg since it contains a set of exercise books. The coefficient of friction between the briefcase and the roof of his car is $\frac{3}{14}$. What happens if he accelerates at:

a $1.8\,\text{m}\,\text{s}^{-2}$ **b** $2\,\text{m}\,\text{s}^{-2}$ **c** $2.1\,\text{m}\,\text{s}^{-2}$ **d** $2.2\,\text{m}\,\text{s}^{-2}$?

9.2 Friction and Inclined Forces

When a heavy trunk is pulled across the floor by a person, the applied force is probably not going to be horizontal. Is it easier to pull the trunk with a horizontal or an inclined force? By looking at the mathematics this situation can be modelled. At present, there are too many unknown quantities. The mass of the trunk, coefficient of friction and the angle at which the trunk is being pulled are not known. To be able to complete a calculation, some assumptions need to be made. These assumptions are:

- $\mu = 0.6$ (a typical value for a carpeted floor)
- the force is applied at an angle of 25° above the horizontal
- mass of the trunk equals M kg
- the trunk will be on the point of moving; it is in limiting equilibrium.

This will give a general result for any mass.

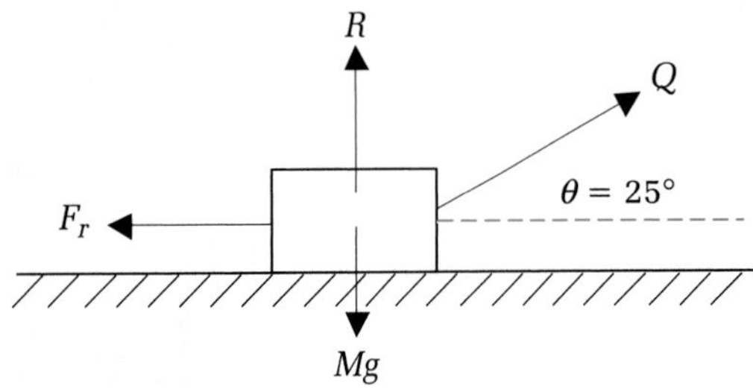

Resolving ↑

$$R + Q\sin 25^\circ - Mg = 0$$

sin is not with the angle.

$$R + 0.423Q - Mg = 0$$

Add Mg.

$$R = Mg - 0.423Q$$

Subtract $0.423Q$.

Applying $F_r \leq \mu R$

$$F_r = \mu R$$
$$F_r = 0.6R$$
$$F_r = 0.6(Mg - 0.423Q)$$

Use $R = Mg - 0.423Q$

Resolving →

$$Q\cos 25^\circ - F_r = 0$$

cos is with the angle.

$$0.906Q = F_r$$

Replace F_r.

$$0.906Q = 0.6(Mg - 0.423Q)$$

Expand the brackets.

$$0.906Q = 0.6Mg - 0.254Q$$

Add $0.254Q$.

$$0.906Q + 0.254Q = 0.6Mg$$
$$1.160Q = 0.6Mg$$

Divide by 1.160.

$$Q = \frac{0.6Mg}{1.160}$$
$$Q = 0.52Mg$$

The analysis is complicated because the force Q affects the reaction force R. For a horizontal force, $Q = 0.6Mg$. This is larger so it is easier to pull at an angle.

Overview of method

Step ① Draw a clear force diagram.
Step ② Resolve the forces vertically to find R or an expression for R.
Step ③ Use $F_r \leq \mu R$.
Step ④ Apply $F = ma$ horizontally.

Example

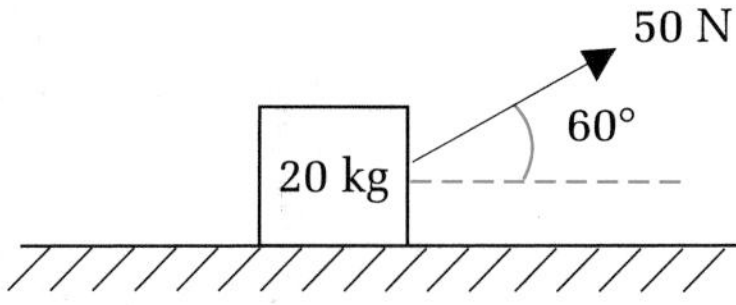

The coefficient of friction between the mass and the surface is 0.8. Taking $g = 10\ \text{m s}^{-2}$, find the value of the frictional force.

Solution

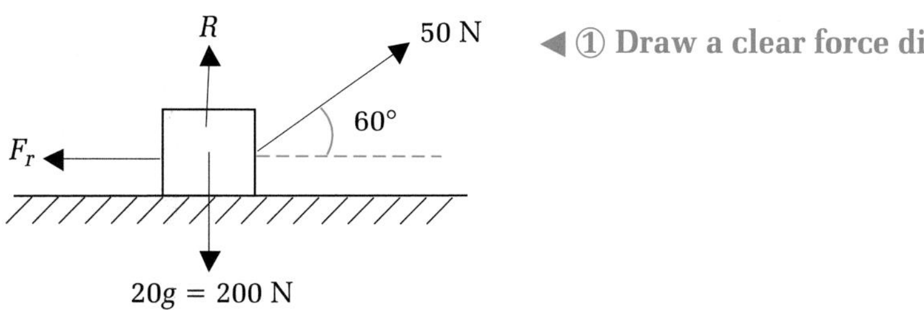

◀ ① Draw a clear force diagram.

Resolving ↑ ◀ ② Resolve the forces vertically to find R.

$$R + 50\sin 60° - 200 = 0$$
$$R = 200 - 50\sin 60°$$
$$R = 157 \text{ N (3 s.f.)}$$

Add 200, subtract 50sin 60°.

Store value for R in the calculator.

Using $F_r \leq \mu R$, ◀ ③ Use $F_r \leq \mu R$.

$$F_r \leq 0.8 \times 157$$
$$F_r \leq 125 \text{ N (3 s.f.)}$$

Use stored value for R from calculator.

Applying $F = ma$ → ◀ ④ Apply $F = ma$ horizontally.

$$50\cos 60° - F_r = 50 \times 0$$
$$25 - F_r = 0$$
$$F_r = 25 \text{ N}$$

Assume mass is at rest. This means the acceleration must be 0.

F_r can equal 25 N and so the mass will remain at rest. $F_r = 25$ N.

9.2 Friction and Inclined Forces

Exercise

Technique

1 Draw a clear force diagram for each of the following situations.

a A mass of 7 kg resting on a rough horizontal plane. A force of 20 N acts on the mass at an angle of 10° above the horizontal.

b A mass of 13 kg being pulled by a force P across a rough horizontal surface. The force P acts at 5° below the horizontal and accelerates the mass at 3 m s^{-2}.

c A mass of 3 kg being pulled across a rough horizontal surface by a force X. The force X acts at 25° above the horizontal. The mass is travelling at a constant velocity of 2 m s^{-1}.

2

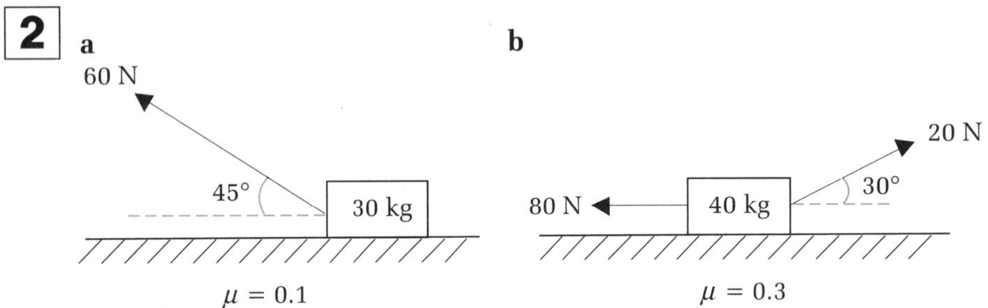

State whether the mass will remain at rest, be in limiting equilibrium or will accelerate. Take $g = 10$ m s^{-2} and find the value of the frictional force in surd form.

3

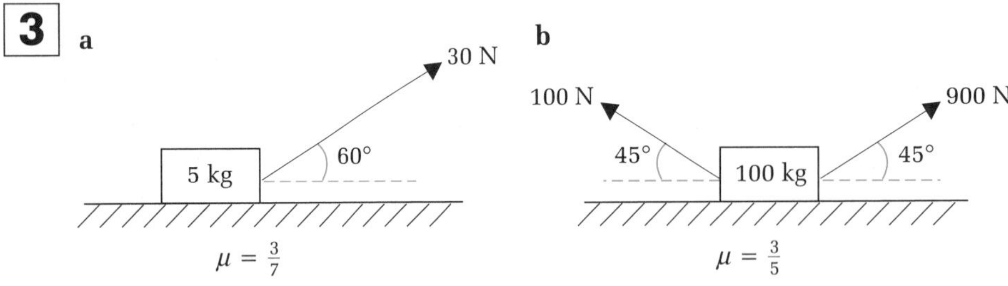

Work out the acceleration of the masses.

4

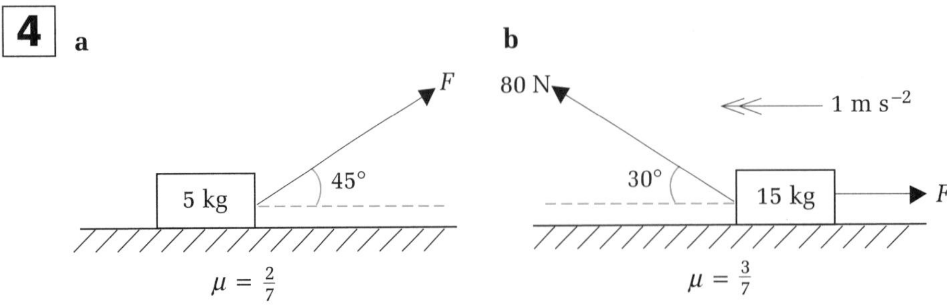

The mass is in limiting equilibrium

Find the force labelled F in the given situations.

5

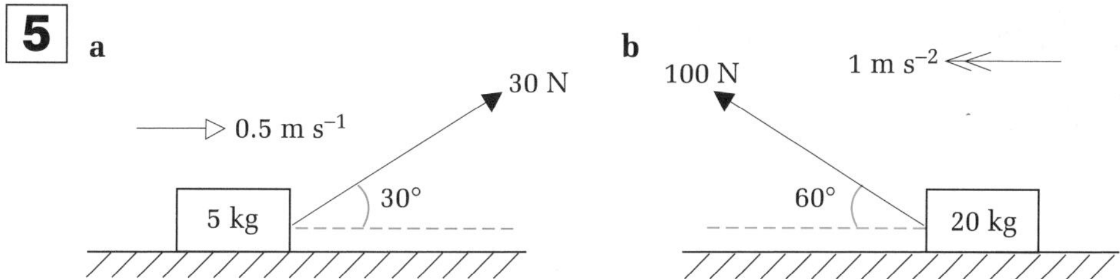

Calculate the value of the coefficient of friction for the situations illustrated.

6 A particle of mass M kg is placed on a rough horizontal plane. The coefficient of friction between the mass and the plane is μ. A force is applied to the particle at an angle of θ above the horizontal. The particle is in limiting equilibrium.

a Draw a clear force diagram for this situation.

b Show that the applied force must be $\dfrac{\mu Mg}{\cos\theta + \mu\sin\theta}$

Contextual

1 A woman pulls a trunk of mass 20 kg along a horizontal floor. The coefficient of friction between the trunk and the floor is $\frac{3}{7}$. Leaving your answers in terms of g, find the value of:

a the horizontal force necessary to move the trunk at constant speed

b the force necessary to move the trunk at constant speed if applied at 30° above the horizontal.

2 A horse pulls a sledge along a horizontal snow field. The horse and sledge move at constant speed. The horse pulls the sledge with a force of 200 N at an angle θ above the horizontal where $\theta = \sin^{-1}\frac{3}{5}$. The sledge has a mass of 80 kg. Show that the coefficient of friction between the sledge and the snow is $\frac{20}{83}$.

$\theta = \arcsin\frac{3}{5}$

9.3 Rough, Inclined Planes

Place a book on a table. Slowly lift one edge of the table to make an inclined plane. At first the book stays still. If the angle is increased then there comes a point when the book begins to move down the plane. Why does this happen? The diagrams show the weight resolved into two perpendicular directions. The directions are parallel and perpendicular (at right angles) to the plane.

Recall that the symbol for parallel is // and the symbol for perpendicular is ⊾.

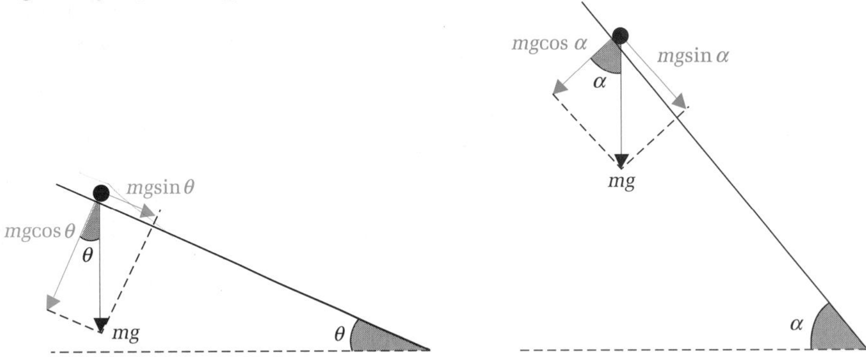

As the angle of inclination is increased you can see that:

- the weight component *parallel* to the plane has *increased*
- the weight component *perpendicular* to the plane has *decreased*.

This means that the *force acting down* the plane has *increased*. At the same time the *reaction force* has *decreased*. This has the effect of *decreasing* the maximum possible value of the *frictional force*. There must then come a point when the weight component down the table is greater than the frictional force. This will cause the book to move.

Overview of method

Step ① Draw a clear force diagram.
Step ② Resolve the forces *perpendicular* to the plane to find R.
Step ③ Use $F_r \leq \mu R$.
Step ④ Apply $F = ma$ *parallel* to the plane, or resolve *parallel* to the plane if the object is stationary.

Example 1

A book of mass 0.5 kg is placed on a slope inclined at 30° to the horizontal. If the book is just on the point of moving down the slope, calculate the value of the coefficient of friction.

Solution

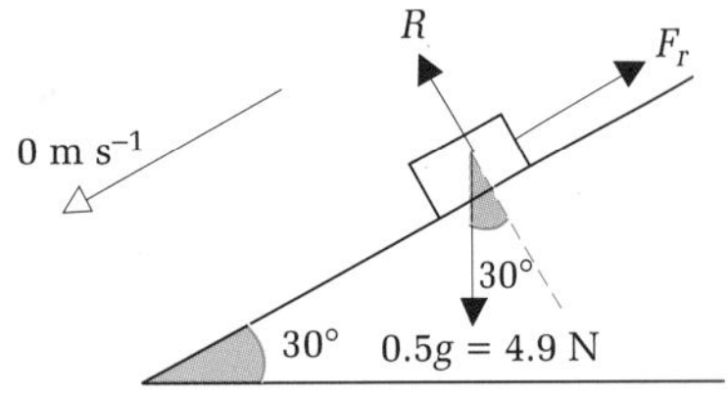

◀ ① Draw a clear force diagram.

Notice that R is perpendicular to the plane and F_r acts up the plane to prevent motion.

Resolving ⊥ to the plane ↖ ◀ ② **Resolve perpendicular to the plane to find R.**

The arrow shows the direction for resolving the forces.

$R - 4.9\cos 30^\circ = 0$

$R = 4.9\cos 30^\circ$ Use trigonometry to resolve.

$R = 4.24$ N (3 s.f.) Store this value for R.

Using $F_r \le \mu R$, ◀ ③ **Use $F_r \le \mu R$.**

$F_r = \mu R$ Since the book is in limiting equilibrium.

$F_r = 4.24\mu$ Use $R = 4.24$ N.

Resolving // to the plane ↙ ◀ ④ **Resolve // to the plane because the object is stationary.**

$4.9\sin 30^\circ - F_r = 0$ Weight resolved // to the plane will be $mg\sin\theta$.

$2.45 - 4.24\mu = 0$ Use $F_r = 4.24\mu$.

$2.45 = 4.24\mu$ Add 4.24μ.

$\mu = \frac{2.45}{4.24}$ Divide by 4.24.

$\mu = 0.577$ (3 s.f.)

Example 2

A mass of 10 kg is pushed *up* a slope at 45° to the horizontal. The acceleration of the mass is 2 m s^{-2} and the coefficient of friction is 0.7. Taking $g = 10\text{ m s}^{-2}$, calculate the value of the applied force if the force is horizontal.

Solution

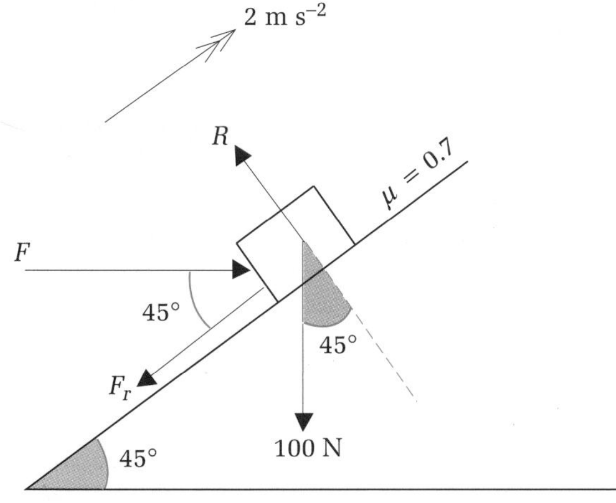

A component of F will affect the reaction R.

Resolving ⊥ to the plane ↖

$R - 100\cos 45^\circ - F\sin 45^\circ = 0$

$R - 100\frac{\sqrt{2}}{2} - F \times \frac{\sqrt{2}}{2} = 0$

$R - 50\sqrt{2} - \frac{\sqrt{2}}{2}F = 0$

$R = 50\sqrt{2} + \frac{\sqrt{2}}{2}F$

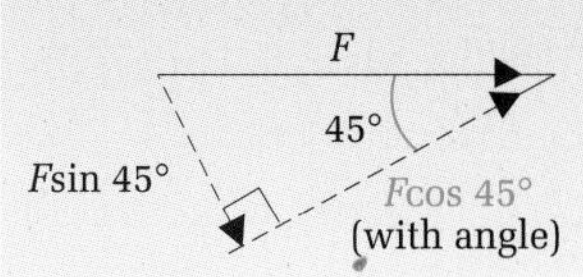

$100\cos 45^\circ = 50\sqrt{2}$

Using $F_r = \mu R$, ◀ ③ Use $F_r = \mu R$.

Since the mass is moving, friction takes on its maximum value.

$$F_r = 0.7(50\sqrt{2} + \tfrac{\sqrt{2}}{2}F)$$

Apply $F = ma$ // to the plane ↗ ◀ ④ Apply $F = ma$.

$$F\cos 45° - F_r - 100\sin 45° = 10 \times 2$$

$$F\tfrac{\sqrt{2}}{2} - 0.7(50\sqrt{2} + \tfrac{\sqrt{2}}{2}F) - 50\sqrt{2} = 20$$

$$0.7071F - 0.7(70.71 + 0.7071F) - 70.71 = 20$$

Multiply out brackets.

$$0.7071F - 49.50 - 0.4950F - 70.71 = 20$$

Simplify by collecting like terms.

$$F(0.7071 - 0.4950) = 20 + 70.71 + 49.5$$

$$0.2121F = 140.21$$

Divide by 0.2121.

$$F = 661 \text{ N (3 s.f.)}$$

In the following exercises assume that any motion takes place *in the plane of the slope*. This means that the motion is straight up or down the slope. The diagrams explain what is meant by moving in the plane of the slope.

This wording is commonly used in examination questions.

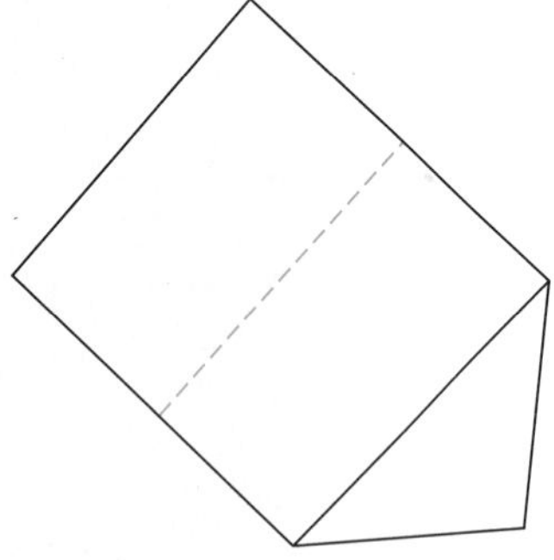

In the plane of the slope

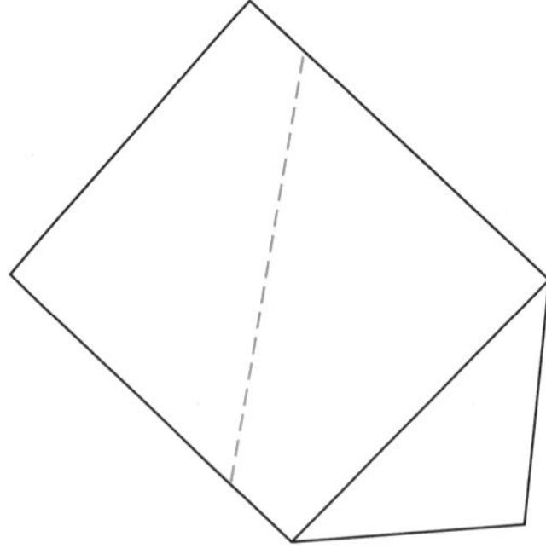

Not in the plane of the slope

Another statement meaning exactly the same is *moving along the line of greatest slope*. If the diagrams represented a mountain side, the most difficult route would be in the plane of the slope. This is also the largest angle up the slope. The line not in the plane of the slope is an easier route to climb because the angle is not as large and so the route must not be as steep. If the motion was not in the plane of the slope the problem would become three dimensional. This would be much more difficult to solve.

9.3 Rough, Inclined Planes

Exercise

Technique

1 **a**

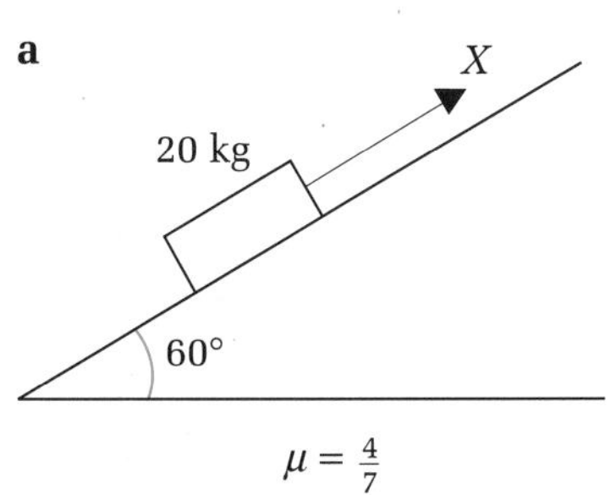

b

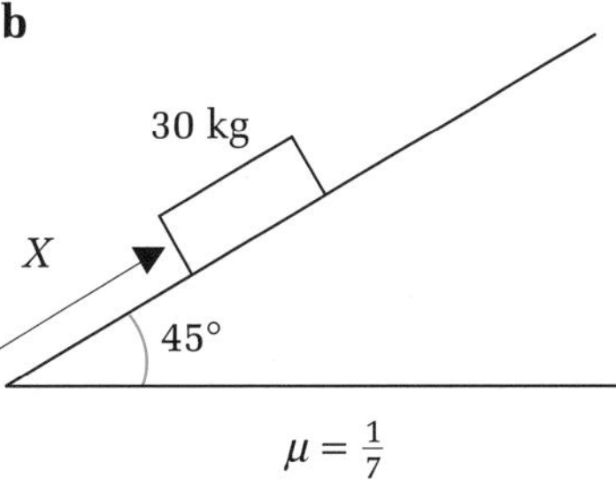

Work out the value of the force X so that motion down the plane is just prevented. Give your answer in surd form.

2 **a**

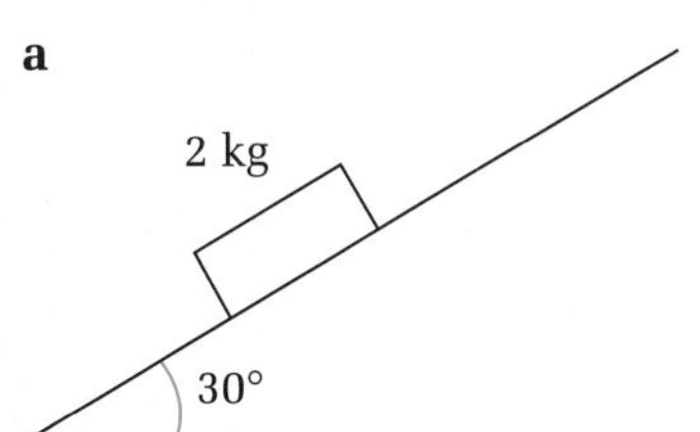

b

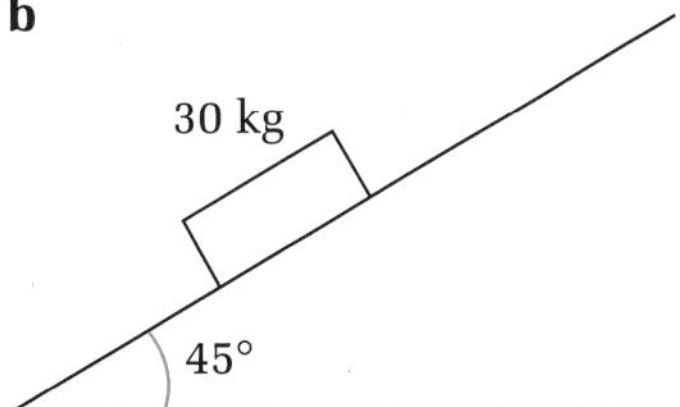

Taking $g = 10\,\text{m}\,\text{s}^{-2}$, calculate the value of the coefficient of friction if the masses are just about to slip down the plane.

3 **a**

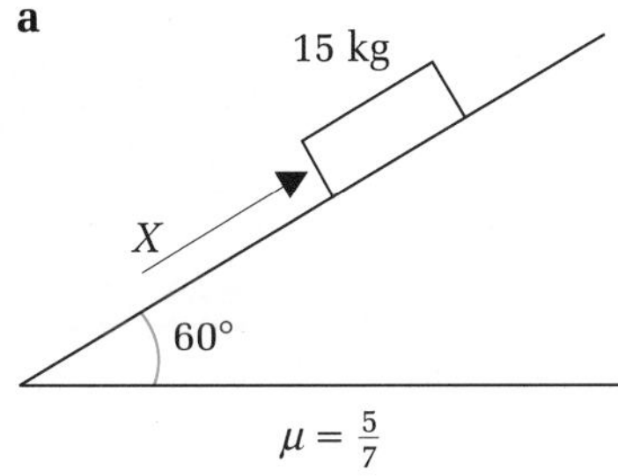

b

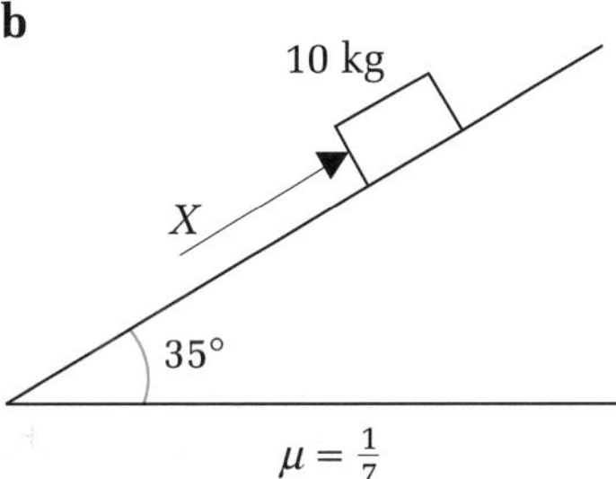

Find the value of the force X if the mass is just on the point of moving *up* the plane.

4 **a**

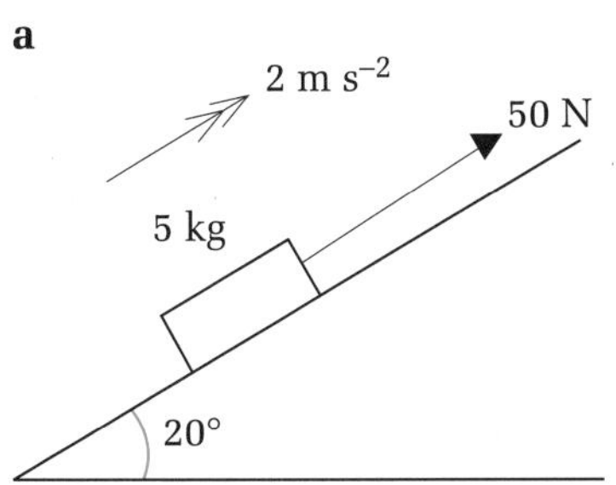

b

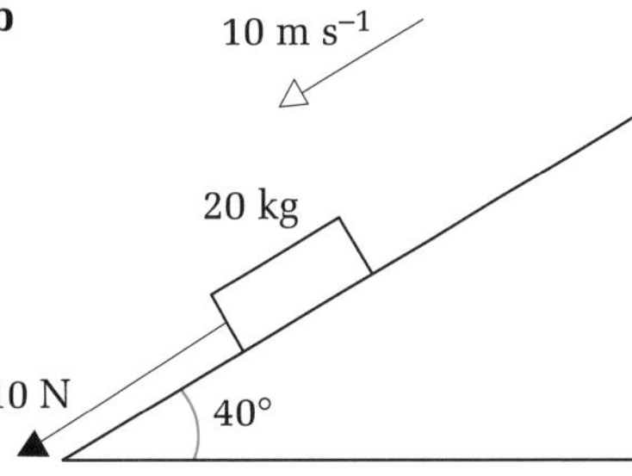

Determine the value of the coefficient of friction between the mass and the plane.

5

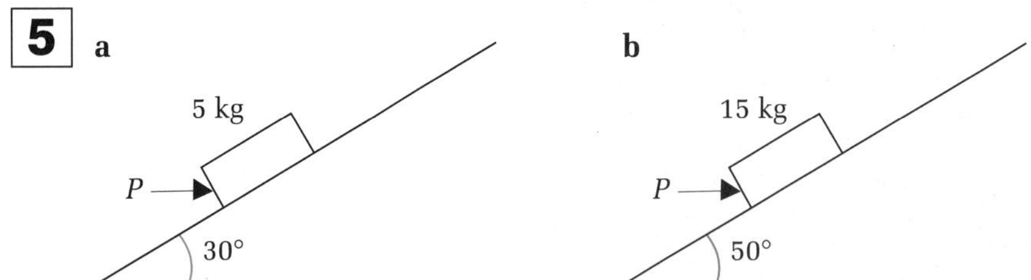

Find the value of the horizontal force P if the mass is just prevented from slipping down the plane. The coefficient of friction between the mass and the inclined plane is $\frac{3}{7}$.

6 A particle of mass m kg is placed on a rough slope inclined at $\theta°$ to the horizontal. The coefficient of friction for the slope is μ. A force parallel to the slope is applied to the particle. This force just prevents the particle from sliding down the plane. Show that the applied force is:

$$mg\sin\theta - \mu mg\cos\theta.$$

Contextual

1 A girl slides down a snow covered slope on a sledge. The girl and the sledge weigh 40 kg in total. The angle of the slope to the horizontal is 10°. The coefficient of friction between the sledge and the snow is 0.1. Find the acceleration of the girl.

2 A boy weighs 30 kg. He is just on the point of moving down a slope on his skis. The slope is inclined at 5° to the horizontal. Taking $g = 10\,\text{m}\,\text{s}^{-2}$, work out the value of the coefficient of friction between his skis and the snow.

3 A woman of mass 60 kg uses a ski lift to go up a slope inclined at 8° to the horizontal. The force of the ski lift acts parallel to the slope and she is pulled up at constant speed. The coefficient of friction is $\frac{2}{7}$. Determine the value of the force exerted by the ski lift on the woman.

9.4 Connected Particles

A roller coaster could use a connected particle system to accelerate the cars. In Chapter 8, you learned how to analyse such a connected particle system. This analysis used a simplified model, and friction was omitted. A better model for a connected particle system would include friction.

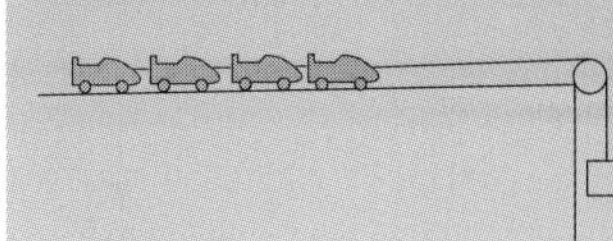

In the following examples and exercises assume that:

- the strings are light and inextensible
- the pulleys are smooth and fixed
- the strings are taut when the system is released
- the masses, pulleys and strings all lie in the same vertical plane
- the strings are parallel to the line of greatest slope for inclined planes.

Wording like this is commonly used in examination questions.

These assumptions keep the motion in two dimensions and make sure that the tensions act parallel to the plane. The light strings mean their mass will not affect the calculations.

Overview of method

Step ① Draw a clear diagram.
Step ② Resolve perpendicular to the rough surface.
Step ③ Use $F_r \leq \mu R$ to find the frictional force.
Step ④ Apply $F = ma$ to each particle.

Steps ③ and ④ can be swapped. This will depend on whether the coefficient of friction is given in the question or is asked to be found.

Example 1

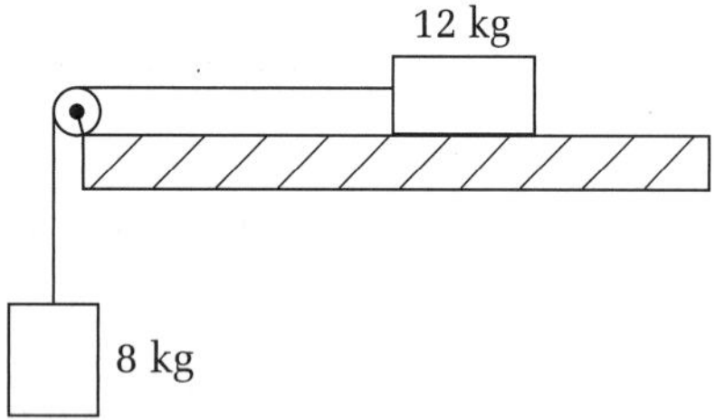

The coefficient of friction is 0.7. Taking $g = 10\,\text{m s}^{-2}$, find the frictional force experienced by the mass on the table. The pulley can be assumed to be smooth and fixed.

Solution

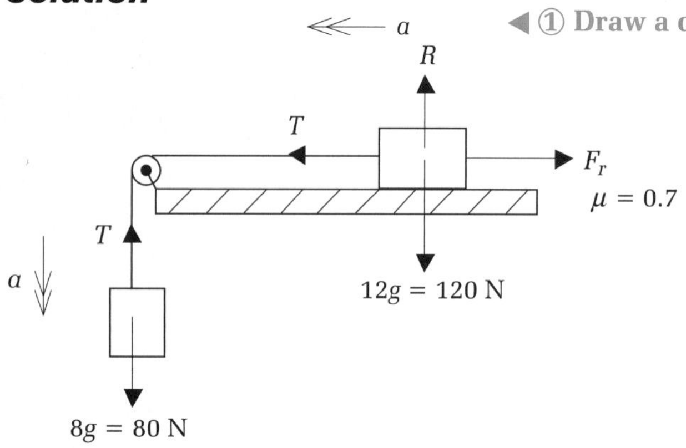

◀ ① Draw a clear diagram.

Assume the acceleration is to the left ⇒ friction is to the right.
Mark on the tensions in the strings. Remember, tension acts inwards.

Resolving ↑ ◀ ② Resolve perpendicular to the rough surface.

$R = 120$ N

Applying $F_r \leq \mu R$, ◀ ③ Use $F_r \leq \mu R$.

$F_r \leq 0.7 \times 120$
$F_r \leq 84$ N

Assume that the masses *do* move.

Applying $F = ma$ to both particles, ◀ ④ Apply $F = ma$ to each particle.

8 kg ↓ $80 - T = 8a$ [1]
12 kg ← $T - F_r = 12a$ [2]

The direction arrows apply to the diagram.

Adding equations [1] and [2],

$$80 - F_r = 8a + 12a$$
$$80 - F_r = 20a \qquad [3]$$

By *adding* the equations the tensions are eliminated (cancelled).

But $F_r = 84$ N if the masses accelerate.

$$80 - 84 = 20a$$
$$-4 = 20a$$
$$a = -\tfrac{1}{5}\,\text{m s}^{-2}$$

Replace F_r in equation [3] with 84.

The acceleration works out to be negative. This means that friction would be pulling the masses. This cannot happen; friction must always oppose motion. Therefore the mass must remain at rest.

Friction must oppose motion – it cannot cause motion.
System at rest $\Rightarrow a = 0$.

Using equation [3] to find F_r

$$80 - F_r = 20a$$
$$80 - F_r = 0$$
$$F_r = 80\text{ N}$$

Use $a = 0\,\text{m s}^{-2}$.

Example 2

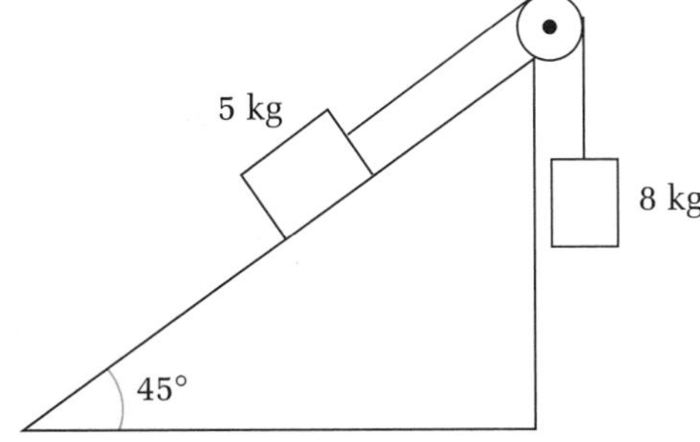

The coefficient of friction is 0.5. Taking $g = 10\,\text{m s}^{-2}$, find the acceleration of this system.

Solution

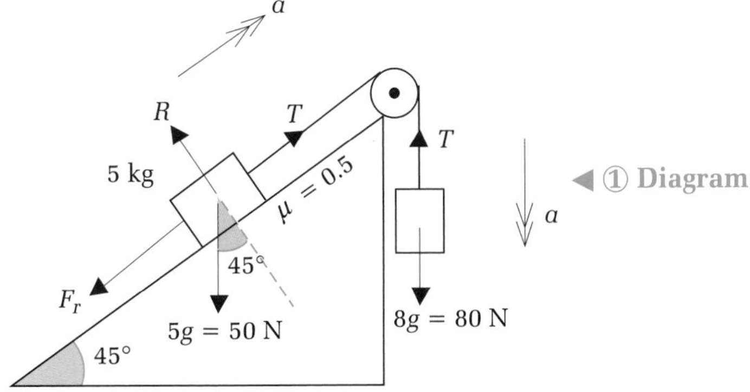

◀ ① Diagram.

Resolving ⊥ to the plane ↖ ◀ ② **Resolve.**

Recall that ⊥ means perpendicular (at right angles).

$$R - 50\cos 45° = 0$$
$$R = 50\cos 45°$$
$$R = 50\tfrac{\sqrt{2}}{2}$$
$$R = 25\sqrt{2}$$

$\cos 45° = \frac{\sqrt{2}}{2}$

Assume that the mass will move.

$$F_r = \mu R$$
$$F_r = 0.5 \times 25\sqrt{2}$$
$$F_r = 12.5\sqrt{2}\,\text{N}$$

◀ ③ **Apply $F \le \mu R$.**

In motion, friction must take its maximum value.

Applying $F = ma$, ◀ ④ **Apply $F = ma$ to each particle.**

8 kg ↓ $80 - T = 8a$ [1]

5 kg ↗ $T - 50\sin 45° - F_r = 5a$ [2]

Remember the weight component acting down the plane.

Adding equations [1] and [2],

$$80 - T + T - 50\sin 45° - F_r = 8a + 5a$$
$$80 - 50\tfrac{\sqrt{2}}{2} - 12.5\sqrt{2} = 13a$$
$$26.967 = 13a$$
$$a = 2.07\,\text{m}\,\text{s}^{-2}\ \text{(3 s.f.)}$$

By adding the equations T is eliminated.

$\sin 45° = \frac{\sqrt{2}}{2}$ and $F_r = 12.5\sqrt{2}$.

9.4 Connected Particles
Exercise

Technique

Assume the pulleys are smooth and rigid and the strings are light and inextensible.

Assume smooth pulleys.

1 **a**

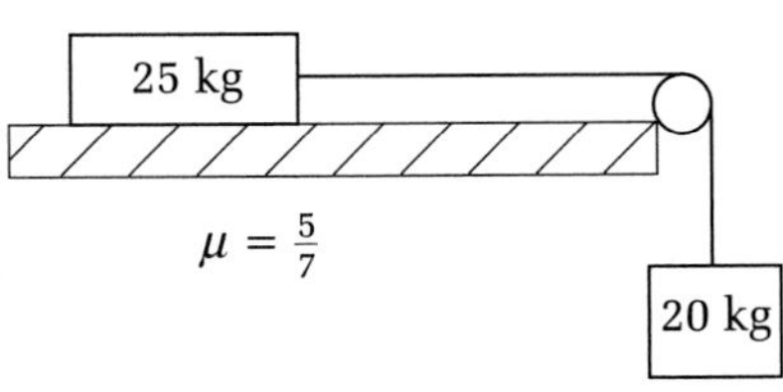

b

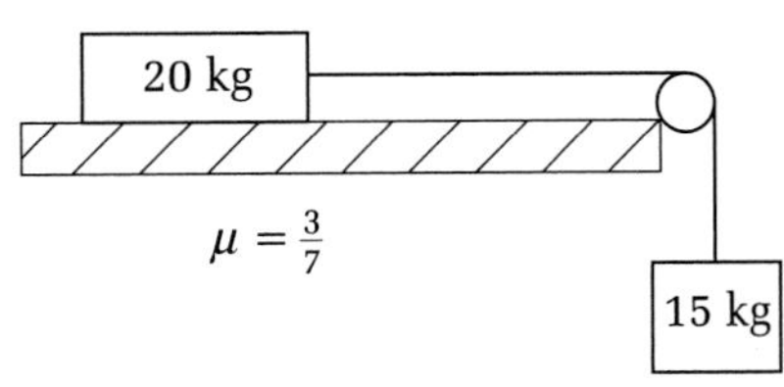

Calculate the acceleration of the masses in these systems.

2 **a**

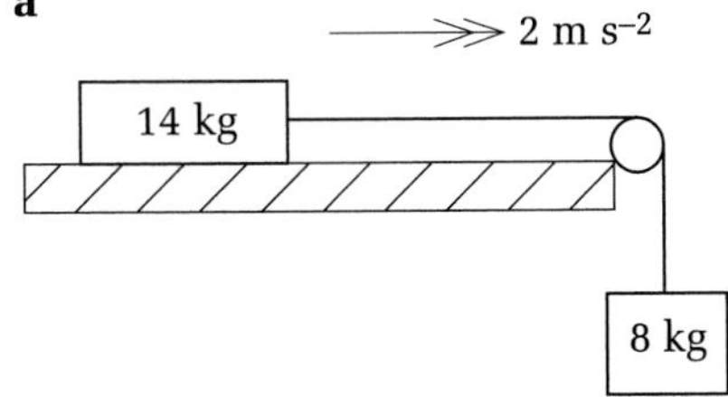

b

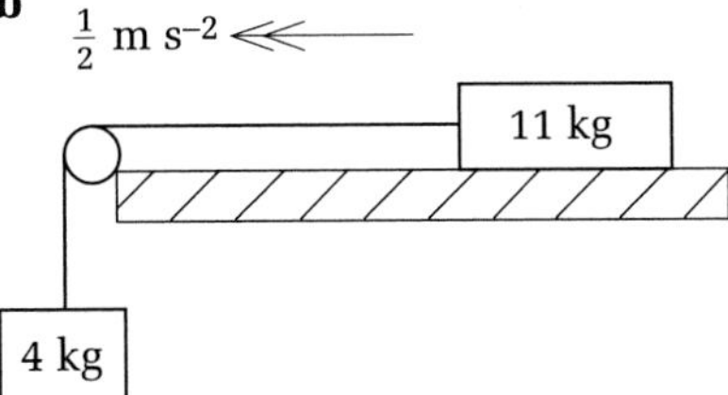

Taking $g = 10\text{ m s}^{-2}$, determine the value of the coefficient of friction between the mass and the table. Leave your answer as a fraction.

3 **a**

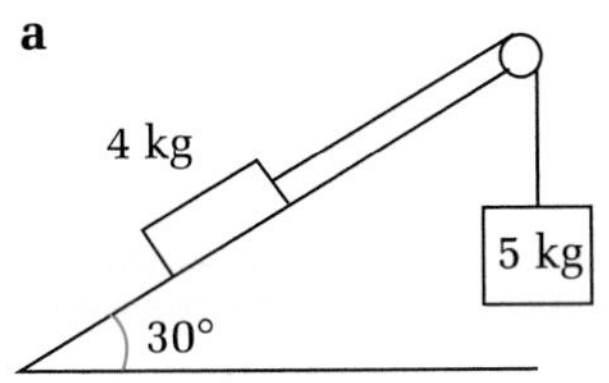

b

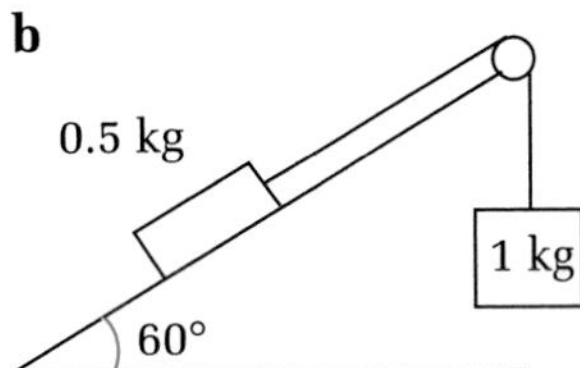

The coefficient of friction between the mass and the surface is 0.3. Taking $g = 10\text{ m s}^{-2}$ and leaving your answer in surd form, find the acceleration of these systems.

4

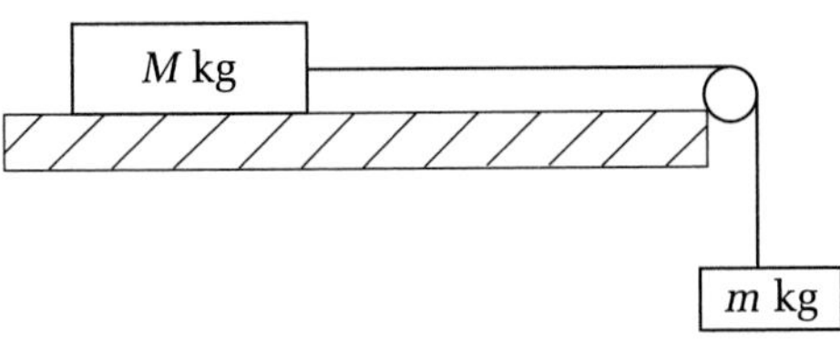

The coefficient of friction between the mass M and the table is μ. Show that the acceleration of the system is given by $\dfrac{g(m - \mu M)}{m + M}$.

9.5 Angle of Friction

Place a book on a table. Slowly lift one edge of the table to make an inclined plane. Continue lifting until the book is just about to move. The book is in **limiting equilibrium**. The angle of inclination of the table is called the **angle of friction**. This is the angle at which friction just prevents the book from moving.

Instead of resolving the weight, a different approach is to replace R and F_r with their resultant. This force is called the **resultant reaction**. R cannot be used to represent the resultant, so the next letter in the alphabet is S.

R is already used for the normal reaction.

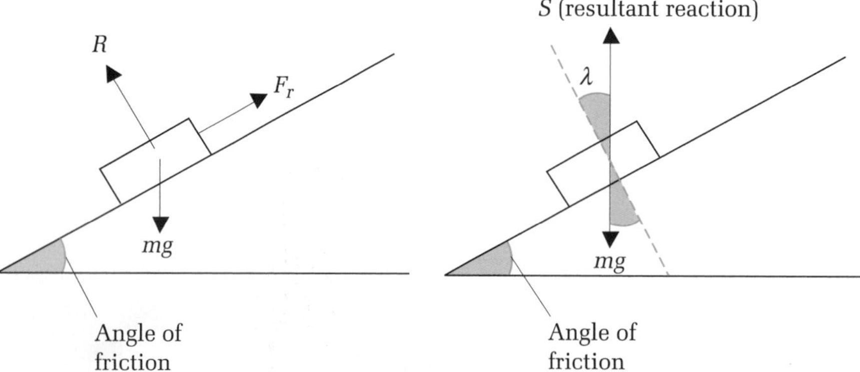

S and mg must be equal but in opposite directions to keep the object in equilibrium.

The *weight* and the *resultant reaction* must be *equal in size* but act in opposite directions. The angle λ and the angle of friction of the slope must be the same size. This means that the angle λ is also called the **angle of friction**.

Where has μ disappeared to? To show where μ has gone S needs to be resolved into two components. If directions parallel and perpendicular to the plane are chosen, these components must be equal to friction and the normal reaction.

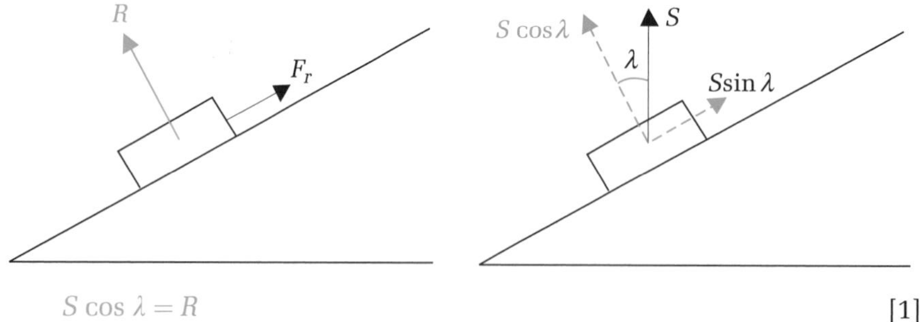

$S \cos \lambda = R$ [1]

$S \sin \lambda = F_r$

$S \sin \lambda = \mu R$ [2]

Resolve ⊥ to the plane.
Resolve // to the plane.

Use $F_r = \mu R$ because the book is in limiting equilibrium.

If equation [2] is divided by equation [1]:

$$\frac{S\sin\lambda}{S\cos\lambda} = \frac{\mu R}{R}$$

S cancels.

$$\frac{\sin\lambda}{\cos\lambda} = \mu$$

Recall that $\frac{\sin\lambda}{\cos\lambda} = \tan\lambda$.

$$\boldsymbol{\mu = \tan\lambda}$$

This shows that μ is related to λ and this formula can be used to convert between them.

Using the resultant reaction (S) is useful for reducing the number of forces by one. In particular, four force systems can be reduced to three force problems and so Lami's theorem or the triangle of forces can be applied. This is often quicker and easier than resolving.

The angle of friction can *only* be used when the object is:

- in limiting equilibrium *or*
- moving with constant velocity.

Overview of method

Step ① Draw a clear force diagram.
Step ② Draw a force diagram with the angles marked between each force.
Step ③ Apply Pythagoras and trigonometry, Lami's theorem or use the triangle of forces.

Example 1

Find the angle of friction if the coefficient of friction is $\frac{3}{7}$.

Solution

$$\mu = \tan\lambda$$
$$\tfrac{3}{7} = \tan\lambda$$
$$\lambda = \tan^{-1}\tfrac{3}{7}$$
$$\lambda = 23.2^\circ \text{ (1 d.p.)}$$

Recall that $\tan^{-1}\frac{3}{7} \equiv \arctan\frac{3}{7}$

Example 2

A sledge of mass 200 kg is pulled along a horizontal snow field by huskies. The sledge travels at constant speed and the applied force is 400 N. Find the angle of friction and the resultant reaction.

Solution

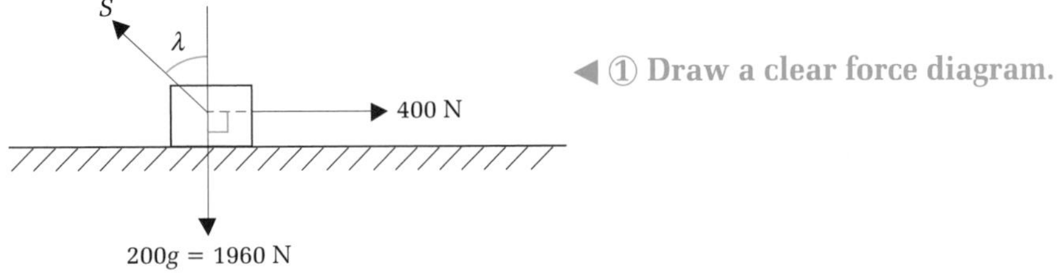

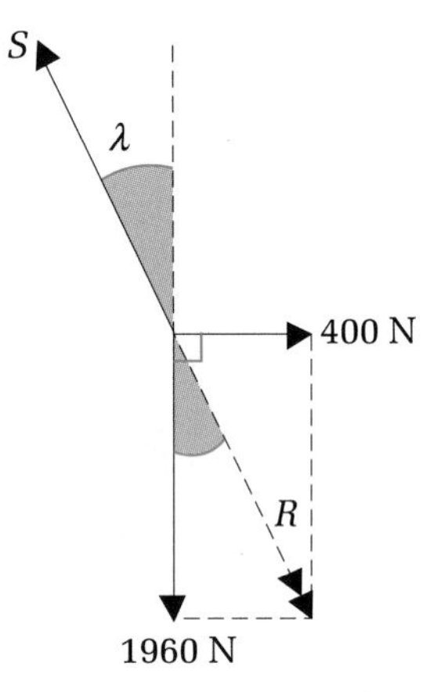

◀ ② **Work out all the angles you can.**

By finding the resultant of the 400 N and 1960 N forces, the system is reduced to two forces. This resultant must be equal but opposite to the reaction force S.

Using Pythagoras' theorem,

◀ ③ **Solve using Pythagoras' theorem because of the right angle.**

$$R^2 = 400^2 + 1960^2$$
$$R^2 = 4\,001\,600$$
$$R = 2000.4 \text{ N}$$

So $S = 2000$ N (3 s.f.).

Since the magnitudes of R and S must be equal.

(adjacent) 1960

R (hypotenuse)

λ

400 (opposite)

$$\tan \lambda = \tfrac{400}{1960}$$
$$\lambda = \tan^{-1} \tfrac{400}{1960}$$
$$\lambda = 11.5^\circ \text{ (1 d.p.)}$$

Use trigonometry to find the angle.
$\tan^{-1} \frac{400}{1960} \equiv \arctan \frac{400}{1960}$

An alternative method would be to use a triangle of forces.

Example 3

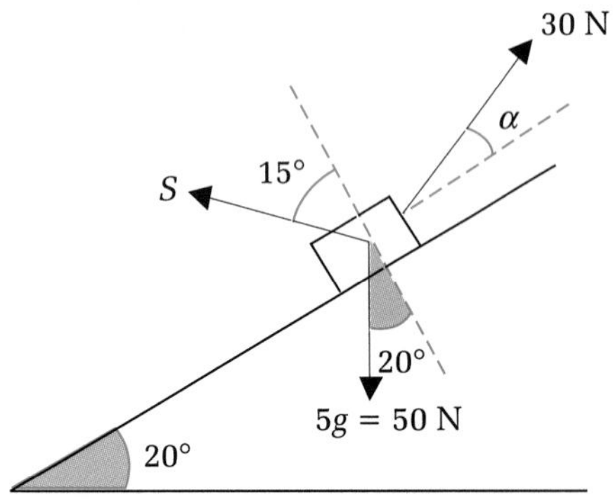

A mass of 5 kg is pulled at constant speed up a slope inclined at 20° to the horizontal. The angle of friction is 15° and the force pulling the mass up the slope is 30 N. Taking $g = 10\,\text{m}\,\text{s}^{-2}$, find the angle between the 30 N force and the slope and the resultant reaction.

Solution

① Draw a diagram. ▶

② Calculate all the angles between the forces. ▶

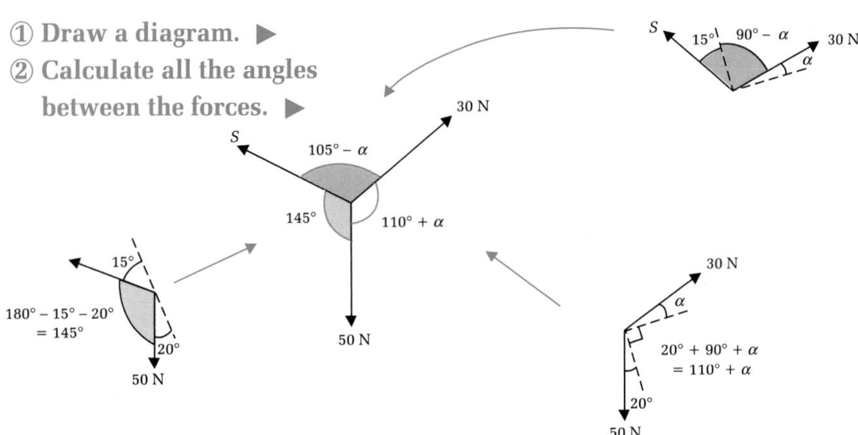

Applying Lami's theorem to find α, ◀ ③ Apply Lami's theorem.

$$\frac{\sin(105^\circ - \alpha)}{50} = \frac{\sin 145^\circ}{30}$$

$$\sin(105^\circ - \alpha) = \frac{\sin 145^\circ}{30} \times 50$$

$$\sin(105^\circ - \alpha) = 0.956$$

$$105^\circ - \alpha = 72.9^\circ$$

$$105^\circ - 72.9^\circ = \alpha$$

$$\alpha = 32.1^\circ \text{ (1 d.p.)}$$

Applying Lami's theorem to find S ◀ ③ Use Lami's theorem.

$$\frac{S}{\sin(110^\circ + \alpha)} = \frac{30}{\sin 145^\circ}$$

$$S = \frac{30}{\sin 145^\circ} \times \sin(110^\circ + \alpha)$$

Use $\alpha = 32.1^\circ$, $S = 32.2$ N

When finding an unknown angle, write the angles on the numerator (the top of the fraction).

When finding the forces, write the forces on the numerator.

9.5 Angle of Friction
Exercise

Technique

1 Find the angle of friction if the coefficient of friction is:

a 0.5 **b** $\frac{1}{7}$ **c** $\frac{1}{\sqrt{3}}$

2 Determine the coefficient of friction if the angle of friction is:

a 20° **b** 15° **c** 60°

3 **a**

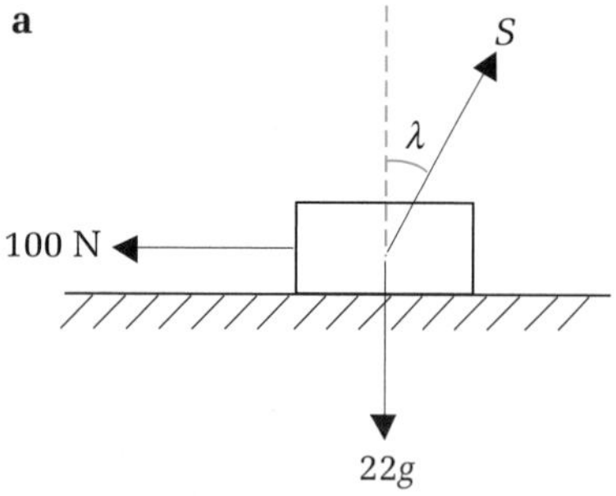

b

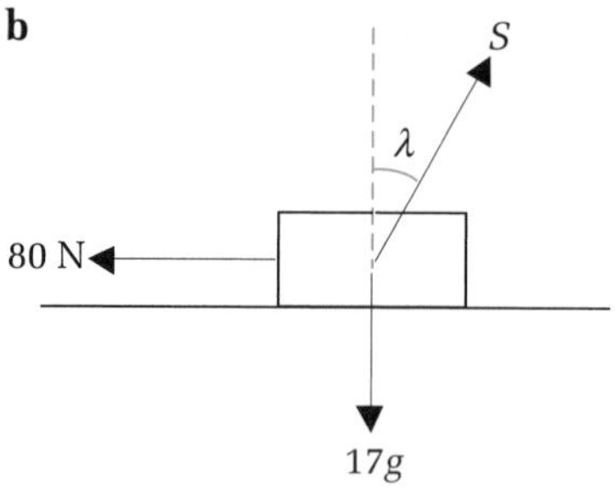

Taking $g = 10\ \text{m s}^{-2}$, work out the magnitude of S and λ if the masses are just about to move.

4 **a**

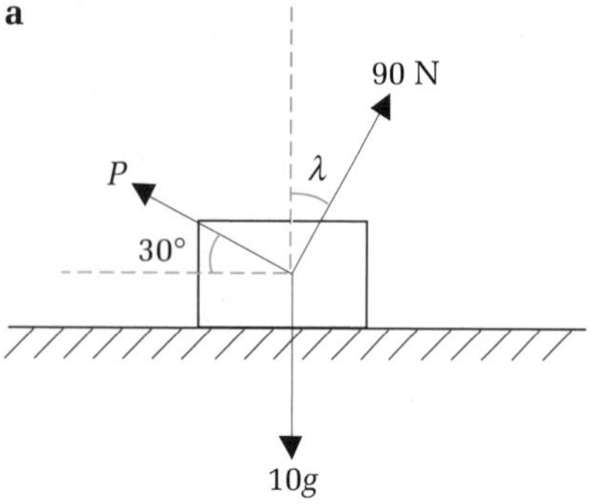

b

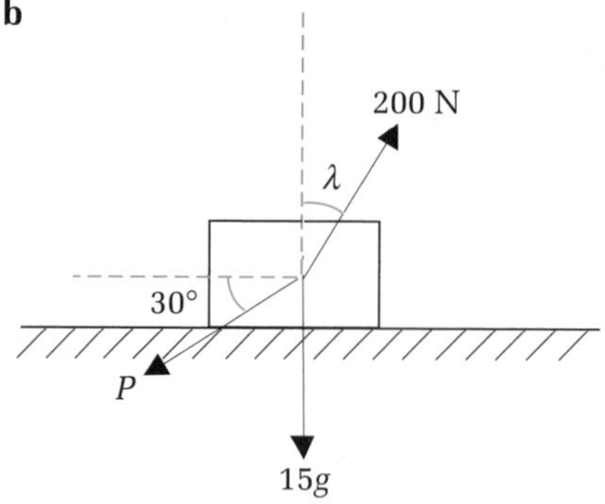

The masses are just about to move. Use Lami's theorem to find λ and P.

5 **a**

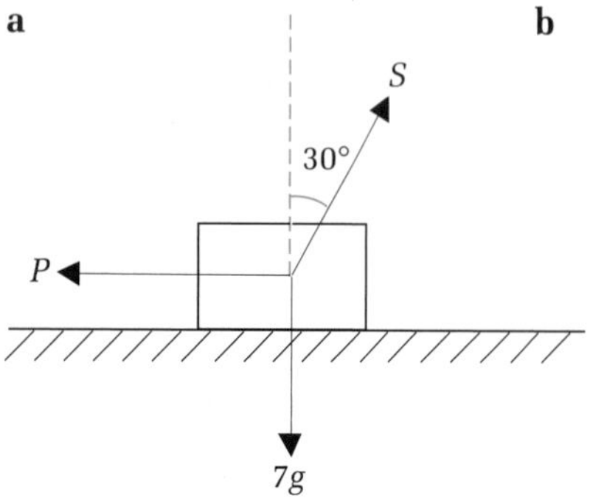

b

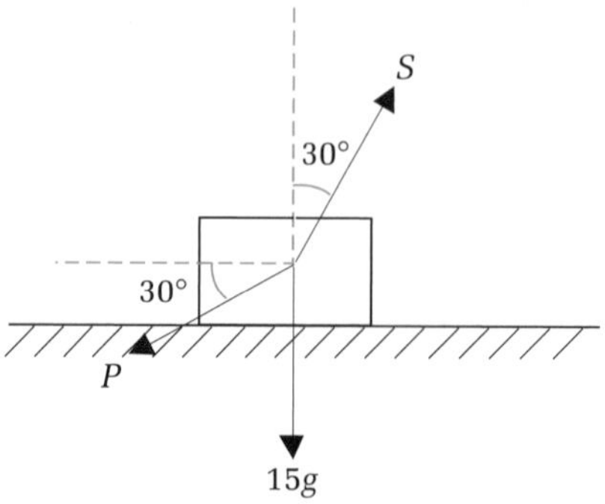

The masses are just on the point of moving. The angle of friction is 30° for each surface. Taking $g = 10\ \text{m s}^{-2}$, calculate the value of P and S.

6 A mass of 15 kg rests in limiting equilibrium on a rough horizontal surface. The mass is being pulled by a horizontal force P. The angle of friction is 30°. Find the resultant reaction acting on the mass and the magnitude of P.

7 A mass of 11 kg rests in limiting equilibrium on a rough inclined plane. The plane is inclined at 32° to the horizontal. Taking $g = 10\,\mathrm{m\,s^{-2}}$, calculate the size of the resultant reaction and the angle of friction.

8 A mass of 100 kg is on the point of being pulled up an inclined plane. The plane is inclined at 20° to the horizontal and the force pulling the mass acts parallel to the plane. The angle of friction is 40°. Find the size of the applied force and the resultant reaction of the plane on the mass.

Contextual

1 A skier of mass 90 kg just starts to move when the slope is 3° to the horizontal. Calculate the angle of friction and the resultant reaction.

2 A bobsleigh has a mass of 400 kg. The angle of friction between the runners and the ice is 4°. During training, the four team members push the bobsleigh at constant speed along a horizontal ice rink. Assuming they push horizontally, determine the force they need to generate and the resultant reaction.

3 A skier is pulled up a slope angled at 5° to the horizontal at constant speed. The mass of the skier is 60 kg and the angle of friction is 10°. Taking $g = 10\,\mathrm{m\,s^{-2}}$, calculate the resultant reaction and the force pulling the skier up the slope if the cable is parallel to the slope.

4 A sled is pulled up a slope of 7° at a constant speed. The sled has a mass of 3 kg and the angle of friction is 4°. The force necessary to pull the sled up the slope is 10 N. Taking $g = 10\,\mathrm{m\,s^{-2}}$, work out the angle the rope makes with the plane.

Consolidation

Exercise A

1 A laundry basket of mass 3 kg is being pulled along a rough horizontal floor by a light rope inclined upward at an angle of 30° to the floor. The tension in the rope is 8 N. Considering the laundry basket as a particle, calculate the magnitude of the normal component of the resultant force exerted on the laundry basket by the floor. (Take $g = 9.81\,\text{m s}^{-2}$.)

Given that the acceleration of the laundry basket is $0.2\,\text{m s}^{-2}$, find the coefficient of friction between the laundry basket and the floor.

(UCLES)

2 A particle P of mass 5 kg rests on a rough horizontal table. The particle is attached, by a light inextensible string passing over a smooth pulley at the edge of the table to a particle Q of mass 3 kg which hangs freely. A horizontal force of magnitude X newtons acting on P just prevents P moving towards the pulley. The coefficient of friction between P and the table is 0.4. (Take $g = 10\,\text{m s}^{-2}$.)

a Calculate the value of X.

b If the force of magnitude X ceases to act, show that the tension in the string is reduced by 12.5%.

(UCLES)

3

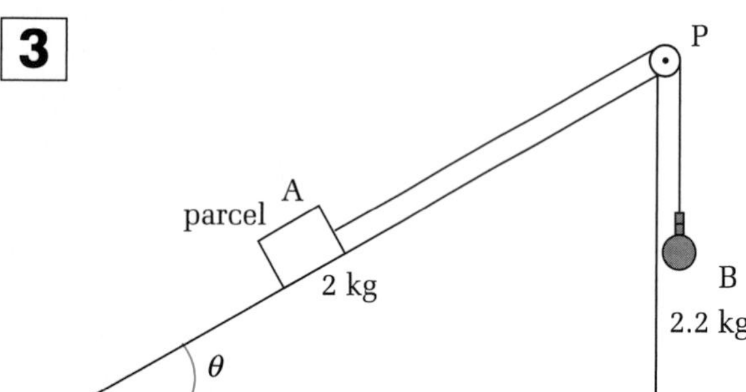

A parcel A of mass 2 kg rests on a rough slope inclined at an angle $\theta°$ to the horizontal, where $\tan\theta = \frac{3}{4}$. A string is attached to A and passes over a small smooth pulley fixed at P. The other end of the string is attached to a weight B of mass 2.2 kg, which hangs freely, as shown. The parcel A is in limiting equilibrium and about to slide up the slope. By modelling A and B as particles and the string as light and inextensible, find:

a the normal contact force acting on A

b the coefficient of friction between A and the slope.

(ULEAC)

Exercise B

1

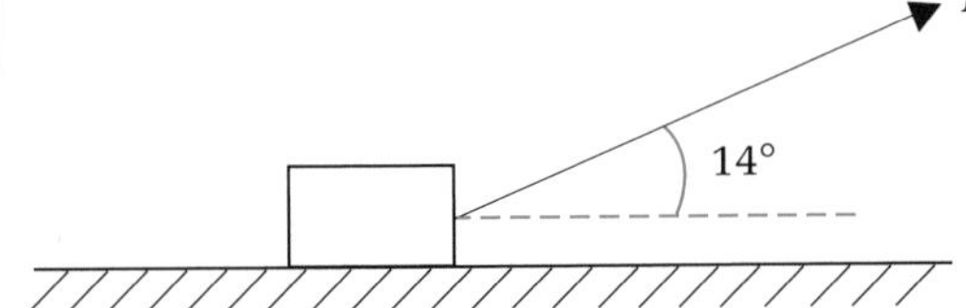

A small box of mass 20 kg rests on a rough horizontal floor. The coefficient of friction between the box and the floor is 0.25. A light inextensible rope is tied to the box and pulled with a force of magnitude P newtons at 14° to the horizontal as shown. Given that the box is on the point of sliding, find the value of P, giving your answer to one decimal place.

(ULEAC)

2

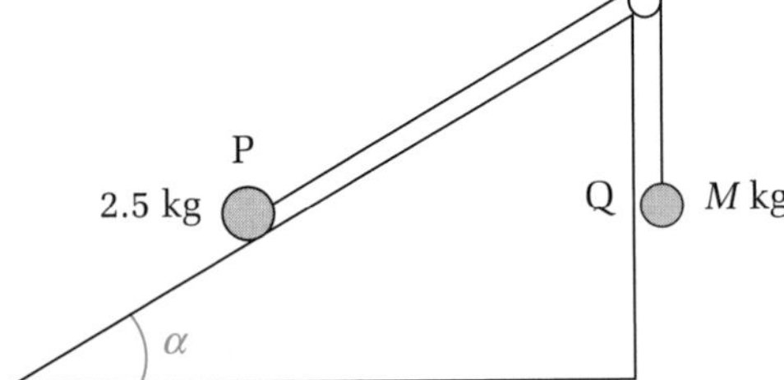

A particle P, of mass 2.5 kg, is placed on a rough plane, inclined to the horizontal at an angle α, where $\tan \alpha = \frac{3}{4}$. The particle P is attached by a light inextensible string, passing over a light pulley, to a particle Q, of mass M kg, which hangs freely as shown in the diagram. The coefficient of friction between P and the plane is 0.4. (Take $g = 10\,\text{m s}^{-2}$.)

a Find the value of M for which P is on the point of sliding:

- **i** up the plane
- **ii** down the plane.

b Given that $M = 0.5$, find the acceleration of P down the plane and the tension in the string.

(UCLES)

3

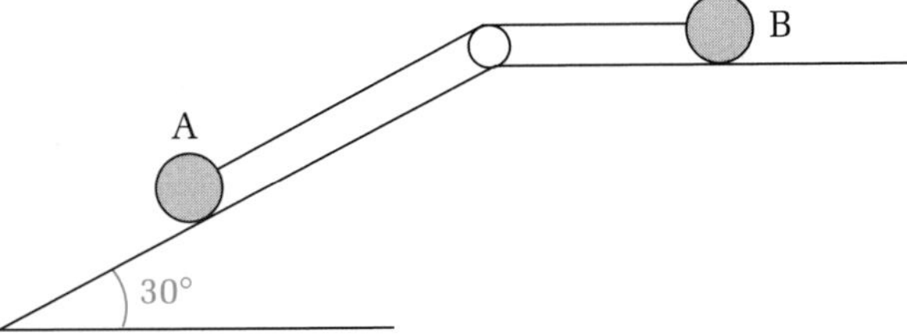

The figure shows two particles A of mass 3 kg, and B of mass 2 kg, connected by a light inextensible string passing over a smooth fixed pulley. The particles are held at rest with A on a smooth slope inclined at 30° to the horizontal, and B on the rough horizontal surface. The coefficient of friction between B and the surface is 0.3. Find the acceleration of the particles and the tension in the string when the system is released from rest. (Take $g = 10\,\text{m s}^{-2}$.)

(UCLES)

Applications and Activities

1

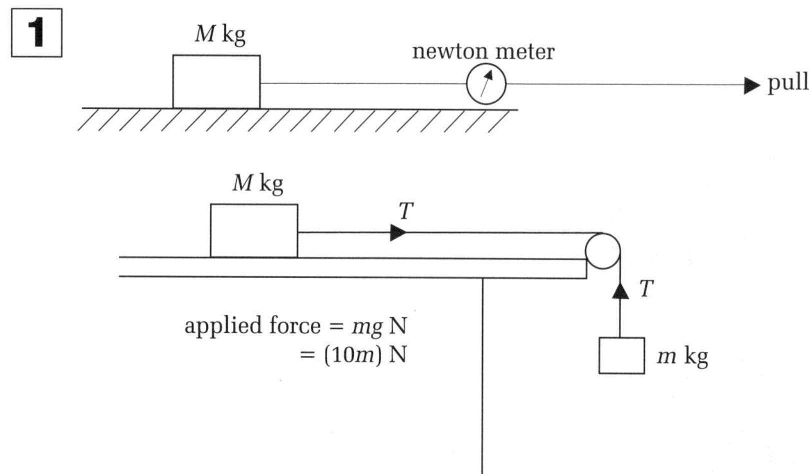

By using either of the two experiments shown in the diagrams, the $F_r \leq \mu R$ relationship can be investigated.

a Record the force required to just move the mass M. Change the mass M and repeat. Does $F_r = \mu R$ for limiting equilibrium?

b Change the surface and find the value of the coefficient of friction for different surfaces, such as carpet or rubber.

2 Place a mass on a table. Lift one end of the table until the mass just starts to move. Record the angle of inclination. Change the mass and repeat. What happens to the angle of friction? Try different surfaces.

3

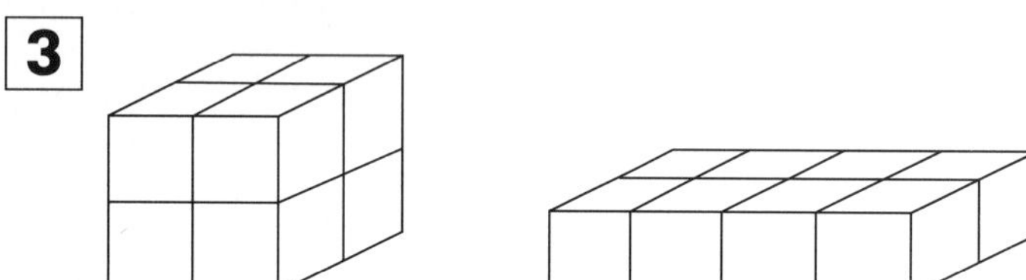

Use wooden blocks to test if friction does depend on contact surface area. Tape the blocks together and place them on a table. Lift one end of the table until the mass just starts to move. Record the angle of inclination and calculate the value of μ. Try to find an explanation for your results.

Summary

- The formula for friction is

$$F_r \leq \mu R$$

- The coefficient of friction can take values in the range $\mu \geq 0$.
- When an object is just about to move on a rough surface it is said to be in **limiting equilibrium** and

$$F_r = \mu R$$

- $$F_r = \mu R$$

  can be used when motion is occurring.
- For problems involving rough horizontal planes we resolve horizontally and vertically and for problems involving rough inclined planes we resolve parallel and perpendicular to the plane.
- The angle of friction λ is related to the coefficient of friction by the formula

$$\mu = \tan \lambda$$

10 Work, Energy and Power

What you need to know

- How to resolve forces into two perpendicular directions.
- How to model friction using $F_r \leq \mu R$.
- How to use dimensional analysis to check formulas.
- How to find a formula using proportion.
- How to use the quadratic formula.

Review

1 A mass of 7 kg rests on a rough plane inclined at 20° to the horizontal.

a Draw a diagram to show the forces acting on the mass.

b Taking $g = 10\,\text{m s}^{-2}$, work out the value of the frictional force and the normal reaction.

2 A sledge of mass 130 kg is pulled across a snow covered field at a constant speed. Assume that the field is horizontal. The coefficient of friction between the runners of the sledge and the snow is 0.15. Calculate the horizontal force that needs to be applied to the sledge to cause this motion.

3 **a** Write down the dimensions of velocity and acceleration.

b Show that the formula $Fs = \frac{1}{2}mv^2$ is dimensionally correct, where F is a force, s is a distance, m is a mass and v is a velocity.

4 **a** A resistance force, R, varies directly with v. When $R = 200$ then $v = 5$.

i Find an equation between R and v.

ii Calculate R when $v = 20$.

iii Work out v when R is 16 000.

b F is proportional to the square of v. When $F = 1620$ then $v = 9$.

i Write down an equation relating F and v.

ii Determine F when v is 15.

iii Calculate v when F is 320.

5 Solve the following equations, giving your answers correct to three significant figures.

a $40v^2 + 672v - 8760 = 0$

b $12v^2 + 950v = 98\,000$

c $\frac{18\,000}{v} - 15v = 540$

10.1 Work Done

On 21 April 1985, Ingrid Kristiansen set a new World and European record at the London marathon. She completed the 26.22 mile course in 2 hours, 21 minutes and 6 seconds. This gives her an average speed of 11.1 mph for the race.

2 h 21 m 6 s =2.352 h

$$\text{speed} = \frac{\text{distance}}{\text{time}} = \frac{26.22}{2.352}$$

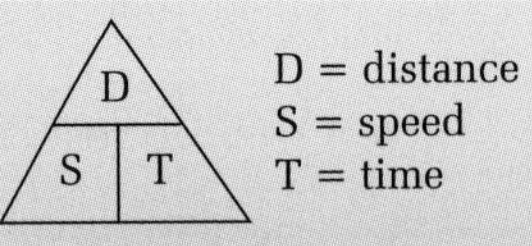

By the end of the race, Ingrid Kristiansen would have been very tired. How could this "tiredness" be measured? To be able to answer this question, several assumptions will have to be made. Ingrid Kristiansen will be modelled as a particle travelling at constant speed. The course will be assumed straight and level. The resistances to motion are assumed constant.

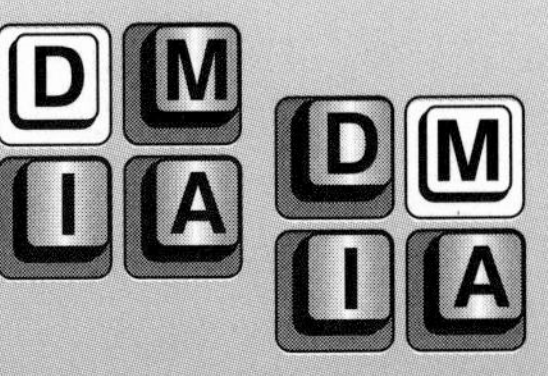

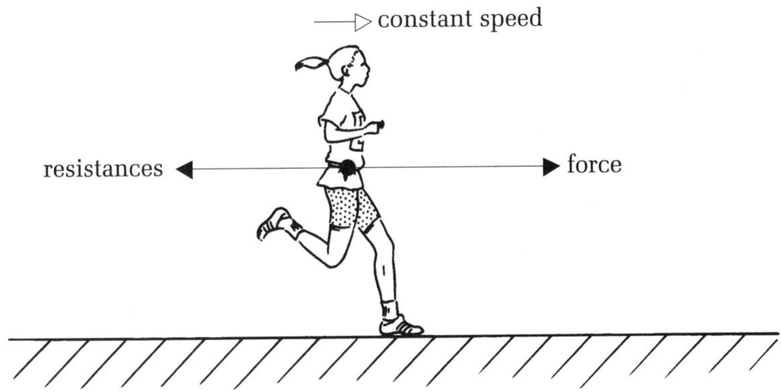

The athelete is in dynamic equilibrium and so there can be no overall force.

Resolve →

$$\text{force} - \text{resistances} = 0$$
$$\text{force} = \text{resistances}$$

Since the resistances are constant then the applied force must also be constant. As she covers more and more distance, she would have become more and more tired. This is because she is applying the same force continuously, over a longer and longer distance. A measure of this effort could be the force multiplied by the distance covered:

$$\text{force} \times \text{distance}$$

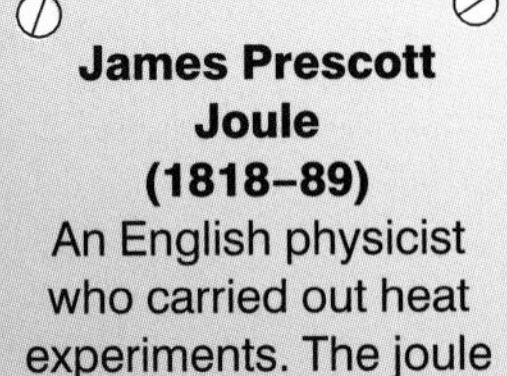

In mechanics, this measurement is called the **work done**. Work is defined as the force multiplied by the distance moved in the direction of the force. This statement can be written as:

work done = force × distance moved

Work is measured in joules (J). The formula for work done can be abbreviated to:

$$W = Fs$$

This formula is only valid when the applied force is constant.

Notation
W = work done (J)
F = applied force (N)
s = distance moved in the direction of the applied force (m)

Work done against resistances

If the resistance forces on Ingrid Kristiansen were 20 N, then the work done against resistance forces could be calculated.

$W = ?$ $\quad F = 20\,\text{N}$ $\quad s = 26.22 \text{ miles} \approx 42\,000\,\text{m}$

$W = Fs$
$W = 20 \times 42\,000$
$W = 840\,000\,\text{J}$
$W = 840\,\text{kJ}$

26.22 miles
$\approx 26.22 \times \frac{8}{5}\,\text{km}$
$= 41.952\,\text{km} = 41\,952\,\text{m}$
$= 42\,000\,\text{m}$ (3 s.f.)
$1000\,\text{J} = 1\,\text{kJ}$

In practice, this will be an underestimate of the work done by the athlete. This is because the resistances are unlikely to be constant. The course will not be level and running uphill is harder than running on a horizontal surface.

Work done against gravity

A vertical wall climb is often one of the activities at an outward bound centre. How much work will a person of mass m kg need to do to get up the wall of height h metres? The person is assumed to climb the wall at a constant speed and the person will be modelled as a particle. A diagram to model this situation is shown.

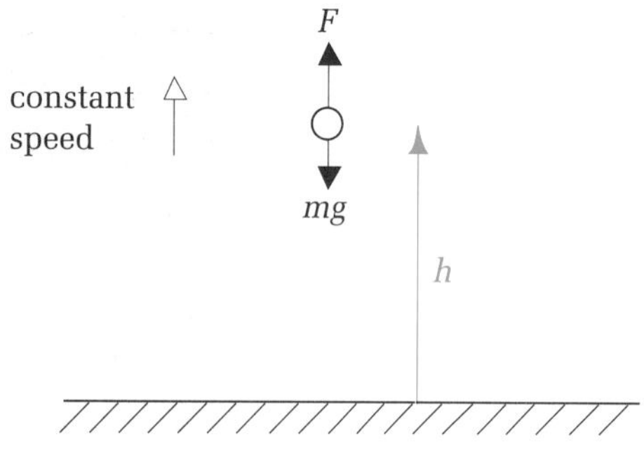

Resolve ↑

$F - mg = 0$

The person is in dynamic equilibrium.

Use $W = Fs$

$W = ?$ $\quad F = mg$ $\quad s = h$

$W = Fs$
$W = mg \times h$
$W = mgh$

The work done this time is to overcome the force of gravity. This is described as the work done against gravity and it is given by:

work done against gravity = mgh

Work done and inclined forces

A 20 kg trunk is pulled across the floor by a 60 N force inclined at 35° above the horizontal for a distance of 3 m. Why is the work done by the

60 N force *not* 180 N? All of the 60 N force does not make the trunk move horizontally. Only a component of the force makes the trunk move horizontally. The definition of work done states that the force and the distance moved must be in the same direction. By resolving the applied force, it is possible to calculate the work done correctly. The motion of the trunk will be assumed to be in a straight line.

DM
IA

Resolve the 60 N force horizontally and vertically.

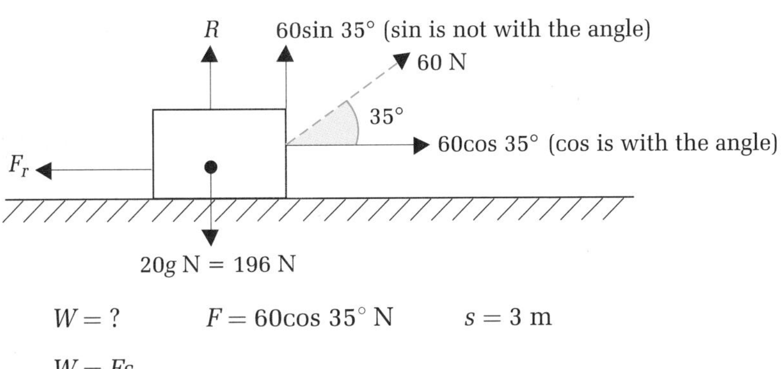

$W = ?$ $\quad F = 60\cos 35°$ N $\quad s = 3$ m

$W = Fs$
$W = 60\cos 35° \times 3$
$W = 147$ J (3 s.f.)

The vertical component of the force does not do any work because the trunk does not move vertically.

However, the vertical component will reduce the normal reaction force. This will reduce the value of the frictional force.

Overview of method

Step ① Draw a clear force diagram.
Step ② Resolve the force along the direction of motion (if necessary).
Step ③ Summarise the information.
Step ④ Apply $W = Fs$.

Example 1

A mass of 2.5 kg is pulled along a smooth horizontal surface by a 25 N force which acts horizontally. The work done by this force is 125 J. Determine the distance covered by the mass.

Solution

▼ ① Draw a clear force diagram.

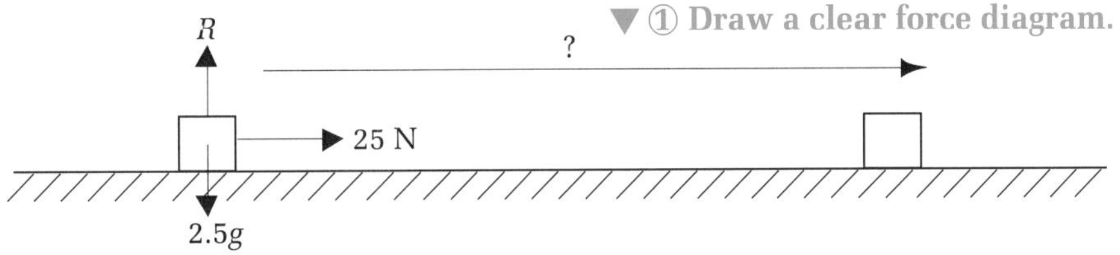

$W = 125$ J $\quad F = 25$ N $\quad s = ?$ ◀ ③ Summarise the information.

$W = Fs$ ◀ ④ Apply $W = Fs$.
$125 = 25 \times s$
$125 = 25s$
$s = 5$ m

Note that ② is not needed because the force and motion are in the same direction.

Example 2

A baby of mass 5 kg is lifted vertically 1.2 m from the ground by her mother. Find the work done against gravity.

Solution

The work done against gravity $= mgh$.

The lifting force is an example of a conservative force because the work done by the force is independent of the route taken (asssuming g remains constant).

$W = ?$ $m = 5\text{ kg}$ $h = 1.2\text{ m}$

$W = mgh$
$W = 5 \times 9.8 \times 1.2$
$W = 58.8\text{ J}$

Example 3

A mass of 10 kg is pulled up a smooth inclined plane for a distance of 10 m. The plane is inclined at $\sin^{-1}\frac{3}{5}$ to the horizontal. Calculate:

Recall that $\sin^{-1}\frac{3}{5} = \arcsin\frac{3}{5}$

a the vertical distance the mass is raised
b the work done against gravity.

Solution

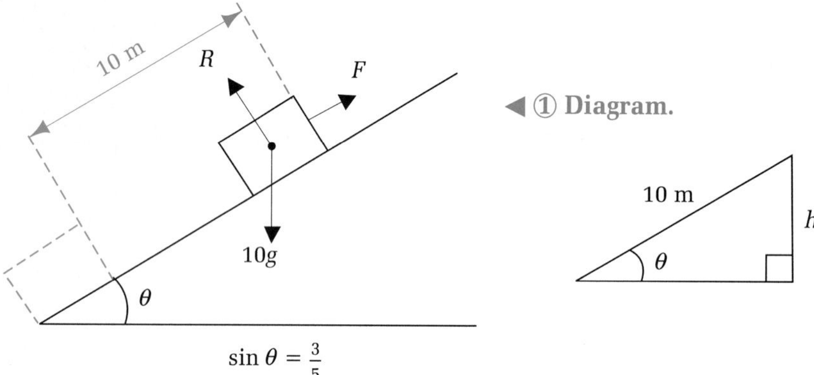

a Use trigonometry to find h.

$h = 10\sin\theta$
$h = 10 \times \frac{3}{5}$
$h = 6\text{ m}$

b $W = ?$ $m = 10\text{ kg}$ $h = 6\text{ m}$ $g = 9.8\text{ m s}^{-2}$ ◀ ③ Summary.

$W = mgh$ ◀ ④ Use $W = mgh$.
$W = 10 \times 9.8 \times 6$
$W = 588\text{ J}$

10.1 Work Done
Exercise

Technique

1 An object is placed on a smooth horizontal surface and pulled by a constant horizontal force of 12 N for a distance of 3 m. Calculate the work done by the 12 N force.

2 A particle is pulled for a distance of 0.2 m. The work done by the applied force is 4 J. Find the applied force if it acts in parallel to the direction of motion.

3 The work done by a force of 1000 N is 900 J. Determine the distance travelled by the object given that the force acts parallel to the direction of motion.

4 A particle of weight 70 N is pulled by a horizontal force along a rough horizontal plane at a constant speed. The coefficient of friction is 0.4 and the distance covered is 3 m. Find the value of:

a the frictional force
b the applied horizontal force
c the work done to overcome friction.

5 A body of mass 4 kg is pulled by a horizontal force along a smooth table. The force is applied for a distance of 12 m and the work done by this force is 30 J. Calculate:

a the magnitude of the applied force
b the acceleration of the body
c the time taken for the mass to cover the 12 m if the body is initially at rest.

6 An object of mass 15 kg is lifted a vertical height of 3 m at a constant speed. Find:

a the weight of the object
b the work done against gravity.

7 A particle of mass 5 kg is pulled across a rough horizontal plane for a distance of 7 m at a constant speed of 2 m s^{-1}. The work done against friction is 28 J and the force acts in the direction of motion. Determine:

a the size of the applied force
b the coefficient of friction.

8 A body of mass 10 kg is pulled by a horizontal force across a rough horizontal plane, at a constant speed. The coefficient of friction between the surfaces is 0.6. The work done against friction is 588 J. Find:

a the frictional force
b the distance covered.

9 A particle is pulled across a smooth horizontal surface by a force of $30\sqrt{3}$ N inclined above the horizontal at 30°. The particle covers a distance of 8 m. Calculate the value of the work done.

10 An object of mass 4 kg is pulled at constant speed along a horizontal plane. The force is applied to the object at 60° to the horizontal and the resistance to motion is 20 N. The work done against the resistance is 90 J. Take $g = 10\text{ m s}^{-2}$ and determine:

a the distance covered by the object
b the magnitude of the applied force.

11

A mass of 7 kg is pulled up a smooth inclined plane. The plane is inclined at $\tan^{-1}\frac{5}{12}$ to the horizontal. Taking $g = 10\text{ m s}^{-2}$, calculate:

Recall that $\tan^{-1}\frac{5}{12} = \arctan\frac{5}{12}$

a the vertical distance the mass is raised
b the work done against gravity.

12

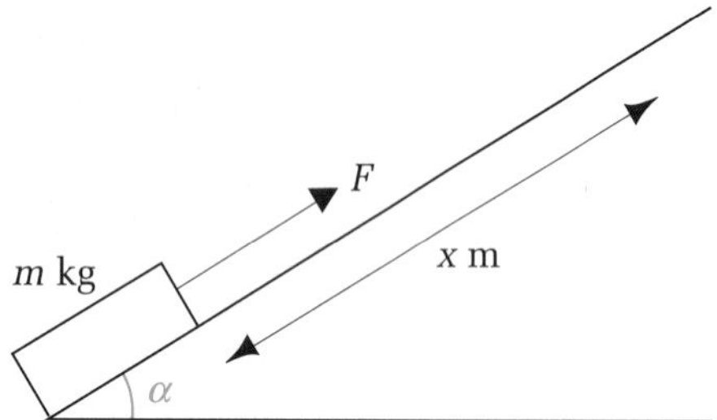

A particle of mass m kg is pulled up a rough inclined plane for a distance of x metres. The angle of inclination is α and the acceleration due to gravity is g. The coefficient of friction between the plane and the particle is μ.

a Show that the work done against gravity is $mgx\sin\alpha$.
b Find the total work done by the force F in terms of m, g, μ, x and α.

13 A particle of mass 10 kg is pulled across a smooth horizontal surface by a force of 50 N inclined at 20° to the horizontal. The particle travels a distance of 4 m along the horizontal surface. Calculate the work done by the 50 N force.

A student's *incorrect* solution is shown. Explain where the mistake has occurred and calculate the correct answer.

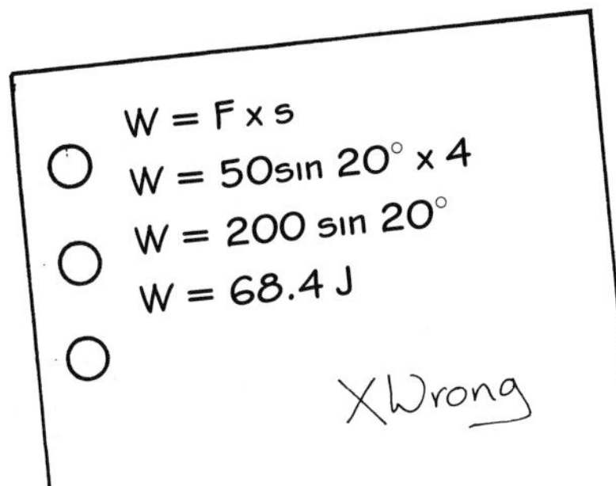

Contextual

1 A cyclist pedals against resistances of 40 N. If the work done by the cyclist is 1000 J, determine the distance travelled. State the assumptions you have made.

2 A mother pulls her son in his new pedal car. The rope makes an angle of 30° to the horizontal. The tension in the rope is 20 N and the car is pulled at constant speed for a distance of 20 m. Find the *exact* values of:

a the resistance forces
b the work done by the mother.

3 A baby of mass 7 kg is lifted 1.5 m vertically upwards by her father. Calculate the work done by the father.

4 A roller coaster of mass 12 tonnes is pulled up an inclined track at a constant speed. The inclination of the track is $\tan^{-1}\frac{3}{4}$ and the resistances to motion are 2400 N. The track is 32 m long. Taking $g = 10\ \text{m s}^{-2}$, find:

a the work done against gravity
b the work done against the resistances.

Recall that $\tan^{-1}\frac{3}{4} = \arctan\frac{3}{4}$

10.2 Energy

Energy is necessary to be able to do work. Ingrid Kristiansen must have had enough energy in her body to be able to complete the marathon. To make sure of this, she would probably have eaten high energy foods before the race. The energy stored in foods is called **chemical energy**.

Near Dinorwic in Wales there is a pumped storage hydroelectric station called Dinorwig. This station uses two reservoirs to generate emergency electricity. Water is pumped into the top reservoir when demand for electicity is low. When electricity is needed, the water is released and flows to the lower reservoir via turbines to make electricity.

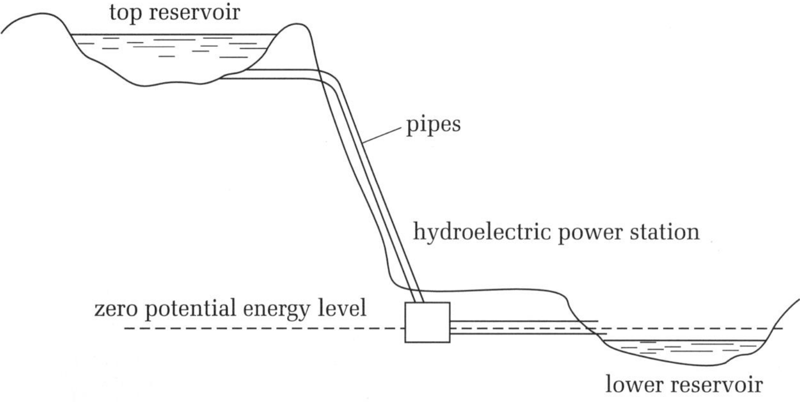

Schematic drawing of Dinorwig pumped storage station

The water has energy in the top reservoir due to its vertical height above the lower reservoir. This type of energy is called **potential energy**. Potential energy must always be measured from a fixed level. In this case, the lower reservoir would be chosen as the **zero potential energy level**. As the water flows down the mountain side its velocity will increase. The water now has **kinetic energy** because it is moving. Kinetic energy and potential energy are types of **mechanical energy**.

Potential energy

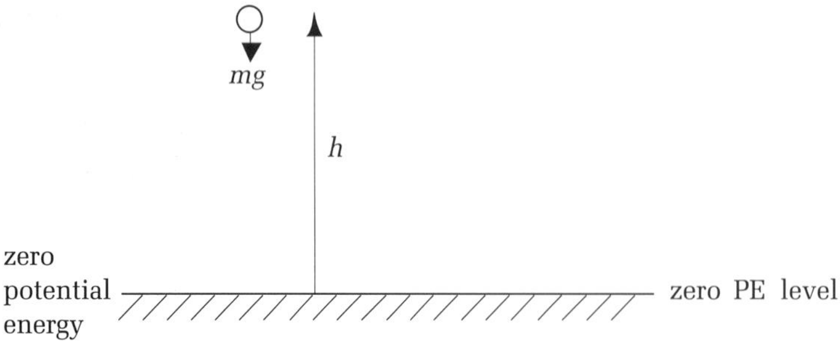

A particle of mass m is lifted slowly to h metres above the ground. The potential energy of the particle is the same as the work which would have to be done against gravity to raise the particle this distance above the ground. Ground level would be the position of **zero potential energy**.

By lifting the mass slowly, the mass will have negligible kinetic energy.

Using the work done equation, a formula for potential energy can be found.

$W = ?$ $\quad F = mg$ $\quad s = h$

The force acting on the particle is its weight, and weight $= mg$.

$W = Fs$
$W = mgh$
$\text{PE} = \text{mgh}$

Notation
PE = potential energy (J)

Potential energy is measured in joules (J). The potential energy will change depending from which point the height of the particle is measured. A fixed level must always be labelled as the *zero potential energy level* so that potential energies can be calculated and compared. The lowest point of the motion of the particle is normally labelled as the *zero potential energy* level.

Kinetic energy

Kinetic energy is the amount of energy a particle possesses because of its motion. A formula can be derived (worked out) by using the equation for work.

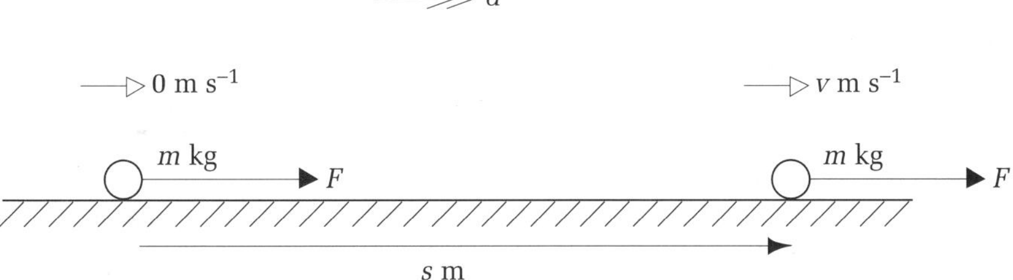

Consider a particle of mass m kg, shown in the diagram moving on a smooth horizontal surface. It is accelerated by a constant force F. After a displacement s, the particle has velocity v. As there is no resistance to motion, *all* the work done by the force must cause the particle to accelerate. This work done must be the same as the increase in the particle's kinetic energy. It can be calculated as follows.

$W = Fs$ — Apply $W = Fs$.
$W = mas$ [1] — Use $F = ma$ to replace F.

Use the uniform acceleration formulas to replace as

$v^2 = u^2 + 2as$
$v^2 = 0 + 2as$ — $u = 0\,\text{m s}^{-1}$
$as = \frac{1}{2}v^2$ [2] — Divide by 2.

Use equation [2] to replace as in equation [1].

$W = mas$
$W = m(\frac{1}{2}v^2)$
$W = \frac{1}{2}mv^2$
$\text{KE} = \frac{1}{2}mv^2$

Notation
KE = kinetic energy (J)

The kinetic energy must be the same as the work done to increase the particle's velocity to $v\,\text{m s}^{-1}$. Memorise the formulas for potential energy and kinetic energy:

$$\textbf{PE} = \boldsymbol{mgh} \quad \text{and} \quad \textbf{KE} = \tfrac{1}{2}\boldsymbol{mv^2}$$

Overview of method

Step ① Draw a clear diagram.

Step ② Label the zero potential energy (PE) level. When potential energies are involved a fixed level must be labelled as the zero level. This enables potential energies to be compared.

Step ③ Write down the information given.

Step ④ Use either or both formulas for KE and PE, as appropriate.

Example 1

A mass of 100 kg accelerates from 2 m s^{-1} to 4 m s^{-1}. Find its gain in kinetic energy.

Solution

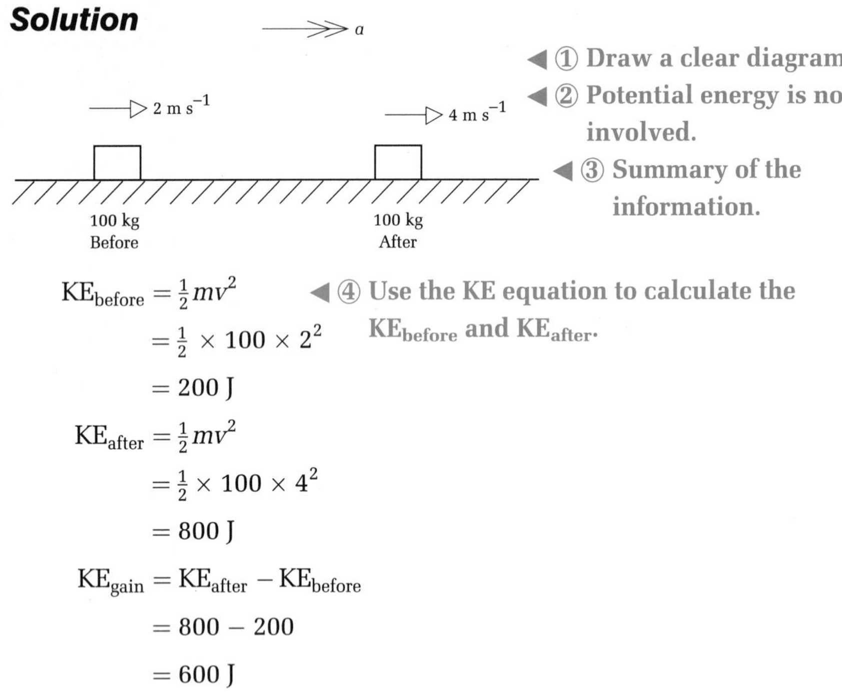

◀ ① Draw a clear diagram.

◀ ② Potential energy is not involved.

◀ ③ Summary of the information.

$$\begin{aligned} KE_{before} &= \tfrac{1}{2}mv^2 \\ &= \tfrac{1}{2} \times 100 \times 2^2 \\ &= 200\text{ J} \end{aligned}$$

◀ ④ Use the KE equation to calculate the KE_{before} and KE_{after}.

$$\begin{aligned} KE_{after} &= \tfrac{1}{2}mv^2 \\ &= \tfrac{1}{2} \times 100 \times 4^2 \\ &= 800\text{ J} \end{aligned}$$

$$\begin{aligned} KE_{gain} &= KE_{after} - KE_{before} \\ &= 800 - 200 \\ &= 600\text{ J} \end{aligned}$$

The KE_{gain} is equal to the difference between the KE_{before} and KE_{after}.

Example 2

An apple of mass 0.1 kg falls from a height of 2 m. Taking $g = 10\text{ m s}^{-2}$, find the loss in potential energy.

Solution

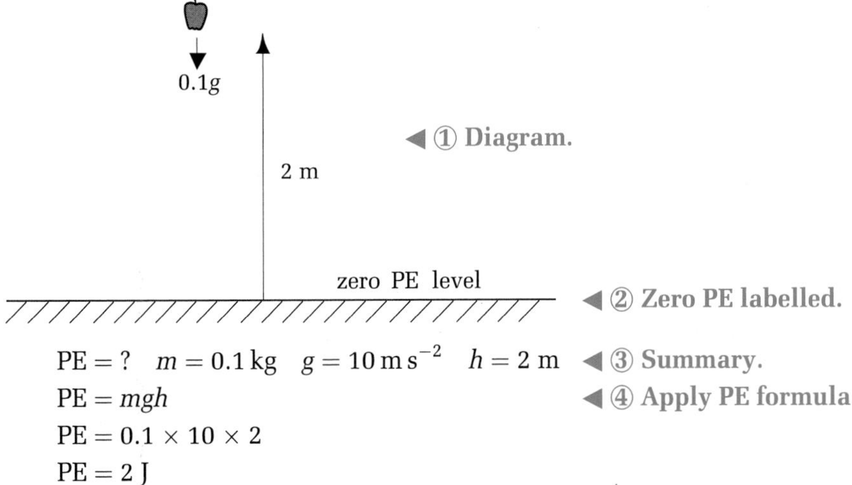

PE = ? $m = 0.1\,\text{kg}$ $g = 10\,\text{m s}^{-2}$ $h = 2\,\text{m}$ ◀ ③ Summary.

PE = mgh ◀ ④ Apply PE formula.

PE = $0.1 \times 10 \times 2$

PE = 2 J

Example 3

A roller coaster train, of mass 8 tonnes, is winched up a slope inclined at 20° to the horizontal. The slope is 80 m long. Determine the increase in potential energy of the roller coaster train from the bottom of the slope.

Solution

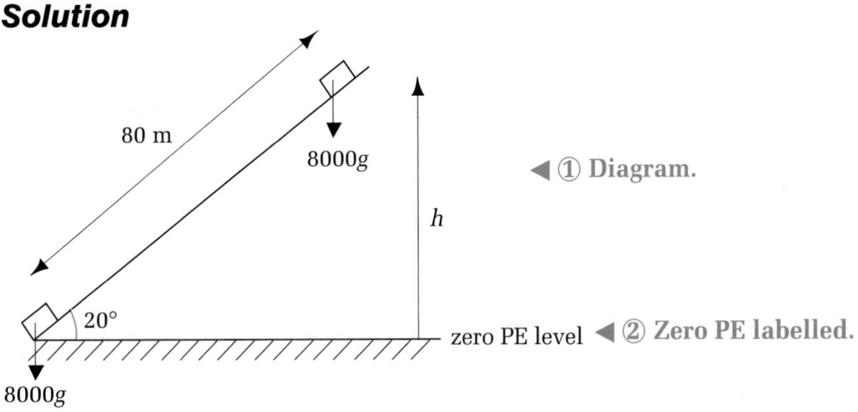

PE = ? $m = 8000\,\text{kg}$ $g = 9.8\,\text{m s}^{-2}$ $h = ?$ ◀ ③ Summarise the information.

From the summary, the formula PE = mgh cannot be used yet. The value for h is not known. To find this out, trigonometry will have to be used.

opp = hyp × sin 20°

$h = 80 \times \sin 20°$

$h = 27.36$ m (4 s.f.)

PE = ? $m = 8000\,\text{kg}$ $g = 9.8\,\text{m s}^{-2}$ $h = 27.36\,\text{m}$

Remember to store the value for h in the calculator's memory.

PE = mgh ◀ ④ Use PE formula.

PE = $8000 \times 9.8 \times 27.36$

PE = 2 145 150.3

PE = 2 150 000 J (3 s.f.)

PE = 2150 kJ (3 s.f.)

10.2 Energy
Exercise

Technique

1 Calculate the potential energy gained when:

a a particle of mass 5 kg is raised 4 m vertically
b an object of mass 9 kg is lifted a vertical distance of 50 cm
c a body of mass 100 grams is raised a vertical distance of 8 m.

2 Find the kinetic energy of the following:

a a body of mass 20 grams travelling at 40 m s^{-1}
b a particle with a mass of 2 kg and speed of 14 m s^{-1}
c an object of mass 8 kg travelling with a velocity of -4 m s^{-1}.

3 The potential energy of a body is increased by 20 J when it is raised 1.5 m vertically. Taking $g = 10 \text{ m s}^{-2}$, calculate the mass of the body.

4 The mass of an object is 5 kg and its potential energy, when measured from a flat surface, is 100 J. Calculate the vertical height of the object above the surface.

5 An object has a kinetic energy of 60 J when its speed is 2 m s^{-1}. Determine the mass of the object.

6 A body has a mass of 3 kg and a kinetic energy of 98 J. Find the *exact* speed of the body.

7 Calculate the kinetic energy gained by a particle of mass 200 grams which speeds up from 3 m s^{-1} to 7 m s^{-1}.

8 An object slows down from 10 m s^{-1} to 2 m s^{-1}. The loss of kinetic energy is 280 J. Determine the mass of the object.

9 A particle of mass 25 kg is lifted a vertical height of 0.5 m. Calculate the gain in potential energy.

10 A body of mass m kg has initial speed $u \text{ m s}^{-1}$ and final speed $6u \text{ m s}^{-1}$. Show that the kinetic energy gained is $\frac{35}{2} mu^2$.

11 Use dimensional analysis to find the dimensions of work done, potential energy and kinetic energy.

Contextual

1 Find the kinetic energy of a 65 kg sprinter when she is travelling at $10\,\mathrm{m\,s^{-1}}$.

2 Concorde has a mass of 185 tonnes and a take-off speed of $112\,\mathrm{m\,s^{-1}}$. Calculate the kinetic energy of Concorde at take-off.

3 A lift of mass 700 kg is raised from ground level to a height of 30 m. Determine the increase in potential energy.

4 A car of mass 900 kg increases its speed from $10\,\mathrm{m\,s^{-1}}$ to $30\,\mathrm{m\,s^{-1}}$. Find the increase in kinetic energy.

5 On a roller coaster, the train drops a vertical height of 13 metres to a helical loop. The mass of the train is 12 tonnes. Work out the decrease in potential energy.

6 A roller coaster train has a mass of 10 tonnes and an initial speed of $4\,\mathrm{m\,s^{-1}}$. Its kinetic energy increases by 300 kJ. Calculate:

a its initial kinetic energy
b its final kinetic energy
c its final speed.

7 A model car slows down from $10\,\mathrm{m\,s^{-1}}$ to $2\,\mathrm{m\,s^{-1}}$. The loss of kinetic energy is 280 J. Determine the mass of the model car.

8 A radiator of mass 25 kg is lifted a vertical height of 0.5 m. Calculate the gain in potential energy.

10.3 Conservation of Energy

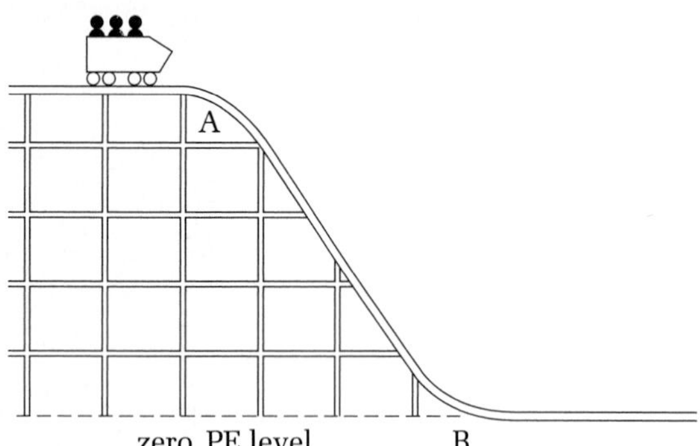

When the 'Big One' roller coaster opened at Blackpool Pleasure Beach, it was the tallest roller coaster in the United Kingdom at that time. The roller coaster uses a steep drop to generate its speed. The roller coaster has potential energy at the top of the slope (point A). As it descends the slope the potential energy is converted into kinetic energy. At the bottom of the slope (point B), the potential energy has been converted into kinetic energy. This can be written as:

$$PE_A = KE_B$$

Notation
PE_A = potential energy at A
KE_B = kinetic energy at B

In general, the total energy at A must equal the total energy at B:

$$\mathbf{PE_A + KE_A = PE_B + KE_B}$$

This principle is known as the **conservation of energy**. The principle of conservation of energy states that energy cannot be created or destroyed but can only be converted from one form to another. In practice, not all the potential energy is converted into kinetic energy. Some of the potential energy must be used to do work to overcome the resistances to motion. An equation for the roller coaster model would be:

$PE_A = KE_B$ + work done against resistances

This is called the **work–energy principle**.

What type of energy do you think the work done against resistances will end up as? Work done against resistances ends up as heat and sound energies. The wheels rolling on the track make sound. The friction between the wheels and the track will cause them to heat up.
Each situation will lead to a different work–energy equation. You need to think about what is happening to the energy during the motion. An overall equation would be:

Resistance forces are sometimes called dissipative forces because they reduce the energy of the system.

$$\mathbf{PE_{start} + KE_{start} + W_{in} = PE_{end} + KE_{end} + W_{out}}$$

Sometimes work done by the external forces (W_{in}) will *increase* the energy of the particle. In this formula weight is not treated as an external force. The work done to overcome resistances (W_{out}) will *decrease* the energy of the particle. Although this appears complicated not all the energies will need to be used in every case. This will make the problem easier to solve.

Notation
W_{in} = the work done by external forces (e.g. engine).
W_{out} = work done to overcome resistances.

Overview of method

Step ① Draw a clear diagram.
Step ② Label a zero potential energy level.
Step ③ Think about what is happening with the energies and work involved and write an equation relating them *or* use $PE_{start} + KE_{start} + W_{in} = PE_{end} + KE_{end} + W_{out}$.

Example 1

A toolbox, of mass 3 kg, is knocked off a table which is 0.3 m above the ground. Using conservation of energy, calculate the vertical speed with which the toolbox lands on the ground.

When told to use conservation of energy, ignore resistance forces.

Solution

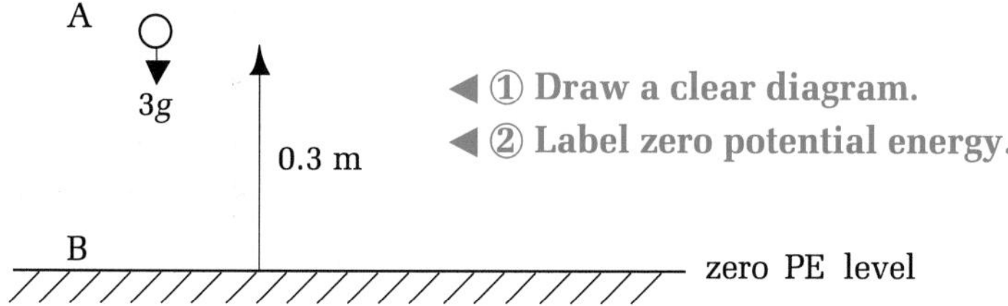

Initially, the toolbox has potential energy. As the box falls, the potential energy is converted to kinetic energy. When it lands on the ground, the potential energy has been converted to kinetic energy. ◀ ③ Think about what is happening to the energies.

The vertical velocity at A is assumed 0.

$$\text{PE}_A = \text{KE}_B$$

$PE_A = mgh$ and $KE_B = \frac{1}{2}mv^2$

$$mgh = \tfrac{1}{2}mv^2$$

Substitute the numbers into the formula.

$$3 \times 9.8 \times 0.3 = \tfrac{1}{2} \times 3 \times v^2$$

Multiply by 2 and divide by 3.

$$2 \times 9.8 \times 0.3 = v^2$$

Calculate LHS.

$$5.88 = v^2$$

Square root.

$$v = 2.42\ \text{m s}^{-1}\ (3\ \text{s.f.})$$

An alternative method is to use

$\text{PE}_{\text{start}} + \text{KE}_{\text{start}} + \text{W}_{\text{in}} = \text{PE}_{\text{end}} + \text{KE}_{\text{end}} + \text{W}_{\text{out}}$

Replacing KE_{start}, W_{in}, PE_{end} and W_{out} by 0 gives the same equation.

Example 2

A 10 kg mass is pulled along a rough horizontal surface by a horizontal force of magnitude 100 N. The mass is initially at rest and it is pulled by the force for a distance of 10 m. The coefficient of friction between the mass and the surface is 0.6. Use the work–energy principle to find the final speed of the mass.

Solution

◀ ① Draw a clear diagram.

◀ ② is not required because the potential energy does not change.

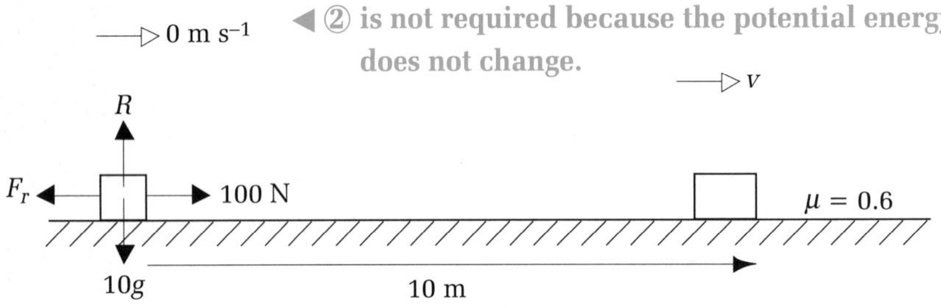

The work done by the 100 N force is needed to overcome the work against the frictional force and to increase the kinetic energy of the mass. ◀ ③ Think about the energy and work done.

$$\text{W}_{\text{in}} = \text{KE}_B + \text{W}_{\text{out}}$$

Remember $W = Fs$ and $KE = \frac{1}{2}mv^2$.

$$Fs = \tfrac{1}{2}mv^2 + F_r s \qquad [1]$$

Substitute the numbers into the formula.

$$100 \times 10 = \tfrac{1}{2} \times 10 \times v^2 + F_r \times 10$$

$$1000 = 5v^2 + 10F_r \qquad [2]$$

We need to calculate F_r.

Resolving ↑ to find R,

$$R - 10g = 0$$

$$R = 10g$$

Using $F_r \leq \mu R$,

$F_r = \mu R$

$F_r = 0.6 \times 10g$

$F_r = 6g$

$\mu = 0.6$ from the question.

Replacing F_r in equation [2],

$$1000 = 5v^2 + 10F_r$$
$$1000 = 5v^2 + 10 \times 6g$$
$$1000 = 5v^2 + 588$$
$$1000 - 588 = 5v^2$$
$$412 = 5v^2$$
$$82.4 = v^2$$
$$v = 9.08\,\mathrm{m\,s^{-1}}\ (3\text{ s.f.})$$

$g = 9.8\,\mathrm{m\,s^{-2}}$.
Subtract 588 from both sides.
Divide both sides by 5.
Square root both sides.

Alternative method

$$\mathrm{PE_{start}} + \mathrm{KE_{start}} + \mathrm{W_{in}} = \mathrm{PE_{end}} + \mathrm{KE_{end}} + \mathrm{W_{out}}$$ ◀ ③
$$0 + 0 + Fs = 0 + \tfrac{1}{2}mv^2 + F_r s$$
$$Fs = \tfrac{1}{2}mv^2 + F_r s$$

PE = 0 because there is no vertical motion and $\mathrm{KE_{start}} = 0$ because it is initially at rest.

This is the same as equation [1]. The procedure to complete the solution is the same as above.

Example 3

A female athlete of mass 65 kg runs up a slope inclined at 5° to the horizontal. Her speed at the bottom of the slope is $4\,\mathrm{m\,s^{-1}}$ and her speed decreases to $3\,\mathrm{m\,s^{-1}}$ at the top of the slope. The slope is 120 m long and the resistances to motion can be assumed constant at 40 N. Determine the constant force she must exert to get to the top of the slope.

Solution

◀ ① Draw a clear diagram.

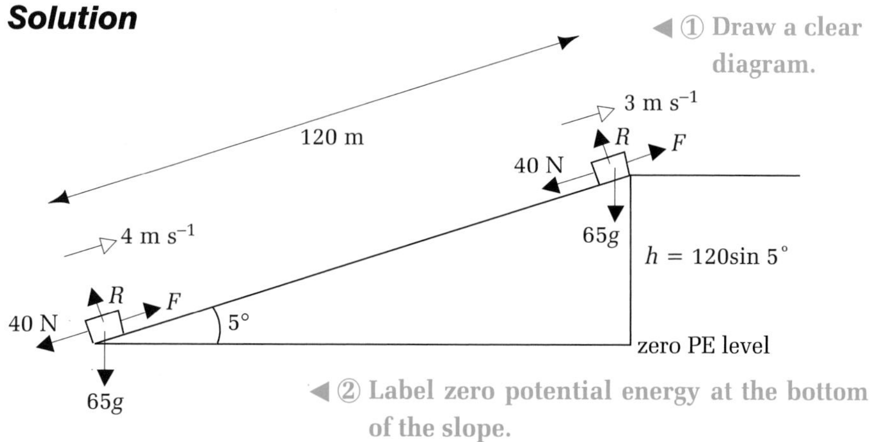

◀ ② Label zero potential energy at the bottom of the slope.

The normal reaction and weight are conservative forces since they do not affect the energy of the system.

Use trigonometry to find h.

The athlete has kinetic energy to start off with and she is putting work into her running. This energy is used to overcome work against resistances and to increase her potential energy. At the top of the slope she still has kinetic energy. ◀ ③ **Think about the energy and work done.**

$$\text{KE}_{\text{start}} + \text{W}_{\text{in}} = \text{W}_{\text{out}} + \text{PE}_{\text{end}} + \text{KE}_{\text{end}}$$

$$\tfrac{1}{2}mu^2 + Fs = 40s + mgh + \tfrac{1}{2}mv^2 \quad [1]$$

u = initial speed.
Substitute the numbers.

$$\tfrac{1}{2} \times 65 \times 4^2 + F \times 120 = 40 \times 120 + 65 \times 9.8 \times 120\sin 5^\circ + \tfrac{1}{2} \times 65 \times 3^2$$

$$520 + 120F = 4800 + 6662.2 + 292.5$$

$$520 + 120F = 11\,754.7$$

Subtract 520.

$$120F = 11\,234.7$$

Divide by 120.

$$F = 93.6 \text{ N (3 s.f.)}$$

Alternative method

$$\text{PE}_{\text{start}} + \text{KE}_{\text{start}} + \text{W}_{\text{in}} = \text{PE}_{\text{end}} + \text{KE}_{\text{end}} + \text{W}_{\text{out}} \quad ◀ ③$$

$\text{PE}_{\text{start}} = 0$

$$0 + \tfrac{1}{2}mu^2 + Fs = mgh + \tfrac{1}{2}mv^2 + 40s$$

$$\tfrac{1}{2}mu^2 + Fs = mgh + \tfrac{1}{2}mv^2 + 40s$$

This is now the same as equation [1] in the above solution.

10.3 Conservation of Energy
Exercise

Technique

1 A particle has a mass of 5 kg. It is held at a height of 3 metres above the ground. Find:

Take zero PE at ground level.

- **a** its potential energy
- **b** its kinetic energy when it hits the ground
- **c** the speed with which the particle hits the ground.

2 An object is pulled by a horizontal force of 20 N along a smooth horizontal surface for a distance of 7 m. The object is initially at rest and has a mass of 2 kg. Calculate:

- **a** the work done by the 20 N force
- **b** the increase in kinetic energy of the body
- **c** the final speed of the body.

3 A body of mass 0.5 kg is thrown vertically upwards with a speed of $10\,\mathrm{m\,s^{-1}}$. Taking $g = 10\,\mathrm{m\,s^{-2}}$, determine:

- **a** the initial kinetic energy of the body
- **b** the gain in potential energy when the body has reached its maximum height
- **c** the maximum height reached above the starting position.

4 A 5 kg mass is pulled across a rough horizontal plane for a distance of 15 m. The horizontal force has a value of 60 N and the coefficient of friction between the plane and the mass is 0.8. Find:

- **a** the work done by the applied force
- **b** the work done against friction
- **c** the final speed of the mass if the mass is initially at rest.

5 A particle of mass 1 kg is dropped. Taking $g = 10\,\mathrm{m\,s^{-2}}$, find the speed of the particle in surd form when it has fallen a distance of:

- **a** 4.8 m
- **b** 15 m

6 A particle has a mass of 20 grams. It is pulled by a horizontal force of 0.4 N along a rough horizontal surface. Its speed increases from $1\,\mathrm{m\,s^{-1}}$ to $10\,\mathrm{m\,s^{-1}}$ over a distance of 4 m. Find the coefficient of friction between the surface and the particle.

7 An object has an initial speed of $8\,\text{m s}^{-1}$ at the bottom of a smooth inclined plane. The plane is inclined at $\tan^{-1}\frac{3}{4}$ to the horizontal and the object has a mass of 100 g. Calculate:

Recall that $\tan^{-1}\frac{3}{4} = \arctan\frac{3}{4}$

- **a** the initial kinetic energy of the particle
- **b** the potential energy when the particle has reached the maximum distance from the bottom of the plane
- **c** the maximum distance the particle travels from the bottom of the plane.

8 A particle of mass 200 g is projected up a rough plane inclined at $\sin^{-1}\frac{4}{5}$ to the horizontal. The particle travels up the slope and stops momentarily at a distance of 3 m from the point of projection. The coefficient of friction between the particle and the plane is $\frac{4}{7}$. Find the speed of projection using the work–energy principle.

Recall that $\sin^{-1}\frac{4}{5} = \arcsin\frac{4}{5}$

Contextual

1 A car, of mass 1100 kg, experiences constant resistances of 400 N. The car accelerates from $10\,\text{m s}^{-1}$ to $30\,\text{m s}^{-1}$ over a distance of 600 m. Calculate:

- **a** the gain in kinetic energy of the car
- **b** the work done against the resistances
- **c** the work done by the engine
- **d** the force produced by the engine.

State one key assumption that you have made.

2 A roller coaster has an initial speed of $3\,\text{m s}^{-1}$ at the top of a slope. The slope drops a vertical distance of 50 m. The mass of the roller coaster train is 2 tonnes. Neglect any resistances. Determine:

- **a** the decrease in potential energy of the roller coaster
- **b** the increase in kinetic energy of the roller coaster
- **c** the final speed of the roller coaster.

3 A cyclist free wheels down a road inclined at an angle of $\sin^{-1}\frac{5}{13}$ to the horizontal. The mass of the cyclist and bicycle is 65 kg. The initial speed of the cyclist is $2\,\text{m s}^{-1}$ and the speed at the bottom of the slope is $16\,\text{m s}^{-1}$. The length of the road is 65 m. Find the resistances to motion assuming that they are constant.

$\sin^{-1}\frac{5}{13} = \arcsin\frac{5}{13}$

4 A ball, of mass 100 g, is dropped from a height of 3 m above the ground. It bounces to a height of 2 m. Calculate the kinetic energy lost in the bounce. What has happened to this energy?

10.4 Power

In 1996, Frank Biela won the British Touring Car Championship in an Audi A4. The team and manufacturer titles were also won by Audi. The winning car was based on a production Audi A4 which produced 144 000 watts (W) of power. This power enabled the car to reach a top speed of 238 km h^{-1} (149 mph). By increasing the power output and decreasing the mass of the car, the engineers could make the race version go even faster.

Or 193 brake horse power (bhp) in Imperial units.

James Watt (1736–1819)
A Scottish engineer who first used the term horse power.
The watt (W) is named after him.

The power of the engine gives an indication of a car's maximum speed. Generally speaking, the more power an engine can develop, the faster the car will be able to travel. Other factors are of course important. Power is also used when describing electrical appliances like heaters, motors and generators. Dinorwig pumped storage hydroelectric power station can produce 1800 MW of electricity.

MW stands for megawatt (1 MW =1 000 000 W).

But what is power? The more power that is available, the more quickly an amount of work can be completed. **Power** is defined as the **rate of doing work**. This means that power is work divided by time if a *constant force* does the work. This definition provides a formula to calculate power.

$$\boldsymbol{P = \frac{W}{t}}$$

Notation
P = power (W)
W = work done (J)
t = time (s)

Another formula can be derived using the work done equation.

$$P = \frac{W}{t}$$

Replace W with Fs.

$$P = \frac{Fs}{t}$$

$$P = F \times \frac{s}{t}$$

Use $v = \frac{s}{t}$.

$$\boldsymbol{P = Fv}$$

Overview of method

Step ① Draw a clear diagram.
Step ② Summarise the information given.
Step ③ It may be necessary to calculate the work done using KE $= \frac{1}{2}mv^2$, PE $= mgh$ and W $= Fs$.
Step ④ Use $P = Fv$ or $P = \frac{W}{t}$.

You may also need to resolve forces or to apply $F = ma$ where F is the *resultant* force.

Example 1

A cyclist travels at a constant speed of 10 m s^{-1} along a straight horizontal road. The power the cyclist develops is 400 W and the mass of the cyclist and bicycle totals 80 kg.

a Find the magnitude of the resistance forces at this speed.

The resistance forces are found to be proportional to the cyclist's speed.

b Write down the equation for the resistance forces.

c Calculate the acceleration of the cyclist when his speed is $2\ \text{m s}^{-1}$ if the power developed remains unchanged.

Solution

a

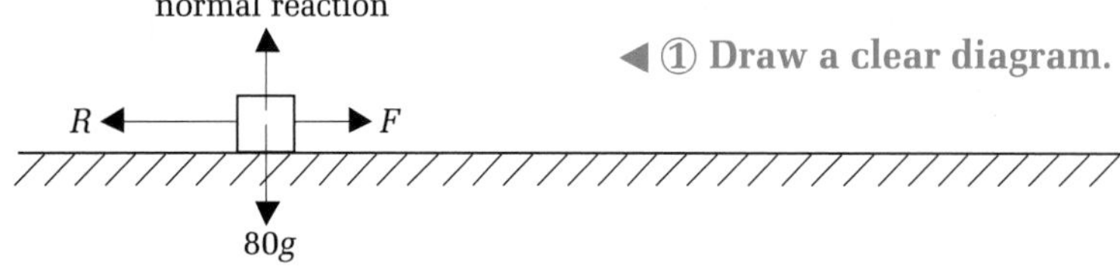

◀ ① **Draw a clear diagram.**

$P = 400$ W $\quad F = ? \quad v = 10\ \text{m s}^{-1}$ ◀ ② **Summarise the information.**

$P = Fv$ ◀ ④ **Use $P = Fv$.**

③ is not necessary because $P = \frac{W}{t}$ does not need to be used.

$400 = F \times 10$

$F = 40$ N

Divide by 10.

The cyclist is in dynamic equilibrium because the speed is constant. Resistances = 40 N.

b $R \propto v$

The resistances vary with speed.

$R = kv$ ◀ **Introduce the constant of proportion.**

$40 = k \times 10$

Substitute the numbers into the formula.

$k = 4$

Divide by 10.

$R = 4v$ ◀ **Replace k by 4 in $R = kv$.**

c

a

$2\ \text{m s}^{-1}$

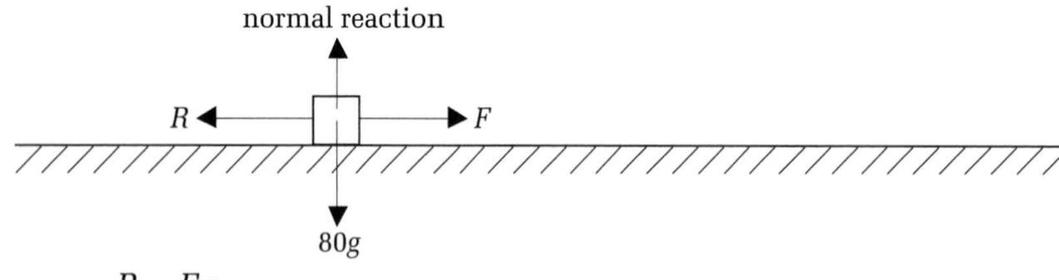

$P = Fv$

$400 = F \times 2$

$F = 200$ N

$R = ? \quad v = 2\ \text{m s}^{-1}$

$R = 4v$

Use the equation for the resistances obtained in **b**.

$R = 4 \times 2$

$R = 8$ N

Apply $F = ma \rightarrow$

$F = ma$ ◀ **Remember this F is the resultant force.**

$200 - 8 = 80a$

$192 = 80a$

$a = 2.4\,\text{m s}^{-2}$

Use $F = ma$ to find the acceleration of the cyclist at $2\,\text{m s}^{-1}$.

Example 2

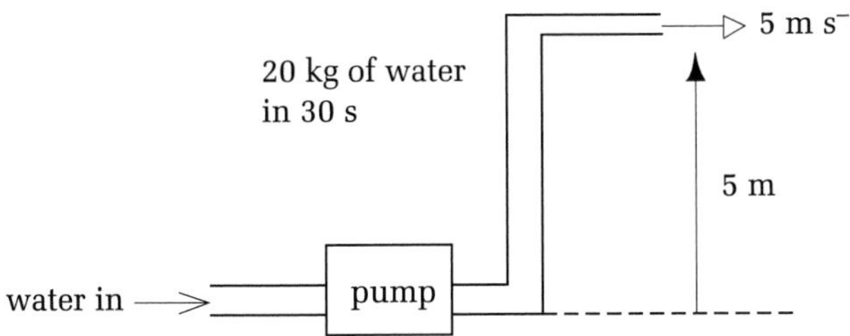

A pump raises 20 kg of water to a height of 5 m in 30 seconds. The water starts at rest and it is issued at $5\,\text{m s}^{-1}$. Calculate:

a the work done by the pump

b the power developed by the pump.

State one key assumption that you have made.

Solution

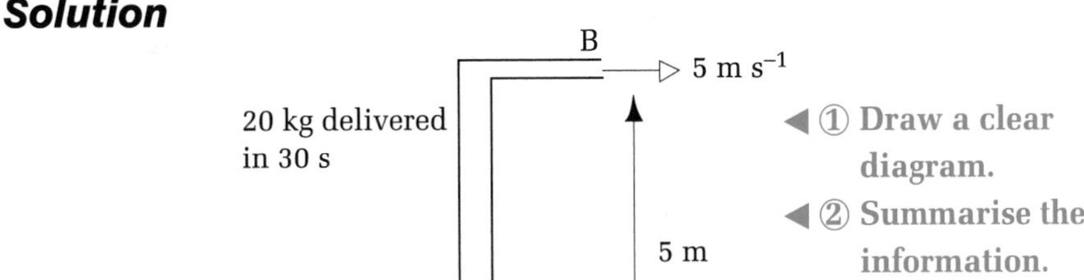

◀ ① **Draw a clear diagram.**

◀ ② **Summarise the information.**

a The work done by the pump is the same as the increase in mechanical energy of the water.

$W = PE_B + KE_B$ ◀ ③ **Use the PE and KE formulas to calculate the work done by the pump.**

$W = mgh + \frac{1}{2}mv^2$

$W = 20 \times 9.8 \times 5 + \frac{1}{2} \times 20 \times 5^2$

$W = 980 + 250$

$W = 1230\,\text{J}$

Assuming no resistances or loss of energy.

The zero level for potential energy is labelled on the diagram.

b $P = ?$ $W = 1230$ $t = 30\,\text{s}$

$P = \frac{W}{t}$ ◀ ④ **Use $P = \frac{W}{t}$ to calculate the power.**

$P = \frac{1230}{30}$

$P = 41\,\text{W}$

The force produced by the pump is assumed to be constant.

If this is not the case, then 41 W is the average power of the pump.

Example 3

A car, of mass 1000 kg, produces 50 kW of power. The resistances to motion are given by $R = 100v$ where v is the speed of the car. Find the maximum speed the car can attain ascending (going up) a road inclined at 10° to the horizontal.

Solution

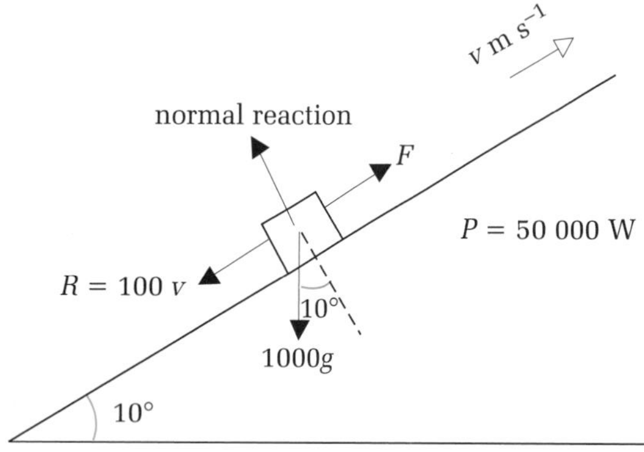

Use $P = Fv$

$50\,000 = Fv$ — Divide by v

$$F = \frac{50\,000}{v} \qquad [1]$$

Resolve // to the plane ↗

$$F - R - 1000g\sin 10^\circ = 0$$ — Remember the weight component.

$$\frac{50\,000}{v} - 100v - 1701.8 = 0$$ — Use equation [1]. Multiply by v.

$$50\,000 - 100v^2 - 1701.8v = 0$$ — Rearrange into a quadratic equation.

$$100v^2 + 1701.8v - 50\,000 = 0$$

$$v = \frac{-b \pm \sqrt{b^2 - 4ac}}{2a}$$ — Use the formula to solve the quadratic equation.

$$v = \frac{-1701.8 \pm \sqrt{1701.8^2 - 4 \times 100 \times (-50\,000)}}{200}$$

$$v = \frac{-1701.8 \pm \sqrt{22\,895\,960.4}}{200}$$

$$v = \frac{-1701.8 \pm 4784.97}{200}$$ — Store both values in calculator memory.

$$v = \frac{-1701.8 + 4784.97}{200}$$ — $v = \frac{-1701.8 - 4784.97}{200}$ will give a negative answer.

$v = 15.4\,\text{m s}^{-1}$ (3 s.f.)

10.4 Power
Exercise

Technique

1 A mass of 20 kg is raised 20 m vertically in 40 s. Find the average power required.

2 A 5 kg mass is accelerated from 4 m s^{-1} to 8 m s^{-1} in 8 s. Determine:

a the gain in kinetic energy
b the power needed to cause this acceleration.

3 A vehicle develops 18 kW of power. The resistances to motion are 600 N and they can be assumed constant. Calculate the maximum speed of the vehicle.

1 kW = 1000 W

4 A vehicle travels at a constant 60 m s^{-1}. The resistances to motion at this speed are 1000 N. Calculate the power developed.

5 The power of a vehicle is 12 kW and its maximum speed is 50 m s^{-1}. Find:

a the tractive force for the vehicle
b the resistances to motion at this speed.

Tractive force is the force developed by the engine.

6 A pump issues 50 kg of water at a speed of 3 m s^{-1} every 10 seconds. The water is initially at rest. Determine:

a the increase in kinetic energy of the water
b the power of the pump.

7 A vehicle's engine develops a power of 75 kW. The mass of the vehicle is 900 kg and the resistances to motion are proportional to the vehicle's speed. At 10 m s^{-1} the resistances are 400 N. Assume the vehicle is travelling along a straight level road.

a Write down an equation for the resistances to motion.
b Calculate the vehicle's maximum speed.

8 A vehicle of mass 800 kg travels up an inclined plane at a constant speed of 20 m s^{-1}. The angle of inclination is 5° to the horizontal and the resistances to motion are 400 N.

a Draw a diagram showing the forces acting on the vehicle.
b Find the power developed by the vehicle at this speed.

9 A vehicle of mass 1200 kg travels along a flat, straight road. Its engine develops 90 kW of power. The resistances to motion are directly proportional to speed. The maximum speed of the vehicle is $50\,\text{m s}^{-1}$.

a Determine the magnitude of the resistances to motion at maximum speed.
b Write down an equation for the resistances to motion.
c The same vehicle now travels up a road inclined at $\sin^{-1}\frac{1}{70}$ to the horizontal. Assume the equation for the resistances remains the same. Work out the maximum speed of the vehicle on the inclined road.

Recall that $\sin^{-1}\frac{1}{70} = \arcsin\frac{1}{70}$

Contextual

1 A sports car develops 320 kW of power at its maximum speed. The resistances to motion at this speed are 3800 N. Find the maximum speed of the car.

2 A small car's engine produces 56 kW at its maximum speed of $44\,\text{m s}^{-1}$ and the resistances to motion are proportional to the speed of the car.

a Find the tractive force of the car at its maximum speed.
b Work out a formula for the resistances to motion.

3 A water fountain pump throws 1 kg of water to a height of 0.75 m every 30 seconds. Work out the power of the pump.

4 A roller coaster ride uses a lift with a power rating of 140 kW. If the mass of the train is 11 tonnes and the angle of inclination of the slope is 30°, find the maximum speed of ascent. State one assumption you have made.

5 A petrol pump raises 5 kg of petrol a height of 3 m and ejects the petrol at $0.5\,\text{m s}^{-1}$ every 10 s. Calculate:

a the work done by the pump
b the power of the pump.

6 Concorde's engines produce 76 000 kW (or 76 MW). Its maximum horizontal speed is $597\,\text{m s}^{-1}$. The resistances to motion vary directly with the square of the aircraft's speed.

a Find an equation for the resistances to motion.
b The take-off speed of the plane is $112\,\text{m s}^{-1}$, the mass of the plane is 185 tonnes and the angle of its ascent is 10° to the horizontal. Determine the maximum acceleration of the aircraft at the start of its ascent.

Consolidation

Exercise A

1 A small block is pulled along a rough horizontal surface at a speed of $2\ \text{m s}^{-1}$ by a constant force. This force has magnitude 25 N and acts at an angle of 30° to the horizontal. Calculate the work done by the force in 10 seconds. (Take $g = 9.81\ \text{m s}^{-2}$.) *(UCLES)*

2 A bead of mass 2 kg moves along a smooth straight horizontal wire from point A to point B under the action of a force **F**. The position vectors of A and B are $(2\mathbf{i} + 3\mathbf{j})$ m and $(5\mathbf{i} + 7\mathbf{j})$ m respectively and $\mathbf{F} = (12\mathbf{i} - 5\mathbf{j})$ N.

a Find the work done by **F** in the motion from A to B.
b Given that the bead was at rest at A, find its speed at B. *(WJEC)*

Hint: draw a clear diagram and work out the angle between the force and displacement. Alternative: use $W = \mathbf{F} \cdot \mathbf{s}$

3 A car of mass 1000 kg has a power output of 30 000 watts and is driving up a slope inclined at 2° to the horizontal. The resistance forces acting on the car are modelled as having a magnitude of $40v$, where v is the speed of the car. (In this question assume $g = 10\ \text{m s}^{-2}$.)

a Show that the maximum speed, to the nearest metre per second, of the car going up the hill is $23\ \text{m s}^{-1}$.
b Find the maximum speed of the car when travelling down the slope.
c Comment on the validity of the model for the resistance forces. *(AEB)*

4 A boy and his racing bike have a total mass of 65 kg. He is cycling along a straight horizontal road with constant speed $7\ \text{m s}^{-1}$ and he is working at a constant rate of 420 W.

a Calculate the magnitude of the force opposing motion.
b The boy now cycles down a straight road which is inclined at an angle α to the horizontal. His work rate is 420 W, the force opposing his motion is of magnitude 120 N and he is moving at a constant speed of $15\ \text{m s}^{-1}$. Calculate the value of α to the nearest degree. *(ULEAC)*

Exercise B

1 A toboggan run is 1213 m long and drops 157 m from the start to the finish. One day a toboggan and its rider with a combined mass of 112 kg, starting from rest, achieved a speed of $119\ \text{km h}^{-1}$ at the finish.

a Calculate the gain in kinetic energy.
b Find the loss in potential energy.
c Determine the work done against the resistive forces. *(WJEC)*

2 A bus of mass 12 tonnes moves with a constant acceleration of $0.5\,\text{m}\,\text{s}^{-2}$ down a hill inclined at an angle of $\sin^{-1}\frac{1}{60}$ to the horizontal. The engine of the bus exerts a tractive force of 7.5 kN and the motion of the bus is opposed by a constant resistance of magnitude R newtons. Taking $g = 10\,\text{m}\,\text{s}^{-2}$, find:

Recall that $\sin^{-1}\frac{1}{60} = \arcsin\frac{1}{60}$

a the rate at which the engine of the bus is working when the speed of the bus is $10\,\text{m}\,\text{s}^{-1}$

b the value of R. *(NEAB)*

3 **a** A metal ball of mass 20 kg is allowed to fall from rest from a point P above a horizontal floor. The ball is brought to rest on impact with the floor and the kinetic energy lost is 1690 joules. Taking $g = 10\,\text{m}\,\text{s}^{-2}$, calculate:

i the speed of the ball immediately before impact

ii the height of P above the floor

iii the work done on the ball when it is lifted from the floor up to the point P.

b The speed of the water at the top of a waterfall of height 60 metres is $5\,\text{m}\,\text{s}^{-1}$. By considering the potential energy and kinetic energy of 1 kg of water, find the speed of the water at the bottom of the waterfall.

Water flows over the waterfall at a rate of $240\,\text{m}^3\,\text{s}^{-1}$. The mass of $1\,\text{m}^3$ of water is 1000 kg. Assuming that 30 percent of the kinetic energy of the water at the bottom of the waterfall can be converted into electricity by suitable generators, calculate the power, in kilowatts, that could be developed. *(UCLES)*

4 A woman of mass 60 kg runs along a horizontal track at a constant speed of $4\,\text{m}\,\text{s}^{-1}$. In order to overcome air resistance, she works at a constant rate of 120 W.

a Find the magnitude of the air resistance which she experiences.

b She now comes to a hill inclined at an angle α to the horizontal where $\sin\alpha = \frac{1}{15}$. To allow for the hill, she reduces her speed to $3\,\text{m}\,\text{s}^{-1}$ and maintains this constant speed as she runs up the slope. In a preliminary model of this situation, the air resistance is modelled as having a constant value obtained in **a** whatever the speed of the woman. Estimate the rate at which the woman has to work against external forces in order to run up the hill.

c In a more refined model, the air resistance experienced by the woman is taken as proportional to the square of her speed. Use your answer to **a** to obtain a revised estimate of the air resistance experienced by the woman when running at $3\,\text{m}\,\text{s}^{-1}$.

d Find a revised estimate of the rate at which the woman has to work against the external forces as she runs up the hill. *(ULEAC)*

Applications and Activities

1

Walk up a flight of stairs. Time how long it takes. Calculate:

a the work done against gravity
b the power you have developed.

2 Using energy considerations, predict the speed of a trolley at the end of a slope. Carry out an experiment and use the uniform acceleration formulas to check your prediction. Suggest an improved model.

Summary

- The formula for **work done** is

  work done = force × distance moved

  where it is the distance moved in the direction of the force

- The formula for **potential energy** is

  $\mathbf{PE} = mgh$

- The formula for **kinetic energy** is

  $\mathbf{KE} = \frac{1}{2}mv^2$

- The **principle of conservation of energy** is

  $\mathbf{PE_{start} + KE_{start} = PE_{end} + KE_{end}}$

- The **work–energy principle** is

  $\mathbf{PE_{start} + KE_{start} + W_{in} = PE_{end} + KE_{end} + W_{out}}$

- **Power** is defined as the rate of doing work. It is given by the formula

  $P = \dfrac{W}{t}$

- For moving vehicles, **power** can be calculated using

  $P = Fv$

11 Hooke's Law and Elasticity

What you need to know

- How to solve quadratic equations using the formula method.
- How to integrate linear expressions.
- How to apply Newton's laws of motion.
- How to find friction.
- How to apply the principle of conservation of energy.
- How to use the work–energy principle.

Review

1 Solve:

a $2x^2 - 7x + 4 = 0$ **b** $3.8x^2 - 8.4x - 2.7 = 0$

2 Find:

a $\int_0^{0.5} 16x \, dx$ **b** $\int_0^3 (15 - 4x) \, dx$

c $\int (3x + 2) \, dx$ **vd** $\int (7 - 9x) \, dx$

3 **a**

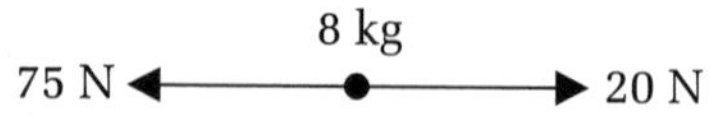

b

125 N 125 N
40° 40°
5 kg
49 N

Find the acceleration of the particles shown in the diagrams.

4 A body of mass 0.7 kg slides down a slope inclined at 40° to the horizontal. The coefficient of friction is 0.3. Find:

a the normal reaction, R

b the friction, F_r

c the acceleration.

5 **a** A particle of mass 3 kg is projected vertically upwards from the ground at a speed of 14 m s^{-1}. Find, using conservation of energy, the height it will reach before falling back to the ground.

b A particle of mass 120 g is dropped from a height of 20 m. What speed will it have reached when it hits the ground?

6 An object of mass 450 g is released from rest at a height of 4 m above the ground. If air resistance is constant and of magnitude 0.8 N, find the speed of the object when it reaches the ground using the work-energy principle.

11.1 Tension in an Elastic String or Spring

Spectators gasped when five people jumped off the roof of the stadium at the opening of the 1994 Commonwealth Games in New Zealand. However, they were not plunging to a certain death. They were introducing the rest of the world to the activity of bungee jumping. A bungee jumper attaches one end of an elastic rope to a fixed point on a high structure, the other end to a belt around his or her ankles and then steps out into thin air. Would you like to try this? It is important to be able to predict how far a bungee jumper will fall. This and other problems involving elastic strings and springs will be solved in this chapter.

Earlier work has involved strings that were inextensible. Any extension of a string due to tension was ignored. This is a reasonable model in many situations where the extension is small in comparison with the unstretched (natural) length of the string. But with some materials the extension is quite large and it is important to take it into account in the model.

Hooke's law

A British physicist, Robert Hooke (1635–1703) discovered, by experiment, that the extension in an elastic string is proportional to the tension. This law can be written as:

As the extension increases, the tension increases in the string.

$$T = kx$$

The value of k varies from one string to another and is called the **stiffness** of the string.

Notation
T = tension (N)
x = extension of the string or spring (m)
k = stiffness (N m^{-1})

The modulus of elasticity

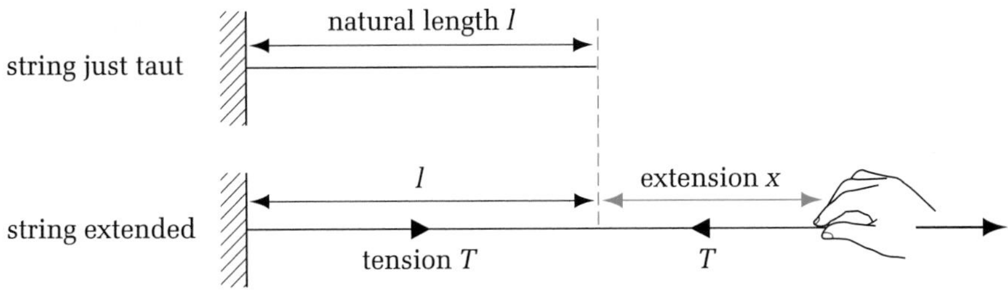

For a particular elastic material the value of k is inversely proportional to the natural (i.e. unstretched) length of the string. This fact can be included in the formula for the tension, giving:

$$T = \frac{\lambda x}{l}$$

This is the formula most often used for tension at this level in mathematics. The **modulus of elasticity,** λ, is equal to the tension required to double the length of the string.

Notation
T = tension (N)
x = extension of the string or spring (m)
λ = modulus of elasticity (N)
l = natural length (m)
i.e. when $x = l$ then total length is $2l$ and $\lambda = T$

The formula can be rearranged to give an equation for λ, the modulus of elasticity.

Recall that 'modulus' is also the magnitude of a vector.

$$T = \frac{\lambda x}{l}$$

Multiply by l.

$$Tl = \lambda x$$

Divide by x.

$$\lambda = \frac{Tl}{x}$$

Dimensional analysis gives:

$$[\lambda] = \frac{[T][l]}{[x]}$$

$[T] = [\text{Force}] = \text{MLT}^{-2}$

$$= \frac{\text{MLT}^{-2}\text{L}}{\text{L}}$$

L cancels

$$= \text{MLT}^{-2}$$

The dimensions of λ are those of a force and the units of λ are newtons.

Springs

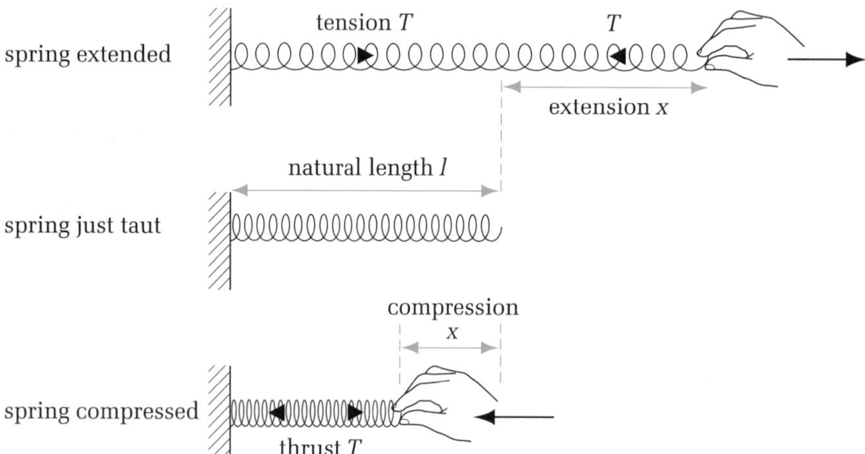

Thrust was introduced in Section 2.4.

When springs are stretched they are also subject to Hooke's law. When springs are **compressed** they exert a **thrust** outwards. Hooke's law still applies, but now T represents the thrust and x is the compression.

Limitations of Hooke's law

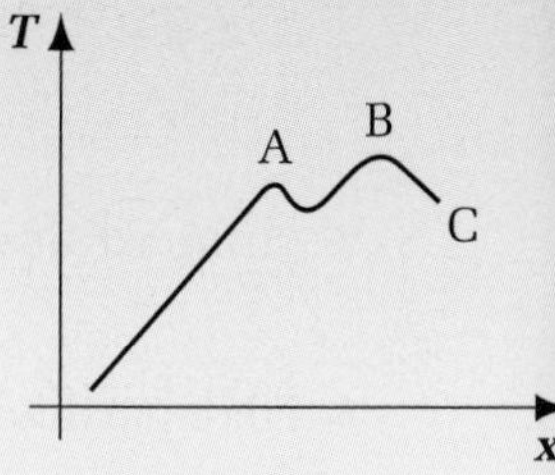

A = elastic limit
A–B = plastic deformation
C = breaking point
Hooke's law does not hold for very small extensions nor extensions beyond the elastic limit.

If an elastic band is stretched too far, it snaps. If a very heavy object is suspended from an elastic spring, the spring may not return to its original length when the object is removed. In these examples the material has been stretched beyond its elastic limit. The string or spring will not regain its original form after the stretching force is removed. When this happens Hooke's law no longer applies. Different materials behave in different ways after the elastic limit and solving problems is more complex. At this level, the work is restricted to examples which have not reached the elastic limit and so Hooke's law will apply.

Overview of method

Step ① Note what you are trying to find.

Step ② Write down the values of T, λ, x, l which are known, converting to SI units if necessary.

Step ③ Write down Hooke's law and substitute the known values.

Step ④ Solve the equation.

Or T, k, x.
The SI units are N and m.

Example 1

An elastic rope is extended by 20% when it is used to secure goods on a lorry. If the tension in the rope is 140 N, find the modulus of elasticity.

Solution

$\lambda = ?$ ◀ ① Note what you are trying to find.

$T = 140$ N ◀ ② Write down the values of T, λ, x, l that are known, converting to SI units if necessary.

l and x are not known, but since x is 20% of l then $x = 0.2l$

$$T = \frac{\lambda x}{l}$$ ◀ ③ Write down Hooke's law and substitute the known values.

$$140 = \frac{\lambda \times 0.2l}{l}$$

l can be cancelled.

$$140 = 0.2\lambda$$

Divide by 0.2.

$$\lambda = \frac{140}{0.2}$$ ◀ ④ Solve the equation.

$$\lambda = 700\,\text{N}$$

The modulus of elasticity is 700 N.

Example 2

The spring in a suspension system exerts a thrust of 3 kN when it is compressed to a length of 17.5 cm. The modulus of elasticity is 24 kN. Find the natural length of the spring.

Solution

$l = ?$ ◀ ① Note what you are trying to find.

$T = 3$ kN $= 3000$ N ◀ ② Write down the values of T, λ, x, l which are known, converting to SI units if necessary.

$x = l - 0.175$ m

$\lambda = 24$ kN $= 24\,000$ N

Although x is not known, it can be written in terms of l.

$$T = \frac{\lambda x}{l}$$

◀ ③ Write down Hooke's law and substitute the known values.

$$3000 = \frac{24\,000 \times (l - 0.175)}{l}$$

◀ ④ Solve the equation to find l.

Multiply by l.

$$3000l = 24\,000 \times (l - 0.175)$$

Divide by 3000.

$$l = 8(l - 0.175)$$

Expand the brackets.

$$l = 8l - 1.4$$

Subtract l and add 1.4.

$$1.4 = 7l$$

$$l = 0.2 \text{ m}$$

The natural length of the spring is 0.2 m, or 20 cm.

Example 3

A tension of 4 N produces an extension of 2.5 cm in an elastic string. Find:

a the stiffness, k

b the tension when the extension is 15 cm.

Questions may be set using the stiffness, k rather than the modulus of elasticity, λ.

Solution

a $k = ?$

Using $T = 4$ when $x = 0.025$,

$$T = kx$$

$$4 = k \times 0.025$$

$$k = \frac{4}{0.025}$$

$$k = 160$$

The stiffness is 160 N m^{-1}.

k is found by dividing the tension in N by the extension in m, so the units of k are N m^{-1}.

b $T = ?$

Using $k = 160$ and $x = 0.15$,

$$T = kx$$

$$T = 160 \times 0.15$$

$$T = 24 \text{ N}$$

When the extension is 15 cm the tension is 24 N.

11.1 Tension in an Elastic String or Spring

Exercise

Technique

1 An elastic string has natural length 2.5 m and modulus of elasticity 160 N. Find the tension when it is extended by 0.3 m.

2 The natural length of an elastic string is 36 cm and when it is extended to 40 cm the tension is 18 N. Find the modulus of elasticity.

3 The modulus of elasticity of an elastic string is 1.5 kN and its natural length is 0.6 m. Find the extension when the tension is 900 N.

4 The thrust in an elastic spring is 5.6 N when it is compressed by 21 mm. If the modulus of elasticity is 20 N, find the natural length of the spring.

5 An elastic string is extended by 25%. If the modulus of elasticity is 48 N, find the tension.

6 When an elastic string is stretched to a length of 1.4 m the tension is 12.5 N. Given that $\lambda = 75$ N, find the natural length of the string.

7 A spring is compressed from its natural length of 30 cm to two-thirds of its natural length. If the modulus of elasticity is 24 N, find the force in the spring and state whether it is a tension or thrust.

8 When an elastic string is extended by 0.2 m the tension is 38 N. Find:

a the stiffness, k, and state its units

b the tension when the extension is 0.5 m.

Contextual

1 A towrope extends by 6 cm when the tension is 240 N. If the modulus of elasticity is 16 kN, calculate the natural length of the towrope.

2 In a children's playground one ride consists of a motorcycle mounted on a spring of natural length 0.8 m. The spring is designed to compress by 15 cm when the thrust exerted is 300 N. Find the modulus of elasticity.

3 A guy rope is extended by 5% when it is used to support a tent. If the tension in the rope is 28 N, determine the modulus of elasticity.

4 **a** Find the stiffness of a climbing rope if it is extended by 0.8 m when the tension is 600 N.

b Calculate the extension in the same rope when the tension is 720 N.

11.2 Equilibrium Problems

Sally would like to buy some elastic rope to make a swing for her younger brother. She intends to attach an old tyre to a length of rope and hang it from a tree. The tyre weighs 10 kg, her brother weighs 50 kg and the branch is 6 m from the ground. The manufacturers of the rope give its modulus of elasticity to be 2.4 kN.

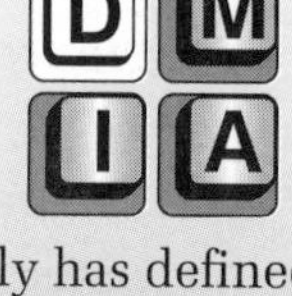

Sally has defined a mechanics problem.

Can Sally work out how much rope she needs to make the swing so that the tyre just touches the ground when her brother stands on it? The problem can be solved by modelling her brother and the tyre as a particle of mass 60 kg in equilibrium. The rope is taken to be an elastic string of unknown length l and modulus 2.4 kN. By treating Sally's brother and the tyre as a particle, they are assumed to have no size. The string is assumed to be light, that is, it has no weight. The tree will be considered to be rigid and so the branch will not bend. For an approximate result, g can be taken to be $10\,\text{m}\,\text{s}^{-2}$.

First a diagram is drawn showing clearly the forces which act. It is useful to note on the sketch those items which are known, and what is to be found.

6 m

T

$\lambda = 2400$ N

$l = ?$

$x = 6 - l$

$60g$

The problem can now be solved using resolution of forces and Hooke's law.

Resolve ↑

$$T - 60g = 0$$

$$T = 60g$$

$$T = 600 \text{ N}$$

Using Hooke's law

$$T = \frac{\lambda x}{l}$$

$$T = \frac{2400(6 - l)}{l}$$

Equating the two expressions for T gives:

$$\frac{2400(6 - l)}{l} = 600$$

$$2400(6 - l) = 600l$$

$$14\,400 - 2400l = 600l$$

$$14\,400 = 3000l$$

$$l = 4.8 \text{ m}$$

The length of rope needed is 4.8 m. Does this answer seem reasonable? As the branch is 6 m from the ground the answer of 4.8 m for the length of the rope looks about right.

There will be other questions Sally should ask before going ahead and buying the rope. How much ground clearance should she allow? When her brother is not standing on the tyre will it be near enough to the ground for him to climb on easily? Will the size and shape of the tyre make a difference? How much extra rope will be needed for attaching the tyre and tying to the branch? Does she want the rope to stretch so much? There is a lot of scope for further mathematical modelling.

Overview of method

Step ① Draw a clear force diagram.
Step ② Note the values given and what you are trying to find.
Step ③ Resolve forces – in one direction or two perpendicular directions.
Step ④ Use Hooke's law.
Step ⑤ Solve the equations.

Sometimes ③ and ④ will be swapped depending on the question asked. You may need to use trigonometry or Pythagoras' theorem.

Example 1

A particle P is attached to the midpoint of a light elastic string of natural length 0.5 m and modulus of elasticity 56 N. The ends of the string are fixed at points A and B which are at the same horizontal level with AB = 0.6 m. When the system hangs in equilibrium AP and BP are inclined at 60° to the horizontal. Find the mass of the particle.

Solution

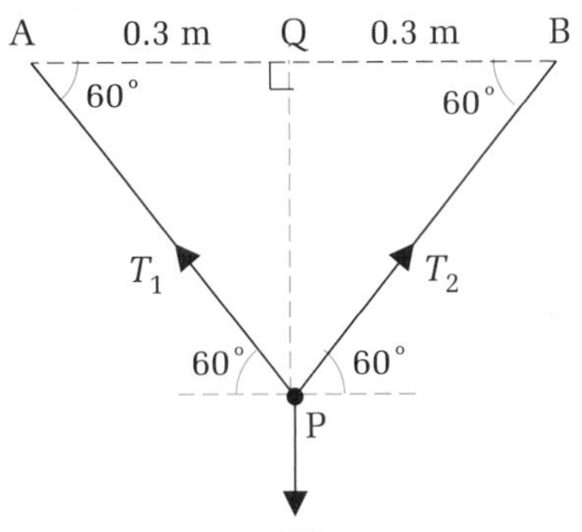

◀ ① Draw a clear force diagram.
◀ ② Note the items given and what you are trying to find.

$\lambda = 56$ N

$l = 0.25$ m (for each part AP, BP)

$m = ?$

Before the mass can be found by resolving forces vertically, it is necessary to find the tension in each part of the string. Are T_1 and T_2 equal?

Resolve → ◀ ③ **Resolve the forces.**

$$T_1\cos 60° - T_2\cos 60° = 0$$

$$T_1\cos 60° = T_2\cos 60°$$

$$T_1 = T_2$$

In symmetrical models like this one, the forces are also symmetrical. Both tensions may now be denoted by T. But what is the value of T? T depends on the extension.

Using trigonometry in triangle APQ to calculate the length of the string,

$$\cos 60° = \frac{0.3}{\text{AP}}$$

$$\text{AP} = \frac{0.3}{\cos 60°}$$

$$\text{AP} = 0.6$$

For string AP, $l = 0.25$ m

Half of the original string.
$\lambda = 56$ N and
$x = 0.6 - 0.25 = 0.35$ m

$$T = \frac{\lambda x}{l}$$ ◀ ④ **Apply Hooke's law.**

$$T = \frac{56 \times 0.35}{0.25}$$

$$T = 78.4 \text{ N}$$

Resolve ↑

$$2T\sin 60° = mg$$

$$2 \times 78.4 \sin 60° = m \times 9.8$$ ◀ ⑤ **Solve the equation.**

$$m = \frac{(2 \times 78.4 \sin 60°)}{9.8}$$

$$m = 13.86$$

The mass of the particle is 13.9 kg (3 s.f.).

Example 2

A tennis ball of mass 60 g is attached to a post in a garden by an elastic string of natural length 3 m. When using this equipment for practice a player holds the ball so that the string is horizontal and stretched by 15 cm. If the force applied to the ball by the player is F newtons acting at 15° above horizontal, find, to two significant figures:

a the value of F

b the modulus of elasticity of the string.

Solution

a

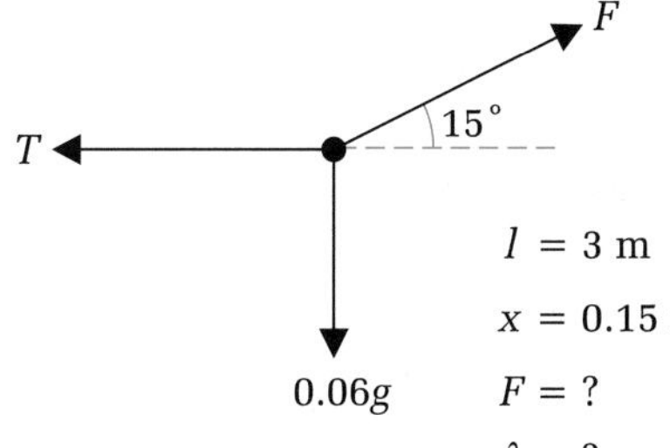

◀ ① **Draw a clear force diagram.**

◀ ② **Note the values given and what you are trying to find.**

$l = 3$ m

$x = 0.15$ m

$F = ?$

$\lambda = ?$

Resolve ↑ ◀ ③ **Resolve the forces.**

$$F\sin 15^\circ - 0.06g = 0$$
$$F\sin 15^\circ = 0.06 \times 9.8$$
$$F = \frac{0.06 \times 9.8}{\sin 15^\circ}$$
$$F = 2.272 \text{ N}$$
$$F = 2.3 \text{ N (2 s.f.)}$$

b The tension is needed before λ can be found.

Resolve ←

$$T - F\cos 15^\circ = 0$$
$$T = F\cos 15^\circ$$
$$T = 2.272 \times \cos 15^\circ$$
$$T = 2.194 \text{ N}$$

$$T = \frac{\lambda x}{l}$$ ◀ ④ **Apply Hooke's law.**

$$2.194 = \frac{\lambda \times 0.15}{3}$$
$$\lambda = \frac{3 \times 2.194}{0.15}$$

Multiply by 3 and divide by 0.15.

$$\lambda = 43.89 \text{ N}$$

The modulus of elasticity of the string = 44 N (2 s.f.).

11.2 Equilibrium Problems Exercise

Technique

1 A particle, P, of mass 1.5 kg is attached to one end of an elastic string whose natural length is 0.6 m. The other end of the string is attached to a fixed point O and the string hangs in equilibrium with P a distance of 0.8 m below O. Taking $g = 10\,\mathrm{m\,s^{-2}}$, find the modulus of elasticity of the string.

2 A spring is fixed at one end and supports a particle of mass 2.7 kg at the other end, as shown in the sketch. The modulus of elasticity of the spring is 45 N. Find the compression of the spring as a percentage of its natural length.

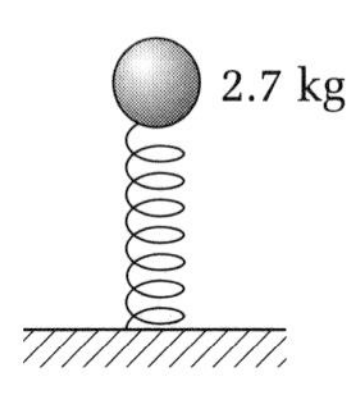

3 An object of mass 1.6 kg is attached to one end, A, of an elastic string of natural length 30 cm and modulus of elasticity 80 N. The other end of the string is attached to a point, B, on a smooth inclined plane. The system rests in equilibrium with AB = 35 cm. Find

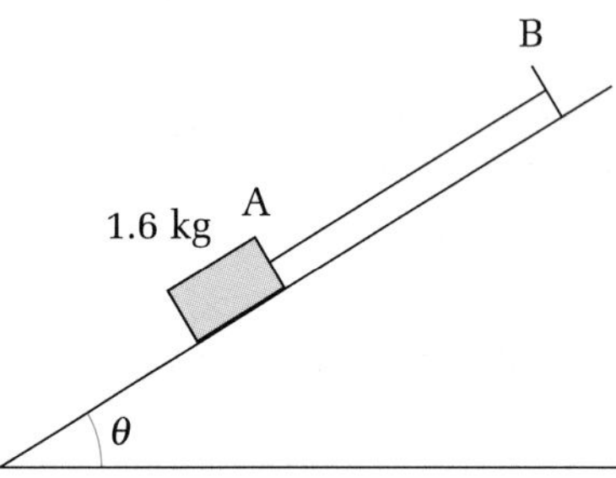

a the tension in the string

b to the nearest degree, the angle of inclination of the plane to the horizontal.

4 A particle, P, of mass 450 g is attached to two identical springs PQ and PR. The system is in equilibrium with Q, P and R in a vertical line as shown with QR = 3 m. The natural length of each spring is 1.25 m and the modulus of elasticity is 24 N.

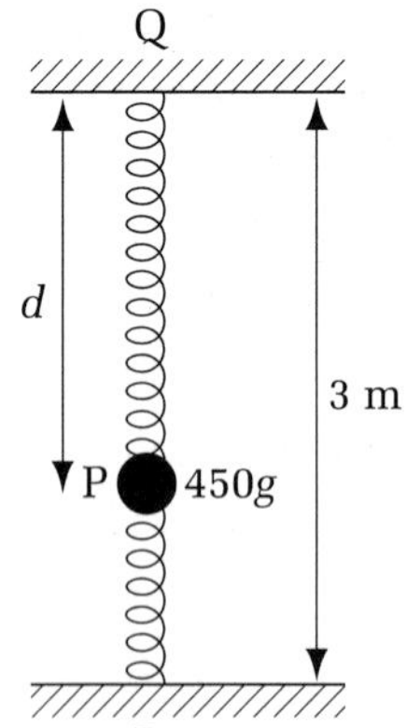

a Denoting the distance QP by d (metres) and assuming both springs are in tension, find formulas in terms of d for:

- **i** the tension in QP
- **ii** the tension in PR.

b Find d.

5 The sketch shows a particle, P, of mass 2 kg which is attached to a light inextensible string PQ and a spring PR. PR is horizontal and PQ is inclined at $60°$ to the vertical.

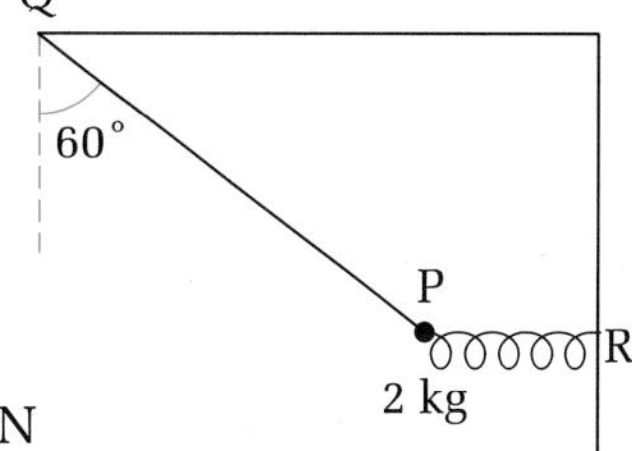

a Find the tension in PQ.

b If the spring has modulus of elasticity 50 N and natural length 16 cm, find the distance PR.

Contextual

1 When a climber of mass 80 kg hangs from a rope the natural length of the rope is increased by 7%. Find the modulus of elasticity of the rope.

2 A Jack-in-the-box consists of a doll of mass 200 g mounted on a spring of natural length 15 cm and modulus 12 N.

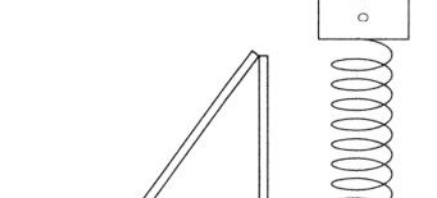

a Find the compression in the spring when the doll is out of the box.

b When the doll is in the box the spring is compressed to a third of its natural length. Find the force exerted on the doll by the lid.

3 Three springs of natural length 25 cm and modulus of elasticity 300 N are attached between two handles to form an exerciser.

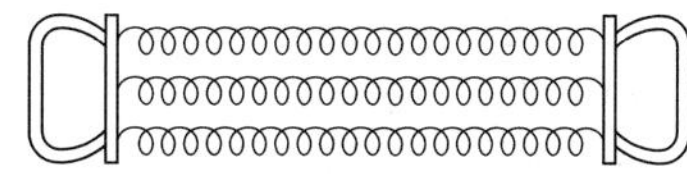

a Find the force that is needed on each handle to extend the springs to:
i 30 cm ii twice their natural length.

b The exerciser is adjusted by removing the central spring. If a force of 420 N is applied outwards to each handle, by how much are the springs extended from their natural length?

4 A hanging basket is suspended by a smooth hook from an elastic rope of natural length 0.6 m and modulus of elasticity 36 N. The ends of the rope are attached to points P and Q which are at the same horizontal level a distance of 0.6 m apart. When the basket hangs in equilibrium the hook is a distance of 0.4 m below the level of PQ. Find:

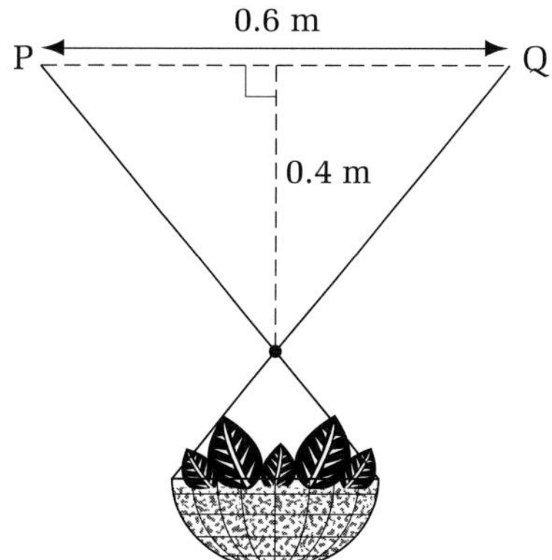

a the tension in the elastic rope

b the mass of the basket.

11.3 Motion involving Elastic Strings and Springs

You may have seen a pinball machine at an amusement arcade. When a coin is inserted, a ball is released. By pulling and releasing a handle the ball is fired into the machine. The ball scores points by colliding with obstacles in the machine before disappearing down a hole.

The firing mechanism for a pinball machine usually involves a spring as shown in the sketch. The spring is compressed and then released to propel the ball into the machine. A relationship between the properties of the spring and the acceleration of the ball can be found by modelling the ball as a particle at the end of a compressed spring. The method for this situation and others involving elastic strings can be summarised:

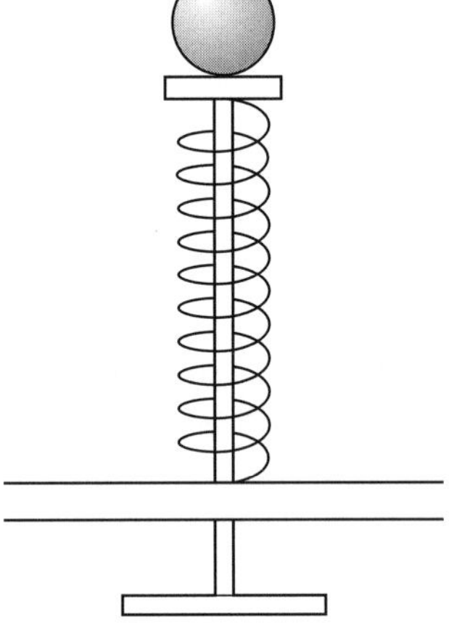

Overview of method

Step ① Draw a clear force diagram.
Step ② Note the values given and what you are trying to find.
Step ③ Use Hooke's law.
Step ④ Use Newton's law, $F = ma$, in the direction of motion.
Step ⑤ Solve the equations.

Sometimes ③ and ④ will need to be swapped to solve the problem. Trigonometry or Pythagoras' theorem may be needed.

Example 1

A particle, P, of mass 2 kg is attached to one end of a light elastic string of natural length 0.5 m and modulus of elasticity 60 N. The other end of the string is attached to a fixed point O. The particle P is held at a distance of 0.7 m vertically below O and then released from rest. Find the acceleration of P when OP = 0.7 m.

When the motion is in a vertical direction the weight of the object must be included.

Solution

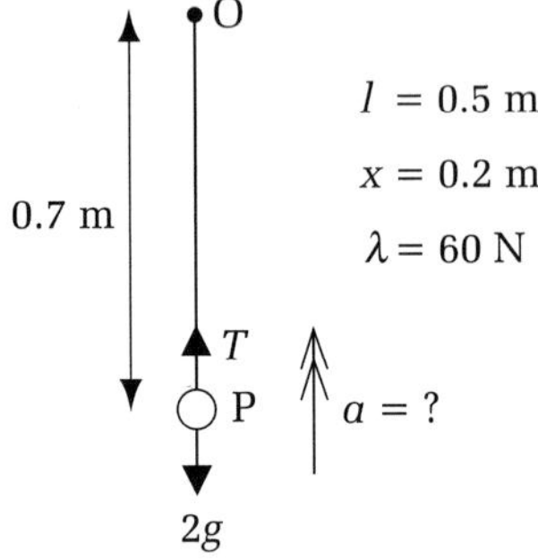

$l = 0.5$ m

$x = 0.2$ m

$\lambda = 60$ N

◀ ① Draw a clear force diagram.
◀ ② Note the values given and what you are trying to find.

Using Hooke's law, ◀ ③ Use Hooke's law.

$$T = \frac{\lambda x}{l}$$

$$T = \frac{60 \times 0.2}{0.5}$$

$$T = 24\,\text{N}$$

Using $F = ma \uparrow$ ◀ ④ Apply $F = ma$

$$F = ma$$

$$T - 2g = 2a$$ ◀ ⑤ Solve the equation.

$$24 - 2 \times 9.8 = 2a$$

$$4.4 = 2a$$

$$a = 2.2\,\text{m s}^{-2}$$

When OP = 0.7 m the acceleration is $2.2\,\text{m s}^{-2}$ upwards.

Example 2

When an aircraft lands on an aircraft carrier it hooks onto an elastic cable of length 40 m and modulus of elasticity 200 kN lying across the deck. As the cable stretches it helps to reduce the speed of the aircraft. In one landing the hook attaches at the centre of the cable and the engines of the aircraft produce a retarding force of 7.2 kN. The mass of the aircraft is 4 tonnes. Find the deceleration of the aircraft after it has travelled 15 m along the deck.

Solution

The aircraft is modelled as a particle, P, of mass 4000 kg and the cable as a light elastic string of natural length 40 m and modulus of elasticity 200 000 N. It is assumed that the cable is just taut before the aircraft hooks onto it. Motion is assumed to be horizontal and perpendicular to the initial position of the cable. Air resistance and friction are ignored.

◀ ① Diagram.

◀ ② Summary.

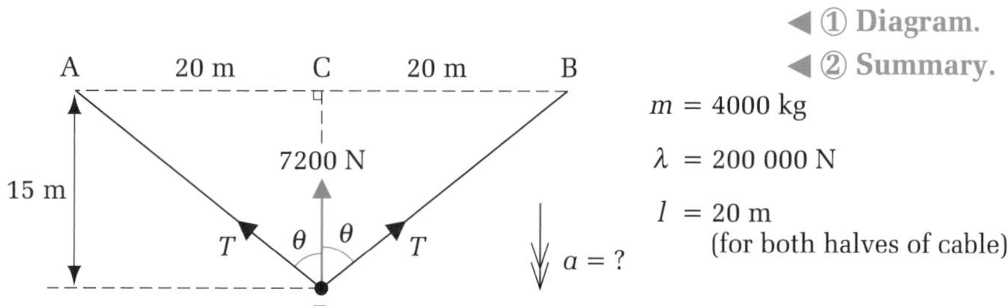

$m = 4000$ kg

$\lambda = 200\,000$ N

$l = 20$ m (for both halves of cable)

Direction of motion is ↓

The sketch shows the model after the aircraft has travelled 15 m along the deck.

Before using Hooke's law it is necessary to find the extension in the cable.

Using Pythagoras' theorem in triangle ACP,

$$AP^2 = 20^2 + 15^2$$
$$AP^2 = 625$$
$$AP = \sqrt{625}$$
$$AP = 25 \text{ m}$$

ACP is an enlargement of the 3, 4, 5 triangle.

The extension in cable AP = 25 − 20 = 5 m.

$$T = \frac{\lambda x}{l}$$ ◀ ③ Hooke's law.

$$T = \frac{200\,000 \times 5}{20}$$
$$T = 50\,000 \text{ N}$$

Using $F = ma$ in the direction of motion, ◀ ④ $F = ma$.

$$-2T\cos\theta - 7200 = 4000a$$
$$-100\,000 \times \tfrac{15}{25} - 7200 = 4000a$$
$$-67\,200 = 4000a$$ ◀ ⑤ Solve the equation.

$$a = \tfrac{-67\,200}{4000}$$
$$a = -16.8 \text{ m s}^{-2}$$

The forces are both negative as they oppose the motion.

The deceleration is 16.8 m s^{-2}. The aircraft is slowing down rapidly, as expected. The further it stretches the cable, the greater will be the deceleration.

Example 2 is a very simplified version of what happens when an aircraft lands on a carrier. In practice more complex cable systems are used and the aircraft's engines continue to provide thrust forwards so that the aircraft can climb again if the landing fails.

11.3 Motion involving Elastic Strings and Springs

Exercise

Technique

1 A particle, P, of mass 2.5 kg, rests on a smooth horizontal table. It is attached to a fixed point O on the table by a spring of natural length 0.3 m and modulus of elasticity 10 N. The particle is held so that the distance OP is 0.9 m and then it is released from rest. Find the acceleration of P when it begins to move.

2 A particle, P, of mass 0.5 kg is attached to one end of a light elastic string of natural length 0.2 m and modulus of elasticity 3 N. The other end of the string is attached to a fixed point O. The particle P released from a distance of 0.6 m vertically below O. Find the upward acceleration of P when:

a OP = 0.6 m **b** OP = 0.4 m

3 A body, B, of mass 3.2 kg, is attached by an elastic string to a fixed point A. The string has natural length 1.2 m and modulus of elasticity 140 N. If the body is dropped from A and falls vertically downwards, find the downward acceleration of the body when:

a AB = 1.2 m **b** AB = 1.45 m **c** AB = 1.6 m

4 A particle is attached to one end of a light elastic string and the other end is attached to a fixed point on a smooth plane inclined at 30° to the horizontal. The natural length of the string is 20 cm and its modulus of elasticity is 36 N. The mass of the particle is 1.8 kg. The particle is pulled down the slope until the length of the string is 30 cm and then it is released from rest. Taking $g = 10\ \text{m s}^{-2}$, find:

a the acceleration when the particle begins to move

b the length of the string when the acceleration of the particle becomes zero.

Assume that the particle travels up the slope when released.

5 A body of mass 2 kg is suspended from two fixed points, A and B, by two identical elastic strings of natural length 0.5 m and modulus of elasticity 26 N. A and B are at the same horizontal level with AB = 1.6 m. The body is pulled down vertically until it is a distance of 0.6 m below the level of AB and then it is released from rest. Find the acceleration when it is released.

Contextual

1 Helen has attached a football of mass 0.25 kg to one end of an elastic rope of natural length 4 m and modulus of elasticity 6 N. The other end of the rope is attached to the base of a washing line post. She pulls the ball along the ground until the rope is 5.2 m long and then releases it. What will be the acceleration of the ball when it starts to move?

Assume the ground is smooth.

2 A model of a bird of mass 0.15 kg hands from the ceiling by an elastic thread. The natural length of the thread is 0.8 m and $\lambda = 3.6$ N. The bird is pulled down so that it is 1.2 m below the ceiling and then released. Find its upward acceleration when:

a the length of the string is 1.2 m
b the length of the string reduces to 1 m.

3 Ian has a doll of mass 0.2 kg, which is mounted on a spring of natural length 5 cm and modulus of elasticity 13 N. Ian pushes down the doll so that the spring compresses to a length of 4 cm and then he releases it.

a With what acceleration will the doll begin to move?
b By how much would Ian need to compress the spring to give the doll an initial acceleration of 15 m s^{-2}?

4

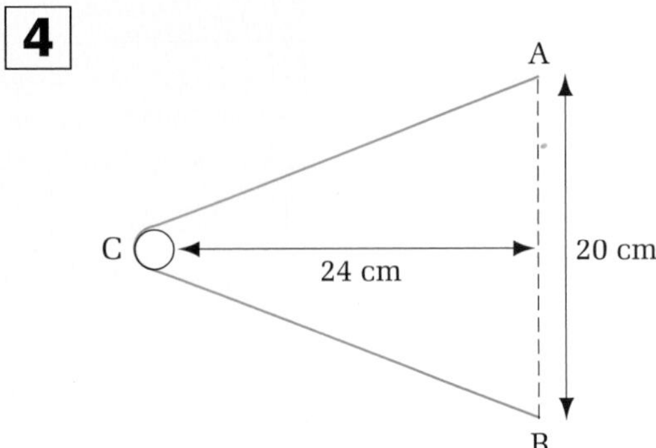

A practice machine uses a catapult to project table tennis balls horizontally towards a player. A ball of mass 25 g is held at the centre of a light elastic belt which has a natural length 20 cm and modulus of elasticity 0.5 N. The ends of the belt are attached to points A and B which are at the same horizontal level, a distance 20 cm apart. The ball is propelled from a point, C, which is 24 cm from AB. The sketch shows the ball in this position when viewed from above.

Find the acceleration of the ball when it is released. Assume that the ball moves horizontally and state other assumptions you make.

11.4 Elastic Potential Energy

A toy consists of a bat and ball attached by an elastic string. This toy is popular with children because they do not have to retrieve the ball. The elastic string does the work for them. This section studies the work done in stretching an elastic string and the energy possessed by a stretched string.

Work and elastic potential energy

When a force stretches an elastic string, the force does work and the string is given potential energy. You have met potential energy before in the form of **gravitational** potential energy. If an object is held at a height above the ground and released, it falls. The potential energy is converted into kinetic energy. An object at the end of a stretched string will also move if it is released. This time the energy which is converted into kinetic energy was the potential energy stored in the stretched string. It is called **elastic** potential energy and can be abbreviated to EPE.

The amount of energy stored in a stretched elastic string depends on the extension and the modulus of elasticity of the string. A formula can be derived by finding the work done when an elastic string is stretched.

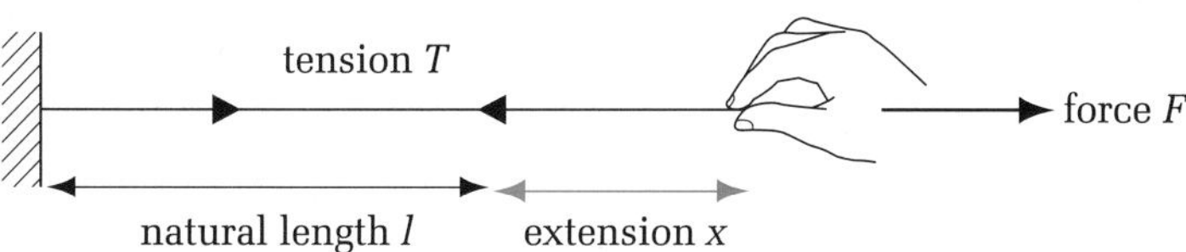

The sketch shows a force F stretching an elastic string. As the extension increases, the force must increase. At each stage the force must be equal and opposite to the tension.

$$F = T$$

$$F = \frac{\lambda x}{l}$$

Use $T = \frac{\lambda x}{l}$

The force is proportional to x. The work done in stretching the string can be found by multiplying the average force by the distance moved in the direction of the force.

As the extension increases from 0 to x, the force increases from 0 to $\frac{\lambda x}{l}$.

So average force $= \left(0 + \frac{\lambda x}{l}\right) \div 2 = \frac{\lambda x}{2l}$ and distance moved $= x$.

So work done $= x \times \frac{\lambda x}{2l} = \frac{\lambda x^2}{2l}$

Using $T = kx$ gives EPE $= \frac{kx^2}{2}$

This formula can also be derived using the area under a force–displacement graph or by integration. When a variable force F moves an object a small distance δx then the work done is given by

$$\text{work done} = F \times \delta x$$

When the force moves the object a total distance x, then the total work done is given by

$$\text{total work done} = \int_0^x F\,\mathrm{d}x$$

The units for elastic potential energy must be the same as for work and energy. Elastic potential energy is measured in joules, abbreviated to J.

For a string or spring: total work done $= \int_0^x T\,\mathrm{d}x = \int_0^x \frac{\lambda x}{l}\,\mathrm{d}x$. $= \left[\frac{\lambda x^2}{2l}\right]_0^x = \frac{\lambda x^2}{2l}$

$$\textbf{EPE} = \frac{\lambda x^2}{2l} \quad \text{or} \quad \frac{kx^2}{2}$$

Notation

EPE = elastic potential energy (J)
x = extension [or compression for a spring] (m)
l = natural length (m)
k = stiffness (N m^{-1})
λ = modulus of elasticity (N)

Overview of method

Step ① Note what you are trying to find.
Step ② Write down the known values, converting to SI units if necessary.
Step ③ Write down the formula you intend to use for EPE or work done.
Usually $\frac{\lambda x^2}{2l}$, occasionally $\frac{kx^2}{2}$ or $\int_0^x T\,\mathrm{d}x$
Step ④ Substitute the known values and find the required value.

Example 1

The firing mechanism in a pinball machine contains a spring of natural length 4 cm whose modulus of elasticity is 10 N. The work done in compressing the spring is 0.05 J. By how much is the spring compressed?

Solution

$x = ?$ ◀ ① Note what you are trying to find.

$l = 0.04$ m $\quad \lambda = 10$ N
work done = EPE = 0.05 J ◀ ② Write down the known values.

$$\text{EPE} = \frac{\lambda x^2}{2l}$$ ◀ ③ Write down the formula.

$$0.05 = \frac{10x^2}{0.08}$$ ◀ ④ Substitute the known values and find the required value.

Multiply by 0.08 and divide by 10.

$$x^2 = \frac{0.05 \times 0.08}{10}$$

$$x^2 = 0.0004$$

$$x = \sqrt{0.0004}$$

$$x = 0.02$$

The spring is compressed by 0.02 m = 2 cm.

Example 2

The stiffness of a string is 200 N m^{-1}. Find the work done when the string is extended by 0.8 m.

Solution

Work done when string is stretched by 0.8 m? ◀ ① **Note what you are trying to find.**

$k = 200$, giving $T = 200x$ ◀ ② **Write down the known values.**

Remember $T = kx$.

$$\text{work done} = \int_0^x T\,dx$$

◀ ③ **Write down the formula for work done.**

$$= \int_0^{0.8} 200x\ dx$$

◀ ④ **Substitute the known values and find the required value.**

Integrate $200x$.

$$= \left[\frac{200x^2}{2}\right]_0^{0.8}$$

$$= [100x^2]_0^{0.8}$$

$$= 100 \times 0.8^2$$

Work done $= 64$ J.

Alternative solution

As the work done must be equal to the EPE given to the string an alternative approach is:

$$\text{EPE} = \frac{\lambda x^2}{2l}$$

Although λ and l are not known, the stiffness k can replace $\frac{\lambda}{l}$, giving:

$$\text{EPE} = \frac{kx^2}{2}$$

$$= \frac{200 \times 0.8^2}{2}$$

$$= 64 \text{ J as before}$$

11.4 Elastic Potential Energy
Exercise

Technique

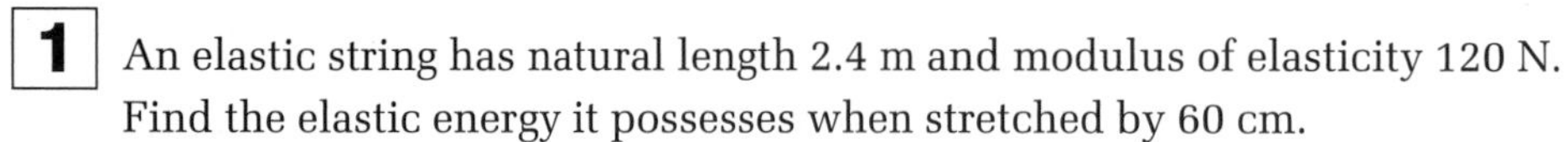

1 An elastic string has natural length 2.4 m and modulus of elasticity 120 N. Find the elastic energy it possesses when stretched by 60 cm.

2 The work done in compressing a spring from its natural length of 8 cm to 6 cm is 0.35 J. Find its modulus of elasticity.

3 An elastic string has a natural length of 1.6 m and modulus of elasticity 2 kN. The work done in stretching the string is 100 J. Find:

a the extension

b the stretched length of the string.

4 The modulus of elasticity of a spring is 250 N. When it is stretched to three times its natural length the work done is 150 J. Find the natural length of the spring.

5 A force of F newtons is used to compress a spring. If $F = 300x$ when the compression is x metres, find the work done by F when the compression is 0.2 m.

6 Find the work done when an elastic string of stiffness 160 N m^{-1} is extended from its natural length by 40 cm.

Contextual

1 A washing line is stretched between two posts a distance of 26 m apart. Find the work done if the natural length of the line is 25 m and its modulus of elasticity is 750 N.

2 A ball-point pen contains a spring of natural length 16 mm and modulus of elasticity 2 N. The spring is compressed by 6 mm when the pen is operated. Find the potential energy in the spring.

3 When a bungee-runner stretches an elastic rope by 15 m the work done is 450 J. If the natural length of the rope is 20 m, find its modulus of elasticity.

4 A Jack-in-the box contains a spring of natural length 20 cm and modulus of elasticity 15 N. The energy used in compressing the spring is 0.24 J. Find the length of the spring when Jack is in the box.

11.5 Conservation of Energy and the Work–Energy Principle

Many problems involving elastic strings and springs can be solved using the principle of conservation of mechanical energy and the work–energy principle.

Consider the energy changes which take place when a bungee-jumper falls. Standing at the top of a high structure, the bungee-jumper has gravitational potential energy. After jumping off, the jumper gradually loses this potential energy. The energy is converted into kinetic energy which increases as the jumper's speed increases. At some point the rope will begin to stretch. Energy is now being converted into elastic potential energy. Eventually the jumper slows down and stops. The kinetic energy has all been converted into elastic potential energy. If external forces such as air resistance are ignored, the principle of conservation of mechanical energy can be used to predict how far the jumper will fall and what the speed will be at any stage. A worked example involving a bungee-jump is included later in this section.

A more refined model could include the effect of air resistance. In this case the work–energy principle would be used to make the predictions.

Overview of method

Step ① Draw clear diagrams showing all the main details.

Step ② Decide on a zero level for potential energy.

Step ③ Find expressions for the total mechanical energy at two points in the motion.

Step ④ Decide whether any external forces should be included. If no external forces are involved, use the principle of conservation of mechanical energy. If external forces are involved, use the work–energy principle.

Total mechanical energy includes gravitational potential energy, elastic potential energy and kinetic energy.

Example 1

A particle, P, of mass 0.5 kg, is attached to one end of a light elastic string of natural length 40 cm and modulus of elasticity 7 N. The other end of the string is attached to a fixed point O. The particle is released from rest at the point A, which is a distance of 1 m vertically below O. Find the velocity of the particle when the string becomes slack.

Solution

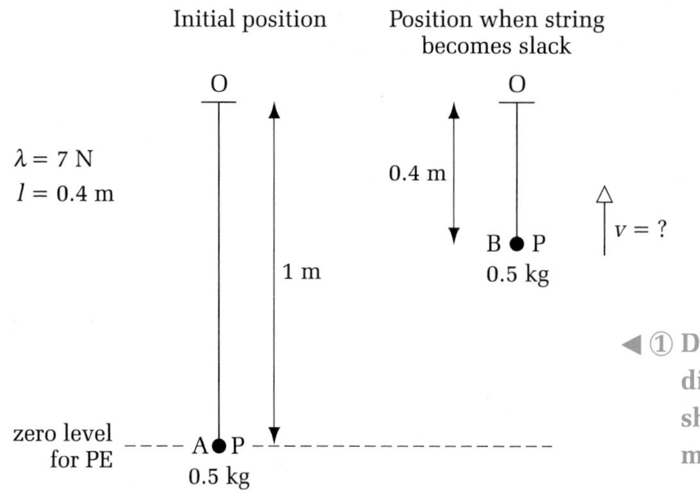

Initial position

Position when string becomes slack

O

O

$\lambda = 7$ N

$l = 0.4$ m

0.4 m

$v = ?$

B ● P

0.5 kg

1 m

◀ ① Draw clear diagrams showing all the main details.

zero level for PE ---- A ● P ----

0.5 kg

The level of A has been chosen as the zero level for potential energy.

◀ ② Decide on a zero level for potential energy.

As an alternative, the level of O could have been used.

For the initial position, A,

$$\text{PE} = 0 \qquad \text{KE} = 0 \qquad \text{EPE} = \frac{\lambda x^2}{2l}$$

$$= \frac{7 \times 0.6^2}{2 \times 0.4}$$

$$= 3.15\,\text{J}$$

$x = 1 - 0.4 = 0.6$ m

Total mechanical energy in position A = 3.15 J.

For the position B, when the string becomes slack:

$$\text{PE} = mgh \qquad \text{KE} = \tfrac{1}{2}mv^2 \qquad \text{EPE} = 0$$

$$= 0.5 \times 9.8 \times 0.6 \qquad = 0.5 \times 0.5v^2$$

$$= 2.94\ \text{J} \qquad = 0.25v^2$$

Total mechanical energy in position B $= 0.25v^2 + 2.94$

◀ ③ Find the total mechanical energy at two points in the motion.

Using the principle of conservation of mechanical energy,

◀ ④ As no external forces are involved, use the principle of conservation of mechanical energy.

$$\text{ME}_B = \text{ME}_A$$

ME = total mechanical energy.

$$0.25v^2 + 2.94 = 3.15$$

Subtract 2.94.

$$0.25v^2 = 0.21$$

Divide by 0.25.

$$v^2 = 0.84$$

Take the square root.

$$v = \sqrt{0.84}$$

$$v = 0.9165\,\text{m s}^{-1}$$

The velocity of the particle when the string becomes slack is 0.917 m s^{-1} (3 s.f.). If the working had given a negative value for v^2 it would have meant that the initial EPE was not sufficient for the particle to rise to a height where the string becomes slack.

Alternative approach

Instead of calculating the total mechanical energy at two positions, the problem could have been solved using changes in energy.

EPE lost = KE gained + PE gained.

Changes in energy as particle moves from A to B.

This method results in equations equivalent to those found in the original solution. Because it is easier to make errors with signs using this alternative method, the original approach will be used for the rest of the examples.

Example 2

A toy engine has a mass of 800 g. When it reaches a buffer at the end of the line it is travelling at 0.1 m s^{-1}. The buffer consists of a spring of natural length 3 cm and modulus of elasticity 4.5 N. Find the compression in the elastic spring when the engine comes to rest.

Solution

The engine is modelled as a particle with $m = 0.8$ kg and the buffer as a spring with $l = 0.03$ m and $\lambda = 4.5$ N.

Friction and air resistance are assumed to be zero.

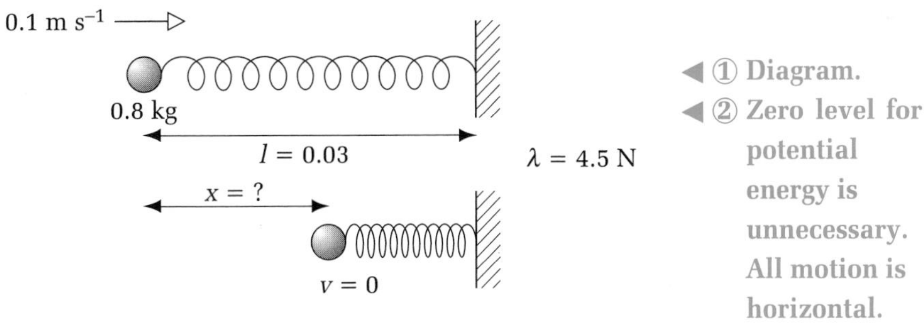

◀ ① Diagram.

◀ ② Zero level for potential energy is unnecessary. All motion is horizontal.

Before engine meets buffer,

$$\begin{aligned} \text{KE} &= \tfrac{1}{2}mv^2 \qquad\qquad \text{EPE} = 0 \\ &= 0.5 \times 0.8 \times 0.1^2 \\ &= 0.004 \text{ J} \end{aligned}$$

Ignore PE when motion is horizontal.

Total mechanical energy before buffer = 0.004 J.

When engine comes to rest, ◀ ③ **Find the total mechanical energy at two points in the motion.**

$$\text{KE} = 0 \qquad \text{EPE} = \frac{\lambda x^2}{2l}$$
$$= \frac{4.5 \times x^2}{2 \times 0.03}$$
$$= 75x^2$$

Using the principle of conservation of mechanical energy, ◀ ④ **As no external forces are given, use conservation of energy.**

$$75x^2 = 0.004$$
$$x^2 = 5.333 \times 10^{-5}$$ Divide by 75.
$$x = \sqrt{5.333 \times 10^{-5}}$$ Take the square root.
$$x = 0.007\,303$$

The compression in the buffer is 7.3 mm (2 s.f.). The answer of 7 mm compression seems reasonable with a spring of natural length 3 cm.

Example 3

A man, of mass 70 kg is going to carry out a sponsored bungee-jump from a bridge. The bridge is 64 m above the river which flows beneath it and the rope he intends to use has a modulus of elasticity of 4 kN. Taking $g = 10\,\text{m}\,\text{s}^{-2}$, and assuming conservation of energy, find the natural length of the rope needed if he plans to fall a distance of 60 m.

Solution

The man can be modelled as a particle of mass 70 kg and the rope as a light elastic string of unknown natural length l and modulus of elasticity 4000 N. Assume that he starts from rest.

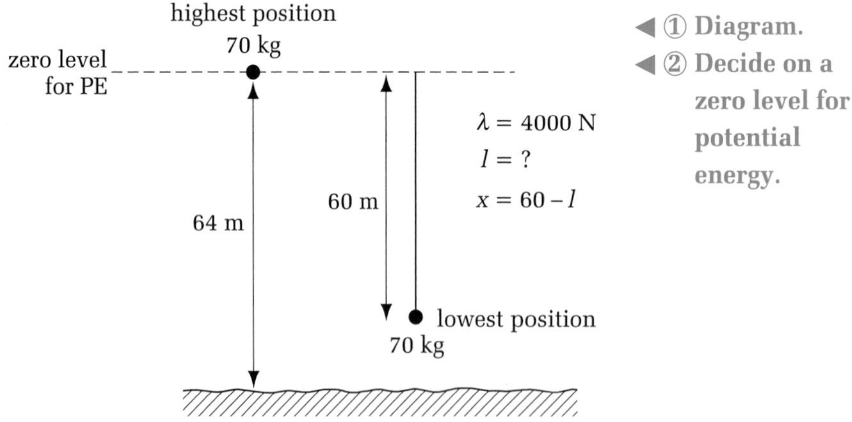

◀ ① **Diagram.**
◀ ② **Decide on a zero level for potential energy.**

This time the level of the bridge has been taken as the zero level for potential energy. When the man is *below* the level of the bridge he has *negative potential energy*.

For the highest position,

PE $= 0$ KE $= 0$ EPE $= 0$

Total mechanical energy $= 0$

For the lowest position, ◀ ③ **Find the total mechanical energy at two points.**

$$\text{PE} = mgh \qquad \text{KE} = 0 \qquad \text{EPE} = \frac{\lambda x^2}{2l}$$

$$= 70 \times 10 \times -60 \qquad\qquad = \frac{4000(60 - l)^2}{2l}$$

$$= -42\,000\ \text{J}$$

h is the distance fallen *not* the height of the bridge.

$$\text{Total mechanical energy} = \left(\frac{4000(60 - l)^2}{2l} - 42\,000\right)\text{J.}$$

Using the principle of conservation of mechanical energy, ◀ ④ **Use this principle as requested.**

$$\frac{4000(60 - l)^2}{2l} - 42\,000 = 0$$

Add 42 000

$$\frac{2000(60 - l)^2}{l} = 42\,000$$

Multiply by *l*.

$$2000(60 - l)^2 = 42\,000l$$

Divide by 2000 to simplify the equation. Expand the brackets.

$$(60 - l)^2 = 21l$$

$$(60 - l)(60 - l) = 21l$$

$$3600 - 120l + l^2 = 21l$$

Subtract 21*l*.

$$l^2 - 141l + 3600 = 0$$

The quadratic equation is solved by the formula method.

$$l = \frac{141 \pm \sqrt{141^2 - 4 \times 3600}}{2}$$

$$l = \frac{141 \pm \sqrt{5481}}{2} = \frac{141 \pm 74.03}{2}$$

$$l = 33.48 \quad \text{or} \quad 107.52$$

Ignore the second answer, which is obviously too long for a 60 m drop. The natural length of rope needed is 33 m (to nearest m).

Work–Energy Principle

Example 3 ignores air resistance. If a constant force of 80 N opposed the motion, the solution would be altered as follows:

$$\text{ME}_\text{H} + \text{W}_\text{in} = \text{ME}_\text{L} + \text{W}_\text{out}$$

$$0 + 0 = \frac{4000(60 - l)^2}{2l} - 42\,000 + 80 \times 60$$

Solve this equation. You should find this revised model suggests the natural length should be 35 m (to the nearest metre).

Notation
ME = total mechanical energy
H = highest position
L = lowest position
W_out = resistance × distance fallen

11.5 Conservation of Energy and the Work–Energy Principle

Exercise

Technique

In questions 1 to 3 a particle, P, of mass m kg is attached by a light elastic string of natural length l m and modulus of elasticity λ N to a fixed point O on a smooth horizontal surface as shown in the diagram.

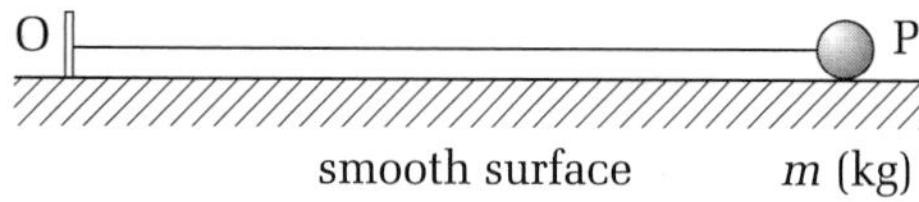

1 $m = 2, l = 0.5, \lambda = 6.$
P is held so that OP = 0.8 m and then released from rest. Find the speed of P when the string becomes slack.

2 $m = 1.2, l = 1, \lambda = 8.$
Initially OP = 1 m and P is projected along the surface, with velocity 3 m s^{-1} away from O. Find the speed of P when OP = 1.5 m.

3 $m = 0.7, l = 2, \lambda = 5.$
P is projected along the surface from O with speed 4 m s^{-1}. Find the length of the string when P comes instantaneously to rest.

In questions 4 and 5 a particle, P, of mass m kg is attached by a light spring of natural length l m and modulus of elasticity λ N to a fixed point O on a horizontal surface as shown. Motion is along the surface and opposed by a constant frictional force F N.

natural length l (m)
modulus of elasticity λ (N)
O P
rough surface m (kg)
friction F (N)

4 $m = 1.5, l = 2.5, \lambda = 40, F = 2.$
P is held so that OP = 3 m and then released from rest. Find the speed of P when the spring reduces to its natural length.

5 $m = 8, l = 1, \lambda = 50, F = 40.$
Initially OP = 1 m and P is projected with a velocity of 5 m s^{-1} away from O. Find the speed of P when OP = 1.4 m.

In questions 6 to 8 a particle, P, of mass m kg is attached to one end of a light elastic string of natural length l m and modulus of elasticity λ N. The other end of the string is attached to a fixed point O as shown in the sketch. The particle moves vertically.

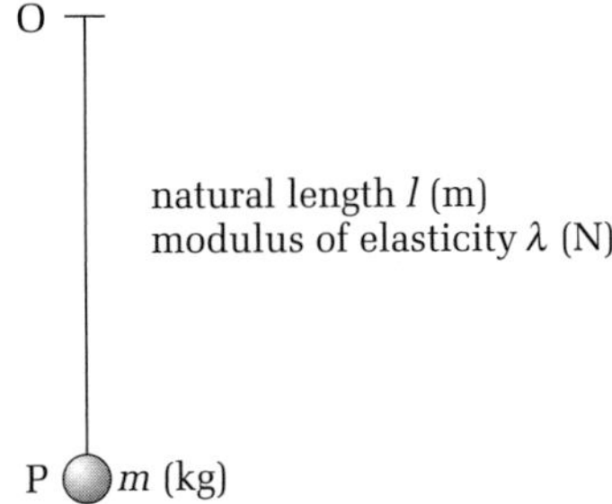

6 $m = 2.5$, $l = 2$, $\lambda = 28$.
P is released from rest at O. Find the speed at which P is falling when OP = 3 m, assuming:

a no air resistance

b the air resistance is constant and of magnitude 4 N.

7 $m = 0.5$, $l = 1.5$, $\lambda = 60$.
P is pulled down until OP = 2 m and then released from rest. Find:

a the speed of P when the string becomes slack

b the distance OP when P comes instantaneously to rest.

8 A particle, P, of mass 0.6 kg is attached to one end of a light elastic string of natural length 50 cm and modulus of elasticity 28 N. The other end of the string is attached to a fixed point O. The particle is released from rest at O. If x m is the extension when P comes instantaneously to rest:

a use the conservation of mechanical energy to find a quadratic equation for x;

b solve the equation and hence find how far P falls before instantaneously coming to rest.

9 A body of mass 2 kg is attached to one end of a light elastic string. The other end of the string is attached to a point O on a rough plane inclined at 30° to the horizontal. The particle is released from O and slides down the plane until it comes to instantaneous rest at a point A. The natural length of the string is 1 m, $\mu = 0.1$ and $\lambda = 40$ N.

a Find the magnitude of the friction force which acts on the body as it moves down the slope.

b Use the work–energy principle to find a quadratic equation for the extension, x m, in the string when the particle comes instantaneously to rest at A.

c Solve the equation and find the distance OA.

Contextual

1 A toy frog of mass 20 g is mounted on a light spring of natural length 5 cm and modulus of elasticity 4 N. A child presses down on the frog until the spring is compressed to half of its natural length and then releases it. To what height will the frog jump before falling to the ground? State any assumptions you make in your mathematical model.

2 Abdul has a toy car of mass 0.3 kg. It is attached to an elastic string of natural length 2.4 m and modulus of elasticity 8 N. Abdul attaches the other end of the string to the base of a wall and then releases the car from rest from a point on the ground 4 m away from the wall. Find the speed with which the car crashes into the wall:

a using the principle of conservation of mechanical energy
b using the work–energy principle, assuming that resistances to motion are constant and of magnitude 0.5 N.

3 A man, of mass 75 kg intends to bungee-jump from a bridge. For safety reasons he wishes to fall no further than 80 m and the rope he intends to use has a modulus of elasticity of 6 kN.

a Assuming conservation of energy find, to three significant figures, the maximum value for the natural length of the rope he should use.
b If air resistance is taken to be 50 N, use the work–energy principle to revise your answer to part **a**.

4 A model parachutist of mass 0.4 kg is attached by an elastic string to a point A on Jenny's ceiling. The string is of natural length 70 cm and modulus of elasticity 25 N. Jenny pulls the model downwards until it is 1 m from the ceiling and then releases it. Find:

a the model's distance from the ceiling when it stops travelling upwards
b the speed with which the model is travelling when the string becomes slack.

5 In a charity event a woman of mass 63 kg is attached to a rope of natural length 55 m and modulus of elasticity 16 kN. The other end of the rope is attached to a platform on a viaduct which is 100 m above the ground. The woman steps off the platform and falls towards the ground. Ignoring air resistance, find:

a the speed at which she is falling when she is 30 m above the ground
b how far above the ground she is when she stops falling.

State briefly whether each answer would be greater or smaller if air resistance were included in the model.

Consolidation

Exercise A

1 A particle of mass 0.5 kg is suspended from a fixed point O by a light elastic string of natural length 1.5 m and modulus of elasticity 40 N. The particle is released from rest at the point A, which is vertically below O and such that OA = 1.5 m. Using the principle of conservation of energy and taking $g = 9.81\ \mathrm{m\,s^{-2}}$, find the distance below A at which the particle comes instantaneously to rest for the first time.

(UCLES)

2 A light, elastic string has natural length 0.5 m and modulus of elasticity 49 N. The end A is attached to a point on a ceiling. A small object of mass 3 kg is attached to the end B of the string and hangs in equilibrium.

a Calculate the length AB.

A second string, identical to the first one, is now attached to the object at B and to a point C on the floor, 2.5 m below the point A. The system is in equilibrium with B a distance x m below A, as shown in the diagram.

b Find the tension in each of the strings in terms of x and hence show that $x = 1.4$ m.

c Calculate the elastic potential energy in the strings when the object hangs in equilibrium.

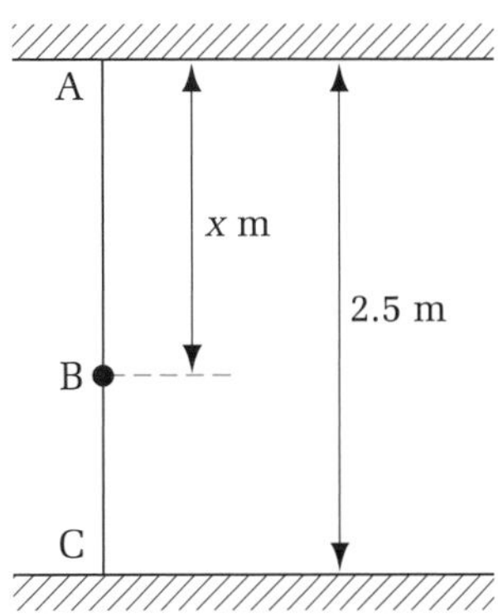

The object is now pulled down 0.1 m from its equilibrium position and released from rest.

d Calculate the speed of the object when it passes through the equilibrium position. Any resistances to motion may be neglected.

(MEI)

3 A small catapult consists of a light elastic string fastened to two fixed points A and B, with the line AB horizontal and the distance AB = 30 cm. The natural length of the string is 20 cm. When the string forms a straight line between A and B, the tension in the string is 150 N.

a Find, in newtons, the modulus of elasticity of the string.

A small light leather pouch P is fixed to the midpoint of the string. The pouch is now pulled back horizontally a distance of 20 cm in a direction perpendicular to AB, so that A, B and P all lie in the same horizontal plane. The figure shows a view of the catapult from above.

The figure is on the next page.

b Find the magnitude of the horizontal force required to hold the pouch in equilibrium in this position.

A small stone of mass 0.1 kg is placed in the pouch and held in the position shown in the figure. The pouch is then released from this position.

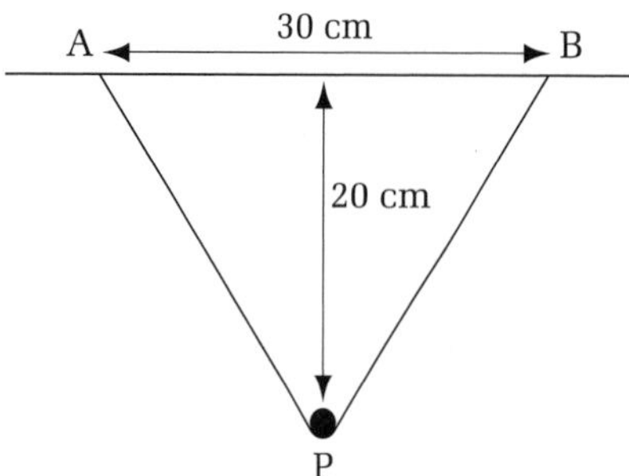

c By considering the energy of the system, find, in m s^{-1}, the horizontal speed which the stone has when it crosses the line AB. (Any vertical motion of the stone can be assumed to be so small that it may be neglected.)

(ULEAC)

4 A particle P of mass 0.2 kg is attached to one end of a light elastic string of natural length 0.5 m and modulus 8 N. The other end of the string is attached to a fixed point O. The particle is initially held at a point A at a distance 0.5 m vertically below O and is then released from rest. When the particle is at a distance x metres below A, the resultant downward force acting on it is F newtons.

a Taking $g = 10\,\text{m s}^{-2}$, show that $F = 2 - 16x$.

b Find the work done by F when x increases from 0 to 0.1.

c Calculate the speed of P when $x = 0.1$.

d Given that the work done by F when x increases from 0 to a is zero, where $a > 0$, find the value of a. Hence, or otherwise, calculate the greatest tension in the string during the motion of P.

(NEAB)

Hint:
WD by F = gain in KE.

5 A bungee-jumper of mass 80 kg attaches one end of his rope to a high bridge, the other end round his ankles, and dives off. At the moment when the rope becomes taut it is vertical and he is travelling vertically downwards at $30\,\text{m s}^{-1}$. He travels a further 40 m before coming instantaneously to rest. Taking $g = 10\,\text{m s}^{-2}$, use a work–energy equation to find the stiffness k_1 of the rope as it extends.

Use EPE $= \frac{kx^2}{2}$

The rope is not perfectly elastic and has a different stiffness value $k_2 = 0.8k_1$ during contraction. Find the speed of the bungee-jumper when he regains the height at which the rope ceases to be in tension.

(OCSEB)

Exercise B

1 A light elastic rope AB of natural length 10 m and modulus 19 600 N has the end A attached to a fixed point. Two children, C_1 and C_2, hold onto the end B of the rope and they are hanging in equilibrium with B vertically below A. Given that C_1 has mass 40 kg and C_2 has mass 60 kg, show that the extension of the rope is 0.5 m. (In this question take g to be 9.8 m s^{-2}.)
The child C_2 now lets go of the rope. Find the upward speed of child C_1, who is still holding on to the rope, at the instant when the rope first becomes slack.

(AEB)

2 A particle, P, of mass 1.04 kg, is attached to two strings AP and BP. The points A and B are on the same horizontal level and are 130 cm apart. The string BP is inextensible and of length 120 cm. The particle hangs in equilibrium with AP = 50 cm, and APB = 90°.

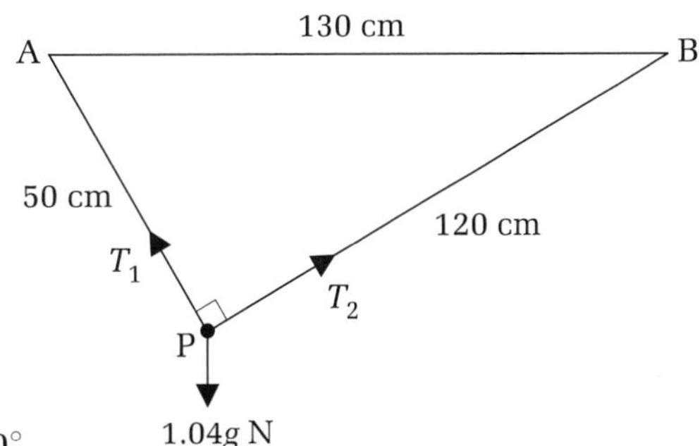

The diagram shows all the external forces acting on the particle.

a Find the tension, in newtons, correct to one decimal place, in each of the strings AP and BP.

b The string AP is elastic and its modulus of elasticity is 9.8 N. Find the natural length, in centimetres, correct to one decimal place, of the string AP.

(NICCEA)

3 A ball, B, of mass 0.5 kg, is attached to a fixed point O by a light elastic string of natural length 2 m and modulus of elasticity λ newtons. The ball is released from rest at O and moves under gravity. In the subsequent motion the effect of air resistance may be ignored. After release, B comes to rest instantaneously at a point R vertically below O, where OR = 2.5 m. Find the loss in gravitational potential energy as B falls from O to R. Find, in terms of λ, the gain in elastic energy as B falls from O to R, and hence find the value of λ. (Use $g = 9.81$ m s^{-2}.)

(UCLES)

4 **a** An elastic rope, of natural length 2 m and modulus 1 N, has one end attached to a fixed support. A load of 40 kg is attached to the other end of the rope and hangs in equilibrium at a distance 2.25 m vertically below the support. Find the value of λ as a multiple of g.

b A similar rope with the same modulus λ N, but of natural length l m, is to be used by a man in the performance of a charity stunt. One end of the rope is attached to his ankles and the other end is fixed to a point A on a bridge which is 35 m above a river. The man will step off the bridge so that he falls vertically from rest and, for safety reasons, it is required that subsequently he first comes to instantaneous rest when the rope has extended to a length of 30 m.

To instantaneous rest means the object stops for a split second.

When the man is standing at A his centre of mass is 1 m above A, and when the rope first brings him to rest his centre of mass will be 31 m below A. The mass of the man is 75 kg:

Model the man as a particle at his centre of mass.

i Use the principle of the conservation of energy to show that:

$$l^2 - 75l + 900 = 0$$

ii Hence find the required value of l.

This means use your previous result to find l.

iii Calculate, in terms of g, the magnitude of the acceleration of the man at the instant when he is first brought to rest.

(*NEAB*)

5 A light elastic string AB has stiffness k and natural length l_0. The end A of the string is fixed to a vertical wall, and the end B to a block of mass M which is supported by a smooth horizontal plane. To the other side of the block is attached an inelastic light string which passes over a smooth pulley and is then tied to a particle of mass m at C, which hangs freely at all times. The block is initially held against the wall and then is moved gently towards the pulley until it is in equilibrium. The elastic string and the part of the other string between the block and the pulley are horizontal, as shown.

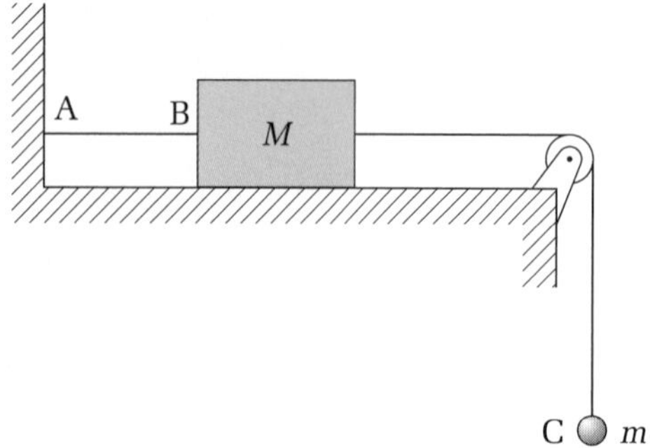

Find expressions for the following in terms of some or all of m, g, k and l_0:

a the extension in the elastic string;

b the potential energy lost by the hanging mass as the system is moved to its equilibrium position;

c the energy stored in the elastic string.

d Compare your answers to parts **b** and **c**. Why is energy not conserved?

e If the string supporting the hanging mass breaks when the system is in equilibrium, show that the block will hit the wall with a speed v given by $v^2 = \frac{m^2g^2}{Mk}$. Find also an expression for the acceleration of the block immediately after the string breaks.

f Show that the two quantities v^2 and $\frac{m^2g^2}{Mk}$ have the same dimensions.

(*MEI*)

Applications and Activities

1 Estimate the modulus of elasticity for one or more of the following items by the method given.
Items to use: a length of elastic, an elastic band, an elastic belt, a pair of braces, a bungee rope (the type used for securing loads to the roof rack of a car), a hairband, a piece of washing line.
Method: In each case suspend the item from a fixed point and measure the extension produced by attaching a selection of weights.

Draw up a table of values for the extension, x m, and the weight attached, T N. Plot a graph of T against x. Draw the line of best fit and find the gradient of this line. The gradient is equal to the stiffness, k, of the elastic string. To find λ you will need to multiply k by the original length, l, of the string.

2 Model a toy bungee-jump and then use dolls or cuddly toys to test your calculations.

Never attempt a real bungee-jump without professional help!

Summary

- The formula for the tension in an elastic string (or spring) is

$$T = \frac{\lambda x}{l} \text{ or } T = kx$$

- The formula for the elastic potential energy in an elastic string (or spring) is

$$\text{EPE} = \frac{\lambda x^2}{2l} \quad \text{or} \quad \frac{kx^2}{2}$$

- The dimensions for the modulus of elasticity are $[\text{MLT}^{-2}]$; the SI units are newtons.
- Work done in stretching a string or spring:

$$\text{work done} = \int_0^x T\,dx$$

- The principle of conservation of energy is

$$\text{ME}_{\text{start}} = \text{ME}_{\text{end}}$$

$$\text{PE}_{\text{start}} + \text{KE}_{\text{start}} + \text{EPE}_{\text{start}} = \text{PE}_{\text{end}} + \text{KE}_{\text{end}} + \text{EPE}_{\text{end}}$$

ME = total mechanical energy

- The work–energy principle is

$$\text{ME}_{\text{start}} + \text{W}_{\text{in}} = \text{ME}_{\text{end}} + \text{W}_{\text{out}}$$

12 Collisions

What you need to know

- How to find the magnitude of a vector quantity.
- How to use vectors.
- How to calculate the kinetic energy of a moving body.
- How to calculate changes in potential energy.
- How to solve simultaneous equations.

Review

1 Find the magnitude, to three significant figures, of:

a the force $\mathbf{F} = (18\mathbf{i} - 35\mathbf{j})$ N
b the velocity $\mathbf{v} = (-6.5\mathbf{i} - 7.2\mathbf{j})$ m s^{-1}
c the acceleration $\mathbf{a} = (0.7\mathbf{i} + 1.1\mathbf{j})$ m s^{-2}.

2 a If $\mathbf{a} = 3\mathbf{i} - 2\mathbf{j}$ and $\mathbf{b} = -2\mathbf{i} + 5\mathbf{j}$, find:
i $\mathbf{a} + \mathbf{b}$ ii $\mathbf{a} - \mathbf{b}$ iii $5\mathbf{a}$ iv $3\mathbf{b}$
b Write down the vector that is twice as long and in the same direction as $2\mathbf{i} + 4\mathbf{j}$.
c Write down the vector that is five times as long as $-7\mathbf{i} + \mathbf{j}$, and is in the opposite direction.

3 Calculate the kinetic energy of each of the following:

a a stone of mass 3 kg, rolling along at 2 m s^{-1}
b a car of mass 850 kg, travelling at 45 km h^{-1}
c a ping pong ball of mass 5 g, moving at 10 m s^{-1}.

Hint: Make sure to convert the units, where necessary, *before* performing the main calculation.

4 a What is the increase in potential energy when a crate of mass 120 kg is raised by a pulley to a height 4 m above its starting position?
b What is the loss in potential energy when a textbook of mass 650 g is dropped from a first floor classroom window to the ground, 3.5 m below?

5 Solve the following simultaneous equations:

a $2v + u = 10$
$4v - 3u = 5$

b $u + 12 = 3v$
$2v - 5u = 8$

12.1 Momentum

There are various sports in which the players must catch a ball. What factors make the ball more difficult to catch? To test your ideas you could drop different balls from a height of 1 m above where it is to be caught. By using the same height the speed at which it is caught will remain the same if air resistance is ignored.

A ball is caught when it is *stopped* and held.

By changing the height that you drop the ball to 1.5 m or 0.5 m, the speed of the ball when it is caught is changed. What effect does this have?

The larger the ball's mass, the more difficult the ball is to stop. The higher the speed of the ball, the harder it is to stop. One measure of how difficult an object is to stop is called **momentum**. A formula for momentum is:

The amount the ball will deform is also important.

$$\text{momentum} = m\mathbf{v}$$

Notation
m = mass of the object (kg)
$\mathbf{v}$ = velocity of the object (m s^{-1})

Is momentum a scalar or a vector quantity? The formula for momentum multiplies mass and velocity. Mass is a scalar and velocity is a vector. A scalar multiplied by a vector produces a vector answer. This means *momentum* is a *vector*. The *momentum* of an object must be in the *same direction* as the *velocity*.

Momentum and velocity must be parallel vectors.

Magnitude of momentum

To find just the magnitude of momentum the speed of the object is used.

This type of momentum is sometimes called linear momentum.

$$\begin{aligned} \text{momentum} &= m\mathbf{v} \\ |\text{momentum}| &= |m\mathbf{v}| = m|\mathbf{v}| \\ |\text{momentum}| &= \text{mass} \times \text{speed} \end{aligned}$$

The units of momentum

The units of momentum can be determined from its formula by using dimensions.

$$\begin{aligned} \text{momentum} &= m\mathbf{v} \\ [\text{momentum}] &= \text{MLT}^{-1} \end{aligned}$$

When using SI units, these dimensions would be $\mathbf{kg\,m\,s^{-1}}$. An alternative approach uses the dimensions of force.

$$\begin{aligned} \mathbf{F} &= m\mathbf{a} \\ [\mathbf{F}] &= \text{MLT}^{-2} \end{aligned}$$

By multiplying the force by time, the same units for momentum can be obtained.

$$[\mathbf{F}t] = \text{MLT}^{-2} \times \text{T} = \text{MLT}^{-1}$$

This gives an equivalent unit for momentum of newton-seconds, or **N s**. The N s is the most commonly used unit for momentum.

A relationship between $\mathbf{F}t$ and momentum is derived in Section 12.2.

Example 1

A body of mass 10 kg is moving with velocity $\mathbf{v}$, where $\mathbf{v} = (16\mathbf{i} + 5\mathbf{j})\,\text{m s}^{-1}$.

a What is the momentum of the body?
b What is the magnitude of this momentum?

Solution

a momentum $= m\mathbf{v}$

$$= 10(16\mathbf{i} + 5\mathbf{j})$$
$$= (160\mathbf{i} + 50\mathbf{j})\text{ N s}$$

b The magnitude of the momentum is the magnitude of the vector $(160\mathbf{i} + 50\mathbf{j})$ N s

$$|160\mathbf{i} + 50\mathbf{j}| = \sqrt{160^2 + 50^2}$$

Using Pythagoras' theorem.

$$= \sqrt{25\,600 + 2500}$$
$$= \sqrt{28\,100}$$
$$= 168\text{ N s (3 s.f.)}$$

Example 2

A moving body has momentum of magnitude 85 N s. If its mass is 5 kg, what is its speed?

Solution

magnitude of momentum = mass × speed

Substitute the values.

$$85 = 5 \times v$$

Divide by 5.

$$v = \frac{85}{5}$$
$$v = 17\text{ m s}^{-1}$$

Example 3

A body has speed 18 m s^{-1} and momentum of magnitude 3.6 N s. What is the mass of the body?

Solution

magnitude of momentum $= mv$

$$3.6 = m \times 18$$

Divide by 18.

$$m = \frac{3.6}{18}$$
$$m = 0.2\text{ kg}$$

12.1 Momentum Exercise

Technique

1 In each of the following cases, work out the momentum of the moving body:

a a body of mass 2.5 kg, with velocity $(4\mathbf{i} - 8\mathbf{j})\,\text{m s}^{-1}$
b a body of mass 0.65 kg, with velocity $(-13\mathbf{i} - 19\mathbf{j})\,\text{m s}^{-1}$
c a body of mass 3.2 tonnes, with velocity $(0.73\mathbf{i} - 0.81\mathbf{j})\,\text{m s}^{-1}$.

Hint: Remember to convert the units, where necessary, before calculating the momentum.

2 Find the magnitude of the momentum in each of the following cases:

a a particle of mass 2 kg travels with speed $6\,\text{m s}^{-1}$
b a particle of mass 350 kg travels with speed $35\,\text{m s}^{-1}$
c a particle of mass 125 g travels with speed $80\,\text{cm s}^{-1}$.

3 a A body has momentum of magnitude 30 N s. What is its speed, if its mass is 0.5 kg?
b A body travelling at a speed of $45\,\text{m s}^{-1}$ has momentum of magnitude 13.5 N s. What is its mass?
c A body of mass 2 tonnes has momentum of magnitude 6400 N s. What is its speed?

4 A particle of mass 65 kg is moving with velocity $(49\mathbf{i} - 12\mathbf{j})\,\text{m s}^{-1}$.

a What is its speed?
b What angle does its direction make with the **i** direction?
c What is the magnitude of its momentum?

5 A particle of mass 0.35 kg has velocity $(-\mathbf{i} + 2.4\mathbf{j})\,\text{m s}^{-1}$.

a What is its momentum?
b What is the magnitude of its momentum?
c What is the angle between the direction of the momentum and the **i** vector?

6 A body of mass 4 kg is dropped from a height of 2 m above the ground.

Take $g = 9.8\,\text{m s}^{-2}$.

a Calculate the speed of the body immediately before it hits the ground.
b Calculate the magnitude of the momentum of the body immediately before it hits the ground.
c What would be the magnitude of the momentum if it had been dropped from a height of 3 m?

Contextual

1 Calculate the momentum of each of the following:

a a ping pong ball of mass 5 g moving with velocity $(8\mathbf{i} + 6\mathbf{j})\ \text{m s}^{-1}$
b a snooker ball of mass 50 g moving with velocity $(-3\mathbf{i} - 5\mathbf{j})\ \text{m s}^{-1}$
c a golf ball of mass 40 g moving with velocity $(15\mathbf{i} - 8\mathbf{j})\ \text{m s}^{-1}$.

2 In each of these cases, find the magnitude of the momentum:

a a pedestrian of mass 90 kg walking at $8\ \text{km h}^{-1}$
b a cyclist of mass 75 kg on a bike of mass 12 kg, moving at $8\ \text{m s}^{-1}$.

3 A fly, of mass 0.07 g is flying with velocity $(-0.6\mathbf{i} - 0.9\mathbf{j})\ \text{m s}^{-1}$.

a What is the fly's speed?
b What is the fly's direction, measured anticlockwise from **i**?
c What is the magnitude of the fly's momentum?

4 A jet aircraft of mass 1.6 tonnes is flying due south-east with speed $80\ \text{m s}^{-1}$ at constant altitude. Take **i** as the unit vector east and **j** as the unit vector north.

a What is the aircraft's velocity vector?
b What is the aircraft's momentum?
c What is the magnitude of the aircraft's momentum?

5 A bungee-jumper of mass 80 kg free-falls a distance of 10 m before her bungee rope becomes taut.

a What is her speed at the moment when her rope becomes taut?
b What is the magnitude of her momentum at that time?

6 A coach of mass 3.5 tonnes moves forward with momentum of magnitude 525 N s. Find its speed.

12.2 Impulse

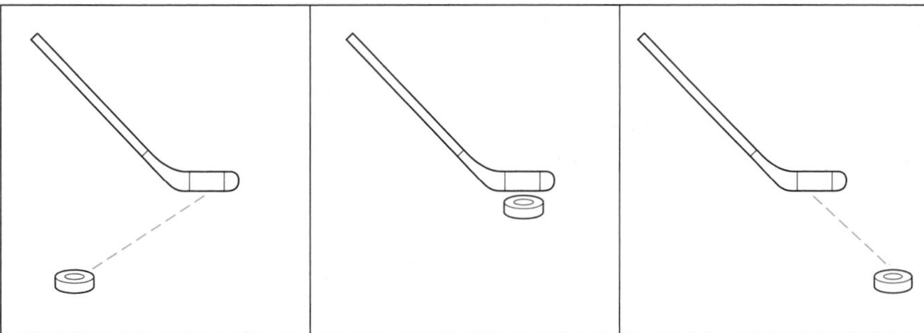

Consider an ice hockey puck sliding across the surface of the ice. When it is struck by the player's hockey stick it changes both speed and direction. As it has a new velocity, its momentum has also changed. What has brought about this change? The contact with the hockey stick was relatively brief, but the force applied during this time had the effect of changing the velocity and also the momentum of the ice puck.

What would have caused a greater change? The effect would have been even greater if either the magnitude of the applied force were increased or if the duration of the contact between the stick and the puck were lengthened. The product of force and time would give a measure of this change and this is called **impulse**.

impulse = force × time

impulse $= \mathbf{F}t$

Impulse is a vector quantity, having the same direction as the applied force. There will be occasions, however, when it is necessary to consider the magnitude of the impulse.

magnitude of impulse $= |\mathbf{F}| \times$ time

$= Ft$

This formula gives the units of impulse as N s. These units are the same as momentum and a relationship between impulse and momentum can be derived.

impulse = force × time
units of impulse = N × s
i.e. Newton-seconds.

The derivation of the impulse–momentum equation

Impulse and momentum are more closely connected than simply sharing the same units.

$$\begin{aligned}\text{impulse} &= \mathbf{F}t\\ &= m\mathbf{a}t\\ &= m(\mathbf{v} - \mathbf{u})\\ &= m\mathbf{v} - m\mathbf{u}\end{aligned}$$

Use $\mathbf{F} = m\mathbf{a}$ to replace $\mathbf{F}$.
Re-arrange $\mathbf{v} = \mathbf{u} + \mathbf{a}t$ to replace $\mathbf{a}t$.
Expand the brackets.

impulse = final momentum − initial momentum

This is known as the impulse–momentum equation. It is also quoted as follows:

impulse = change in momentum

This relationship will only apply to uniformly accelerated objects because we have used the uniform acceleration formulas. This means the force must also be constant. Even if this is not the case, then this type of motion must be assumed to be taking place so that the impulse–momentum equation can be used.

Can this assumption be made for a racquet hitting a tennis ball? The ball will be deformed by the impact and so the force is unlikely to be constant. However the time of contact is likely to be very short and so the idea of *average* force enables this assumption to be made.

Overview of method

Step ① Draw *before* and *after* diagrams with a positive direction clearly indicated.

Step ② Show all the known information on these diagrams.

Step ③ Substitute the information into the impulse–momentum equation and/or impulse = $\mathbf{F}t$.

Step ④ Calculate the required quantities stating clearly their direction.

Often this direction will be the same as the original velocity.

Example 1

A body of mass 5 kg is travelling at $3\,\text{m}\,\text{s}^{-1}$. It is brought to rest by an impulse. Find the magnitude of this impulse.

Solution

Where no direction is specified, choose the positive direction to be shown to the right.

This is like x-coordinates.

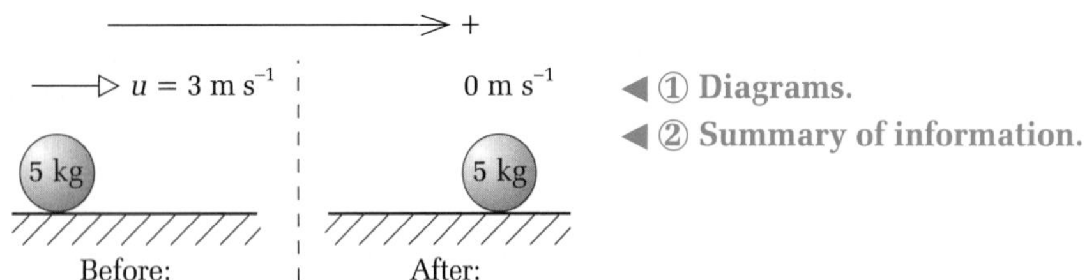

◀ ① **Diagrams.**

◀ ② **Summary of information.**

Note that *brought to rest* means $v = 0\,\text{m}\,\text{s}^{-1}$.

$$\begin{aligned}\text{impulse} &= mv - mu \\ &= 5 \times 0 - 5 \times 3 \\ &= 0 - 15\end{aligned}$$
◀ ③ **Impulse–momentum equation.**

$$\text{impulse} = -15\,\text{N}\,\text{s}$$
◀ ④ **Required quantity.**

The magnitude of the impulse is 15 N s. The negative sign means that the impulse acts in the opposite direction to the original motion.

Example 2

A body with initial velocity $(2\mathbf{i} - 7\mathbf{j})\,\mathrm{m\,s^{-1}}$ is given an impulse causing its velocity to change to $(-8\mathbf{i} + \mathbf{j})\,\mathrm{m\,s^{-1}}$. The mass of the body is 0.5 kg. If the duration of the impulse is 0.2 seconds, calculate the magnitude of the constant force involved.

Solution

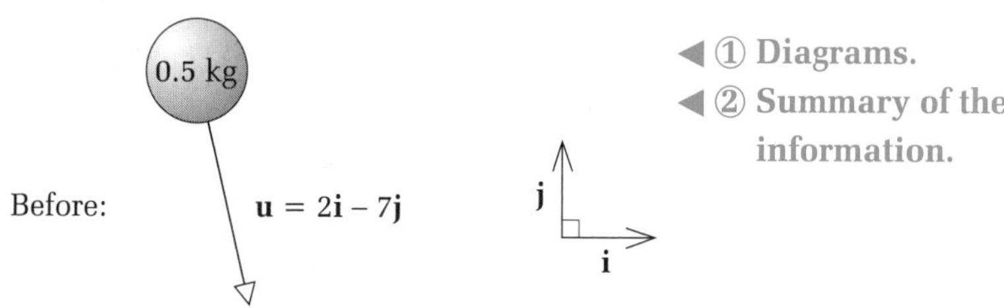

◀ ① Diagrams.

◀ ② Summary of the information.

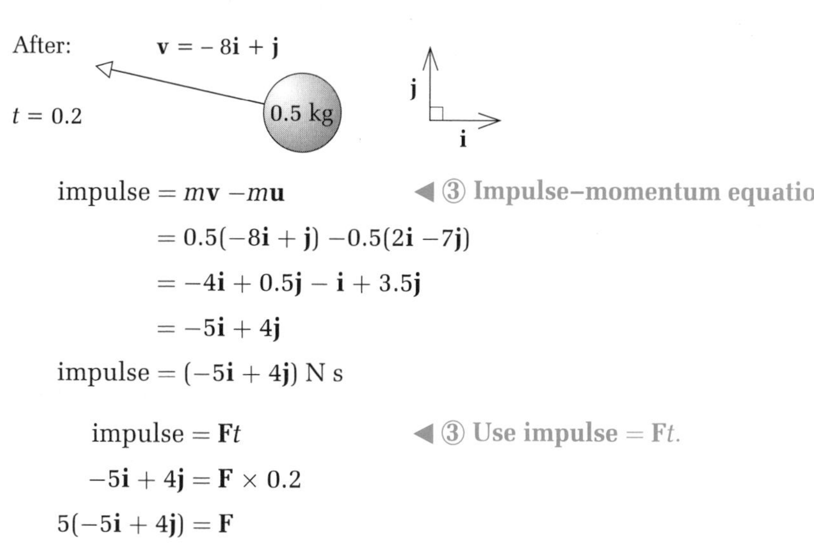

$$\text{impulse} = m\mathbf{v} - m\mathbf{u}$$ ◀ ③ Impulse–momentum equation.

$$= 0.5(-8\mathbf{i} + \mathbf{j}) - 0.5(2\mathbf{i} - 7\mathbf{j})$$ Expand brackets.

$$= -4\mathbf{i} + 0.5\mathbf{j} - \mathbf{i} + 3.5\mathbf{j}$$ Simplify by collecting components.

$$= -5\mathbf{i} + 4\mathbf{j}$$

$$\text{impulse} = (-5\mathbf{i} + 4\mathbf{j})\ \mathrm{N\,s}$$

$$\text{impulse} = \mathbf{F}t$$ ◀ ③ Use impulse = $\mathbf{F}t$.

$$-5\mathbf{i} + 4\mathbf{j} = \mathbf{F} \times 0.2$$ Multiply both sides by 5 since $5 \times 0.2 = 1$.

$$5(-5\mathbf{i} + 4\mathbf{j}) = \mathbf{F}$$

$$\mathbf{F} = (-25\mathbf{i} + 20\mathbf{j})\ \mathrm{N}$$

The constant force involved is $\mathbf{F} = (-25\mathbf{i} + 20\mathbf{j})$ N.

$$|\mathbf{F}| = \sqrt{(-25)^2 + 20^2}$$ ◀ ④ Calculate the required quantity. Use Pythagoras' theorem

$$= \sqrt{1025}$$

$$= 32.0\ \mathrm{N}\ (3\ \text{s.f.})$$

The magnitude of the constant force is 32.0 N.

12.2 Impulse
Exercise

Technique

1 A body of mass 3 kg is initially travelling with velocity $(5\mathbf{i} + 2\mathbf{j})\,\text{m s}^{-1}$. After it receives an impulse its new velocity is $(11\mathbf{i} - \mathbf{j})\,\text{m s}^{-1}$.

a Find the impulse given to the body.
b If the impulse lasted for 0.2 seconds, find the magnitude of the constant force involved.

2 A body of mass 10 kg is moving initially with a velocity of $(3\mathbf{i} - 2\mathbf{j})\,\text{m s}^{-1}$, when it receives an impulse of $6\mathbf{j}$ N s. What will be the new velocity of the body?

3 A particle of mass 0.75 kg is initially at rest. After an impulse lasting 0.3 seconds, its speed is $12\,\text{m s}^{-1}$.

a What is the magnitude of the impulse on the particle?
b What is the magnitude of the constant force acting on the particle?

4 A particle has an initial velocity of $3u$. After the action of an impulse its direction is reversed and its speed is u.
If the mass of the particle is $\frac{1}{2}m$, find:

a the magnitude of the impulse
b the duration of the impulse if a constant force of $8mu$ was acting.

5 A body is at rest on a smooth horizontal surface. A force of 12 N acts on the body for 0.5 seconds. If, after the impulse, the body moves with a constant speed of $3.6\,\text{m s}^{-1}$, what must be the mass of the body?

6 A constant force of $(a\mathbf{i} + b\mathbf{j})$ acts for 4 seconds on a body of mass 8 kg. If the initial velocity of the body is $(-0.3\mathbf{i} + 0.9\mathbf{j})\,\text{m s}^{-1}$ and the velocity after the impulse is $(0.1\mathbf{i} + 2.5\mathbf{j})\,\text{m s}^{-1}$, find the value of a and b.

7 A body travelling with a constant velocity of $1.8\mathbf{i}\,\text{m s}^{-1}$ is brought to rest by an impulse due to a force $\mathbf{F}$ acting for 0.1 seconds. Find the constant force, $\mathbf{F}$ if the mass of the body is 500 grams.

8 The effect of an impulse $\mathbf{F}t$ is to change the velocity of a particle from $(3.6\mathbf{i} + 2.8\mathbf{j})\,\text{m s}^{-1}$ to $(-1.2\mathbf{i} + 4.2\mathbf{j})\,\text{m s}^{-1}$.

a Find the impulse if the mass of the particle is 0.2 kg.
b Find t if the magnitude of $\mathbf{F}$ is 2.5 N.

9 The speed of a body of mass $5m$ is reduced from $6u$ to $2u$ by an impulse.

a What is the magnitude of this impulse?
b If the same impulse acted upon a body of mass $4m$, moving with constant speed $4u$, what would be the result?

10 A force of magnitude 7 N acts for 6 seconds on a body mass 7 kg. This impulse reverses the direction of motion of the body. If the new speed is $4\,\mathrm{m\,s^{-1}}$, what was the speed of the body before the impulse?

Contextual

1 A professional tennis player serves a 50 g tennis ball at a speed of 100 mph. What impulse is required for the ball to be returned with a speed of 80 mph? State any assumptions that you have made.

Hint: Convert mph to $\mathrm{m\,s^{-1}}$.

2 A space shuttle uses a 30 second burst of its manoeuvring thrusters to reduce its forward velocity from $15\,\mathrm{m\,s^{-1}}$ to $12\,\mathrm{m\,s^{-1}}$. Given that the mass of the space shuttle is 45 000 kg, what is the magnitude of the constant force produced by the firing of the thrusters?

3 A jeep of mass 1 tonne is travelling across an open stretch of safari country with a velocity of $10\mathbf{j}\,\mathrm{m\,s^{-1}}$, when it is charged by a rhino. The impact deflects the jeep such that its velocity immediately after the impact is $(4\mathbf{i} + 9\mathbf{j})\,\mathrm{m\,s^{-1}}$.

a Calculate the magnitude of the impulse.
b Find the angle between the original direction of the jeep and the direction of the impulse.

4 Two schoolboys are hitting a marble of mass 8 g across the surface of their desk, using their rulers. At one point the marble is rolling with velocity $(0.15\mathbf{i} - 0.2\mathbf{j})\,\mathrm{m\,s^{-1}}$ when it receives an impulse of $(0.003\,76\mathbf{i} - 0.0004\mathbf{j})\,\mathrm{N\,s}$ from contact with one boy's ruler. Find the velocity of the marble immediately after it is hit.

12.3 Conservation of Linear Momentum

Collisions between two bodies

When two snooker balls collide, their velocities will change. These changes are caused by impulses acting on both balls. How could the velocities of the snooker balls be calculated after the collision? The snooker balls can be modelled as particles, denoting their initial speeds as u_1 and u_2 and their final speeds as v_1 and v_2. The masses of the snooker balls will be taken to be m_1 and m_2 and the collision is assumed to be direct (i.e. head-on). This will give a general formula for collisions between two particles. The snooker balls will be called A and B. A diagram to show this situation is shown.

A positive direction must be stated

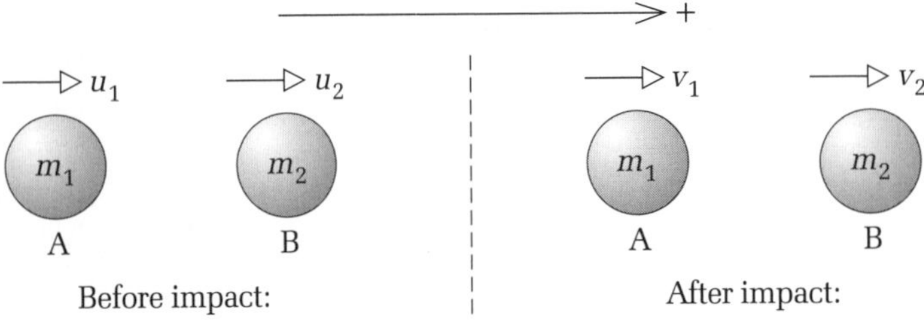

For the impact to take place in the first instance, $u_1 > u_2$. For the particles to separate after impact, $v_1 < v_2$. There is an impulse on B, due to its impact with A and there must be an impulse on A due to its impact with B.

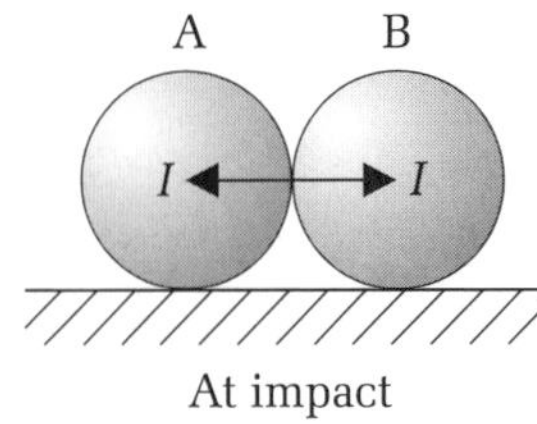

At impact

Whatever happens, both balls are affected.

Using Newton's third law, the two forces will be equal in magnitude and opposite in direction. These forces will act for the same amount of time and so the impulses acting on the snooker balls will be equal but opposite.

Forces occur in equal and opposite pairs. Since $\mathbf{I} = \mathbf{F}t$

impulse on A = −(impulse on B) ◀ Use impulse = $m\mathbf{v} - m\mathbf{u}$.

$$m_1v_1 - m_1u_1 = -(m_2v_2 - m_2u_2)$$

$$m_1v_1 - m_1u_1 = -m_2v_2 + m_2u_2$$

$$m_1v_1 + m_2v_2 = m_1u_1 + m_2u_2$$

Expand the brackets. Add m_1u_1 and m_2v_2.

$$\boldsymbol{m_1u_1 + m_2u_2 = m_1v_1 + m_2v_2}$$

total momentum before collision = total momentum after collision

Notation
m_1, m_2 = masses
u_1, u_2 = initial speeds
v_1, v_2 = final speeds

This is known as the **principle of conservation of linear momentum** (PCLM).

Although the principle of conservation of linear momentum applies equally well for bodies moving in two dimensions, only direct collisions in a straight line will be considered in this chapter. To make sure this is the case, the radii of the spheres must be the same.

Radii is the plural of radius.

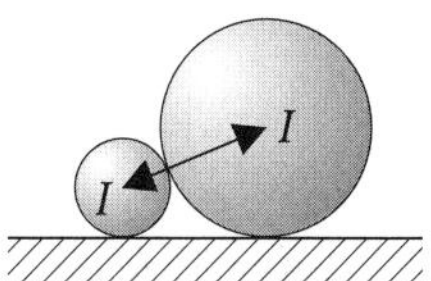

When this is not the case, the impulse will be inclined to the horizontal. This type of collision is beyond the scope of this book.

Particles that coalesce

If the two particles **coalesce**, then the speeds of both particles after collision will be the same. This is because coalesce means the particles will *stick together*.

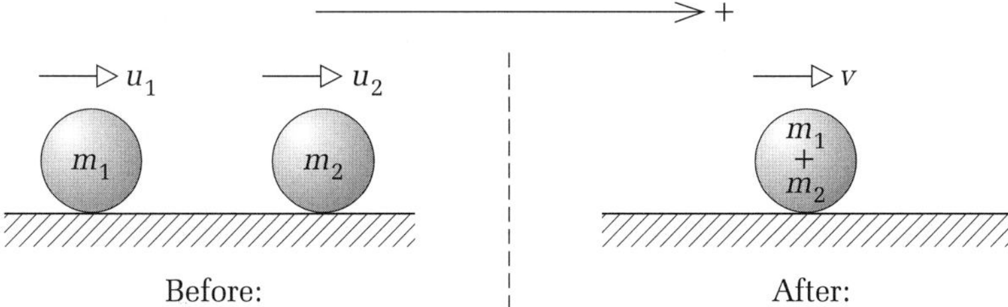

For this situation, PCLM becomes:

$$\boldsymbol{m_1 u_1 + m_2 u_2 = (m_1 + m_2)v}$$

Notation

v = speed of both particles after collision.

Two bodies joined by a string

A special case of impulse occurs where two bodies are joined by a string, which is initially slack. If one body is projected with a certain velocity, its movement does not affect the stationary body straight away. However, once the string becomes taut, the second body will move. From that point onwards the two bodies will move with the same speed.

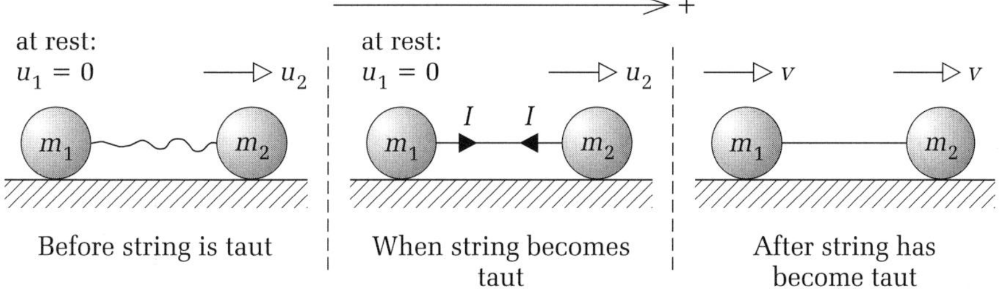

There is an impulsive tension in the string acting on both particles at the moment that the string becomes taut. In other words, there will be an impulse due to this tension, which will affect both bodies. This type of problem can still be solved using PCLM. The momentum before and after the string becomes taut must be equal.

Loss of mechanical energy

Although momentum is conserved during impacts like these, the system of particles changes in other ways. In particular, kinetic energy is *lost*. Why is it incorrect to say that it is *lost*? Where does it go?

Theoretically, energy is never lost, only changed from one form into another. In the case of collisions, some of the kinetic energy is transformed into sound and heat energy. This loss of kinetic energy from the system can be calculated by subtracting the total kinetic energy of the particles after impact from the total kinetic energy of the particles before impact. This gives the formula:

$$\mathbf{KE_{loss} = KE_{before} - KE_{after}}$$

This equation for kinetic energy loss assumes that all surfaces are smooth and that the bodies do not rotate. The kinetic energy is independent of the direction of motion. When a negative speed is squared, a positive answer will result.

Notation
KE_{loss} = loss of kinetic energy due to impact.
KE_{before} = kinetic energy before impact.
KE_{after} = kinetic energy after impact.
i.e. $\frac{1}{2}m(-v)^2 = \frac{1}{2}mv^2$

Overview of method

Step ① Draw *before* and *after* diagrams, with a clearly indicated positive direction.

Step ② Show all the known information on these diagrams.

Step ③ Substitute the information into the conservation of linear momentum equation:

$$m_1u_1 + m_2u_2 = m_1v_1 + m_2v_2$$

Step ④ Calculate the required quantities, stating the directions of vectors.

Step ⑤ Find the kinetic energy lost during the collision by using:

$$KE_{loss} = KE_{before} - KE_{after}$$

Assume left to right to be the positive direction.

Take particular care with the use of signs.

Example 1

A sphere of mass 0.1 kg is moving with speed 3 m s^{-1}, when it collides directly with a second sphere of mass 0.2 kg, which is moving at 1 m s^{-1} in the same direction. After the impact, the speed of the second sphere is doubled. What will be the speed of the other sphere? Determine the loss in kinetic energy due to the impact.

Solution

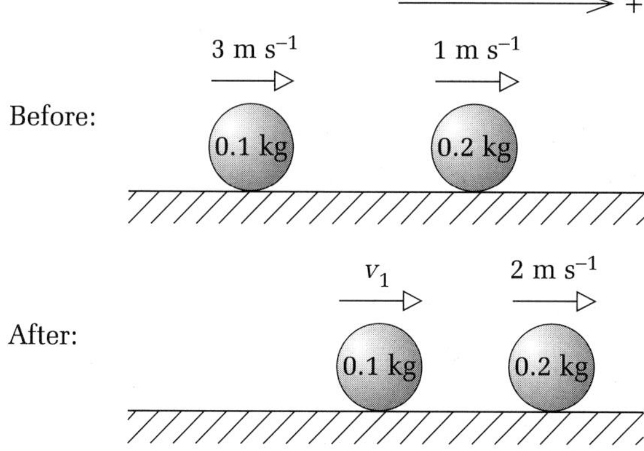

◀ ① Before and after diagrams.

◀ ② Summary of the information.

Using PCLM,

momentum before = momentum after ◀ ③ Substitute momentum values.

PCLM stands for principle of conservation of linear momentum.

$$0.1 \times 3 + 0.2 \times 1 = 0.1 \times v_1 + 0.2 \times 2$$

Remember momentum = mv.

$$0.3 + 0.2 = 0.1v_1 + 0.4$$

Subtract 0.4.

$$0.1 = 0.1v_1$$

Divide by 0.1.

$$v_1 = 1 \text{ m s}^{-1}$$

◀ ④ Calculate the required quantity.

The final speed of the first sphere is 1 m s^{-1} in the same direction as its original velocity.

$$\text{KE}_{\text{loss}} = \text{KE}_{\text{before}} - \text{KE}_{\text{after}}$$

Use KE $= \frac{1}{2}mv^2$ where m is the mass and v is the speed.

$$\begin{aligned}\text{KE}_{\text{before}} &= \tfrac{1}{2} \times 0.1 \times 3^2 + \tfrac{1}{2} \times 0.2 \times 1^2 \\ &= 0.45 + 0.1 \\ &= 0.55 \text{ J}\end{aligned}$$

◀ Calculate kinetic energy before and after impact.

$$\begin{aligned}\text{KE}_{\text{after}} &= \tfrac{1}{2} \times 0.1 \times 1^2 + \tfrac{1}{2} \times 0.2 \times 2^2 \\ &= 0.05 + 0.4 \\ &= 0.45 \text{ J}\end{aligned}$$

$$\begin{aligned}\text{KE}_{\text{loss}} &= 0.55 - 0.45 \\ &= 0.1 \text{ J}\end{aligned}$$

Example 2

Two bodies, P and Q, are lying on a smooth horizontal table. Their masses are 1 kg and 3 kg respectively. The two bodies are connected by a light inextensible string which is initially slack. Body P is projected horizontally with velocity 4 m s^{-1} away from Q. Find:

a the speed of P and Q after the string becomes taut

b the magnitude of the impulse due to the tension in the string.

Solution

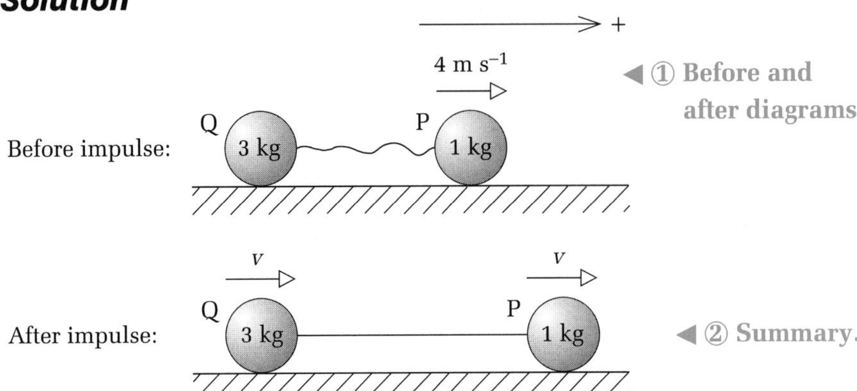

a Applying PCLM,

momentum before = momentum after ◀ ③ Substitute values.

$$1 \times 4 = (3 + 1) \times v$$

$$4 = 4v$$ ◀ ④ Calculate required quantity.

$$v = 1\text{ m s}^{-1}$$

Simplify both sides.
Divide by 4.

So after the impulse both bodies travel with speed 1 m s^{-1}.

b impulse = change in momentum of Q

$$= 3 \times v - 0$$
$$= 3 \times 1$$
$$= 3\text{ N s}$$

Use Q since its initial speed is zero.

Example 3

A body, of mass m, is travelling with speed $2u$ when it collides directly with a body of mass $3m$ travelling in the opposite direction with speed u. If the impact reduces the second body to rest, what will be the speed of the first body after impact?

Solution

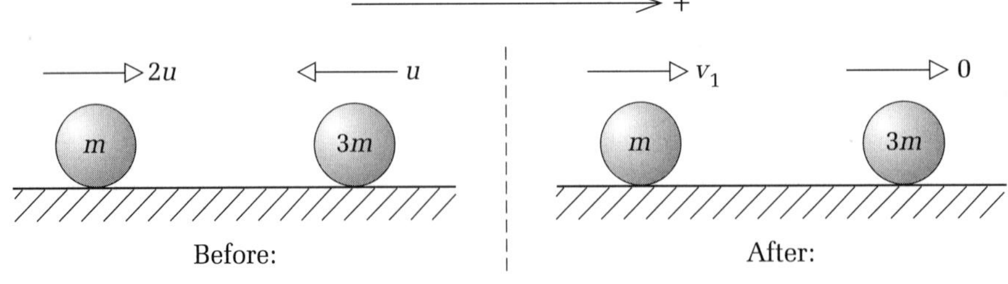

① Before and after diagrams.
② Summary of the information.
Assume unknown velocity is in the positive direction.

Using PCLM ◀ ③ Use PCLM.

momentum before = momentum after

$$m(2u) + 3m(-u) = m(v_1) + 3m(0)$$

$$2mu - 3mu = mv_1$$ ◀ ④ Calculate the required quantity.

$$-mu = mv_1$$

$$v_1 = -u \text{ so speed} = u$$

Use momentum = mv.
Simplify by removing brackets.
Divide by m.

12.3 Conservation of Linear Momentum

Exercise

Technique

Except where stated, each of the following questions concerns direct collisions between two smooth spheres of equal radii, moving on a smooth horizontal surface.

1 Sphere A has mass 1 kg and is projected towards B with speed 2 m s^{-1}. Sphere B has mass 0.5 kg and is already moving in the same direction with speed 1 m s^{-1}. After the collision, B has speed 2 m s^{-1}. Find the speed of A.

2 Sphere C has mass 0.3 kg and is projected towards D with speed 1.6 m s^{-1}. Sphere D has mass 0.4 kg and is at rest. After the collision, C is reduced to rest. What is the speed of D after the collision?

3 Spheres E and F have masses 800 g and 200 g respectively. They are travelling directly towards each other with speeds 0.5 m s^{-1} and 1.5 m s^{-1} respectively. After the collision, the direction of F is reversed and its new speed is 1 m s^{-1}.

Hint: take great care with the signs.

a What is the new speed and direction of E?
b Find also the magnitude of the impulse exerted on F by E.

4 Spheres G and H have masses 2.0 kg and 2.5 kg respectively. Sphere H is initially at rest and G is projected directly towards it with speed $5u \text{ m s}^{-1}$. The collision reduces the speed of G to $2u \text{ m s}^{-1}$; the direction of G remains unchanged. What will be the speed of H after the collision?

5 A particle of mass 300 g is projected with speed 5 m s^{-1} directly towards a particle of mass 700 g moving with speed 2 m s^{-1} in the same direction. After impact the two particles coalesce and move with speed $v \text{ m s}^{-1}$. Determine:

a the magnitude of v
b the loss in kinetic energy due to the collision.

6 Particle R has mass 4.5 kg and S has mass 0.5 kg. They are joined by a light inextensible string with R being projected with speed 2 m s^{-1} and S being initially at rest.

a When the string becomes taut, what will be the speed of the two particles?
b Calculate the loss in kinetic energy after the string becomes taut.

7 Two bodies, each of mass $2m$, are travelling with respective speeds $(u + 2)$ and $(u - 2)$ directly towards each other. After the impact they both reverse their directions, travelling with speed v and $2v$ respectively. Calculate the value of v.

8 Particle P has mass 0.5 kg and is projected with speed $4.5\ \text{m s}^{-1}$ towards a stationary particle, Q, of mass 0.4 kg. The two particles coalesce.

a With what speed do they move after the impact?

The new single particle made from P and Q continues to move with this same speed until it hits another stationary particle, R, with mass 1 kg. This second impact reduces the new particle to rest.

b What is the speed of R after this latter collision?

c Find the total loss in kinetic energy since the beginning of the motion.

9 A body of mass $6m$ and a body of $2m$ are projected towards each other with speeds $7u$ and $5u$ respectively. At the moment of impact the two bodies coalesce.

a Find the speed with which the combined mass moves after the impact.

b Show that the loss in kinetic energy is given by $108mu^2$.

Contextual

1 A hotel waiter is momentarily distracted and walks into a stationary serving trolley. The mass of the waiter and the trolley are 90 kg and 40 kg respectively. Before the collision the waiter is walking at $1.5\ \text{m s}^{-1}$ and afterwards his speed is reduced to $0.9\ \text{m s}^{-1}$.

a What will the speed of the trolley be immediately after the impact?

b What is the total loss in kinetic energy?

2 Two metric weights with masses 100 g and 200 g have been tied together with a 50 cm piece of string. The string can be assumed to be light and inextensible. Both weights are placed on the very edge of a high wall.

a After the 200 g weight has been pushed off the wall, what will its speed be at the moment the string becomes taut?

b What will the speed of both weights be immediately after the impulsive tension in the string?

c Calculate the magnitude of the impulsive tension in the string.

12.4 Newton's Law of Restitution

Elastic collisions

A ball is dropped from a certain height and it bounces on the floor. What happens to the ball? Will the ball return to its original height? What types of ball will bounce highest? How could this situation be modelled? We could treat the ball as a particle and ignore air resistance. The height of the ball after the bounce is less than the height before the bounce.

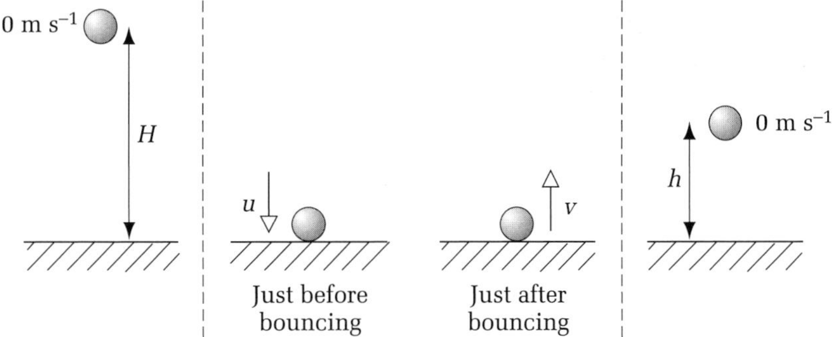

Dropped means initial velocity is zero.

Will the speed of the ball after bouncing be greater or less than the speed just before impact? After the impact, the speed of the ball must have decreased. The value of this speed can be calculated using the formula:

$$\boldsymbol{v = eu}$$

Notation
v = speed after impact
u = speed before impact
e = coefficient of restitution

This formula describes **Newton's law of restitution** (NLR) or **Newton's experimental law**. The value of the coefficient of restitution will depend on the structure of the body and the surface with which the body collides. The coefficient of restitution, e, must be smaller than 1 otherwise the ball would rebound with a larger speed. This leads to the inequality:

$$0 \leq e \leq 1$$

If $e = 1$, this means the rebound speed will equal the speed before impact. This type of collision is described as **perfectly elastic**, meaning there is no loss in speed.

A superball has a value of e close to 1.

If $0 < e < 1$, the speed on rebound is less than the speed before impact. This is called an elastic collision and the smaller the value of e, the slower the speed after impact.

A tennis ball or snooker ball would fall into this category.

If $e = 0$, the *rebound speed* is zero and the collision is describe as **inelastic**. If this applied to a dropped ball, the ball would simply remain on the floor. When two moving objects are involved, they would not separate after collision, but would stick together, or coalesce.

A bean bag falling on the floor would have a value of e close to 0.

Using Newton's law of restitution

When two objects are involved, Newton's law of restitution is most commonly used in the forms:

$$\boldsymbol{e} = \frac{\textbf{speed of separation}}{\textbf{speed of approach}}$$

or **speed of separation = $\boldsymbol{e}$ × (speed of approach)**

Alternative formula: $-e(u_1 - u_2) = v_1 - v_2$ A positive direction must be stated.

More complex problems

The most demanding questions may require the application of all the principles covered in this chapter. Generally, this will require the solution of simultaneous equations.

Overview of method

Step ① Draw before and after diagrams, with a clearly indicated positive direction.
Step ② Show all the known information on these diagrams.
Step ③ Apply the principle of conservation of linear momentum.
Step ④ Use Newton's law of restitution.
Step ⑤ Solve the resulting simultaneous equations.
Step ⑥ Calculate the loss in kinetic energy, if required.

PCLM is only used when two bodies collide.

Some examples only need one or two of these steps.

Example 1

The diagrams illustrate collisions between smooth spheres with identical radii. Calculate e, the coefficient of restitution between each pair of spheres.

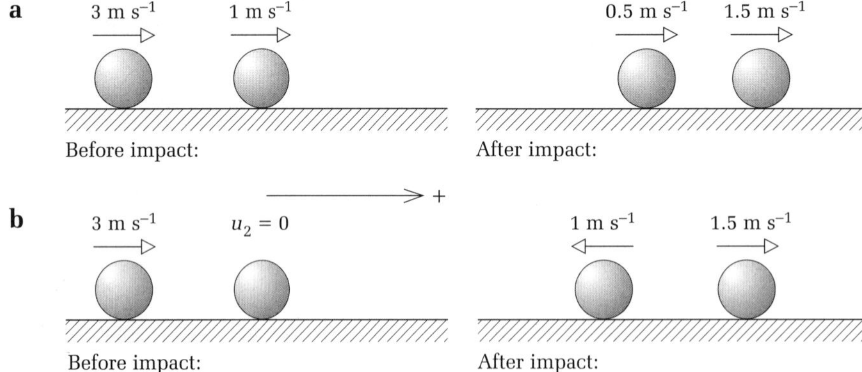

Solution

a Applying NLR

NLR stands for Newton's law of restitution.

$$e = \frac{\text{speed of separation}}{\text{speed of approach}}$$

$$e = \frac{(1.5 - 0.5)}{(3 - 1)}$$ ◀ **Substitute values.**

Simplify fraction.

$$e = \tfrac{1}{2}$$

Or 0.5.

b Apply NLR

$$e = \frac{\text{speed of separation}}{\text{speed of approach}}$$

$$e = \frac{(1 + 1.5)}{3}$$ ◀ Substitute the values.

Work out values for numerator and denominator.

$$e = \frac{2.5}{3}$$

$$e = \tfrac{5}{6}$$

Multiply numerator and denominator by 2.
Or $0.8\dot{3}$.

Example 2

Two smooth spheres A and B are travelling towards each other with speeds of $0.1\,\text{m s}^{-1}$ and $0.4\,\text{m s}^{-1}$ respectively. After impact, the direction of A is reversed and its speed doubled. If $e = 0.6$, what is the speed of B?

Solution

▼ ① Before and after diagrams.

▼ ② Summary of information.

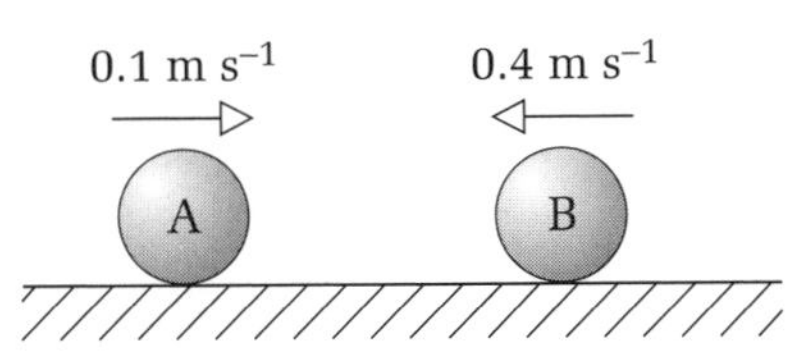
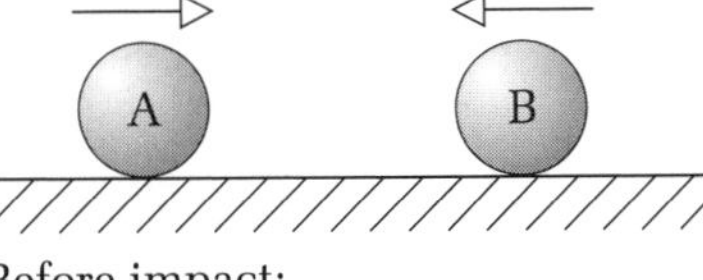

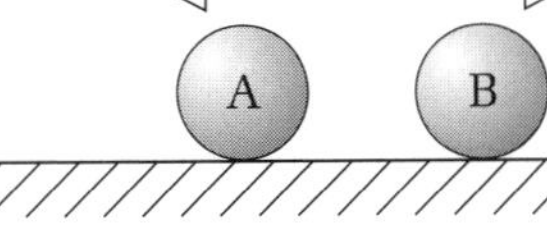

Apply NLR ◀ ④ Use Newton's law of restitution.

speed of separation $= e \times$ (speed of approach)

$$0.2 + v_2 = 0.6 \times (0.1 + 0.4)$$ ◀ Substitute the values.

$$0.2 + v_2 = 0.3$$

$$v_2 = 0.1\,\text{m s}^{-1}$$

Work out RHS ($0.6 \times 0.5 = 0.3$).
Subtract 0.2 from both sides.

Example 3

A smooth sphere is travelling with a speed of $5\,\text{m s}^{-1}$ towards a vertical wall. After impact with the wall, it rebounds with an initial speed of $4\,\text{m s}^{-1}$. Calculate the value of the coefficient of restitution, e.

Solution

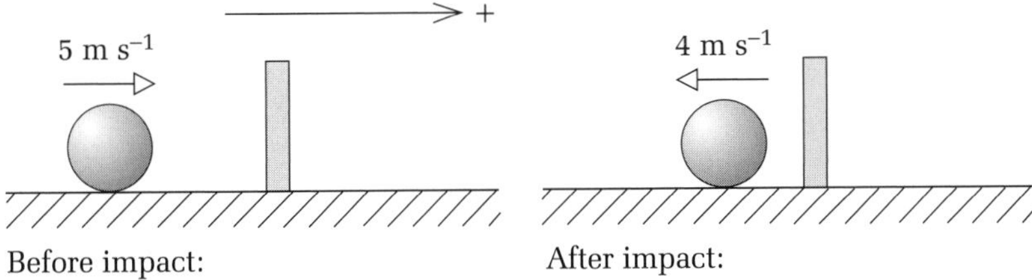

① Diagrams.
② Summary.

Using NLR, ◀ ④ Use Newton's law of restitution.

$$e = \frac{\text{speed of separation}}{\text{speed of approach}}$$

$$e = \tfrac{4}{5}$$ ◀ Substitute the values.

Or $e = 0.8$.

Example 4

A smooth sphere of mass $4m$ is travelling in a straight line on a horizontal table. It collides with another sphere with an identical radius and mass $8m$ moving in the same straight line directly towards it. Before collision, the speed of the first sphere is $u\,\text{m s}^{-1}$ and the speed of the second is $0.6\,\text{m s}^{-1}$. After the collision, the speed of the first sphere is doubled and its direction reversed. Given that $e = \frac{1}{2}$, determine the speeds of both spheres after impact.

Solution

▼ ① Before and after diagrams.

▼ ② Summary of information.

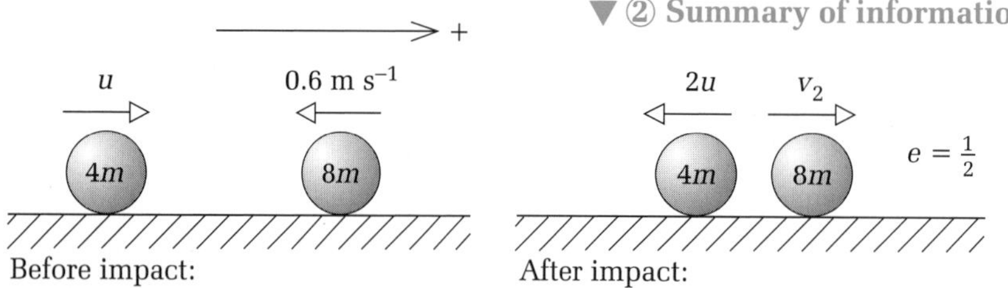

The positive direction is to the right.

Always mark any unknown quantities in the positive direction. A negative answer will mean it is actually travelling in the opposite direction.

Applying PCLM, ◀ ③ Apply principle of conservation of linear momentum.

$$4m \times u - 8m \times 0.6 = 8m \times v_2 - 4m \times 2u$$

momentum before = momentum after

$$4mu - 4.8m = 8mv_2 - 8mu$$

$$u - 1.2 = 2v_2 - 2u$$

Divide by $4m$ to simplify.

$$3u - 2v_2 = 1.2 \qquad [1]$$

Add $2u$ and 1.2, subtract $2v_2$.

This equation by itself is insufficient to solve for u or v_2. A second equation can be generated by applying Newton's law of restitution.

Applying NLR, ◀ ④ Use Newton's law of restitution.

$$2u + v_2 = \tfrac{1}{2}(u + 0.6)$$

speed of separation = $e\times$(speed of approach)

$$4u + 2v_2 = u + 0.6$$

Multiply by 2.

$$3u + 2v_2 = 0.6 \qquad [2]$$

Subtract u from both sides.

Solving equations [1] and [2] simultaneously,

$$3u - 2v_2 = 1.2$$ ◀ ⑤ Solve simultaneous equations.

$$3u + 2v_2 = 0.6$$

Adding, $6u = 1.8$

$u = 0.3$

Add the equations and divide by 6.

Now $3 \times 0.3 + 2v_2 = 0.6$

$0.9 + 2v_2 = 0.6$

$2v_2 = -0.3$

$v_2 = -0.15$

Use equation [2] with u replaced by 0.3.

Therefore $v_2 = -0.15\,\text{m s}^{-1}$ and after the collision the two spheres are moving to the left, with speeds of $0.6\,\text{m s}^{-1}$ and $0.15\,\text{m s}^{-1}$ respectively.

This will be opposite to the direction for v_2 shown in the diagram.

12.4 Newton's Law of Restitution

Exercise

Technique

1

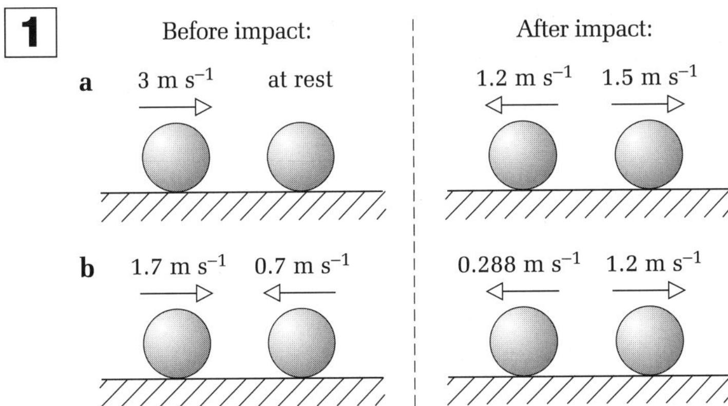

The diagram shows the speeds and directions before and after collisions for two different pairs of smooth spheres. Calculate the value of e, the coefficient of restitution, in each case.

2 A ball hits the ground with a speed of $8\,\text{m s}^{-1}$ and rebounds with a speed of $6\,\text{m s}^{-1}$.

a Calculate the value of the coefficient of restitution between this ball and the ground.

On another occasion the same ball strikes the ground with speed $2.6\,\text{m s}^{-1}$.

b What will be the rebound speed?

3 Two balls, P and Q collide directly with speeds $1.8\,\text{m s}^{-1}$ and $2.1\,\text{m s}^{-1}$. The coefficient of restitution between them is known to be 0.7 and the speed of Q is reduced to zero by the impact. What will be the speed of P?

4 Two balls, A and B, are projected in the same direction along the same straight line with speeds $2.9\,\text{m s}^{-1}$ and $1.8\,\text{m s}^{-1}$ respectively, so that they collide. The coefficient of restitution is 0.3 for these two balls. If the speed of A is reduced to $1.9\,\text{m s}^{-1}$ after the collision, what will be the speed of B?

5 Two smooth spheres, P and Q, of masses 3 kg and 2 kg respectively, are travelling towards each other. Sphere P has speed $0.8\,\text{m s}^{-1}$ and Q has speed $0.5\,\text{m s}^{-1}$. After the impact both spheres move in the same direction as the original direction of P.

a If the speed of Q after the collision is twice the speed of P, find the new speed of each sphere.

b Calculate the value of the coefficient of restitution, giving your answer as a fraction.

6 Two smooth spheres with equal radii are projected directly towards each other. The first has mass $2m$ and speed $u\,\mathrm{m\,s^{-1}}$, the second has mass $3m$ and speed $1.3\,\mathrm{m\,s^{-1}}$. The collision reverses the direction of motion of both spheres. The first has speed $u\,\mathrm{m\,s^{-1}}$ and the second has speed $v\,\mathrm{m\,s^{-1}}$.

a Given that $e = 0.6$, use Newton's law of restitution and the principle of conservation of linear momentum to write a pair of simultaneous equations involving u and v.

b Solve these equations to find out the speed of each ball after the collision.

7 A smooth ball, P, is projected with speed $4.8\,\mathrm{m\,s^{-1}}$ across a smooth horizontal surface towards a second smooth ball, Q, of the same radius. The masses of P and Q are $5m$ and $8m$ and Q is initially stationary. After the impact, the direction of P is reversed and its speed is $1.2\,\mathrm{m\,s^{-1}}$.

a What will be the speed of Q after the collision?

b Ball Q subsequently collides with a vertical wall perpendicular to its path. The coefficient of restitution between the wall and Q is e. Show that for Q to collide again with P, $e > \frac{8}{25}$.

Contextual

1 The greatest value of e, the coefficient of restitution, is 1.

a Explain what it would mean for the coefficient between a ball and a surface to be 1.

b Can you give an example?

c Rank the following in order according to your estimate of their coefficient of restitution with a hard surface, from lowest to highest: snooker ball; inflatable beach ball; juggler's bean bag; tennis ball.

2 Two identical toy trains are propelled along a straight track so that they collide *head-on*. Just before the impact they are both travelling with speed $0.5\,\mathrm{m\,s^{-1}}$. Their speeds on separation are $0.12\,\mathrm{m\,s^{-1}}$ and $0.11\,\mathrm{m\,s^{-1}}$.

a Should the speeds after the impact be the same? How might the difference be explained?

b Use Newton's experimental law to calculate a coefficient of restitution.

c Why might it not be realistic to model the situation in this way?

3 A tennis ball and a cricket ball are rolled towards each other and collide directly, with the tennis ball changing direction. The mass of the tennis ball is 50 g, while the mass of the cricket ball is 250 g. The initial speed of the tennis ball is $2\,\mathrm{m\,s^{-1}}$ and of the cricket ball is $1\,\mathrm{m\,s^{-1}}$. The coefficient of restitution between them is believed to be 0.4. Find the speed of each ball after the collision.

Consolidation

Exercise A

1 Particle A has mass 0.2 kg and particle B has mass 0.5 kg. The particles are travelling towards each other in the same line and they collide. Immediately before the collision the speed of A is $6\,\mathrm{m\,s^{-1}}$ and the speed of B is $4\,\mathrm{m\,s^{-1}}$. Particle B is brought to rest by the collision. Find:

a the speed of A immediately after the collision

b the kinetic energy lost in the collision, stating the units in which your answer is measured. *(ULEAC)*

2 **a** A particle A of mass $3m$ is travelling with speed u across a smooth horizontal floor when it collides directly with a particle B of mass $2m$ which is at rest. After impact, B moves with speed u.

i Find the speed of A after the collision.

ii Find the magnitude of the impulse on B due to the collision.

iii Write down the magnitude of the impulse on A due to the collision and indicate its direction.

b The particle B subsequently strikes a wall which is at right angles to its direction of motion. It rebounds from the wall with a speed w and collides directly with A again, bringing both particles to rest.

i Show that $w = \frac{1}{2}u$.

ii Find the magnitude of the impulse of the wall on B. *(NEAB)*

3 A spaceship of mass 80 000 kg docks with a space station of mass 400 000 kg. The space station is travelling at $200\,\mathrm{m\,s^{-1}}$ immediately before docking takes place, and the space ship is travelling $0.6\,\mathrm{m\,s^{-1}}$ faster. In a model for the docking, two particles, moving in the same direction in the same straight line, collide and coalesce.

a Show that the speed of the spaceship is reduced by $0.5\,\mathrm{m\,s^{-1}}$ by the docking.

b Calculate the total loss in kinetic energy during the docking.

(UCLES)

4 A particle P, of mass $2m$, is moving in a straight line with speed u at the instant when it collides directly with a particle Q, of mass m, which is at rest. The coefficient of restitution between P and Q is e.

a Show that, after the collision, P is moving with speed $\frac{1}{3}(2 - e)u$.

b Show that the loss of kinetic energy due to the collision is $\frac{1}{3}mu^2(1 - e^2)$.

c Find, in terms of m, u and e, the impulse exerted by P on Q in the collision. *(ULEAC)*

Exercise B

1 A car of mass 1.2 tonnes collides with a stationary van of mass 2.4 tonnes. After the collision the two vehicles become entangled and skid 15 m before stopping. Police accident investigators estimate that the magnitude of the friction force during the skid was 2880 N. Assume the road is horizontal and that all the motion takes place in a straight line.

a Find the speed of the vehicles just after the collision.

b Find the speed of the car before the collision. *(AEB)*

2 A particle A of mass m is moving with speed $2u$ in a straight line on a smooth horizontal table. It collides with another particle B of mass km which is moving in the same straight line on the table with speed u and in the opposite direction to A. In the collision, the particles form a single particle which then moves with speed $\frac{2}{3}u$ in the original direction of A's motion. Find the value of k. *(ULEAC)*

3 An unloaded railway wagon A, of mass 800 kg, and a loaded wagon B, of mass 3000 kg, are free to move on a straight horizontal track. Wagon A is travelling at a speed of 8 m s^{-1} when it runs into B, which is stationary, causing B to start to move with a speed of 2 m s^{-1}. Calculate:

a the speed of A immediately after the impact

b the loss of kinetic energy due to the impact. *(UCLES)*

4 A particle P of mass $3m$ lies at rest on the surface of a horizontal ice rink. The particle is attached to a fixed point O by a light inextensible string of length l with OP horizontal and the string just taut. An ice hockey puck, Q, of mass $4m$ moves across the ice at speed u along a line perpendicular to OP and collides directly with P. The speed of Q is reduced by 60% on impact with P.

a Find, in terms of u, the speed of P immediately after the collision.

After its collision with P, the puck Q travels a distance d before striking a smooth vertical barrier at right angles to its path and rebounds with speed $\frac{3u}{10}$. Subsequently Q collides directly with P when P first returns to its starting point.

b Find d in terms of l.

c Comment briefly on one assumption in your model of the motion.

(NEAB)

5 A smooth sphere, A, of mass $4m$ which is travelling with a speed u collides directly with a stationary smooth sphere, B, of mass m. The coefficient of restitution between the two spheres is e.

a Find the velocity of sphere A immediately after the collision.

b Find the kinetic energy lost by sphere A in the collision.

c Find the maximum and minimum possible velocities of sphere A immediately after the collision. *(NICCEA)*

Applications and Activities

1

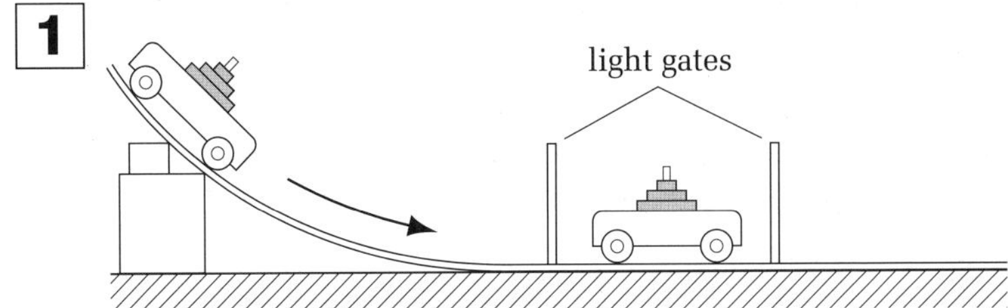

Investigate different collisions between different trolleys. Model the situations mathematically and comment on your results.

2 By dropping a ball onto a surface from different heights, find the coefficient of restitution between the ball and the surface. Change the surface. Try table tops, carpeted floor, concrete surface and tiled floor.

3 Professional tennis players can serve a tennis ball at speeds of over 100 mph. Calculate the coefficient of restitution between a tennis ball and a tennis racket by experiment. Find out the fastest serves for men and women tennis players. Model the collision between racket head and ball to determine the speed of the racket head at impact.

Summary

- The formula for momentum is

  momentum $= m\mathbf{v}$

- Impulse is given by the formula

  impulse = force × time

- The impulse–momentum equation is

  impulse = final momentum − initial momentum,

  and we assume that the objects have uniform acceleration.

- The principle of conservation of linear momentum is

  total momentum before collision = total momentum after collision

- The loss in kinetic energy due to a collision is

  $$\mathbf{KE_{loss} = KE_{before} - KE_{after}}$$

- Newton's law of restitution is

  $$v = eu \text{ or } e = \frac{\textbf{speed of separation}}{\textbf{speed of approach}}$$

  and the inequality for the coefficient of restitution is

  $$0 \le e \le 1$$

13 Moments

What you need to know

- How to add vectors in **i** and **j** form.
- When a particle is in equilibrium.
- How to find the resultant of two or more forces.

Review

1 Vectors **a** and **b** are given by $\mathbf{a} = 7\mathbf{i} - 10\mathbf{j}$ and $\mathbf{b} = -3\mathbf{i} + 8\mathbf{j}$. Find:

a $\mathbf{a} + \mathbf{b}$ **b** $2\mathbf{a} - 3\mathbf{b}$

2 **a** Explain what is meant by static and dynamic equilibrium.

b

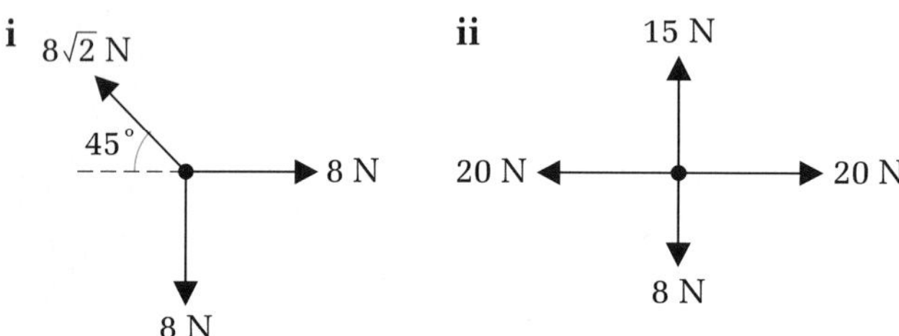

State whether the particles shown are in equilibrium or not.

3 **a**

10 N

5 N

b

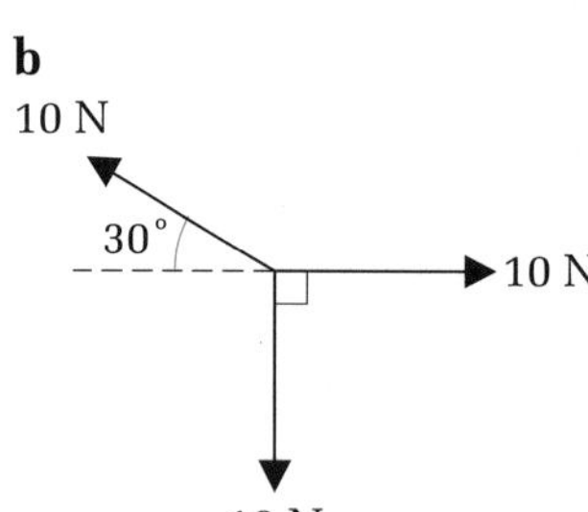

Find the resultant of the forces shown. State both the magnitude and direction of the resultant.

13.1 The Moment of a Force

Some refrigerators have a handle running the whole width of the door. If you were to open such a door, where would you hold to pull it open? Which position would be the most difficult to hold when trying to open the door? Try out your ideas on an ordinary classroom door.

At a *small* distance from the hinge, a *large* force must be applied to make the door turn. At a *large* distance from the hinge, only a *small* force is necessary to make the door open. The turning of the door must depend on the force applied and the distance from the hinge. A measure of the turning effect of a force is called the **moment**.

Definition

The moment of a force is the product of the force and its perpendicular distance away from the hinge.

Product means multiplication.

A **pivot** will also allow an object to turn or rotate.

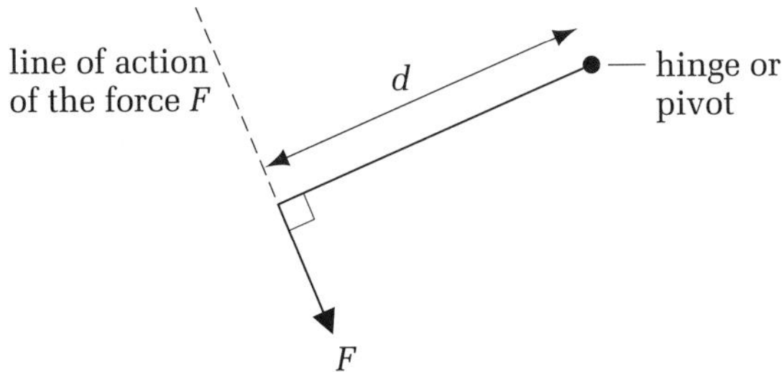

This statement can be written as:

$$M = Fd$$

Notation
M = moment of the force (N m)
F = force (N)
d = perpendicular distance (m)

The perpendicular distance is measured from the **line of action** of the force to the hinge or pivot. The units for a moment must be the same as the unit of force multiplied by the unit for distance. This means the newton metre (N m) is the unit used for a moment.

A force can cause a clockwise turning moment or an anticlockwise turning moment. This means the direction of the moment is important and therefore the moment of a force is a **vector** quantity.

Overview of method

The process of finding the moment of a force is called *taking moments about a point.*

Step ① Draw a diagram showing the forces and distances.
Step ② Calculate the perpendicular distance to the force (if necessary).
Step ③ Take moments about the hinge, pivot or the point stated in the question.

Example 1

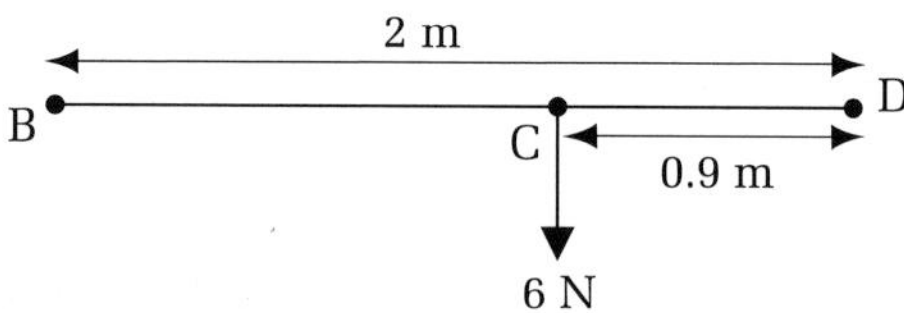

Find the moment of the 6 N force about the points B, C and D.

Solution

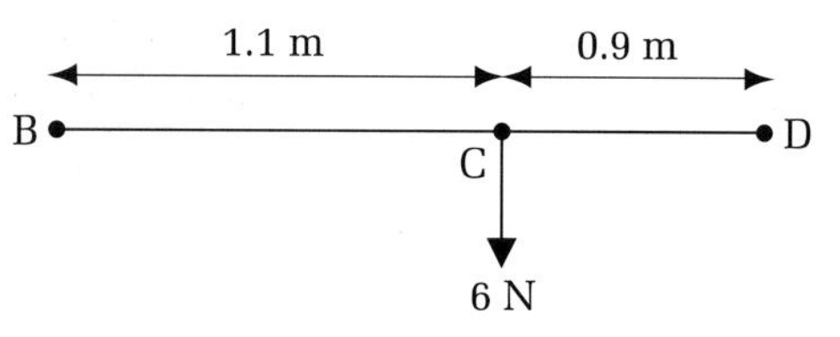

◀ ① Draw a diagram.
◀ ② Mark on all the perpendicular distances.

$2 - 0.9 = 1.1$ m

↻B Clockwise ◀ ③ Take moments about the point B.

$M = Fd$

$M = 6 \times 1.1$

$M = 6.6$ N m clockwise

↻B is shorthand for taking moments about B.

↻C Clockwise ◀ ③ Take moments about the point C.

$M = Fd$

$M = 6 \times 0$

$M = 0$ N m clockwise

$M = 0$ N m

This is similar to trying to open the door by pushing on the hinge. The perpendicular distance will be zero and so the turning effect will be zero. In general, if any force acts through the pivot or hinge, its moment will be zero.

The direction does not need to be stated when the moment is zero because there will be *no* turning effect.

↻D Anticlockwise

$M = Fd$

$M = 6 \times 0.9$

$M = 5.4$ N m anticlockwise

The turning effect of this force will be anticlockwise and so moments are taken in this direction.

Example 2

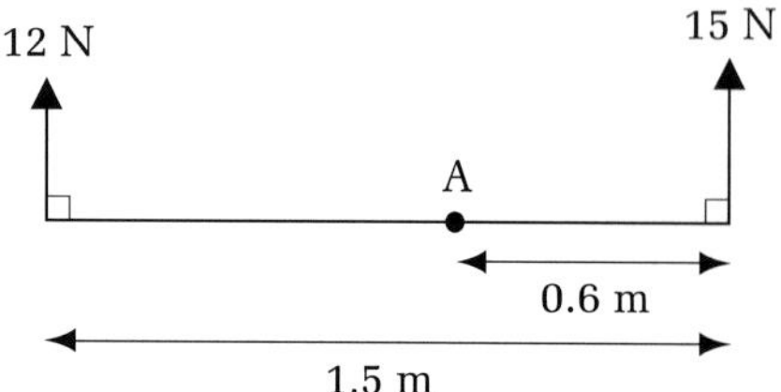

Find the total moment about the point A.

Solution

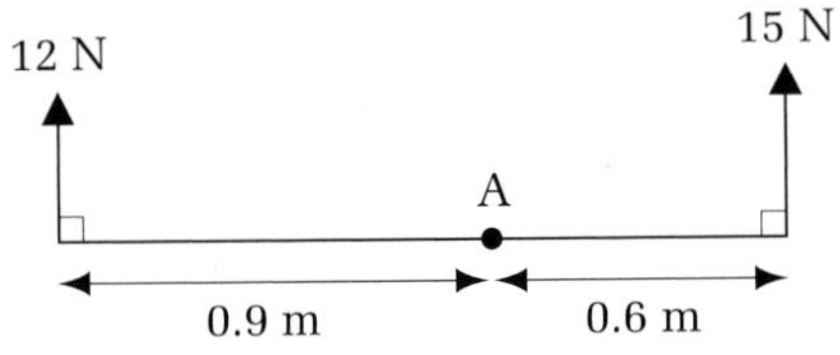

◀ ① Draw a diagram.
◀ ② Mark on all the perpendicular distances.

1.5 − 0.6 = 0.9 m

The moments of both forces can be written on the same line. To make sure the overall moment is calculated correctly, a positive direction is stated.

This is similar to stating a positive direction for uniform acceleration problems. The positive direction will be clockwise.

↻A Clockwise ◀ ③ Take moments.

$M = 12 \times 0.9 - 15 \times 0.6$ ◀ The 15 N force acts anticlockwise and so it is negative.

$M = 10.8 - 9$

$M = 1.8$ N m clockwise

Example 3

Find the moment of the force (3**i** − 5**j**) N acting through the point with position vector (6**i** + 3**j**) m about the origin.

Moments will be taken about the origin.

Solution

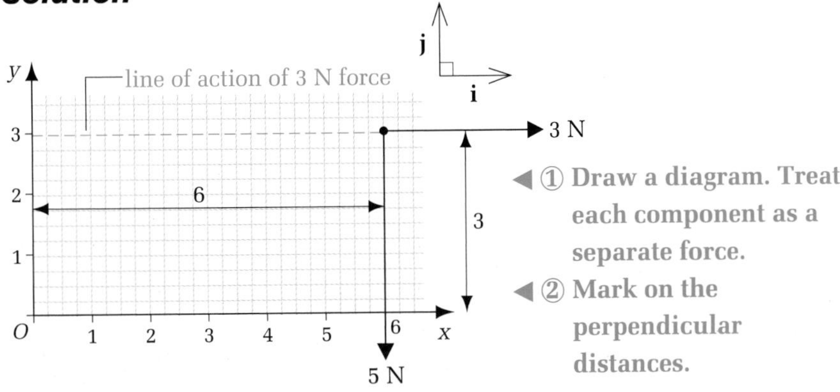

◀ ① Draw a diagram. Treat each component as a separate force.
◀ ② Mark on the perpendicular distances.

↻O Clockwise ◀ ③ Take moments about O.

$M = 3 \times 3 + 5 \times 6$

$M = 9 + 30$

$M = 39$ N m clockwise

Both forces are turning in a clockwise direction. Check this using a piece of paper.

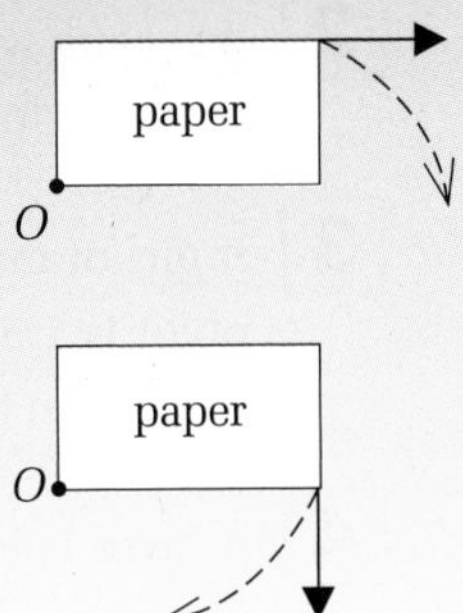

13.1 The Moment of a Force
Exercise

Technique

1

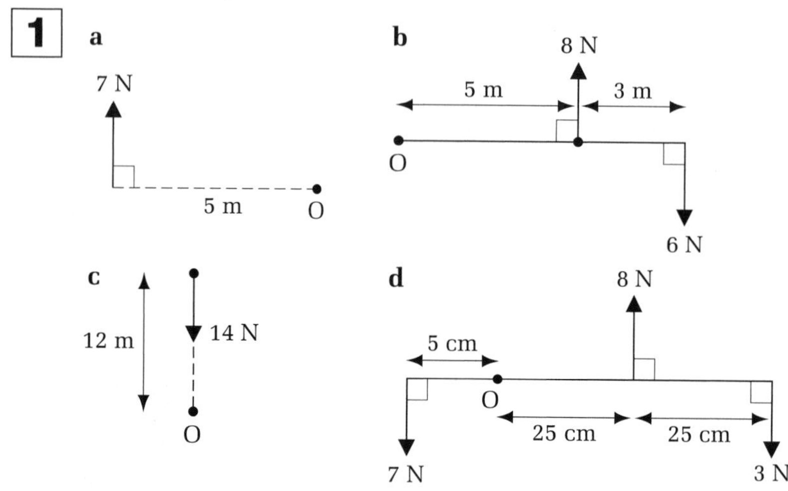

For *each* diagram, find the total moment about the point O.

2 A force of $10\mathbf{j}$ N acts at the point $(6\mathbf{i} + 8\mathbf{j})$ m. Find the moment of this force about the origin.

3 A force of $6\mathbf{i}$ N acts at the point $(-4\mathbf{i} + 7\mathbf{j})$ m. What is the moment of the force about the origin?

4 A $(6\mathbf{i} + 8\mathbf{j})$ N force acts at the point $(3\mathbf{i} + 4\mathbf{j})$ m. Determine the moment of the force about O, the origin.

5 A force of $(8\mathbf{i} + 5\mathbf{j})$ N acts at the point $(13\mathbf{i} + 4\mathbf{j})$ m and a second force of $(7\mathbf{i} + 4\mathbf{j})$ N acts at the point $(6\mathbf{i} - \mathbf{j})$ m. Work out the total moment of these two forces about the origin.

Contextual

1 A fridge door is pulled with a force of 7 N. The distance from the hinge to the handle is 0.4 m. Calculate the magnitude of the moment produced by the 7 N force.

Assume that the forces and distances given are perpendicular.

2 A torque wrench has a rating of 20 N m. The length of its handle is 40 cm. Find the force that needs to be applied to produce a torque of 20 N m.

Torque is the same as a moment.

3 A girl of mass 40 kg sits on a see-saw. The distance from the girl to the pivot is 1.5 m. Determine the size of the moment produced by the girl's weight on the see-saw.

4 A lever is to be used to apply a torque of 50 N m. The maximum force that can be applied is 40 N. Work out the length of the lever from the hinge.

13.2 Moments with Forces Applied at an Angle

Whenever you open a door, you pull the handle at right angles to the door. Why do you do this automatically? The design of the handle makes you apply your force at right angles. Why has someone designed the door handle like this? Attach a piece of string to the door handle. Try opening the classroom door by pulling the string at different angles.

A force applied perpendicular to the door creates a larger turning effect than one which is applied at a different angle. By drawing a diagram, the difference in the moments can be modelled.

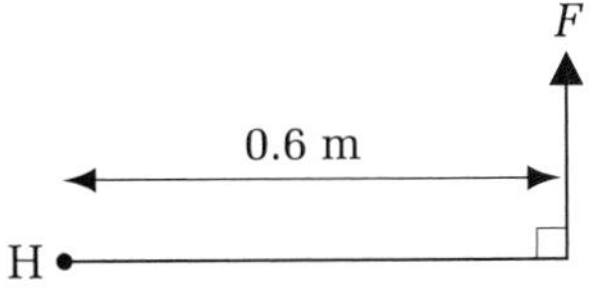

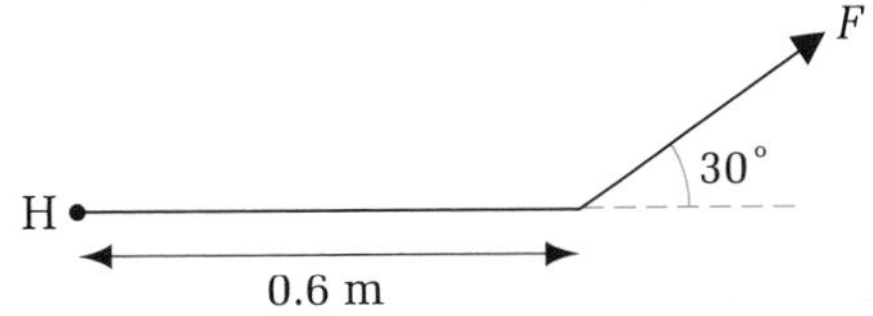

The line of action of the angled force is extended backwards. A line is drawn from the hinge perpendicular to this line of action. The perpendicular distance to this force is d. This distance, d, must be smaller than 0.6 m because 0.6 m is the length of the hypotenuse of the right-angled triangle.

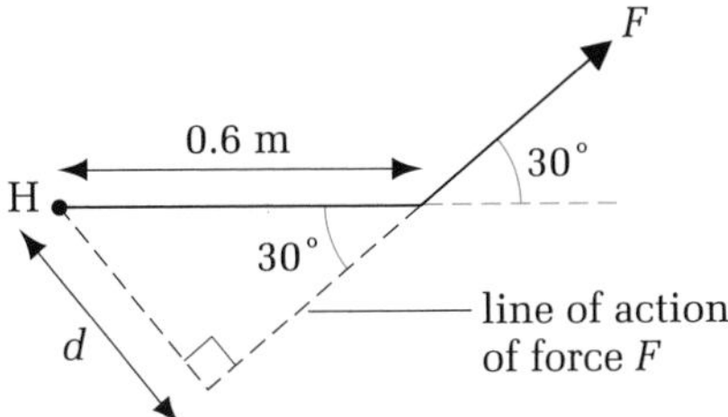

$\circlearrowleft$H Anticlockwise

Perpendicular force:

$$M = F \times 0.6$$

$$M = 0.6F \text{ N m}$$

Force at 30°:

$$M = Fd$$

$$M = F \times 0.6\sin 30^\circ$$

$$M = F \times 0.6 \times \tfrac{1}{2}$$

$$M = 0.3F \text{ N m}$$

Use trigonometry.
$d = 0.6\sin 30^\circ$

Another way of modelling this situation is to resolve the force acting at 30° into two components.

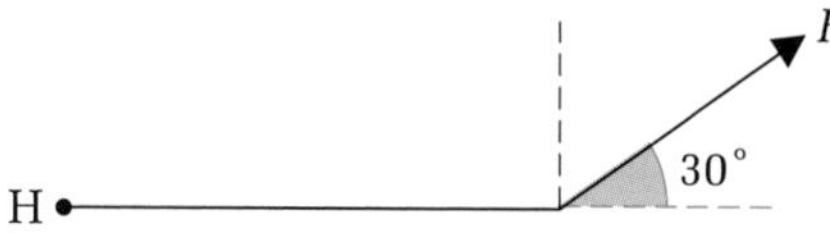

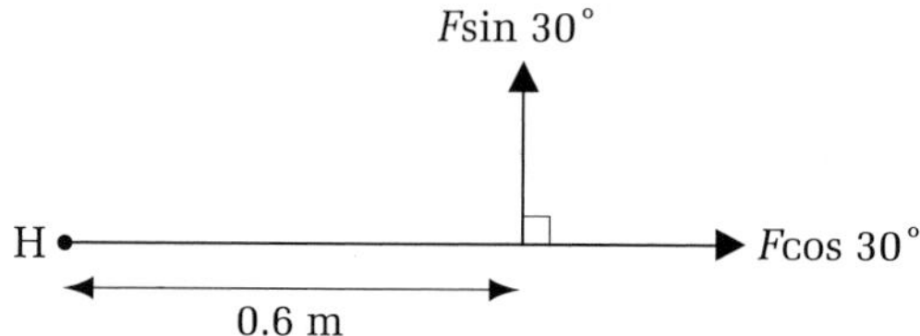

Recall cos is *with* the angle, sin is *not with* the angle.

The turning effect of the $F\cos 30°$ component must be zero because the perpendicular distance from $F\cos 30°$ to H is zero. The perpendicular distance for the $F\sin 30°$ force is 0.6 m.

If the line of action of $F\cos 30°$ is extended it passes through H.

↶H Anticlockwise

$M = F\sin 30° \times 0.6$

$M = F \times \frac{1}{2} \times 0.6$

$M = 0.3F$ N m

Notice that this is the same answer as considering the perpendicular distance of the whole force. This comparison shows that the angle at which forces act is very important when calculating their moments.

Overview of method

Step ① Draw a clear force diagram.
Step ② Resolve any angled forces into two components.
Choose directions parallel and perpendicular to the line joining the hinge (or pivot) to the point where the force acts. The moment of the parallel component is always zero.
Step ③ Mark on the perpendicular distances.
Step ④ Use $M = Fd$ to calculate the moment of the force.

or

Step ① Draw a clear force diagram.
Step ② Extend the line of action of the force.
Draw a line from the hinge (or pivot) perpendicular to the line of action of the force.
Step ③ Calculate the perpendicular distance to the force using Pythagoras' theorem or trigonometry.
Step ④ Use $M = Fd$ to calculate the moment of the force.

Resolving the forces into two components will usually prove to be the easier method.

Example 1

A crane holds a 200 kg concrete block. The angle the crane arm makes with the horizontal is 60°. The length of the crane arm is 40 m. Determine the moment about the hinge caused by the concrete mass.

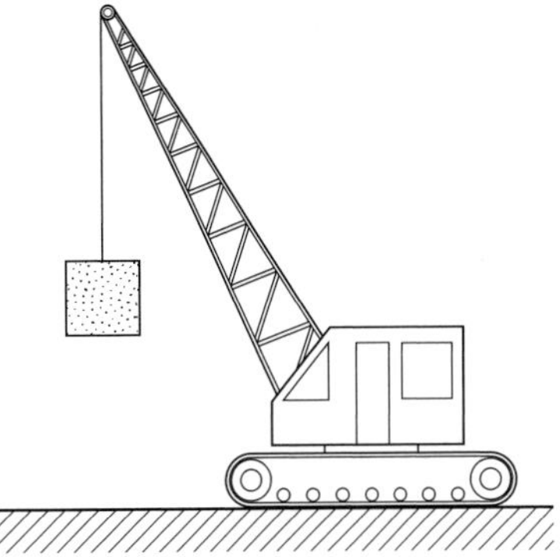

Solution

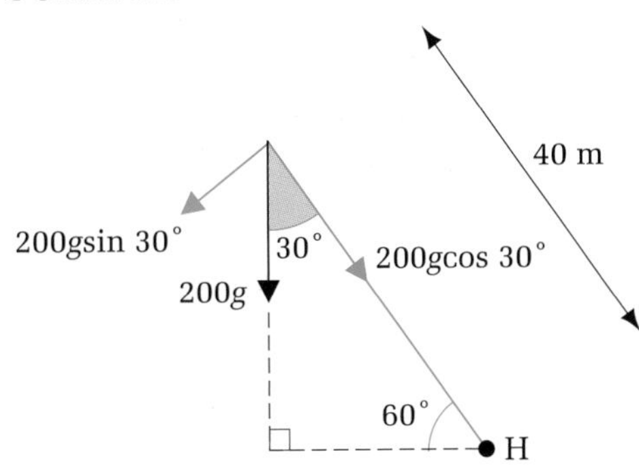

◀ ① Draw a clear force diagram.

◀ ② Resolve the force parallel and perpendicular to the crane arm.

◀ ③ Mark on the perpendicular distances.

↶H Anticlockwise ◀ ④ Take moments about H using $M = Fd$.

$M = Fd$

$M = 200g \sin 30° \times 40$

$M = 200g \times \frac{1}{2} \times 40$

$M = 39\,200$ N m anticlockwise

$\sin 30° = \frac{1}{2}$

$g = 9.8\,\text{m s}^{-2}$

Alternative Method

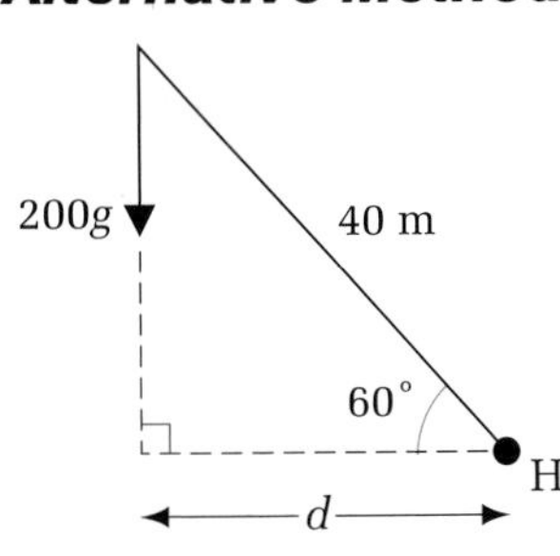

◀ ① Draw a clear force diagram.

◀ ② Draw in the perpendicular distance to the line of action of the force.

$d = 40\cos 60°$ ◀ ③ Calculate the perpendicular distance using trigonometry.

$d = 40 \times \frac{1}{2}$

$d = 20\,\text{m}$

↶H Anticlockwise ◀ ④ Take moments about H.

$M = Fd$

$M = 200g \times 20$

$M = 39\,200\,\text{N m}$ anticlockwise

The force acting on the arm is the weight of the block.
weight $= mg = 200g$
$g = 9.8\,\text{m s}^{-2}$

Example 2

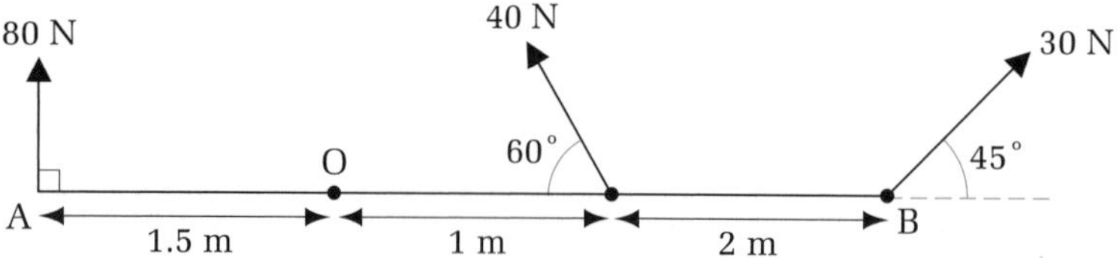

Calculate the total moment of the forces on the bar AB about the pivot O.

Solution

This problem will be most easily solved by resolving the forces. This is because drawing on the construction lines for the perpendicular distances can lead to a cluttered diagram making solving the problem difficult.

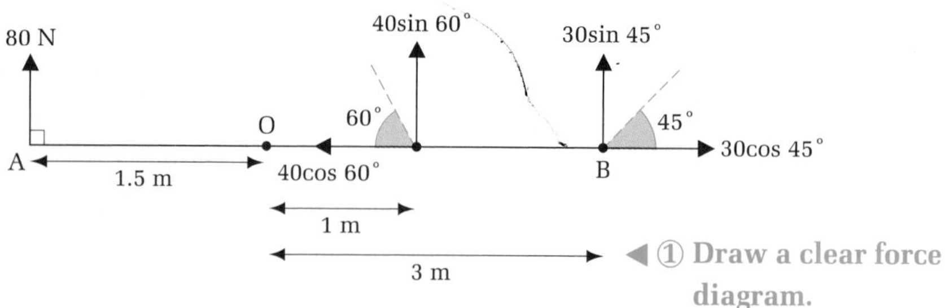

cos is with the angle.
sin is not with the angle.

◀ ① Draw a clear force diagram.

▲ ② Resolve the forces parallel and perpendicular to AB.

▲ ③ Mark on the perpendicular distances.

↻O Clockwise ◀ ④ Take moments about O using $M = Fd$.

$M = 80 \times 1.5 - (40\sin 60° \times 1) - (30\sin 45° \times 3)$

$M = 120 - (40 \times \frac{\sqrt{3}}{2}) - (30 \times \frac{\sqrt{2}}{2} \times 3)$

$M = 120 - 20\sqrt{3} - 45\sqrt{2}$

$M = 21.7$ N m (3 s.f.) clockwise

$\sin 60° = \frac{\sqrt{3}}{2}$ and $\sin 45° = \frac{\sqrt{2}}{2}$

By assuming clockwise moments as positive, then all the anticlockwise moments are negative. The positive answer means the overall moment is clockwise.

13.2 Moments with Forces Applied at an Angle

Exercise

Technique

1

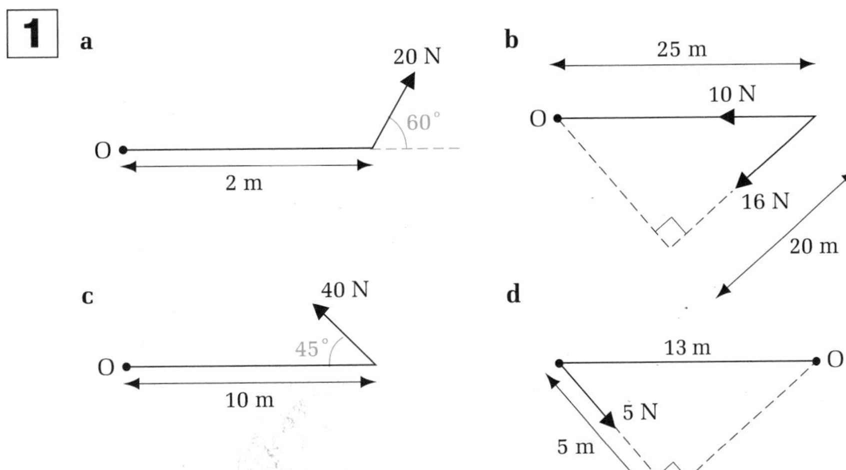

By calculating the perpendicular distances to the forces for each diagram, work out the moment the forces produce about O, the origin.

2

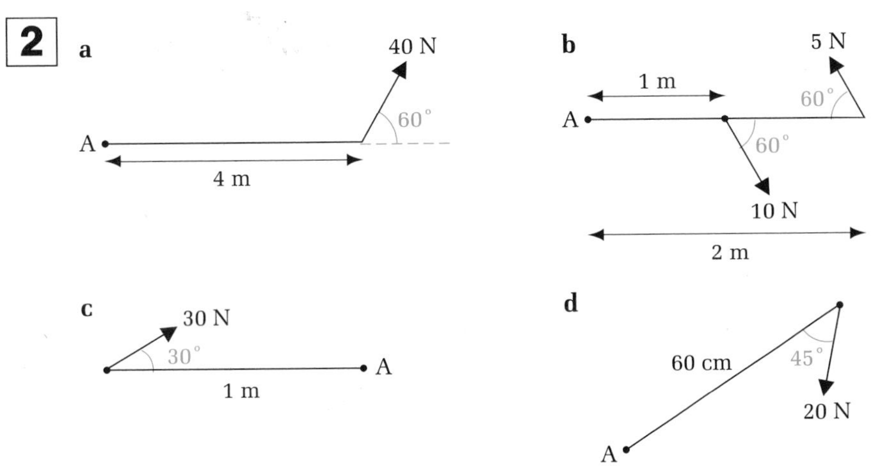

By resolving each force into two components for each diagram, determine the moment produced about A.

3

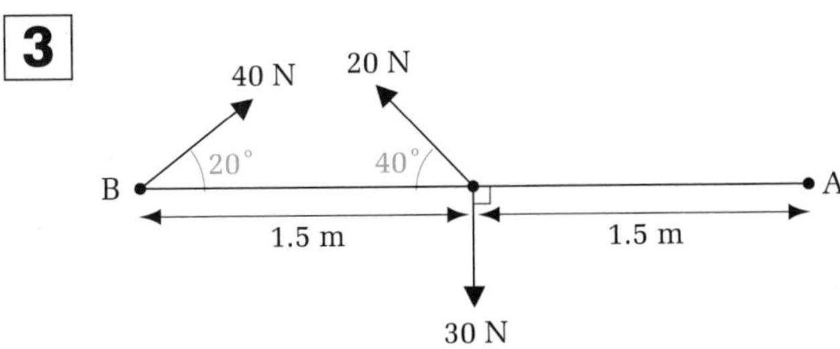

Find the total moment acting on the bar AB about the pivot A.

4

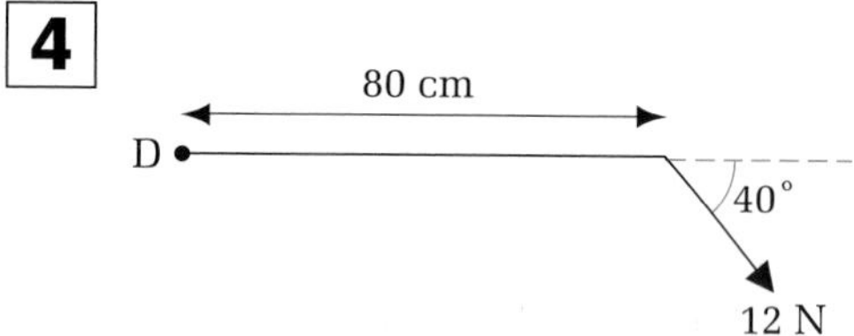

Find the moment of the 12 N force about D. A student's solution is shown below. Explain why this answer is *wrong* and determine the correct answer.

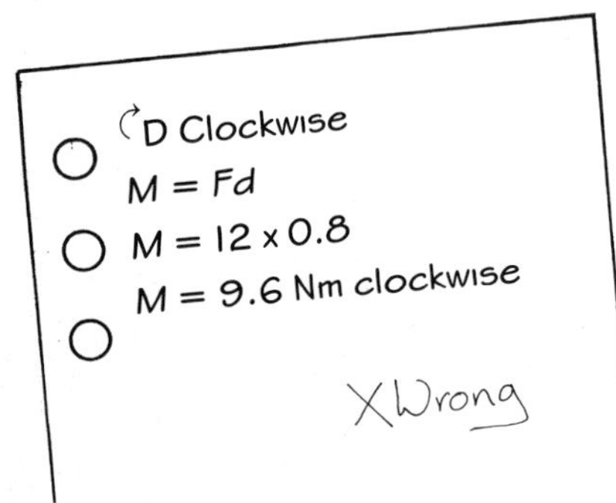

Contextual

1

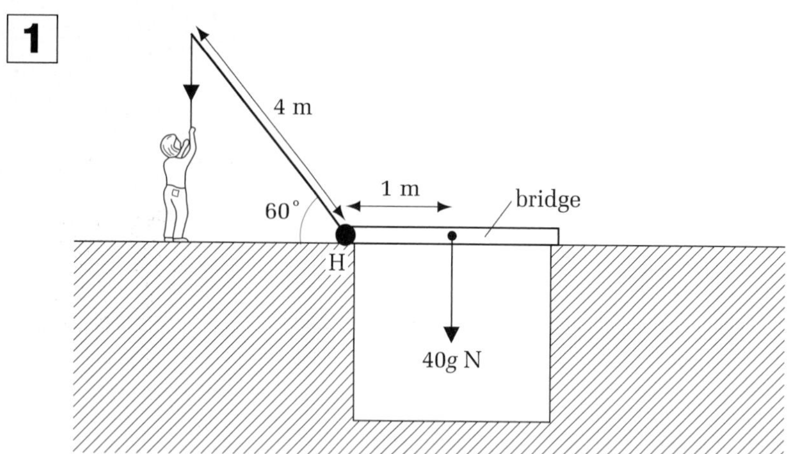

The diagram shows a mechanism for raising a bridge. Calculate the overall moment acting on the bridge about the hinge H, if $g = 10\,\text{m}\,\text{s}^{-2}$ and the person pulls with a force of:

a 100 N **b** 200 N **c** 300 N

13.3 Balances

The set of scales shown can be used to weigh different objects. A 1 kg mass could be put in the pan on one side of the scales. In the other pan, flour could be added until the scales balanced. What is the mass of the flour in the other scale pan? Assume the distance from the pivot, P, to each mass is the same and it is 0.1 m. The objects are modelled as particles and the mass of the bar is ignored. The mass in the other scale pan is assumed to be m kg. What do you think the overall moment should be for a balanced set of scales? In this situation, the scales are stationary and there is no overall turning effect. This means that the overall moment acting on the scales is *zero*.

The pivot is sometimes called the **fulcrum** of the balance.

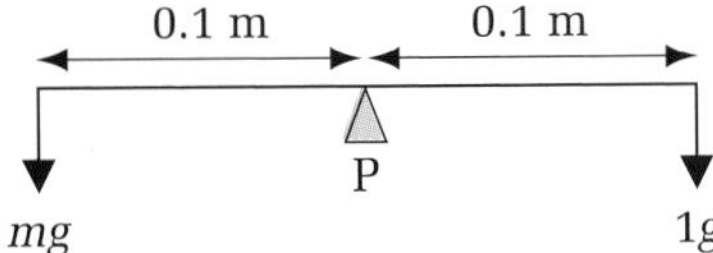

$\curvearrowleft$P Anticlockwise ◀ **Take moments about P in an anticlockwise direction.**

$$M = mg \times 0.1 - (1g \times 0.1)$$ ◀ $M = 0$.

$$0 = 0.1 \times mg - 0.1g$$

$$0.1g = 0.1mg$$ 0.1g added.

$$m = 1 \text{ kg}$$ Divided by 0.1.

This answer confirms that the masses in each scale pan will be the same. If the scale pans are not moving then there must be no resultant force acting on the system.

At first sight there seems to be an overall downward force. The balance, in theory, should accelerate downwards. What force prevents the balance from doing this? The bar and fulcrum are in contact and so there must be a contact force.

Resolve ↑

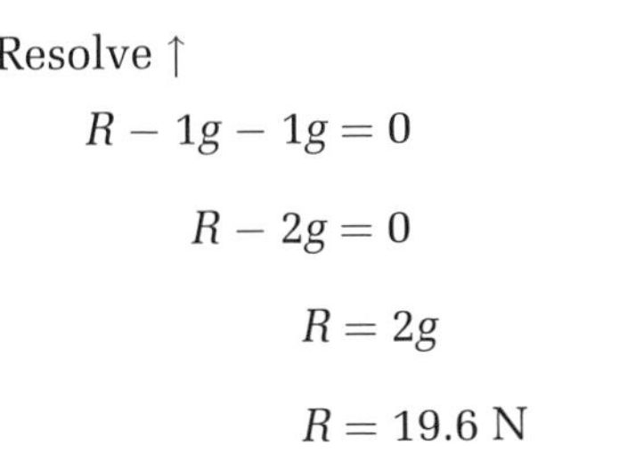

$$R - 1g - 1g = 0$$ Resultant force should be zero for equilibrium.

$$R - 2g = 0$$ Add $2g$.

$$R = 2g$$ $2g = 2 \times 9.8 = 19.6$

$$R = 19.6 \text{ N}$$

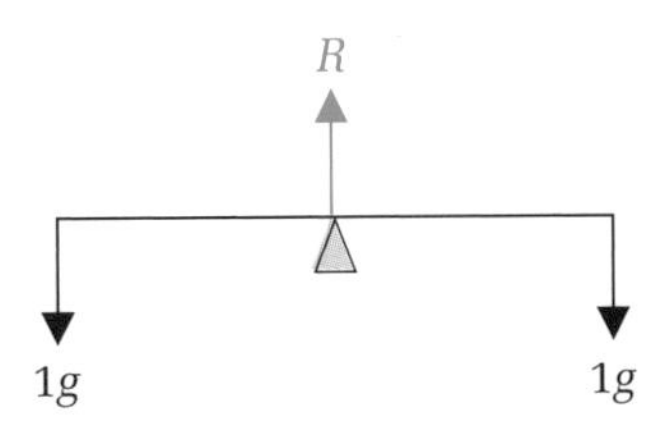

This reaction does not affect the moments because it acts through the pivot. The perpendicular distance between R and the fulcrum is zero.

Uniform bars and beams

In the scales model, the mass of the bar was ignored. The bar would probably be made of cast iron and so the weight of such a bar would be significant. Neglecting the mass of the bar is not a valid mathematical assumption. However, the mass of the bar *could* have no effect on the moments calculation. What condition must occur for this to be true?

If the weight of the bar acted through the fulcrum then this would have no effect on the moments. The weight of a **uniform** bar or beam acts at its midpoint. Instead of neglecting the mass of the bar, it must be assumed **uniform** for the above calculations to be valid.

The point at which the weight of an object can be taken to act is called the **centre of gravity**. It should be noted that the weight of the bar *will* increase the reaction at the fulcrum.

A **non-uniform** bar or beam will *not* have its centre of gravity at its midpoint.

Overview of method

Step ① Draw a clear diagram, marking all the forces.
Step ② Mark on the perpendicular distances.
Resolve any angled forces.
Step ③ Take moments about the pivot or supports.
For balanced beams or rods, the total moment about any point must equal zero.
Step ④ Resolve forces.

In some questions steps ③ and ④ will need to be swapped.

Example 1

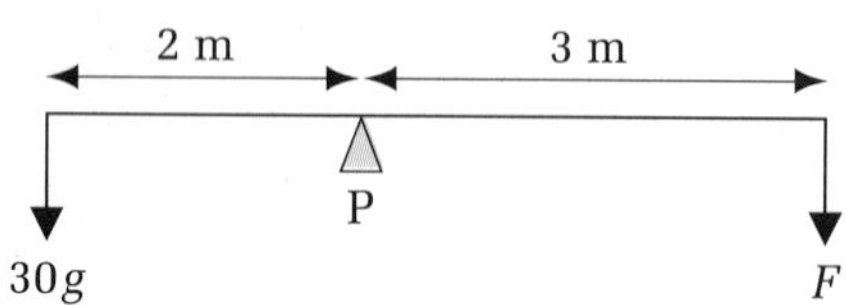

The bar has a length of 5 m and can be assumed to be light. Find the size of the force F and the magnitude of the reaction at the pivot P when the bar is balanced.

Solution

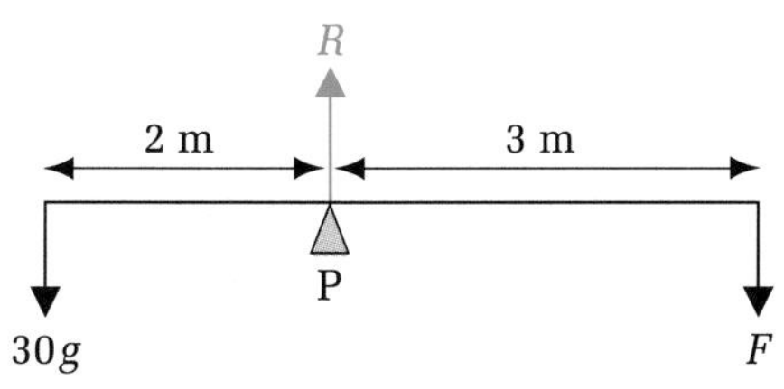

◀ ① Draw a clear force diagram, marking all the forces.

◀ ② Mark on the perpendicular distances.

↻P Clockwise ◀ ③ Take moments about P clockwise.

$M = F \times 3 - 30g \times 2$

$0 = 3F - 60g$

$60g = 3F$

$F = 20g$

$F = 196$ N

Anticlockwise moments are negative because clockwise moments are positive.

Resolve ↑ ◀ ④ Resolve forces.

$R - 30g - F = 0$

$R - 30g - 20g = 0$

$R - 50g = 0$

$R = 50g$

$R = 490$ N

$F = 20g$ N from above.

$-30g - 20g = -50g$

Add $50g$.

$g = 9.8\ \mathrm{m\,s^{-2}}$

Example 2

A uniform bar of mass 20 kg is supported at each end so that it is horizontal. The bar is 4 m long and a mass of 10 kg is placed 1 m from one end. Find the reactions at each support.

Solution

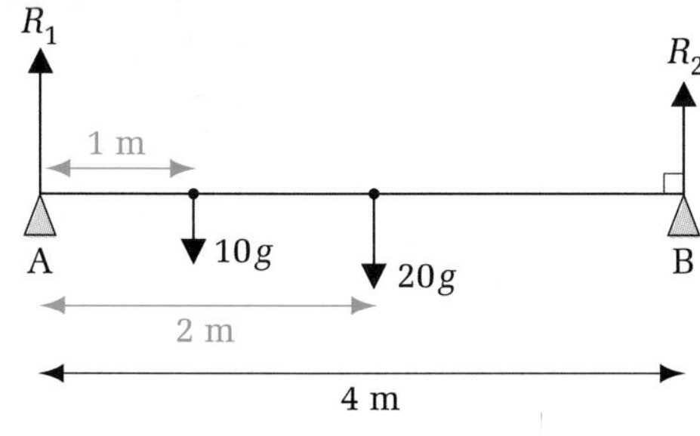

◀ ① Draw a diagram, marking all the forces.

◀ ② Mark on the perpendicular distances.

Label the ends A and B to make it easier to state the point about which moments are taken. If moments are taken about A, then the reaction R_2 can be found. R_2 creates an anticlockwise moment.

↻A Clockwise ◀ ③ Take moments about A clockwise.

$M = 10g \times 1 + 20g \times 2 - R_2 \times 4$

$0 = 10g + 40g - 4R_2$

$4R_2 = 50g$

$R_2 = 12.5g$

$R_2 = 122.5$ N

$M = 0$ for equilibrium.

Rearrange to find R_2.

Divide by 4.

$g = 9.8\ \mathrm{m\,s^{-2}}$

↻B Anticlockwise ◀ ③ **Take moments about B anticlockwise.**

$M = 20g \times 2 + 10g \times 3 - R_1 \times 4$ — $M = 0$ for equilibrium.

$0 = 40g + 30g - 4R_1$ — Add $4R_1$.

$4R_1 = 70g$ — Divide by 4.

$R_1 = 17.5g$ — $g = 9.8\,\text{m s}^{-2}$

$R_1 = 171.5\text{ N}$

These answers can be checked by resolving.

Resolve ↑ ◀ ④ **Resolve to check the answers.**

resultant force $= R_1 + R_2 - 10g - 20g$ — Replace R_1 and R_2.

$= 17.5g + 12.5g - 30g$ — $17.5g + 12.5g = 30g$

$= 30g - 30g$

$= 0$

The resultant force should equal zero because the system is in equilibrium.

Alternatively, instead of taking moments about B, resolving could have been used to find R_1. Then, taking moments could have been used as a check.

Example 3

A non-uniform bar of length 6 m has a mass of 30 kg. The bar is pivoted at one end and is held in equilibrium by a $10g$ N force acting vertically upwards at the other end. Find the distance from the pivot to the centre of gravity of the bar if the bar is horizontal.

The centre of gravity of the bar is the position where the total weight of the bar can be assumed to act.

Solution

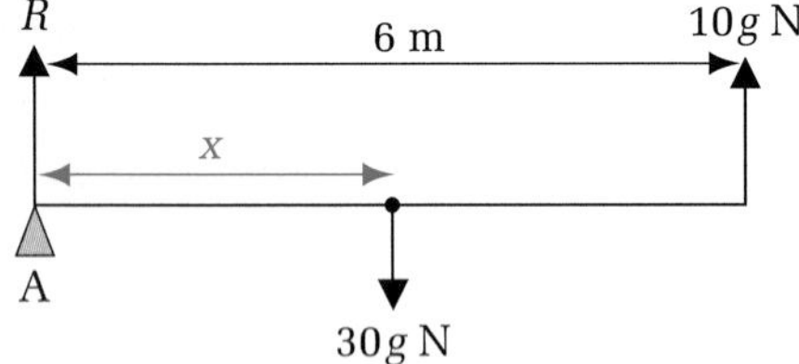

◀ ① **Diagram.**

◀ ② **Label the perpendicular distances.**

Let x be the distance from A to the centre of gravity.

↻A Clockwise ◀ ③ **Take moments about A clockwise.**

$M = 30g \times x - 10g \times 6$ — Total moment must be zero because the bar is balanced.

$0 = 30gx - 60g$ — Add $60g$.

$60g = 30gx$ — Divide by $30g$.

$2 = x$

$x = 2\text{ m}$

13.3 Balances

Exercise

Technique

1 **a** **b**

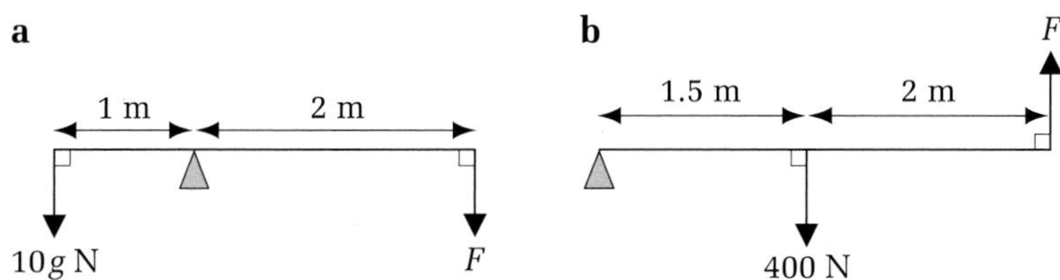

The beams in the diagrams are balanced. Find the value of the force labelled F and the reaction at the pivot.

2 **a** **b**

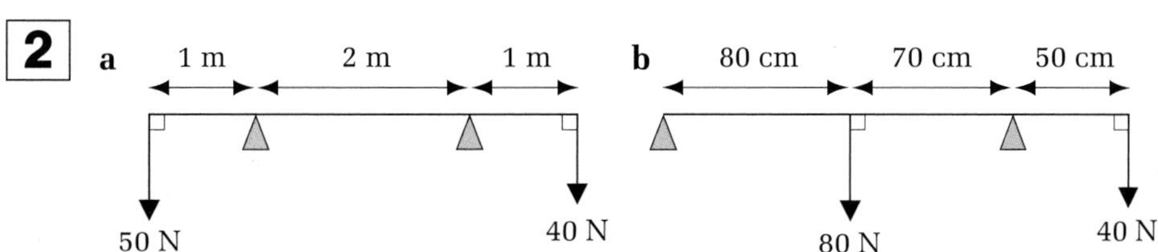

Calculate the reactions at the supports given that the beams are in equilibrium.

3

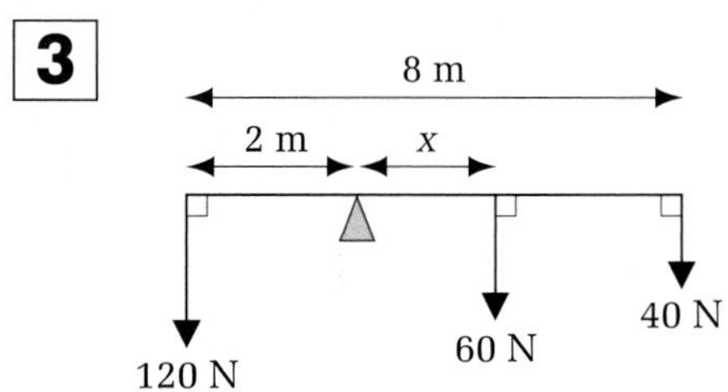

Work out the value of the distance x and the reaction at the pivot when the bar is in equilibrium.

4

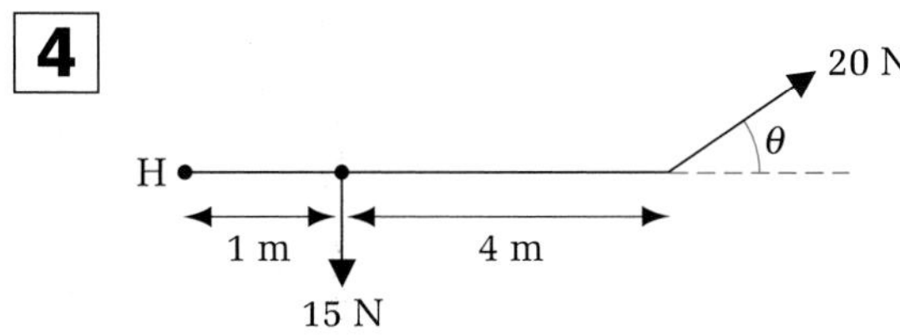

The bar shown is hinged at H and it is in equilibrium. Find the angle θ.

5

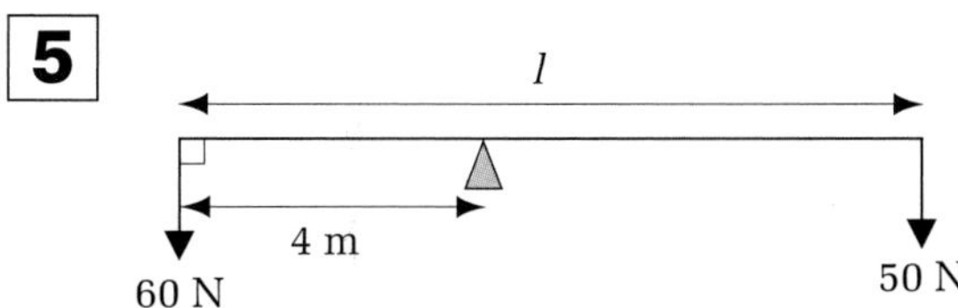

Determine the length, l, of the light uniform bar given that it is balanced.

6 A uniform bar of length 5 m and mass 20 kg rests horizontally on two supports, one at each end. A mass of 10 kg is placed 2 m from one end. Work out the values of the vertical reactions at each end.

7 A light beam, AB, is 3 m long. It is pivoted 1 m from end A. A 2 kg mass is placed at end A and g can be taken as $10\,\mathrm{m\,s^{-2}}$. If the system is to balance, what mass needs to be placed at:

a end B **b** 0.5 m from end B?

8 A non-uniform beam of mass 15 kg is 6 m in length. It is held horizontally by two supports placed 1m from each end. The reaction at one of the supports is 63 N. Determine:

a the reaction in the other support

b the position of the centre of gravity for the beam.

9

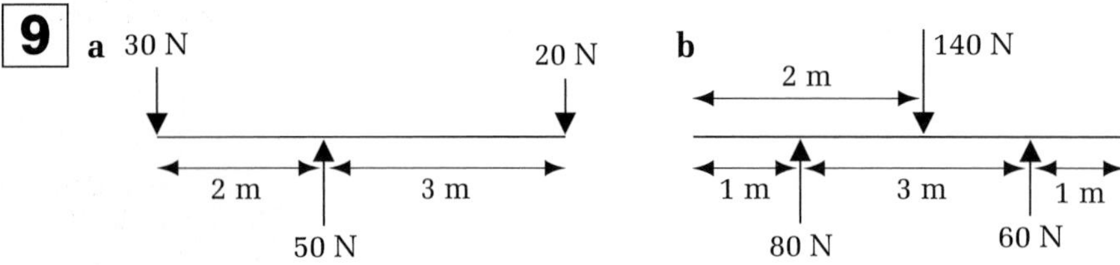

State which of these systems are in equilibrium.

Contextual

1

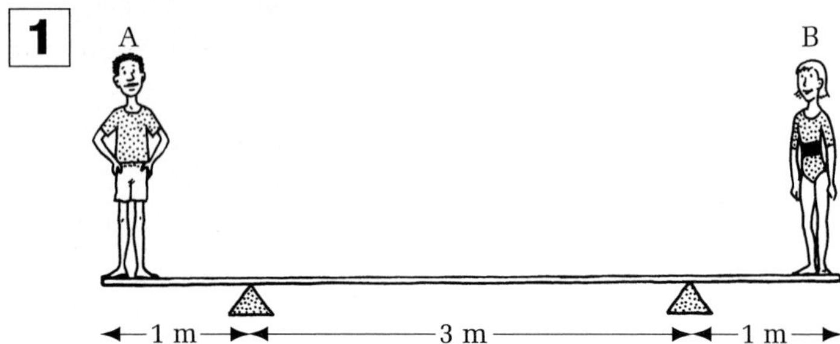

The diagram shows a balance beam with two gymnasts standing on it, labelled A and B. The balance beam has a mass of 40 kg and is assumed to be uniform. Gymnast A weighs 35 kg and gymnast B weighs 30 kg. Determine the reaction at *each* support.

2 A woman and a man support a non-uniform plank, AB, of mass 10 kg and length 4 m. The woman holds the plank 1 m from A and the man holds the plank at B. The vertical reaction force provided by the woman is 56 N. Find:

a the vertical reaction force provided by the man

b the position at which the weight of the plank acts, measured from A.

The woman now holds the plank by herself. Where should she hold the plank to keep it balanced horizontally?

13.4 Couples

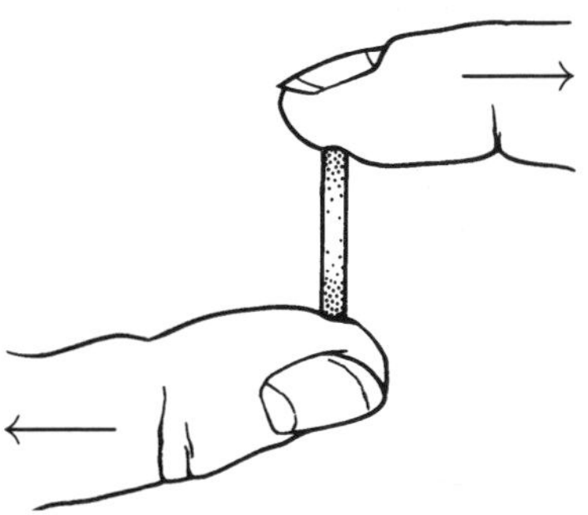

A coin can be spun using the forefinger on the right hand and the thumb on the left hand (or vice versa). By moving the forefinger and thumb in the directions shown by the arrows, the coin can be made to spin. With practice, the coin can be made to spin only on one spot. Why does this occur?

The coin is assumed to be uniform and capable of spinning on an axis of symmetry. Its weight will act through its axis of rotation and so the weight will have no effect on the moments. If there is no sideways motion of the coin, there must be no resultant force acting on the coin. Let d be the diameter of the coin.

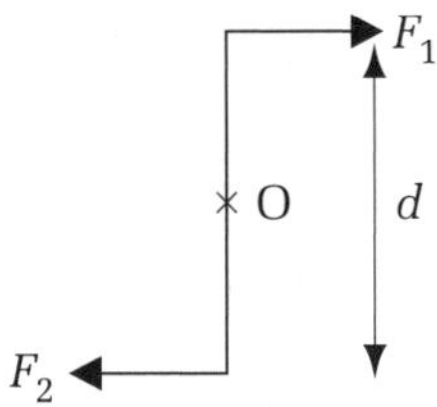

Resolve → ◀ **Resolve the forces horizontally.**

$$F_1 - F_2 = 0$$
$$F_1 = F_2$$

No sideways motion ⇒ no overall force.
F_1 and F_2 must be balanced.
Let $F = F_1 = F_2$.

↻O Clockwise ◀ **Take moments about O clockwise.**

$$M = F \times \tfrac{1}{2}d + F \times \tfrac{1}{2}d$$
$$M = \tfrac{1}{2}Fd + \tfrac{1}{2}Fd$$
$$M = Fd \text{ clockwise}$$

There is an overall turning effect and this is what causes the coin to spin. These forces are called a **couple**. A couple has no resultant force but it does produce an overall turning effect. The moment of a couple is the same regardless of where moments are taken about.
The moment of a couple is given by:

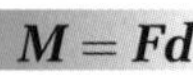

$$\boldsymbol{M = Fd}$$

Notation
F = value of one of the forces in the couple (N)
d = perpendicular distance between the forces (m)

A couple has:

- a resultant force of zero
- an overall moment which is not zero.

Overview of method

Step ① Resolve the forces. The resultant force must be zero for a couple.
Step ② Take moments about a point. Use $M = Fd$ where relevant. The moment of a couple will be non-zero.

These two steps can be swapped depending on how the question is asked.

Example 1

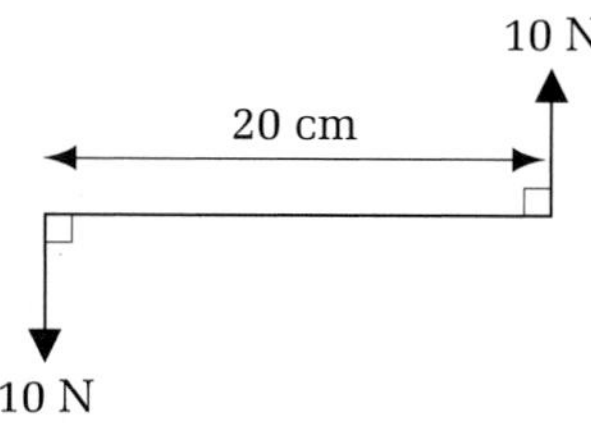

Calculate the moment of the couple shown.

Solution

① is not needed because the question states that the forces form a couple.

Take moments anticlockwise. ◀ ② Take moments about a point.

$M = Fd$ — Formula.

$M = 10 \times 0.2$ — Convert 20 cm into 0.2 m.

$M = 2$ N m anticlockwise

Example 2

Two forces of $(2\mathbf{i} - 5\mathbf{j})$ N and $(-2\mathbf{i} + 5\mathbf{j})$ N act at the points with positions $(4\mathbf{i} + 2\mathbf{j})$ m and $(2\mathbf{i})$ m respectively. Show that the forces reduce to a couple and state the moment of the couple which needs to be applied in order to produce equilibrium.

Solution

$$\text{resultant force} = 2\mathbf{i} - 5\mathbf{j} + (-2\mathbf{i} + 5\mathbf{j})$$
$$= \mathbf{0}$$

◀ ① Find the resultant force.

The forces are already in component form and so resolving is not required.

There is no resultant force.

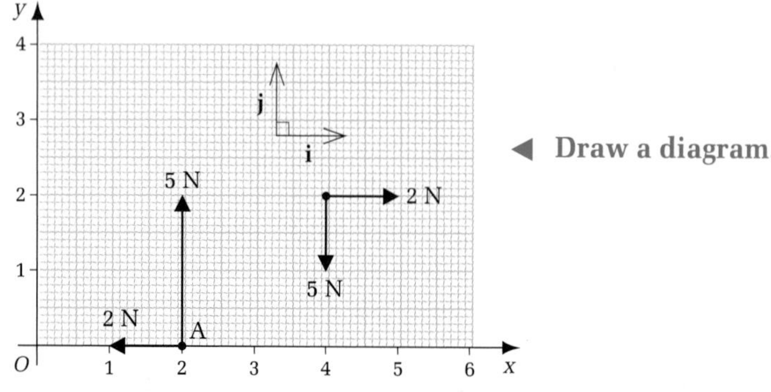

◀ Draw a diagram.

Keep the forces in component form.

↻A Clockwise ◀ ② **Take moments about A.**

$M = 2 \times 2 + 5 \times 2 + 5 \times 0 + 2 \times 0$

$M = 4 + 10$

$M = 14$ N m clockwise

A is chosen because two of the forces go through A. This means two of the moments will turn out to be zero.

There is an overall turning effect of 14 N m clockwise and no resultant force. The system will reduce to a couple. To produce equilibrium, the overall moment must be zero. A couple whose moment is 14 N m anticlockwise must be applied to produce equilibrium.

Example 3

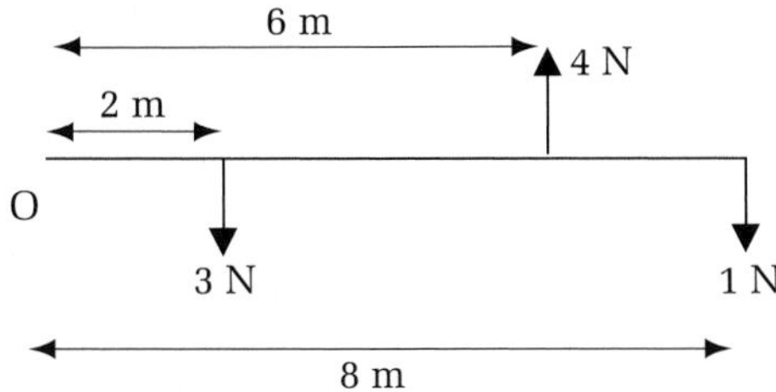

Does the system reduce to a couple? If so, find the moment of the couple.

Solution

Use the two conditions for a couple. First, is the resultant force zero?

Resolve ↑ ◀ ① **Resolve the forces vertically.**

$$\text{resultant} = 4 - 3 - 1$$
$$= 0$$

Next, is the overall moment non-zero?

↻O Clockwise ◀ ② **Take moments about the origin, O.**

$M = 3 \times 2 + 1 \times 8 - 4 \times 6$

$M = 6 + 8 - 24$

$M = 14 - 24$

$M = -10$ N m clockwise

$M = 10$ N m anticlockwise

There is an overall turning effect but no resultant force. These are the two conditions for a couple. The moment of the couple is 10 N m anticlockwise.

Example 4

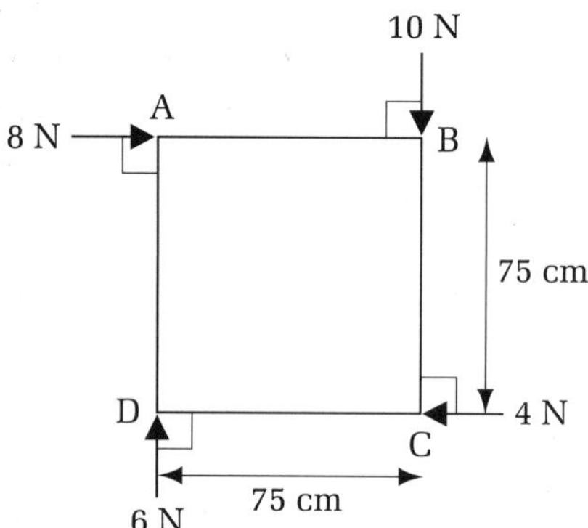

The diagram shows a square ABCD of side 75 cm, which has forces acting on it as shown. If the system is reduced to a force acting through C and a couple, find the magnitude and direction of the force. Also determine the moment of the couple.

Solution

Resolve ↑ ◀ ① **Resolve to find the resultant force.**

$Y = 6 - 10$
$Y = -4$ N

Resolve →

$X = 8 - 4$
$X = 4$ N

$R^2 = 4^2 + 4^2$
$R^2 = 16 + 16$
$R^2 = 32$
$R = 5.66$ N (3 s.f.)

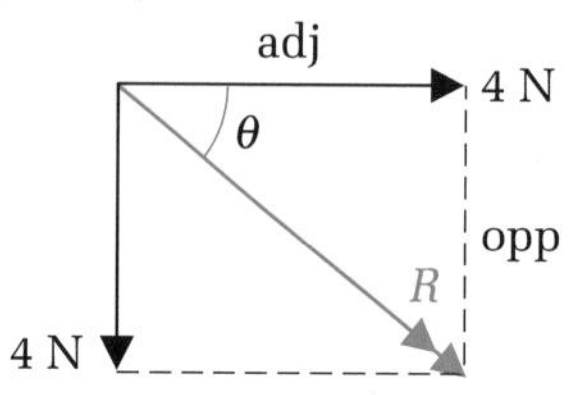

Use Pythagoras' theorem to find the resultant force.

$\tan\theta = \frac{\text{opp}}{\text{adj}}$
$\tan\theta = \frac{4}{4}$
$\tan\theta = 1$
$\theta = 45°$

Use trigonometry to find the angle.

The resultant force is 5.66 N acting at 45° to the 8 N force in an anticlockwise direction.

If moments are taken about C, the resultant moment must be the moment of the couple. This is because the resultant force acts through C and so its moment must be zero.

↻C Clockwise ◀ ② **Take moments about C.**

$M = 6 \times 0.75 + 8 \times 0.75 + 4 \times 0 + 10 \times 0$
$M = 4.5 + 6$
$M = 10.5$ N m clockwise

The 4 N and 10 N forces act through point C and so their perpendicular distances must be zero.

13.4 Couples
Exercise

Technique

1

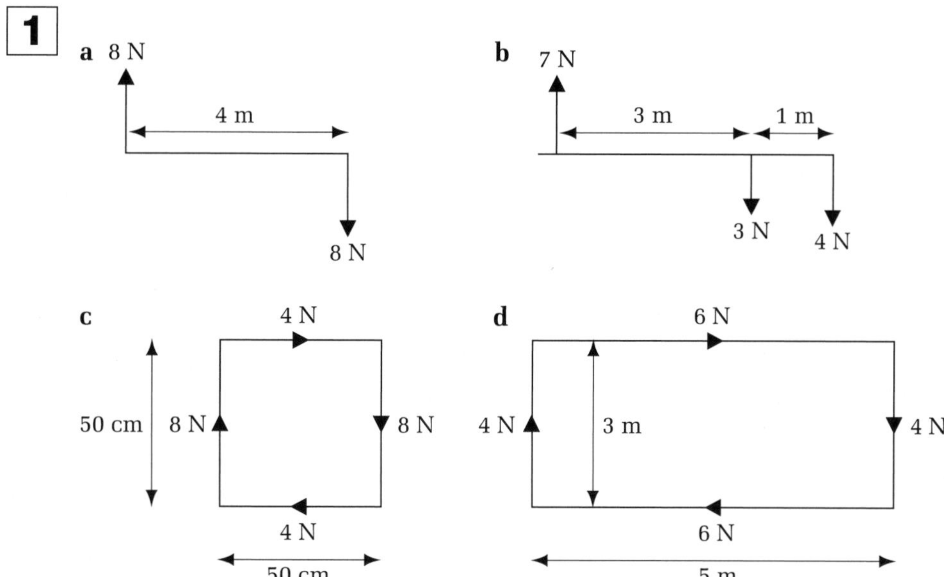

Find out which of the systems reduce to a couple. If they do reduce to a couple, give the moment of the couple.

2 ABCD is a square of side 60 cm. Forces of 6 N, 2 N, 6 N and 2 N act along the sides AB, CB, CD and AD respectively in the directions indicated by the order of the letters. Show that the forces reduce to a couple. State the moment of the couple that must be applied to the system to produce equilibrium.

3 Forces of $(\mathbf{i} + \mathbf{j})$ N, $(-4\mathbf{i} + \mathbf{j})$ N and $(3\mathbf{i} - 2\mathbf{j})$ N act at the points having positions $(2\mathbf{i} + 2\mathbf{j})$ m, $(-\mathbf{i} + 4\mathbf{j})$ m and $(4\mathbf{i} - 2\mathbf{j})$ m respectively. Show that these forces reduce to a couple and find the moment of this couple.

4 The diagram shows a square ABCD of side 25 cm. The system will reduce to a force acting through D and a couple. Find the magnitude and direction of the force and the moment of the couple.

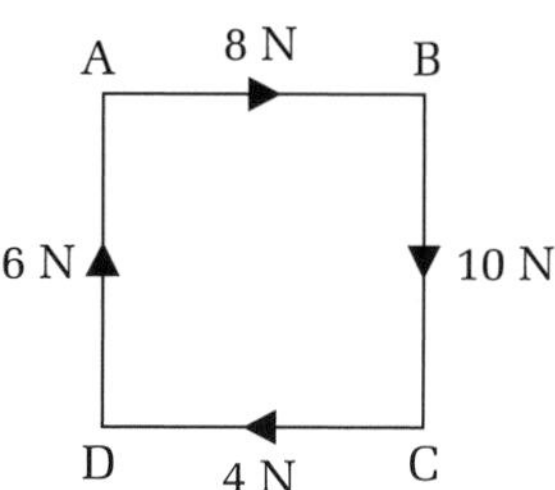

Consolidation

Exercise A

1

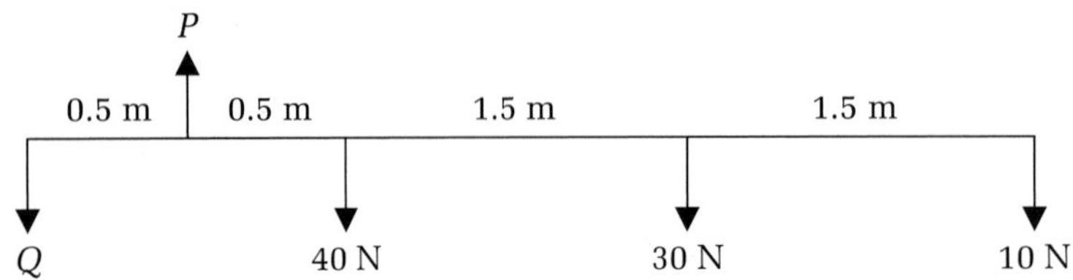

Find the value of P and Q if the system is in equilibrium.

2

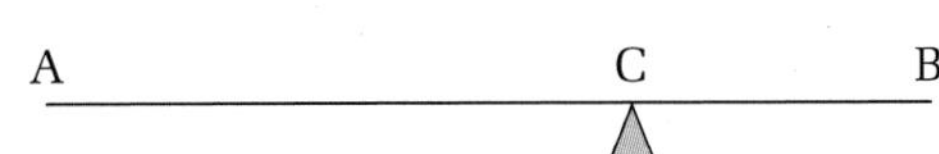

A uniform rod AB has length 8 m and mass 12 kg. A particle of mass 8 kg is attached to the rod at B. The rod is supported at a point C and is in equilibrium in a horizontal position, as shown. Find the length of AC.

(*ULEAC*)

3 A uniform rod AB, of length 90 cm and weight 20 N, rests horizontally on two smooth supports at C and D, where AC = 20 cm and AD = 60 cm.

a Given that a particle of weight 6 N is suspended from B, find the magnitudes of the reactions at C and D.

b Find the greatest weight of a particle that may be suspended from B without disturbing the equilibrium of AB. (*WJEC*)

4

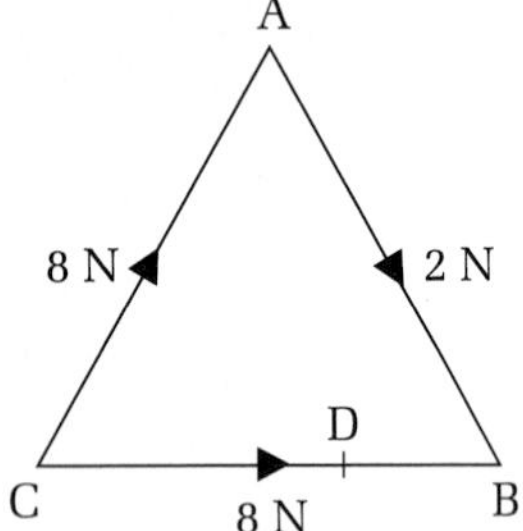

Forces of 8 N, 8 N and 2 N act along the edges CA, CB, and AB respectively of the triangle ABC where AB = BC = AC = 4 cm, as shown. The three forces can be replaced by a single force **F** acting through a point D which lies on the edge CB and a clockwise couple of magnitude 0.2 N m.

a Find the magnitude and the direction of the force **F**.

b Find the distance CD in centimetres, correct to two decimal places.

(*NICCEA*)

Exercise B

1

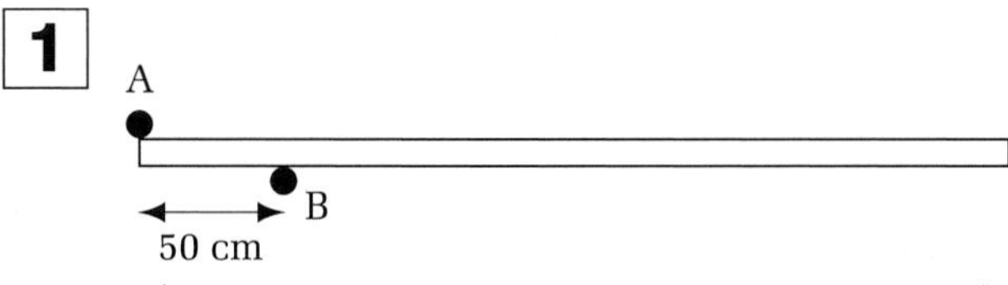

A large uniform plank of wood of length 8 m and mass 30 kg is held in equilibrium by two small steel rollers A and B, ready to be pushed into a saw-mill. The centres of the rollers are 50 cm apart. One end of the plank presses against roller A from underneath, and the plank rests on top of roller B, as shown. The rollers are adjusted so that the plank remains horizontal and the force exerted on the plank by each roller is vertical.

a Suggest a suitable model for the plank to determine the forces exerted by the rollers.

b Find the magnitude of the force exerted on the plank by the roller at B.

c Find the magnitude of the force exerted on the plank by the roller at A.

(*ULEAC*)

2 In the diagram, AB is a uniform rod of mass 2.5 kg and length 0.8 m which is smoothly hinged at B to a fixed vertical wall. The rod is held in equilibrium, making an angle of 40° with the wall, by means of a force of magnitude T newtons acting at A. The force acts in a direction making an angle of 110° with the rod. By taking moments about B, or otherwise, find T. Take $g = 9.81\ \text{m s}^{-2}$.

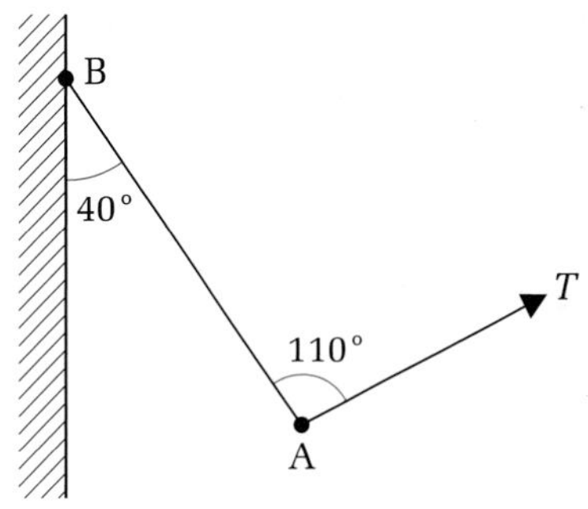

(*UCLES*)

3 A woman of mass 80 kg crosses a garden stream by using, as a bridge, a plank of length 4 m and mass 120 kg. Assume that:

- the plank can be modelled as a rod with its weight acting at its centre
- the woman can be modelled as a particle
- the reactions of the banks act at the ends of the plank.

Find the reactions of the banks on the plank given that the woman is 0.5 m along the plank.

What further information would you need to find the reactions when the woman is pushing a wheelbarrow along the plank?

(*WJEC*)

Applications and Activities

1 Design a set of simple scales to weigh 100 g to 500 g using five 10 g masses. Design the scales for different mass ranges. Comment on your design. How could you make it easier for a non-mathematician to use your device?

Summary

- The moment of a force is the product of the magnitude of the force and its perpendicular distance from the point about which moments are taken.
- The formula for finding the moment of a force is:

  $\boldsymbol{M = Fd}$

  where d is the perpendicular distance from the point to the line of action of the force.
- A body is in equilibrium if:
  1. the total sum of the forces acting equals zero
  2. the total moment equals zero.
- A couple has no resultant force, but it does produce a turning effect.
- The moment of a couple is given by

  $\boldsymbol{M = Fd}$

  where d is the perpendicular distance between the forces.

14 Centre of Mass

What you need to know

- How to calculate the moment of a force about a fixed point.
- How to add and subtract vectors in **i** and **j** form.
- How to calculate the volume of cylinders, cones and hemispheres.
- How to use radian measure to calculate arc lengths and sector areas.
- How to integrate x^n, $\sin n\theta$ and $\cos n\theta$.

Review

1

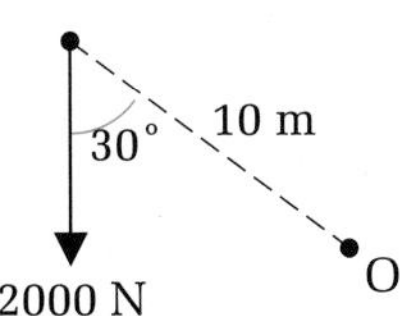

Calculate the moment of the force about the fixed point, O.

2 Vectors **a** and **b** are given by $\mathbf{a} = -7\mathbf{i} + 5\mathbf{j}$ and $\mathbf{b} = 3\mathbf{i} - 6\mathbf{j}$. Find:

a $\mathbf{a} + \mathbf{b}$ **b** $\mathbf{b} - \mathbf{a}$

3 **a** A cylinder has a radius of 10 cm and a height of 20 cm. Calculate the volume of the cylinder.

b A right circular cone has a base radius of 1 m and a height of 1 m. Determine the volume of the cone.

c Calculate the volume of the hemisphere with a base radius of 2 m.

4 **a** Write down the formulas for arc length and sector area.

b An arc has a radius of 10 cm and an angle of $\frac{\pi}{3}$. Find the arc length.

c A sector has an angle of $\frac{\pi}{6}$ and a radius of 2 m. Determine the area of the sector.

5 Find:

a $\int_0^4 x^3\,dx$ **b** $\int_1^2 x^{\frac{3}{2}}\,dx$ **c** $\int_0^{\frac{\pi}{2}} \sin 2\theta\,d\theta$ **d** $\int_{-\frac{\pi}{2}}^{\frac{\pi}{2}} \cos\theta\,d\theta$

14.1 Centre of Mass of Particle Systems

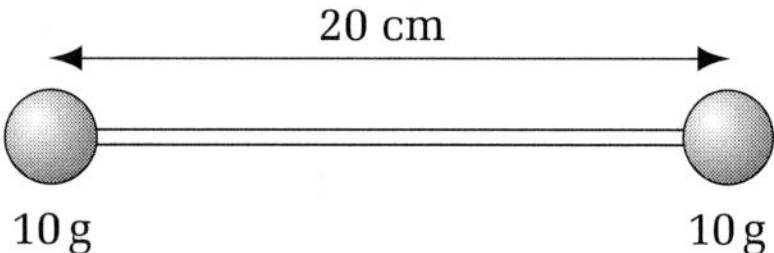

The diagram shows two 10 gram masses tied to a plastic rod. This system of masses is to be modelled by replacing the 10 gram masses by a single 20 gram mass. Where do you think the 20 gram mass should be placed to model this mass system? Assume the plastic rod has a negligible mass.

The 20 gram mass must be placed at the centre of the rod. This is because the initial diagram has two lines of symmetry. The point where they cross, is the same place at which the rod would balance if pivoted. This position is called the **centre of mass**. It is defined as the single point at which the total mass of the system can be placed and still have the same *characteristics*. The moments caused by the single mass must be the same as the moments caused by the separate masses.

Centre of mass and centre of gravity

The terms *centre of mass* and *centre of gravity* are often used to mean the same thing. However this is not strictly true. The centre of gravity can be different from the centre of mass. This is caused by the fact that the acceleration due to gravity can vary at different points in space. This means that the weights for particles of the same mass will vary depending on their position. This effect will only be important for large objects, for example a planet. For small objects, the acceleration due to gravity will change so slightly over its length that this effect can be neglected.

Overview of method

Step ① Draw a diagram and label the point (or axes) about which moments will be taken.

Step ② Draw a table of masses and positions of the masses.

Step ③ Equate moments for the masses and the equivalent system.

Check whether the answer is reasonable using the diagram.

Example 1

Four masses of 2 kg, 3 kg, 4 kg and 5 kg are placed at the coordinates (0, 2), (4, 4), (4, 0) and (1, 1) respectively. Determine the centre of mass of the system.

Solution

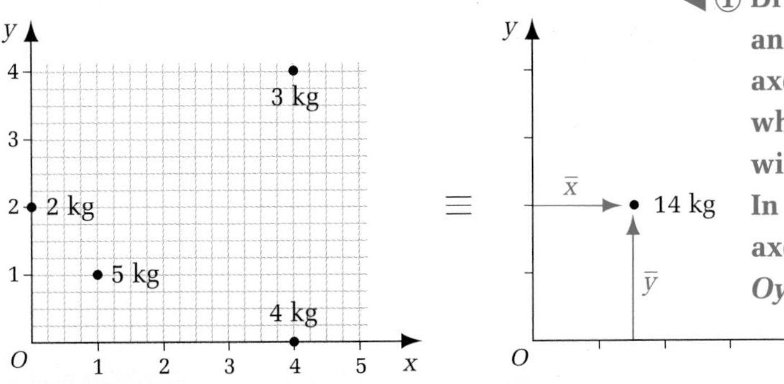

◀ ① **Draw a diagram and label the axes about which moments will be taken. In this case, the axes are *Ox* and *Oy*.**

Notice the coordinates of the centre of mass are $(\bar{x}, \bar{y})$.

Mass	Weight	*x*-coordinate Distance from *Oy*	*y*-coordinate Distance from *Ox*
2 kg	$2g$	0	2
3 kg	$3g$	4	4
4 kg	$4g$	4	0
5 kg	$5g$	1	1
14 kg	$14g$	$\bar{x}$	$\bar{y}$

◀ ② **Draw a table.**

Recall that the *x*-coordinate is defined as the distance from *Oy*.

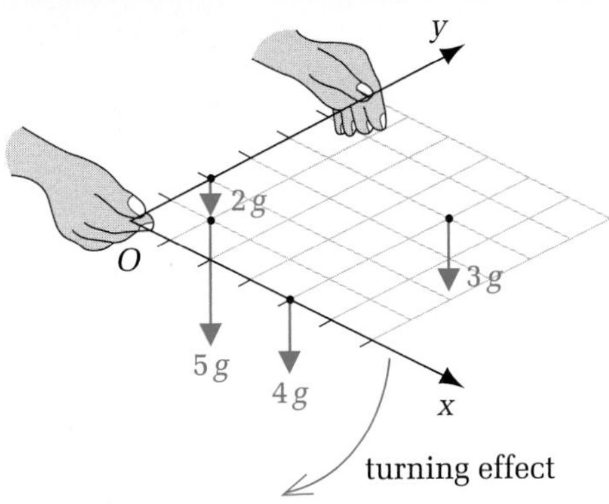

Think of the masses as being on a thin sheet of metal held along *Oy* (or *Ox*). The weights will cause a moment to act about *Oy* (or *Ox*).

↻*Oy* ◀ ③ **Equate moments.**

$$2g \times 0 + 3g \times 4 + 4g \times 4 + 5g \times 1 = 14g\bar{x}$$

Divide by g.

$$0 + 12 + 16 + 5 = 14\bar{x}$$

$$33 = 14\bar{x}$$

Divide by 14.

$$\bar{x} = \tfrac{33}{14}$$

$$\bar{x} = 2\tfrac{5}{14} \text{ units}$$

↻*Ox*

$$2g \times 2 + 3g \times 4 + 4g \times 0 + 5g \times 1 = 14g\bar{y}$$

Divide by g.

$$4 + 12 + 0 + 5 = 14\bar{y}$$

$$21 = 14\bar{y}$$

Divide by 14.

$$\bar{y} = 1\tfrac{1}{2} \text{ units}$$

The centre of mass is at $(2\tfrac{5}{14}, 1\tfrac{1}{2})$.

Find this point on the grid. Is the answer sensible?

Example 2

Masses of 10 kg and 20 kg are placed at the points with position vectors $-6\mathbf{i} - 8\mathbf{j}$ and $3\mathbf{i} + 2\mathbf{j}$ respectively. Find the position vector of the centre of mass.

Solution

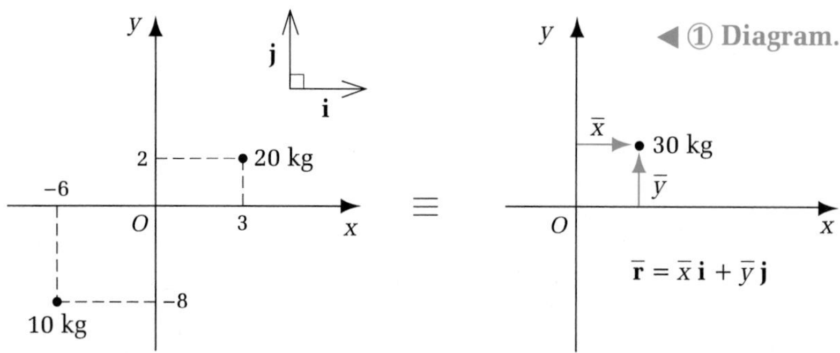

◀ ① Diagram.

▼ ② Table.

Mass	Weight	*x*-coordinate Distance from *Oy*	*y*-coordinate Distance from *Ox*
10 kg	$10g$	-6	-8
20 kg	$20g$	3	2
30 kg	$30g$	$\bar{x}$	$\bar{y}$

↻*Oy* ◀ ② Equate moments.

$$10g \times (-6) + 20g \times 3 = 30g\bar{x}$$

Divide by g.
Simplify LHS.

$$-60 + 60 = 30\bar{x}$$

$$\bar{x} = 0$$

↻*Ox* ◀ ③ Equate moments.

$$10g \times (-8) + 20g \times 2 = 30g\bar{y}$$

Divide by g.
Simplify LHS.
Divide by 30.

$$-80 + 40 = 30\bar{y}$$

$$-40 = 30\bar{y}$$

$$\bar{y} = -1\tfrac{1}{3}$$

The position vector is $\bar{\mathbf{r}} = -1\frac{1}{3}\,\mathbf{j}$.

Example 3

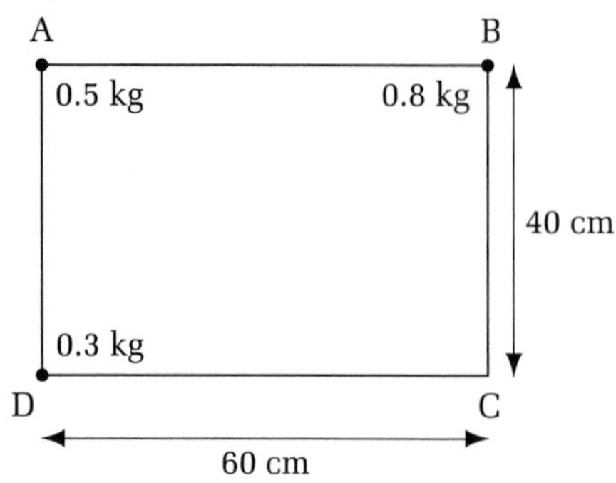

A mass is added at C to make the centre of mass lie on a line equidistant from AB and DC.

a Calculate the value of the mass to be added.

b Find the distance of the centre of mass from AD.

Solution

◀ ① Diagram.

A B 0.5 kg 0.8 kg 0.4 m 0.3 kg m kg D C 0.6 m ≡ A B $\bar{x}$ $(1.6 + m)$ kg 0.2 m D C

◀ ② Table.

Mass	Weight	Distance from AD	Distance from DC
0.5 kg	$0.5g$	0	0.4
0.8 kg	$0.8g$	0.6	0.4
m kg	mg	0.6	0
0.3 kg	$0.3g$	0	0
$1.6 + m$	$(1.6 + m)g$	$\bar{x}$	0.2

total mass $= 0.5 + 0.8 + 0.3 + m.$ $= (1.6 + m)$ kg

↻DC ◀ ③ Equate moments about DC.

This will enable m to be found since it is the only unknown.

$$0.5g \times 0.4 + 0.8g \times 0.4 + mg \times 0 + 0.3g \times 0 = (1.6 + m)g \times 0.2$$ Divide by g.

$$0.2 + 0.32 + 0 + 0 = 0.32 + 0.2m$$ Simplify LHS.

$$0.52 = 0.32 + 0.2m$$ Subtract 0.32.

$$0.2 = 0.2m$$ Divide by 0.2.

$$m = 1$$

1 kg needs to be added at C.

↻AD ◀ ③ Equate moments about AD.

$$0.8g \times 0.6 + mg \times 0.6 = (1.6 + m)g \times \bar{x}$$ Divide by g and replace m by 1.

$$0.48 + 1 \times 0.6 = (1.6 + 1)\bar{x}$$ Simplify RHS.

$$0.48 + 0.6 = 2.6\bar{x}$$ Simplify LHS.

$$1.08 = 2.6\bar{x}$$ Divide by 2.6.

$$\bar{x} = 0.415 \text{ m (3 s.f.)}$$

Centre of mass of rod systems

When shapes are made up of uniform rods, the centre of mass of each rod will be at its centre. The weight of each rod will depend on its length. The weight of a unit length of rod can be taken to be W.

Example 4

A 60 cm metal rod is bent into a triangle. Two of the sides are of length 10 cm and 26 cm.

a Calculate the length of the third side.

b Determine the position of the centre of mass.

Solution

a third side $= 60 - 10 - 26 = 24$ cm

b Sides of the triangle are 10 cm, 24 cm, 26 cm. This is a special triangle. It is a 5, 12, 13 triangle and this means it will be right angled. This will make the centre of mass easier to find.

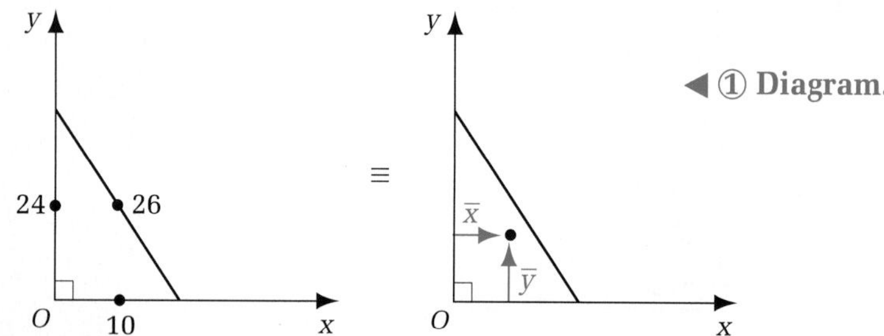

◀ ① Diagram.

Rod	Weight	x-coordinate Distance from *Oy*	y-coordinate Distance from *Ox*
26 cm	$26W$	5	12
24 cm	$24W$	0	12
10 cm	$10W$	5	0
60 cm	$60W$	$\bar{x}$	$\bar{y}$

◀ ② Table.

↻ Oy ◀ ③ Equate moments.

$$26W \times 5 + 24W \times 0 + 10W \times 5 = 60W\bar{x}$$ Divide by W.

$$130 + 0 + 50 = 60\bar{x}$$ Simplify LHS.

$$180 = 60\bar{x}$$ Divide by 60.

$$\bar{x} = 3 \text{ cm}$$

↻ Ox

$$26W \times 12 + 24W \times 12 + 10W \times 0 = 60W\bar{y}$$ Divide by W.

$$312 + 288 + 0 = 60\bar{y}$$ Simplify LHS.

$$600 = 60\bar{y}$$ Divide by 60.

$$\bar{y} = 10 \text{ cm}$$

General formula for centre of mass

In the above examples, it should be noted that the acceleration due to gravity always cancels when moments are taken. An alternative way of calculating the centre of mass for masses $m_1, m_2, m_3, \ldots, m_n$ acting at the coordinates $(x_1, y_1), (x_2, y_2), (x_3, y_3), \ldots, (x_n, y_n)$ can be stated without including g.

Taking moments:

$$m_1gx_1 + m_2gx_2 + m_3gx_3 + \ldots + m_ngx_n = (m_1g + m_2g + m_3g + \ldots + m_ng)\bar{x}$$

Divide by g.

$$m_1x_1 + m_2x_2 + m_3x_3 + \ldots + m_nx_n = (m_1 + m_2 + m_3 + \ldots + m_n)\bar{x}$$

Write the additions as summations.

$$\sum_1^n m_ix_i = \left(\sum_1^n m_i\right)\bar{x}$$

◀ **Divide by $\sum_1^n m_i$.**

$$\bar{x} = \frac{\sum_1^n m_ix_i}{\sum_1^n m_i}$$

Similarly for $\bar{y}$:

$$\bar{y} = \frac{\sum_1^n m_iy_i}{\sum_1^n m_i}$$

14.1 Centre of Mass of Particle Systems

Exercise

Technique

1 **a**

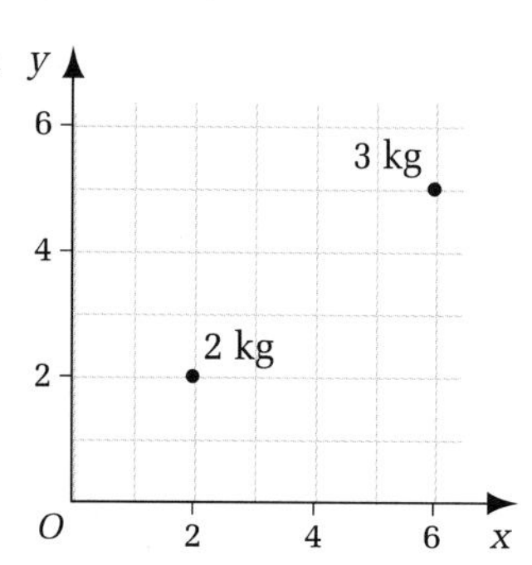

b

4 kg
8 kg
8 kg

Find the coordinates of the centres of mass for the point mass systems shown.

2 **a**

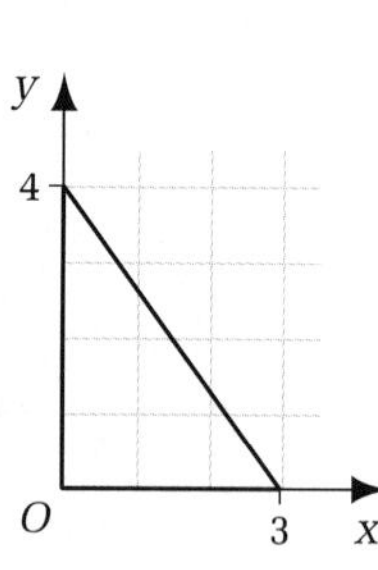

b

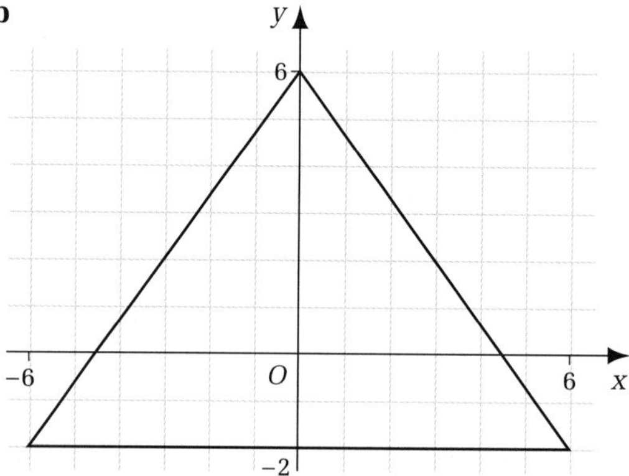

Determine the coordinates of the centres of mass for the rod systems shown.

3 Calculate the coordinates of the centre of mass for the following masses:

a 2 kg, 3 kg and 5 kg placed at (2, 4), (3, 3) and (1, 2) respectively

b 70 g, 20 g and 10 g placed at (−1, 4), (15, −10) and (−20, −20) respectively

c 10 kg, 15 kg, 20 kg, 5 kg placed at (2, 2), (4, 6), (−3, −2), (−6, −10) respectively

d m_1, m_2, m_3 and m_4 placed at (x_1, y_1), (x_2, y_2), (x_3, y_3) and (x_4, y_4) respectively.

4 Determine the position vectors for the centres of mass for the following particle systems:

a Masses of 2 kg and 6 kg at $3\mathbf{i} + 6\mathbf{j}$ and $-\mathbf{i} + 2\mathbf{j}$ respectively

b Masses of 4 kg, 5 kg and 6 kg at $-3\mathbf{i} + 9\mathbf{j}$, $3\mathbf{i} - 6\mathbf{j}$ and $2\mathbf{i} - \mathbf{j}$ respectively.

5 Two masses of 2 kg and 4 kg are positioned at the coordinates (3, 2) and (−1, −2) respectively. Another mass of 4 kg is added to the system so that the centre of mass is located at (−1, 1). Determine the location of the 4 kg mass.

Hint: Let the position of the 4 kg mass be (a, b).

6

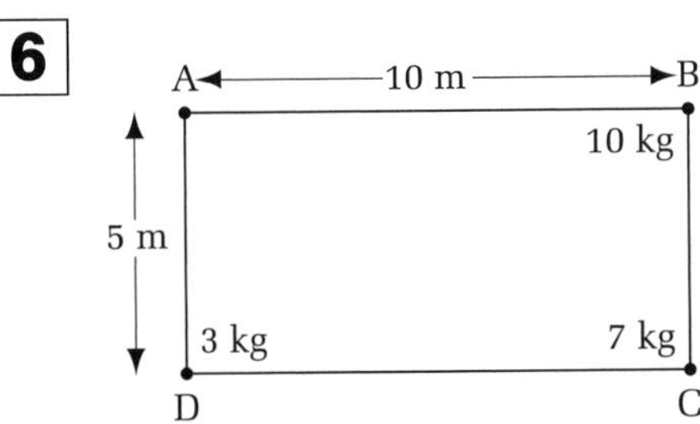

A mass is added to the system at A to make the centre of mass lie along the line equidistant from the lines BC and AD. Calculate:

a the mass to be added

b the distance of the centre of mass from AB.

7 Three masses of 3 kg, 7 kg and 10 kg are placed at (−3, 3), (−2, 3) and (1, −1) respectively. A mass of 5 kg is positioned so that the centre of mass is located at the origin. Find the position of the 5 kg mass.

Contextual

1 A weight-lifting bar has masses of 70 kg and 30 kg placed at each end. The length of the bar is 1.5 m.

a Find the position of the centre of mass, if the mass of the bar is negligible.

b Determine the position of the centre of mass if the bar is uniform and has a mass of 20 kg.

2

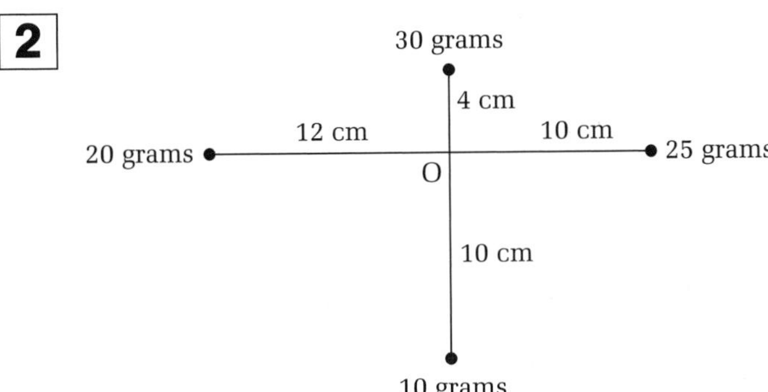

The mobile shown is made up of two uniform rods and four masses. Determine the masses of the two rods if the centre of mass of the mobile is to be at O.

14.2 Centre of Mass of Uniform Laminas and Solids

Hold a piece of A4 card at one corner. What happens to the card? Why does this happen to the card? The card swings into its equilibrium position. The weight of the card can be treated as acting at one point, its centre of mass. This weight causes a turning effect on the card about the corner being held. The card will rotate until the weight no longer causes a moment about the corner A. No moment is produced by the weight of the card when the line of action of the weight passes through corner A.

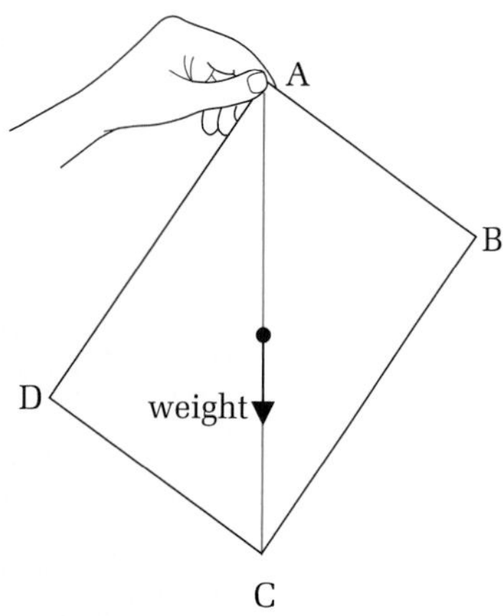

Suspend the card from corner A. Draw a vertical line from the corner onto the card. A piece of string with a weight attached will act as a plumb line. Hold the card from corner B and draw the vertical line from corner B. The lines on the card will cross at the centre of gravity of the card.

When the value of g remains constant for all parts of the card, this point will be the same as the centre of mass.

Where is the centre of gravity for the card? The lines should cross at the centre of the rectangle *if* the card is a **uniform** lamina. A uniform lamina means that the mass of the card is spread evenly over its surface. If two tiny pieces of card with exactly the same area were cut from any part of the card, they will have exactly the same mass.

The lines of symmetry of a rectangle cross at its centre of mass. By using their lines of symmetries, the centres of mass of different laminas can be found.

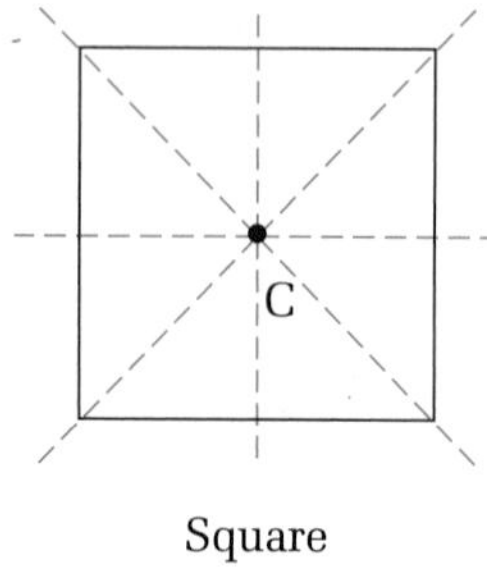

Square

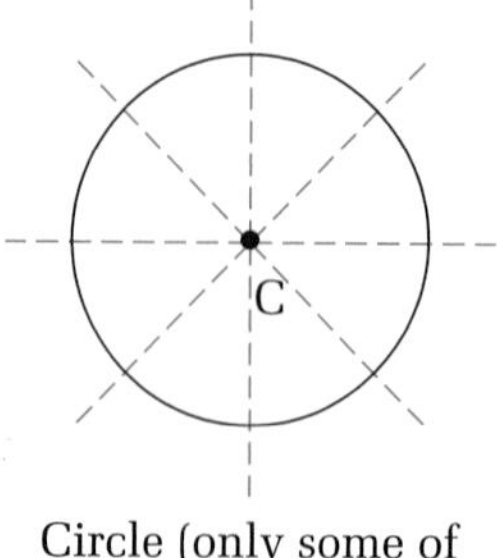

Circle (only some of the lines of symmetry are shown)

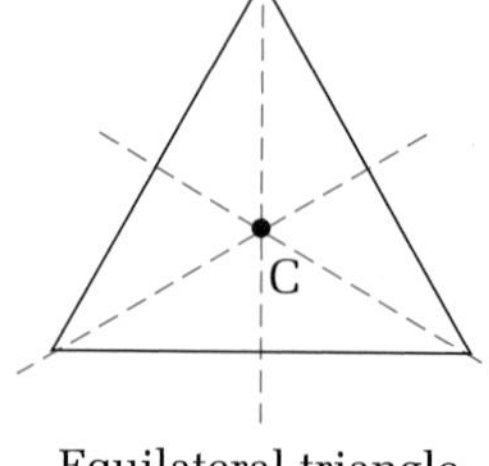

Equilateral triangle

Triangular laminas

The centre of mass for an equilateral triangular lamina can be found using its lines of symmetry. However, this method will not work with any other type of triangle. How can the centre of mass be found for any triangle? The lamina could be suspended and the position located using a plumb line. This is time consuming and requires the lamina to be constructed. Instead the triangle can be split into thin slices. Each thin slice is approximately the same as a rectangle. The centre of mass of each rectangle is at its centre. The centres of mass of all the rectangles lie along a line. This line is called a **median** because it joins one vertex with the middle of the opposite side. The centre of mass must lie along the median. When this is repeated with all the corners of the triangle, the crossing of the three medians coincide. This point is the centre of mass.

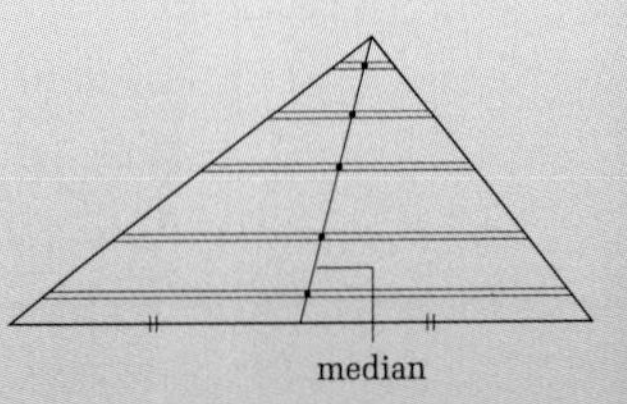

Draw a triangle. Draw on the three medians. Measure the distances marked on the diagram. What do you notice?

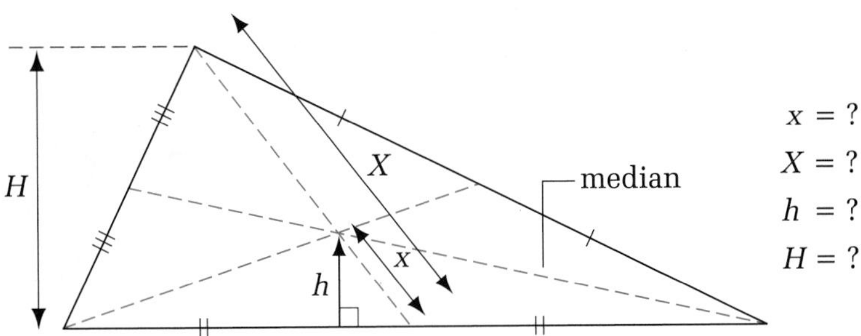

The position of the centre of mass is one third of the way from the base of the triangle along the median. This coincides with being one third of the height of the triangle measured from the base.

Example 1

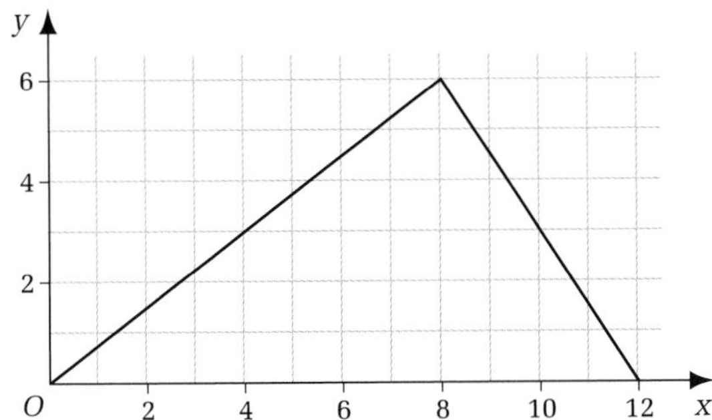

Find the centre of mass of the uniform triangular lamina.

Solution

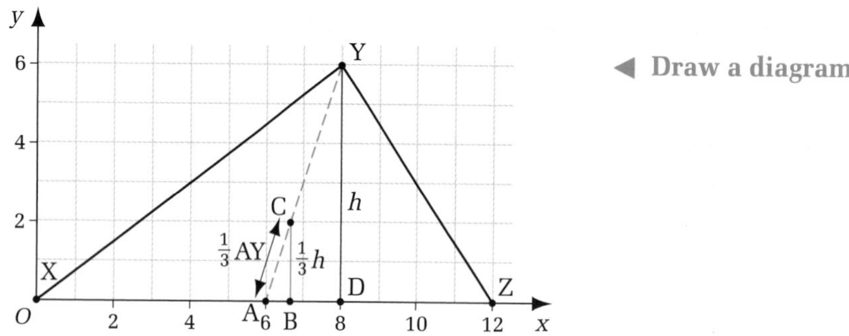

◀ Draw a diagram.

Triangles ACB and AYD are similar triangles, where C is the centre of mass.

$$AC = \tfrac{1}{3}AY$$

$$\begin{aligned} CB &= \tfrac{1}{3}YD \\ &= \tfrac{1}{3} \times 6 \\ &= 2 \end{aligned}$$

Position of centre of mass of the triangle is $\frac{1}{3}$ along the median from the base.

$$\begin{aligned} AB &= \tfrac{1}{3}AD \\ &= \tfrac{1}{3} \times 2 \\ &= \tfrac{2}{3} \end{aligned}$$

The triangles are similar.

The coordinates of the centre of mass are $(6\frac{2}{3}, 2)$.

Composite laminas

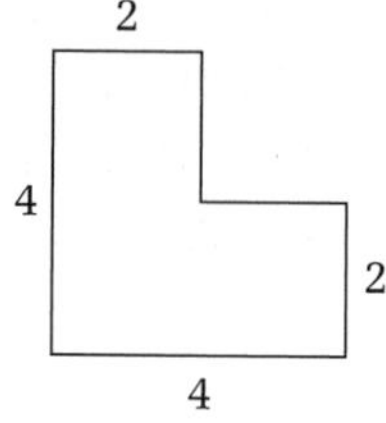

The diagram shows a composite lamina. It is made up of two shapes, a rectangle and a square. Each shape can be replaced by a mass at a single point and then the composite lamina can be treated as a particle system.

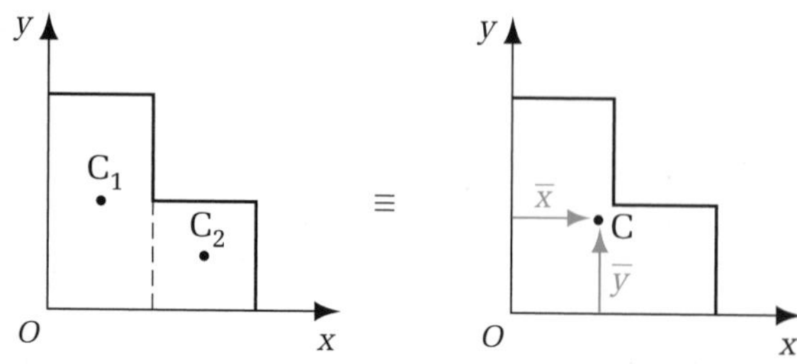

This shape has a diagonal line of symmetry. Although this line does not give any specific values for $\bar{x}$ and $\bar{y}$, it does mean $\bar{x}$ must equal $\bar{y}$.

Overview of method

Step ① Draw a diagram of the shape and mark on axes Ox and Oy.
Step ② Split the shape up into rectangles, squares, circles and/or triangles.
Step ③ Are there any lines of symmetry?
Step ④ Draw a table of shape, area, weight, and distances from two axes.
Step ⑤ Take moments about two axes.

Example 2

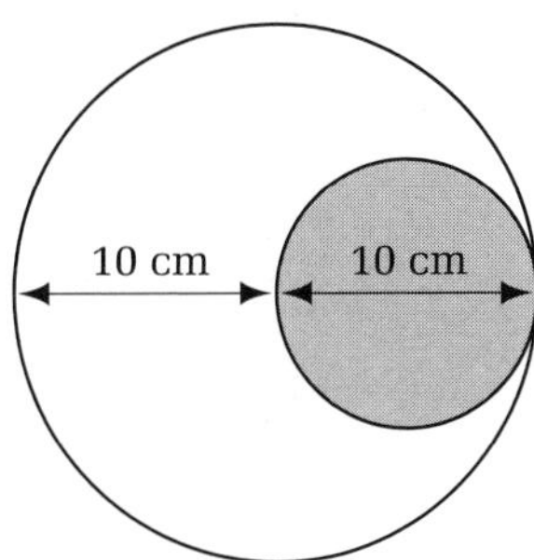

A shape is formed by cutting a small circle out of a larger one, as shown in the diagram. Determine the centre of mass of the lamina.

Solution

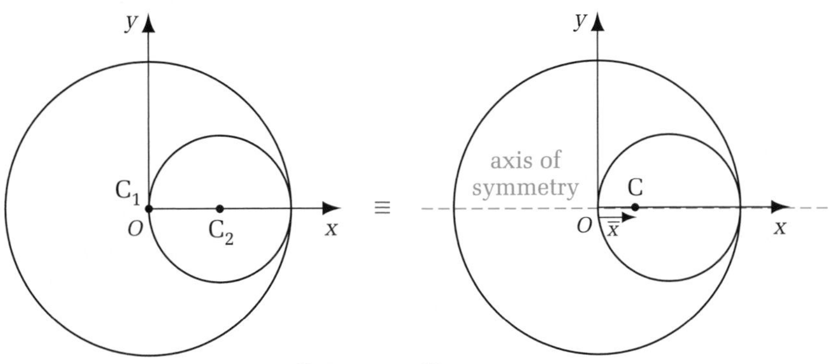

▲ ① Draw a diagram.
▲ ② Split the shape up into two circles.
▲ ③ Are there any axes of symmetry?

Mark on the axes Ox and Oy.

▼ ④ Draw a table.

Shape	Area	Weight	x-coordinate Distance from Oy
Big circle	$\pi \times 10^2 = 100\pi$	$100\pi W$	0
Small circle	$-\pi \times 5^2 = -25\pi$	$-25\pi W$	5
Whole shape	75π	$75\pi W$	$\bar{x}$

The weight of the small circle is negative because this circle is cut away.

$\curvearrowright Oy$ ◀ ⑤ **Equate moments.**

$$100\pi W \times 0 + (-25\pi W) \times 5 = 75\pi W \times \bar{x}$$

Divide by πW.

$$0 - 125 = 75\bar{x}$$
$$-\tfrac{125}{75} = \bar{x}$$
$$\bar{x} = -1\tfrac{2}{3}$$

The position of the centre of mass is along the axis of symmetry, $1\frac{2}{3}$ cm from the centre of the 20 cm diameter circle, away from the smaller cut out circle.

Check that this answer is sensible.

Centres of mass of solids

This time the planes of symmetry can be used to find the centres of mass.

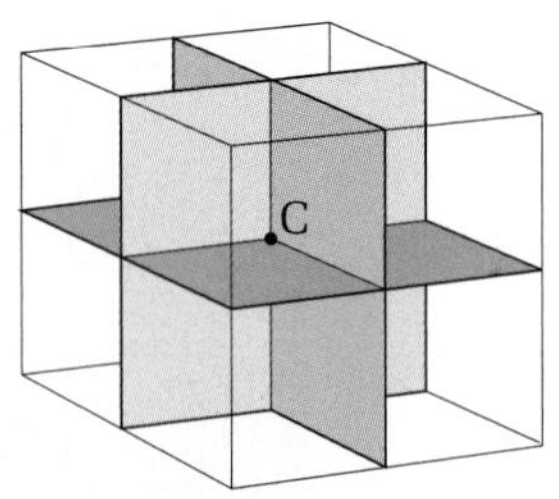

Cube with planes of symmetry shown and C marked at the point where they cross

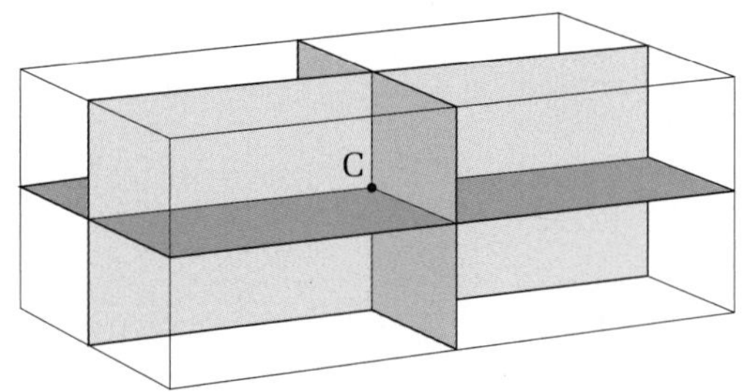

Cuboid with planes of symmetry

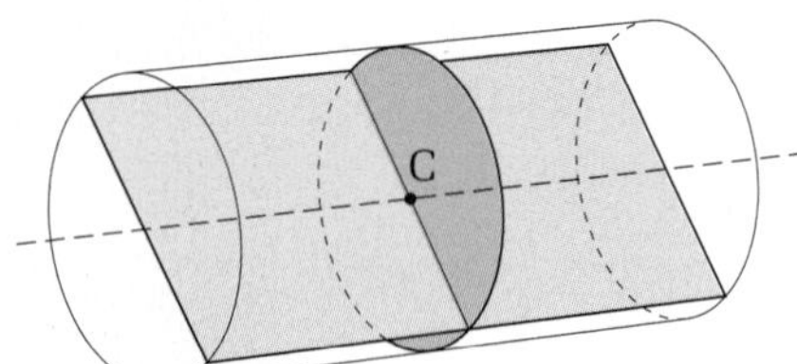

Cylinder showing centre of mass C and two planes of symmetry

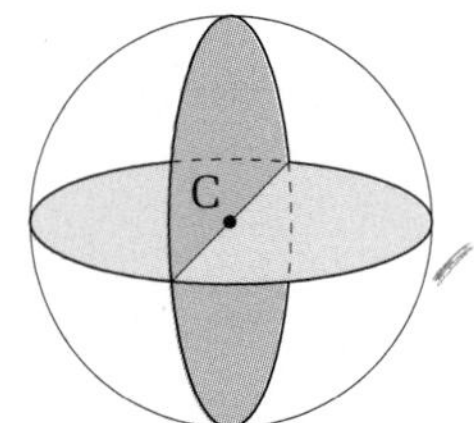

Sphere with two of the planes of symmetry shown

Example 3

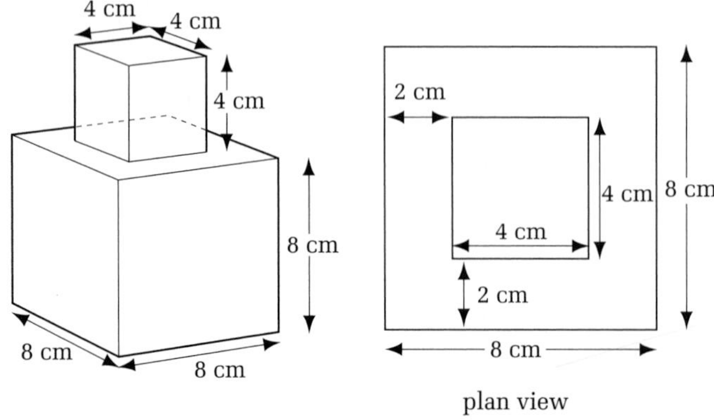

Find the centre of mass of the solid.

Solution

In 3D shapes, moments could need to be taken about three axes.
The planes of symmetry will often help reduce this to only one or two axes.

◀ ① **Draw a diagram. Mark on the axes *Ox* and *Oy*.**

◀ ② **Split the shape into two cubes.**

The diagram is a 2D representation of the cubes. The weight will depend on the volume this time and *not* the area.

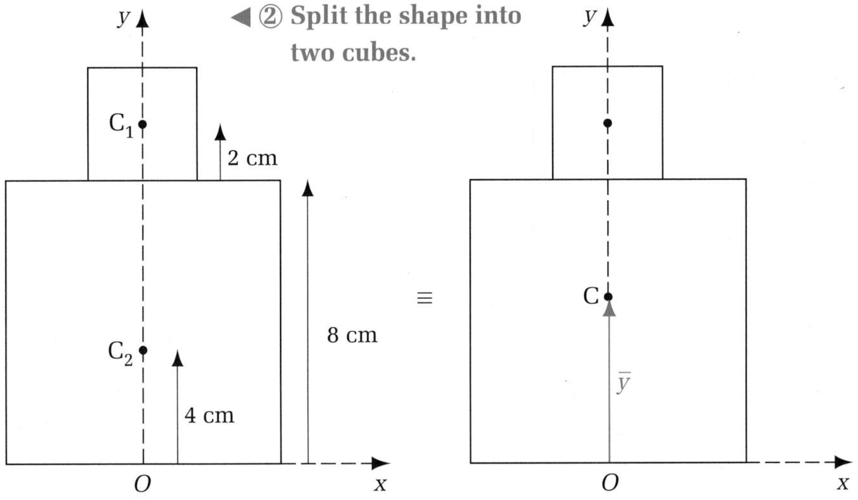

The centre of mass must lie along the line where the planes of symmetry cross. This means only the height above the base needs to be found.

▲ ③ **Symmetry.**

Shape	Volume	Weight	*y*-coordinate Distance from *Ox*
Small cube	64 cm^3	$64W$	10 cm
Large cube	512 cm^3	$512W$	4 cm
Whole shape	576 cm^3	$576W$	$\bar{y}$

◀ ④ **Table.**

The weight per unit volume is W.
The units are consistent although SI units are not being used. The answer for $\bar{y}$ will be given in cm.

$\curvearrowright Ox$ ◀ ⑤ **Equate moments about *Ox*.**

$$64W \times 10 + 512W \times 4 = 576W\bar{y}$$

$$640 + 2048 = 576\bar{y}$$

Divide by W.

$$2688 = 576\bar{y}$$

$$\bar{y} = 4.67 \text{ cm (3 s.f.)}$$

The centre of mass is 4.67 cm (3 s.f.) above the base. This seems to make sense, the small cube will raise the centre of mass above the centre of mass of the large cube.

14.2 Centre of Mass of Uniform Laminas and Solids

Exercise

Technique

1

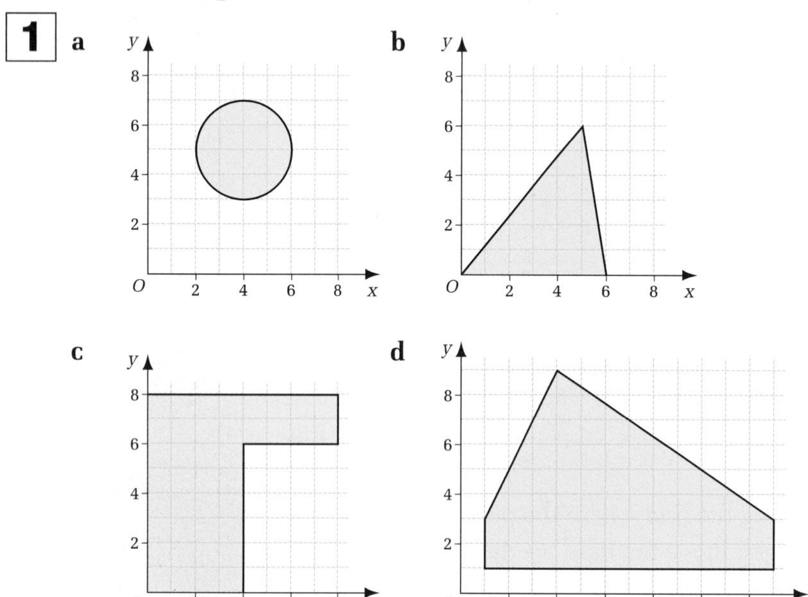

Determine the centre of mass of each uniform lamina.

2

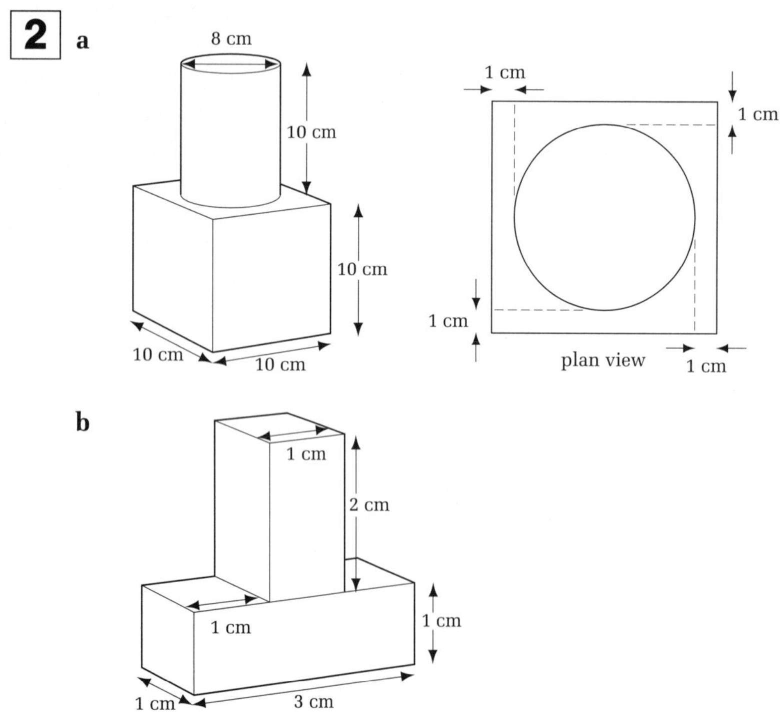

Find the position of the centre of mass of each uniform solid shown.

3

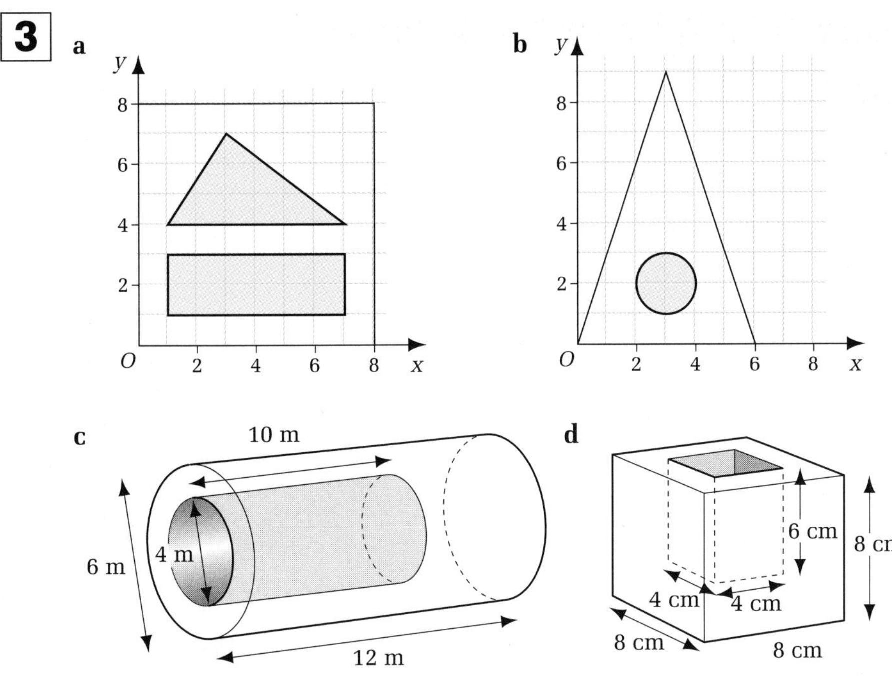

Work out the centres of mass of each uniform lamina or solid shown. The shaded parts have been cut away to form the shapes.

Contextual

1 An earring has been made from a thin sheet of silver. Calculate the position of the centre of mass.

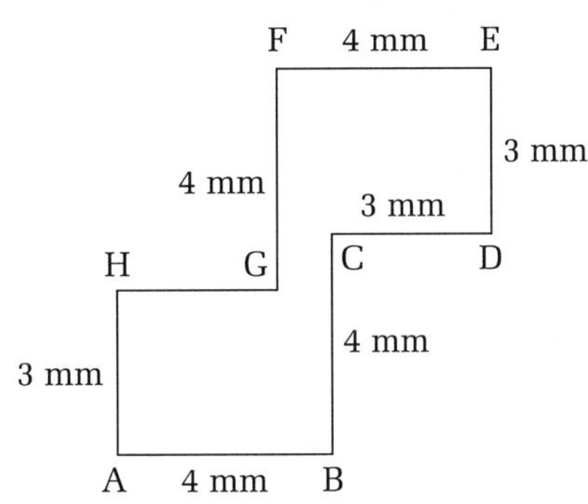

2 A holder for a candle has been made by drilling a cylindrical hole in a large cylinder. Find the centre of mass for the shape.

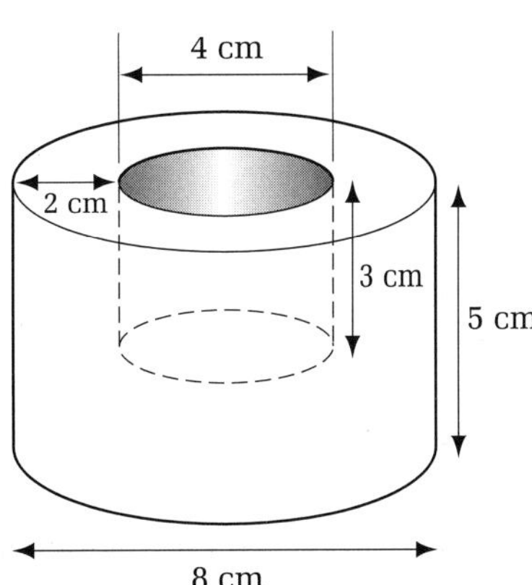

14.3 Suspended Laminas and Rods

A rectangular lamina, such as an A4 piece of card, is suspended from a corner. What angle do the sides make with the downward vertical? The lamina is assumed uniform. The lines of symmetry cross in the middle of the rectangle. The centre of mass must also be in the centre if the card is uniform. The triangle ABC can be used to calculate the angles the sides make with the downward vertical.

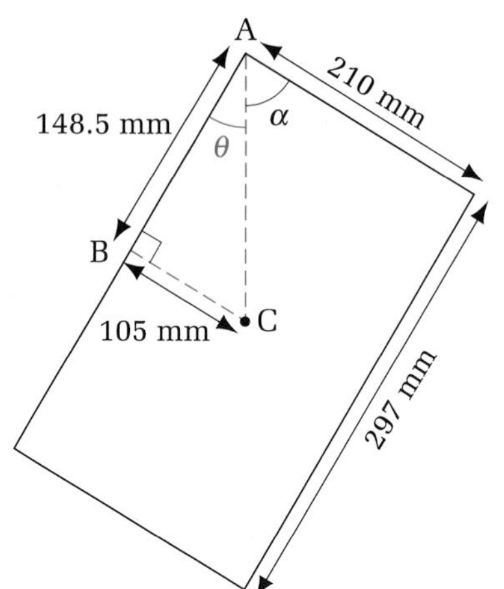

$$\tan\theta = \frac{\text{opp}}{\text{adj}} = \frac{105}{148.5}$$
$$\theta = 35.3^\circ$$

$\theta = \tan^{-1}\left(\frac{105}{148.5}\right)$, or $\arctan\left(\frac{105}{148.5}\right)$

$$\alpha = 90^\circ - 35.3^\circ = 54.7^\circ \text{ (1 d.p.)}$$

The angle between the longer side and the vertical is 35.3°. The angle between the shorter side and the vertical is 54.7°.

Example

The uniform triangular lamina is suspended from A. Calculate the angle that AB makes with the downward vertical.

Solution

The centre of mass is located one third of the distance from the base, along the axis of symmetry.

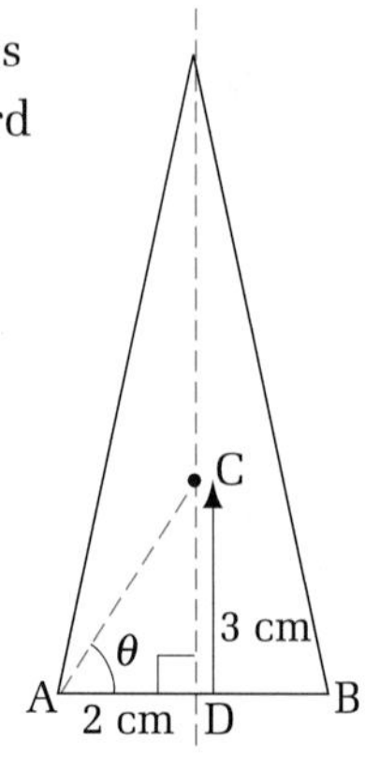

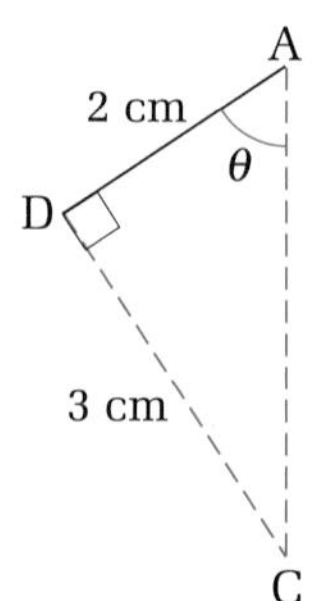

When the lamina is suspended AC must be vertical.

$$\tan\theta = \tfrac{3}{2} \Rightarrow \theta = 56.3^\circ \text{ (1 d.p.)}$$

14.3 Suspended Laminas and Rods

Exercise

Technique

1

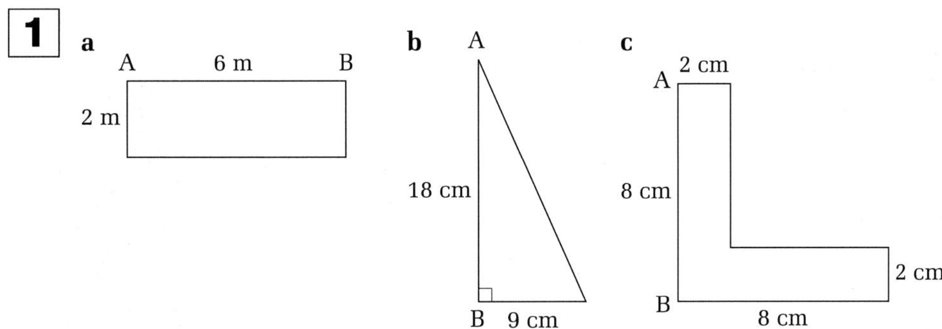

Calculate the angle the side AB makes with the downward vertical when the uniform laminas are suspended from A.

Contextual

1

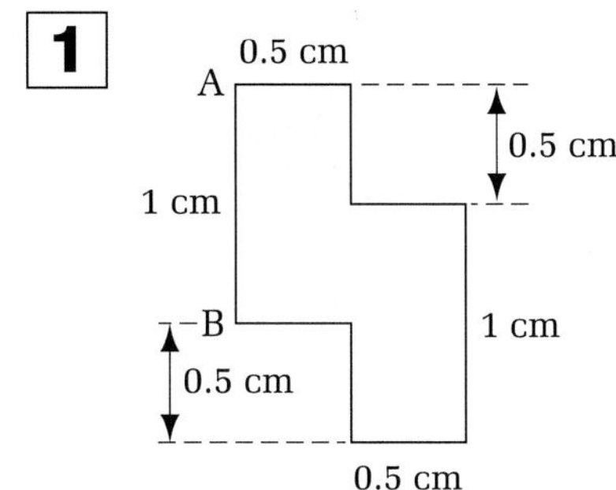

The earring shown is suspended from point A. Determine the angle AB makes with the downward vertical.

2

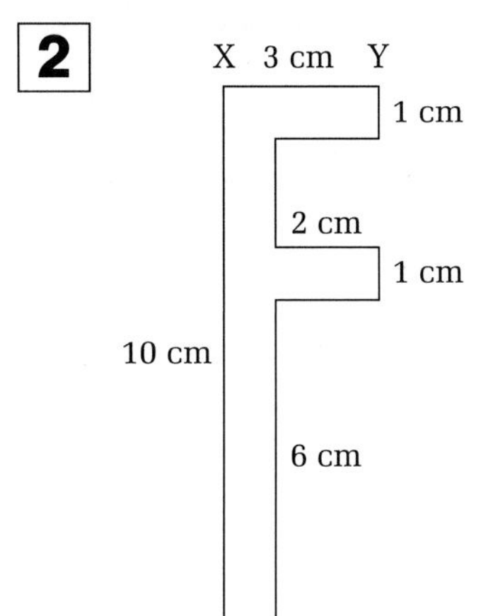

A uniform lamina in the shape of the letter F is made for a mobile. The letter is hung on the mobile using string attached to point X. Find the angle XY makes with the horizontal.

14.4 Centre of Mass using Integration

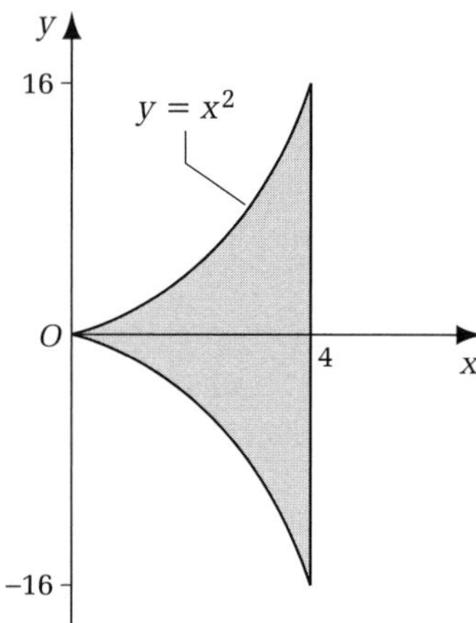

The lamina shown cannot be treated as a composite lamina in the normal way. The lamina is not made up of rectangles or triangles. This means that an alternative method must be used. The lamina can be divided into thin slices. Each slice will be approximately equal to a rectangle. The area can be found and the weight will be proportional to this area. The weight of each rectangle can be added together to find the whole mass of the lamina.

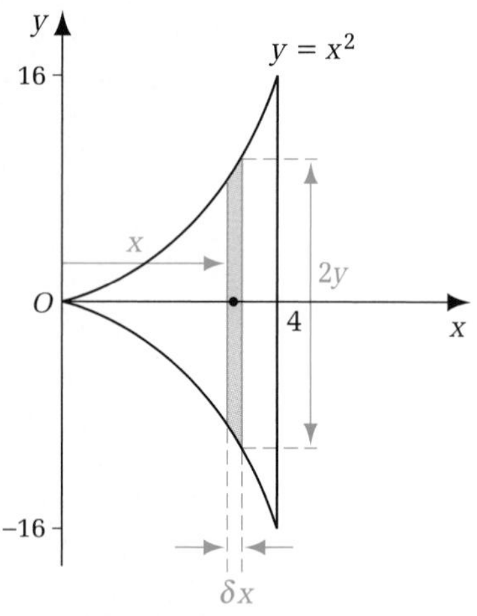

Shape	Area	Weight	x-coordinate Distance from *Oy*
Small rectangle	$2y\delta x = 2x^2\delta x$	$(2x^2\delta x)W = 2Wx^2\delta x$	x
Whole shape	$\sum_0^4 2x^2\delta x$	$\sum_0^4 2Wx^2\delta x$	$\bar{x}$

The height of each rectangle is $2y$ and $y = x^2$. The weight per unit area is W. The area must be found in terms of x because the rectangles are δx wide.

The moment of each rectangle can be calculated and all such moments added together. Equating moments can then be used. This will give an approximate answer for the centre of mass but by letting the width of each strip get smaller and smaller, the answer will become more and more accurate. The exact answer of the centre of mass is obtained when the summation is done by integration. This occurs when the slice width tends to 0.

$\circlearrowright Oy$ ◀ **Equate the moments.**

$$\left(\sum_0^4 2Wx^2\delta x\right)\bar{x} = \sum_0^4 (2Wx^2\delta x)x$$

$$2W\left(\sum_0^4 x^2\delta x\right)\bar{x} = 2W\sum_0^4 (x^3\delta x)$$

Take constants outside the summation sign ($2W$).

As $\delta x \to 0$, the summations will become integrals:

$$2W\left(\int_0^4 x^2 \mathrm{d}x\right)\bar{x} = 2W\int_0^4 x^3\,\mathrm{d}x$$

Divide by $2W$.
$\bar{x}$ is a constant.

$$\bar{x}\int_0^4 x^2\mathrm{d}x = \int_0^4 x^3\,\mathrm{d}x$$

◀ **Integrate the expressions.**

$$\bar{x}\left[\frac{x^3}{3}\right]_0^4 = \left[\frac{x^4}{4}\right]_0^4$$

Insert the limits.

$$\bar{x}\left(\frac{4^3}{3} - \frac{0^3}{3}\right) = \left(\frac{4^4}{4} - \frac{0^4}{4}\right)$$

$$\tfrac{64}{3}\bar{x} = 64$$

Divide by $\frac{64}{3}$.

$$\bar{x} = \tfrac{3}{64} \times 64$$

$$\bar{x} = 3$$

Overview of method

Step ① Draw a diagram.
Step ② Split the shape into thin slices.
Step ③ Draw a table with areas, weights and distances.
Step ④ Equate moments.
Step ⑤ Let the width of the slice tend to 0 and change the summations into integrals.
Step ⑥ Integrate and insert limits.

It should be noted that this technique can also be used to find the centres of mass of uniform rods and solids. In these cases, the weight will depend on the length of the rod or the volume of the solid.

Example 1

Find the centre of mass of a circular arc with radius r and angle 2α. Use this result to show that the centre of mass of a semicircular arc is a distance of $\frac{2r}{\pi}$ from the centre of the circle.

Solution

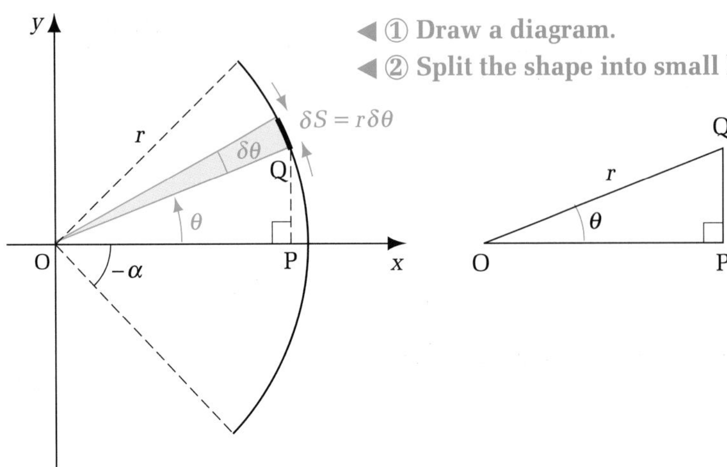

◀ ① Draw a diagram.

◀ ② Split the shape into small lengths.

Each small length is $r\delta\theta$ long. The distance of the centre of mass from Oy will be OP since the length $r\delta\theta$ will be extremely small and so the centre and end of this arc will be a negligible distance apart. This is calculated using trigonometry, OP = $r\cos\theta$.

Length of arc $= r\theta$.

▼ ③ Table of values.

Shape	Length	Weight	x-coordinate Distance from *Oy*
Small arc	$r\delta\theta$	$Wr\delta\theta$	$r\cos\theta$
Whole shape	$r(2\alpha) = 2r\alpha$	$2Wr\alpha$	$\bar{x}$

The weight per unit length is W.

$\circlearrowright Oy$ ◀ ④ Equate moments.

$$(2Wr\alpha)\bar{x} = \sum_{-\alpha}^{\alpha}(Wr\delta\theta \times r\cos\theta)$$

Take constants outside the summation sign.

$$2Wr\alpha\bar{x} = Wr^2\sum_{-\alpha}^{\alpha}\cos\theta\delta\theta$$

Divide by Wr.

$$2\alpha\bar{x} = r\sum_{-\alpha}^{\alpha}\cos\theta\delta\theta$$

Let $\delta\theta \to 0$ ◀ ⑤ As $\delta\theta \to 0$, the summations will become integrals.

$$2\alpha\bar{x} = r\int_{-\alpha}^{\alpha}\cos\theta\,d\theta$$ ◀ ⑥ Integrate expression.

$$2\alpha\bar{x} = r[\sin\theta]_{-\alpha}^{\alpha}$$ ◀ ⑥ Insert limits.

$$2\alpha\bar{x} = r[\sin\alpha - \sin(-\alpha)]$$

$\sin(-\alpha) = -\sin\alpha$

$\sin\alpha - (-\sin\alpha) = 2\sin\alpha$

$$2\alpha\bar{x} = 2r\sin\alpha$$

Divide by 2α.

$$\bar{x} = \frac{r\sin\alpha}{\alpha}$$

For a semicircle, $\alpha = \frac{\pi}{2}$

$$\bar{x} = \frac{r\sin\frac{\pi}{2}}{\frac{\pi}{2}}$$

$\sin\left(\frac{\pi}{2}\right) = 1$

◀ Invert the fraction (turn upside down) and multiply.

$$\bar{x} = r \times \frac{2}{\pi}$$

$$\bar{x} = \frac{2r}{\pi}$$

Example 2

Find the centre of mass of a solid hemisphere with radius r.

Solution

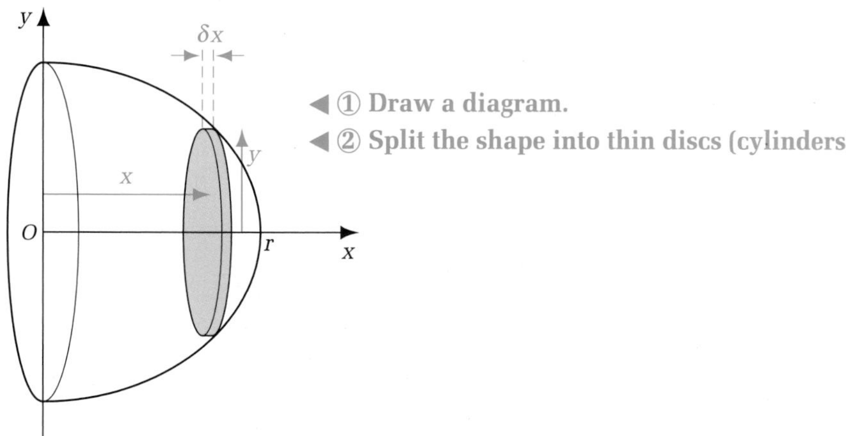

◀ ① Draw a diagram.

◀ ② Split the shape into thin discs (cylinders).

Each cylinder has its centre of mass on the axis, Ox. The radius of each cylinder is y and the thickness of each disc will be δx. So the volume of each cylinder will be $\pi y^2 \delta x$. Using the equation of a circle with centre O, y^2 can be found in terms of x

$$x^2 + y^2 = r^2$$

$$y^2 = r^2 - x^2$$

▼ ③ Table of values.

Shape	Volume	Weight	x-coordinate Distance from Oy
Small cylinder	$\pi y^2 \delta x = \pi(r^2 - x^2)\delta x$	$\pi W(r^2 - x^2)\delta x$	x
Whole shape	$\frac{2}{3}\pi r^3$	$\frac{2}{3}\pi W r^3$	$\bar{x}$

Volume of sphere $= \frac{4}{3}\pi r^3$ and the hemisphere is half this value.
The weight per unit volume is W.

$\curvearrowright Oy$ ◀ ④ **Equate moments.**

$$\tfrac{2}{3}\pi W r^3 \bar{x} = \sum_0^r \left(\pi W (r^2 - x^2)\delta x \times x\right)$$

Multiply the brackets by x.

$$\tfrac{2}{3}\pi W r^3 \bar{x} = \pi W \sum_0^r (xr^2 - x^3)\delta x$$

Divide by πW.

$$\tfrac{2}{3} r^3 \bar{x} = \sum_0^r (xr^2 - x^3)\delta x$$

Let $\delta x \to 0$ ◀ ⑤ **The summations will become integrals as $\delta x \to 0$.**

$$\tfrac{2}{3} r^3 \bar{x} = \int_0^r (xr^2 - x^3)\,dx$$ ◀ ⑥ **Integrate.**

$$\tfrac{2}{3} r^3 \bar{x} = \left[\frac{x^2 r^2}{2} - \frac{x^4}{4}\right]_0^r$$ ◀ ⑥ **Insert limits.**

$$\tfrac{2}{3} r^3 \bar{x} = \left[\frac{r^4}{2} - \frac{r^4}{4}\right] - 0$$

$$\tfrac{2}{3} r^3 \bar{x} = \frac{r^4}{4}$$

$$\bar{x} = \frac{r^4}{4} \times \frac{3}{2r^3}$$

Multiply by 3 and divide by $2r^3$ to find $\bar{x}$.

$$\bar{x} = \frac{3r}{8}$$

Example 3

Find the centre of mass of a solid right circular cone with radius r and height h.

Solution

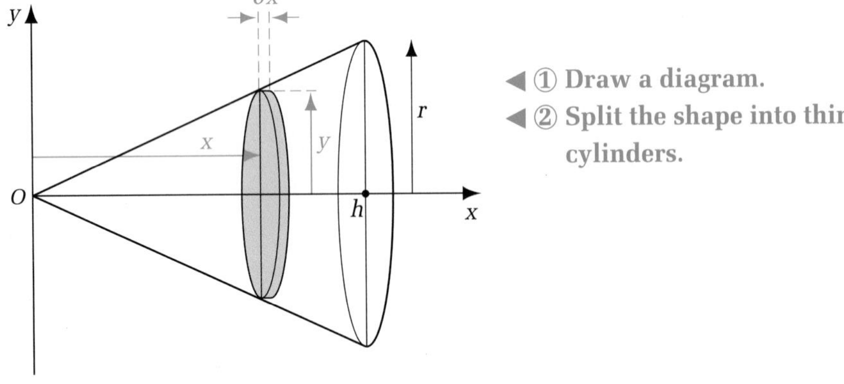

◀ ① **Draw a diagram.**
◀ ② **Split the shape into thin cylinders.**

Each cylinder has its centre of mass on the axis, Ox. The radius of each cylinder is y and the thickness of each cylinder will be δx. So the volume of each cylinder will be $\pi y^2 \delta x$. Using similar triangles, y can be found in terms of x.

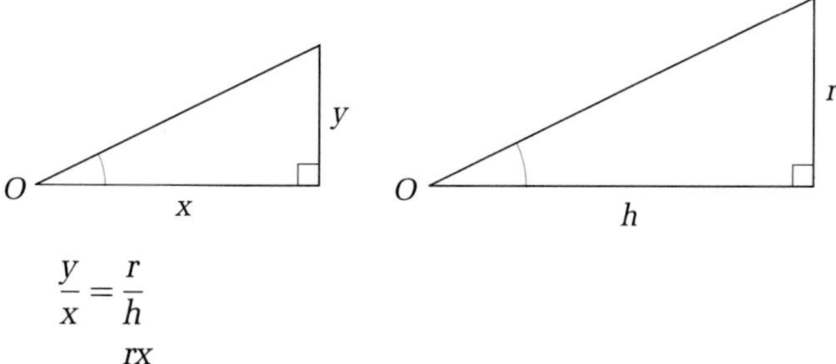

$$\frac{y}{x} = \frac{r}{h}$$

$$y = \frac{rx}{h}$$

▼ ③ Table of values.

Shape	Volume	Weight	x-coordinate Distance from Oy
Small cylinder	$\pi y^2 \delta x = \pi\left(\frac{r^2x^2}{h^2}\right)\delta x$	$\pi W\left(\frac{r^2x^2}{h^2}\right)\delta x$	x
Whole shape	$\frac{1}{3}\pi r^2 h$	$\frac{1}{3}\pi W r^2 h$	$\bar{x}$

The weight per unit volume is W.

$\curvearrowright Oy$ ◀ ④ Equate moments.

$$\tfrac{1}{3}\pi W r^2 h\bar{x} = \sum_0^h \left(\pi W\left(\frac{r^2x^2}{h^2}\right)\delta x \times x\right)$$

Take out a common factor of $\frac{\pi W r^2}{h^2}$.

$$\tfrac{1}{3}\pi W r^2 h\bar{x} = \frac{\pi W r^2}{h^2}\sum_0^h x^3 \delta x$$

Divide by $\pi W r^2$.

$$\tfrac{1}{3}h\bar{x} = \frac{1}{h^2}\sum_0^h x^3 \delta x$$

Let $\delta x \to 0$ ◀ ⑤ The summations will become integrals as $\delta x \to 0$.

$$\tfrac{1}{3}h\bar{x} = \frac{1}{h^2}\int_0^h x^3 \, dx$$ ◀ ⑥ Integrate.

$$\tfrac{1}{3}h\bar{x} = \frac{1}{h^2}\left[\frac{x^4}{4}\right]_0^h$$

Insert limits.

$$\tfrac{1}{3}h\bar{x} = \frac{1}{h^2}\left[\frac{h^4}{4}\right] - 0$$

$$\tfrac{1}{3}h\bar{x} = \frac{h^2}{4}$$

Multiply by 3 and divide by h to find $\bar{x}$.

$$\bar{x} = \frac{h^2}{4} \times \frac{3}{h}$$

$$\bar{x} = \frac{3h}{4}$$

The centre of mass is $\frac{3}{4}h$ from the vertex.

14.4 Centre of Mass using Integration

Exercise

Technique

1 Determine the centre of mass of the lamina enclosed by the lines $y = 6x$, $x = 3$ and the x-axis using integration.

2 Find the centre of mass of the lamina enclosed between the curve $y = x^3$, the line $x = 2$ and the x-axis.

3 A uniform lamina is formed by the curve $y = 6x^2$, the line $x = 1$ and the x-axis. Determine the centre of mass of the lamina.

4 Determine the centre of mass of the solid formed when the area enclosed by the curve $y = x^2$ and the line $x = 3$ is rotated $360°$ about the x-axis.

5 An area is formed by the curve $y^2 = x$, $x = 2$ and the x-axis. This area is rotated about the x-axis for one revolution to form a uniform solid. Find the centre of mass of this solid.

6 The curve $y = x^2$ and the lines $x = 2$, $x = 4$ and the x-axis enclose an area that forms a uniform lamina.

a Determine the centre of mass of this lamina.

b The lamina is now rotated about the x-axis to form a solid shape. Find the centre of mass of this solid shape.

7 Show that the centre of mass of a uniform semicircular lamina is $\frac{4r}{3\pi}$ from the centre of the diameter, where r is the radius.

8 Show that the centre of mass of a circular arc, of angle 2α and radius r, is $\frac{r \sin \alpha}{\alpha}$ measured from the centre of the circle. Use this result to obtain the position of the centre of mass of a semicircular arc.

9 Find an expression for the position of the centre of mass of a solid right circular cone in terms of the height h.

10 Show that the centre of mass of a uniform hemispherical shell is $\frac{1}{2}r$ from the base, where r is the radius of the hemisphere.

11 Find a formula for the position of the centre of mass of a uniform solid hemisphere with radius R.

14.5 Standard Results for Centres of Mass

During the last section, integration was used to find formulas for the centre of mass of common shapes. These results can often be used straight from tables instead of being proved by integration each time. The table of standard results is shown below.

Shape	Centre of mass
Circular arc, radius r and angle 2α	$\dfrac{r\sin\alpha}{\alpha}$ from the centre, O
Semicircular arc, radius r	$\dfrac{2r}{\pi}$ from the centre, O
Sector of a circle, radius r and angle 2α	$\dfrac{2r\sin\alpha}{3\alpha}$ from the centre, O
Semicircular lamina, radius r	$\dfrac{4r}{3\pi}$ from the centre, O
Hemispherical shell, radius r	$\dfrac{r}{2}$ from the centre, O
Solid hemisphere, radius r	$\dfrac{3r}{8}$ from the centre, O
Solid right circular cone, height h (or pyramid)	$\dfrac{3h}{4}$ from the vertex, V or $\dfrac{h}{4}$ from the base
Hollow cone, height h	$\dfrac{h}{3}$ from the base

These results can be used to calculate the centres of mass of composite shapes.

Overview of method

Step ① Draw a diagram of the shape and mark on axes Ox and Oy.
Step ② Are there any lines of symmetry?
Step ③ Split into shapes with standard results.
Step ④ Draw a table of shape, length/area/volume, weight, distances from the axes.
Step ⑤ Take moments about the axes.

Remember to check that the answer is sensible.

Example 1

Find the centre of gravity of the lamina made of three semicircles, as shown. State any assumptions that you have made.

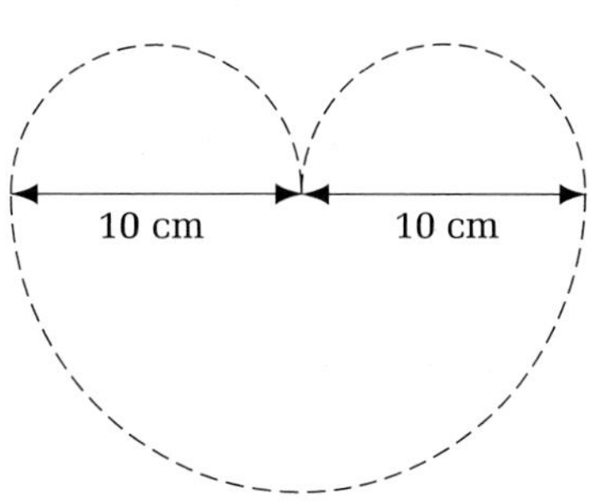

Solution

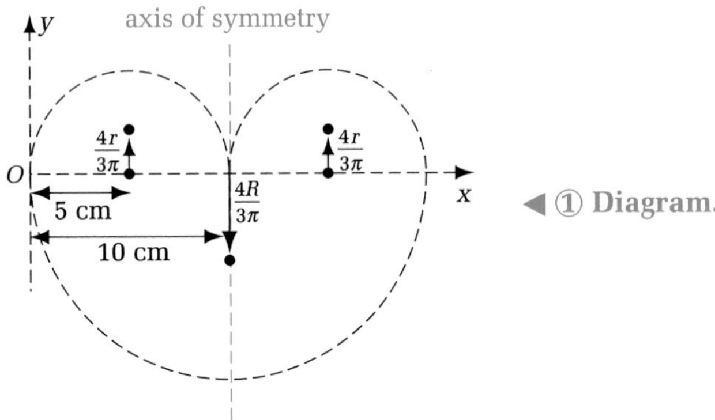

◀ ① Diagram.

There is an axis of symmetry and so the centre of gravity must lie along it. ◀ ② Symmetry.

▼ ③ Split shape up. ▼ ④ Table.

Shape	Area	Weight	Distance from Ox
Small semicircle	$\frac{1}{2}\pi \times 5^2 = 12.5\pi$	$12.5\pi W$	$\frac{4r}{3\pi} = \frac{20}{3\pi}$
Small semicircle	12.5π	$12.5\pi W$	$\frac{4r}{3\pi} = \frac{20}{3\pi}$
Large semicircle	$\frac{1}{2}\pi \times 10^2 = 50\pi$	$50\pi W$	$-\frac{4R}{3\pi} = -\frac{40}{3\pi}$
Whole shape	75π	$75\pi W$	$\bar{y}$

The distance for the large semicircle is negative because it is below Ox.

↻Ox ◀ ⑤ Equate moments.

$$12.5\pi W \times \frac{20}{3\pi} + 12.5\pi W \times \frac{20}{3\pi} + 50\pi W \times \left(-\frac{40}{3\pi}\right) = 75\pi W\bar{y}$$

Divide by πW.

$$\frac{250}{3\pi} + \frac{250}{3\pi} - \frac{2000}{3\pi} = 75\bar{y}$$

Simplify by adding the fractions.

$$-\frac{1500}{3\pi} = 75\bar{y}$$

Simplify the fraction by cancelling by 3.

$$75\bar{y} = -\frac{500}{\pi}$$

Divide by 75.

$$\bar{y} = -\frac{500}{75\pi}$$

$$\bar{y} = -\frac{20}{3\pi} \text{ cm}$$

The centre of mass is $\frac{20}{3\pi}$ cm below the line Ox.

Check the diagram. Is this answer sensible?

The assumptions that we have made are that the lamina is uniform and that the acceleration due to gravity remains the same over the whole lamina.

Example 2

The diagram shows a frustrum. It is the shape left when a small cone is cut from the top of a large cone. Find the centre of mass of the frustrum.

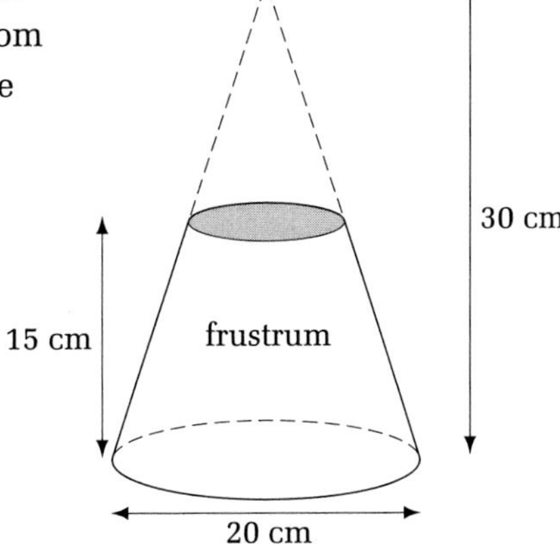

Solution

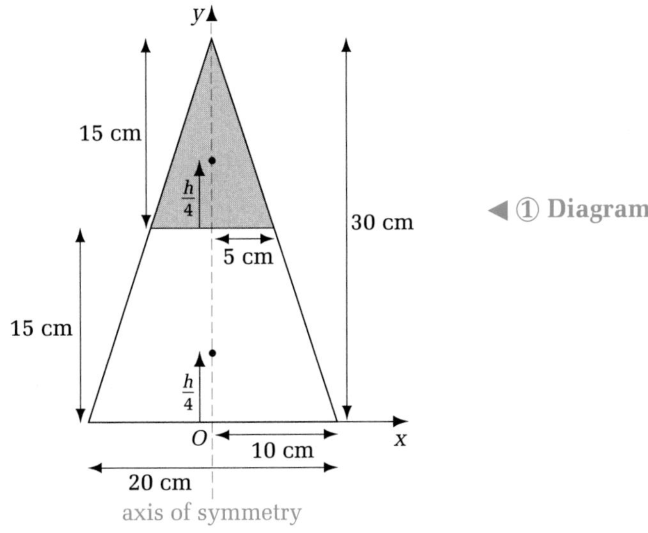

◀ ① Diagram.

The frustrum has an axis of symmetry. This is shown as a dotted line on the diagram. ◀ ② Symmetry.

▼ ③ Split shape up. ▼ ④ Table.

Shape	Volume	Weight	Distance from Ox
Large cone	$\frac{1}{3}\pi \times 10^2 \times 30 = 1000\pi$	$1000\pi W$	$\frac{h}{4} = \frac{30}{4} = 7.5$
Small cone	$-\frac{1}{3}\pi \times 5^2 \times 15 = -125\pi$	$-125\pi W$	$\frac{15}{4} + 15 = 18.75$
Whole shape	875π	$875\pi W$	$\bar{y}$

Small cone has a negative volume and weight because it is cut away.

$\circlearrowright Ox$ ◀ ⑤ Equate moments.

$$1000\pi W \times 7.5 - 125\pi W \times 18.75 = 875\pi W\bar{y}$$ Divide by πW.

$$7500 - 2343.75 = 875\bar{y}$$

$$5156.25 = 875\bar{y}$$

$$\bar{y} = 5.89 \text{ cm (3 s.f.)}$$ Check the answer is sensible.

Example 3

A child's toy is formed by gluing a cylinder onto a hemisphere. The centre of mass of the toy lies on the glued edge. Calculate the height of the cylinder.

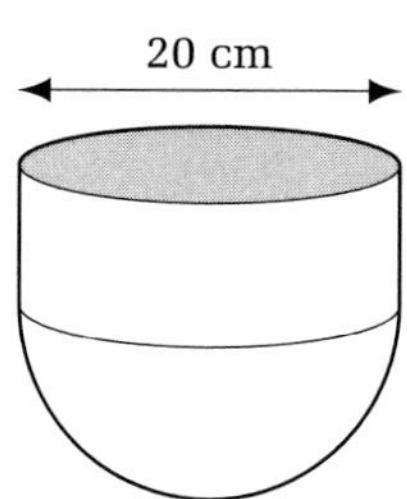

Solution

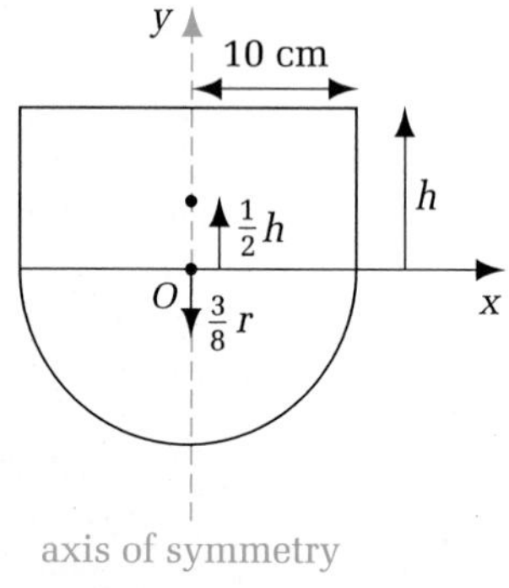

◀ ① Diagram.
◀ ② Symmetry.

▼ ③ Split shape up. ▼ ④ Table.

Shape	Volume	Weight	Distance from *Ox*
Cylinder	$\pi \times 10^2 \times h = 100\pi h$	$100\pi hW$	$\frac{h}{2}$
Hemisphere	$\frac{2}{3}\pi \times 10^3 = \frac{2000}{3}\pi$	$\frac{2000}{3}\pi W$	$-\frac{3r}{8} = -\frac{30}{8}$ $= -3.75$
Whole shape	$100\pi h + \frac{2000}{3}\pi$	$100\pi hW + \frac{2000}{3}\pi W$	$\bar{y} = 0$

The centre of mass of the hemisphere is below *Ox* so it is negative.

$\circlearrowright Ox$ ◀ ⑤ Equate moments

$$100\pi hW \times \frac{h}{2} + \tfrac{2000}{3}\pi W \times (-3.75) = \left(100\pi hW + \tfrac{2000}{3}\pi W\right) \times 0$$ Divide by πW.

$$50h^2 - 2500 = 0$$ Add 2500.

$$50h^2 = 2500$$ Divide by 50.

$$h^2 = 50$$ Take the square root.

$$h = \sqrt{50} = 5\sqrt{2} \text{ cm}$$

14.5 Standard Results for Centres of Mass

Exercise

Technique

1 **a** **b**

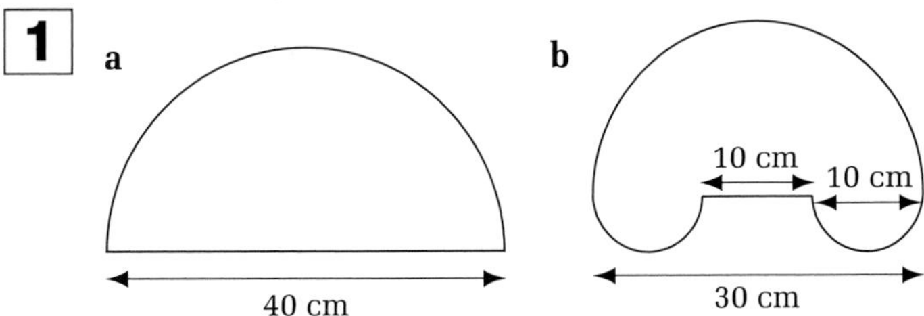

Find the centres of mass of the uniform rods shown. The shapes are made from semicircles and straight lines.

2 **a** **b**

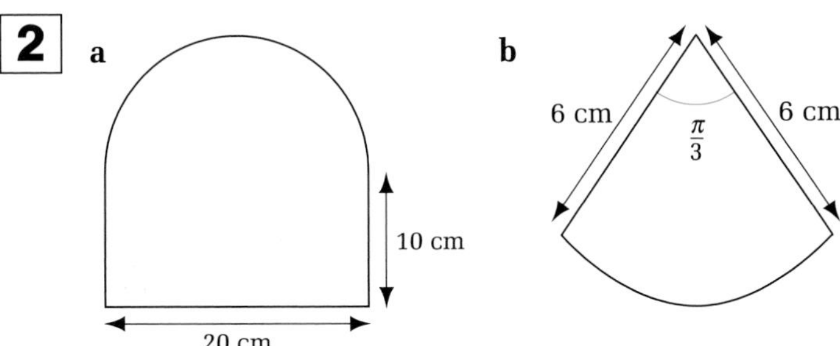

Determine the centres of mass of the uniform laminas shown.

3 **a** **b**

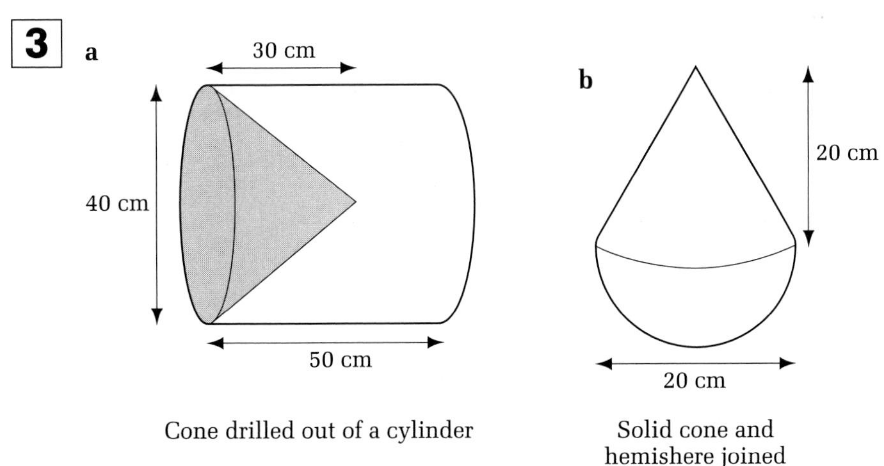

Cone drilled out of a cylinder

Solid cone and hemishere joined

Calculate the position of the centres of mass of the uniform solids.

Contextual

1

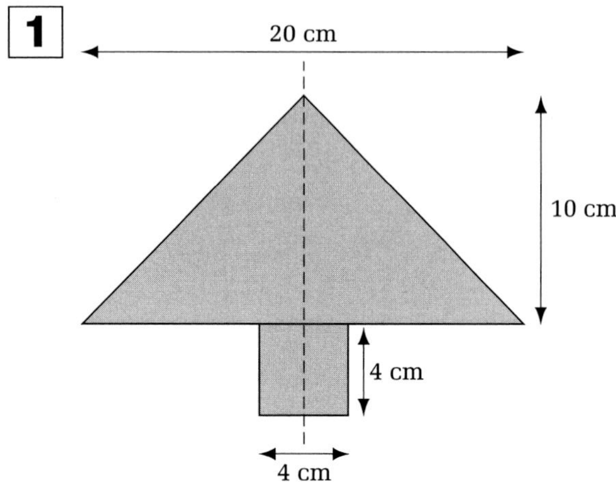

A child's spinner is made from a solid right circular cone and a cylinder of the same material. Find the centre of gravity of the spinner, stating any assumptions made.

2

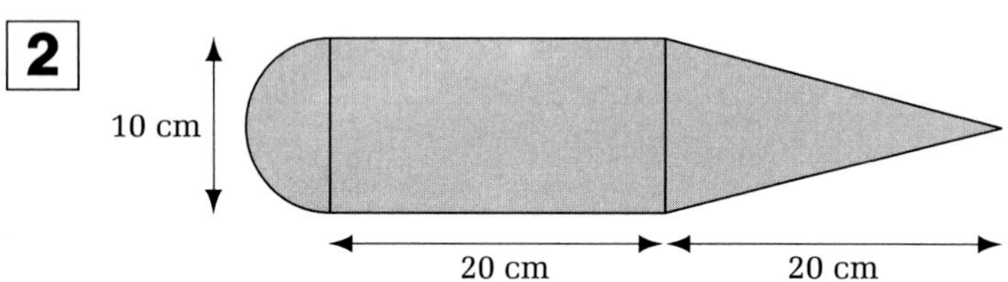

A spike is made from a hemisphere, a cylinder and a cone. Determine the centre of mass of the spike.

14.6 Sliding and Toppling

Four cubes are taped together to form a block. The block is set on a table as shown in the diagram. The table is inclined. What will happen to the block?

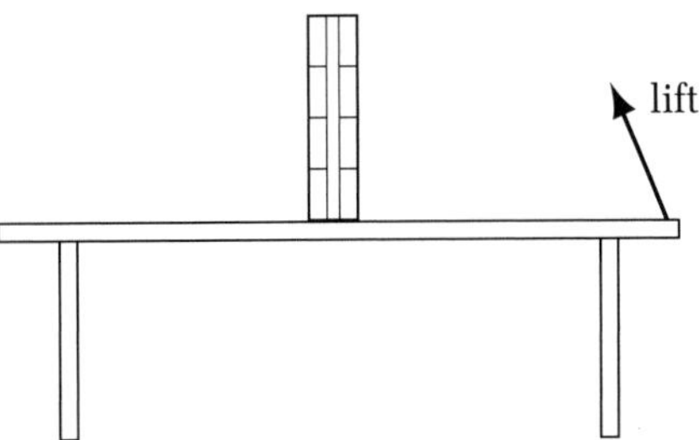

The same block of four cubes is now set on the table lengthways. The table is inclined again. What happens to the block this time? Why do different outcomes occur?

Toppling

In the first situation, the block topples. By looking at what happens to the weight force, the reason for toppling can be seen.

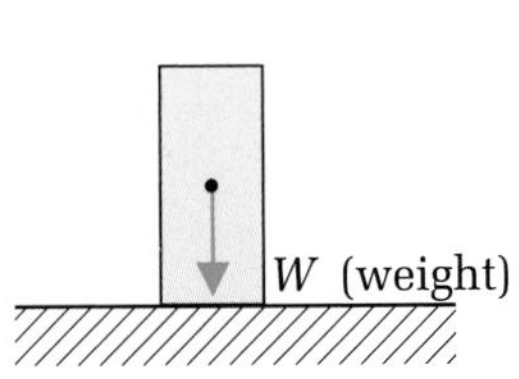

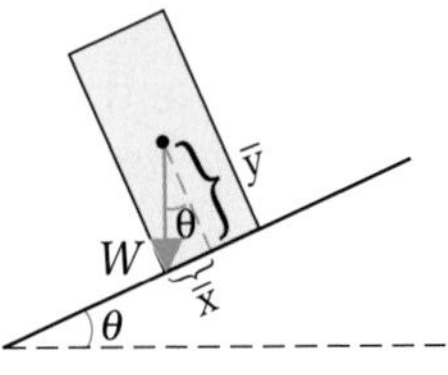

The block is just about to topple

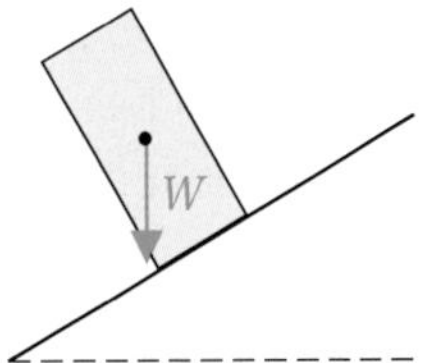

The block will topple

When the weight force acts outside the base of the object, the object will topple. This is because the resultant reaction force can no longer act in the same line as the weight. The weight and reaction produce an overall moment on the blocks, causing them to topple.

For the block to begin to topple:

$$\tan\theta = \frac{\bar{x}}{\bar{y}}$$

Note that when the weight force acts at the corner, the object is just about to topple.

Sliding

In the second situation, the block slides before it will be able to topple. The weight of the block will overcome the frictional force before the *toppling angle* is reached. The block will slide when the angle of friction is exceeded.

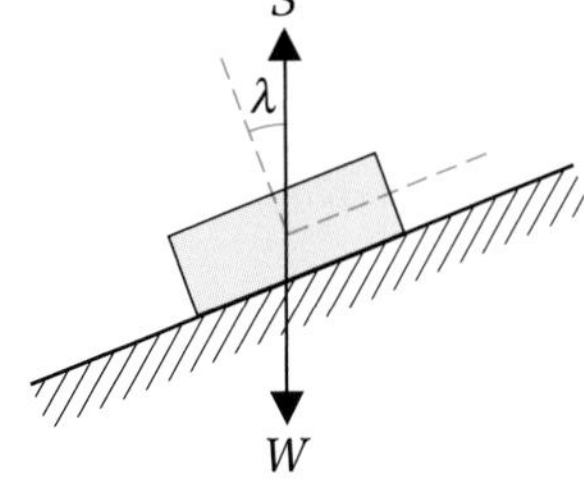

Remember $\tan\lambda = \mu$.
λ = angle of friction

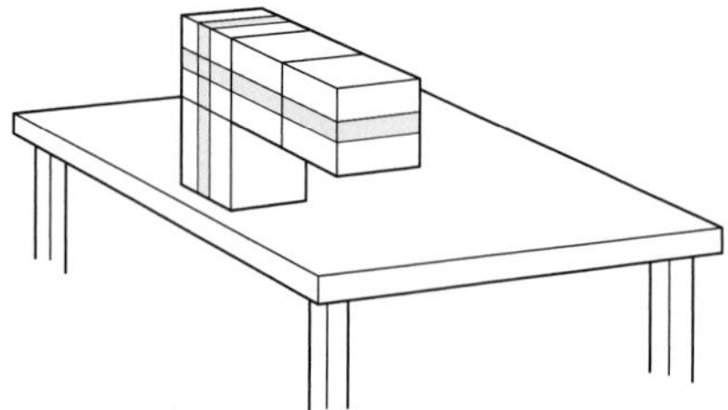

Toppling can also occur on a horizontal surface. The four blocks are taped in a different arrangement. When this is placed on a horizontal table will it topple? Why does this happen? The weight acts outside the base and the normal reaction can no longer act in the same line as the weight. The weight and reaction produce an overall moment on the blocks and they topple.

Example 1

At a fairground, one of the games is to knock over a solid right circular cone of mass 5 kg. The cone has a base radius of 20 cm and a height of 40 cm. If the cone is struck at its vertex (point), find the force necessary to make the cone topple.

Solution

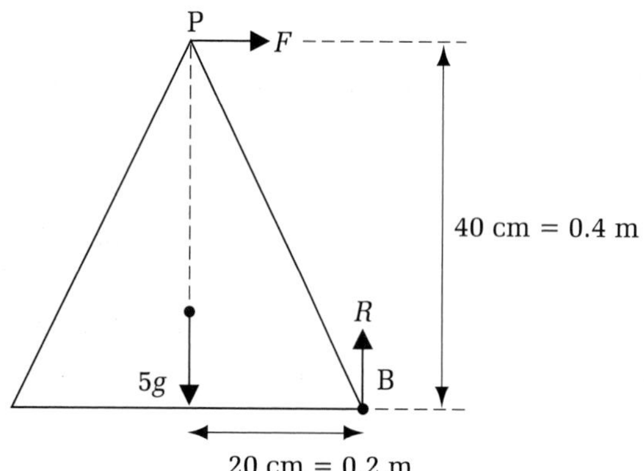

When the cone turns about B then only the point B will be in contact with the surface. So the reaction force must act at point B.

The cone will turn about B and so moments must be taken about B. The cone will topple when the moment of the force acting at the point P is greater than the moment of the weight.

↻B

Take moments about B, so the reaction force at B has no effect.

$$F \times 0.4 > 5g \times 0.2$$

$$0.4F > 9.8$$

$$F > 24.5 \text{ N}$$

The force applied must be greater than 24.5 N. This assumes that the cone is of uniform construction and that the cone does not slide first.

Example 2

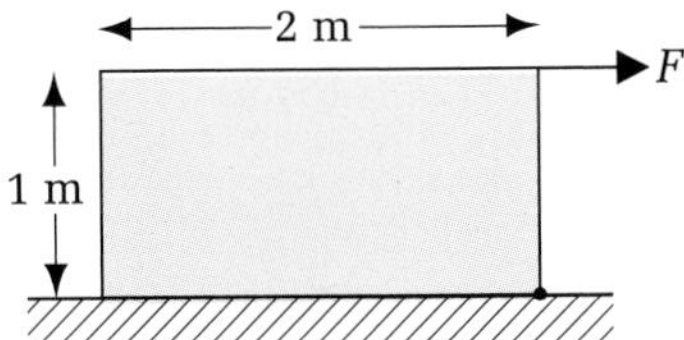

A block rests on a horizontal surface where the coefficient of friction is 0.7. Determine whether the block will topple or slide as the force F is increased.

Solution

When the block is just about to topple the reaction acts through X.

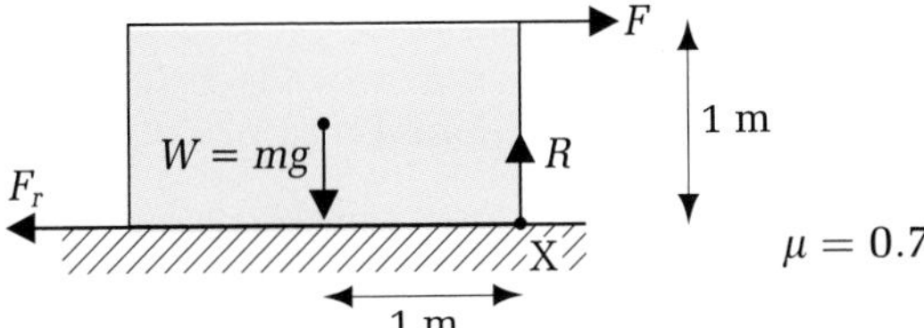

When the block is just about to topple, the moment caused by the force F about X must be equal but opposite to the moment caused by the weight. Equate moments.

$$F \times 1 = mg \times 1$$
$$F = mg$$

Let the mass of the block be m.

When the block is just about to slide the force F and friction must be equal in magnitude but opposite in direction.

$$F = F_r$$
$$F = \mu R = \mu mg$$
$$F = 0.7mg$$

Remember $F_r = \mu R$ for limiting equilibrium. $\mu = 0.7$ from the question.

The block will slide because less force is needed to make the block slide.

14.6 Sliding and Toppling
Exercise

Technique

1 **a**

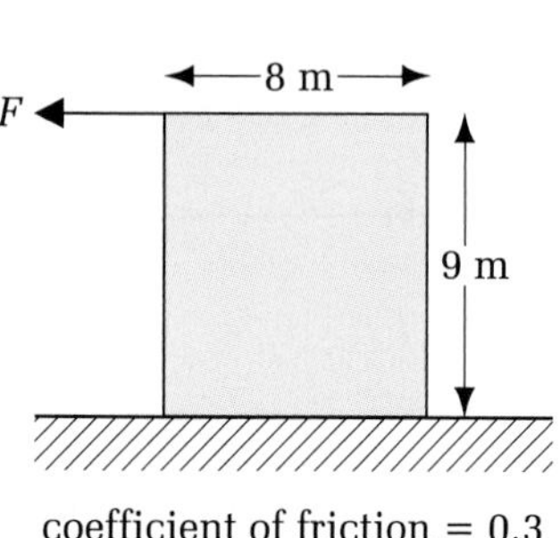

coefficient of friction = 0.3

b

5 m
F
10 m

coefficient of friction = 0.8

Will the uniform cuboids shown slide or topple as the force F is increased?

2 A solid right circular cone has a mass of 10 kg, a radius of 20 cm and a height of 40 cm. A horizontal force P, acts at its vertex as shown.

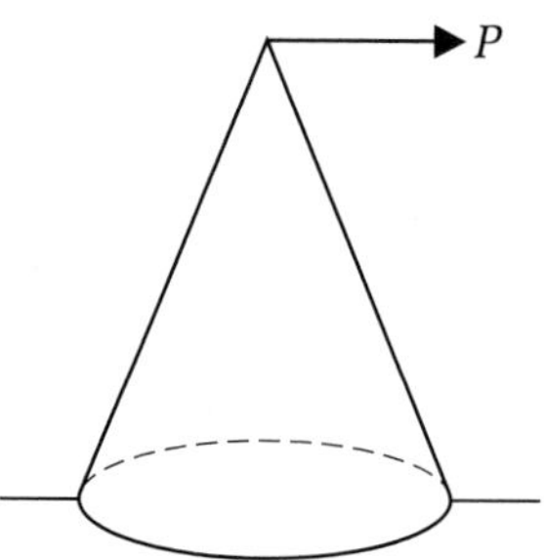

a Calculate the force P when the cone is about to topple.

b Find P, in terms of μ, when the cone is about to slide.

3

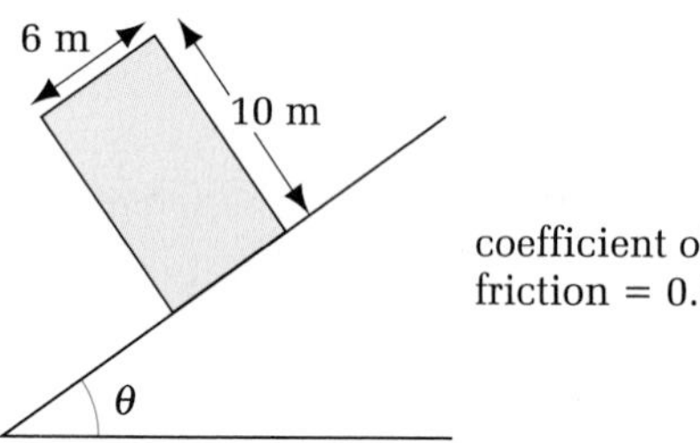

coefficient of friction = 0.7

Does the block slide or topple as θ is increased?

4 **a**

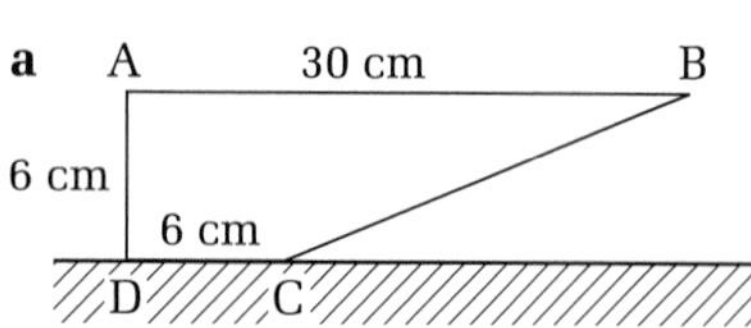

b

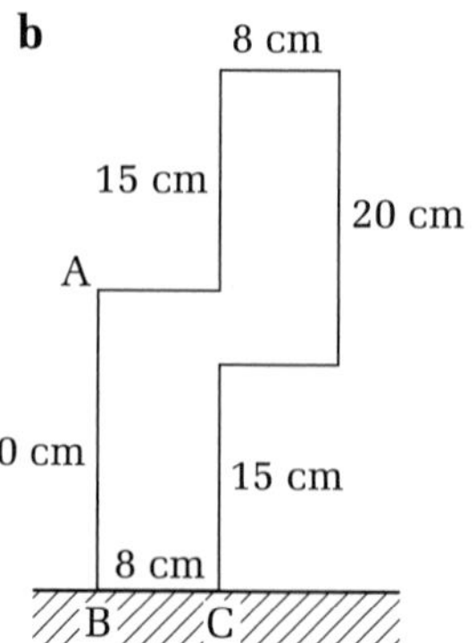

i Find the position of the centres of mass for the laminas shown.

ii Determine whether the laminas will topple.

Consolidation

Exercise A

1 A uniform triangular lamina ABC is in equilibrium, suspended from a fixed point O by a light inelastic string attached to the point B of the lamina, as shown in the diagram. AB = 45 cm, BC = 60 cm and angle ABC = 90°. Calculate the angle θ between BC and the downward vertical.

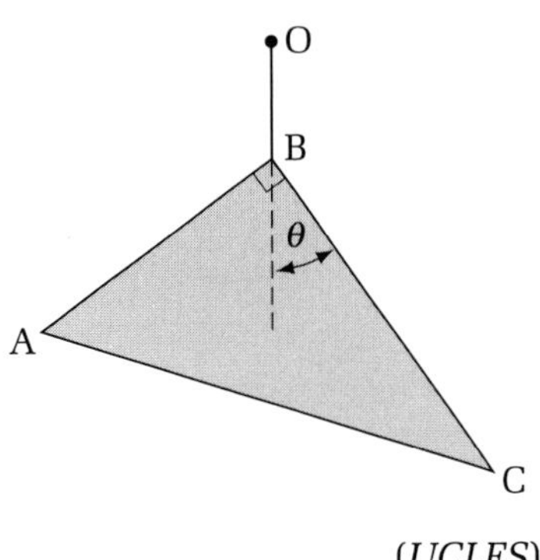

(*UCLES*)

2 A thin uniform rectangular metal plate ABCD of mass M rests on a rough plane inclined at an angle α to the horizontal. The plate lies in a vertical plane containing a line of greatest slope of the inclined plane, with the edge CD in contact with the plane and C further up the plane than D, as shown. The lengths of AB and BC are 10 cm and 30 cm respectively. The plane is sufficiently rough to prevent the plate from slipping.

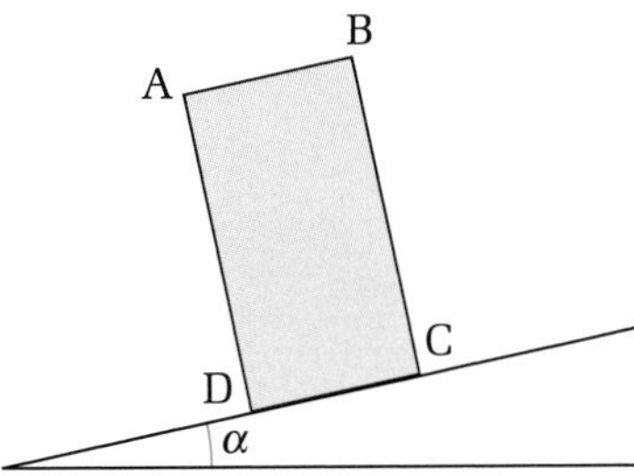

a Find to the nearest degree, the greatest value which α can have if the plate does not topple.

A small stud of mass m is fixed to the plate at the point C.

b Given that $\tan \alpha = \frac{1}{2}$, find, in terms of M, the smallest value of m which will enable the plate to stay in equilibrium without toppling.

(*ULEAC*)

3 A uniform right circular solid cone has height h. Find, by integration, the distance of the centre of mass of the cone from its vertex. (*WJEC*)

4 A uniform rectangular metal plate ABCD, where AB = 6 cm and BC = 2 cm, has mass M. Four particles of mass m, m, $3m$ and $3m$ are attached to the points A, B, C and D respectively. When the loaded plate is suspended freely from the point A and hangs in equilibrium, AB makes an angle α with the downward vertical, as shown, where $\sin \alpha = \frac{5}{13}$.

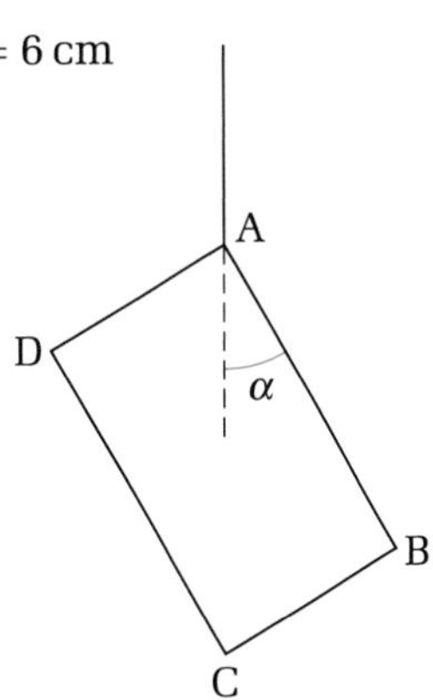

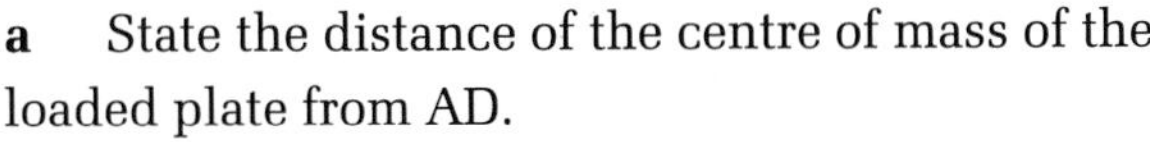
a State the distance of the centre of mass of the loaded plate from AD.

b Show that the distance of the centre of mass of the loaded plate from AB is 1.25 cm.

c Hence find m in terms of M.

(*ULEAC*)

5 A solid is made from a uniform, right circular cylinder of height h and radius r and a uniform, right circular cone of height h and radius r, joined as shown in the diagram. The density of the cone is twice that of the cylinder.

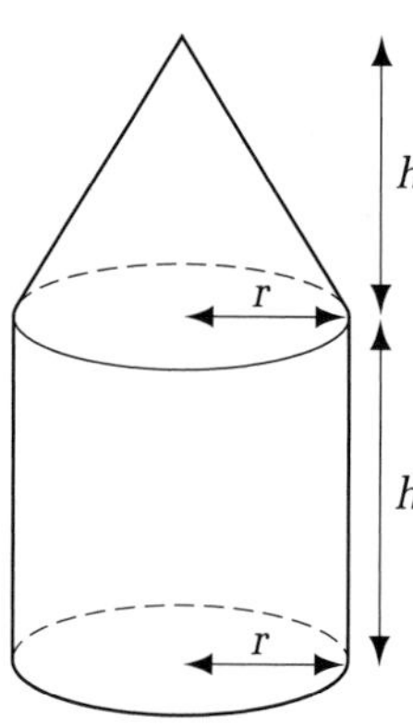

a Show that the centre of gravity of the solid is at a distance $\frac{4}{5}h$ from the centre of the circular base of the cylinder.

The solid is placed with its circular base on a horizontal plane, which is tilted gradually. The plane is rough enough to prevent sliding.

b Given that $h = 2r$, find the angle the plane makes with the horizontal when the solid begins to topple. *(NICCEA)*

Exercise B

1 The diagram shows four light rods which are rigidly joined together to form a square OBCD of side $2a$. Particles of mass $2m$ are attached to the midpoints of OB, BC and DO, particles of mass $5m$ and m are attached at O and B respectively. The centre of mass of the five particles is G $(\bar{x}, \bar{y})$.

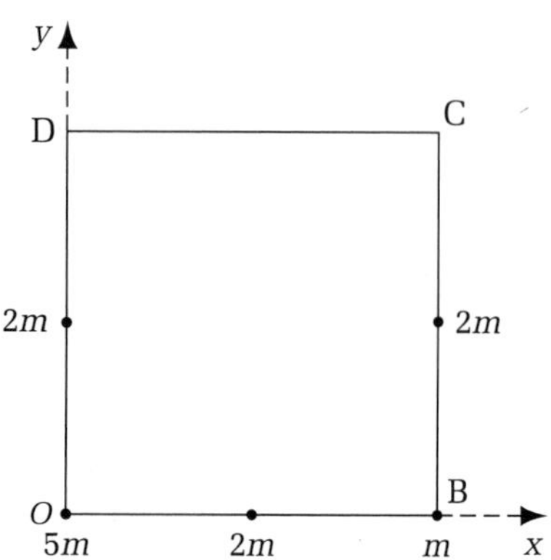

a Prove that $\bar{x} = \frac{2}{3}a$.

b Find the distance OG.

The system is freely suspended from O and hangs in equilibrium with OB inclined at an angle θ to the downward vertical. Prove that $\tan\theta = 0.5$. *(AEB)*

2 A uniform solid cylinder, of base radius r and height h, has the same density as a uniform solid hemisphere of radius r. The plane face of the hemisphere is joined to a plane face of the cylinder to form the composite solid S shown in the diagram. The point O is the centre of the plane base of S.

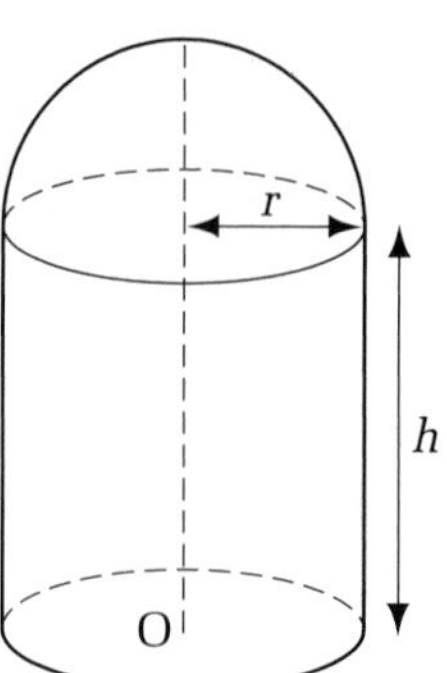

a Show that the distance from O of the centre of mass of S is

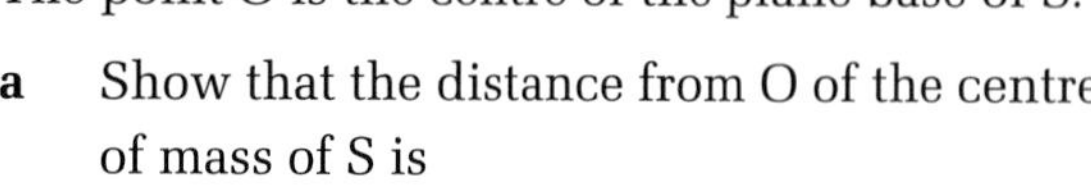

$$\frac{6h^2 + 8hr + 3r^2}{4(3h + 2r)}$$

The solid is placed on a rough plane which is inclined at an angle α to the horizontal. The plane base of S is in contact with the inclined plane.

b Given that $h = r$, and that S is on the point of toppling, find α, to the nearest degree. *(ULEAC)*

3 The diagram, which is not drawn to scale, shows a uniform lamina formed by drilling a circular hole of radius 2 cm in a rectangle ABCD with length AB $= 8\pi$ cm and breadth BC $= 12$ cm. The centre of the hole is 9 cm from AB and is equidistant from AD and BC. Find the distance of the centre of mass of the lamina from AB.

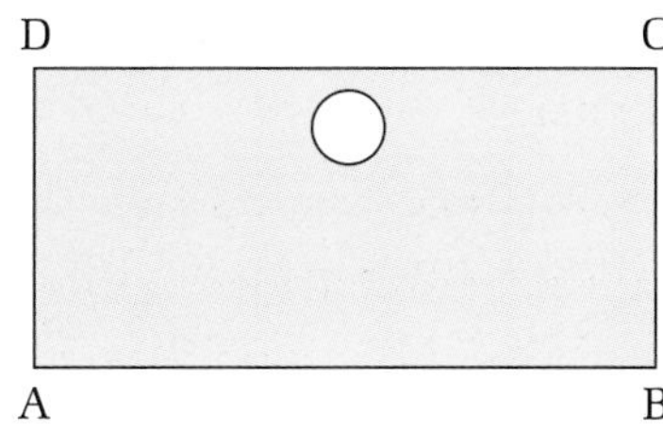

(WJEC)

4 A lamina, in the shape of a letter T, is made of uniform material of density 1 kg m^{-2}. The dimensions of the shape are shown.

a Find the distance of the centre of mass of the lamina from the edges OA and OG.

The lamina is freely suspended from B.

b Find the mass of the particle which must be attached to the lamina at C so that it will hang in equilibrium with AB vertical.

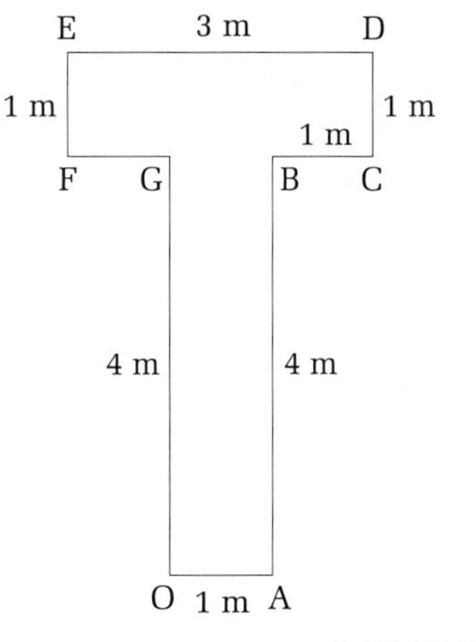

(NICCEA)

Density is mass per unit area for laminas, mass per unit volume for solids.

5 A uniform solid cylinder has height 30 cm and radius 10 cm. The cylinder is held on a rough plane, with its base in contact with the plane, as shown in the diagram. The plane is inclined at a fixed angle α to the horizontal. The cylinder is released. The coefficient of friction between the cylinder and the plane is μ. Given that the cylinder remains in equilibrium show that $\tan \alpha \leq \frac{2}{3}$ and $\tan \alpha \leq \mu$.

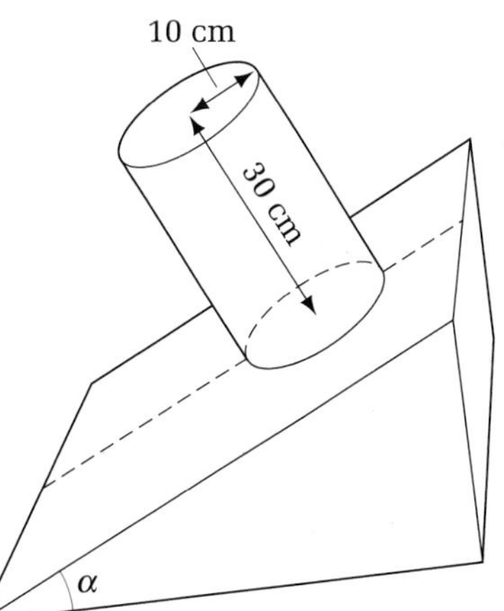

Describe briefly, giving reasons, what, if anything, happens when the cylinder is released in each of the following cases:

a $\mu = \frac{1}{3}$ and $\tan \alpha = \frac{1}{2}$ **b** $\mu = \frac{4}{5}$ and $\tan \alpha = \frac{3}{4}$.

(UCLES)

Applications and Activities

1

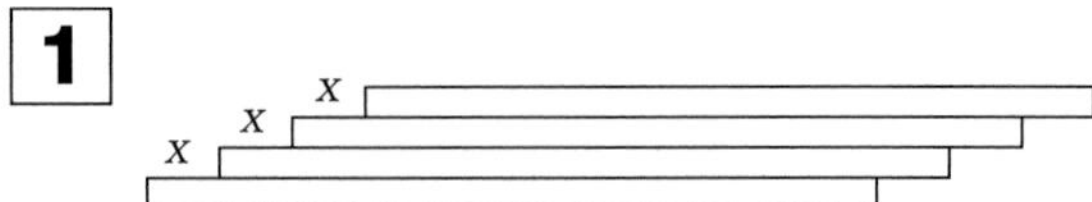

Rulers are stacked as shown in the diagram. How many rulers can be stacked with $x = 5$ cm. Try to explain why this happens using centres of gravity.

2

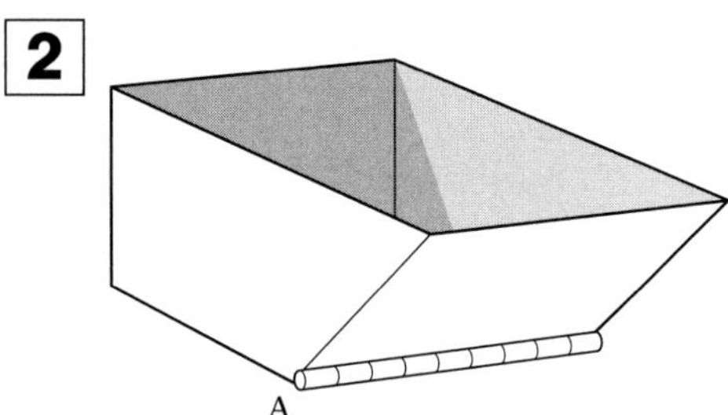

A container at a water park fills up with water. It is pivoted at A. When the container fills up, it tilts and when it is empty it topples back to its original position. Design the container. Make and test it using rice or sand to model the water.

Summary

- The centre of mass is found by constructing a table of masses and the position of the centre of each mass, and then taking moments.
- The centre of mass can also be found by integration.
- When a body is suspended the centre of mass is always positioned vertically below the point of suspension and this result is used to determine the angle of suspension.
- Standard results for the position of centres of mass can be used to solve problems.
- An object will *topple* if the line of action of the weight force acts *outside* the base of the object.
- An object will *slide* if the line of action of the weight force acts *inside* the base of the object and the angle of friction is exceeded.

15 Equilibrium of a Rigid Body

What you need to know

- How to calculate moments.
- How to model friction.
- How to mark reaction forces on a diagram.
- How to find the centre of mass for uniform shapes.

Review

1 **a**

8 m
A
$15g$ N

b

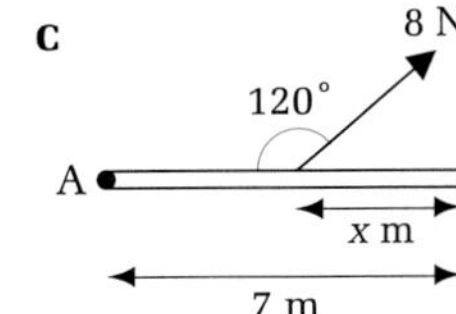

c

8 N
120°
A
x m
7 m

Write an expression for the moment of the force about the point A, in each of the cases shown.

2 A block of mass 5 kg is placed on a horizontal surface. The coefficient of friction between the block and the surface is $\frac{2}{5}$. A horizontal force acts on the block.

a Taking $g = 10\,\text{m s}^{-2}$, find the magnitude of the frictional force when the horizontal force is:

i 8 N **ii** 20 N **iii** 30 N

b In which case is the block said to be in *limiting equilibrium*?

Remember the normal reaction force acts at right angles to the continuous surface.

3 **a**

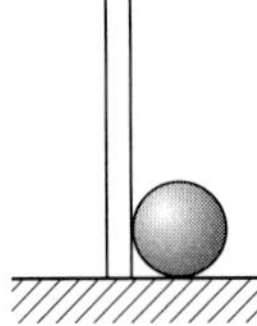

b

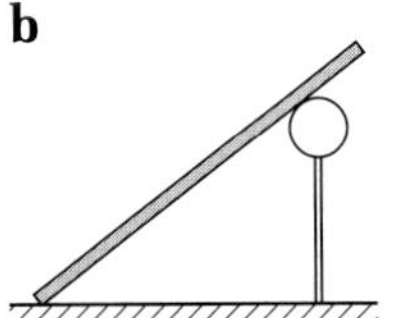

c

Copy these three diagrams and draw in the direction of the normal reaction forces due to contact.

4 **a**

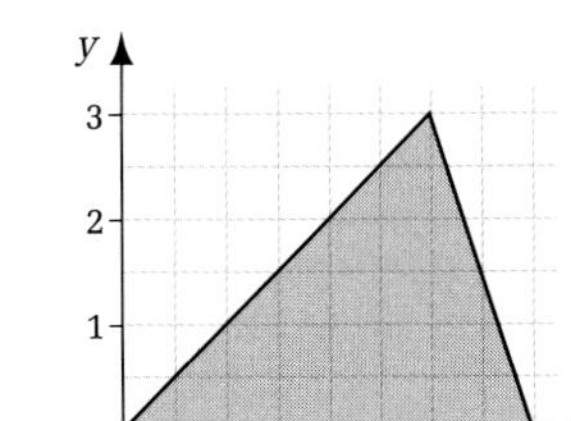

b

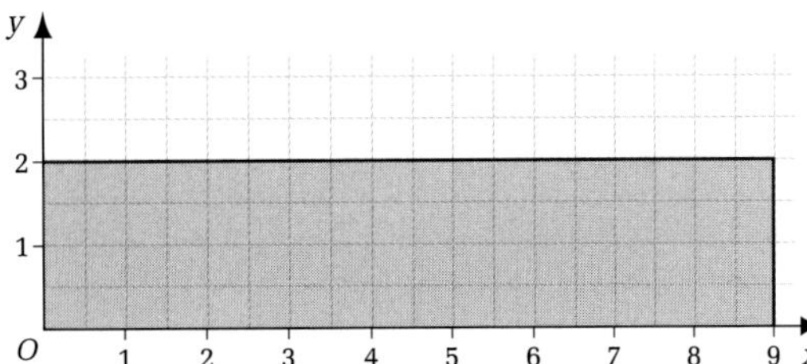

State the coordinates of the centre of mass of these uniform laminas.

Equilibrium of Rigid Bodies

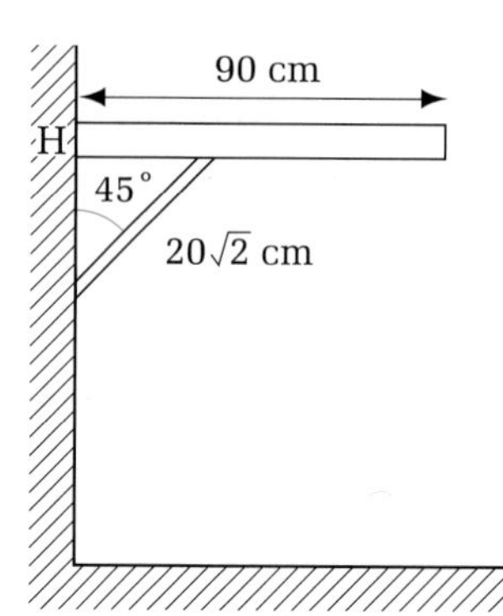

... design for a folding table is shown in the diagram. The table top has a mass of 8 kg, a length of 90 cm, and the support has a length of $20\sqrt{2}$ cm.

How strong does the support have to be? The table top is assumed uniform and rigid. Rigid means that the table top will not bend. The support is light and the table will be assumed to be in static equilibrium. The acceleration due to gravity will be taken as $10\ \text{m s}^{-2}$. The table top and the support cannot be treated as a particle because their lengths are important. None of the parts of the table top are moving, so the resultant force acting on the table top must be zero. A second condition must be that the *moments* acting on the table top must be *zero*. This makes sure the table top will *not rotate*.

The compression force or thrust T in the rod will have a horizontal component $T\cos 45°$ so there must be another horizontal force acting. This force is a **reaction force** at the hinge.

Consider the forces acting on the table top.

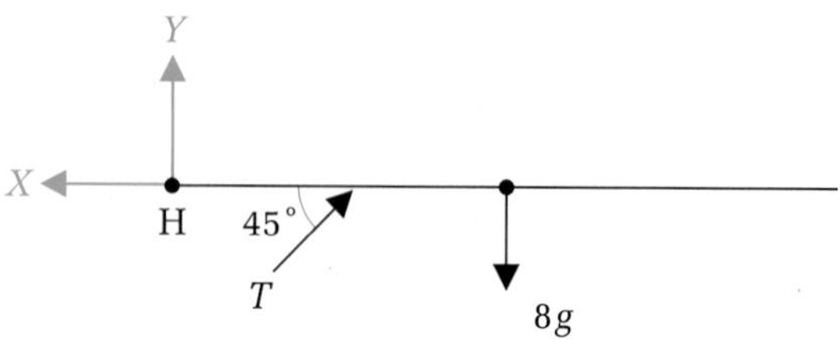

Resolve ↑ $\quad Y + T\sin 45° - 80 = 0 \quad$ [1]

Resolve→ $\quad T\cos 45° - X = 0 \quad$ [2]

There are three unknowns in these two equations. Another equation needs to be found to be able to obtain a solution. Not only must the *overall force* be *zero*, the *overall moment acting on the table top must be zero*. Moments could be taken about any point. However, by choosing the point H, two forces (X and Y) will have no effect.

Perpendicular distances for these forces will be zero.

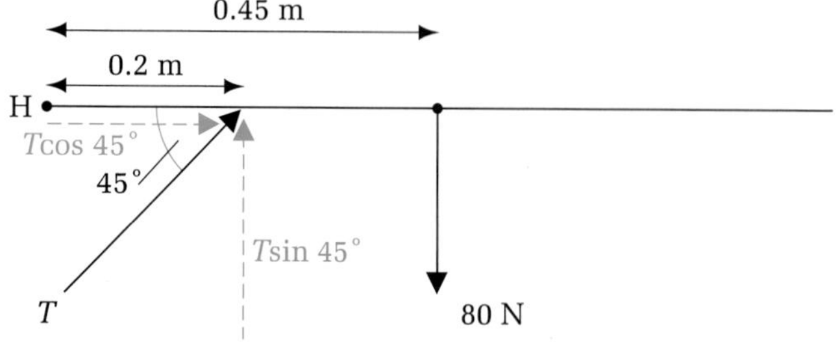

↻H clockwise

$$80 \times 0.45 - T\sin 45^\circ \times 0.2 = 0$$

Use $\sin 45^\circ = \frac{\sqrt{2}}{2}$

$$36 - T(0.1\sqrt{2}) = 0$$

Add $T(0.1\sqrt{2})$.

$$36 = T(0.1\sqrt{2})$$

Divide by $0.1\sqrt{2}$.

$$T = \frac{36}{(0.1\sqrt{2})}$$

$$T = 255 \text{ N (3 s.f.)}$$

Equations [1] and [2] can now be used to find the reaction forces acting at the hinge.

Using equation [2].

$$T\cos 45^\circ = X$$

$$255 \times \frac{\sqrt{2}}{2} = X$$

$$X = 180 \text{ N}$$

Using equation [1].

$$Y = 80 - T\sin 45^\circ$$

$$Y = 80 - 180$$

$$Y = -100$$

$$Y = 100 \text{ N downwards}$$

Overview of method

Step ① Draw a clear diagram, marking all forces including reaction forces at hinges.

Step ② Resolve the forces in two perpendicular directions (usually horizontally and vertically).

Step ③ Take moments about a point (either the hinge, pivot or point with the most unknown forces acting).

Step ④ Solve the equations to find unknown quantities.

Example 1

The diagram shows a uniform rod AB of mass 7 kg and length 1 m which is hinged at A. The rod is held in equilibrium by a string which is attached to the rod at C, where BC = 0.25 m. Taking $g = 10\text{ m s}^{-2}$, determine the tension in the string and the magnitude of the reaction at the hinge.

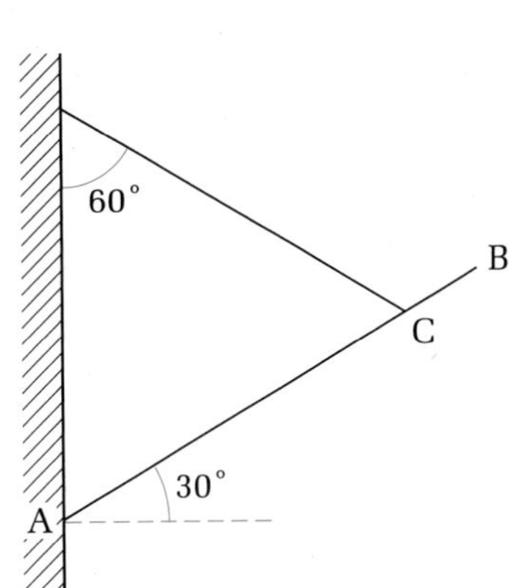

Solution

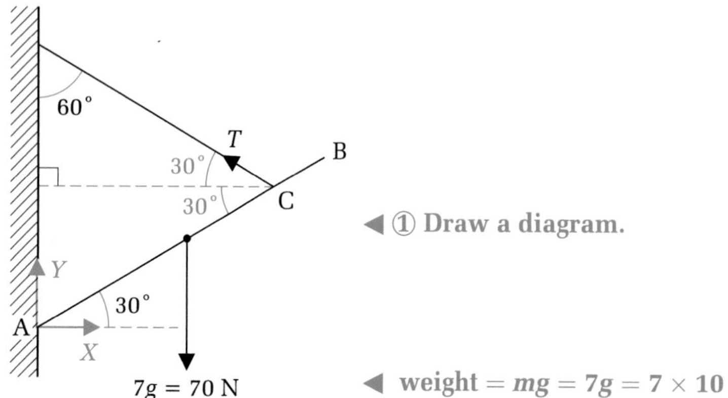

◀ ① Draw a diagram.

Mark on the reactions at hinge.

◀ weight $= mg = 7g = 7 \times 10$

The rod is in equilibrium, so consider only the forces acting on the rod.

Resolve ↑ ◀ ② Resolve the forces

$$Y + T\sin 30° - 70 = 0$$

Use $\sin 30° = 0.5$.

$$Y + 0.5T - 70 = 0 \quad [1]$$

Resolve →

$$X - T\cos 30° = 0 \quad [2]$$

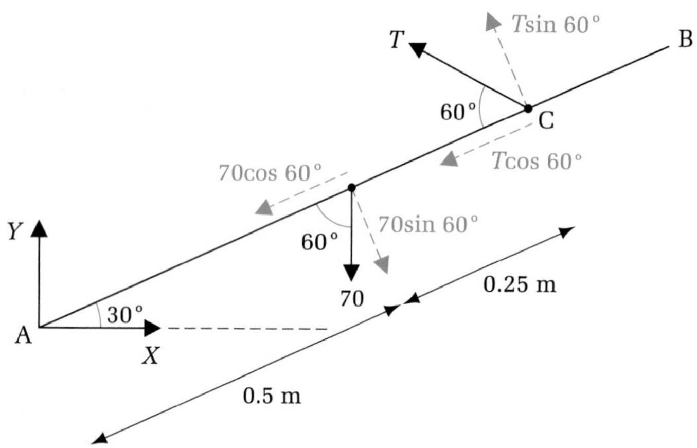

Resolve forces parallel and perpendicular to the rod to help with taking moments.

↻A clockwise ◀ ③ Take moments about hinge.

$$70\sin 60° \times 0.5 - T\sin 60° \times 0.75 = 0$$

◀ Divide by sin 60°.

$$70 \times 0.5 - T \times 0.75 = 0$$

Add $T \times 0.75$.

$$35 = T \times 0.75$$

Divide by 0.75.

$$\frac{35}{0.75} = T$$

$$T = 46.\dot{6}\ \text{N}$$

Use equations [1] and [2] to find X and Y.

◀ ④ **Solve the equations to find the unknown quantities.**

Rearrange equation [1].

$$Y + 0.5 \times 46.\dot{6} - 70 = 0$$

$$Y = 70 - 0.5 \times 46.\dot{6}$$

$$Y = 70 - 23.\dot{3}$$

$$Y = 46.\dot{6} \text{ N}$$

Rearrange equation [2]. Use $\cos 30° = \frac{\sqrt{3}}{2}$ and the value of T.

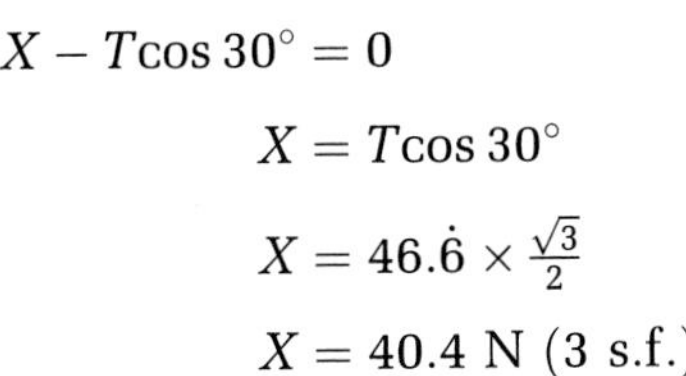

$$X - T\cos 30° = 0$$

$$X = T\cos 30°$$

$$X = 46.\dot{6} \times \frac{\sqrt{3}}{2}$$

$$X = 40.4 \text{ N (3 s.f.)}$$

Magnitude of the reaction:

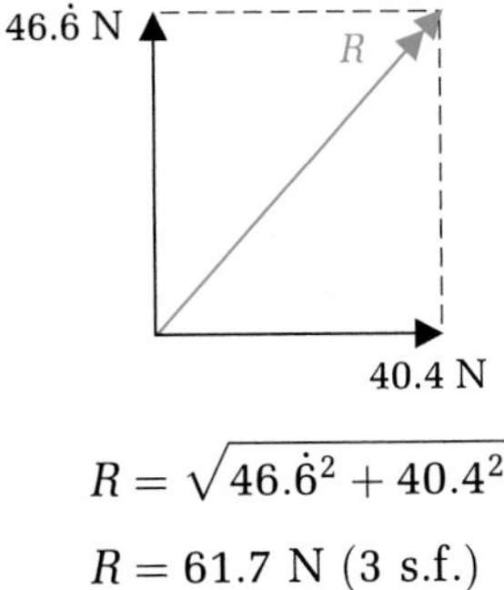

$$R = \sqrt{46.\dot{6}^2 + 40.4^2}$$

$$R = 61.7 \text{ N (3 s.f.)}$$

Example 2

A uniform ladder of mass 5 kg and length 4 m is placed on a rough horizontal floor and against a smooth vertical wall. A woman of mass 60 kg goes up the ladder. The ladder makes an angle of 60° with the horizontal and the coefficient of friction between the floor and the ladder is 0.5. How far up the ladder can the woman go before the ladder will start to slip?

Solution

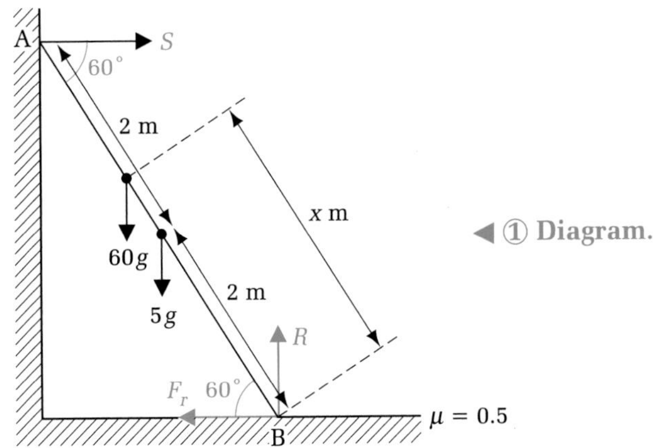

◀ ① **Diagram.**

The woman will get a distance x m from the bottom of the ladder.

Resolve ↑ ◀ ② **Resolve.**

$$R - 5g - 60g = 0$$
$$R = 65g$$
$$R = 637 \text{ N}$$

Resolve →

$$S - F_r = 0$$
$$S = \mu R$$
$$S = 0.5 \times 637$$
$$S = 318.5 \text{ N}$$

↻B clockwise ◀ ③ **Moments.**

$$S\sin 60° \times 4 - 60g \times \sin 30° \times x - 5g \times \sin 30° \times 2 = 0$$
$$318.5 \times \tfrac{\sqrt{3}}{2} \times 4 - 294x - 49 = 0$$
$$1054.32 - 294x = 0$$
$$1054.32 = 294x$$
$$x = 3.59 \text{ m (3 s.f.)}$$

Alternatively calculate the perpendicular distances.

The woman can get 3.59 m up the ladder from its base. The exact distance in reality will depend on the spacing of the rungs.

15.1 Equilibrium of Rigid Bodies

Exercise

Technique

1 **a**

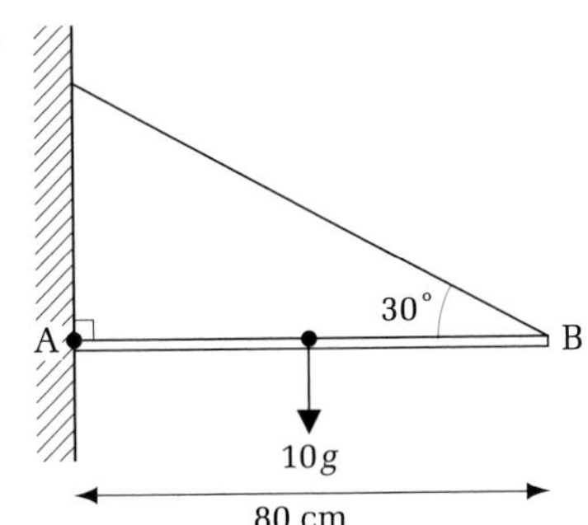

b

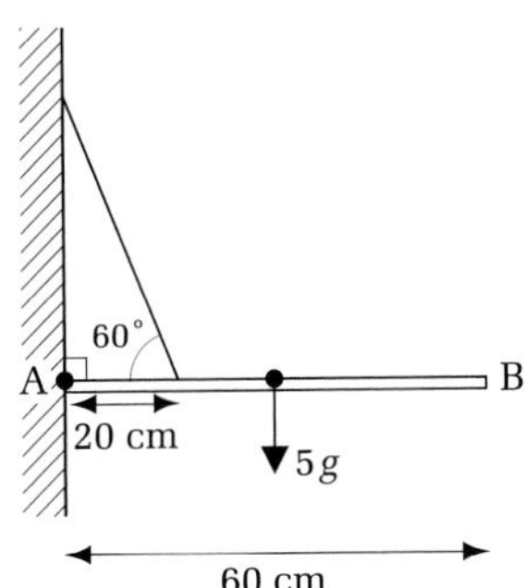

The diagrams show *uniform* rods AB hinged at A being held in equilibrium by a piece of string. For each one, determine:

i the tension in the string
ii the horizontal and vertical components of the reaction at the hinge
iii the magnitude and direction of the reaction at the hinge A.

2 **a**

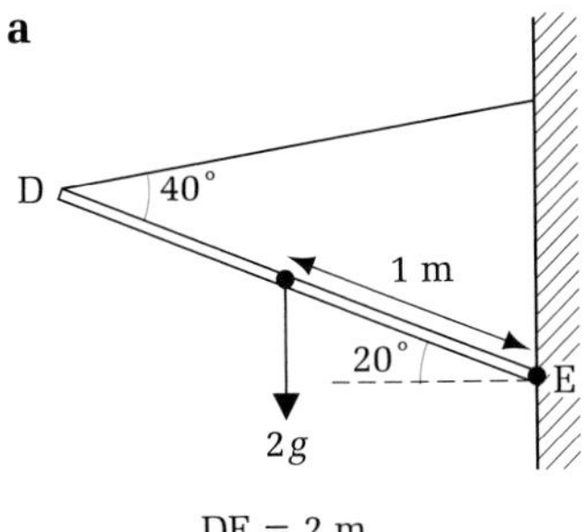

b

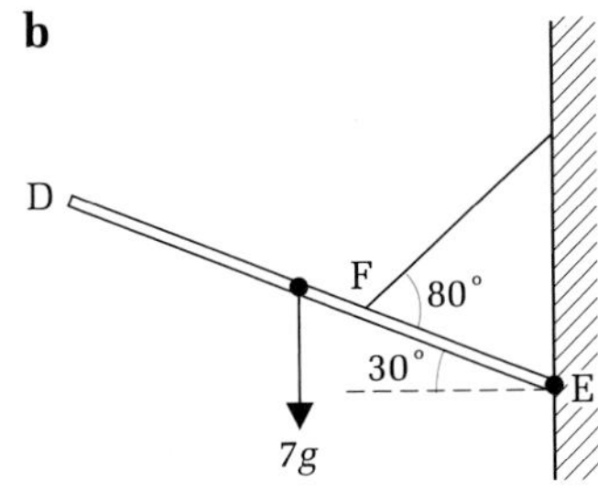

The diagrams show uniform rods DE hinged at E and being held in equilibrium by a light inextensible wire. Taking $g = 10\text{ m s}^{-2}$, calculate:

i the tension in the wire
ii the horizontal and vertical components of the reaction at the hinge
iii the reaction at the hinge E in magnitude and direction form.

3

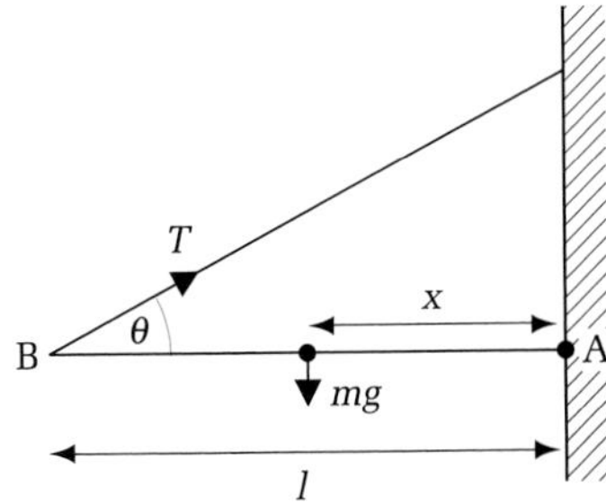

The diagram shows a rod AB with mass m and length l hinged at A. It is held in equilibrium by a wire with tension T and inclined at angle θ to the rod. The position of the centre of mass of the rod is a distance x from A.

a For $m = 7$ kg, $l = 3.5$ m, $x = 2$ m and $T = 90$ N find:
 i the angle θ
 ii the magnitude of the reaction at the hinge.

b For $m = 2$ kg, $l = 20$ cm, $x = 5$ cm and $T = 24$ N, calculate the angle θ.

c For $l = 1.2$ m, $x = 0.5$ m, $T = 80$ N and $\theta = 30°$, determine the mass m of the rod.

4 A uniform rod MN is placed against a horizontal and vertical surface as shown in the diagram. The horizontal surface is rough and the vertical surface is smooth. Take $g = 10\,\text{m s}^{-2}$.

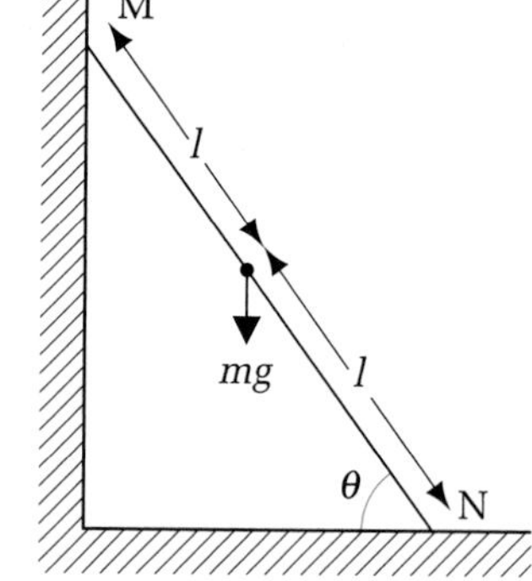

a Calculate the normal reaction forces at M and N and the frictional force at N when:
 i $\theta = 50°$ and $m = 8$ kg
 ii $\theta = 60°$ and $m = 5$ kg
 iii $\theta = 70°$ and $m = 15$ kg.

b The rod is now in limiting equilibrium and has mass 8 kg. Determine the angle θ when the coefficient of friction between the rod and the horizontal surface is:
 i 0.4 **ii** 0.5 **iii** 0.8

5 A uniform rod of length 4 m and mass 10 kg is supported by a smooth circular bar at B, as shown in the diagram. The end A of the rod rests on a rough horizontal surface.

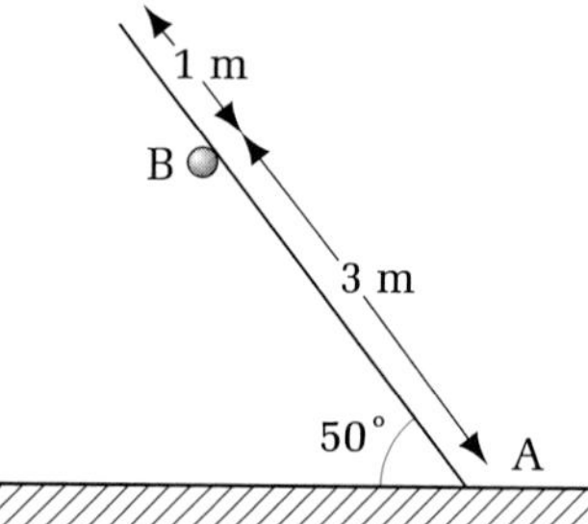

a State the direction of the reaction of the bar on the rod.

b Find:
 i the size of the reaction of the bar on the rod at B
 ii the size of the reaction on the rod at A
 iii the frictional force acting on the rod at A
 iv the coefficient of friction between the rod and the surface, if the rod is in limiting equilibrium.

6 A uniform rod is placed against a rough vertical surface and on a rough horizontal surface so that it is in limiting equilibrium. The rod is inclined at an angle of θ to the horizontal. The coefficient of friction of the vertical surface is 0.3 and the horizontal surface is 0.7. Find the angle θ.

Contextual

1

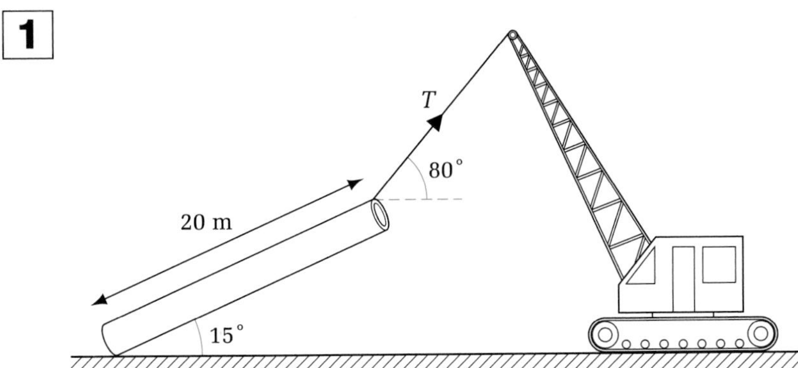

A uniform water pipe of mass 2 tonnes is being held in the position shown by a crane. Determine:

a the tension in the wire

b the normal reaction between the ground and the pipe

c the frictional force acting on the pipe

d the coefficient of friction between the ground and the pipe if the pipe is in limiting equilibrium.

2 A uniform ladder, of mass of 15 kg and length 6 m, is placed against a smooth vertical wall and on a rough horizontal floor. The ladder makes an angle of 70° with the horizontal. Work out all the forces acting on the ladder.

3 A person of mass 55 kg goes up a uniform ladder of mass 5 kg and length 3 m, which makes an angle of 55° with the horizontal. The ladder rests against a smooth vertical wall and on a rough horizontal floor. The coefficient of friction between the floor and the ladder is 0.5. Determine how far up the ladder the person can go before the ladder starts to slip.

4 A uniform ladder has a length of 7 m and a mass of 8 kg. It is placed against a rough vertical wall with coefficient of friction 0.4 and on a rough horizontal floor of coefficient of friction 0.8. Calculate the acute angle the ladder makes with the horizontal if the ladder is in limiting equilibrium.

15.2 Three Force Principle

An alternative approach for solving the folding table problem is called the **three force principle**.

See Section 15.1.

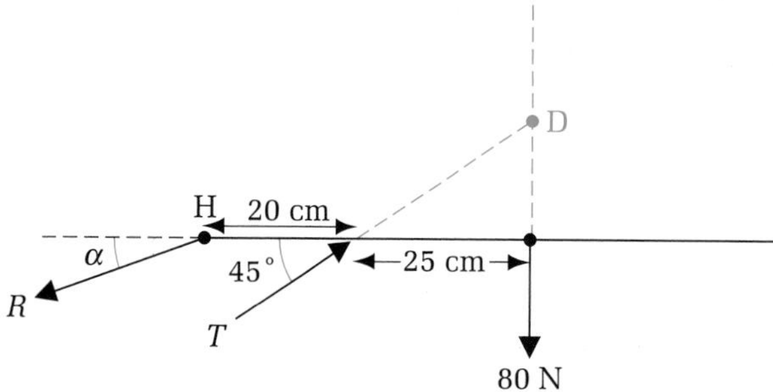

When the lines of action of the thrust and weight are extended, they cross at a point, D. The reaction at H could be represented by a force R acting at an angle α to the horizontal. The overall moment of this system of forces must be zero because the system is still in equilibrium. If moments are taken about D, then the only way that the system can have an overall moment of zero is if the line of action of R passes through the point D, as shown.

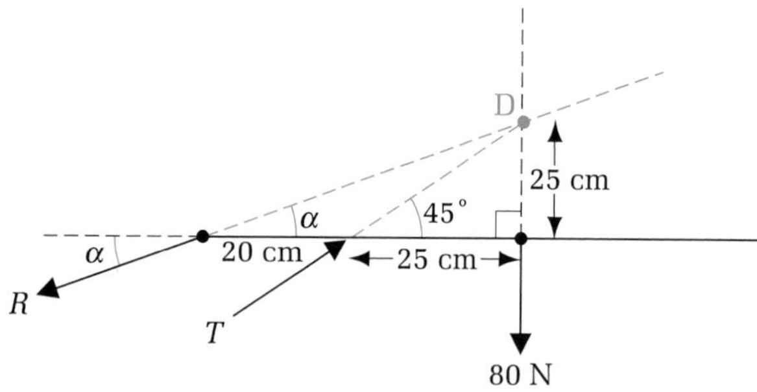

By using trigonometry the angle α can be calculated:

$$\tan\alpha = \tfrac{25}{45}$$

$$\alpha = 29.1^\circ \text{ (1 d.p.)}$$

$\alpha = \tan^{-1}\left(\tfrac{25}{45}\right)$ or $\arctan\left(\tfrac{25}{45}\right)$

The magnitudes of the forces can be calculated using Lami's theorem, the triangle of forces or resolving. For example, to find the tension:

$$\frac{T}{\sin 60.9^\circ} = \frac{80}{\sin 164.1^\circ}$$

$$T = \frac{80 \times \sin 60.9^\circ}{\sin 164.1^\circ}$$

$$T = 255 \text{ N (3 s.f.)}$$

Multiply by sin 60.9°.

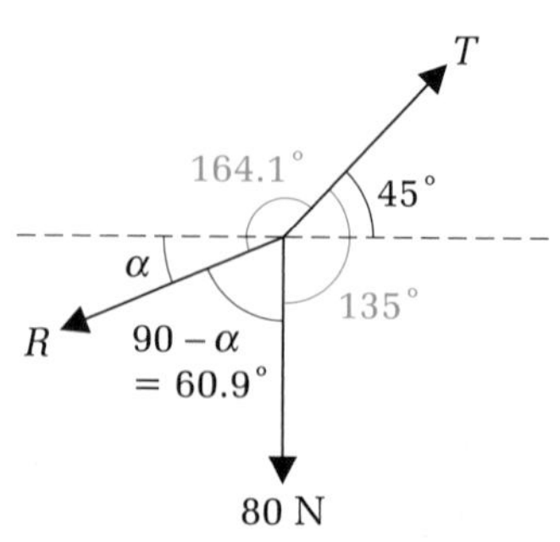

Overview of method

Step ① Draw a diagram with the lines of action of the three forces extended to cross at one point.

Step ② Calculate any angles from the lengths on the diagram.

Step ③ Use Lami's theorem, triangle of forces or resolving of forces as appropriate.

Example

A uniform ladder has a mass of 30 kg and is placed on a rough horizontal floor and against a smooth vertical wall. The ladder is placed at an angle of 30° to the horizontal and it is just about to slip. Determine the angle of friction by using the three force principle. Calculate the resultant reaction between the ladder and the floor.

Solution

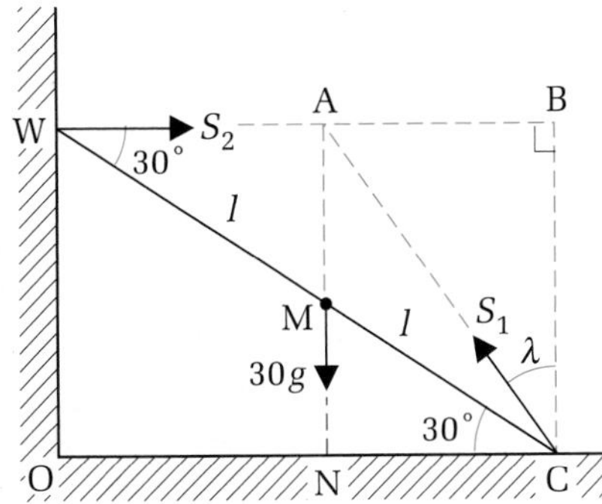

Let the ladder's length be $2l$. The triangle ABC can be used to find the angle of friction λ.

Using trigonometry in triangles CMN and CWO.

$$AB = l\cos 30^\circ$$

$$BC = 2l\sin 30^\circ$$

Substitute for AB and BC.

$$\tan\lambda = \frac{AB}{BC}$$

$$= \frac{l\cos 30^\circ}{2l\sin 30^\circ}$$

Use $\cos 30^\circ = \frac{\sqrt{3}}{2}$ and $\sin 30^\circ = \frac{1}{2}$.

$$= \frac{\frac{\sqrt{3}}{2}}{2 \times \frac{1}{2}}$$

$$\tan\lambda = \frac{\sqrt{3}}{2}$$

$$\lambda = 40.9^\circ \text{ (1 d.p.)}$$

Resolve ↑

$$S_1\cos\lambda - 30g = 0$$

Add $30g$.

$$S_1\cos 40.9^\circ = 30g$$

Divide by $\cos 40.9^\circ$.

$$S_1 = \frac{30 \times 9.8}{\cos 40.9^\circ}$$

$$S_1 = 389 \text{ N (3 s.f.)}$$

15.2 Three Force Principle
Exercise

Technique

1 **a**

b

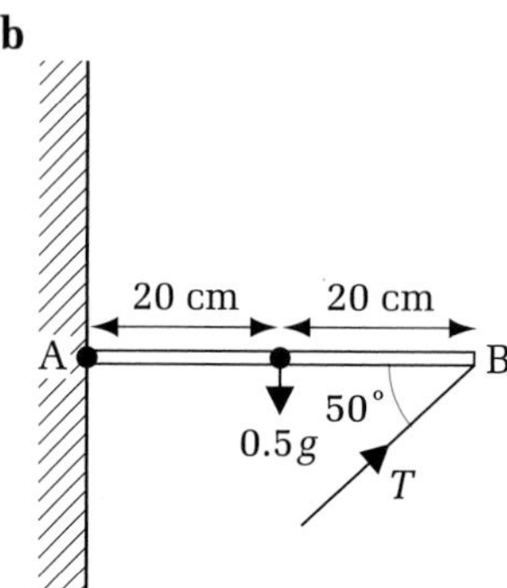

The diagrams above show a rod AB held horizontally by a force T.

i Using the three force principle, determine the direction and magnitude of the reaction at the hinge A.

ii Determine the magnitude of T.

2 A rod of length 8 m and mass 10 kg rests against a smooth vertical surface and a rough horizontal surface. Calculate:

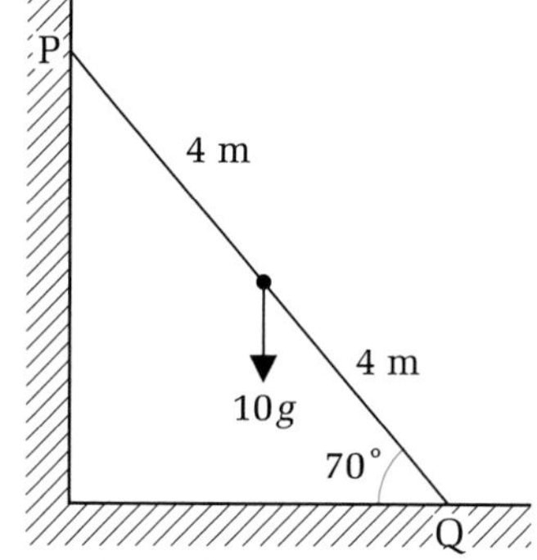

a the direction of the resultant reaction at Q

b the magnitude of the resultant reaction at Q

c the normal reaction at P.

3 A uniform rod of length $4l$ and mass m is placed against a smooth vertical surface and on a rough horizontal surface. The angle between the rod and the horizontal is $60°$ when the rod is just on the point of slipping. Determine:

a the angle of friction

b the coefficient of friction

c the resultant reaction between the horizontal surface and the rod.

15.3 Frameworks

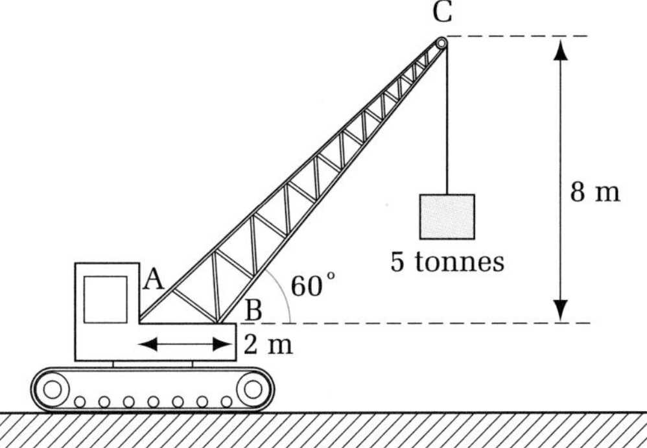

A crane is holding a mass of 5 tonnes as shown. How strong do the members AC and BC have to be? Assume the members AC and BC are light and rigid. The structure is taken to be in equilibrium. All the joints are assumed to be smoothly pin-jointed. This enables the joint to move freely.

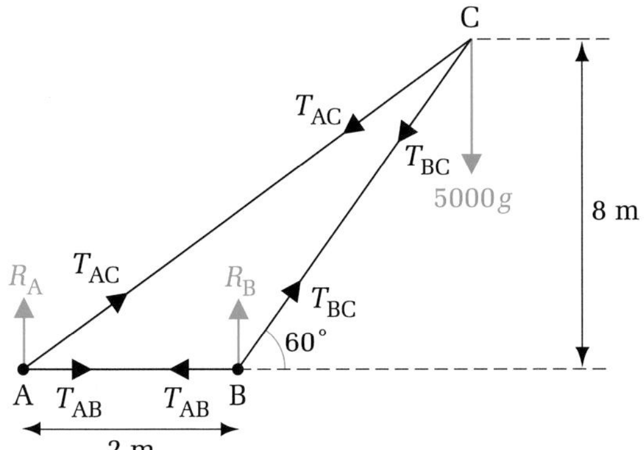

R_A and R_B are external forces. They must be vertical to balance the $5000g$. The horizontal forces at A and B are internal forces.

The diagram has been simplified to a three rod problem. There must be reactions at points A and B. Mark on all the forces in the rods as tensions. If the tensions turn out to be negative, then they will be thrusts.

The problem can now be solved by resolving the forces for the whole system and then by taking moments. The tensions and thrusts in the rods can be found by resolving at each joint. This can be done because each joint must also be in equilibrium.

Overview of method

Step ① Diagram marking on all the forces in the members as tensions.

Step ② Resolve the forces into two perpendicular directions (usually horizontally and vertically).

Step ③ Take moments about hinge (or point with most unknown forces acting on it).

Step ④ Resolve at each point to determine each force in the member.

Example

The framework shown is hinged at A. The rods can be assumed light and pin-jointed. Work out:

a the value of Q

b the forces in BC, AB, CD, CA and AD, stating whether they are tensions or thrusts

c the magnitude and direction of the reaction at A.

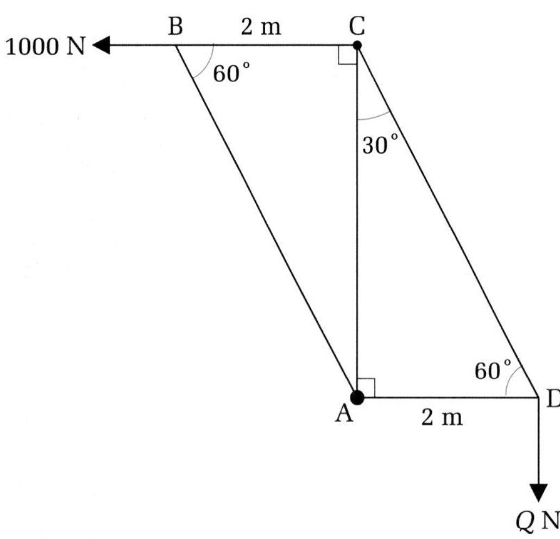

Solution

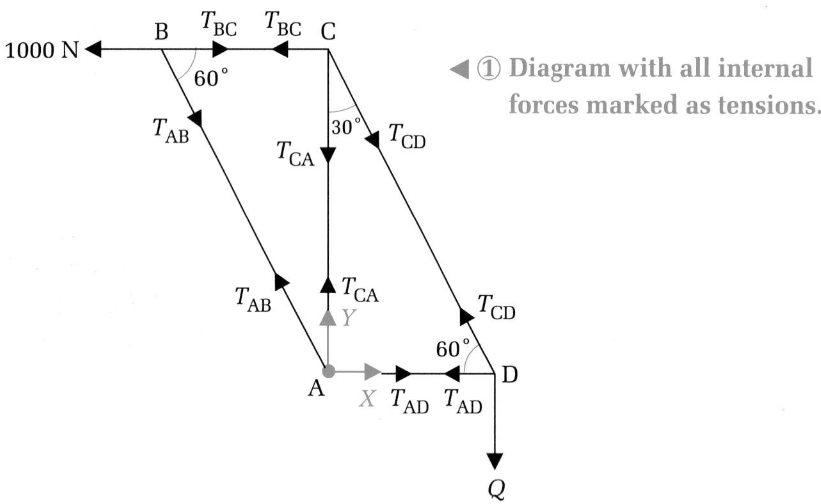

◀ ① Diagram with all internal forces marked as tensions.

a Resolve ↑ for whole framework.

◀ ② Resolve the forces for the whole framework.

$$Y - Q = 0$$

$$Y = Q \qquad [1]$$

Internal forces can be ignored (since they are in equal and opposite pairs).

Resolve →

$$X - 1000 = 0$$

$$X = 1000\ \text{N}$$

This information is not needed for part **a** but it will be used later in the solution.

↻A clockwise ◀ ③ Take moments about hinge.

$$2 \times Q - 1000 \times CA = 0$$

$$2Q = 1000 \times CA$$

$$Q = 500 \times CA$$

Calculate the distance CA using trigonometry.

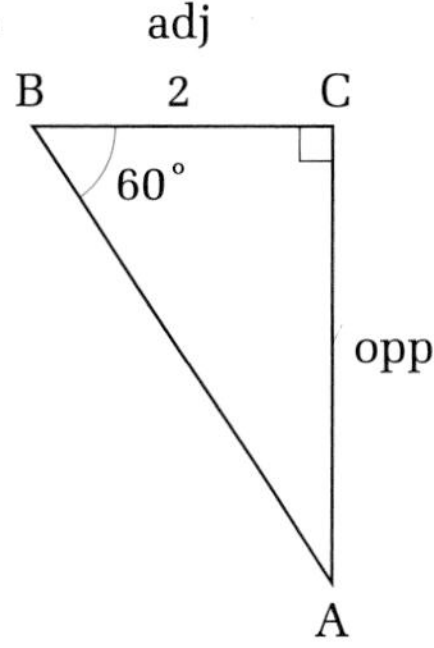

$$CA = 2 \times \tan 60°$$

$$CA = 2\sqrt{3}$$

Substitute for CA to find Q

$$Q = 500 \times 2\sqrt{3}$$

$$Q = 1000\sqrt{3}$$

No units since these were stated with Q in the question.

b Resolve at point B: ◀ ④ Resolve forces at each point to find the tensions (or thrusts).

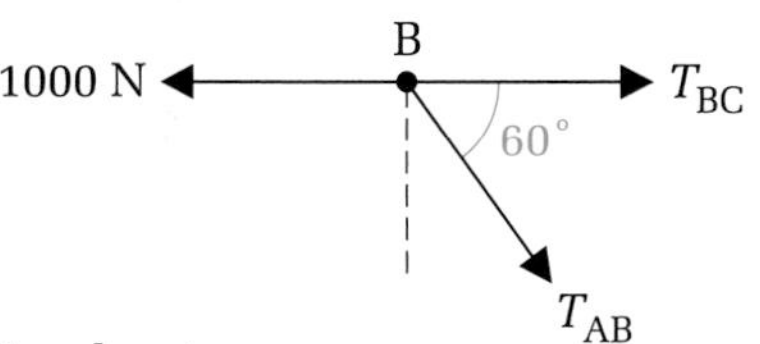

Resolve ↑

$$-T_{AB} \sin 60° = 0$$

$$T_{AB} = 0$$

Resolve →

$$T_{BC} - 1000 = 0$$

$$T_{BC} = 1000 \text{ N (tension)}$$

Resolve at point A:

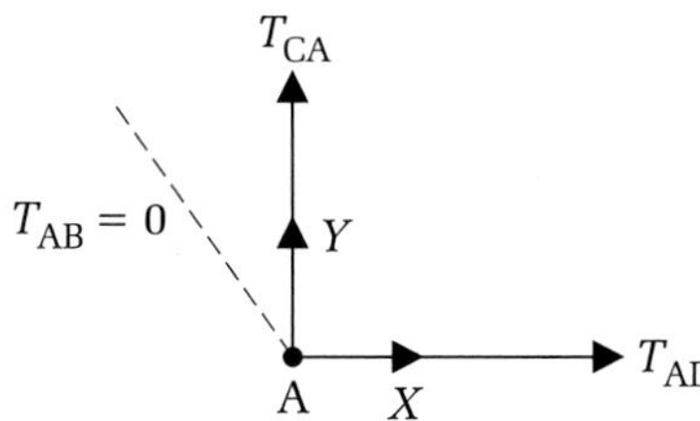

An alternative involves resolving at C since T_{BC} is known.

Resolve →

$$X + T_{AD} = 0$$

$$T_{AD} = -X$$

$$T_{AD} = -1000 \text{ N}$$

$$T_{AD} = 1000 \text{ N (thrust)}$$

Resolve ↑

$$Y + T_{CA} = 0$$

$$T_{CA} = -Y$$

$$T_{CA} = -1000\sqrt{3}$$

$$T_{CA} = 1000\sqrt{3} \text{ N (thrust)}$$

From equation [1], $Y = Q = 1000\sqrt{3}$

Resolve at point D:

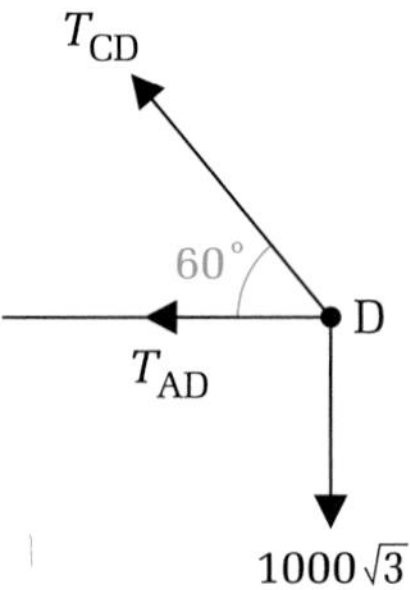

Resolve ←

$$
\begin{aligned}
T_{AD} + T_{CD}\cos 60° &= 0 \\
-1000 + T_{CD} \times \tfrac{1}{2} &= 0 \\
T_{CD} \times \tfrac{1}{2} &= 1000 \\
T_{CD} &= 2000 \text{ N (tension)}
\end{aligned}
$$

So the forces in the rods are:

$T_{AB} = 0$ N (rod could be removed)

$T_{BC} = 1000$ N (tension)

$T_{CD} = 2000$ N (tension)

$T_{AC} = 1000\sqrt{3}$ N (thrust)

$T_{AD} = 1000$ N (thrust)

c Magnitude and direction of reaction at hinge.

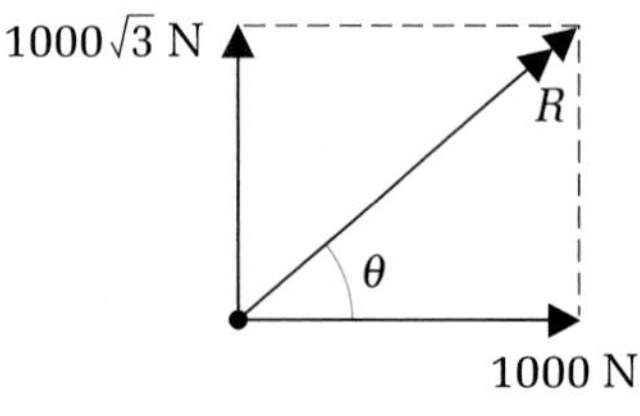

$$
\begin{aligned}
R &= \sqrt{(1000\sqrt{3})^2 + 1000^2} \\
&= 2000 \text{ N}
\end{aligned}
$$

$$
\begin{aligned}
\tan\theta &= \frac{1000\sqrt{3}}{1000} \\
\tan\theta &= \sqrt{3} \\
\theta &= 60°
\end{aligned}
$$

Reaction at the hinge is 2000 N acting at 60° to AD (anticlockwise).

15.3 Frameworks
Exercise

Technique

All the frameworks in this exercise are in equilibrium.

1 **a** Find the reaction forces at A and C.

b Find the forces acting in the rods AB, BC and AC, stating whether they are tensions or thrusts.

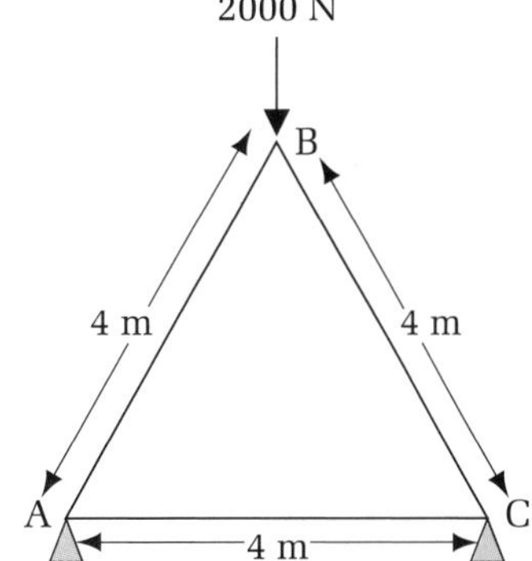

2 **a** Determine the reactions at A and D.

b Determine the forces in all the rods, stating whether they are tensions or thrusts.

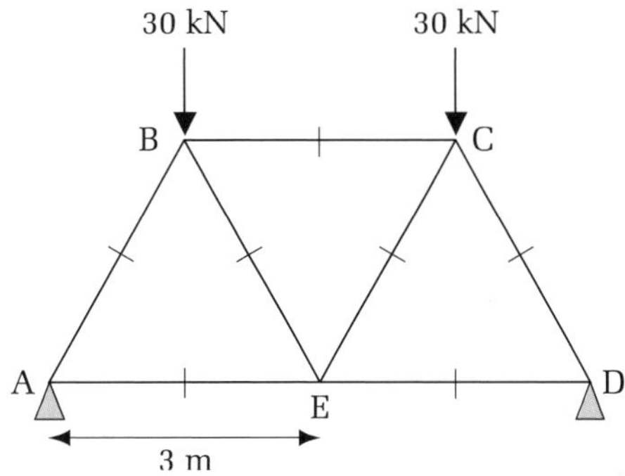

3 A rod system is hinged at A.
Calculate:

a the magnitude of the force P

b the angle ABC

c the forces acting in all the rods

d the magnitude and direction of the reaction at the hinge A.

State which rods are in tension and which rods could be replaced by inextensible strings. Are there any rods which could be removed?

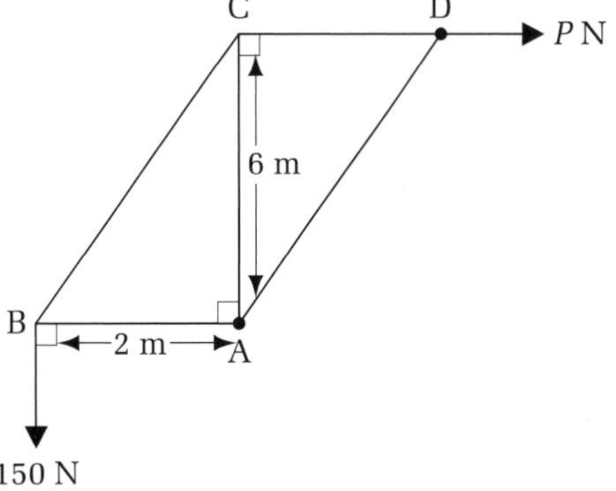

4 Determine the forces in the rods AB, BC, AC and BD. State which of the rods are in tension.

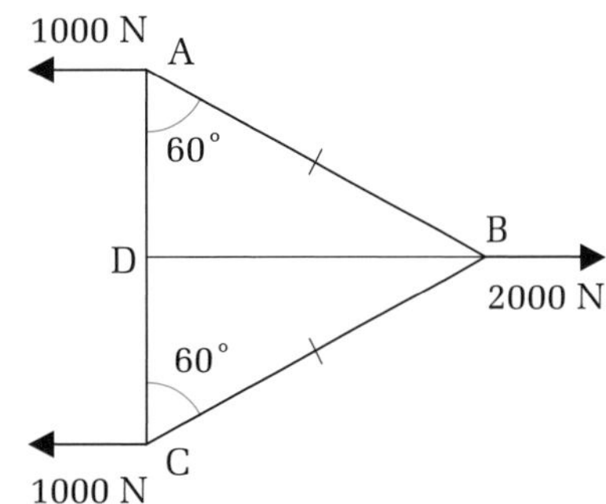

Contextual

1

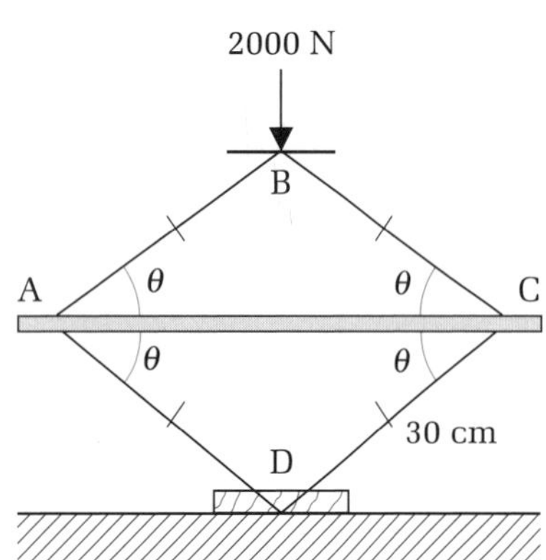

A jack is used to raise a car. Calculate the forces in the rods when:

a $\theta = 60^\circ$ **b** $\theta = 40^\circ$ **c** $\theta = 10^\circ$

State any assumptions that you have made.

2

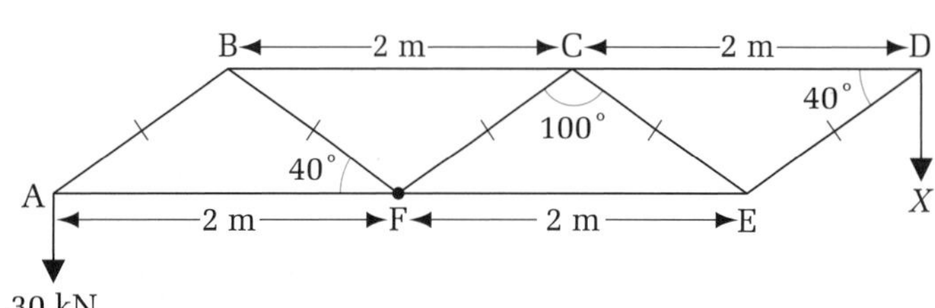

The diagram shows a model of a crane where F is the pivot. The crane can be assumed to be stationary. Calculate:

a the value of the load X

b the forces in all the rods, stating which ones are in compression (thrust).

3

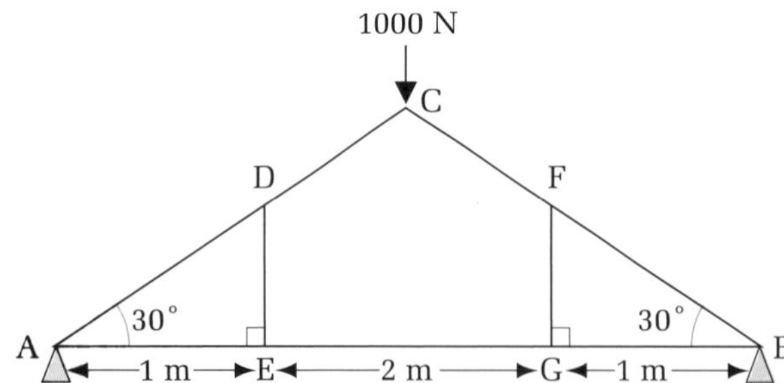

The diagram shows the design for a roof support in equilibrium. Determine:

a the reactions at A and B

b the forces in each member stating whether they are tensions or thrusts.

Consolidation

Exercise A

1 Tom and Peter carry a uniform ladder, which remains horizontal. The ladder is 7 m long and has mass 45 kg. Tom holds one end of the ladder and Peter holds it at a point x metres from the other end.

a Peter carries $\frac{2}{3}$ of the weight of the ladder.

i Draw a diagram that models this situation.

ii Use the model to find the value of x.

b Explain briefly what would happen if $x > 3.5$.

(*NICCEA*)

2

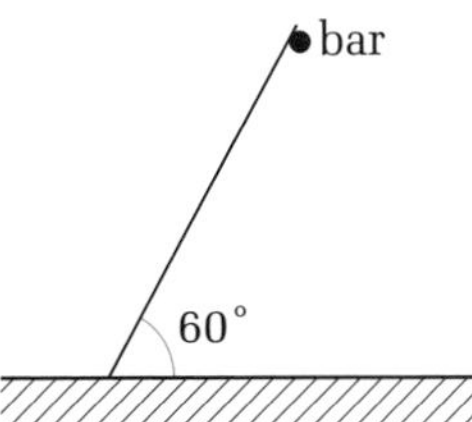

A uniform plank, of mass m and length $2a$, has one end resting on rough ground and the other resting on a smooth horizontal bar. The plank makes an angle of 60° with the ground, which is horizontal.

a Draw a clear diagram to show the forces acting on the plank. Clearly label each force.

b Show that the magnitude of the force that the bar exerts on the plank is $\frac{1}{4}mg$.

c Find the minimum value of the coefficient of friction between the plank and the ground if the plank is to remain at rest.

(*AEB*)

3

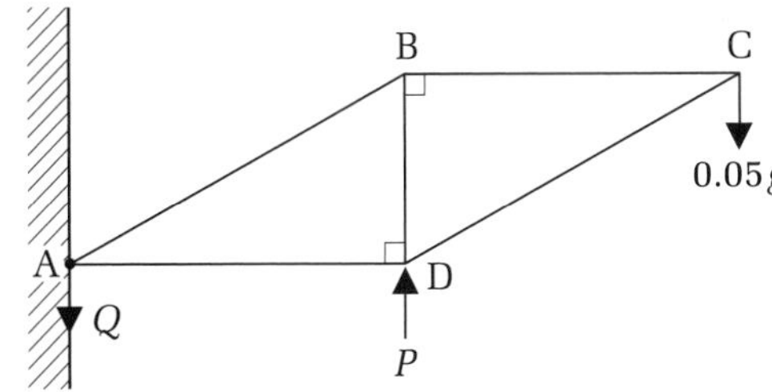

The figure shows a system of light pin-jointed rods resting in a vertical plane. The system is smoothly hinged to a vertical wall at A and supported at D by a vertical force P. A particle of mass of 0.05 kg is suspended from C. Rods AB and CD are each 0.13m long. Rods BC and AD are each 0.12 m long and horizontal. The vertical rod BD is 0.05 m long. Take $g = 10\text{ m s}^{-2}$.

a Explain why the reaction, Q, at the hinge A must be a vertical force. Find P and Q in newtons.

b Name one rod in which the force is a tension.

c Find the forces in each of the rods BC, DC, AB and BD.

(*NICCEA*)

Exercise B

1 A uniform plank AB, of length 4 m and weight 200 N, rests horizontally on two supports at C and D, where AC = 0.5 m and AD = 3.2 m, when a load of W N is attached at B.

a Given that $W = 84$, find the reactions on the plank at C and D.
b Find the greatest value of W for which the plank remains in equilibrium. *(WJEC)*

2 The foot of a uniform ladder of mass m rests on rough horizontal ground and the top of the ladder rests against a smooth vertical wall. When a man of mass $4m$ stands at the top of the ladder the system is in equilibrium with the ladder inclined at 60° to the horizontal. Show that the coefficient of friction between the ladder and the ground is greater than or equal to $\frac{3\sqrt{3}}{10}$. *(AEB)*

3

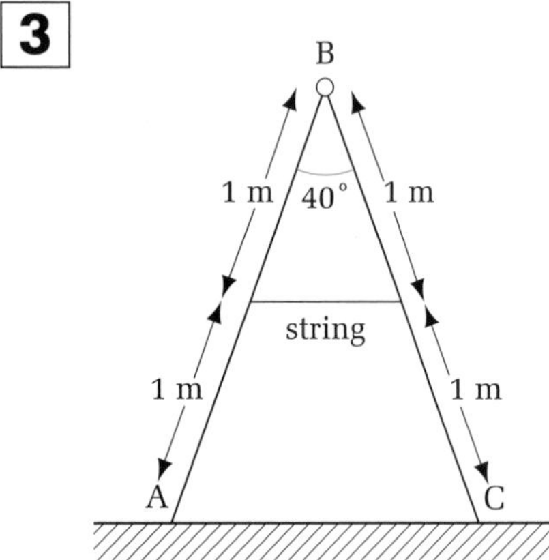

A step ladder may be modelled as two equal uniform rods AB and BC each of length 2 m and of mass 10 kg, freely hinged at B and braced by a light, inextensible string attached to the midpoint of each rod. The step ladder is resting on a smooth horizontal floor and the angle ABC is 40°.

a Explain briefly why the internal forces in the hinge at B are horizontal.
b Draw a diagram showing all four forces acting on the rod BC, including those acting in the hinge and the string.
c By resolving and by taking moments about a suitable point, or otherwise, calculate the tension in the string.
d Suppose that the floor is rough and the string is cut. What is the least value of the coefficient of friction between the rods and the floor so that the step ladder remains in equilibrium with the same angle ABC? *(OCSEB)*

Applications and Activities

1

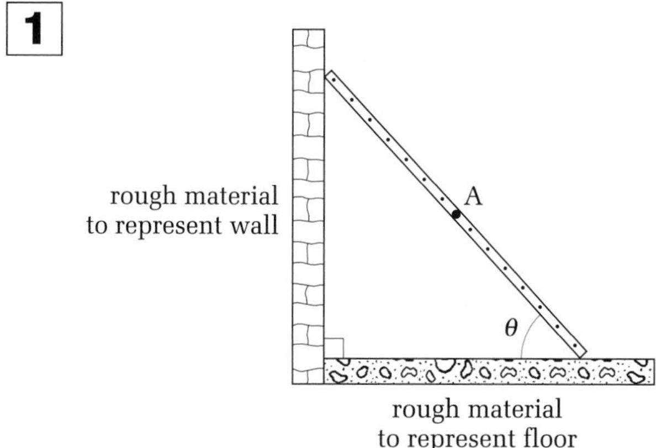

An experimental model for a ladder is shown. Increase the mass at point A to simulate a person on the ladder. Record the mass that makes the ladder slide. Try different starting angles. Is there a best angle at which to erect a ladder? Use another mass to simulate a person standing at the bottom of the ladder. How does this affect your results?

2

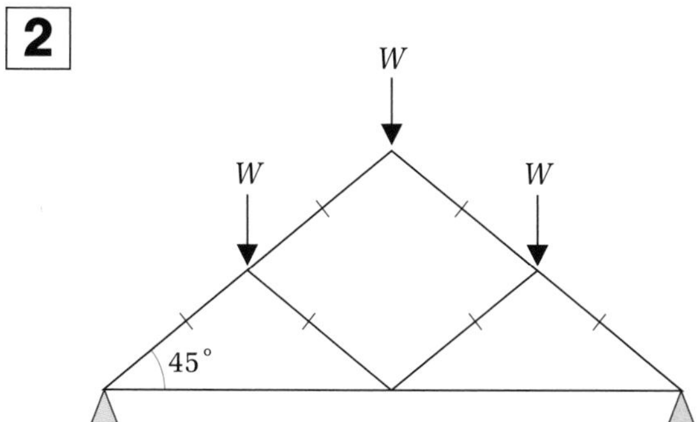

The framework shown is one design for a roof support. Investigate the tensions and thrusts in this framework. How do your findings compare with theoretical results. Try to design your own roof support.

Summary

- The two conditions for a rigid body to be in equilibrium are

  1. The overall force must be zero.
  2. The overall moment must be zero.

- The three force principle states that three forces in equilibrium must have their lines of action passing through the same point.

16 Projectiles

What you need to know

- How to solve quadratic equations.
- How to solve problems using the uniform acceleration formulas.
- How to resolve velocities into two perpendicular directions.

Review

1 Solve the quadratic equations given below.

a $20t - 5t^2 = 0$ **b** $20 = 25t - 5t^2$ **c** $30 = 35t - 4.9t^2$

2 **a** A ball is thrown vertically upwards with a speed of $20\,\text{m s}^{-1}$. Calculate the time the ball takes to return to its starting position.

b A train has an initial velocity of $10\,\text{m s}^{-1}$ which increases to $50\,\text{m s}^{-1}$ over a distance of 400 m. Determine the acceleration of the train.

c A ball is dropped. What is the speed of the ball after 3 seconds?

3 **a**

b

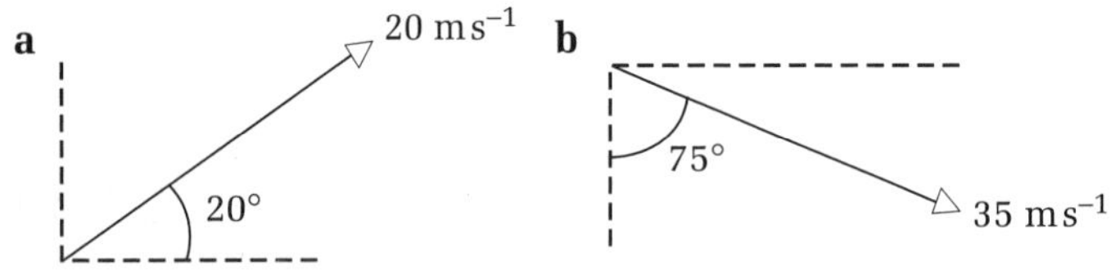

Resolve the velocities shown into horizontal and vertical components.

Additional pure

For this chapter you will also need to know the following trigonometrical identities:

$$2\sin\theta\cos\theta = \sin 2\theta$$

$$\sec\theta = \frac{1}{\cos\theta}$$

$$1 + \tan^2\theta = \sec^2\theta$$

16.1 Horizontal Projection

Hardraw Force is the tallest waterfall in England. The water drops a height of 29.3 metres. How long does the water take to fall? How far does the water travel horizontally? The speed of the water will be assumed to be $2\ \mathrm{m\,s^{-1}}$ horizontally at the top of the fall. Air resistance will be neglected. The vertical speed of the water will be zero at the top of the waterfall.

Hardraw Force is near Hawes in Wensleydale, North Yorkshire.

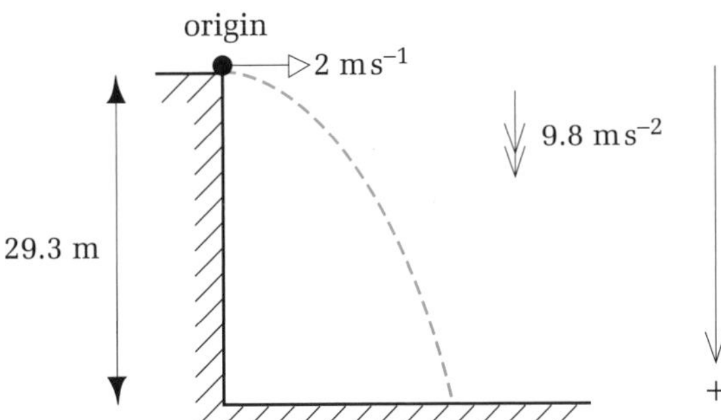

The motion of the water will be treated in two perpendicular directions, horizontally and vertically. It will be helpful to summarise the information in horizontal and vertical directions.

Horizontal $\rightarrow$	Vertical $\downarrow$
$s = ?$	$s = 29.3$ m
$u = 2\ \mathrm{m\,s^{-1}}$	$u = 0$
$t = ?$	$v = ?$
$a = 0$	$a = 9.8\ \mathrm{m\,s^{-2}}$
	$t = ?$

◀ **Take vertically downwards as positive.**

Air resistance is being neglected. This means that the horizontal velocity will always be $2\ \mathrm{m\,s^{-1}}$. The horizontal velocity will remain constant. The vertical motion will be used to find the time, t, to fall to the bottom of the waterfall.

$$s = ut + \tfrac{1}{2}at^2$$
$$29.3 = 0 \times t + \tfrac{1}{2} \times 9.8 \times t^2$$
$$29.3 = 4.9t^2$$
$$5.98 = t^2$$
$$t = 2.445\ \mathrm{s}$$

Write the uniform acceleration equation.
Substitute the values.
Divide by 4.9.
Take the square root.

This time can be used to calculate the horizontal distance travelled.

$$s = ut + \tfrac{1}{2}at^2$$
$$s = 2 \times 2.445 + \tfrac{1}{2} \times 0 \times 2.445^2$$
$$s = 4.89\ \mathrm{m}$$

Write down the uniform acceleration formula. Remember $a = 0\ \mathrm{m\,s^{-2}}$ horizontally.

This horizontal distance seems quite large. The initial assumption of $2\ \mathrm{m\,s^{-1}}$ for the horizontal speed could represent a river after a heavy fall of rain.

How far would the water travel horizontally, if the initial speed was $0.5\ \mathrm{m\,s^{-1}}$ or $1\ \mathrm{m\,s^{-1}}$?

D M
I A

What difference would air resistance make? Air resistance would act to decelerate the water in both directions. This would have the effect of increasing the time for the water to fall and reducing the speed.

Overview of method

Step ① Sketch a diagram. Choose point of projection as the origin and state the positive direction.
Step ② Summarise the information, horizontally and vertically.
Step ③ Use the uniform acceleration formulas vertically.
Step ④ Use $s = ut$ (constant velocity formula) horizontally.

Steps ③ and ④ can be swapped depending on the information that is given. If two pieces of information about the horizontal motion are given, then Step ④ will come before Step ③.

Example

A particle is projected horizontally. It travels 4 m horizontally and 10 m vertically downwards in time T seconds. Taking $g = 10\text{ m s}^{-2}$, determine:

a the value of T
b the initial speed of projection
c the final speed of the particle
d the angle at which the ball hits the ground.

Solution

a

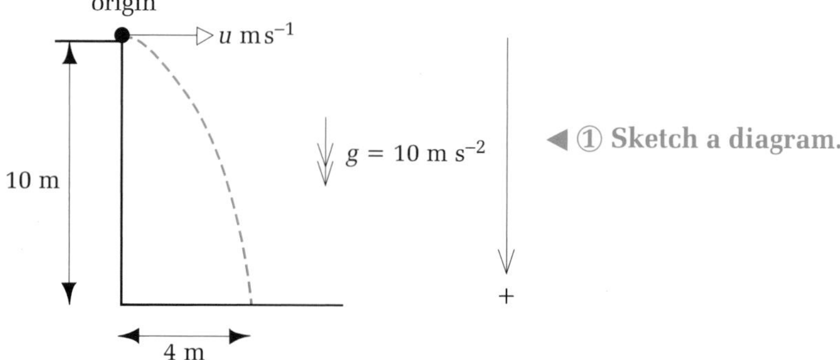

◀ ① Sketch a diagram.

The positive direction is chosen as downwards because the vertical motion of the particle will be downwards.

Horizontal →	Vertical ↓
$s = 4\text{ m}$	$s = 10\text{ m}$
$u = ?$	$u = 0\text{ m s}^{-1}$
$t = T$	$a = 10\text{ m s}^{-2}$
	$t = T$

◀ ② Summary.

Use vertical motion to find T:

$s = ut + \frac{1}{2}at^2$ ◀ ③ Use uniform acceleration formula vertically.

$10 = 0 + \frac{1}{2} \times 10 \times T^2$ Substitute the numbers.

$10 = 5T^2$ Divide by 5.

$2 = T^2$ Take the square root.

$T = \sqrt{2}$

No units are included for T because the units were stated in the question. So T is just a number.

b Use horizontal motion.

$s = ut$ ◀ ④ Use $s = ut$ horizontally.

$4 = uT$ — Substitute the numbers. Use $T = \sqrt{2}$.

$4 = u\sqrt{2}$ — Divide by $\sqrt{2}$.

$\frac{4}{\sqrt{2}} = u$ ◀ Rationalise the denominator $\left(\times \frac{\sqrt{2}}{\sqrt{2}}\right)$.

$u = \frac{4\sqrt{2}}{2}$ — Cancel by 2 in the fraction.

$u = 2\sqrt{2}\,\text{m s}^{-1}$

c The final speed of the particle must combine the horizontal and vertical components. The horizontal component is $2\sqrt{2}\,\text{m s}^{-1}$ from part **b**. Use vertical motion to find v

$v^2 = u^2 + 2as$ — Use $v^2 = u^2 + 2as$ just in case the value of T is incorrect.

$v^2 = 0^2 + 2 \times 10 \times 10$

$v^2 = 200$

$v = \sqrt{200}$ — Square root. $\sqrt{200} = \sqrt{100 \times 2} = 10\sqrt{2}$

$v = 10\sqrt{2}\,\text{m s}^{-1}$

For the final speed, use Pythagoras' theorem

$\text{speed}^2 = (10\sqrt{2})^2 + (2\sqrt{2})^2$

$\text{speed}^2 = 200 + 8$

$\text{speed} = \sqrt{208}$ — $\sqrt{208} = \sqrt{16 \times 13} = 4\sqrt{13}$

$\text{speed} = 4\sqrt{13}\,\text{m s}^{-1}$

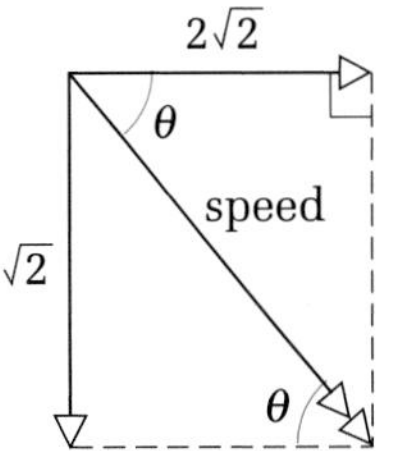

The final speed of the ball is $4\sqrt{13}\,\text{m s}^{-1}$.

d For the angle at which the ball hits the ground, use trigonometry

$\tan\theta = \frac{10\sqrt{2}}{2\sqrt{2}}$

$\tan\theta = 5$

$\theta = 78.7°$

The ball hits the ground at $78.7°$.

16.1 Horizontal Projection
Exercise

Technique

1 An object is projected horizontally with a speed of $5\,\mathrm{m\,s^{-1}}$. It hits the ground 3 s later. Calculate:

a the horizontal distance covered
b the vertical distance fallen.

2 A body, of mass 50 g, is thrown horizontally with a speed of $8\,\mathrm{m\,s^{-1}}$. The body hits the ground after dropping a vertical distance of 20 m. Determine:

a the time taken for the body to hit the ground
b the horizontal distance travelled by the body
c the vertical speed of the body as it hits the ground.

3 A particle is projected horizontally. In 3 seconds it has travelled a horizontal distance of 3 m. Taking $g = 10\,\mathrm{m\,s^{-2}}$, work out:

a the particle's speed of projection
b the particle's vertical speed after 3 seconds
c the particle's overall speed after 3 seconds, in surd form.

4 A body is projected horizontally. It covers a horizontal distance of 6 m and drops a vertical distance of 30 m at the same time. Find:

a the time taken
b the speed of projection
c the final velocity of the particle, in magnitude and direction form.

5 A particle is projected with a horizontal speed of $2U\,\mathrm{m\,s^{-1}}$. The particle hits the ground with a vertical speed of $6U\,\mathrm{m\,s^{-1}}$. The acceleration due to gravity is $g\,\mathrm{m\,s^{-2}}$. Find expressions for:

a the time taken for the particle to hit the ground
b the horizontal distance covered
c the vertical distance fallen
d the speed of the particle as it hits the ground.

6 A particle is projected horizontally with a speed of $10\,\mathrm{m\,s^{-1}}$. It hits the ground with a vertical speed of $20\,\mathrm{m\,s^{-1}}$. Calculate:

a the time taken for the particle to hit the ground
b the horizontal distance travelled
c the overall speed, in surd form, with which the particle hits the ground
d the angle at which the particle hits the ground, measured from the horizontal.

Contextual

1 In a film, a car is driven off a horizontal bridge at $15\ \mathrm{m\,s^{-1}}$. The bridge is 40 m above the water. Calculate:

a the time taken for the car to hit the water after leaving the bridge
b the horizontal distance travelled by the car
c the overall speed of the car when it hits the water.

State two key assumptions that you have made during your analysis.

2 A stone is thrown horizontally off a cliff, with a speed of $4\ \mathrm{m\,s^{-1}}$. It takes 4 s for the stone to land on the beach below. Find:

a the horizontal distance travelled by the stone
b the height of the cliff
c the velocity, in magnitude and direction form, of the stone as it lands on the beach.

3 A pencil case is thrown horizontally out of a classroom window. The window is 5 m above the ground and the pencil case lands 1.5 m from the wall. Taking $g = 10\ \mathrm{m\,s^{-2}}$ find:

a the speed with which the pencil case was thrown
b the angle at which the pencil case hit the ground, measured from the horizontal.

4 The Angel Falls in Venezuela is the highest waterfall in the world at 979 m. If the water lands 30 m from the foot of the waterfall, determine:

a the initial speed of the water, assuming it is horizontal
b the final speed of the water
c the angle at which it hits the surface of the water at the bottom of the waterfall.

16.2 Inclined Projection

In 1986, Paul Thorburn set a new record for the longest kick in a Rugby Union International. His kick covered a distance of 64.22 m when Wales played Scotland in the Five Nations Championship. What was the initial speed of the ball?

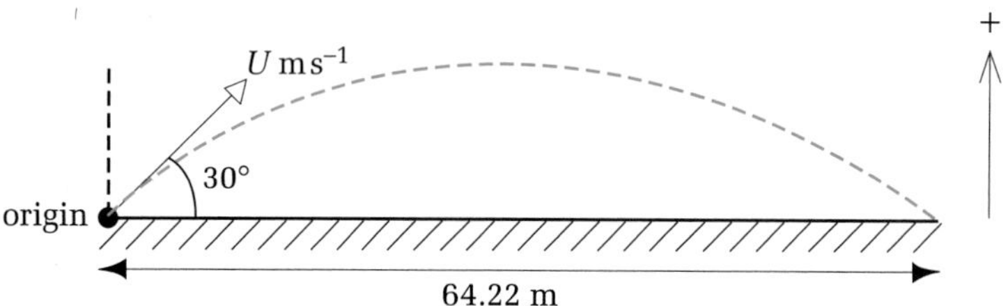

Let the initial speed be $U\,\text{m s}^{-1}$. Assume that the angle of projection was 30°.

The approach will be to resolve the velocity into two components. The uniform acceleration formulas will then be used to solve the problem.

Horizontal →	Vertical ↑
$u = U\cos 30°\,\text{m s}^{-1}$	$u = U\sin 30°\,\text{m s}^{-1}$
$s = 64.22$ m	$s = 0$ m
$t = ?$	$t = ?$
	$a = -9.8\,\text{m s}^{-2}$

Note the positive direction for vertical motion is now upwards. This is because the ball is kicked upwards initially. This means $a = -9.8\,\text{m s}^{-2}$.

When the ball lands on the ground, the vertical displacement is zero again. The ball has returned to the same vertical level as its starting position. The ground is assumed level.

For vertical motion:

$$s = ut + \tfrac{1}{2}at^2$$ ◀ Use uniform acceleration formula.

$$0 = U\sin 30°t + \tfrac{1}{2}(-9.8)t^2$$

Substitute the values. $\sin 30° = \frac{1}{2}$

$$0 = \tfrac{1}{2}Ut - 4.9t^2$$

Factorise by taking out a common factor of t.

$$0 = t(\tfrac{1}{2}U - 4.9t)$$ ◀ Put bracketed expression equal to zero to find other solution.

$$t = 0 \text{ or } \tfrac{1}{2}U - 4.9t = 0$$ ◀ Add $4.9t$

$$\tfrac{1}{2}U = 4.9t$$

Divide by 4.9.

$$t = \frac{U}{9.8}$$

For horizontal motion:

$$s = ut$$

$$64.22 = U\cos 30^\circ\left(\frac{U}{9.8}\right)$$

$$\frac{64.22 \times 9.8}{\cos 30^\circ} = U^2$$

$$726.7 = U^2$$

$$26.96 = U$$

$$U = 27.0$$

Replace t by $\frac{U}{9.8}$. Multiply by 9.8 and divide by cos 30°.

Square root.

This speed will be an underestimate for the angle of 30° because air resistance will need to be overcome.

Overview of method

The steps remain the same as for horizontal projection except the initial velocity must be resolved into two perpendicular components.

Step ① Diagram. State origin and positive direction.
Step ② Summarise the information. Resolve the velocity into two components.
Step ③ Use the uniform acceleration formulas for vertical motion.
Step ④ Use $s = ut$ for horizontal motion.

Example 1

A javelin is thrown at 20 m s^{-1} at an angle of 40°. Calculate:

a the maximum height reached
b the time taken to reach its maximum height
c the distance travelled horizontally when it reaches the ground.

Assume javelin starts at ground level.

Solution

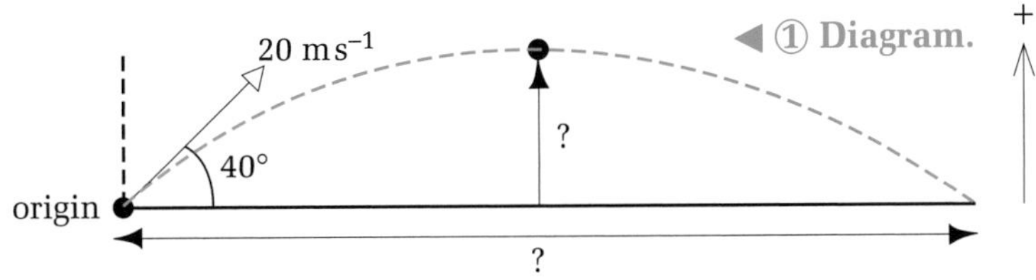

The initial vertical motion will be upwards so choose this as the positive direction.

a Horizontal → ◀ ② Summarise the information.

$u = 20\cos 40^\circ$ m s^{-1}
$t = ?$
$s = ?$

Vertical ↑

$u = 20\sin 40^\circ$ m s^{-1}
$v = 0$ m s^{-1}
$s = ?$
$t = ?$
$a = -9.8$ m s^{-2}

Resolve the velocities. For maximum height $v = 0$.

For vertical motion:

$v^2 = u^2 + 2as$ ◀ ③ Use a uniform acceleration formula.

$0 = (20\sin 40°)^2 + 2 \times (-9.8)s$

Add 19.6s.

$19.6s = (20\sin 40°)^2$

Divide by 19.6.

$s = \dfrac{(20\sin 40°)^2}{19.6}$

$s = 8.43\text{ m}$

b $t = ?$

$v = u + at$ ◀ Formula.

$0 = 20\sin 40° - 9.8t$

Add 9.8t.

$9.8t = 20\sin 40°$

Divide by 9.8.

$t = \dfrac{20\sin 40°}{9.8}$

$t = 1.31\text{ s}$

c

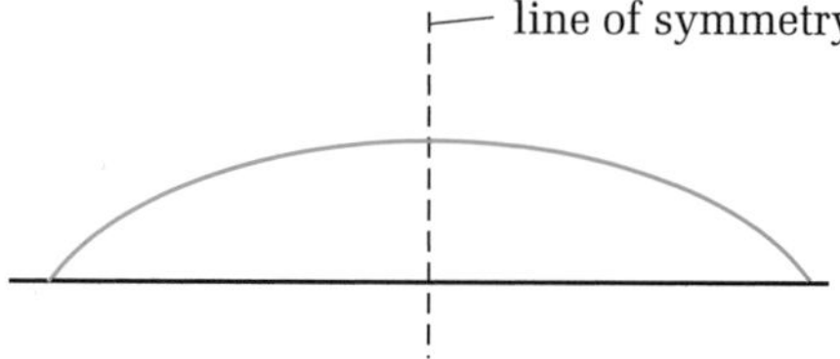

The sketch shows that the projectile path, or *trajectory*, looks symmetrical. If this is the case then the time to reach the ground will be double the time to reach its maximum height.

Vertical ↑

$u = 20\sin 40°\text{ m s}^{-1}$

$s = 0\text{ m}$

$t = ?$

$a = -9.8\text{ m s}^{-2}$

$s = ut + \frac{1}{2}at^2$ ◀ Formula.

$0 = (20\sin 40°)t - 4.9t^2$ ◀ Factorise.

$0 = t(20\sin 40° - 4.9t)$

$t = 0$ or $20\sin 40° - 4.9t = 0$ ◀ Add 4.9t.

Put expression in brackets equal to zero.

$4.9t = 20\sin 40°$

Divide by 4.9t.

$t = \dfrac{20\sin 40°}{4.9}$

$t = 2.62\text{ s}$

This shows that the projectile trajectory is symmetrical.
For the horizontal motion:

However, it is always better to calculate values than assume the path is symmetrical.

$s = ut$

$s = (20\cos 40°) \times 2.62$

$s = 40.2\text{ m}$

Example 2

A gun fires a shell from a cliff top, 100 m above the sea. The shell is projected at 200 m s^{-1} at an angle of $45°$ above horizontal. Taking $g = 10 \text{ m s}^{-2}$, find:

a the time taken for the shell to land in the sea

b the horizontal distance the shell travels.

Solution

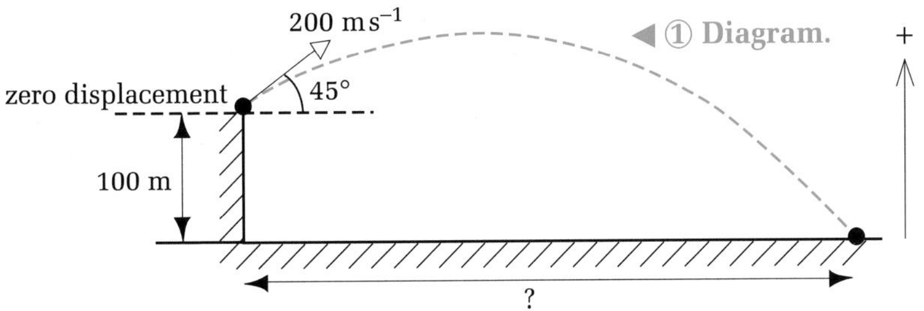

The starting position is the zero level for displacement.

a Horizontal →

$u = 200\cos 45° \text{ m s}^{-1}$

$t = ?$

$s = ?$

Vertical ↑

$u = 200\sin 45° \text{ m s}^{-1}$

$s = -100 \text{ m}$

$a = -10 \text{ m s}^{-2}$

$t = ?$

◀ ② Summary.

The final displacement is negative because it is below the shell's starting position.

For vertical motion:

◀ ③ Use uniform acceleration formula.

$$s = ut + \tfrac{1}{2}at^2$$

$$-100 = (200\sin 45°)t + \tfrac{1}{2} \times (-10)t^2$$

$$-100 = 200\frac{\sqrt{2}}{2}t - 5t^2$$

$$-100 = 100\sqrt{2}t - 5t^2$$

$$5t^2 - 100\sqrt{2}t - 100 = 0$$

$$t^2 - 20\sqrt{2}t - 20 = 0$$

Substitute and use $\sin 45° = \frac{\sqrt{2}}{2}$

$200\frac{\sqrt{2}}{2} = 100\sqrt{2}$

Add $5t^2$ and subtract $100\sqrt{2}t$ to simplify.

Divide by 5.

◀ Solve using the quadratic formula.

$$t = \frac{20\sqrt{2} \pm \sqrt{(-20\sqrt{2})^2 - 4 \times 1 \times (-20)}}{2 \times 1}$$

$$t = \frac{20\sqrt{2} \pm \sqrt{800 + 80}}{2}$$

$$t = \frac{20\sqrt{2} \pm 29.66}{2}$$

$$t = -0.69 \text{ or } t = 28.97$$

The solution $t = -0.69$ s can be ignored.

$t = 29.0$ s (3 s.f.)

The shell cannot reach the sea 0.69 s *before* it was fired.

b For horizontal motion:

◀ ④ Use $s = ut$ horizontally.

$s = ut$

$s = (200\cos 45°) \times 28.97$

$s = 4098$ m (nearest metre)

In this case, the motion of the shell from its starting position is *not* symmetrical. A diagram is always useful to check on what is happening.

16.2 Inclined Projection

Exercise

Technique

1 A particle is projected at an angle of $60°$ above the horizontal with a speed of $40\ \text{m s}^{-1}$. Calculate:

- **a** the maximum height reached
- **b** the time taken to reach the maximum height
- **c** the time taken to return to the horizontal surface
- **d** the horizontal distance travelled.

2

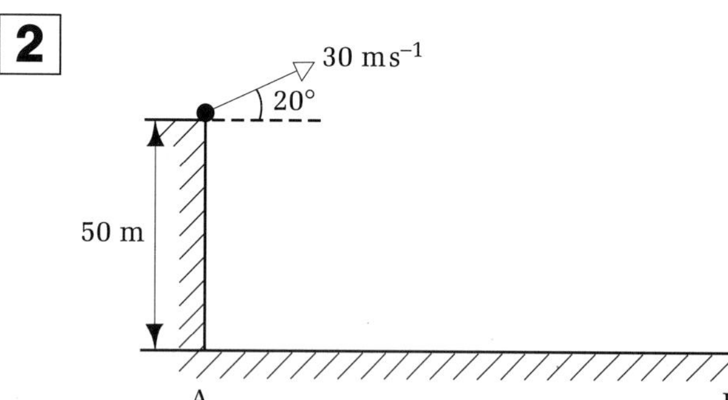

An object is projected as shown in the diagram. Find:

- **a** the time taken to reach the horizontal surface AB
- **b** the horizontal distance travelled
- **c** the speed of the particle as it lands on AB.

3

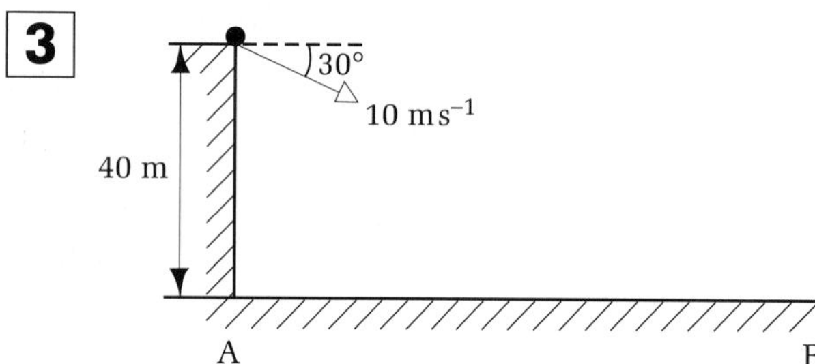

A body is projected as shown. Determine:

- **a** the horizontal distance covered
- **b** the velocity of the body as it lands on the surface AB.

4 A body is projected at an angle of $45°$ above the horizontal from a horizontal surface. The body lands on the horizontal surface after travelling a horizontal distance of 50 m. Taking $g = 10\ \text{m s}^{-2}$, work out the speed of projection leaving your answer in surd form.

5 A particle is projected from a horizontal surface with an initial velocity of $(20\mathbf{i} + 39.2\mathbf{j})\ \text{m s}^{-1}$ where **i** and **j** are horizontal and vertical unit vectors respectively. Calculate:

- **a** the time taken to return to the horizontal surface
- **b** the horizontal distance covered.

Hint:
$\rightarrow\ u = 20\ \text{m s}^{-1}$
$\uparrow\ u = 39.2\ \text{m s}^{-1}$

Contextual

1 A javelin is thrown at an angle of 40° above the horizontal with a speed of $30\,\mathrm{m\,s^{-1}}$. Find:

- **a** the maximum height reached by the javelin
- **b** the time taken to reach its maximum height
- **c** the horizontal distance travelled when the javelin is at its maximum height
- **d** the time taken for the javelin to land on the ground
- **e** the horizontal distance covered by the javelin.

State three key assumptions that you have made.

2 A long jumper jumps a horizontal distance of 7 m when she takes off at an angle of 30° above the horizontal. By modelling the long jumper as a particle, determine estimates for:

- **a** her initial speed
- **b** the length of time she was in the air.

Explain why her initial speed is likely to be an underestimate.

3 A tennis ball is hit at a height of 2.5 m above the ground. The ball is hit at $25\,\mathrm{m\,s^{-1}}$ at an angle of 5° below the horizontal. Calculate:

- **a** the horizontal distance covered when the ball first bounces
- **b** the speed with which the ball hits the ground.

4 A golfer hits a golf ball from a tee which is raised 5 m above ground level (assume horizontal). The ball is hit with a speed of $40\,\mathrm{m\,s^{-1}}$ at an angle of $\tan^{-1}\left(\frac{3}{4}\right)$ above the horizontal. By modelling the golf ball as a particle and taking $g = 10\,\mathrm{m\,s^{-2}}$, determine:

or $\arctan\left(\frac{3}{4}\right)$

- **a** the time taken for the ball to hit the ground
- **b** the distance between the tee and the position of the golf ball's first bounce.

5 A rugby ball is kicked at an angle of 45° above the horizontal. The ball rebounds off the bar which is 3.2 m above the ground and a horizontal distance of 20 m from where the ball was kicked. Work out:

- **a** the speed with which the ball was kicked
- **b** the time taken for the ball to hit the bar.

16.3 General Formulas for Projectile Motion

When preparing athletes, calculations can be carried out to find out the **range** for different angles of projection. Instead of calculating each range for each angle, a general formula would enable these calculations to be carried out more quickly. Other important quantities are the maximum height and the time to reach it.

The range is the horizontal distance covered.

Equation for the range and time of flight

What is the range when an object is projected with a speed $U\,\mathrm{m\,s^{-1}}$ at an angle of $\theta\,°$? The object will be modelled as a particle, the ground will be assumed horizontal and air resistance will be ignored. Assume the object is projected from *ground level.*

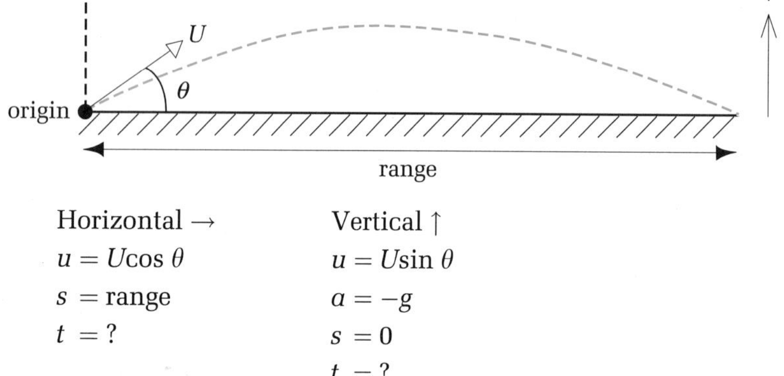

g is used to represent the acceleration due to gravity instead of using 9.8 or 10.

Horizontal →	Vertical ↑
$u = U\cos\theta$	$u = U\sin\theta$
$s = \text{range}$	$a = -g$
$t = ?$	$s = 0$
	$t = ?$

For vertical motion:

$$s = ut + \tfrac{1}{2}at^2$$ ◀ ③ Use uniform acceleration formula.

$$0 = (U\sin\theta)t + \tfrac{1}{2}(-g)t^2$$ Substitute the expressions.

$$0 = t(U\sin\theta - \tfrac{1}{2}gt)$$ Factorise.

$$U\sin\theta - \tfrac{1}{2}gt = 0 \text{ or } t = 0$$ Solve the equation.

$$U\sin\theta = \tfrac{1}{2}gt$$ Divide by g and multiply by 2.

$$\frac{2U\sin\theta}{g} = t$$

$$\textbf{time of flight} = \frac{2U\sin\theta}{g}$$

For horizontal motion:

$$s = ut$$

Replace t by $\frac{2U\sin\theta}{g}$

$$\text{range} = \frac{(U\cos\theta)(2U\sin\theta)}{g}$$

Collect $2\sin\theta\cos\theta$ together, because $2\sin\theta\cos\theta = \sin 2\theta$.

$$\text{range} = \frac{U^2(2\sin\theta\cos\theta)}{g}$$

$$\textbf{range} = \frac{U^2\sin(2\theta)}{g}$$

Maximum range and angle of projection

What do you think is the best angle for projection? What is the maximum horizontal distance covered? For the maximum range, $\sin 2\theta$ must take its maximum value.

$$\sin 2\theta = 1$$

$$2\theta = 90^\circ$$

$$\boldsymbol{\theta = 45^\circ}$$

The maximum value for a sine curve is 1.

The best angle for projection is 45° but remember this *only* applies when the ground is *level* and the object is *projected from ground level*. The range equation can now be used to find an equation for the maximum range.

$$\text{range} = \frac{U^2 \sin 2\theta}{g}$$

$$\textbf{maximum range} = \frac{U^2}{g}$$

$\sin 2\theta = 1$ when $\theta = 45^\circ$

In reality a javelin will need to be thrown at less than 45° to obtain maximum distance because the javelin is not launched from ground level.

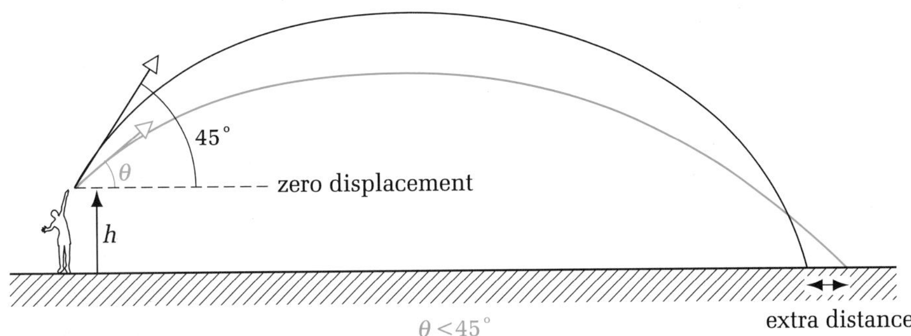

Maximum height

A formula for the maximum height and the time taken to reach it can be found. Remember that the maximum height occurs when the *vertical velocity is zero*.

Horizontal →	Vertical ↑
$u = U\cos\theta$	$u = U\sin\theta$
	$a = -g$
	$v = 0$
	$s = H$
	$t = ?$

For vertical motion:

$$v^2 = u^2 + 2as$$ ◀ **Formula.**

$$0 = (U\sin\theta)^2 + 2 \times (-g) \times H$$

$$0 = U^2\sin^2\theta - 2gH$$

$$2gH = U^2\sin^2\theta$$

$$\boldsymbol{H = \frac{U^2\sin^2\theta}{2g}}$$

Substitute the expressions into the formula.
Add $2gH$.
Divide by $2g$.

The time at which this maximum height occurs can also be found.
For vertical motion:

$$v = u + at$$

$$0 = U\sin\theta - gt$$

$$gt = U\sin\theta$$

$$\boldsymbol{t = \frac{U\sin\theta}{g}}$$

Substitute the expressions into the formula.
Add gt.
Divide by g.

Notice that the *time to reach the maximum height is half the time of flight*.

Equation of trajectory

During much of the analysis for projectiles, the time had to be calculated. To remove this step, an equation can be formed to relate the horizontal and vertical displacements. This equation will enable the path or trajectory of the projectile to be plotted without the need to calculate any times.

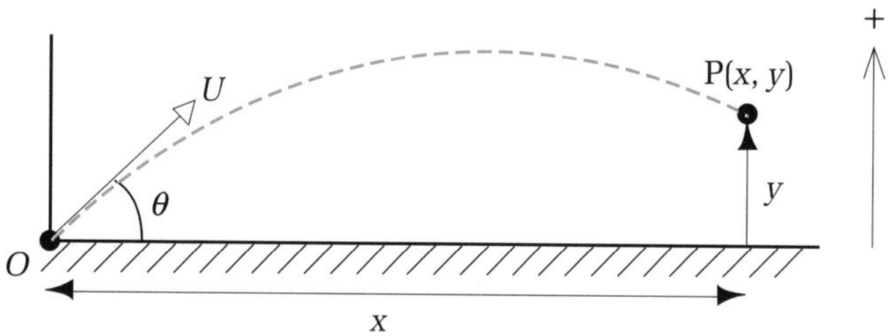

The equation of the trajectory is formed by eliminating time from the horizontal and vertical equations.

Horizontal →	Vertical ↑
$u = U\cos\theta$	$u = U\sin\theta$
$s = x$	$s = y$
$t = ?$	$a = -g$
	$t = ?$

For horizontal motion:

$$s = ut$$

$$x = (U\cos\theta)t$$

$$t = \frac{x}{U\cos\theta} \qquad [1]$$

Divide by $U\cos\theta$.

For vertical motion:

$$s = ut + \tfrac{1}{2}at^2$$

$$y = (U\sin\theta)t + \tfrac{1}{2}(-g)t^2$$

$$y = (U\sin\theta)t - \tfrac{1}{2}gt^2$$

Now t can be replaced with $\dfrac{x}{U\cos\theta}$ from equation [1]

$$y = U\sin\theta\left(\frac{x}{U\cos\theta}\right) - \frac{1}{2}g\left(\frac{x}{U\cos\theta}\right)^2$$

◀ U cancels and $\dfrac{\sin\theta}{\cos\theta} = \tan\theta$.

$$y = x\tan\theta - \frac{gx^2}{2U^2\cos^2\theta}$$

◀ $\dfrac{1}{\cos\theta} = \sec\theta$ so $\dfrac{1}{\cos^2\theta} = \sec^2\theta$.

$$y = x\tan\theta - \frac{gx^2(\sec^2\theta)}{2U^2}$$

Use $\sec^2\theta = 1 + \tan^2\theta$.

$$\boldsymbol{y = x\tan\theta - \frac{gx^2}{2U^2}(1 + \tan^2\theta)}$$

For given values of U, θ and y the equation is a quadratic in x. When U, x and y are given it is a quadratic in $\tan\theta$.

This equation is known as the **equation of the trajectory**. It is most commonly used for calculating the speed of projection or the angle of projection.

General equations for projectile motion

The equations you are expected to be able to prove are:

$$\textbf{range} = \frac{U^2\sin(2\theta)}{g}$$

$$\textbf{time of flight} = \frac{2U\sin\theta}{g}$$

$$\textbf{maximum height} = \frac{U^2\sin^2\theta}{2g}$$

$$\textbf{time to reach maximum height} = \frac{U\sin\theta}{g}$$

$$\textbf{maximum range} = \frac{U^2}{g} \textbf{ when } \theta = 45^\circ$$

Notation

U = initial speed of projection (m s^{-1})

θ = angle of projection (degrees)

g = value for the acceleration due to gravity (m s^{-2})

$$\mathbf{y = x\tan\theta - \frac{gx^2}{2U^2}(1 + \tan^2\theta)}$$

x = horizontal distance from starting position (m)
y = vertical distance from starting position (m)

The examples in this section will use the equations which have been proved. In some of the questions in the exercises, you will be asked to prove the equation before it can be used.

Overview of method

Step ① Draw a diagram.
Step ② Summarise the information.
Step ③ Use the appropriate formula.

Example 1

The range of a projectile is given by $R = \frac{V^2\sin(2\alpha)}{g}$, where V = initial speed; α = angle of projection; g = acceleration due to gravity. The range of the projectile is 200 m when it is fired at an angle of 20°. Calculate the initial speed of projection.

Solution

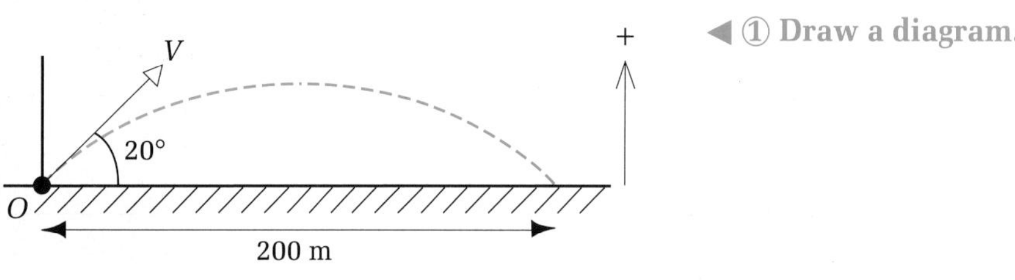

◀ ① Draw a diagram.

$R = 200$ m $\quad V = ?\quad \alpha = 20° \quad g = 9.8\,\text{m s}^{-2}$ ◀ ② Summarise the information.

$$R = \frac{V^2\sin(2\alpha)}{g}$$ ◀ ③ Use range equation.

$$200 = \frac{V^2\sin(2 \times 20°)}{9.8}$$

Substitute the numbers. g must be positive for these formulas.

$$200 = 0.0656V^2$$

Divide by 0.0656.

$$V^2 = \frac{200}{0.0656}$$

Take the square root.

$$V = 55.2\,\text{m s}^{-1}$$

Example 2

The equation for the trajectory for a projectile is given by:

$$y = x\tan\theta - \frac{gx^2}{2U^2}(1 + \tan^2\theta)$$

where y is the vertical displacement, x is the horizontal displacement, U is the speed of projection, θ is the angle of projection and g is the acceleration due to gravity. A tennis ball is hit at a height of 30 cm above the ground with a speed of $10\,\mathrm{m\,s^{-1}}$. The ball just clears the net which is 8 m away and is 1.2 m high. Taking $g = 10\,\mathrm{m\,s^{-2}}$, find the angle of projection.

Solution

◀ ① Diagram.

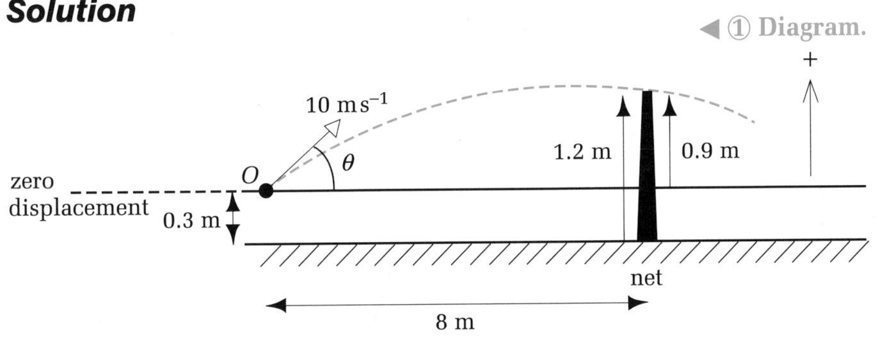

Take the starting position as the origin.

▼ ② Summary of the information.

$x = 8$ m $\quad y = 0.9$ m $\quad U = 10\,\mathrm{m\,s^{-1}}$ $\quad g = 10\,\mathrm{m\,s^{-2}}$ $\quad \theta = ?$

g taken as positive.

◀ ③ Write down equation of trajectory.

$$y = x\tan\theta - \frac{gx^2}{2U^2}(1 + \tan^2\theta)$$

Substitute the numbers.

$$0.9 = 8\tan\theta - \frac{10 \times 8^2}{2 \times 10^2}(1 + \tan^2\theta)$$

$$0.9 = 8\tan\theta - 3.2(1 + \tan^2\theta)$$

Multiply out the brackets.

$$0.9 = 8\tan\theta - 3.2 - 3.2\tan^2\theta$$

Rearrange to form a quadratic equation in $\tan\theta$.

$$3.2\tan^2\theta - 8\tan\theta + 4.1 = 0$$

The equation can be solved by using the quadratic formula.

$$\tan\theta = \frac{8 \pm \sqrt{(-8)^2 - 4 \times 3.2 \times 4.1}}{2 \times 3.2}$$

$$\tan\theta = \frac{8 \pm \sqrt{11.52}}{6.4}$$

$$\tan\theta = 1.78 \text{ or } 0.7197$$

$$\theta = 60.7^\circ \text{ or } 35.7^\circ$$

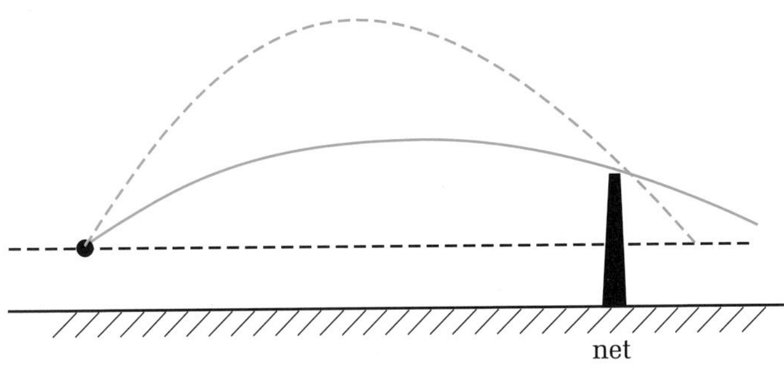

There are two possible answers for the angle of projection. From the diagram both can be seen to be sensible.

16.3 General Formulas for Projectile Motion

Exercise

Technique

1 A particle is projected from a horizontal surface with a speed V and an angle α measured from the horizontal. The acceleration due to gravity is g.

a Find expressions for:

i the time of flight (the time taken for the particle to return to the horizontal surface)

ii the range of the projectile

iii the maximum range and the corresponding angle of projection

iv the maximum height and the time to reach the maximum height.

b The coordinates of the particle at any instant are (x, y) where the origin is the starting position for the particle. Show that the equation of trajectory is:

$$y = x\tan\alpha - \frac{gx^2}{2V^2}(1 + \tan^2\alpha)$$

For the remainder of the questions in this exercise, the projectile equations can be used without proof.

2 An object is projected from a horizontal plane. It takes 10 s to return to the plane when the angle of projection is 60° to the horizontal. Calculate:

a the speed of projection

b the range of the projectile.

3 A projectile has a maximum horizontal range of 1 km.

a State the angle of projection.

b Determine the speed of projection.

4 A body is fired from a horizontal surface. Its range is 120 m when the speed of projection is $60\,\text{m}\,\text{s}^{-1}$. Find the two possible angles of projection.

5

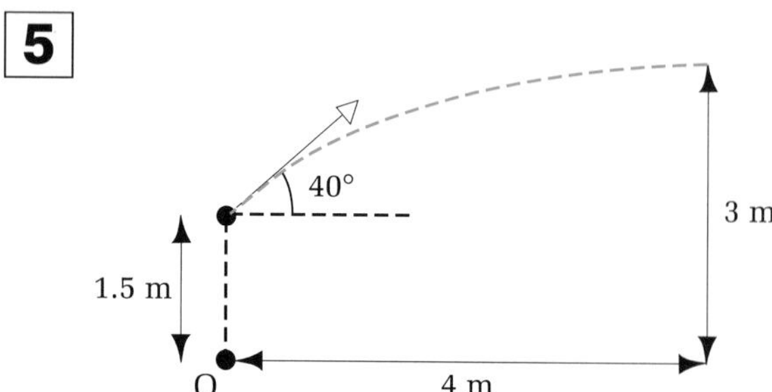

Find the speed of projection.

6 A particle is projected with a speed of $20\ \text{m s}^{-1}$ and reaches a maximum height of 10 m. Work out the angle of projection.

Contextual

1 A rugby ball is kicked into the air from a height h m above the ground, with a speed of $U\ \text{m s}^{-1}$ at an angle of $\alpha°$ above the horizontal.

a Find expressions for the maximum height the ball reaches and the time taken.

b A player kicks the ball at $30\ \text{m s}^{-1}$ from a height of 0.5 m above the ground. The ball reaches a maximum height of 40 m above the ground. Determine:

i the angle of projection

ii the time taken to reach the maximum height.

2 A cricket ball is hit with a speed of $V\ \text{m s}^{-1}$ at an angle of $\alpha°$ to the horizontal.

a Find an equation for T, the time of flight for the projectile.

b Show that an expression for the range of the ball is $\frac{V^2 \sin(2\alpha)}{g}$. State *three* assumptions that you have made.

3 A netball is thrown from a height h above the ground at an angle β to the horizontal. The initial speed of the ball is V and the acceleration due to gravity is g.

a Show that the equation of trajectory of the ball is

$$y = h + x\tan\beta - \frac{gx^2}{2V^2}(1 + \tan^2\beta)$$

b The player throws the ball from 1.2 m above the ground and it goes through a loop that is 2.5 m above the ground and 3 m from the player measured horizontally. The ball has an initial speed of $8\ \text{m s}^{-1}$. Find the two possible angles of projection.

Consolidation

Exercise A

1 A golfer hits a golf ball so that it moves with an initial speed of $40\,\text{m s}^{-1}$ at an angle of $20°$ above the horizontal.

a State two essential assumptions that you should make if you are to estimate the horizontal distance between the point where the ball was hit and the point where it hits the ground for the first time.

b Taking $g = 10\,\text{m s}^{-2}$, find this distance to the nearest metre.

c The ball is actually hit on a raised area that is higher than the ground where the ball lands for the first time. How would this affect the answer that you obtained in **b**?

(*AEB*)

2 A boy stands 5 m from a house and throws a ball towards an open window, the sill of which is 6 m above the point of projection. He projects the ball with speed $13\,\text{m s}^{-1}$ at an angle of $45°$ to the horizontal in a plane at right angles to the window.

a Using the equation of the path of a projectile, or otherwise, find at what distance below the sill the ball strikes the wall.

b If the ball had been projected by the boy at $14\,\text{m s}^{-1}$ from the same position, find, correct to one decimal place, the two possible angles of projection for the ball to just clear the sill.

c State *two* assumptions that are made in the modelling of the projectile motion of the ball.

(*NICCEA*)

3 A projectile is launched at ground level with speed V at an angle θ above the horizontal.

a Show that the range of the projectile is $\frac{V^2\sin(2\theta)}{g}$, and state any essential assumptions that you have to make to obtain this result.

b It is estimated that a good shot-putter tries to launch the shot at an angle of $45°$ above the horizontal, at a speed of $13\,\text{m s}^{-1}$ and from a height of 2 m. Taking $g = 10\,\text{m s}^{-2}$, find the range of the shot launched in this way.

c Also find the range of the shot of **b**, but ignoring the height of release and using the formula found in **a**. State whether or not the formula gives a good prediction, giving a reason for your answer.

(*AEB*)

Exercise B

1 A golf ball is hit from a point A and lands at a point B. The distance from A to B is 100 m and the ground between A and B is horizontal. During its flight, the golf ball just clears the top of a tree 20 m high situated midway between A and B. At A, the horizontal and vertical components of the velocity of the ball are $u\,\mathrm{m\,s^{-1}}$ and $v\,\mathrm{m\,s^{-1}}$, respectively. In this question, take $g = 10\,\mathrm{m\,s^{-2}}$.

a Show that $v = 20$.

b Find the time taken for the ball to travel from A to B.

c Find the value of u.

(NEAB)

2 A child hits a tennis ball.

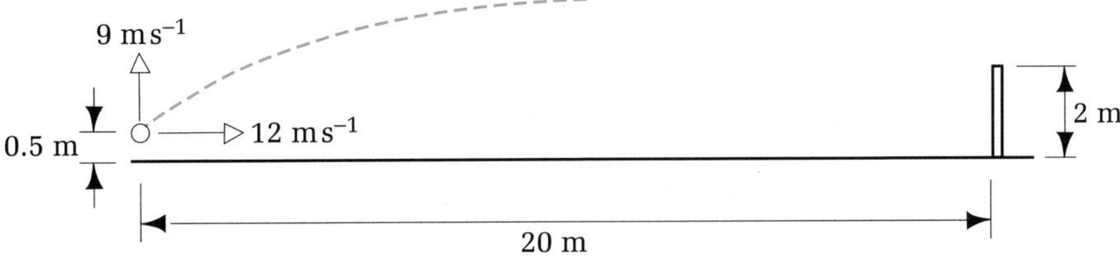

a When the ball is hit its horizontal component of velocity is $12\,\mathrm{m\,s^{-1}}$. Find how long it takes to cover a horizontal distance of 20 m.

b The ball is 0.5 m above the ground when it is hit. It is given a vertical component of velocity of $9\,\mathrm{m\,s^{-1}}$ upwards and has an acceleration of $9.8\,\mathrm{m\,s^{-2}}$ downwards. Find an expression for its height above the ground t seconds after being hit.

The child hits the ball towards a wall 2 m high and 20 m away with the given components of velocity. Determine whether or not the ball will go over the wall. (You should neglect air resistance).

(OCSEB)

3 **a** A projectile is fired from a point O, with initial speed V at an angle α above the horizontal. Find an expression for the range on a horizontal plane and hence find, in terms of V and g, the maximum range as α varies.

b In this part of the question take the value of g to be $10\,\mathrm{m\,s^{-2}}$. A Roman ballista was capable of catapulting rocks as projectiles. For a particular ballista the speed of projection was $40\,\mathrm{m\,s^{-1}}$. Rocks were fired so as just to clear a vertical wall of height 10 m at a distance of 100 m from the point of projection. The plane of the trajectory was perpendicular to the wall. Denoting the angle of projection by θ, show that:

$$25\tan^2\theta - 80\tan\theta + 33 = 0$$

Hence find the two possible angles of projection, giving your answers to the nearest 0.1°. Using the principle of conservation of energy, or otherwise, find the speed of a rock at the instant it passed over the wall.

(UCLES)

Applications and Activities

1

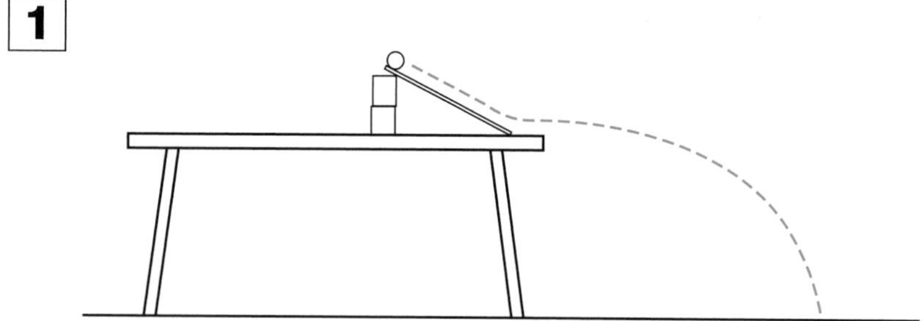

A ball is given an initial speed using a ramp on a table. How far does the ball travel horizontally before hitting the floor? What is the initial speed of projection?

2

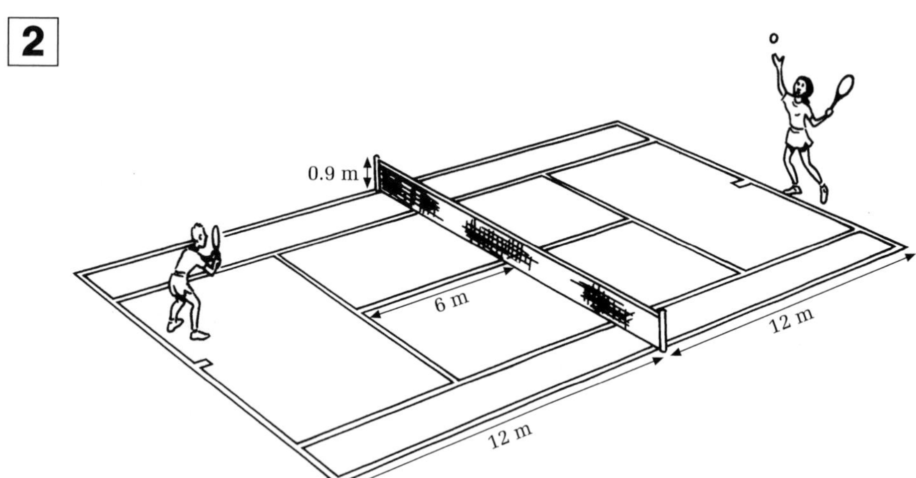

A tennis ball is served from the baseline. It goes over the net and lands inside the fault line. Determine the maximum speed at which the tennis ball can be served. How can tennis players serve the tennis ball faster than this speed?

$x_{min} = 0$, $x_{max} = 20$, scl $= 1$

$y_{min} = 0$, $y_{max} = 5$, scl $= 1$

Graph

Summary

- Projectile problems are solved by considering the horizontal and vertical motion separately.

  For horizontal motion use

  $$s = ut$$

  For vertical motion use

  $$v = u + at$$

  $$s = ut + \tfrac{1}{2}at^2$$

  $$s = \tfrac{1}{2}(u + v)t$$

  $$v^2 = u^2 + 2as$$

  with $a = g$ or $a = -g$ as appropriate.

- The range and time of flight of a projectile (projected from a horizontal plane) are:

  $$\textbf{range} = \frac{U^2 \sin(2\theta)}{g}$$

  $$\textbf{time of flight} = \frac{2U\sin\theta}{g}$$

- The maximum height of a projectile is:

  $$\textbf{maximum height} = \frac{U^2\sin^2\theta}{2g}$$

  and it occurs at time:

  $$\textbf{time to reach maximum height} = \frac{U\sin\theta}{g}$$

- The maximum range on a horizontal plane is given by:

  $$\textbf{maximum range} = \frac{U^2}{g}$$

- The angle which gives the maximum range on a horizontal plane is 45°.
- The equation of trajectory is:

  $$y = x\tan\theta - \frac{gx^2}{2U^2}(1 + \tan^2\theta)$$

17 Circular Motion

What you need to know

- A relationship between $\sin\theta$, $\cos\theta$ and $\tan\theta$.
- How to solve problems using energy considerations.
- How to resolve forces into two perpendicular directions.
- How to apply $F = ma$.

Review

1 Write down a relationship between $\sin\theta$, $\cos\theta$ and $\tan\theta$.

2
- **a** Write down the formulas for kinetic energy and potential energy.
- **b** A ball, of mass 20 grams, is released from a height of 3 m and it rebounds to a height of 2.2 m.
  - **i** Calculate the kinetic energy lost in the bounce.
  - **ii** Determine the speed of the ball as it hits the ground using energy considerations.

3 Resolve the following forces into horizontal and vertical components:

- **a** 200 N acting to the right at 40° above the horizontal
- **b** R N acting to the left at 50° to the upward vertical.

4

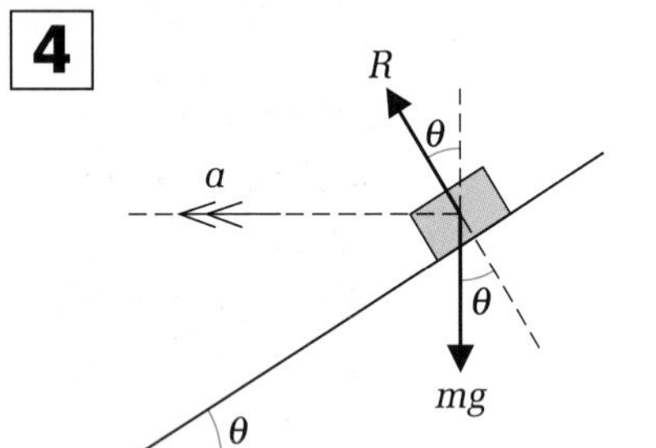

Write down an equation relating R, m, a and θ.

17.1 Radians

How do you calculate the minor arc length AB? First the whole of the circumference must be calculated. Then the portion for the angle β can be worked out.

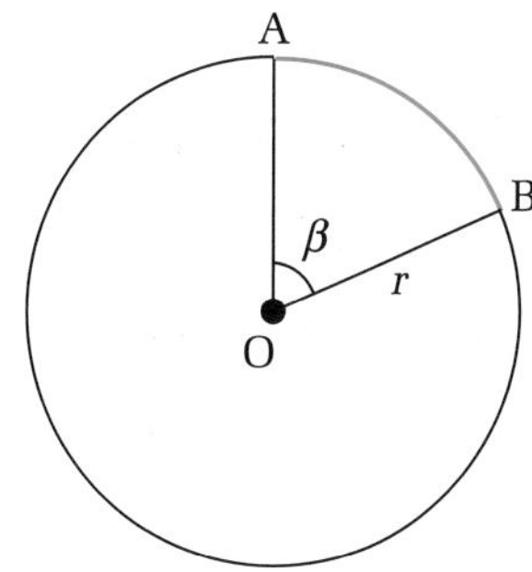

$$C = 2\pi r$$

$$\text{arc of } 1^\circ = \frac{2\pi r}{360}$$

$$\text{arc}_{AB} = \frac{2\pi r}{360} \times \beta$$

Formula for the circumference of a circle.
Divide by 360 to find arc length of 1°.
Multiply by β to find arc length AB.

The circumference is divided by 360° to find the part corresponding to 1° and then multiplied by β. To avoid this conversion, a different measurement for angle can be used. *One radian* is the angle that gives an arc length equal to the radius of the circle.

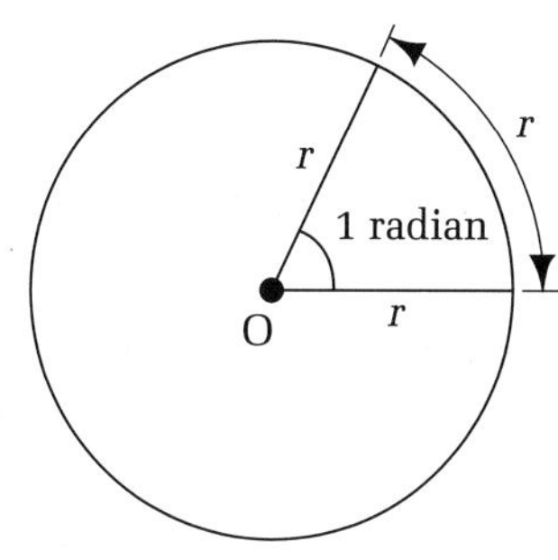

1 radian = 1 rad = 1^c. The small c stands for circular measure. Write down the arc lengths when the angle is 2 radians, 3 radians or 4 radians in terms of the radius.

Answers, $2r$, $3r$, $4r$.

By using radians a simpler formula is obtained for calculating arc length:

$$s = r\theta$$

Notation
s = arc length (m)
r = radius (m)
θ = angle in radians (rad)

The next problem is how to convert between radians and degrees. If the circumference is used, then the number of radians equal to 360° can be found:

$$r\theta = C$$

$$r\theta = 2\pi r$$

$$r\theta = r(2\pi)$$

Let arc length = circumference of a circle.
The angle for the circumference of a circle is 360°.

For an angle of 360°, the radian angle is 2π

$$360^\circ \to 2\pi \text{ radians}$$

Write down what 180° and 90° would be in radians.

Converting degrees to radians

To convert 60° into radians,

$$360^\circ \to 2\pi \text{ radians}$$

$$1^\circ \to \frac{2\pi}{360} \text{ rad}$$

$$60^\circ \to \frac{2\pi}{360} \times 60 \text{ rad}$$

$$= \frac{\pi}{3}$$

When π is contained in the answer then the 'c' is left out. The π shows that the angle is in radians.

A general conversion formula can be written as:

$$\theta = \frac{2\pi}{360} \times \alpha \quad \text{or} \quad \theta = \frac{\pi}{180} \times \alpha \qquad [1]$$

Notation
$\theta =$ angle in radians
$\alpha =$ angle in degrees

Converting radians to degrees

By rearranging equation [1], a radians to degrees conversion can be found.

$$\theta = \frac{\pi}{180} \times \alpha$$

$$180\theta = \pi \times \alpha$$

$$\frac{180}{\pi} \times \theta = \alpha$$

Notation
$\alpha =$ angle in degrees
$\theta =$ angle in radians

Example 1

Convert the following angles into radians:

a 30° **b** 85°

Solution

a
$$\theta = \frac{\pi}{180} \times \alpha$$
$$\theta = \frac{\pi}{180} \times 30$$
$$\theta = \frac{\pi}{6}$$

b
$$\theta = \frac{\pi}{180} \times \alpha$$
$$\theta = \frac{\pi}{180} \times 85$$
$$\theta = \frac{17\pi}{36}$$
$$\theta = 1.48^{c} \text{ (3 s.f.)}$$

Example 2

Convert the following angles into degrees:

a $\frac{3\pi}{4}$ **b** $\frac{2\pi}{3}$ **c** 1^{c} **d** 2^{c}

Solution

a
$$\alpha = \frac{180}{\pi} \times \theta$$
$$\alpha = \frac{180}{\pi} \times \frac{3\pi}{4}$$
$$\alpha = 135^\circ$$

b
$$\alpha = \frac{180}{\pi} \times \theta$$
$$\alpha = \frac{180}{\pi} \times \frac{2\pi}{3}$$
$$\alpha = 120^\circ$$

c
$$\alpha = \frac{180}{\pi} \times \theta$$
$$\alpha = \frac{180}{\pi} \times 1$$
$$\alpha = 57.3^\circ \text{ (1 d.p.)}$$

d
$$\alpha = \frac{180}{\pi} \times \theta$$
$$\alpha = \frac{180}{\pi} \times 2$$
$$\alpha = 114.6^\circ \text{ (1 d.p.)}$$

17.1 Radians

Exercise

Technique

1 Change the following angles into angles measured in radians. Leave your answers in terms of π where appropriate.

a	150°	**e**	72°	**i**	360°
b	120°	**f**	270°	**j**	720°
c	60°	**g**	90°	**k**	74.3°
d	80°	**h**	180°	**l**	57.3°

2 Change the following angles into degrees:

a	4π	**e**	$\frac{5\pi}{6}$	**i**	5^c
b	8π	**f**	$\frac{3\pi}{4}$	**j**	3^c
c	$\frac{\pi}{6}$	**g**	$\frac{\pi}{4}$	**k**	π
d	$\frac{\pi}{20}$	**h**	$\frac{\pi}{3}$	**l**	3.5^c

17.2 Angular Speed

In many power stations in the United Kingdom, the generator rotor rotates at 50 revolutions every second or 3000 revolutions per minute (rpm). Revolutions per minute (rpm) is one of the ways to measure angular speed. Angular speed is a measure of how fast an object is rotating. Can you think of anything else which is measured in revolutions per minute?

$50 \times 60 = 3000\,\text{rpm}$

Another measure of angular speed is radians per second (rad s^{-1}). What would 3000 rpm be in radians per second?

This is the SI unit for measuring angular speed.

$$\begin{aligned} 3000 \text{ rpm} &= 50 \text{ revolutions per second} \\ &= 50 \times 2\pi \text{ radians per second} \\ &= 100\pi \text{ rad s}^{-1} \end{aligned}$$

1 revolution $= 360° = 2\pi$ radians

Time period

The time period is the time taken for the object to complete one revolution. One revolution is equivalent to a rotation of 2π radians. How long will the generator rotor take to complete one revolution? The rotor rotates at 100π rad s^{-1}

$$\text{time} = \frac{2\pi}{100\pi}$$

$$\text{time} = \frac{1}{50}\text{ s}$$

Check: Rotor completes 50 revolutions in 1 second from the description at the start of the section.

This leads to a formula for the time period:

$$T = \frac{2\pi}{\omega}$$

Notation

$T =$ time period (s)

$\omega =$ angular speed (rad s^{-1})

Linear speed

If the generator rotor has a radius of 0.6 metres, what is the speed of the outside edge in metres per second? How fast a point on the outer edge travels is termed **linear speed** even though the point will be moving on a circular path.

In 1 second the generator rotates 100π radians. In 1 second, the point on the generator's circumference must move:

$$\begin{aligned} s &= r\theta \\ s &= 0.6 \times 100\pi \\ s &= 60\pi\,\text{m} \\ s &= 188\,\text{m (3 s.f.)} \end{aligned}$$

This distance is travelled in 1 second. The linear speed of a point on the generator's rotor circumference is 188 m s^{-1}. This method gives a formula to calculate linear speed:

$188\,\text{m s}^{-1} \approx 423$ mph

$$\boldsymbol{v = \omega r} \quad \text{or} \quad s = r\theta$$

$$\frac{ds}{dt} = r\frac{d\theta}{dt}$$

$$\boldsymbol{v = \omega r}$$

Notation

$v =$ linear speed (m s^{-1})

$\omega =$ angular speed (rad s^{-1})

$r =$ radius (m)

Overview of method

Step ① Summarise the information. Convert angular speed into rad s^{-1}, if necessary.

Step ② Write down the formula $v = \omega r$ or $T = \frac{2\pi}{\omega}$.

Step ③ Substitute the values into the formula and calculate the quantity required.

Example 1

The angular speed of a camshaft on an engine is 15 000 rpm. Find the angular speed in radians per second.

Solution

$$15\,000\text{ rpm} = 15\,000 \div 60 \text{ revolutions per second}$$
$$= 250 \times 2\pi \text{ rad s}^{-1}$$
$$= 500\pi \text{ rad s}^{-1}$$

Example 2

A car travels around a circular curve at 40 m s^{-1}. The radius of the curve is 20 m. Determine:

a the car's angular speed

b the time the car takes to complete one circuit.

Solution

a $v = 40\text{ m s}^{-1} \quad \omega = ? \quad r = 20\text{ m}$ ◀ ① Summarise the information.

$v = \omega r$ ◀ ② Write down the formula.

$40 = \omega \times 20$ ◀ ③ Substitute the known values.

Divide by 20.

$\omega = 2\text{ rad s}^{-1}$

b $\omega = 2\text{ rad s}^{-1} \qquad T = ?$

$$T = \frac{2\pi}{\omega}$$

$$T = \frac{2\pi}{2}$$

$$T = \pi$$

$$T = 3.14\text{ s (3 s.f.)}$$

17.2 Angular Speed
Exercise

Technique

1 A particle rotates at 2000 rpm. Calculate the angular speed in radians per second.

2 An object has an angular speed of 8 rad s^{-1} around a circle of radius 20 m. Determine the object's linear speed.

3 A body rotates at 6 rpm around a circle of radius 60 cm. Find the body's linear speed.

4 A particle has a linear speed of 60 m s^{-1} around a circle of radius 8 m. Work out:

- **a** the particle's angular speed in radians per second
- **b** the time taken to complete one circle.

5 A body moves around a circle of radius 2 km, with a linear speed of 200 m s^{-1}. Determine the body's angular speed in:

- **a** radians per second
- **b** revolutions per minute.

Find the time taken for the body to complete one circle.

Contextual

1 A centrifuge, of radius 10 cm, rotates at 100 rad s^{-1}. Calculate the linear speed at its outer edge.

Biologists use a machine called a centrifuge to separate solids and liquids. To do this, the centrifuge rotates at high speeds.

2 A power station turbine rotates 30 times each second. The radius of the turbine is 1.5 m. Find:

- **a** the angular speed in radians per second
- **b** the linear speed at the outer edge of the turbine.

3 A fairground ride has a radius of 4 m and a speed of 10 m s^{-1} at its outer edge.

- **a** Determine the angular speed of the ride in:
  - **i** rad s^{-1}
  - **ii** rpm
- **b** Work out the time for the fairground ride to complete 10 complete rotations.

17.3 Acceleration for Circular Motion with Constant Speed

A car travels around a corner at a constant *speed* of $20\,\mathrm{m\,s^{-1}}$ and the radius of the corner is 50 m. Explain why the velocity *cannot be constant*. Why must the car be accelerating? What is the acceleration of the car?

Acceleration is a vector quantity and so if the direction is changing, there must be an acceleration.

The direction of the car is *always changing*. This will mean the velocity is always changing and so the car must be *accelerating*. By looking at a small section of the curve, the size and direction of the acceleration can be found.

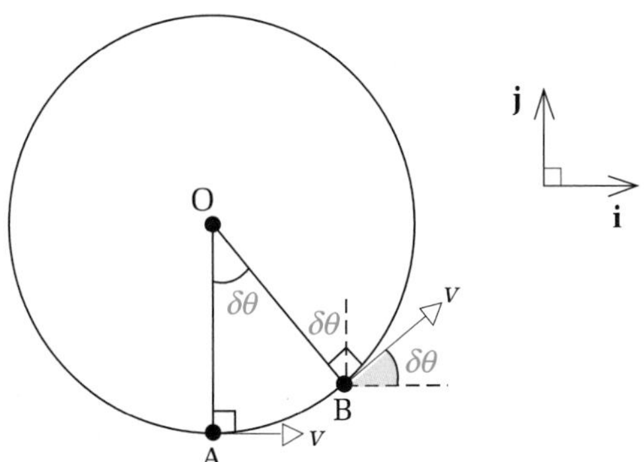

$\delta\theta$ is small but sketched large so that the changes can be seen clearly.

The object has a constant speed of $v\,\mathrm{m\,s^{-1}}$. It travels an angle $\delta\theta$ in time δt where $\delta\theta$ and δt are small. By resolving horizontally and vertically at points A and B the velocity at both points can be found.

Point A:

Resolve ↑ $\quad 0$

Resolve → $\quad v$

$$\mathbf{v}_\mathrm{A} = v\mathbf{i} + 0\mathbf{j}$$

$$\mathbf{v}_\mathrm{A} = v\mathbf{i}$$

Point B:

Resolve ↑ $\quad v\sin\delta\theta$

Resolve → $\quad v\cos\delta\theta$

$$\mathbf{v}_\mathrm{B} = (v\cos\delta\theta)\mathbf{i} + (v\sin\delta\theta)\mathbf{j}$$

Since acceleration is the rate of change of velocity with time,

$$\text{acceleration} = \frac{\mathbf{v}_\mathrm{B} - \mathbf{v}_\mathrm{A}}{\delta t}$$

$$\mathbf{a} = \frac{(v\cos\delta\theta)\mathbf{i} + (v\sin\delta\theta)\mathbf{j} - v\mathbf{i}}{\delta t}$$

$$\mathbf{a} = \frac{(v\cos\delta\theta - v)\mathbf{i} + (v\sin\delta\theta)\mathbf{j}}{\delta t}$$

As $\delta\theta \to 0$, the acceleration at point A will be given.

When $\delta\theta \to 0$, then $\cos\delta\theta \to 1$ and $\sin\delta\theta \to \delta\theta$.
So,

$$\mathbf{a} = \frac{(v \times 1 - v)\mathbf{i} + (v \times \delta\theta)\mathbf{j}}{\delta t}$$

$$\mathbf{a} = \frac{0\mathbf{i} + v\delta\theta\mathbf{j}}{\delta t}$$

$$\mathbf{a} = v\frac{\delta\theta}{\delta t}\mathbf{j}$$

$$\mathbf{a} = v\omega\mathbf{j}$$

Put your calculator into radian mode and try cos (0.01), cos (0.02), cos (0.03) and sin (0.01), sin (0.02), sin (0.03). What do you notice? Replace $\cos\delta\theta$ with 1 and $\sin\delta\theta$ with $\delta\theta$.

$v - v = 0$

$\frac{\delta\theta}{\delta t} = \frac{\text{radians}}{\text{time}}$ = angular speed

The acceleration has a magnitude of $v\omega$ and a *direction towards the centre of the circle*. This formula uses both linear and angular speed. It is more useful to have formulas involving v or ω but not both. This can be achieved by using the linear speed formula, $v = \omega r$.

$$a = v\omega$$

$$a = (\omega r)\omega$$

$$\boldsymbol{a = \omega^2 r}$$

Replace v with ωr.

$\omega \times \omega = \omega^2$.

and

$$a = v\omega$$

$$a = v\left(\frac{v}{r}\right)$$

$$\boldsymbol{a = \frac{v^2}{r}}$$

$v = \omega r$ so $\omega = \frac{v}{r}$

$v \times v = v^2$

This gives two formulas for the acceleration of a particle at constant speed around a circle:

$$\boldsymbol{a = \omega^2 r}$$

$$\boldsymbol{a = \frac{v^2}{r}}$$

Notation
a = acceleration (m s^{-2})
v = *constant* linear speed (m s^{-1})
ω = *constant* angular speed (rad s^{-1})
r = radius (m)

The direction of the acceleration is always towards the centre of the circle. The acceleration for the car can now be calculated.

v m s^{-1}
a
v m s^{-1}
a
O
a
v m s^{-1}

$$a = \frac{v^2}{r} = \frac{20^2}{50}$$

$$a = 8\text{ m s}^{-2}$$

The force causing the acceleration is the friction between the tyres and the road.

Overview of method

Step ① Summarise the information. Convert the angular speed into rad s^{-1} if necessary.

Step ② Use either $a = \omega^2 r$ or $a = \frac{v^2}{r}$.

Step ③ Use $F = ma$ or $v = \omega r$.

Example 1

A coin, of mass 20 grams, is placed on a horizontal turntable. The coin is 20 cm from the centre of the turntable when it rotates at a constant speed of 5 revolutions per minute.

a Calculate the acceleration of the coin and state its direction.
b Find the force causing this acceleration and state what causes it.

Solution

a 5 rev per minute = 10π radians per minute

$= \frac{10\pi}{60}$ rad s^{-1} ◀ ① Summarise the information. Convert the angular speed into rad s^{-1}.

$= \frac{\pi}{6}$ rad s^{-1}

$\omega = \frac{\pi}{6}$ rad s^{-1} $\quad r = 0.2$ m

$a = \omega^2 r$ ◀ ② Select formula.

$a = \left(\frac{\pi}{6}\right)^2 \times 0.2$

$a = 0.0548$ m s^{-2} (3 s.f.)

The acceleration of 0.0548 m s^{-2} acts towards the centre of the circle.

b Use $F = ma$ ◀ ③ Use $F = ma$ to calculate the force.

$F = 0.02 \times 0.0548$

$F = 0.001\,10$ N (3 s.f.)

This force will be caused by the friction between the coin and the turntable.

Example 2

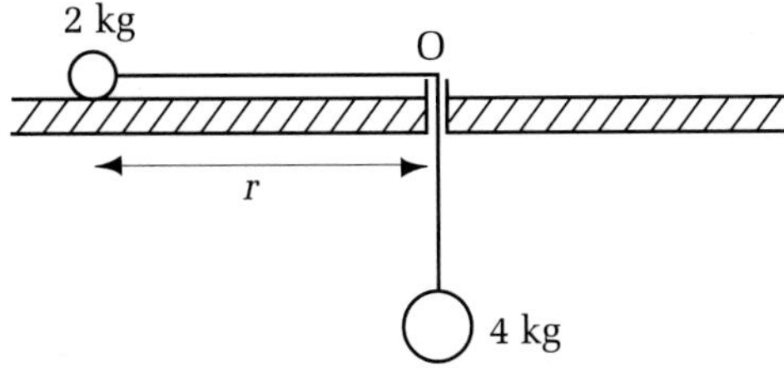

The diagram shows a mass of 2 kg on a smooth horizontal surface attached by a light inextensible string to a 4 kg mass which hangs vertically in equilibrium. The 2 kg mass moves in a horizontal circle with centre O and radius r m. The angular speed of the 2 kg mass is 20 rad s^{-1}. Taking $g = 10$ m s^{-2}, calculate the value of r.

Solution

$a = ?$ $\omega = 20 \text{ rad s}^{-1}$ $r = ?$

There are too many unknowns. The acceleration needs to be calculated first.

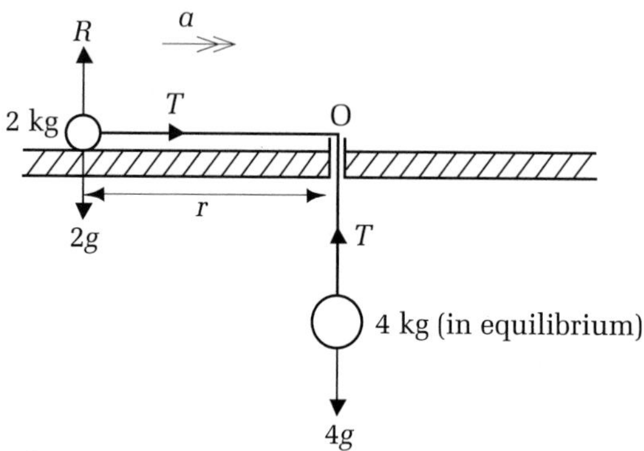

The force causing the acceleration towards the centre is the tension in the string.

Resolve ↑ for 4 kg mass:

$$T - 4g = 0$$
$$T = 4g$$
$$T = 40 \text{ N}$$

Apply $F = ma$ to the 2 kg mass towards the centre of the circle.

$$T = 2a$$ ◀ ③ Use $F = ma$ to find a.

$$40 = 2a$$
$$a = 20 \text{ m s}^{-2}$$

From the above working, $T = 40$ N. Divide by 2.

$a = 20 \text{ m s}^{-2}$ $\omega = 20 \text{ rad s}^{-1}$ $r = ?$ ◀ ① Summarise the information.

$$a = \omega^2 r$$ ◀ ② Select formula.

Substitute the numbers.

$$20 = 20^2 r$$
$$20 = 400r$$

Divide by 400.

$$r = \tfrac{1}{20} = 0.05$$

No units are written for r because the units were given in the question.

17.3 Acceleration for Circular Motion with Constant Speed

Exercise

Technique

1 A particle of mass 2 kg travels in a circle of radius 0.5 m with a constant angular speed of 10 rad s^{-1}. Find:

- **a** the magnitude and direction of the acceleration of the particle
- **b** the size of the force causing this acceleration.

2 An object rotates at 20 revolutions per second around a circle of diameter 10 cm. Calculate the acceleration of the object, stating one key assumption.

3 A body of mass 500 grams travels around a circle with a constant linear speed of 8 m s^{-1}. The acceleration of the body towards the centre of the circle is 6 m s^{-2}. Determine the radius of the circle.

4 A 5 kg mass rotates at 1.5 m about a fixed point, O. The mass accelerates towards the centre of the circle at 3 m s^{-2}. Work out:

- **a** the constant linear speed of the mass
- **b** the constant angular speed of the mass.

5 A particle, of mass 10 kg, travels around a smooth horizontal circular loop. The radius of the loop is 80 cm and the particle completes 0.5 revolutions every second. Determine:

- **a** the horizontal reaction between the particle and the loop
- **b** the resultant reaction acting on the particle.

6

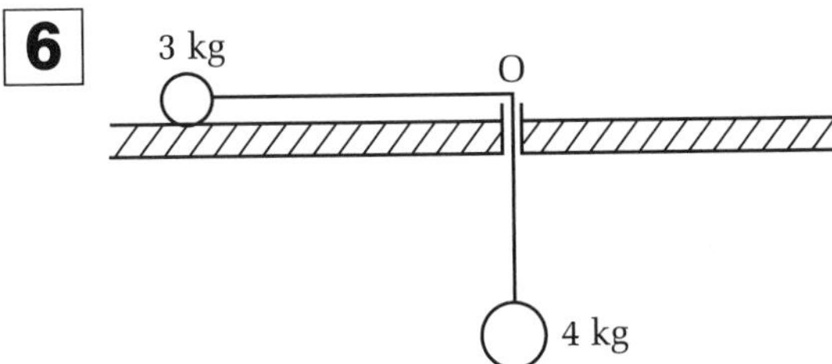

A particle of mass 3 kg is attached by a 1 m length of light inextensible string to a particle of mass 4 kg. The 4 kg particle hangs in equilibrium 40 cm below the horizontal surface. The 3 kg mass rotates in a horizontal circle with centre O, on a smooth horizontal surface. Calculate:

- **a** the tension in the string
- **b** the constant angular speed of the 3 kg mass.

7 An object, of mass 200 grams, is set on the rough surface of a circular disc. The disc is rotated at a constant angular speed of 5 rad s^{-1} and the object is 0.2 m from the centre of the disc. The surface of the disc is horizontal. Find:

a the force keeping the particle moving in a circular motion
b the normal reaction acting on the object
c the coefficient of friction, if the object is just about to slip.

8 A particle of mass m kg is attached to a particle of mass $2m$ kg by a light inelastic string. The $2m$ kg particle hangs in equilibrium below a horizontal surface. The particle of mass m kg rotates with constant angular speed of ω rad s^{-1} on the smooth horizontal surface. Find, in terms of ω and g, an expression for the radius for the circular motion.

Contextual

1 A 20 tonne train travels around a corner at a constant linear speed of 20 m s^{-1}. The radius of the corner is 500 m. Determine:

a the acceleration of the train
b the horizontal reaction between the wheels and the track.

2 A car, of mass 1000 kg, goes around a corner of radius 50 m. The coefficient of friction between the tyres and the road is 0.8. Find:

a the maximum frictional force that can act on the car
b the maximum acceleration of the car around the corner if its speed remains constant
c the maximum linear speed with which the car can travel around the corner.

3 A train, of mass 10 tonnes, travels around a bend in the track with a radius of 200 m. For safety reasons, the maximum horizontal reaction between the rails and the wheels is 90 000 N. Work out the maximum speed of the train around the bend.

4 An athlete, of mass 70 kg, runs around a bend at a constant linear speed of 8 m s^{-1}. The coefficient of friction between the athlete's training shoes and the track is 0.7. Taking $g = 10$ m s^{-2}, calculate the smallest radius of the bend around which the athlete can run.

17.4 Conical Pendulums

Attach a mass of 1 kg to a length of string measuring 30 cm. Make the mass rotate in a horizontal circle with radius 10 cm. This is an example of a **conical pendulum**. What is the angular speed of the conical pendulum? How long does the mass take to complete one revolution? The mass is modelled as a particle and the string is assumed to be light and inextensible. Air resistance will be neglected.

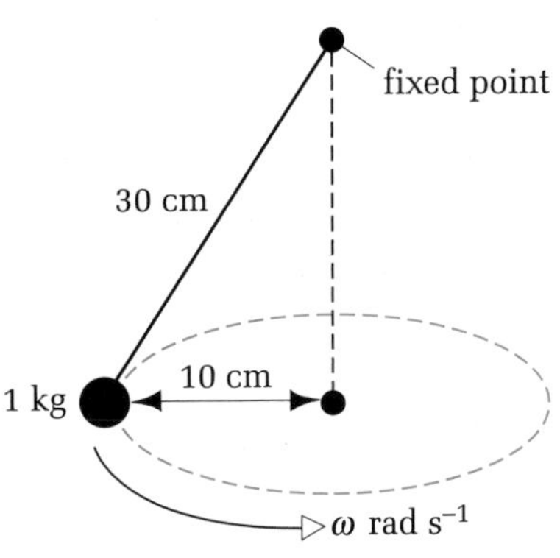

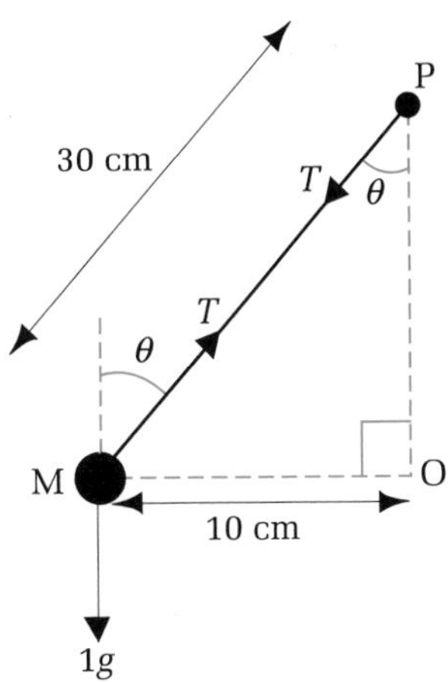

Find θ using trigonometry.

$$\sin\theta = \tfrac{10}{30}$$

$$\theta = 19.5° \text{ (3 s.f.)}$$

Resolve ↑ at M

$$T\cos 19.5° = 1g$$

$$T = \frac{9.8}{\cos\ 19.5°}$$

$$T = 10.4 \text{ N (3 s.f.)}$$

Apply $F = ma \rightarrow$

$$T\sin 19.5° = 1 \times a$$

$$10.4\sin 19.5° = a$$

$$3.46 = \omega^2 r$$

$$3.46 = \omega^2 \times 0.1$$

$$34.6 = \omega^2$$

$$\omega = 5.89 \text{ rad s}^{-1} \text{ (3 s.f.)}$$

$F = ma$ is applied towards the centre of the circle.
$T = 10.4$ N
Use $a = \omega^2 r$.
$r = 10\,\text{cm} = 0.1\,\text{m}$
Divide by 0.1.
Take the square root.

One revolution is 2π:

$$\text{time period} = \frac{2\pi}{\omega}$$

$$\text{time period} = \frac{2\pi}{5.89}$$

$$\text{time period} = 1.07 \text{ s (3 s.f.)}$$

The pendulum could be tried by experiment to check this answer.

Overview of method

Step ① Draw a clear diagram.

Step ② Resolve vertically.

Step ③ Apply $F = ma$ towards the centre of the circle.

Step ④ Use $a = \omega^2 r$ or $a = \frac{v^2}{r}$.

Example 1

A mass of 2 kg is attached to a string of length 20 cm. The string is fixed at the other end and it is made to rotate at 10 rad s^{-1} to form a conical pendulum. Find:

a the tension in the string

b the angle between the string and the downward vertical.

Solution

a

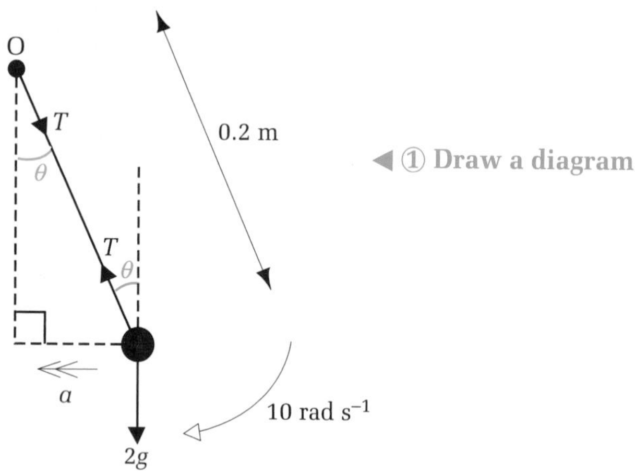

◀ ① Draw a diagram.

Resolve ↑ ◀ ② Resolve vertically.

$$T\cos\theta - 2g = 0$$

$$T\cos\theta = 2g$$ Add $2g$.

$$T\cos\theta = 19.6 \quad [1]$$ $g = 9.8$.

Apply $F = ma$ ← ◀ ③ Apply $F = ma$ towards the centre of the circle.

$$T\sin\theta = 2a$$ ◀ ④ Replace a with $\omega^2 r$

$$T\sin\theta = 2\omega^2 r$$

$$T\sin\theta = 2 \times 10^2 \times r \quad [2]$$ $\omega = 10 \text{ rad s}^{-1}$

Use trigonometry to find r

$$\sin\theta = \frac{r}{0.2}$$

$$0.2\sin\theta = r$$

Replace r by $0.2\sin\theta$ in equation [2]

$$T\sin\theta = 200 \times 0.2\sin\theta$$

Divide by $\sin\theta$.

$$T = 200 \times 0.2$$

$$T = 40\,\text{N}$$

b Use equation [1]

$$T\cos\theta = 19.6$$

Replace T by 40.

$$40\cos\theta = 19.6$$

Divide by 40.

$$\cos\theta = \frac{19.6}{40}$$

$\cos^{-1}(\frac{19.6}{40})$ or arccos $(\frac{19.6}{40})$

$$\theta = 60.7^\circ \text{ (3.s.f.)}$$

Example 2

The mass is 10 kg, the radius is 0.4 m and the linear speed of the conical pendulum is $4\,\text{m}\,\text{s}^{-1}$. Determine:

a the angle between the string and the downward vertical

b the tension in the string.

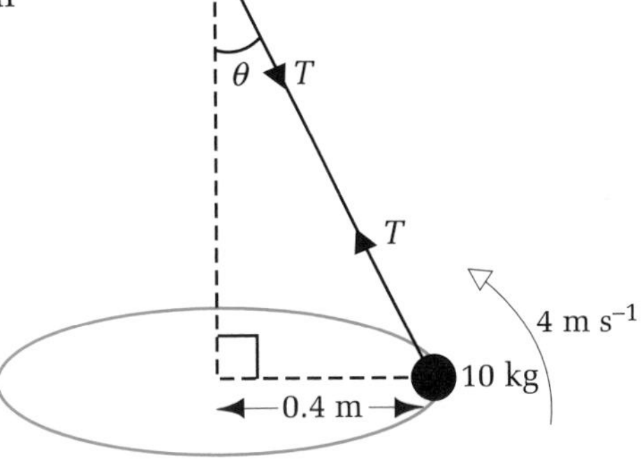

Solution

a

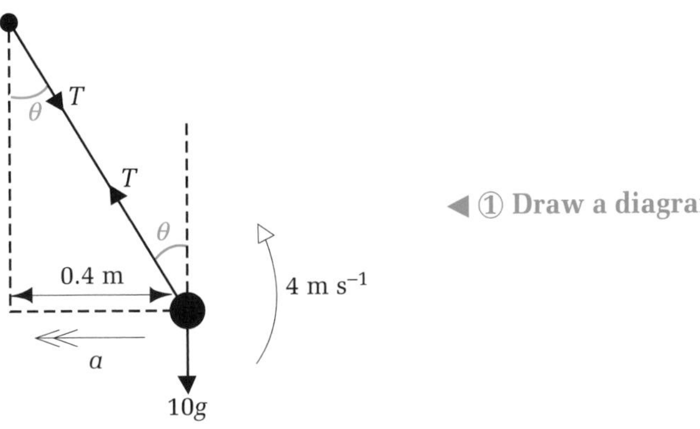

◀ ① Draw a diagram.

Resolve ↑ ◀ ② **Resolve vertically.**

$T\cos\theta = 10g$

$T\cos\theta = 98$ [1]

Apply $F = ma$ ← ◀ ③ **Apply $F = ma$ towards the centre of the circle.**

$T\sin\theta = 10a$

Replace a with $\frac{v^2}{r}$.

$T\sin\theta = 10 \times \dfrac{v^2}{r}$

$v = 4$ and $r = 0.4$.

$T\sin\theta = 10 \times \dfrac{4^2}{0.4}$

$T\sin\theta = 400$ [2]

Divide equation [2] by equation [1]:

$\dfrac{T\sin\theta}{T\cos\theta} = \dfrac{400}{98}$

T cancels and $\frac{\sin\theta}{\cos\theta} = \tan\theta$.

$\tan\theta = 4.08$

$\theta = 76.2°\ (3\text{ s.f.})$

b Use equation [2] to find T:

$T\sin 76.2° = 400$

$T = \dfrac{400}{\sin 76.2°}$

$T = 412\text{ N}\ (3\text{ s.f.})$

The tension in the string is $T = 412$ N. The angle between the string and the downward vertical is $\theta = 76.2°$.

17.4 Conical Pendulums

Exercise

Technique

1 The diagram shows a 6 kg mass performing horizontal circles. Taking $g = 10\,\text{m}\,\text{s}^{-2}$, determine:

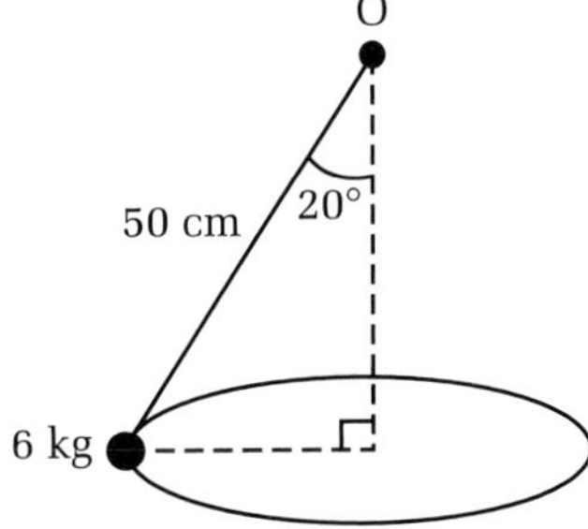

- **a** the radius of the circle
- **b** the tension in the string
- **c** the acceleration towards the centre of the circle
- **d** the angular speed of the 6 kg mass
- **e** the time period of the conical pendulum.

2 The 10 kg mass performs horizontal circles about A. Find:

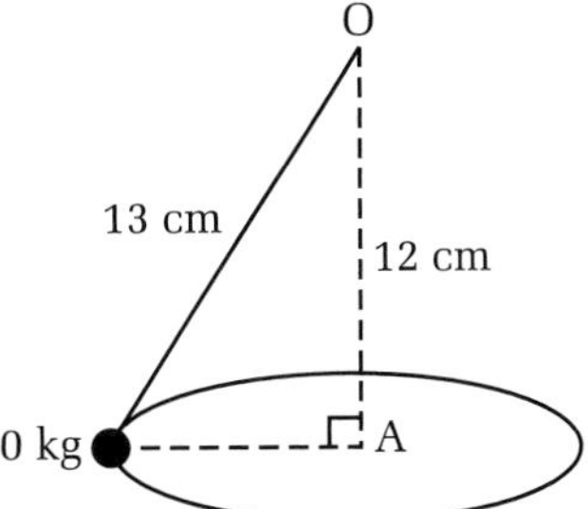

- **a** the radius of the circle
- **b** the tension in the string
- **c** the constant linear speed of the 10 kg mass.

3 A 5 kg mass is attached to a light inextensible string of length 80 cm. The other end of the string is fixed to a point A. The mass is then made to complete horizontal circles with a constant angular speed of 8 rad s^{-1}.

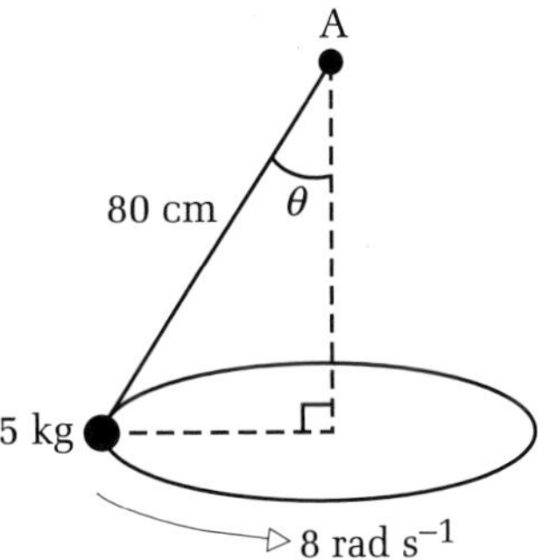

- **a** Find an expression for the radius in terms of θ.
- **b** Work out the tension in the string and the angle the string makes with the downward vertical.

4 The mass shown completes horizontal circles about O. Taking $g = 10\,\text{m}\,\text{s}^{-2}$, calculate the angle the string makes with the downward vertical and the tension in the string.

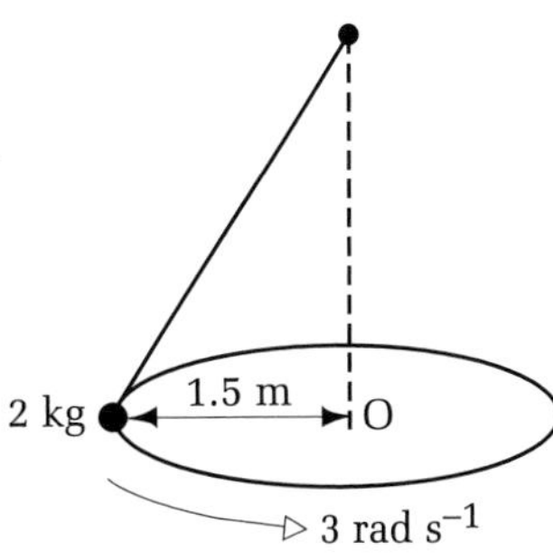

Contextual

1 A sling shot is shown in the diagram. It has a stone of mass 80 grams placed in it. The sling is rotated at 3 revolutions every second with a radius of 50 cm. Calculate:

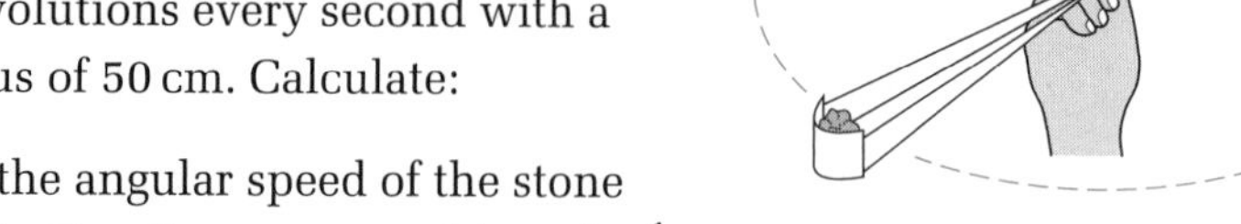

a the angular speed of the stone in the sling, measured in rad s^{-1}

b the angle the sling makes with the downward vertical and the tension in the sling.

2 A chair-o-plane ride consists of a wire, of length 5 m, connected to a circular disc of radius 10 m. The mass of the person and chair at A is 80 kg. Determine:

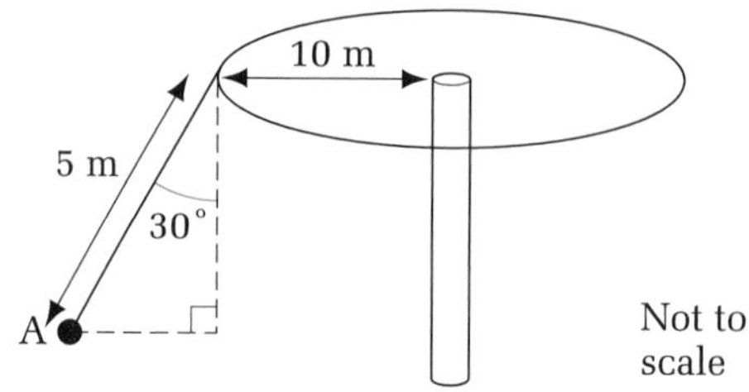

a the tension in the wire

b the radius of the circle that A describes

c the constant linear speed of the person at A.

17.5 Banked Tracks

On 21 June 1992, the Jaguar XJ220 set a new record for the highest speed achieved by a standard production car. The Jaguar reached 217.1 mph at the Nardo Circuit in Italy. This circuit uses a banked track to help the cars to corner faster. If the car is travelling around the corner at the maximum possible speed, friction will become involved.

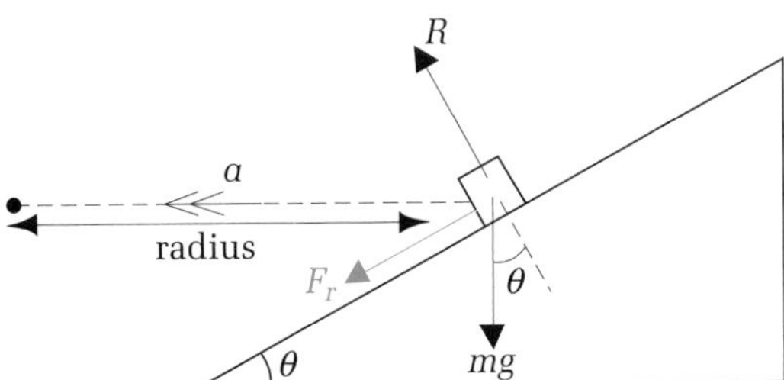

The car will tend to *slide up* the bank if it is travelling too fast. This means *friction* must act *down* the bank.

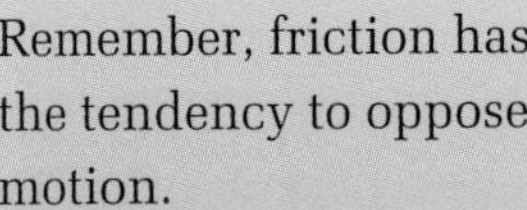
Remember, friction has the tendency to oppose motion.

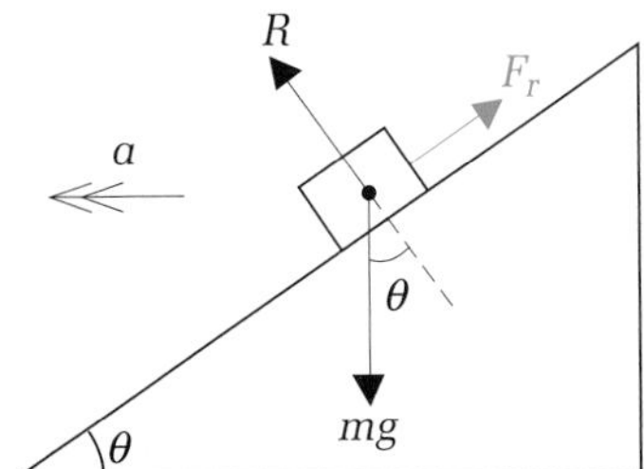

If the banking is steep and the car moves too slowly a different situation arises. The car would tend to *slip down* the banking. When this happens *friction* will act *up* the banking.

Trains on banked tracks

A runaway mine train ride uses a banked track for the curves. Again, this will help the train corner faster. Three situations arise with the train which are similar to the car.

Reaction acts parallel to banking.

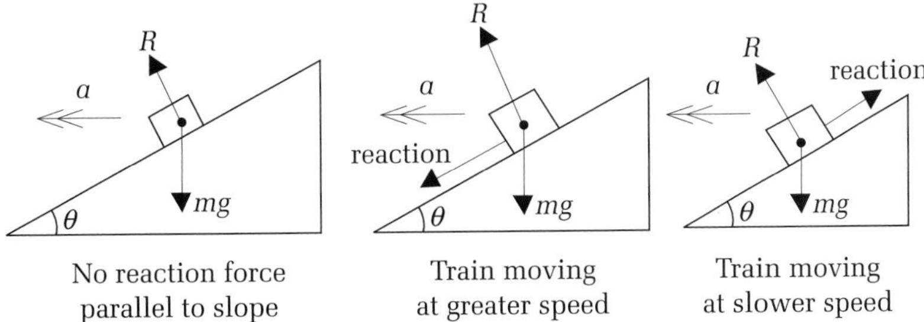

No reaction force parallel to slope

Train moving at greater speed

Train moving at slower speed

This time the force acting parallel to the banked track is a reaction force not friction. This is because of the design of the rails and the tracks.

Overview of method

Step ① Draw a clear force diagram, marking on the acceleration towards the centre of the circle.
Step ② Resolve the forces vertically.
Step ③ Apply $F = ma$ horizontally towards the centre of the circle.
Step ④ Solve the equations simultaneously.

Example 1

A car, of mass 1200 kg, travels around a banked curve at a constant speed. The curve has a radius of 100 m and is angled at 50° to the horizontal. Find the car's maximum speed if the frictional force acting parallel to the banking is zero.

Solution

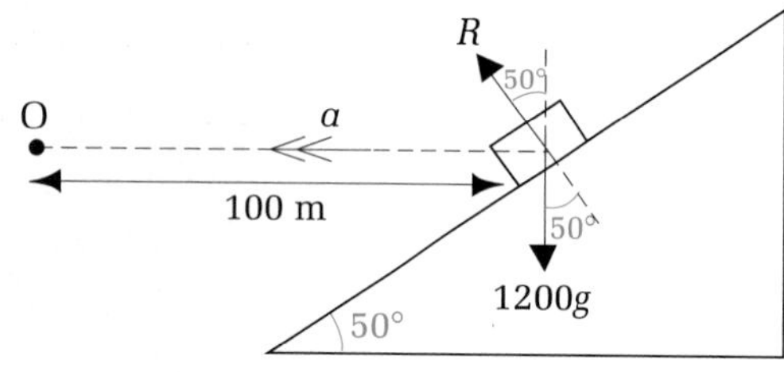

◀ ① Draw a clear force diagram.

Resolve ↑ ◀ ② Resolve vertically.

$$R\cos 50° - 1200g = 0$$

$$R\cos 50° = 1200g$$

Divide by cos 50°.

$$R = \frac{11\,760}{\cos 50°}$$

$$R = 18\,295\text{ N}$$

The reaction force is larger than the weight of the car because of the banking.

Apply $F = ma$ ← ◀ ③ Apply $F = ma$ towards the centre of the circle.

$$R\sin 50° = 1200 \times \left(\frac{v^2}{r}\right)$$

◀ ④ Solve the equations by using $R = 18\,295$ N.

$$18\,295 \times \sin 50° = 1200 \times \frac{v^2}{100}$$

Simplify.

$$14\,015 = 12v^2$$

Divide by 12.

$$1167.9 = v^2$$

Take the square root.

$$v = 34.2\text{ m s}^{-1}\ (3\text{ s.f.})$$

Example 2

A car of mass 800 kg travels at a maximum speed of 100 m s^{-1} around a banked curve of radius 80 m. The coefficient of friction between the tyres and the road is 0.9. Determine the angle of inclination of the banking to the horizontal.

Solution

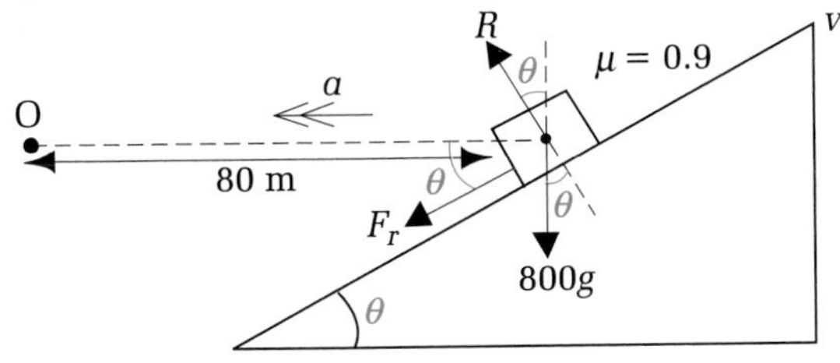

◀ ① **Draw a clear force diagram.**

Let the angle be θ.

Resolve ↑ ◀ ② **Resolve vertically.**

$$R\cos\theta - F_r\sin\theta - 800g = 0$$

Use $F_r = \mu R$ and $\mu = 0.9$.

$$R\cos\theta - 0.9R\sin\theta = 800g$$

Take out R as a common factor.

$$R(\cos\theta - 0.9\sin\theta) = 7840 \qquad [1]$$

Apply $F = ma$ ← ◀ ③ **Apply $F = ma$ and use $a = \frac{v^2}{r}$.**

$$F_r\cos\theta + R\sin\theta = 800 \times \frac{100^2}{80}$$

$F_r = 0.9R$

$$0.9R\cos\theta + R\sin\theta = 100\,000$$

Take R out as a common factor.

$$R(0.9\cos\theta + \sin\theta) = 100\,000 \qquad [2]$$

Divide equation [1] by equation [2] to eliminate R ◀ ④ **Solve the equations.**

$$\frac{R(\cos\theta - 0.9\sin\theta)}{R(0.9\cos\theta + \sin\theta)} = \frac{7840}{100\,000}$$ ◀ **Cancel R.**

$$\frac{(\cos\theta - 0.9\sin\theta)}{(0.9\cos\theta + \sin\theta)} = \frac{7840}{100\,000}$$

Cross multiply.

$$100\,000(\cos\theta - 0.9\sin\theta) = 7840(0.9\cos\theta + \sin\theta)$$

Expand brackets.

$$100\,000\cos\theta - 90\,000\sin\theta = 7056\cos\theta + 7840\sin\theta$$

Collect sines and cosines.

$$92\,944\cos\theta = 97\,840\sin\theta$$

Divide by $\cos\theta$ and 97 840.

$$\frac{92\,944}{97\,840} = \frac{\sin\theta}{\cos\theta}$$

Remember $\frac{\sin\theta}{\cos\theta} = \tan\theta$.

$$0.950 = \tan\theta$$

$$\theta = 43.5^\circ \text{ (3 s.f.)}$$

17.5 Banked Tracks

Exercise

Contextual

1 A car travels around a banked curve, of radius 50 m. The car has a mass of 800 kg and the curve is banked at an angle of 20° to the horizontal. There is no frictional force acting perpendicular to the motion of the car (i.e. up or down the bank). What is the constant linear speed of the car?

2 A 2 tonne train travels around a banked curve with a constant speed of $15\ \text{m s}^{-1}$. The angle of the banking to the horizontal is 5°. There is no reaction force acting parallel to the banked curve. Calculate the radius of the curve.

3 A car, of mass 1200 kg, travels around a bend of radius 60 m. The bend is banked at 50° to the horizontal and the coefficient of friction between the tyres and the bend is 0.8.

a Draw a clear force diagram, if the car is travelling at the maximum speed around the curve.

b What is the car's maximum speed around the curve?

c Draw a clear force diagram if the car is travelling at the minimum speed around the curve

d Determine the minimum speed of the car around the curve.

4 A car has a mass of 900 kg and it travels around a banked curve with a maximum speed of $80\ \text{m s}^{-1}$. The radius of the curve is 60 m and the coefficient of friction between the tyres and the road is 0.85. What is the angle of inclination of the track?

5 The diagram shows the forces acting on an aeroplane banking. The lift force, L, acts at right angles to the wings. The mass of the aeroplane is 200 tonnes and the aeroplane travels at a constant speed of $200\ \text{m s}^{-1}$. The radius of the circle is 1.5 km. Determine the angle of the wings to the horizontal and the lift force acting on the aeroplane.

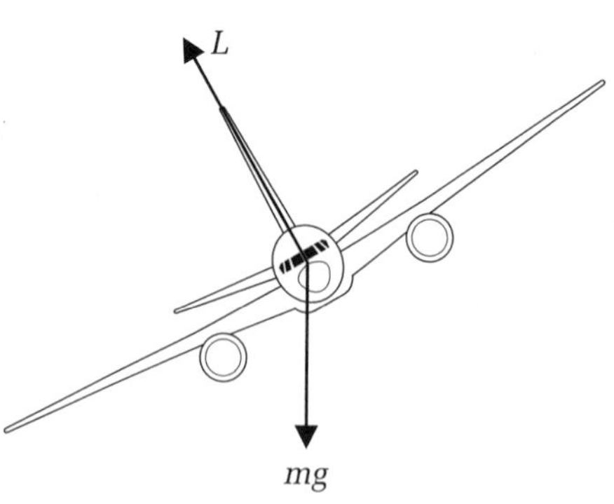

17.6 Vertical Circles

A roller coaster is to have a vertical loop of radius 20 m. Find the speed the roller coaster needs to have at the bottom of the loop to make sure the roller coaster completes the loop. The mass of the roller coaster will be m kg and all resistances will be ignored. The circular motion is not at constant speed anymore. Energy considerations will be used to solve this problem.

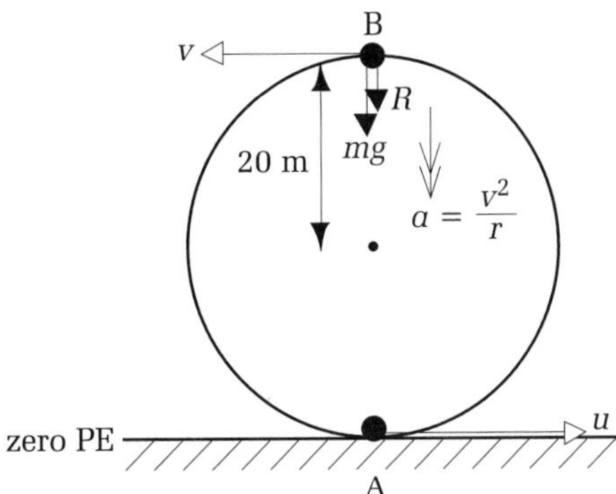

Using energy considerations.

$$KE_A = KE_B + PE_B$$ ◀ **Write energy equation.**

$$\tfrac{1}{2}mu^2 = \tfrac{1}{2}mv^2 + mgh$$

$$u^2 = v^2 + 2gh$$

Multiply by 2 and divide by m.
$h = 2 \times 20 = 40$ m

$$u^2 = v^2 + 2g(40)$$

$$u^2 = v^2 + 80g$$ [1]

Apply $F = ma \downarrow$ at B

$$mg + R = ma$$

$$mg + R = \frac{mv^2}{r}$$

Apply $F = ma$ towards the centre of the circle. Replace a with $\frac{v^2}{r}$.

If the roller coaster loses contact with the track then there will be no reaction force between the roller coaster and the track. It is this condition, $R = 0$, *not* $v = 0$ that determines when the roller coaster will leave the track.

This assumes that nothing else is holding the roller coaster to the track.

$$mg = \frac{mv^2}{20}$$

Divide by m.

$$g = \frac{v^2}{20}$$

Multiply by 20.

$$20g = v^2$$

Replace v^2 in equation [1] with $20g$

$$u^2 = 20g + 80g$$

Simplify RHS.

$$u^2 = 100g$$

$g = 9.8$ and take the square root.

$$u = \sqrt{980}$$

$$u = 31.3\ \text{m s}^{-1}\ (3\ \text{s.f.})$$

This speed will enable the roller coaster to get to the top of the loop. The speed will need to be greater than or equal to $31.3\ \text{m s}^{-1}$ for the roller coaster to complete vertical circles successfully. To improve the model resistance forces could be taken into account.

Overview of method

Step ① Draw a clear force diagram.
Step ② Use conservation of energy.
Step ③ Apply $F = ma$, usually towards the centre of the circle.
Step ④ Solve the equations.

Example

A child, of mass 40 kg, is on a swing. She is pulled back until the rope makes an angle of 20° to the vertical and then given a push. The child's initial speed is $3\ \text{m s}^{-1}$ and the rope is 3 m long. Determine:

a the child's maximum speed
b the tension in the rope at this point
c the angle of the rope when the child stops momentarily and the tangential acceleration at this point.

Solution

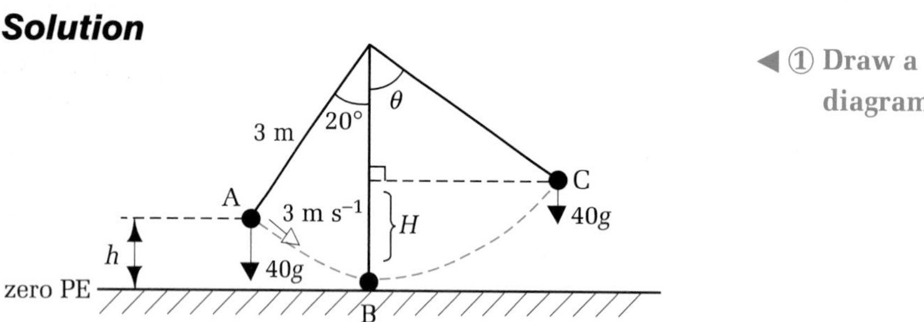

◀ ① Draw a diagram.

a The child's maximum speed will occur at point B. The PE has been changed into KE.

At B, the potential energy is a minimum.

Conservation of energy ◀ ② Use conservation of energy.

$$PE_A + KE_A = KE_B$$

$$mgh + \tfrac{1}{2}mu^2 = \tfrac{1}{2}mv^2$$

$$40 \times 9.8 \times h + \tfrac{1}{2} \times 40 \times 3^2 = \tfrac{1}{2} \times 40v^2$$

Divide by 20 to simplify equation.

$$19.6h + 9 = v^2$$

We find h from the diagram and substitute.

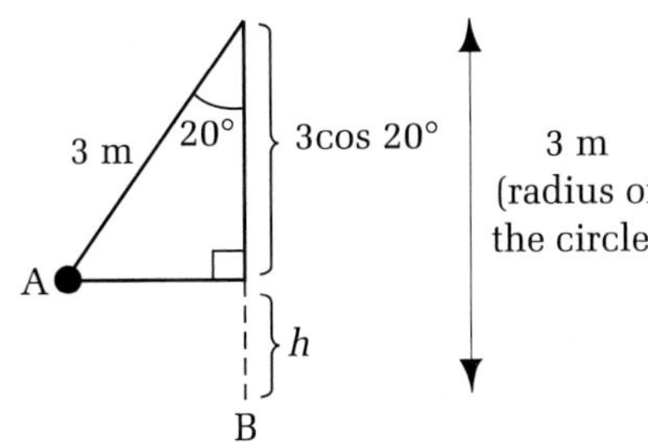

$$19.6(3 - 3\cos 20°) + 9 = v^2$$

$$12.55 = v^2$$

$$v = 3.54\ \text{m s}^{-1}\ (3\ \text{s.f.})$$

$h = 3 - 3\cos 20°$

b Apply $F = ma$ ↑ at B ◀ ③ Apply $F = ma$ towards the centre of the circle.

$$T - mg = ma$$

$$T - 40 \times 9.8 = 40 \times \frac{v^2}{r}$$ ◀ ④ Solve the equation.

$$T - 392 = 40 \times \frac{12.55}{3}$$

$$T = 392 + 167.3$$

$$T = 559\ \text{N}\ (3\ \text{s.f})$$

$v^2 = 12.55$ from **a** and $r = 3$.
Add 392.

This is the maximum value of the tension.

c Use conservation of energy.

$$PE_A + KE_A = PE_C$$

$$40 \times 9.8 \times h + \tfrac{1}{2} \times 40 \times 3^2 = 40 \times 9.8 \times H$$

$$19.6h + 9 = 19.6H$$

$$12.55 = 19.6H$$

$$H = 0.640\ \text{m}\ (3\ \text{s.f.})$$

At C, $v = 0$ so $KE_C = 0$.
Energy equation.
Divide by $20 = \frac{1}{2} \times 40$.

$19.6h + 9 = 12.55$ from **a**.
Divide by 19.6.

$$\cos\theta = \frac{2.36}{3}$$

$$\cos\theta = 0.787$$

$$\theta = 38.1°\ (3\ \text{s.f.})$$

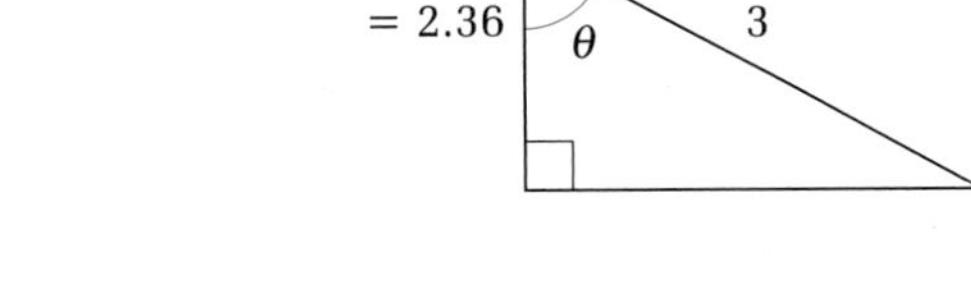

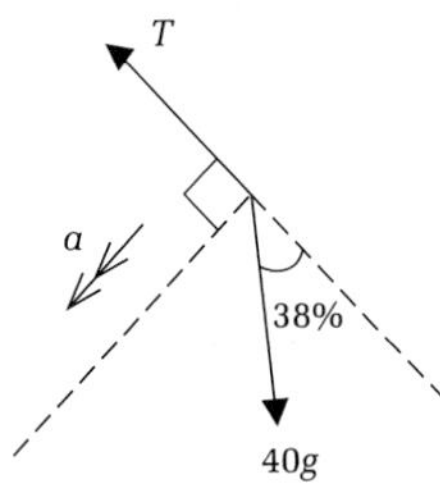

Apply $F = ma$ ↙

$$40g\sin 38.1° = 40a$$

$$9.8\sin 38.1° = a$$

$$a = 6.05\ \text{m s}^{-2}\ (3\ \text{s.f.})$$

Divide by 40.

17.6 Vertical Circles

Exercise

Technique

1 A particle, of mass 200 grams, is released from the top of a smooth circular surface of radius 50 cm. The particle leaves the surface when OA makes an angle of θ with the vertical. State the condition which means the particle has lost contact with the surface.

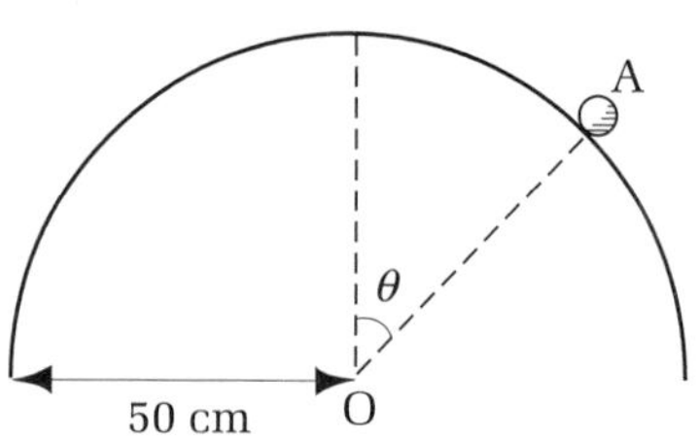

Determine θ when:

a the particle is displaced just enough to start it moving

b the particle starts at the top with a horizontal speed of:

i 0.5 m s^{-1}

ii 1 m s^{-1}

2 A particle of mass 500 grams is attached to a string of length 1 m and the particle is given an initial horizontal speed as shown in the diagram. State two key assumptions that you need to make about the string.

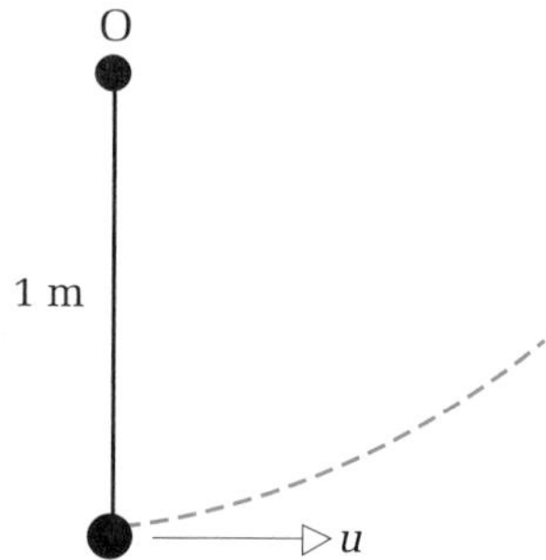

a The particle is projected with a horizontal speed of 2 m s^{-1}.
Find the angle the string makes with the downward vertical when the particle comes to rest.

b The particle is to complete vertical circles. State the values of u for which this will occur.

3 A particle of mass m is attached to one end of a light inextensible string of length 1.5 m and the other end is fixed at a point O. The particle is held so that the string makes an angle θ with the downward vertical and then released.

a Calculate the particle's maximum speed when:

i $\theta = 30°$

ii $\theta = 60°$

iii $\theta = 90°$

b State the position of the particle when the maximum tension occurs in the string and find this tension in terms of m for the angles given in **a**.

4 A body of mass m is placed at the top of a smooth spherical surface of radius r, and centre O. The body is displaced just enough to start it moving and the body leaves the surface at a point A, where OA makes an angle of α with the vertical. Find $\cos\alpha$ and the tangential acceleration at this point.

5 An object of mass m is attached to a string of length a and the other end is attached to a fixed point O. The mass is projected with a horizontal speed u when the string is vertical with the mass below O. Determine an expression for u if the object just completes vertical circles.

Contextual

1 A ball bearing of mass 50 grams is placed inside a circular tube. It is projected from the lowest position and it just completes vertical circles. The radius of the tube is 50 cm. Determine the initial speed of the ball bearing.

2 A solid smooth hemisphere, of radius 30 cm, is set with its flat surface on a horizontal surface. A marble, of mass 20 grams, is placed at the highest point on the hemisphere and released. Given that the marble starts to move, find the angle at which the marble leaves the hemisphere.

3 A football, of mass 300 grams, is attached to one end of a light inextensible string. The other end of the string is attached to a fixed point. Initially, the football hangs in equilibrium. It is kicked with a horizontal speed of $15\ \text{m s}^{-1}$ and it just completes a vertical circle. Work out the length of the string.

4

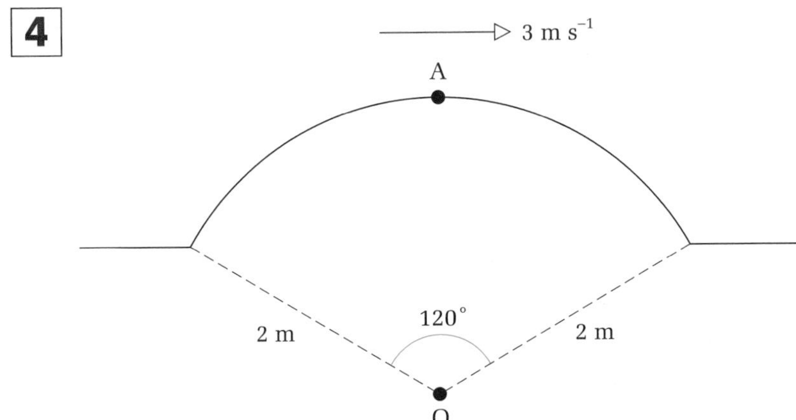

The diagram shows the dimensions of a ramp. A cyclist has reached point A and has a speed of $3\ \text{m s}^{-1}$ as shown. The cyclist then freewheels down the other side of the ramp. Show that the cyclist leaves the ramp and find the angle from the vertical at which this occurs. State two key assumptions that you have made.

Consolidation

Exercise A

1 A car of mass 1.2 tonnes is travelling around a roundabout, at a steady speed of $12\,\text{m s}^{-1}$. The friction force that is acting on the car has a magnitude equal to 90% of the magnitude of the normal reaction on the car. Assume that the car can be modelled as a particle and that the road surface is horizontal. (Assume $g = 10\,\text{m s}^{-2}$.)

a Draw a diagram to show the forces acting on the car if there is assumed to be no air resistance.

b Find the radius of the circle described by the car as it travels around the roundabout.

c The diagram shows the air resistance force that actually acts on the car as it moves on the roundabout, but that has been ignored in **a** and **b**. *On a copy of the diagram* draw a vector to show the resultant force on the car, and hence a vector to show the direction of the friction force on the car (i.e. the force between the tyres and the road).

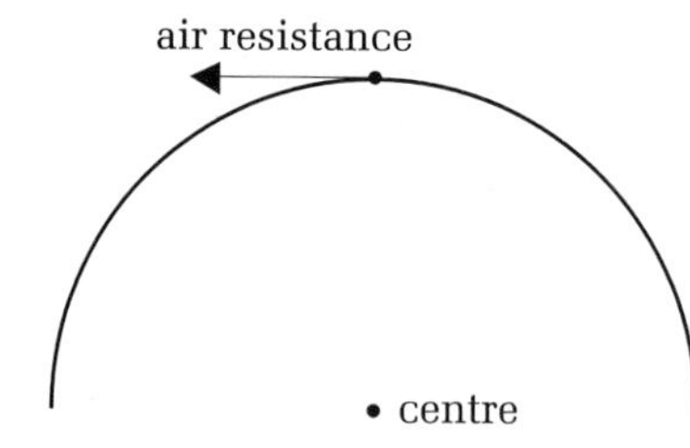

(AEB)

2 A particle of mass 0.2 kg is attached to one end of a light inextensible string of length 0.6 m. The other end of the string is attached to a fixed point O. The string is taut and the particle describes, with constant speed, horizontal circles about the vertical axis through O. The string makes an angle of 30° with the downward vertical. Find:

a the tension in the string

b the speed of the particle.

(WJEC)

3 The diagram represents a motorcycle of mass m kg travelling round a banked track of radius 50 m and shows all the external forces acting on it. The coefficient of friction between the tyres and the track is 0.5. The track is inclined at an angle α to the horizontal.

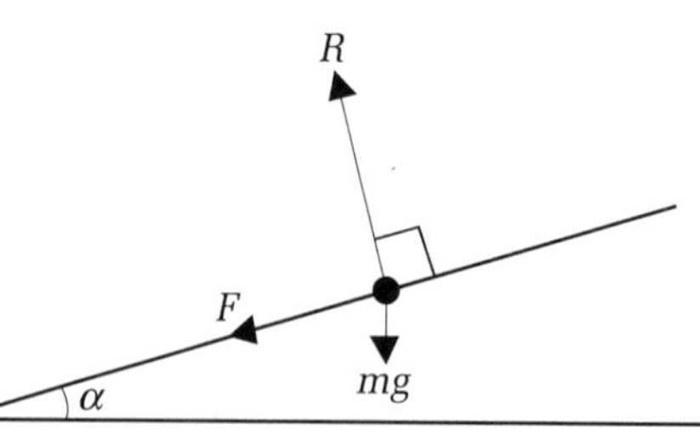

In this question F represents friction.

a If the motorcycle travels round this track at a maximum speed of $20\,\text{m s}^{-1}$, without skidding, find α, the inclination of the track to the horizontal. (Take $g = 10\,\text{m s}^{-2}$.)

b With the aid of a sketch, indicate how the track might be banked to cater for variable speeds.

(NICCEA)

4 A particle P, of mass m, is suspended by a light inextensible string of length a from a fixed point O. The particle is projected horizontally with initial speed u and starts to move in a vertical circle of centre O and radius a.

a Show that if the particle just reaches the level of O then $u^2 = 2ag$.

b Given that $u^2 = 3ag$, show that when the string is still taut and inclined at an angle θ to the *upward* vertical, the velocity of P is given by $v^2 = ag(1 - 2\cos\theta)$. Find, in terms of m, g and θ, the tension of the string in this position. Calculate, correct to the nearest degree, the value of θ when the string first becomes slack.

(*NEAB*)

Exercise B

1 A strip of smooth metal, in the shape of a semicircle of radius 20 cm, is fixed on a smooth horizontal surface. A marble of mass 20 grams is fired into the semicircle and travels at a speed of $5\ \text{m s}^{-1}$. Part of the path of the marble is shown by the broken line in the diagram. (Take $g = 10\ \text{m s}^{-2}$.)

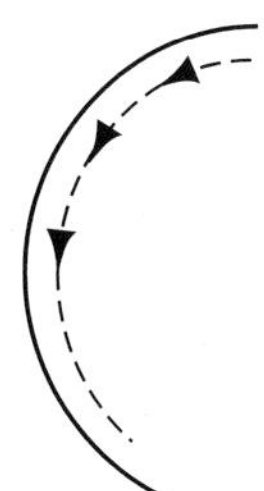

a Find the magnitude of the acceleration of the marble in m s^{-2}.

b Show that the magnitude of the resultant of the reaction forces acting on the marble is approximately 2.51 N.

c Copy the diagram and show the path of the marble when it leaves the semicircle.

(*AEB*)

2

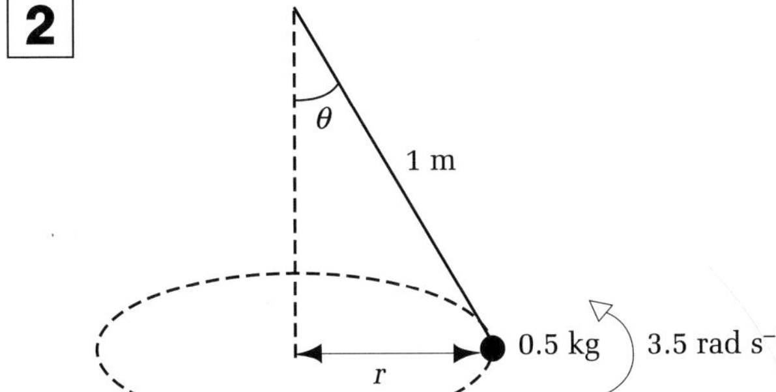

A light, inextensible string of length 1 m has one end attached to a fixed point. A particle of mass 0.5 kg is attached to the other end of the string. The particle is made to rotate uniformly in a horizontal circle, as a conical pendulum, with an angular speed of 3.5 radians per second, as shown in the diagram.

a Show that the tension in the string is 6.125 N.

b Find the angle, θ, which the string of the conical pendulum makes with the downward vertical.

c Explain briefly why it is not possible, in such an arrangement, for θ to be 90°.

(*NICCEA*)

3

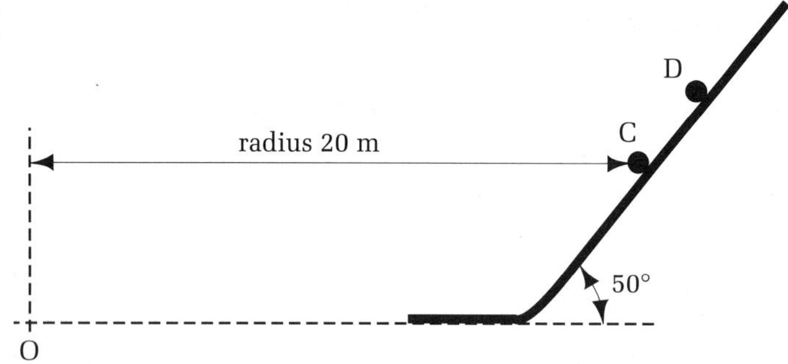

The diagram shows the cross-section of a banked circular cycle racing track, in a vertical plane through its centre O. A cyclist C moves at a constant speed on the steepest part of the track in a horizontal circular path of radius 20 m. The mass of the cyclist and his machine is 80 kg and the angle between the steepest part of the track and the horizontal is 50°. By using a model in which the cyclist and his machine are considered as a single particle and in which the track is smooth, and taking $g = 9.81\,\text{m}\,\text{s}^{-2}$:

a calculate the normal component of the contact force on the machine due to the track

b show that the magnitude of the acceleration of C is $11.7\,\text{m}\,\text{s}^{-2}$, correct to three significant figures

c calculate the speed of C.

Another cyclist D moves at constant speed on the steepest part of the track in a higher horizontal circular path. Determine which of the cyclists C and D completes one circuit of the track in the shorter time.

(*UCLES*)

4 A particle of mass m is attached to one end of a light, inelastic string of length, l. The other end B of the string is attached to a ceiling so that the particle is free to swing in a vertical plane; the angle between the string and the downward vertical is θ radians. You may assume that the air resistance on the particle is negligible.

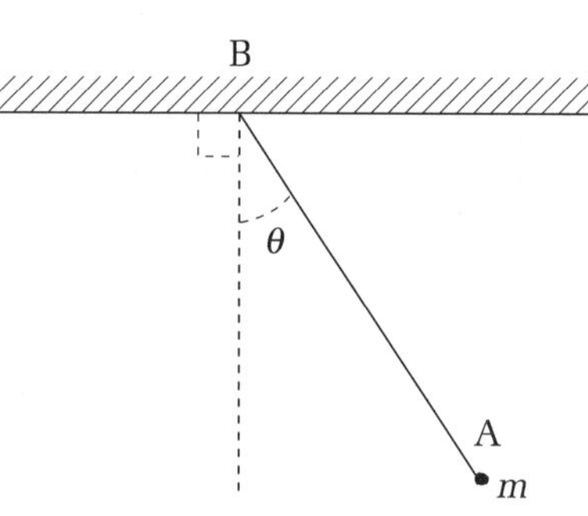

Initially $\theta = \frac{\pi}{3}$ and the particle is released from rest.

a Show that the potential energy lost by the particle since leaving its initial position is $\frac{mgl}{2}(2\cos\theta - 1)$. Hence find an expression for v^2, where v is the linear speed of the particle, in terms of l, g and θ.

b Show that the tension in the string at any point of the motion is $mg(3\cos\theta - 1)$.

c Find the greatest tension in the string. What is the position of the particle when the tension in the string is greatest?

(*MEI*)

Applications and Activities

1 A hammer is made up of a mass of 7.3 kg attached to a 1 m length of wire. The hammer thrower can make two complete revolutions per second. What is the linear speed of the mass and the tension in the wire?

The Enterprise is a ride that initially rotates horizontally. The ride is then angled until it completes vertical circles. Investigate the minimum speed necessary for the passengers to complete vertical circles.

3 A tumble drier is designed so that the clothes have to fall the maximum distance. At what speed should the tumble drier rotate for this to happen?

4 Design a conical pendulum with a time period of 1 second. Test out your design.

Summary

- The formula for linear speed in a horizontal circle is

  $$\mathbf{v} = \omega \mathbf{r}$$

- The formula to calculate the time to complete one revolution is

  $$T = \frac{2\pi}{\omega}$$

- The two formulas for the acceleration for motion at a constant speed in a horizontal circle are

  $$\mathbf{a} = \frac{\mathbf{v}^2}{\mathbf{r}}$$

  $$\mathbf{a} = \omega^2 \mathbf{r}$$

18 Variable Acceleration

What you need to know

- How to *differentiate* algebraic, trigonometric and exponential functions.
- How to *integrate* algebraic, trigonometric and exponential functions.
- How to sketch graphs of simple algebraic functions.
- How to write vectors in component form given the magnitude and direction.
- How to find the magnitude and direction of vectors from their component form.
- How to find the scalar product of two vectors and use it to prove vectors are perpendicular.
- How to solve differential equations by separating the variables.

Review

1 Differentiate the following functions:

a $y = 5x(x^3 - 3)$ **b** $y = 1 + \frac{7}{x^2}$

c $y = 5\sin 3x - 2\cos 3x$ **d** $y = 2(1 - e^{-9x})$

2 Find the following integrals:

a $\int 6x^2(2 - x)\,dx$ **d** $\displaystyle\int \frac{6x}{(10 - 3x^2)}\,dx$

b $\displaystyle\int \left(3 - \frac{5}{x}\right) dx$ **e** $\int (4\cos 2x + 7\sin 2x)\,dx$

c $\displaystyle\int \frac{4}{2x + 3}$ **f** $\int (2x + 5e^{-0.1x} + 30)\,dx$

3 Sketch the graphs of:

a $y = x^3 - 1$ **b** $y = 9 - x^2$ **c** $y = x^2 - 7x + 12$

4 Write the following vector in the form $a\mathbf{i} + b\mathbf{j}$:

Remember to underline vectors.

a

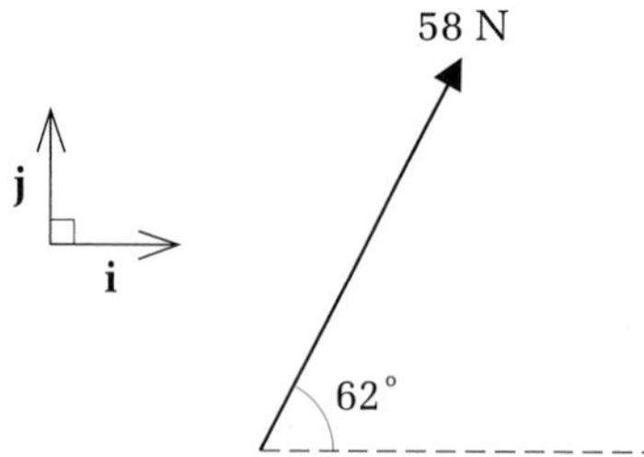

A force of 58 newtons at an angle of 62° to the horizontal as shown.

b A velocity of 25 m s^{-1} on a bearing of 310°, using **i** to represent a unit vector to the east and **j** a unit vector to the north.

5 **a** Calculate the magnitude of the force:

$$\mathbf{F} = 8\mathbf{i} - 6\mathbf{j} + 24\mathbf{k} \text{ newtons}$$

b The velocity of a ship is given by the vector $\mathbf{v} = 11\mathbf{i} - 7\mathbf{j}\text{ km h}^{-1}$ where **i** is a unit vector to the east and **j** is a unit vector to the north. Find the speed and the bearing on which the ship is travelling.

6 **a** Find the scalar product of the vectors:

$\mathbf{v}_1 = 3\mathbf{i} + 2\mathbf{j} - 4\mathbf{k}$ and $\mathbf{v}_2 = 5\mathbf{i} - 6\mathbf{j} - \mathbf{k}$

b Find the values of t for which the forces $\mathbf{F}_1 = t\mathbf{i} - 2\mathbf{j}$ and $\mathbf{F}_2 = 2t\mathbf{i} + (t + 6)\mathbf{j}$ are perpendicular.

7 Solve the following differential equations by separating the variables:

a $\dfrac{dy}{dx} = \dfrac{1}{y}$, given that $y = 2$ when $x = 1$

b $y\dfrac{dy}{dx} = 4x$, given that $y = 4$ when $x = 0$

c $\dfrac{dy}{dx} = y^2(x + 1)$ given that $y = 1$ when $x = 2$

d $\dfrac{dy}{dx} = 2y$, given that $y = 5$ when $x = 0$.

18.1 Using Differentiation to find Velocity and Acceleration

When acceleration is constant, problems involving motion in a straight line can be solved using the uniform acceleration formulas. *When acceleration is not constant these formulas do not apply.*

See Chapter 6.

Travel graphs may also be used to solve problems involving motion in a straight line. The graphs used previously involved *straight* line segments. Again this means that the acceleration was uniform. Often motion is more complex. When a car travels down a city street its velocity and acceleration are constantly changing and the (t, x) and (t, v) graphs would consist of curves rather than straight lines.

See Chapter 4.

Remember:
x = displacement
v = velocity
t = time

Some of the ideas used in travel graphs can be developed for use with motion where the acceleration is not constant. Remember that for an object travelling in a straight line:

Kinematics with variable acceleration.

Velocity is equal to the gradient of a displacement–time graph.
Acceleration is equal to the gradient of a velocity–time graph.

It is possible to find the gradient of a curve by drawing a tangent and measuring its gradient as shown in the sketch.

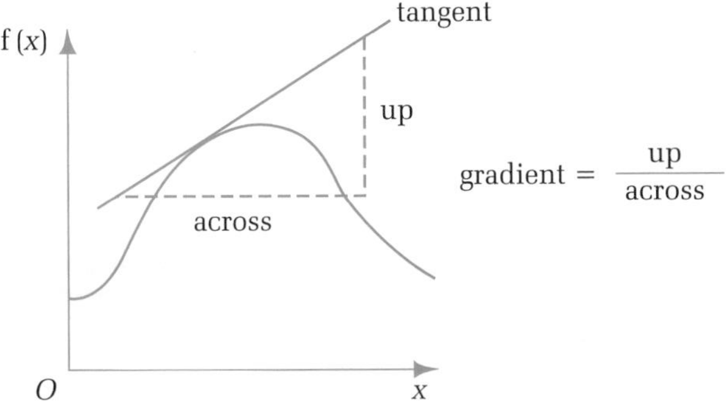

$$\text{gradient} = \frac{\text{up}}{\text{across}}$$

If the equation of the curve is known, differentiation gives a more accurate value for the gradient. If displacement is given as a function of time, differentiating once gives a formula for velocity and differentiating again gives a formula for acceleration. Using x to denote displacement, t time, v velocity and a acceleration,

$$v = \frac{dx}{dt}$$

and $$a = \frac{dv}{dt} = \frac{d^2x}{dt^2}$$

Velocity is the rate of change of displacement. Acceleration is the rate of change of velocity.

If the mass of the moving object is known, Newton's law, $F = ma$, can be used to find the force producing the acceleration.

Dot notation

Sometimes a dot is used above a letter to show that the quantity represented by that letter has been differentiated with respect to time. A double dot means that the quantity has been differentiated twice.

$\dot{x}$ means the same as $\dfrac{dx}{dt}$

and $\ddot{x}$ means the same as $\dfrac{d^2x}{dt^2}$

Differentiate x with respect to t.
Differentiate x with respect to t twice.

Overview of method

Step ① Differentiate to find formulas for the quantities needed.

$$v = \frac{dx}{dt} \qquad a = \frac{dv}{dt} \qquad F = ma = m\frac{dv}{dt} \quad \text{or} \quad F = m\frac{d^2x}{dt^2}$$

Step ② Substitute the given values and evaluate the items required.
Step ③ Draw a sketch or graph if helpful or requested.

Example 1

A particle, P, of mass 2 kg, moves along a straight line so that its displacement from a fixed point, O, on the line after t seconds is given by $x = 5 - t^3$ (metres). Find the magnitude and direction of the force acting on the object when $t = 2$.

Solution

$x = 5 - t^3$

$\dot{x} = -3t^2$ ◀ ① Differentiate to find formulas for the quantities needed.

$\ddot{x} = -6t$

$F = m\ddot{x} = -12t$

$v = \dot{x}$
$a = \ddot{x}$
$F = ma = m\ddot{x}$

When $t = 2$, $F = -12 \times 2 = -24$ ◀ ② Substitute the given values and evaluate the items required.

The force is of magnitude 24 N and acts *towards* O. The negative sign means the force is acting in the opposite direction to x.

Since x is measured *from* O, the force acts *towards* O.

Sometimes s is used to denote displacement rather than x.

Example 2

A truck of mass 500 kg is moving along a track so that its displacement from a signal after t seconds is $s = 120(1 - e^{-0.04t})$ metres.

a Find the displacement, velocity and acceleration of the truck after 5 seconds.

b Explain briefly what will happen to the displacement and velocity as t increases.

Solution

The truck is modelled as a particle moving in a straight line.

a $s = 120(1 - e^{-0.04t}) = 120 - 120e^{-0.04t}$

$v = \dfrac{ds}{dt} = 4.8e^{-0.04t}$ ◀ ① **Differentiate to find formulas for the quantities needed.**

$a = \dfrac{dv}{dt} = -0.192e^{-0.04t}$

$v = \dfrac{ds}{dt}$

$a = \dfrac{dv}{dt}$

When $t = 5$

$s = 120(1 - e^{-0.2})$

$s = 120(1 - 0.8187)$

$s = 120 \times 0.1813$

$s = 21.75$

$-0.04t = -0.04 \times 5$
$= -0.2$

So after 5 s, displacement = 22 m (to the nearest metre).

When $t = 5$

$v = 4.8e^{-0.2}$

$v = 4.8 \times 0.8187$

$v = 3.9299$

So after 5 s, velocity = 3.9 m s^{-1} (2 s.f.)

When $t = 5$

$a = -0.192e^{-0.2}$ ◀ ② **Substitute the given values and evaluate the items required.**

$a = -0.192 \times 0.8187$

$a = -0.1572$

So after 5 s, acceleration = -0.16 m s^{-2} (2 s.f.)

b As $t \to \infty$, $e^{-0.04t} \to 0$

$s = 120(1 - e^{-0.04t}) \to 120$

and $v = 4.8e^{-0.04t} \to 0$

As t increases the displacement approaches 120 m and the velocity reduces towards zero.

Calculate $e^{-0.04t}$ for $t = 10, 20, 30, 40$

Example 3

A particle moves along a straight line. Its displacement from a fixed point, O, on the line after t seconds is given by $x = t^3 - 9t^2 + 15t$ (metres).

a Find a formula for the velocity.

b Find the times at which the particle is at rest.

Solution

a $v = \dfrac{dx}{dt} = 3t^2 - 18t + 15$ ◀ ① **Differentiate to find the velocity.**

$v = \dfrac{dx}{dt}$

b The particle is at rest when $v = 0$

$3t^2 - 18t + 15 = 0$ ◀ ② **Substitute and divide by 3 to simplify.**

$t^2 - 6t + 5 = 0$

$(t - 1)(t - 5) = 0$

$t = 1$ or $t = 5$

Factorise the quadratic.

Solve the quadratic.

The particle is at rest after 1 second and 5 seconds.

18.1 Using Differentiation to find Velocity and Acceleration

Exercise

Technique

1 For each of the following displacement formulas, find formulas in terms of t for the velocity and acceleration:

a $x = t^5 + 4t^2 - 3t + 1$ **b** $x = 5 - \frac{3}{t}$

c $x = 7\sin 2t$ **d** $x = 6e^{5t}$

2 The displacement, s metres, of an object from a fixed point, O, at time t seconds is $s = 5\cos 3t$. If the mass of the object is 0.2 kg, find the magnitude and direction of the force acting on the object when:

a $t = 0$ **b** $t = 0.5$

(Assume the motion is in a straight line and remember to use radians.)

3 A particle moves along the x-axis so that its displacement from the origin after t seconds is $x = t^3 + 1$.

a Find an expression for the velocity in terms of t.

b Sketch the (t, x) and (t, v) graphs of the motion for $t \geq 0$.

4 The equation $x = 2t^3 - 15t^2 + 36t$ gives the displacement in metres of a particle from a fixed point, O, in terms of the time, t seconds.

a Find the values of t for which the particle is at rest.

b Find the distance moved by the particle between these values of t.

c Find the total distance travelled in time interval $0 \leq t \leq 4$.

Take care – the velocity changes direction. Find the distance travelled in *each part* of the motion.

Contextual

1 A man watches his daughter on a fairground ride. The girl travels in a straight line and her displacement in metres from her father is given by the formula $x = 5 + 3\cos 2t$ where t is the time in seconds after the ride begins.

a Find formulas for $\dot{x}$ and $\ddot{x}$ and explain what information is given by these formulas.

b Find the displacement and velocity of the girl when:

i $t = 0$ **ii** $t = 1$ **iii** $t = 2$

c What are the maximum and minimum displacements?

d What are the maximum values of the speed and acceleration?

2 When a package is dropped from an aircraft the distance it falls in t seconds is $x = 75t + 750e^{-\frac{t}{10}} - 750$ metres.

a Find formulas for the velocity, v, and the acceleration, a, in terms of t.

b Find the velocity and acceleration when $t = 0$.

c What happens to v and a as $t \to \infty$?

d Use your answers to **b** and **c** to describe briefly the motion of the package.

18.2 Using Integration to find Velocity and Displacement

Integration is the opposite of differentiation. By reversing the process introduced in the last section, formulas for velocity and displacement can be found from an expression for acceleration.

If acceleration a is given as a function of time t, then the velocity v and the displacement x are

Velocity is the integral of acceleration. Displacement is the integral of velocity.

$$v = \int a \, dt$$

$$x = \int v \, dt$$

You may remember that displacement is given by the area under the velocity–time graph. Since integrating gives the area under a curve, this confirms the fact that integrating the formula for velocity gives the displacement.

See Chapter 4.

Indefinite integration always introduces an arbitrary constant. This constant can only be found if more information is given about the motion. Often questions will give the initial velocity and displacement. These values are called **boundary conditions**.

Boundary or *initial conditions.*

Overview of method

Step ① Use integration to find the formula needed;

$$v = \int a \, dt \quad \text{and} \quad x = \int v \, dt$$

Step ② Substitute the boundary conditions and evaluate the constant of integration.

Step ③ Substitute any other values given and find the items requested.

Follow this procedure more than once if both velocity and displacement are required. If a formula for the force is given use Newton's law, $F = ma$, first to find a formula for acceleration.

Example 1

A particle, P, moving along a straight line, passes through a point O on the line with velocity $2\ \text{m s}^{-1}$. The acceleration of the particle is given by $a = 2(3t + 1)\ \text{m s}^{-2}$ where t is the time in seconds after the particle passes through O. Find expressions in terms of t for the velocity and displacement of the particle from O.

Solution

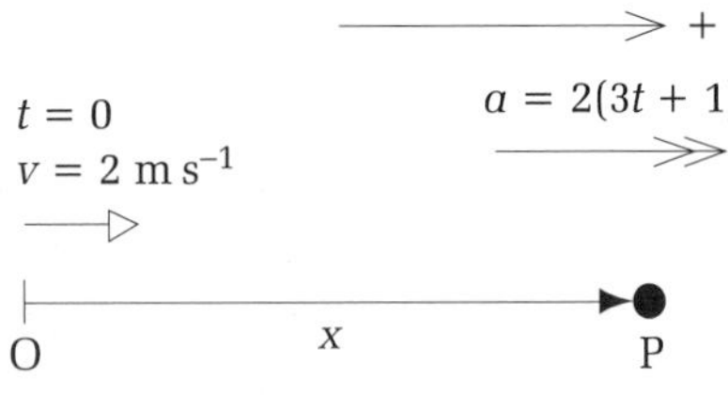

$v = \int a\,dt$

$v = \int 2(3t + 1)\,dt$

$v = \int (6t + 2)\,dt$

$v = 3t^2 + 2t + c$

◀ ① **Use integration to find the formula needed; $v = \int a\,dt$.**

Replace a.
Expand brackets and integrate.

When $t = 0$, $v = 2$

$2 = 3 \times 0^2 + 2 \times 0 + c$

$2 = c$

$v = 3t^2 + 2t + 2$

◀ ② **Substitute the boundary conditions and evaluate the constant of integration.**

$x = \int v\,dt$

$x = \int (3t^2 + 2t + 2)\,dt$

$x = t^3 + t^2 + 2t + k$

◀ ① **Use integration to find the formula needed; $x = \int v\,dt$.**

When $t = 0$, $x = 0$ since the particle is passing through O

$0 = 0^3 + 0^2 + 2 \times 0 + k$

$0 = k$

$x = t^3 + t^2 + 2t$

$x = t(t^2 + t + 2)$

◀ ② **Substitute the boundary conditions and evaluate the constant of integration.**

Factorise by taking out t as a common factor.

Example 2

A manufacturer of fireworks has invented a new rocket of mass 0.2 kg. For the first four seconds of motion, a force of magnitude $F = 8 - 2t$ newtons propels the rocket vertically upwards (where t is the time in seconds after it leaves the ground). The motion is resisted by the rocket's weight. Taking $g = 10$ m s^{-2}, estimate the velocity and height of the rocket at the end of the first four seconds of motion when F becomes zero.

Solution

The sketch shows the rocket modelled as a particle of mass 0.2 kg moving vertically upwards under the action of the propulsion force, F and the force of gravity. The mass is assumed to be constant.

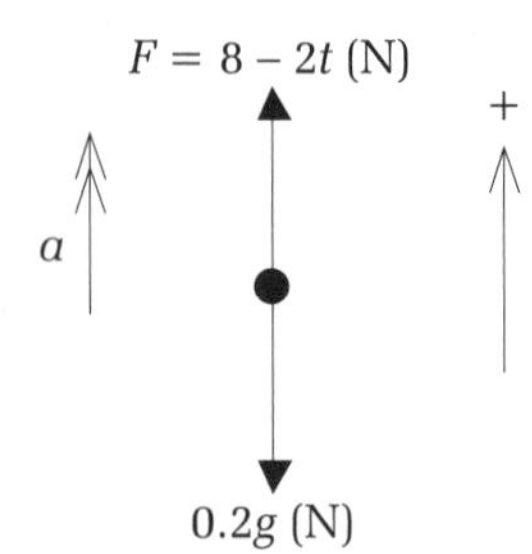

Applying $F = ma \uparrow$

$$8 - 2t - 0.2g = 0.2a$$
$$8 - 2t - 2 = 0.2a$$
$$6 - 2t = 0.2a$$
$$a = \frac{6 - 2t}{0.2} = 30 - 10t, \text{ for } 0 \le t \le 4$$

Recall that the F in Newton's law stands for the *resultant* force in the direction of motion. Take care not to confuse it with the propulsion force, F, given in the question.

After finding a formula for the acceleration a, the usual steps of the method can be used to find the velocity and displacement.

$v = \int a\,dt$ ◀ ① **Use integration to find v.**

$v = \int (30 - 10t)\,dt$

$v = 30t - 5t^2 + c$

When $t = 0$, $v = 0 \Rightarrow c = 0$. ◀ ② **Find the constant of integration.**

The formula for the velocity is $v = 30t - 5t^2$.

$x = \int v\,dt$ ◀ ① **Use integration to find x.**

$x = \int (30t - 5t^2)\,dt$

$x = 15t^2 - \frac{5}{3}t^3 + k$

When $t = 0$, $x = 0 \Rightarrow k = 0$. ◀ ② **Find the constant of integration.**

The formula for the displacement is $x = 15t^2 - \frac{5}{3}t^3$.

When $t = 4$

$v = 30t - 5t^2$ ◀ ③ **Substitute any given values and find the items requested.**

$v = 30 \times 4 - 5 \times 4^2$

$v = 120 - 80 = 40$

$x = 15t^2 - \frac{5}{3}t^3$

$x = 15 \times 4^2 - \frac{5}{3} \times 4^3$

$x = 240 - \frac{320}{3}$

$x = 133\frac{1}{3}$

After 4 seconds the rocket is travelling upwards at $40\,\text{m}\,\text{s}^{-1}$ and has reached a height of $133\frac{1}{3}$ m.

In practice, the mass of the rocket will reduce as fuel is used. The reduction in weight would lead to an increase in acceleration. On the other hand, as the rocket's speed increased, air resistance would cause a decrease in acceleration.

18.2 Using Integration to find Velocity and Displacement

Exercise

Technique

1 A particle, P, moves in a straight line with acceleration $a = (9t^2 - 1)\,\text{m s}^{-2}$ where t is the time in seconds. O is a fixed point on the line. When $t = 0$, the particle is at rest and OP = 2 m. Find formulas, in terms of t, for the velocity and displacement from O.

2 A particle moving along the x-axis passes through the origin with velocity $2\,\text{m s}^{-1}$ (in the positive direction) when $t = 0$. Find formulas for the velocity and displacement after t seconds if:

a $a = 15\sqrt{t}\,\text{m s}^{-2}$ **b** $a = 3\sin(\frac{1}{2}t)\,\text{m s}^{-2}$

3 After t seconds of motion on a straight line, the acceleration of a particle is given by $a = 6(2t - 1)^2\,\text{m s}^{-1}$. Initially the particle is at rest at a fixed point, O, on the line. Find the velocity and displacement of the particle from O when $t = 2$.

4 When $t = 0$, a particle is moving through the origin with velocity $6\,\text{m s}^{-1}$ in the positive x direction. A resultant force $F = 5 - 3t$ newtons acts on the particle when $t \geq 0$. If the mass of the particle is 0.5 kg, find the time at which the particle returns to O.

Contextual

1 When a lorry travelling at $15\,\text{m s}^{-1}$ joins a motorway, it accelerates for 10 seconds. During this time the acceleration is $a = \frac{1}{4}(16 - t)\,\text{m s}^{-2}$ where t is the time in seconds after it begins to accelerate.

a Find the lorry's speed at the end of this 10 s period.

b Find the distance travelled by the lorry whilst it accelerates and hence find its average speed during this period.

Remember: average speed $= \dfrac{\text{total distance}}{\text{total time}}$

2 A car is travelling at $16\,\text{m s}^{-1}$ when it accelerates to overtake a coach. The driving force of the engine increases with time according to the formula $F = 120(t^2 + 2)$ N. The mass of the car is 1 tonne and the resistance to motion is 240 N. If the car accelerates for 6 seconds find its velocity at the end of this period and the distance it has travelled.

3 A spacecraft is 100 m from a space station when it begins a docking procedure in which it travels in a straight line with velocity $2e^{-0.02t}\,\text{m s}^{-1}$ towards the space station, where t is the time in seconds.

a Find a formula in terms of t for the displacement of the spacecraft during the manoeuvre, measured from its original position.

b The spacecraft is secured to the space station when it has travelled 99 m. Find the time taken to achieve this.

18.3 Vectors

Previous sections of this chapter have applied differentiation and integration to motion in a straight line – in other words, motion in one dimension. Many objects move in two or three dimensions. If the Earth's surface is modelled as a plane, cars, ships, and people travel on the plane in two dimensions. Bodies such as aircraft, birds and fish, which also move upwards or downwards from this plane, move in three dimensions. How can two or three dimensional motion be modelled? The answer is with time-dependent vectors.

In Chapters 3 and 5, three dimensional quantities such as forces and velocities were written in the form $x\mathbf{i} + y\mathbf{j} + z\mathbf{k}$ where $\mathbf{i}$, $\mathbf{j}$ and $\mathbf{k}$ are unit vectors in the x, y and z directions. The three components x, y and z were constants.

For a two dimensional quantity, z was zero giving a vector of the form $x\mathbf{i} + y\mathbf{j}$.

For problems involving motion, the components, x, y and z, may be constant or functions of time. The acceleration, $\mathbf{a}$, the velocity, $\mathbf{v}$, and any force, $\mathbf{F}$, will now be in vector form. The position of the object will be given by its position vector, $\mathbf{r}$, and differentiation and integration again relate these quantities. In vector form the results are:

Differentiation $\mathbf{v} = \dfrac{\mathrm{d}\mathbf{r}}{\mathrm{d}t}$ and $\mathbf{a} = \dfrac{\mathrm{d}\mathbf{v}}{\mathrm{d}t} = \dfrac{\mathrm{d}^2\mathbf{r}}{\mathrm{d}t^2}$

Integration $\mathbf{v} = \int \mathbf{a}\,\mathrm{d}t$ and $\mathbf{r} = \int \mathbf{v}\,\mathrm{d}t$

Dot notation may be used: $\mathbf{v} = \dot{\mathbf{r}}$ and $\mathbf{a} = \ddot{\mathbf{r}}$.

This time the *constant of integration* must be a *vector*.
Newton's law, $\mathbf{F} = m\mathbf{a}$, can be used in problems involving forces.

The examples and exercises include a wide variety of problems requiring differentiation or integration as well as other techniques you have met earlier in the course. The general approach is given below.

Overview of method

Step ① Use differentiation or integration to find expressions, in terms of t, for the quantities needed.

Step ② If given a value of t, substitute this into general expressions to find the particular values required.

Step ③ Use vector techniques or other methods from mechanics to find other items or provide proofs.

Example 1

A particle starts from the point whose position vector is $2\mathbf{i} + \mathbf{j} - \mathbf{k}$ (m) and moves with velocity $\mathbf{v} = 8t^3\mathbf{i} - 3t^2\mathbf{j} + 2t\mathbf{k}$ (m s^{-1}). Find the velocity, acceleration and position vector of the particle after 2 seconds of motion.

Solution

Given $\mathbf{v} = 8t^3\mathbf{i} - 3t^2\mathbf{j} + 2t\mathbf{k}$ ◀ ① Use differentiation or integration to find the quantities needed.

$$\mathbf{a} = \frac{d\mathbf{v}}{dt} = 24t^2\mathbf{i} - 6t\mathbf{j} + 2\mathbf{k}$$

$$\mathbf{r} = \int \mathbf{v}\, dt$$

$$\mathbf{r} = \int (8t^3\mathbf{i} - 3t^2\mathbf{j} + 2t\mathbf{k})\, dt$$

$\mathbf{r} = 2t^4\mathbf{i} - t^3\mathbf{j} + t^2\mathbf{k} + \mathbf{c}$, where $\mathbf{c}$ is a vector constant of integration.

Substituting the boundary condition $\mathbf{r} = 2\mathbf{i} + \mathbf{j} - \mathbf{k}$ when $t = 0$ gives

$$2\mathbf{i} + \mathbf{j} - \mathbf{k} = \mathbf{c}$$

$$\mathbf{r} = 2t^4\mathbf{i} - t^3\mathbf{j} + t^2\mathbf{k} + 2\mathbf{i} + \mathbf{j} - \mathbf{k}$$

$$\mathbf{r} = 2(t^4 + 1)\mathbf{i} + (1 - t^3)\mathbf{j} + (t^2 - 1)\mathbf{k}$$

When $t = 2$,

$$\text{velocity} = 8 \times 2^3\mathbf{i} - 3 \times 2^2\mathbf{j} + 2 \times 2\mathbf{k}$$
$$= 64\mathbf{i} - 12\mathbf{j} + 4\mathbf{k} \quad (\text{m s}^{-1})$$

◀ ② Substitute value given for t.

$$\text{acceleration} = 24 \times 2^2\mathbf{i} - 6 \times 2\mathbf{j} + 2\mathbf{k}$$
$$= 96\mathbf{i} - 12\mathbf{j} + 2\mathbf{k} \quad (\text{m s}^{-2})$$

$$\text{position vector} = 2(2^4 + 1)\mathbf{i} + (1 - 2^3)\mathbf{j} + (2^2 - 1)\mathbf{k}$$
$$= 34\mathbf{i} - 7\mathbf{j} + 3\mathbf{k} \ (\text{m})$$

Example 2

The position vector of a particle at time t seconds is given by $\mathbf{r} = \sin 2t\,\mathbf{i} + \cos 2t\,\mathbf{j}$ (metres).

a Find the velocity and acceleration as functions of t.

b Show that the speed of the particle is constant and that its direction of motion is perpendicular to $\mathbf{r}$.

Solution

a $\mathbf{r} = \sin 2t\,\mathbf{i} + \cos 2t\,\mathbf{j}$ ◀ ① Use differentiation or integration to find the quantities needed.

$\mathbf{v} = 2\cos 2t\,\mathbf{i} - 2\sin 2t\,\mathbf{j}$

$\mathbf{a} = -4\sin 2t\,\mathbf{i} - 4\cos 2t\,\mathbf{j}$

b speed of particle is $|\mathbf{v}| = \sqrt{(2\cos 2t)^2 + (2\sin 2t)^2}$

$$= \sqrt{4(\cos^2 2t + \sin^2 2t)}$$
$$= \sqrt{4} = 2$$

For any angle, θ, $\sin^2\theta + \cos^2\theta = 1$.

The speed of the particle, 2 m s^{-1}, is constant.

The scalar product can be used to show that the direction of motion is perpendicular to $\mathbf{r}$:

$$\mathbf{v}.\mathbf{r} = (2\cos 2t\,\mathbf{i} - 2\sin 2t\,\mathbf{j}).(\sin 2t\,\mathbf{i} + \cos 2t\,\mathbf{j})$$
$$\mathbf{v}.\mathbf{r} = 2\cos 2t \sin 2t - 2\sin 2t \cos 2t$$
$$\mathbf{v}.\mathbf{r} = 0$$

◀ ③ Use vector techniques to provide proofs.

This particle is moving in a circle at a constant linear speed of 2 m s^{-1}.

A scalar product of zero proves that $\mathbf{v}$ is perpendicular to $\mathbf{r}$.

18.3 Vectors
Exercise
Technique

1 Find expressions for the velocity and acceleration of a particle if its displacement is given in metres after t seconds by:

a $\mathbf{r} = t^3\mathbf{i} + (6t - 4)\mathbf{j} - (5 - t^2)\mathbf{k}$

b $\mathbf{r} = 2\sin 5t\,\mathbf{i} - \cos 5t\,\mathbf{j} + e^{-2t}\mathbf{k}$

Remember to *underline* all vectors in your solutions.

2 The acceleration of a particle is $\mathbf{a} = 6t\mathbf{i} + 4\mathbf{j}\ \text{m s}^{-2}$. When $t = 0$, the velocity $\mathbf{v} = -3\mathbf{j}\ \text{m s}^{-1}$ and the displacement of the particle from the origin is $2\mathbf{i} - \mathbf{j}$ m.

a Find the acceleration, velocity and displacement of the particle when $t = 2$.

b Find the speed and the angle between the direction of motion and the direction of $\mathbf{i}$ at this time.

Remember speed is the magnitude of the velocity vector.

3 A particle of mass 0.5 kg is acted upon by a force $\mathbf{F} = 2\mathbf{i} - t\mathbf{j} + 6(t^2 - 2)\mathbf{k}$ where t is the time in seconds. When $t = 0$ the particle is at rest at the point with position vector $4\mathbf{i} + 7\mathbf{j} - 10\mathbf{k}$. Find the speed, kinetic energy and position vector of the particle when $t = 3$.

4 The velocity of a particle is given by $\mathbf{v} = 7(t - 5)\mathbf{i} + 24t\,\mathbf{j}\ \text{m s}^{-1}$ where t is the time in seconds.

a Show that when $t = 0$ the particle is moving parallel to the x-axis and find the time at which the particle is moving parallel to the y-axis.

b What is the speed with which the particle moves parallel to the y-axis?

c Show that the acceleration is constant.

d If the mass of the particle is 2 kg, find the magnitude of the force acting on the particle and the angle between the force and the $\mathbf{j}$ direction.

5 The velocity of a particle, at time t seconds, is given by $\mathbf{v} = 2\mathbf{i} + 8t\mathbf{j}\ \text{m s}^{-1}$. When $t = 0$ the particle passes through the point whose position vector is $\mathbf{r} = -5\mathbf{j}$.

a Find $\mathbf{r}$ in terms of t.

b Show that $\mathbf{r}$ and $\mathbf{v}$ are perpendicular when $t = 0$ and find the other value of t for which this occurs, giving your answer as a surd.

Contextual

1 A speedboat passes a buoy and after t seconds its displacement from the buoy is given in metres, by the position vector $\mathbf{r} = t^2\mathbf{i} - 7t\mathbf{j}$ where $\mathbf{i}$ is a unit vector to the east and $\mathbf{j}$ is a unit vector to the north.

a Find an expression for the velocity and show that the acceleration is constant.

b Find the distance and bearing of the boat from the buoy when $t = 4$.

c Find the speed and direction of motion when $t = 4$.

2 The acceleration of a helicopter, at time t seconds during take-off, is given by $\mathbf{a} = -10t\mathbf{i} + 4t^2\mathbf{j} + 6(3 - t)\mathbf{k}\,\text{m s}^{-2}$, where $\mathbf{i}$ and $\mathbf{j}$ are unit vectors to the east and north and $\mathbf{k}$ is a unit vector upwards. When $t = 0$ the helicopter is at rest and its displacement from an observer, O, on the ground is $\mathbf{r} = 15\mathbf{i} - 20\mathbf{j}$ metres.

a Find expressions for the velocity and displacement of the helicopter from the observer after t seconds of motion.

b Find the height above the ground and the distance between the helicopter and the observer when $t = 3$.

3

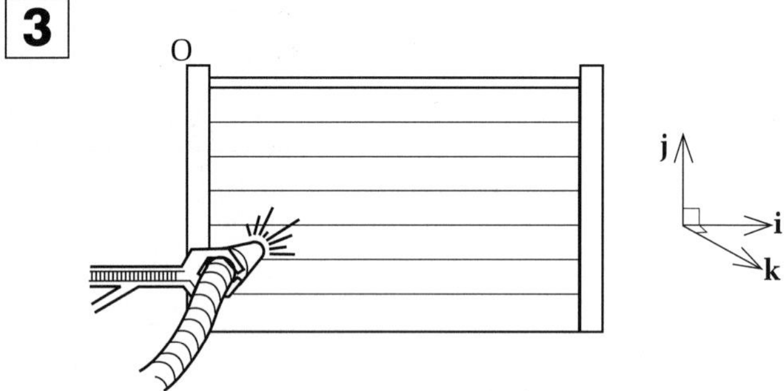

A robot arm is used to spray fence panels with wood preservative. The velocity of the spray gun after t seconds is given by $\mathbf{v} = \sin\left(\frac{1}{2}t\right)\mathbf{i} - \frac{1}{12}\mathbf{j}\,\text{m s}^{-1}$ where $\mathbf{i}$ and $\mathbf{j}$ are horizontal and vertical unit vectors as shown in the sketch. When $t = 0$ the nozzle of the spray gun is at the point $\mathbf{r} = 1.5\mathbf{k}$ relative to the origin, O, which is situated at the top left-hand corner of the panel.

a Find $\mathbf{r}$ as a function of t.

b Spraying continues until the spray gun reaches the bottom of the panel. If this occurs when the $\mathbf{j}$ component of its position vector is $-3\mathbf{j}$, find the time taken to spray the panel.

c Find also the speed with which the spray gun is moving when it completes the operation.

4

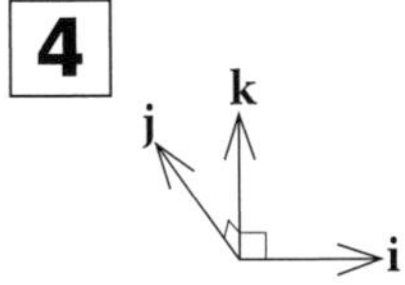

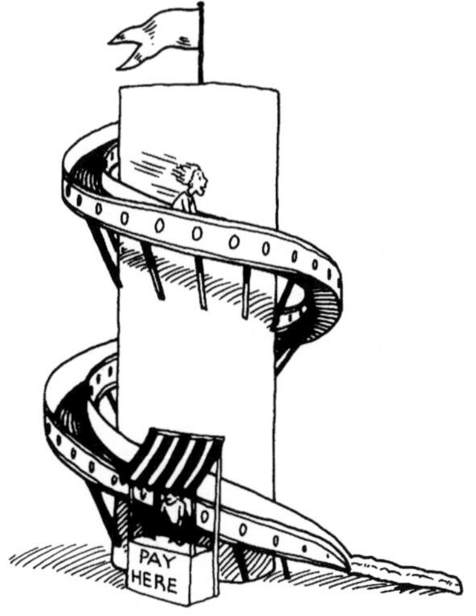

A girl of mass 30 kg is given a push and slides down a helter-skelter as shown in the sketch. The helter-skelter is designed so that after t seconds of motion the displacement of the girl from the pay kiosk at ground level is given by $\mathbf{r} = \sin 2t\,\mathbf{i} + \cos 2t\,\mathbf{j} + (9 - \frac{1}{4}t^2)\mathbf{k}$, where $\mathbf{i}$ and $\mathbf{j}$ are perpendicular horizontal unit vectors and $\mathbf{k}$ is a vertical unit vector.

a Find expressions for the velocity, acceleration and force acting on the girl after t seconds.

b Show that the girl reaches ground level after 6 seconds.

c Find the kinetic energy of the girl when she reaches the bottom.

d Show that the magnitude of her acceleration is constant throughout the motion.

5 A small motor boat, of mass 250 kg, starts from rest to cross a lake. During the first 5 seconds of motion the motor produces a force of magnitude $80 + 30t$ newtons to the north. A current from the direction 300° exerts a force of magnitude 48 N on the motor boat.

a Write each force in terms of $\mathbf{i}$ and $\mathbf{j}$ where $\mathbf{i}$ is a unit vector to the east and $\mathbf{j}$ is a unit vector to the north and find the resultant horizontal force.

b Find the speed of the boat and its direction of motion after 5 seconds.

6 The position of a boy on a roundabout, relative to its centre O at time t seconds, is $\mathbf{r} = a\sin(\omega t)\mathbf{i} + a\cos(\omega t)\mathbf{j}$(m).

a Find his velocity.

b Show that his acceleration is $\omega^2 a$ towards.

This is the general form for the position vector of a point moving around a circle of radius a and angular speed ω.

18.4 Acceleration as a Function of Velocity

Until now forces, acceleration, velocity and displacement have been modelled as functions of time. In practice, many situations occur in which the force and acceleration depend on the velocity or displacement. When a car travels along the motorway the air resistance increases as the velocity increases. Football supporters, who hang their scarves out of the window, can see this happening.

In mathematical modelling, air resistance is usually taken to be proportional to a power of the velocity. This is also true of the resistance experienced by objects moving through water or other fluids. The expression used for this resistance is often of the form $R = kv$ or $R = kv^2$, where k is a constant.

Resistance $\propto v^n$ where n is a number and v is the velocity.

This section concentrates on motion where resultant force and acceleration are functions of velocity. We will continue to use the fact that $a = \frac{dv}{dt}$, but in order to find a formula for v in terms of t it is now necessary to solve a differential equation using separation of variables. The main steps are given below. As the examples all involve motion in a straight line, vector notation is not needed.

Overview of method

Newton's law is not necessary if the question gives an expression for a.

Step ① Use $F = ma$ (if necessary) and replace a by $\frac{dv}{dt}$ to give a differential equation of the form $\frac{dv}{dt} = f(v)$.

Step ② Separate the variables and insert integral signs at each side.

Step ③ Carry out the integration, remembering to include a constant at one side.

Step ④ Use boundary conditions (usually the initial values of v and t) to evaluate the constant of integration.

Step ⑤ Write down the equation relating v and t and, if necessary, use it to answer questions.

Step ⑥ If the displacement, x, is needed, find a formula for v in terms of t and integrate. (As usual include and evaluate the constant of integration.)

When integrals involve logarithms, the law $\ln a - \ln b = \ln\left(\frac{a}{b}\right)$ is often useful. Such examples can be written in exponential form, often involving exponential decay. Note that questions may also require the use of other techniques you have met previously in mechanics.

Example

A skydiver of mass m falls from rest from an aeroplane. During the fall the air resistance is of magnitude mkv where k is a constant and v is the speed.

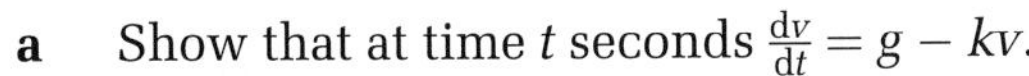

a Show that at time t seconds $\frac{dv}{dt} = g - kv$.

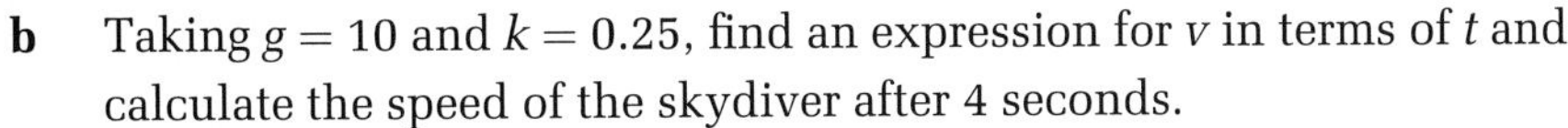

b Taking $g = 10$ and $k = 0.25$, find an expression for v in terms of t and calculate the speed of the skydiver after 4 seconds.

c Find also the distance fallen during this time.

Solution

a The skydiver is modelled as a particle of mass m falling vertically downwards. The forces are the air resistance mkv upwards and weight downwards.

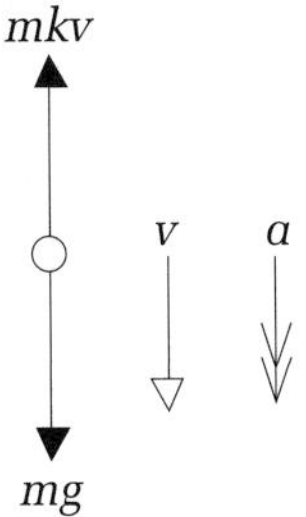

Using $F = ma$ downwards

$$mg - mkv = m\frac{dv}{dt}$$

◀ ① **Use $F = ma$ and replace a by $\frac{dv}{dt}$ to give a differential equation.**

Divide by m.

$$\frac{dv}{dt} = g - kv$$

b Substituting $g = 10$ and $k = 0.25$

$$\frac{dv}{dt} = 10 - 0.25v$$

$$\frac{dv}{dt} = 0.25(40 - v) \quad [1]$$

Take out 0.25 (the coefficient of v) as a common factor.

$$dv = 0.25(40 - v)dt$$

◀ ② **Separate the variables.**

$$\frac{dv}{40 - v} = 0.25dt$$

$$\int \frac{1}{40 - v} dv = \int 0.25\, dt$$

◀ ③ **Carry out the integration, remembering the constant.**

$$-\ln|40 - v| = 0.25t + c$$

When $t = 0$, $v = 0$ gives $-\ln 40 = c$

◀ ④ **Use boundary conditions to evaluate the constant.**

$$-\ln|40 - v| = 0.25t - \ln 40$$

$$\ln|40 - v| = -0.25t + \ln 40$$

◀ **Note the negative t term. This gives an exponential decay term later.**

Changing the signs gives a more convenient form to transpose for v.

$$\ln|40 - v| - \ln 40 = -0.25t$$

$$\ln\left(\frac{|40 - v|}{40}\right) = -0.25t$$

$$\frac{40 - v}{40} = e^{-0.25t}$$

The logarithm terms are collected at one side and the law $\ln a - \ln b = \ln(\frac{a}{b})$ is used to combine them.

$$40 - v = 40e^{-0.25t}$$

◀ ⑤ **Find the equation relating v and t.**

$$40 - 40e^{-0.25t} = v$$

$$v = 40(1 - e^{-0.25t})$$

As $t \to \infty$, $v \to 40$. The velocity approaches a constant value called the terminal velocity. From [1], this is the value of v for which the acceleration, $\frac{dv}{dt} = 0$.

When $t = 4$

$$v = 40(1 - e^{-1})$$

$$v = 40(1 - 0.3679)$$

$$v = 25.3\,\text{m s}^{-1} \text{ (3 s.f.)}$$

c Displacement:

$$x = \int v\, dt$$

◀ ⑥ **For displacement integrate v.**

$$x = \int (40 - 40e^{-0.25t})\, dt$$

$$x = 40t + 160e^{-0.25t} + c$$

When $t = 0$, $x = 0$

$$0 = 160 + c$$

$e^0 = 1$

$$c = -160$$

$$x = 40t + 160e^{-0.25t} - 160$$

When $t = 4$

$$x = 160 + 160e^{-1} - 160$$

$$x = 58.9\,\text{m} \quad \text{(3 s.f.)}$$

18.4 Acceleration as a Function of Velocity

Exercise

Technique

1 A particle of mass 400 g moves horizontally along the x-axis. When $t = 0$ the particle passes through O with velocity $7\ \mathrm{m\,s^{-1}}$. Subsequently the motion is resisted by a force whose magnitude is $0.2v$ newtons where v is the velocity in $\mathrm{m\,s^{-1}}$.

a Derive a formula for v in terms of t and hence predict the velocity of the particle after 2 seconds.
b Find the distance moved by the particle in this time.

2 A particle moves in a straight line with acceleration $\frac{dv}{dt} = 6\sqrt{v}\ \mathrm{m\,s^{-2}}$. The particle passes through a point O on the line with velocity $1\ \mathrm{m\,s^{-1}}$.

a Deduce formulas for the velocity and displacement from O, t seconds later.
b Calculate the particle's speed and distance from O when $t = 3$.

3 A particle of mass 2.5 kg moves along the x-axis, passing through O with velocity $15\ \mathrm{m\,s^{-1}}$ when $t = 0$. The only force acting on the particle is air resistance which has magnitude $0.5v^2$ newtons.

a Find a formula for v in terms of t and predict the velocity after 3 seconds.
b Calculate the distance moved by the particle in this time.

4 An object of mass 4 kg falls from rest through a fluid which resists the motion with a force equal to $16v$ newtons where v is the velocity of the object after t seconds. (Take $g = 10\ \mathrm{m\,s^{-2}}$.)

a Show that $\frac{dv}{dt} = 4(2.5 - v)$ and hence prove that $v = 2.5(1 - e^{-4t})$.
b Find the velocity when $t = 0.2$.
c How long will it take for the velocity to reach $2\ \mathrm{m\,s^{-1}}$?
d State the terminal velocity of the object.

Contextual

1

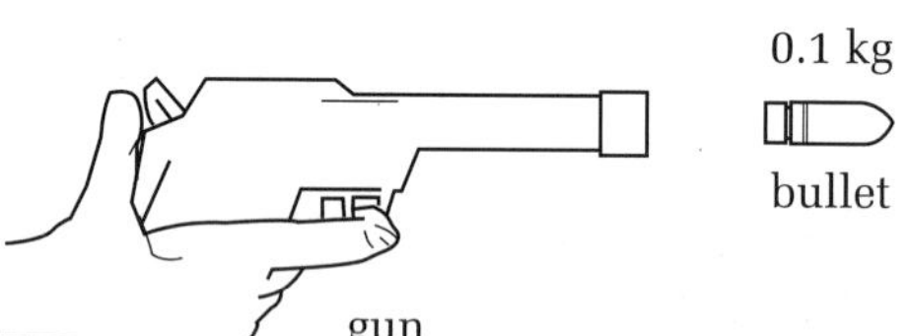

1 millisecond $= \frac{1}{1000}$ second

A bullet of mass 0.1 kg is fired into a block of wood. It is travelling at $100\,\text{m s}^{-1}$ when it enters the block and its motion is then resisted by a force of $20v^2$ newtons, where $v\,\text{m s}^{-1}$ is the velocity of the bullet.

a Show that the relationship between v and t can be written as $200t = \frac{1}{v} - \frac{1}{100}$, where t is the time in seconds after the bullet enters the block.

b Find, in milliseconds, the time taken for the velocity to reduce from $100\,\text{m s}^{-1}$ to $1\,\text{m s}^{-1}$.

2 When a rock, of mass 2.5 kg, is dropped from rest into a deep lake the resistance to motion is $5v$ newtons where v is the velocity in m s^{-1}.

a Taking $g = 10\,\text{m s}^{-2}$, show that the acceleration of the rock is given by $\frac{dv}{dt} = 2(5 - v)$.

b Prove that $v = 5(1 - e^{-2t})$ and find a formula for the displacement, x.

c Calculate:

i the velocity and distance fallen when $t = 1$

ii the time taken for the rock to reach a speed of $2\,\text{m s}^{-1}$

iii the terminal velocity of the rock.

3 A parachutist, of mass 80 kg, jumps from a plane and is travelling vertically downwards at $25\,\text{m s}^{-1}$ when her parachute opens. The resistance to motion whilst the parachute is open is $160v$ newtons.

a Taking $g = 10\,\text{m s}^{-2}$, show that $\frac{dv}{dt} = -2(v - 5)$.

b Derive an expression for v in terms of the time, t seconds, after the parachute opens and hence find the speed when $t = 1.5$.

c What is the parachutist's terminal velocity?

d Find the distance travelled in the first four seconds after the parachute opens.

18.5 Acceleration and Velocity as Functions of Displacement

The gravitational force of attraction that keeps a planet in orbit around the Sun depends on the planet's distance from the Sun. The tension in the elastic rope that supports a bungee-jumper depends on the extension of the rope. In these, and many other cases, a force depends on the position of an object.

When the force, and hence the acceleration, is a function of displacement it is not useful to use $\frac{dv}{dt}$ for the acceleration. This would give a differential equation of the form $\frac{dv}{dt} = f(x)$. There are three variables in this equation, v, t and x, and it cannot be solved by separating the variables as before. Another form for the acceleration is more useful.

Alternative form for acceleration

Using the chain (function of a function) rule for differentiation:

$$a = \frac{dv}{dt} = \frac{dv}{dx} \times \frac{dx}{dt}$$

However $\frac{dx}{dt}$ is the velocity. Substituting this into the equation above, and rearranging gives:

$$\boldsymbol{a = v\frac{dv}{dx}}$$

It is essential to use this form in problems where acceleration is a function of the displacement, x. It is also useful when the acceleration is a function of velocity. In both cases, separating the variables and integrating gives the relationship between v and x.

In this section many problems involve only the relationship between a, v and x and the time, t, is not needed. In the small number of questions where t does arise, either $a = \frac{dv}{dt}$ or $v = \frac{dx}{dt}$ can be used.

Overview of method

Step ① Use $F = ma$ and replace a by $v\frac{dv}{dx}$ to give a differential equation in v and x.

Step ② Separate the variables and integrate, remembering to include a constant at one side.

Step ③ Use boundary conditions (usually the initial values of v and x) to evaluate the constant of integration.

Newton's law may not be necessary if the question gives an expression for a.

Step ④ Write down the equation relating v and x and, if necessary, use it to answer questions.

Step ⑤ If necessary, use $a = \frac{dv}{dt}$ or $v = \frac{dx}{dt}$ to find formulas involving time.

Step ⑥ If a question gives the velocity, v, as a function of x, differentiating and then using $a = v\frac{dv}{dx}$ will give a formula for the acceleration.

Example 1

A particle, P, of mass 3 kg moves in a straight line. P is acted upon by a force of magnitude $\frac{12}{x^2}$ newtons, directed towards a fixed point, O, on the line, where x is the displacement in metres from O to P. Initially P is released from rest from a point A on the line where OA = 2 m.

a Find an equation relating the velocity, v, of the particle to x.

b Find the velocity when $x = 1$.

c Find the position of P when it reaches a speed of 4 m s^{-1}.

Solution

a

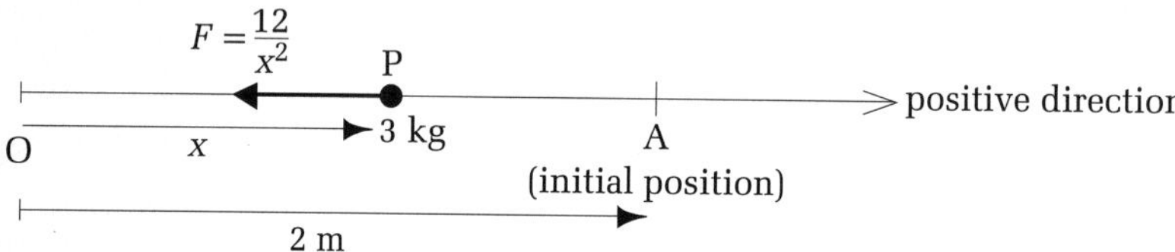

The positive direction is shown in the sketch. Since the force acts towards O, the force is in the negative direction and the particle, P, will move towards O when it is released from A.

Using $F = ma$,

$$-\frac{12}{x^2} = 3v\frac{dv}{dx}$$

◀ ① Use $F = ma$ and replace a by $v\frac{dv}{dx}$.

$$-\frac{4}{x^2} = v\frac{dv}{dx}$$

◀ ② Separate the variables and integrate, remembering the constant.

$$\int -4x^{-2}\,dx = \int v\,dv$$

$$4x^{-1} = \tfrac{1}{2}v^2 + c$$

$$\frac{4}{x} = \tfrac{1}{2}v^2 + c$$

Initially, when $x = 2$, $v = 0$

$$\tfrac{4}{2} = c$$

$$c = 2$$

◀ ③ Use boundary conditions (usually the initial values of v and x) to evaluate the constant of integration.

The equation relating x and v is $\quad \dfrac{4}{x} = \tfrac{1}{2}v^2 + 2$

This could be simplified to $\frac{8}{x} = v^2 + 4$ or other forms.

b When $x = 1$

$\frac{4}{1} = \frac{1}{2}v^2 + 2$ ◀ ④ **Write down the equation relating v and x, and use it to answer questions.**

$2 = \frac{1}{2}v^2$

$4 = v^2$

$v = \pm 2$

Since P is moving *towards* O, the velocity is $-2\,\text{m}\,\text{s}^{-1}$.

Remember to give the direction, as well as the magnitude, when asked for velocity.
Minus sign indicates *towards* O.

c When $v = -4\,\text{m}\,\text{s}^{-1}$

$\frac{4}{x} = \frac{1}{2}v^2 + 2$

$\frac{4}{x} = \frac{1}{2} \times (-4)^2 + 2$

$\frac{4}{x} = 10$

$4 = 10x$

$x = 0.4$

The displacement of P from O is 0.4 m when P reaches a speed of $4\,\text{m}\,\text{s}^{-1}$.

Example 2

A body of mass 4 kg moves in a straight line with velocity $v = \sqrt{x}$ where x is its displacement from a point A on the line. Find:

a the force producing this motion
b a formula for t in terms of x if $x = 1$ when $t = 0$.

Solution

a $v = \sqrt{x} = x^{\frac{1}{2}}$

$\frac{dv}{dx} = \frac{1}{2}x^{-\frac{1}{2}}$ ◀ ⑥ **Differentiate v and use $a = v\frac{dv}{dx}$.**

$F = ma$

$F = mv\frac{dv}{dx} = 4 \times x^{\frac{1}{2}} \times \frac{1}{2}x^{-\frac{1}{2}}$

$F = 2\text{ N}$

b $v = \frac{dx}{dt} = x^{\frac{1}{2}}$ ◀ ⑤ $v = \frac{dx}{dt}$.

$\frac{dx}{x^{\frac{1}{2}}} = dt$

$\int x^{-\frac{1}{2}}\,dx = \int dt$

$2x^{\frac{1}{2}} = t + c$

When $t = 0$, $x = 1$ then $c = 2$

$2x^{\frac{1}{2}} = t + 2$

$t = 2x^{\frac{1}{2}} - 2$ or $t = 2(x^{\frac{1}{2}} - 1)$

Factorise.

18.5 Acceleration and Velocity as Functions of Displacement

Exercise

Technique

1 A particle, P, of mass 4 kg, is initially at rest at a distance of 1 m from a fixed point, O. Subsequently P is acted upon by a force of magnitude $3x$ newtons directed away from O, where x denotes the displacement of P from O in metres.

a Using $v\,\text{m s}^{-1}$ to represent the velocity of P, derive a formula for v^2 in terms of x.

b Calculate:

i the velocity when OP $= 5$ m, giving your answer as a surd

ii the distance OP when the velocity reaches $6\,\text{m s}^{-1}$.

2 An object of mass 3 kg is projected from a point O with velocity $2\,\text{m s}^{-1}$. When the velocity is $v\,\text{m s}^{-1}$, the motion is resisted by a force of magnitude $\frac{2}{v}$ newtons. How far will the object travel before coming to rest?

3 A particle of mass 0.5 kg moves along the positive x-axis under the influence of a single force of magnitude $\frac{1}{4x}$ newtons directed towards the origin, O. Two points, A and B lie on the x-axis where OA $= 1$ m and OB $= 4$ m. If the particle passes through A with velocity $1.5\,\text{m s}^{-1}$, find its velocity when it reaches B.

4 A particle, P, moves along the positive x-axis with velocity $v = 2(1 - x^2)^{\frac{1}{2}}$.

a Show that the acceleration is proportional to x and in the opposite direction.

b Find the displacement and acceleration of P when $v = 1.6$.

Contextual

In this exercise, take $g = 10\,\text{m s}^{-2}$ and remember to convert to SI units where necessary.

1 A rocket is launched from the surface of the Earth. When it reaches a distance x metres from the centre of the Earth the acceleration due to gravity, towards the centre of the Earth, has magnitude $(4 \times 10^{14})x^{-2}\,\text{m s}^{-2}$. The rocket is travelling at $4\,\text{km s}^{-1}$ when it reaches a distance of 200 000 km from the centre of the Earth.

a Find a formula for v^2 in terms of x.

b Find the velocity of the rocket when it is 500 000 km from the centre of the Earth.

c Explain briefly what will happen to the velocity as the rocket gets further and further away from the Earth.

2 In a charity bungee jump a man of mass 72 kg is attached to one end of an elastic rope whose modulus of elasticity is 4.5 kN. The other end of the rope is attached to a high bridge and the natural length of the rope is 25 m. When the rope becomes taut the man is travelling vertically downwards at a speed of $30\,\mathrm{m\,s^{-1}}$.

a If the downward velocity of the man is $v\,\mathrm{m\,s^{-1}}$ when the extension in the rope is x m, show that $2v\frac{\mathrm{d}v}{\mathrm{d}x} = 20 - 5x$.

b By solving this differential equation, find

i the velocity of the man when the rope has extended to 40 m

ii the total distance fallen by the man when he comes to rest instantaneously.

3 A toy car of mass 0.2 kg is projected from a point A along a horizontal floor with speed $5\,\mathrm{m\,s^{-1}}$.

a In a model of this situation the floor is assumed to be smooth. Air resistance is taken to be a force of magnitude $0.1v$ newtons where v is the velocity of the car in $\mathrm{m\,s^{-1}}$. Use this model to find a differential equation relating v and the displacement, x m from A. Solve the equation and hence predict the velocity of the car when it has travelled a distance of 7 m.

N.B. You will need to use $\dfrac{2v}{v+1} \equiv 2 - \dfrac{2}{v+1}$.

b It is found in practice that the car stops before it has travelled 7 m. Show that if the model is adapted to include friction with $\mu = 0.05$, the new model will predict that the car will come to rest before it has travelled 7 m. Find the distance travelled by the car.

4 A ball of mass 0.1 kg is projected vertically upwards with a speed of $10\,\mathrm{m\,s^{-1}}$.

a Ignoring all forces except that due to gravity, calculate the maximum height reached above the point of projection.

b If the model is refined to include air resistance of magnitude $0.0025v^2$, where v is the velocity in $\mathrm{m\,s^{-1}}$, find a revised answer for the maximum height reached above the point of projection.

Consolidation

Exercise A

1 A particle P moves along the x-axis. It passes through the origin O at time $t = 0$ with speed $15\ \text{m s}^{-1}$ in the direction of x increasing. At time t seconds the acceleration of P in the direction of x increasing is $(6t - 18)\ \text{m s}^{-2}$.

a Find the values of t at which P is instantaneously at rest.

b Find the distance between the points at which P is instantaneously at rest.

(ULEAC)

2 A particle follows a path so that its position at time t is given by $\mathbf{r} = 4\cos(2t)\,\mathbf{i} + 3\sin(2t)\,\mathbf{j}$.

a Find the position, velocity and acceleration of the particle when $t = \frac{\pi}{2}$.

b Show that the magnitude of the acceleration at time t is $\sqrt{144 + 112\cos^2(2t)}$, and find its maximum and minimum values.

(AEB)

3 A particle of mass 2.5 kg falls vertically under gravity against a resistance to motion of $5v$ newtons, where $v\ \text{m s}^{-1}$ is the speed of the particle at time t seconds. Take $g = 10\ \text{m s}^{-2}$.

a Express the acceleration of the particle in terms of v.

b Given that the speed approaches a constant value $V\ \text{m s}^{-1}$, find V.

(NEAB)

4 An ice puck of mass 0.4 kg is struck and has an initial speed of $30\ \text{m s}^{-1}$ along a horizontal icy surface. During the time the puck is in motion a horizontal force of resistance acts on it. The magnitude of this force is $0.004v^2$ N, where $v\ \text{m s}^{-1}$ is the speed of the puck.

a By modelling the puck as a particle, show that its equation of motion can be written as $v\,\frac{dv}{dx} = -0.01v^2$.

b By solving this differential equation, show that, after it has travelled a distance of 20 m, the speed of the puck is approximately $24.6\ \text{m s}^{-1}$.

(NICCEA)

Exercise B

1 A particle moves in a straight line in such a way that its acceleration is $(2 - 2t)\ \text{m s}^{-2}$, where t is the time in seconds. The velocity is $3\ \text{m s}^{-1}$ when $t = 0$. Show that the particle comes instantaneously to rest when $t = 3$. Find the distance moved between $t = 0$ and $t = 3$.

(UCLES)

2 A particle P moves along the x-axis with a variable velocity $v\,\mathrm{m\,s^{-1}}$. When $\mathrm{OP} = x$ metres, the acceleration of P is $-2v\,\mathrm{m\,s^{-2}}$. Given that $v = 10$ when $x = 0$, find v in terms of x.

(*AEB*)

3 At time t seconds, the force $\mathbf{F}$ newtons acting on a particle P is given by $\mathbf{F} = (t + 3)\mathbf{i} - 2t\mathbf{j}$, where $\mathbf{i}$ and $\mathbf{j}$ are perpendicular horizontal unit vectors. P has mass 2 kg, and its velocity, when $t = 0$, is $-\frac{1}{2}(\mathbf{i} + 3\mathbf{j})\,\mathrm{m\,s^{-1}}$. Find:

a the velocity of P at time t seconds

b the values of t when P is moving in a direction parallel to the vector $\mathbf{i} - \mathbf{j}$.

(*ULEAC*)

4 The motion of an electric train on the straight stretch of track between two stations is given by $x = 11\left[t - \frac{45}{\pi}\sin\left(\frac{\pi}{45}t\right)\right]$, where x metres is the distance covered t seconds after leaving the first station. The train stops at these two stations and nowhere between them.

a Find the velocity, $v\,\mathrm{m\,s^{-1}}$, in terms of t. Hence find the time taken for the journey between the two stations.

b Calculate the distance between the two stations. Hence find the average velocity of the train.

c Find the acceleration of the train 30 seconds after leaving the first station.

(*OCSEB*)

5 A body falls vertically, the forces acting being gravity and air resistance. The air resistance is proportional to v, where v is the body's speed at time t. The value of v for which the acceleration is zero is known as the *terminal velocity* for the motion, and is denoted by U. Show that the equation of motion of the body may be expressed as:

$$\frac{\mathrm{d}v}{\mathrm{d}t} = \frac{g}{U}(U - v)$$

A parachutist jumps from a helicopter which is hovering at a height of several hundred metres, and falls vertically. Assume that, before the parachute is opened, the terminal velocity for the motion is $50\,\mathrm{m\,s^{-1}}$. Assume also that, after the parachute is opened, the terminal velocity for the motion is $10\,\mathrm{m\,s^{-1}}$. The parachutist opens the parachute 10 s after jumping. (Take $g = 9.81\,\mathrm{m\,s^{-2}}$.)

a For the parachutist's motion before the parachute opens, express the velocity in terms of the time, and hence show that the parachutist is falling at approximately $43\,\mathrm{m\,s^{-1}}$ just before the parachute opens.

b Assuming that the time taken for the parachute to open fully is negligible, find the parachutist's speed 2 s after the parachute opens.

c Sketch the (t, v) graph for the parachutist's descent.

(*UCLES*)

Applications and Activities

When an object falls subject to the force due to gravity and a resistance proportional to the velocity, the general formulas for velocity and displacement are:

$$v = \frac{g}{k}(1 - e^{-kt}) \text{ and } x = \frac{g}{k^2}(kt + e^{-kt} - 1)$$

where g is the acceleration due to gravity and k is a constant that depends on the size and shape of the object.

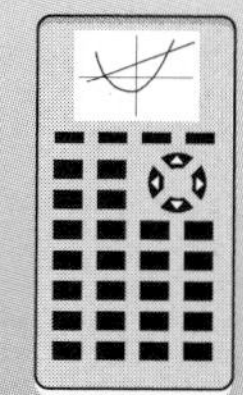

From example in Section 18.4.

1 Use a graphical calculator to explore the shapes of the graphs of these expressions for different values of k. Use $g = 10$ and start with easy values for k (such as 1, 2). What features do the graphs have in common? How do the graphs vary as k varies?
Draw $v = 40(1 - e^{-0.25t})$ and $x = 160(0.25t + e^{-0.25t} - 1)$.

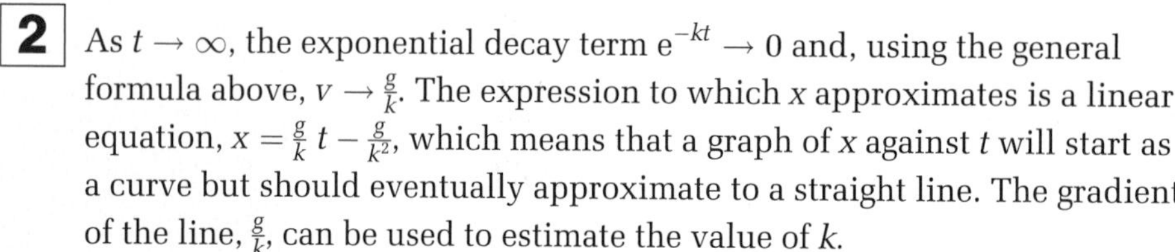

2 As $t \to \infty$, the exponential decay term $e^{-kt} \to 0$ and, using the general formula above, $v \to \frac{g}{k}$. The expression to which x approximates is a linear equation, $x = \frac{g}{k}t - \frac{g}{k^2}$, which means that a graph of x against t will start as a curve but should eventually approximate to a straight line. The gradient of the line, $\frac{g}{k}$, can be used to estimate the value of k.

Experiment

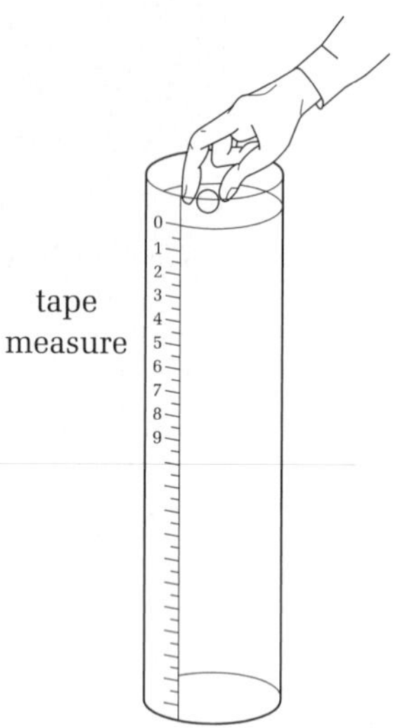

Fill a long container with thick oil (the thicker, the better). Attach a tape measure to the side of the container with the start of the scale against the surface of the oil. Drop a small object (such as a peanut, marble or ball bearing) into the oil, releasing it from rest at the surface. Draw up a table of corresponding values for x and t. Draw a graph of x against t. If the graph has a straight section at the end, measure its gradient and hence estimate the value of k. Compare the values of k for different objects.

Summary

- Displacement, velocity and acceleration are related through differentiation by the formulas

  $$v = \frac{dx}{dt}$$

  $$a = \frac{dv}{dt} = \frac{d^2x}{dt^2}$$

  when they are given in terms of time.

Alternative notation:
$v = \dot{x}$
$a = \dot{v} = \ddot{x}$

- Displacement, velocity and acceleration are related through integration by the formulas

  $$v = \int a \, dt$$

  $$r = \int v \, dt$$

  when they are given in terms of time.

- Vectors are used for motion in 2 or 3 dimensions.

  $$\mathbf{v} = \frac{d\mathbf{r}}{dt} = \int \mathbf{a} \, dt$$

  $$\mathbf{r} = \frac{d\mathbf{v}}{dt} = \frac{d^2\mathbf{r}}{dt^2} = \int \mathbf{v} \, dt$$

- The acceleration can be found using

  $$a = v\frac{dv}{dx}$$

  when velocity is given as a function of displacement.

- Differential equations can be solved by *separation of variables* when force or acceleration is given as a function of velocity or displacement.

- Newton's law $F = ma$ can be used in the forms

  $$F = m\frac{dv}{dt} = m\frac{d^2x}{dt^2}$$

  or $$F = mv\frac{dv}{dx}$$

  In terms of vectors

  $$\mathbf{F} = m\frac{d\mathbf{v}}{dt} = m\frac{d^2\mathbf{r}}{dt^2}$$

19 Simple Harmonic Motion

What you need to know

- Hooke's law.
- How to apply $F = ma$.
- How to differentiate trigonometric expressions.
- The graphs of $y = \sin\theta$ and $y = \cos\theta$.
- How to solve trigonometric equations, giving answers in radians.

Review

1 For a spring of natural length 20 cm and modulus of elasticity 15 N, calculate:

a the tension in the spring when it is extended by 4 cm

b the thrust exerted by the spring when it is compressed to 12 cm.

2 Find the acceleration of the particle.

3 **a** If $x = 7\cos 4t$, evaluate $\dot{x}$ and $\ddot{x}$ when $t = 0.2$.

b If $x = 5\sin(2\pi t + 0.63)$ evaluate $\dot{x}$ and $\ddot{x}$ when $t = 0.6$.

Recall that $\dot{x} = \frac{dx}{dt}$ and $\ddot{x} = \frac{d^2x}{dt^2}$. Use radians.

4 Sketch the graphs of $y = \sin\theta$ and $y = \cos\theta$ for $-2\pi \leq \theta \leq 2\pi$.

5 Solve the following equations, in radians, giving the smallest positive value of t:

a $5\cos 2t = 0.6$

b $4\sin \pi t = 1$

c $1.6\cos(\frac{1}{2}\pi t + 1.7) = -1$

d $25\sin(0.2\pi t - 2.7) = -15$

19.1 Basic Equation of Simple Harmonic Motion

Here are descriptions of three situations. What will happen in each case when the object is released?

- A model plane is attached to the ceiling by a spring. The plane is pulled down and then released.
- A child is sitting on a swing. An adult pulls the swing back and then releases it.
- A cork is floating in a glass of wine. It is pushed down a little further into the wine and then released.

Although the situations described are all different, they have much in common.

In each case the object starts in an equilibrium position. It is then displaced from the equilibrium position and released from rest. In all cases the object will travel backwards and forwards (or up and down) along a path through the equilibrium position. In practice, resistance to motion will eventually bring the object to rest, but if there were no resistance the object would continue to oscillate for ever. This type of repetitive motion is called **simple harmonic motion**, often abbreviated to **SHM**. In SHM, an object travels between two extreme positions at either side of a central, equilibrium position. The distance between the centre of the motion and one end of the path is called the amplitude, denoted by a.

Since the letter a now represents the amplitude of the motion, the symbol $\ddot{x}$ will be used for acceleration. This will avoid any confusion between the two.

In SHM the resultant force acts towards the centre of motion. The further the object is from the centre, the larger is this force and hence the acceleration.

Linear simple harmonic motion

Linear simple harmonic motion is motion in which the acceleration is directed towards a fixed point and is proportional to the distance from the fixed point.

Linear SHM means simple harmonic motion in a straight line.

Basic equation of simple harmonic motion

In SHM the acceleration is given by:

$$\ddot{\mathbf{x}} = -\omega^2 \mathbf{x}$$

where x is the displacement from the equilibrium position and ω is a constant.

Notation
$\ddot{x}$ = acceleration (m s^{-2})
ω = constant
x = displacement (m)

Using ω^2 (which is always positive) together with a – sign means x and $\ddot{x}$ are always opposite in sign.

If you are asked to prove that motion is simple harmonic, you must show that the acceleration of the object can be written in the form $\ddot{x} = -\omega^2 x$.

This is sometimes called the equation of motion.

Minimum and maximum magnitude of the acceleration

The minimum and maximum acceleration can be deduced from $\ddot{x} = -\omega^2 x$. At the centre of the motion, when $x = 0$, the acceleration must be zero.

$\ddot{x} = -\omega^2 x$

$\ddot{x} = -\omega^2(0)$

$\ddot{x} = 0$

At the extremities of the motion, when $x = \pm a$, the magnitude of the acceleration takes its maximum value of $\omega^2 a$. The resultant force on the particle will also be at its maximum value of $m\omega^2 a$.

Using $F = m\ddot{x}$.

Overview of method

In the examples in this section all the objects will start from rest at one end of the path. Some or all of the following steps will be used.

Other starting points will be considered later in the chapter.

Step ① Find the equilibrium position. This is the centre of the motion.
Step ② Draw a diagram of the general position with x representing the displacement from the equilibrium position.
Step ③ Use $F = m\ddot{x}$ in the direction of increasing x.
Step ④ Show that this gives an equation of the form $\ddot{x} = -\omega^2 x$, proving SHM.
Step ⑤ Find the amplitude, a, the distance between the end of the path and the equilibrium position.
Step ⑥ Calculate the maximum acceleration $\omega^2 a$, or the maximum force $m\omega^2 a$ if required.

If x is not measured from the centre but from some other point then the equation of motion will be of the form $\ddot{x} = -\omega^2(x + k)$ where k is a constant. The substitution $y = x + k$ gives $\dot{y} = \dot{x}$ and $\ddot{y} = \ddot{x}$ and so $\ddot{y} = -\omega^2 y$

Example

A particle, P, of mass 1.5 kg is attached to one end of a spring of natural length 50 cm and modulus of elasticity 6 N. The other end, O, of the spring is attached to a point on a smooth horizontal surface. P is held at rest on the surface with OP = 75 cm and then released from rest. Show that P performs SHM and find the maximum acceleration.

Solution

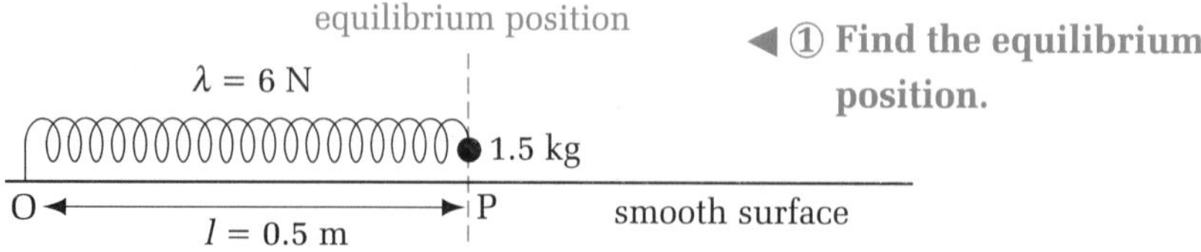

◀ ① **Find the equilibrium position.**

The surface is smooth, so there is no friction. The particle will be in equilibrium when the tension in the spring is zero. This occurs when the spring is at its natural length.

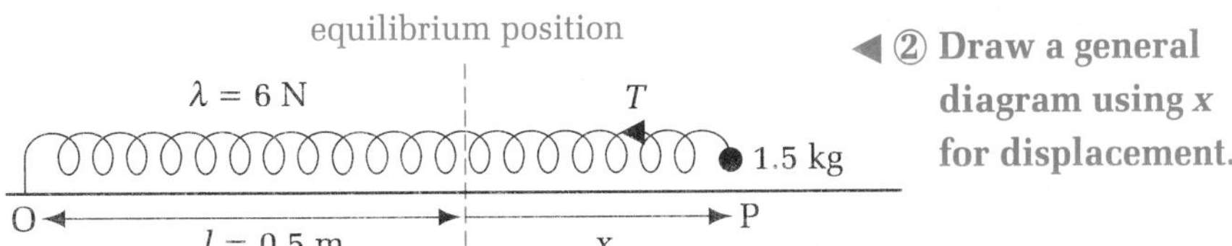

◀ ② **Draw a general diagram using x for displacement.**

In the general position, the displacement, x, is equal to the extension in the spring.

Using $F = m\ddot{x}$ → ◀ ② **Use $F = m\ddot{x}$ in the direction of increasing x.**

$$-T = m\ddot{x}$$

Use Hooke's law to replace T.

$$-\frac{\lambda x}{l} = m\ddot{x}$$

$$-\frac{6x}{0.5} = 1.5\ddot{x}$$

Substitute values.

$$-12x = 1.5\ddot{x}$$

Divide by 1.5.

$$-\frac{12}{1.5} = \ddot{x}$$

Simplify.

$$\ddot{x} = -8x$$

◀ ④ **Compare with $\ddot{x} = -\omega^2 x$ for SHM.**

This is the basic equation of SHM with:

$$\omega^2 = 8$$

Take the square root.

$$\omega = \sqrt{8}$$

$\sqrt{8} = \sqrt{4 \times 2} = 2\sqrt{2}$

$$\omega = 2\sqrt{2}$$

▼ ⑤ **Find the amplitude, a.**

The amplitude is the maximum value of x. Displacement from the equilibrium position is greatest at the start when the spring is extended to 75 cm and the extension is 25 cm. Amplitude, $a = 0.25$ m.

Note that the initial position of the particle is used only to find the amplitude. This is done *after* the equilibrium and general positions have been considered.

$$\text{maximum acceleration} = \omega^2 a$$

◀ ⑥ **Calculate the maximum acceleration $\omega^2 a$.**

$$= 8 \times 0.25$$

Substitute values.

$$= 2 \text{ m s}^{-2}$$

Alternative general position

In the general position used above, the spring was extended. The method works equally well if the spring is compressed instead. The sketch shows an alternative general position.

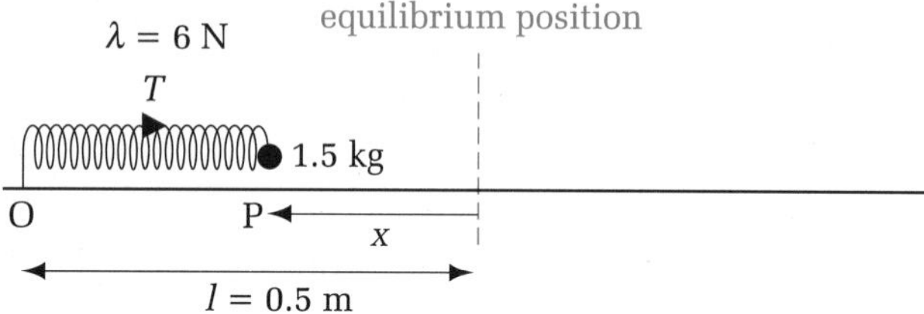

A spring in compression exerts a thrust, T. Using $F = m\ddot{x}$ in the direction of increasing x gives:

$$-T = m\ddot{x}$$

$$-\frac{\lambda x}{l} = m\ddot{x}$$

By Hooke's law, $T = \frac{\lambda x}{l}$.

The rest of the working is exactly the same as before.

In SHM it does not matter which side of the equilibrium position is chosen for the general position.

Partial SHM

Occasionally motion occurs which is only partly simple harmonic. If the spring in the Example was replaced by an elastic string, the motion would only be simple harmonic whilst the string was stretched. Once the string became slack, there would be no tension. As the surface is smooth there would be no horizontal force at all. The particle would travel at a constant speed until it passed O and travelled far enough to stretch the string at the other side. The motion would then become simple harmonic again.

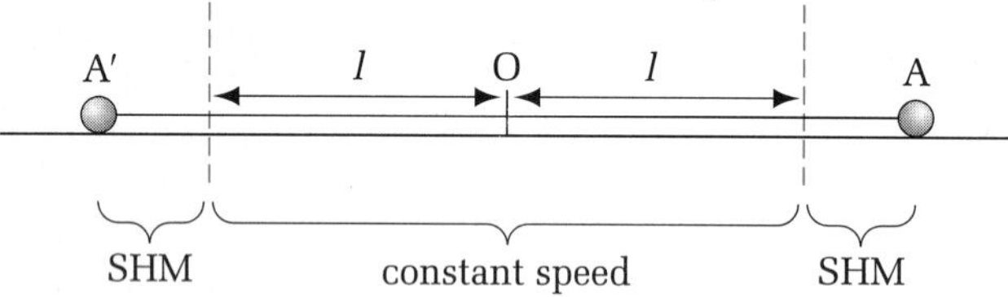

In the absence of any resistance, the particle would travel to and fro between A and A′, but this time only part of the motion would be simple harmonic.

19.1 Basic Equation of Simple Harmonic Motion

Exercise

Technique

1 One end of a spring of natural length 40 cm and modulus of elasticity 12 N is attached to a fixed point, O, on a smooth horizontal surface. The other end of the spring is attached to a particle, P, of mass 2 kg. Initially P is held at rest at a point on the surface 65 cm from O. Show that when P is released it moves with simple harmonic motion and state the amplitude of the motion.

2 A body, B, of mass 3 kg is attached to one end of a light elastic string of natural length 1.2 m and modulus of elasticity 14 N. The other end of the string is attached to a fixed point, A, and B hangs in equilibrium vertically below A.

a Calculate the extension in the string.

b The object, B, is lifted vertically until AB = 2 m and then released from rest. Show that the subsequent motion is SHM and find the magnitude of the maximum acceleration.

Hint: Use e for the extension in equilibrium position so that x can be used for the extra extension in general position.

3 The ends of a spring of natural length one metre, are attached to points A and B which are one metre apart on a smooth horizontal surface. A particle, P, of mass 40 g, is attached to the centre of the spring. P is held on the surface at a point between A and B a distance of 70 cm from A and then released from rest. Given that the modulus of elasticity of the spring is 9 N

a derive the equation of motion of the particle

b find the maximum force which acts on the particle during motion.

4 A particle of mass 4 kg moves on a straight line between two fixed points, A and B. When the particle is at a point P, where AP = d metres, it is acted on by forces of $2d$ newtons towards A and $6(4 - d)$ newtons towards B. The distance AB is 4 metres.

a Find the point on AB at which the particle is in equilibrium.

The particle is released from rest from a point C where AC = 2.5 m.

b Prove that the particle performs SHM and find its maximum acceleration.

Contextual

1

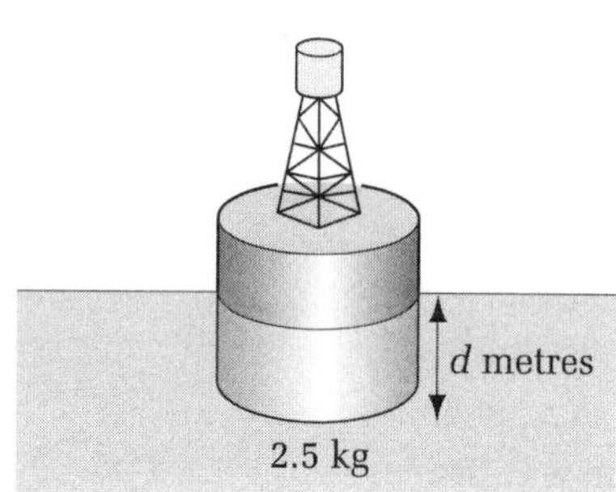

When a cylindrical buoy is placed in water, the upward force exerted on it by the water is proportional to d metres, the depth of its lower face below the surface of the water.

a If the buoy has mass 2.5 kg and floats when immersed to a depth of 35 cm, show that the upward force due to the water is given by $U = 70d$ newtons.

b Show also that the buoy will move with simple harmonic motion if it is displaced slightly from the equilibrium position in a vertical direction and released from rest.

A slight displacement means that the buoy is not lifted out of the water nor completely immersed in it.

2 A climber of mass 72 kg is climbing down a vertical training wall. The climber is attached to the ceiling by an elastic rope of natural length 6 m and modulus of elasticity 2.7 kN. When the rope is just taut the climber releases his hold on the wall and falls from rest. Taking $g = 10\,\text{m s}^{-2}$, and assuming that air resistance is negligible and that the climber does not come into contact with the wall or floor, show that the climber will move with simple harmonic motion and find the maximum resultant force on the climber during this motion. What difference would it make to the type of motion, if the climber let go of the wall whilst the rope was still slack?

3 A Jack-in-the-box consists of a doll of mass 150 g mounted on a spring of natural length 12 cm and modulus of elasticity 9 N. When the doll is in the box the spring is compressed to a length of 4 cm. By modelling the doll as a particle and taking $g = 10\,\text{m s}^{-2}$:

a calculate the length of the spring when the doll rests in equilibrium out of his box

b show that, if the doll is initially in the box which is then opened, the equation of motion is $\frac{d^2x}{dt^2} = -500x$

c find the magnitude of the maximum acceleration.

Note $\frac{d^2x}{dt^2}$ is $\ddot{x}$.

19.2 Velocity as a Function of Displacement

Imagine any of the examples of SHM you have met. What happens to the velocity as the object moves backwards and forwards? The object travels most quickly at the centre of the motion and slows down to come to rest at each end of the path. When it changes direction its velocity changes sign from positive to negative, or vice versa. A formula relating the velocity to displacement can be derived by replacing $\ddot{x}$ in the basic SHM equation by $v\frac{dv}{dx}$.

$$\ddot{x} = -\omega^2 x$$

Replace $\ddot{x}$.

$$v\frac{dv}{dx} = -\omega^2 x$$

$$\int v\,dv = -\omega^2 \int x\,dx$$

$$\tfrac{1}{2}v^2 = -\tfrac{1}{2}\omega^2 x^2 + c$$

Separate the variables and then integrate. Remember the constant.

The velocity is zero when the object reaches one end of its path.
The displacement, x, is then equal to the amplitude.
Substituting $v = 0$ when $x = a$ gives:

$$0 = -\tfrac{1}{2}\omega^2 a^2 + c$$

Add $\frac{1}{2}\omega^2 a^2$.

$$c = \tfrac{1}{2}\omega^2 a^2$$

$$\tfrac{1}{2}v^2 = -\tfrac{1}{2}\omega^2 x^2 + \tfrac{1}{2}\omega^2 a^2$$ ◀ **Replace c with $\frac{1}{2}\omega^2 a^2$.**

Multiply by 2.

$$v^2 = \omega^2 a^2 - \omega^2 x^2$$

Factorise.

$$\mathbf{v^2 = \omega^2(a^2 - x^2)}$$

Taking the square root gives

$$\mathbf{v = \pm\omega\sqrt{a^2 - x^2}}$$

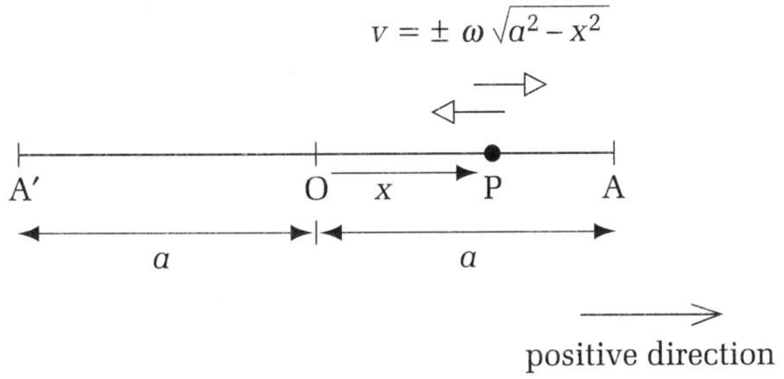

$v = \pm\,\omega\sqrt{a^2 - x^2}$

A′ O x P A

a a

positive direction

For each value of x there are two equal and opposite values of the velocity. The positive value will apply when the object is travelling in the positive direction, from A′ to A. The negative value will apply on the return journey from A to A′. When the object is at A or A′ the value of x^2 is a^2 and the velocity is zero. When the object is at the centre of the motion, $x = 0$ and the speed takes its maximum value of ωa:

$$\mathbf{v_{max} = \omega a}$$

Overview of method

The main steps in the worked examples are given below. Other ideas from earlier in the course are occasionally needed.

Step ① Sketch the situation and write down any of ω a, x, v which are known.

Step ② Substitute known values into $v^2 = \omega^2(a^2 - x^2)$ and calculate the value required.

Step ③ Apply any other formulas that are needed. A list is given below:

equation of motion, $\ddot{x} = -\omega^2 x$

maximum acceleration $= \ddot{x}_{max} = \omega^2 a$

maximum force $= m\omega^2 a$

maximum speed $= v_{max} = \omega a$

Example 1

A particle of mass 2 kg is on a horizontal surface which moves with simple harmonic motion in a vertical direction. If the amplitude is 6 m and $\omega = 5$, find:

a the velocity when $x = 4$

b the distance of the particle from the centre of the motion when it is travelling at $10\ \text{m s}^{-1}$

c the maximum resultant force acting on the particle during the motion

d the maximum vertical reaction on the particle due to the surface.

Solution

a

upper end of path

R

$v = ?$

$a = 6$ m

$x = 4$

$2g$

$\omega = 5$

centre of motion

$a = 6$ m

lower end of path

◀ ① **Sketch the situation and summarise the information.**

$$v^2 = \omega^2(a^2 - x^2)$$
$$v^2 = 5^2(6^2 - 4^2)$$
$$v^2 = 25(36 - 16)$$
$$v^2 = 500$$
$$v = \pm\sqrt{500}$$
$$v = \pm 10\sqrt{5} \text{ or } \pm 22.4\ \text{m s}^{-1} \text{ (3 s.f.)}$$

◀ ② **Substitute known values into $v^2 = \omega^2(x^2 - a^2)$.**

$\pm$ since the particle could be moving in either direction.

b When $v = 10$

$$v^2 = \omega^2(a^2 - x^2)$$ ◄ ② **Substitute the values**

$$10^2 = 5^2(6^2 - x^2)$$

Work out the squares.

$$100 = 25(36 - x^2)$$

Divide by 25 to simplify.

$$4 = 36 - x^2$$

Add x^2 and subtract 4.

$$x^2 = 36 - 4$$

Work out RHS.

$$x^2 = 32$$

Square root.

$$x = \pm\sqrt{32}$$

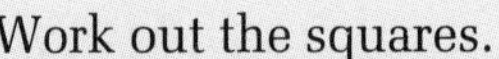

$\sqrt{32} = \sqrt{16 \times 2} = 4\sqrt{2}$

$$x = \pm 4\sqrt{2} \quad \text{or} \quad \pm 5.66\,\text{m}\ (3\text{ s.f.})$$

The particle is 5.66 m (to 3 s.f.) from the centre of the motion.

c Maximum resultant force

$F_{max} = m\ddot{x}_{max}$

$$F_{max} = m\omega^2 a$$ ◄ ③ **Apply any other formulas which are needed.**

$$F_{max} = 2 \times 5^2 \times 6$$

$$F_{max} = 300\,\text{N}$$

d Resultant force upwards, $F = R - 2g$

Add $2g$.

$$F + 2g = R$$

$$R_{max} = F_{max} + 2g$$

$$R_{max} = 300 + 2 \times 9.8$$

$$R_{max} = 320\ \text{N}\ (3\text{ s.f.})$$

Example 2

The sketch shows a piston, P, which performs simple harmonic oscillations between the ends, A and B, of a cylindrical tube. When P is 5 cm from the centre of the tube the piston is travelling at $1\,\text{m}\,\text{s}^{-1}$. When P is 4 cm from the centre of the tube the piston is travelling at $2\,\text{m}\,\text{s}^{-1}$. Find the length of the tube and the maximum speed of the piston.

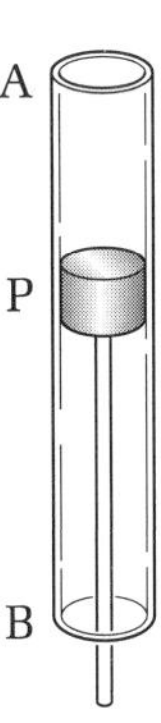

Solution

The piston is modelled as a particle travelling in a straight line with SHM.

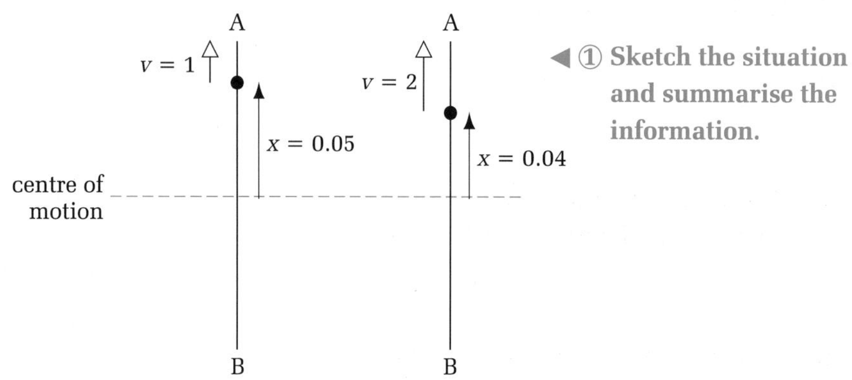

◀ ① **Sketch the situation and summarise the information.**

When $x = 0.05$ m, $v = 1\,\text{m s}^{-1}$ and when $x = 0.04$ m, $v = 2\,\text{m s}^{-1}$. Substituting these into $v^2 = \omega^2(a^2 - x^2)$ gives a pair of simultaneous equations:

$$1^2 = \omega^2(a^2 - 0.05^2)$$

$$1 = \omega^2(a^2 - 0.0025) \qquad [1]$$

$$2^2 = \omega^2(a^2 - 0.04^2)$$

$$4 = \omega^2(a^2 - 0.0016) \qquad [2]$$

Dividing equation [2] by equation [1] eliminates ω.

◀ ② **Calculate the value required.**

$$\frac{4}{1} = \frac{a^2 - 0.0016}{a^2 - 0.0025}$$

Multiply by $(a^2 - 0.0025)$.

$$4(a^2 - 0.0025) = a^2 - 0.0016$$

Expand brackets.

$$4a^2 - 0.01 = a^2 - 0.0016$$

Add 0.01 and subtract a^2.

$$3a^2 = 0.0084$$

Divide by 3.

$$a^2 = 0.0028$$

Take the square root.

$$a = \sqrt{0.0028} = 0.052\,915$$

$$\text{AB} = 2a = 0.105\,83$$

The length of the tube is 10.6 cm (3 s.f.).

To determine the maximum speed, ωa, the value of ω is needed. Substituting $a^2 = 0.0028$ into equation [1] gives:

$$1 = \omega^2(0.0028 - 0.0025)$$

$$1 = 0.0003\omega^2$$

Divide by 0.0003.

$$\omega^2 = \frac{1}{0.0003}$$

Calculate RHS.

$$\omega^2 = 3333.\dot{3}$$

Take the square root.

$$\omega = 57.735 \text{ (3 d.p.)}$$

◀ ③ **Apply any other formulas which are needed.**

$$\text{maximum speed} = \omega a$$

$$\text{maximum speed} = 57.735 \times 0.052\,915$$

$$\text{maximum speed} = 3.06\,\text{m s}^{-1} \text{ (3 s.f.)}$$

19.2 Velocity as a Function of Displacement

Exercise

Technique

1 The motion of a particle is simple harmonic with $\omega = 7$ and $a = 5$ (metres). Find the speed when the particle is 4 m from the centre of the motion.

2 A particle, P, performs SHM with amplitude 2 m. The velocity of P is 3 m s^{-1} when its displacement from the centre of the motion is 1.5 m. Find the value of ω.

3 An object is moving with SHM between two points A and B which are 5 m apart. If $\omega = 2$ calculate:

a v when $x = 2$ **b** x when $v = 4$

4 When a body of mass 3 kg oscillates, its equation of motion is $\ddot{x} = -16x$ where x is its displacement from a fixed point O. The body travels at a speed of 8 m s^{-1} when $x = 3$. Determine:

a the value of ω
b the amplitude of the motion
c the maximum force which acts on the body during its motion.

5 A particle, P, moves with SHM about a fixed point O. When OP = 1 m, P is moving at 5 m s^{-1}. When OP = 2 m, P is moving at 3 m s^{-1}.

a Use simultaneous equations to find the values of a and ω.
b What is
  i the maximum speed
  ii the maximum acceleration?

Contextual

1 A package of mass 12 kg is dropped onto a platform which is supported by a spring as shown in the sketch. If the package then performs simple harmonic motion with amplitude, $a = 2$ cm and $\omega = 3$, find:

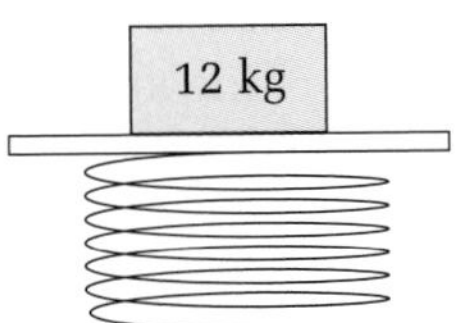

a the velocity of the package when it is 1 cm from the centre of the motion
b the maximum resultant force on the package
c the maximum force on the package due to the platform.

2 The end of a prong of a tuning fork oscillates between two fixed points which are 0.2 mm apart. If $\omega = 1500$, calculate:

a the speed of the end of the prong when it is 0.05 mm from the centre of its motion

b the maximum speed of the end of the prong

c the maximum acceleration of the end of the prong.

3 A machine component performs oscillations of amplitude 4 cm and its equation of motion is $\ddot{x} = -25x$. Find:

a the maximum speed

b the component's distance from the centre of motion when it is moving at half the maximum speed.

4

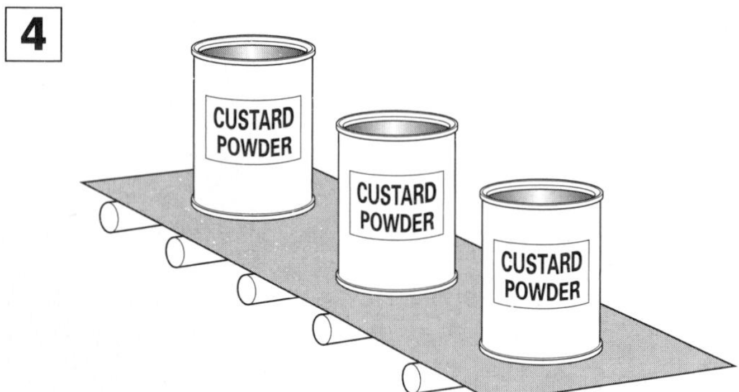

A factory produces tins of custard powder. After the tins are filled, they stand on a conveyer belt which performs SHM, with $a = 5$ cm and $\omega = 6$, to settle the contents.

a Calculate the speed of a tin when it is 3 cm from its centre of motion.

b What is the maximum acceleration of a tin?

c The force on the tin which produces the motion is friction. Find the minimum value of the coefficient of friction if the tin is not to slide along the belt.

5 A girl of mass 30 kg sits on a seat on a fairground ride. The seat performs vertical SHM, travelling from a point 0.5 m above the ground to a maximum height of h metres above the ground. When the seat is 1 m from its centre of motion it is travelling at $6\ \text{m s}^{-1}$, and when it is 2 m from the centre of motion it is travelling at $2\ \text{m s}^{-1}$. Calculate:

a the value of h

b the maximum reaction on the girl due to the seat.

19.3 Particular Solutions for Displacement in Terms of Time

There is a relationship between circular motion and simple harmonic motion which is useful in deriving formulas.

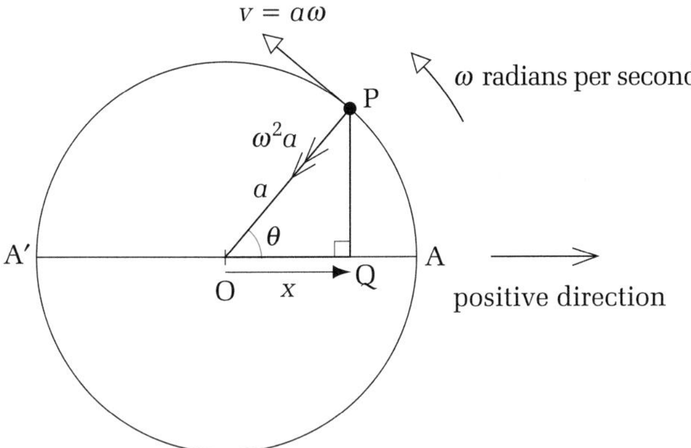

Acceleration towards centre of circle of radius a, equals $\omega^2 a$. (see Chapter 17.)

Suppose a particle P is moving round a circle of radius a at a constant rate of ω radians per second (rad s^{-1}). The acceleration of P is $\omega^2 a$ towards the centre of the circle, O. In the diagram, Q is the foot of the perpendicular from P to a diameter AA′. As P moves around the circle, Q moves backwards and forwards along AA′. The acceleration of Q is the component of P's acceleration in the direction AA′.

Acceleration of Q $= \omega^2 a\cos\theta$ towards O.
If x is the displacement OQ, then $\cos\theta = \frac{x}{a}$.

$$\text{acceleration of Q} = -\omega^2 a \times \frac{x}{a}$$
$$\ddot{x} = -\omega^2 x$$

$\cos\theta = \frac{\text{adj}}{\text{hyp}}$.
a cancels.
Negative because the acceleration is towards O.

As P moves around the circle at a constant angular speed of ω rads s^{-1}, Q moves along the diameter AA′ with SHM.

Period

The time taken for Q to perform one complete oscillation is called the **periodic time** (or **period**), usually denoted by T. This is the same as the time taken for P to travel around the circle once. As one revolution is 2π radians and P is travelling at ω rad s^{-1}

$$T = \frac{2\pi}{\omega} \text{ seconds}$$

Notation
T = time period

If Q is performing n oscillations per second, $T = \frac{1}{n}$ seconds.
The symmetry of the motion means that the time taken for Q to travel from one end of the path to the other is $\frac{1}{2}T$ seconds. Also, since P always takes the same time to travel round a quarter of the circle, the time taken for Q to travel between the centre and one end of the path is $\frac{1}{4}T$ seconds.

Solutions for *x* in terms of *t*

There are a variety of forms which may be used. The best form for a particular question depends on what is happening at $t = 0$. Two particular cases that are very common will be studied in this section.

Particle starting from rest at the positive end of the path when $t = 0$

This was the case in all examples in Section 19.1.

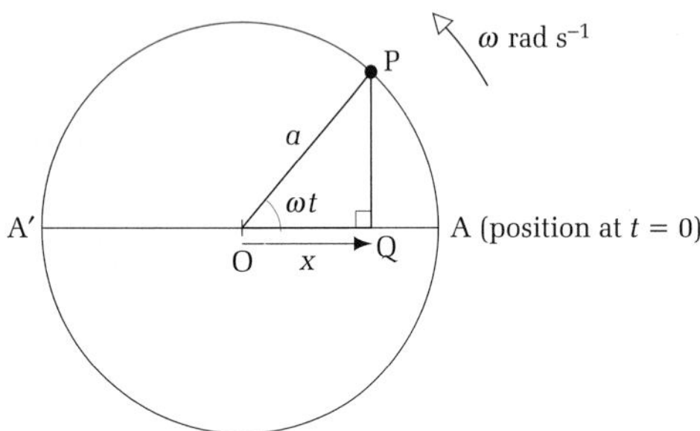

P and Q both start from A when $t = 0$. After t seconds OP has turned through an angle ωt radians, as shown. Using trigonometry in triangle OPQ gives:

$$\boldsymbol{x = a\cos\omega t}$$

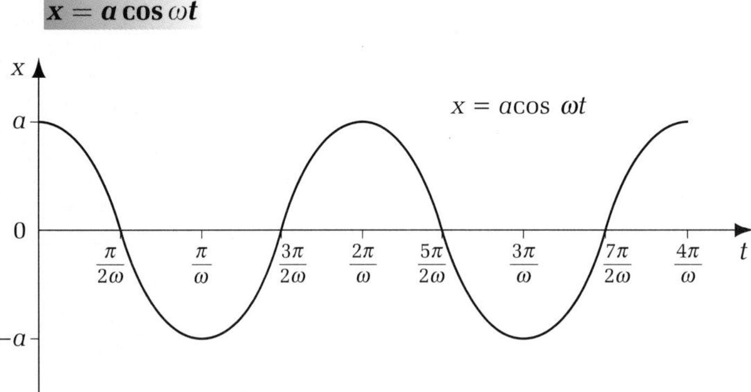

The sketch shows the (t, x) graph for this solution. Note the repetitive nature of the graph corresponding to the repeated oscillations in the motion. One complete oscillation takes place in a time interval of $\frac{2\pi}{\omega}$ seconds.

Remember: period $= \frac{2\pi}{\omega}$ seconds.

Particle travelling through the centre of the path when $t = 0$

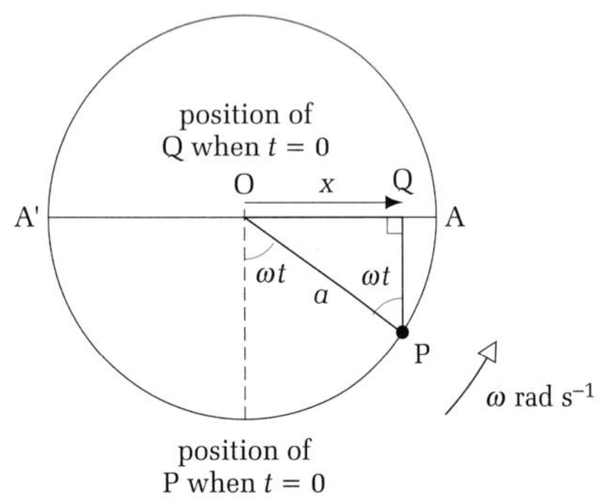

Suppose Q is travelling through O in the direction OA when $t = 0$. P would then be moving through the lowest point on the circle. After t seconds P and Q would be in the positions shown in the sketch. Using trigonometry in triangle OPQ gives:

$$x = a\sin \omega t$$

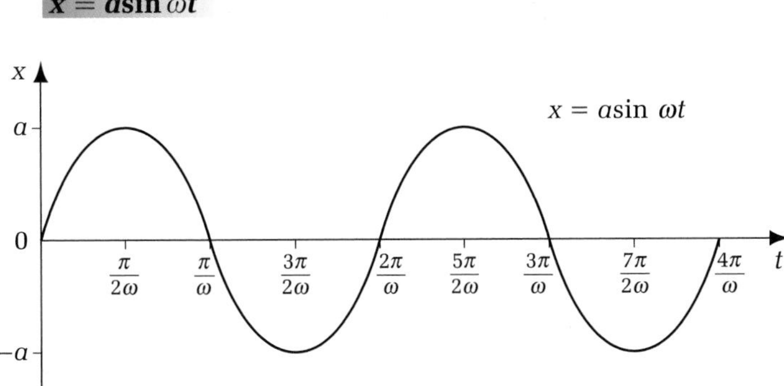

The sketch shows the (t, x) graph for this solution. Again the shape clearly shows the oscillations and one complete oscillation takes place in a time interval of $\frac{2\pi}{\omega}$ seconds.

The two graphs are identical except for the fact that they start at different points of the motion.

Other forms of the solution

Zero time could be taken at any point during an oscillation. Other forms of the solution will be studied in Section 19.4.

Overview of method

Step ① Sketch the motion and write down known values of a, ω and T (or other information which is given).

Step ② Use period $T = \frac{2\pi}{\omega}$ or $\frac{1}{n}$ where n is the number of oscillations per second.

Step ③ To find a formula for displacement in terms of time use:

- $x = a\cos \omega t$ if the particle is at rest at the positive end of the path when $t = 0$.
- $x = a\sin \omega t$ if the particle is travelling through the centre in the positive direction when $t = 0$.

Questions normally require just a few of these steps.

Step ④ For time taken to traverse part of the path use:

- time to travel from one end of path to the other $= \frac{1}{2}T$
- time to travel between one end and the centre (or vice versa) $= \frac{1}{4}T$
- time taken to travel between any other points can be found using $x = a\cos \omega t$ or $x = a\sin \omega t$

Step ⑤ Derive a formula for velocity in terms of time by differentiating the formula for x.

Step ⑥ Use $v = \pm\omega\sqrt{a^2 - x^2}$ to relate velocity to displacement.

Step ⑦ Use the fact that the velocity at the centre of motion $= a\omega$. (This is often used to find a or ω.)

Step ⑧ Derive a formula for acceleration by differentiating the formula for velocity or using $\ddot{x} = -\omega^2 x$.

Example 1

A particle performs vertical simple harmonic motion of period 4 seconds and amplitude 5 m. The ends of the path are points A and A′, with A above A′, and O is the centre of the motion.

a Find the time taken to travel:

i from A to A′ **ii** from O to A.

b If the particle starts from rest at A when $t = 0$, determine its position when:

i $t = 0.5$ **ii** $t = 1.3$

Solution

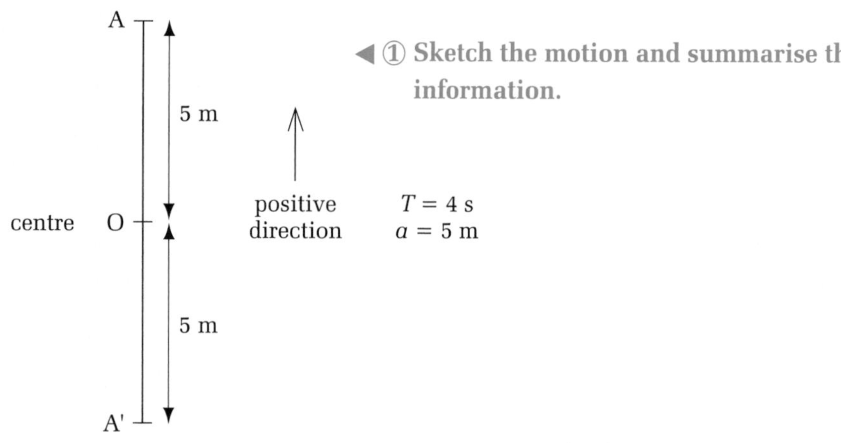

◀ ① Sketch the motion and summarise the information.

a i Time taken to travel from A to A′ $= \frac{1}{2}T = \frac{1}{2} \times 4 = 2$ s.

◀ ④ $AA' = \frac{1}{2}$ of oscillation
$OA = \frac{1}{4}$ of oscillation.

ii Time taken to travel from O to A $= \frac{1}{4}T = \frac{1}{4} \times 4 = 1$ s.

b The solution for x in terms of t is $x = a\cos\omega t$, where $a = 5$ and ω can be found from its relationship with the periodic time, T.

◀ ③ Use $x = a\cos\omega t$.

Particle is at rest at the positive end of path when $t = 0$.

$$T = \frac{2\pi}{\omega}$$

◀ ② Use period $T = \frac{2\pi}{\omega}$.

$$\omega = \frac{2\pi}{T}$$

Rearrange formula.

$$\omega = \frac{2\pi}{4}$$

Substitute value for T.

$$\omega = \frac{\pi}{2}$$

ω is normally left in terms of π rather than decimals.

The formula for displacement is $x = 5\cos(\frac{1}{2}\pi t)$.

i When $t = 0.5$

$x = 5\cos(\frac{1}{2}\pi \times 0.5)$

$x = 5\cos 0.7854$

$x = 3.54$ m (3 s.f.)

Substitute values. Remember to use radians.

When $t = 0.5$ the particle is 3.54 m (to 3 s.f.) above O.

ii When $t = 1.3$

$x = 5\cos(\frac{1}{2}\pi \times 1.3)$

$x = 5\cos 2.042$

$x = -2.27$ m (3 s.f.)

Remember to use radians.

When $t = 1.3$ the particle is 2.27 m (to 3 s.f.) below O.

Example 2

An object performs simple harmonic motion at a rate of 20 oscillations per second between two points A and B which are 12 cm apart. If C is the midpoint of AB calculate the time taken to travel directly:

a from A to C **b** from C to the midpoint of CB.

Solution

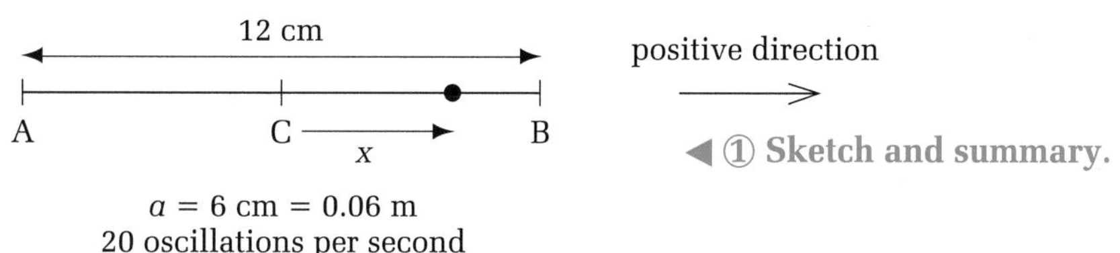

$a = 6$ cm $= 0.06$ m
20 oscillations per second

a Time taken to travel from A to C $= \frac{1}{4}T$, ◀ ④ Time for $\frac{1}{4}$ of oscillation $= \frac{1}{4}T$.

where $T = \frac{1}{n}$ ◀ ② Use period $T = \frac{1}{n}$.

$= \frac{1}{20}$

$= 0.05$ s

$n = 20$ (number of oscillations per second)

Time taken to travel from A to C $= \frac{1}{4} \times 0.05 = 0.0125$ s.
Time taken to travel from A to C $= 12.5$ ms (milliseconds).

1 millisecond $= \frac{1}{1000}$ s

b To find the time taken to move from C to the midpoint of CB it is necessary to use one of the formulas for x in terms of t. As the question does not give the position of the object when $t = 0$, it can be assumed to be at C moving in the direction CB. The corresponding formula for x is:

$x = a\sin \omega t$ ◀ ③ Use $x = a\sin\omega t$.

Particle is initially travelling through centre in positive direction.

where $a = 0.06$ and ω can be found from the period.

$$T = \frac{2\pi}{\omega}$$ ◀ ② Use period $T = \frac{2\pi}{\omega}$.

Rearrange formula.

$$\omega = \frac{2\pi}{T}$$

Substitute values.

$$\omega = \frac{2\pi}{0.05} = 40\pi$$

The formula for displacement is:

$$x = 0.06\sin 40\pi t$$

When the object is at the midpoint of CB, $x = 0.03$. Substituting this into the formula:

$$0.03 = 0.06 \sin 40\pi t$$

Divide by 0.06.

$$\sin 40\pi t = 0.5$$

$$40\pi t = \sin^{-1}(0.5)$$

Or arcsin(0.5). Calculate the angle in radians.

$$40\pi t = 0.5236$$

Divide by 40π.

$$t = \frac{0.5236}{40\pi} = 0.004\,17\text{ s}$$

The time taken to move from C to the midpoint of CB = 4.17 ms.

Example 3

The equation of motion of a particle, P, is $\ddot{x} = -4x$ where x is the displacement in metres from a fixed point O. When $t = 0$, P is moving through O at 6 m s^{-1}. Find formulas for

a x in terms of t

b v in terms of t

c v in terms of x.

Solution

a ◀ ① Sketch and summary.

O x P

$v = 6$ m s^{-1} when $t = 0$

$\ddot{x} = -4x$ gives $\omega^2 = 4$ so $\omega = 2$

Compare with $\ddot{x} = -\omega^2 x$.

At the centre of motion

$$v = a\omega$$ ◀ ⑦ Velocity at centre of motion $= a\omega$.

$$6 = a \times 2$$

$$a = 3$$

The formula for x is $x = 3 \sin 2t$.

b Differentiating gives $v = \dot{x} = 6 \cos 2t$. ◀ ⑤ Derive v in terms of t.

c $v^2 = \omega^2(a^2 - x^2)$ ◀ ⑥ $v = \pm\omega\sqrt{a^2 - x^2}$.

$$v^2 = 2^2(3^2 - x^2)$$

$$v = \pm 2\sqrt{9 - x^2}$$

19.3 Particular Solutions for Displacement in Terms of Time

Exercise

Technique

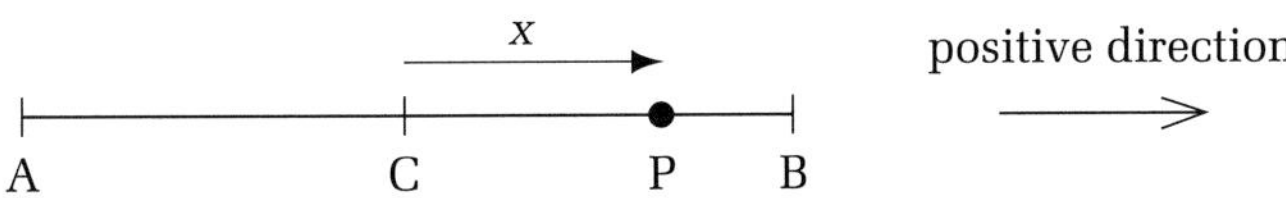

For questions [1] to [5] the diagram shows the path of a particle P which is performing SHM between the fixed points A and B. The point C is the centre of motion.

1 If the period is 3 seconds, find the time taken for P to travel

a from A to B **b** from A to C **c** from C to B.

2 P performs two oscillations per second. Calculate:

a the period
b the time taken to travel from:
  i A to C
  ii B to A.

3 The amplitude of the motion is 7 metres and the period is 8 seconds. When $t = 0$, P is passing through the centre of motion C in the positive direction.

a Find ω in terms of π.
b Write down a formula for the displacement, x, in terms of t.
c Determine the position of P when
  i $t = 1$
  ii $t = 2$
  iii $t = 5$

Remember to use radians.

4 Initially P is at rest at B. The distance AB is 4 metres and P performs 5 oscillations per second.

a Derive an equation which relates the displacement, x, to the time, t, after the particle leaves B.
b Determine the time taken for P to reach:
  i the midpoint of BC
  ii the midpoint of AC
  iii the point D on AB where AD = 3.5 m.

Find the smallest positive value of t.

5 AB = 10 m and when $t = 0$, P is travelling through C with velocity $20\,\text{m}\,\text{s}^{-1}$.

a Deduce the values of a and ω.

b Find formulas for the displacement, velocity and acceleration after t seconds.

c Calculate the displacement, velocity and acceleration when $t = 1$.

Contextual

1 When a heavy case is put into the boot of a car with poor shock absorbers its motion can be modelled as simple harmonic motion with period 0.6 seconds. What is the time taken for the case to travel:

a from the highest point in the motion to the lowest point

b from the lowest point in the motion to the equilibrium position?

2

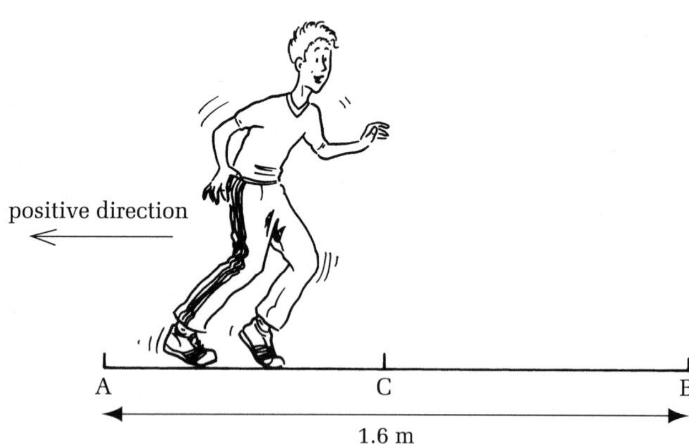

A section of floor in a fairground House of Fun moves horizontally with simple harmonic motion when anyone steps onto it. A person standing on this floor starts from rest at a point A and 2 seconds later comes to rest instantaneously at another point B where AB = 1.6 m. The point C is the midpoint of AB.

a Find the value of :

i a **ii** ω

b Using t to denote the time in seconds since the person started from A, derive a formula, in terms of t, for:

i the displacement, x, of the person from C

ii the velocity.

c Determine the position and velocity of the person when:

i $t = 0.6$ **ii** $t = 1.2$ **iii** $t = 2.4$ **iv** $t = 3.2$

d Find the velocity when the person is 1.2 m from A.

19.4 General Solutions for Displacement in Terms of Time

The previous section involved SHM which began with the object at the centre or end of its path. However, the object may pass through some other point when $t = 0$. The relationship between circular motion and simple harmonic motion can be used to derive more general formulas to be used in such cases.

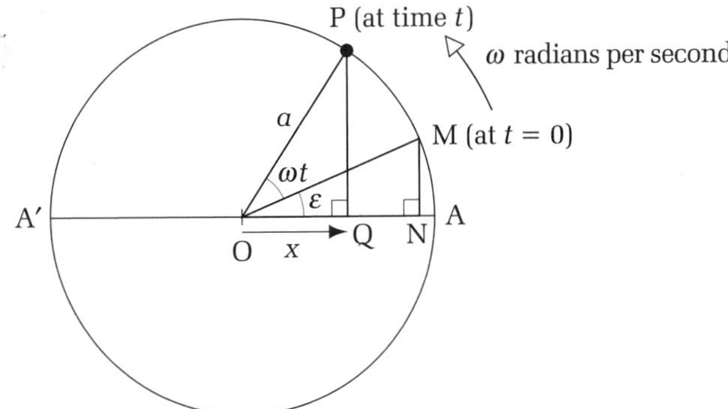

P is moving round a circle of radius a at a constant rate of ω radians per second. As P moves around the circle, Q moves backwards and forwards with SHM along AA′. Suppose when $t = 0$, P is at the point marked M and Q is at N where $\angle MON = \varepsilon$. In the sketch, ε is shown as an acute angle, but by varying ε from 0 to 2π (or $-\pi$ to π), the starting point of P could be anywhere on the circle and that of Q anywhere on the diameter.

After t seconds OP has turned through an angle ωt radians as shown.

Using trigonometry in triangle OPQ,

$$x = a\cos(\omega t + \varepsilon)$$

ε is sometimes called the phase angle.

This is a general solution for the displacement of Q after t seconds.

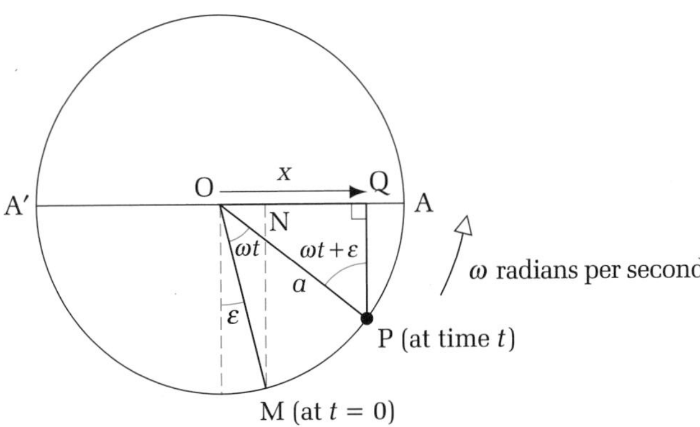

An alternative solution can be derived by measuring angles from a vertical line.

The initial positions of P and Q are M and N, as shown in the second sketch. In this case the relationship between x and t is:

$$x = a\sin(\omega t + \varepsilon)$$

For SHM the general solution for displacement can be written as

$$\mathbf{x = a\cos(\omega t + \varepsilon)} \quad \text{or} \quad \mathbf{x = a\sin(\omega t + \varepsilon)}$$

Expanding either of these gives the alternative formula: $x = A\sin(\omega t) + B\cos(\omega t)$

Both expressions give a graph with the same sinusoidal shape as those met in Section 19.3. The period is $\frac{2\pi}{\omega}$. If the object is at the positive end or centre of the path when $t = 0$ the general expressions simplify to:

$$x = a\cos\omega t \quad \text{or} \quad x = a\sin\omega t$$

As used in Section 19.3.

Overview of method

Step ① Draw a sketch of the motion, noting any information given.

Step ② If required, show the motion is simple harmonic by proving $\ddot{x} = -\omega^2 x$.

For method, see Section 19.1.

Step ③ To find a general formula for displacement in terms of time use $x = a\cos(\omega t + \varepsilon)$ or $x = a\sin(\omega t + \varepsilon)$, where the constants a, ω, ε should be found using the information given.

NB: Use an easier formula if given the choice.

Step ④ Use period $T = \dfrac{2\pi}{\omega} = \dfrac{1}{n}$ to find ω (where n is the number of oscillations per second).

Step ⑤ Use $v^2 = \omega^2(a^2 - x^2)$ to find a.

Step ⑥ Differentiate the formula for x to find velocity in terms of time.

Step ⑦ Use the initial conditions to find a value of ε between $-\pi$ and π (or between 0 and 2π).

Step ⑧ Derive a formula for acceleration by differentiating the formula for velocity or using $\ddot{x} = -\omega^2 x$.

Some of these steps may not be required.

Example 1

One end of a spring is attached to a fixed point O and the other end is attached to a particle which is hanging freely in equilibrium at a point C vertically below O. When $t = 0$ the particle is pulled downwards by 0.1 m from C and projected downwards with a speed of $4\ \text{m s}^{-1}$. In the subsequent motion the particle performs SHM with period 1 s.

a Write the displacement x from C, at time t, in the form $x = a\cos(\omega t + \varepsilon)$.

b Derive formulas for the velocity and acceleration in terms of t.

Solution

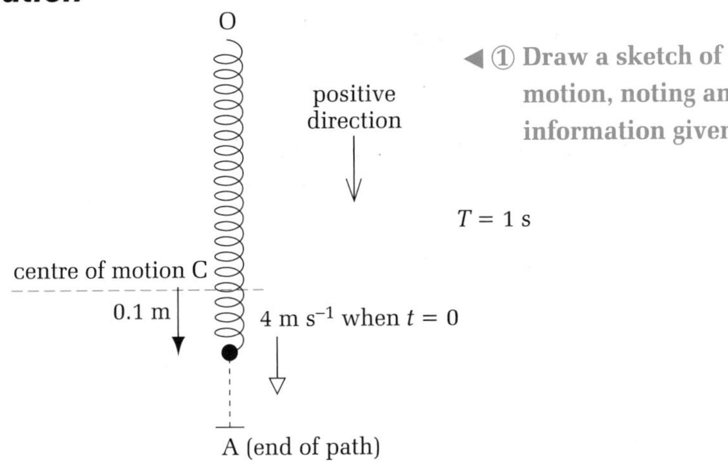

a $x = a\cos(\omega t + \varepsilon)$ where x and t are the variables and a, ω and ε are constants to be found. ◀ ③ Use $x = a\cos(\omega t + \varepsilon)$.

$$T = \frac{2\pi}{\omega}$$ ◀ ④ Use period $T = \frac{2\pi}{\omega}$ to find ω.

Rearrange formula.

$$\omega = \frac{2\pi}{T}$$

$$\omega = \frac{2\pi}{1} = 2\pi$$

Initially $x = 0.1$ and $v = 4$

$$v^2 = \omega^2(a^2 - x^2)$$ ◀ ⑤ Use $v^2 = \omega^2(a^2 - x^2)$ to find a.

$$16 = 4\pi^2(a^2 - 0.01)$$

Divide by $4\pi^2$.

$$\frac{4}{\pi^2} = a^2 - 0.01$$

Add 0.01.

$$0.4053 = a^2 - 0.01$$

Take the square root.

$$a^2 = 0.4153$$

$$a = 0.6444$$

The formula for displacement is:

$$x = 0.6444\cos(2\pi t + \varepsilon) \qquad [1]$$

Using $x = 0.1$ when $t = 0$ gives: ◀ ⑦ Use initial conditions to find ε.

Divide by 0.6444.

$$0.1 = 0.6444\cos\varepsilon$$

$$\cos\varepsilon = \frac{0.1}{0.6444} = 0.1552$$

$\varepsilon = \pm 1.41^c$

There are two values of ε between $-\pi$ and π for which this is true. Finding a formula for velocity allows the correct one to be identified. Differentiating [1]

$$v = \dot{x} = \frac{dx}{dt} = -2\pi \times 0.6444\sin(2\pi t + \varepsilon)$$ ◀ ⑥ Differentiate x to find velocity.

$$v = \dot{x} = -4.049\sin(2\pi t + \varepsilon) \qquad [2]$$

When $t = 0$, $v = -4.049 \sin \varepsilon$.
Initially v is positive. This means ε must be negative.

$$\varepsilon = \cos^{-1}(0.1552) = -1.41 \text{ (3 s.f.)}$$

Taking ε between $-\pi$ and π.

arccos(0.1552)

The formula for displacement is:

$$x = 0.644 \cos(2\pi t - 1.41) \text{ (3 s.f.)}$$

Other values may be used for ε. An alternative positive value is $-1.41 + 2\pi = 4.87$. Giving $x = 0.644 \times \cos(2\pi t + 4.87)$.

b From equation [2] the velocity is:

$$\dot{x} = -4.05 \sin(2\pi t - 1.41) \quad \text{(3 s.f.)}$$

Differentiating:

$$\ddot{x} = -4.05 \times 2\pi \cos(2\pi t - 1.41)$$

◀ ⑧ **Differentiate v (or $\dot{x}$).**

$$\ddot{x} = -25.4 \cos(2\pi t - 1.41) \text{ (3 s.f.)}$$

Alternatively $\ddot{x} = -\omega^2 x$ gives: $-4\pi^2 x = -25.4\cos(2\pi t - 1.41)$

Example 2

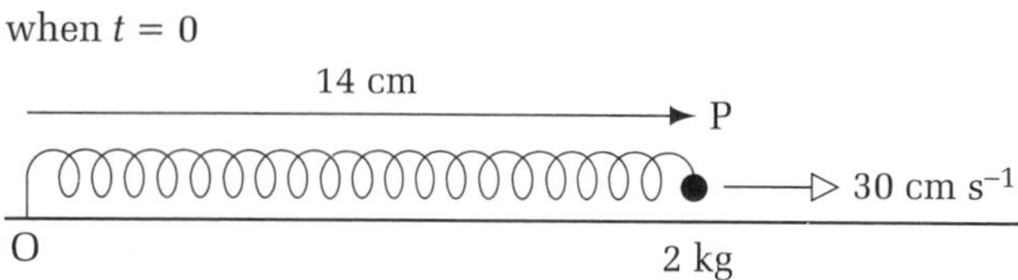

A particle, P, of mass 2 kg is attached to one end of a spring of natural length 10 cm and modulus 20 N. The other end of the spring is attached to a fixed point O on a smooth horizontal surface. The particle P is initially held on the surface at a distance of 14 cm from O and then projected away from O at 30 cm s^{-1}, as shown.

a Prove that P moves with SHM and find the value of ω.

b Find a formula for the displacement from the centre of motion in the form $x = a \sin(\omega t + \varepsilon)$.

Solution

a The surface is smooth, so there is no friction. The particle will be in equilibrium when the tension in the spring is zero. This occurs when the spring is at its natural length.

Identify the equilibrium position, then consider the general position.

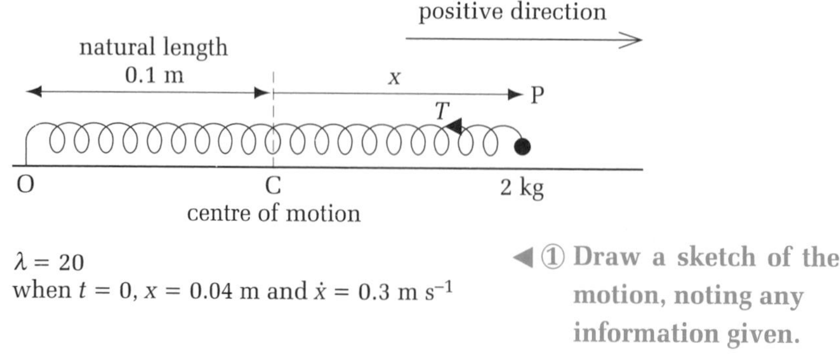

$\lambda = 20$
when $t = 0$, $x = 0.04$ m and $\dot{x} = 0.3$ m s^{-1}

◀ ① **Draw a sketch of the motion, noting any information given.**

The diagram shows the general position with x representing the displacement from the equilibrium position. In the general position, the displacement, x, is equal to the extension in the spring.

Using $F = m\ddot{x} \rightarrow$

Use $F = m\ddot{x}$ in the direction of increasing x.

$$-T = m\ddot{x}$$

◀ Use Hooke's Law, $T = \frac{\lambda x}{l}$.

◀ ② Show the motion is simple harmonic by proving $\ddot{x} = -\omega^2 x$.

$$-\frac{\lambda x}{l} = m\ddot{x}$$

Substitute the values.

$$-\frac{20x}{0.1} = 2\ddot{x}$$

Divide by 2.

$$-200x = 2\ddot{x}$$

$$\ddot{x} = -100x$$

This is the basic equation of SHM with $\omega = 10$.

b The formula for displacement is

$$x = a\sin(\omega t + \varepsilon)$$

◀ ③ Use $x = a\sin(\omega t + \varepsilon)$ for displacement.

Use the value for ω.

$$x = a\sin(10t + \varepsilon)$$

Using the initial values $x = 0.04$, $v = 0.3$ and $\omega = 10$ in $v^2 = \omega^2(a^2 - x^2)$ gives

$$0.09 = 100(a^2 - 0.0016)$$

◀ ⑤ Use $v^2 = \omega^2(a^2 - x^2)$ to find a.

Substitute values.

Divide by 100.

$$0.0009 = a^2 - 0.0016$$

Add 0.0016.

$$a^2 = 0.0025$$

Square root.

$$a = 0.05$$

The displacement $x = 0.05\sin(10t + \varepsilon)$. [1]

Using $x = 0.04$ when $t = 0$ gives ◀ ⑦ Use initial conditions to find ε.

$$0.04 = 0.05\sin\varepsilon$$

Divide by 0.05.

$$\sin\varepsilon = \frac{0.04}{0.05} = 0.8$$

Again there are two values of ε between $-\pi$ and π for which this is true. Finding a formula for velocity allows the correct one to be identified.

Differentiating [1]

$$v = \dot{x} = \frac{dx}{dt} = 0.5\cos(10t + \varepsilon) \quad [2]$$

◀ ⑥ Differentiate the formula for x to find velocity in terms of time.

Using $v = 0.3$ when $t = 0$ gives

$$0.3 = 0.5\cos\varepsilon$$

$$\cos\varepsilon = \frac{0.3}{0.5} = 0.6$$

So $\cos\varepsilon$ and $\sin\varepsilon$ are both positive. This is true if ε is an acute positive angle. Now ε can be found from $\varepsilon = \arcsin(0.8) = 0.9273$.

or $\varepsilon = \arccos(0.6) = 0.9273$

The formula for displacement is

$$x = 0.05\sin(10t + 0.927) \quad \text{(3 s.f.)}$$

Do not rush to use general solutions. Wherever possible use an easier formula.

Example 3

A particle performs SHM with $\omega = 1$ (rad s^{-1}). When the displacement $x = 3$ (m), the velocity $v = 4$ (m s^{-1}). Find how long it takes for the particle to come to rest from this speed of 4 m s^{-1}.

Solution

Let Q be position of particle when $x = 3$ (m) and $v = 4$ (m s^{-1})

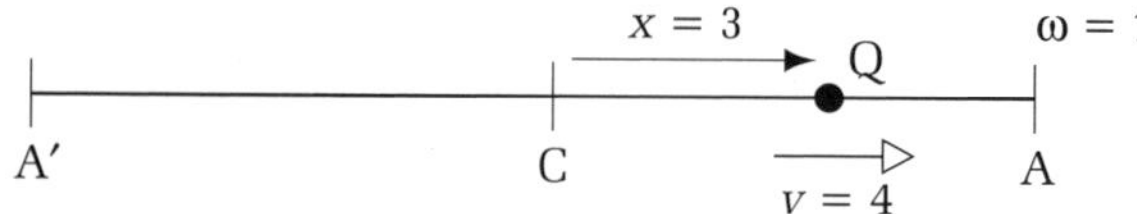

Assume $t = 0$ at the centre of motion

$$x = a\sin\omega t = a\sin t$$

Since $\omega = 1$
Use $x = a\sin\omega t$ or $x = a\cos\omega t$ where possible.

To find a use:

$$v^2 = \omega^2(a^2 - x^2)$$

$$4^2 = 1^2(a^2 - 3^2)$$

$$16 = a^2 - 9$$

$$25 = a^2$$

$$a = 5$$

$$x = 5\sin t$$

The time taken to come to rest is the time taken to travel from Q to A.

When $x = 3$, $\quad 3 = 5\sin t$

$$\sin t = \tfrac{3}{5}$$

$$t = \sin^{-1}(\tfrac{3}{5}) = 0.6435 \text{ s}$$

Time to travel from C to Q $= 0.6435$ s.
Time to travel from C to A $= \frac{1}{4}T = \frac{1}{4} \times 2\pi = \frac{\pi}{2}$.
Time to travel from Q to A $= \frac{\pi}{2} - 0.6435 = 0.927$ s

$T = \frac{2\pi}{\omega}$

19.4 General Solutions for Displacement in Terms of Time

Exercise

Technique

1 A particle, P, performs SHM of period π seconds. When $t = 0$ the displacement of P from the centre of motion is 0.5 m and P is travelling in the positive direction with speed $1\ \text{m s}^{-1}$. Evaluate ω, a and ε and hence write x in the form $x = a\sin(\omega t + \varepsilon)$.

2 A body is performing SHM at a rate of 2 oscillations per second. The body travels through the point where $x = 2$ with velocity $-25\ \text{m s}^{-1}$ and t seconds later the displacement from the centre of motion is x metres.

a Write x in the form $x = a\cos(\omega t + \varepsilon)$.

b Deduce formulas for the velocity and acceleration of the body.

3

when $t = 0$

$20\ \text{cm s}^{-1}$

P

150 g

O

12 cm

A particle, P, of mass 150 g, is attached to one end of a spring of natural length 15 cm and modulus of elasticity 9 N. The other end of the spring is attached to a point, O, on a smooth horizontal surface. The particle is held on the surface with the spring compressed to a length of 12 cm and an impulsive force is applied so that P begins to move towards O at a speed of $20\ \text{cm s}^{-1}$. Prove that P's motion is simple harmonic, and find the time for:

a P to come to rest for the first time

b the spring to reach its natural length for the first time.

Contextual

1 When a voltage is applied to an oscilloscope it causes a spot of light to move vertically up and down a fluorescent screen. The vertical motion of the spot of light is simple harmonic at a rate of 4 oscillations per second. When the displacement of the spot of light from its central position is 2.5 cm, it is moving at a velocity of $50\ \text{cm s}^{-1}$. The positive direction is vertically upwards. Find the time taken for the spot to travel from this position to the lowest point in its motion.

19.5 The Simple Pendulum

The pendulum on a grandfather clock moves backwards and forwards with simple harmonic motion, but in this case the motion is not in a straight line. The pendulum moves to and fro along an arc of a circle.

Basic equation of angular SHM

The basic equation of SHM may be proved using the model of a heavy particle, P, of mass m, attached to one end of a light inextensible string of length l. The other end of the string is attached to a fixed point, O. In the equilibrium position, the string lies along the line OA. Imagine the particle (often called the bob) is pulled to one side so that $\angle$AOP is a *small* angle, and then released.

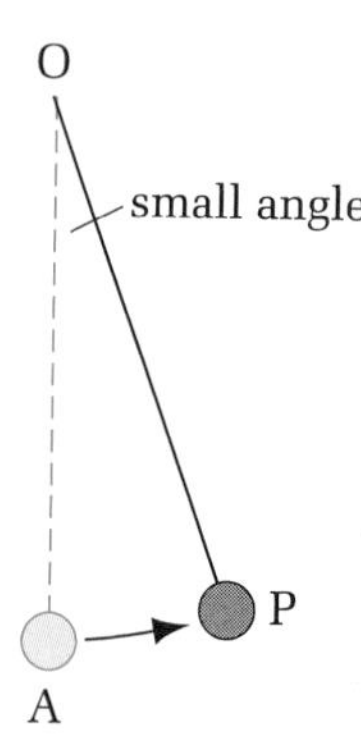

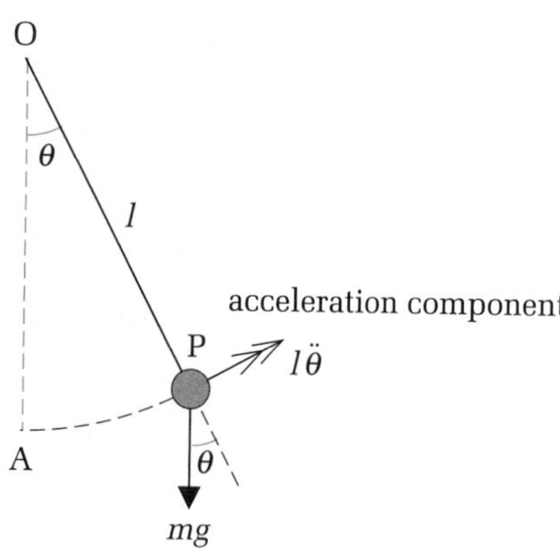

The sketch shows the pendulum in a general position when the angle between OP and the vertical is θ.

Assuming θ is in radians.

The displacement = length of arc AP = $l\theta$.

Differentiating with respect to t:

velocity of the particle along the tangent $= l\dot{\theta}$

l is constant.

Differentiating again:

acceleration along the tangent $= l\ddot{\theta}$

Using $F = m\ddot{x}$ along the tangent in the direction of increasing θ

$$-mg\sin\theta = ml\ddot{\theta}$$

$$-g\sin\theta = l\ddot{\theta}$$

For small values of θ, $\sin\theta \approx \theta$.

$$-g\theta \approx l\ddot{\theta}$$

$$\ddot{\theta} \approx -\frac{g}{l}\theta$$

Try sin(0.1), sin(0.15) and sin(0.2) in radians. What do you notice? Compare with $\ddot{x} = -\omega^2 x$.

This is the basic equation for angular SHM with $\omega = \sqrt{\frac{g}{l}}$. Notice that the motion of the simple pendulum is only approximately SHM. This approximation only works when the bob is *displaced by a small angle*.

The period of the motion is

$$T = \frac{2\pi}{\omega} \approx 2\pi\sqrt{\frac{l}{g}}$$

Again this will only be an approximation for the time period.

Note that the period does not depend on the mass of the bob. For a particular location on the Earth's surface, g is a constant. Since 2π is also constant, the period is proportional to the square root of the length of the string. The longer the string, the longer the period.

The seconds pendulum

If a pendulum takes 1 second to travel from one end of its path to the other it is called a seconds pendulum. The pendulum is often said to *beat* seconds. The period of such a pendulum is *2 seconds* and the length of string required can be calculated using the formula for period:

$$2 = 2\pi\sqrt{\frac{l}{g}}$$

Dividy by 2.

$$1 = \pi\sqrt{\frac{l}{g}}$$

Divide by π.

$$\frac{1}{\pi} = \sqrt{\frac{l}{g}}$$

Square both sides.

$$\frac{1}{\pi^2} = \frac{l}{g}$$

Multiply by g.

$$\frac{g}{\pi^2} = l$$

The length of string needed to produce a seconds pendulum depends on the acceleration due to gravity. At a location where g is exactly $9.8\ \text{m s}^{-2}$, the length of string needed $= \frac{9.8}{\pi^2} = 0.993$ m. As g varies, depending on the distance from the centre of the Earth, the length of the seconds pendulum varies. The length of a seconds pendulum is greater at the bottom of a mountain than it is at the top.

Overview of method

Step ① Prove the basic equation of SHM, $\ddot{\theta} \approx -\frac{g}{l}\theta$, if required.
Step ② Write down $T = 2\pi\sqrt{\frac{l}{g}}$ and rearrange if necessary.

Step ③ Substitute the known values and find the value required.
Step ④ If asked for a pendulum which beats seconds use $T = 2$.

Example 1

Calculate, to the nearest tenth of a second, the period of a pendulum of length 2.1 m at a location where $g = 9.81\ \text{m s}^{-2}$.

Solution

$$T = 2\pi\sqrt{\frac{l}{g}}$$

◀ ② Write down $T = 2\pi\sqrt{\frac{l}{g}}$.

Substituting $l = 2.1$, $g = 9.81$,

$$T = 2\pi\sqrt{\frac{2.1}{9.81}}$$

$$T = 2\pi\sqrt{0.214\,07}$$

$$T = 2.907$$

◀ ③ Substitute the known values and find the value required.

The period of the pendulum is 2.9 s to the nearest tenth of a second.

Example 2

A grandfather clock loses 1 minute in 8 hours. Find the percentage change in the length of the pendulum which is necessary to correct the clock.

Solution

Number of seconds in 8 hours $= 8 \times 60 \times 60 = 28\,800$. As the clock loses 60 seconds, the number of *half-oscillations* performed $= 28\,740$.

$$\text{Time taken for half an oscillation} = \frac{28\,800}{28\,740} = 1.002\,088.$$

$$\text{Period} = 2.004\,175$$

Use the calculator's memory to hold as many figures as possible (7 s.f. are shown). Multiply 1.002 088 by 2.

To answer the question, it is necessary to compare the actual length of the pendulum, with the length required to keep the correct time.

$$T = 2\pi\sqrt{\frac{l}{g}}$$

◀ ② Write down $T = 2\pi\sqrt{\frac{l}{g}}$ and transpose if necessary.

Divide by 2π.

$$\frac{T}{2\pi} = \sqrt{\frac{l}{g}}$$

Square both sides.

$$\frac{T^2}{4\pi^2} = \frac{l}{g}$$

Multiply by g.

$$\frac{gT^2}{4\pi^2} = l$$

The original length of the pendulum:

$$l_0 = \frac{gT^2}{4\pi^2}$$ ◀ ③ Substitute the known values.

$$= \frac{g \times 2.004\,18^2}{4\pi^2}$$

$$= \frac{4.016\,72g}{4\pi^2}$$

Simplify.
It is not necessary to use a value for g since it cancels later.

The required length for correct time:

$$l_c = \frac{gT^2}{4\pi^2}$$ ◀ ④ If asked for a pendulum which beats seconds use $T = 2$.

$$= \frac{g \times 2^2}{4\pi^2}$$

$$= \frac{4g}{4\pi^2}$$

Simplify.

Dividing the expressions for l_c and l_0 gives:

$$\frac{l_c}{l_0} = \frac{4}{4.016\,72} = 0.995\,84$$

$$l_c = 0.995\,84\ l_0$$

To find the % change needed in the original length, l_c must be found as a % of l_0.

$100 - 99.584 = 0.416$

The correct length $l_c = 99.584\%$ of the actual length. The length should be reduced by 0.42% (2 s.f.).

Example 3

When a rope swing is displaced through a small angle and released from rest it oscillates with period T seconds. When a girl sits on the swing, the length of the rope is increased by 18%. What will be the percentage change in the period of small oscillations?

Solution

The swing is modelled as a simple pendulum

$$T = 2\pi\sqrt{\frac{l}{g}}$$ ◀ ② Write down $T = 2\pi\sqrt{\frac{l}{g}}$.

When the girl sits on the swing the length becomes $1.18l$. Using T_n to denote the new period:

$$T_n = 2\pi\sqrt{\frac{1.18l}{g}}$$ ◀ ③ Substitute the known values and find the value required.

Collect $2\pi\sqrt{\frac{l}{g}}$ together (T).

$$T_n = \sqrt{1.18} \times 2\pi\sqrt{\frac{l}{g}}$$

Replace $2\pi\sqrt{\frac{l}{g}}$ with T.

$$T_n = 1.086T$$

$\frac{1.086-1}{1} \times 100 = 8.6\%$

The period is increased by 8.6% (2 s.f.)

Since the length has increased, the period has increased.

19.5 The Simple Pendulum

Exercise

Technique

1 The length of a pendulum is 1.5 m and it is located at a place where $g = 9.806\ \text{m s}^{-2}$. Find the period.

2 If $g = 9.8\ \text{m s}^{-2}$, find the length of a pendulum whose period is 2.4 seconds.

3 A pendulum of length 2236 mm has a period of 3 seconds. Calculate, to three decimal places, the value of g.

4 The length of a pendulum is reduced by 30%. Find the percentage change in the period.

5 The period of a pendulum is T seconds. If the length of the pendulum is doubled, write the new period in terms of T.

Contextual

1 Calculate, to the nearest mm, the length required for a seconds pendulum at a place where $g = 9.802\ \text{m s}^{-2}$.

2 A grandfather clock keeps perfect time when the length of its pendulum is 994 mm. Determine, to three significant figures, the value of g.

3 A seconds pendulum beats exact seconds at a location where $g = 9.80\ \text{m s}^{-2}$. If it is taken to a place where $g = 9.81\ \text{m s}^{-2}$, find:

a by how many seconds per day it will be wrong
b by how much the length should be altered to correct it.

4 A light, of mass m, hangs from the ceiling by a flex which is l m long.

a Show that when the light is accidentally knocked and displaced slightly, the motion can be modelled as SHM and derive a formula for the period of oscillations.
b Calculate the period if the length of the wire is 20 cm.

Consolidation

Exercise A

1 A machine component consists of a small piston of mass 0.2 kg moving inside a fixed horizontal cylinder. The piston, which is modelled as a particle moves with simple harmonic motion and the total distance from one end of each oscillation to the other is 0.05 m. Given that the speed of the piston must not exceed $20\ \text{m s}^{-1}$, find:

a the maximum number of oscillations per second which the piston can perform;

b the maximum horizontal force that can be experienced by the piston.

(ULEAC)

2

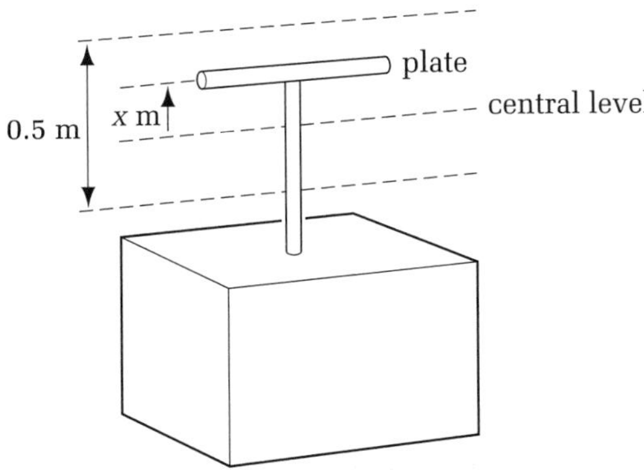

A thin horizontal plate is being driven by a mechanism so that its vertical motion is simple harmonic. It moves through two complete oscillations per second and the distance from the lowest to the highest point of the motion is 0.5 m. At the instant from which time is measured the plate is moving upwards through the centre of its motion. At a time t seconds later the plate is x metres above this central level, as shown in the diagram.

a Show that the acceleration, $\ddot{x}$, of the plate is given by $\ddot{x} = -16\pi^2 x$.

b Find an expression for x at time t.

c Find an expression for v^2 in terms of x, where $v\ \text{m s}^{-1}$ is the speed of the plate.

When the plate is at its lowest point, it picks up a small piece of grit of mass m kg.

d Draw a diagram showing the forces acting on the piece of grit while it is in contact with the plate, and derive the equation of motion for the piece of grit. Explain why the grit leaves the plate when $\ddot{x} = -g$.

e How far does the piece of grit travel while in contact with the plate? What is its speed when it leaves the plate?

f For how long is the piece of grit in contact with the plate?

(MEI)

3 A simple pendulum consists of a heavy mass, m kilogrammes, which is attached to one end of a light, inextensible string of length l metres. The other end of the string is suspended from a fixed point. The mass is drawn to the side and held so that the string is taut and makes a small angle θ with the vertical. It is then released from rest. (Take $g = 10\,\text{m}\,\text{s}^{-2}$.)

a **i** Prove that the motion of the mass, m, is approximately simple harmonic.

ii Show that the periodic time for the motion is $2\pi\sqrt{\frac{l}{10}}$ seconds.

iii State one modelling assumption you have made.

A particle whose motion is also simple harmonic, oscillates about a point O in time with a simple pendulum of length 40 cm. At a particular instant the particle is moving through a point P which is 4 cm from O with a velocity of $15\,\text{cm}\,\text{s}^{-1}$ towards O.

b **i** Find the amplitude of the motion of the particle.

ii Find the time which elapses from the instant when the particle leaves P until it passes through O for the first time. (*NICCEA*)

Exercise B

1 A particle, P, of mass 2 kg, moves along a straight line and it is known that its motion is simple harmonic. It is observed to come instantaneously to rest at the points A and B. The distance AB is measured as 1.6 m and the time taken for P to travel once from A to B is recorded as 1.2 s.

a Write down the amplitude and the period of the motion.

b Calculate the greatest speed achieved by P during the motion.

c Show that the greatest magnitude of the force acting on P which causes its motion is approximately 11 N. (*NEAB*)

2 A particle P is suspended from a fixed point O by a light inextensible string of length 4 m. The particle is displaced so that the taut string makes an angle α with the downward vertical through O. The particle is then released from rest. By considering the transverse component of acceleration of the particle at time t seconds after release, when the string makes an angle θ with the downward vertical through O (see diagram), obtain a differential equation expressing $\frac{d^2\theta}{dt^2}$ in terms of θ.

O
θ
4 m
P

By using an approximation based on the assumption that α is small, and ignoring air resistance, deduce that the motion of the particle will be approximately simple harmonic, and calculate its approximate period. (*UCLES*)

Transverse component of acceleration is the acceleration along the tangent, i.e. $l\ddot{\theta}$.

$\frac{d^2\theta}{dt^2} \equiv \ddot{\theta}$

3 A particle P of mass 0.1 kg is attached to one end of a light elastic spring of natural length 0.5 m. The other end of the spring is attached to a fixed point O. The particle is hanging freely in equilibrium at the point B where $OB = 0.598$ m.

a Find the elastic modulus of the spring.

At time $t = 0$ the particle is pulled down to a point 0.15 m vertically below B and then released from rest. The subsequent downwards displacement of P from B at time t s is denoted by x m and air resistance is to be neglected.

b Express, in terms of x, the force exerted by the spring.

c Show that $\frac{d^2x}{dt^2} + 100x = 0$.

d Find the time when P is next at a distance of 0.15 m below B.

e Find the speed of P when at a distance of 0.05 m below B.

f Without further calculation, explain why the answer to **d** would be different if the spring were replaced by a string of the same modulus.

(*WJEC*)

4 A light elastic string of natural length a and modulus mg has one end fixed to a particle, P, of mass m, and the other end to a fixed point A. The particle is held with the string vertical, at a point O which is at a distance a below A. At a given instant, P is projected vertically downwards.

a Write down the equation of motion of P when it is at a distance x, $(x > 0)$, below O.

b Show that, whilst the string is taut, P performs simple harmonic motion centred on a point B, distance a below O.

c Given that the initial speed at O is $\sqrt{8ga}$, use the principle of conservation of energy to show that when the string has total length $a + x$, where $x > 0$, the speed of P is given by v, where:

$av^2 = 2ag(x + 4a) - gx^2$

d Hence, or otherwise, find the maximum distance of P below O, and find the magnitude of the greatest tension in the string.

(*AEB*)

Applications and Activities

1 Tie a heavy object to the end of a piece of string. Use this as a simple pendulum and time how long it takes to perform a number of oscillations. Calculate the period. Measure the length of the string and use $T = 2\pi\sqrt{\frac{l}{g}}$ to find the value of g.

2 Repeat Activity 1, finding the period for different lengths of string. Plot a graph of T against $\sqrt{l}$ and draw the line of best fit. Use the gradient of the graph to find an estimate of g.

3 Make a seconds pendulum.

A simple pendulum where $T = 2$ s.

4 Attach a weight to the end of a spring (or elastic string) and measure the extension in the string when it hangs vertically in equilibrium. Use Hooke's law to find the modulus of elasticity. Apply the theory of SHM to predict the period of oscillations when the weight is pulled down and then released. Test the theory by timing a number of oscillations and comparing the actual period with that predicted.

Summary

- Motion is simple harmonic if the acceleration can be written in the form

  $$\ddot{\mathbf{x}} = -\omega^2\mathbf{x}$$

- Maximum acceleration is given by $\omega^2 a$.
- The period of SHM is

  $$T = \frac{2\pi}{\omega}$$

- The formula that relates velocity and displacement is

  $$v^2 = \omega^2(a^2 - x^2)$$

- Maximum speed $= \omega a$
- When the object is initially at the end of the path the displacement (in terms of time) is

  $$x = a\cos\omega t$$

- When the object is initially at the centre of the path the displacement (in terms of time) is

  $$x = a\sin\omega t$$

- The general forms for displacement in terms of time are

  $$x = a\cos(\omega t + \varepsilon)$$

  $$x = a\sin(\omega t + \varepsilon)$$

- The equation of motion of a simple pendulum is

  $$\ddot{\theta} \approx -\frac{g}{l}\theta$$

  This is approximately simple harmonic motion.

- The time period of a simple pendulum is

  $$T = 2\pi\sqrt{\frac{l}{g}}$$

20 Resultant and Relative Velocities

What you need to know

- How to find the resultant of two vectors.
- How to add and subtract vectors in **i, j** form.
- How to use the sine and cosine rules.
- How to use and calculate bearings.

Review

1 Calculate the resultant of the two vectors shown.

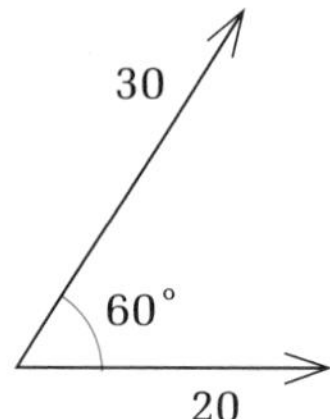

2 $\mathbf{a} = -7\mathbf{i} + 8\mathbf{j}$ and $\mathbf{b} = 10\mathbf{i} - 5\mathbf{j}$

Determine:

a $\mathbf{a} + \mathbf{b}$

b $4\mathbf{a} - 3\mathbf{b}$

3 **a**

B
10 cm 130° 20 cm
A C

Find *AC*.

b

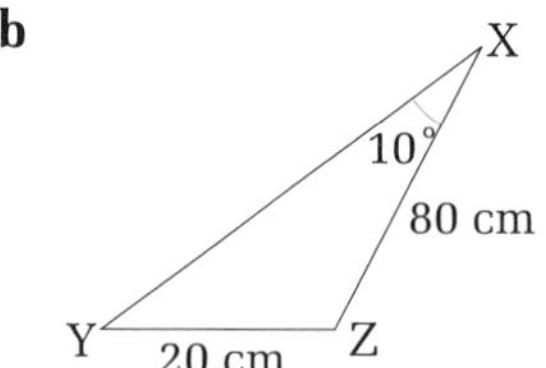

Determine the acute angle XYZ.

4 **a** Point B is 060° from point A. Work out the bearing of point A from point B.

b Point Y is on a bearing of 130° from point X and 270° from point Z. Determine the angle XYZ.

20.1 Resultant Velocity

An airport near Edinburgh is 300 km due north of an airport at Liverpool. A wind of 50 km h^{-1} blows from the west and an aircraft can maintain a speed of 400 km h^{-1} in still air. In which direction must the aircraft fly, to arrive at Edinburgh? The wind's speed will be assumed constant. The aircraft will be treated as a particle and its speed during the flight will be assumed constant. Take-off and landing times will be ignored.

The aircraft's speed of 400 km h^{-1} will be affected by the speed and direction of the wind. A velocity vector diagram will help. The resultant velocity of the aircraft will have to act from Liverpool to Edinburgh.

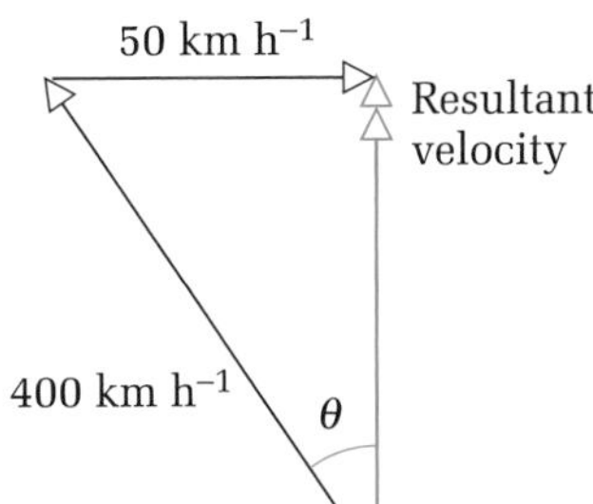

Using trigonometry:

$$\tan\theta = \tfrac{50}{400}$$

$$\tan\theta = \tfrac{1}{8}$$

$$\theta = \tan^{-1}\left(\tfrac{1}{8}\right)$$

or $\arctan(\tfrac{1}{8})$

$$\theta = 7.1^\circ$$

This angle can be used to calculate the bearing of the aircraft.

$$\text{bearing} = 360^\circ - 7.1^\circ$$
$$= 352.9^\circ$$

How long would this journey take? First the speed of the aircraft can be calculated using Pythagoras' theorem.

$$400^2 = |\mathbf{v}|^2 + 50^2$$

$$400^2 - 50^2 = |\mathbf{v}|^2$$

Subtract 50^2.

$$157\,500 = |\mathbf{v}|^2$$

Calculate LHS.

$$|\mathbf{v}| = \sqrt{157\,500}$$

Take the square root.

$$|\mathbf{v}| = 397\,\text{km h}^{-1}\ (3\ \text{s.f.})$$

Use the speed, distance, time formula.

$$T = \frac{D}{S}$$

Substitute the values.

$$T = \tfrac{300}{397}$$

Calculate the value in hours.

$$T = 0.756\,\text{h}$$

Convert into minutes and seconds.

$$T = 45\ \text{minutes}\ 21\ \text{seconds}$$

This seems the correct order of magnitude. The journey time is quite short so take-off and landing times will be significant.

Overview of method

Step ① Draw a clear diagram.
Step ② Mark on the resultant velocity using the velocity triangle.
Step ③ Use trigonometry and Pythagoras' theorem *or* use sine rule and cosine rule.

Example

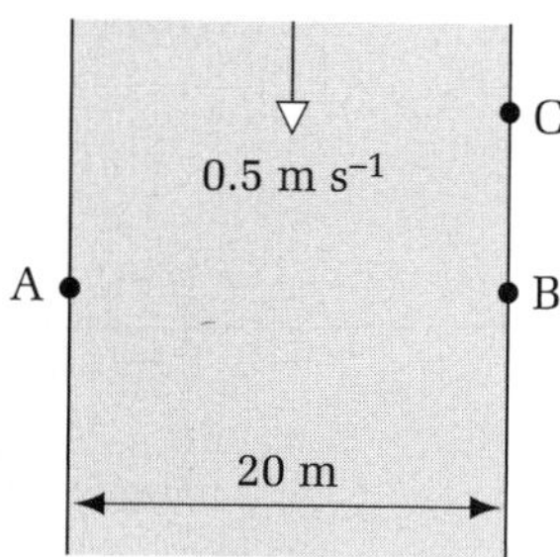

A river is 20 m wide. A woman can swim at 2 m s^{-1} in still water. The current in the river flows at 0.5 m s^{-1}.

a The woman swims at right angles to the river bank, starting at A.
  i How long does it take her to cross the river?
  ii When she reaches the other bank, how far is she from B?

b In which direction should she swim to arrive at C, 10 m upstream from B?

Solution

a

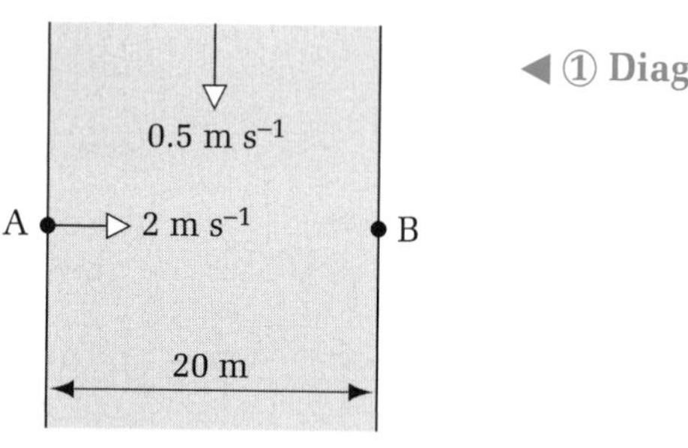

◀ ① Diagram.

This route gives the shortest possible crossing time.

i Time to travel from one bank to the other.

$$T = \frac{D}{S}$$

$$T = \frac{20}{2}$$

$$T = 10\text{ s}$$

Use speed, distance, time triangle.
The distance and speed perpendicular to the bank are used to calculate the time to cross the river.

ii Distance travelled downstream

$D = S \times T$

$D = 0.5 \times 10$

$D = 5\text{ m}$

The speed parallel to the bank is used.

The woman is 5 m downstream of B.

b

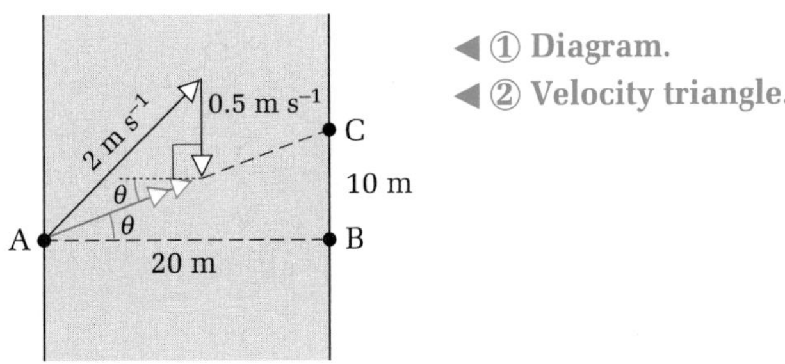

◀ ① **Diagram.**

◀ ② **Velocity triangle.**

The resultant velocity must act along AC. There is no right angle in the velocity triangle and so the sine and cosine rules must be used. First calculate angle θ using trigonometry in triangle ABC.

$\tan\theta = \frac{10}{20}$

$\tan\theta = 0.5$

$\theta = 26.6°$

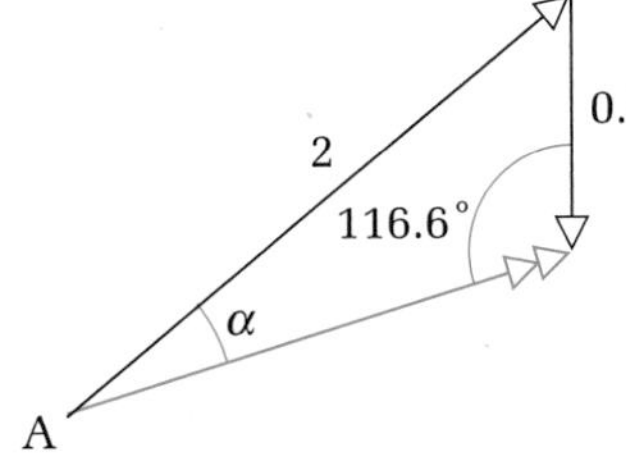

$\theta + 90° = 26.6° + 90°$

$= 116.6°$

Use the sine rule to find α ◀ ③ **Use sine rule.**

$$\frac{\sin\alpha}{0.5} = \frac{\sin 116.6°}{2}$$

Multiply by 0.5

$$\sin\alpha = \frac{0.5 \times \sin 116.6°}{2}$$

Work out RHS.

$\sin\alpha = 0.2236$

$\alpha = 12.9°$

$\alpha = \sin^{-1}(0.2236)$ or $\arcsin(0.2236)$

Angle upstream $= 12.9° + 26.6° = 39.5°$ (from AB)

20.1 Resultant Velocity
Exercise
Contextual

1

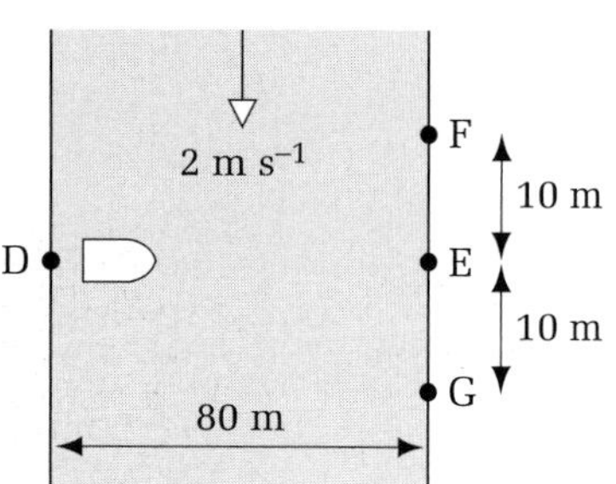

A boat can be rowed at a steady speed of 5 m s^{-1} in still water. The current in the river flows at 2 m s^{-1}.

a The boat is rowed directly towards E.
  i How long will the boat take to cross the river?
  ii How far from E will the boat be when it reaches the other side?

b Find the direction that the boat must be rowed if it is it reach
  i point E **ii** point F **iii** point G.

c The boat is rowed upstream at 45° to the bank.
  i When it reaches the opposite bank, how far from E is the boat?
  ii At what speed must the boat be rowed if it is to reach point E?

2 An aeroplane has to fly from airport A to airport B, where B is 1500 km due south of A. A wind of 100 km h^{-1} blows from the east and the aeroplane can fly at 400 km h^{-1} in still air.

a Find the direction in which the aeroplane needs to travel to reach airport B.

b How long does the journey take?

3 A canoeist wants to cross a river as quickly as possible. The river is 130 m wide and the water in it flows at a constant speed of 2 m s^{-1}. The canoeist can paddle at a maximum speed of 4 m s^{-1} in still water.

a State the course the canoeist must take.

b Calculate the time taken for the canoeist to reach the other bank.

c Determine where on the opposite bank the canoeist will land.

4 A helicopter can fly at 200 km h^{-1} in still air. It has to travel from an airport to a hospital. The hospital is 600 km from the airport on a bearing of 250°. Work out the course for the helicopter if:

a the wind speed is 50 km h^{-1} and blows from the east

b the wind speed is 80 km h^{-1} and blows from the south west

c the wind speed is 130 km h^{-1} and blows from the north east.

20.2 Relative Velocity

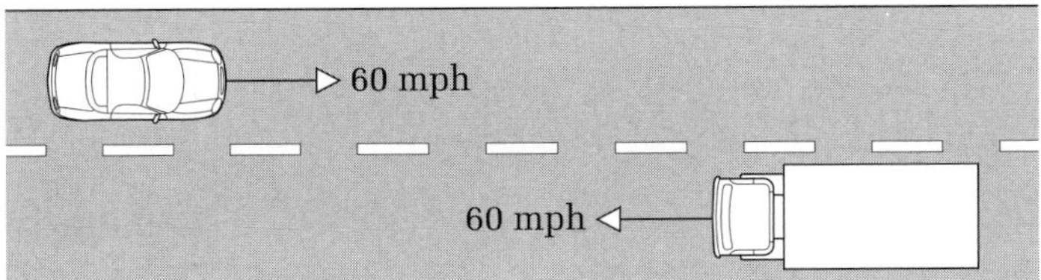

A car and a van are travelling in opposite directions along a straight road. The velocity of the car is 60 mph towards the van, and the velocity of the van is 60 mph towards the car. How fast does the van appear to be travelling to the car driver? The car driver sees the van appearing to travel much faster than 60 mph. Treat the car and van as particles. Assume the speed of both vehicles remain constant.

The velocity of the van **relative** to the car driver is what the car driver sees. This means the car should be treated as stationary. To do this, a velocity of −60 mph must be applied to the car. The same velocity must be applied to the van. This has the effect of *stopping* the car but increasing the *apparent* speed of the van. The van appears to be travelling at 120 mph towards the car. This is the **velocity of the van relative to the car**.

For a general formula, two particles A and B moving with $\mathbf{v}_A$ and $\mathbf{v}_B$ will be used.

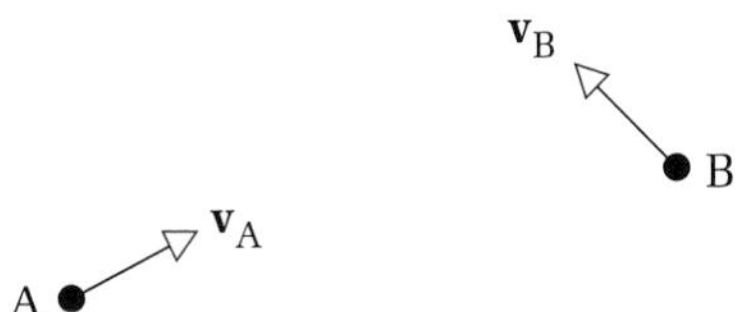

Stop particle B by applying $-\mathbf{v}_B$ to both particles.

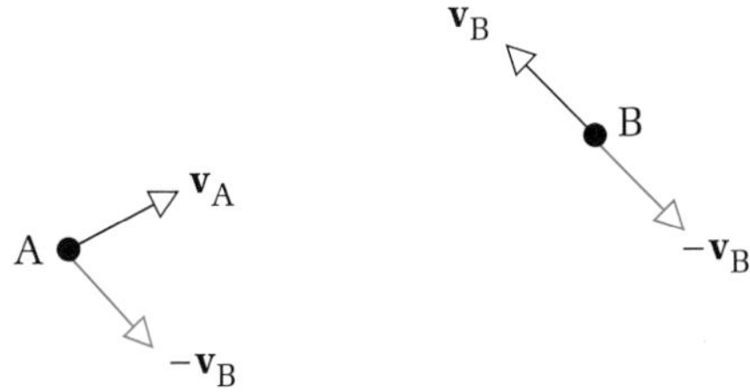

This gives the velocity of A relative to B as:

$$_A\mathbf{v}_B = \mathbf{v}_A - \mathbf{v}_B$$

Notice that the order of the letters to state the velocity of A relative to B gives the order of the letters for the subtraction.

Notation

$_A\mathbf{v}_B$ = velocity of A relative to B

$\mathbf{v}_A$ = velocity of A

$\mathbf{v}_B$ = velocity of B

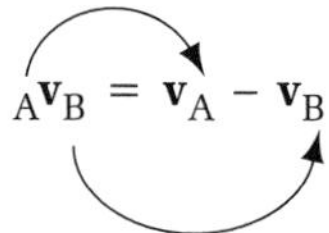

This can be used to write a formula for the velocity of B relative to A

$$_B\mathbf{v}_A = \mathbf{v}_B - \mathbf{v}_A$$

Notation

$_B\mathbf{v}_A$ = velocity of B relative to A.

By taking out a minus one as a common factor on the right hand side of the equation, a relationship between the relative velocities can be found.

$$_B\mathbf{v}_A = \mathbf{v}_B - \mathbf{v}_A$$

$$_B\mathbf{v}_A = -(\mathbf{v}_A - \mathbf{v}_B)$$

$$_B\mathbf{v}_A = -_A\mathbf{v}_B$$

Take out a minus one as a common factor.

Replace $\mathbf{v}_A - \mathbf{v}_B$ with $_A\mathbf{v}_B$.

Example 1

A plane P flies at 600 km h^{-1} on a bearing of 300° and a helicopter H flies at 200 km h^{-1} on a bearing of 060°. Calculate the velocity of the plane relative to the helicopter.

Solution

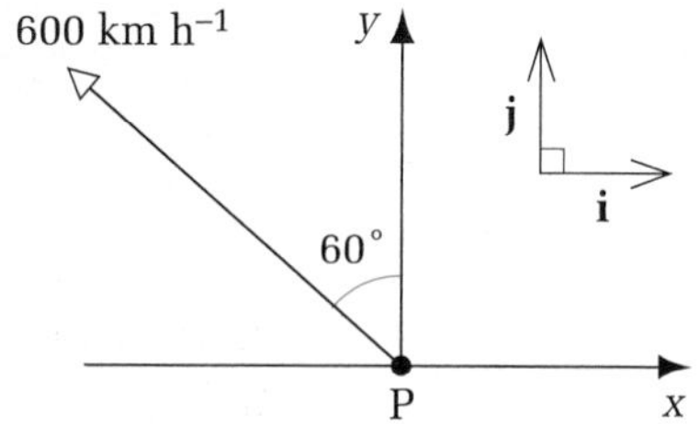

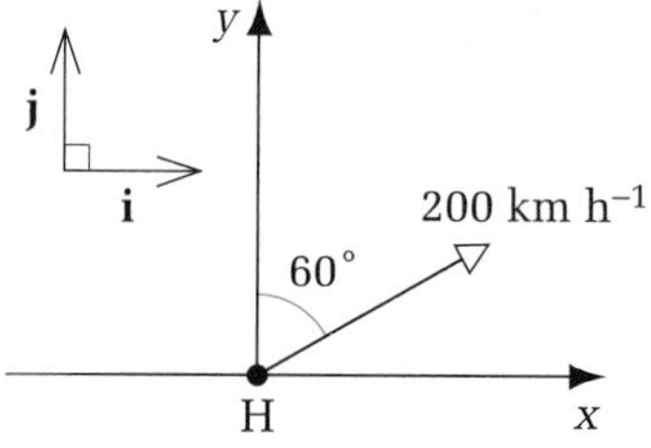

$\mathbf{v}_P$: Resolve → $\quad -600\sin 60° = -519.6$

↑ $\quad 600\cos 60° = 300$

$$\mathbf{v}_P = -519.6\mathbf{i} + 300\mathbf{j}$$

$\mathbf{v}_H$: Resolve → $\quad 200\sin 60° = 173.2$

↑ $\quad 200\cos 60° = 100$

$$\mathbf{v}_H = 173.2\mathbf{i} + 100\mathbf{j}$$

$$_P\mathbf{v}_H = \mathbf{v}_P - \mathbf{v}_H$$

$$_P\mathbf{v}_H = (-519.6\mathbf{i} + 300\mathbf{j}) - (173.2\mathbf{i} + 100\mathbf{j})$$

$$_P\mathbf{v}_H = -519.6\mathbf{i} + 300\mathbf{j} - 173.2\mathbf{i} - 100\mathbf{j}$$

$$_P\mathbf{v}_H = -692.8\mathbf{i} + 200\mathbf{j}$$

Insert vector values.

Expand the bracket.

Convert back into magnitude and direction.

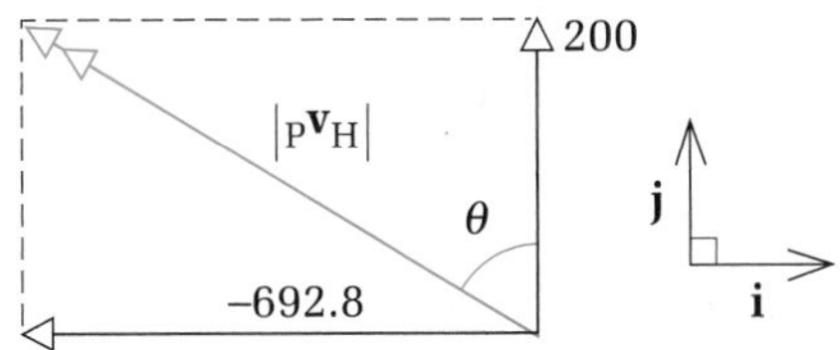

$|_P\mathbf{v}_H| = \sqrt{(-692.8)^2 + 200^2}$

$|_P\mathbf{v}_H| = 721\,\text{km h}^{-1}$ (3 s.f.)

Use Pythagoras' theorem.

$\tan\theta = \frac{692.8}{200}$

$\tan\theta = 3.464$

$\theta = 73.9°$

Use trigonometry.
$\theta = \tan^{-1}(3.464)$ or $\arctan(3.464)$

bearing $= 360° - 73.9°$

$= 286.1°$ (1 d.p.)

The plane appears to be travelling at 721 km h^{-1} on a bearing of 286.1°.

Example 2

A car is travelling at 50 mph along a straight motorway. A lorry overtakes the car but only appears to be travelling at 10 mph by the driver of the car. Find the actual speed of the lorry.

Solution

The velocity of the lorry relative to the car is what the car driver sees.

$_L\mathbf{v}_C = \mathbf{v}_L - \mathbf{v}_C$

$10 = \mathbf{v}_L - 50$

$60 = \mathbf{v}_L$

Write formula and substitute the values.
Add 50.

Speed of lorry = 60 mph.

20.2 Relative Velocity
Exercise

Technique

1 Find the velocity of A relative to B for:

a $\mathbf{v}_A = 3\mathbf{i} + 7\mathbf{j}$
$\mathbf{v}_B = 2\mathbf{i} + 5\mathbf{j}$

b $\mathbf{v}_A = -3\mathbf{i} - 5\mathbf{j}$
$\mathbf{v}_B = -8\mathbf{i} - 11\mathbf{j}$

2 Determine the velocity of Q relative to P when the velocities of P and Q are:

a $\mathbf{v}_P = -7\mathbf{i} + 8\mathbf{j}$
$\mathbf{v}_Q = -2\mathbf{i} - \mathbf{j}$

b $\mathbf{v}_P = -7\mathbf{i} + 2\mathbf{j}$
$\mathbf{v}_Q = 40\mathbf{i} - 7\mathbf{j}$

3 Calculate the velocity of R relative to S for:

	Velocity of R	Velocity of S
a	$30\,\text{km}\,\text{h}^{-1}$ due north	$50\,\text{km}\,\text{h}^{-1}$ due west
b	$60\,\text{m}\,\text{s}^{-1}$ on a bearing of 045°	$50\,\text{m}\,\text{s}^{-1}$ on a bearing of 120°

4 The velocity of A is $40\,\text{km}\,\text{h}^{-1}$ on a bearing of 060°. The velocity of B is $20\,\text{km}\,\text{h}^{-1}$ on a bearing of 240°. The velocity of C is $50\,\text{km}\,\text{h}^{-1}$ on a bearing of 300°. Determine:

a the velocity of C relative to A

b the velocity of B relative to C.

5 The velocity of A is $(x_1\mathbf{i} + y_1\mathbf{j})\,\text{m}\,\text{s}^{-1}$ and the velocity of B is $(x_2\mathbf{i} + y_2\mathbf{j})\,\text{m}\,\text{s}^{-1}$. Find:

a the velocity of A relative to B

b the velocity of B relative to A.

Comment on your answers to **a** and **b**.

Contextual

In this exercise, take **i** to represent a unit vector to the east and **j** to represent a unit vector to the north whenever **i** and **j** are used.

1 A car travels at $50\,\text{km}\,\text{h}^{-1}$ along a straight road and a van travels in the opposite direction with a speed of $100\,\text{km}\,\text{h}^{-1}$. Work out:

a the velocity of the car relative to the van

b the velocity of the van relative to the car.

2 A tractor is overtaken by a car along a straight road. The tractor is travelling at 25 mph and the car appears to be travelling at 20 mph to the tractor driver. Calculate the *actual* speed of the car.

3 An aircraft appears to be travelling at $(400\mathbf{i} - 300\mathbf{j})\,\text{km}\,\text{h}^{-1}$ relative to a pilot in a helicopter. This helicopter is travelling with a velocity of $(-200\mathbf{i} + 100\mathbf{j})\,\text{km}\,\text{h}^{-1}$. Find the *true* velocity of the aircraft.

20.3 Interception and Collision

A yacht is drifting with a constant velocity. A coastguard plots a course to rescue the yacht. The starting positions of the yacht and the coastguard are $\mathbf{s}_Y$ and $\mathbf{s}_C$ respectively. The velocity of the yacht is $\mathbf{v}_Y$ and the velocity of the coastguard's boat is $\mathbf{v}_C$. How long will the coastguard take to reach the yacht? Treat both vessels as particles. Assume the water is completely still.

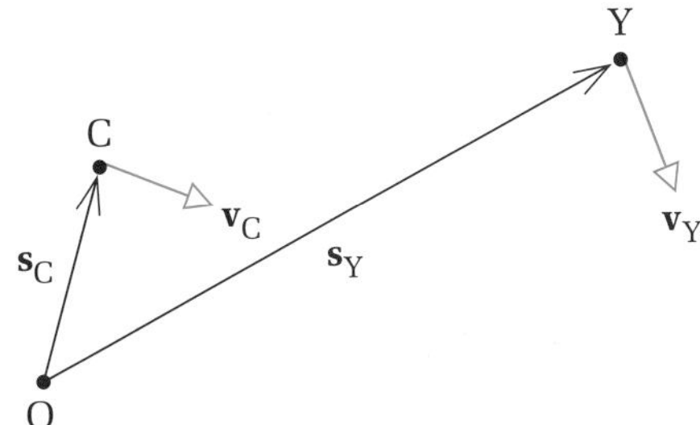

The starting positions for the yacht and the coastguard are given by $\mathbf{s}_Y$ and $\mathbf{s}_C$. This information can be used to find an expression for the position vector of both boats at any time *t*.

$$\mathbf{r}_Y = \mathbf{s}_Y + \mathbf{v}_Y t$$
$$\mathbf{r}_C = \mathbf{s}_C + \mathbf{v}_C t$$

Notation
$\mathbf{r}_Y$ = position vector of Y (yacht) at time *t*.
$\mathbf{s}_Y$ = starting position vector of Y (yacht).

When the coastguard reaches the yacht, the displacements of both vessels must be equal.

$$\mathbf{r}_Y = \mathbf{r}_C$$
$$\mathbf{s}_Y + \mathbf{v}_Y t = \mathbf{s}_C + \mathbf{v}_C t$$

Overview of method

Step ① Draw a clear diagram.
Step ② Use $\mathbf{r} = \mathbf{s} + \mathbf{v}t$ for both objects.
Step ③ For interception or collision the displacements for both objects must be equal.

Example

A particle A is initially 4 km due north of a particle B. Particle A has a velocity of $10\sqrt{3}\,\text{km h}^{-1}$ due east and particle B has a speed of $20\,\text{km h}^{-1}$ on a bearing of 060°.

a Show that the particles collide.
b How long does it take for the particles to collide?
c Determine the location of the collision. Give your answer as a distance and bearing from B's initial position.

Solution

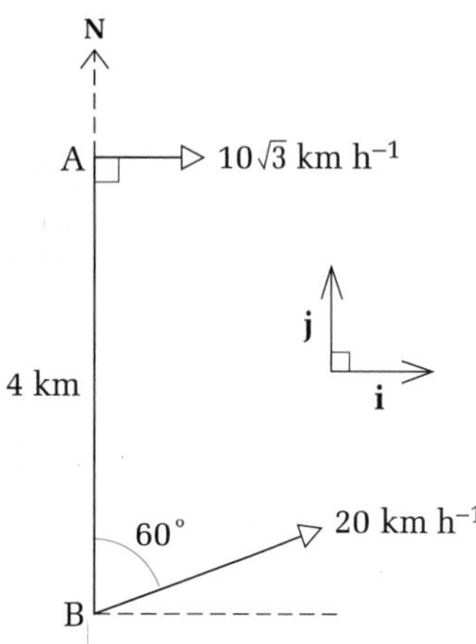

a $\mathbf{v}_A = 10\sqrt{3}\mathbf{i}$

Resolve the velocity for B

Resolve → $20\sin 60° = 20 \times \frac{\sqrt{3}}{2} = 10\sqrt{3}$

Resolve ↑ $20\cos 60° = 20 \times \frac{1}{2} = 10$

$\mathbf{v}_B = 10\sqrt{3}\mathbf{i} + 10\mathbf{j}$

Take the position of B to be the origin.

Use $\mathbf{r} = \mathbf{s} + \mathbf{v}t$

$\mathbf{r}_A = 4\mathbf{j} + (10\sqrt{3}\mathbf{i})t$

$\mathbf{r}_B = \mathbf{0} + (10\sqrt{3}\mathbf{i} + 10\mathbf{j})t$

For collision, $\mathbf{r}_A = \mathbf{r}_B$

$4\mathbf{j} + (10\sqrt{3}\mathbf{i})t = \mathbf{0} + (10\sqrt{3}\mathbf{i} + 10\mathbf{j})t$

$10\sqrt{3}t\mathbf{i} + 4\mathbf{j} = 10\sqrt{3}t\mathbf{i} + 10t\mathbf{j}$

Equate the **i** components

$10\sqrt{3}t = 10\sqrt{3}t$

For any value of t the **i** components must be equal.

Compare the speeds of A and B in the **i** direction.

Equate the **j** components:

$4 = 10t$

$t = 0.4$

Particles collide at $t = 0.4$ h (or 24 minutes).

b $t = 0.4$ h

c The position:

$D = S \times T$

$D = 20 \times 0.4$

$D = 8$ km

The collision is 8 km on a bearing of 060° from the initial position of B.

Use particle B to calculate the position of the collision.

20.3 Interception and Collision

Exercise

Technique

1 A particle A has a position vector $(20\mathbf{i} + 30\mathbf{j})$ m and a velocity of $(10\mathbf{i} - 5\mathbf{j})\text{ m s}^{-1}$. A second particle B starts at $(35\mathbf{i} + 75\mathbf{j})$ m with a velocity of $(7\mathbf{i} - 14\mathbf{j})\text{ m s}^{-1}$.

- **a** Show that the two particles will collide.
- **b** Find the time at which they will collide.
- **c** Determine the position vector of the collision.

2 Two objects, X and Y, are initially at $(10\mathbf{i} + 30\mathbf{j})$ m and $(-59\mathbf{i} + 191\mathbf{j})$ m respectively. Their velocities are $\mathbf{v}_X$ and $\mathbf{v}_Y$. The two objects collide at the position vector $(56\mathbf{i} + 122\mathbf{j})$ m, 23 seconds later.

- **a** Write down expressions for the displacements of the two objects in terms of $\mathbf{v}_X$ and $\mathbf{v}_Y$.
- **b** Find $\mathbf{v}_X$ and $\mathbf{v}_Y$.

3 A particle has an initial position vector of $(300\mathbf{i} - 200\mathbf{j})$ m and moves with a constant velocity of $(-8\mathbf{i} - 15\mathbf{j})\text{ m s}^{-1}$. A second particle starts at $(124\mathbf{i} - 508\mathbf{j})$ m and moves with a constant velocity. The two particles collide after 11 seconds. Find:

- **a** the position vector of the collision
- **b** the velocity of the second particle.

4 Two particles, M and N, have constant velocities of $(20\mathbf{i} + 30\mathbf{j})\text{ m s}^{-1}$ and $(-30\mathbf{i} + 40\mathbf{j})\text{ m s}^{-1}$ respectively. The particles M and N collide at $(-80\mathbf{i} + 1030\mathbf{j})$ m after 21 seconds. Determine the initial positions of the two particles.

5 An object starts at a point X and it moves with a constant speed of $10\sqrt{2}\text{ m s}^{-1}$ on a bearing of 135°. A second particle, initially at a point Y, moves with a uniform speed of 10 m s^{-1} due east. Point X is 40 m due north of point Y.

- **a** Show that the particles collide.
- **b** Determine the position of the collision measured from Y.

Contextual

In this exercise, take **i** to represent a unit vector to the east and **j** to represent a unit vector to the north whenever **i** and **j** are used.

1 A supply ship starts from a position of $(-133\mathbf{i} + 121\mathbf{j})$ km and travels with a uniform velocity of $(8\mathbf{i} - 8\mathbf{j})\,\mathrm{km\,h^{-1}}$. Another ship starts at $(-70\mathbf{i} + 100\mathbf{j})$ km and sails with a constant velocity of $(-7\mathbf{i} - 3\mathbf{j})\,\mathrm{km\,h^{-1}}$.

- **a** Show that the two ships will meet after 4.2 hours.
- **b** Find the position vector of the meeting point.

2 A jet aircraft and a refuelling aeroplane start from position vectors of $(100\mathbf{i} + 70\mathbf{j})$ km and $(1600\mathbf{i} + 130\mathbf{j})$ km respectively. They meet at $(700\mathbf{i} + 370\mathbf{j})$ km after 6 hours has passed. The aircraft can be assumed to remain at the same altitude throughout their motion. Determine the velocities of the jet aircraft and the refuelling aeroplane.

3 A missile is fired at a jet aircraft from another aircraft at the same altitude. The missile starts from a position $(4000\mathbf{i} + 1400\mathbf{j})$ m and travels with a constant velocity of $(300\mathbf{i} - 100\mathbf{j})\,\mathrm{m\,s^{-1}}$. The jet aircraft is initially at $(8000\mathbf{i} - 1000\mathbf{j})$ m and flies with a constant velocity of $(-200\mathbf{i} + 200\mathbf{j})\,\mathrm{m\,s^{-1}}$.

- **a** Show that the aircraft and the missile collide, provided their courses remain unchanged.
- **b** Determine the time at which the missile and aircraft collide.
- **c** Find the position vector of the collision.

4 At 15.00 hours, a helicopter is 150 km due east of an aeroplane. The helicopter sets off at $100\sqrt{2}\,\mathrm{km\,h^{-1}}$ due north and the aeroplane travels at a speed of $200\,\mathrm{km\,h^{-1}}$ on a bearing of 045°.

- **a** Show that if the courses of both aircraft remain unchanged, they will collide.
- **b** Find the time of collision.
- **c** State one key assumption you have made.

5 Take **i**, **j** and **k** to be unit vectors to the east, to the north and vertically upwards respectively. At 09.00 hours, an aircraft A has a position vector of $(500\mathbf{i} + 700\mathbf{j} + 3\mathbf{k})$ km and a velocity of $(200\mathbf{i} - 50\mathbf{j} + 2\mathbf{k})\,\mathrm{km\,h^{-1}}$. A second aircraft has a position vector of $(1250\mathbf{i} + 75\mathbf{j} + 10.5\mathbf{k})$ km and a velocity of $(-100\mathbf{i} + 200\mathbf{j} - \mathbf{k})\,\mathrm{km\,h^{-1}}$.

- **a** Show that if the velocities remain unchanged, the aircraft will collide.
- **b** Determine the time and position vector of the collision.

20.4 Course for Interception and Collision

The diagram shows the positions of a battleship B, and a submarine S. The velocity of the battleship is $\mathbf{v}_B$ and the maximum speed of the torpedo is $|\mathbf{v}_T|$. In which direction should the torpedo be fired to hit the battleship? Treat the battleship and the torpedo as particles. Assume the velocities of both will remain constant throughout. The sea is perfectly still.

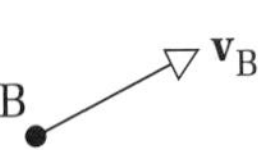

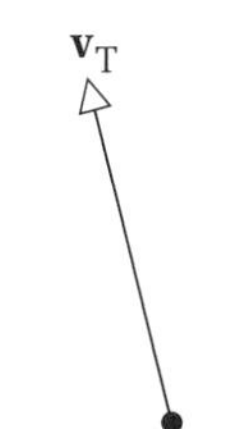

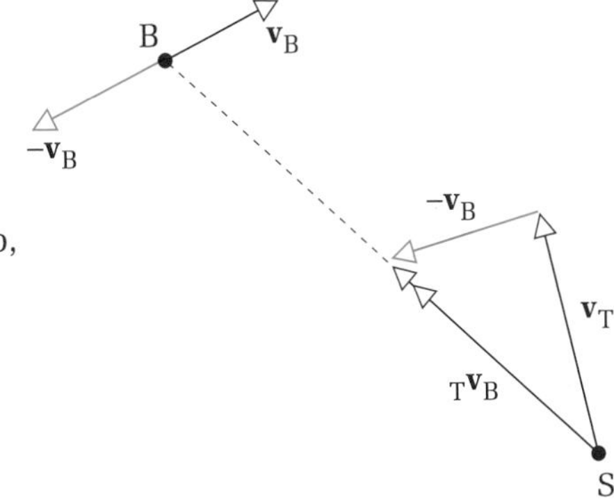

By applying the velocity of $-\mathbf{v}_B$ to both the battleship and the torpedo, the battleship is *stopped*.

For the torpedo to hit the ship the velocity of the torpedo relative to the battleship must travel along $\overrightarrow{SB}$. The velocity triangle can then be used to calculate the direction of $\mathbf{v}_T$ using the sine and cosine rules.

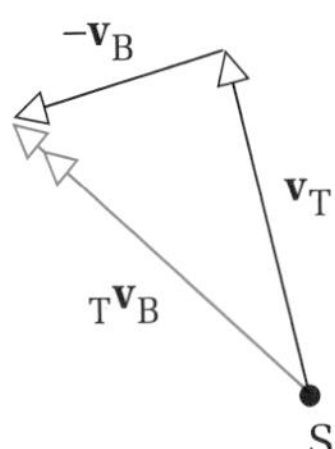

Overview of method

Step ① Draw a clear diagram.

Step ② *Stop* one of the objects by applying a negative velocity.

Step ③ Draw a velocity triangle to represent the relative velocity

$${}_A\mathbf{v}_B = \mathbf{v}_A - \mathbf{v}_B$$

Step ④ Calculate the direction of the course for collision using the sine and cosine rules.

Example

A clay pigeon is released from a point which is at a distance of 80 m on a bearing of 300° from a shooter. The clay pigeon travels with a constant speed of 40 m s^{-1} on a bearing of 050°. As soon as the clay pigeon is released, the gun is fired and the bullet has a speed of $200\,\mathrm{m\,s^{-1}}$. Any vertical motion of the objects can be ignored.

a In which direction must the gun be fired for the bullet to hit the clay pigeon?

b How long after the gun is fired, does the bullet hit the clay pigeon?

Solution

a

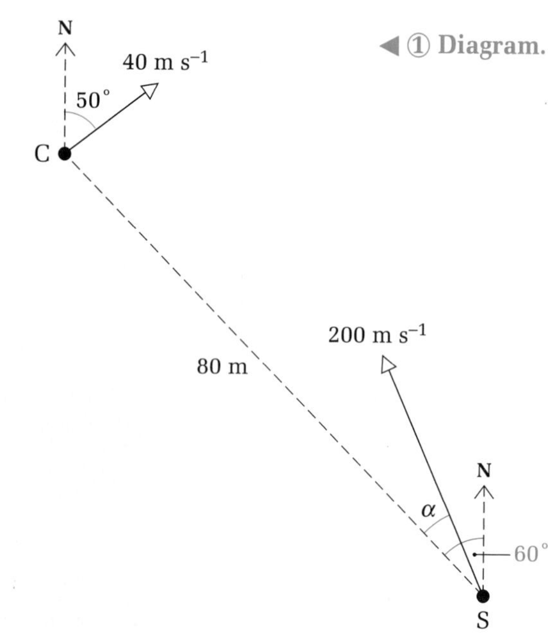

◀ ① **Diagram.**

Stop the clay pigeon by applying $40\,\mathrm{m\,s^{-1}}$ in the opposite direction.

▲ ② ***Stop* one of the objects.**

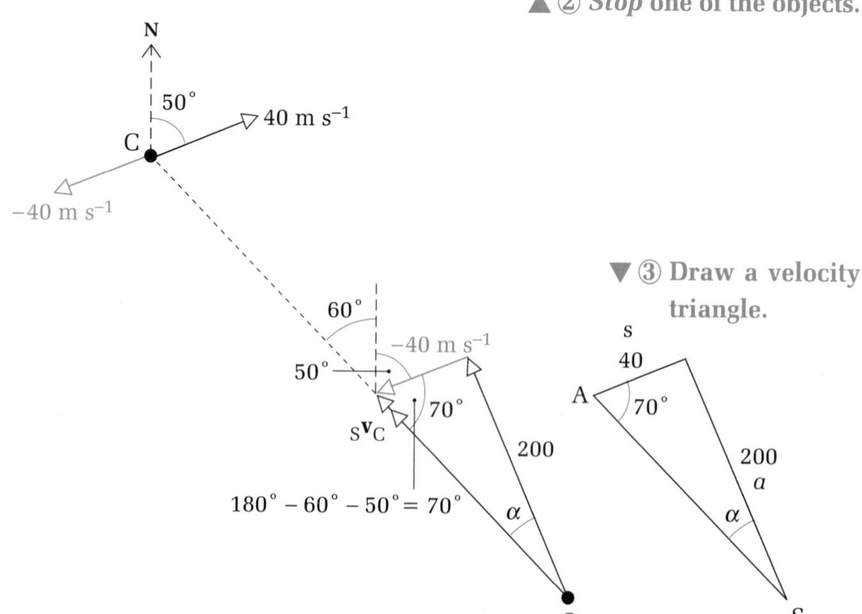

▼ ③ **Draw a velocity triangle.**

$$\frac{\sin S}{s} = \frac{\sin A}{a}$$

$$\frac{\sin\alpha}{40} = \frac{\sin 70°}{200}$$

◀ ④ **Use the sine rule.**

Multiply by 40.

$$\sin\alpha = \frac{40 \times \sin 70°}{200}$$

$$\sin\alpha = 0.1879$$

$\alpha = \sin^{-1}(0.1879)$ or $\arcsin(0.1879)$

$$\alpha = 10.8°$$

bearing $= 300° + 10.8° = 310.8°$ (1 d.p.)

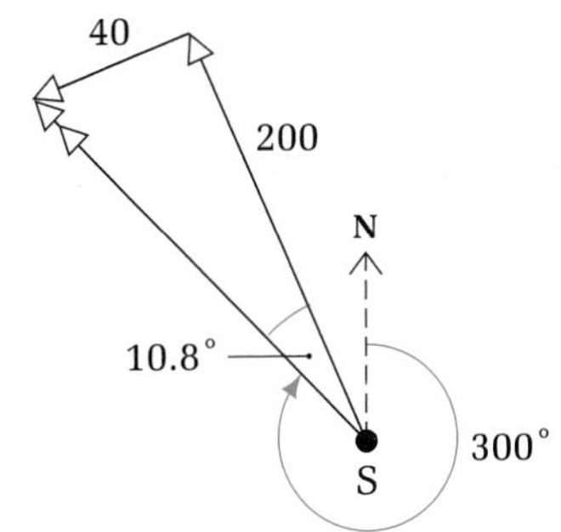

b Calculate the magnitude of ${}_S\mathbf{v}_C$ using the sine rule.

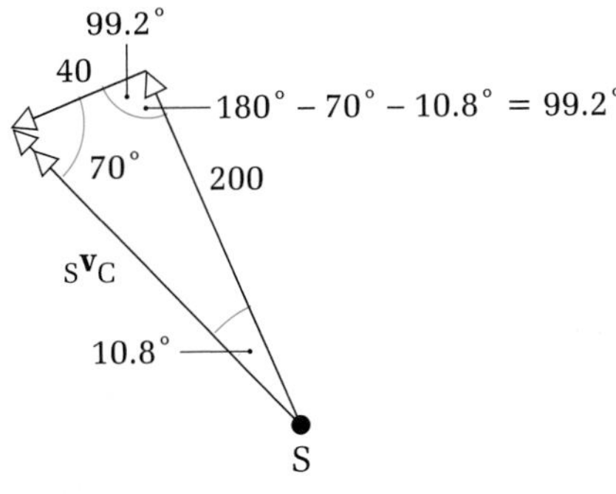

$$\frac{|{}_S\mathbf{v}_C|}{\sin 99.2°} = \frac{200}{\sin 70°}$$

Multiply by sin 99.2°.

$$|{}_S\mathbf{v}_C| = \frac{200 \times \sin 99.2°}{\sin 70°}$$

$$|{}_S\mathbf{v}_C| = 210\,\text{m s}^{-1} \text{ (3 s.f.)}$$

$$t = \frac{SC}{|{}_S\mathbf{v}_C|}$$

time $= \frac{\text{distance}}{\text{speed}}$.

$$t = \tfrac{80}{210}$$

$$t = 0.381\,\text{s (3 s.f.)}$$

20.4 Course for Interception and Collision

Exercise

Technique

1 Initially, a body M is 30 km due west of a second body N. The body N has a speed of $3\,\text{km}\,\text{h}^{-1}$ due north and the body M has a maximum speed of $5\,\text{km}\,\text{h}^{-1}$. Work out:

- **a** the course for M to intercept N
- **b** the length of time which passes before this occurs
- **c** the position of the interception (measured from N's initial position).

2 A particle X is 40 m on a bearing of 150° from a particle Y. The particle X has a constant speed of $5\,\text{m}\,\text{s}^{-1}$ on a bearing of 220°. The maximum speed of the particle Y is $8\,\text{m}\,\text{s}^{-1}$. Determine:

- **a** the direction of the course for particle Y if the two particles are to collide as quickly as possible
- **b** how long it takes for the particles to collide
- **c** the position of the collision, measured from Y's initial position.

3 An object A has an initial position vector of $(30\mathbf{i} - 70\mathbf{j})$ m and a velocity of $(4\mathbf{i} + 2\mathbf{j})\,\text{m}\,\text{s}^{-1}$. A second object B has an initial position vector of $(-40\mathbf{i} + 50\mathbf{j})$ m and a maximum speed of $6\,\text{m}\,\text{s}^{-1}$. Find:

The unit vector **i** acts to the east and the unit vector **j** acts to the north.

- **a** the velocity of A in magnitude and direction form
- **b** the distance and bearing of A from B
- **c** the course object B must take for the two objects to collide in the shortest possible time
- **d** the length of time that elapses before the collision takes place
- **e** the position vector of the collision.

Contextual

1 An aircraft carrier is travelling at $5\,\text{km}\,\text{h}^{-1}$ due north. A Harrier jump jet is 300 km due west of the aircraft carrier and it can travel at $200\,\text{km}\,\text{h}^{-1}$. Determine the course the jump jet needs to take so that it can land on the aircraft carrier. How long does the jet take to reach the carrier?

2 An aircraft carrier has an initial position of $(200\mathbf{i} - 1000\mathbf{j})$ m and a uniform velocity of $(-4\mathbf{i} + 3\mathbf{j})\,\text{m}\,\text{s}^{-1}$. A helicopter has an initial position of $(-8000\mathbf{i} + 4000\mathbf{j})$ m and it can travel at a maximum speed of $150\,\text{m}\,\text{s}^{-1}$. Work out:

The unit vector **i** acts to the east and the unit vector **j** acts to the north.
Make sure you store answers in your calculator's memory.

- **a** the velocity of the aircraft carrier in magnitude and direction form
- **b** the distance and bearing of the carrier from the helicopter
- **c** the course the helicopter should take to reach the carrier as quickly as possible
- **d** the length of time the helicopter takes to reach the carrier.

20.5 Closest Approach

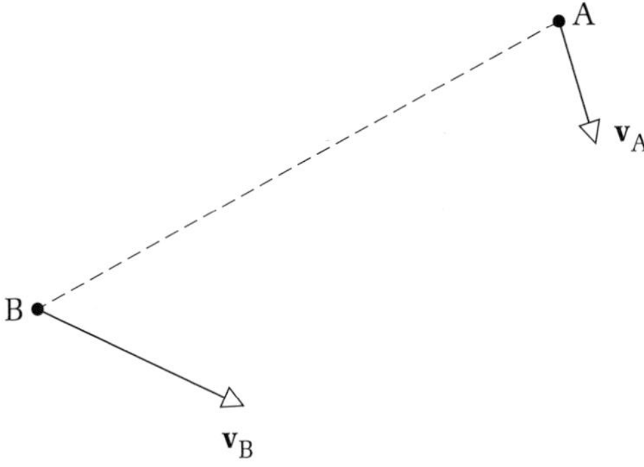

Two aircraft have positions at A and B initially. They are travelling with constant velocities of $\mathbf{v}_A$ and $\mathbf{v}_B$ respectively. How can the closest distance between them be calculated? The aircraft are treated as particles and the wind speed is assumed negligible. The altitudes of both aircraft are assumed to be the same.

One of the aircraft can be *stopped* by applying its velocity in the opposite direction to both aircraft. We *stop* aircraft A by applying $-\mathbf{v}_A$.

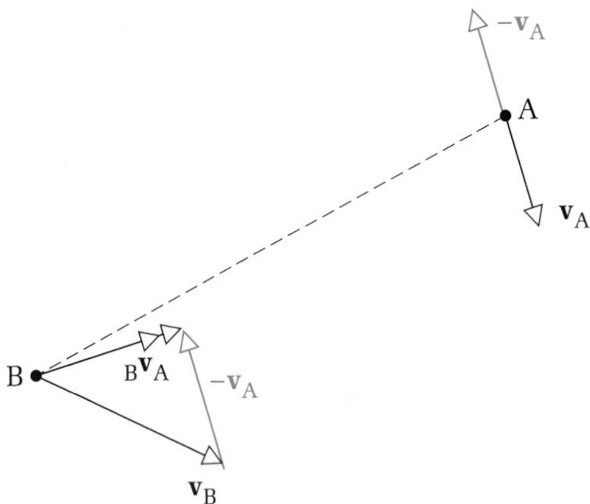

The **velocity** of aircraft **B relative to A** can be used to plot the course of aircraft B relative to aircraft A.

The velocity of B relative to A is written as ${}_B\mathbf{v}_A$.

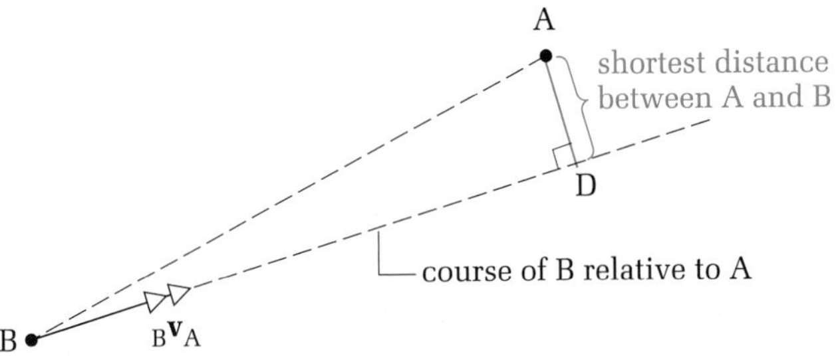

The shortest distance between the two aircraft will occur at the point D, where AD and BD are perpendicular.

Perpendicular means at right angles.

To see why AD gives the shortest distance look at a point either side of D. AX and AY will be longer than AD because they are hypotenuses of the triangles ADX and ADY respectively.

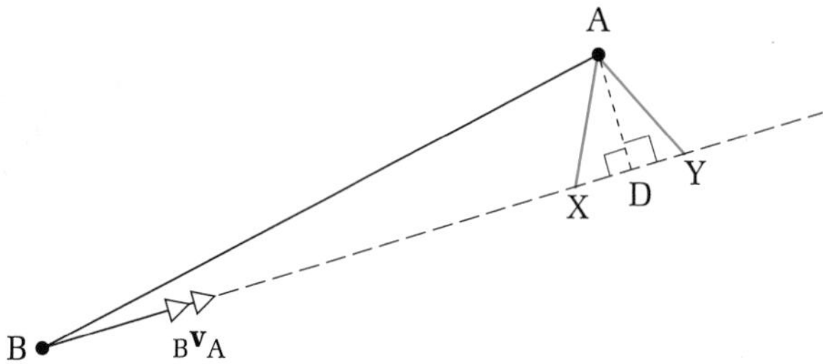

The right-angled triangle ABD can be used to calculate the shortest distance, AD. The time to arrive at point D can be found using:

$$\text{time} = \frac{BD}{\text{speed of B relative to A}}$$

$$t = \frac{BD}{|_B\mathbf{v}_A|}$$

time $= \frac{\text{distance}}{\text{speed}}$

speed $= |\mathbf{v}|$

Overview of method

Step ① Draw a diagram of the situation.
Step ② *Stop* one of the objects by applying its velocity in the opposite direction.
Step ③ Form a right-angle triangle for the relative course and the shortest distance.
Step ④ Use trigonometry to find the shortest distance between the objects.

Example

The diagram shows the velocities and initial positions of two particles A and B. Find the closest distance between the particles and how long they take to reach this position.

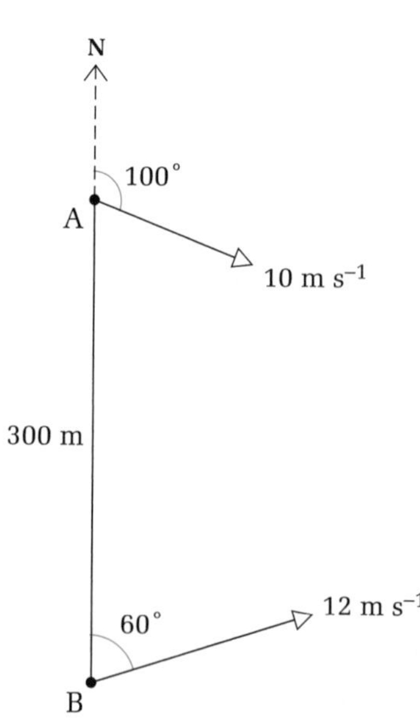

Solution

◀ ① Diagram.

◀ ② Stop A.

◀ ③ Draw the triangle for the shortest distance.

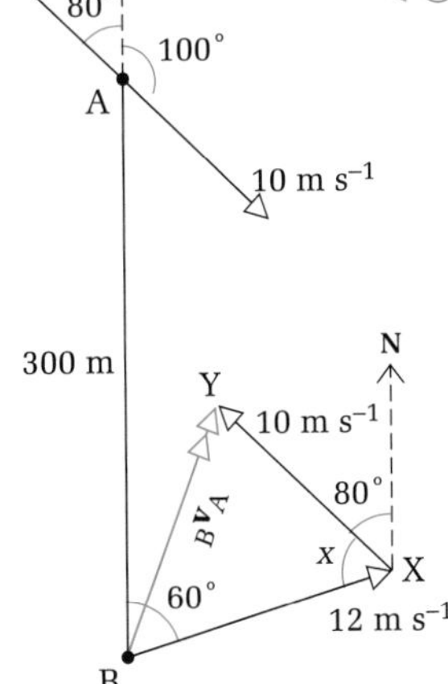

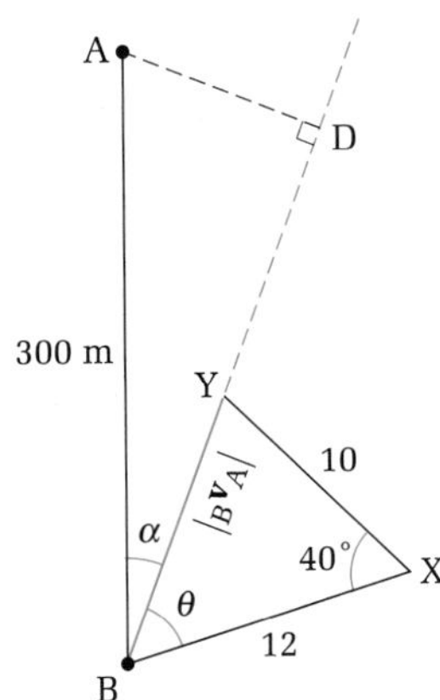

Not to scale.

$60° + 80° + x = 180°$ (interior angles)

$x = 40°$

Find $|{}_B\mathbf{v}_A|$ and angle θ. This will enable angle α, AD and then the time to be found.

Use the cosine rule on triangle BXY

$$|{}_B\mathbf{v}_A|^2 = 10^2 + 12^2 - 2 \times 10 \times 12 \cos 40°$$

$$|{}_B\mathbf{v}_A|^2 = 60.149$$

$$|{}_B\mathbf{v}_A| = 7.756$$

Use $a^2 = b^2 + c^2 - 2bc\cos A$. Take the square root.

Use sine rule to find θ

$$\frac{\sin\theta}{10} = \frac{\sin 40°}{7.756}$$

Multiply by 10.

$$\sin\theta = \frac{10 \times \sin 40°}{7.756}$$

$$\sin\theta = 0.8288$$

$$\theta = 56.0°$$

Work out RHS. $\theta = \sin^{-1}(0.8288)$ or $\arcsin(0.8288)$

$$\alpha = 60° - 56.0°$$

$$\alpha = 4.0°$$

$$AD = 300 \times \sin 4.0°$$

◀ ④ Use trigonometry to find *AD*.

$$AD = 21.1\,\text{m}$$

The shortest distance is 21.1 m (3 s.f.).

Time to reach point D is given by:

$$t = \frac{BD}{|{}_B\mathbf{v}_A|}$$

Find *BD* using trigonometry

$$BD = 300 \cos 4.0°$$

$$BD = 299.3\text{ m}$$

$$t = \frac{299.3}{7.756}$$

$$t = 38.6\text{ s}$$

Time taken is 38.6 s.

20.5 Closest Approach

Exercise

Technique

1

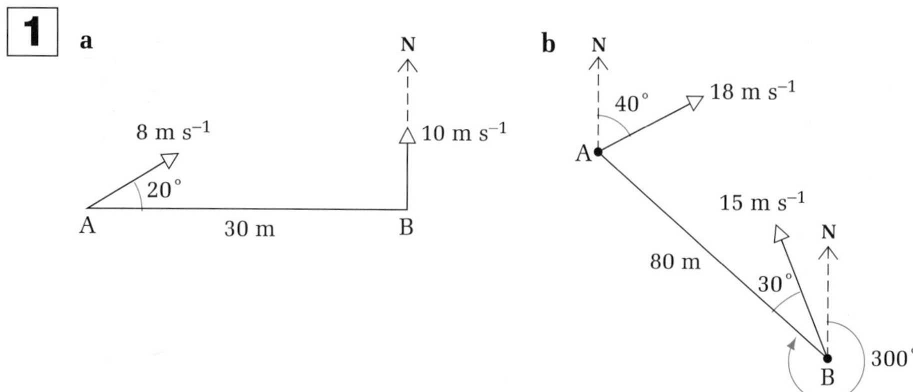

In the diagrams, the points A and B represent the initial positions of two particles and the velocities of the particles remain constant. For each diagram, determine:

i the shortest possible distance between the two particles

ii the length of time the particles take to reach this position from their starting positions.

2 A particle Q is 200 m on a bearing of 040° from a particle P. Particle Q has a uniform speed of $25\,\text{m s}^{-1}$ due south and particle P has a speed of $30\,\text{m s}^{-1}$ on a bearing of 070°. Find the smallest distance between the particles and the time at which this occurs.

Contextual

1 An aeroplane has a speed of $300\,\text{km h}^{-1}$ due west. A helicopter is 50 km due south of the aeroplane and it travels at $250\,\text{km h}^{-1}$ on a bearing of 320°. Calculate the closest distance between the aeroplane and the helicopter. How long does it take for the aircraft to reach this position?

2 At 06.00 hours, a ferry is 80 km on a bearing of 290° from a tanker. The ferry travels with a constant speed of $15\,\text{km h}^{-1}$ on a bearing of 030° and the tanker travels at $12\,\text{km h}^{-1}$ on a bearing of 300°. Determine the closest distance between the ferry and the tanker and the time at which this occurs.

3 A jet aeroplane is 500 m on a bearing of 100° from an anti-aircraft gun. The aeroplane is flying with a speed of $300\,\text{m s}^{-1}$ due west. A shell is fired from the gun on a bearing of 120° with a speed of $400\,\text{m s}^{-1}$. What is the closest distance between the shell and the aeroplane?

20.6 Course for Closest Approach

A camera crew are in a small speedboat and they are trying to get as close as possible to a yacht to photograph a pop star. The yacht starts at a point Y and travels with a velocity of $\mathbf{v}_Y$. The speedboat starts at point S and has a maximum speed of $|\mathbf{v}_S|$. Suppose this speed is *not fast enough* to allow the *speedboat to intercept the yacht*. How can the best direction for the speedboat to take be worked out? The boats will be treated as particles and their velocities will be assumed to remain constant.

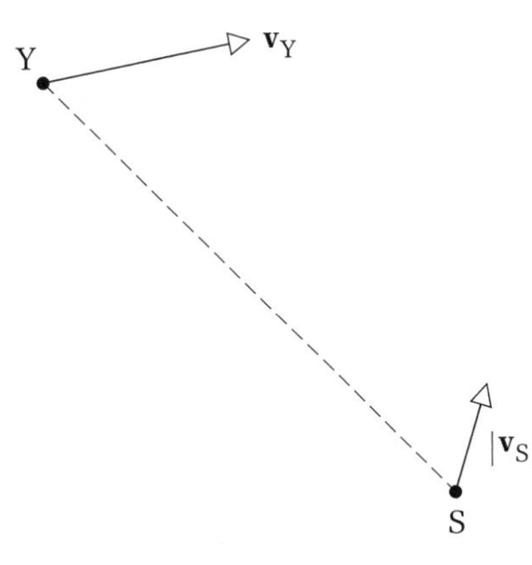

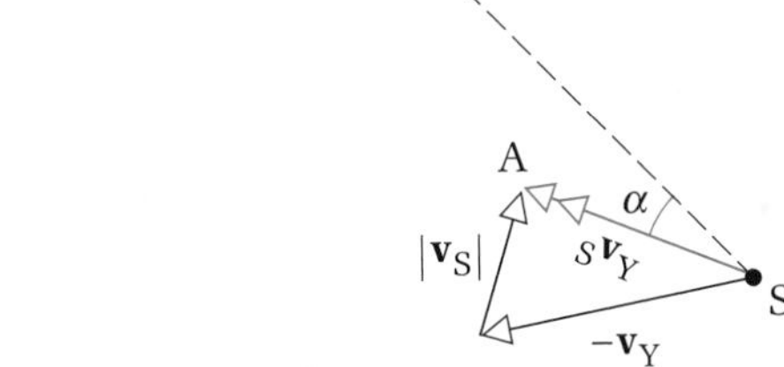

The yacht will be *stopped* by applying $-\mathbf{v}_Y$ to both boats.

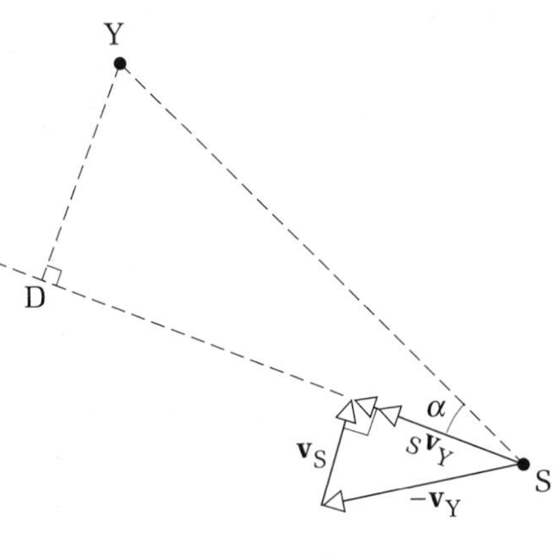

To get as close as possible to the yacht, the angle (α) between ${}_S\mathbf{v}_Y$ and SY must be as small as possible. To achieve this, $\mathbf{v}_S$ and ${}_S\mathbf{v}_Y$ must be perpendicular. If the direction of the speed $|\mathbf{v}_S|$ is moved so that the angle is not 90° then the angle between ${}_S\mathbf{v}_Y$ and SY is *not* as small as possible. This condition enables the direction of $\mathbf{v}_S$ to be found using trigonometry. The closest distance will occur when ${}_S\mathbf{v}_Y$ and the line SY are perpendicular.

Y

D

α

$\mathbf{v}_S$

${}_S\mathbf{v}_Y$

S

$-\mathbf{v}_Y$

The time to reach this position can be found using:

$$t = \frac{DS}{|{}_S\mathbf{v}_Y|}$$

See Section 20.5.

Overview of method

Step ① Draw a diagram of the situation.

Step ② *Stop* the object whose velocity is known by applying its velocity in the opposite direction.

Step ③ Form a right angled velocity triangle for the course for closest approach.

Step ④ Use trigonometry to calculate the direction for closest approach.

Step ⑤ Form a right angled triangle for the relative course and the shortest distance.

Step ⑥ Use trigonometry to find the shortest distance between the objects.

Example 1

A safari vehicle is 100 m on a bearing of 050° from a rhinoceros. The safari vehicle is travelling at a constant speed of $10\,\text{m s}^{-1}$ due south. The rhinoceros charges at the vehicle and runs with a steady speed of $6\,\text{m s}^{-1}$. In which direction should the rhinoceros run to get as close to the vehicle as possible? What will be the least distance between the rhinoceros and the vehicle? How long will the rhinoceros take to reach this distance?

Solution

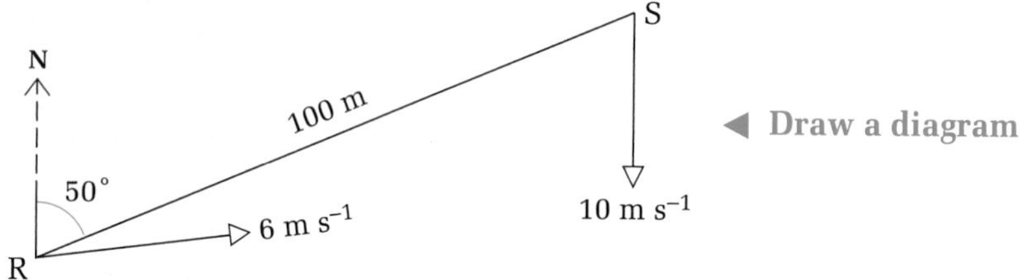

◀ Draw a diagram.

Guess initial direction for R.

Stop the vehicle. ◀ ② *Stop* the object whose velocity is known.

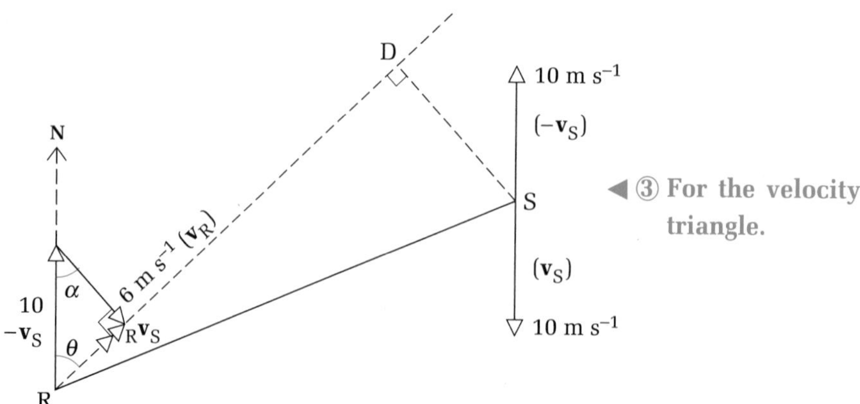

◀ ③ For the velocity triangle.

$\sin\theta = \frac{6}{10}$ ◀ ④ **Use trigonometry to find the course for closest approach.**

$\sin\theta = 0.6$

$\theta = 36.9°$

$\alpha = 180° - 90° - 36.9°$

$\alpha = 53.1°$

$\text{bearing} = 180° - 53.1°$

$= 126.9°$

Closest distance occurs at point D

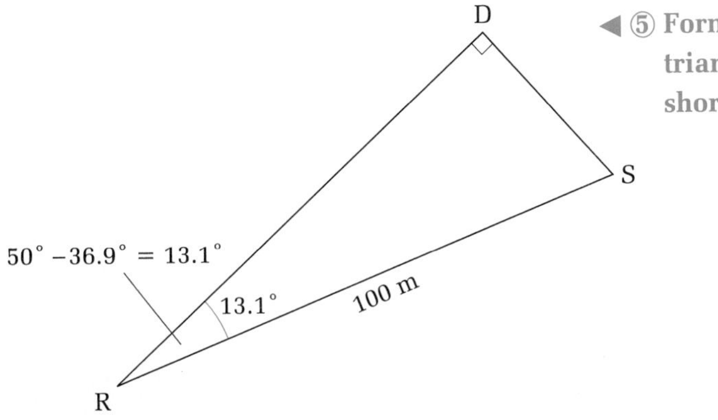

◀ ⑤ **Form a right angled triangle for the shortest distance.**

$DS = 100 \times \sin 13.1°$ ◀ ⑥ **Use trigonometry to find the closest distance.**

$DS = 22.7\,\text{m}\ (3\ \text{s.f.})$

Time to reach this position

$$t = \frac{DR}{|_R\mathbf{v}_S|}$$

First calculate $|_R\mathbf{v}_S|$ then DR.

$|_R\mathbf{v}_S| = \sqrt{10^2 - 6^2}$

$|_R\mathbf{v}_S| = 8\,\text{m}\,\text{s}^{-1}$

Use Pythagoras' theorem.

$DR = 100 \times \cos 13.1°$

$DR = 97.4\,\text{m}\ (3\ \text{s.f.})$

$$t = \frac{DR}{|_R\mathbf{v}_S|}$$

$$t = \frac{97.4}{8}$$

$t = 12.2\ (3\ \text{s.f.})$

Time taken is 12.2 s (3 s.f.).

Example 2

At 9 a.m., a fishing boat is 10 km on a bearing of 110° from a trawler. The trawler travels with a speed of 8 km h^{-1} on a bearing of 060°. The fishing boat has a top speed of 6 km h^{-1}. Determine the route of the fishing boat if its captain wants to get as close to the trawler as possible. Find the distance between the two boats at this point and the time at which it will occur.

Solution

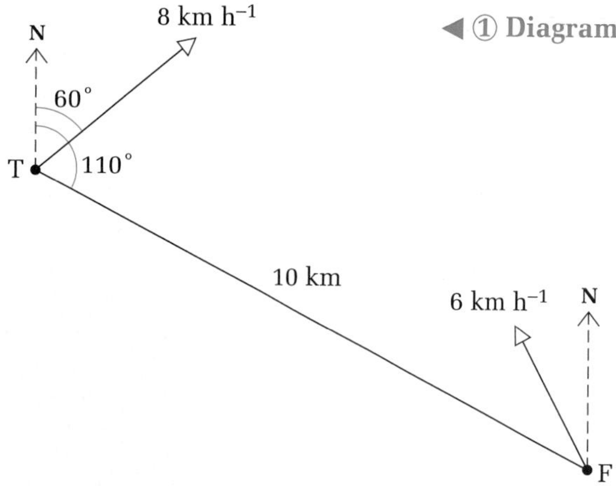

◀ ① Diagram.

Stop the trawler.

◀ ② Stop the object whose velocity is known.

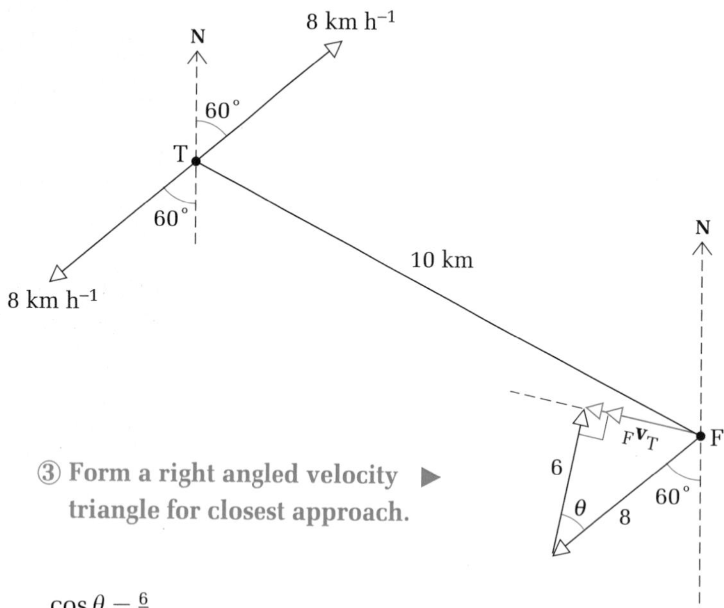

③ Form a right angled velocity triangle for closest approach. ▶

$\cos\theta = \frac{6}{8}$

$\cos\theta = 0.75$

$\theta = 41.4°$

◀ ④ Use trigonometry to calculate the course of closest approach.

bearing $= 90° - 30° - 41.4°$

$= 018.6°$

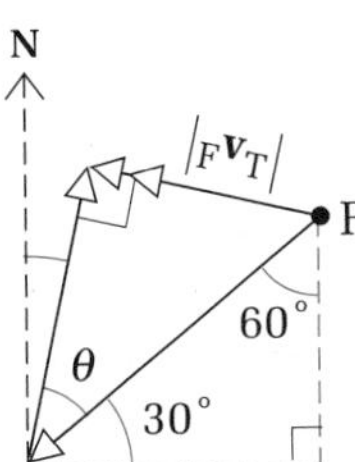

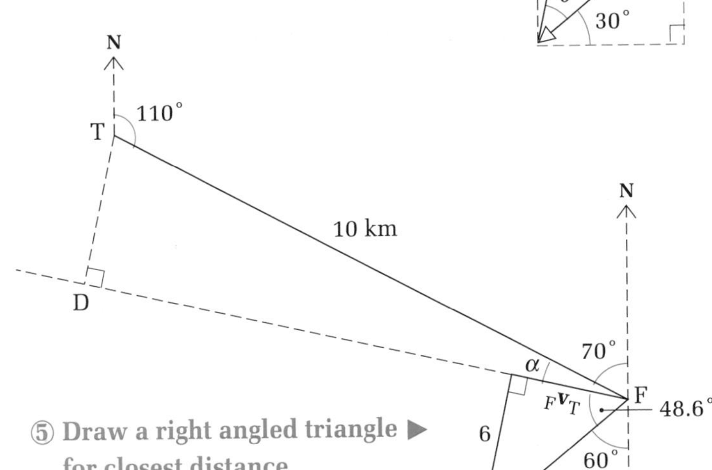

⑤ **Draw a right angled triangle for closest distance** ▶

$\alpha = 180° - 70° - 60° - 48.6°$

$\alpha = 1.41°$

$DT = 10 \times \sin 1.41°$

◀ ⑥ **Use trigonometry to calculate the shortest distance.**

$DT = 0.246$ km (3 s.f.)

Shortest distance = 0.246 km (3 s.f.).

Time taken will be given by $t = \dfrac{FD}{|_F\mathbf{v}_T|}$. Both FD and $|_F\mathbf{v}_T|$ need to be found.

$|_F\mathbf{v}_T| = \sqrt{8^2 - 6^2}$

$= 5.292 \text{ km h}^{-1}$

$FD = 10 \times \cos 1.41°$

$= 9.997$ km

$t = \frac{9.997}{5.292}$

$t = 1.89 \text{ h} = 1 \text{ h } 53 \text{ min}$

This position occurs at 10.53 a.m.

Use Pythagoras' theorem to calculate $|_F\mathbf{v}_T|$.
Use trigonometry to calculate FD.

20.6 Course for Closest Approach

Exercise

Technique

1 A particle at point A travels on a bearing of 060° at $12\,\text{m}\,\text{s}^{-1}$. A second particle starts at point B, which is 30 m due east of point A, and has a maximum speed of $5\,\text{m}\,\text{s}^{-1}$. Find:

a the course that the second particle must set to get as close as possible to the first particle

b the closest distance between the particles and the time at which this will occur.

2 Two bodies X and Y start at two points P and Q respectively. Point P is 100 m on a bearing of 150° away from Q. Body X moves with a constant speed of $30\,\text{m}\,\text{s}^{-1}$ on a bearing of 090°. Body Y has a maximum speed of $22\,\text{m}\,\text{s}^{-1}$.

a Determine the course for Y to get as close to X as possible.

b Calculate the time taken to reach this position and this distance between the two bodies.

3 Two objects P and Q are initially 20 m apart, with P being south west of Q. Object P has a speed of $16\,\text{m}\,\text{s}^{-1}$ due north and Q can have a maximum speed of $10\,\text{m}\,\text{s}^{-1}$. How close can Q get to P?

Contextual

1 A yacht is 300 m on a bearing of 080° from a small speedboat. The yacht travels with a speed of $18\,\text{m}\,\text{s}^{-1}$ on a bearing of 190°. The speedboat has a maximum speed of $15\,\text{m}\,\text{s}^{-1}$. Find the bearing of the course which the speedboat should take to get as close as possible to the yacht. Work out this minimum distance between the boats and the time at which it occurs.

2 At 11 a.m., a jet aeroplane is 120 km due east of a helicopter. The aeroplane is flying at a constant speed of $800\,\text{km}\,\text{h}^{-1}$ on a bearing of 240° and the helicopter has a maximum speed of $400\,\text{km}\,\text{h}^{-1}$. Find:

a the course that gets the helicopter as close as possible to the jet aeroplane

b this least distance between the aircraft and the time at which this occurs.

Assume the aircraft are at the same altitude.

Consolidation

Exercise A

1

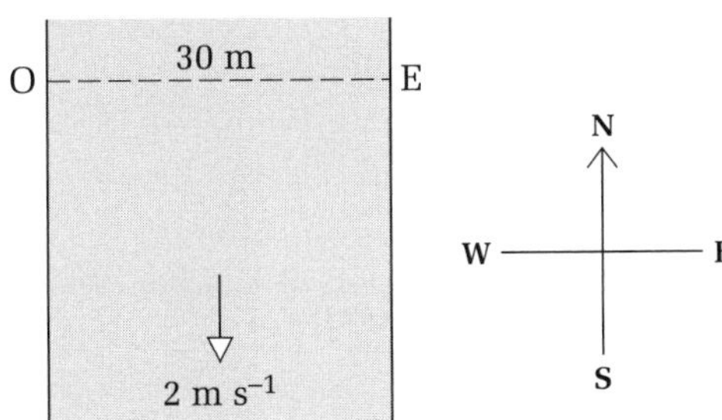

A river with parallel banks flows due south with a uniform speed of $2\,\text{m}\,\text{s}^{-1}$. A man capable of rowing at a maximum speed of $2.5\,\text{m}\,\text{s}^{-1}$ in still water launches a rowing boat from a point O on the west bank of the river. The point E due east of O, on the opposite bank is 30 m from O (see diagram). The man rows in such a way that his boat travels directly from O to E. Show that he can complete his journey in 20 s.

He returns from E to the west bank as quickly as possible. Show that this takes 12 s, and calculate the distance between the point where he lands and the point O.

(UCLES)

2 A missile is launched from a point O and targeted at a point A which is 400 km horizontally from O, so that its position vector at time t seconds after launch is given by

$$\mathbf{r}_m = t\mathbf{i} + kt(400 - t)\mathbf{j}\ \text{km},$$

where $\mathbf{i}$, $\mathbf{j}$ are unit vectors measured horizontally and vertically respectively, and k is constant.

a Find k so that the maximum height of the trajectory is 32 km. An anti-missile missile is launched from A when the missile is detected by radar, at which time it is above a point B on the ground 100 km from A. The velocity of the anti-missile missile is $-1.5\mathbf{i} + 0.408\mathbf{j}\,\text{km}\,\text{s}^{-1}$.

b **i** Show that the position vector of the anti-missile missile is given by:

$$\mathbf{r}_a = (850 - 1.5t)\mathbf{i} + 0.408(t - 300)\mathbf{j},\ \text{for}\ t > 300$$

ii Determine whether the anti-missile missile intercepts the missile.

(AEB)

3 A ship, P, is moving due north at a speed of $10.5\,\text{km}\,\text{h}^{-1}$. At noon a second ship, Q, which has a maximum speed of $14\,\text{km}\,\text{h}^{-1}$, is 8 km away on a bearing of $300°$.

a Sketch a diagram to show the position of Q relative to P at noon.

b If Q were to move due east at its maximum speed, determine the magnitude and direction of the velocity of Q relative to P.

c Hence, or otherwise:

i calculate the shortest distance between the ships in the motion that would follow, and

ii show that the time at which this position would be reached is 12.27 p.m. approximately.

Instead, Q decides to intercept P and, while maintaining maximum speed, takes a course which will allow it to reach P as soon as possible.

d **i** Find the bearing that Q should steer to intercept P; and

ii show that the time at which Q reaches P is 12.30 p.m. approximately.

(NICCEA)

Exercise B

1 An ice-hockey player strikes a puck and it splits into two fragments. These begin to move across the ice in two directions at right angles to each other, with speeds of $23.4\ \text{m s}^{-1}$ and $8.8\ \text{m s}^{-1}$. By modelling the fragments as particles moving with constant horizontal velocities, calculate:

a the relative speed of the two particles

b how far apart the two particles will be after 0.3 s.

Give a reason why, after 0.3 s, the fragments of the puck might not actually be separated by the distance calculated in **a**.

(UCLES)

2 Two particles A and B move simultaneously through the points which have position vectors $(3\mathbf{i} + 2\mathbf{j} + 7\mathbf{k})$ m and $(-2\mathbf{i} + 2\mathbf{j} - 3\mathbf{k})$ m respectively, referred to an origin O. The velocities of A and B are constant and equal to $(2\mathbf{i} - \mathbf{j} + 3\mathbf{k})\ \text{m s}^{-1}$ and $(4\mathbf{i} - \mathbf{j} + 7\mathbf{k})\ \text{m s}^{-1}$ respectively.

a Show that A and B collide.

b Find the position vector of the collision point.

(ULEAC)

3 Two cars travelling with constant speeds $30\ \text{m s}^{-1}$ and $20\ \text{m s}^{-1}$ on perpendicular straight roads are approaching O, the point of intersection of the roads. At time $t = 0$ both are at a distance of 442 m from O. Determine their displacements from O at any subsequent time t seconds and find the value of t when the cars are closest together.

(WJEC)

Applications and Activities

1

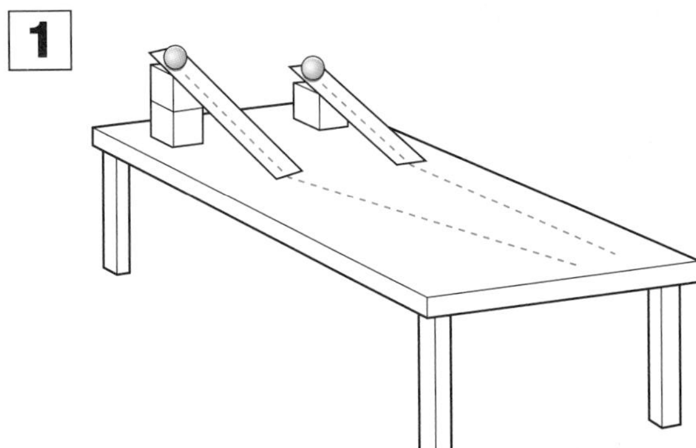

Set up the apparatus as shown. Adjust the directions at which the balls move until they collide. Record the directions. How does this compare with the theory. Try to explain your results.

2 Find out the speeds of the bullets and the clay pigeons in clay pigeon shooting. Find out typical distances between the clay pigeon and the gun. Produce recommendations on the lead angle the shooter should use when trying to hit a clay pigeon.

Summary

- The velocity of A relative to B is

  $${}_{A}\mathbf{v}_{B} = \mathbf{v}_{A} - \mathbf{v}_{B}$$

- The velocity of B relative to A is

  $${}_{B}\mathbf{v}_{A} = \mathbf{v}_{B} - \mathbf{v}_{A}$$

  $${}_{B}\mathbf{v}_{A} = -{}_{A}\mathbf{v}_{B}$$

- The position vector of a particle travelling with constant velocity is given by

  $$\mathbf{r} = \mathbf{s} + \mathbf{v}t$$

Answers

All angle answers are given correct to one decimal place. All other answers are either exact or are given to three significant figures.

1 Principles of Mechanics

1.1 Contextual (p. 5)

1. Possible answers include running, and motion involving cars, aeroplanes, roller coasters, bicycles.
2. Possible answers include bridges, roller coaster track, roads, supports for roofs and walls.
3. Define, Model, Analyse, Interpret
4. Define: What sort of party? What food is needed? What drink is needed? What music is needed? How much can be spent? Will people be charged? Does a profit need to be made? How many people will there be? How much will be charged?
   Model: Assume 50 people attend and they each pay £2. Other assumptions about expenses.
   Analyse: Calculate the income and expenses.
   Interpret: Is the profit big enough? Do the figures seem sensible?
   Change the assumptions and repeat.
5. **a** yes **b** no **c** no **d** yes
6. Advantage: The size of the ball can be ignored.
   Disadvantage: Any spin on the ball will also be ignored.
7. The golf ball's spin will affect the flight of the ball.
8. Air resistance on the shuttlecock will be significant.

2 Forces

Review (p. 7)

1. **a i** 4 **ii** $\pm 2\sqrt{10}$ or ± 6.32
   b i 60 **ii** 490 **iii** ± 5
   c i 5 **ii** 112 **iii** ± 50
2. **a i** 1.93×10^{8} **ii** 1.62×10^{-4}
   b i 2 370 000 **ii** 0.000 015 9
3. **a** $y = 5x$ **b** $y = 10x^2$ **c** $y = 2x^2$

2.2 Technique (p. 13)

1. 3.34×10^{-8} N
2. 2.07×10^{32} kg
3. 1.03×10^{5} m

2.2 Contextual (p. 13)

1. 3.53×10^{22} N
2. 98.4 kg
3. 2.28×10^{11} m

2.3 Technique (p. 16)

1. **a** 70 N **b** 2000 N **c** 0.02 N
   d 100 000 N **e** 4×10^{-4} N
2. **a** 313.6 N **b** 3400 N **c** 0.245 N
   d 73 500 N **e** 1.18×10^{-4} N
3. **a** 17 kg **b** 3 g or 0.003 kg
   c 1200 kg
4. **a** 5 kg **b** 0.02 kg **c** 100 t or 100 000 kg

2.3 Contextual (p. 16)

1. **a** 15 000 N **b** 5 N **c** 1.5×10^{-4} N
2. **a** 392 000 N **b** 7.84 N **c** 4.9×10^{-4} N

2.4 Contextual (p. 23)

1. 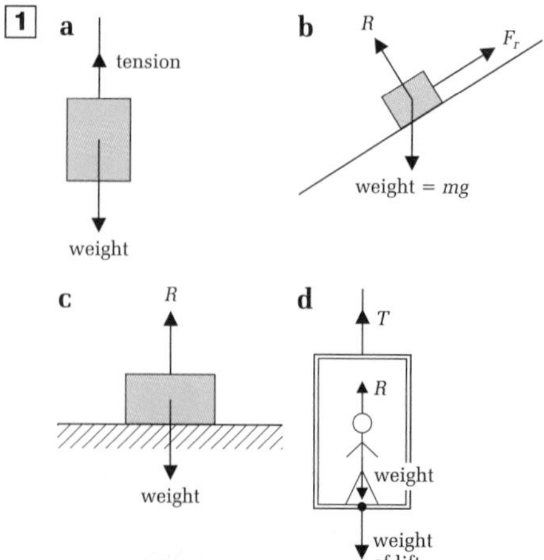

2 a

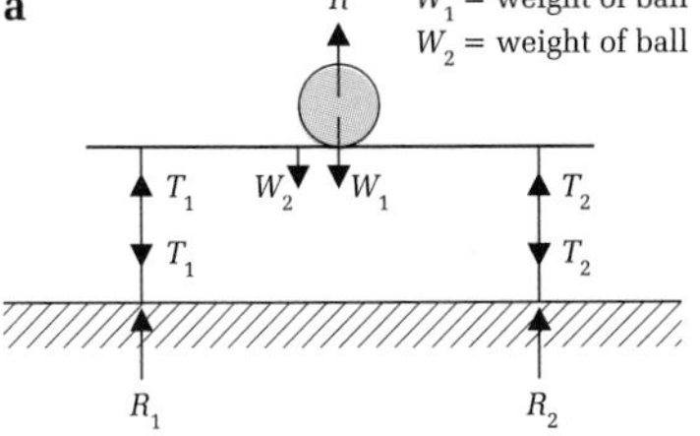

b

R
F_r
weight

c

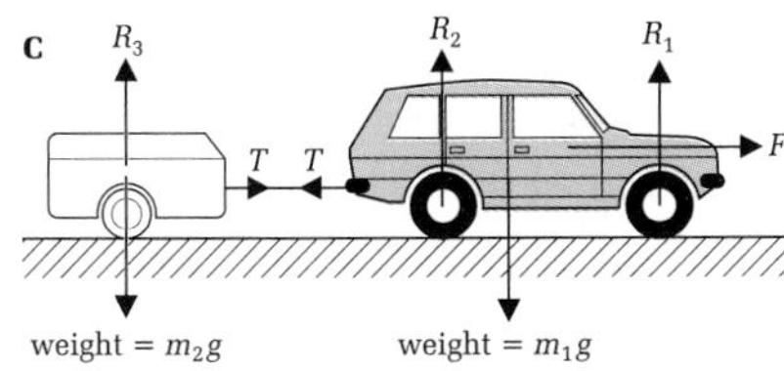

3

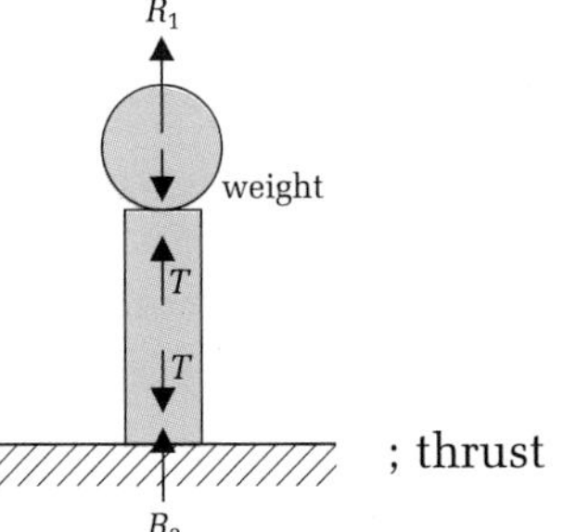

; thrust

2.5 Technique (p. 26)

1 **a** $R = 40v$ **b** 280 N **c** $7.5\,\mathrm{m\,s^{-1}}$

2 **a** $R = 10v^2$ **b** $60\,\mathrm{m\,s^{-1}}$ **c** 12 250 N

2.5 Contextual (p. 26)

1 **a** $R_a \propto v$; $R_a \propto v^2$
b $R_a = 150v$; $R_a = 10v^2$
c $R_a = 150v$

2 **a** $R_{\mathrm{oil}} = 0.25v$ **b** $0.4\,\mathrm{m\,s^{-1}}$ **c** 0.375 N

3 Vectors I

Review (p. 28)

1 **a** 32° **b** parallelogram, $y = 139°$, $z = 41°$
c square, parallelogram, rhombus, rectangle
d i 120° **ii** 60°

2 **a** $5\sqrt{2}$ **b** $4\sqrt{2}$ **c** $3\sqrt{5}$ **d** $\sqrt{72}$

3 **a** $\sqrt{58}$ cm **b** 6.24 cm

4 **a** $x = 3.90$ cm, $y = 7.33$ cm **b** $z = 44.3$ m

5

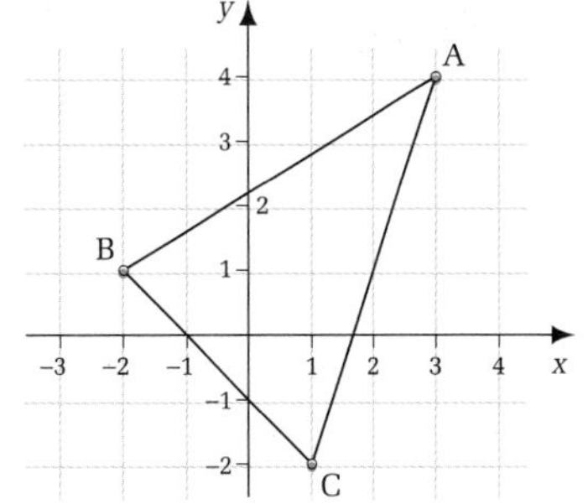

a area = 12 square units
b $(\frac{1}{2}, 2\frac{1}{2})$ **c** $\sqrt{40} = 6.32$

3.1 Technique (p.34)

1

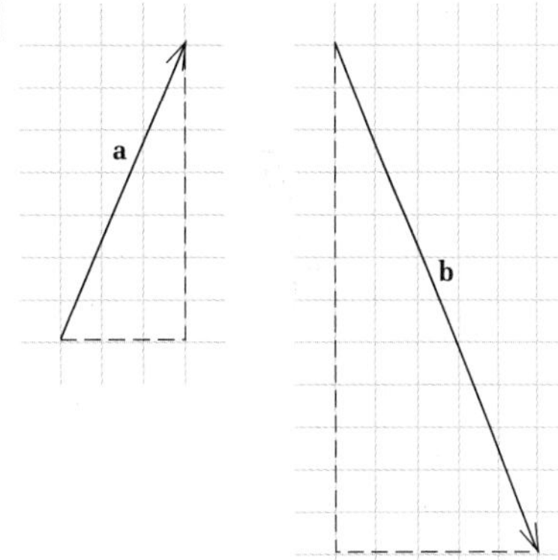

2

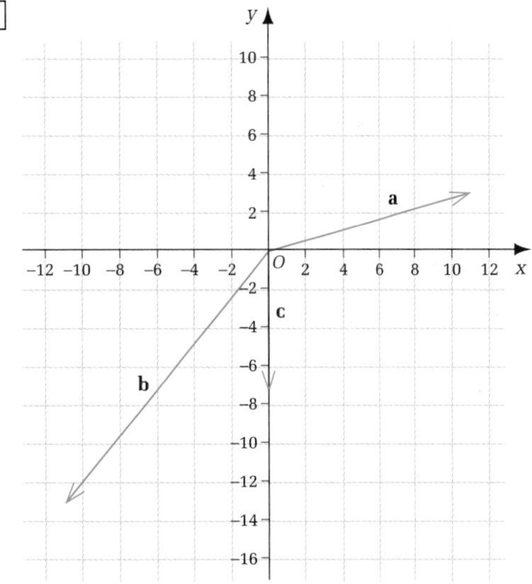

3

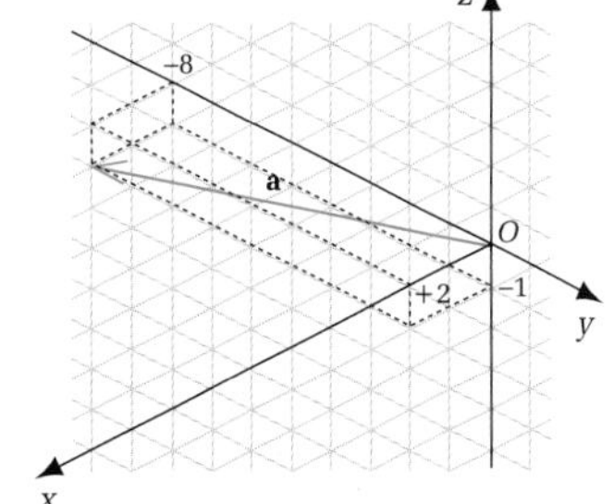

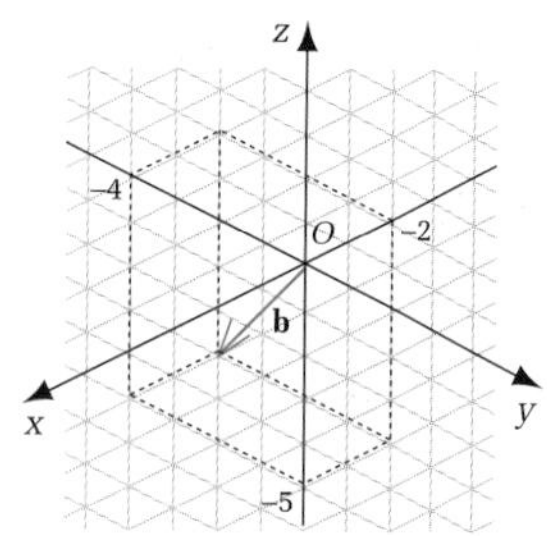

4 a $\mathbf{a} = -7\mathbf{i} - 4\mathbf{j}$
$\mathbf{b} = -3\mathbf{i} - 2\mathbf{j} - 4\mathbf{k}$

5 $\mathbf{a} = \begin{pmatrix} 11 \\ 3 \end{pmatrix}$ $\mathbf{b} = \begin{pmatrix} 5 \\ -17 \end{pmatrix}$ $\mathbf{c} = \begin{pmatrix} 0 \\ -7 \end{pmatrix}$
$\mathbf{d} = \begin{pmatrix} 6 \\ -11 \\ 7 \end{pmatrix}$

3.1 Contextual (p. 34)

1 $\mathbf{a} = \begin{pmatrix} 6 \\ 10 \end{pmatrix}$ km $\mathbf{b} = \begin{pmatrix} -2 \\ -5 \end{pmatrix}$ km

2 $\mathbf{a} = (18\mathbf{i} + 12\mathbf{j})$ m $\mathbf{b} = (-7\mathbf{i} + 2\mathbf{j})$ km

3.2 Technique (p. 37)

1 a $\begin{pmatrix} -8 \\ 7 \end{pmatrix}$ b $\begin{pmatrix} -5 \\ -16 \end{pmatrix}$ c $\begin{pmatrix} 2 \\ -19 \end{pmatrix}$

2 a $11\mathbf{i} - 4\mathbf{j}$ b $-9\mathbf{i} - 13.3\mathbf{j}$ c $16\mathbf{i} - 14\mathbf{j}$

3 a $2\mathbf{r} = \begin{pmatrix} 4 \\ 6 \end{pmatrix}$ $3\mathbf{r} = \begin{pmatrix} 6 \\ 9 \end{pmatrix}$ $5\mathbf{r} = \begin{pmatrix} 10 \\ 15 \end{pmatrix}$
$\frac{1}{2}\mathbf{r} = \begin{pmatrix} 1 \\ 1\frac{1}{2} \end{pmatrix}$ $-\mathbf{r} = \begin{pmatrix} -2 \\ -3 \end{pmatrix}$ $-2\mathbf{r} = \begin{pmatrix} -4 \\ -6 \end{pmatrix}$

b

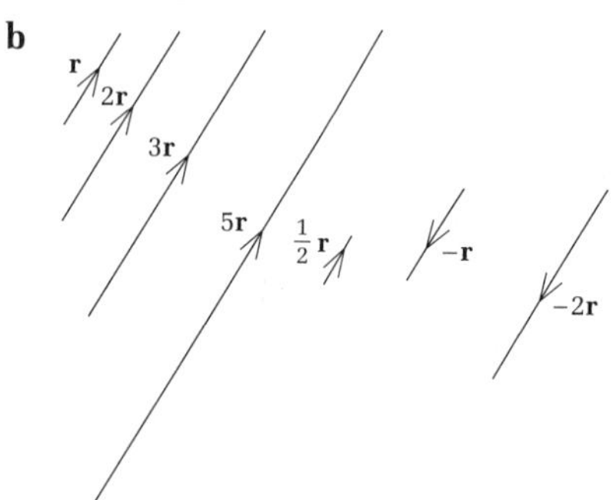

c All the vectors are parallel.

4 a $2\mathbf{s} = -8\mathbf{i} + 16\mathbf{j}$
b $10\mathbf{s} = -40\mathbf{i} + 80\mathbf{j}$
c $-\frac{1}{2}\mathbf{s} = 2\mathbf{i} - 4\mathbf{j}$
d $-25\mathbf{s} = 100\mathbf{i} - 200\mathbf{j}$

5 a i $36\mathbf{i} - 4\mathbf{j} - 12\mathbf{k}$
ii $31\mathbf{i} - 19\mathbf{j} - 11\mathbf{k}$
iii $12\mathbf{i} - 53\mathbf{j} + 41\mathbf{k}$

b i $\begin{pmatrix} -10 \\ -10 \\ 100 \end{pmatrix}$ ii $\begin{pmatrix} 22 \\ 2 \\ 12 \end{pmatrix}$ iii $\begin{pmatrix} 74 \\ -10 \\ 208 \end{pmatrix}$

3.3 Technique (p. 41)

1 $|\mathbf{p}| = 19.9$, angle $= 325.8°$ or $-34.2°$
$|\mathbf{q}| = 13.7$, angle $= 270°$
$|\mathbf{r}| = 21.4$, angle $= 98.2°$
$|\mathbf{s}| = 20.1$, angle $= 71.7°$
$|\mathbf{t}| = 12.0$, angle $= 259.9°$ or $-100.1°$
$|\mathbf{u}| = 0.885$, angle $= 10.4°$

2 $|\mathbf{a}| = 6\sqrt{6} = 14.7$, angle $= 35.3°$
$|\mathbf{b}| = 8$, angle $= 315°$ or $-45°$
$|\mathbf{c}| = 0.326$, angle $= 259.4°$ or $-100.6°$
$|\mathbf{d}| = 630$, angle $= 2.8°$
$|\mathbf{e}| = 8.2$, angle $= 180°$

3 a 10.3 b 11.8 c 2.45

3.3 Contextual (p. 41)

1 a 8.04 km, 128.4°
b 4.43 km, 018.4°
c 10.6 km, 284.8°

2 $|\mathbf{a}| = 21.6$ m; bearing = 056.3°
$|\mathbf{b}| = 91$ km; bearing = 157.4°
$|\mathbf{c}| = 12$ m; bearing = 225°

3 $|\mathbf{F}_1| = 26$ N; angle = 0°
$|\mathbf{F}_2| = 38.1$ N; angle = 87.0°
$|\mathbf{F}_3| = 21.6$ N; angle = 236.3°
$|\mathbf{F}_4| = 16.3$ N; angle = 169.4°
$|\mathbf{F}_5| = 21$ N; angle = 270°

3.4 Technique (p. 45)

1 $\hat{\mathbf{a}} = \begin{pmatrix} 0.394 \\ 0.919 \end{pmatrix}$ $\hat{\mathbf{b}} = \begin{pmatrix} -1 \\ 0 \end{pmatrix}$
$\hat{\mathbf{c}} = 0.965\mathbf{i} + 0.263\mathbf{j}$
$\hat{\mathbf{d}} = -0.989\mathbf{i} + 0.148\mathbf{j}$

2 a $\begin{pmatrix} -17.4 \\ 9.92 \end{pmatrix}$ b $-4.52\mathbf{i} - 5.34\mathbf{j}$

3 **a**, **b**, **e**, **f** are parallel and **d**, **g**, **h** are parallel.

4 $t = -4$

5 $t = 5.6$

3.5 Technique (p. 51)

1 a $\mathbf{a} = 2\mathbf{i} + 5\mathbf{j}$
b $|\mathbf{a}| = \sqrt{29}$
c $\mathbf{b} = -2\mathbf{i} - 5\mathbf{j}$
d $\mathbf{a} + \mathbf{b} = \mathbf{0}$
e $a^2 = 29$
f $\overrightarrow{AB} = \mathbf{b} - \mathbf{a}$
g $\mathbf{b} = -\mathbf{a}$
h $\overrightarrow{OA} = \mathbf{a}$

2 a $a = \sqrt{58}$
b $|\mathbf{b}| = \sqrt{5}$
c $b^2 = 5$
d $|\mathbf{a} + \mathbf{b}| = \sqrt{61}$
e $a^4 = 3364$
f $\mathbf{a} + 2\mathbf{b} = 7\mathbf{i} + 5\mathbf{j}$
g $a \times b = \sqrt{290}$

2 True: **b c h**.
False: **a d e f g**.

4 **a** B= $\begin{pmatrix}4\\5\end{pmatrix}$, C= $\begin{pmatrix}3\\1\end{pmatrix}$, D= $\begin{pmatrix}-2\\-1\end{pmatrix}$
b $\overrightarrow{AC} = \begin{pmatrix}4\\-2\end{pmatrix}$ $\overrightarrow{BD} = \begin{pmatrix}-6\\-6\end{pmatrix}$
c $\overrightarrow{AB} = \begin{pmatrix}5\\2\end{pmatrix}$ $\overrightarrow{DC} = \begin{pmatrix}5\\2\end{pmatrix}$, i.e. $\overrightarrow{AB} = \overrightarrow{DC}$

5 $t = \frac{15}{2} = 7.5$

6 **a** $|\mathbf{p}| = 10.6, |\mathbf{q}| = 11.1, |\mathbf{p}+\mathbf{q}| = 16.3$
b Resultant of two vectors is the direct/shortcut route so will generally be shorter than the sum of the two individual lengths.
$|\mathbf{a}| + |\mathbf{b}| = |\mathbf{a}+\mathbf{b}|$ when **a** and **b** are parallel and in the same direction.

7 **a** $|\overrightarrow{AB}| = 10, |\overrightarrow{AC}| = 30$
b Since $|\overrightarrow{BA}| + |\overrightarrow{AC}| = |\overrightarrow{BC}|$, B, A, C are collinear. $\overrightarrow{BC} = -24\mathbf{i} + 32\mathbf{j}$

8 $|\overrightarrow{EF}| = 20$ or $|\overrightarrow{EF}| = 72$

Consolidation A (p. 52)

1 **a** 6.40 N **b** 38.7°

2 5.66N, 45°; $a = 1$ or 7; 143.1° or 216.9° from Ox

3 **a** 8.77 **b** $\lambda = 4, \mu = -4\frac{1}{2}$

4 **a** 17.5 N **b** 66°
c $\mathbf{P} = (3\mathbf{i} + 12\mathbf{j})$ N, $\mathbf{Q} = (4\mathbf{i} + 4\mathbf{j})$ N

Consolidation B (p. 53)

1 $|\mathbf{P}| = 4$ N, $|\mathbf{Q}| = 2.83$ N

2 **a** $|\mathbf{F}_1| = 10.8$ N
b 303.7° anticlockwise from Ox or 56.3° clockwise from Ox
c $(5\mathbf{i} - 12\mathbf{j})$ N
d $|\mathbf{F}_3| = 13$ N

3 $\lambda = 9$ or $\lambda = -10$

4 $((\lambda - 4)\mathbf{i} + 4\mathbf{j})$ N; $\sqrt{\lambda^2 - 8\lambda + 32}$ N; $\lambda = 1$ or 7; $\frac{4}{3}$

4 Travel Graphs

Review (p. 56)

1 **a** scalar **b** vector **c** vector

2 **a** 1.5 **b** −3.2

3 $12.5\ \mathrm{m\,s^{-1}}$

4 46.7 mph

5 **a** $26\ \mathrm{m^2}$ **b** $210\ \mathrm{mm^2}$

6 **a** a^7 **b** b^{-5} **c** f^{24} **d** x^3
e $y^0 = 1$ **f** p^3q^{-1} **g** $x^{-2}y^3$ **h** $a^2b^{-2}c^{-4}$

7 **a i** $m = 1, c = 5$ **ii** $m = -2, c = 5$
b i $y = 2x + 4$ **ii** $y = 4 - x$

8 The size and shape of the object are ignored.

4.1 Technique (p. 62)

1 **a** $230\ \mathrm{km\,h^{-1}}$ **b** $8.4\ \mathrm{km\,h^{-1}}$

2 **a** $44.4\ \mathrm{m\,s^{-1}}$ **b** $23.6\ \mathrm{m\,s^{-1}}$

3 **a** OA $14\ \mathrm{m\,s^{-1}}$; AB $0\ \mathrm{m\,s^{-1}}$
b AB $5\ \mathrm{cm\,s^{-1}}$; BC $0\ \mathrm{cm\,s^{-1}}$; CD $8\ \mathrm{cm\,s^{-1}}$

4 **a**

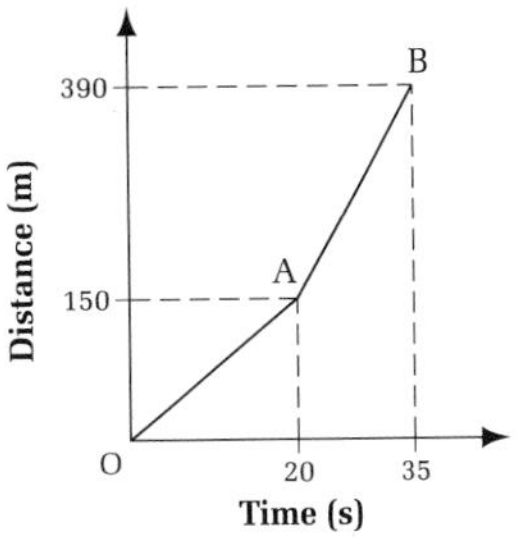

b OA **i** $7.5\ \mathrm{m\,s^{-1}}$ **ii** $27\ \mathrm{km\,h^{-1}}$
AB **i** $16\ \mathrm{m\,s^{-1}}$ **ii** $57.6\ \mathrm{km\,h^{-1}}$
c i $11.1\ \mathrm{m\,s^{-1}}$ **ii** $40.1\ \mathrm{km\,h^{-1}}$

4.1 Contextual (p. 62)

1 **a** $34.6\ \mathrm{km\,h^{-1}}$ **b** $27\ \mathrm{km\,h^{-1}}$

2 **a** $88.9\ \mathrm{m\,s^{-1}}$ **b** $1.81\ \mathrm{m\,s^{-1}}$

3 **a** OA $42\ \mathrm{km\,h^{-1}}$, AB $105\ \mathrm{km\,h^{-1}}$, BC $0\ \mathrm{km\,h^{-1}}$, CD $72\ \mathrm{km\,h^{-1}}$
b $72\ \mathrm{km\,h^{-1}}$

4 **a**

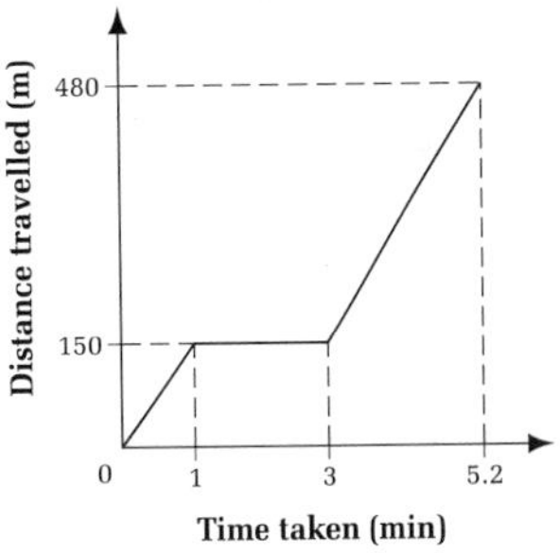

b $5.54\ \mathrm{km\,h^{-1}}$

5 **a i** $95.7\ \mathrm{km\,h^{-1}}$ **ii** $26.6\ \mathrm{m\,s^{-1}}$
b i $84.8\ \mathrm{km\,h^{-1}}$ **ii** $23.6\ \mathrm{m\,s^{-1}}$

4.2 Technique (p. 68)

1 **a** AB $4\ \mathrm{m\,s^{-1}}$, BC $0\ \mathrm{m\,s^{-1}}$
b AB $-2\ \mathrm{m\,s^{-1}}$, BC $0\ \mathrm{m\,s^{-1}}$
CD $-2\ \mathrm{m\,s^{-1}}$, DE $2\ \mathrm{m\,s^{-1}}$

2 **a**

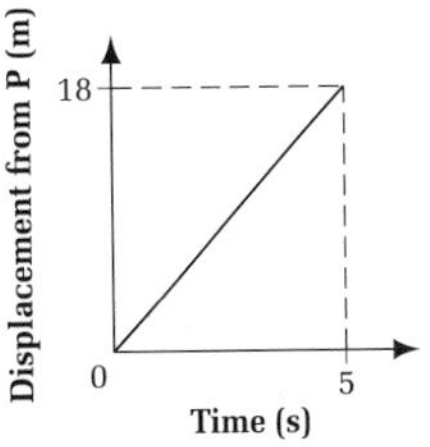

b

3 **a i** $1.47\ \mathrm{m\,s^{-1}}$ **ii** $-0.4\ \mathrm{m\,s^{-1}}$
b i $4.8\ \mathrm{cm\,s^{-1}}$ **ii** $2.4\ \mathrm{cm\,s^{-1}}$

4 **a i** AB $12\ \mathrm{m\,s^{-1}}$ **b i** BC $1.7\ \mathrm{cm\,s^{-1}}$

a ii

b ii

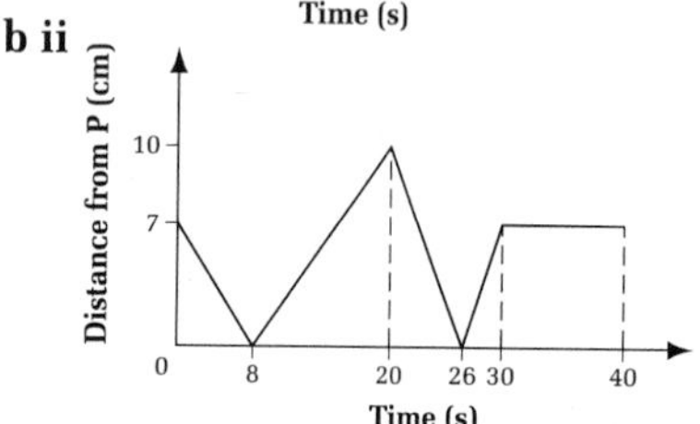

5 **a i**

b i

c i

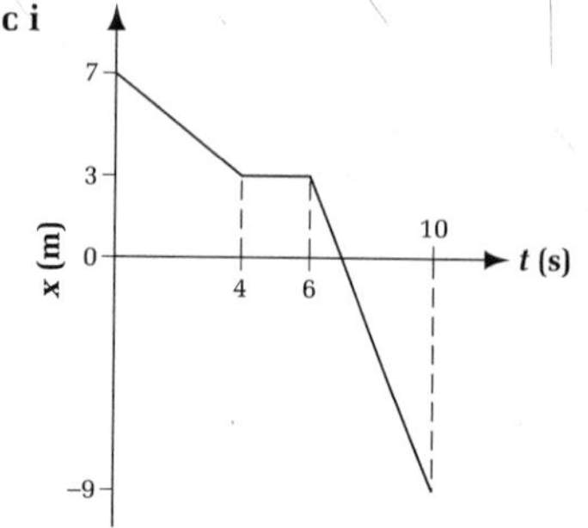

a ii $4\ \mathrm{m\,s^{-1}}$ **iii** 40 m
b ii $2\ \mathrm{m\,s^{-1}}, -1\ \mathrm{m\,s^{-1}}$ **iii** 15 m
c ii $-1\ \mathrm{m\,s^{-1}}, 0\ \mathrm{m\,s^{-1}}, -3\ \mathrm{m\,s^{-1}}$
iii 16 m

4.2 Contextual (p. 69)

1 **a**

b $0.4\ \mathrm{m\,s^{-1}}$ **c** $0\ \mathrm{m\,s^{-1}}$

2

3 **a** 25 m
b 1st length $3.125\ \mathrm{m\,s^{-1}}$; 2nd length $-2.08\ \mathrm{m\,s^{-1}}$; 3rd length $2.5\ \mathrm{m\,s^{-1}}$
c 75 m
d $2.5\ \mathrm{m\,s^{-1}}$
e $0.833\ \mathrm{m\,s^{-1}}$
f Sonja is unlikely to continue at the same speed when she turns. A more realistic graph would be curved, especially at the points where the direction of motion changes.

4 **a**

b $-0.98\ \mathrm{m\,s^{-1}}$ (2 s.f.)

5 **a** After 9.5 s at the first floor.
b Lift P **i** $1.09\ \mathrm{m\,s^{-1}}$ **ii** $0\ \mathrm{m\,s^{-1}}$
Lift Q **i** $0.75\ \mathrm{m\,s^{-1}}$ **ii** $0.75\ \mathrm{m\,s^{-1}}$

4.3 Technique (p. 79)

1 **a i** $5\ \mathrm{m\,s^{-1}}$ **ii** $15\ \mathrm{m\,s^{-1}}$ **iii** 55 m
iv 55 m **v** $2.5\ \mathrm{m\,s^{-2}}$
b i $-4\ \mathrm{m\,s^{-1}}$ **ii** $8\ \mathrm{m\,s^{-1}}$ **iii** 36 m
iv 60 m **v** $\frac{2}{3}\ \mathrm{m\,s^{-2}}$
c i $30\ \mathrm{cm\,s^{-1}}$ **ii** $-30\ \mathrm{cm\,s^{-1}}$ **iii** 6 m
iv 9 m **v** $-3\ \mathrm{cm\,s^{-2}}$
d i $-4\ \mathrm{m\,s^{-1}}$ **ii** $6\ \mathrm{m\,s^{-1}}$ **iii** -2.75 m
iv 7.25 m **v** $8\ \mathrm{m\,s^{-2}}$

2 **a**

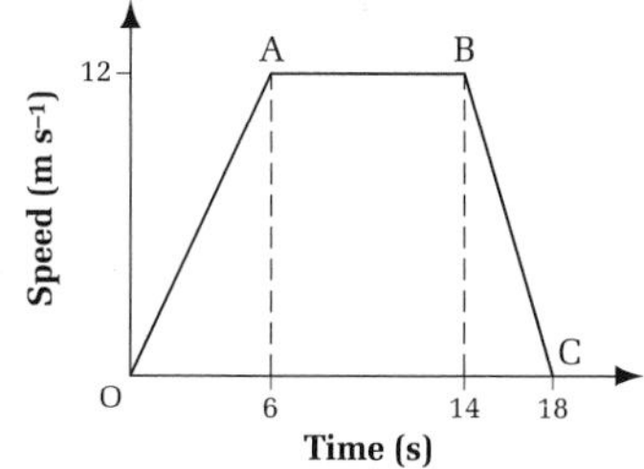

b distance = 156 m; acceleration = $2\,\text{m s}^{-2}$; deceleration = $3\,\text{m s}^{-2}$.

3 **a**

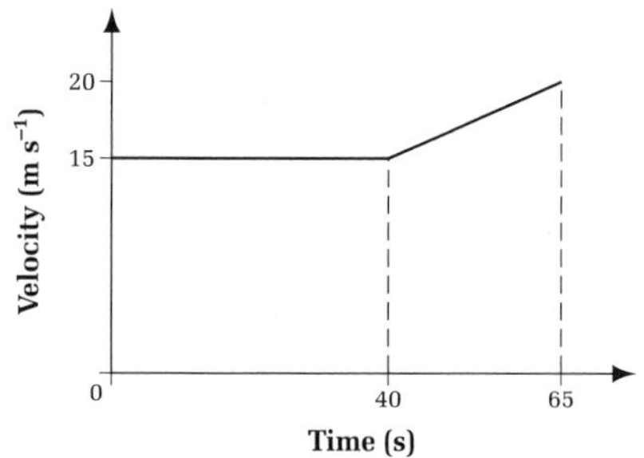

b 1037.5 m **c** $16.0\,\text{m s}^{-1}$

4 **a**

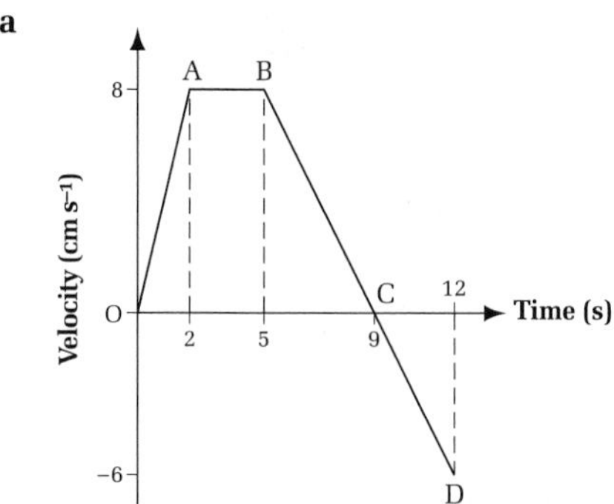

b 39 cm **c** 57 cm
d OA $4\,\text{cm s}^{-2}$; AB $0\,\text{cm s}^{-2}$; BC and CD $-2\,\text{cm s}^{-2}$

5 **a** 12.5 **b** $0.32\,\text{m s}^{-2}$

6 **a** 10 **b** $0\,\text{m s}^{-2}$, $3.5\,\text{m s}^{-2}$

4.3 Contextual (p. 81)

1 **a** $2\,\text{m s}^{-2}$ **b** $2.5\,\text{m s}^{-2}$ **c** 8 s
d 25 m **e** 20 m

2 **a** Ball is thrown up at $12\,\text{m s}^{-1}$. Speed reduces steadily until it stops after 1.2 s and begins to fall downwards. It is caught after a total time of 2.4 s.
b $-10\,\text{m s}^{-2}$
c 7.2 m

3 **a**

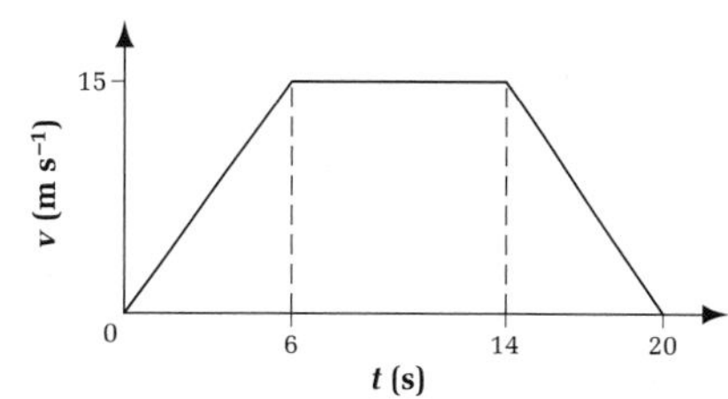

b $2.5\,\text{m s}^{-2}$ **c** $2.5\,\text{m s}^{-2}$ **d** 210 m

4 **a** 10 m **b** 3 s **c** 20

5 **a**

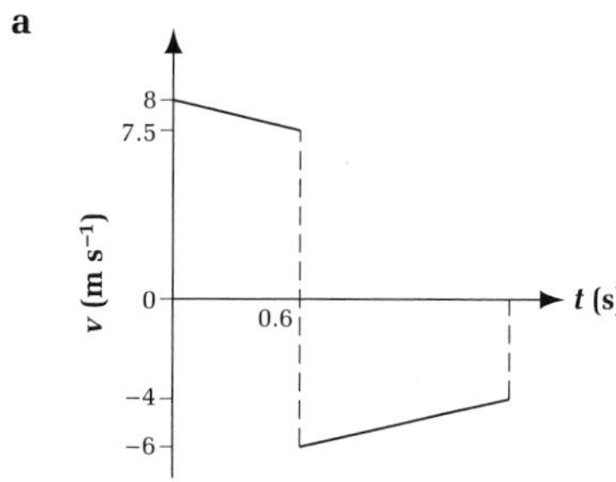

b 4.65 m **c** 0.93 s

6 **a**

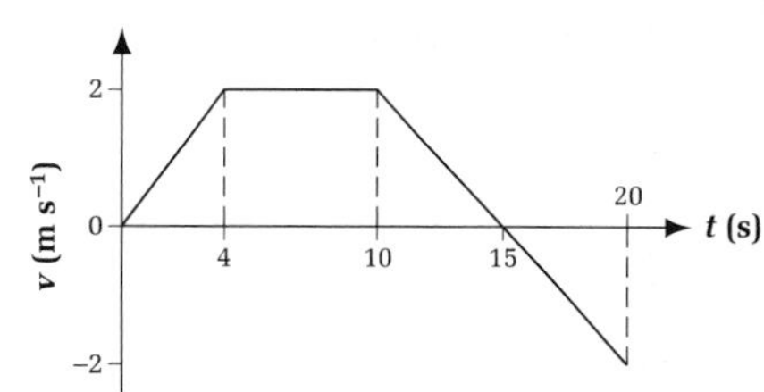

b Car starts from rest ($v = 0$ when $t = 0$) and accelerates to $2\,\text{m s}^{-1}$ in 4 s. It travels at a constant velocity of $2\,\text{m s}^{-1}$ for 6 s, then decelerates and comes to rest after a further 5 s ($v = 0$ when $t = 15$). The car then moves in the opposite direction, accelerating in the next 5 s to its final speed of $2\,\text{m s}^{-1}$.
c 26 m
d 16 m from the starting position in the direction of the initial motion.

4.4 Technique (p. 86)

1 **a** **i** L^2 **ii** L^3
b **i**, **iii**, **iv** are correct and **ii** is incorrect.

2 **a** ML^{-3} **b** MLT^{-1} **c** ML^2T^{-2}
d ML^2T^{-3} **e** ML^2T^{-2} **f** $ML^{-1}T^{-2}$

4 Yes, it is a possible formula.

5 $a = 1, b = 2$

6 **a** MT^{-1} **b** $ML^{-2}T$

7 $M^{-1}L^3T^{-2}$

Consolidation A (p. 87)

1 **a** $1\,\text{m s}^{-1}$
b $-\frac{2}{3}\,\text{m s}^{-1}$; snooker ball hit cushion.

2 a

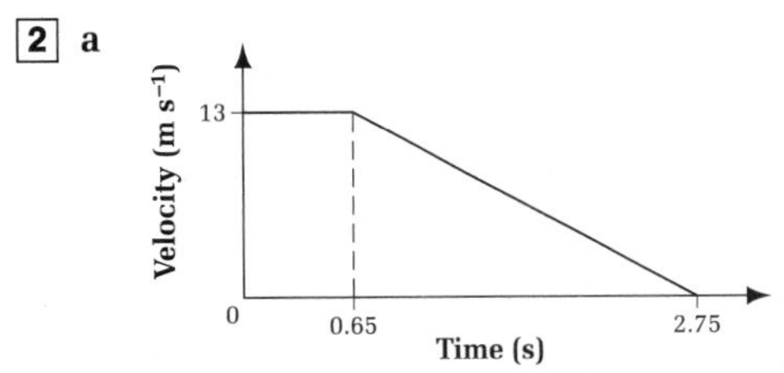

3 a i $1\frac{1}{3}\,\text{m s}^{-2}$ ii $\frac{2}{3}\,\text{m s}^{-2}$ iii 60 s
iv 600 m v 1200 m
b 105 s
c curves where the velocity changes

Consolidation B (p. 88)

1 a 4 b $0.125\,\text{m s}^{-2}$

2 $0.2\,\text{m s}^{-1}$; $0\,\text{m s}^{-1}$; $0.15\,\text{m s}^{-1}$

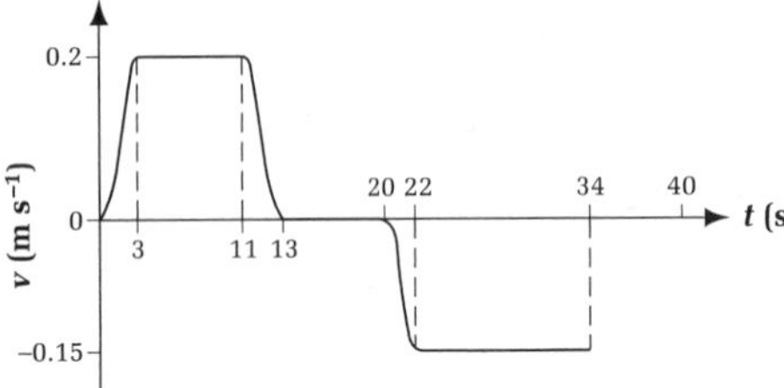

Train starts from rest and accelerates to $0.2\,\text{m s}^{-1}$ in 3 s whilst travelling 0.2 m. It travels at $0.2\,\text{m s}^{-1}$ for 8 s travelling a further 1.6 m. It then slows down and comes to rest after a total of 13 s when its displacement from the starting point is 2 m. It stops here for 7 s and then begins to move in the opposite direction.
After 2 s it is travelling at $0.15\,\text{m s}^{-1}$ and it continues back along the track at this speed for 12 s. It has then returned to its starting position. It immediately stops there and remains stationary for 6 s.

3 a

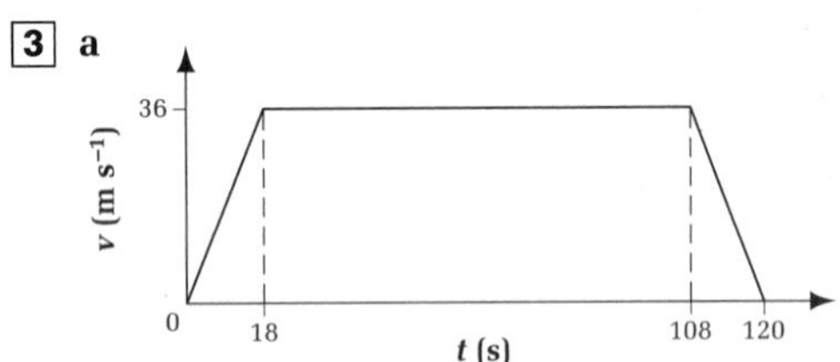

b 120 s c 3.78 km

4 a

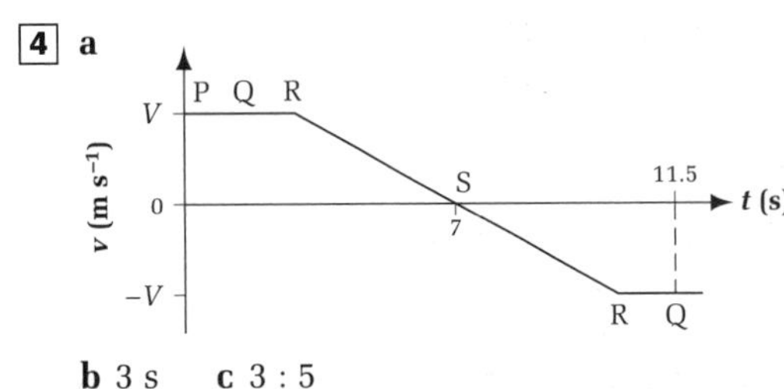

b 3 s c 3 : 5

5 Vectors II

Review (p. 91)

1 a $x = 10.3$ cm
b $y = 8.12$ cm, $z = 4.32$ cm

2 a AC should measure 20.2 cm (nearest 0.1 cm).
b PR should measure 21.5 cm (nearest 0.1 cm).

3 a $\mathbf{a} + \mathbf{b} = 3\mathbf{i} - 10\mathbf{j}$; $\mathbf{a} - \mathbf{b} = 9\mathbf{i} - 6\mathbf{j}$
b $\mathbf{p} + \mathbf{q} = \begin{pmatrix} -6 \\ 9 \end{pmatrix}$; $\mathbf{p} - \mathbf{q} = \begin{pmatrix} 18 \\ 5 \end{pmatrix}$

4 a 12.7 cm
b i $B = 51.7°$
ii ($C = 72.6°$) $c = 11.7$ cm
c i 61.0° or 119.0°
ii 119.0°

5 C(−1, 2, 0), D(−1, 0, 0), E(3, 0, 5), F(3, 2, 5), G(−1, 2, 5), H(−1, 0, 5)

6 $|\mathbf{a}| = 20$ $|\mathbf{b}| = 3\sqrt{10}$ $|\mathbf{c}| = \sqrt{61}$ $|\mathbf{d}| = 17$

7 **b** and **c**

5.1 Technique (p. 99)

1 a $\begin{pmatrix} 6.86 \\ 5.36 \end{pmatrix}$ b $\begin{pmatrix} 3.68 \\ 11.3 \end{pmatrix}$ c $\begin{pmatrix} 4.53 \\ -2.11 \end{pmatrix}$
d $\begin{pmatrix} -14.2 \\ 11.1 \end{pmatrix}$ e $\begin{pmatrix} -0.611 \\ -0.382 \end{pmatrix}$ f $\begin{pmatrix} -62.4 \\ -19.1 \end{pmatrix}$
g $\begin{pmatrix} -2.59 \\ -9.66 \end{pmatrix}$ h $\begin{pmatrix} 31.4 \\ -29.3 \end{pmatrix}$

2 a $(11.4\mathbf{i} + 3.71\mathbf{j})$ m
b $(-1.92\mathbf{i} + 1.61\mathbf{j})$ km

3 a $(-13.6\mathbf{i} - 77.2\mathbf{j})$ N
b $(-40.6\mathbf{i} - 151\mathbf{j})$ N
c $(-21.4\mathbf{i} - 244\mathbf{j})$ N

4 a $(-6.16\mathbf{i} - 16.9\mathbf{j})$ N
b $(7.31\mathbf{i} - 6.82\mathbf{j})$ N
c $(-2.28\mathbf{i} + 6.62\mathbf{j})$ N
d $(5.94\mathbf{i} + 2.64\mathbf{j})$ N

5.1 Contextual (p. 100)

1 $\mathbf{v}_1 = (10.8\mathbf{i} - 5.26\mathbf{j})\,\text{km h}^{-1}$
$\mathbf{v}_2 = (7.36\mathbf{i} + 3.13\mathbf{j})\,\text{km h}^{-1}$
$\mathbf{v}_3 = (9.38\mathbf{i} + 22.1\mathbf{j})\,\text{km h}^{-1}$
$\mathbf{v}_4 = (-13.3\mathbf{i} - 4.33\mathbf{j})\,\text{km h}^{-1}$
$\mathbf{v}_5 = (1.26\mathbf{i} - 18.0\mathbf{j})\,\text{km h}^{-1}$
(note, to 4 s.f. $\mathbf{v}_5 = 1.256\mathbf{i} - 17.96\mathbf{j}$)

2 $\begin{pmatrix} -18.7 \\ -61.2 \end{pmatrix}\,\text{km h}^{-1}$

3 a $(-2.08\mathbf{i} - 11.8\mathbf{j})$ N
b $(-4.14\mathbf{i} - 15.5\mathbf{j})$ N
c $(4.23\mathbf{i} - 9.06\mathbf{j})$ N
d $(20.8\mathbf{i} - 54.1\mathbf{j})$ N

5.2 Technique (p. 103)

1 a 11.6 cm, 41° (nearest degree)
b 9.1 cm (2 s.f.), 95° (nearest degree)

2 12.6 units, 82° (nearest degree)

3 **a** 55, 48° (nearest degree)
b 1.3, 171° (nearest degree)

4 8.1 km, 262° (nearest degree)

5.3 Technique (p. 106)

1 **a** 25.8 cm, +20.3° **b** 0.701 cm, +281.5° or −78.5°

2 6.40 units, 109.3°

3 598 m, bearing = 305.2°

5.3 Contextual (p. 106)

1 31.4 m, 161.0°

2 **a** 10.6 km **b** 308.8°

3 043.6°, 0.901 km

5.4 Technique (p. 109)

1 **a** 19.5 units, +154.1°
b 20.5 cm, 253.1° or −106.9°

2 21.7 units, +36.0°

3 **a** $4.59\mathbf{i} + 6.55\mathbf{j}$, $6.58\mathbf{i} - 2.39\mathbf{j}$, $-7.43\mathbf{i} + 6.69\mathbf{j}$ resultant $= 3.74\mathbf{i} + 10.9\mathbf{j}$
b $8\mathbf{j}$, $14.7\mathbf{i} + 3.12\mathbf{j}$, $9.83\mathbf{i} - 6.88\mathbf{j}$, $-11.9\mathbf{i} - 7.42\mathbf{j}$; resultant $= 12.6\mathbf{i} - 3.18\mathbf{j}$

4 6.70 units, 70.0°

5.5 Technique (p. 112)

1

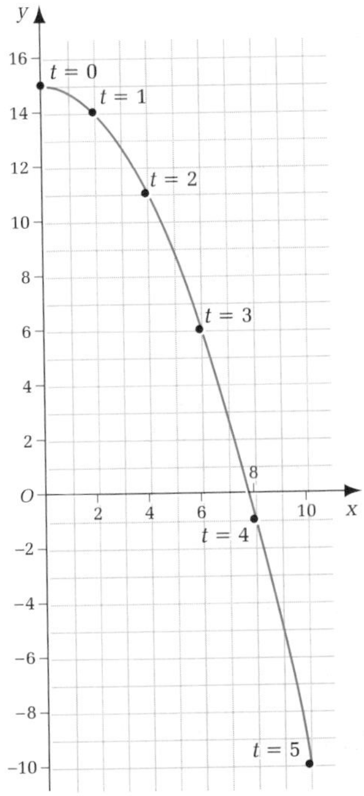

2 $y = (x - 3)^2$ or $y = x^2 - 6x + 9$

3 **a** $k = -\frac{1}{2}$
b $\lambda = 0$ or $\lambda = 2$. $\lambda = 2$ gives $4\mathbf{i} + 4\mathbf{j}$ which is clearly parallel to $2\mathbf{i} + 2\mathbf{j}$. $\lambda = 0$ gives $0\mathbf{i} + 0\mathbf{j}$. This cannot be parallel to $2\mathbf{i} + 2\mathbf{j}$.

4 **a** $\sqrt{34}$ **b** $\sqrt{157}$ **c** 3.25

5 **a** $t = -\frac{1}{5}$, $t = -1$
b $|\mathbf{a}| = \sqrt{5((t + \frac{3}{5})^2 + \frac{36}{25})}$ least value $\frac{6\sqrt{5}}{5}$
c Solutions of $12t^2 - 10t - 5 = 0$ are $t = 1.18$ and $t = -0.352$

5.6 Technique (p. 116)

1 **a** 1 **b** −12 **c** 8

2 **a** 13 **b** 0 **c** 3

3 **a** 7.5 **b** −46.3 **c** 20.7

4 **a** 11.9° **b** 4.4° **c** 69.8°

5 **a** 108.0° **b** 79.8°

5.7 Technique (p. 119)

1 **a** and **f**, **b** and **h**, **c** and **g**, **d** and **e**.

2 **a** 3.62 **b** −4.67

3 **a** −12 **b** 6.5 **c** 1.29, −5.79

4 **a** **i** 26.6° **ii** 47.4°
b $t = -\frac{2}{3}$, ($t = 0$, trivial solution)

5 **a** $\lambda = -3$
b $\lambda = -0.935, -47.1$

Consolidation A (p. 120)

1 **a** $\mathbf{R} = (20\mathbf{i} + 21\mathbf{j})$ N
b $R = 29$ N
c $\cos\theta = 0.905$

2 26 N, 57.8°

3 **a** $\begin{pmatrix} 23.8 \\ 7.73 \end{pmatrix}$ km
b $\begin{pmatrix} -8.28 \\ -30.9 \end{pmatrix}$ km
c $\begin{pmatrix} 15.5 \\ -23.2 \end{pmatrix}$ km
d 27.9 km, 326°

Consolidation B (p. 120)

1 53.9 N

2 **a** $2\mathbf{i} - \mathbf{j} - 4\mathbf{k}$ **b** 147.7°

3 **a** $(1.46\mathbf{i} - 6.85\mathbf{j})$ km
b $(-9.40\mathbf{i} - 3.42\mathbf{j})$ km
c $(-7.94\mathbf{i} - 10.3\mathbf{j})$ km
d 13.0 km, 037.7°

6 Motion in a Straight Line

Review (p. 123)

1

Term	Definition	SI units	Vector or scalar
Displacement	Distance in a specified direction	m	vector
Speed	Rate of change of distance	$m\,s^{-1}$	scalar
Velocity	Rate of change of displacement or speed in a specified direction	$m\,s^{-1}$	vector
Acceleration	Rate of change of velocity	$m\,s^{-2}$	vector

2 **a**

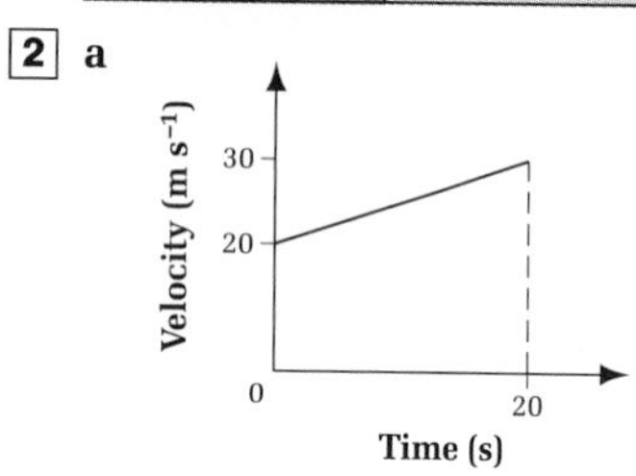

b $0.5\,m\,s^{-2}$ **c** 500 m

3 **a** 30 **b** 2 **c** −24 or 24 **d** −4 or 4

4 **a** $t = 0$ or $t = 7$
b $t = -5$ or $t = 10$
c $t = 6$ or $t = -2$

5 **a** $x = -9.80$ or $x = -0.204$
b $x = -1.10$ or $x = 9.10$
c $x = -2.12$ or $x = 0.786$

6 **a** $5\sqrt{2}$ **b** $3\sqrt{3}$ **c** $16\sqrt{7}$ **d** $\frac{7}{8}$

7 **a** $\begin{pmatrix}1\\0\end{pmatrix}$ **b** $\begin{pmatrix}-12\\8\end{pmatrix}$ **c** $11\mathbf{j} - 15\mathbf{k}$

8 **a** $2\sqrt{5}=4.47$ **b** $\sqrt{29}=5.39$

6.1 Technique (p. 130)

1 **a** $33\,m\,s^{-1}$ **b** $\pm 40\,m\,s^{-1}$
c 21 m **d** 2025 m or 2.025 km

2 **a** $12\,m\,s^{-1}$ **b** $0.2\,m\,s^{-2}$

3 **a** 7 s **b** 73.5 m

4 2 s

5 **a** 8 s **b** $1\,m\,s^{-2}$

6 **a** 5 s **b** $30\,m\,s^{-1}$

7 **a** $\sqrt{11} - 1$ s **b** $\sqrt{21} - 1$ s

8 $4 + \sqrt{15}$ s

6.1 Contextual (p. 131)

1 $0.5\,m\,s^{-2}$

2 $7\frac{1}{7}$ s; $3\frac{23}{25}\,m\,s^{-2}$

3 **a** 50 s **b** $-1.2\,m\,s^{-2}$

4 **a** $5\sqrt{5}\,m\,s^{-1}$ **b** $50 - 10\sqrt{5}$ s

5 **a** $\frac{6\sqrt{14}-2}{5}$ s **b** $6\sqrt{14}\,m\,s^{-1}$

6 $\frac{5}{12}\,m\,s^{-2}$

7 $11 + 2\sqrt{30}$ s after being passed.

6.2 Technique (p. 134)

1 **a** 4.47 s **b** $43.8\,m\,s^{-1}$

2 **a** 28.8 m **b** $-24\,m\,s^{-1}$ or $24\,m\,s^{-1}$ downwards
c $24\,m\,s^{-1}$ **d** 4.8 s

3 **a** 125 m **b** 5 s

4 **a** $35\,m\,s^{-1}$ **b** 61.25 m

5 **a i** 1 s **ii** 3 s **b** 2 s

6 **a** 1.683 km **b** $184\,m\,s^{-1}$

7 3 s

6.2 Contextual (p. 135)

1 **a** 1.43 s **b** $14\,m\,s^{-1}$

2 **a** 31.25 m **b** $25\,m\,s^{-1}$

3 **a** $24.0\,m\,s^{-1}$ **b** 29.4 m

4 **a** 45 m **b** $30\,m\,s^{-1}$
Assumptions: straight line motion, no air resistance, vertical speed is initially zero.

5 **a** $5\,m\,s^{-1}$ **b** $3\,m\,s^{-1}$

6 **a** $4.17\,m\,s^{-1}$ **b** 0.868 m **c** $10.8\,m\,s^{-1}$

7 **a** $5.42\,m\,s^{-1}$ **b** 1.11 s

6.3 Technique (p. 138)

1 $15\,m\,s^{-1}$

2 **a** $(-3\mathbf{i} + 51\mathbf{j})$ m
b $(2\mathbf{i} + 29\mathbf{j})\,m\,s^{-1}$
c $29.1\,m\,s^{-1}$

3 **a** 7 s **b** $(91\mathbf{i} + 122.5\mathbf{j} - 220.5\mathbf{k})$ m

4 **a** $\begin{pmatrix}1\\2\end{pmatrix}\,m\,s^{-2}$ **b** $\begin{pmatrix}8\\2\end{pmatrix}$ m

5 12 s

6 **a** $\begin{pmatrix}-2\\5\\-3\end{pmatrix}\,m\,s^{-1}$ **b** $\sqrt{38}\,m\,s^{-1}$
c $\sqrt{146}\,m\,s^{-1}$

6.3 Contextual (p. 139)

1 **a** $(0.5\mathbf{i} - \mathbf{j} - 2\mathbf{k})\,m\,s^{-2}$ **b** 100 m

2 **a** $(8.6\mathbf{i} - 4\mathbf{k})\,m\,s^{-1}$ **b** $9.48\,m\,s^{-1}$ **c** 7.04 m

3 a 5 s b $\begin{pmatrix} 125 \\ 187.5 \\ -112.5 \end{pmatrix}$ m

4 $(3\mathbf{i} - 12\mathbf{j} + 8\mathbf{k})\,\mathrm{m\,s^{-1}}$

5 a $\begin{pmatrix} 9.2 \\ -4 \end{pmatrix}\mathrm{m\,s^{-1}}$ b $10.0\,\mathrm{m\,s^{-1}}$ c 7.68 m

Consolidation A (p. 140)

1 a 50 s b $24.2\,\mathrm{m\,s^{-1}}$

2 a 36 m
b 38 to 40 m. Wheelbase measurement is not taken into account. This measurement can be between about 2 and 4 m. The car cannot accelerate until both wheels are over the ramp.

3 a 11.025 m b 1.5 s c $4.9\,\mathrm{m\,s^{-1}}$

4 a $\begin{pmatrix} 15 \\ 24 - 9.8t \end{pmatrix}\mathrm{m\,s^{-1}}$, $\begin{pmatrix} 15t \\ 24t - 4.9t^2 + 1 \end{pmatrix}$m
b 4.94 s, 74.1 m
c $24.6\,\mathrm{m\,s^{-1}}$

Consolidation B (p. 141)

1 13.0 m

2 2.02 s

3 a i $\begin{pmatrix} 4 \\ -10t \end{pmatrix}\mathrm{m\,s^{-1}}$ ii $\begin{pmatrix} 4t \\ -5t^2 \end{pmatrix}$m
b $\mathbf{v} = \begin{pmatrix} 4 \\ -10\sqrt{5} \end{pmatrix}\mathrm{m\,s^{-1}}$
This vector is parallel to the direction vector from A to the sack.
A to the sack $= \begin{pmatrix} 4\sqrt{5} \\ -50 \end{pmatrix}$ m.

4 $2.5\,\mathrm{m\,s^{-2}}$, 16 s

7 Equilibrium

Review (p. 144)

1 a translation b enlargement
c rotation d reflection

2 a $x = \sqrt{108} = 6\sqrt{3}$
b $y = \sqrt{340} = 2\sqrt{85}$

3 $x = 8.73$ cm, $y = 15.7$ cm, $z = 5.32$ cm

4 a $\mathbf{a} + \mathbf{b} = \begin{pmatrix} 2 \\ -6 \end{pmatrix}$

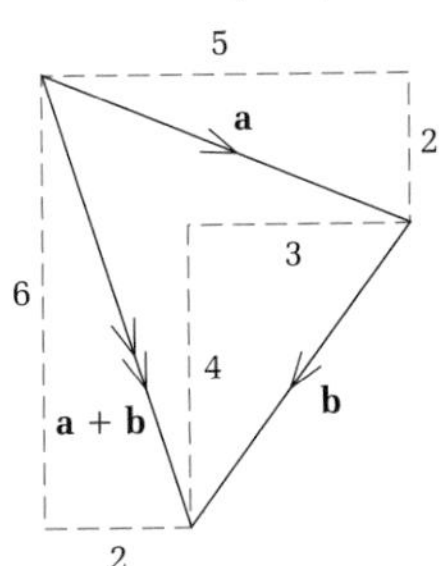

b 9.11 units, bearing 126.7°
c 9.54 units, 93.0°

5 a $x = 8.91$ cm, $y = 15.8$ cm
b 9.36 m
c $\theta = 59.4°$, R = 85.6°, $PQ = 6.95$ cm or $\theta = 120.6°$, R = 24.4°, $PQ = 2.88$ cm

7.1 Technique (p. 149)

1 a −17, −5 b 17.7 N

2 a −4, −3 b 7.28 N, 6.40 N, 4.24 N

3 a $(-4\mathbf{i} + 16\mathbf{j})$ N b 16.5 N, 104.0°

4 a $\begin{pmatrix} -14 \\ -16 \end{pmatrix}$ b 21.3 c 228.8°
d

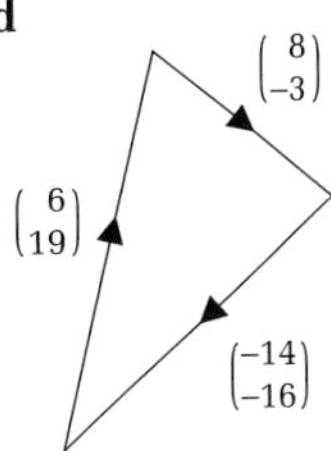

5 a $a = -17, b = 10$ b 19.7 N c 149.5°

6 a $(-5\mathbf{i} + 5\mathbf{j})$ N b 135°

7 a $a = 6, b = -1, c = -3$ b 6.78 N

8 a $\mathbf{Z} = (-20\mathbf{i} + 8\mathbf{j} - 2\mathbf{k})$ N
b 159.7°, 104.9°

7.1 Contextual (p. 150)

1 a $(-5\mathbf{i} - 4\mathbf{j})$ N b 6.40 N c 218.7°

2 a $a = -3, b = 21$ b 21.2 N

3 a $(-\mathbf{i} - 4\mathbf{j} - 7\mathbf{k})$ N b 8.12 N c 30.5°

4 a $(-20\mathbf{i} + 2\mathbf{j})$ N
b

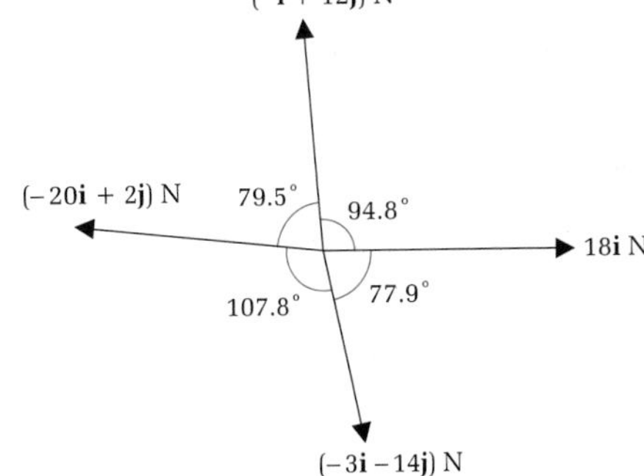

c $(-\mathbf{i} + 12\mathbf{j})$ N

7.2 Technique (p. 154)

1 a

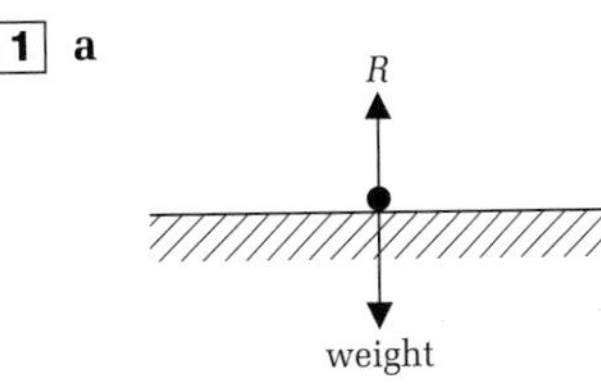

b two c 49 N

2 Since resultant force is zero, the particle is in equilibrium.

3 **a**

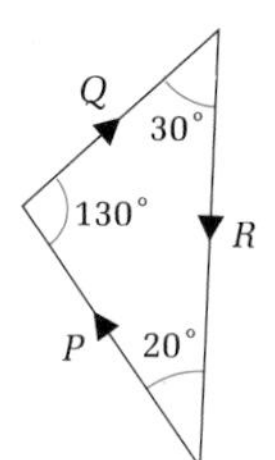

b

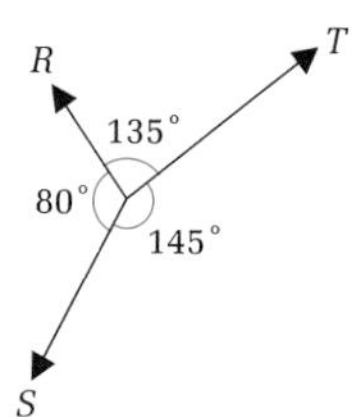

4 **a**

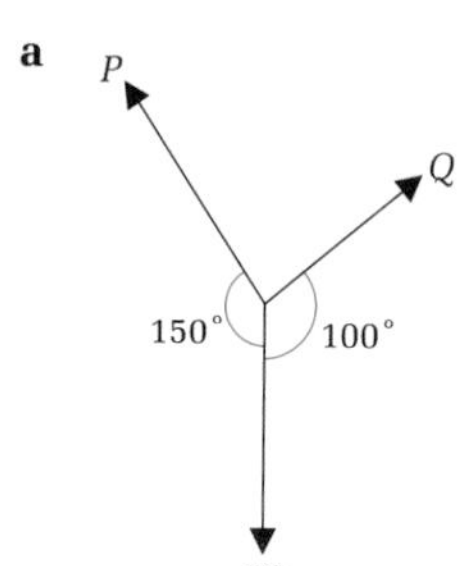

b

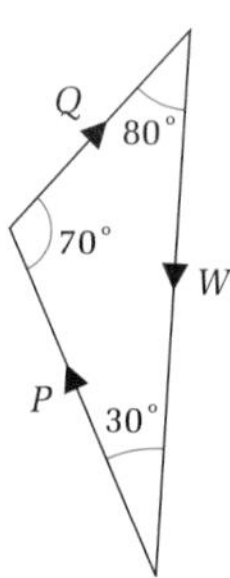

5 **b** **i** 15.7 N **ii** 139°

6 148°, 145°, 67°

7.2 Contextual (p. 155)

1 **a**

thrust

weight

b 98 N, 98 N

c Object can be modelled as a particle. No current flow; still water.

2 **a**

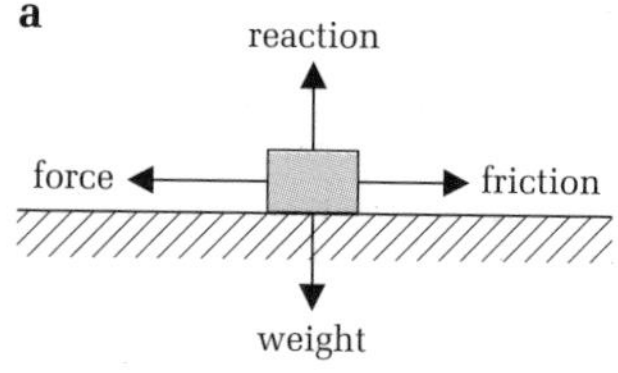

b constant velocity ⇒ dynamic equilibrium. Therefore magnitude of friction equals magnitude of horizontal force.

c 392 N downwards (weight). 392 N upwards (reaction).

3 **a**

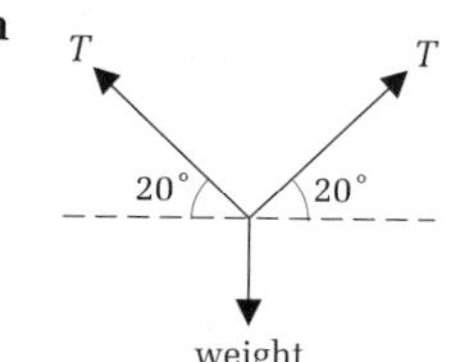

b

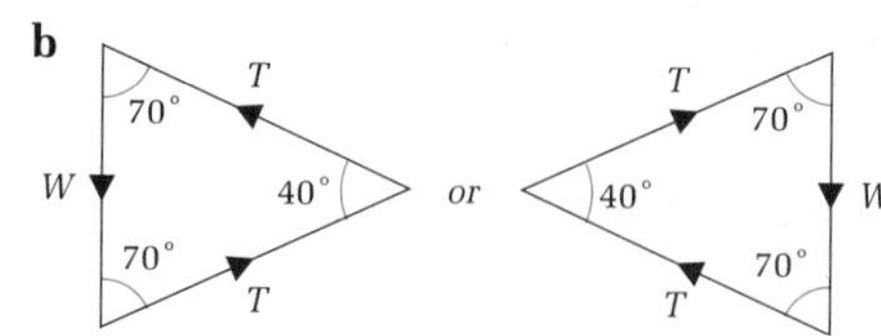

4 24.7 N, 17°

7.3 Technique (p. 159)

1 **a** 17 N, 151.9°
b 15.8 N, 161.6°

2 $\sqrt{549 + 270\sqrt{2}}\,\text{N} = 3\sqrt{61 + 30\sqrt{2}}\,\text{N}$, 159.7°

3 148.9°, 129.2°, 81.9°

4 **a** **i** 15.9 N **ii** 13.4 N **iii** 10.4 N
b **i** 123.7° **ii** 58.1° **iii** 0°

7.3 Contextual (p. 160)

1 18.8 N, 138.2°

2 **a** 15.2 N **b** 135.6°

3 134.9°, 125.2°, 99.9°

4 0.001 35 N, 0.001 41 N

5 943 N, 9.2°

7.4 Technique (p. 163)

1 **a** $|\mathbf{P}| = 9.50$ N; $|\mathbf{Q}| = 4.48$ N
b $|\mathbf{R}| = 174.8$ N; $|\mathbf{S}| = 280.8$ N

2 **a** **i** 13.9 N **ii** 17.9 N **iii** 17.9 N
b **i** 41.2° (or 138.8°)
ii 81.4° (or 98.6°)
iii 19.2° (or 160.8°)

3 30.1 N, 35.7 N

4 **a** 286.8 N, 265.7 N **b** 69.4 N, 64.3 N

7.4 Contextual (p. 164)

1 **a** 320 N, 757 N **b** 303 N, 886 N
c Child and tyre can be modelled as a particle. Rope has negligible mass. No other forces involved (wind?).

2 **a** 143.1°, 126.9°
b 1.76 N, 2.35 N
c 1.85 N, 2.47 N

3 **a** 90.8 kg **b** 50.2 N

7.5 Technique (p. 169)

1 **a** $T\cos\theta = 18.2$ **b** $T\sin\theta = 10.7$
c $\theta = 30.5°$, $T = 21.1$ N

2 18.4 N, 40.6°

3 **a** $X = 50$ N, $Y = 86.6$ N
b $X = 70.7$ N, $Y = 70.7$ N
c $X = 76.6$ N, $Y = 64.3$ N
d $X = 98.5$ N, $Y = 17.4$ N

4 **a** $|\mathbf{Y}| = 20.8$ N **b** $|\mathbf{X}| = 10.7$ N

5 **i** component is 4.96, **j** component is −5.38. For equilibrium both must be zero.

6 **a** 146.7° **b** 33.3 N

7 11.5 N, 56.1°

8 $\sqrt{73 + 20\sqrt{3}}$, 55° (nearest degree)

7.5 Contextual (p. 171)

1 **a** 22.6°, 67.4° **b** 4.52 N, 10.9 N

2 106 N, 305 N. The child is treated as a particle, the rope is light and inextensible and it remains straight.

3 **a** 504 N **b** 13.5° **c** 512 N, 17.0°

4 $|\mathbf{X}| = 22.3$ N, $|\mathbf{Y}| = 37.5$ N

Consolidation A (p. 172)

1 $P = 10.3$ N; $Q = 28.2$ N

2 $\mathbf{T}_1 = 13.6$ N; $\mathbf{T}_2 = 5.7$ N

3 $T = 61$ N; $\theta = 10.4°$

Consolidation B (p. 173)

1 **a** $p = 2, q = -6$ **b** 6.32 N **c** 18°

2 $T\cos 40° = T\cos\theta \Rightarrow \theta = 40°$; $T = 0.763$ N

3 **a** $AC^2 + BC^2 = AB^2$
b $T_1 = 23.5$ N, $T_2 = 9.81$ N

8 Newton's Laws of Motion

Review (p. 176)

1 **a** $(43.3\mathbf{i} + 25\mathbf{j})$ N **b** $(46.0\mathbf{i} - 46.0\mathbf{j})$ N

2 **a** **i** 13 N **ii** 22.6°
b **i** 5 N **ii** 126.9°

3 **a** $2\mathbf{i} + 9\mathbf{j}$ **b** $-11\mathbf{i} + 12\mathbf{j}$ **c** $7\mathbf{i} + 52\mathbf{j}$

4 **a** $v = u + at$
$s = ut + \frac{1}{2}at^2$
$v^2 = u^2 + 2as$
$s = \frac{1}{2}(u + v)t$
b 2.5 m s^{-2} **c** 1.01 s
d 24 m **e** 225 m

5 **a** $a = 5$; $T = 25$ **b** $a = 10$; $T = 20$

6 **a** 49 N **b** 0.98 N **c** 19 600 N

7 **a** 1 **b** $\frac{1}{2}$ **c** $\frac{1}{\sqrt{2}} = \frac{\sqrt{2}}{2}$
d $\sqrt{3}$ **e** $\frac{\sqrt{3}}{2}$ **f** $\frac{1}{2}$

8.1 Technique (p. 182)

1 **a** $F = 8$ N; $R = 16$ N **b** $S = 15$ N

2 **a** $F = 60$ N; $R = 30$ N
b $P = 250$ N; $R = 200$ N

3 90 N, 98 N

4 4**j** N

5 18.8 N

6 **a** 35 N **b** $25\sqrt{3}$ N

8.1 Contextual (p. 183)

1 **a**

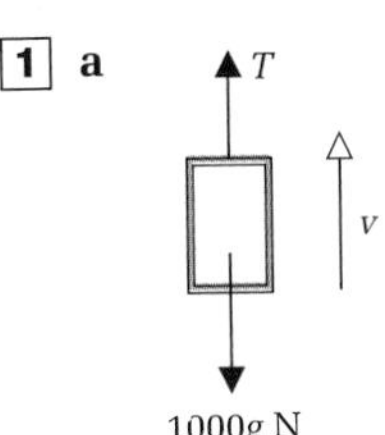

b 9800 N

2 **a**

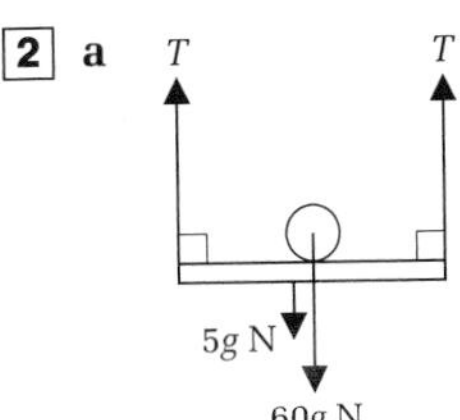

b 319 N

3 **a** 98 N **b** 50 N

4 $40\sqrt{3}$ N

5 485 N

6 277 N

7 **a** 133 kN **b** 464 kN

8.2 Technique (p. 187)

1 7 N

2 3.6 m s^{-2}

3 3.77 kg

4 6 m s^{-2}

5 $(12\mathbf{i} + 15\mathbf{j})$ N

6 $(20\mathbf{i} - 30\mathbf{j}) \text{ m s}^{-2}$

7 $\frac{1}{3}$ kg

8 **a** $(100\mathbf{i} + 200\mathbf{j}) \text{ m s}^{-2}$ **b** 224 m s^{-2}
c 63.4° from **i**

9 **a** $(-21\mathbf{i} - 28\mathbf{j})$ N **b** 35 N
c 233.1° from **i**

10 **a** 5 m s^{-2}, 2.5 m s^{-2} **b** 10 m s^{-1} **c** 70 m

8.2 Contextual (p. 188)

1 12 N

2 **a** 9440 N **b** 0.351 m s^{-2}

3 5 m s^{-2} assuming no resistance forces.

4 4170 kg assuming no resistance forces and horizontal motion.

5 **a** 6 m s^{-2} **b** 4800 N **c** 5600 N

6 6 m s^{-2}

7 800 kN

8 **a** 2 m s^{-2} **b** 275 kN

8.3 Technique (p. 193)

1 **a** 17.3 m s^{-2} **b** 1.20 m s^{-2}

2 **a** 237 N **b** 56.8 N

3 **a** 2.27 kg **b** 50 kg

4 5.1 m s^{-2}

5 $(5\sqrt{2}-3) \text{ m s}^{-2}$

6 **a** 3.35 m s^{-2} **b** 57.3 m

7 537 N

8 **a i** 1.66 N **ii** 0.830 m s^{-2}
iii opposite direction to 7 N force.
b i 40.1 N **ii** 10.0 m s^{-2}
iii 20.6° clockwise from 80 N force.

8.3 Contextual (p. 194)

1 4220 N

2 0.798 m s^{-2}

3 **a** 4.275 m s^{-2} **b** 20.8 m s^{-1}

4 **a**

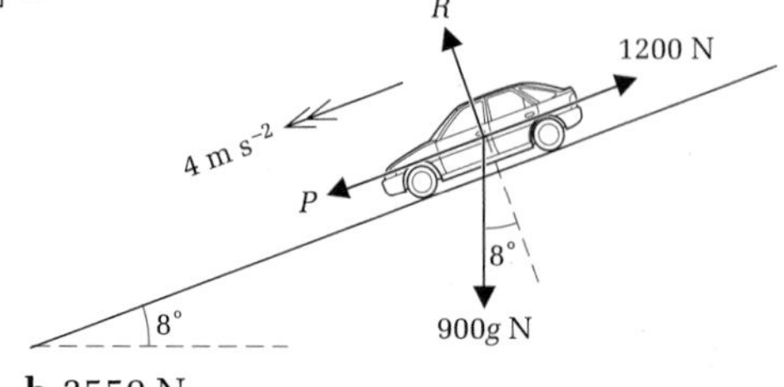

b 3550 N

8.4 Technique (p. 200)

1 **a i** 4.9 m s^{-2} **ii** 0.147 N
b i 0.891 m s^{-2} **ii** 26.7 N

2 **a** 6.125 m s^{-2}; 18.4 N **b** 8.71 m s^{-2}; 8.71 N

3 **a** 3.97 m s^{-2} **b** 0.854 m s^{-2}

4 3.68 m s^{-2}; 18.4 N

5 **a** 4.29 m s^{-2} **b** 3.79 m s^{-2}

8.4 Contextual (p. 201)

1 **a** 1.49 m s^{-2} **b** 1360 N
c

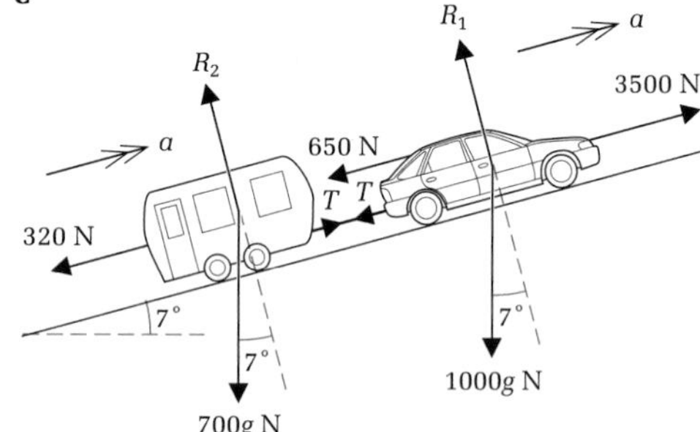

d Car:
$3500 - 650 - 1000g\sin 7° - T = 1000a$
Caravan: $T - 320 - 700g\sin 7° = 700a$
e 0.294 m s^{-2}

2 **a** 0.933 m s^{-2} **b** 2150 N **c** 21.4 s

3 **a** 11.3 kN **b** 7.54 m s^{-2}
c 38.8 m s^{-1} **d** 5.15 s

Consolidation A (p. 202)

1 **a i**

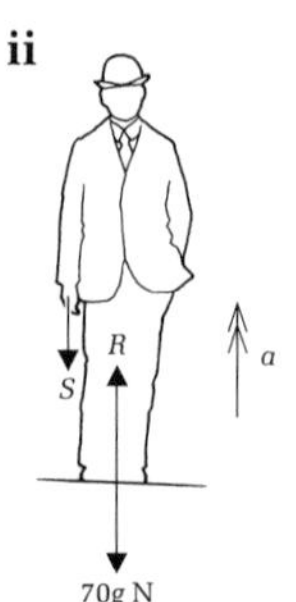

ii

b 936 N, 96 N

2 1640 N

3 **a** $\frac{g}{10}$ **b** $\frac{9mg}{5}$

Consolidation B (p. 203)

1 a

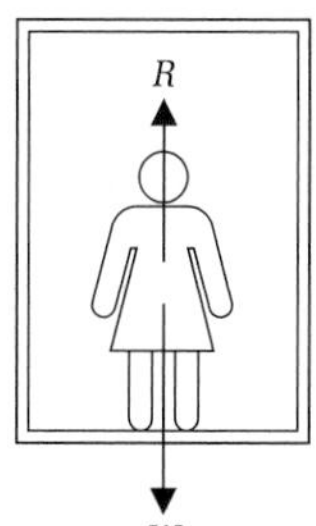

b 588 N **c** 708 N **d** 468 N
e 708 N **f** maximum: 8 people

2 **a** $\mathbf{P}+\mathbf{Q}+\mathbf{R}=\mathbf{0}$
b $(5\mathbf{i}-3\mathbf{j})$ N, $\sqrt{34}$ N $= 5.83$ N
c $(\mathbf{i}-\frac{3}{5}\mathbf{j})\,\text{m s}^{-2}$; $(10\mathbf{i}-6\mathbf{j})\,\text{m s}^{-1}$
d $\mathbf{a}=(\frac{3}{5}\mathbf{i}+\frac{4}{5}\mathbf{j})\,\text{m s}^{-2}$;
$\mathbf{v}=[(10+\frac{3}{5}t)\mathbf{i}+(\frac{4}{5}t-6)\mathbf{j}]\,\text{m s}^{-1}$
e 7.5 s

3 **a** $400-250=12000a$; $\frac{1}{80}\,\text{m s}^{-2}$
b $\frac{1}{2}\,\text{m s}^{-1}$; 40 s
c **i** 15 s **ii** $13\frac{3}{4}$ m **iii** 55 s

4 **b** 96.9 kg

9 Friction

Review (p. 207)

1 **a** $X=40$ N; $Y=100$ N **b** 40 N

2

A	30°	45°	60°
Sin A	$\frac{1}{2}$	$\frac{\sqrt{2}}{2}$ or $\frac{1}{\sqrt{2}}$	$\frac{\sqrt{3}}{2}$
Cos A	$\frac{\sqrt{3}}{2}$	$\frac{\sqrt{2}}{2}$ or $\frac{1}{\sqrt{2}}$	$\frac{1}{2}$
Tan A	$\frac{1}{\sqrt{3}}$	1	$\sqrt{3}$

3 **a** $a=2\,\text{m s}^{-2}$; $T=8$ N
b $a=1\frac{1}{4}\,\text{m s}^{-2}$; $T=22\frac{1}{2}$ N

4 **a** **i** $\lambda=46.3°$; $S=161$ N
ii $S=39.7$ N; $P=42.4$ N
b **i** $S=108$ N; $\theta=68.2°$
ii $\alpha=112.6°$; $\beta=90°$ (5, 12, 13 triangle)

5 **a** $-0.1\,\text{m s}^{-2}$ **b** $0.5\,\text{m s}^{-2}$
c $33\frac{1}{3}$ s **d** $8\,\text{m s}^{-1}$

9.1 Technique (p. 215)

1

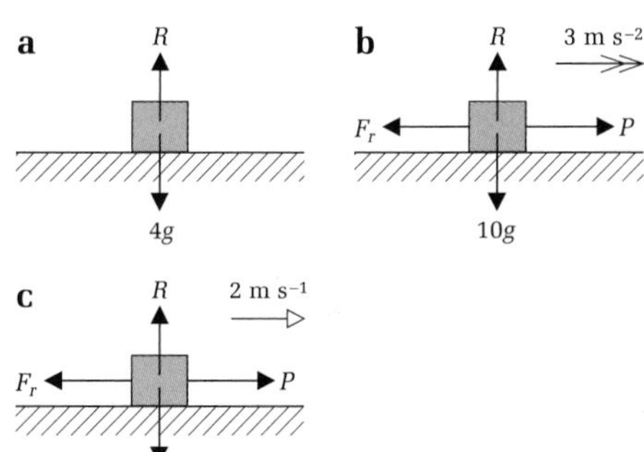

2 **a** Accelerate, $F_r=8$ N.
b Limiting equilibrium, $F_r=100$ N.
c Accelerates, $F_r=30$ N.

3 **a** $9.8\,\text{m s}^{-2}$ **b** $0.7\,\text{m s}^{-2}$

4 **a** 28 N **b** 66 N **c** 25 N

5 **a** Remains on the surface, $F_r=8$ N.
b Remains on the surface, $F_r=50$ N.
c Slides off the surface, $F_r=20$ N.

6 **a** $\frac{1}{7}$ **b** $\frac{1}{2}$ **c** $\frac{2}{7}$

7 24 N

9.1 Contextual (p. 217)

1 **a** 240 N **b** 324 N

2 **a** 10920 N **b** $9.1\,\text{m s}^{-2}$

3 **a** 40320 N **b** 0.7

4 **a** Remains on roof.
b Remains on roof.
c Remains on roof–limiting equilibrium.
d Slides off roof.

9.2 Technique (p. 220)

1

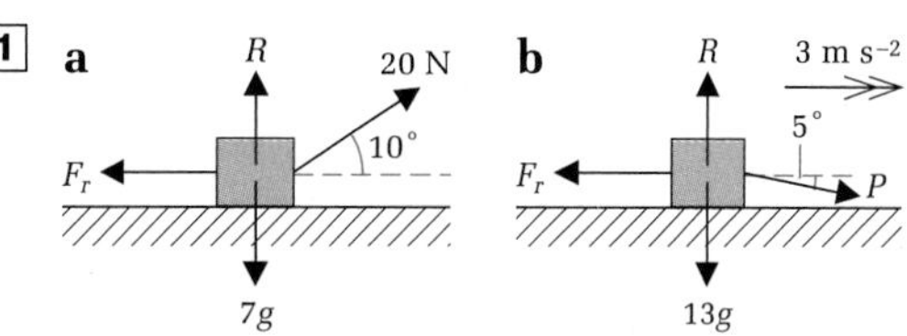

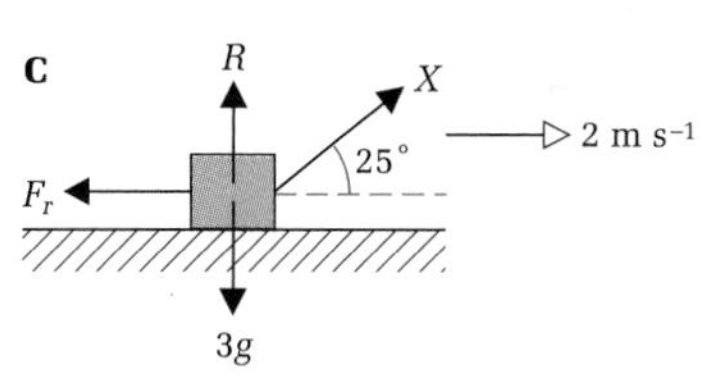

2 **a** Accelerate, $F_r=3(10-\sqrt{2})$ N
b At rest, $F_r=10(8-\sqrt{3})$ N

3 **a** $1.03\,\text{m s}^{-2}$ **b** $4.02\,\text{m s}^{-2}$

4 **a** 15.4 N **b** 8.42 N

5 **a** 0.764 **b** 0.274

6 **a**

R
F
θ
F_r
Mg

9.2 Contextual (p. 221)

1 **a** $\frac{60}{7}g$ **b** $\frac{20(7\sqrt{3}-3)g}{23}$ N $\left[\text{or } \frac{120g}{7\sqrt{3}+3}\right]$

9.3 Technique (p. 225)

1 **a** $14(7\sqrt{3}-4)$ N **b** $(126\sqrt{2})$ N

2 **a** 0.577 **b** 1

3 a 180 N b 67.7 N

4 a 0.505 b 0.906

5 a 5.84 N b 74.3 N

9.3 Contextual (p. 226)

1 $0.737\ \text{m s}^{-2}$

2 0.0875

3 248 N

9.4 Technique (p. 231)

1 a $0.467\ \text{m s}^{-2}$ b $1.8\ \text{m s}^{-2}$

2 a $\frac{9}{35}$ b $\frac{13}{44}$

3 a $\frac{10-2\sqrt{3}}{3}\ \text{m s}^{-2}$ b $\frac{37-10\sqrt{3}}{6}\ \text{m s}^{-2}$

9.5 Technique (p. 236)

1 a 26.6° b 8.1° c 30°

2 a 0.364 b 0.268 c 1.73 or $\sqrt{3}$

3 a $S = 242$ N; $\lambda = 24.4°$
b $S = 188$ N; $\lambda = 25.2°$

4 a $\lambda = 10.6°$ (or 49.4°); $P = 19.1$ N (or 78.9 N)
b $\lambda = 20.5°$; $P = 80.8$ N

5 a $P = 40.4$ N; $S = 80.8$ N
b $P = 150$ N; $S = 260$ N

6 $S = 170$ N; $P = 84.9$ N

7 $S = 110$ N; $\lambda = 32°$

8 $F = 1110$ N; $S = 1200$ N

9.5 Contextual (p. 237)

1 3°; 882 N

2 274 N; 3930 N

3 607 N; 158 N

4 59.1° (or −51.1°)

Consolidation A (p. 238)

1 25.43 N, 0.249

2 a 10 N

3 a 15.68 N b 0.625

Consolidation B (p. 239)

1 $P = 47.5$ N (1 d.p.)

2 a i $M = 2.3$ ii $M = 0.7$
b $a = 0.667\ \text{m s}^{-2}$; $T = 5.33$ N

3 $a = 1.8\ \text{m s}^{-2}$; $T = 9.6$ N

10 Work, Energy and Power

Review (p. 242)

1 a

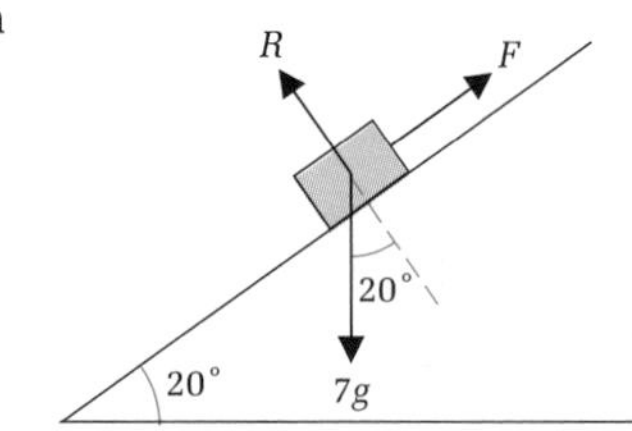

b 23.9 N, 65.8 N

2 191.1 N

3 a $[v] = \text{LT}^{-1}$; $[a] = \text{LT}^{-2}$
b $[Fs] = \text{ML}^2\text{T}^{-2}$; $[mv^2] = \text{ML}^2\text{T}^{-2}$

4 a i $R = 40v$ ii 800 iii 400
b i $F = 20v^2$ ii 4500 iii ±4

5 a −25.4, 8.62 b −138, 59.1
c −57.0, 21.0

10.1 Technique (p. 247)

1 36 J

2 20 N

3 0.9 m

4 a 28 N b 28 N c 84 J

5 a 2.5 N b $0.625\ \text{m s}^{-2}$ c 6.20 s

6 a 147 N b 441 J

7 a 4 N b $\frac{4}{49}$ or 0.0816

8 a 58.8 N b 10 m

9 360 J

10 a 4.5 m b 40 N

11 a 5 m b 350 J

12 b $mgx(\mu\cos\alpha + \sin\alpha)$

13 Should be cos 20° not sin 20°, 188 J.

10.1 Contextual (p. 249)

1 25 m, cyclist travels at a constant speed along horizontal ground.

2 a $10\sqrt{3}$ N b $200\sqrt{3}$ J

3 103 J

4 a 2304 kJ b 76.8 kJ

10.2 Technique (p. 254)

1 a 196 J b 44.1 J c 7.84 J

2 a 16 J b 196 J c 64 J

3 1.33 kg

4 2.04 m

5 30 kg

6 $\frac{14\sqrt{3}}{3}$ m s^{-1}

7 4 J

8 5.83 kg

9 122.5 J

11 [W] = ML^2T^{-2}, [PE] = ML^2T^{-2}, [KE] = ML^2T^{-2}

10.2 Contextual (p. 255)

1 3250 J

2 1 160 000 kJ

3 205.8 kJ

4 360 kJ

5 1530 kJ

6 **a** 80 kJ **b** 380 kJ **c** 8.72 m s^{-1}

7 5.83 kg

8 122.5 J

10.3 Technique (p. 261)

1 **a** 147 J **b** 147 J **c** 7.67 m s^{-1}

2 **a** 140 J **b** 140 J **c** 11.8 m s^{-1}

3 **a** 25 J **b** 25 J **c** 5 m

4 **a** 900 J **b** 588 J **c** 11.2 m s^{-1}

5 **a** $4\sqrt{6}$ m s^{-1} **b** $10\sqrt{3}$ m s^{-1}

6 0.778

7 **a** 3.2 J **b** 3.2 J **c** 5.44 m

8 8.20 m s^{-1}

10.3 Contextual (p. 262)

1 **a** 440 kJ **b** 240 kJ **c** 680 kJ **d** 1130 N
The force produced by the engine is assumed constant.

2 **a** 980 kJ **b** 980 kJ **c** 31.4 m s^{-1}

3 119 N

4 0.98 J, kinetic energy is converted into sound (and heat in the surface of the ball).

10.4 Technique (p. 267)

1 98 W

2 **a** 120 J **b** 15 W

3 30 m s^{-1}

4 60 kW

5 **a** 240 N **b** 240 N

6 **a** 225 J **b** 22.5 W

7 **a** $R = 40v$ **b** 43.3 m s^{-1}

8 **a**

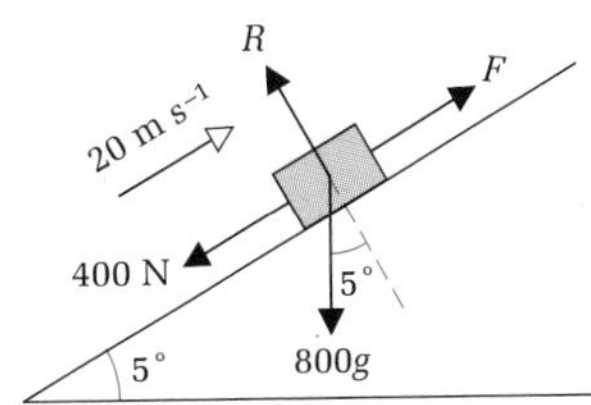

b 21.7 kW

9 **a** 1800 N **b** $R = 36v$ **c** 47.7 m s^{-1}

10.4 Contextual (p. 268)

1 84.2 m s^{-1}

2 **a** 1270 N **b** $R = 28.9v$

3 0.245 W

4 2.60 m s^{-1}. Resistance forces are assumed negligible.

5 **a** 148 J **b** 14.8 W

6 **a** $R = 0.357v^2$ **b** 1.94 m s^{-2}

Consolidation A (p. 269)

1 433 J

2 **a** 16 J **b** 4 m s^{-1}

3 **a** 23.4 m s^{-1} **b** 32.1 m s^{-1}
c The model seems to be reasonable.

4 **a** 60 N **b** 8°

Consolidation B (p. 269)

1 **a** 61 200 J
b 172 000 J
c 111 000 J

2 **a** 75 kW **b** 3500 N

3 **a i** 13 m s^{-1} **ii** 8.45 m **iii** 1690 J
b 35 m s^{-1}, 44 100 kW

4 **a** 30 N **b** 208 W **c** 16.9 **d** 168 W

11 Hooke's Law and Elasticity

Review (p. 272)

1 **a** 0.72, 2.78 (2 d.p.)
b −0.28, 2.50 (2 d.p.)

2 **a** 2 **b** 27 **c** $\frac{3}{2}x^2 + 2x + c$
d $7x - \frac{9}{2}x^2 + c$

3 **a** 6.875 m s^{-2} to left
b 28.5 m s^{-2}, upwards

4 a 5.26 N
b 1.58 N
c 4.05 m s^{-2}

5 a 10 m b 19.8 m s^{-1}

6 8.01 m s^{-1}

11.1 Technique (p. 277)

1 19.2 N

2 162 N

3 0.36 m

4 75 mm

5 12 N

6 1.2 m

7 8 N, thrust

8 a 190 N m^{-1} b 95 N

11.1 Contextual (p. 277)

1 4 m

2 1.6 kN

3 560 N

4 a 750 N m^{-1} b 0.96 m

11.2 Technique (p. 282)

1 45 N

2 58.8%

3 a 13.$\dot{3}$ N b 58° (nearest °)

4 a i (19.2d – 24) N
ii (33.6 – 19.2d) N
b 1.61 m

5 a 39.2 N b 26.9 cm

11.2 Contextual (p. 283)

1 11.2 kN

2 a 2.45 cm b 6.04 N

3 a i 180 N ii 900 N
b 17.5 cm

4 a 24 N b 3.92 kg

11.3 Technique (p. 287)

1 8 m s^{-2}

2 a 2.2 m s^{-2} b –3.8 m s^{-2}

3 a 9.8 m s^{-2}
b 0.69 m s^{-2} (2 d.p.)
c – 4.78 m s^{-2} (2 d.p.)

4 a 5 m s^{-2} b 25 cm

5 5.8 m s^{-2}, upwards

11.3 Contextual (p. 288)

1 7.2 m s^{-2}

2 a 2.2 m s^{-2} b –3.8 m s^{-2}

3 a 3.2 m s^{-2} b 1.9 cm (2 s.f.)

4 59 m s^{-2} (2 s.f.) Assume that there is no air resistance.

11.4 Technique (p. 292)

1 9 J

2 140 N

3 a 0.4 m b 2 m

4 0.3 m or 30 cm

5 6 J

6 12.8 J

11.4 Contextual (p. 292)

1 15 J

2 0.002 25 J

3 80 N

4 12 cm

11.5 Technique (p. 298)

1 0.735 m s^{-1}

2 2.71 m s^{-1}

3 4.12 m

4 1.15 m s^{-1}

5 4.47 m s^{-1}

6 a 7.29 m s^{-1} b 6.60 m s^{-1}

7 a 3.19 m s^{-1} b 0.980 m

8 a $28x^2 - 5.88x - 2.94 = 0$ (or alternatives)
b 0.946 m

9 a 1.70 N
b $20x^2 - 8.103x - 8.103 = 0$ (3 d.p.) (or alternatives)
c 1.87 m

11.5 Contextual (p. 300)

1 12.8 cm

2 a 5.33 m s^{-1} b 3.89 m s^{-1}

3 a 49.0 m b 49.8 m

4 a 59.0 cm b 1.47 m s^{-1}

5 a 18.2 m s^{-1} (smaller) b 27.5 m (greater)

Consolidation A (p. 301)

1 0.368 m

2 a 0.8 m b $T_{AB} = (98x - 49)$ N; $T_{BC} = (196 - 98x)$ N
c AB 39.7 J; BC 17.6 J d 0.808 m s^{-1}

3 **a** 300 N **b** 720 N **c** 34.6 m s^{-1}

4 **b** 0.12 J **c** 1.10 m s^{-1}
d $a = 0.25$, greatest tension = 4 N.

5 85 N m^{-1}, 23.7 m s^{-1}

Consolidation B (p. 303)

1 1.57 m s^{-1}

2 **a** $T_1 = 9.4$ N (1 d.p.); $T_2 = 3.9$ N (1 d.p.)
b 25.5 cm (1 d.p.)

3 Loss in PE = 12.3 J,
Gain EPE = 0.0625λ J, $\lambda = 196$ N

4 **a** $320g$ N **b ii** 15 **iii** $\frac{49}{15}g$

5 **a** $\frac{mg}{k}$ **b** $mgl_0 + \frac{(mg)^2}{k}$ **c** $\frac{(mg)^2}{2k}$
d The system does not move freely – work is done against the motion by an external force moving the block gently towards the pulley.
e acceleration = $\frac{mg}{M}$

12 Collisions

Review (p. 306)

1 **a** 39.4 N **b** 9.7 m s^{-1} **c** 1.30 m s^{-2}

2 **a i** $\mathbf{i} + 3\mathbf{j}$ **ii** $5\mathbf{i} - 7\mathbf{j}$
iii $15\mathbf{i} - 10\mathbf{j}$ **iv** $-6\mathbf{i} + 15\mathbf{j}$
b $4\mathbf{i} + 8\mathbf{j}$ **c** $35\mathbf{i} - 5\mathbf{j}$

3 **a** 6 J **b** 66.4 kJ **c** 0.25 J

4 **a** 4700 J **b** 22.3 J

5 **a** $u = 3$, $v = 3.5$ **b** $u = 0$, $v = 4$

12.1 Technique (p. 309)

1 **a** $(10\mathbf{i} - 20\mathbf{j})$ N s
b $(-8.45\mathbf{i} - 12.35\mathbf{j})$ N s
c $(2336\mathbf{i} - 2592\mathbf{j})$ N s

2 **a** 12 N s **b** 12 250 N s **c** 0.1 N s

3 **a** 60 m s^{-1} **b** 0.3 kg **c** 3.2 m s^{-1}

4 **a** 50.4 m s^{-1}
b 346.2° anticlockwise from **i**
c 3280 N s

5 **a** $(-0.35\mathbf{i} + 0.84\mathbf{j})$ N s
b 0.91 N s
c 112.6° anticlockwise from **i**

6 **a** 6.26 m s^{-1} **b** 25.0 N s **c** 30.7 N s

12.1 Contextual (p. 310)

1 **a** $(0.04\mathbf{i} + 0.03\mathbf{j})$ N s **b** $(-0.15\mathbf{i} - 0.25\mathbf{j})$ N s
c $(0.6\mathbf{i} - 0.32\mathbf{j})$ N s

2 **a** 200 N s **b** 696 N s

3 **a** 1.08 m s^{-1} **b** 236.3° **c** 7.57×10^{-5} N s

4 **a** $(56.6\mathbf{i} - 56.6\mathbf{j})$ m s^{-1}
b $(90\,500\mathbf{i} - 90\,500\mathbf{j})$ N s
c 128 000 N s

5 **a** 14 m s^{-1} **b** 1120 N s

6 0.15 m s^{-1}

12.2 Technique (p. 314)

1 **a** $(18\mathbf{i} - 9\mathbf{j})$ N s **b** 101 N

2 $\mathbf{v} = (3\mathbf{i} - 1.4\mathbf{j})$ m s^{-1}

3 **a** 9 N s **b** 30 N

4 **a** $2mu$ (in opposite direction to initial velocity)
b 0.25 s (assuming SI units)

5 $1\frac{2}{3}$ kg

6 $a = 0.8$, $b = 3.2$

7 $\mathbf{F} = -9\mathbf{i}$ N

8 **a** $(-0.96\mathbf{i} + 0.28\mathbf{j})$ N s **b** 0.4 s

9 **a** $20mu$
b New speed is u; direction reversed.

10 2 m s^{-1}

12.2 Contextual (p. 315)

1 4 N s; no loss of speed due to air resistance, racquet is perpendicular to direction of motion of the ball.

2 4500 N

3 **a** 4120 N **b** 104.0°

4 $(0.62\mathbf{i} - 0.25\mathbf{j})$ m s^{-1}

12.3 Technique (p. 321)

1 1.5 m s^{-1}

2 1.2 m s^{-1}

3 **a** 0.125 m s^{-1}; reverse direction **b** 0.5 N s

4 $2.4u$ m s^{-1}

5 **a** 2.9 m s^{-1} **b** 0.945 J

6 **a** 1.8 m s^{-1} **b** 0.9 J

7 $v = 4$

8 **a** 2.5 m s^{-1} **b** 2.25 m s^{-1} **c** 2.53 J

9 **a** $4u$

12.3 Contextual (p. 322)

1 **a** 1.35 m s^{-1} **b** 28.35 J

2 **a** 3.13 m s^{-1} **b** 2.09 m s^{-1} **c** 0.209 N s

12.4 Technique (p. 327)

1 **a** 0.9 **b** 0.62

2 **a** 0.75 **b** 1.95 m s^{-1}

3 2.73 m s^{-1}

4 $2.23\,\text{m}\,\text{s}^{-1}$

5 **a** $0.2\,\text{m}\,\text{s}^{-1}$, $0.4\,\text{m}\,\text{s}^{-1}$ **b** $\frac{2}{13}$

6 **a** $4u - 3v = 3.9$ and $4u + 10v = 7.8$ or equivalent.
b $u = 1.2\,\text{m}\,\text{s}^{-1}$, $v = 0.3\,\text{m}\,\text{s}^{-1}$

7 **a** $3.75\,\text{m}\,\text{s}^{-1}$

12.4 Contextual (p. 328)

1 **a** Perfect elastic collision; no loss of speed.
b No! Superballs come close.
c Bean bag, snooker ball, tennis ball, beach ball.

2 **a** Yes. Possibly different frictional forces at wheels.
b 0.23
c Model overlooks friction; not smooth rolling.

3 Tennis ball: $1.5\,\text{m}\,\text{s}^{-1}$, reverse direction.
Cricket ball: $0.3\,\text{m}\,\text{s}^{-1}$, same direction.

Consolidation A (p. 329)

1 **a** $4\,\text{m}\,\text{s}^{-1}$ **b** 6 J

2 **a** **i** $\frac{1}{3}u$ **ii** $2mu$ **iii** $2mu$ towards A.
b **ii** $3mu$

3 **a** $v = 200.1\,\text{m}\,\text{s}^{-1}$ **b** 12 kJ

4 **c** $\frac{2}{3}mu(1 + e)$ towards Q.

Consolidation B (p. 330)

1 **a** $4.90\,\text{m}\,\text{s}^{-1}$ **b** $14.7\,\text{m}\,\text{s}^{-1}$

2 $\frac{4}{5}$

3 **a** $\frac{1}{2}\,\text{m}\,\text{s}^{-1}$ **b** 19.5 kJ

4 **a** $\frac{8}{15}u$ **b** $\frac{3}{4}\pi l$
c Assumptions: no friction ($\therefore$ no loss of speed), rebound assumed instantaneous

5 **a** $\frac{u}{5}(4 - e)$ **b** $\frac{2mu^2}{25}(9 + 8e - e^2)$
c Maximum $\frac{4}{5}u$, minimum $\frac{3}{5}u$.

13 Moments

Review (p. 332)

1 **a** $4\mathbf{i} - 2\mathbf{j}$ **b** $23\mathbf{i} - 44\mathbf{j}$

2 **a** Static equilibrium – no resultant force, at rest.
Dynamic equilibrium – no resultant force, moving with constant velocity.
b **i** Yes, resultant force is zero
ii No, resultant force of 7 N upwards.

3 **a** $5\sqrt{5}$ N or 11.2 N at 63.4° from 5 N force in an anticlockwise direction.
b 5.18 N at 75° from horizontal 10 N force in a clockwise direction.

13.1 Technique (p. 336)

1 **a** 35 N m, clockwise
b 8 N m, clockwise
c 0 N m
d 0.85 N m, anticlockwise.

2 60 N m, anticlockwise.

3 42 N m, clockwise.

4 0 N m

5 64 N m, anticlockwise.

13.1 Contextual (p. 336)

1 2.8 N m

2 50 N

3 588 N m

4 1.25 m

13.2 Technique (p. 341)

1 **a** $20\sqrt{3}$ N m, anticlockwise
b 240 N m, clockwise
c $200\sqrt{2}$ N m, anticlockwise
d 60 N m, anticlockwise.

2 **a** $80\sqrt{3}$ N m, anticlockwise
b 0 N m
c 15 N m, clockwise
d $6\sqrt{2}$ N m, clockwise.

3 15.3 N m, clockwise.

4 The force needs to be resolved; 6.17 N m, clockwise.

13.2 Contextual (p. 342)

1 **a** 200 N m, clockwise **b** 0 N m
c 200 N m, anticlockwise

13.3 Technique (p. 347)

1 **a** 49 N, 147 N **b** 171 N, 229 N

2 **a** 55 N, 35 N **b** 24 N, 96 N

3 0 m, 220 N

4 8.6°

5 8.8 m

6 156.8 N, 137.2 N

7 **a** 1 kg **b** $1\frac{1}{3}$ kg

8 **a** 84 N **b** 2.29 m from the 63 N support.

9 **a** Yes **b** No, overall moment.

13.3 Contextual (p. 348)

1 555 N, 474 N

2 **a** 42 N **b** 2.29 m, 2.29 m from A.

13.4 Technique (p. 353)

1. a Couple, 32 N m clockwise
   b Couple, 25 N m clockwise
   c Couple, 6 N m clockwise.
   d Couple, 38 N m clockwise.
2. 2.4 N m, direction DCBA.
3. 13 N m, anticlockwise.
4. $4\sqrt{2}$ N at 45° from DC clockwise; 4.5 N m clockwise.

Consolidation A (p. 354)

1. $P = 310$ N, $Q = 230$ N
2. 5.6 m
3. a 3 N, 23 N b 10 N
4. a 14 N, 21.8° measured anticlockwise from CB.
   b 2.52 cm

Consolidation B (p. 355)

1. a The plank will not bend and the thickness of the plank can be neglected.
   b 2352 N c 2058 N
2. 8.38 N
3. 1274 N, 686 N. The weight of the wheelbarrow, its angle of inclination, its dimensions and its centre of gravity.

14 Centre of Mass

Review (p. 357)

1. 10 000 N m, anticlockwise
2. a $-4\mathbf{i} - \mathbf{j}$ b $10\mathbf{i} - 11\mathbf{j}$
3. a 6280 cm^3 b 1.05 m^3 c 16.8 m^3
4. a $S = r\theta, A = \frac{1}{2}r^2\theta$, where θ is in radians
   b 10.5 cm c 1.05 m^2
5. a 64 b 1.86 c 1 d 2

14.1 Technique (p. 364)

1. a (4.4, 3.8) b (0, −0.8)
2. a (1, 1.5) b (0, 0.5)
3. a (1.8, 2.7) b (0.3, −1.2) c (−0.2, 0.4)
   d $\left(\frac{m_1x_1 + m_2x_2 + m_3x_3 + m_4x_4}{m_1 + m_2 + m_3 + m_4}, \frac{m_1y_1 + m_2y_2 + m_3y_3 + m_4y_4}{m_1 + m_2 + m_3 + m_4}\right)$

   or $\left(\frac{\sum_1^4 m_ix_i}{\sum_1^4 m_i}, \frac{\sum_1^4 m_iy_i}{\sum_1^4 m_i}\right)$
4. a 3**j** b **i**
5. (−3, 3.5)
6. a 14 kg b 1.47 m
7. (2.6, −4)

14.1 Contextual (p. 365)

1. a 0.45 m from 70 kg mass.
   b 0.5 m from 70 kg mass.
2. 14 cm rod, 6.67 g;
   22 cm rod, 10 g.

14.2 Technique (p. 372)

1. a (4, 5) b $(3\frac{2}{3}, 2)$
   c (2.8, 4.6) d (6.4, 3.8)
2. a 8.35 cm above base on axis of symmetry
   b 1.1 cm above base on axis of symmetry.
3. a (4.07, 4.35) b (3, 3.13)
   c 6.59 m from open end
   d 4.23 cm from open end.

14.2 Contextual (p. 373)

1. 3.5 mm up from AB,
   3.5 mm across from AH.
2. 2.68 cm from open end.

14.3 Technique (p. 375)

1. a 18.4° b 14.0° c 27.2°

14.3 Contextual (p. 375)

1. 33.7°
2. 12.6°

14.4 Technique (p. 382)

1. (2, 6)
2. (1.6, 2.29)
3. (0.75, 1.8)
4. (2.5, 0)
5. (1.33, 0)
6. a (3.21, 5.31) Hint: For each rectangle the centre of mass is $\frac{y}{2}$ from x-axis.
   b (3.39, 0)
8. $\frac{2r}{\pi}$
9. $\frac{3}{4}h$ from vertex or $\frac{1}{4}$h from base.
11. $\frac{3}{8}R$

14.5 Technique (p. 387)

1. a 7.78 cm above straight rod
   b 3.95 cm above straight rod.

2 **a** 9.07 cm from bottom of shape
b $\frac{12}{\pi}$ cm from vertex.

3 **a** 29.375 cm from open end
b 0.625 cm above joined faces.

14.5 Contextual (p. 388)

1 2.29 cm above join.

2 28.0 cm from the vertex of the cone.

14.6 Technique (p. 392)

1 **a** Slide **b** Topple

2 **a** 49 N **b** 98μ N

3 Topples at 31.0°

4 **a i** 10.3 cm from AD horizontally and 3.67 cm from DC vertically
ii Topples
b i 8 cm from AB horizontally and 17.5 cm from BC vertically
ii Does not topple (just about to topple)

Consolidation A (p. 393)

1 36.9°

2 **a** 18° **b** $m = \frac{1}{4}M$

3 $\frac{3}{4}h$

4 **a** 3 cm **c** $m = \frac{1}{8}M$

5 **b** 32.0°

Consolidation B (p. 394)

1 **b** $\frac{\sqrt{5}}{3}a$

2 **b** 50°

3 5.87 cm

4 **a** 3.07 m, 0.5 m **b** 3.5 kg

5 **a** Slides, angle of friction is less than the angle for toppling to occur.
b Topples, angle for toppling is exceeded and friction is large enough to prevent sliding.

15 Equilibrium of a Rigid Body

Review (p. 397)

1 **a** $120g$ N m, clockwise
b $25\sqrt{3}$ N m, anticlockwise
c $4\sqrt{3}(7 - x)$ N m, anticlockwise

2 **a i** 8 N **ii** 20 N **iii** 20 N
b case **ii**

3 **a** **b**

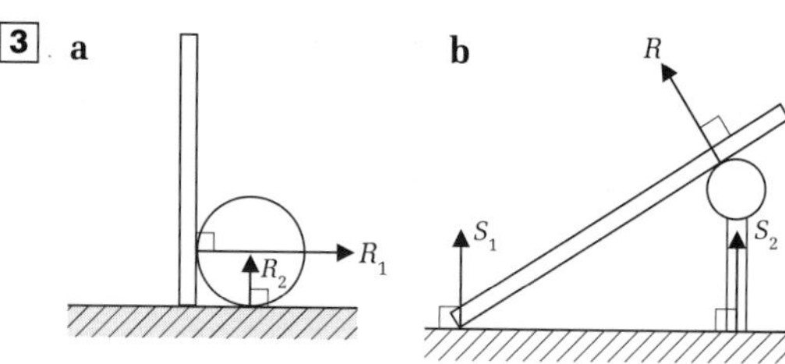

c

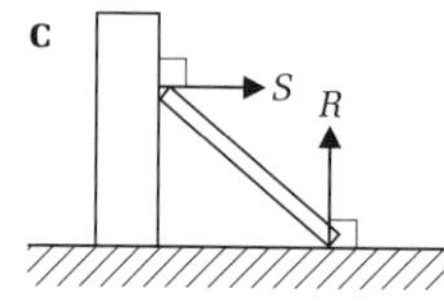

4 **a** $(2\frac{1}{3}, 1)$ **b** $(4\frac{1}{2}, 1)$

15.1 Technique (p. 403)

1 **a i** 98 N
ii 84.9 N, 49 N
iii 98 N at 30° from AB anticlockwise.
b i 84.9 N
ii 42.4 N, 24.5 N
iii 49 N at 30° from AB clockwise.

2 **a i** 14.6 N
ii 13.7 N, 15 N
iii 20.3 N at 27.5° from ED clockwise.
b i 123 N
ii 79.1 N, 24.3 N
iii 82.8 N at 47.1° from ED anticlockwise.

3 **a i** 25.8° **ii** 86.2 N
b 11.8° **c** 9.80 kg

4 **a i** 33.6 N, $R = 80$ N, $F_r = 33.6$ N
ii 14.4 N, $R = 50$ N, $F_r = 14.4$ N
iii 27.3 N, $R = 150$ N, $F_r = 27.3$ N
b i 51.3° **ii** 45° **iii** 32.0°

5 **a** Perpendicular to the rod.
b i 42.0 N **ii** 71.0 N
iii 32.2 N **iv** 0.453

6 29.4°

15.1 Contextual (p. 405)

1 **a** 10 400 N **b** 9310 N
c 1810 N **d** 0.195

2 Weight = 147 N, $S_{\text{wall}} = 26.8$ N, $F_r = 26.8$ N, $R = 147$ N.

3 2.20 m from the base of the ladder.

4 23.0°

15.2 Technique (p. 408)

1 **a i** 78.4 N, at 30° from AB anticlockwise
ii 78.4 N
b i 3.20 N, at 130° from AB anticlockwise
ii 3.20 N

[2] a 10.3° from vertical b 99.6 N c 17.8 N

[3] a 16.1° b 0.289 c $\frac{\sqrt{39}mg}{6}$ or 1.04 mg

15.3 Technique (p. 413)

[1] a 1000 N, 1000 N
b $\frac{2000\sqrt{3}}{3}$ N (thrust), $\frac{2000\sqrt{3}}{3}$ N (thrust), $\frac{1000\sqrt{3}}{3}$ N (tension)

[2] a 30 kN, 30 kN
b $T_{AB} = T_{CD} = 34.6$ kN (thrust)
$T_{AE} = T_{DE} = 17.3$ kN (tension)
$T_{CE} = T_{BE} = 0$ kN
$T_{BC} = 17.3$ kN (thrust)

[3] a 50 N b 71.6°
c $T_{BC} = 158$ N (tension)
$T_{AB} = 50$ N (thrust)
$T_{AD} = 0$ N
$T_{CD} = 50$ N (tension)
$T_{AC} = 150$ N (thrust)
d 158 N, 71.6° from AB clockwise. Rods in tension: CD and BC. Rods that could be replaced by strings are CD and BC. AD can be removed.

[4] $T_{DB} = 0$ N, $T_{AB} = 1150$ N,
$T_{BC} = 1150$ N, $T_{AD} = 577$ N
tension: AB, BC

15.3 Contextual (p. 414)

[1] a $T_{AB} = T_{BC} = T_{AD} = T_{DC} = 1150$ N
$T_{AC} = 1150$ N
b $T_{AB} = T_{BC} = T_{AD} = T_{DC} = 1560$ N
$T_{AC} = 2380$ N
c $T_{AB} = T_{BC} = T_{AD} = T_{DC} = 5760$ N
$T_{AC} = 11\,300$ N
Assumptions: smooth pin-joints, jack is in equilibrium, light rods.

[2] a 20 kN
b $T_{AB} = 46.7$ kN, $T_{AF} = 35.8$ kN
$T_{BF} = 46.7$ kN, $T_{BC} = 71.5$ kN
$T_{CE} = 31.1$ kN, $T_{DC} = 23.8$ kN
$T_{DE} = 31.1$ kN, $T_{FE} = 47.7$ kN
$T_{FC} = 31.1$ kN
Rods in compression: AF, BF, DE, FE, FC.

[3] a 500 N, 500 N
b $T_{DE} = T_{FG} = 0$ N
$T_{AC} = 1000$ N (thrust)
$T_{AB} = 500\sqrt{3}$ N (tension)
$T_{BC} = 1000$ N (thrust)

Consolidation A (p. 415)

[1] a i

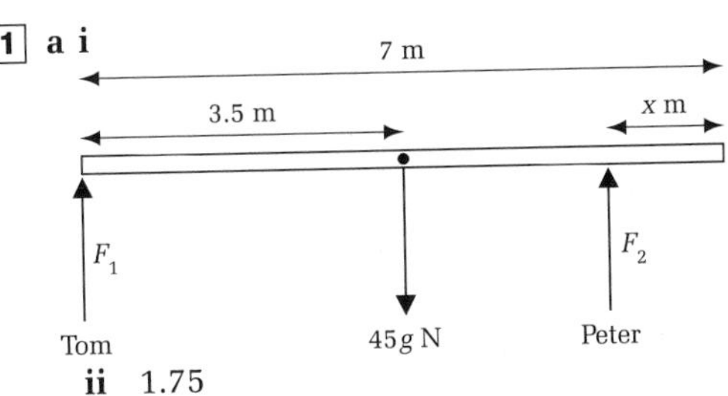

ii 1.75

b The ladder would topple as Tom and Peter would both be on the same side of the centre of mass.

[2] a

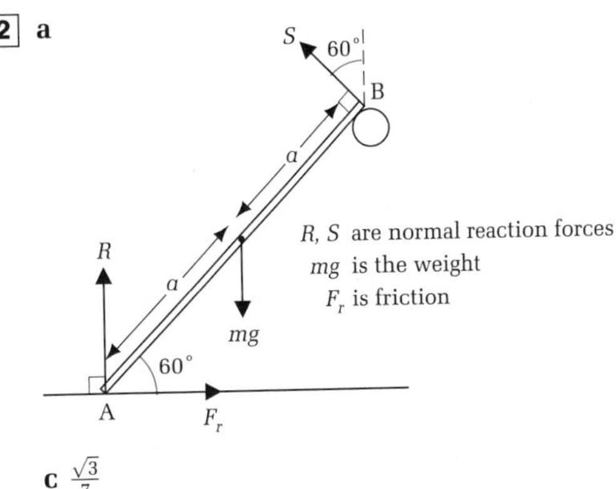

c $\frac{\sqrt{3}}{7}$

[3] a Treating the framework as whole, there are no horizontal forces. Therefore Q must be vertical. (The only non-vertical forces are internal). $P = 1$ N, $Q = 0.5$ N
b AB or BC
c 1.2 N in BC, 1.3 N in DC and AB, 0.5 N in BD.

Consolidation B (p. 416)

[1] a 64 N and 220 N b 300 N

[3] a Neither rod has an upwards or downwards action on the other
b

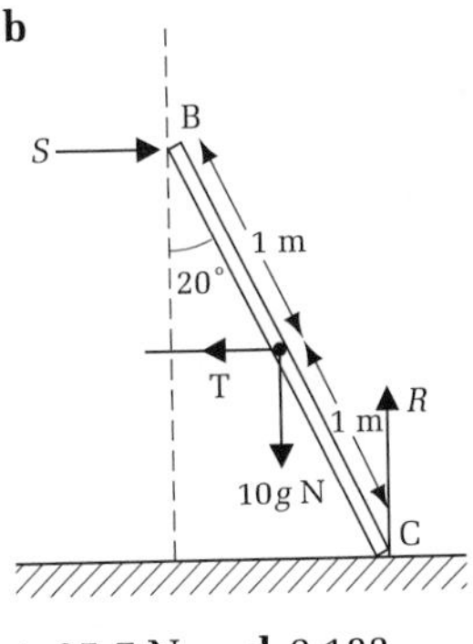

c 35.7 N d 0.182

16 Projectiles

Review (p. 418)

[1] a 0, 4 b 1, 4 c 0.996, 6.15

[2] a 4.08 s b 3 m s^{-2} c 29.4 m s^{-1}

[3] a ↑ 6.84 m s^{-1} → 18.8 m s^{-1} b ↓ 9.06 m s^{-1} → 33.8 m s^{-1}

16.1 Technique (p. 422)

[1] a 15 m b 44.1 m

[2] a 2.02 s b 16.2 m c 19.8 m s^{-1}

3 **a** $1\,\text{m}\,\text{s}^{-1}$ **b** $30\,\text{m}\,\text{s}^{-1}$ **c** $\sqrt{901}\,\text{m}\,\text{s}^{-1}$

4 **a** 2.47 s **b** $2.42\,\text{m}\,\text{s}^{-1}$
c $24.4\,\text{m}\,\text{s}^{-1}$ at 84.3° below the horizontal

5 **a** $\frac{6U}{g}$ **b** $\frac{12U^2}{g}$ **c** $\frac{18U^2}{g}$ **d** $2U\sqrt{10}$

6 **a** 2.04 s **b** 20.4 m
c $10\sqrt{5}\,\text{m}\,\text{s}^{-1}$ **d** 63.4°

16.1 Contextual (p. 423)

1 **a** 2.86 s **b** 42.9 m **c** $31.8\,\text{m}\,\text{s}^{-1}$
Air resistance is neglected, car is treated as a particle and so its size is neglected.

2 **a** 16 m **b** 78.4 m
c $39.4\,\text{m}\,\text{s}^{-1}$ at 84.2° to the horizontal.

3 **a** $1.5\,\text{m}\,\text{s}^{-1}$ **b** 81.5°

4 **a** $2.12\,\text{m}\,\text{s}^{-1}$ **b** $139\,\text{m}\,\text{s}^{-1}$
c 89.1° to the horizontal

16.2 Technique (p. 428)

1 **a** 61.2 m **b** 3.53 s **c** 7.07 s **d** 141 m

2 **a** 4.41 s **b** 124 m **c** $43.4\,\text{m}\,\text{s}^{-1}$

3 **a** 20.7 m **b** $29.7\,\text{m}\,\text{s}^{-1}$ at 73.1° to AB

4 $10\sqrt{5}\,\text{m}\,\text{s}^{-1}$

5 **a** 8 s **b** 160 m

16.2 Contextual (p. 429)

1 **a** 19.0 m **b** 1.97 s **c** 45.2 m
d 3.94 s **e** 90.4 m
Particle model, the field is flat, the javelin starts at ground level.

2 **a** $8.90\,\text{m}\,\text{s}^{-1}$, **b** 0.908 s.
Her initial speed needs to be higher to overcome air resistance.

3 **a** 13.1 m **b** $26.0\,\text{m}\,\text{s}^{-1}$

4 **a** 5 s **b** 160 m

5 **a** $15.3\,\text{m}\,\text{s}^{-1}$ **b** 1.85 s

16.3 Technique (p. 436)

1 **a** **i** $T = \frac{2V\sin\alpha}{g}$
ii $R = \frac{V^2\sin(2\alpha)}{g}$
iii $R_{\text{max}} = \frac{V^2}{g}$ when $\alpha = 45°$
iv $H = \frac{V^2\sin^2\alpha}{2g}$ at $t = \frac{V\sin\alpha}{g}$

2 **a** $56.6\,\text{m}\,\text{s}^{-1}$ **b** 283 m

3 **a** 45° **b** $99.0\,\text{m}\,\text{s}^{-1}$

4 9.5° or 80.5°

5 $8.48\,\text{m}\,\text{s}^{-1}$

6 44.4°

16.3 Contextual (p. 437)

1 **a** $H = h + \frac{U^2\sin^2\alpha}{2g}$ at $T = \frac{U\sin\alpha}{g}$
b **i** 68.0° **ii** 2.84 s

2 **a** $\frac{2V\sin\alpha}{g}$
Neglect air resistance, ground is level, ball is hit at ground level.

3 **b** 39.2°, 74.2°

Consolidation A (p. 438)

1 **a** No air resistance, the ground is level.
b 103 m
c The answer would be larger than the answer in **b**.

2 **a** 2.45 m **b** 59.2°, 81.0°
c No air resistance, the size of the ball is neglected.

3 **a** Assumptions: Level ground, starts at ground level and no air resistance.
b 18.7 m **c** 16.9 m
Not a good prediction because the release height is significant.

Consolidation B (p. 438)

1 **b** 4 s **c** 25

2 **a** $1\frac{2}{3}$ s
b $0.5 + 9t - 4.9t^2$; 1.89 m so the ball hits the wall

3 **a** $R = \frac{V^2\sin 2\alpha}{g}$; $R_{\text{max}} = \frac{V^2}{g}$
b 25.9°, 69.8° **c** $37.4\,\text{m}\,\text{s}^{-1}$

17 Circular Motion

Review (p. 442)

1 $\tan\theta = \frac{\sin\theta}{\cos\theta}$

2 **a** $\text{KE} = \frac{1}{2}mv^2$; $\text{PE} = mgh$
b **i** 0.1568 J
ii $7.67\,\text{m}\,\text{s}^{-1}$

3 **a** → 153 N
↑ 129 N
b ← $R\sin 50°$
↑ $R\cos 50°$

4 $R\sin\theta = ma$

17.1 Technique (p. 445)

1 **a** $\frac{5\pi}{6}$ **b** $\frac{2\pi}{3}$ **c** $\frac{\pi}{3}$ **d** $\frac{4\pi}{9}$ **e** $\frac{2\pi}{5}$ **f** $\frac{3\pi}{2}$
g $\frac{\pi}{2}$ **h** π **i** 2π **j** 4π **k** 1.30^c **l** 1.00^c

2 **a** 720° **b** 1440° **c** 30° **d** 9° **e** 150°
f 135° **g** 45° **h** 60° **i** 286.5° **j** 171.9°
k 180° **l** 200.5°

17.2 Technique (p. 448)

1 $209\,\text{rad}\,\text{s}^{-1}$

2 $160\,\text{m}\,\text{s}^{-1}$

3 $0.377\,\text{m}\,\text{s}^{-1}$

4 **a** $7.5\,\text{rad}\,\text{s}^{-1}$ **b** 0.838 s

5 **a** $0.1\,\text{rad}\,\text{s}^{-1}$ **b** 0.955 rpm; 62.8 s

17.2 Contextual (p. 448)

1 $10\,\text{m}\,\text{s}^{-1}$

2 **a** $60\pi\,\text{rad}\,\text{s}^{-1}$ **b** $90\pi\,\text{m}\,\text{s}^{-1}$

3 **a** **i** $2.5\,\text{rad}\,\text{s}^{-1}$ **ii** 23.9 rpm
b 25.1 s

17.3 Technique (p. 453)

1 **a** $50\,\text{m}\,\text{s}^{-2}$ towards the centre of the circle.
b 100 N

2 $790\,\text{m}\,\text{s}^{-2}$. Angular speed is constant.

3 10.7 m

4 **a** $2.12\,\text{m}\,\text{s}^{-1}$ **b** $1.41\,\text{rad}\,\text{s}^{-1}$

5 **a** 79.0 N **b** 126 N

6 **a** 39.2 N **b** $4.67\,\text{rad}\,\text{s}^{-1}$

7 **a** 1 N **b** 1.96 N **c** 0.510

8 $\frac{2g}{\omega^2}$

17.3 Contextual (p. 454)

1 **a** $0.8\,\text{m}\,\text{s}^{-2}$ **b** 16 kN

2 **a** 7840 N **b** $7.84\,\text{m}\,\text{s}^{-2}$ **c** $19.8\,\text{m}\,\text{s}^{-1}$

3 $42.4\,\text{m}\,\text{s}^{-1}$

4 9.14 m

17.4 Technique (p. 459)

1 **a** 17.1 cm **b** 63.9 N **c** $3.64\,\text{m}\,\text{s}^{-2}$
d $4.61\,\text{rad}\,\text{s}^{-1}$ **e** 1.36 s

2 **a** 5 cm **b** 106 N **c** $0.452\,\text{m}\,\text{s}^{-1}$

3 **a** $0.8\sin\theta$ **b** 256 N, 79.0°

4 53.5°, 33.6 N

17.4 Contextual (p. 460)

1 **a** $6\pi\,\text{rad}\,\text{s}^{-1}$ **b** 86.8°, 14.2 N

2 **a** 905 N **b** 12.5 m **c** $8.41\,\text{m}\,\text{s}^{-1}$

17.5 Contextual (p. 464)

1 $13.4\,\text{m}\,\text{s}^{-1}$

2 262 m

3 **a**

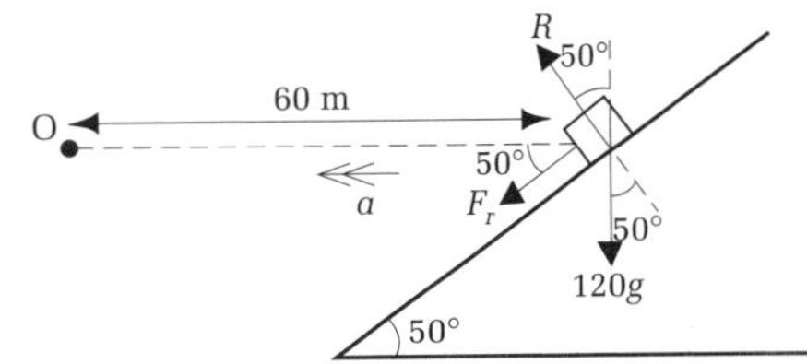

b $159\,\text{m}\,\text{s}^{-1}$

c

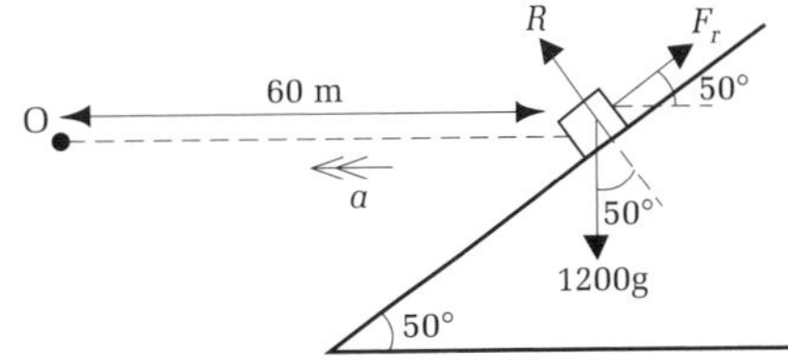

d $10.9\,\text{m}\,\text{s}^{-1}$

4 44.4°

5 69.8°, 5680 kN

17.6 Technique (p. 468)

1 $R = 0$
a 48.2° **b** **i** 46.9° **ii** 42.7°

2 **a** 37.3° **b** $u \geq 7\,\text{m}\,\text{s}^{-1}$

3 **a** **i** $1.98\,\text{m}\,\text{s}^{-1}$
ii $3.83\,\text{m}\,\text{s}^{-1}$
iii $5.42\,\text{m}\,\text{s}^{-1}$
b Maximum tension occurs at the bottom of the circle.
i $12.4m$ N
ii $19.6m$ N
iii $29.4m$ N

4 $\cos\alpha = \frac{2}{3}, \frac{\sqrt{5}}{3}g$

5 $\sqrt{5ga}$

17.6 Contextual (p. 469)

1 $4.95\,\text{m}\,\text{s}^{-1}$

2 48.2°

3 4.59 m

4 34.9° to the vertical, so the cyclist leaves the ramp. Particle model; no resistances.

Consolidation A (p. 470)

1 **a**

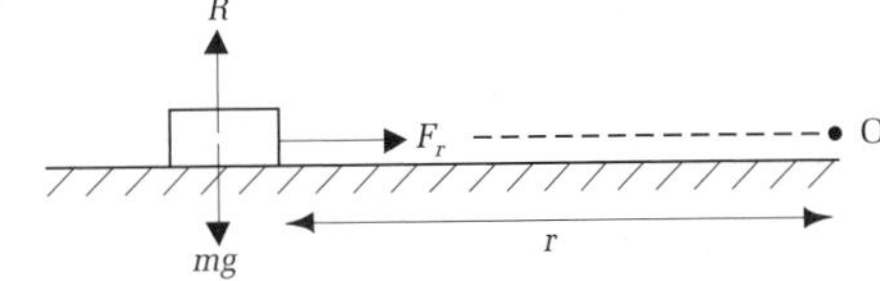

b 16 m

c 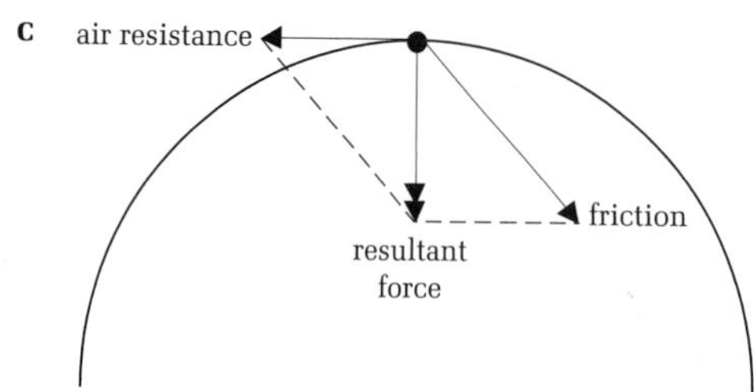

2 a 2.26 N b $1.30\,\mathrm{m\,s^{-1}}$

3 a 12.1°
b
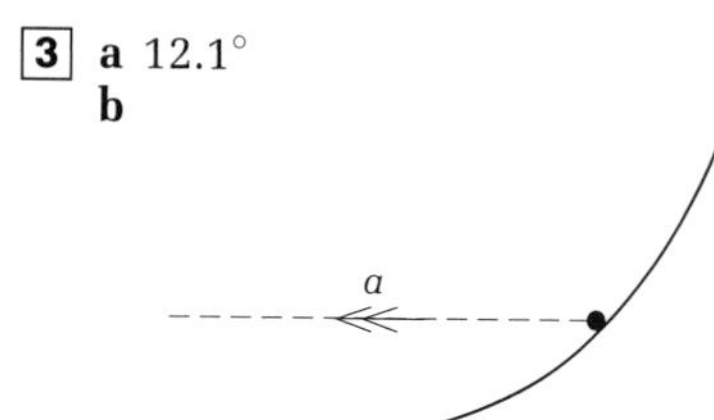

4 $mg(1 - 3\cos\theta)$, $\theta = 71°$

Consolidation B (p. 471)

1 a $125\,\mathrm{m\,s^{-2}}$
c
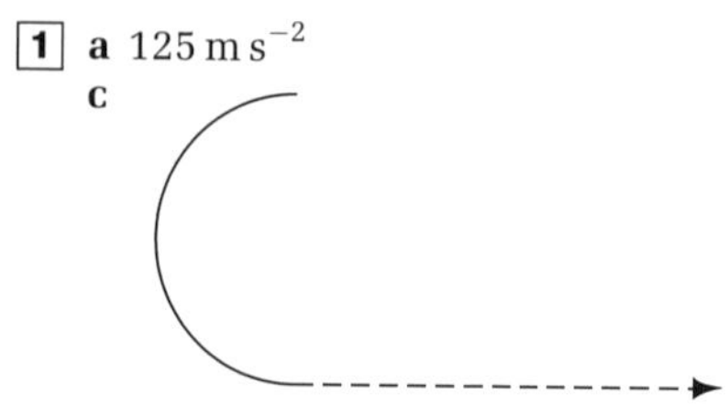

2 b 36.9°
c $T\cos\theta = 0.5g$. If $\theta = 90°$, then $\cos\theta = 0$, but $T \times 0 \neq 0.5g$.

3 a 1220 N c $15.3\,\mathrm{m\,s^{-1}}$; cyclist C.

4 a $gl(2\cos\theta - 1)$
c $2mg$, particle is at its lowest point on the circular arc.

18 Variable Acceleration

Review (p. 475)

1 a $\frac{dy}{dx} = 20x^3 - 15$
b $\frac{dy}{dx} = -\frac{14}{x^3}$
c $\frac{dy}{dx} = 15\cos 3x + 6\sin 3x$
d $\frac{dy}{dx} = 18e^{-9x}$

2 a $4x^3 - \frac{3}{2}x^4 + c$
b $3x - 5\ln|x| + c$
c $2\ln|2x + 3| + c$
d $-\ln|10 - 3x^2| + c$
e $2\sin 2x - \frac{7}{2}\cos 2x + c$
f $x^2 - 50e^{-0.1x} + 30x + c$

3
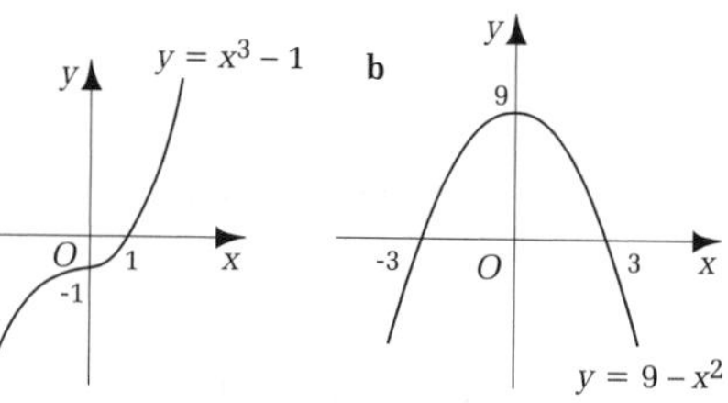

c
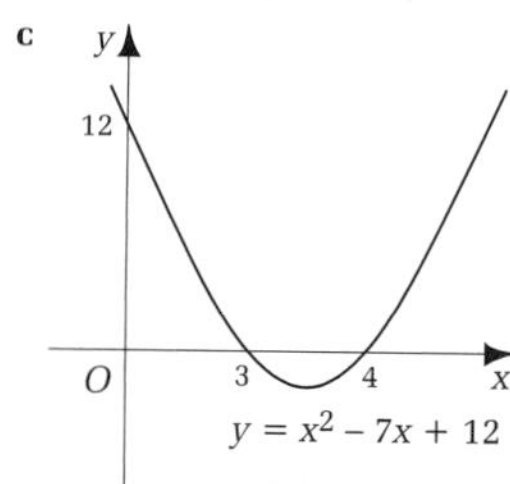

4 a $27.2\mathbf{i} + 51.2\mathbf{j}$ newtons
b $-19.2\mathbf{i} + 16.1\mathbf{j}\,\mathrm{m\,s^{-1}}$

5 a 26 newtons
b $13.0\,\mathrm{km\,h^{-1}}$ on bearing 122° (nearest °).

6 a 7 b −2, 3

7 a $y^2 = 2(x + 1)$ or $y = \pm\sqrt{2(x + 1)}$
b $y^2 = 4(x^2 + 4)$ or $y = \pm 2\sqrt{x^2 + 4}$
c $y = \frac{2}{10 - 2x - x^2}$
d $y = 5e^{2x}$

18.1 Technique (p. 480)

1 a $v = 5t^4 + 8t - 3$, $a = 20t^3 + 8$
b $v = 3t^{-2}$, $a = -6t^{-3}$
c $v = 14\cos 2t$, $a = -28\sin 2t$
d $v = 30e^{5t}$, $a = 150e^{5t}$

2 a 9 N towards O b 0.637 N towards O

3 a $v = 3t^2$
b
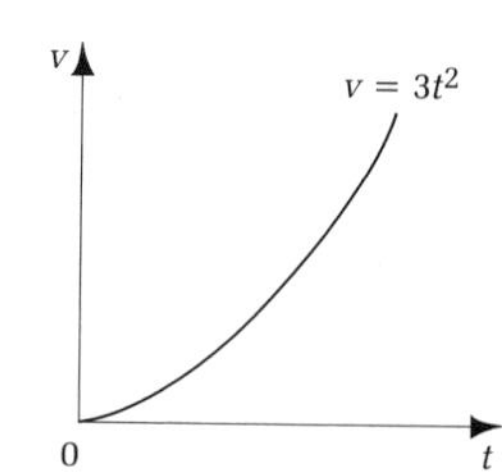

4 a $t = 2, 3$ b 1 m c 34 m

18.1 Contextual (p. 480)

1 a $\dot{x} = -6\sin 2t$, velocity;
$\ddot{x} = -12\cos 2t$, acceleration
b i 8 m, $0\,\mathrm{m\,s^{-1}}$
ii 3.75 m, $-5.46\,\mathrm{m\,s^{-1}}$
iii 3.04 m, $4.54\,\mathrm{m\,s^{-1}}$
c Maximum 8 m, minimum 2 m
d Maximum speed $6\,\mathrm{m\,s^{-1}}$, maximum acceleration $12\,\mathrm{m\,s^{-2}}$

2 **a** $v = 75 - 75e^{-t/10}$, $a = 7.5e^{-t/10}$
b $0\,\mathrm{m\,s^{-1}}$, $7.5\,\mathrm{m\,s^{-2}}$
c $v \to 75\,\mathrm{m\,s^{-1}}$, $a \to 0\,\mathrm{m\,s^{-2}}$
d The package starts from rest and accelerates (at a decreasing rate) to a final velocity of $75\,\mathrm{m\,s^{-1}}$.

18.2 Technique (p. 484)

1 **a** $v = 3t^3 - t$, $x = \frac{3}{4}t^4 - \frac{1}{2}t^2 + 2$

2 **a** $v = 10t^{\frac{3}{2}} + 2$, $x = 4t^{\frac{5}{2}} + 2t$
b $v = 8 - 6\cos(\frac{1}{2}t)$, $x = 8t - 12\sin(\frac{1}{2}t)$

3 $28\,\mathrm{m\,s^{-1}}$, 12 m

4 6 s

18.2 Contextual (p. 484)

1 **a** $42.5\,\mathrm{m\,s^{-1}}$
b $308\frac{1}{3}$ m, $30\frac{5}{6}\,\mathrm{m\,s^{-1}}$

2 $24.6\,\mathrm{m\,s^{-1}}$, 109 m

3 **a** $x = 100(1 - e^{-0.02t})$
b 230 s (nearest second)

18.3 Technique (p. 487)

1 **a** $\mathbf{v} = 3t^2\mathbf{i} + 6\mathbf{j} + 2t\mathbf{k}$, $\mathbf{a} = 6t\mathbf{i} + 2\mathbf{k}$
b $\mathbf{v} = 10\cos(5t)\,\mathbf{i} + 5\sin(5t)\,\mathbf{j} - 2e^{-2t}\mathbf{k}$,
$\mathbf{a} = -50\sin(5t)\,\mathbf{i} + 25\cos(5t)\,\mathbf{j} + 4e^{-2t}\mathbf{k}$

2 **a** $\mathbf{a} = (12\mathbf{i} + 4\mathbf{j})\,\mathrm{m\,s^{-2}}$, $\mathbf{v} = (12\mathbf{i} + 5\mathbf{j})\,\mathrm{m\,s^{-1}}$,
$\mathbf{r} = (10\mathbf{i} + \mathbf{j})$ m
b $13\,\mathrm{m\,s^{-1}}$ at $22.6°$ to $\mathbf{i}$

3 $39\,\mathrm{m\,s^{-1}}$, 380 J, $\mathbf{r} = (22\mathbf{i} - 2\mathbf{j} - 37\mathbf{k})$ m

4 **a** 5 s **b** $120\,\mathrm{m\,s^{-1}}$ **d** 50 N, 16° (nearest °)

5 **a** $\mathbf{r} = 2t\mathbf{i} + (4t^2 - 5)\mathbf{j}$ **b** $\frac{3\sqrt{2}}{4}$ s

18.3 Contextual (p. 488)

1 **a** $\mathbf{v} = 2t\mathbf{i} - 7\mathbf{j}\,\mathrm{m\,s^{-1}}$, $\mathbf{a} = 2\mathbf{i}\,\mathrm{m\,s^{-2}}$
b 32.2 m, 150° (nearest °)
c $10.6\,\mathrm{m\,s^{-1}}$, 131° (nearest °)

2 **a** $\mathbf{v} = -5t^2\mathbf{i} + \frac{4}{3}t^3\mathbf{j} + (18t - 3t^2)\mathbf{k}$
$\mathbf{r} = (15 - \frac{5}{3}t^3)\mathbf{i} + (\frac{1}{3}t^4 - 20)\mathbf{j} + (9t^2 - t^3)\mathbf{k}$
b 54 m, 62.2 m

3 **a** $\mathbf{r} = 2[1 - \cos(\frac{1}{2}t)]\mathbf{i} - \frac{1}{12}t\mathbf{j} + 1.5\mathbf{k}$
b 36 s **c** $0.76\,\mathrm{m\,s^{-1}}$ (2 s.f.)

4 **a** $\mathbf{v} = 2\cos(2t)\,\mathbf{i} - 2\sin(2t)\,\mathbf{j} - \frac{1}{2}t\mathbf{k}$
$\mathbf{a} = -4\sin(2t)\,\mathbf{i} - 4\cos(2t)\,\mathbf{j} - \frac{1}{2}\mathbf{k}$
$\mathbf{F} = -120\sin(2t)\,\mathbf{i} - 120\cos(2t)\,\mathbf{j} - 15\mathbf{k}$
c 195 J

5 **a** $24\sqrt{3}\mathbf{i} + (56 + 30t)\mathbf{j}$ N
b $2.75\,\mathrm{m\,s^{-1}}$ on a bearing of 017.6°

6 **a** $v = a\omega\cos(\omega t)\mathbf{i} - a\omega\sin(\omega t)\mathbf{j}$

18.4 Technique (p. 493)

1 **a** $v = 7e^{-0.5t}$, $2.58\,\mathrm{m\,s^{-1}}$
b 8.85 m

2 **a** $v = (3t + 1)^2$, $x = \frac{1}{9}(3t + 1)^3 - \frac{1}{9}$
b $100\,\mathrm{m\,s^{-1}}$, 111 m

3 **a** $v = \frac{15}{1+3t}$, $1.5\,\mathrm{m\,s^{-1}}$
b 11.5 m

4 **b** $1.38\,\mathrm{m\,s^{-1}}$
c 0.402 s
d $2.5\,\mathrm{m\,s^{-1}}$

18.4 Contextual (p. 493)

1 **b** 4.95 m s

2 **b** $x = 2.5(2t + e^{-2t} - 1)$
c **i** $4.32\,\mathrm{m\,s^{-1}}$, 2.84 m
ii 0.255 s
iii $5\,\mathrm{m\,s^{-1}}$

3 **b** $v = 20e^{-2t} + 5$, $6.00\,\mathrm{m\,s^{-1}}$
c $5\,\mathrm{m\,s^{-1}}$ **d** 30.0 m

18.5 Technique (p. 498)

1 **a** $v^2 = \frac{3}{4}(x^2 - 1)$
b **i** $3\sqrt{2}\,\mathrm{m\,s^{-1}}$
ii 7 m

2 4 m

3 $0.93\,\mathrm{m\,s^{-1}}$ (2 s.f.)

4 **b** ± 0.6, ∓ 2.4

18.5 Contextual (p. 498)

1 **a** $v^2 = \frac{8\times10^{14}}{x} + 1.2 \times 10^7$
b $3.69\,\mathrm{km\,s^{-1}}$
c It will approach the terminal velocity of $3.46\,\mathrm{km\,s^{-1}}$ unless it comes under the influence of other gravitational forces.

2 **b** **i** $25.2\,\mathrm{m\,s^{-1}}$ **ii** 48.4 m

3 **a** $1.5\,\mathrm{m\,s^{-1}}$ **b** 6.42 m

4 **a** 5 m **b** 4.46 m

Consolidation A (p. 500)

1 **a** $t = 1, 5$ **b** 32 m

2 **a** $\mathbf{r} = -4\mathbf{i}$, $\mathbf{v} = -6\mathbf{j}$, $\mathbf{a} = 16\mathbf{i}$
b Maximum $16\,\mathrm{m\,s^{-2}}$, minimum $12\,\mathrm{m\,s^{-2}}$

3 **a** $a = 10 - 2v$ **b** $V = 5$

Consolidation B (p. 500)

1 9 m

2 $v = 10 - 2x$

3 **a** $\mathbf{v} = \frac{1}{2}[(\frac{1}{2}t^2 + 3t - 1)\mathbf{i} - (t^2 + 3)\mathbf{j}]$ **b** 2, 4

4 **a** $v = 11[1 - \cos(\frac{\pi}{45}t)]$, 90 s
b 990 m, $11\,\mathrm{m\,s^{-1}}$
c $0.665\,\mathrm{m\,s^{-2}}$

5 **a** $v = 50(1 - e^{-0.196t})$
b $14.6\,\text{m s}^{-1}$
c

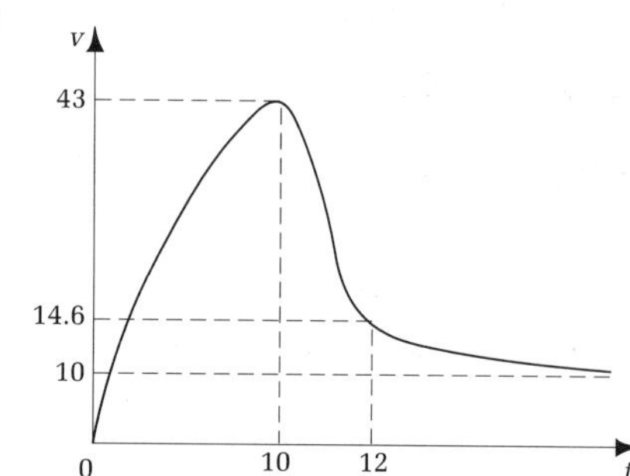

19 Simple Harmonic Motion

Review (p. 504)

1 **a** 3 N **b** 6 N

2 $4.2\,\text{m s}^{-2}$ upwards

3 **a** $\dot{x} = -20.1$, $\ddot{x} = -78.0$
b $\dot{x} = -9.66$, $\ddot{x} = 188$

4

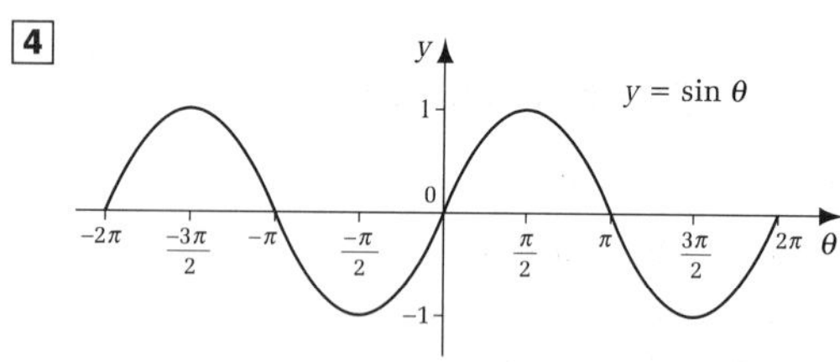

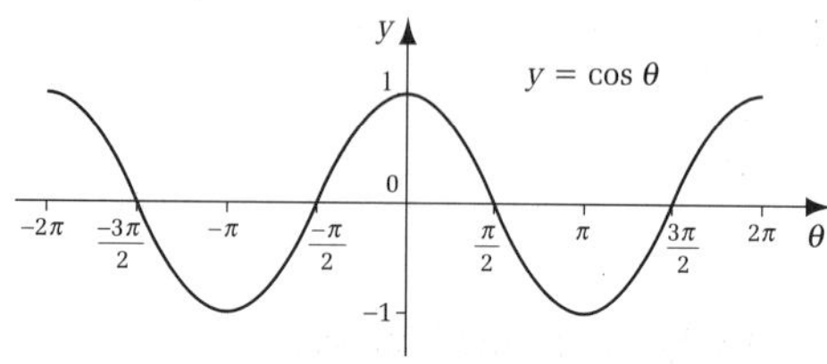

5 **a** 0.725^c **b** 0.0804^c **c** 0.348^c **d** 0.321^c

19.1 Technique (p. 509)

1 25 cm

2 **a** 2.52 m **b** $6.69\,\text{m s}^{-2}$

3 **a** $\ddot{x} = -900x$ **b** 7.2 N

4 **a** 3 m from A **b** $1\,\text{m s}^{-2}$

19.1 Contextual (p. 510)

2 720 N. The motion would not be simple harmonic until the rope became taut. The first part of the motion would be that of a body in free fall, subject to gravity.

3 **a** 10 cm **c** $30\,\text{m s}^{-2}$

19.2 Technique (p. 515)

1 $21\,\text{m s}^{-1}$

2 2.27

3 **a** $\pm 3\,\text{m s}^{-1}$ **b** ± 1.5 m

4 **a** 4 **b** 3.61 m **c** 173 N

5 **a** $a = 2.38$ m, $\omega = 2.31$
b **i** $5.51\,\text{m s}^{-1}$ **ii** $12.7\,\text{m s}^{-2}$

19.2 Contextual (p. 515)

1 **a** $5.20\,\text{cm s}^{-1}$ **b** 2.16 N **c** 120 N

2 **a** $0.130\,\text{m s}^{-1}$ **b** $0.15\,\text{m s}^{-1}$ **c** $225\,\text{m s}^{-2}$

3 **a** $0.2\,\text{m s}^{-1}$ **b** 3.46 cm

4 **a** $0.24\,\text{m s}^{-1}$ **b** $1.8\,\text{m s}^{-2}$ **c** $\frac{9}{49}$

5 **a** 4.68 **b** 963 N

19.3 Technique (p. 523)

1 **a** 1.5 s **b** 0.75 s **c** 0.75 s

2 **a** 0.5 s **b** **i** 0.125 s
ii 0.25 s

3 **a** $\frac{1}{4}\pi$ **b** $x = 7\sin(\frac{1}{4}\pi t)$
c **i** On CB, 4.95 m from C
ii at B
iii On AC, 4.95 m from C

4 **a** $x = 2\cos 10\pi t$
b **i** $\frac{1}{30}$ or $0.0\dot{3}$ s
ii $\frac{1}{15}$ or $0.0\dot{6}$ s
iii 0.023 s (2 s.f.)

5 **a** $a = 5$, $\omega = 4$
b $x = 5\sin 4t$; $\dot{x} = 20\cos 4t$; $\ddot{x} = -80\sin 4t$
c -3.78 m; $-13.1\,\text{m s}^{-1}$; $60.5\,\text{m s}^{-2}$

19.3 Contextual (p. 524)

1 **a** 0.3 s **b** 0.15 s

2 **a** $a = 0.8$, $\omega = \frac{\pi}{2}$
b **i** $x = 0.8\cos(\frac{\pi}{2}t)$
ii $\dot{x} = -0.4\pi\sin(\frac{\pi}{2}t)$
c **i** Between A and C, 0.470 m from C travelling towards C at $1.02\,\text{m s}^{-1}$.
ii Between C and B, 0.247 m from C travelling towards B at $1.20\,\text{m s}^{-1}$.
iii Between C and B, 0.647 m from C travelling towards C at $0.739\,\text{m s}^{-1}$.
iv Between A and C, 0.247 m from C travelling towards A at $1.20\,\text{m s}^{-1}$.
d $\pm 1.09\,\text{m s}^{-1}$

19.4 Technique (p. 531)

1 $\omega = 2$, $a = \frac{\sqrt{2}}{2}$ m, $\varepsilon = \frac{\pi}{4}$
$x = \frac{\sqrt{2}}{2}\sin(2t + \frac{\pi}{4})$ or
$x = 0.707\sin(2t + 0.785)$

2 **a** $x = 2.82\cos(4\pi t + 0.783)$
b $\dot{x} = -35.4\sin(4\pi t + 0.783)$,
$\ddot{x} = -445\cos(4\pi t + 0.783)$

3 **a** 0.0161 s
b 0.0946 s

19.4 Contextual (p. 531)

1 0.152 s

19.5 Technique (p. 536)

1 2.46 s

2 1.43 m

3 $9.808\ \text{m s}^{-2}$

4 16.3% reduction

5 $\sqrt{2}T$

19.5 Contextual (p. 536)

1 993 mm

2 $9.81\ \text{m s}^{-2}$

3 **a** Gain 44 s **b** Increase by 1.01 mm

4 **a** $T = 2\pi\sqrt{\frac{l}{g}}$ **b** 0.898 s

Consolidation A (p. 537)

1 **a** 127 **b** 3.2 kN

2 **b** $0.25\sin(4\pi t)$ **c** $v^2 = \pi^2(1 - 16x^2)$
d Leaves plate when $R = 0$.

R

mg

e 0.312 m; $3.04\ \text{m s}^{-1}$ **f** 0.145 s

3 **a iii** Air resistance negligible
b i 5 cm
ii 0.185 s

Consolidation B (p. 538)

1 **a** $a = 0.8$ m; $T = 2.4$ s **b** $\frac{2\pi}{3}$ or $2.09\ \text{m s}^{-1}$

2 $\frac{d^2\theta}{dt^2} = \frac{-g}{4}\sin\theta$, $T = 4$ s

3 **a** 5 N **b** Tension $= 10x + 0.98$ newtons
d $\frac{\pi}{5}$ or 0.628 s **e** $\sqrt{2}$ or $1.41\ \text{m s}^{-1}$
f When string becomes slack motion will no longer be SHM.

4 **a** $\ddot{x} = g(1 - \frac{x}{a})$
b Maximum distance $= 4a$, greatest tension $= 4mg$

20 Resultant and Relative Velocities

Review (p. 542)

1 43.6 at 36.6° anticlockwise from vector 20.

2 **a** $3\mathbf{i} + 3\mathbf{j}$ **b** $-58\mathbf{i} + 47\mathbf{j}$

3 **a** 27.5 cm **b** 44.0°

4 **a** 240° **b** 140° (or 220°)

20.1 Contextual (p. 546)

1 **a i** 16 s **ii** 32 m
b i 23.6° from DE (upstream)
ii 30.5° from DE (upstream)
iii 16.3° from DE (upstream).
c i 34.7 m from E
ii $2\sqrt{2}$ or $2.83\ \text{m s}^{-1}$

2 **a** 165.5° **b** 3 h 52 min (or 3.87 h)

3 **a** 90° to the bank. **b** 32.5 s
c 65 m downstream from the starting position

4 **a** 245.1° **b** 240.3° **c** 265.9°

20.2 Technique (p. 550)

1 **a** $\mathbf{i} + 2\mathbf{j}$ **b** $5\mathbf{i} + 6\mathbf{j}$

2 **a** $5\mathbf{i} - 9\mathbf{j}$ **b** $47\mathbf{i} - 9\mathbf{j}$

3 **a** $58.3\ \text{km h}^{-1}$, 059.0°
b $67.4\ \text{m s}^{-1}$, 359.3°

4 **a** $78.1\ \text{km h}^{-1}$, 273.7°
b $43.6\ \text{km h}^{-1}$, 143.4°

5 **a** $(x_1 - x_2)\mathbf{i} + (y_1 - y_2)\mathbf{j}$
b $(x_2 - x_1)\mathbf{i} + (y_2 - y_1)\mathbf{j}$; ${}_A\mathbf{v}_B = -{}_B\mathbf{v}_A$

20.2 Contextual (p. 550)

1 **a** $150\ \text{km h}^{-1}$ (car's direction is assumed positive)
b $-150\ \text{km h}^{-1}$

2 45 mph

3 $(200\mathbf{i} - 200\mathbf{j})\ \text{km h}^{-1}$

20.3 Technique (p. 553)

1 **b** 5 s **c** $(70\mathbf{i} + 5\mathbf{j})$ m

2 **a** $10\mathbf{i} + 30\mathbf{j} + 23\mathbf{v}_X$, $-59\mathbf{i} + 191\mathbf{j} + 23\mathbf{v}_Y$
b $(2\mathbf{i} + 4\mathbf{j})\ \text{m s}^{-1}$; $(5\mathbf{i} - 3\mathbf{j})\ \text{m s}^{-1}$

3 **a** $(212\mathbf{i} - 365\mathbf{j})$ m **b** $(8\mathbf{i} + 13\mathbf{j})\ \text{m s}^{-1}$

4 $(-500\mathbf{i} + 400\mathbf{j})$ m; $(550\mathbf{i} + 190\mathbf{j})$ m

5 **a** Show $\mathbf{r}_A = \mathbf{r}_B$ when $t = 4$ s.
b 40 m due east of Y.

20.3 Contextual (p. 554)

1 **b** $(-99.4\mathbf{i} + 87.4\mathbf{j})$ km

2 $(100\mathbf{i} + 50\mathbf{j})$ km h^{-1}, $(-150\mathbf{i} + 40\mathbf{j})$ km h^{-1}

3 **b** 8 s
c $(6400\mathbf{i} + 600\mathbf{j})$ m

4 **a** Show $\mathbf{r}_H = \mathbf{r}_A$ after 1.06 h
b 16.04 (nearest minute)
c No wind or same altitude.

5 **b** 11.30 hours; $(1000\mathbf{i} + 575\mathbf{j} + 8\mathbf{k})$ km

20.4 Technique (p. 558)

1 **a** 053.1° **b** 7.5 h **c** 22.5 km north of N.

2 **a** 186.0° **b** 8.39 s **c** 67.2 m at 186.0°

3 **a** 4.47 m s^{-1} at 063.4°
b 138.9 m at 149.7°
c 101.7° **d** 37.3 s
e $(179\mathbf{i} + 4.64\mathbf{j})$ m

20.4 Contextual (p. 558)

1 088.6°, 1.5 h

2 **a** 5 m s^{-1} at 53.1° anticlockwise from the **j** vector. (Bearing 306.9°.)
b 9600 m at 121.4° clockwise from the **j** vector. (Bearing 121.4°.)
c 121.2° clockwise from the **j** vector. (Bearing 121.2°.)
d 62.0 s

20.5 Technique (p. 562)

1 **a i** 20.8 m **ii** 2.06 s
b i 42.9 m **ii** 3.54 s

2 4.74 m, 4.43 s

20.5 Contextual (p. 562)

1 29.4 km, 10 minutes 15 seconds (0.171 h)

2 52.8 km, 09.08 (nearest minute)

3 62.6 m

20.6 Technique (p. 568)

1 **a** 354.6° **b** 2.81 m, 2.74 s later

2 **a** 132.8° **b** 1.45 s, 95.5 m

3 2.20 m

20.6 Contextual (p. 568)

1 156.4°, 70.3 m, 29.3 s later.

2 **a** 180° **b** 0 km, 11.10 a.m. (nearest minute)

Consolidation A (p. 569)

1 24 m

2 **a** 0.0008
b ii Interception takes place at 340 s.

3 **a**

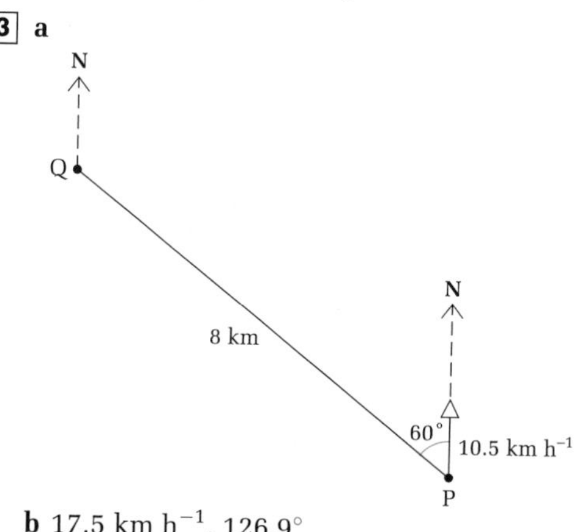

b 17.5 km h^{-1}, 126.9°
c i 0.957 km
d i 079.5°

Consolidation B (p. 570)

1 **a** 25 m s^{-1} **b** 7.5 m
Slowed down by friction because the surfaces will not be perfectly smooth.

2 **a** Collision at 2.5 s
b $r = 8\mathbf{i} - 0.5\mathbf{j} + 14.5\mathbf{k}$

3 $\mathbf{r}_A = (442 - 30t)\mathbf{i}$ or $\mathbf{r}_A = (442 - 30t)\mathbf{j}$
$\mathbf{r}_B = (442 - 20t)\mathbf{j}$ $\mathbf{r}_B = (442 - 20t)\mathbf{i}$
17 s

Formulas

This is a list of formulas you should **remember.** Each formula has been referenced to the chapter in which it **first appears** in the text.

TOPIC	FORMULA	CHAPTER
Newton's Law of Gravitation	$F = \dfrac{Gm_1m_2}{d^2}$	2
Weight	$W = mg$	2
Vectors	2D vector $\mathbf{a} = x\mathbf{i} + y\mathbf{j}$	
	Magnitude $\lvert\mathbf{a}\rvert = \sqrt{x^2 + y^2}$	3
	Direction $\tan\theta = \dfrac{y}{x}$	3
	where θ is angle with x-axis or $\mathbf{i}$	
	3D vector $\mathbf{a} = x\mathbf{i} + y\mathbf{j} + z\mathbf{k}$	3
	Magnitude $\lvert\mathbf{a}\rvert = \sqrt{x^2 + y^2 + z^2}$	3
	Unit Vector $\hat{\mathbf{a}} = \dfrac{\mathbf{a}}{\lvert\mathbf{a}\rvert}$	3
	Vector $\mathbf{a}$ of magnitude r at an angle θ to $\mathbf{i}$	
	$\mathbf{a} = r\cos\theta\,\mathbf{i} + r\sin\theta\,\mathbf{j}$	5
	For vectors $\mathbf{a} = x_1\mathbf{i} + y_1\mathbf{j} + z_1\mathbf{k}$ and $\mathbf{b} = x_2\mathbf{i} + y_2\mathbf{j} + z_2\mathbf{k}$	
	Resultant Vector $\mathbf{R} = \mathbf{a} + \mathbf{b} = (x_1 + x_2)\mathbf{i} + (y_1 + y_2)\mathbf{j} + (z_1 + z_2)\mathbf{k}$	5
	Scalar (Dot) Product $\mathbf{a}.\mathbf{b} = x_1x_2 + y_1y_2 + z_1z_2 = ab\cos\theta$	5
	Parallel Vectors $\mathbf{a} \,//\, \mathbf{b} \Leftrightarrow \mathbf{a} = k\mathbf{b}$	3
	Perpendicular Vectors $\mathbf{a}.\mathbf{b} = 0 \Leftrightarrow \mathbf{a} \perp \mathbf{b}$ (assuming non-zero vectors)	5
	Angle between Vectors $\cos\theta = \dfrac{\mathbf{a}.\mathbf{b}}{\lvert\mathbf{a}\rvert\lvert\mathbf{b}\rvert}$	5
Travel Graphs	Velocity = gradient of displacement–time graph	4
	Average speed $= \dfrac{\text{total distance travelled}}{\text{total time taken}}$	4
	Average velocity $= \dfrac{\text{total displacement}}{\text{total time taken}}$	4
	Acceleration = gradient of velocity–time graph	4
	Displacement = area between a velocity–time graph and the time axis	4

TOPIC	FORMULA	CHAPTER
Motion with Constant Acceleration	$v = u + at$ $s = \frac{1}{2}(u+v)t$ $s = ut + \frac{1}{2}at^2$ $v^2 = u^2 + 2as$	**6** **6** **6** **6**
Lami's Theorem	$\dfrac{P}{\sin\alpha} = \dfrac{Q}{\sin\beta} = \dfrac{R}{\sin\gamma}$	**7**
Newton's Second Law	$F = ma$ in one direction and $\mathbf{F} = m\mathbf{a}$ in two or three dimensions	**8** **8**
Friction	$F_r \le \mu R$	**9**
Angle of Friction	$\mu = \tan\lambda$	**9**
Component of Weight down plane	$mg\sin\theta$	**9**
Component of Weight perpendicular to plane	$mg\cos\theta$	**9**
Work (constant force)	$W = Fs$ where s is the distance moved in the direction of the force	**10**
Potential Energy	$\text{PE} = mgh$	**10**
Kinetic Energy	$\text{KE} = \frac{1}{2}mv^2$	**10**
Power	$P = Fv$ or $P = \dfrac{W}{t}$	**10**
Hooke's Law	$T = \dfrac{\lambda x}{l}$ or $T = kx$	**11**
Elastic Potential Energy	$\text{EPE} = \dfrac{\lambda x^2}{2l}$ or $\text{EPE} = \dfrac{kx^2}{2}$ or $\text{EPE} = \int_0^x T\,dx$	**11**
Conservation of Energy	$\text{PE}_{\text{start}} + \text{KE}_{\text{start}} + \text{EPE}_{\text{start}} = \text{PE}_{\text{end}} = \text{KE}_{\text{end}} + \text{EPE}_{\text{end}}$	**11**

TOPIC	FORMULA	CHAPTER
Work–Energy Principle	$\text{ME}_{\text{start}} + \text{W}_{\text{in}} = \text{ME}_{\text{end}} + \text{W}_{\text{out}}$	11
Impulse	$\mathbf{I} = m\mathbf{v} - m\mathbf{u}$ or $\mathbf{I} = \mathbf{F}t$	12
Principle of Conservation of Linear Momentum	$m_1u_1 + m_2u_2 = m_1v_1 + m_2v_2$	12
Newton's Law of Restitution	$v = eu$ $0 \le e \le 1$ $e = \dfrac{\text{speed of separation}}{\text{speed of approach}}$	12 12 12
Moment of a Force	$M = Fd$ where the distance d is perpendicular to F	13
Centre of Mass (particle system)	$\bar{x} = \dfrac{\sum_i m_i x_i}{\sum_i m_i}$ and $\bar{y} = \dfrac{\sum_i m_i y_i}{\sum_i m_i}$	14
Centres of Mass	Triangular Lamina: $\frac{2}{3}$ distance along median from vertex	14
	Circular Arc, radius r and angle 2α: $\dfrac{r \sin\alpha}{\alpha}$ from centre	14
	Semicircular Arc: $\dfrac{2r}{\pi}$ from centre	14
	Sector, radius r and angle 2α: $\dfrac{2r\sin\alpha}{3\alpha}$ from centre	14
	Semicircular Lamina: $\dfrac{4r}{3\pi}$ from centre	14
	Solid Cone/Pyramid: $\frac{1}{4}h$ from centre of base	14
	Solid Hemisphere: $\frac{3}{8}r$ from centre	14
Projectiles	$\text{Range} = \dfrac{U^2 \sin(2\theta)}{g}$	16
	$\text{Maximum range} = \dfrac{U^2}{g}$ when $\theta = 45^\circ$	16
	$\text{Maximum height} = \dfrac{U^2 \sin^2\theta}{2g}$	16
	$\text{Time to reach maximum height} = \dfrac{U\sin\theta}{g}$	16
	$\text{Time of flight} = \dfrac{2U\sin\theta}{g}$	

TOPIC	FORMULA	CHAPTER
Equation of Trajectory	$y = x\tan\theta - \frac{gx^2}{2U^2}(1+\tan^2\theta)$	16
Circular Motion	$v = \omega r$ $T = \frac{2\pi}{\omega}$	17
Acceleration towards Centre	$\omega^2 r$ or $\frac{v^2}{r}$	17
Variable Acceleration [For vectors replace *x* by r]	$v = \frac{\mathrm{d}x}{\mathrm{d}t} = \dot{x}$	18
	$a = \frac{\mathrm{d}v}{\mathrm{d}t} = \frac{\mathrm{d}^2x}{\mathrm{d}t^2} = \ddot{x}$ or $a = v\frac{\mathrm{d}v}{\mathrm{d}x}$	18
	$F = m\ddot{x}$	18
	$v = \int a\,\mathrm{d}t$	18
	$x = \int v\,\mathrm{d}t$	18
Simple Harmonic Motion	$\ddot{x} = -\omega^2 x$	19
	Maximum acceleration $= \omega^2 a$	19
	$v^2 = \omega^2(a^2 - x^2)$	19
	Maximum speed $= \omega a$	19
	Object initially at End of Path $x = a\cos\omega t$	19
	Object initially at Centre of Path $x = a\sin\omega t$	19
	General Forms $x = a\cos(\omega t + \varepsilon)$ or $x = a\sin(\omega t + \varepsilon)$ or $x = A\sin(\omega t) + B\cos(\omega t)$	19
	Periodic Time $T = \frac{2\pi}{\omega}$	19
	Simple Pendulum $\ddot{\theta} = -\frac{g}{l}\theta$	19
	$T = 2\pi\sqrt{\frac{l}{g}}$	19
Relative Velocity	${}_{\mathrm{A}}\mathbf{v}_{\mathrm{B}} = \mathbf{v}_{\mathrm{A}} - \mathbf{v}_{\mathrm{B}}$	20
	${}_{\mathrm{A}}\mathbf{v}_{\mathrm{B}} = -{}_{\mathrm{B}}\mathbf{v}_{\mathrm{A}}$	20

Arrow Notation

Arrow Notation used in this Book		
	——▶ Force	——▶▶—— Resultant force
	——▷ Velocity	——▷▷—— Resultant velocity
	——> Displacement	——>>—— Resultant displacement
	——>> Acceleration	◀——▶ Distance, dimensions

Index